Street by Street

CW00326506

LONDON

4th edition May 2005
© Automobile Association Developments Limited 2005

Original edition printed May 2001

Ordnance Survey® This product includes map data licensed from Ordnance Survey® with the permission of the Controller of Her Majesty's Stationery Office. © Crown copyright 2005. All rights reserved. Licence number 399221.

Published by AA Publishing (a trading name of Automobile Association Developments Limited, whose registered office is Southwood East, Apollo Rise, Farnborough, Hampshire, GU14 0JW. Registered number 1878835).

Mapping produced by the Cartography Department of The Automobile Association. (A02254)

A CIP Catalogue record for this book is available from the British Library.

Printed by Oriental Press in Dubai

The contents of this atlas are believed to be correct at the time of the latest revision. However, the publishers cannot be held responsible for loss occasioned to any person acting or refraining from action as a result of any material in this atlas, nor for any errors, omissions or changes in such material. This does not affect your statutory rights. The publishers would welcome information to correct any errors or omissions and to keep this atlas up to date. Please write to Publishing, The Automobile Association, Fanum House (FH17), Basing View, Basingstoke, Hampshire, RG21 4EA.

Ref: ML038x

Key to map pages	ii-iii
Key to map symbols	iv–1
Enlarged map pages	2-19
Main map pages	20-217
Index – towns & villages	218-219
Index – streets	220-307
Index – featured places	307-328
Acknowledgements	328

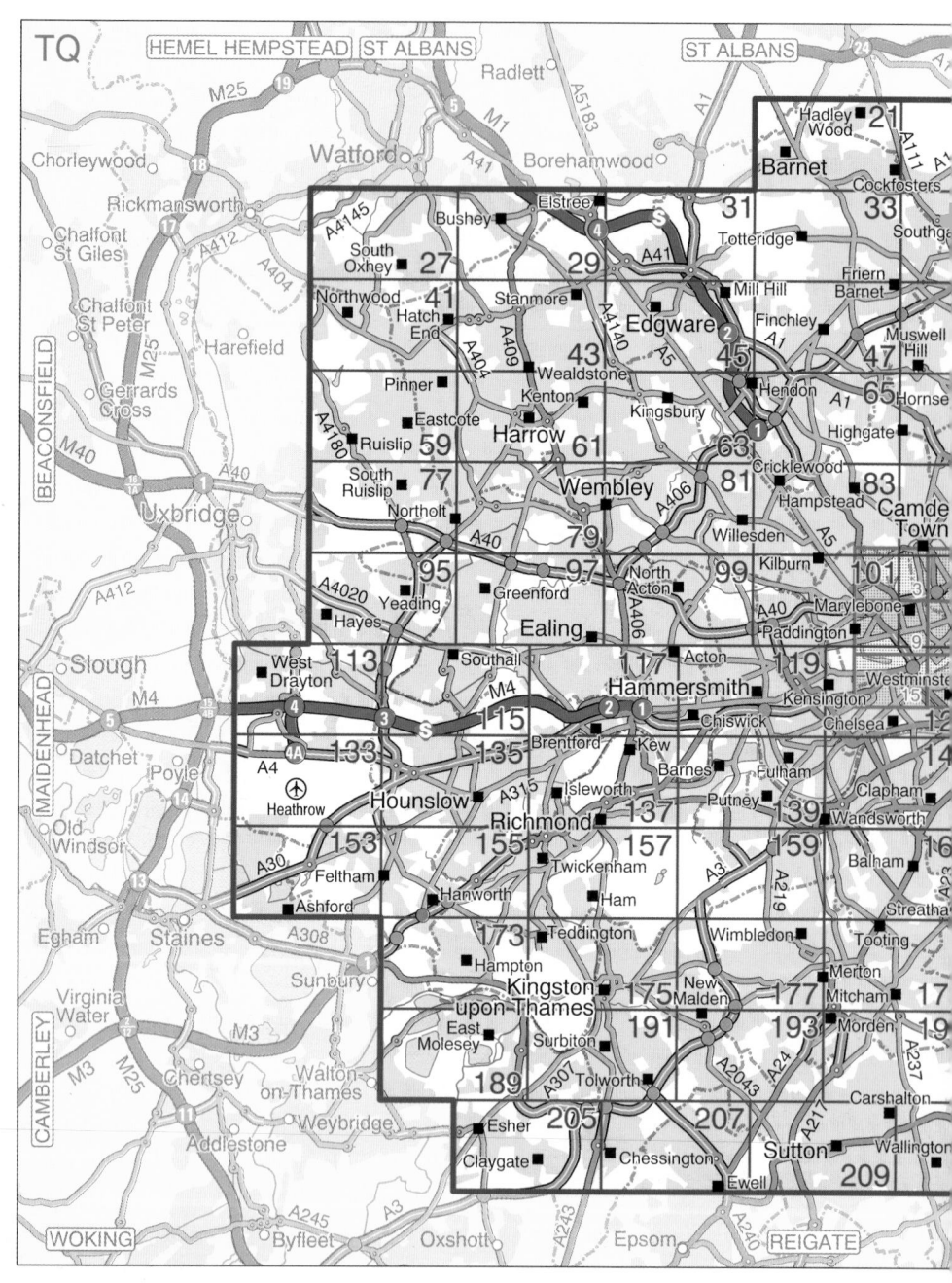

ii

TQ

HEMEL HEMPSTEAD ST ALBANS   ST ALBANS

Radlett

Chorleywood   Watford   Borehamwood   Barnet   Hadley 21
                                                                    Wood
                                                    Cockfosters
Rickmansworth   Elstree   31   33 Southga
Chalfont   Bushey   Totteridge
St Giles   South   29   A41   Mill Hill   Friern 47
                                  Oxhey 27   Barnet
Chalfont   Northwood 41 Stanmore   Edgware 45 Finchley Muswell
St Peter   Hatch   Hill
        Harefield End   43 Wealdstone   Hendon 65 Hornse
Gerrards   Pinner   Kenton   Kingsbury   Highgate
Cross   Eastcote Harrow 61 63   Cricklewood 83
                          Ruislip 59   81 Hampstead Camde
Uxbridge   South   Wembley   Willesden   Town
                  Ruislip 77 Northolt 79   North 99 Kilburn 101
                          95 Yeading 97 Greenford Acton   Marylebone
                  Hayes   Ealing   A40 Paddington
Slough   West 113 Southall 117 Acton   119   Westminste
        Datchet   Drayton   Hammersmith Kensington   15
                          133 135 Brentford Chiswick Chelsea
        Poyle   A4   Kew   Fulham   14
                  Heathrow Hounslow Isleworth Barnes   Clapham 139
Old   Richmond 137 Putney   Wandsworth
Windsor   153 155 157 159 Balham 16
        Feltham   Twickenham   Streatha
        Ashford   Ham   Wimbledon Tooting
Egham Staines   173 Teddington   Merton
                  Hampton   Kingston 175 New 177 Mitcham 17
Virginia   Sunbury upon-Thames   Malden 193 Morden 19
Water   East 191 Surbiton
        Chertsey Walton- Molesey   189 Tolworth 207 Carshalton
        Weybridge on-Thames   205   Sutton 209
Addlestone   Byfleet Esher Chessington Wallington
                  Claygate   Ewell
WOKING   Oxshott   Epsom REIGATE

Scale of enlarged map pages 1:10,000   6.3 inches to 1 mile

0   1/4   miles   1/2
0   1/4   1/2 kilometres 3/4   1

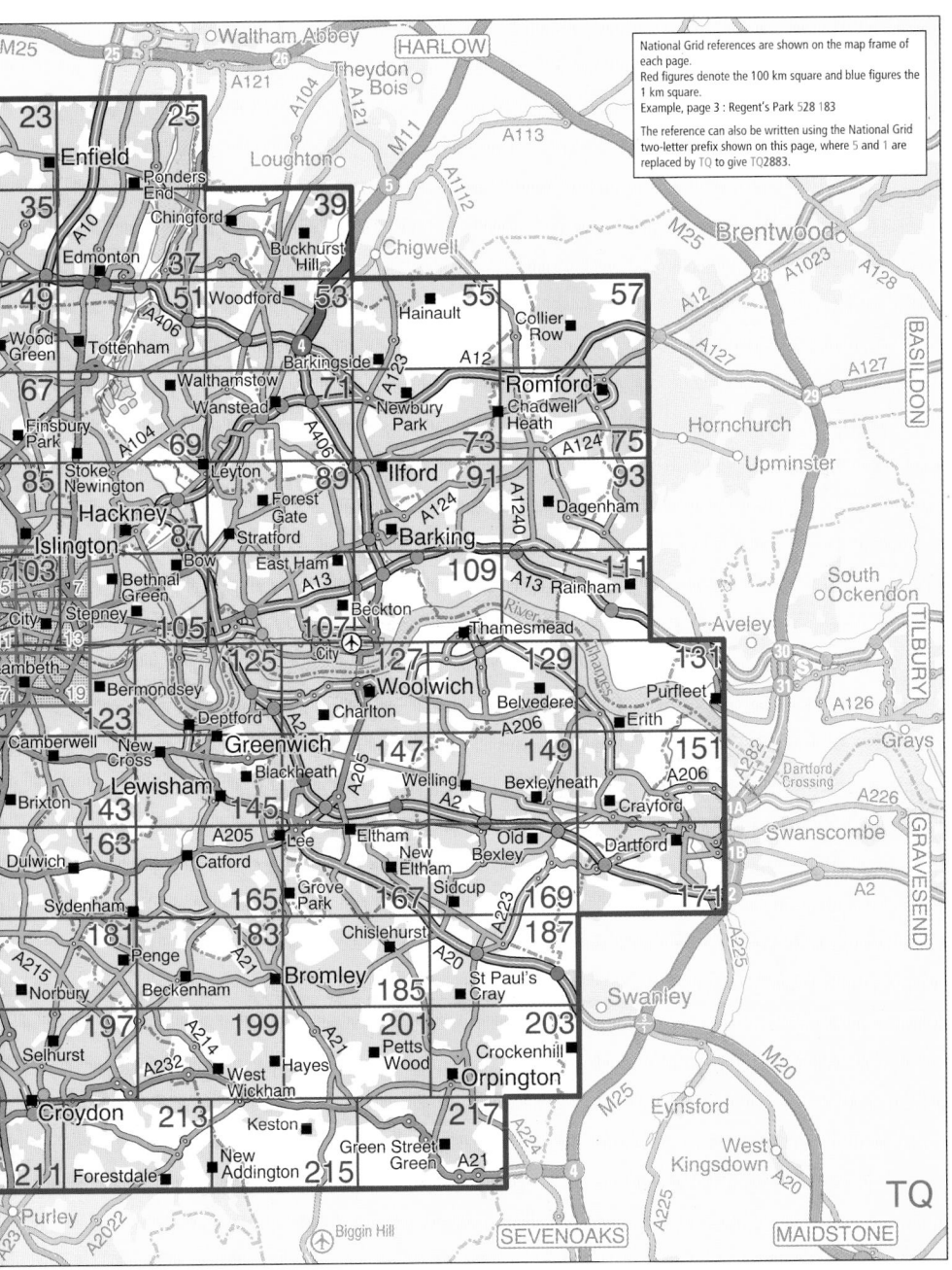

National Grid references are shown on the map frame of each page.
Red figures denote the 100 km square and blue figures the 1 km square.
Example, page 3 : Regent's Park 528 183

The reference can also be written using the National Grid two-letter prefix shown on this page, where 5 and 1 are replaced by TQ to give TQ2883.

3.6 inches to 1 mile

Scale of main map pages 1:17,500

miles
0   1/2   1

kilometres
0   1/2   1   1 1/2

Junction 9	Motorway & junction
Services	Motorway service area
	Primary road single/dual carriageway
Services	Primary road service area
	A road single/dual carriageway
	B road single/dual carriageway
	Other road single/dual carriageway
	Minor/private road, access may be restricted
← ←	One-way street
	Pedestrian area
==========	Track or footpath
	Road under construction
	Road tunnel
P	Parking
P+	Park & Ride
	Bus/coach station
	Railway & main railway station
	Railway & minor railway station
⊖	Underground station
⊖	Light railway & station

+++++++++	Preserved private railway
LC	Level crossing
•—•—•—	Tramway
---------	Ferry route
....	Airport runway
— · — · — ·	County, administrative boundary
	Congestion Charging Zone *
▼▼▼▼▼▼▼▼	Mounds
93	Page continuation 1:17,500
7	Page continuation to enlarged scale 1:10,000
	River/canal, lake, pier
	Aqueduct, lock, weir
465 ▲ Winter Hill	Peak (with height in metres)
	Beach
	Woodland
	Park
† † † † †	Cemetery
	Built-up area
	Featured building
⊓⊔⊓⊔⊓	City wall

* The AA central London Congestion Charging map is also available

A&E	Hospital with 24-hour A&E department	🏛	Historic house or building
PO	Post Office	Wakehurst Place NT	National Trust property
📖	Public library	Ⓜ	Museum or art gallery
i	Tourist Information Centre	🦅	Roman antiquity
i	Seasonal Tourist Information Centre	⊥	Ancient site, battlefield or monument
🅿🅿	Petrol station, 24 hour Major suppliers only	🏭	Industrial interest
†	Church/chapel	✼	Garden
🚻	Public toilets	⚙	Garden Centre Garden Centre Association Member
♿	Toilet with disabled facilities	🌷	Garden Centre Wyevale Garden Centre
PH	Public house AA recommended	🌳	Arboretum
🍴	Restaurant AA inspected	🛒	Farm or animal centre
Madeira Hotel	Hotel AA inspected	🦌	Zoological or wildlife collection
🎭	Theatre or performing arts centre	🦜	Bird collection
🎥	Cinema	🐋	Nature reserve
⚑	Golf course	🐟	Aquarium
▲	Camping AA inspected	🄵	Visitor or heritage centre
🚐	Caravan site AA inspected	♈	Country park
▲🚐	Camping & caravan site AA inspected	⌒	Cave
⚒	Theme park	🎐	Windmill
🏰	Abbey, cathedral or priory	🛢	Distillery, brewery or vineyard
♟	Castle	**IKEA**	IKEA store

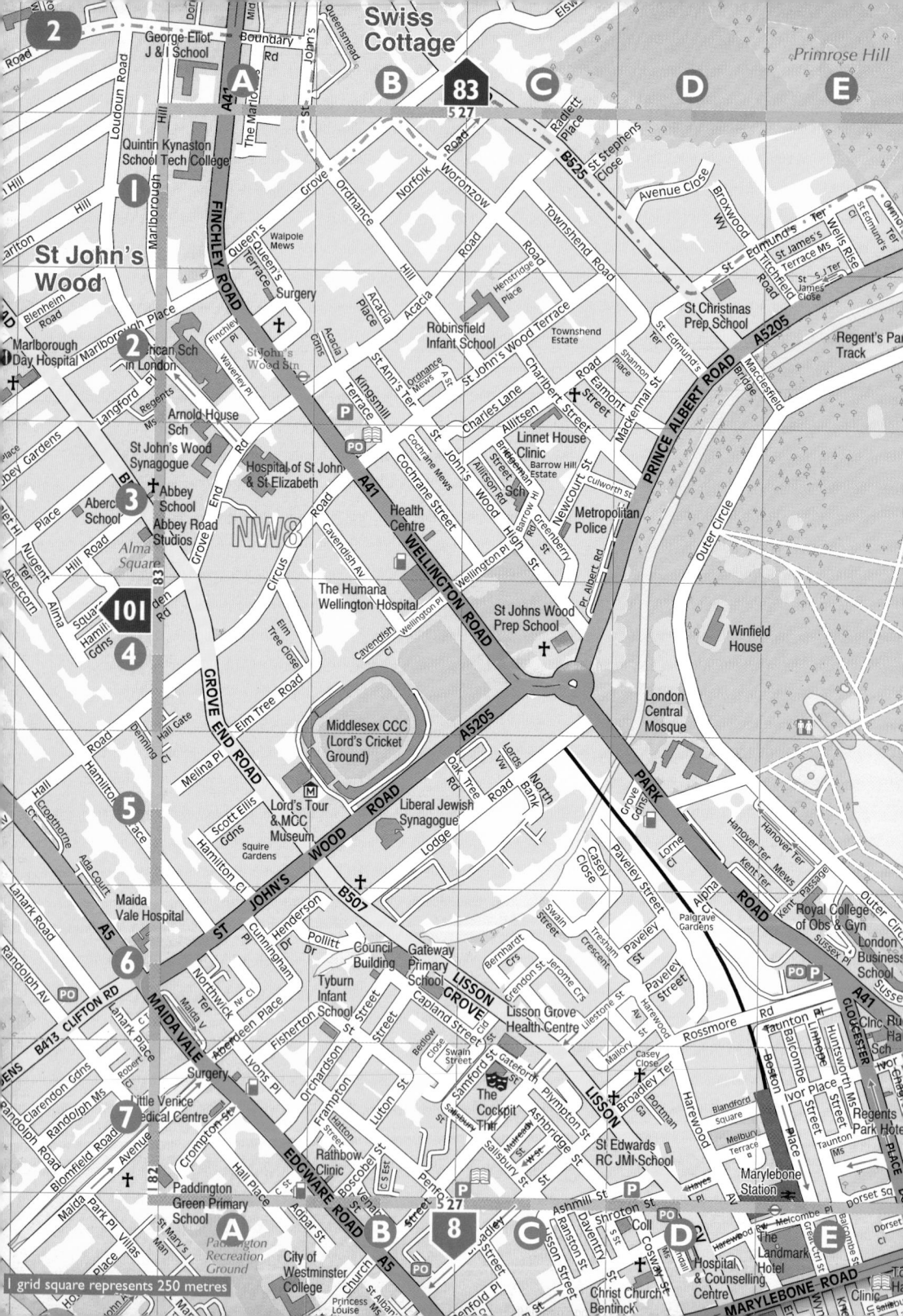

Swiss Cottage

Primrose Hill

2

George Eliot J & I School

Boundary Rd

Queensmead

Elsworthy

A41

The Marlboro

St John's

Queensmead

Radlett Place

B525

St Stephens Close

Avenue Close

Broxwood Wy

St Edmunds Ter

St James's Terrace Ms

St Edmund's

St J Ter

Qwner Cir

A   **B**   **83** 5 27   **C**   **D**   **E**

1

Quintin Kynaston School Tech College

Loudoun Road

Marlborough

Finchley Hill

Hill

Grove End Road

Ordnance Hill

Norfolk Rd

Woronzow Rd

Townshend Road

St James's Close

Wells Rise

Itchfield

St John's Wood

Blenheim Road

Marlborough Day Hospital

Marlborough Place

American Sch in London

Finchley Road

St John's Wood Stn

Queen's Terrace

Queen's

Walpole Mews

Surgery

Acacia Place

Acacia Gdns

Acacia Rd

Robinsfield Infant School

St John's Wood Terrace

Townshend Estate

St Christinas Prep School

A5205

Regent's Park Track

Regent's Park

2

Langford Pl

Regents

Waverley Pl

St John's Wd Stn

Kingsmill Terrace

Ordnance Mews

Charles Lane

Allitsen Rd

St John's Wood

Eamont Street

Mackennal St

Shannon Place

3

Abbey Gardens

Nugent Pl

Abercorn Place

Grove End Rd

Arnold House Sch

St John's Wood Synagogue

Aberc School

Abbey School

Hospital of St John & St Elizabeth

Cochrane Mews

Cochrane Street

Allitsen Rd

Barrow Hill

Linnet House Clinic

Barrow Hill Estate

Newcourt St

Culworth St

Greenberry

Metropolitan Police

Prince Albert Rd

Marchesford

NW8

Abbey Road Studios

Alma Square

Abercorn

Alma

Hamilton

Circus

Cavendish Av

Health Centre

Wellington Pl

Wellington Rd

St John's Wood High St

Pr Albert Rd

Outer Circle

Winfield House

3

4

101

Hamilt Gdns

Square

den Rd

Elm Tree Close

Elm Tree Road

The Humana Wellington Hospital

Cavendish Cl

Wellington Pl

St Johns Wood Prep School

5

Hall Place

Crogmorne

Melina Pl

Hall Gate

Lord's Tour & MCC Museum

Squire Gardens

Scott Ellis Gdns

Hamilton Cl

Middlesex CCC (Lord's Cricket Ground)

Liberal Jewish Synagogue

A5205

Lodge

Oak Tree Rd

North Bank

Lorne Cl

Vw

Lord's Vw

London Central Mosque

PARK

Grove End

Hanover Ter Ms

Hanover

Outer Cir

ROAD

Kent Passage

Royal College of Obs & Gyn

London Business School

6

Maida Vale

A5

Lanark Road

Maida Vale Hospital

Denning

Henderson Dr

Cunningham

Pollitt Dr

Council Building

Gateway Primary School

Tyburn Infant School

B507

Capland Street

LISSON GROVE

Bernhardt Crs

Grendon St

Jerome Cr

Swain Street

Trechan Crs

Ulestone St

Paveley Street

Casey Close

Paveley St

Harewood Av

Palgrave Gardens

Alpha Cl

Sussex Pl

PO P

Rossmore Rd

Kent Ter

Regents Park Hse

7

Randolph Av

Clifton Rd

PO

B413 CLIFTON RD

Blomfield Road

Maida Park Pl

Randolph Ms

Clarendon Gdns

Clarendon Rd

Robert Cl

Lanark Place

Maida V

Little Venice Medical Centre

Surgery

Aberdeen Place

Nlr Cl

Fisherton Street

Orchardson Street

Frampton St

Hatton

Rathbow Clinic

Boscobel St

Venart St

Frampton St

Luton St

Bell St

Bedow

Gateforth St

Samford

Salisbury St

Lisson Grove Health Centre

Lisson St

Mallory

Plympton St

Ashbridge St

Ashmill St

Daventry St

Shroton St

Coll

Harewood

Melbury Terrace

St Edwards RC JMI School

LISSON

Broadley Ter

Bentinck

Christ Church

Portman

Blandford Square

Balcombe St

Linhope Street

Huntsworth Ms

Ivor Place

Regents Park Ho

Marylebone Station

Harewood Av

A41 GLOUCESTER

Clinic

Taunton Pl

Taunton Rd

Boston Pl

Ivor Street

Dorset Cl

Melcombe Pl

Marylebone Station

Clinic Ru

Sch

Dorset

A   **B**   **8** 5 27   **C**   **D** 2   **E**

MAIDA VALE

EDGWARE ROAD

A5

Church St

Hall Place

Adpar St

Ashmill St

PO

Penfold St

Lisson St

Ranston St

Coxwell

Rossmore Rd

The Landmark Hotel

Hospital & Counselling Centre

MARYLEBONE ROAD

Clinic

Paddington Green Primary School

St Mary's Man

Paddington Recreation Ground

City of Westminster College

Princess Louise

Church St

enfold Court

Bell St

Crawford St

Christ Church Bentinck

1 grid square represents 250 metres

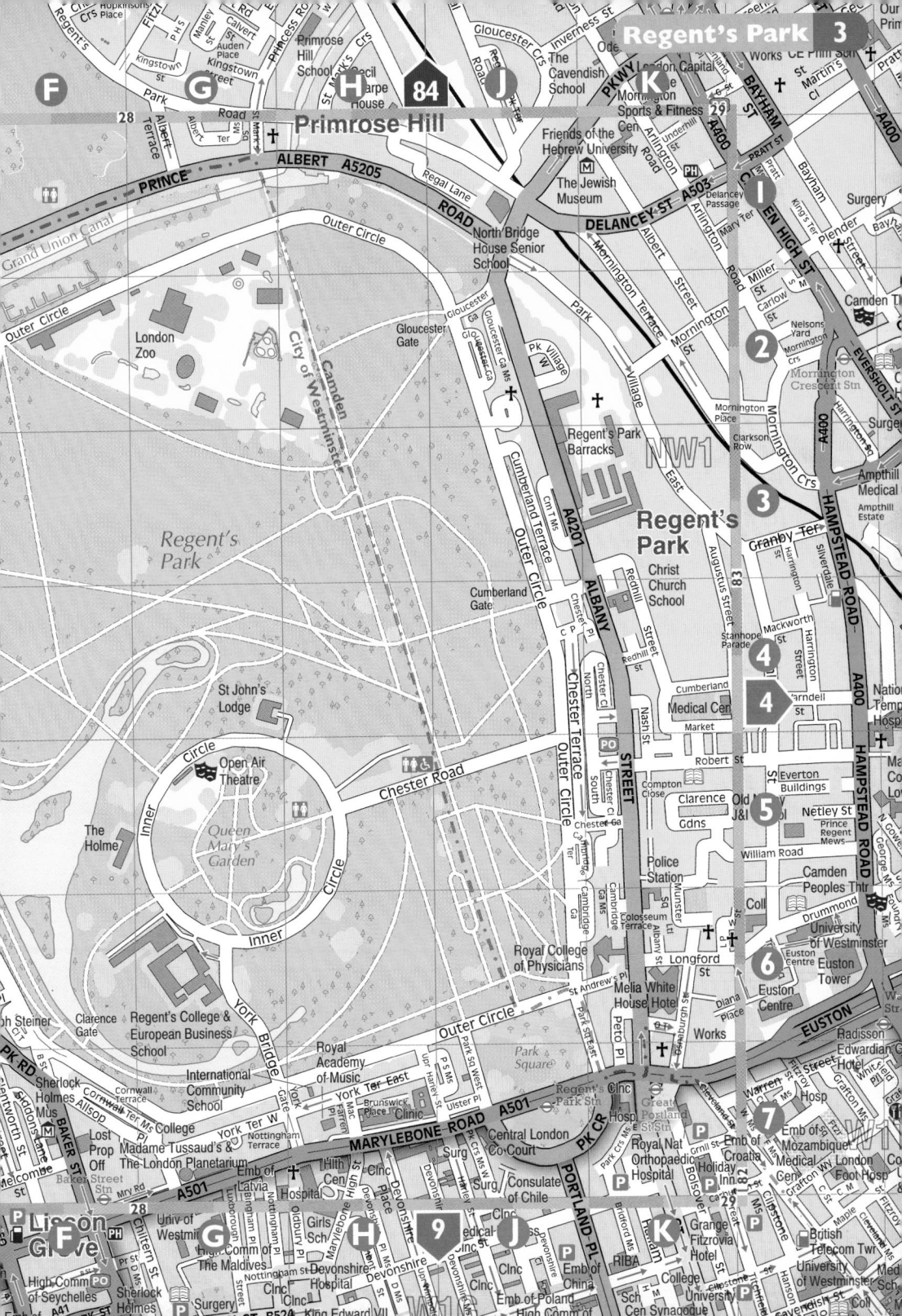

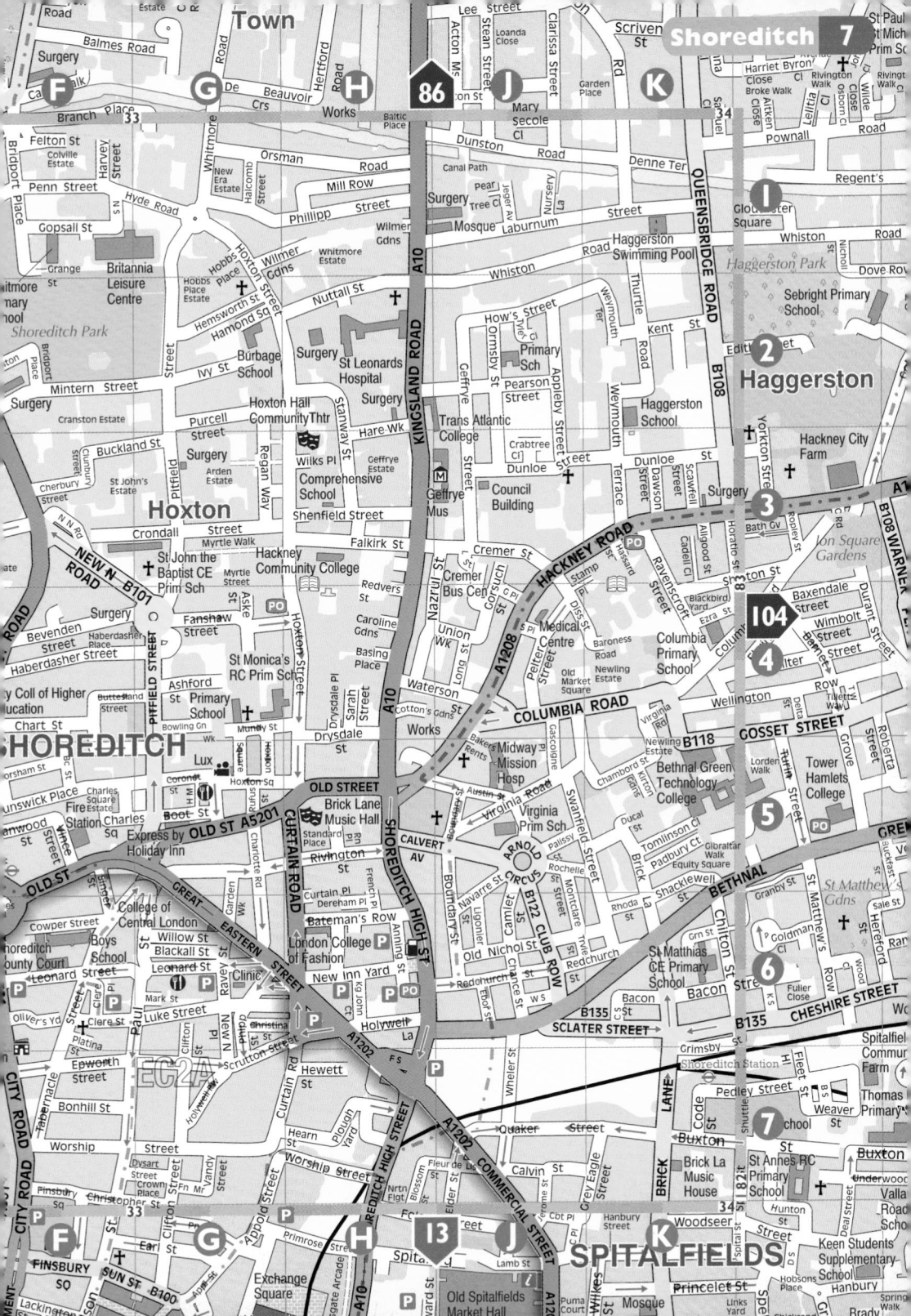

1 grid square represents 250 metres

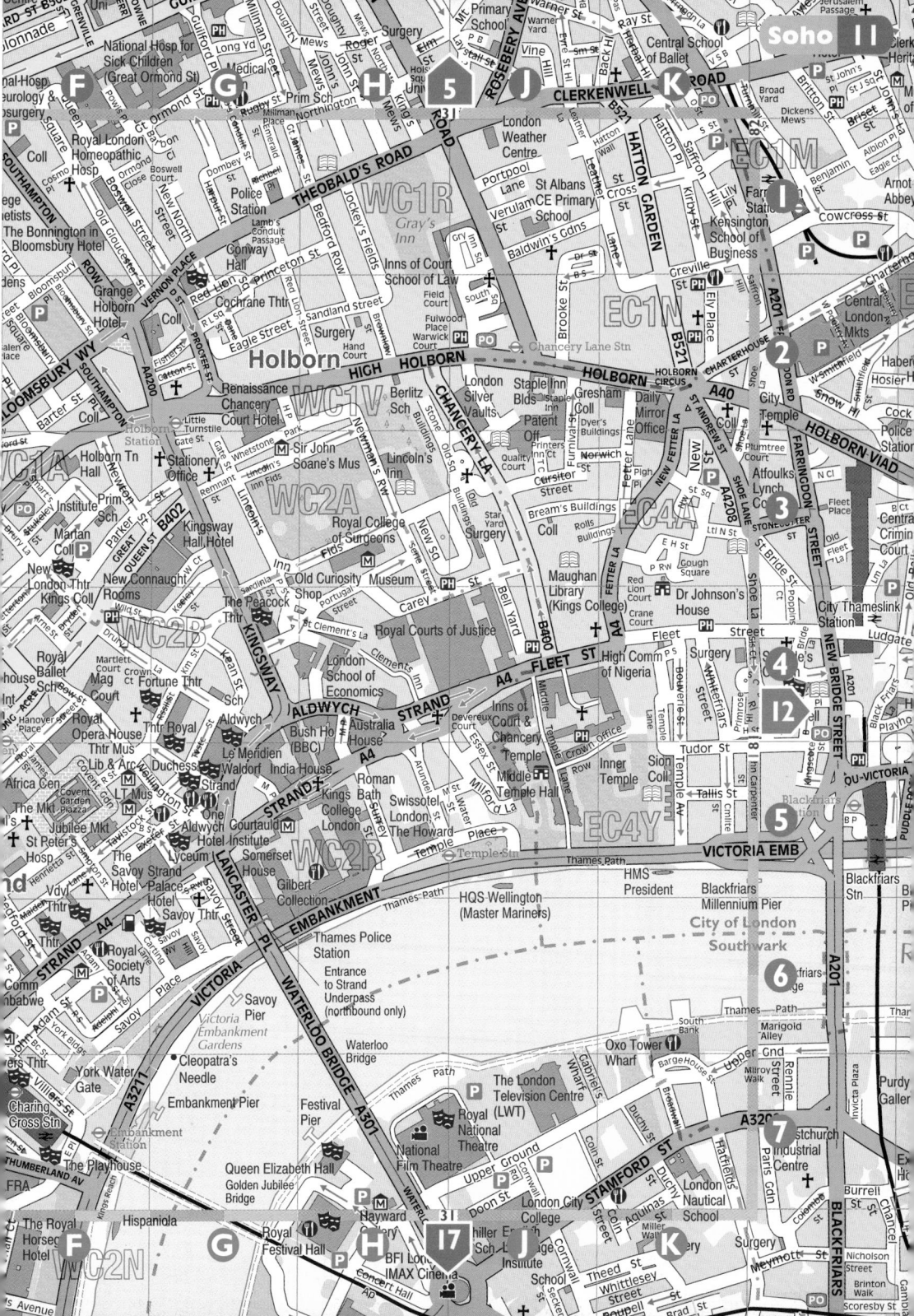

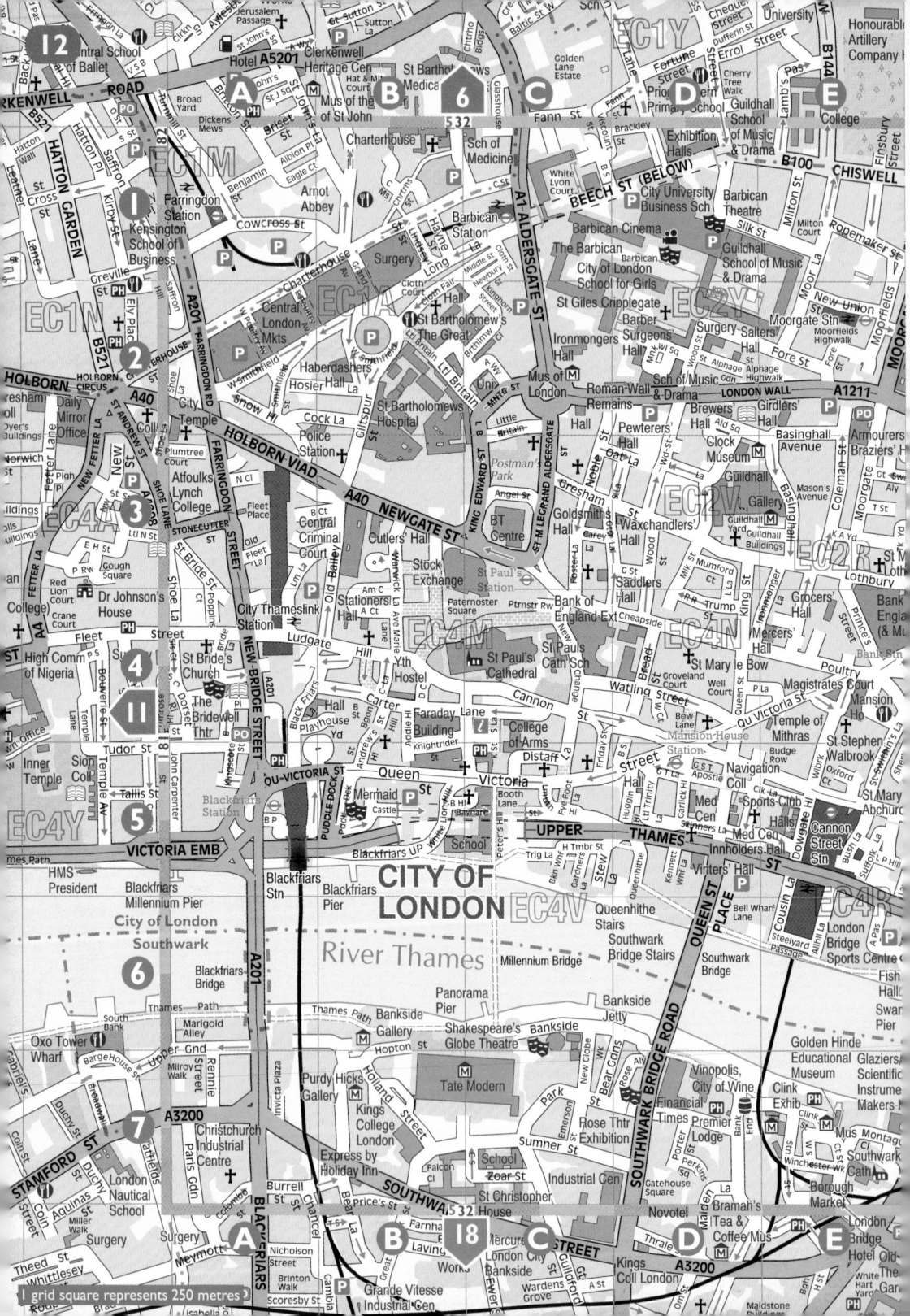

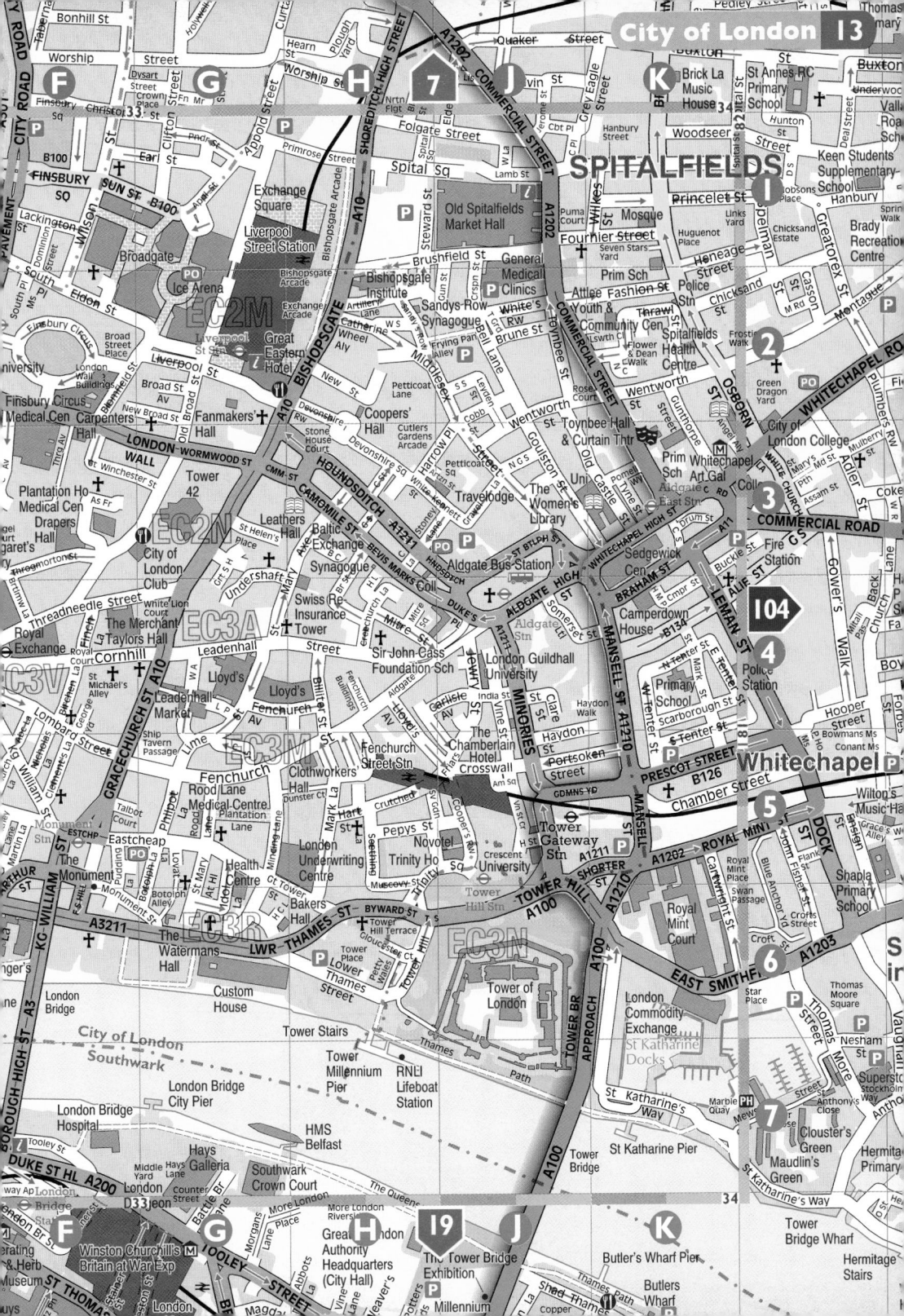

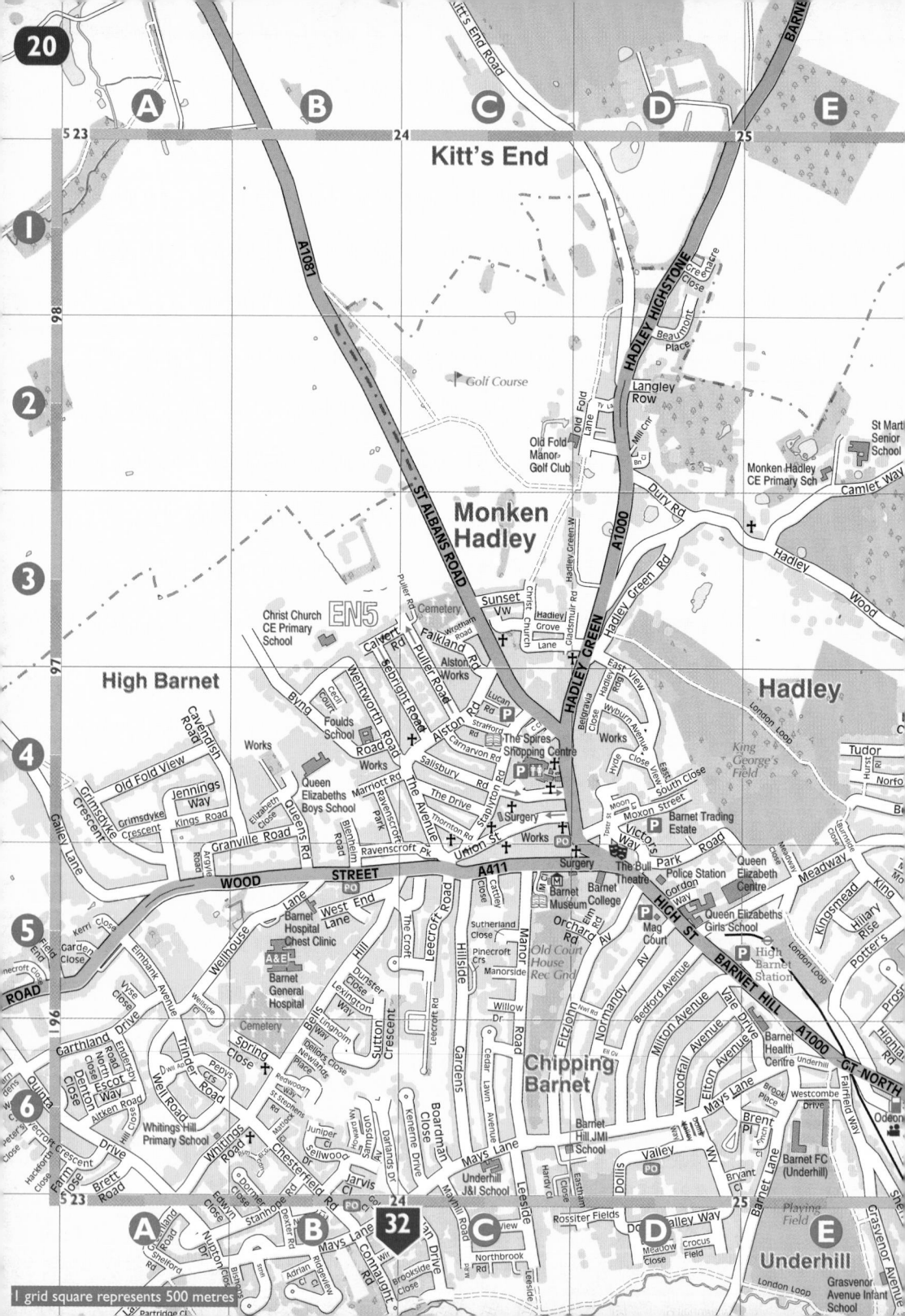

A · B · C · D · E

5 28 · 29 · 30 · A1005

London Loop · Th

I

London Loop

Hill

Hadley Road

Park Farm

Hadley

98

2

London Loop

3

University of Middlesex

21

COCKFOS

Trent Country Park

Snakes Lane

Snakes Lane

4

Golf Course

ROAD

Cockfosters Sports Ground

Trent Park Cemetery

Southgate Compton CC Lane

Chalk

Cockfosters Station

ENFIELD ROAD

ENFIELD RD

A110

Lakeside

Greystoke Gdns

Lowther Drive

5

Belmont Close

PO

A111

School

easant

Mount Close

Galway

Close

Surgery

Norfolk Close

West Close

Ridge

East Close

Bramley Close

PO

South Lodge Drive

Lonsdale

Lonsdale Drive

Grosvenor Gdns

Netherby

Culgaith Gardens

Merryhills Drive

Clifton Gardens

Longdale

Branton Gdns

Curthwaite Gdns

Brantwood Gardens

Longdale Drive

Nor

Trent Park Golf Club

Westpole

Avenue

Oakwood Station

Prince

Carlton Av

South Lodge Drive

Penni

Ch.

Road

96

on Court

Avenue

Preston Gardens

Leys Gdns

Gloucester Gardens

Kent Drive

Southgate School

Sussex Way

Oakwood Medical Cen

Harper Cl

Gerrards

Stafford Cl

Tregenna Cl

George

Sheringham Av

Lakenheath

Surgery

Merrivale

South Ldg Dr

Overton Road Dr

6

HILL

Museum of Domestic Design & Architecture

A111

Chicken Shed Theatre

De Bohun Primary School

BRAMLEY ROAD

A110

The Poplars

Priory Close

Peake

Reservoir Road

Wolverton Wy Close

Chestnut

The Vineries

Ashmead

Merrivale

South Ldg Dr

Sheringham Avenue

Oakwood

5 28

A · B · **34** · C · D · E

29 · 30

lesey University

CHASE SIDE

Green

The Fairway

Cowper Gardens

De Bo

Saxon Wy

Oakwood Park

1 grid square represents 500 metres

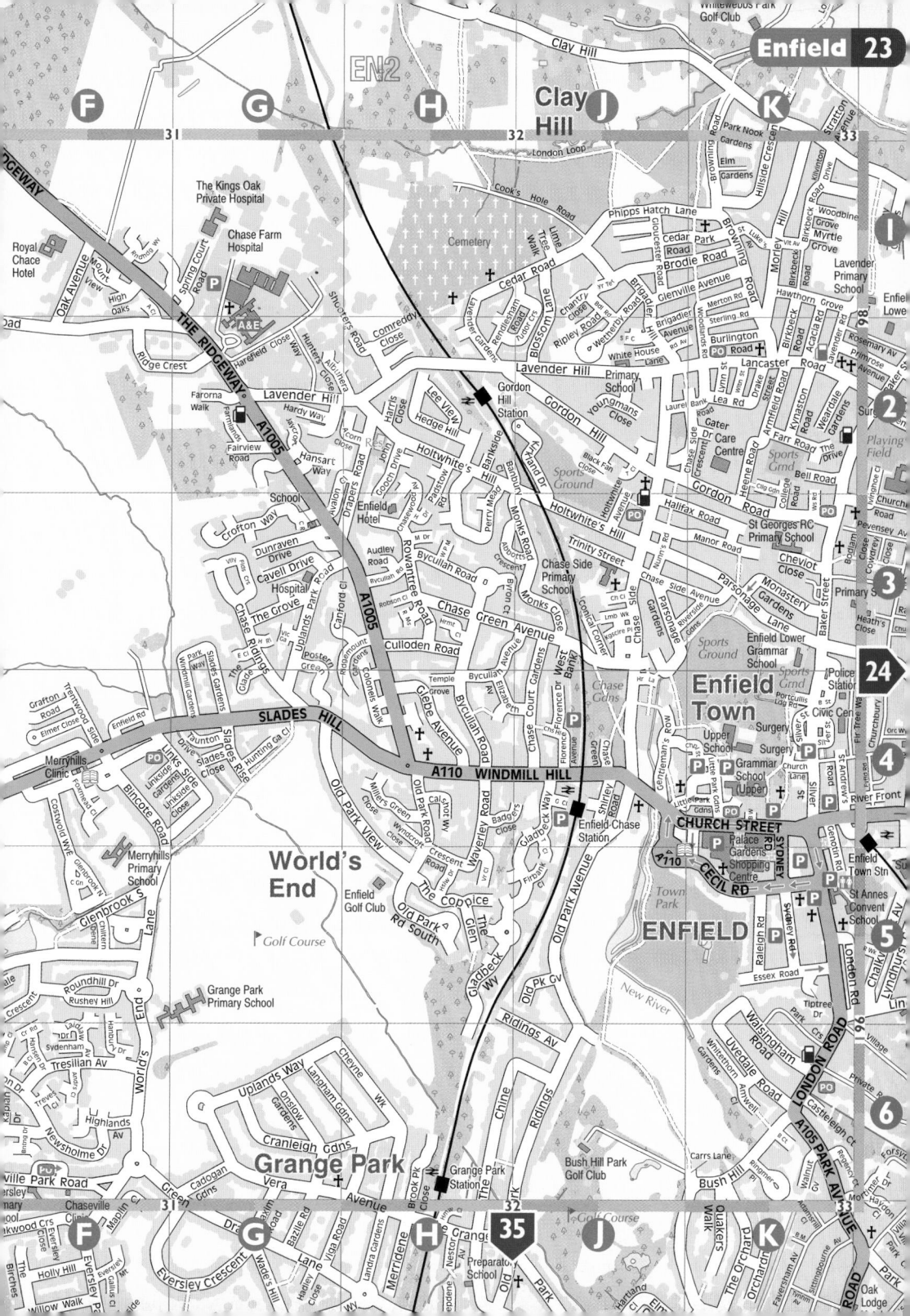

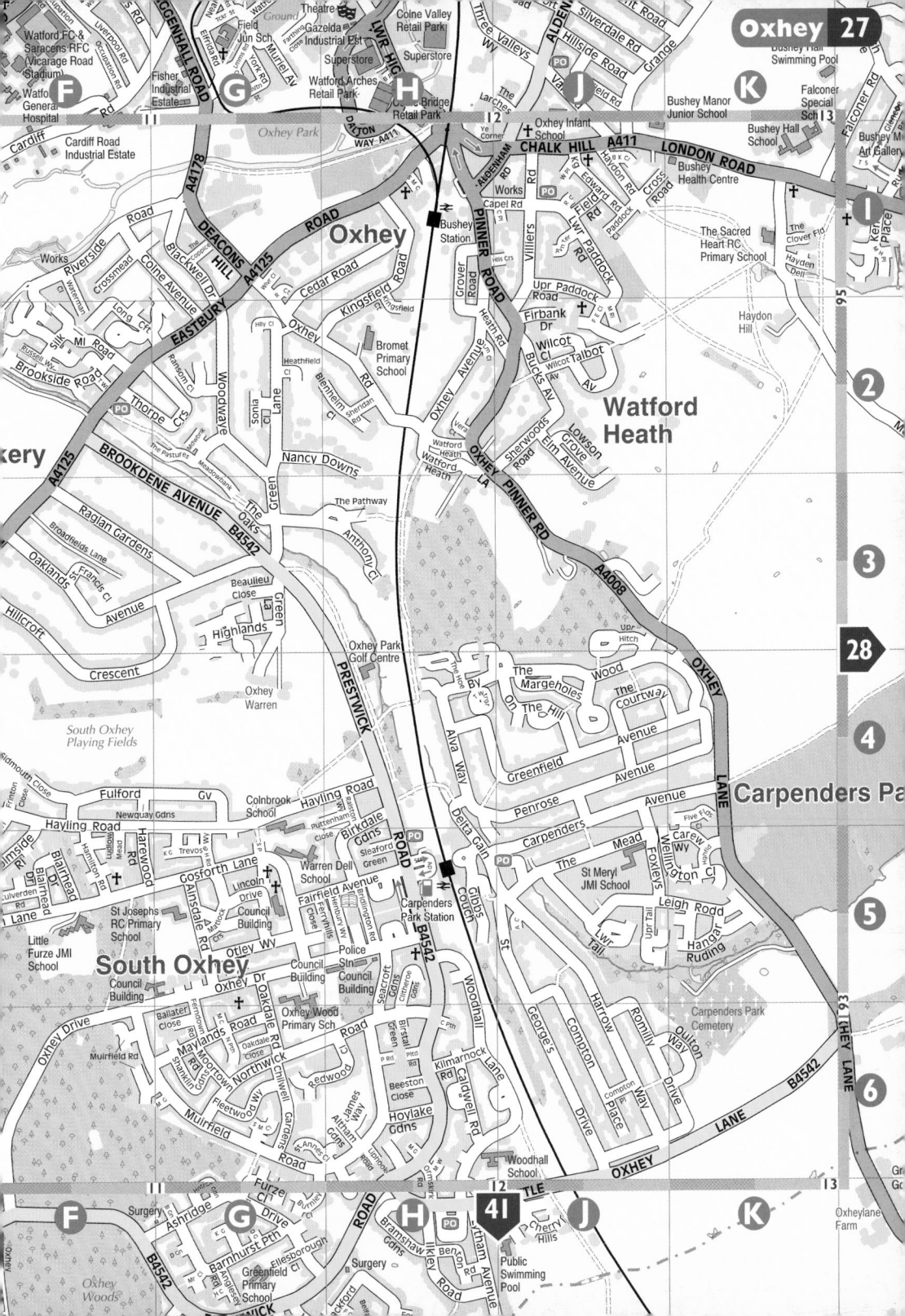

I grid square represents 500 metres

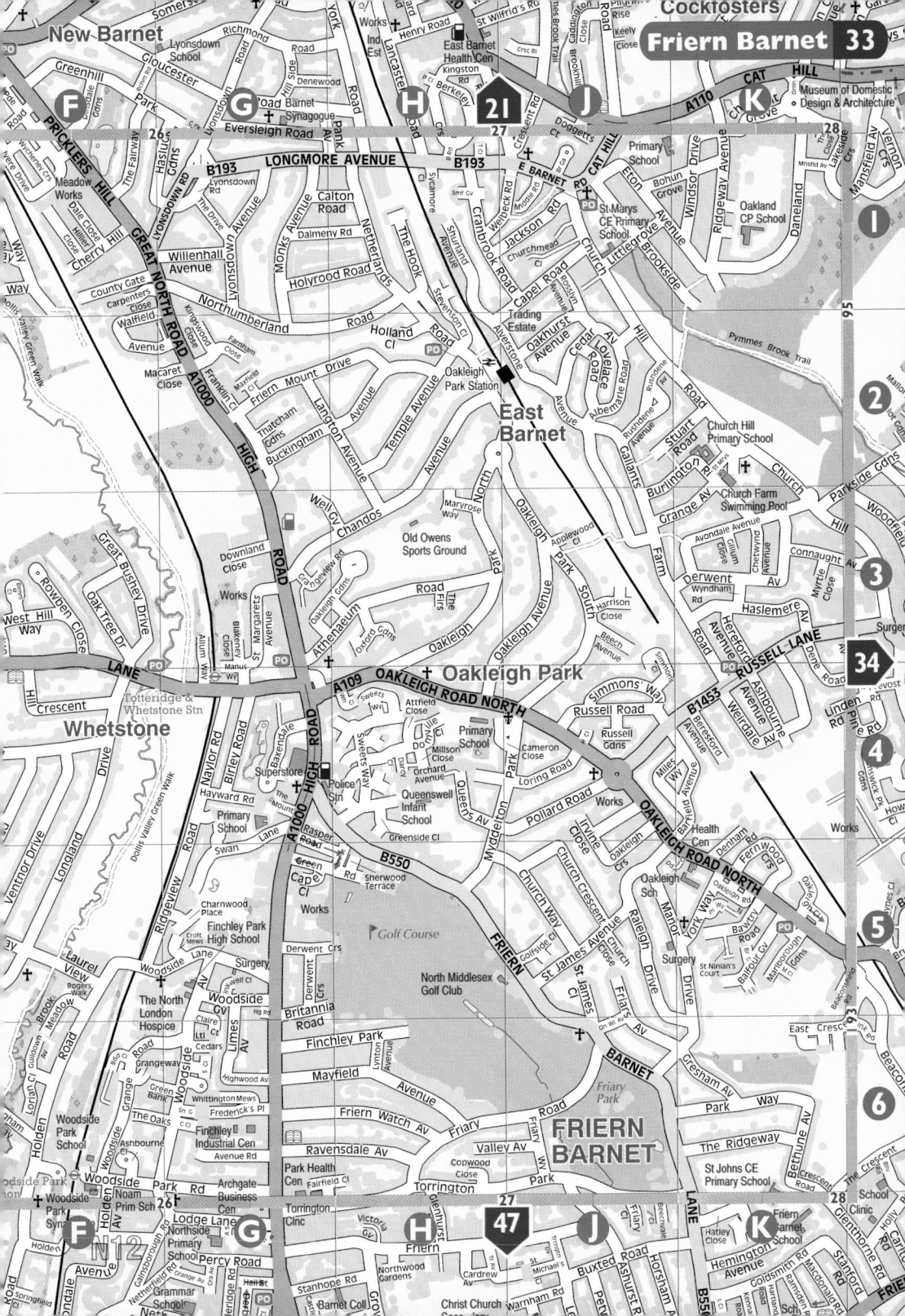

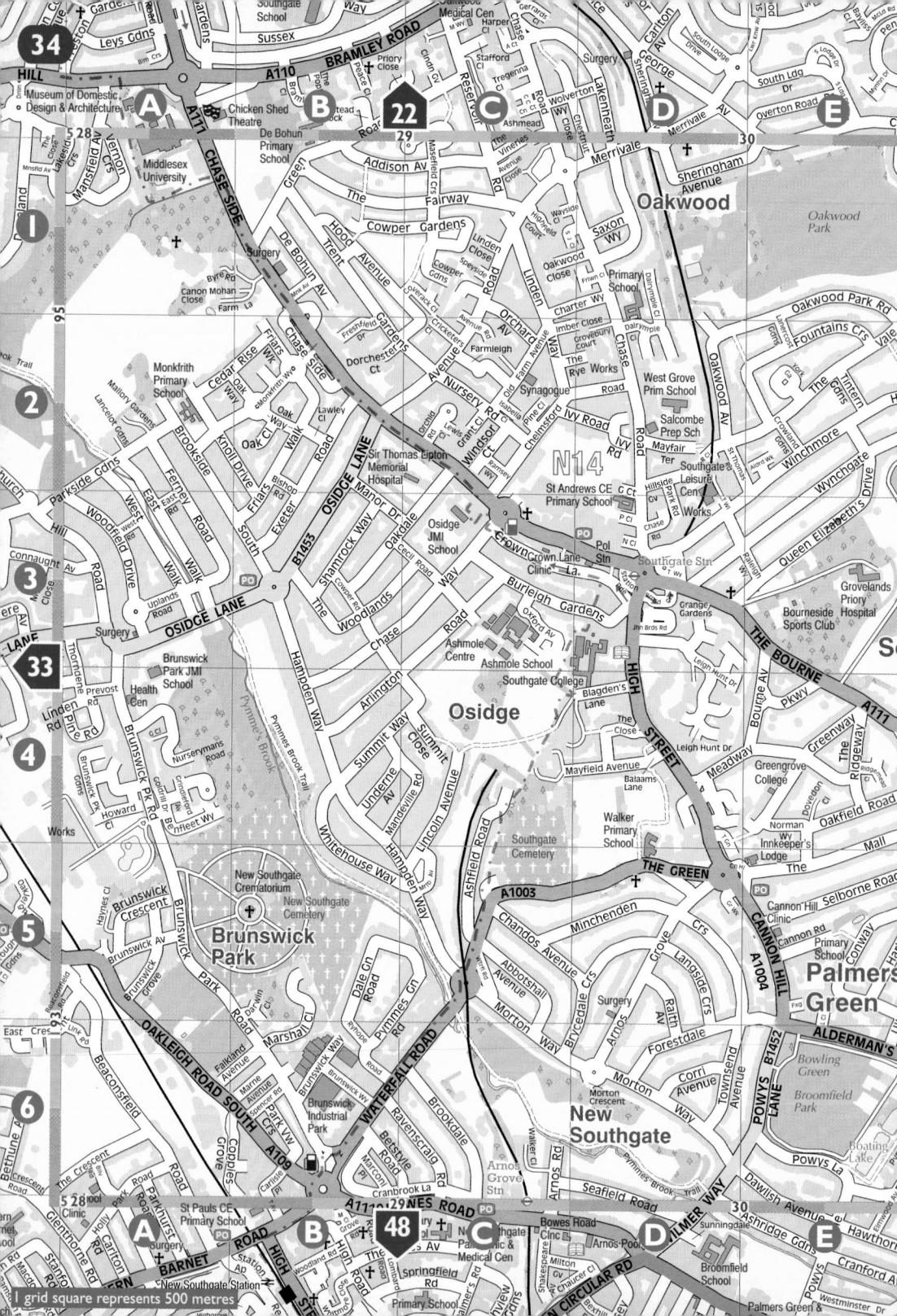

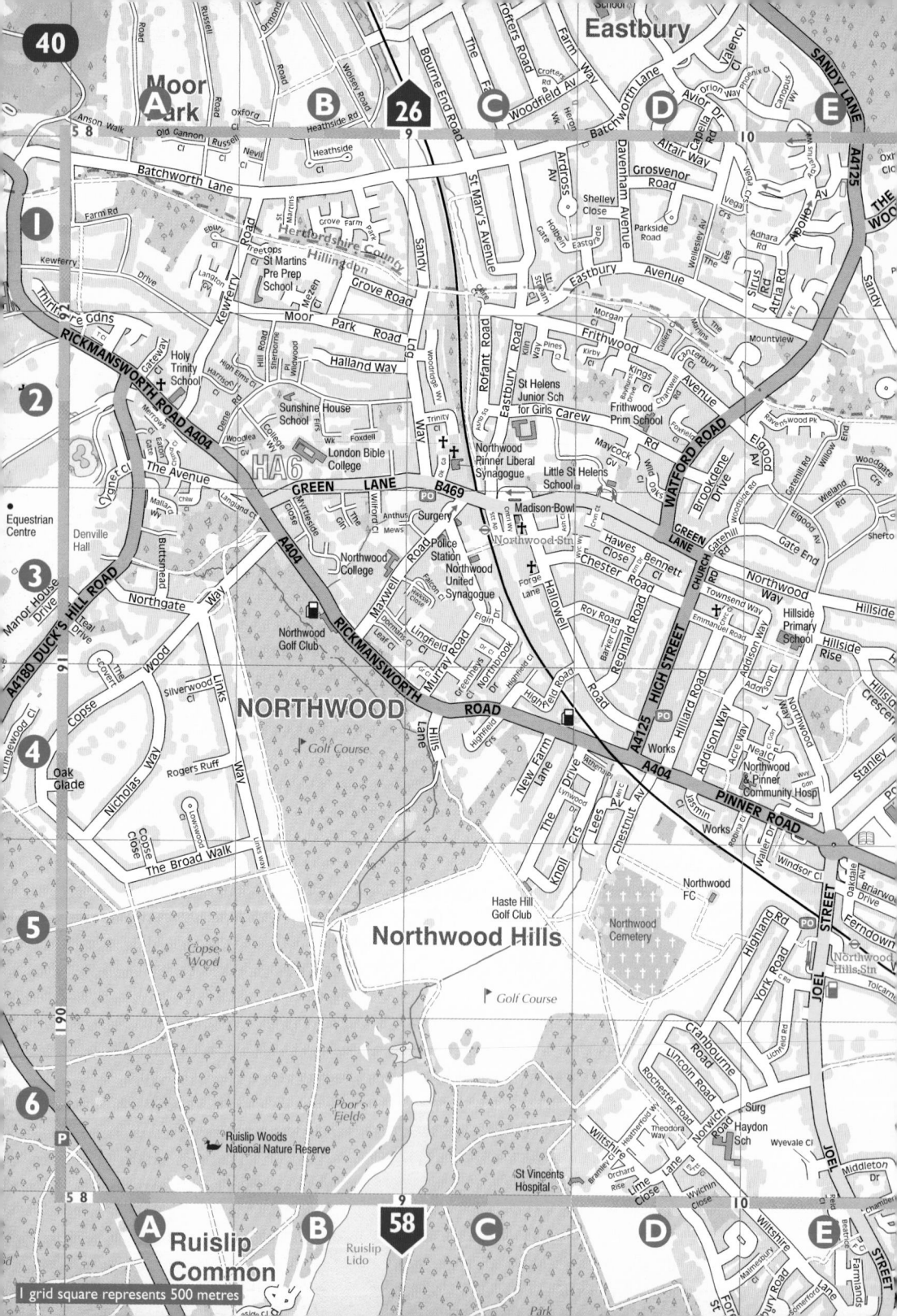

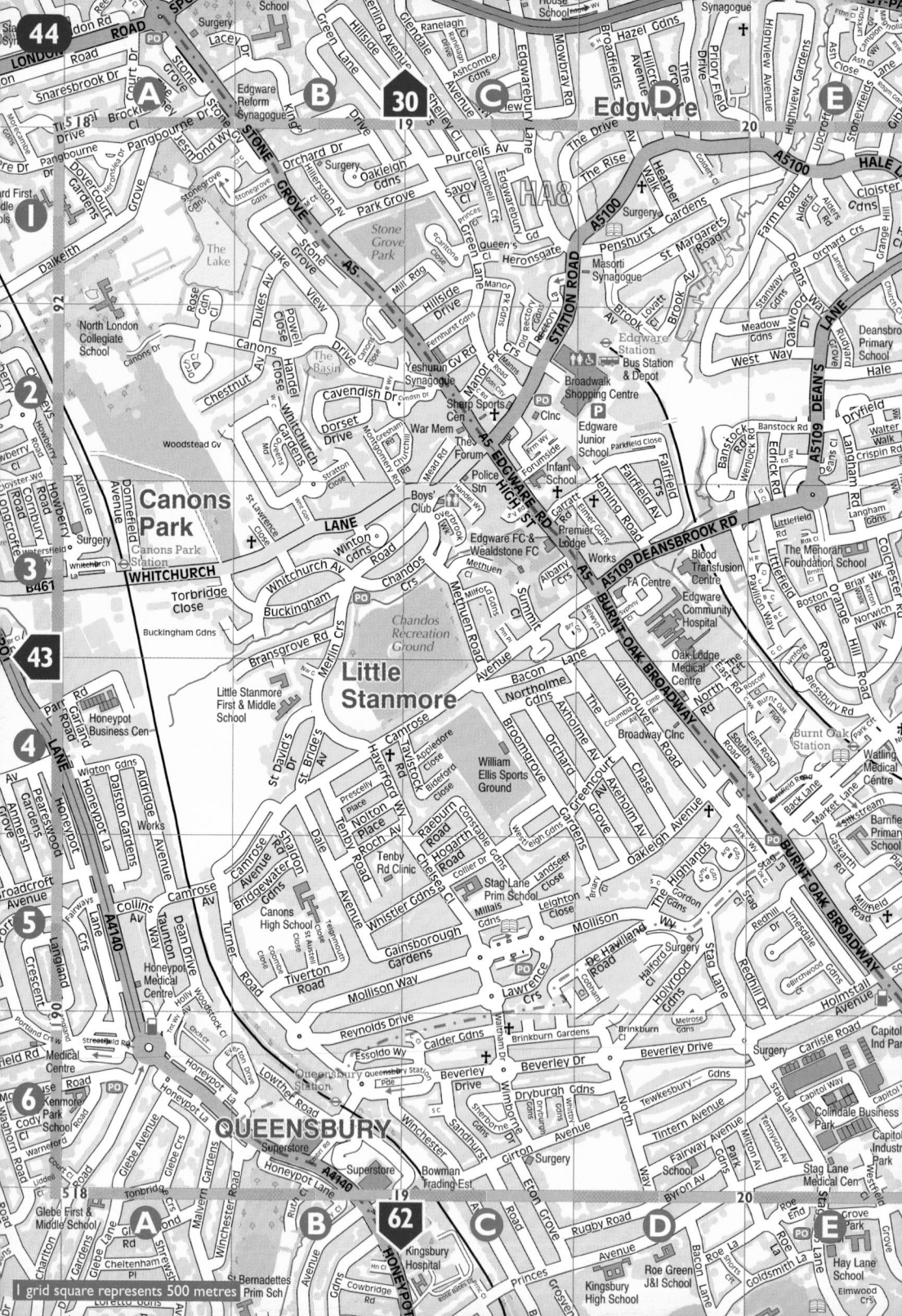

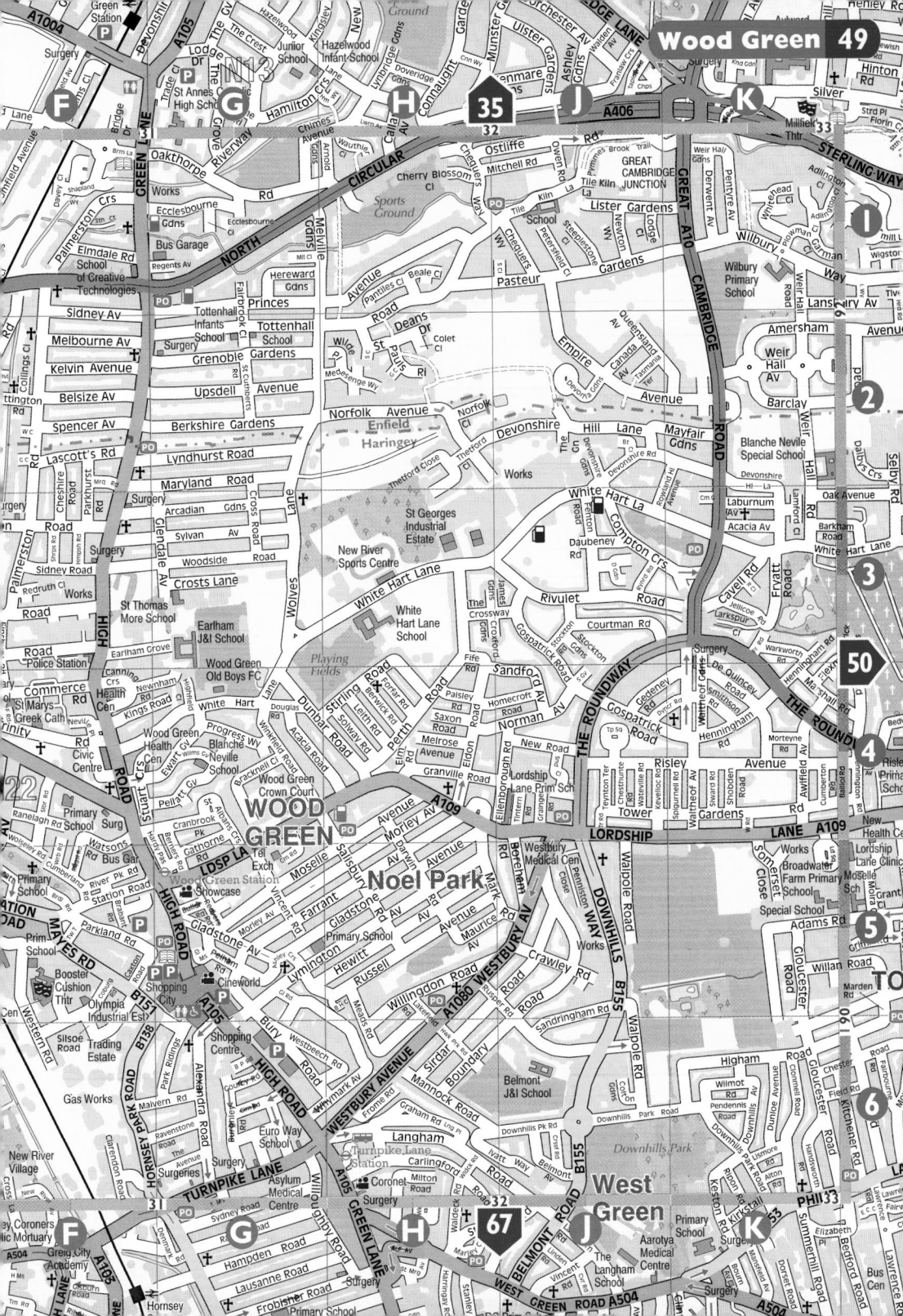

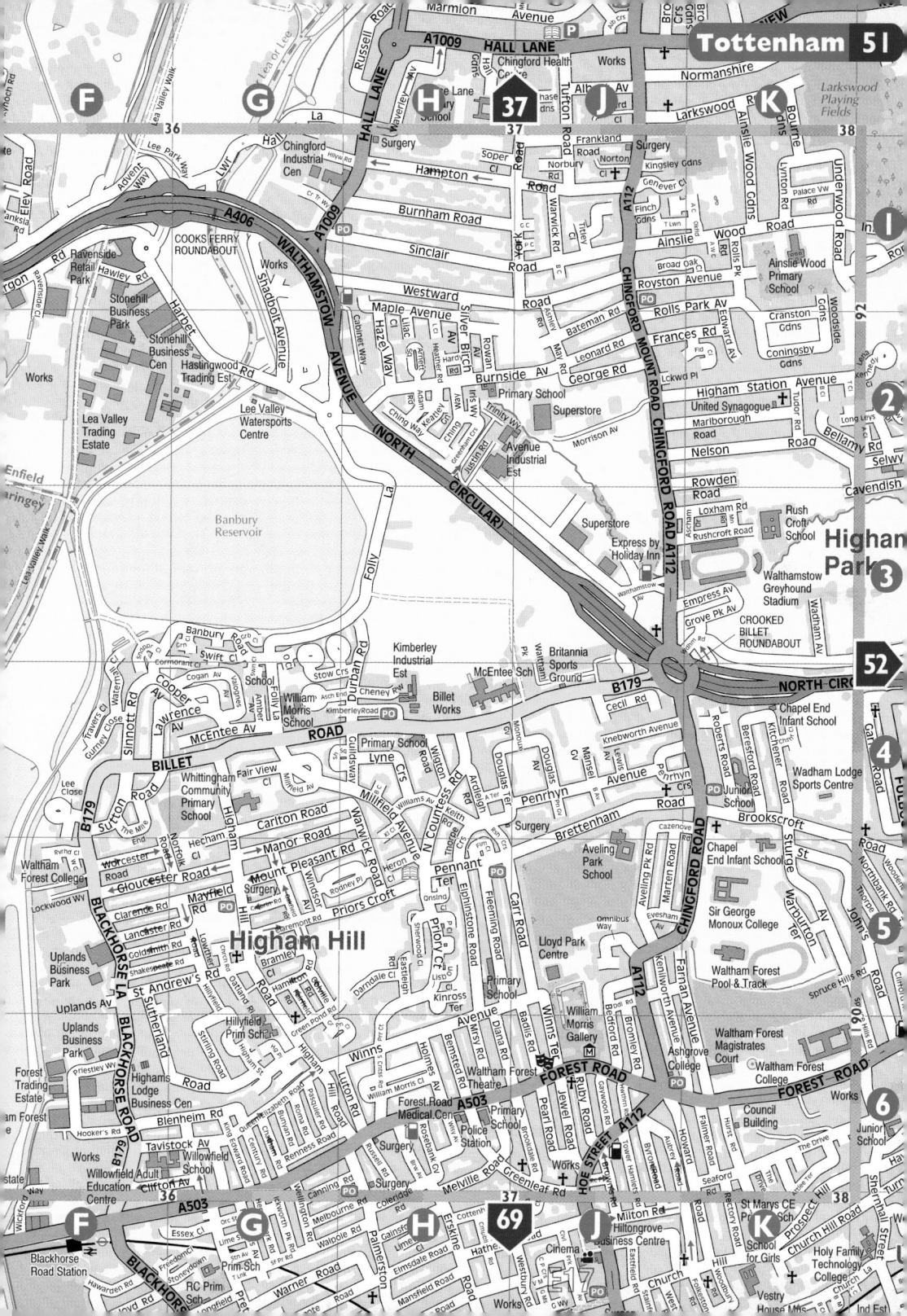

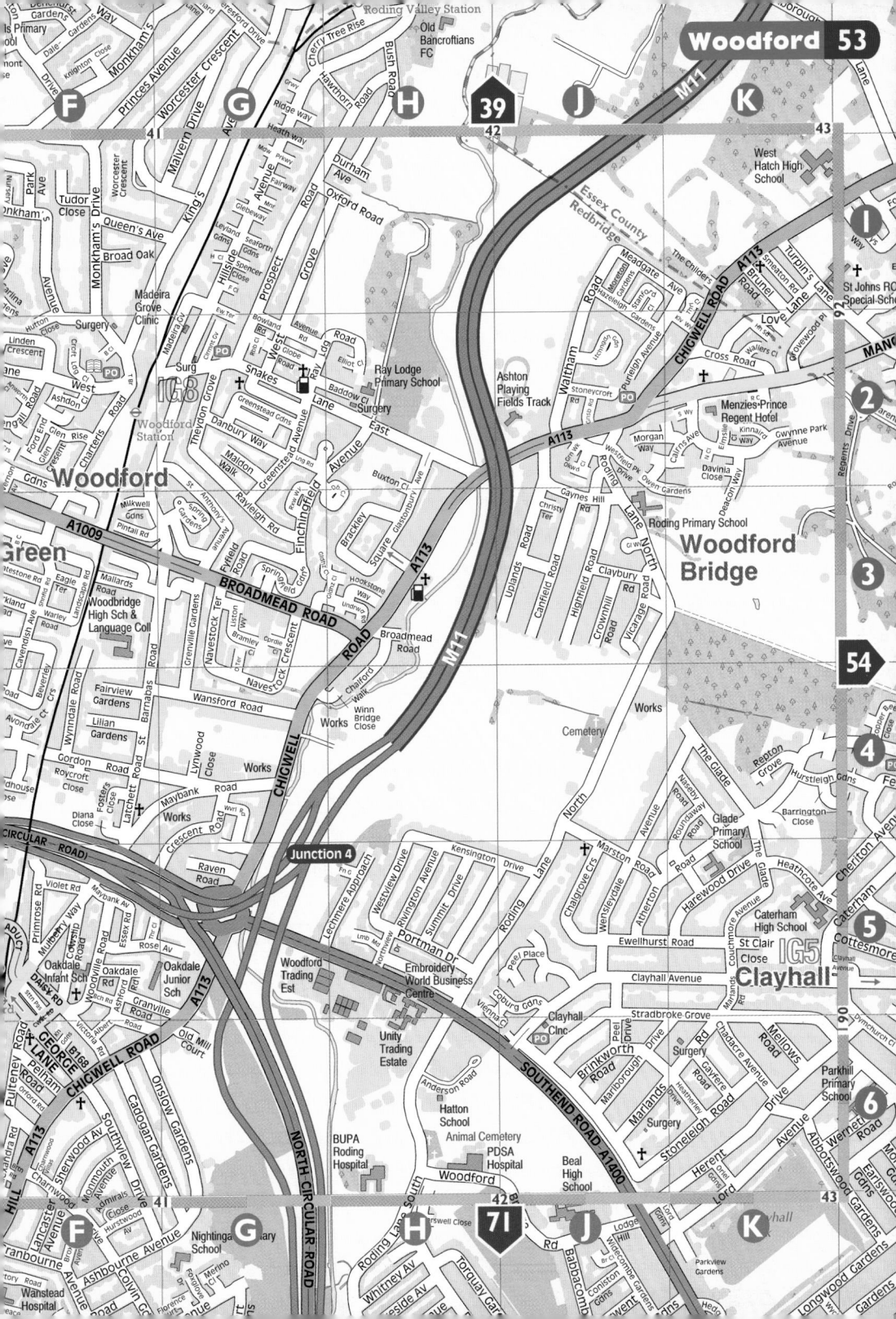

1 grid square represents 500 metres

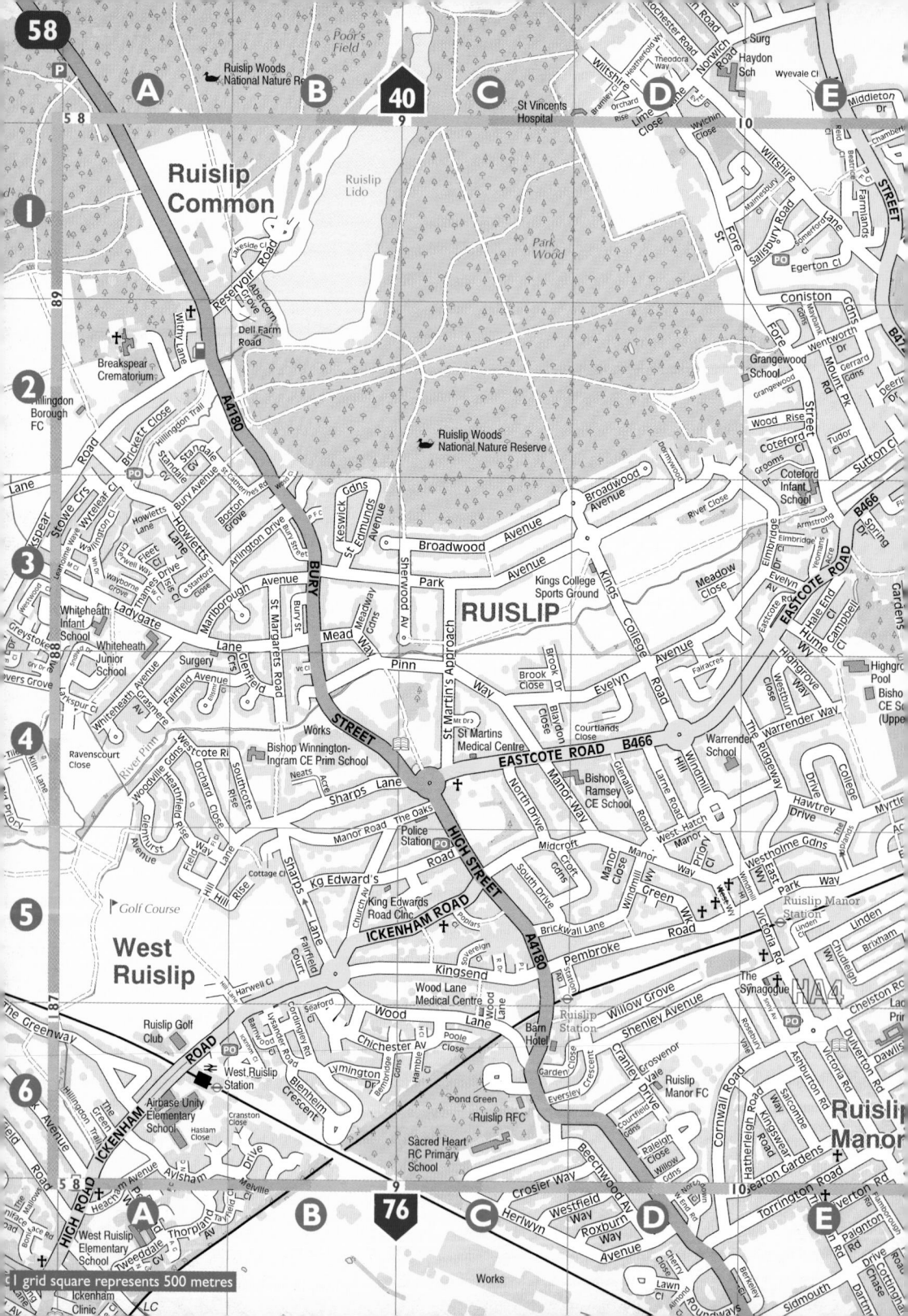

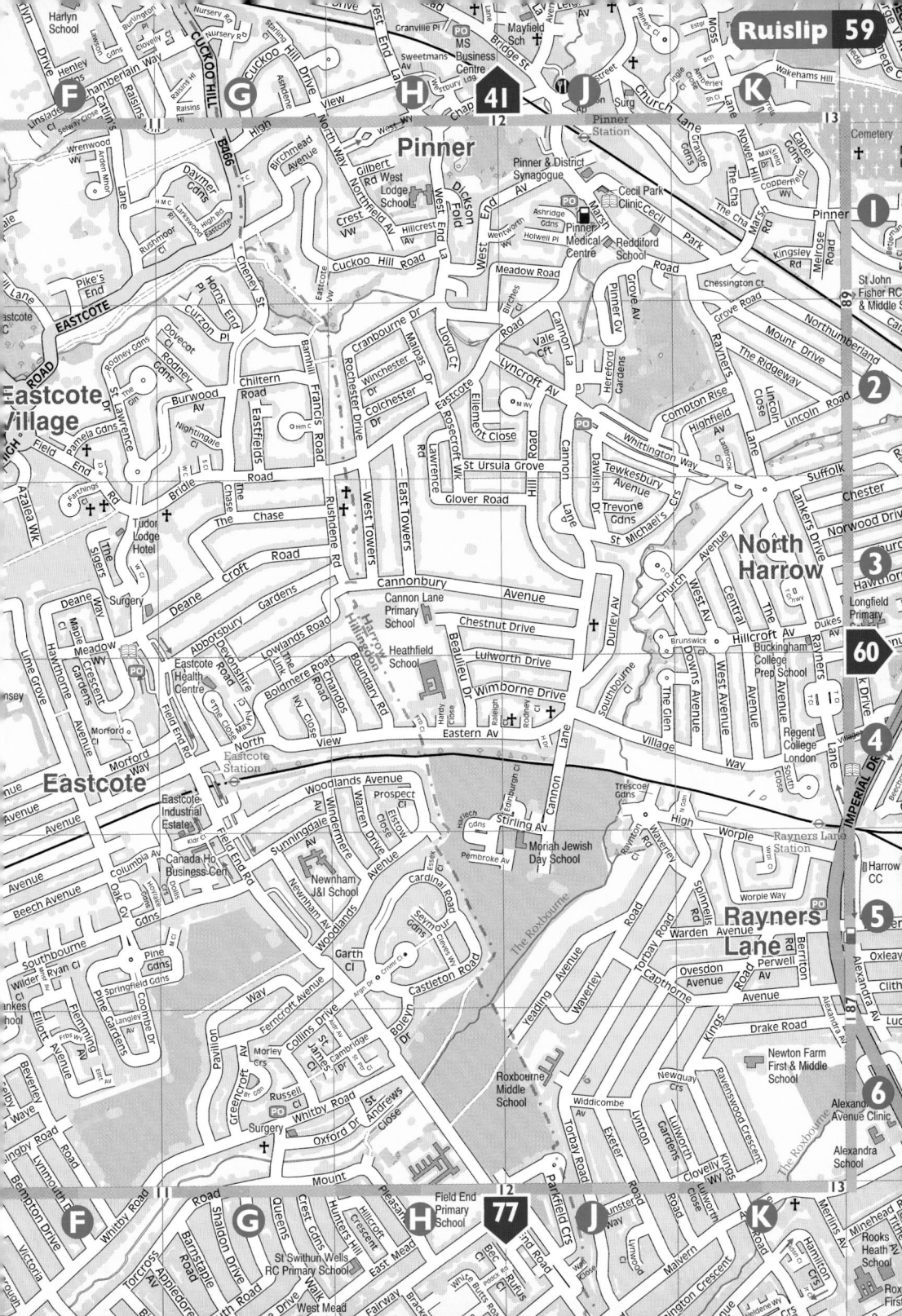

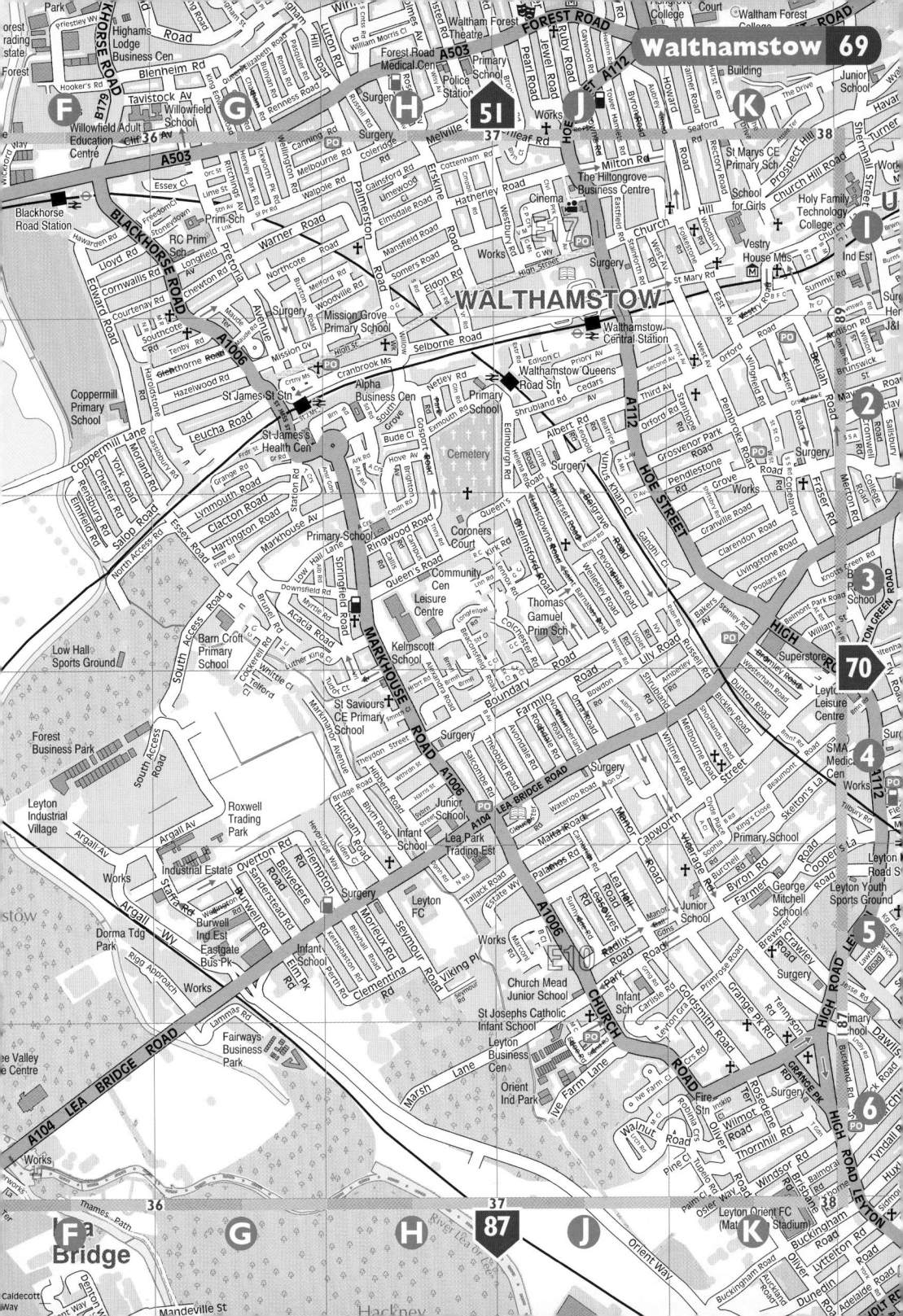

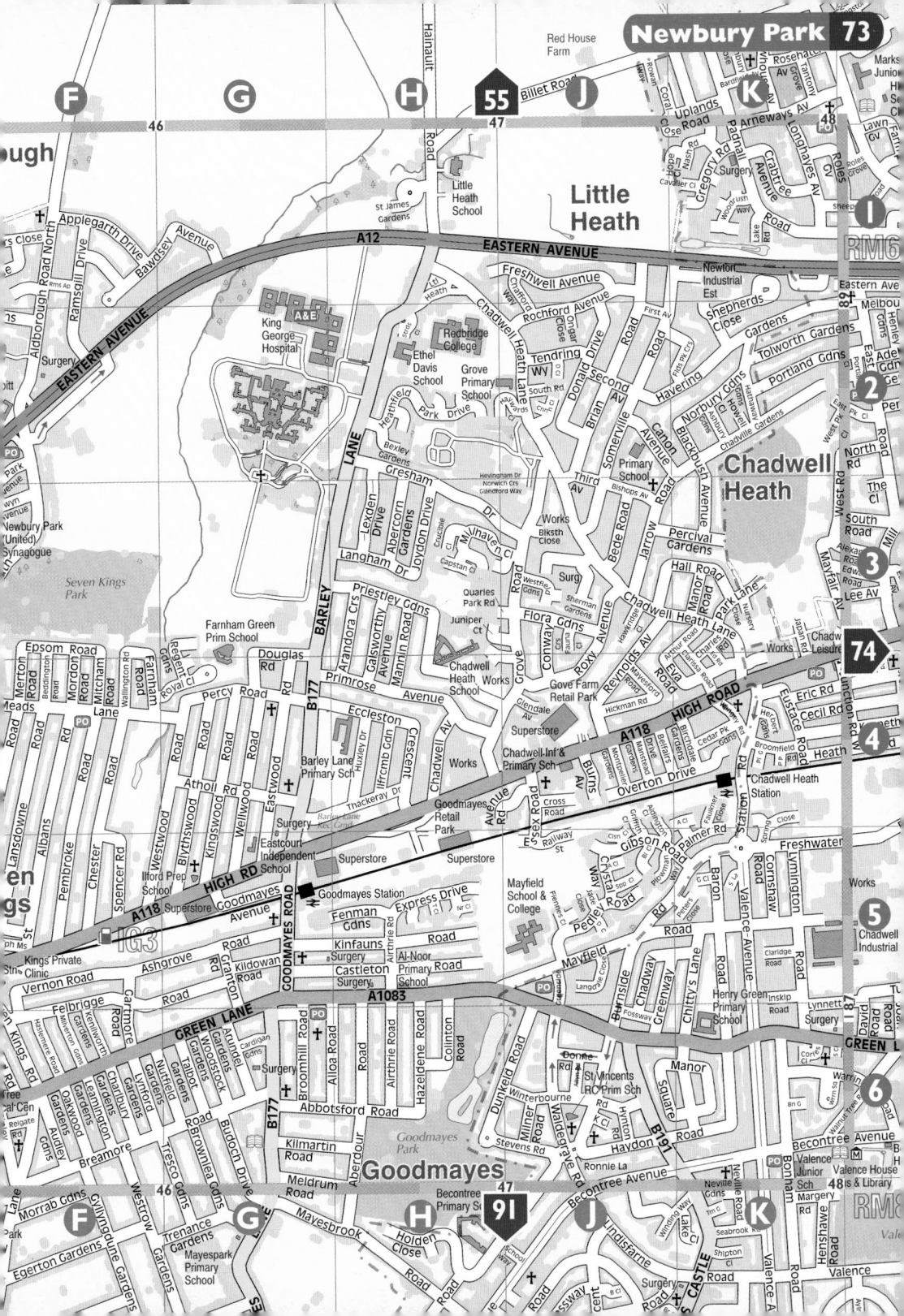

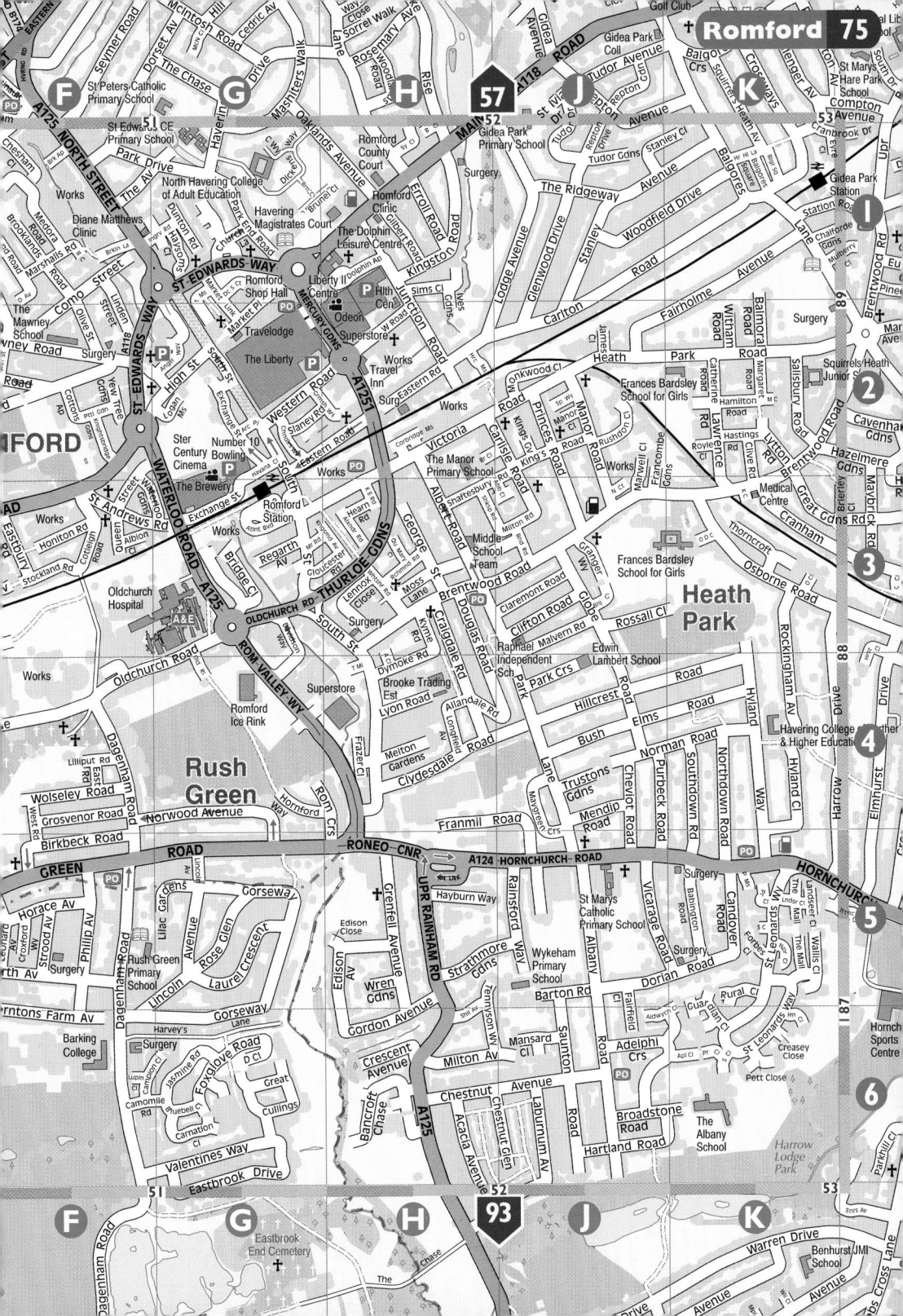

I grid square represents 500 metres

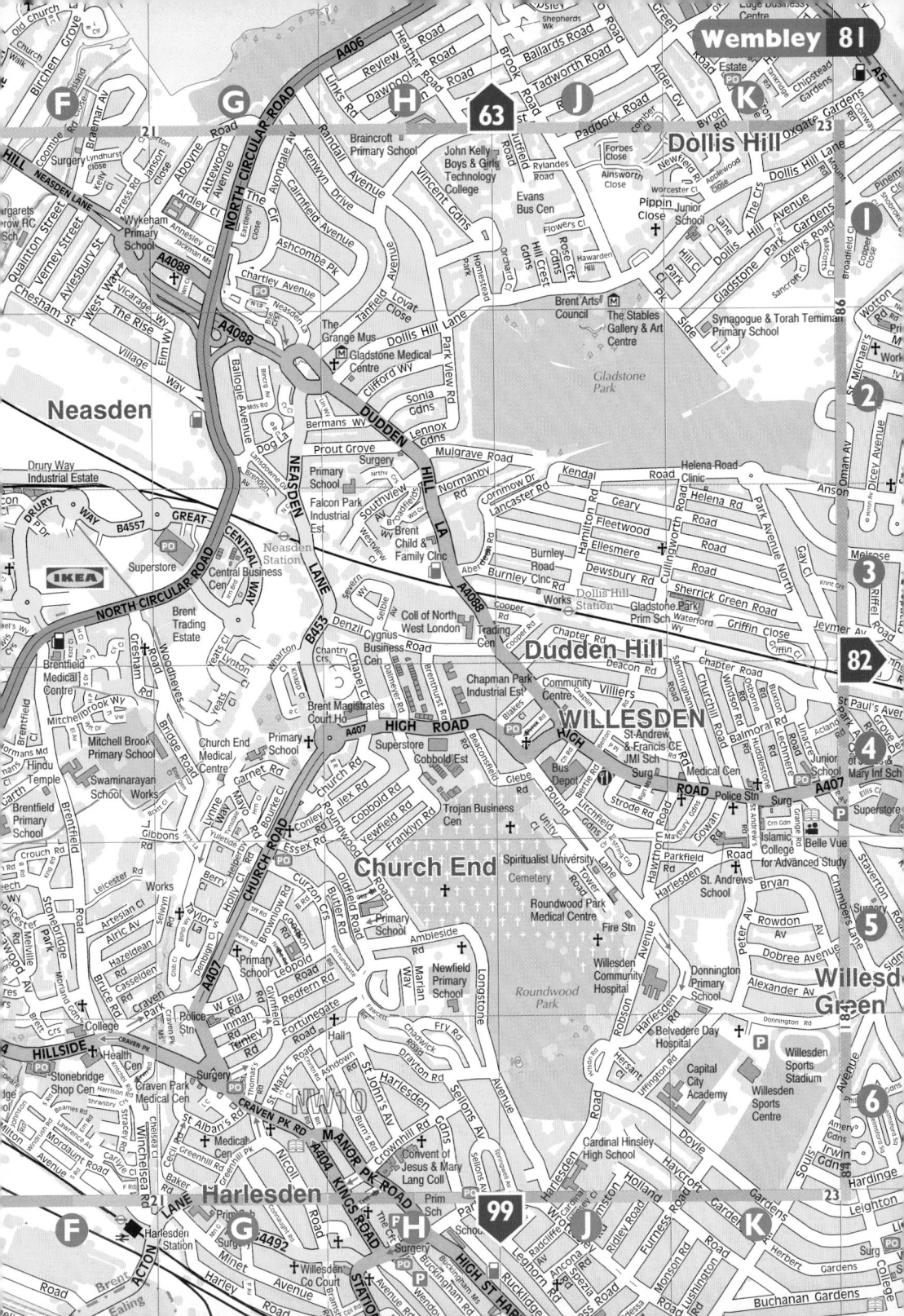

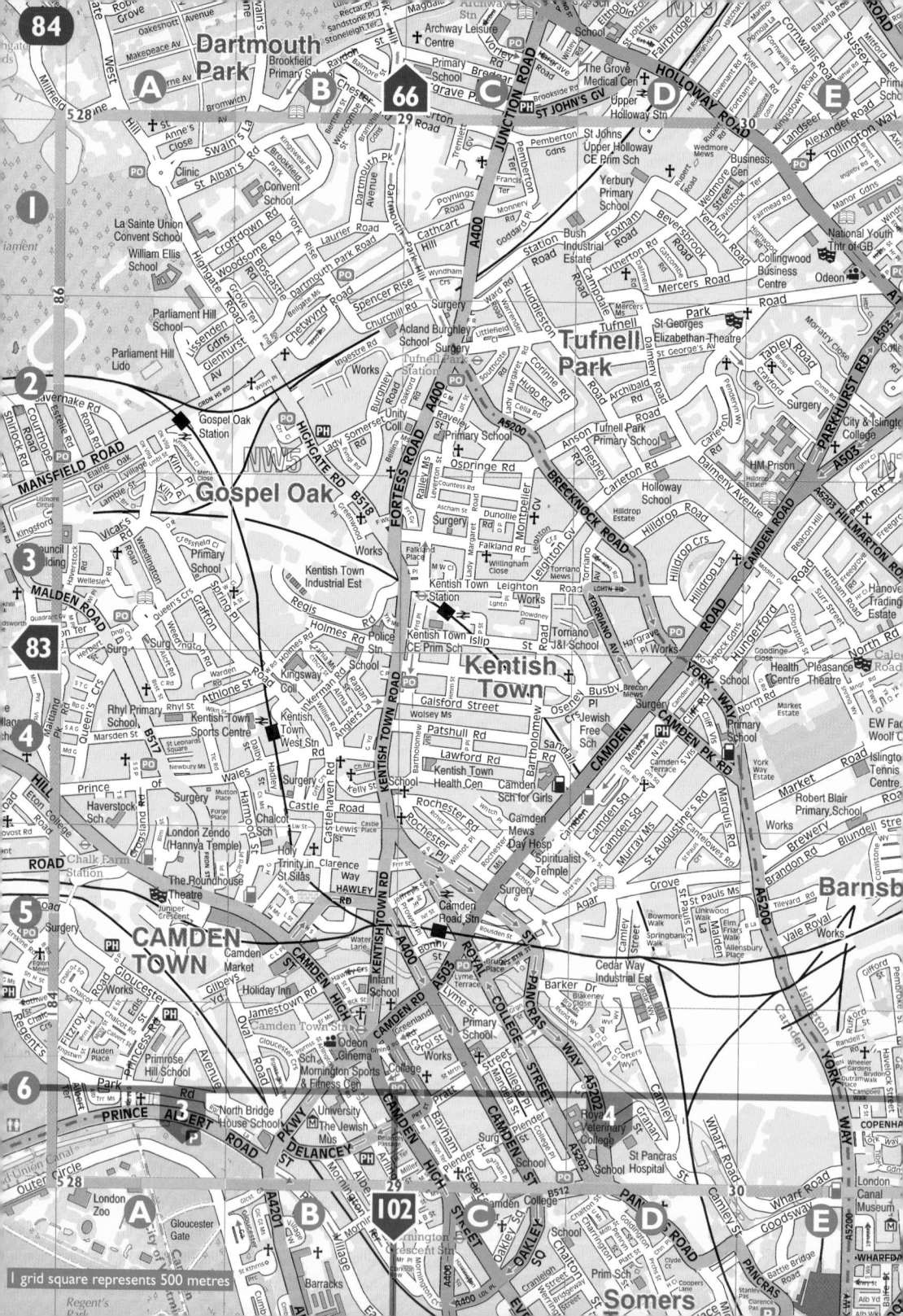

grid square represents 500 metres

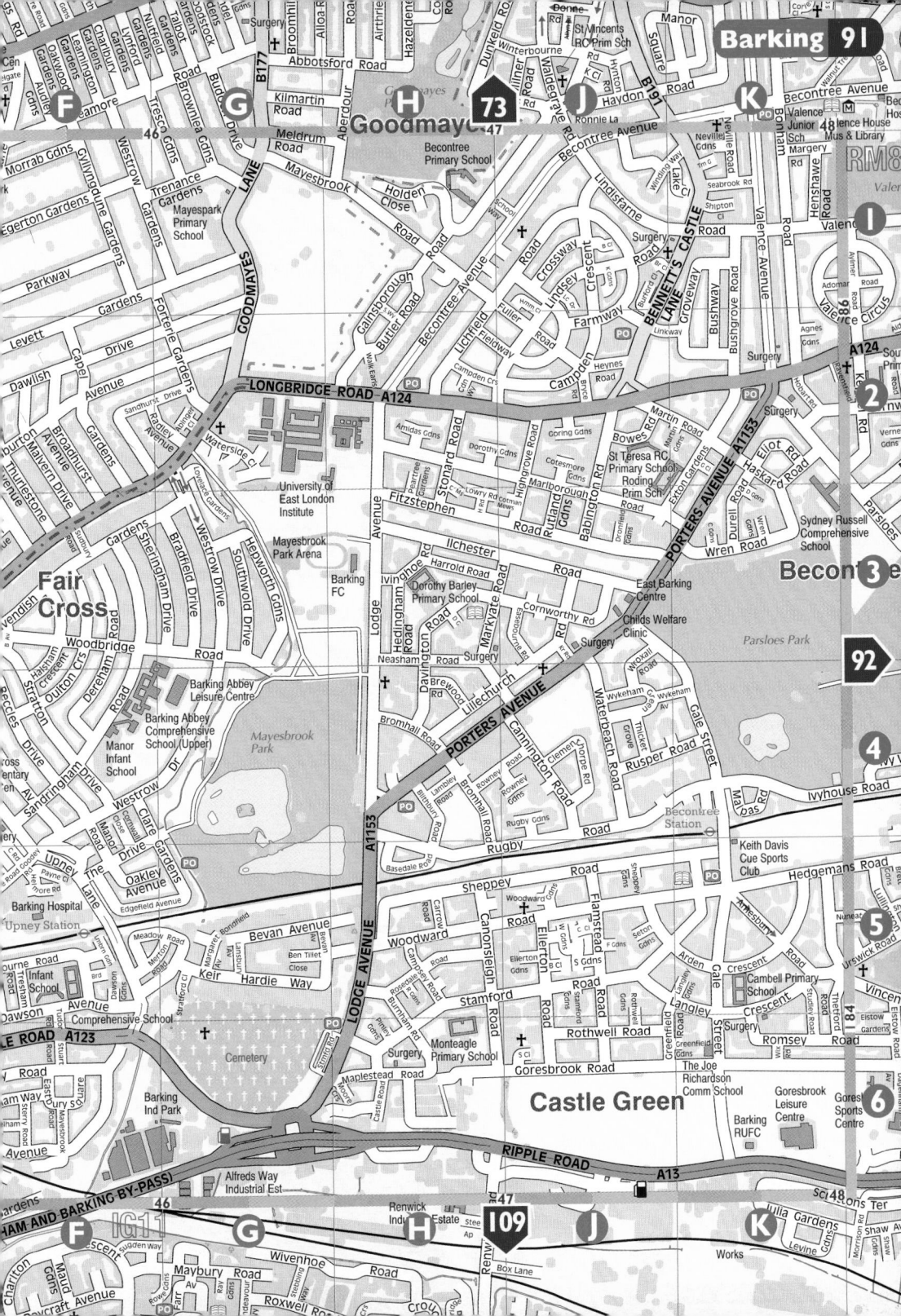

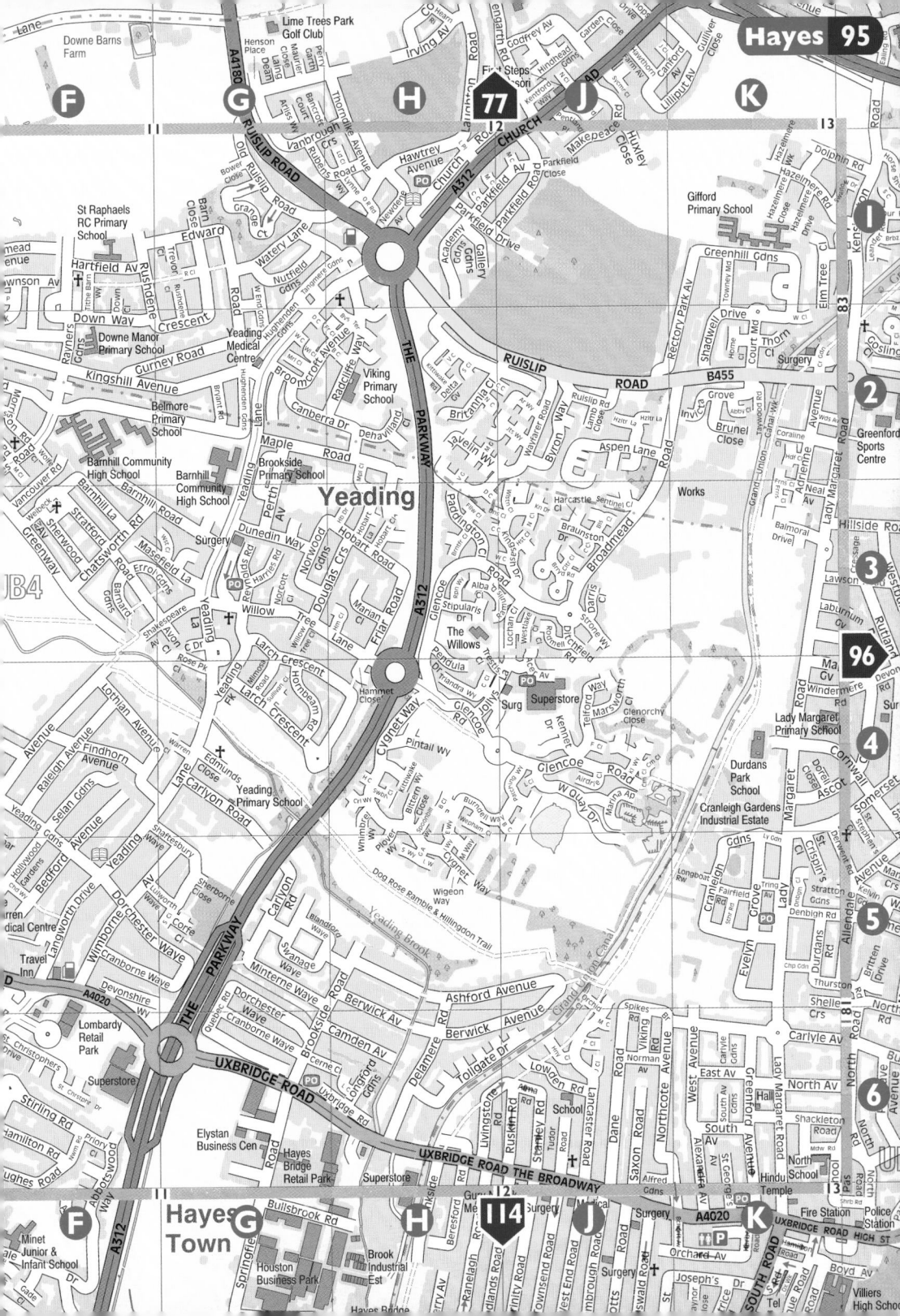

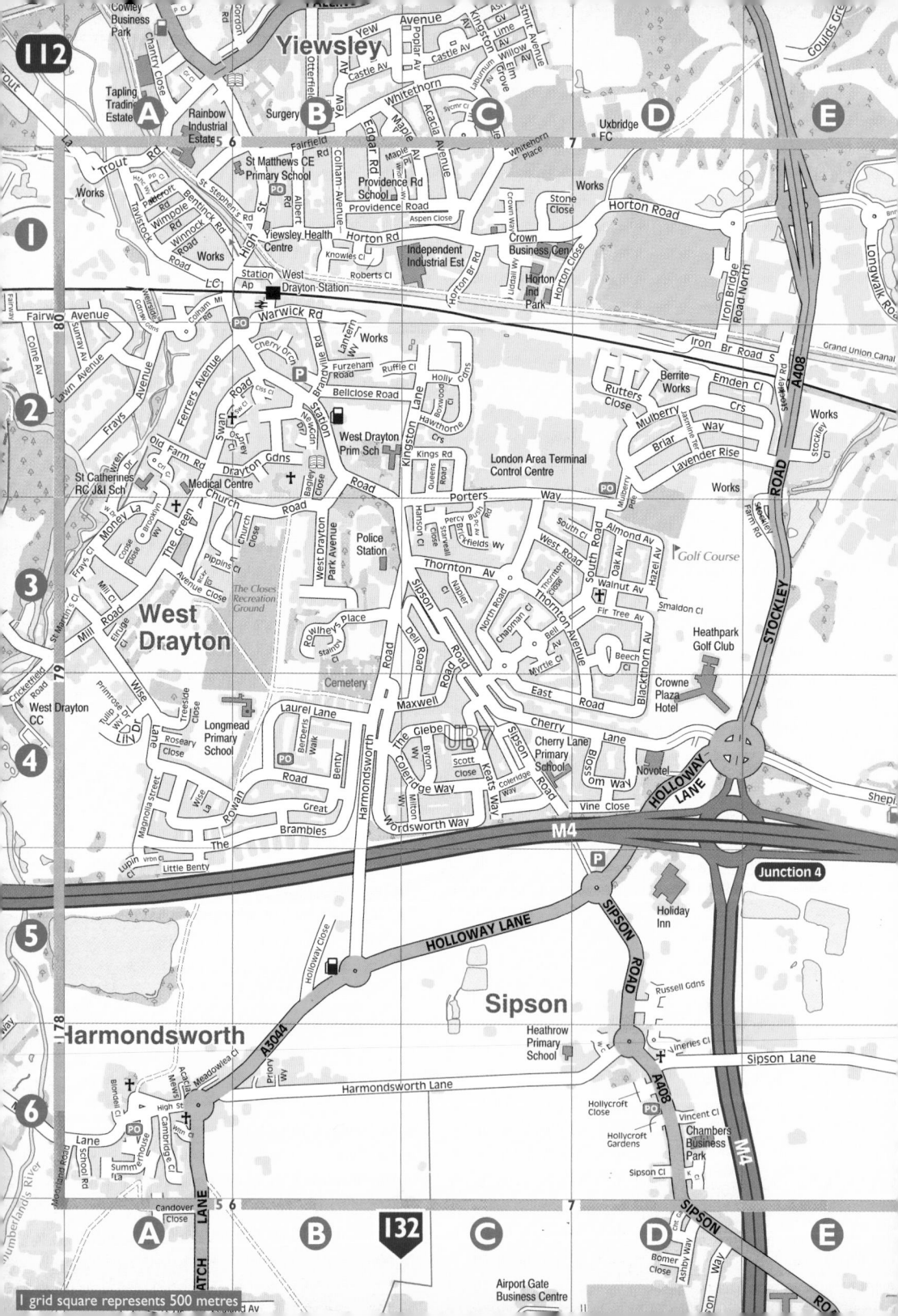

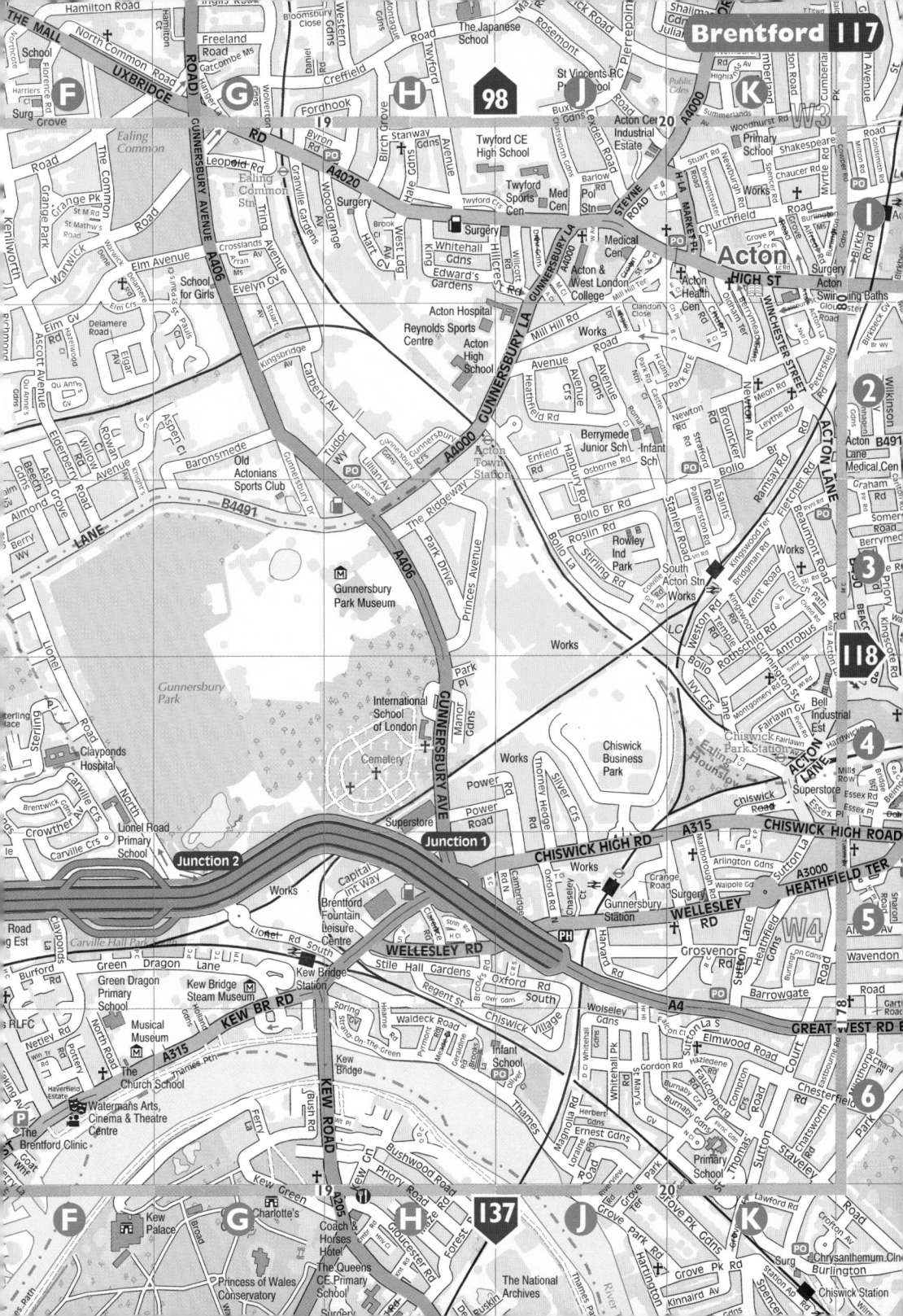

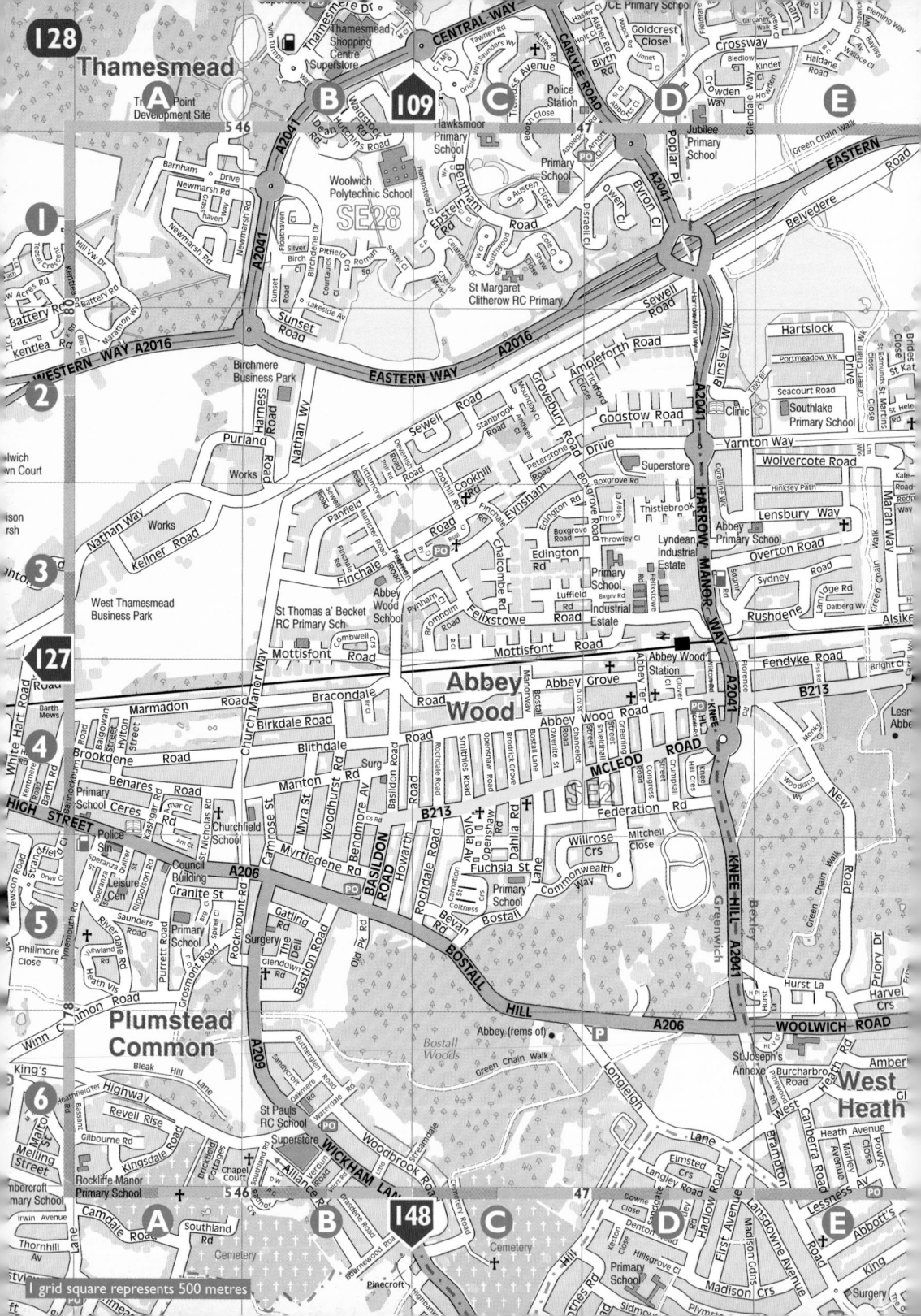

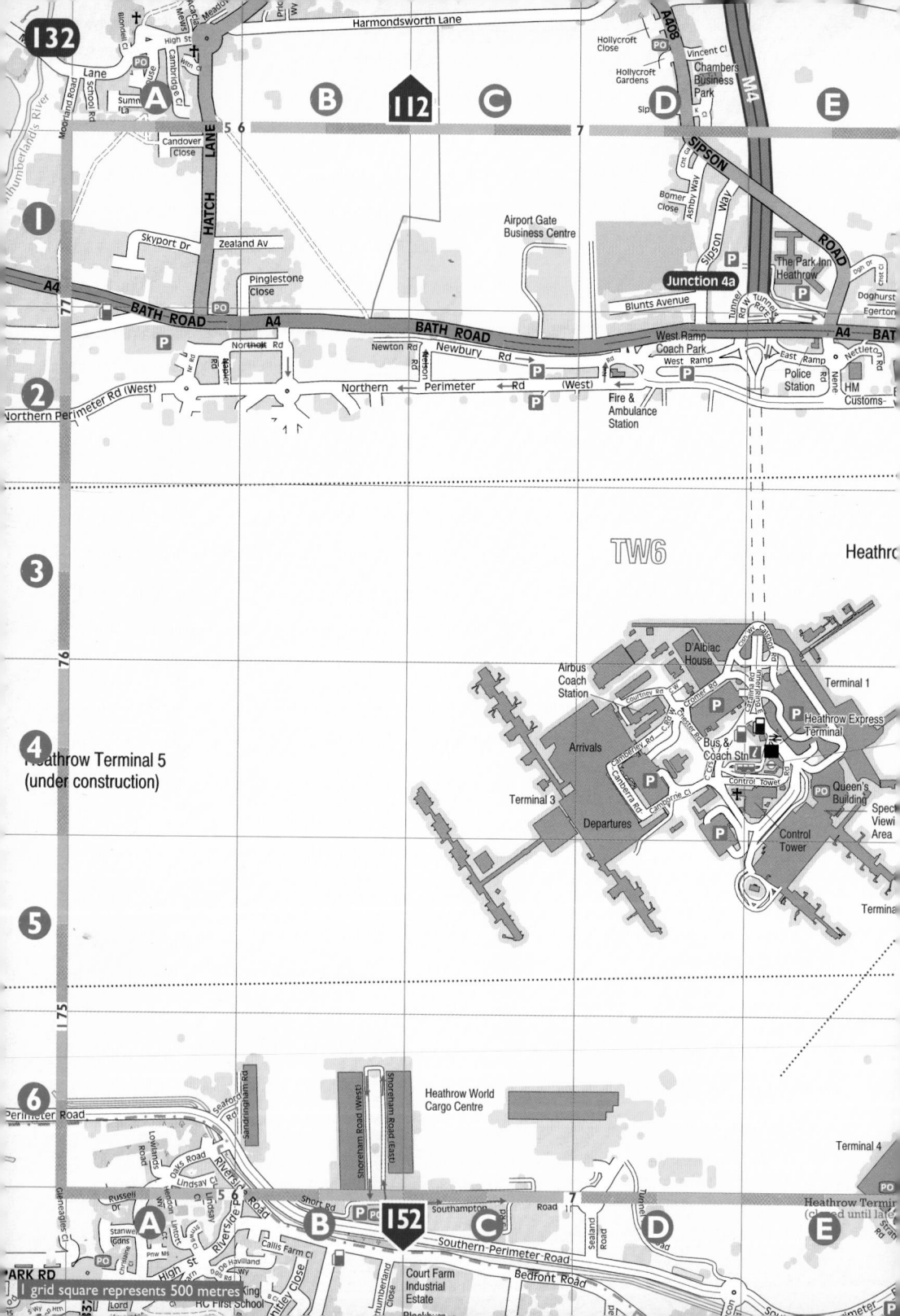

132

A B **112** C D E

Harmondsworth Lane

Blondell Way
Meadow
Price Wy
A408
Hollycroft Close
Vincent Cl
Hollycroft Gardens
Chambers Business Park
M4

High St
Candover Close
Cambridge Cl
Summerhouse
HATCH LANE
5 6
Sip

SIPSON ROAD

I

Skyport Dr
Zealand Av
Pinglestone Close
Airport Gate Business Centre
Bomer Close
Ashby Way
Sipson Way
The Park Inn Heathrow
Doghurst
Egerton

A4
77
BATH ROAD
A4
Northolt Rd
Newton Rd
Newbury Rd
BATH ROAD
West Ramp Coach Park
West Ramp
Junction 4a
Blunts Avenue
A4
BAT
East Ramp
Nettleto
Nene

2
Northern Perimeter Rd (West)
Northolt Rd
Northern ← Perimeter → Rd (West)
Police Station
HM Customs

Fire & Ambulance Station

TW6
Heathro

3
76

Airbus Coach Station
D'Albiac House
P
Terminal 1
Heathrow Express Terminal

4
Heathrow Terminal 5
(under construction)
Arrivals
Courtney Rd
Cromer Rd
Camborne Rd
Bus & Coach Stn
Control Tower
P
P
Queen's Building
Speci Viewi Area

Terminal 3
Camborne Cl
P
Departures
P
Control Tower
Terminal

5
175

6
Perimeter Road
Oaks Road
Lowlands Road
Seaforth Rd
Saunders Rd
Riverside Rd
Shoreham Road (West)
Shoreham Road (East)
Heathrow World Cargo Centre
Terminal 4

A
Russell Dr
Stanwell Gdns
Lindsay Dr
High St
River Rd
B
Short Rd
P
152
Southampton
C
Road
Tunne
Sealand Road
D
E
Heathrow Termin (closed until late)

PARK RD
Callis Farm Cl
Southern Perimeter Road
Bedfont Road
Court Farm Industrial Estate

grid square represents 500 metres

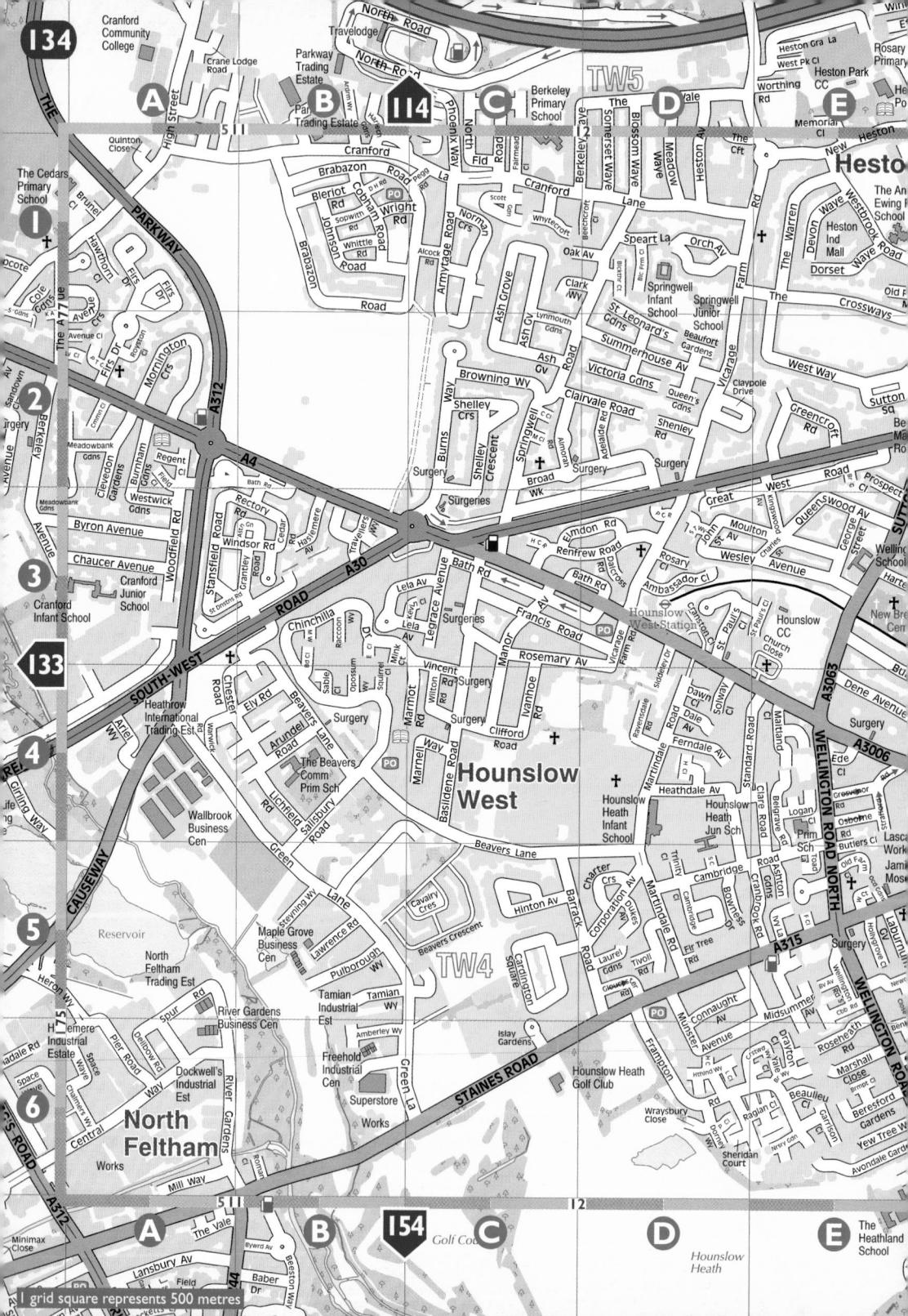

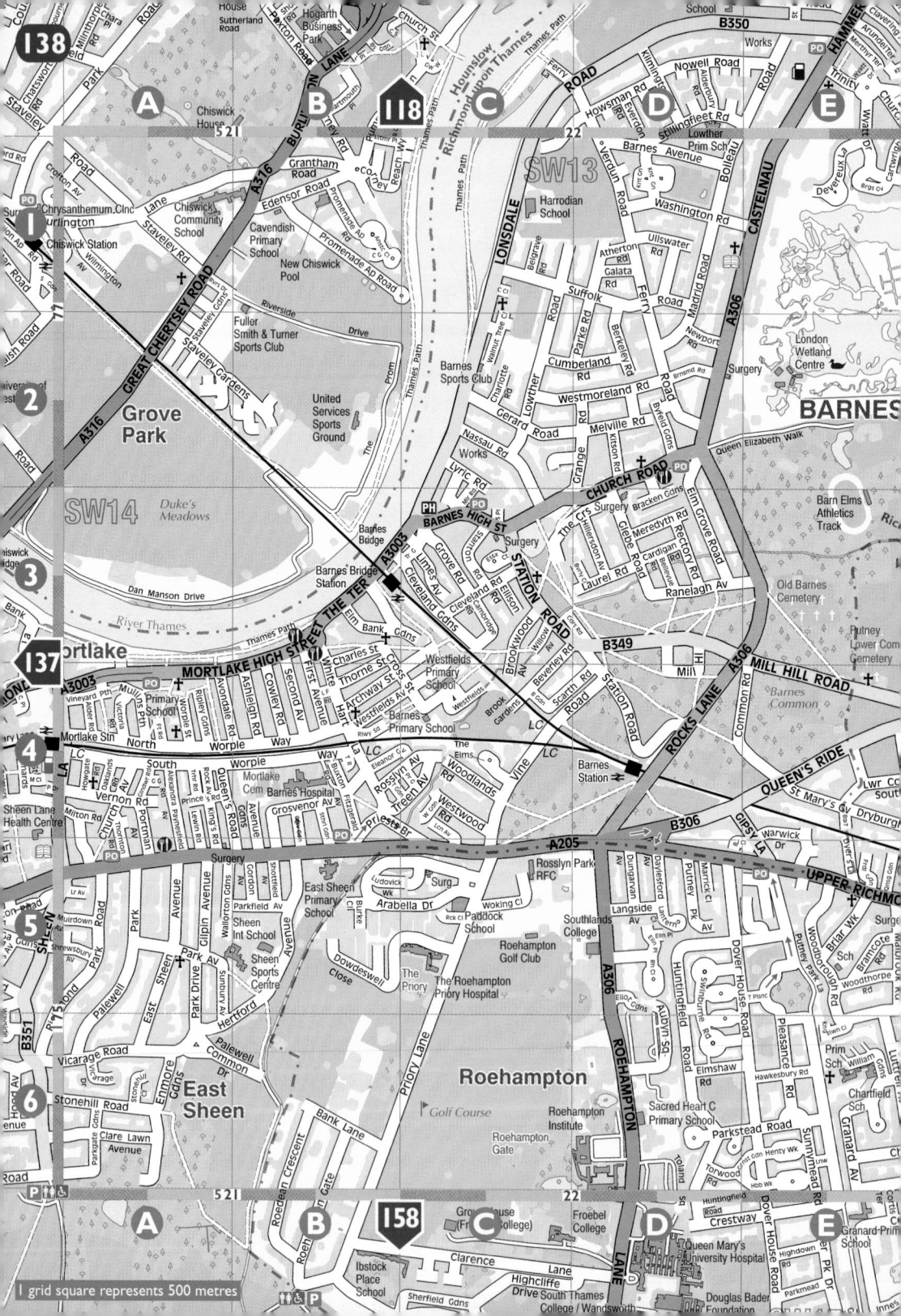

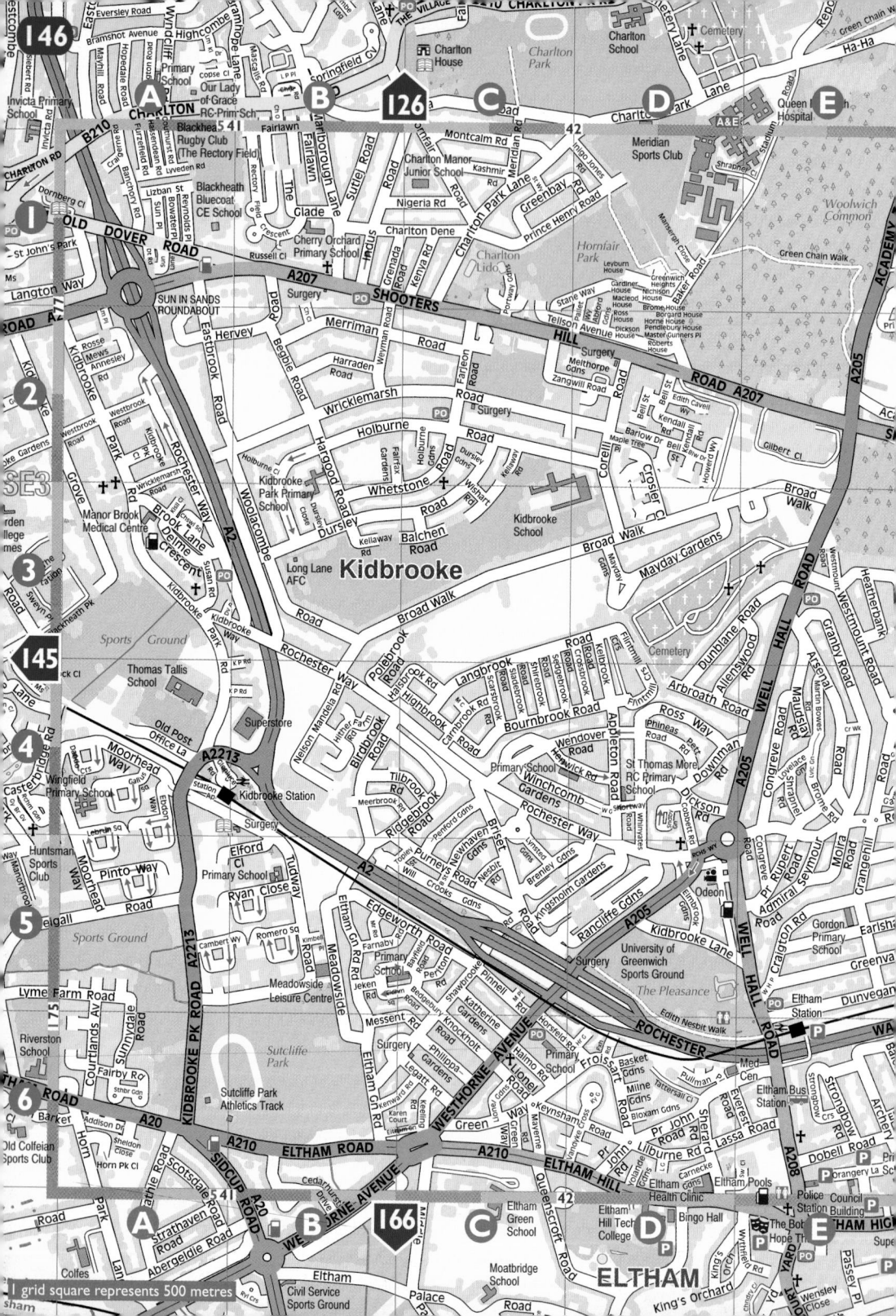

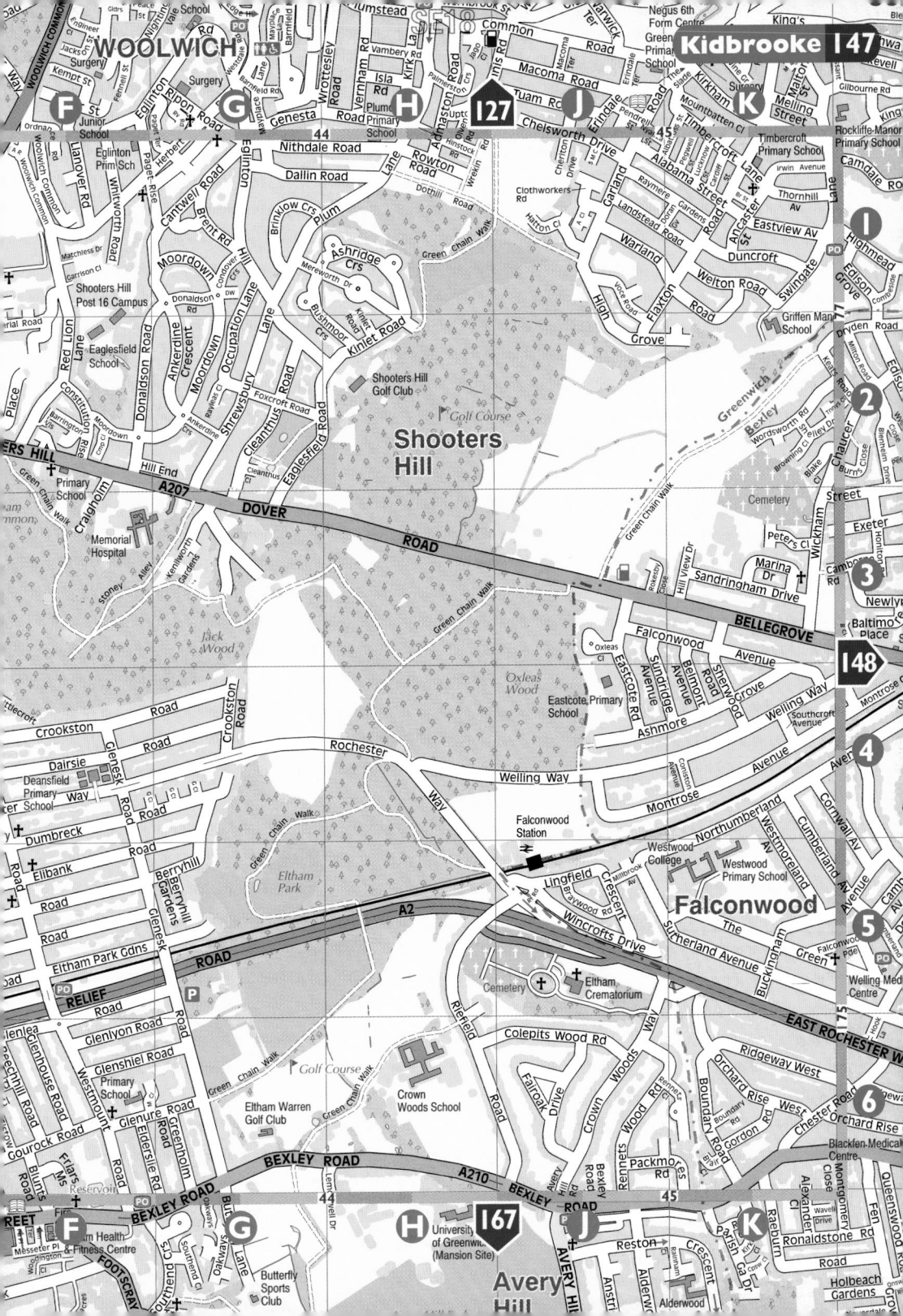

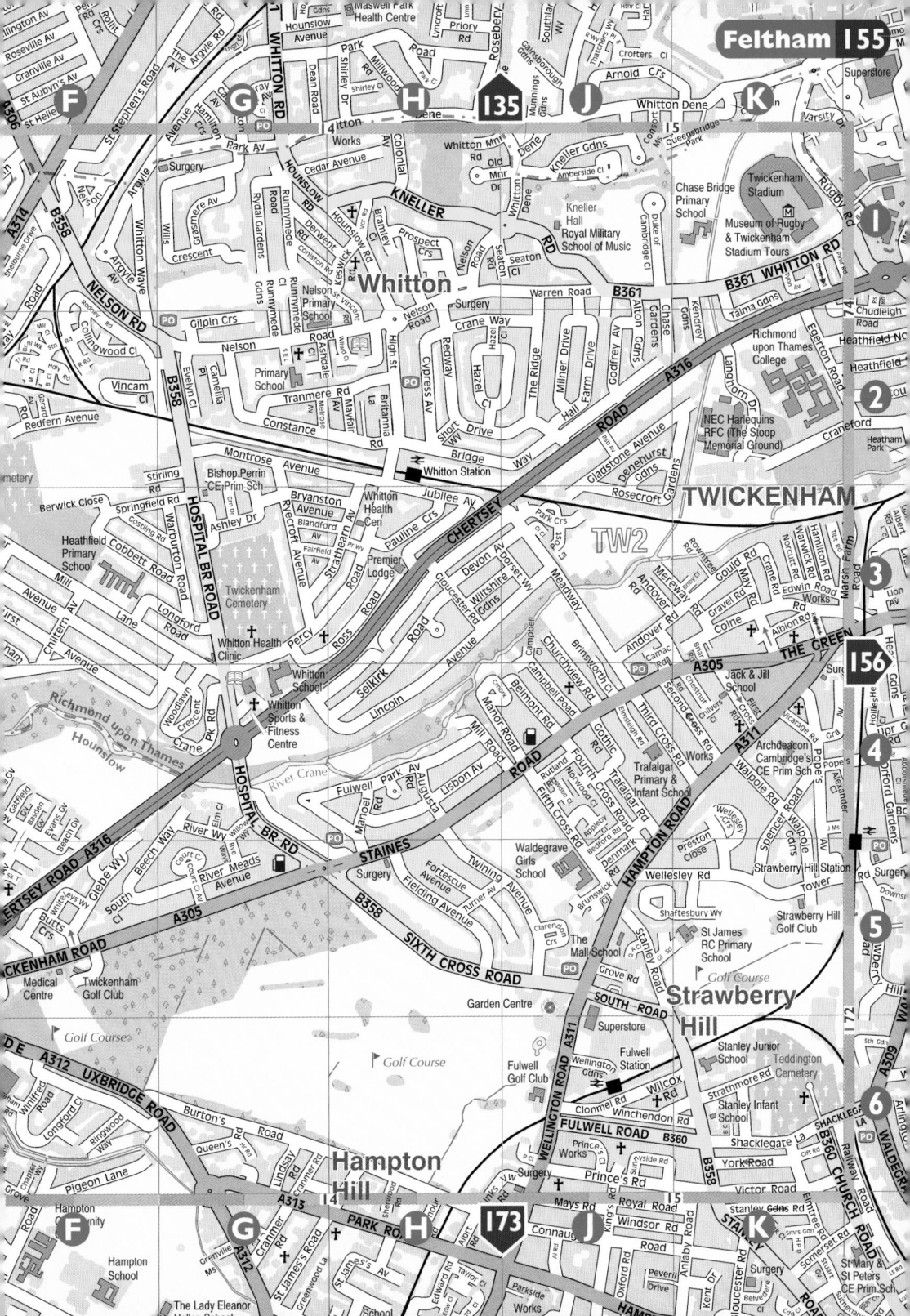

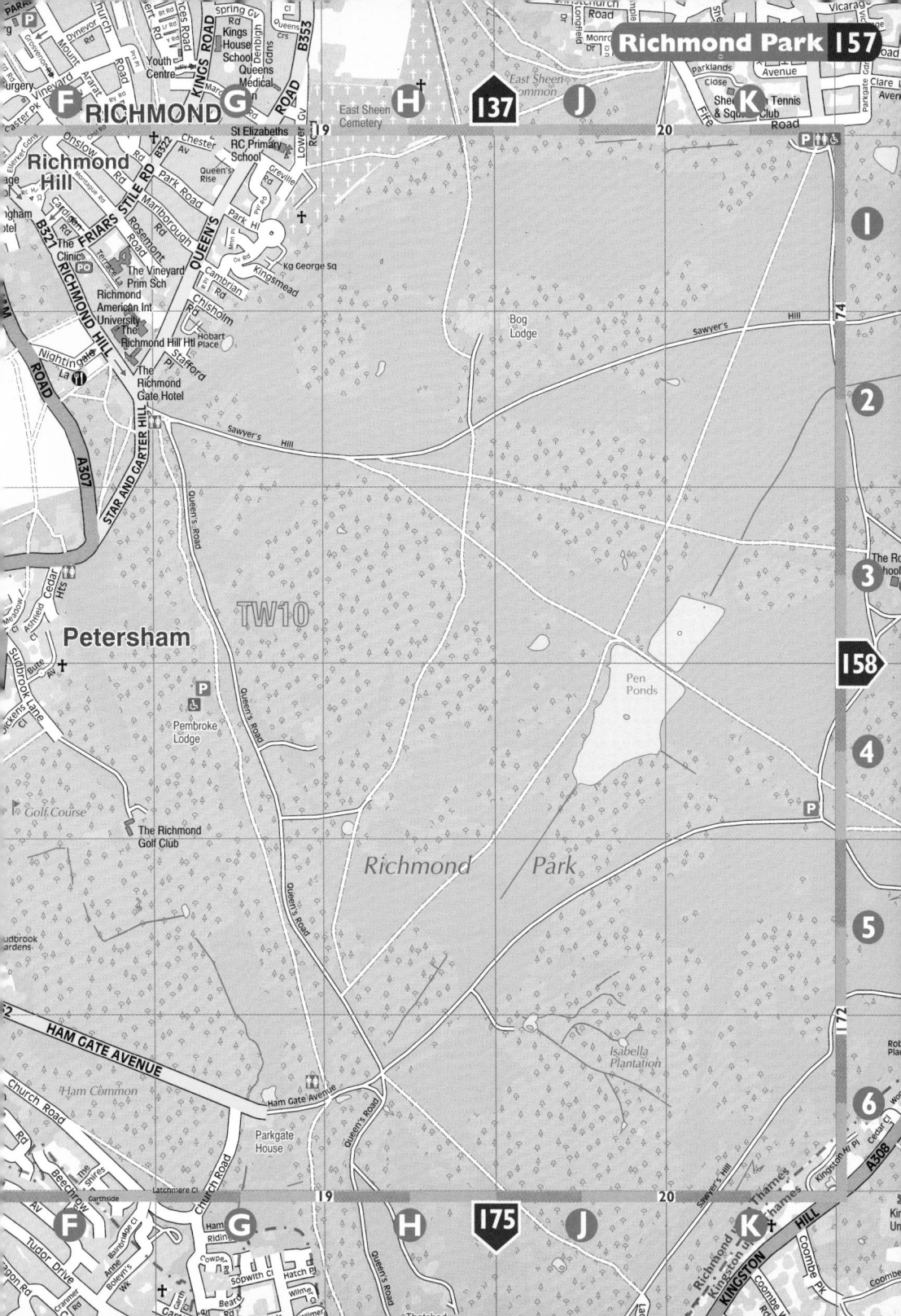

F RICHMOND

G

H

137

J

K

Richmond
Hill

I

St Elizabeths
RC Primary
School

Youth
Centre

Kings
House
School

Queens
Medical
Centre

East Sheen
Cemetery

East Sheen
Common

Shene
& Sq

Tennis
Club

2

Onslow
Rd

Park Road

Queen's
Rise

Chester
Av

Marlborough
Rd

Park Hl

Chisholm
Rd

Richmond
American Int
University

The
Richmond Hill Htl

Hobart
Place

Stafford

Bog
Lodge

Sawyer's

Hill

3

The
Richmond
Gate Hotel

Sawyer's

Hill

2

TW10

158

Petersham

Pen
Ponds

4

P

Pembroke
Lodge

Queen's Road

Golf Course

The Richmond
Golf Club

Richmond   Park

5

HAM GATE AVENUE

Isabella
Plantation

172

Ham Common

Ham Gate Avenue

6

Church Road

Parkgate
House

Queen's Road

Sawyer's Hill

Richmond
Gate Hotel

Tudor Drive

F

G

H

175

J

K

Kingston upon Thames

Kingston

HILL

A308

Coombe

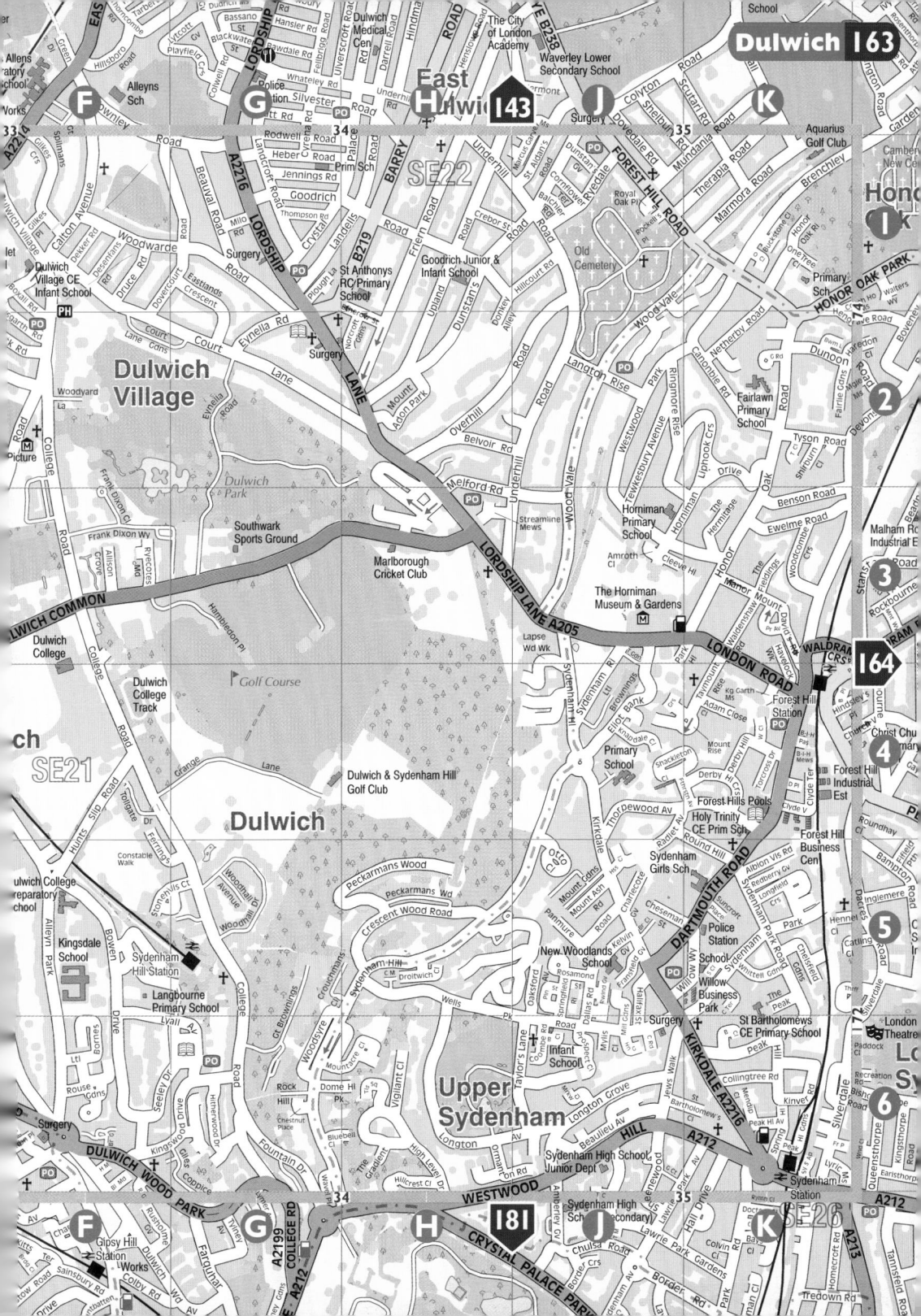

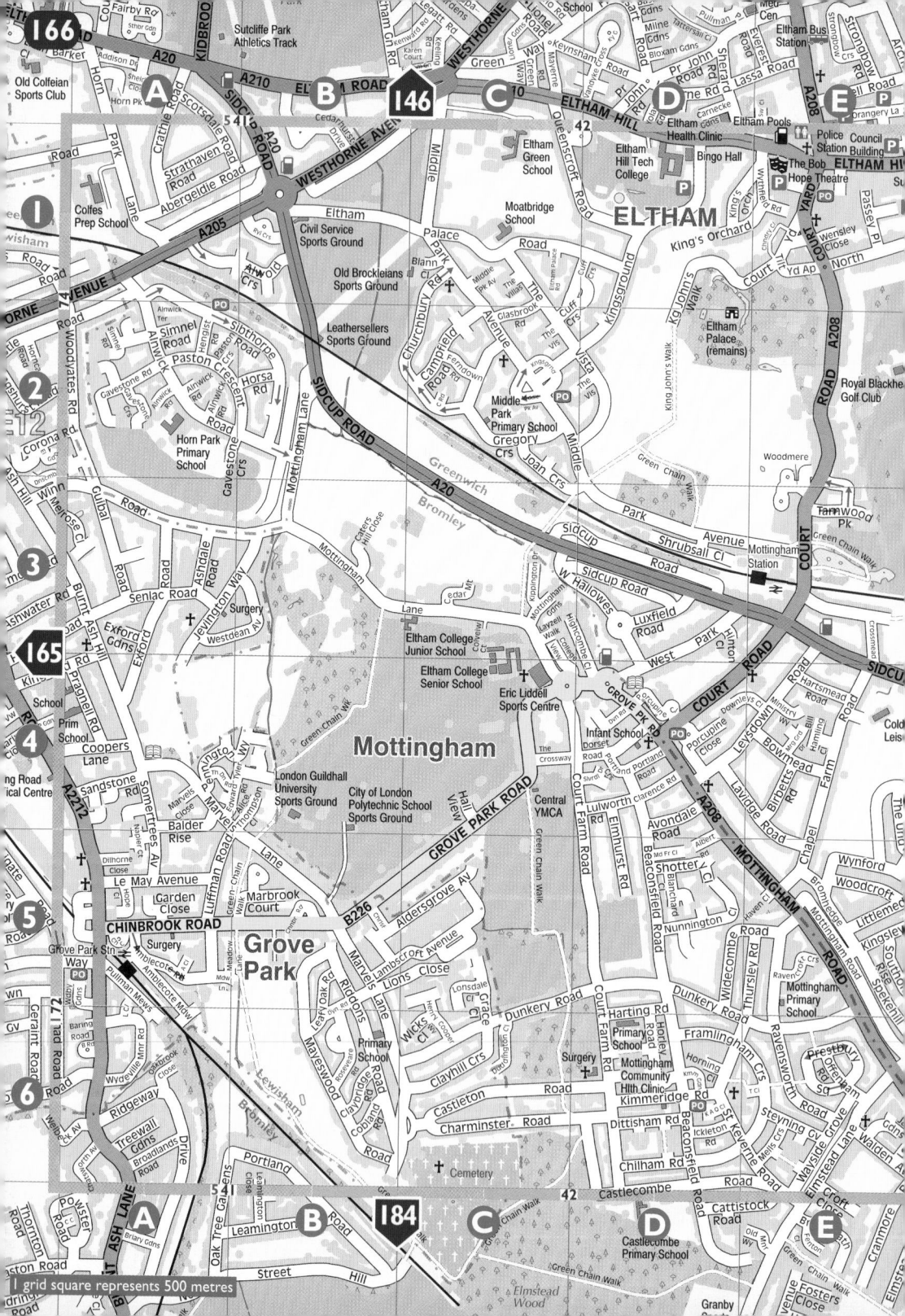

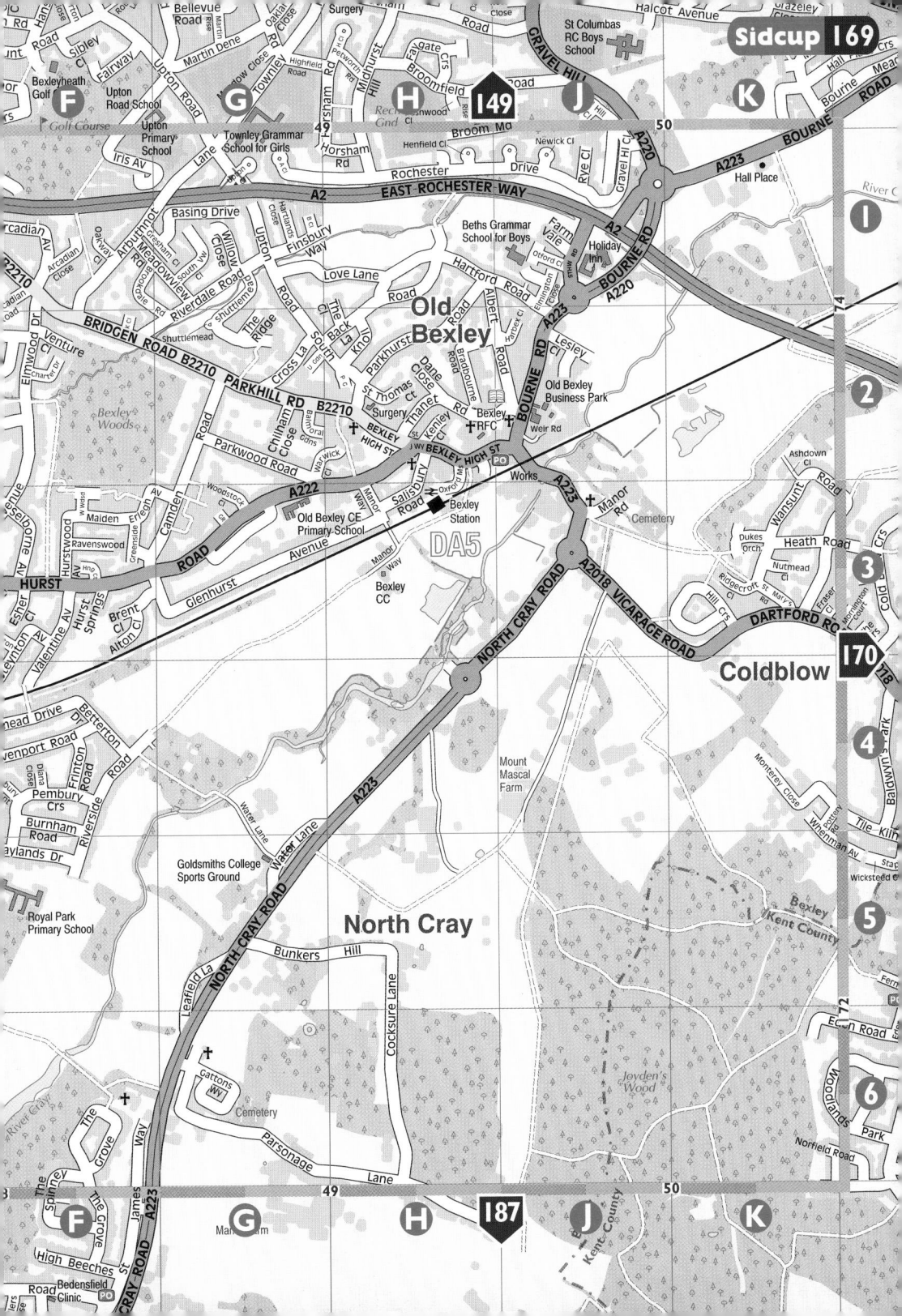

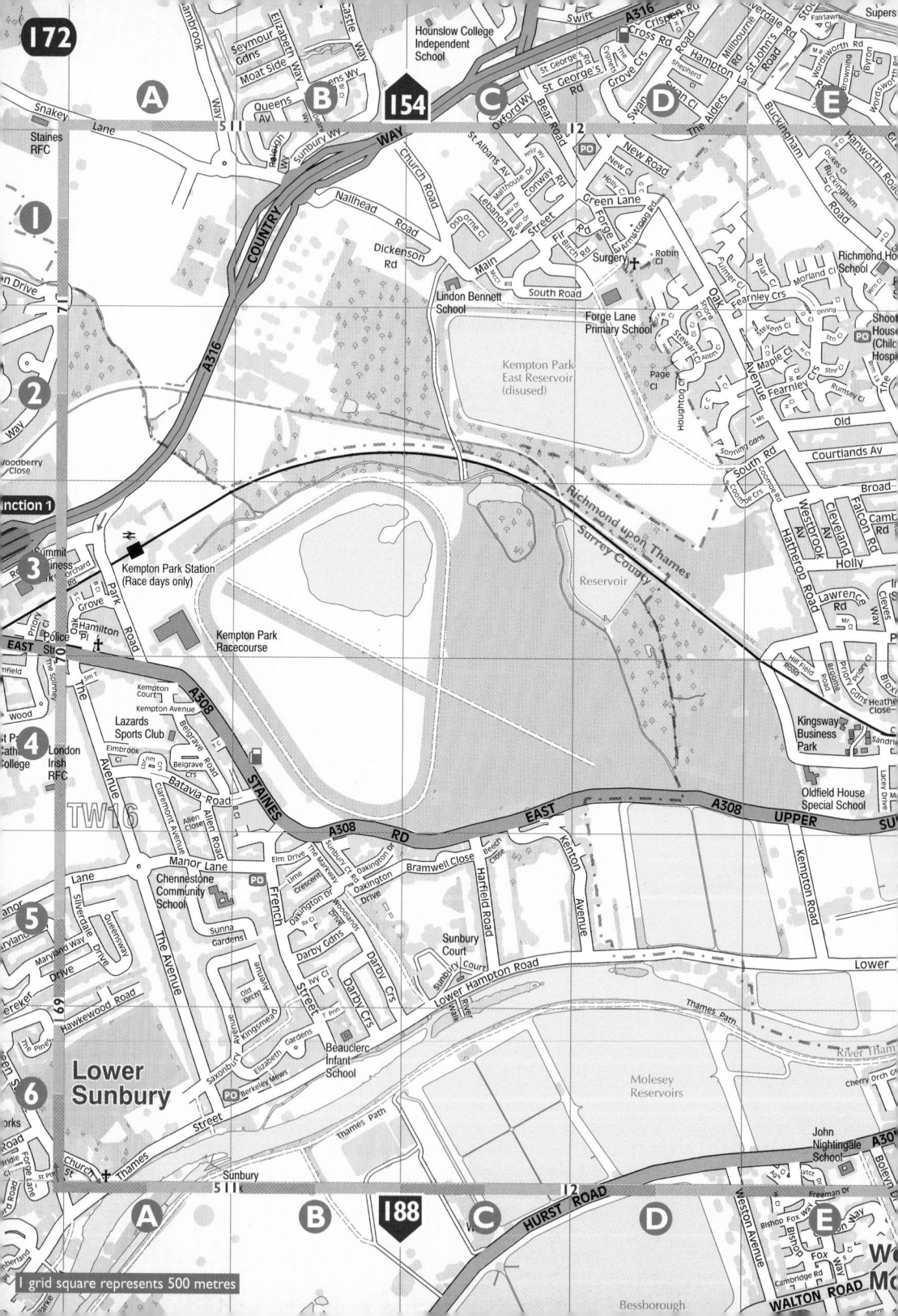

172

A B 154 C D E

I

2

3

Kempton Park Station
(Race days only)

4

TW16

5

6

Lower
Sunbury

A B 188 C HURST ROAD D E

1 grid square represents 500 metres

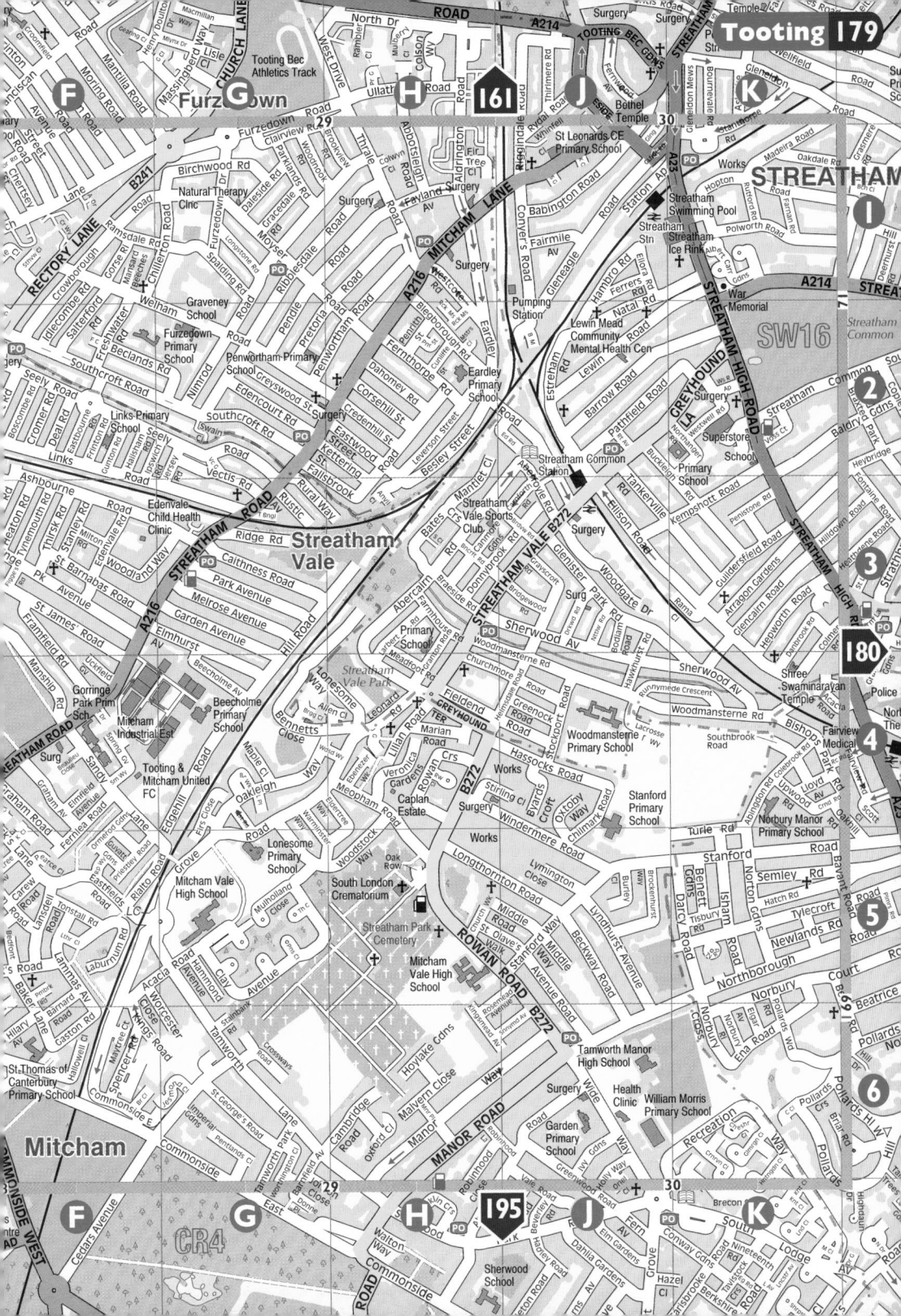

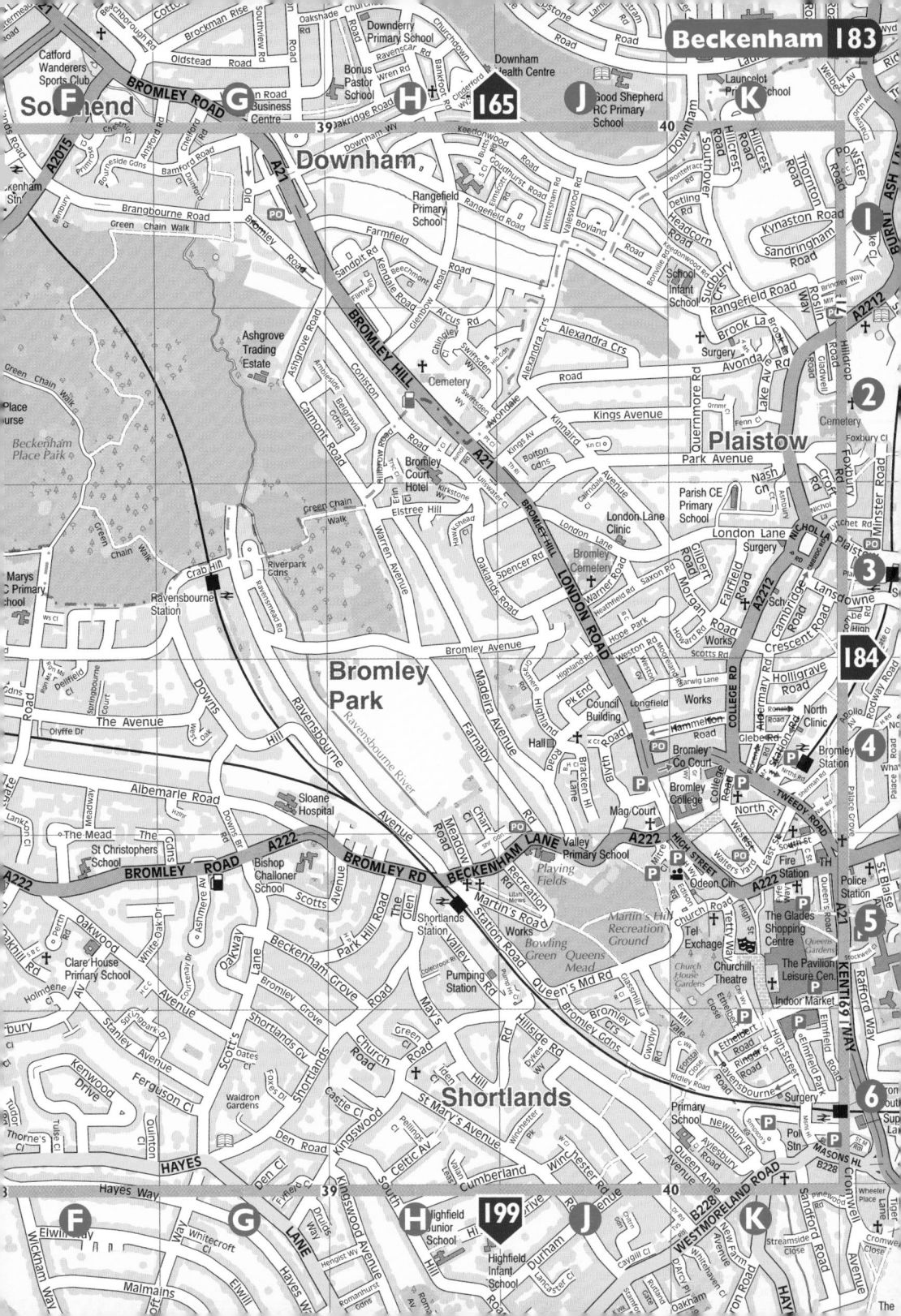

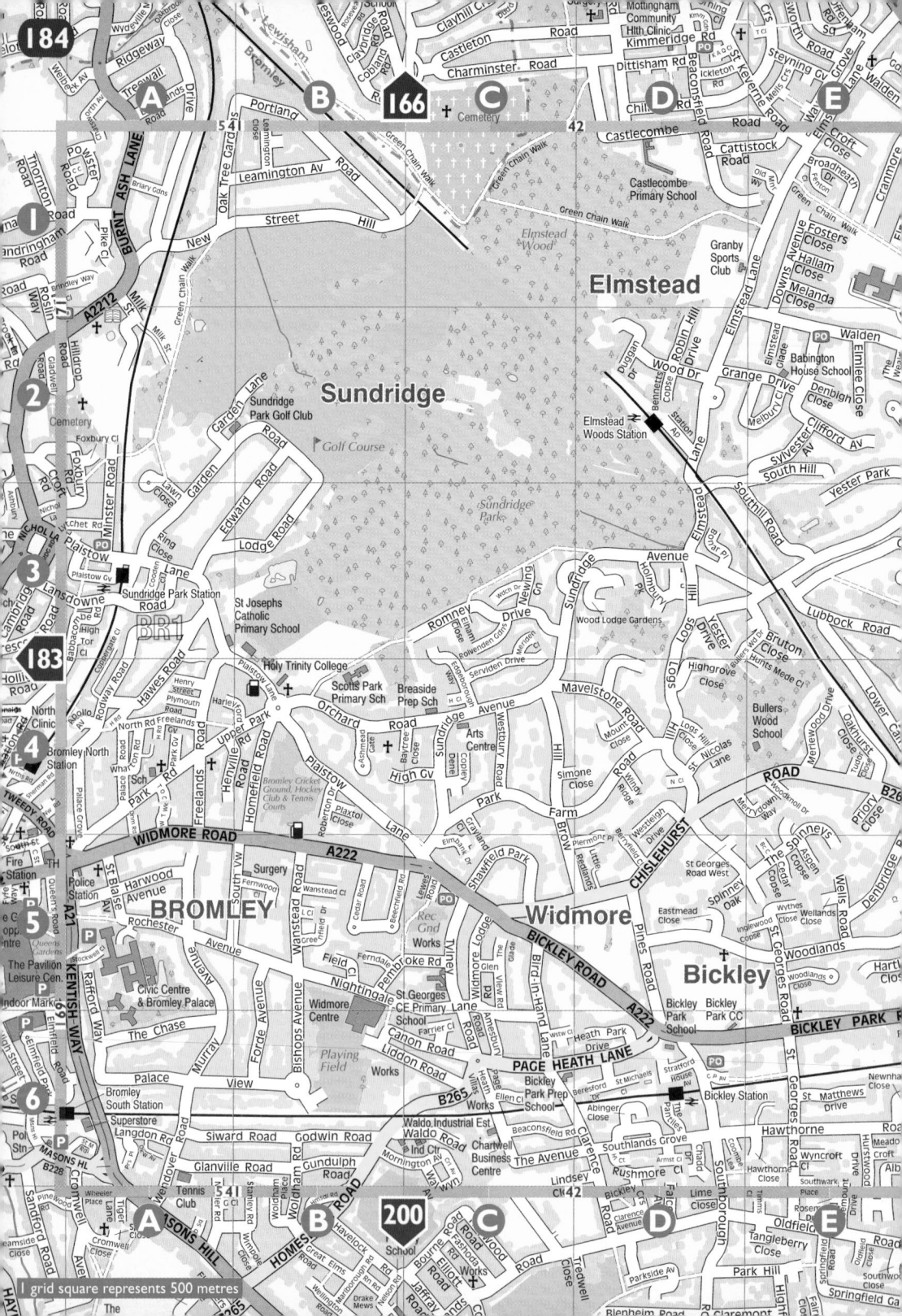

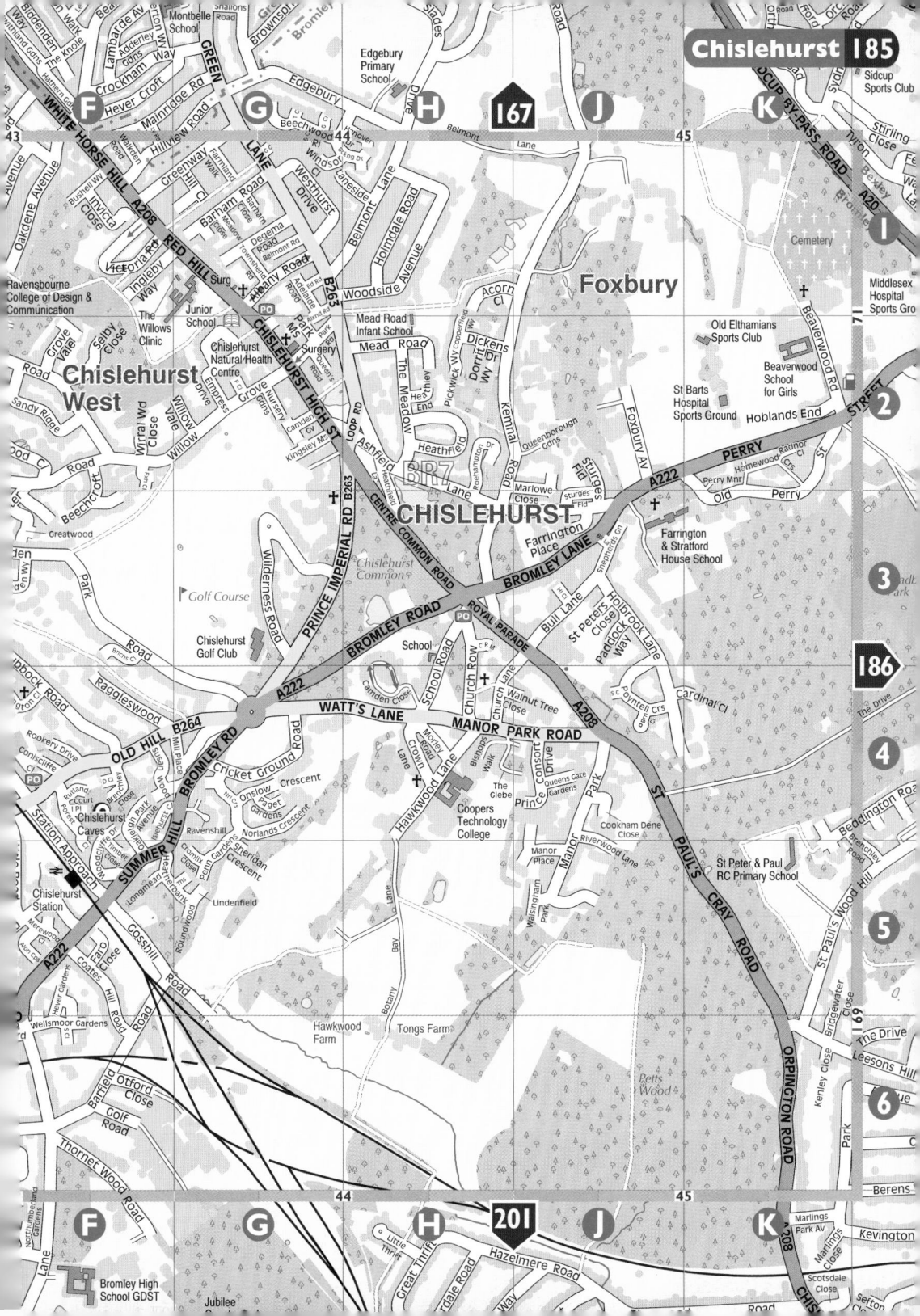

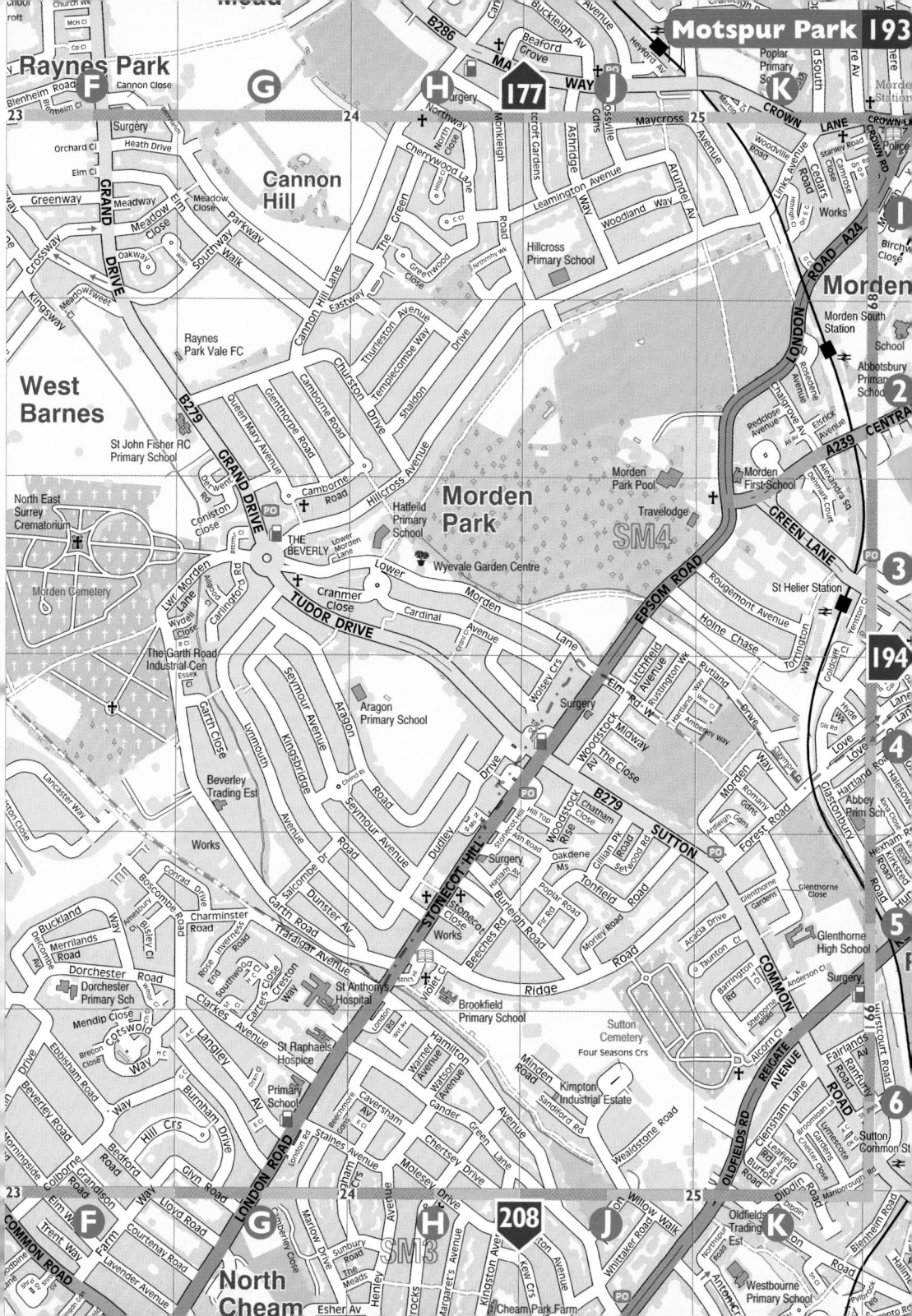

1 grid square represents 500 metres

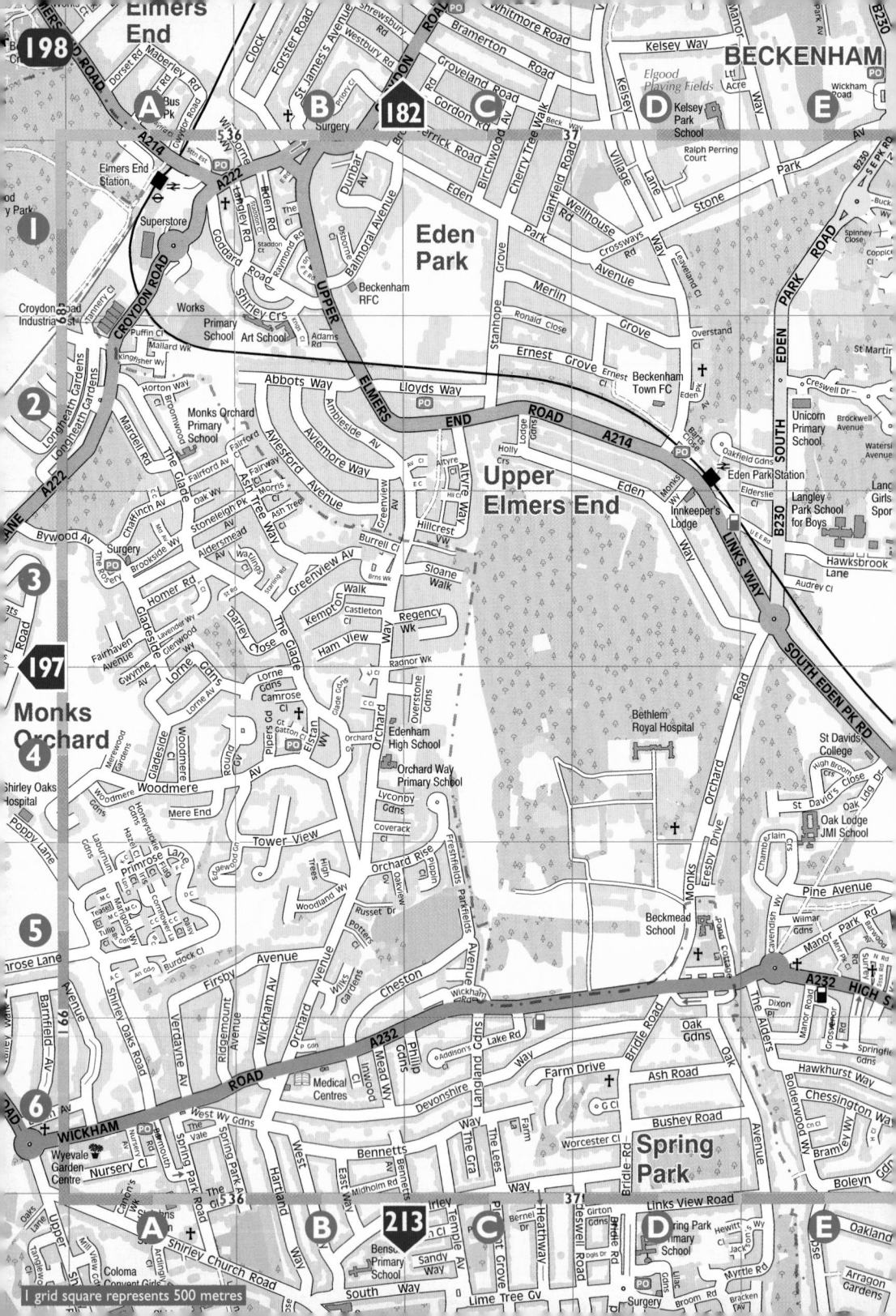

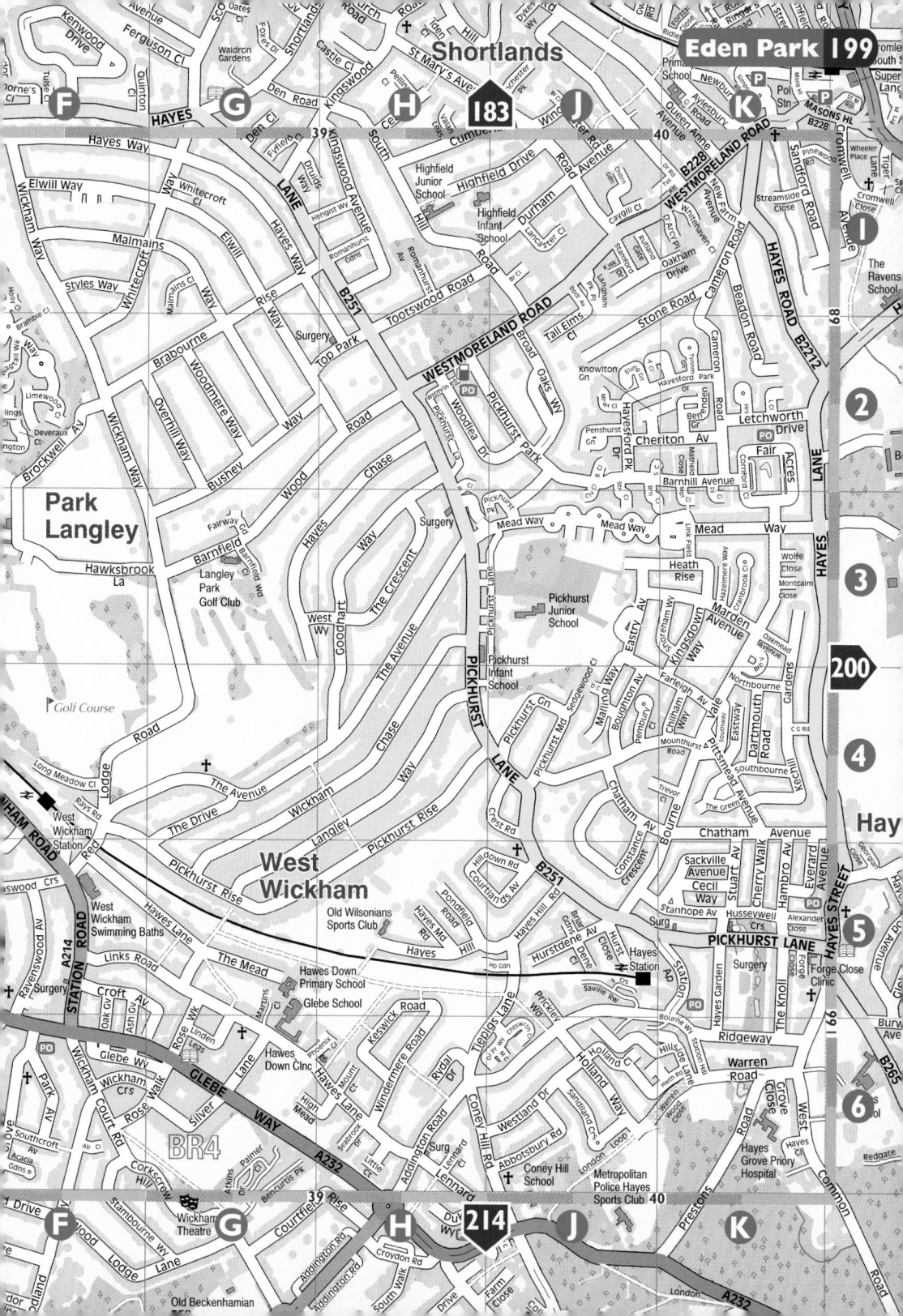

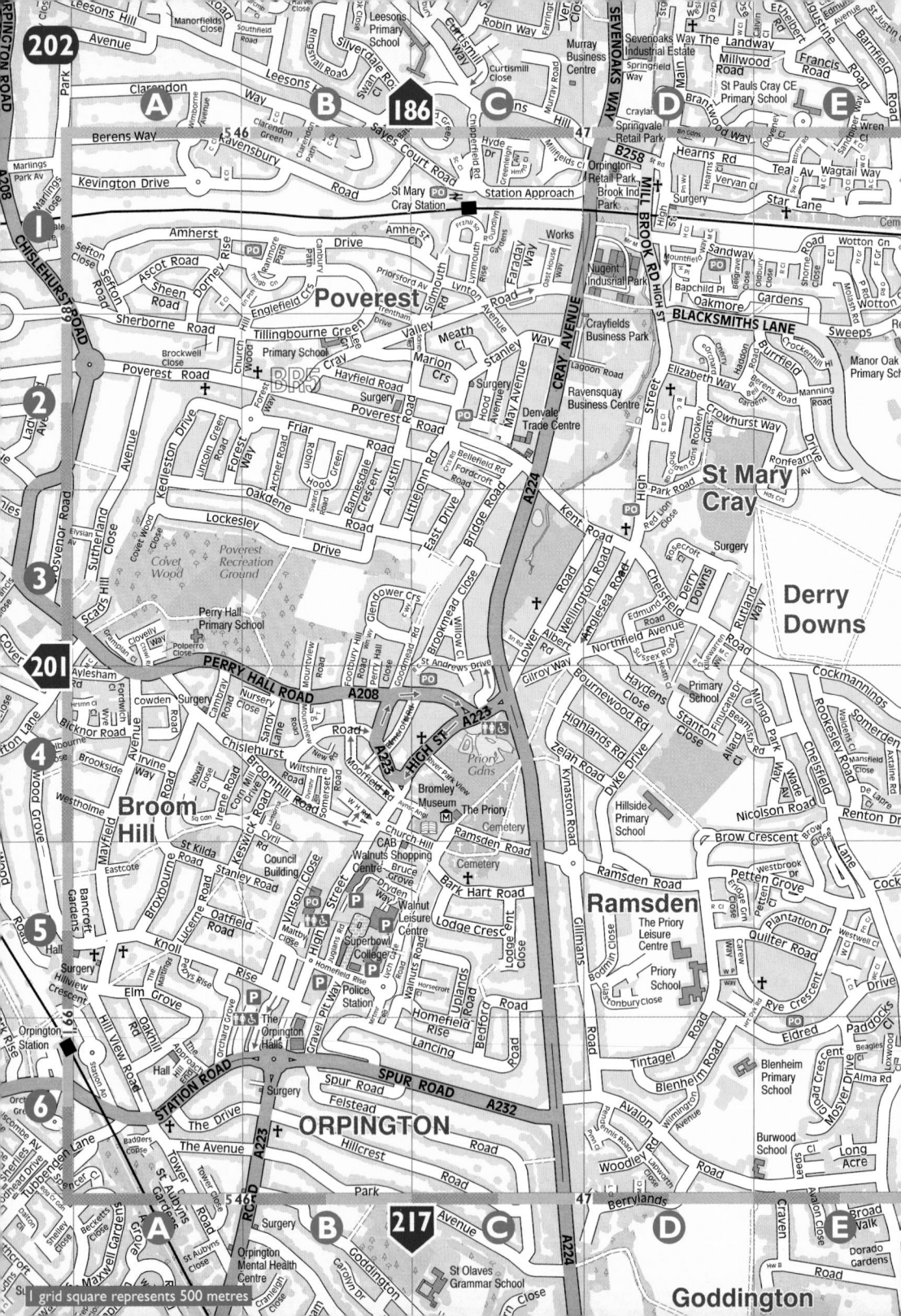

F   G   H   **187**   J   K

Star Lane

49   50

Lynden

Cherry Avenue

1

Bourne Wood

Sheepcote Lane

Sheepcote Farm

Furness Swanley

Bromley Kent County

Stones Cross Road

Cf Road

2

Shawcroft School

KENHILL ROAD

Kevingtown

B258

Crouch Farm

Crockenhill Primary School

seven Acres

GREEN COURT ROAD

3

Crockenhill

PO

Waldens Road

Bransell Close

CRAY ROAD B258   MAIN RD

Tudor Court

Church Road

East Hall Road

Lane

gs

Kibbs Lane

Lone Barn

Tylers Hill

Darns Hill

Green Road

Old Chapel Road

Newport

4

Woodmount

5

66

Daltons Road

Gorse Road

6

Crown Wood

Skeet Hill Lane

49   50

F   G   H   J   K

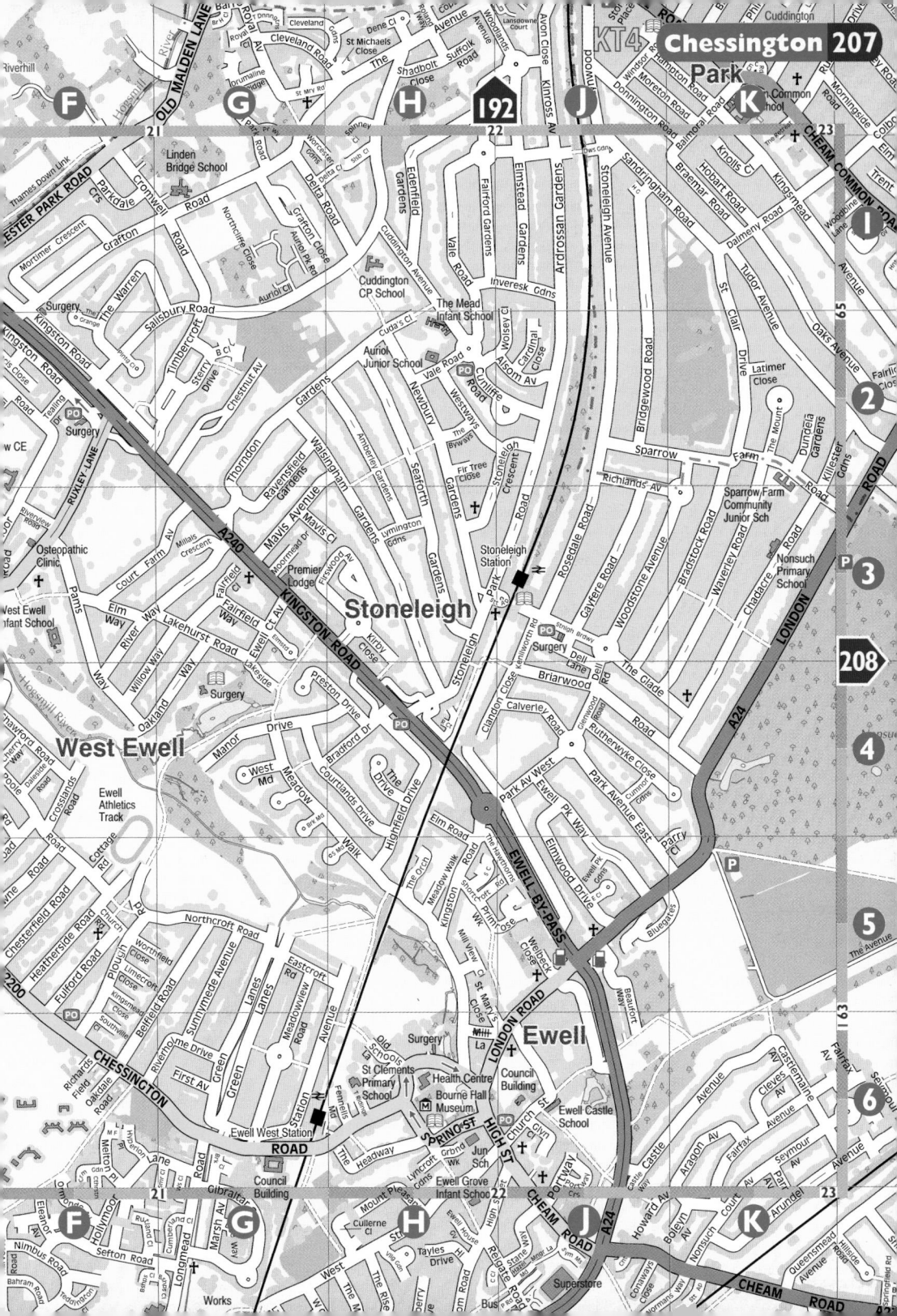

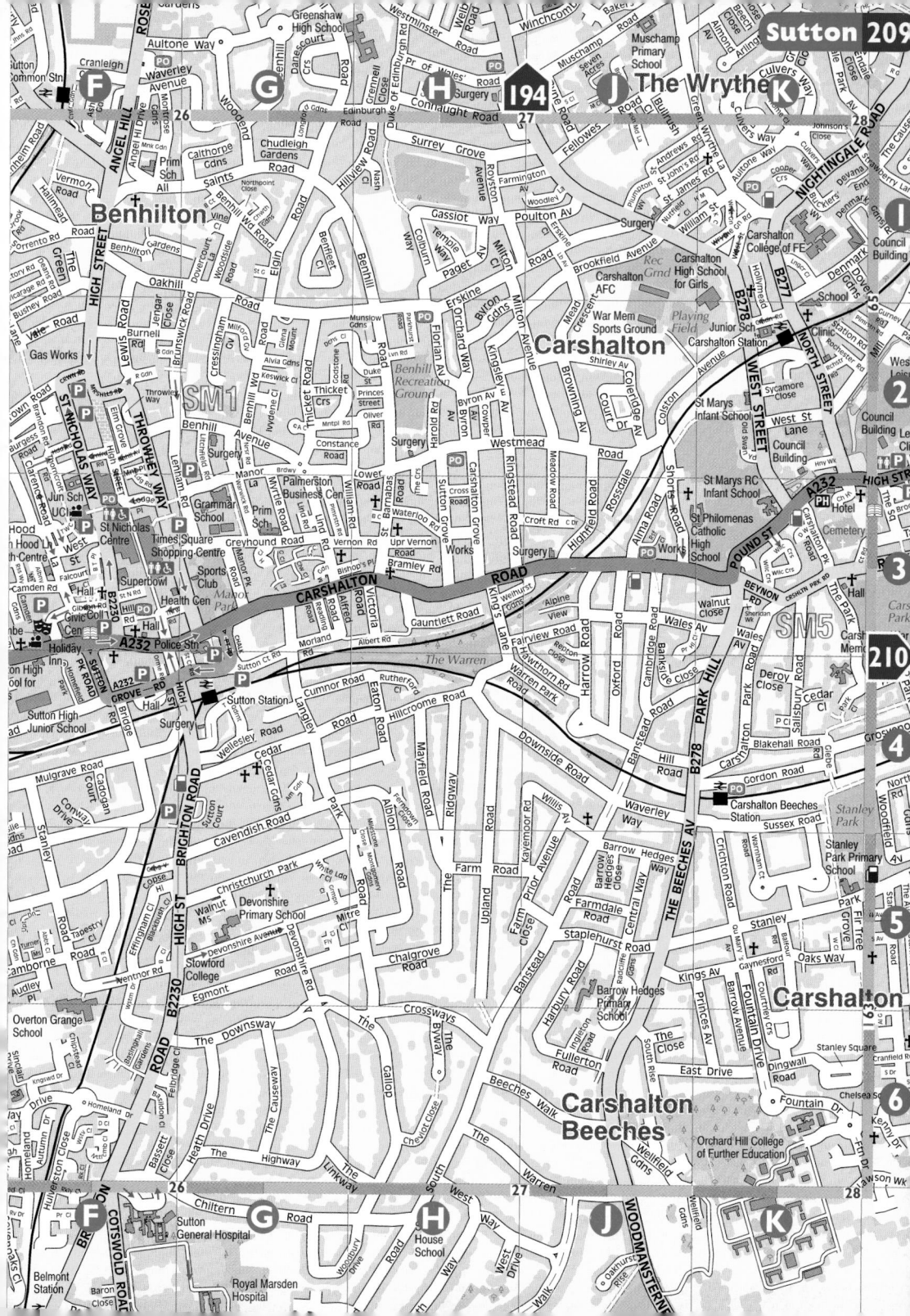

I grid square represents 500 metres

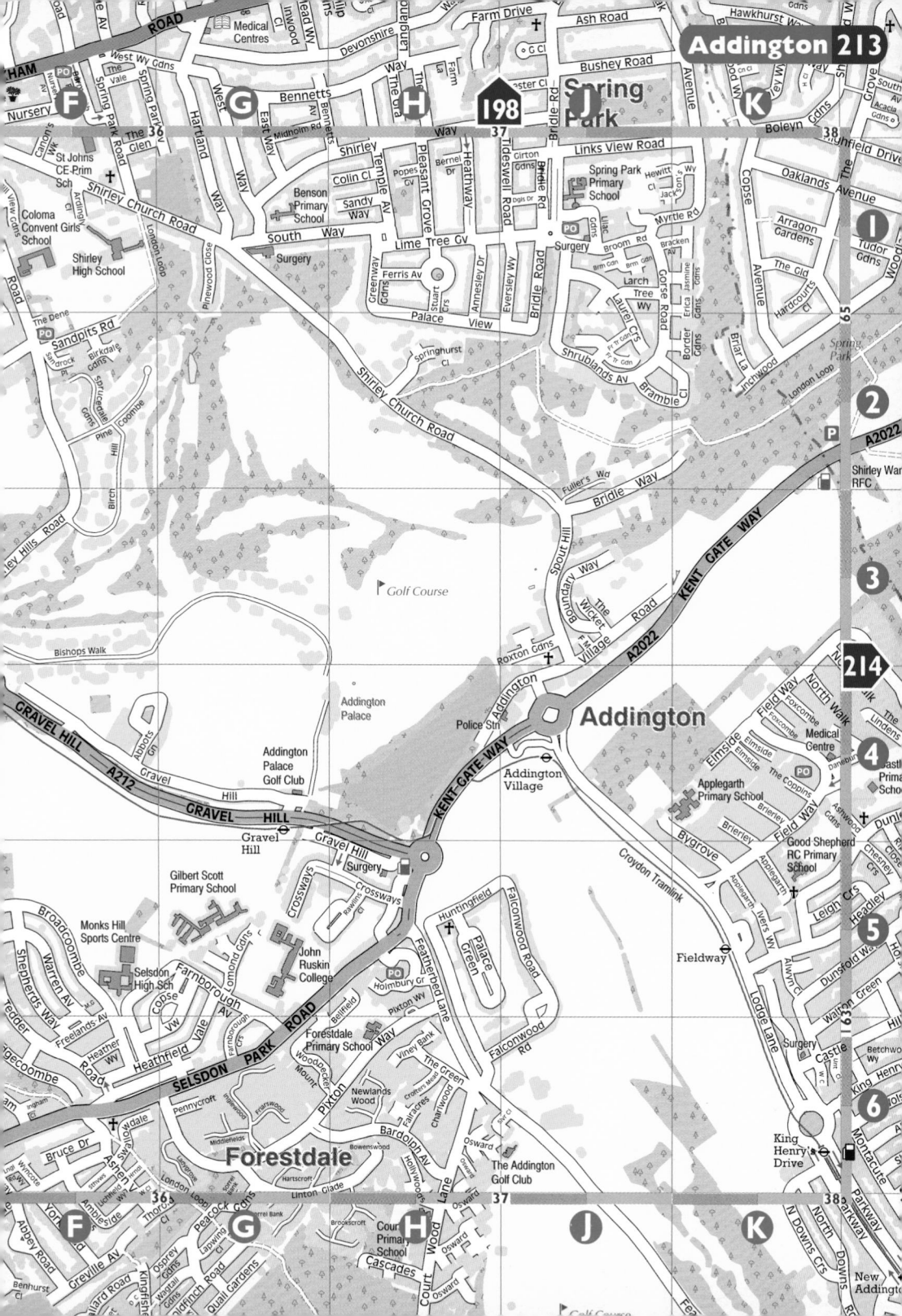

Abbey Wood ...128 C4
Acton ...117 K1
Acton Green ...118 A4
Addington ...213 J4
Addiscombe ...197 G4
Adborough Hatch ...72 E1
Aldersbrook ...71 G5
Alperton ...80 A6
Anerley ...181 H5
Ashford ...153 D6
Avery Hill ...167 H1
Balham ...160 E2
Bandonhill ...210 D3
Barking ...90 D5
Barkingside ...54 B6
Barnehurst ...150 A4
Barnes ...138 E2
Barnes Cray ...150 E5
Barnet ...32 D1
Barnet Gate ...31 G1
Barnsbury ...84 E5
Barwell ...205 J5
Battersea ...140 E1
Bayswater ...101 F6
Beckenham ...182 D6
Beckton ...107 K5
Becontree ...91 K3
Beddington ...195 K6
Beddington Corner ...195 F4
Bedford Park ...118 C3
Belgravia ...15 G6
Bell Green ...164 C5
Bellingham ...164 D6
Belmont ...43 J6
Belmont ...208 E6
Belvedere ...129 J5
Benhilton ...209 F1
Berrylands ...191 G3
Bethnal Green ...104 D2
Bexley ...148 D5
Bexleyheath ...149 G5
Bickley ...184 D5
Blackfen ...168 A1
Blackheath ...145 J3
Blackheath Park ...145 K5
Blackwall ...106 B6
Bloomsbury ...10 D1
The Borough ...18 D3
Bow ...105 J1
Bow Common ...105 J4
Bowes Park ...48 E2
Bowmans ...170 C2
Brentford ...116 E6
Brentford End ...116 C6
Brimsdown ...25 G3
Brixton ...142 B5
Broad Green ...196 C4
Brockley ...144 C6
Bromley ...105 K2
Bromley ...184 A5
Bromley Common ...200 C3
Bromley Park ...183 H4
Brompton ...14 C5
Brondesbury ...82 C4
Brondesbury Park ...82 B6
Brook Green ...119 F3
Broom Hill ...202 A4
Brunswick Park ...34 A5
Buckhurst Hill ...39 G5
Burnt Oak ...45 F3
Bushey ...28 C2
Bushey Heath ...28 E2
Bushey Mead ...177 G6
Bush Hill Park ...36 A1
Caldecote Hill ...29 F2
Camberwell ...143 J2
Camden Town ...84 A5
Canary Wharf ...124 D1
Canning Town ...107 F4
Cannon Hill ...193 G1
Canonbury ...85 J4
Canons Park ...44 A3
Carpenders Park ...27 K4
Carshalton ...209 J2
Carshalton Beeches ...209 J6
Carshalton on the Hill ...209 K5
Castle Green ...91 J6
Catford ...165 F1
Chadwell Heath ...73 K2
Charlton ...126 C5
Chase Cross ...57 G2
Chattern Hill ...152 E6
Cheam ...208 C5
Chelsea ...23 J1
Chessington ...206 A4
Child's Hill ...64 C6
China Town ...10 C5
Chingford ...38 B3
Chingford Green ...38 A2
Chingford Hatch ...38 C6
Chipping Barnet ...20 C6
Chislehurst ...185 H3
Chislehurst West ...185 F2
Chiswick ...118 C4
Church End ...46 E5
Church End ...50 E4
City of London ...12 B5
Clapham ...141 G3
Clapham Park ...161 J1
Clapton Park ...87 H2
Claremont Park ...204 A5
Claygate ...205 F4
Clayhall ...53 J5
Clerkenwell ...5 J6
Cockfosters ...21 J6
Coldblow ...169 K4
Coldharbour ...130 D4
Cole Park ...156 B1
Colindale ...45 G6
College Park ...99 J2
Collier Row ...56 E4
Collier's Wood ...177 J3
Coney Hatch ...47 J1
Coney Hall ...214 C2
Coombe ...176 B3
Copse Hill ...176 D3

Cottenham Park ...176 E4
Cranbrook ...72 A4
Cranford ...133 K1
Cranley Gardens ...66 A1
Crayford ...150 D6
Creekmouth ...108 E4
Cricklewood ...82 B2
Crockenhill ...203 K3
Crofton ...201 J6
Crooked Billet ...176 E2
Crouch End ...66 C3
Croydon ...211 K1
Crystal Palace ...181 H2
Cubitt Town ...125 F4
Custom House ...107 J6
Dagenham ...92 D5
Dalston ...86 B5
Dartford ...171 F2
Dartmouth Park ...66 A6
Deacons Hill ...30 C1
De Beauvoir Town ...86 A6
Deptford ...124 C6
Derry Downs ...202 E3
Dollis Hill ...81 K1
Dormer's Wells ...96 B6
Downham ...183 G1
Ducks Island ...32 B2
Dudden Hill ...81 J3
Dulwich ...163 G4
Dulwich Village ...163 F2
Ealing ...97 J6
Earl's Court ...119 K5
Earlsfield ...160 B3
East Acton ...99 H6
East Barnet ...33 H2
East Bedfont ...152 E2
Eastbury ...26 D6
Eastcote ...59 F4
Eastcote Village ...59 F2
East Dulwich ...143 H6
East Finchley ...47 H6
East Ham ...107 J1
East Molesey ...189 H2
East Sheen ...138 A6
East Wickham ...148 B2
Eden Park ...198 C1
Edgware ...30 D6
Edmonton ...36 A6
Elmers End ...182 A6
Elm Park ...93 K3
Elmstead ...184 D1
Elstree ...30 A1
Eltham ...166 D1
Enfield ...23 J3
Enfield Highway ...24 E3
Enfield Town ...23 K4
Enfield Wash ...25 G1
Erith ...130 C5
Esher ...204 C3
Ewell ...207 J6
Fair Cross ...91 J6
Fairlop ...54 E4
Falconwood ...147 K5
Farnborough ...216 B3
Feltham ...154 A4
Field Common ...188 E4
Finchley ...46 E4
Finsbury ...5 J4
Finsbury Park ...67 F6
Foots Cray ...186 C2
Forestdale ...213 G6
Forest Gate ...88 E3
Forest Hill ...164 A3
Fortis Green ...65 K1
Forty Hill ...24 B2
Foxbury ...185 J1
Friday Hill ...38 B5
Friern Barnet ...33 J6
Fulham ...139 G1
Fullwell Cross ...54 D4
Furzedown ...161 G6
Gants Hill ...71 K3
Gidea Park ...57 H5
Giggshill ...190 B4
Globe Town ...105 F2
Goddington ...217 J1
Golders Green ...64 C5
Goodmayes ...73 H6
Gospel Oak ...84 A3
Grange Hill ...54 D1
Grange Park ...23 G6
Greenford ...96 D3
Greenhill ...61 F2
Green Street Green ...216 E5
Greenwich ...125 G5
Grove Park ...138 A2
Grove Park ...166 B5
Hackbridge ...195 G6
Hackney ...86 D2
Hackney Wick ...87 J4
Hadley ...20 E4
Hadley Wood ...21 H1
Haggerston ...104 B1
Hainault ...55 G2
Hale End ...52 B2
Ham ...156 E5
Hammersmith ...118 E4
Hampstead ...83 H2
Hampstead Garden Suburb ...65 F2
Hampton ...173 G4
Hampton Hill ...155 H6
Hampton Wick ...174 C4
Hanwell ...115 K1
Hanworth ...154 C5
Harlesden ...99 G3
Harlington ...113 F6
Harringay ...67 G2
Harrow ...60 D3
Harrow on the Hill ...60 E5
Harrow Weald ...42 E3
Hatch End ...41 J3
Hatton ...133 H5
Hayes ...98 E3
Hayes ...200 A4
Hayes End ...94 B3
Hayes Town ...114 B1

Headstone ...60 B1
Heath Park ...75 K3
Heath Side ...170 C4
Hendon ...64 K2
Herne Hill ...162 D1
Heston ...134 E1
Higham Hill ...51 G5
Highams Park ...51 K3
High Barnet ...20 A4
Highbury ...85 H3
Highgate ...65 K4
Highwood Hill ...31 H4
Hinchley Wood ...205 F1
Hither Green ...165 H1
Hockenden ...187 J6
Holborn ...11 G2
Holders Hill ...46 B4
Holwell ...26 C1
Homerton ...87 F4
Honor Oak ...164 A1
Honor Oak Park ...164 B1
Hook ...206 A3
Hook Green ...170 C6
Hornsey ...66 E1
Hornsey Vale ...67 F2
Hounslow ...135 F3
Hounslow West ...134 C4
Hoxton ...7 G3
Hurst Park ...173 H5
The Hyde ...63 H2
Ilford ...90 B1
Isle of Dogs ...125 F4
Isleworth ...136 C4
Islington ...85 K5
Joyden's Wood ...170 C6
Kenley ...121 K6
Kensal Green ...100 A1
Kensal Rise ...100 C3
Kensal Town ...100 C3
Kensington ...119 K3
Kentish Town ...84 C4
Kenton ...61 J2
Keston ...215 H2
Keston Mark ...215 H1
Kevingtown ...203 G3
Kew ...137 G1
Kidbrooke ...146 B3
Kilburn ...82 C6
Kingsbury ...62 D3
Kingsland ...86 A5
Kingston upon Thames ...191 H1
Kingston Vale ...176 A1
Kitt's End ...20 C1
Knightsbridge ...14 D2
Knight's Hill ...162 D3
Ladywell ...144 D5
Lambeth ...17 J4
Lampton ...135 G2
Lea Bridge ...87 F1
Lee ...165 J1
Lessness Heath ...129 J6
Lewisham ...145 F5
Leyton ...88 B1
Leytonstone ...70 D5
Limehouse ...105 G6
Lisson Grove ...9 F1
Little Heath ...73 J1
Little Ilford ...90 A3
Little Stanmore ...44 B4
Locksbottom ...216 B1
Long Ditton ...190 C5
Longlands ...167 H5
Lower Clapton ...86 E2
Lower Edmonton ...36 A4
Lower Feltham ...153 H5
Lower Green ...189 G6
Lower Holloway ...84 E3
Lower Place ...98 E1
Lower Sunbury ...172 A6
Lower Sydenham ...164 A6
Loxford ...90 C3
Maida Vale ...100 E2
Maitland Park ...83 K4
Manor Park ...89 J2
Marks Gate ...56 A5
Marylebone ...9 G2
Mayfair ...9 J6
Maypole ...170 B5
Merry Hill ...28 B3
Merton ...177 K4
Merton Park ...177 J5
Mile End ...105 G3
Mill Hill ...31 K5
Mill Meads ...106 B1
Millwall ...124 D3
Mitcham ...179 F6
Monken Hadley ...20 C3
Monks Orchard ...197 K4
Moor Park ...26 A6
Morden ...193 K1
Morden Park ...193 H3
Mortlake ...137 K3
Motspur Park ...192 D3
Mottingham ...166 B4
Muswell Hill ...48 A4
Nash ...215 F4
Neasden ...81 F2
New Addington ...214 B5
New Barnet ...21 F6
New Beckenham ...182 B2
New Malden ...72 D5
Newbury Park ...72 D1
New Charlton ...126 C4
New Cross ...144 B3
New Cross Gate ...144 B2
New Eltham ...167 G4
Newington ...17 K5
New Malden ...176 C6
New Southgate ...34 C6
New Town ...171 J1
Noel Park ...49 H5
Norbiton ...175 G5
Norbury ...180 C5
North Acton ...98 E3
North Cheam ...208 B1
North Cray ...169 H5
North End ...65 G5

North End ...150 C2
North Feltham ...134 A6
North Finchley ...47 G2
North Harrow ...59 K3
North Hyde ...114 D4
North Kensington ...100 B4
Northolt ...78 A5
North Sheen ...137 J3
Northumberland Heath ...149 K1
North Wembley ...61 H5
Northwood ...40 A4
Northwood Hills ...40 B5
North Woolwich ...126 D2
Norwood Green ...115 F4
Norwood New Town ...180 E2
Notting Hill ...100 C6
Nunhead ...143 K5
Oakleigh Park ...33 H4
Oakwood ...34 D1
Old Bexley ...169 H2
Old Ford ...87 G6
Old Malden ...192 A4
Old Oak Common ...99 H5
Orpington ...202 B6
Osidge ...34 C4
Osterley ...135 H1
Oxhey ...27 H1
Paddington ...8 A2
Palmers Green ...34 E5
Park Langley ...199 F3
Park Royal ...98 C2
Parsons Green ...139 K3
Peckham ...143 J3
Penge ...181 K5
Pentonville ...5 H3
Perivale ...79 J6
Petersham ...157 F3
Petts Wood ...201 J1
Pimlico ...121 H5
Pinner ...59 H1
Pinner Green ...41 G5
Pinnerwood Park ...41 G3
Plaistow ...106 D2
Plaistow ...183 K2
Plashet ...89 H4
Plumstead ...127 H5
Plumstead Common ...128 A6
Ponders End ...24 E6
Poplar ...105 J6
Poverest ...202 B1
Preston ...61 K5
Primrose Hill ...3 H1
Purfleet ...131 K5
Putney ...139 G6
Putney Heath ...159 F2
Putney Vale ...158 D5
Queensbury ...44 A6
Queens Park ...100 C1
Rainham ...111 K2
Ramsden ...202 D5
Rayners Lane ...59 K5
Raynes Park ...177 F6
Redbridge ...71 G2
Regent's Park ...3 K3
Richmond ...137 F6
Richmond Hill ...157 F1
Rise Park ...57 G4
Roehampton ...158 C6
Romford ...56 E6
The Rookery ...26 E2
Roundshaw ...211 F4
Roxeth ...60 C6
Ruislip ...58 C3
Ruislip Common ...58 B2
Ruislip Gardens ...76 C1
Ruislip Manor ...58 E6
Rush Green ...75 G4
Ruxley ...187 F2
Rydens ...188 C2
St George in the East ...104 C6
St Giles ...10 D3
St Helier ...194 B5
St James's ...16 C1
St Johns ...144 D5
St John's Wood ...101 H1
St Luke's ...6 D6
St Margarets ...156 D1
St Mary Cray ...202 D2
St Pancras ...5 F5
St Paul's Cray ...186 B5
Sands End ...140 B2
Seething Wells ...190 C3
Selhurst ...196 E2
Seven Kings ...72 E5
Shacklewell ...86 C2
Shadwell ...104 E6
Shepherd's Bush ...118 E1
Shirley ...197 K6
Shooters Hill ...147 H2
Shoreditch ...7 F5
Shortlands ...183 H6
Sidcup ...168 C6
Silvertown ...126 C3
Sipson ...112 C5
Slade Green ...150 D3
Soho ...10 C4
Somers Town ...5 F4
Southall ...114 C2
South Beddington ...210 D4
Southborough ...200 E3
South Bromley ...106 B5
South Croydon ...211 H4
Southend ...165 F6
Southfields ...159 K3
Southgate ...34 C2
South Hackney ...86 E6
South Hampstead ...83 G5
South Harrow ...78 B1
South Hornchurch ...93 J5
South Kensington ...120 B5
South Lambeth ...141 K1
South Norwood ...180 E6
South Oxhey ...27 F5
South Ruislip ...77 H2

South Tottenham ...68 A2
South Wimbledon ...178 B1
South Woodford ...52 E5
Spitalfields ...13 J1
Spring Grove ...135 J2
Spring Park ...198 D6
Stamford Hill ...68 B4
Stanmore ...43 H1
Stanwell ...152 A1
Stepney ...104 E4
Stockwell ...141 K4
Stoke Newington ...68 B6
Stonehill Green ...187 K2
Stoneleigh ...207 H3
Strand ...10 E5
Stratford ...88 A5
Stratford Marsh ...87 K6
Stratford New Town ...88 A4
Strawberry Hill ...155 J5
Streatham ...179 K1
Streatham Hill ...161 K3
Streatham Park ...161 G6
Streatham Vale ...179 G3
Stroud Green ...67 G3
Sudbury ...79 F3
Summerstown ...160 C4
Sundridge ...184 B2
Surbiton ...190 E5
Sutton ...208 E3
Swiss Cottage ...83 H6
Sydenham ...182 A1
Teddington ...173 J2
Temple Hill ...151 G5
Temple Mills ...87 K5
Thames Ditton ...190 A3
Thamesmead ...109 F6
Thornton Heath ...180 C5
Tokyngton ...80 D4
Tolworth ...191 H5
Tooting ...178 C1
Tooting Graveney ...178 C1
Tottenham ...50 A5
Tottenham Hale ...50 B6
Totteridge ...32 E3
Totteridge Green ...32 A3
Tufnell Park ...84 C2
Tulse Hill ...162 C3
Twickenham ...155 K3
Underhill ...32 E1
Upper Clapton ...68 E5
Upper Edmonton ...36 C6
Upper Elmers End ...198 C2
Upper Holloway ...66 C6
Upper Norwood ...180 E4
Upper Shirley ...212 E2
Upper Sydenham ...163 H6
Upper Tooting ...160 D5
Upper Walthamstow ...70 A1
Upton ...89 F5
Upton Park ...89 G5
Vale of Health ...83 H1
Vauxhall ...121 K5
Waddon ...195 K6
Walham Green ...139 K2
Wallend ...90 A6
Wallington ...210 B3
Walthamstow ...51 J6
Walworth ...122 D6
Wandle Park ...196 B6
Wandsworth ...139 K5
Wanstead ...71 F4
Wapping ...123 J1
Watford Heath ...27 J2
Wealdstone ...43 J2
Welling ...148 C4
Welsh Harp ...63 F5
Wembley ...80 A2
Wembley Park ...80 C1
West Acton ...98 C5
West Barnes ...193 F2
West Bedfont ...132 E2
Westbourne Green ...100 E3
West Brompton ...120 A6
West Drayton ...112 A3
West Dulwich ...162 E4
West Ealing ...116 B1
West Ewell ...207 F4
West Green ...49 J6
West Hampstead ...82 E3
West Harrow ...60 C4
West Heath ...65 F6
West Hendon ...128 E6
West Hill ...159 H2
West Kensington ...119 G5
West Kilburn ...100 C2
Westminster ...16 B5
West Molesey ...188 C1
West Norwood ...162 D6
Weston Green ...189 K5
West Ruislip ...58 A3
West Wickham ...199 G5
Whetstone ...33 F4
Whitechapel ...104 D4
Whitton ...155 F1
Widmore ...184 C5
Willesden ...81 K5
Willesden Green ...81 K6
Wilmington ...170 E6
Wimbledon ...177 H1
Winchmore Hill ...35 H5
Wood End ...94 C4
Wood End Green ...94 C4
Woodford ...52 D3
Woodford Bridge ...53 K3
Woodford Green ...52 E3
Woodford Wells ...52 E1
Wood Green ...49 G5
Woodlands ...135 J4
Woodside ...197 H3
Woodside Park ...32 C6
Woolwich ...127 F6
Worcester Park ...192 E6
World's End ...23 J6
The Wrythe ...194 D6
Yeading ...95 G3

USING THE STREET INDEX

Street names are listed alphabetically. Each street name is followed by its postal town or area locality, the Postcode District, the page number, and the reference to the square in which the name is found.

Standard index entries are shown as follows:

Aaron Hill Rd *EHAM* E6 ....**108** A4

Street names and selected addresses not shown on the map due to scale restrictions are shown in the index with an asterisk:

Abbeville Ms *CLAP* SW4 * **141** J6

GENERAL ABBREVIATIONS

ACC	ACCESS	CTYD	COURTYARD	HLS	HILLS	MWY	MOTORWAY	SE	SOUTH EAST
ALY	ALLEY	CUTT	CUTTINGS	HO	HOUSE	N	NORTH	SER	SERVICE AREA
AP	APPROACH	CV	COVE	HOL	HOLLOW	NE	NORTH EAST	SH	SHORE
AR	ARCADE	CYN	CANYON	HOSP	HOSPITAL	NW	NORTH WEST	SHOP	SHOPPING
ASS	ASSOCIATION	DEPT	DEPARTMENT	HRB	HARBOUR	O/P	OVERPASS	SKWY	SKYWAY
AV	AVENUE	DL	DALE	HTH	HEATH	OFF	OFFICE	SMT	SUMMIT
BCH	BEACH	DM	DAM	HTS	HEIGHTS	ORCH	ORCHARD	SOC	SOCIETY
BLDS	BUILDINGS	DR	DRIVE	HVN	HAVEN	OV	OVAL	SPR	SPUR
BND	BEND	DRO	DROVE	HWY	HIGHWAY	PAL	PALACE	SPG	SPRING
BNK	BANK	DRY	DRIVEWAY	IMP	IMPERIAL	PAS	PASSAGE	SQ	SQUARE
BR	BRIDGE	DWGS	DWELLINGS	IN	INLET	PAV	PAVILION	ST	STREET
BRK	BROOK	E	EAST	IND EST	INDUSTRIAL ESTATE	PDE	PARADE	STN	STATION
BTM	BOTTOM	EMB	EMBANKMENT	INF	INFIRMARY	PH	PUBLIC HOUSE	STR	STREAM
BUS	BUSINESS	EMBY	EMBASSY	INFO	INFORMATION	PK	PARK	STRD	STRAND
BVD	BOULEVARD	ESP	ESPLANADE	INT	INTERCHANGE	PKWY	PARKWAY	SW	SOUTH WEST
BY	BYPASS	EST	ESTATE	IS	ISLAND	PL	PLACE	TDG	TRADING
CATH	CATHEDRAL	EX	EXCHANGE	JCT	JUNCTION	PLN	PLAIN	TER	TERRACE
CEM	CEMETERY	EXPY	EXPRESSWAY	JTY	JETTY	PLNS	PLAINS	THWY	THROUGHWAY
CEN	CENTRE	EXT	EXTENSION	KG	KING	PLZ	PLAZA	TNL	TUNNEL
CFT	CROFT	F/O	FLYOVER	KNL	KNOLL	POL	POLICE STATION	TOLL	TOLLWAY
CH	CHURCH	FC	FOOTBALL CLUB	L	LAKE	PR	PRINCE	TPK	TURNPIKE
CHA	CHASE	FK	FORK	LA	LANE	PREC	PRECINCT	TR	TRACK
CHYD	CHURCHYARD	FLD	FIELD	LDG	LODGE	PREP	PREPARATORY	TRL	TRAIL
CIR	CIRCLE	FLDS	FIELDS	LGT	LIGHT	PRIM	PRIMARY	TWR	TOWER
CIRC	CIRCUS	FLS	FALLS	LK	LOCK	PROM	PROMENADE	U/P	UNDERPASS
CL	CLOSE	FLS	FLATS	LKS	LAKES	PRS	PRINCESS	UNI	UNIVERSITY
CLFS	CLIFFS	FM	FARM	LNDG	LANDING	PRT	PORT	UPR	UPPER
CMP	CAMP	FT	FORT	LTL	LITTLE	PT	POINT	V	VALE
CNR	CORNER	FWY	FREEWAY	LWR	LOWER	PTH	PATH	VA	VALLEY
CO	COUNTY	FY	FERRY	MAG	MAGISTRATE	PZ	PIAZZA	VIAD	VIADUCT
COLL	COLLEGE	GA	GATE	MAN	MANSIONS	QD	QUADRANT	VIL	VILLA
COM	COMMON	GAL	GALLERY	MD	MEAD	QU	QUEEN	VIS	VISTA
COMM	COMMISSION	GDN	GARDEN	MDW	MEADOWS	QY	QUAY	VLG	VILLAGE
CON	CONVENT	GDNS	GARDENS	MEM	MEMORIAL	R	RIVER	VLS	VILLAS
COT	COTTAGE	GLD	GLADE	MKT	MARKET	RBT	ROUNDABOUT	VW	VIEW
COTS	COTTAGES	GLN	GLEN	MKTS	MARKETS	RD	ROAD	W	WEST
CP	CAPE	GN	GREEN	ML	MALL	RDG	RIDGE	WD	WOOD
CPS	COPSE	GND	GROUND	ML	MILL	REP	REPUBLIC	WHF	WHARF
CR	CREEK	GRA	GRANGE	MNR	MANOR	RES	RESERVOIR	WK	WALK
CREM	CREMATORIUM	GRG	GARAGE	MS	MEWS	RFC	RUGBY FOOTBALL CLUB	WKS	WALKS
CRS	CRESCENT	GT	GREAT	MSN	MISSION	RI	RISE	WLS	WELLS
CSWY	CAUSEWAY	GTWY	GATEWAY	MT	MOUNT	RP	RAMP	WY	WAY
CT	COURT	GV	GROVE	MTN	MOUNTAIN	RW	ROW	YD	YARD
CTRL	CENTRAL	HGR	HIGHER	MTS	MOUNTAINS	S	SOUTH	YHA	YOUTH HOSTEL
CTS	COURTS	HL	HILL	MUS	MUSEUM	SCH	SCHOOL		

POSTCODE TOWNS AND AREA ABBREVIATIONS

ABYW	Abbey Wood	CAMTN	Camden Town	EA	Ealing	GPK	Gidea Park	LBTH	Lambeth
ACT	Acton	CAN/RD	Canning Town/	EBAR	East Barnet	GSTN	Garston	LEE/GVPK	Lee/Grove Park
ALP/SUD	Alperton/Sudbury		Royal Docks	EBED/NFELT	East Bedfont/	GTPST	Great Portland Street	LEW	Lewisham
ARCH	Archway	CANST	Cannon Street station		North Feltham	GWRST	Gower Street	LEY	Leyton
ASHF	Ashford (Surrey)	CAR	Carshalton	ECT	Earl's Court	HACK	Hackney	LINN	Lincoln's Inn
BAL	Balham	CAT	Catford	ED	Edmonton	HAMP	Hampstead	LOTH	Lothbury
BANK	Bank	CAVSQ/HST	Cavendish Square/	EDGW	Edgware	HAYES	Hayes	LSQ/SEVD	Leicester Square/
BAR	Barnet		Harley Street	EDUL	East Dulwich	HBRY	Highbury		Seven Dials
BARB	Barbican	CDALE/KGS	Colindale/	EFNCH	East Finchley	HCH	Hornchurch	LVPST	Liverpool Street
BARK	Barking		Kingsbury	EHAM	East Ham	HCIRC	Holborn Circus	MANHO	Mansion House
BARK/HLT	Barkingside/Hainault	CEND/HSY/T	Crouch End/	ELTH/MOT	Eltham/Mottingham	HDN	Hendon	MBLAR	Marble Arch
BARN	Barnes		Hornsey/Turnpike Lane	EMB	Embankment	HDTCH	Houndsditch	MHST	Marylebone High Street
BAY/PAD	Bayswater/	CHARL	Charlton	EMPK	Emerson Park	HEST	Heston	MLHL	Mill Hill
	Paddington	CHCR	Charing Cross	EN	Enfield	HGDN/ICK	Hillingdon/Ickenham	MNPK	Manor Park
BCTR	Becontree	CHDH	Chadwell Heath	ENC/FH	Enfield Chase/Forty Hill	HGT	Highgate	MON	Monument
BECK	Beckenham	CHEAM	Cheam	ERITH	Erith	HHOL	High Holborn	MORT/ESHN	Mortlake/
BELMT	Belmont	CHEL	Chelsea	ERITHM	Erith Marshes	HMSMTH	Hammersmith		East Sheen
BELV	Belvedere	CHIG	Chigwell	ESH/CLAY	Esher/Claygate	HNHL	Herne Hill	MRDN	Morden
BERM/RHTH	Bermondsey/	CHING	Chingford	EW	Ewell	HNWL	Hanwell	MTCM	Mitcham
	Rotherhithe	CHSGTN	Chessington	FARR	Farringdon	HOL/ALD	Holborn/Aldwych	MUSWH	Muswell Hill
BETH	Bethnal Green	CHST	Chislehurst	FBAR/BDGN	Friern Barnet/	HOLWY	Holloway	MV/WKIL	Maida Vale/
BFN/LL	Blackfen/Longlands	CHSWK	Chiswick		Bounds Green	HOM	Homerton		West Kilburn
BGVA	Belgravia	CITYW	City of London west	FELT	Feltham	HOR/WEW	Horton/West Ewell	MYFR/PICC	Mayfair/Piccadilly
BKHH	Buckhurst Hill	CLAP	Clapham	FENCHST	Fenchurch Street	HPTN	Hampton	MYFR/PKLN	Mayfair/Park Lane
BKHTH/KID	Blackheath/	CLAY	Clayhall	FITZ	Fitzrovia	HRW	Harrow	NFNCH/WDSPK	North Finchley/
	Kidbrooke	CLKNW	Clerkenwell	FLST/FETLN	Fleet Street/	HSLW	Hounslow		Woodside Park
BLKFR	Blackfriars	CLPT	Clapton		Fetter Lane	HSLWW	Hounslow west	NKENS	North Kensington
BMLY	Bromley	CMBW	Camberwell	FNCH	Finchley	HTHAIR	Heathrow Airport	NOXST/BSQ	New Oxford Street/
BMSBY	Bloomsbury	CONDST	Conduit Street	FSBYE	Finsbury east	HYS/HAR	Hayes/Harlington		Bloomsbury Square
BORE	Borehamwood	COVGDN	Covent Garden	FSBYPK	Finsbury Park	IL	Ilford	NRWD	Norwood
BOW	Bow	CRICK	Cricklewood	FSBYW	Finsbury west	ISL	Islington	NTGHL	Notting Hill
BROCKY	Brockley	CROY/NA	Croydon/	FSTGT	Forest Gate	ISLW	Isleworth	NTHLT	Northolt
BRXN/ST	Brixton north/		New Addington	FSTH	Forest Hill	KENS	Kensington	NTHWD	Northwood
	Stockwell	CRW	Collier Row	FUL/PGN	Fulham/	KIL/WHAMP	Kilburn/	NWCR	New Cross
BRXS/STRHM	Brixton south/	DAGE	Dagenham east		Parsons Green		West Hampstead	NWDGN	Norwood Green
	Streatham Hill	DAGW	Dagenham west	GDMY/SEVK	Goodmayes/	KTBR	Knightsbridge	NWMAL	New Malden
BRYLDS	Berrylands	DART	Dartford		Seven Kings	KTN/HRWW/WS	Kenton/	OBST	Old Broad Street
BTFD	Brentford	DEN/HRF	Denham/Harefield	GFD/PVL	Greenford/Perivale		Harrow Weald/Wealdstone	ORP	Orpington
BTSEA	Battersea	DEPT	Deptford	GINN	Gray's Inn	KTTN	Kentish Town	OXHEY	Oxhey
BUSH	Bushey	DUL	Dulwich	GLDGN	Golders Green	KUT/HW	Kingston upon Thames/	OXSTW	Oxford Street west
BXLY	Bexley	E/WMO/HCT	East & West	GNTH/NBYPK	Gants Hill/		Hampton Wick	PECK	Peckham
BXLYHN	Bexleyheath north		Molesey/		Newbury Park	KUTN/CMB	Kingston upon	PEND	Ponders End
BXLYHS	Bexleyheath south		Hampton Court	GNWCH	Greenwich		Thames north/Coombe	PGE/AN	Penge/Anerley

PIM....Pimlico
PIN....Pinner
PLMGR....Palmers Green
PLSTW....Plaistow
POP/IOD....Poplar/Isle of Dogs
PUR....Purfleet
PUR/KEN....Purley/Kenley
PUT/ROE....Putney/Roehampton
RAIN....Rainham (Gt Lon)
RCH/KEW....Richmond/Kew
RCHPK/HAM....Richmond Park/Ham
RDART....Rural Dartford
REDBR....Redbridge
REGST....Regent Street
RKW/CH/CXG....Rickmansworth/Chorleywood/Croxley Green
ROM....Romford
ROMW/RG....Romford West/Rush Green
RSLP....Ruislip
RSQ....Russell Square

RYLN/HDSTN....Rayners Lane/Headstone
RYNPK....Raynes Park
SAND/SEL....Sanderstead/Selsdon
SCUP....Sidcup
SDTCH....Shoreditch
SEVS/STOTM....Seven Sisters/South Tottenham
SHB....Shepherd's Bush
SHPTN....Shepperton
SKENS....South Kensington
SNWD....South Norwood
SOCK/AV....South Ockendon/Aveley
SOHO/CST....Soho/Carnaby Street
SOHO/SHAV....Soho/Shaftesbury Avenue
SRTFD....Stratford
STAN....Stanmore
STBT....St Bart's
STHGT/OAK....Southgate/Oakwood
STHL....Southall

STHWK....Southwark
STJS....St James's
STJSPK....St James's Park
STJWD....St John's Wood
STKPK....Stockley Park
STLK....St Luke's
STMC/STPC....St Mary Cray/St Paul's Cray
STNW/STAM....Stoke Newington/Stamford Hill
STP....St Paul's
STPAN....St Pancras
STRHM/NOR....Streatham/Norbury
STWL/WRAY....Stanwell/Wraysbury
SUN....Sunbury
SURB....Surbiton
SUT....Sutton
SWFD....South Woodford
SYD....Sydenham
TEDD....Teddington
THDIT....Thames Ditton
THHTH....Thornton Heath
THMD....Thamesmead

TOOT....Tooting
TOTM....Tottenham
TPL/STR....Temple/Strand
TRDG/WHET....Totteridge/Whetstone
TWK....Twickenham
TWRH....Tower Hill
UED....Upper Edmonton
UX/CGN....Uxbridge/Colham Green
VX/NE....Vauxhall/Nine Elms
WALTH....Walthamstow
WALW....Walworth
WAN....Wanstead
WAND/EARL....Wandsworth/Earlsfield
WAP....Wapping
WAT....Watford
WATN....Watford north
WATW....Watford west
WBLY....Wembley
WBPTN....West Brompton
WCHMH....Winchmore Hill
WCHPL....Whitechapel

WDGN....Wood Green
WDR/YW....West Drayton/Yiewsley
WEA....West Ealing
WELL....Welling
WEST....Westminster
WESTW....Westminster west
WFD....Woodford
WHALL....Whitehall
WHTN....Whitton
WIM/MER....Wimbledon/Merton
WKENS....West Kensington
WLGTN....Wallington
WLSDN....Willesden
WNWD....West Norwood
WOOL/PLUM....Woolwich/Plumstead
WOT/HER....Walton-on-Thames/Hersham
WPK....Worcester Park
WWKM....West Wickham
YEAD....Yeading

Index - streets

1 Av - Ado

1 Av WOOL/PLUM SE18....127 G3

A

Aaron Hill Rd EHAM E6....108 A4
Abbess Cl BRXS/STRHM SW2....162 C3
Abbeville Ms CLAP SW4 *....141 J6
Abbeville Rd CEND/HSY/T N8....66 D1
CLAP SW4....161 H1
Abbey Av ALP/SUD HA0....98 A1
Abbey Cl HYS/HAR UB3....95 K2
NTHLT UB5....41 F6
PIN HA5....47 J4
ROM RM1....75 H5
Abbey Crs BELV DA17....129 H4
Abbeydale Rd ALP/SUD HA0....80 B6
Abbey Dr BXLY DA5....169 K4
TOOT SW17....179 F1
Abbeyfield Cl MTCM CR4....178 D5
Abbeyfield Est
BERM/RHTH SE16....123 K4
Abbeyfield Rd
BERM/RHTH SE16....123 K4
Abbey fields Cl WLSDN NW10....98 C2
Abbey Gdns
BERM/RHTH SE16....123 H4
HMSMTH W6....119 H6
STJWD NW8....101 G1
Abbey Gv ABYW SE2....128 C4
Abbey Ms WALTH E17....69 J2
Abbey Mt BELV DA17....129 G5
Abbey Orchard St WEST SW1P....16 D4
Abbey Pk BECK BR3....182 D3
Abbey Pl DART DA1 *....151 G6
Abbey Rd BARK IG11....90 C6
BELV DA17....128 E4
BXLYHS DA6....149 F5
CROY/NA CRO....211 H1
EN EN1....24 A6
GNTH/NBYPK IG2....72 D2
KIL/WHAMP NW6....83 F6
SRTFD E15....106 B1
WIM/MER SW19....178 B3
WLSDN NW10....80 D6
Abbey Ter ABYW SE2....128 D3
Abbey Vw MLHL NW7....31 H5
Abbey Wk E/WMO/HCT KT8....173 G5
Abbey Wood Rd ABYW SE2....128 C4
Abbot Cl RSLP HA4....77 H1
Abbotsbury Cl SRTFD E15....106 A1
WKENS W14 *....119 J2
Abbotsbury Gdns PIN HA5....59 G3
Abbotsbury Ms PECK SE15....143 K4
Abbotsbury Rd MRDN SM4....194 A1
WKENS W14....119 H2
WWKM BR4....199 J6
Abbots Cl STMC/STPC BR5....201 H5
Abbots Dr RYLN/HDSTN HA2....60 A6
Abbotsford Av
SEVS/STOTM N15....67 J1
Abbotsford Gdns WFD IG8....52 E3
Abbotsford Rd
CDMY/SEVK IG3....73 G6
Abbots Gdns EFNCH N2....65 H1
Abbots Gn CROY/NA CRO....213 F4
Abbotshade Rd
BERM/RHTH SE16 *....124 A1
Abbotshall Av
STHGT/OAK N14....34 C5
Abbotshall Rd CAT SE6....165 G3
Abbots La STHWK SE1....19 H1
Abbotsleigh Cl BELMT SM2....209 F5
Abbotsleigh Rd
STRHM/NOR SW16....161 H6
Abbots Mnr PIM SW1V *....121 G5
Abbotsmede Cl TWK TW1....156 A4

Abbots Pk BRXS/STRHM SW2....162 B3
Abbot's Pl KIL/WHAMP NW6....83 F6
Abbots Rd CHEAM SM3....208 C2
EDGW HA8....45 F3
EHAM E6....89 H6
Abbots Ter CEND/HSY/T N8....66 E3
Abbott Rd POP/IOD E14....106 B5
Abbott Av RYNPK SW20....177 G5
Abbott Cl HPTN TW12....172 D2
NTHLT UB5....77 K4
Abbotts Cl IS N1 *....85 J5
ROMW/RG RM7....56 D6
THMD SE28....109 J6
Abbotts Crs CHING E4....38 B6
ENC/FH EN2....23 H5
Abbotts Dr ALP/SUD HA0....61 H6
WALTH E17....51 F5
Abbotts Md RCHPK/HAM TW10 *....156 D6
Abbotts Park Rd LEY E10....70 A4
Abbotts Rd BAR EN5....21 F5
MTCM CR4....195 H1
STHL UB1....114 D1
Abbott's Wk BXLYHN DA7....148 E1
Abchurch La MANHO EC4N....13 F5
Abdale Rd SHB W12....118 E1
Abercairn Rd
STRHM/NOR SW16....179 H3
Aberconway Rd MRDN SM4....178 A6
Abercorn Cl MLHL NW7....46 C3
STJWD NW8....101 G2
Abercorn Crs RYLN/HDSTN HA2....60 B5
Abercorn Gdns CHDH RM6....73 H4
KTN/HRWW/W HA3....61 K4
Abercorn Gv RSLP HA4....58 B1
Abercorn Pl STJWD NW8....101 G2
Abercorn Rd MLHL NW7....46 C3
STAN HA7....43 J3
Abercorn Wy STHWK SE1....123 H5
Abercrombie Dr EN EN1....24 C2
Abercrombie St BTSEA SW11....140 D3
Aberdare Cl WWKM BR4....199 F6
Aberdare Gdns
KIL/WHAMP NW6....83 F5
MLHL NW7....46 B3
Aberdare Rd PEND EN3....24 E5
Aberdeen La HBRY N5....85 H3
Aberdeen Pde UED N18 *....50 D1
Aberdeen Pk HBRY N5....85 J3
Aberdeen Pl STJWD NW8....2 A7
Aberdeen Rd CROY/NA CRO....211 J3
HBRY N5....85 J2
KTN/HRWW/W HA3....43 F6
UED N18....50 D1
WLSDN NW10....81 H5
Aberdeen Ter BKHTH/KID SE3....145 G3
Aberdour Rd BCTR RM8....91 H1
Aberdour St STHWK SE1....19 G6
Aberfeldy St POP/IOD E14....106 A5
Aberford Gdns
WOOL/PLUM SE18....146 D2
Aberfoyle Rd
STRHM/NOR SW16....179 J3
Abergeldie Rd
LEE/GVPK SE12....166 A1
Abernethy Rd LEW SE13....145 H5
Abersham Rd HACK E8....86 B3
Abery St WOOL/PLUM SE18....127 K4
Abingdon Cl STHWK SE1 *....19 K7
WIM/MER SW19....178 B1
Abingdon Rd FNCH N3....47 G5
KENS W8....119 K3
STRHM/NOR SW16....179 K4
Abingdon St WEST SW1P....16 E3

Abingdon Vls KENS W8....119 K3
Abingdon Wy ORP BR6....217 H2
Abinger Av BELMT SM2....208 A6
Abinger Cl BMLY BR1....184 D6
CROY/NA CRO....214 A4
RYNPK SW20....91 G2
Abinger Dr NRWD SE19....180 D3
Abinger Gdns ISLW TW7....135 K4
Abinger Gv DEPT SE8....124 C6
Abinger Ms MV/WKIL W9....100 E3
Abinger Rd CHSWK W4....118 B3
Abney Park Ter
STNW/STAM N16 *....68 B6
Aboyne Dr RYNPK SW20....176 D5
Aboyne Rd TOOT SW17....160 C5
WLSDN NW10....81 G1
Abridge Gdns CRW RM5....56 C2
Abridge Wy BARK IG11....109 H1
Abyssinia Cl BTSEA SW11....140 D5
Abyssinia Rd BTSEA SW11....140 D5
Acacia Av BTFD TW8....136 C1
HCH RM12....75 H6
RSLP HA4....58 E5
TOTM N17....49 K3
WBLY HA9....80 A3
YEAD UB4....94 D5
Acacia Cl DEPT SE8....124 B4
KTN/HRWW/W HA3....42 E2
STMC/STPC BR5....201 J2
Acacia Dr CHEAM SM3....193 J5
Acacia Gdns STJWD NW8....2 B2
WWKM BR4....199 F6
Acacia Gv DUL SE21....162 E4
NWMAL KT3....176 B6
Acacia Ms WDR/YW UB7....112 A6
Acacia Pl STJWD NW8....2 B2
Acacia Rd ACT W3....98 E6
BECK BR3....182 C6
DART DA1....171 F3
ENC/FH EN2....23 K2
HPTN TW12....173 F2
MTCM CR4....179 F5
STJWD NW8....2 B2
STRHM/NOR SW16....179 K4
WALTH E17....69 G3
WAN E11....70 C6
WDGN N22....49 G4
Acacia Wy BFN/LL DA15....168 A3
Academy Gdns CROY/NA CRO....197 G5
NTHLT UB5....95 H1
Academy Pl
WOOL/PLUM SE18....146 E2
Academy Rd
WOOL/PLUM SE18....146 E1
Acanthus Dr STHWK SE1....123 H5
Acanthus Rd BTSEA SW11....141 F4
Accommodation Rd
GLDGN NW11....64 D4
Ace Pde CHSGTN KT9....206 A1
Acer Av RYAD UB4....95 J3
Acfold Rd FUL/PGN SW6....140 A2
Achilles Cl STHWK SE1....123 H5
Achilles Rd KIL/WHAMP NW6....82 E3
Achilles St NWCR SE14....144 B1
Acklam Rd NKENS W10....100 D4
Acklington Dr CDALE/KGS NW9....45 G4
Ackmar Rd FUL/PGN SW6....139 K2
Ackroyd Dr BOW E3....105 J4
Ackroyd Rd FSTH SE23....164 A2
Acland Cl WOOL/PLUM SE18....147 J1
Acland Crs CMBW SE5....142 E5
Acland Rd CRICK NW2....81 K4
Acock Gv NTHLT UB5....78 B2
Acol Crs RSLP HA4....77 F3
Acol Rd KIL/WHAMP NW6....82 E5
Acorn Cl CHING E4....51 K1
CHST BR7....185 H1
ENC/FH EN2....23 G2
HPTN TW12....173 G2
STAN HA7....43 H3
Acorn Gdns ACT W3....99 F4
NRWD SE19....181 G4
Acorn Gv HYS/HAR UB3....133 J1

RSLP HA4....76 D2
Acorn Pde PECK SE15 *....143 J1
Acorn Rd DART DA1....150 C6
Acorns Wy ESH/CLAY KT10....204 C5
Acorn Wy FSTH SE23....164 A5
ORP BR6....216 B2
Acre Dr EDUL SE22....143 H5
Acre La BRXS/STRHM SW2....142 A5
CAR SM5....210 A2
Acre Rd DAGE RM10....92 D5
KUTN/CMB KT2....175 F4
WIM/MER SW19....178 C2
Acre Wy NTHWD HA6....40 D4
Acris St WAND/EARL SW18....140 B6
Acton Cl ED N9....36 C4
Acton Hill Ms ACT W3....117 J1
Acton La ACT W3....117 K2
WLSDN NW10....98 E2
Acton Ms HACK E8....86 B6
Acton St FSBYW WC1X....5 G5
Acuba Rd WAND/EARL SW18....160 A4
Acworth Cl DART DA1 *....139 J1
Acworth Pl DART DA1 *....151 G6
Ada Gdns POP/IOD E14....106 B5
SRTFD E15....88 D6
Adair Cl SNWD SE25....181 J6
Adair Rd NKENS W10....100 C3
Adam Cl CAT SE6....163 K4
FSTH SE23....183 K1
Adam & Eve Ms KENS W8....119 K3
Adam Rd CHING E4....51 H2
Adams Cl BRYLDS KT5....191 G3
CDALE/KGS NW9....62 E5
FNCH N3....46 C5
Adams Ms TOOT SW17....160 E4
WDGN N22 *....49 F5
Adamson Rd CAN/RD E16....106 E5
HAMP NW3....83 H5
Adamson Wy BECK BR3....199 F2
Adams Pl HOLWY N7....85 F3
Adamsrill Rd SYD SE26....164 A6
Adams Rd BECK BR3....198 B2
TOTM N17....49 K5
Adam's Rw MYFR/PKLN W1K....9 H6
Adams Sq BXLYHS DA6....149 F4
Adam St TPL/STR WC2R....11 F5
Adams Wk KUT/HW KT1....175 F5
Adams Wy SNWD SE25....197 G3
Adam Wk FUL/PGN SW6 *....139 F1
Ada Pl BETH E2....86 C6
Adare Wk STRHM/NOR SW16....161 K4
Ada Rd ALP/SUD HA0 *....79 K5
CMBW SE5....143 F1
Ada St HACK E8....86 D6
Adderley Gdns
ELTH/MOT SE9....167 F6
Adderley Gv BTSEA SW11....141 F6
Adderley Rd
KTN/HRWW/W HA3....43 F4
Adderley St POP/IOD E14....106 A5
Addington Dr
NFNCH/WDSP N12....47 H2
Addington Gv SYD SE26....164 B6
Addington Rd BOW E3....105 J2
CAN/RD E16....106 C3
CROY/NA CRO....196 B5
FSBYPK N4....67 G4
SAND/SEL CR2....214 A2
WWKM BR4....214 A2
Addington Sq
CMBW SE5....142 D1
Addington Village Rd
CROY/NA CRO....213 H4
Addis Cl PEND EN3....25 F2
Addiscombe Av
CROY/NA CRO....197 H4
Addiscombe Cl
KTN/HRWW/W HA3....61 J2
Addiscombe Court Rd
CROY/NA CRO....197 F5
Addiscombe Gv
CROY/NA CRO....196 E6
Addiscombe Rd
CROY/NA CRO....197 F6
Addison Av HSLW TW3....135 H2
NTGHL W11....119 H1

STHGT/OAK N14....34 B1
Addison Bridge Pl WKENS W14....119 J4
Addison Cl NTHWD HA6....40 E4
STMC/STPC BR5....201 H3
Addison Crs WKENS W14....119 H3
Addison Dr LEE/GVPK SE12....146 A6
Addison Gdns BRYLDS KT5....191 G1
WKENS W14....119 G3
Addison Gv CHSWK W4....118 B3
Addison Pl NTGHL W11....119 H1
Addison Rd BARK/HLT IG6....54 C4
HAYES BR2....200 C2
NTGHL W11....119 H2
PEND EN3....24 E2
SNWD SE25....197 H1
TEDD TW11....174 C2
WALTH E17....69 K2
WAN E11....70 E5
Addison's Cl CROY/NA CRO....198 B5
Addison Ter CHSWK W4 *....117 K4
Addison Wy GLDGN NW11....64 D1
NTHWD HA6....40 E4
YEAD UB4....94 E5
Addle Hl BLKFR EC4V....12 B5
Addle St CITYW EC2V *....12 D3
Adecroft Wy
E/WMO/HCT KT8....173 H6
Adela Av NWMAL KT3....192 E2
Adelaide Av BROCKY SE4....144 C5
Adelaide Cl EN EN1....24 A1
STAN HA7....43 G1
Adelaide Ct HNWL W7....116 A2
Adelaide Gdns CHDH RM6....74 A2
Adelaide Gv SHB W12....118 D1
Adelaide Rd CHST BR7....185 G1
HAMP NW3....83 K5
HEST TW5....134 D2
IL IG1....88 A1
LEY E10....88 A1
NWDGN UB2....114 D4
RCH/KEW TW9....137 G5
SURB KT6....191 F2
TEDD TW11....174 A2
WAND/EARL SW18....116 B2
WEA W13....116 B2
Adelaide St CHCR WC2N *....10 E5
Adelaide Ter BTFD TW8 *....116 E5
Adela St NKENS W10....100 C3
Adelina Gv WCHPL E1....104 E4
Adelina Ms BAL SW12....161 J3
Adeline Pl RSQ WC1B....10 D2
Adeliza Cl BARK IG11....90 C5
Adelphi Crs HCH RM12....75 J4
YEAD UB4....94 C2
Adelphi Ter CHCR WC2N....11 F6
Adelphi Wy YEAD UB4....94 C2
Adeney Cl HMSMTH W6....119 G6
Aden Gv STNW/STAM N16....85 K2
Adenmore Rd CAT SE6....164 D2
Aden Rd IL IG1....72 B4
PEND EN3....25 G5
Adhara Rd NTHWD HA6....40 E1
Adie Rd HMSMTH W6....119 F3
Adine Rd PLSTW E13....106 E3
Adler St WCHPL E1....104 C4
Adley St HOM E9....87 G3
Adlington Cl UED N18....49 K1
Admaston Rd
WOOL/PLUM SE18....147 H1
Admiral Cl STMC/STPC BR5....202 E1
Admiral Ms NKENS W10....100 B3
Admiral Pl BERM/RHTH SE16....124 B1
Admirals Cl SWFD E18....71 F1
Admiral Seymour Rd
ELTH/MOT SE9....146 E5
Admiral's Ga GNWCH SE10....144 E2
Admiral Sq WBPTN SW10 *....140 B2
Admiral St DEPT SE8....144 D2
Admiral's Wk HAMP NW3....83 G1
Admirals Wy POP/IOD E14....124 E2
Admiralty Rd TEDD TW11....174 A2
WAN E11 *....70 A4
WIM/MER SW19....178 A4
Adnams Wk RAIN RM13....93 J3
Adolf St CAT SE6....164 D6
Adolphus Rd FSBYPK N4....67 H1
Adolphus St DEPT SE8....144 C1

Adomar Rd BCTR RM8 91 K1
Adpar St BAY/PAD W2 8 A1
Adrian Cl BAR EN5 32 B1
Adrian Ms WBPTN SW10 120 A6
Adrienne Av STHL UB1 95 K3
Advance Rd WNWD SE27 162 D6
Advent Wy UED N18 51 F1
Adys Lawn CRICK NW2 81 K4
Adys Rd PECK SE15 143 G4
Aerodrome Rd
CDALE/KGS NW9 45 H6
Aerodrome Wy HEST TW5 114 B6
Affleck St IS N1 * 5 H3
Afghan Rd BTSEA SW11 140 D3
Aftab Ter WCHPL E1 * 104 D3
Agamemnon Rd
KIL/WHAMP NW6 82 D3
Agar Cl SURB KT6 191 G6
Agar Gv CAMTN NW1 84 D5
Agar St CHCR WC2N 10 E6
Agate Cl CAN/RD E16 107 H5
Agate Rd HMSMTH W6 119 F3
Agatha Cl WAP E1W 123 J1
Agaton Rd ELTH/MOT SE9 167 H4
Agave Rd CRICK NW2 82 A2
Agdon St FSBYE EC1V 6 A6
Agincourt Rd HAMP NW3 83 K2
Agister Rd CHIG IG7 55 G1
Agnes Av IL IG1 90 A2
Agnes Cl EHAM E6 108 A6
Agnesfield Cl
NFNCH/WDSP N12 47 J2
Agnes Gdns BCTR RM8 91 K2
Agnes Riley Gdns
CLAP SW4 * 161 H2
Agnes Rd ACT W3 118 C2
Agnes St POP/IOD E14 105 H5
Agnew Rd FSTH SE23 164 B2
Agricola Pl EN EN1 24 B6
Aidan Cl DAGW RM9 92 A2
Ailsa Av TWK TW1 136 B6
Ailsa Rd TWK TW1 136 C6
Ailsa St POP/IOD E14 106 A4
Ainger Rd HAMP NW3 83 K5
Ainsdale Cl ORP BR6 201 J5
Ainsdale Crs PIN HA5 42 A6
Ainsdale Dr STHWK SE1 123 H5
Ainsdale Rd EA W5 97 K3
OXHEY WD19 27 G5
Ainsley Av ROMW/RG RM7 74 E3
Ainsley Cl ED N9 36 A3
Ainsley St BETH E2 104 D2
Ainslie Wood Crs CHING E4 51 K1
Ainslie Wood Gdns CHING E4 37 K6
Ainslie Wood Rd CHING E4 51 J1
Ainsty St BERM/RHTH SE16 * 123 K2
Ainsworth Cl CMBW SE5 * 143 F3
CRICK NW2 81 J1
Ainsworth Rd CROY/NA CR0 196 C5
HOM E9 86 E5
Ainsworth Wy STJWD NW8 83 G6
Aintree Av EHAM E6 89 J6
Aintree Crs BARK/HLT IG6 54 C5
Aintree Rd GFD/PVL UB6 97 H1
Aintree St FUL/PGN SW6 139 H1
Airdrie Cl IS N1 * 85 F5
YEAD UB4 95 J4
Airedale Av CHSWK W4 118 C5
Airedale Av South
CHSWK W4 * 118 C5
Airedale Rd BAL SW12 160 E2
EA W5 116 D3
Airfield Wy HCH RM12 93 K4
Airlie Gdns IL IG1 72 B5
KENS W8 119 K2
Air St REGST W1B 10 B6
Airthrie Rd GDMY/SEVK IG3 73 H5
Aisgill Av WKENS W14 119 J5
Aisher Rd THMD SE28 109 J6
Aislibie Rd LEW SE13 145 H5
Aiten Pl HMSMTH W6 118 D4
Aitken Cl HACK E8 86 C6
MTCM CR4 194 E4
Aitken Rd BAR EN5 20 A6
CAT SE6 164 E4
Aitman Dr CHSWK W4 * 117 H5
Ajax Av CDALE/KGS NW9 45 G6
Ajax Rd KIL/WHAMP NW6 82 D2
Akabusi Cl SNWD SE25 197 H3
Akehurst St PUT/ROE SW15 158 D1
Akenside Rd HAMP NW3 83 H3
Akerman Rd CMBW SE5 142 C2
SURB KT6 190 D3
Alabama St
WOOL/PLUM SE18 147 J1
Alacross Rd EA W5 116 D2
Alan Cl DART DA1 151 F5
Alandale Dr PIN HA5 41 F4
Alan Dr BAR EN5 32 C1
Alan Gdns ROMW/RG RM7 74 C4
Alan Hocken Wy SRTFD E15 106 C1
Alan Rd WIM/MER SW19 177 H1
Alanthus Cl LEE/GVPK SE12 165 J1
Alaska St STHWK SE1 17 J1
Alba Cl YEAD UB4 95 H3
Albacore Crs LEW SE13 164 E1
Alba Gdns GLDGN NW11 64 C3
Albain Crs ASHF TW15 152 B4
Albany Cl BUSH WD23 28 D1
BXLY DA5 168 D2
ESH/CLAY KT10 204 A6
MORT/ESHN SW14 137 J5
SEVS/STOTM N15 67 H1
Albany Ctyd MYFR/PICC W1J 10 B6
Albany Crs EDGW HA8 44 C3
ESH/CLAY KT10 204 E4
Albany Ms BMLY BR1 183 K2
IS N1 * 85 G5
KUTN/CMB KT2 * 174 E2
SUT SM1 209 F3
WALW SE17 122 D6
Albany Pde BTFD TW8 * 117 F6
PEND EN3 25 F1
Albany Pk PEND EN3 * 25 F1
Albany Park Av PEND EN3 24 E2
Albany Park Rd
KUTN/CMB KT2 174 E2
Albany Pl BTFD TW8 116 E6
HOLWY N7 85 G2
Albany Rd BELV DA17 129 G6
BTFD TW8 116 E6
BXLY DA5 168 D2
CHDH RM6 74 B3
CHST BR7 185 G1
CMBW SE5 122 E6
FSBYPK N4 67 F3
HCH RM12 75 J5
MNPK E12 89 H2
NWMAL KT3 192 A1
RCHPK/HAM TW10 * 137 G6
UED N18 50 D1
WALTH E17 69 G3
WEA W13 97 H6
WIM/MER SW19 178 A1
Albany Rw EFNCH N2 * 65 J1
Albany St CAMTN NW1 3 K4
Albany Ter
RCHPK/HAM TW10 * 137 G6
The Albany KUTN/CMB KT2 174 E2
Albany Vw BKHH IG9 38 E3
Alba Pl NTGHL W11 100 D5
Albatross Cl EHAM E6 107 K3
Albatross St
WOOL/PLUM SE18 147 K1
Albemarle Ap
GNTH/NBYPK IG2 72 B3
Albemarle Av WHTN TW2 154 E3
Albemarle Gdns
GNTH/NBYPK IG2 72 B3
NWMAL KT3 192 A1
Albemarle Pk BECK BR3 * 182 E4
STAN HA7 * 43 J1
Albemarle Rd BECK BR3 182 E4
EBAR EN4 33 J2
Albemarle St CONDST W1S 10 A6
Albemarle Wy FARR EC1M 6 A7
Alberon Gdns GLDGN NW11 64 D1
Alberta Av SUT SM1 208 C2
Alberta Est WALW SE17 122 C5
Alberta Rd BXLYHN DA7 149 K2
EN EN1 36 B1
Alberta St WALW SE17 122 C5
Albert Av CHING E4 37 J6
VX/NE SW8 142 A1
Albert Br BTSEA SW11 140 D1
Albert Bridge Ga BTSEA SW11 140 E1
Albert Bridge Rd BTSEA SW11 140 E2
CHEL SW3 120 D6
Albert Carr Gdns
STRHM/NOR SW16 179 K1
Albert Cl HOM E9 86 D6
WDGN N22 48 D4
Albert Crs CHING E4 37 J6
Albert Dr WIM/MER SW19 159 H4
Albert Emb LBTH SE11 121 K5
Albert Gdns WCHPL E1 105 F5
Albert Ga KTBR SW1X 15 F2
Albert Gv
WIM/MER SW19 177 G4
Albert Ms BROCKY SE4 * 144 C5
FSBYPK N4 * 67 F5
KENS W8 120 B3
POP/IOD E14 * 105 G6
Albert Pl FNCH N3 46 E4
KENS W8 120 A2
Albert Rd BCTR RM8 74 B5
BELMT SM2 209 H3
BELV DA17 129 G5
BKHH IG9 39 H4
BXLY DA5 169 H1
CAN/RD E16 126 D1
EA W5 97 H3
EBAR EN4 21 H5
ELTH/MOT SE9 166 D5
FSBYPK N4 67 F5
HAYES BR2 200 C2
HDN NW4 64 B1
HPTN TW12 173 H1
HSLW TW3 135 F5
HYS/HAR UB3 113 H3
IL IG1 90 C1
KIL/WHAMP NW6 100 D1
KUT/HW KT1 175 G5
LEY E10 70 A6
MLHL NW7 45 H1
MTCM CR4 178 E6
NWDGN UB2 114 C3
NWMAL KT3 192 C1
ORP BR6 217 G3
PGE/AN SE20 182 A3
RCHPK/HAM TW10 137 F6
RDART DA2 171 F5
ROM RM1 75 H3
RYLN/HDSTN HA2 42 C6
SEVS/STOTM N15 68 A3
SNWD SE25 197 J1
STMC/STPC BR5 202 C3
SWFD E18 53 F6
TEDD TW11 174 A2
TWK TW1 156 A3
WALTH E17 69 J2
WDGN N22 48 D4
WDR/YW UB7 112 B1
Albert Sq SRTFD E15 88 C3
VX/NE SW8 142 A1
Albert St CAMTN NW1 3 K1
NFNCH/WDSP N12 47 G1
Albert Ter CAMTN NW1 84 A6
EA W5 * 97 H3
WLSDN NW10 * 81 F6
Albert Wy PECK SE15 143 J1
Albion Av MUSWH N10 48 A4
VX/NE SW8 141 J3
Albion Cl BAY/PAD W2 8 D5
ROMW/RG RM7 75 F3
Albion Dr HACK E8 86 C5
Albion Est
BERM/RHTH SE16 * 123 K2
Albion Gdns HMSMTH W6 118 E4
Albion Ga BAY/PAD W2 8 D5
Albion Gv STNW/STAM N16 86 A2
Albion Ms BAY/PAD W2 8 D4
IS N1 * 85 G5
Albion Pl FARR EC1M 12 A1
HMSMTH W6 118 E4
SNWD SE25 * 181 H6
Albion Riverside BTSEA SW11 140 D1
Albion Rd BELMT SM2 209 H4
BXLYHS DA6 149 G5
HSLW TW3 135 F5
HYS/HAR UB3 94 C5
KUTN/CMB KT2 175 K4
STNW/STAM N16 85 K3
TOTM N17 50 B5
WALTH E17 52 A6
WHTN TW2 155 K3
Albion Sq HACK E8 86 B5
Albion St BAY/PAD W2 8 D4
BERM/RHTH SE16 123 K2
CROY/NA CR0 196 C5
Albion Ter CHING E4 * 25 K5
HACK E8 86 B5
Albion Villas Rd FSTH SE23 163 K5
Albion Wk IS N1 5 F3
Albion Wy LEW SE13 145 F5
STBT EC1A 12 C2
WBLY HA9 80 C1
Albion Yd IS N1 5 F3
Albrighton Rd EDUL SE22 143 F4
Albuhera Cl ENC/FH EN2 23 G2
Albury Av BELMT SM2 208 A6
BXLYHN DA7 149 F3
ISLW TW7 136 A1
Albury Cl HOR/WEW KT19 206 D6
HPTN TW12 173 F2
Albury Dr PIN HA5 41 G4
Albury Ms MNPK E12 71 G5
Albury Rd CHSGTN KT9 206 A3
Albury St DEPT SE8 124 D6
Albyfield BMLY BR1 184 E6
Albyn Rd DEPT SE8 144 E3
Alcester Crs CLPT E5 68 D6
Alcester Rd WLGTN SM6 210 B2
Alcock Cl WLGTN SM6 210 D5
Alcock Rd HEST TW5 134 C1
Alconbury Rd CLPT E5 68 C6
Alcorn Cl CHEAM SM3 193 K6
Alcott Cl HNWL W7 97 F4
Aldborough Rd DAGE RM10 92 E4
Aldborough Rd North
GNTH/NBYPK IG2 73 F2
Aldborough Rd South
GDMY/SEVK IG3 72 E5
Aldbourne Rd ACT W3 118 C1
Aldbridge St WALW SE17 123 F5
Aldburgh Ms MHST W1U 9 H3
Aldbury Av WBLY HA9 80 D5
Aldbury Ms ED N9 35 K2
Aldebert Ter VX/NE SW8 142 A1
Aldeburgh Pl WFD IG8 38 E6
Aldeburgh St GNWCH SE10 125 K5
Alden Av SRTFD E15 106 D2
Aldenham Rd OXHEY WD19 27 H1
Aldenham St CAMTN NW1 4 B3
Alden Md PIN HA5 * 42 A3
Aldensley Rd HMSMTH W6 118 E3
Alderbrook Rd BAL SW12 161 G1
Alderbury Rd BARN SW13 118 D6
Alder Cl PECK SE15 123 G6
Alder Gv CRICK NW2 63 J6
Alderholt Wy PECK SE15 * 143 F1
Alderman Av BARK IG11 109 G2
Aldermanbury CITYW EC2V * 12 D3
Aldermanbury Sq CITYW EC2V 12 D2
Alderman Cl DART DA1 170 B2
Alderman Judge Ml
KUT/HW KT1 * 175 F5
Alderman's Hl PLMGR N13 34 E6
Aldermary Rd BMLY BR1 183 K4
Aldermoor Rd CAT SE6 164 C5
Alderney Av HEST TW5 135 G1
Alderney Gdns NTHLT UB5 77 K5
Alderney Ms STHWK SE1 18 E4
Alderney Rd ERITH DA8 150 D1
WCHPL E1 105 F3
Alderney St PIM SW1V 15 J7
Alder Rd MORT/ESHN SW14 138 A4
SCUP DA14 167 K5
Alders Av WFD IG8 52 C2
Aldersbrook Av EN EN1 24 A3
Aldersbrook Dr KUTN/CMB KT2 175 G2
Aldersbrook La MNPK E12 89 K1
Aldersbrook Rd MNPK E12 71 G6
Alders Cl EA W5 116 E3
EDGW HA8 44 E1
WAN E11 71 F6
Aldersey Gdns BARK IG11 90 D4
Aldersford Cl BROCKY SE4 144 A5
Aldersgate St STBT EC1A 12 C3
Aldersgrove E/WMO/HCT KT8 189 J2
Aldersgrove Av
ELTH/MOT SE9 166 B5
Aldershot Rd KIL/WHAMP NW6 82 D6
Aldershot Ter
WOOL/PLUM SE18 * 147 F1
Aldersmead Av CROY/NA CR0 198 A3
Aldersmead Rd BECK BR3 182 B3
Alderson Pl NWDGN UB2 115 H1
Alderson St NKENS W10 100 C3
Alders Rd EDGW HA8 44 E1
The Alders FELT TW13 172 D1
NWDGN UB2 114 E6
STRHM/NOR SW16 * 161 H6
WCHMH N21 35 G1
WWKM BR4 198 E5
Alderton Cl WLSDN NW10 63 F6
Alderton Crs HDN NW4 63 K2
Alderton Rd CROY/NA CR0 197 G4
HNHL SE24 142 D4
Alderton Wy HDN NW4 63 K2
Alderville Rd FUL/PGN SW6 139 J3
Alderwick Dr HSLW TW3 135 J4
Alderwood Ms EBAR EN4 21 G1
Alderwood Rd ELTH/MOT SE9 167 J1
Aldford St MYFR/PKLN W1K 9 G7
Aldgate FENCHST EC3M 13 H4
Aldgate Barrs WCHPL E1 * 13 K3
Aldgate High St TWRH EC3N 13 J4
Aldine St SHB W12 119 F2
Aldingham Gdns HCH RM12 93 J3
Aldington Cl CHDH RM6 73 J4
Aldington Rd
WOOL/PLUM SE18 126 C3
Aldis Ms TOOT SW17 178 D1
Aldis St TOOT SW17 178 D1
Aldred Rd KIL/WHAMP NW6 82 E3
Aldren Rd TOOT SW17 160 B5
Aldrich Crs CROY/NA CR0 214 A6
Aldriche Wy CHING E4 52 A2
Aldrich Gdns CHEAM SM3 208 D1
Aldrich Ter WAND/EARL SW18 160 B4
Aldridge Av EDGW HA8 30 D5
PEND EN3 25 J1
RSLP HA4 59 G6
STAN HA7 44 A4
Aldridge Ri NWMAL KT3 192 B4
Aldridge Road Vls
NTGHL W11 100 D4
Aldridge Wk STHGT/OAK N14 34 E2
Aldrington Rd
STRHM/NOR SW16 179 H1
Aldsworth Cl MV/WKIL W9 101 F3
Aldwick Cl CHST BR7 167 J5
Aldwick Rd CROY/NA CR0 211 F1
Aldworth Gv LEW SE13 165 F1
Aldworth Rd SRTFD E15 88 C5
Aldwych HOL/ALD WC2B 11 G4
Aldwych Av BARK/HLT IG6 72 C1
Aldwych Cl HCH RM12 75 J6
Alers Rd BXLYHS DA6 148 E6
Alesia Cl WDGN N22 48 E3
Alestan Beck Rd CAN/RD E16 107 H5
Alexander Av WLSDN NW10 81 K5
Alexander Cl BFN/LL DA15 147 K6
EBAR EN4 21 H5
HAYES BR2 199 K5
NWDGN UB2 115 H1
WHTN TW2 155 K4
Alexander Evans Ms
FSTH SE23 164 A4
Alexander Ms BAY/PAD W2 101 F5
Alexander Pl SKENS SW7 14 C6
Alexander Rd ARCH N19 84 E1
BXLYHN DA7 148 E3
CHST BR7 185 G2
Alexander Sq CHEL SW3 14 C6
Alexander St BAY/PAD W2 100 E5
Alexander Ter ABYW SE2 * 128 C5
Alexandra Av BTSEA SW11 * 141 F2
RYLN/HDSTN HA2 59 K5
STHL UB1 95 K6
SUT SM1 208 E1
WDGN N22 48 D4
Alexandra Cl RYLN/HDSTN HA2 78 A1
Alexandra Cottages
NWCR SE14 144 C2
Alexandra Ct STHGT/OAK N14 22 C6
Alexandra Crs BMLY BR1 183 J2
Alexandra Dr BRYLDS KT5 191 H4
NRWD SE19 181 F1
Alexandra Gdns CAR SM5 210 A6
HSLW TW3 135 G3
MUSWH N10 66 B1
Alexandra Ga SKENS SW7 14 A2
Alexandra Gv FSBYPK N4 67 H5
NFNCH/WDSP N12 47 F1
Alexandra Ms EFNCH N2 47 K6
Alexandra Palace Wy
CEND/HSY/T N8 66 C1
Alexandra Pde
RYLN/HDSTN HA2 * 78 B2
Alexandra Park Rd MUSWH N10 48 B5
Alexandra Pl CROY/NA CR0 197 F5
SNWD SE25 196 E2
STJWD NW8 83 G6
Alexandra Rd BTFD TW8 * 116 E6
CEND/HSY/T N8 49 G6
CHDH RM6 73 K3
CHSWK W4 118 A2
CROY/NA CR0 197 F5
ED N9 * 36 D2
EHAM E6 108 A2
ERITH DA8 130 C6
HDN NW4 64 B1
HSLW TW3 135 G3
KUTN/CMB KT2 175 H3
LEY E10 88 A1
MORT/ESHN SW14 138 A4
MUSWH N10 48 B4
PEND EN3 25 F5
RAIN RM13 93 H6
RCH/KEW TW9 137 G3
ROM RM1 75 H3
SEVS/STOTM N15 67 K2
STJWD NW8 83 G5
SWFD E18 53 F6
SYD SE26 182 A2
THDIT KT7 190 A2
TWK TW1 156 D1
WALTH E17 69 H3
WIM/MER SW19 177 K1
WIM/MER SW19 178 D3
Alexandra Sq MRDN SM4 193 K2
Alexandra St CAN/RD E16 106 E4
NWCR SE14 144 B1
Alexandria Rd WEA W13 97 G6
Alexis St BERM/RHTH SE16 123 H4
Alfearn Rd CLPT E5 86 E2
Alford Gn CROY/NA CR0 214 B4
Alford Pl IS N1 * 6 D3
Alford Rd ERITH DA8 129 K5
Alfoxton Av SEVS/STOTM N15 67 H1
Alfreda St BTSEA SW11 141 G2
Alfred Cl CHSWK W4 118 A4
Alfred Gdns STHL UB1 95 J6
Alfred Ms FITZ W1T 10 C1
Alfred Pl FITZ W1T 10 C1
Alfred Rd ACT W3 117 K1
BAY/PAD W2 100 E4
BELV DA17 129 G5
BKHH IG9 39 H4
FELT TW13 154 B4
KUT/HW KT1 175 F6
RDART DA2 171 J6
SNWD SE25 197 H2
SRTFD E15 88 D3
SUT SM1 209 G3
Alfred's Gdns BARK IG11 108 E1
Alfred St BOW E3 105 H2
Alfred's Wy (East Ham &
Barking By-Pass) BARK IG11 108 E1
Alfred Vls WALTH E17 * 70 A1
Alfreton Cl WIM/MER SW19 159 G5
Alfriston BRYLDS KT5 191 G3
Alfriston Av CROY/NA CR0 195 K4
RYLN/HDSTN HA2 60 A3
Alfriston Cl BRYLDS KT5 191 G3
DART DA1 170 B1
Alfriston Rd CLAP SW4 140 E6
Algar Cl STAN HA7 43 F1
Algar Rd ISLW TW7 136 B4
Algarve Rd WAND/EARL SW18 160 A3
Algernon Rd HDN NW4 63 J3
KIL/WHAMP NW6 82 E6
LEW SE13 144 E5
Algiers Rd LEW SE13 144 D5
Alguin Ct STAN HA7 * 43 J2
Alibon Gdns DAGE RM10 92 C3
Alibon Rd DAGE RM10 92 C3
Alice La BOW E3 87 H6
Alice St STHWK SE1 19 G5
Alice Thompson Cl
LEE/GVPK SE12 166 B4
Alice Walker Cl HNHL SE24 * 142 C5
Alice Wy HSLW TW3 135 G5
Alicia Av KTN/HRWW/W HA3 61 H1
Alicia Cl KTN/HRWW/W HA3 61 J1
Alicia Gdns KTN/HRWW/W HA3 61 H1
Alie St WCHPL E1 13 K4
Alington Crs CDALE/KGS NW9 62 E5
Alington Gv WLGTN SM6 210 D6
Alison Cl CROY/NA CR0 198 A5
EHAM E6 108 A5
Aliwal Ms BTSEA SW11 * 140 D5
Aliwal Rd BTSEA SW11 140 D5
Alkerden Rd CHSWK W4 118 B5
Alkham Rd STNW/STAM N16 68 B6
Allan Barclay Cl
STNW/STAM N16 68 B3
Allan Cl NWMAL KT3 192 A2
Allandale Av FNCH N3 46 C6
Allandale Pl ORP BR6 217 K1
Allandale Rd EMPK RM11 75 H4
Allan Wy ACT W3 98 E4
Allard Cl STMC/STPC BR5 202 D4
Allard Crs BUSH WD23 28 C4
Allardyce St BRXN/ST SW9 142 A5
Allbrook Cl TEDD TW11 173 K1
Allcot Cl EBED/NFELT TW14 153 J3
Allcroft Rd KTTN NW5 84 A4
Allder Wy SAND/SEL CR2 211 H5
Allenby Av SAND/SEL CR2 211 J6
Allenby Cl GFD/PVL UB6 96 A2
Allenby Rd FSTH SE23 164 B5
STHL UB1 96 A5
Allen Cl MTCM CR4 179 G4
SUN TW16 172 A4
Allendale Av STHL UB1 96 A5
Allendale Cl CMBW SE5 142 E3
SYD SE26 182 A1
Allendale Rd GFD/PVL UB6 79 H4
Allen Edwards Dr VX/NE SW8 141 K2
Allen Rd BECK BR3 182 A5
BOW E3 105 H1
CROY/NA CR0 196 A4
STNW/STAM N16 86 A2
SUN TW16 172 A4
Allensbury Pl CAMTN NW1 84 D5
Allens Rd PEND EN3 24 E6
Allen St KENS W8 119 K3
Allenswood Rd
ELTH/MOT SE9 146 D4
Allerford Rd CAT SE6 164 E6
Allerton Rd STNW/STAM N16 67 J6
Allestree Rd FUL/PGN SW6 139 H1
Alleyn Crs DUL SE21 162 E4
Alleyndale Rd BCTR RM8 73 J6
Alleyn Pk DUL SE21 162 E4
NWDGN UB2 114 E5
Alleyn Rd DUL SE21 162 E5
Allfarthing La
WAND/EARL SW18 160 B1
Allgood Cl MRDN SM4 193 G3
Allgood St BETH E2 7 K3
Allhallows La CANST EC4R 12 E6
Allhallows Rd EHAM E6 107 J5
All Hallows Rd TOTM N17 50 A4
Alliance Cl ALP/SUD HA0 79 K2
Alliance Rd ACT W3 98 D3
PLSTW E13 107 G3
WOOL/PLUM SE18 128 B6
Allied Wy ACT W3 * 118 B2
Allingham Cl HNWL W7 97 F6
Allington Av TOTM N17 50 A2
Allington Cl GFD/PVL UB6 78 C5
WIM/MER SW19 177 G1
Allington Rd HDN NW4 63 K2
NKENS W10 100 C2
ORP BR6 201 K6
RYLN/HDSTN HA2 60 C2
Allington St WESTW SW1E 15 K5
Allison Cl GNWCH SE10 145 F2
Allison Gv DUL SE21 163 F3
Allison Rd ACT W3 98 E5
CEND/HSY/T N8 67 G2
Allitsen Rd STJWD NW8 2 C3
Allitson Rd STJWD NW8 2 C3
Allnutt Wy CLAP SW4 141 J6
Alloa Rd DEPT SE8 124 A5
GDMY/SEVK IG3 73 H6
Allonby Gdns WBLY HA9 61 J5
Alloway Rd BOW E3 105 G2
Allport Ms WCHPL E1 * 104 E4
All Saints' Cl ED N9 36 B4
All Saints Dr BKHTH/KID SE3 145 J3

All Saints Ms
KTN/HRWW/W HA3 42 E2
All Saints Pas
WAND/EARL SW18 * 139 K6
All Saints' Rd ACT W3 117 K3
NTGHL W11 100 D4
SUT SM1 209 F1
WIM/MER SW19 178 B3
All Saints St IS N1 5 G2
Allsop Pl CAMTN NW1 3 F7
All Souls' Av WLSDN NW10 99 K1
All Souls' Pl REGST W1B 9 K2
Allum Wy TRDG/WHET N20 33 G3
Allwood Cl SYD SE26 164 A6
Alma Av CHING E4 52 A3
Almack Rd CLPT E5 86 E2
Alma Cl MUSWH N10 * 48 B4
Alma Ct RYLN/HDSTN HA2 * 60 D6
Alma Crs SUT SM1 208 C3
Alma Gv STHWK SE1 19 K7
Alma Pl NRWD SE19 181 G3
THHTH CR7 196 B2
WLSDN NW10 99 K2
Alma Rd CAR SM5 209 J3
ESH/CLAY KT10 189 K5
MUSWH N10 48 A3
PEND EN3 25 G6
SCUP DA14 168 B5
STHL UB1 95 J6
STMC/STPC BR5 202 E6
WAND/EARL SW18 140 B6
Alma Rw KTN/HRWW/W HA3 * 42 D4
Alma Sq STJWD NW8 101 G2
Alma St KTTN NW5 84 B4
SRTFD E15 88 B4
Alma Ter BOW E3 87 H6
KENS W8 * 119 K3
WAND/EARL SW18 160 C2
Almeida St IS N1 85 H6
Almeric Rd BTSEA SW11 140 E5
Almer Rd RYNPK SW20 176 D3
Almington St FSBYPK N4 * 66 E5
Almond Av CAR SM5 194 E6
EA W5 117 F3
WDR/YW UB7 112 D3
Almond Cl FELT TW13 153 K3
HAYES BR2 201 F4
HYS/HAR UB3 94 C6
RSLP HA4 76 D1
Almond Gv BTFD TW8 136 C1
Almond Rd BERM/RHTH SE16 123 J4
TOTM N17 50 C3
Almonds Av BKHH IG9 38 E4
Almond Wy HAYES BR2 201 F4
MTCM CR4 195 J2
RYLN/HDSTN HA2 42 C5
Almorah Rd HEST TW5 134 C2
IS N1 85 K5
Almshouse La CHSGTN KT9 205 J6
Alnwick Gv MRDN SM4 194 A1
Alnwick Rd CAN/RD E16 107 G5
LEE/GVPK SE12 166 A2
Alnwick Ter LEE/GVPK SE12 166 A2
Alperton La ALP/SUD HA0 97 K2
Alperton St NKENS W10 100 C3
Alphabet Gdns CAR SM5 194 C3
Alpha Cl CAMTN NW1 2 D6
Alpha Est HYS/HAR UB3 * 113 H2
Alpha Gv POP/IOD E14 124 D2
Alpha Pl CHEL SW3 120 D6
KIL/WHAMP NW6 100 E1
MRDN SM4 * 193 G4
Alpha Rd BRYLDS KT5 191 G3
CHING E4 37 J5
CROY/NA CR0 197 F5
HPTN TW12 173 J1
NWCR SE14 144 C2
PEND EN3 25 G5
UED N18 50 C2
Alpha St PECK SE15 143 H3
Alphea Cl WIM/MER SW19 178 D3
Alpine Av BRYLDS KT5 191 K6
Alpine Cl CROY/NA CR0 212 A1
Alpine Copse BMLY BR1 185 F5
Alpine Gv HOM E9 * 86 E5
Alpine Rd BERM/RHTH SE16 123 K4
Alpine Vw SUT SM1 209 J3
Alpine Wk BUSH WD23 28 E4
Alpine Wy EHAM E6 108 A4
Alric Av NWMAL KT3 176 B6
WLSDN NW10 81 F5
Alroy Rd FSBYPK N4 67 G4
Alsace Rd WALW SE17 123 F5
Alscot Rd BERM/RHTH SE16 19 K5
Alscot Wy STHWK SE1 19 J6
Alsike Rd BELV DA17 128 E3
Alsom Av HOR/WEW KT19 207 H2
Alston Cl THDIT KT7 190 C4
Alston Rd BAR EN5 20 C4
TOOT SW17 160 C6
UED N18 50 D1
Altair Cl UED N18 50 B2
Altair Wy NTHWD HA6 40 D1
Altash Wy ELTH/MOT SE9 166 E4
Altenburg Av WEA W13 116 C3
Altenburg Gdns BTSEA SW11 140 E5
Alt Gv WIM/MER SW19 177 J3
Altham Ct RYLN/HDSTN HA2 * 42 B4
Altham Gdns OXHEY WD19 27 H6
Altham Rd PIN HA5 41 J3
Althea St FUL/PGN SW6 140 A3
Althorne Gdns SWFD E18 70 D1
Althorne Wy DAGE RM10 74 C6
Althorp Cl TRDG/WHET N20 31 J2
Althorpe Rd HRW HA1 * 60 C2
Althorp Rd TOOT SW17 160 E3
Altmore Av EHAM E6 89 K5
Alton Av STAN HA7 43 F3
Alton Cl BXLY DA5 169 F3
ISLW TW7 136 A3
Alton Gdns BECK BR3 182 D3
WHTN TW2 155 J1
Alton Rd CROY/NA CR0 211 G2
PUT/ROE SW15 158 D3
RCH/KEW TW9 137 F5
TOTM N17 49 K6
Alton St POP/IOD E14 105 K4
Altyre Cl BECK BR3 198 C2
Altyre Rd CROY/NA CR0 196 E6
Altyre Wy BECK BR3 198 C2
Alvanley Gdns HAMP NW3 83 F3
Alva Wy OXHEY WD19 27 H4
Alverstone Av EBAR EN4 33 H2
WAND/EARL SW18 159 K4
Alverstone Gdns
ELTH/MOT SE9 167 G3
Alverstone Rd CRICK NW2 82 A5
MNPK E12 90 A2
NWMAL KT3 192 C1
WBLY HA9 62 B5
Alverston Gdns SNWD SE25 197 F2
Alverton St DEPT SE8 124 C5
Alveston Av
KTN/HRWW/W HA3 43 H6
Alveston Sq SWFD E18 52 E5
Alvey St WALW SE17 123 F5
Alvia Gdns SUT SM1 209 G2
Alvington Crs HACK E8 86 B3
Alway Av HOR/WEW KT19 206 E3
Alwold Crs LEE/GVPK SE12 166 B1
Alwyn Av CHSWK W4 118 A5
Alwyn Cl BORE WD6 30 B1
CROY/NA CR0 213 K5
Alwyne La IS N1 * 85 H5
Alwyne Pl IS N1 85 J4
Alwyne Rd HNWL W7 96 E6
IS N1 85 J5
WIM/MER SW19 177 J2
Alwyne Sq IS N1 85 J4
Alwyne Vls IS N1 85 H5
Alwyn Gdns ACT W3 98 D5
Alyn Bank CEND/HSY/T N8 * 66 D3
Alyth Gdns GLDGN NW11 64 D3
Amalgamated Dr BTFD TW8 116 B6
Amanda Cl CHIG IG7 54 D2
Amanda Ms ROMW/RG RM7 74 E2
Amar Ct WOOL/PLUM SE18 128 A4
Amardeep Ct
WOOL/PLUM SE18 128 A5
Amazon St WCHPL E1 104 D5
Ambassador Cl HSLW TW3 134 D3
Ambassador Gdns EHAM E6 107 K4
Ambassador Sq POP/IOD E14 124 E4
Amber Av WALTH E17 51 G4
Amberden Av FNCH N3 46 E6
Ambergate St WALW SE17 122 C5
Amber Gv CRICK NW2 64 B5
Amberley Cl ORP BR6 217 F3
PIN HA5 41 K6
Amberley Ct SCUP DA14 186 D1
Amberley Gdns
HOR/WEW KT19 207 H2
Amberley Gv CROY/NA CR0 197 G4
SYD SE26 163 J6
Amberley Rd ABYW SE2 128 E6
BKHH IG9 39 G3
EN EN1 36 B2
LEY E10 69 J4
MV/WKIL W9 100 E4
PLMGR N13 35 F4
Amberley Wy HSLWW TW4 134 B6
MRDN SM4 193 J4
ROMW/RG RM7 74 D1
Amberside Cl ISLW TW7 155 J1
Amber St SRTFD E15 * 88 B4
Amberwood Cl WLGTN SM6 210 E3
Amberwood Ri NWMAL KT3 192 B3
Amblecote Cl LEE/GVPK SE12 166 A5
Amblecote Meadow
LEE/GVPK SE12 166 A5
Amblecote Rd LEE/GVPK SE12 166 A5
Ambler Rd FSBYPK N4 85 H1
Ambleside BMLY BR1 183 G2
Ambleside Av BECK BR3 198 B2
HCH RM12 93 K3
STRHM/NOR SW16 161 J6
WOT/HER KT12 188 B5
Ambleside Cl HOM E9 86 E3
LEY E10 69 K4
TOTM N17 50 B6
Ambleside Crs PEND EN3 25 F4
Ambleside Dr
EBED/NFELT TW14 153 J3
Ambleside Gdns BELMT SM2 209 G4
REDBR IG4 71 J1
WBLY HA9 61 K5
Ambleside Rd BXLYHN DA7 149 H3
WLSDN NW10 81 H5
Ambrey Wy WLGTN SM6 210 D6
Ambrook Rd BELV DA17 129 H3
Ambrosden Av WEST SW1P 16 B5
Ambrose Av GLDGN NW11 64 D3
Ambrose Cl DART DA1 150 C5
ORP BR6 217 F1
Ambrose St
BERM/RHTH SE16 123 J4
Amelia Cl ACT W3 117 J1
Amelia St WALW SE17 122 C5
Amen Cnr STP EC4M 12 B4
Amen Ct STP EC4M 12 B4
America Sq TWRH EC3N 13 J5
America St STHWK SE1 18 C1
Ameriand Rd
WAND/EARL SW18 159 J1
Amersham Av UED N18 49 K2
Amersham Gv NWCR SE14 144 C1
Amersham Rd CROY/NA CR0 196 D3
NWCR SE14 144 C2
Amersham V NWCR SE14 144 C1
Amery Gdns WLSDN NW10 81 K6
Amery Rd HRW HA1 61 G6
Amesbury Av
BRXS/STRHM SW2 161 K4
Amesbury Cl WPK KT4 193 F5
Amesbury Dr CHING E4 37 K1
Amesbury Rd BMLY BR1 184 C6
DAGW RM9 91 K5
FELT TW13 154 C4
Amethyst Ct ORP BR6 216 E4
Amethyst Rd WAN E11 88 B2
Amherst Av WEA W13 97 J5
Amherst Cl STMC/STPC BR5 202 B1
Amherst Dr STMC/STPC BR5 202 A1
Amherst Gdns WEA W13 * 97 J5
Amherst Rd WEA W13 97 J5
Amhurst Gdns ISLW TW7 136 A2
Amhurst Pde
STNW/STAM N16 * 68 B4
Amhurst Pk STNW/STAM N16 68 A4
Amhurst Rd HACK E8 86 D4
Amhurst Ter HACK E8 86 C2
Amidas Gdns BCTR RM8 91 H2
Amiel St WCHPL E1 104 E3
Amies St BTSEA SW11 140 E4
Amina Wy BERM/RHTH SE16 123 H3
Amis Av HOR/WEW KT19 206 C4
Amity Gv RYNPK SW20 177 F4
Amity Rd SRTFD E15 88 D5
Ammanford Gn
CDALE/KGS NW9 * 63 G3
Amner Rd BTSEA SW11 161 F1
Amor Rd HMSMTH W6 119 F3
Amott Rd PECK SE15 143 H4
Ampere Wy CROY/NA CR0 195 K4
Ampleforth Cl ORP BR6 217 J2
Ampleforth Rd ABYW SE2 128 C2
Ampthill Est CAMTN NW1 4 A3
Ampthill Sq CAMTN NW1 4 B3
Ampton St FSBYW WC1X 5 G5
Amroth Cl FSTH SE23 163 J3
Amroth Gn CDALE/KGS NW9 * 63 G3
Amsterdam Rd POP/IOD E14 125 F3
Amwell Cl WCHMH N21 23 K6
Amwell St CLKNW EC1R 5 J4
Amyand Cottages TWK TW1 156 C1
Amyand Park Gdns TWK TW1 156 C2
Amyand Park Rd TWK TW1 156 B2
Amy Cl WLGTN SM6 210 E5
Amyruth Rd BROCKY SE4 144 D6
Amy Warne Cl EHAM E6 107 J4
Ancaster Crs NWMAL KT3 192 D3
Ancaster Rd BECK BR3 182 A6
Ancaster St
WOOL/PLUM SE18 147 K1
Anchorage Cl
WIM/MER SW19 177 K1
Anchor & Hope La CHARL SE7 126 B4
Anchor Cl BARK IG11 109 H2
Anchor Dr RAIN RM13 111 K2
Anchor St BERM/RHTH SE16 123 J4
Anchor Ter WCHPL E1 * 104 E3
Anchor Yd FSBYE EC1V * 6 D6
Ancill Cl HMSMTH W6 119 G6
Ancona Rd WLSDN NW10 99 J1
WOOL/PLUM SE18 127 J5
Andace Park Gdns
BMLY BR1 * 184 B4
Andalus Rd BRXN/ST SW9 141 K4
Ander Cl ALP/SUD HA0 79 K2
Anderson Cl ACT W3 99 F5
CHEAM SM3 193 K5
WCHMH N21 23 F6
Anderson Dr ASHF TW15 153 F6
Anderson Rd HOM E9 87 F4
WFD IG8 53 H6
Anderson's Pl HSLW TW3 135 G5
Anderson Sq IS N1 6 A1
Anderson St CHEL SW3 120 E5
Anderson Wy BELV DA17 129 J2
Andover Av CAN/RD E16 107 H5
Andover Cl
EBED/NFELT TW14 153 J3
GFD/PVL UB6 96 B3
Andover Pl KIL/WHAMP NW6 101 F1
Andover Rd HOLWY N7 67 F6
ORP BR6 201 K5
WHTN TW2 155 J3
Andover Ter HMSMTH W6 * 118 E4
Andre St HACK E8 86 C3
Andrew Borde St
LSQ/SEVD WC2H * 10 D3
Andrew Cl BARK/HLT IG6 54 D3
DART DA1 150 A6
Andrewes Gdns EHAM E6 107 J5
Andrew Pl VX/NE SW8 141 J2
Andrews Cl BKHH IG9 39 G4
HRW HA1 60 D4
STMC/STPC BR5 186 E6
WPK KT4 193 G6
Andrews Pl BXLY DA5 170 B4
RDART DA2 170 D6
Andrews Rd HACK E8 86 D6
Andrew St POP/IOD E14 106 A5
Andrews Wk WALW SE17 122 C6
Andwell Cl ABYW SE2 128 C2
Anerley Gv NRWD SE19 181 G3
Anerley Hl NRWD SE19 181 G2
Anerley Pk PGE/AN SE20 181 J3
Anerley Park Rd
PGE/AN SE20 181 J3
Anerley Rd NRWD SE19 181 H3
Anerley Station Rd
PGE/AN SE20 181 J4
Anerley V NRWD SE19 181 G3
Anfield Cl BAL SW12 161 H2
Angel Aly WCHPL E1 13 K2
Angel Cl UED N18 50 B1
Angel Corner Pde UED N18 * 50 C1
Angel Ct LOTH EC2R 13 F3
Angelfield HSLW TW3 135 G6
Angel Hl SUT SM1 209 F1
Angel Hill Dr SUT SM1 209 F1
Angelica Dr EHAM E6 108 A4
Angelica Gdns CROY/NA CR0 198 A5
Angel La HYS/HAR UB3 94 B4
SRTFD E15 88 B4
Angell Park Gdns
BRXN/ST SW9 142 B4
Angell Rd BRXN/ST SW9 142 C4
Angell Town Est
BRXN/ST SW9 * 142 B3
Angel Ms WCHPL E1 104 D6
Angel Pas CANST EC4R 12 E6
Angel Rd HRW HA1 60 E3
THDIT KT7 190 B5
Angel Rd (North Circular)
UED N18 50 C1
Angel Sq FSBYE EC1V * 6 A3
Angel St STBT EC1A 12 C3
Angel Wk HMSMTH W6 119 F4
Angel Wy ROM RM1 75 G2
Angerstein La BKHTH/KID SE3 145 J1
Anglers La KTTN NW5 84 B4
Anglers Reach SURB KT6 * 190 E2
Anglesea Av
WOOL/PLUM SE18 127 G4
Anglesea Rd KUT/HW KT1 190 E1
STMC/STPC BR5 202 D3
WOOL/PLUM SE18 127 G4
Anglesey Cl ASHF TW15 152 D6
Anglesey Court Rd CAR SM5 210 A4
Anglesey Dr RAIN RM13 111 J3
Anglesey Gdns CAR SM5 210 A4
Anglesey Rd OXHEY WD19 41 G1
PEND EN3 24 D5
Anglesmede Crs PIN HA5 42 A6
Anglesmede Wy PIN HA5 41 K6
Angles Rd STRHM/NOR SW16 161 K6
Anglia Cl TOTM N17 50 D3
Anglian Rd WAN E11 88 B1
Anglo Rd BOW E3 105 H1
Angus Cl CHSGTN KT9 206 C3
Angus Dr RSLP HA4 77 G2
Angus Gdns CDALE/KGS NW9 45 F4
Angus Rd PLSTW E13 107 G2
Angus St NWCR SE14 144 B1
Anhalt Rd BTSEA SW11 140 D1
Ankerdine Crs
WOOL/PLUM SE18 147 G2
Anlaby Rd TEDD TW11 173 K1
Anley Rd HMSMTH W6 119 G2
Anmersh Gv STAN HA7 43 K4
Annabel Cl POP/IOD E14 105 K5
Anna Cl HACK E8 86 B6
Annandale Gv HGDN/ICK UB10 76 A1
Annandale Rd BFN/LL DA15 167 K2
CHSWK W4 118 B4
CROY/NA CR0 197 H6
GNWCH SE10 125 J6
Anna Neagle Cl FSTGT E7 88 E2
Annan Wy ROM RM1 57 F4
Anne Boleyn's Wk
BELMT SM2 208 B5
KUTN/CMB KT2 175 F1
Anne Case Ms NWMAL KT3 * 176 A6
Anne Compton Ms
LEE/GVPK SE12 165 J2
Anne of Cleves Rd DART DA1 151 G6
Annesley Av CDALE/KGS NW9 45 G6
Annesley Cl WLSDN NW10 81 G1
Annesley Dr CROY/NA CR0 213 H1
Annesley Rd BKHTH/KID SE3 146 A2
Anne St PLSTW E13 106 E3
Annette Cl KTN/HRWW/W HA3 42 E5
Annette Rd HOLWY N7 85 F2
Anne Wy BARK/HLT IG6 54 C2
Annie Besant Cl BOW E3 * 87 H6
Anning St SDTCH EC2A 7 H6
Annington Rd EFNCH N2 47 K6
Annis Rd HOM E9 87 G4
Ann La WBPTN SW10 140 C1
Ann Moss Wy
BERM/RHTH SE16 123 K3
Ann's Cl KTBR SW1X 15 F3
Ann St WOOL/PLUM SE18 127 J5
Annsworthy Av THHTH CR7 180 E6
Ansar Gdns WALTH E17 69 G2
Ansdell Rd PECK SE15 143 K3
Ansdell St KENS W8 120 A3
Ansdell Ter KENS W8 120 A3
Ansell Gv CAR SM5 194 E5
Ansell Rd TOOT SW17 160 D5
Anselm Cl CROY/NA CR0 212 B1
Anselm Rd FUL/PGN SW6 119 K6
PIN HA5 41 K3
Ansford Rd BMLY BR1 183 F1
Ansleigh Pl NTGHL W11 100 B6
Anson Cl ROMW/RG RM7 56 D5
Anson Rd CRICK NW2 81 K3
HOLWY N7 84 C2
Anson Wk NTHWD HA6 26 A6
Anstead Dr RAIN RM13 111 J1
Anstey Rd PECK SE15 143 H4
Anstice Cl CHSWK W4 138 B1
Anstridge Rd ELTH/MOT SE9 167 J1
Antelope Rd
WOOL/PLUM SE18 126 E3
Anthony Cl OXHEY WD19 27 H3
Anthony Rd GFD/PVL UB6 96 E1
SNWD SE25 197 H3
WELL DA16 148 B2
Anthony's Cl WAP E1W 123 H1
Anthony St WCHPL E1 104 D5
Anthus Ms NTHWD HA6 40 B3
Antill Rd BOW E3 105 G2
SEVS/STOTM N15 68 C1
Antill Ter WCHPL E1 105 F5
Antlers Hl CHING E4 25 K6
Anton Crs SUT SM1 208 E1
Antoneys Cl PIN HA5 41 H5
Anton Pl WBLY HA9 80 D1
Anton St HACK E8 86 C3
Antrim Rd HAMP NW3 83 K4
Antrobus Cl SUT SM1 208 D3
Antrobus Rd CHSWK W4 117 K4
Anvil Cl STRHM/NOR SW16 179 H3
Anworth Cl WFD IG8 53 F2
Apeldoorn Dr WLGTN SM6 210 E6
Aperfield Rd ERITH DA8 130 C6
Apex Cl BECK BR3 182 E4
Apex Pde MLHL NW7 * 31 F6
Aplin Wy ISLW TW7 135 K2
Apollo Av BMLY BR1 184 A4
NTHWD HA6 40 E1
Apollo Cl EMPK RM11 75 K6
Apollo Pl WAN E11 88 C1
WBPTN SW10 * 140 C1
Apollo Wy WOOL/PLUM SE18 127 J3
Apostle Wy THHTH CR7 180 C5
Apothecary St BLKFR EC4V * 12 A4
Appach Rd BRXS/STRHM SW2 142 B6
Apple Blossom Ct VX/NE SW8 141 J1
Appleby Cl CHING E4 52 A2
SEVS/STOTM N15 67 K2
WHTN TW2 155 J4
Appleby Gdns
EBED/NFELT TW14 * 153 J3
Appleby Rd CAN/RD E16 106 E5
HACK E8 86 C5
Appleby St BETH E2 7 J2
Appledore Av BXLYHN DA7 149 K2
RSLP HA4 77 F1
Appledore Cl EDGW HA8 44 C4
HAYES BR2 199 J2
TOOT SW17 160 E4
Appledore Crs BFN/LL DA15 167 K5
Appledore Wy MLHL NW7 46 B3
Appleford Rd NKENS W10 100 C3
Apple Garth BTFD TW8 116 E4
Applegarth CROY/NA CR0 213 K5
ESH/CLAY KT10 205 F3
Applegarth Dr DART DA1 171 H4
GNTH/NBYPK IG2 73 F1
Applegarth Rd THMD SE28 128 C1
WKENS W14 * 119 G3
Apple Gv CHSGTN KT9 206 A2
EN EN1 24 A4
Apple Ldg ALP/SUD HA0 * 79 J1
Apple Market KUT/HW KT1 174 E5
Apple Rd WAN E11 88 C1
Appleton Cl BXLYHN DA7 149 J3
Appleton Dr RDART DA2 170 E5
Appleton Gdns NWMAL KT3 192 D3
Appleton Rd ELTH/MOT SE9 146 D4
Appletree Cl PGE/AN SE20 181 J4
Appletree Gdns EBAR EN4 21 J5
Apple Tree Yd STJS SW1Y 10 B7
Applewood Cl CRICK NW2 81 K1
TRDG/WHET N20 33 J3
Applewood Dr PLSTW E13 107 F3
Appold St ERITH DA8 130 C6
SDTCH EC2A 13 G1
Apprentice Wy CLPT E5 86 D2
Approach La MLHL NW7 46 C1
Approach Rd BETH E2 104 E1
E/WMO/HCT KT8 189 F2
EBAR EN4 21 G5
RYNPK SW20 177 F5
The Approach ACT W3 99 F5
EN EN1 24 D3
HDN NW4 64 B2
ORP BR6 202 A6
Aprey Gdns HDN NW4 64 A1
April Cl FELT TW13 153 K5
HNWL W7 96 E6
ORP BR6 217 F3
April Gln FSTH SE23 164 A5
April St STNW/STAM N16 86 B2
Apsley Cl HRW HA1 60 C2
Apsley Rd NWMAL KT3 175 K6
SNWD SE25 197 J1
Apsley Wy CRICK NW2 63 J6
MYFR/PICC W1J * 15 J1
Aquarius TWK TW1 * 156 C3
Aquarius Wy NTHWD HA6 40 E1
Aquila St STJWD NW8 2 B2
Aquinas St STHWK SE1 17 K1
Arabella Dr PUT/ROE SW15 138 B5
Arabia Cl CHING E4 38 A2
Arabin Rd BROCKY SE4 144 B5
Aragon Av EW KT17 207 K6
THDIT KT7 190 A2
Aragon Cl ENC/FH EN2 23 F1
HAYES BR2 200 E5
LOU IG10 39 J1
Aragon Dr BARK/HLT IG6 54 C3
RSLP HA4 59 H5
Aragon Rd KUTN/CMB KT2 175 F1
MRDN SM4 193 G4
Arandora Crs CHDH RM6 73 H4
Arbery Rd BOW E3 105 G2
Arbor Cl BECK BR3 182 E5
Arborfield Cl
BRXS/STRHM SW2 162 A3
Arbor Rd CHING E4 38 B5
Arbour Rd PEND EN3 25 F5
Arbour Sq WCHPL E1 104 E5
Arbour Wy HCH RM12 93 K3
Arbroath Gn OXHEY WD19 26 E5
Arbroath Rd ELTH/MOT SE9 146 D4
Arbrook Cl STMC/STPC BR5 186 B6
Arbrook La ESH/CLAY KT10 204 D4
Arbuthnot La BXLY DA5 169 F1
Arbuthnot Rd NWCR SE14 144 A3
Arbutus St HACK E8 86 B6
Arcade Chambers
ELTH/MOT SE9 * 167 F1
Arcade Pde CHSGTN KT9 * 206 A2
Arcade Pl ROM RM1 75 G2
The Arcade ELTH/MOT SE9 * 167 F1
LVPST EC2M * 13 G2
WALTH E17 * 69 J1
Arcadia Av FNCH N3 46 E4
Arcadia Cl CAR SM5 210 A2
Arcadian Av BXLY DA5 169 F1
Arcadian Cl BXLY DA5 169 F1
Arcadian Gdns WDGN N22 49 G3
Arcadian Pl
WAND/EARL SW18 159 J2
Arcadian Rd BXLY DA5 169 F2
Arcadia St POP/IOD E14 105 J5
Archangel St
BERM/RHTH SE16 124 A2
Archbishop's Pl
BRXS/STRHM SW2 162 A1
Archdale Ct SHB W12 118 E1
Archdale Pl NWMAL KT3 175 J6
Archdale Rd EDUL SE22 143 G6
Archel Rd WKENS W14 119 J6
Archer Cl KUTN/CMB KT2 175 F3
Archer Rd SNWD SE25 197 J1
STMC/STPC BR5 202 B3
Archers Dr PEND EN3 24 E3
Archer Sq DEPT SE8 124 B6
Archer St SOHO/SHAV W1D 10 C5

Archery CI *BAY/PAD* W2 ....8 D4
KTN/HRWW/W HA5 ....43 F6
Archery Rd *CHCR* WC2N * 146 E6
The Arches *CHCR* WC2N * 11 F7
RYLN/HDSTN HA2 ....60 B6
Archibald Ms *MYFR/PICC* W1J 9 H6
Archibald Rd *HOLWY* N7 ....84 D2
Arch St *STHWK* SE1 ....18 C5
Archway CI *ARCH* N19 * 57 K2
CROY/NA CRO * 210 E1
NKENS W10 ....100 B4
WIM/MER SW19 ....160 A6
Archway Rd *HGT* N6 ....65 K2
Archway St *BARN* SW13 ....138 B4
Arcola St *HACK* E8 ....86 B3
Arctic St *KTTN* NW5 ....84 B3
Arcus Rd *BMLY* BR1 ....183 H2
Ardbeg Rd *HNHL* SE24 ....162 E1
HRW HA1 ....78 D1
THMD SE28 ....37 H5
Arden Court Gdns *EFNCH* N2 ....65 H4
Arden Crs *DAGW* RM9 ....91 J5
POP/IOD E14 ....124 D4
Arden Est *IS* N1 ....7 G3
Arden Gv *ORP* BR6 ....216 B2
Arden Mhor *PIN* HA5 ....59 F1
Arden Rd *FNCH* N3 ....46 D6
WEA W13 ....97 J6
Ardent CI *SNWD* SE25 ....181 F6

Ardfern Av
STRHM/NOR SW16 ....180 B6
Ardfillan Rd *CAT* SE6 ....165 G3
Ardgowan Rd *CAT* SE6 ....165 H3
Ardilaun Rd *HBRY* N5 ....85 J2
Ardingly CI *CROY/NA* CR0 ....213 F1
Ardleigh Gdns *CHEAM* SM3 ....193 K5
Ardleigh Rd *IS* N1 ....86 A4
WALTH E17 ....51 H4
Ardleigh Ter *WALTH* E17 ....51 H4
Ardley CI *FSTH* SE23 ....164 A4
WLSDN NW10 ....81 G1
Ardlui Rd *WNWD* SE27 ....162 D4
Ardmay Gdns *SURB* KT6 ....191 F2
Ardmere Rd *LEW* SE13 ....165 G1
Ardmore La *BKHH* IG9 ....39 F3
Ardmore PI *BKHH* IG9 * 39 F2
Ardoch Rd *CAT* SE6 ....165 G2
Ardra Rd *ED* N9 ....37 F5
Ardrossan Gdns *WPK* KT4 ....207 J1
Ardross Av *NTHWD* HA6 ....40 C1
Ardshiel CI *PUT/ROE* SW15 ....139 G4
Ardwell Av *BARK/HLT* IG6 ....72 C2
Ardwell Rd *BRXS/STRHM* SW2 ......161 K4
Ardwick Rd *CRICK* NW2 ....82 E2
Arena Est *FSBYPK* N4 * 67 H3
The Arena *STKPK* UB11 * 113 F1
Argall Av *LEY* E10 ....69 G4
Argall Wy *LEY* E10 ....69 F5
Argenta Wy *WLSDN* NW10 ....80 D5
Argosy La *STWL/WRAY* TW19 ....152 A2
Argosy Wy *NTHLT* UB5 ....95 J2
Argus CI *ROMW/RG* RM7 ....56 D4
Argus Wy *NTHLT* UB5 ....95 J1
Argyle CI *WEA* W13 ....97 F3
Argyle Cnr *WEA* W13 * 97 H6
Argyle PI *HMSMTH* W6 ....118 E4
Argyle Rd *BAR* EN5 ....20 A5
CAN/RD E16 ....107 F5
GFD/PVL UB6 ....96 E3
HSLW TW3 ....135 G6
IL IG1 ....72 A6
NFNCH/WDSP N12 ....46 E1
RYLN/HDSTN HA2 ....60 B3
SRTFD E15 ....88 C2
TOTM N17 ....50 C4
UED N18 ....36 C6
WCHPL E1 ....105 F5
Argyle Sq *STPAN* WC1H * 5 F4
Argyle St *CAMTN* NW1 ....4 E4
STPAN WC1H 5 F5
Argyle Wk *STPAN* WC1H * 5 F4
Argyll Av *STHL* UB1 ....115 G1
Argyll CI *BRXN/ST* SW9 ....142 A4
Argyll Gdns *EDGW* HA8 ....44 D5
Argyll Rd *KENS* W8 ....119 K2
WOOL/PLUM SE18 ....127 H3
Argyll St *REGST* W1B 10 A4
Arica Rd *BROCKY* SE4 ....144 B5
Ariel Rd *KIL/WHAMP* NW6 ....82 E4
Ariel Wy *HSLWW* TW4 ....134 A4
SHB W12 ....119 F1
Aristotle Rd *CLAP* SW4 ....141 J4
Arkell Gv *NRWD* SE19 ....180 C3
Arkindale Rd *CAT* SE6 ....165 F5
Arkley Crs *WALTH* E17 ....69 H2
Arkley Rd *WALTH* E17 ....69 H2
Arklow Rd *NWCR* SE14 ....124 C6
Arkwright Rd *HAMP* NW3 ....83 G3
Arlesford Rd *BRXN/ST* SW9 ....141 K4

Arlingford Rd
BRXS/STRHM SW2 ....162 B1
Arlington *NFNCH/WDSP* N12 ....32 E5
Arlington Av *IS* N1 ....6 D1
Arlington CI *BFN/LL* DA15 ....167 K2
LEW SE13 ....145 G6
SUT SM1 ....193 K6
TWK TW1 ....156 A6
Arlington Ct *HYS/HAR* UB3 ....113 G5
Arlington Dr *CAR* SM5 ....194 E6
RSLP HA4 ....58 B3
Arlington Gdns *CHSWK* W4 ....117 K5
IL IG1 ....71 K4

Arlington Pde
BRXS/STRHM SW2 ....142 A5
Arlington Rd *CAMTN* NW1 ....3 K1
STHGT/OAK N14 ....34 B4
SURB KT6 ....190 E4
TWK TW1 ....156 A6

TWK TW1 ....156 D1
WEA W13 ....97 H5
WFD IG8 ....52 E4
Arlington St *MYFR/PICC* W1J 9 K7
Arlington Wy *CLKNW* EC1R 5 K4
Arliss Wy *NTHLT* UB5 ....77 G6
Arlow Rd *WCHMH* N21 ....35 G3
Armadale CI *TOTM* N17 ....68 D1
Armadale Rd
EBED/NFELT TW14 ....133 K6
FUL/PGN SW6 ....139 K1
Armada St *DEPT* SE8 ....124 D6
Armada Wy *EHAM* E6 ....108 C5
Armagh Rd *BOW* E3 ....87 H6
Armfield CI *E/WMO/HCT* KT8 ....188 E2
Armfield Crs *MTCM* CR4 ....178 E5
Armfield Rd *ENC/FH* EN2 ....23 K2
Arminger Rd *SHB* W12 ....118 E1
Armitage Rd *GLDGN* NW11 ....64 C5
GNWCH SE10 ....125 J5
Armour CI *HOLWY* N7 ....85 F4
Armoury Rd *DEPT* SE8 ....144 E3
Armoury Wy
WAND/EARL SW18 ....139 K6
Armstead Wk *DAGE* RM10 ....92 C5
Armstrong Av *WFD* IG8 ....52 C2
Armstrong Rd *BCTR* RM8 ....73 K4
BMLY BR1 ....184 D6
EHAM E6 ....107 K5
RSLP HA4 ....58 E3
Armstrong Crs *EBAR* EN4 ....21 H4
Armstrong Rd *ACT* W3 ....118 C1
FELT TW13 ....172 D1
WOOL/PLUM SE18 ....127 H3
Armstrong Wy *NWDGN* UB2 ....115 H2
Armytage Rd *HEST* TW5 ....134 C1
Arnal Crs *WAND/EARL* SW18 ....159 H2
Arncliffe CI *FBAR/BDGN* N11 ....48 A2
Arne Gv *ORP* BR6 ....217 F1
Arne St *LSQ/SEVD* WC2H 11 F4
Arnett Sq *CHING* E4 ....51 H2
Arne Wk *BKHTH/KID* SE3 ....145 J5
Arneways Av *CHDH* RM6 ....73 K1
Arneway St *WEST* SW1P 16 D5
Arnewood CI *PUT/ROE* SW15 ....158 D3
Arney's La *MTCM* CR4 ....195 F5
Arngask Rd *CAT* SE6 ....165 G2
Arnham PI *POP/IOD* E14 ....124 D5
Arnison Rd *E/WMO/HCT* KT8 ....189 J1
Arnold Av East *PEND* EN3 ....25 J1
Arnold Av West *PEND* EN3 ....25 H1
Arnold Circ *BETH* E2 ....7 J5
Arnold Ct *KTN/HRWW/W* HA3 ....62 D4
Arnold Crs *ISLW* TW7 ....135 J6
Arnold Dr *CHSGTN* KT9 ....205 K4
Arnold Est *STHWK* SE1 ....19 K3
Arnold Gdns *PLMGR* N13 ....49 H1
Arnold Rd *BOW* E3 ....105 J2
DAGW RM9 ....92 B5
NTHLT UB5 ....77 J4
TOOT SW17 ....178 E3
TOTM N17 ....50 B6
Arnold Ter *STAN* HA7 * 43 F1
Arnos Gv *STHGT/OAK* N14 ....34 D6
Arnos Rd *FBAR/BDGN* N11 ....48 C1
Arnott CI *CHSWK* W4 ....118 A4
THMD SE28 ....128 D1
Arnould Av *CMBW* SE5 ....142 E5
Arnsberg Wy *BXLYHN* DA7 ....149 H5
Arnside Gdns *WBLY* HA9 ....61 K5
Arnside Rd *BXLYHN* DA7 ....149 H2
Arnside St *WALW* SE17 ....122 D6
Arnulf St *CAT* SE6 ....164 E6
Arnull's Rd *STRHM/NOR* SW16 ....180 C2
Arodene Rd
BRXS/STRHM SW2 ....162 A1
Arosa Rd *TWK* TW1 ....156 E1
Arragon Gdns
STRHM/NOR SW16 ....179 K3
WWKM BR4 ....213 K1
Arragon Rd *EHAM* E6 ....89 H6
TWK TW1 ....156 B1
WAND/EARL SW18 ....159 K3
Arran CI *ERITH* DA8 ....130 A6
Arran Dr *MNPK* E12 ....71 H6
STAN HA7 ....29 J6
Arran Gn *OXHEY* WD19 * 27 H6
Arran Ms *ACT* W3 ....117 G1
Arran Rd *CAT* SE6 ....164 E4
Arran Wk *IS* N1 ....85 J5
Arran Wy *ESH/CLAY* KT10 ....189 G6
Arras Av *MRDN* SM4 ....194 B2
Arrol Rd *BECK* BR3 ....181 K6
Arrow Rd *BOW* E3 ....105 K2
Arrowsmith Rd *CHIG* IG7 ....55 F1
Arsenal Rd *ELTH/MOT* SE9 ....146 E3
Arsenal Wy *CAN/RD* E16 ....127 F2
Arterberry Rd *RYNPK* SW20 ....177 F3
Artesian CI *ROM* RM1 ....75 H3
WLSDN NW10 ....81 F5
Artesian Gv *BAR* EN5 ....21 G5
Artesian Houses
NTGHL W11 * 100 E5
Artesian Rd *BAY/PAD* W2 ....100 E5
Arthingworth St *SRTFD* E15 ....88 C6
Arthurdon Rd *LEW* SE13 ....144 D6
Arthur Rd *CHDH* RM6 ....73 J2
ED N9 ....36 B4
EHAM E6 ....107 K1
HOLWY N7 ....85 F2
KUTN/CMB KT2 ....175 H3
NWMAL KT3 ....192 E2
WIM/MER SW19 ....159 K6
Arthur St *CANST* EC4R 13 F6
ERITH DA8 ....150 C1
Artichoke HI *WAP* E1W 104 D6
Artichoke PI *CMBW* SE5 * 142 E2
Artillery La *LVPST* EC2M 13 H2
SHB W12 ....99 J5
Artillery Pas *WCHPL* E1 * 13 H2
Artillery PI *WOOL/PLUM* SE18 ....126 E5

Artillery Rw *WEST* SW1P 16 C5
Artington CI *ORP* BR6 ....216 C2
Artizan St *WCHPL* E1 ....13 H3
Arundel Av *MRDN* SM4 ....193 J1
Arundel CI *BTSEA* SW11 ....140 D6
BXLY DA5 ....169 G1
CROY/NA CR0 * 211 H1
HPTN TW12 ....173 G1
SRTFD E15 ....69 F3
Arundel Dr *ORP* BR6 ....217 H3
RYLN/HDSTN HA2 ....77 K2
WFD IG8 ....52 E3
Arundel Gdns *EDGW* HA8 ....45 G5
GDMY/SEVK IG3 ....73 G6
NTGHL W11 ....100 D6
WCHMH N21 ....35 G3
Arundel Gv *STNW/STAM* N16 ....86 A3
Arundel PI *IS* N1 ....85 G4
Arundel Rd *BELMT* SM2 ....208 D5
CROY/NA CR0 ....196 E3
DART DA1 ....151 F5
EBAR EN4 ....21 J4
HSLWW TW4 ....134 B4
KUT/HW KT1 ....175 K5
Arundel Sq *HOLWY* N7 ....85 G4
Arundel St *TPL/STR* WC2R 11 H5
Arundel Ter *BARN* SW13 ....118 E6
Arvon Rd *HBRY* N5 ....85 G3
Asbaston Ter *IL* IG1 ....90 C4
Ascalon St *VX/NE* SW8 ....141 H1
Ascension Rd *CRW* RM5 ....56 E2
Ascham Dr *CHING* E4 ....51 K3
Ascham End *WALTH* E17 ....51 G4
Ascham St *KTTN* NW5 ....84 C3
Aschurch Rd *CROY/NA* CR0 ....197 G4
Ascot CI *BARK/HLT* IG6 ....54 C2
NTHLT UB5 ....78 A3
Ascot Gdns *STHL* UB1 ....95 K4
Ascot Ms *WLGTN* SM6 ....210 C6
Ascot Pde *CLAP* SW4 * 141 K5
Ascot Rd *EBED/NFELT* TW14 ....152 D5
EHAM E6 ....107 K2
SEVS/STOTM N15 ....67 K2
STMC/STPC BR5 ....202 A1
TOOT SW17 ....179 F2
UED N18 ....36 C6
WATW WD18 ....26 C1
Ascott Av *EA* W5 ....117 F2
Ascott Ct *PIN* HA5 * 58 E1
Ashanti Ms *HACK* E8 ....86 D4
Ashbourne Sq *NTHWD* HA6 ....40 C2
Ashbourne Av *BXLYHN* DA7 ....149 F7
GLDGN NW11 ....64 D2
RYLN/HDSTN HA2 ....71 F1
SWFD E18 ....53 F2
TRDG/WHET N20 ....33 K4
Ashbourne CI *EA* W5 ....98 B4
NFNCH/WDSP N12 ....47 F1
Ashbourne Gv *CHSWK* W4 ....118 B5
EDUL SE22 ....143 G5
MLHL NW7 ....45 F1
Ashbourne Pde *EA* W5 * 98 B3
GLDGN NW11 * 64 D2
Ashbourne Ri *ORP* BR6 ....216 D2
Ashbourne Rd *EA* W5 ....98 B3
MTCM CR4 ....179 F2
Ashbourne Ter
WIM/MER SW19 ....177 K3
Ashbourne Wy *GLDGN* NW11 ....64 D2
Ashbridge Rd *WAN* E11 ....70 C4
Ashbridge St *STJWD* NW8 ....2 C7
Ashbrook *EDGW* HA8 ....44 B1
Ashbrook Rd *ARCH* N19 ....66 D5
DAGE RM10 ....92 D1
Ashburn Gdns *SKENS* SW7 ....120 B4
Ashburnham Av *HRW* HA1 ....61 F4
Ashburnham CI *EFNCH* N2 ....47 H6
OXHEY WD19 * 26 E5
Ashburnham Gdns *HRW* HA1 ....61 F5
Ashburnham Gv *GNWCH* SE10 ....144 E1
Ashburnham Pk
ESH/CLAY KT10 ....204 C2
Ashburnham PI *GNWCH* SE10 ....144 E1
Ashburnham Retreat
GNWCH SE10 ....144 E1
Ashburnham Rd *BELV* DA17 ....129 K4
RCHPK/HAM TW10 ....156 C5
WBPTN SW10 ....140 B6
WLSDN NW10 ....100 A2
Ashburn PI *SKENS* SW7 ....120 B4
Ashburton Av *CROY/NA* CR0 ....197 J5
GDMY/SEVK IG3 ....91 F2
Ashburton CI *CROY/NA* CR0 ....197 J5
Ashburton Gdns
CROY/NA CR0 ....197 H6
Ashburton Gv *HOLWY* N7 ....85 G2
Ashburton Rd *CAN/RD* E16 ....106 E5
CROY/NA CR0 ....197 H6
RSLP HA4 ....58 E6
Ashbury Dr *BMLY* BR1 ....183 K3
Ashbury Gdns *CHDH* RM6 ....73 K2
Ashbury PI *WIM/MER* SW19 ....178 B2
Ashbury Rd *BTSEA* SW11 ....140 E4
Ashby Av *CHSGTN* KT9 ....206 C4
Ashby Gv *IS* N1 ....85 J5
Ashby Ms *BROCKY* SE4 ....144 C4
Ashby Rd *BROCKY* SE4 ....144 C3
SEVS/STOTM N15 ....68 C2
Ashby St *FSBYE* EC1V 6 B5
Ashby Wk *CROY/NA* CR0 ....196 D3
Ashby Wy *WDR/YW* UB7 ....132 D1
Ashchurch Gv *SHB* W12 ....118 D2
Ashchurch Park Vls *SHB* W12 ....118 D3
Ashchurch Ter *SHB* W12 ....118 C3
Ash CI *CAR* SM5 ....194 E6
EDGW HA8 ....30 E6
NWMAL KT3 ....176 A5
PGE/AN SE20 ....181 K5
ROMW/RG RM7 ....56 D3
SCUP DA14 ....168 C5
STAN HA7 ....43 G3
STMC/STPC BR5 ....201 J2
SWLY BR8 ....187 K5
Ashcombe Av *SURB* KT6 ....190 E4

Ashcombe Gdns *EDGW* HA8 ....30 C6
Ashcombe Pk *CRICK* NW2 ....81 G1
Ashcombe Rd *CAR* SM5 ....210 A4
WIM/MER SW19 ....177 K1
Ashcombe Sq *NWMAL* KT3 ....175 K6
Ashcombe St *FUL/PGN* SW6 * 140 A3
Ash Ct *HOR/WEW* KT19 ....206 E2
Ashcroft *PIN* HA5 ....42 A2
Ashcroft Av *BFN/LL* DA15 ....168 B1
Ashcroft Crs *BFN/LL* DA15 ....168 B1
Ashcroft Rd *BOW* E3 ....105 G2
CHSGTN KT9 ....206 B1
Ashdale CI *STWL/WRAY* TW19 ......152 C2
WHTN TW2 ....155 G2
Ashdale Gv *STAN* HA7 ....43 F2
Ashdale Rd *LEE/GVPK* SE12 ....166 A3
Ashdene *PIN* HA5 ....41 G6
Ashdon CI *WFD* IG8 ....53 F2
Ashdon Rd *BECK* BR5 ....182 E5
BXLY DA5 ....170 D1
Ashdown WEA W13 * 97 H4
Ashdown CI *BECK* BR3 ....182 D5
RCHPK/HAM TW10 ....157 F3
Ashdown Crs *KTTN* NW5 ....84 A3
Ashdown Dr *DART* DA1 ....170 D1
Ashdown Gn *WHLCF* KT1 ....85 J4
Ashdown Rd *CROY/NA* CR0 ....197 G5
PEND EN3 ....25 F1
WLSDN NW10 ....81 G6
Ashdown Wk *ROMW/RG* RM7 ....56 D4
Ashdown Wy *TOOT* SW17 ....161 F4
Ashenden Rd *CLPT* E5 ....87 G3
Ashen Dr *DART* DA1 ....170 D1
Ashen Gv *WIM/MER* SW19 ....159 K5
Ashen V *SAND/SEL* CR2 ....213 F6
Asher Loftus Wy
FBAR/BDGN N11 ....47 K2
Asher Wy *WAP* E1W 123 H1
Ashfield Av *BUSH* WD23 ....28 B1
FELT TW13 ....154 A3
Ashfield CI *BECK* BR3 ....182 D3
RCHPK/HAM TW10 ....157 F3
Ashfield Ct *EA* W5 * 98 A6
Ashfield La *CHST* BR7 ....185 H2
Ashfield Rd *ACT* W3 ....118 C1
FSBYPK N4 ....67 J5
STHGT/OAK N14 ....34 C5
Ashfield St *WCHPL* E1 ....104 E4
Ashfield Yd *WCHPL* E1 * 104 E4
Ashford Av *CEND/HSY/T* N8 ....66 E1
YEAD UB4 ....95 H5
Ashford CI *ASHF* TW15 ....152 B6
WALTH E17 ....69 H3
Ashford Crs *ASHF* TW15 ....152 B5
PEND EN3 ....25 F2
Ashford Gn *OXHEY* WD19 ....41 H1
Ashford Rd *CRICK* NW2 ....82 B2
EHAM E6 ....89 K6
FELT TW13 ....153 H5
SWFD E18 ....53 F5
Ash Gv *EA* W5 ....117 F2
EBED/NFELT TW14 ....153 H1
EN EN1 ....24 B6
HACK E8 ....86 D6
HEST TW5 ....134 C1
HYS/HAR UB3 ....94 B6
PGE/AN SE20 ....181 K5
PLMGR N13 ....35 H5
STHL UB1 ....96 A4
WBLM BR4 ....199 F6
Ashgrove Rd *BMLY* BR1 ....183 G2
GDMY/SEVK IG3 ....73 F5
Ash HI *BUSH* WD23 * 29 A3
Ash Hill Dr *PIN* HA5 ....41 G6
Ashingdon CI *CHING* E4 ....38 A4
Ashington Rd *FUL/PGN* SW6 * 139 J3
Ashlake Rd
STRHM/NOR SW16 ....161 K6
Ashland PI *MHST* W1U 3 G7
Ashlar PI *WOOL/PLUM* SE18 ....127 G4
Ashleigh Gdns *SUT* SM1 ....194 A6
Ashleigh Rd
MORT/ESHN SW14 ....138 B4
PGE/AN SE20 ....181 J5
Ashley Av *BARK/HLT* IG6 ....54 B5
MRDN SM4 ....193 K2
Ashley CI *HDN* NW4 ....45 F5
PIN HA5 ....41 F5
Ashley Crs *BTSEA* SW11 ....141 F4
WDGN N22 ....49 G5
Ashley Dr *ISLW* TW7 ....115 K6
WHTN TW2 ....155 G3
Ashley Gdns *ORP* BR6 ....216 E3
PLMGR N13 ....35 J6
RCHPK/HAM TW10 ....156 E5
WBLY HA9 ....62 B6
Ashley La *CROY/NA* CR0 ....211 H2
MLHL NW7 ....31 J4
Ashley PI *WEST* SW1P 16 A5
Ashley Rd *ARCH* N19 ....66 E5
CHING E4 ....51 K2
FSTGT E7 ....89 H4
HPTN TW12 ....173 F4
PEND EN3 ....25 F1
RCH/KEW TW9 ....137 F5
THDIT KT7 ....190 A3
THHTH CR7 ....196 A1
TOTM N17 ....68 C3
WIM/MER SW19 ....178 A2
Ashling Rd *CROY/NA* CR0 ....197 H5
Ashlin Rd *SRTFD* E15 ....88 B2
Ashlone Rd *PUT/ROE* SW15 ....139 G3
Ashlyns Wy *CHSGTN* KT9 ....205 K4
Ashmead *STHGT/OAK* N14 ....22 C6
Ashmead Ga *BMLY* BR1 ....184 B4
Ashmead Ms *DEPT* SE8 * 144 D3
Ashmead Rd *DEPT* SE8 ....144 D3
EBED/NFELT TW14 ....154 A3
Ashmere Av *BECK* BR3 ....183 G5
Ashmere CI *CHEAM* SM3 ....208 A3
Ashmere Gv *CLAP* SW4 ....141 H3
Ash Ms *KTTN* NW5 ....84 C3
Ashmill St *STJWD* NW8 ....2 C7
Ashmole PI *VX/NE* SW8 ....122 A6
Ashmole St *VX/NE* SW8 ....122 A6

Ashmore Gv *WELL* DA16 ....147 J4
Ashmore Rd *MV/WKIL* W9 ....100 D2
Ashmount Rd *HGT* N6 ....66 C4
SEVS/STOTM N15 ....68 B2
Ashmour Gdns *ROM* RM1 ....57 F5
Ashneal Gdns *HRW* HA1 ....78 D1
Ashness Gdns *GFD/PVL* UB6 ....79 H4
Ashness Rd *BTSEA* SW11 ....140 E6
Ashridge CI
KTN/HRWW/W HA3 ....61 J3
Ashridge Crs
WOOL/PLUM SE18 ....147 H1
Ashridge Dr *OXHEY* WD19 ....41 G1
Ashridge Gdns *PIN* HA5 ....59 J1
PLMGR N13 ....48 E1
Ashridge Wy *MRDN* SM4 ....193 J1
Ash Rd *CROY/NA* CR0 ....213 J1
DART DA1 ....171 G3
MRDN SM4 ....193 K4
ORP BR6 ....217 G5
RDART DA2 ....171 J6
SRTFD E15 ....88 C3
Ash Rw *HAYES* BR2 ....201 F3
Ashtead Rd *CLPT* E5 ....68 C4
Ashton CI *SUT* SM1 ....208 E2
Ashton Gdns *CHDH* RM6 ....74 A3
HSLWW TW4 ....134 E5
Ashton Rd *SRTFD* E15 ....88 B3
Ashton St *POP/IOD* E14 ....106 A6
Ashtree Av *MTCM* CR4 ....178 C5
Ash Tree CI *CROY/NA* CR0 ....198 B3
SURB KT6 ....191 F1
Ashtree CI *ORP* BR6 ....216 B2
Ash Tree Dell *CDALE/KGS* NW9 ....62 E2
Ash Tree Wy *CROY/NA* CR0 ....198 B2
Ashurst CI *DART* DA1 ....150 C4
NTHWD HA6 ....40 C3
PGE/AN SE20 ....181 J4
Ashurst Dr *BARK/HLT* IG6 ....72 C2
Ashurst Gdns
BRXS/STRHM SW2 ....162 B3
NFNCH/WDSP N12 ....47 J6
Ashurst Wk *CROY/NA* CR0 ....197 J6
Ashvale Gdns *CRW* RM5 ....57 F1
Ashvale Rd *TOOT* SW17 ....178 E1
Ashville Rd *WAN* E11 ....70 B6
Ash Wk *ALP/SUD* HA0 ....79 J2
Ashwater Rd *LEE/GVPK* SE12 ....165 K3
Ashwin St *HACK* E8 ....86 B4
Ashwood Av *RAIN* RM13 ....111 J4
Ashwood Gdns *CROY/NA* CR0 ....213 K4
HYS/HAR UB3 ....113 J4
Ashwood Rd *CHING* E4 ....38 B5
Ashworth CI *CMBW* SE5 ....142 E3
Ashworth Rd *MV/WKIL* W9 ....101 F2
Askern CI *BXLYHS* DA6 ....148 E5
Aske St *IS* N1 ....7 G4
Askew Crs *SHB* W12 ....118 C2
Askew Rd *NTHWD* HA6 ....26 B4
SHB W12 ....118 C2
Askew VIs *PLMGR* N13 * 35 H5
Askham Rd *SHB* W12 ....118 D1
Askill Dr *PUT/ROE* SW15 ....139 H6
Askwith Rd *RAIN* RM13 ....111 F1
Asland Rd *SRTFD* E15 ....88 B6
Aslett St *WAND/EARL* SW18 ....160 A2
Asmara Rd *CRICK* NW2 ....82 C3
Asmuns HI *GLDGN* NW11 ....64 D2
Asmuns PI *GLDGN* NW11 ....64 C2
Aspen CI *EA* W5 ....117 G2
ORP BR6 ....217 G3
WDR/YW UB7 ....112 C1
Aspen Copse *BMLY* BR1 ....184 E5
Aspen Dr *ALP/SUD* HA0 ....79 G1
Aspen Gdns *MTCM* CR4 ....195 F1
Aspen Gn *ERITH* DA18 ....129 G3
Aspen La *NTHLT* UB5 ....95 J2
Aspenlea Rd *HMSMTH* W6 ....119 G6
Aspen Wy *FELT* TW13 ....154 A5
POP/IOD E14 ....106 A6
Aspern Gv *HAMP* NW3 ....83 J3
Aspinall Rd *BROCKY* SE4 ....144 A4
Aspinden Rd
BERM/RHTH SE16 ....123 J4
Aspley Rd *WAND/EARL* SW18 ....140 A6
Asplins Rd *TOTM* N17 ....50 C4
Asplins VIs *TOTM* N17 * 50 C4
Asquith CI *BCTR* RM8 ....73 J5
Assam St *WCHPL* E1 ....104 C5
Assata Ms *IS* N1 ....85 H4
Assembly Pas *WCHPL* E1 ....104 E4
Assembly Wk *CAR* SM5 ....194 D4
Ass House La
KTN/HRWW/W HA3 ....28 B6
Astall CI *KTN/HRWW/W* HA3 ....42 D4
Astbury Rd *PECK* SE15 ....143 K2
Astell St *CHEL* SW3 ....120 D5
Asteys Rw *IS* N1 ....85 H5
Astle St *BTSEA* SW11 ....141 F3
Aston Av *KTN/HRWW/W* HA3 ....62 A3
Aston CI *BUSH* WD23 ....28 C1
SCUP DA14 ....168 B5
Aston Gn *HEST* TW5 ....134 B3
Aston Rd *EA* W5 ....97 K5
ESH/CLAY KT10 ....204 E4
RYNPK SW20 ....177 F5
Astons Rd *NTHWD* HA6 ....26 A3
Aston St *POP/IOD* E14 ....105 G5
Aston Ter *BAL* SW12 * 161 G1
Astonville St
WAND/EARL SW18 ....159 K3
Astor Av *RG* RM7 ....74 D3
Astor CI *KUTN/CMB* KT2 ....175 J2
Astoria Pde *ASHF* TW15 * 152 D6
STRHM/NOR SW16 ....161 K5
Astoria Wk *BRXN/ST* SW9 ....142 B4
Astra CI *HCH* RM12 ....93 K4
Astrop Ms *HMSMTH* W6 ....119 F3
Astrop Ter *HMSMTH* W6 ....119 F2
Astwood Ms *SKENS* SW7 ....120 A4
Asylum Rd *PECK* SE15 ....143 J1
Atalanta St *FUL/PGN* SW6 ....139 G2

Atbara Rd TEDD TW11 174 C2
Atcham Rd HSLW TW3 135 H5
Atcost Rd BARK IG11 109 G4
Atheldene Rd
WAND/EARL SW18 160 A3
Athelney St CAT SE6 164 D5
Athelstane Gv BOW E3 105 H1
Athelstane Ms FSBYPK N4 67 G5
Athelstan Gdns
KIL/WHAMP NW6 * 82 C5
Athelstan Rd KUT/HW KT1 191 G1
Athelstan Wy
STMC/STPC BR5 186 B4
Athelstone Rd
KTN/HRWW/W HA3 42 D5
Athena Cl KUT/HW KT1 175 G6
RYLN/HDSTN HA2 60 D6
Athenaeum Pl MUSWH N10 48 B6
Athenaeum Rd
TRDG/WHET N20 33 G3
Athena Pl NTHWD HA6 40 D4
Athenlay Rd PECK SE15 144 A6
Athens Gdns MV/WKIL W9 * 100 E3
Atherden Rd CLPT E5 86 E2
Atherfold Rd BRXN/ST SW9 141 K4
Atherley Wy HSLWW TW4 154 E2
Atherstone Ms SKENS SW7 * 120 B4
Atherton Cl STWL/WRAY TW19 152 A1
Atherton Dr WIM/MER SW19 159 G6
Atherton Hts ALP/SUD HA0 79 J4
Atherton Ms FSTGT E7 88 D4
Atherton Pl RYLN/HDSTN HA2 42 C6
STHL UB1 96 A6
Atherton Rd BARN SW13 138 D1
CLAY IG5 53 J5
FSTGT E7 88 D3
Atherton St BTSEA SW11 140 D3
Athlone ESH/CLAY KT10 204 E4
Athlone Cl CLPT E5 86 D3
Athlone Ct WALTH E17 52 B6
Athlone Rd BRXS/STRHM SW2 162 A2
Athlone St KTTN NW5 84 A4
Athlon Rd ALP/SUD HA0 97 K1
Athol Cl PIN HA5 41 F4
Athole Gdns EN EN1 24 A6
Athol Gdns PIN HA5 41 F4
Atholl Rd GDMY/SEVK IG3 73 G4
Athol Rd ERITH DA8 129 K5
Athol Sq POP/IOD E14 106 A5
Atkins Dr WWKM BR4 214 B1
Atkinson Cl ORP BR6 217 G3
Atkinson Rd CAN/RD E16 107 G4
Atkins Rd BAL SW12 161 H2
LEY E10 69 K3
Atlanta Bvd ROM RM1 75 G3
Atlantic Rd BRXN/ST SW9 142 B5
Atlantis Cl BARK IG11 109 H2
Atlas Gdns CHARL SE7 126 B4
Atlas Ms HACK E8 86 B4
Atlas Rd DART DA1 151 J4
FBAR/BDGN N11 48 A2
PLSTW E13 106 E1
WBLY HA9 80 E2
WLSDN NW10 99 G2
Atley Rd BOW E3 87 J6
Atlip Rd ALP/SUD HA0 80 A6
Atney Rd PUT/ROE SW15 139 H5
Atria Rd NTHWD HA6 40 E1
Attenborough Cl OXHEY WD19 27 J5
Atterbury Rd FSBYPK N4 67 G3
Atterbury St WEST SW1P 16 D7
Attewood Av CRICK NW2 81 G1
Attewood Rd NTHLT UB5 77 J4
Attfield Cl TRDG/WHET N20 33 H4
Attlee Cl CROY/NA CR0 196 D3
NTHLT UB5 * 95 F2
Attlee Dr DART DA1 151 K6
Attlee Rd THMD SE28 109 H6
YEAD UB4 94 E2
Attlee Ter WALTH E17 69 K1
Attneave St FSBYW WC1X 5 J6
Atwell Rd PECK SE15 * 143 H3
Atwood Av RCH/KEW TW9 137 H3
Atwood Rd HMSMTH W6 118 E4
Aubert Pk HBRY N5 85 G2
Aubert Rd HBRY N5 85 H2
Aubrey Pl STJWD NW8 101 G1
Aubrey Rd CEND/HSY/T N8 * 66 E2
KENS W8 119 J1
WALTH E17 51 J6
Aubrey Wk KENS W8 119 J1
Auburn Cl NWCR SE14 144 B1
Aubyn Hl WNWD SE27 162 D6
Aubyn Sq PUT/ROE SW15 138 D5
Auckland Av RAIN RM13 111 H2
Auckland Cl NRWD SE19 181 G4
Auckland Hl WNWD SE27 162 D6
Auckland Ri NRWD SE19 181 F4
Auckland Rd BTSEA SW11 140 D5
IL IG1 72 B5
KUT/HW KT1 191 G1
LEY E10 87 K1
NRWD SE19 181 G4
Aucklands Gdns NRWD SE19 181 F4
Auckland St LBTH SE11 122 A5
Aucuba Vls WELL DA16 * 148 C4
Audax CDALE/KCS NW9 * 45 H5
Auden Pl CAMTN NW1 84 A6
CHEAM SM3 * 208 A2
Audleigh Pl CHIG IG7 54 A2
Audley Cl MUSWH N10 48 B3
Audley Ct PIN HA5 41 G5
SWFD E18 70 D1
Audley Dr CAN/RD E16 126 A1
Audley Gdns GDMY/SEVK IG3 73 F6
Audley Pl BELMT SM2 209 F5
Audley Rd EA W5 98 B4
ENC/FH EN2 23 H3
HDN NW4 63 J3
RCHPK/HAM TW10 137 G6
Audley Sq MYFR/PKLN W1K * 9 H7
Audrey Cl BECK BR3 198 E3
Audrey Gdns ALP/SUD HA0 61 H6
Audrey Rd IL IG1 90 B1
Audrey St BETH E2 104 C1
Audric Cl KUTN/CMB KT2 175 H4
Augurs La PLSTW E13 107 F2
Augusta Cl E/WMO/HCT KT8 172 E6
Augusta Rd WHTN TW2 155 H4
Augustine Rd
KTN/HRWW/W HA3 42 B4
STMC/STPC BR5 186 E6
WKENS W14 119 G3
Augustus Cl BTFD TW8 136 E1
SHB W12 118 E2
STAN HA7 29 J5
Augustus Rd WIM/MER SW19 159 H3
Augustus St CAMTN NW1 3 K3
Aultone Wy CAR SM5 209 K1
SUT SM1 194 A6
Aulton Pl LBTH SE11 122 B5
Aurelia Gdns THHTH CR7 196 A2
Aurelia Rd CROY/NA CR0 195 K3
Auriel Av DAGE RM10 93 F4
Auriga Ms IS N1 85 K3
Auriol Cl HOR/WEW KT19 207 G1
Auriol Dr GFD/PVL UB6 78 D5
Auriol Park Rd WPK KT4 207 G1
Auriol Rd WKENS W14 119 H4
Austell Gdns MLHL NW7 31 G5
Austen Cl THMD SE28 128 C1
Austen Rd ERITH DA8 149 J1
RYLN/HDSTN HA2 60 B6
Austin Av HAYES BR2 200 D3
Austin Cl CAT SE6 164 B2
Austin Friars OBST EC2N 13 F3
Austin Friars Sq OBST EC2N * 13 F3
Austin Rd BTSEA SW11 141 F2
HYS/HAR UB3 113 J2
STMC/STPC BR5 202 B3
Austin's La HGDN/ICK UB10 76 B2
Austin St BETH E2 7 J5
Austral Cl BFN/LL DA15 168 A5
Australia Rd SHB W12 99 K6
Austral St LBTH SE11 18 A6
Austyn Gdns BRYLDS KT5 * 191 J5
Autumn Cl EN EN1 24 D3
WIM/MER SW19 178 B2
Autumn Dr BELMT SM2 209 F6
Autumn St BOW E3 87 J6
Avalon Cl ENC/FH EN2 23 G3
ORP BR6 202 E6
RYNPK SW20 177 H5
WEA W13 97 G4
Avalon Rd FUL/PGN SW6 140 A2
ORP BR6 202 D6
WEA W13 97 G3
Avard Gdns ORP BR6 216 C2
Avarn Rd TOOT SW17 178 E2
Avebury Pk SURB KT6 * 190 E3
Avebury Rd ORP BR6 216 D1
WAN E11 70 B5
WIM/MER SW19 177 J4
Avebury St IS N1 6 E1
Aveley Cl ERITH DA8 130 C6
Aveline St LBTH SE11 122 A5
Aveling Park Rd WALTH E17 51 J5
Avelon Rd CRW RM5 57 F2
RAIN RM13 93 J6
Ave Marie La STP EC4M 12 B4
Avenell Rd HBRY N5 85 H1
Avening Rd
WAND/EARL SW18 159 K2
Avening Ter
WAND/EARL SW18 159 K1
Avenons Rd PLSTW E13 106 E4
Avenue Cl HEST TW5 134 A2
STHGT/OAK N14 34 C1
STJWD NW8 2 D1
WDR/YW UB7 112 A3
Avenue Crs ACT W3 117 J2
HEST TW5 134 A2
Avenue Elmers SURB KT6 191 F2
Avenue Gdns ACT W3 117 J2
HEST TW5 * 133 K1
MORT/ESHN SW14 138 B4
TEDD TW11 174 A3
Avenue Ga LOU IG10 39 G1
Avenue Ms MUSWH N10 48 B6
Avenue Pde SUN TW16 * 172 A6
WCHMH N21 * 35 K2
Avenue Park Rd WNWD SE27 162 C4
Avenue Rd ACT W3 117 J2
BTFD TW8 116 D5
BXLYHS DA6 149 F4
ERITH DA8 149 K1
FELT TW13 153 J5
FSTGT E7 89 F3
GDMY/SEVK IG3 73 H4
HGT N6 66 C4
HPTN TW12 173 G4
ISLW TW7 135 K2
KUT/HW KT1 175 F6
NFNCH/WDSP N12 33 G6
NWMAL KT3 176 B6
PGE/AN SE20 181 K4
PIN HA5 41 J6
RYNPK SW20 176 E5
SEVS/STOTM N15 67 K2
SNWD SE25 181 H5
STHGT/OAK N14 34 C2
STHL UB1 114 E1
STJWD NW8 83 H6
STRHM/NOR SW16 179 J5
TEDD TW11 174 B3
WFD IG8 53 G2
WLGTN SM6 210 C5
WLSDN NW10 99 H1
Avenue South BRYLDS KT5 191 G4
Avenue Ter NWMAL KT3 175 K6
OXHEY WD19 27 J1
The Avenue BAR EN5 20 C4
BECK BR3 182 E4
BELMT SM2 208 D6
BMLY BR1 184 C6
BRYLDS KT5 191 G3
BXLY DA5 168 E2
CAR SM5 210 A5
CEND/HSY/T N8 49 G6
CHING E4 52 B2
CHSWK W4 118 B3
CLAP SW4 141 F6
CROY/NA CR0 212 A1
ESH/CLAY KT10 204 E4
EW KT17 208 A5
FBAR/BDGN N11 48 B1
GNWCH SE10 145 G1
HEST TW5 133 K2
HPTN TW12 172 E2
HSLW TW3 135 G6
KIL/WHAMP NW6 82 C6
KTN/HRWW/W HA3 43 F4
LOU IG10 39 J1
MUSWH N10 48 C5
NTHWD HA6 40 A2
ORP BR6 202 A6
PIN HA5 41 K2
PIN HA5 59 K3
RCH/KEW TW9 137 G3
ROM RM1 75 F1
STMC/STPC BR5 186 C3
SUN TW16 172 A5
TOTM N17 50 A5
TWK TW1 156 C1
WAN E11 71 F3
WBLY HA9 62 B6
WEA W13 97 H6
WPK KT4 192 C6
WWKM BR4 199 G4
Averil Gv STRHM/NOR SW16 180 C2
Averill St HMSMTH W6 119 G6
Avern Gdns E/WMO/HCT KT8 189 G1
Avern Rd E/WMO/HCT KT8 189 G1
Avery Farm Rw BGVA SW1W * 15 J7
Avery Gdns GNTH/NBYPK IG2 71 K2
Avery Hill Rd ELTH/MOT SE9 167 H3
Avery Rw MYFR/PKLN W1K 9 J5
Aviary Cl CAN/RD E16 106 D4
Aviemore Cl BECK BR3 198 C2
Aviemore Wy BECK BR3 198 B2
Avignon Rd BROCKY SE4 144 A4
Avington Gv PGE/AN SE20 181 K3
Avington Wy PECK SE15 * 143 G1
Avion Crs CDALE/KGS NW9 45 J5
Avior Dr NTHWD HA6 26 D6
Avis Sq WCHPL E1 105 F5
Avoca Rd TOOT SW17 161 F6
Avocet Cl STHWK SE1 123 G5
Avocet Ms THMD SE28 127 J3
Avon Cl SUT SM1 209 G2
WPK KT4 192 D6
YEAD UB4 95 G3
Avon Ct PIN HA5 * 42 A3
Avondale Av CRICK NW2 81 G1
EBAR EN4 33 K3
ESH/CLAY KT10 205 G1
NFNCH/WDSP N12 47 F1
WPK KT4 192 C5
Avondale Cl LOU IG10 39 K2
Avondale Ct WFD IG8 53 F4
Avondale Crs PEND EN3 25 G4
REDBR IG4 71 H2
Avondale Dr HYS/HAR UB3 113 K1
LOU IG10 39 K1
Avondale Gdns HSLWW TW4 134 E6
Avondale Park Gdns
NTGHL W11 * 100 C6
Avondale Park Rd
NTGHL W11 100 C6
Avondale Pavement
STHWK SE1 * 123 H5
Avondale Ri PECK SE15 143 G4
Avondale Rd ASHF TW15 152 A5
BMLY BR1 183 H2
CAN/RD E16 106 C4
ELTH/MOT SE9 166 D4
FNCH N3 47 G4
KTN/HRWW/W HA3 43 F6
MORT/ESHN SW14 138 A4
PLMGR N13 35 G4
SAND/SEL CR2 211 J4
SEVS/STOTM N15 67 H2
WALTH E17 69 J4
WELL DA16 148 D3
WIM/MER SW19 178 A1
Avondale Sq STHWK SE1 123 H5
Avonley Rd NWCR SE14 143 K1
Avonmore Gdns
WKENS W14 * 119 J4
Avonmore Pl WKENS W14 119 H4
Avonmore Rd WKENS W14 119 J4
Avonmouth Rd DART DA1 151 G6
Avonmouth St STHWK SE1 18 C4
Avon Rd BROCKY SE4 144 D4
GFD/PVL UB6 96 A3
WALTH E17 52 B6
Avonstowe Cl ORP BR6 216 C1
Avon Wy SWFD E18 70 E1
Avonwick Rd HSLW TW3 135 G3
Avril Wy CHING E4 52 A1
Avro Wy WLGTN SM6 210 E5
Awberry Ct WATW WD18 * 26 B1
Awlfield Av TOTM N17 49 K4
Awliscombe Rd WELL DA16 148 A3
Axeholm Av EDGW HA8 44 D4
Axe St BARK IG11 90 C6
Axholme Av EDGW HA8 44 C4
Axis Ct GNWCH SE10 125 H6
Axminster Crs WELL DA16 148 D2
Axminster Rd HOLWY N7 84 E1
Axon Pl IL IG1 72 C6
Axtaine Rd STMC/STPC BR5 202 E4
Aybrook St MHST W1U 9 G2
Aycliff Ct KUT/HW KT1 * 175 H5
Aycliffe Cl BMLY BR1 200 E1
Aycliffe Rd SHB W12 118 C1
Aylands Cl WBLY HA9 62 A6
Aylesbury Cl FSTGT E7 88 D4
Aylesbury Rd HAYES BR2 183 K6
WALW SE17 122 E5
Aylesbury St CLKNW EC1R 6 A7
WLSDN NW10 81 F1
Aylesford Av BECK BR3 198 B2
Aylesford St PIM SW1V 121 J5
Aylesham Cl MLHL NW7 45 J3
Aylesham Rd ORP BR6 201 K4
Ayles Rd YEAD UB4 95 F2
Aylestone Av KIL/WHAMP NW6 82 B5
Aylett Rd ISLW TW7 135 K3
SNWD SE25 197 J1
Ayley Cft EN EN1 24 C6
Ayliffe Cl KUT/HW KT1 175 H5
Aylmer Cl STAN HA7 29 G6
Aylmer Dr STAN HA7 29 G6
Aylmer Pde EFNCH N2 * 65 K2
Aylmer Rd BCTR RM8 92 A1
EFNCH N2 65 J2
SHB W12 118 B2
WAN E11 70 D4
Ayloffe Rd DAGW RM9 92 B4
Aylsham Dr HGDN/ICK UB10 58 A6
Aylton Est
BERM/RHTH SE16 * 123 K2
Aylward Rd FSTH SE23 164 A4
RYNPK SW20 177 J5
Aylwards Ri STAN HA7 29 G6
Aylward St WCHPL E1 * 104 E5
Aynhoe Rd WKENS W14 119 G4
Aynscombe Angle ORP BR6 202 B4
Ayres Cl PLSTW E13 106 E2
Ayres Crs WLSDN NW10 81 F5
Ayres St STHWK SE1 18 D2
Ayr Gn ROM RM1 57 G4
Ayrsome Rd STNW/STAM N16 86 A1
Ayrton Rd SKENS SW7 14 A4
Ayr Wy ROM RM1 57 G4
Aysgarth Rd DUL SE21 162 E1
Aytoun Pl BRXN/ST SW9 142 A3
Aytoun Rd BRXN/ST SW9 142 A3
Azalea Cl HNWL W7 116 A1
IL IG1 90 B3
Azalea Ct WFD IG8 * 52 C3
Azalea Wk PIN HA5 59 F3
Azania Ms KTTN NW5 84 B3
Azenby Rd PECK SE15 143 G3
Azof St GNWCH SE10 125 H4

B

Baalbec Rd HBRY N5 85 H3
Babbacombe Cl CHSGTN KT9 205 K3
Babbacombe Gdns REDBR IG4 71 J1
Babbacombe Rd BMLY BR1 184 A4
Baber Bridge Pde
EBED/NFELT TW14 * 154 B1
Baber Dr EBED/NFELT TW14 154 B1
Babington Ri WBLY HA9 80 C4
Babington Rd BCTR RM8 91 J3
HCH RM12 75 K5
HDN NW4 63 K1
STRHM/NOR SW16 179 J1
Babmaes St STJS SW1Y 10 C7
Bache's St IS N1 7 F5
Back Church La WCHPL E1 104 C5
Back Hl CLKNW EC1R 5 K7
Back La BTFD TW8 136 E1
BXLY DA5 169 H2
CEND/HSY/T N8 66 E2
CHDH RM6 74 A4
EDGW HA8 44 E4
HAMP NW3 83 G2
RCHPK/HAM TW10 156 D5
Backley Gdns SNWD SE25 197 H3
Back Rd SCUP DA14 168 B6
TEDD TW11 173 K3
Bacon Gv STHWK SE1 19 J6
Bacon La CDALE/KGS NW9 62 E2
EDGW HA8 44 C4
Bacon Link CRW RM5 56 D2
Bacon's La HGT N6 66 A5
Bacon St BETH E2 7 K6
Bacton St BETH E2 104 E2
Baddow Cl DAGE RM10 92 C6
WFD IG8 53 H2
Baden Pl STHWK SE1 18 E2
Baden Powell Cl DAGW RM9 92 A6
SURB KT6 191 G6
Baden Rd CEND/HSY/T N8 66 D1
IL IG1 90 B3
Bader Wy HCH RM12 93 J4
Badger Cl FELT TW13 154 A5
HSLWW TW4 134 B4
Badgers Cl ENC/FH EN2 23 H4
HRW HA1 60 D3
HYS/HAR UB3 94 C6
Badgers Copse ORP BR6 202 A6
WPK KT4 192 C6
Badgers Ct WPK KT4 * 192 C6
Badgers Cft ELTH/MOT SE9 167 F5
TRDG/WHET N20 32 C2
Badgers Wk NWMAL KT3 176 B5
Badlis Rd WALTH E17 51 J5
Badlow Cl ERITH DA8 150 B1
Badminton Cl HRW HA1 * 60 E1
NTHLT UB5 78 A4
Badminton Ms CAN/RD E16 125 K1
Badminton Rd BAL SW12 161 F1
Badsworth Rd CMBW SE5 142 D1
Bagley Cl WDR/YW UB7 112 B2
Bagley's La FUL/PGN SW6 140 A2
Bagleys Spring CHDH RM6 74 A1
Bagshot Ct
WOOL/PLUM SE18 * 147 F2
Bagshot Rd EN EN1 36 B2
Bagshot St WALW SE17 123 F5
Baildon St DEPT SE8 144 C1
Bailey Cl WDGN N22 48 D4
Bailey Crs CHSGTN KT9 205 K5
Bailey Pl SYD SE26 181 K2
Baillie Cl RAIN RM13 111 K3
Bainbridge Cl KUTN/CMB KT2 175 F1
Bainbridge Rd DAGW RM9 92 B2
Bainbridge St
NOXST/BSQ WC1A 10 D3
Baines Cl SAND/SEL CR2 211 K3
Baird Av STHL UB1 96 B6
Baird Cl BUSH WD23 28 B1
CDALE/KGS NW9 62 E3
LEY E10 69 J5
Baird Gdns NRWD SE19 163 F6
Baird Rd EN EN1 24 D4
Baird St STLK EC1Y 6 D6
Baizdon Rd BKHTH/KID SE3 145 H3
Baker La MTCM CR4 179 F5
Baker Ms ORP BR6 217 F4
Baker Rd WLSDN NW10 81 G6
WOOL/PLUM SE18 146 D1
Bakers Av WALTH E17 69 K3
Bakers End RYNPK SW20 177 H5
Bakers Gdns CAR SM5 194 D6
Bakers Hl BAR EN5 21 F3
CLPT E5 68 D5
Baker's Ms MHST W1U 9 G3
Bakers Rents BETH E2 7 J4
Baker's Rw CLKNW EC1R 5 J7
SRTFD E15 106 C1
Baker St CAMTN NW1 3 F7
EN EN1 23 K3
MHST W1U 9 G2
Baker's Yd CLKNW EC1R 5 J7
Bakery Cl BRXN/ST SW9 * 142 A1
Bakewell Wy NWMAL KT3 176 B5
Balaams La STHGT/OAK N14 34 D4
Balaam St PLSTW E13 106 E2
Balaclava Rd STHWK SE1 19 K7
SURB KT6 190 D4
Bala Gn CDALE/KGS NW9 * 63 G3
Balcaskie Rd ELTH/MOT SE9 146 E6
Balchen Rd BKHTH/KID SE3 146 C3
Balchier Rd EDUL SE22 163 J1
Balcombe Cl BXLYHS DA6 148 E5
Balcombe St CAMTN NW1 8 E1
Balcorne St HOM E9 86 E5
Balder Ri LEE/GVPK SE12 166 A4
Balderton St MYFR/PKLN W1K 9 H4
Baldock St BOW E3 105 K1
Baldry Gdns
STRHM/NOR SW16 179 K2
Baldwin Crs CMBW SE5 142 D2
Baldwin Gdns HSLW TW3 135 H2
Baldwin's Gdns FSBYW WC1X 11 J1
Baldwin St FSBYE EC1V 6 E5
Baldwin Ter IS N1 6 C2
Baldwyn Gdns ACT W3 98 E6
Baldwyn's Pk BXLY DA5 170 A4
Baldwyn's Rd BXLY DA5 170 A4
Bale Rd WCHPL E1 105 G4
Bales Ter ED N9 * 36 B5
Balfern Gv CHSWK W4 118 B5
Balfern St BTSEA SW11 140 D3
Balfe St IS N1 5 F3
Balfour Av HNWL W7 116 A1
Balfour Gv TRDG/WHET N20 33 K5
Balfour Ms ED N9 36 C5
MYFR/PKLN W1K 9 H7
Balfour Pl MYFR/PKLN W1K 9 H6
Balfour Rd ACT W3 98 E4
CAR SM5 209 K5
HAYES BR2 200 C2
HBRY N5 85 J2
HRW HA1 60 D2
HSLW TW3 135 G4
IL IG1 72 B6
NWDGN UB2 114 C3
SNWD SE25 197 H1
WEA W13 116 C2
WIM/MER SW19 178 A3
Balfour St STHWK SE1 18 E6
Balgonie Rd CHING E4 38 B3
Balgores Crs GPK RM2 57 K6
Balgores La GPK RM2 75 K1
Balgores Sq GPK RM2 75 K1
Balgowan Cl NWMAL KT3 192 B1
Balgowan Rd BECK BR3 182 B6
Balgowan St
WOOL/PLUM SE18 128 A4
Balham Gv BAL SW12 161 F2
Balham High Rd BAL SW12 161 G3
Balham Hl BAL SW12 161 G2
Balham New Rd BAL SW12 161 G2
Balham Park Rd TOOT SW17 160 E3
Balham Rd ED N9 36 C4
Balham Station Rd BAL SW12 161 F3
Balkan Wk WAP E1W * 104 D6
Balladier Wk POP/IOD E14 105 K4
Ballamore Rd BMLY BR1 165 K5
Ballance Rd HOM E9 87 F4
Ballantine St WAND/EARL SW18 140 B5
Ballard Cl KUTN/CMB KT2 176 A3
Ballards Cl DAGE RM10 92 D6
Ballards Farm Rd
SAND/SEL CR2 212 C4
Ballards La FNCH N3 47 F3
Ballards Ri SAND/SEL CR2 212 C4
Ballards Rd CRICK NW2 63 J6
DAGE RM10 92 E5
Ballards Wy SAND/SEL CR2 212 C4
Ballast Quay GNWCH SE10 125 G5
Ballater Cl OXHEY WD19 27 G6
Ballater Rd CLAP SW4 141 K5
SAND/SEL CR2 212 B3
Ballina St FSTH SE23 164 A2
Ballingdon Rd BTSEA SW11 161 F1
Balliol Av CHING E4 38 B6
Balliol Rd NKENS W10 100 A5
TOTM N17 50 A4
WELL DA16 148 C3
Balloch Rd CAT SE6 165 G3
Ballogie Av WLSDN NW10 81 G2
Ballow Cl CMBW SE5 * 142 E1
Ball's Pond Pl IS N1 * 85 K4
Balls Pond Rd IS N1 85 K4
Balmain Cl EA W5 116 E1
Balmer Rd BOW E3 105 H1
Balmes Rd IS N1 85 K6
Balmoral Av BECK BR3 198 B1
FBAR/BDGN N11 48 A2
Balmoral Cl PUT/ROE SW15 * 159 G1
Balmoral Crs
E/WMO/HCT KT8 173 F6

Balmoral Dr STHL UB1 .....95 K3
YEAD UB4 .....94 C3
Balmoral Gdns BXLY DA5 .....169 G2
HNWL W7 .....116 B3
Balmoral Gv HOLWY N7 .....85 F4
Balmoral Ms SHB W12 .....118 C3
Balmoral Rd CRICK NW2 .....81 K4
FSTGT E7 .....89 G2
GPK RM2 .....75 K1
KUT/HW KT1 .....191 G1
LEY E10 .....69 K6
RYLN/HDSTN HA2 .....78 A2
WPK KT4 .....207 K1
Balmore Crs EBAR EN4 .....22 B6
Balmore St ARCH N19 .....66 B6
Balmuir Gdns PUT/ROE SW15 .....139 F5
Balnacraig Av WLSDN NW10 .....81 G2
Balniel Ga PIM SW1V 121 J5
Baltic Cl WIM/MER SW19 .....178 C3
Baltic Pl IS N1 .....86 A6
Baltic St East STLK EC1Y 6 C7
Baltic St West EAR EC1M 6 C7
Baltimore Pl WELL DA16 .....148 A3
Balvaird Pl PIM SW1V 121 J5
Balvernie Gv WAND/EARL SW18 .....159 J2
Bamborough Gdns SHB W12 .....119 F2
Bamford Av ALP/SUD HA0 .....80 B6
Bamford Rd BMLY BR1 .....183 G1
Bampfylde Cl CRW RM5 .....56 D1
Bampton Dr MLHL NW7 .....45 J3
Bampton Rd FSTH SE23 .....164 A5
Banavie Gdns BECK BR3 .....182 E4
Banbury Cl ENC/FH EN2 .....23 H2
Banbury Ct BELMT SM2 * 208 E5
COVGDN WC2E * 10 E5
WALTH E17 .....51 G3
Banbury Rd HOM E9 .....87 F5
Banbury St BTSEA SW11 * 140 D3
Banchory Rd BKHTH/KID SE3 .....146 A1
Bancroft Av EFNCH N2 .....65 J2
Bancroft Ct NTHLT UB5 .....77 G6
Bancroft Gdns KTN/HRWW/W HA3 .....42 C4
ORP BR6 .....201 J5
Bancroft Rd KTN/HRWW/W HA3 .....42 C5
WCHPL E1 .....104 E3
Bandon Ri WLGTN SM6 .....210 D4
Banfield Rd PECK SE15 .....143 J4
Bangalore St PUT/ROE SW15 .....139 F4
Bangor Ct NTHLT UB5 .....78 B3
Banim St HMSMTH W6 .....118 E3
Banister Rd NKENS W10 .....100 B2
Bank Av MTCM CR4 .....178 C5
Bank Blds CHING E4 * 51 J1
Bankfoot Rd BMLY BR1 .....165 H6
Bankhurst Rd CAT SE6 .....164 C2
Bank La KUTN/CMB KT2 .....175 F3
PUT/ROE SW15 .....138 B6
Banksia Rd UED N18 .....50 E1
Bankside ENC/FH EN2 .....23 H2
SAND/SEL CR2 .....212 D4
STHL UB1 .....114 C1
STHWK SE1 .....12 C6
Bankside Av NTHLT UB5 .....94 E1
Bankside Cl CAR SM5 .....209 J5
ISLW TW7 .....136 A5
RDART DA2 .....170 A6
Bankside Dr THDIT KT7 .....190 C6
Bankside Rd IL IG1 .....90 C3
Banks La BXLYHS DA6 .....149 G5
The Bank HGT N6 .....66 B5
Bankton Rd BRXS/STRHM SW2 .....142 B5
Bankwell Rd LEW SE13 .....145 H5
Bank Willow RCHPK/HAM TW10 .....156 C5
Banner St STLK EC1Y 6 D7
Banning St GNWCH SE10 .....125 H5
Bannister Cl BRXS/STRHM SW2 .....162 B3
GFD/PVL UB6 .....78 D3
Bannister Gdns STMC/STPC BR5 .....186 D6
Bannockburn Rd WOOL/PLUM SE18 .....127 K4
Banstead Gdns ED N9 .....35 K5
Banstead Rd BELMT SM2 .....209 H5
PECK SE15 * 143 K4
Banstead Wy WLGTN SM6 .....210 E3
Banstock Rd EDGW HA8 .....44 E2
Banting Dr WCHMH N21 .....23 F4
Banton Cl EN EN1 .....24 D3
Bantry St CMBW SE5 .....142 E1
Banwell Rd BXLY DA5 .....168 E1
Banyard Rd BERM/RHTH SE16 .....123 J3
Bapchild Pl STMC/STPC BR5 .....202 D1
Baptist Gdns HNWL NW5 .....84 A4
Barandon Wk NTGHL W11 * 100 B6
Barbara Hucklesby Cl WDGN N22 .....49 H5
Barbauld Rd STNW/STAM N16 .....86 A1
Barber Cl WCHMH N21 .....35 G2
Barbers Rd SRTFD E15 .....105 K1
Barbican BARB EC2Y 12 D1
Barbican Rd GFD/PVL UB6 .....96 B5
Barb Ms HMSMTH W6 .....119 F3
Barbon Cl BMSBY WC1N 11 H1
Barchard St WAND/EARL SW18 .....140 A6
Barchester Cl HNWL W7 .....116 A1
Barchester Rd KTN/HRWW/W HA3 .....42 D4
Barchester St POP/IOD E14 .....105 K4
Barclay Cl FUL/PGN SW6 * 139 K1
WATW WD18 .....26 E1
Barclay Ov WFD IG8 .....38 E6
Barclay Rd CROY/NA CRO 211 K1
FUL/PGN SW6 .....139 K1
PLSTW E13 .....107 G3
UED N18 .....49 K2
WALTH E17 .....70 A2
WAN E11 .....70 D5
Barcombe Av BRXS/STRHM SW2 .....161 K4
Barcombe Cl STMC/STPC BR5 .....186 B6
Barden St WOOL/PLUM SE18 .....147 K1
Bardfield Av CHDH RM6 .....55 K6
Bardney Rd MRDN SM4 .....194 A1
Bardolph Av CROY/NA CRO 213 H6
Bardolph Rd HOLWY N7 .....84 E2
RCH/KEW TW9 .....137 G3
Bard Rd NKENS W10 .....100 B6
Bardsey Pl WCHPL E1 * 104 E4
Bardsey Wk IS N1 * 85 J4
Bardsley Cl CROY/NA CRO 212 B1
Bardsley La GNWCH SE10 .....125 F6
Barfett St NKENS W10 .....100 D3
Barfield Av TRDG/WHET N20 .....33 K2
Barfield Rd BMLY BR1 .....185 F6
WAN E11 * 70 D5
Barfleur La DEPT SE8 .....124 C4
Barford Cl HDN NW4 .....45 J5
Barford St IS N1 .....5 K1
Barforth Rd PECK SE15 .....143 J4
Barfreston Wy PGE/AN SE20 .....181 J4
Bargate Cl NWMAL KT3 .....192 D4
WOOL/PLUM SE18 .....128 A5
Barge House Rd CAN/RD E16 .....127 G2
Barge House St STHWK SE1 .....11 K7
Bargery Rd CAT SE6 .....164 E3
Barge Wk KUT/HW KT1 .....174 E5
Bargrove Cl PGE/AN SE20 .....181 H3
Bargrove Crs CAT SE6 .....164 C4
Barham Cl ALP/SUD HA0 .....79 H4
CHST BR7 .....185 G1
HAYES BR2 .....200 D5
ROMW/RG RM7 .....56 D5
Barham Ct ALP/SUD HA0 .....79 J4
Barham Rd CHST BR7 .....185 G1
CROY/NA CRO 211 J2
DART DA1 .....171 K2
RYNPK SW20 .....176 C5
Baring Cl LEE/GVPK SE12 .....165 K4
Baring Rd CROY/NA CRO 197 H5
EBAR EN4 .....21 H4
LEE/GVPK SE12 .....165 K3
LEE/GVPK SE12 .....166 A6
Baring St IS N1 .....6 E1
Barker Cl KUT/HW KT1 .....191 J1
NTHWD HA6 .....40 D3
RCH/KEW TW9 .....137 J3
Barker Dr CAMTN NW1 .....84 C5
Barkham Rd TOTM N17 .....49 K3
Bark Hart Rd ORP BR6 .....202 C5
Barking Rd POP/IOD E14 .....106 C5
Park Pl BAY/PAD W2 .....101 F6
Barkston Gdns ECT SW5 .....120 A5
Barkway Dr ORP BR6 .....216 A1
Barkwood Cl ROMW/RG RM7 .....74 E2
Barkworth Rd BERM/RHTH SE16 .....123 J5
Barlby Gdns NKENS W10 .....100 B3
Barlby Rd NKENS W10 .....100 A4
Barley La GDMY/SEVK IG3 .....73 G3
Barley Mow Pas CHSWK W4 .....118 A5
Barlow Cl WLGTN SM6 .....210 E4
Barlow Dr BKHTH/KID SE3 .....146 D2
Barlow Pl MYFR/PICC W1J 9 K6
Barlow Rd ACT W3 .....117 J1
CRICK NW2 .....82 D4
HPTN TW12 .....173 F3
Barlow St WALW SE17 .....19 F7
Barlow Wy DAGW RM9 .....111 F5
Barlow Wy South DAGW RM9 .....111 F5
Barmeston Rd CAT SE6 .....164 E4
Barmor Cl RYLN/HDSTN HA2 .....42 B5
Barmouth Av GFD/PVL UB6 .....97 F1
Barmouth Rd CROY/NA CRO 198 A6
WAND/EARL SW18 .....160 B1
Barnabas Rd HOM E9 .....87 F4
Barnaby Cl RYLN/HDSTN HA2 .....60 C6
Barnaby Pl SKENS SW7 .....14 A7
Barnard Cl CHST BR7 .....185 J4
SUN TW16 .....172 A3
Barnard Gdns NWMAL KT3 .....192 D1
YEAD UB4 .....95 F3
Barnard Hl MUSWH N10 .....48 B5
Barnard Ms BTSEA SW11 .....140 D5
Barnardo Dr BARK/HLT IG6 .....72 C1
Barnardo Gdns WCHPL E1 * 105 F5
Barnardo St WCHPL E1 .....105 F5
Barnard Rd BTSEA SW11 .....140 D5
EN EN1 .....24 D3
MTCM CR4 .....179 F6
Barnards Pl SAND/SEL CR2 .....211 H6
Barnby Sq SRTFD E15 * 88 C6
Barnby St CAMTN NW1 .....4 B3
SRTFD E15 .....88 C6
Barn Cl KTTN NW5 * 84 D3
Barn Crs STAN HA7 .....43 J2
Barneby Cl WHTN TW2 .....155 K3
Barnehurst Av BXLYHN DA7 .....149 K2
Barnehurst Cl ERITH DA8 .....149 K2
Barnehurst Rd BXLYHN DA7 .....149 K3
Barn End Dr RDART DA2 .....171 K6
Barnes Av BARN SW13 .....138 D1
NWDGN UB2 .....114 E4
Barnes Cl MNPK E12 .....89 H2
Barnes Cray Rd DART DA1 .....150 D5
Barnesdale Crs STMC/STPC BR5 .....202 B3
Barnes End NWMAL KT3 .....192 D2
Barnes High St BARN SW13 .....138 C3
Barnes Rd IL IG1 .....90 C3
UED N18 .....36 E6
Barnes St POP/IOD E14 .....105 G5
Barnes Ter DEPT SE8 .....124 C5
Barnet Dr HAYES BR2 .....200 D6
Barnet Gate La BAR EN5 .....31 H1
Barnet Gv BETH E2 .....104 C2
Barnet Hl BAR EN5 .....20 D5
Barnet La BORE WD6 .....30 B1
TRDG/WHET N20 .....32 D3
Barnet Rd MLHL NW7 .....31 G1
Barnett Cl ERITH DA8 .....150 C3
Barnetts Ct RYLN/HDSTN HA2 * 78 B1
Barnett St WCHPL E1 .....104 D5
Barnet Wy (Barnet By-Pass) MLHL NW7 .....31 F2
Barnet Wood Rd HAYES BR2 .....200 B6
Barney Cl CHARL SE7 .....126 B5
Barn Fld HAMP NW3 * 83 K3
Barnfield NWMAL KT3 .....192 B3
Barnfield Av CROY/NA CRO 197 K5
KUTN/CMB KT2 .....156 E6
MTCM CR4 .....195 G1
Barnfield Cl SWLY BR8 .....203 K4
TOOT SW17 * 160 B5
Barnfield Gdns KUTN/CMB KT2 .....175 F1
WOOL/PLUM SE18 * 127 G6
Barnfield Rd BELV DA17 .....129 G6
EA W5 .....97 J3
HGDN/ICK UB10 .....94 A4
SAND/SEL CR2 .....212 A6
STMC/STPC BR5 .....186 E6
WOOL/PLUM SE18 .....127 G6
Barnfield Wood Cl BECK BR3 .....199 G3
Barnfield Wood Rd BECK BR3 .....199 G3
Barnham Dr THMD SE28 .....128 A1
Barnham Rd GFD/PVL UB6 .....96 C2
Barnham St STHWK SE1 .....19 H2
Barnhill PIN HA5 .....59 F3
Barnhill Av HAYES BR2 .....199 K2
Barnhill La YEAD UB4 .....95 F2
Barnhill Rd WBLY HA9 .....80 E1
Barnhurst Pth OXHEY WD19 .....41 G1
Barningham Wy CDALE/KGS NW9 .....63 F3
Barnlea Cl FELT TW13 .....154 D4
Barnmead Gdns DAGW RM9 .....92 B3
Barnmead Rd BECK BR3 .....182 A4
DAGW RM9 .....92 B3
Barnock Cl DART DA1 .....170 B2
Barn Ri WBLY HA9 .....62 C5
Barnsbury Cl NWMAL KT3 .....191 K1
Barnsbury Cr BRYLDS KT5 .....191 K5
Barnsbury Est IS N1 * 5 H1
Barnsbury Gv HOLWY N7 .....85 F5
Barnsbury La BRYLDS KT5 .....191 K5
Barnsbury Pk IS N1 .....85 G5
Barnsbury Rd IS N1 .....5 J2
Barnsbury Sq IS N1 .....85 G5
Barnsbury St IS N1 .....85 G5
Barnsbury Ter IS N1 .....85 F5
Barnscroft RYNPK SW20 .....176 E6
Barnsdale Av POP/IOD E14 .....124 E4
Barnsdale Rd MV/WKIL W9 .....100 D3
Barnsley St WCHPL E1 .....104 D3
Barnstaple La LEW SE13 .....145 F5
Barnstaple Rd RSLP HA4 .....77 G1
Barnston Wk IS N1 * 6 A1
Barn Wy WBLY HA9 .....62 C5
Barnwell Rd BRXS/STRHM SW2 .....142 B6
DART DA1 .....151 J4
Barnwood Cl MV/WKIL W9 .....101 F3
RSLP HA4 .....58 B6
Baron Cl FBAR/BDGN N11 .....48 A1
Baroness Rd BETH E2 .....7 K4
Baronet Gv TOTM N17 .....50 C4
Baronet Rd TOTM N17 .....50 C4
Baron Gdns BARK/HLT IG6 .....54 C6
Baron Gv MTCM CR4 .....194 D1
Baron Rd BCTR RM8 .....73 K5
Barons Cl IS N1 * 5 J2
Barons Court Rd WKENS W14 .....119 H5
Baronsfield Rd TWK TW1 * 156 C1
Barons Ga EBAR EN4 .....33 J1
Barons Keep WKENS W14 * 119 H5
Baronsmead Rd BARN SW13 .....138 D2
Baronsmede EA W5 .....117 G2
Baronsmere Ct BAR EN5 * 20 C5
Baronsmere Rd EFNCH N2 .....65 J1
Baron's Pl STHWK SE1 .....17 K3
The Barons TWK TW1 .....156 C1
Baron St IS N1 .....5 K3
Baron's Wk CROY/NA CRO 198 B5
Barque Ms DEPT SE8 * 124 D6
Barrack Rd HSLWW TW4 .....134 C5
Barra Hall Rd HYS/HAR UB3 .....94 C6
Barratt Av WDGN N22 .....49 F5
Barratt Wy KTN/HRWW/W HA3 .....42 D6
Barrenger Rd MUSWH N10 .....47 K4
Barrett Rd WALTH E17 .....70 A1
Barrett's Green Rd WLSDN NW10 .....98 E1
Barrett's Gv STNW/STAM N16 .....86 A3
Barrfield Rd MLHL NW7 .....46 B1
Barriedale NWCR SE14 .....144 B3
Barrier Point Rd CAN/RD E16 .....126 B2
Barringer Sq TOOT SW17 .....161 F6
Barrington Cl CLAY IG5 .....53 K4
KTTN NW5 .....84 A3
Barrington Rd BRXN/ST SW9 .....142 C4
BXLYHN DA7 .....149 F2
CEND/HSY/T N8 .....66 D2
CHEAM SM3 .....193 K5
MNPK E12 .....90 A4
Barrington Vls WOOL/PLUM SE18 .....147 F2
Barrow Av CAR SM5 .....209 K6
Barrow Cl WCHMH N21 .....35 H5
Barrowdene Cl PIN HA5 .....41 J5
Barrowell Gn WCHMH N21 .....35 H4
Barrowfield Cl ED N9 .....36 D5
Barrowgate Rd CHSWK W4 .....117 K5
Barrow Hedges Cl CAR SM5 .....209 J5
Barrow Hedges Wy CAR SM5 .....209 J5
Barrow Hill WPK KT4 .....192 B6
Barrow Hill Est STJWD NW8 .....2 C3
Barrow Hill Rd STJWD NW8 .....2 C3
Barrow Point Av PIN HA5 .....41 J5
Barrow Point La PIN HA5 .....41 J5
Barrow Rd CROY/NA CRO 211 G3
STRHM/NOR SW16 .....179 J2
Barrs Rd WLSDN NW10 .....81 F5
Barry Av BXLYHN DA7 .....149 F1
SEVS/STOTM N15 .....68 B3
Barry Cl ORP BR6 .....216 E1
Barry Pde EDUL SE22 .....143 H5
Barry Rd EDUL SE22 .....163 H1
EHAM E6 .....107 J5
WLSDN NW10 .....80 E5
Barry Ter ASHF TW15 * 152 C1
Barset Rd PECK SE15 .....143 K4
Barsons Cl PGE/AN SE20 .....181 K3
Barston Rd WNWD SE27 .....162 D4
Barstow Crs BRXS/STRHM SW2 .....162 A3
Barter St NOXST/BSQ WC1A 11 F2
Bartholomew Cl STBT EC1A 12 C2
WAND/EARL SW18 .....140 B5
Bartholomew La LOTH EC2R 13 F3
Bartholomew Rd KTTN NW5 .....84 C4
Bartholomew Sq FSBYE EC1V 6 D6
Bartholomew St STHWK SE1 .....18 E5
Bartholomew Vls KTTN NW5 .....84 C4
Bartle Av EHAM E6 .....107 J1
Bartle Rd NTGHL W11 .....100 B5
Bartlett Cl POP/IOD E14 .....105 J5
Bartlett Ct FLST/FETLN EC4A * 11 K3
Bartlett St SAND/SEL CR2 .....211 K3
Bartlow Gdns CRW RM5 .....57 F4
Barton Av DAGE RM10 .....92 C6
Barton Cl BXLYHS DA6 .....149 F6
HDN NW4 .....63 J2
HOM E9 .....86 E4
SCUP DA14 .....168 C6
Barton Gn NWMAL KT3 .....175 E6
Barton Mdw BARK/HLT IG6 .....72 B1
Barton Rd HCH RM12 .....75 J5
SCUP DA14 .....187 F2
WKENS W14 .....119 H5
The Bartons BORE WD6 .....29 K1
Barton St WEST SW1P 16 E5
Bartram Rd BROCKY SE4 .....144 B6
Bartrams La EBAR EN4 .....21 G1
Bartrip St HOM E9 .....87 G4
Barward Cl WOOL/PLUM SE18 .....127 F4
Barwell Ct CHSGTN KT9 * 205 J5
Barwick Rd FSTGT E7 .....89 F2
Barwood Av WWKM BR4 .....198 E5
Bascombe Gv DART DA1 .....170 B2
Bascome St BRXS/STRHM SW2 .....162 B1
Basden Gv FELT TW13 .....155 F4
Basedale Rd DAGW RM9 .....91 H6
Baseing Cl EHAM E6 .....108 B6
Basevi Wy DEPT SE8 .....124 E6
Bashley Rd WLSDN NW10 .....99 F3
Basil Av EHAM E6 .....107 J2
Basildon Av CLAY IG5 .....54 A4
Basildon Cl BELMT SM2 .....209 F6
WATW WD18 .....26 A1
Basildon Rd ABYW SE2 .....128 B5
Basil Gdns CROY/NA CRO 198 D1
Basil St CHEL SW3 .....14 E4
Basin Ap POP/IOD E14 .....105 G5
Basing Cl THDIT KT7 .....190 A4
Basingdon Wy CMBW SE5 .....142 E5
Basing Dr BXLY DA5 .....169 G1
Basingfield Rd THDIT KT7 .....190 A4
Basinghall Av CITYW EC2V 12 E2
Basinghall Gdns BELMT SM2 .....209 F6
Basinghall St CITYW EC2V 12 E3
Basing Hl GLDGN NW11 .....64 D5
WBLY HA9 .....62 B6
Basing House Yd BETH E2 * 7 H4
Basing Pl BETH E2 .....7 H4
Basing St NTGHL W11 .....100 D5
Basing Wy FNCH N3 .....46 E6
THDIT KT7 .....190 A4
Basire St IS N1 .....85 J6
Baskerville Gdns WLSDN NW10 * 81 G2
Baskerville Rd WAND/EARL SW18 .....160 D2
Basket Gdns ELTH/MOT SE9 .....146 D6
Baslow Cl KTN/HRWW/W HA3 .....42 D3
Baslow Wk CLPT E5 .....87 F2
Basnett Rd BTSEA SW11 .....141 F4
Basque Ct BERM/RHTH SE16 .....124 A2
Bassano St EDUL SE22 .....143 G6
Bassant Rd WOOL/PLUM SE18 .....128 A6
Bassein Park Rd SHB W12 .....118 C2
Bassett Gdns ISLW TW7 .....135 G1
Bassett Rd NKENS W10 .....100 B5
ORP BR6 .....216 D2
Bassetts Cl ORP BR6 .....216 B2
Bassett St KTTN NW5 .....84 A4
Bassett Wy GFD/PVL UB6 .....96 B5
Bassingham Rd ALP/SUD HA0 .....79 K6
WAND/EARL SW18 .....160 B2
Bastable Av BARK IG11 .....109 F1
Bastion Rd ABYW SE2 .....128 B5
Baston Manor Rd WWKM BR4 .....215 F5
Baston Rd HAYES BR2 .....200 A6
Bastwick St FSBYE EC1V 6 C7
Basuto Rd FUL/PGN SW6 .....139 K2
Batavia Cl SUN TW16 .....172 B4
Batavia Ms NWCR SE14 .....144 B1
SUN TW16 .....172 B5
Batchelor St IS N1 .....5 J2
Batchwood Gn STMC/STPC BR5 .....202 B1
Batchworth La NTHWD HA6 .....40 A1
Bateman Cl BARK IG11 .....90 C4
Bateman Rd CHING E4 .....51 J2
Batemans Cnr CHSWK W4 * 118 A5
Bateman's Rw SDTCH EC2A 7 H6
Bateman St SOHO/SHAV W1D 10 C4
Bates Crs CROY/NA CRO 211 G4
STRHM/NOR SW16 .....179 H5
Bate St POP/IOD E14 .....105 H6
Bath Cl PECK SE15 .....143 J1
Bathgate Rd WIM/MER SW19 .....159 G5
Bath Gv BETH E2 .....104 C1
Bath House Rd CROY/NA CRO 195 K5
Bath Pas KUT/HW KT1 .....174 E5
Bath Pl IS N1 * 7 G5
Bath Rd CHSWK W4 .....118 A4
DART DA1 .....170 E2
ED N9 .....36 D4
FSTGT E7 .....89 H4
WDR/YW UB7 .....112 A1
Baths Ap FUL/PGN SW6 .....139 J1
Bath St FSBYE EC1V 6 D5
Bath Ter STHWK SE1 .....18 C4
Bathurst Av WIM/MER SW19 .....178 A4
Bathurst Gdns WLSDN NW10 .....99 K1
Bathurst Ms BAY/PAD W2 .....8 B5
Bathurst Rd IL IG1 .....72 B5
Bathurst St BAY/PAD W2 .....8 B5
Bathway WOOL/PLUM SE18 .....127 F4
Batley Cl MTCM CR4 .....194 E4
Batley Pl STNW/STAM N16 .....86 B1
Batley Rd STNW/STAM N16 .....86 B1
Batman Cl SHB W12 .....118 E1
Batoum Gdns HMSMTH W6 .....119 F3
Batson St SHB W12 .....118 D2
Batsworth Rd MTCM CR4 .....178 C6
Batten Cl EHAM E6 .....107 K5
Batten St BTSEA SW11 .....140 D4
Battersby Rd CAT SE6 .....165 G4
Battersea Br BTSEA SW11 * 140 C5
Battersea Bridge Rd BTSEA SW11 .....140 D1
Battersea Church Rd BTSEA SW11 .....140 C3
Battersea High St BTSEA SW11 * 140 C3
Battersea Park Rd BTSEA SW11 .....141 F2
Battersea Ri BTSEA SW11 .....140 D6
Battersea Sq BTSEA SW11 * 140 C1
Battery Rd THMD SE28 .....128 A2
Battishill St IS N1 .....85 H5
Battle Bridge La STHWK SE1 .....19 G1
Battle Bridge Rd CAMTN NW1 .....4 E3
Battle Cl WIM/MER SW19 .....178 B2
Battledean Rd HBRY N5 .....85 H3
Batty St WCHPL E1 .....104 C4
Baudwin Rd CAT SE6 .....165 H4
Baugh Rd SCUP DA14 .....186 D1
Bavant Rd STRHM/NOR SW16 .....179 K5
Bavaria Rd ARCH N19 .....85 G2
Bavent Rd CMBW SE5 .....142 D3
Bawdale Rd EDUL SE22 .....143 G6
Bawdsey Av GNTH/NBYPK IG2 .....73 F1
Bawtree Rd NWCR SE14 .....144 B1
Bawtry Rd TRDG/WHET N20 .....33 K5
Baxendale TRDG/WHET N20 .....33 G4
Baxendale St BETH E2 .....104 C2
Baxter Cl NWDGN UB2 .....115 G3
Baxter Rd CAN/RD E16 .....107 G5
IL IG1 .....90 B3
IS N1 .....86 B4
UED N18 .....50 D1
Bay Ct EA W5 .....117 F3
Baycroft Cl PIN HA5 .....41 G6
Bayfield Rd ELTH/MOT SE9 .....146 C5
Bayford Ms HACK E8 * 86 D5
Bayford Rd WLSDN NW10 .....100 B2
Bayford St HACK E8 .....86 D5
Bayham Pl CAMTN NW1 .....4 A1
Bayham Rd CHSWK W4 .....118 A3
MRDN SM4 .....194 A1
WEA W13 .....97 H6
Bayham St CAMTN NW1 .....4 A1
Bayhurst Dr NTHWD HA6 .....40 D2
Bayleaf Cl HPTN TW12 .....173 J1
Bayley St FITZ W1T 10 C2
Baylis Rd STHWK SE1 .....17 J4
Bayliss Av THMD SE28 .....109 K6
Bayliss Cl STHGT/OAK N14 .....22 B6
Bayly Rd DART DA1 .....171 K1
Bayne Cl EHAM E6 .....107 K5
Baynes Cl EN EN1 .....24 D3
Baynes Ms HAMP NW3 .....83 H4
Baynes St CAMTN NW1 .....84 C5
Baynham Cl BXLY DA5 .....169 G1
Bayonne Rd FUL/PGN SW6 .....119 H6
Bays Cl SYD SE26 .....181 K1
Bayswater Rd BAY/PAD W2 .....101 G6
Baythorne St BOW E3 .....105 H4
Baytree Cl BFN/LL DA15 .....168 A3
BMLY BR1 .....184 C4
Baytree Rd BRXS/STRHM SW2 .....142 A5
Bazalgette Cl NWMAL KT3 .....191 K2
Bazalgette Gdns NWMAL KT3 .....191 K2
Bazely St POP/IOD E14 .....106 A6
Bazile Rd WCHMH N21 .....35 G1
Beacham Cl CHARL SE7 .....126 C5
Beachborough Rd BMLY BR1 .....165 F6
Beachcroft Rd WAN E11 .....88 C1
Beach Gv FELT TW13 .....155 F5
Beachy Rd BOW E3 .....87 J5
Beacon Ga PECK SE15 .....144 A4
Beacon Hl HOLWY N7 .....84 E3
Beacon Rd ERITH DA8 .....150 E1
HTHAIR TW6 .....152 D1
LEW SE13 .....165 G1
Beaconsfield Cl BKHTH/KID SE3 .....125 K6
CHSWK W4 .....117 K5

Beaconsfield Gdns
ESH/CLAY KT10 204 E5
Beaconsfield Rd
BKHTH/KID SE3 125 K6
BMLY BR1 184 C6
BRYLDS KT5 191 G4
BXLY DA5 170 B4
CAN/RD E16 106 D3
CHSWK W4 118 A3
CROY/NA CR0 196 E3
EA W5 116 D2
ED N9 36 C5
ELTH/MOT SE9 166 D5
ESH/CLAY KT10 204 E5
FBAR/BDGN N11 34 A6
HYS/HAR UB3 114 B1
LEY E10 * 88 A1
NWMAL KT3 176 A5
SEVS/STOTM N15 68 A1
TRDG/WHET N20 33 K5
TWK TW1 156 C2
WALTH E17 69 H3
WALW SE17 122 E6
WLSDN NW10 81 H4
Beaconsfield Terrace Rd
WKENS W14 119 H3
Beaconsfield Wk
FUL/PGN SW6 139 J2
Beacontree Av WALTH E17 52 B4
Beacontree Rd WAN E11 70 D4
Beadlow Cl MRDN SM4 194 C3
Beadman Pl WNWD SE27 * 162 C6
Beadman St WNWD SE27 162 C6
Beadnell Rd FSTH SE23 164 A3
Beadon Rd HAYES BR2 199 K1
HMSMTH W6 119 F4
Beaford Gv RYNPK SW20 177 H6
Beagle Cl FELT TW13 154 A6
Beagles Cl STMC/STPC BR5 202 E6
Beak St REGST W1B 10 A5
Beal Cl WELL DA16 148 B2
Beale Cl PLMGR N13 49 H1
Beale Pl BOW E3 105 H1
Beale Rd BOW E3 87 H6
Beal Rd IL IG1 72 A6
Beam Av DAGE RM10 92 D6
Beames Rd WLSDN NW10 81 F6
Beaminster Gdns
BARK/HLT IG6 54 B6
Beamish Dr BUSH WD23 28 C3
Beamish Rd ED N9 36 C3
STMC/STPC BR5 202 D4
Beamway DAGE RM10 93 F5
Beanacre Cl HOM E9 87 H4
Bean Rd BXLYHS DA6 148 E5
Beanshaw ELTH/MOT SE9 167 F6
Beansland Gv CHDH RM6 56 A5
Bear Cl ROMW/RG RM7 74 D3
Beardell St NRWD SE19 181 G2
Beardow Gv STHGT/OAK N14 * 34 C1
Beard Rd RCHPK/HAM TW10 175 G1
Beardsfield PLSTW E13 88 E6
Beard's Hl HPTN TW12 173 F4
Beard's Hill Cl HPTN TW12 173 F4
Beardsley Wy ACT W3 118 A2
Bearfield Rd KUTN/CMB KT2 175 F3
Bear Gdns STHWK SE1 12 C7
Bear La STHWK SE1 12 B7
Bear Rd FELT TW13 154 C6
Bearstead Ri BROCKY SE4 144 C6
Bearstead Ter BECK BR3 * 182 D4
Bear St LSQ/SEVD WC2H 10 D5
Beatrice Av
STRHM/NOR SW16 180 A6
WBLY HA9 80 A3
Beatrice Cl PIN HA5 58 E1
PLSTW E13 106 E3
Beatrice Pl KENS W8 120 A3
Beatrice Rd ED N9 36 E2
FSBYPK N4 67 G4
RCHPK/HAM TW10 137 G6
STHL UB1 114 E1
STHWK SE1 123 H4
WALTH E17 69 J2
Beattie Cl EBED/NFELT TW14 153 J3
Beattock Ri MUSWH N10 66 B1
Beatty Rd STAN HA7 43 J2
STNW/STAM N16 86 A2
Beatty St CAMTN NW1 * 4 A2
Beattyville Gdns CLAY IG5 54 A6
Beauchamp Pl CHEL SW3 14 D5
Beauchamp Rd BTSEA SW11 140 D5
E/WMO/HCT KT8 189 G2
FSTGT E7 89 F5
SUT SM1 208 E3
THHTH CR7 180 E4
TWK TW1 156 B2
Beauchamp St HCIRC EC1N 11 J2
Beauchamp Ter
PUT/ROE SW15 138 E4
Beauclerc Rd HMSMTH W6 118 E3
Beauclerk Cl FELT TW13 154 A3
Beaufort EHAM E6 108 A4
Beaufort Av
KTN/HRWW/W HA3 61 G1
Beaufort Cl CHING E4 51 K2
EA W5 98 B4
PUT/ROE SW15 159 F3
ROMW/RG RM7 74 E1
Beaufort Dr GLDGN NW11 64 E1
Beaufort Gdns CHEL SW3 14 D4
HDN NW4 64 A3
HEST TW5 134 D2
IL IG1 72 A5
STRHM/NOR SW16 180 A3
Beaufort Rd EA W5 98 B4
KUT/HW KT1 191 F1
RCHPK/HAM TW10 156 D6
RSLP HA4 * 58 B6
TWK TW1 156 D2
Beaufort St CHEL SW3 120 C6
Beaufort Wy EW KT17 207 J5
Beaufoy Rd TOTM N17 50 A3
Beaufoy Wk LBTH SE11 17 H7
Beaulieu Av CAN/RD E16 126 A1
SYD SE26 163 J6
Beaulieu Cl CDALE/KGS NW9 63 G1
CMBW SE5 142 E4
HSLWW TW4 134 E6
MTCM CR4 179 F4
OXHEY WD19 27 G3
TWK TW1 156 E1
Beaulieu Dr PIN HA5 59 H3
Beaulieu Gdns WCHMH N21 35 J2
Beaulieu Pl CHSWK W4 117 K3
Beauly Wy ROM RM1 57 G4
Beaumaris Gn
CDALE/KGS NW9 * 63 G3
Beaumont Av ALP/SUD HA0 79 J3
RCH/KEW TW9 137 G4
RYLN/HDSTN HA2 60 B3
WKENS W14 119 J5
Beaumont Cl
KUTN/CMB KT2 * 175 H3
Beaumont Ct ALP/SUD HA0 79 J3
Beaumont Crs RAIN RM13 93 J4
WKENS W14 119 J5
Beaumont Gdns HAMP NW3 82 E1
Beaumont Gv WCHPL E1 105 F3
Beaumont Ms MHST W1U * 9 H1
PIN HA5 * 41 J6
Beaumont Pl BAR EN5 20 D2
FITZ W1T 4 B6
ISLW TW7 136 A6
Beaumont Ri ARCH N19 66 D5
Beaumont Rd CHSWK W4 117 K3
LEY E10 69 K4
NRWD SE19 180 D2
PLSTW E13 107 F2
STMC/STPC BR5 201 J3
WAND/EARL SW18 159 H2
Beaumont Sq WCHPL E1 105 F4
Beaumont St MHST W1U 9 H1
Beaumont Ter LEW SE13 * 165 H2
Beaumont Wk HAMP NW3 83 K5
Beauvais Ter NTHLT UB5 95 H2
Beauval Rd EDUL SE22 163 G1
Beaverbank Rd
ELTH/MOT SE9 167 J3
Beaver Cl HPTN TW12 173 G4
PGE/AN SE20 * 181 H3
Beaver Rd BARK/HLT IG6 55 J1
Beavers Crs HSLWW TW4 134 C5
Beavers La HSLWW TW4 134 B4
Beaverwood Rd CHST BR7 185 K1
Beavor La HMSMTH W6 118 D4
Bebbington Rd
WOOL/PLUM SE18 * 127 K4
Beblets Cl ORP BR6 217 F3
Beccles Dr BARK IG11 91 F4
Beccles St POP/IOD E14 105 H5
Bec Cl RSLP HA4 77 H1
Beck Cl LEW SE13 144 E2
Beck Ct BECK BR3 182 A6
Beckenham Gdns ED N9 36 A5
Beckenham Gv HAYES BR2 183 G5
Beckenham Hill Rd BECK BR3 182 E2
Beckenham La HAYES BR2 183 H5
Beckenham Place Pk
BECK BR3 182 E3
Beckenham Rd BECK BR3 182 A4
WWKM BR4 198 E4
Becket Av EHAM E6 108 A2
Becket Cl SNWD SE25 197 H3
WIM/MER SW19 * 178 A4
Becket Fold HRW HA1 * 61 F2
Becket Rd UED N18 36 E6
Becket St STHWK SE1 18 E4
Beckett Cl BELV DA17 129 F3
STRHM/NOR SW16 161 J4
WLSDN NW10 81 F4
Becketts Cl
EBED/NFELT TW14 154 A1
ORP BR6 217 F1
Becketts Pl KUT/HW KT1 174 E4
Beckett Wk BECK BR3 182 B2
Beckford Cl WKENS W14 119 J4
Beckford Dr STMC/STPC BR5 201 J4
Beckford Pl WALW SE17 * 122 D5
Beckford Rd CROY/NA CR0 197 G3
Beck La BECK BR3 182 A6
Becklow Rd SHB W12 118 D2
Beck River Pk BECK BR3 182 C4
Beck Rd HACK E8 86 D6
Becks Rd SCUP DA14 168 B5
Beck Wy BECK BR3 182 C6
Beckway Rd
STRHM/NOR SW16 179 J5
Beckway St WALW SE17 19 G7
Beckwith Rd HNHL SE24 162 E1
Beclands Rd TOOT SW17 179 F2
Becmead Av KTN/HRWW/W HA3 61 H2
STRHM/NOR SW16 161 J6
Becondale Rd NRWD SE19 181 F1
Becontree Av BCTR RM8 91 H2
Bective Rd FSTGT E7 88 E2
PUT/ROE SW15 139 H5
Becton Pl ERITH DA8 149 J1
Bedale Rd ENC/FH EN2 23 J1
Bedale St STHWK SE1 * 18 E1
Beddington Farm Rd
CROY/NA CR0 195 K5
Beddington Gdns CAR SM5 210 A4
Beddington Gn
STMC/STPC BR5 186 A4
Beddington Gv WLGTN SM6 210 D3
Beddington La MTCM CR4 195 H2
Beddington Rd
GDMY/SEVK IG3 73 F4
STMC/STPC BR5 185 K4
Beddington Ter
CROY/NA CR0 * 196 A4
Bede Cl PIN HA5 41 H4
Bedens Rd SCUP DA14 187 F2
Bede Rd CHDH RM6 73 J3
Bedfont Cl
EBED/NFELT TW14 153 F1
MTCM CR4 179 F5
Bedfont Green Cl
EBED/NFELT TW14 153 F3
Bedfont La
EBED/NFELT TW14 153 H2
Bedfont Rd
EBED/NFELT TW14 153 F3
STWL/WRAY TW19 152 C1
Bedford Av BAR EN5 20 D6
FITZ W1T 10 D2
YEAD UB4 95 F5
Bedfordbury CHCR WC2N 10 E5
Bedford Cl CHSWK W4 118 B6
MUSWH N10 48 A3
Bedford Cnr CHSWK W4 * 118 B4
Bedford Ct CHCR WC2N 10 E6
Bedford Gdns KENS W8 119 K1
Bedford Hl BAL SW12 161 G4
Bedford Pk CROY/NA CR0 196 D5
Bedford Pl CROY/NA CR0 196 E5
RSQ WC1B 10 E1
Bedford Rd BFN/LL DA15 167 K5
CEND/HSY/T N8 66 D3
CHSWK W4 118 A3
CLAP SW4 141 K5
DART DA1 171 K2
ED N9 36 D2
EFNCH N2 47 J6
EHAM E6 90 A6
HRW HA1 60 C3
IL IG1 90 B1
MLHL NW7 31 G4
NTHWD HA6 26 B6
ORP BR6 202 C6
RSLP HA4 76 D2
SEVS/STOTM N15 67 K1
SWFD E18 52 E5
WALTH E17 51 J5
WDGN N22 48 E4
WEA W13 97 H6
WHTN TW2 155 J5
WPK KT4 193 F6
Bedford Rw FSBYW WC1X 11 H1
Bedford Sq RSQ WC1B 10 D3
Bedford St COVGDN WC2E 10 E5
Bedford Vls KUT/HW KT1 * 175 G5
Bedford Wy STPAN WC1H 4 D7
Bedgebury Gdns
WIM/MER SW19 159 H4
Bedgebury Rd ELTH/MOT SE9 146 C5
Bedivere Rd BMLY BR1 165 K5
Bedlow Cl STJWD NW8 2 B7
Bedlow Wy CROY/NA CR0 211 F2
Bedonwell Rd BELV DA17 129 F6
Bedser Cl THHTH CR7 180 D6
VX/NE SW8 * 122 A6
Bedser Dr GFD/PVL UB6 78 D3
Bedster Gdns
E/WMO/HCT KT8 173 G5
Bedwardine Rd NRWD SE19 181 F3
Bedwell Gdns HYS/HAR UB3 113 H5
Bedwell Rd BELV DA17 129 H5
TOTM N17 50 A4
Beeby Rd CAN/RD E16 107 F4
Beech Av ACT W3 118 B1
BFN/LL DA15 168 B2
BKHH IG9 39 F4
BTFD TW8 136 C1
RSLP HA4 59 F5
TRDG/WHET N20 33 J3
Beech Cl CAR SM5 194 E6
DEPT SE8 124 C6
ED N9 36 C1
HCH RM12 93 K1
PUT/ROE SW15 158 D2
RYNPK SW20 177 F2
STWL/WRAY TW19 152 A2
SUN TW16 172 C5
WDR/YW UB7 112 D3
Beech Copse BMLY BR1 184 E5
SAND/SEL CR2 212 A3
Beech Ct ELTH/MOT SE9 * 166 D1
Beechcroft CHST BR7 185 F3
Beechcroft Av BXLYHN DA7 150 A2
GLDGN NW11 64 D4
NWMAL KT3 175 K4
RKW/CH/CXG WD3 26 A1
RYLN/HDSTN HA2 60 A4
STHL UB1 114 E1
Beechcroft Cl HEST TW5 134 D1
ORP BR6 216 D2
STRHM/NOR SW16 180 A1
Beechcroft Gdns WBLY HA9 80 B1
Beechcroft Rd CHSGTN KT9 206 B2
MORT/ESHN SW14 * 137 K4
ORP BR6 216 D2
SWFD E18 53 F5
TOOT SW17 160 E5
Beechdale WCHMH N21 35 F4
Beechdale Rd
BRXS/STRHM SW2 162 A1
Beech Dell HAYES BR2 215 K2
Beech Dr EFNCH N2 47 K6
Beechen Cliff Wy ISLW TW7 136 A3
Beechengrove PIN HA5 41 K6
Beechen Pl FSTH SE23 163 K4
The Beeches Av CAR SM5 209 J5
Beeches Cl PGE/AN SE20 181 K4
Beeches Rd CHEAM SM3 193 H5
TOOT SW17 160 D5
The Beeches CHING E4 * 38 B3
HNWL W7 * 116 A2
Beeches Wk CAR SM5 209 H6
Beechfield Gdns
ROMW/RG RM7 74 E4
Beechfield Rd BMLY BR1 184 B5
CAT SE6 164 C3
ERITH DA8 150 B1
FSBYPK N4 67 J3
Beech Gdns DAGE RM10 92 D5
EA W5 117 F2
Beech Gv BARK/HLT IG6 54 E2
MTCM CR4 195 J2
NWMAL KT3 176 A6
Beech Hall Crs CHING E4 52 B3
Beech Hall Rd CHING E4 52 A3
Beech Hl EBAR EN4 21 H1
Beech Hill Av EBAR EN4 21 G2
Beechhill Rd ELTH/MOT SE9 147 F6
Beech House Rd
CROY/NA CR0 211 K1
Beech Lawns
NFNCH/WDSP N12 * 47 H1
Beechmont Cl BMLY BR1 183 H1
Beechmore Gdns CHEAM SM3 193 G6
Beechmore Rd BTSEA SW11 140 E2
Beechmount Av HNWL W7 96 D4
Beecholme Av MTCM CR4 179 G4
Beecholme Est CLPT E5 * 86 E1
Beech Rd DART DA1 171 G3
EBED/NFELT TW14 153 H2
FBAR/BDGN N11 48 E2
ORP BR6 217 G5
STRHM/NOR SW16 179 K5
Beechrow KUTN/CMB KT2 157 F6
Beech St ROMW/RG RM7 74 E1
Beech St (Below) BARB EC2Y 12 C1
Beech Tree Cl IS N1 85 G5
STAN HA7 43 J1
Beech Tree Gld CHING E4 38 D3
Beech Tree Pl SUT SM1 209 F3
Beechvale Cl
NFNCH/WDSP N12 47 J1
Beech Wk DART DA1 150 D5
MLHL NW7 45 F2
Beechway BXLY DA5 168 E1
Beech Wy FELT TW13 155 F5
WLSDN NW10 81 F5
Beechwood Av FNCH N3 46 D6
GFD/PVL UB6 96 B2
HYS/HAR UB3 94 B6
ORP BR6 216 E4
RCH/KEW TW9 137 H2
RSLP HA4 58 D6
RYLN/HDSTN HA2 78 B1
THHTH CR7 196 C1
Beechwood Cl EFNCH N2 * 65 K1
MLHL NW7 45 G1
SURB KT6 190 D4
Beechwood Crs BXLYHN DA7 148 E4
Beechwood Dr HAYES BR2 215 H2
WFD IG8 52 D1
Beechwood Gdns CLAY IG5 71 K2
RAIN RM13 111 K4
RYLN/HDSTN HA2 78 B1
Beechwood Gv ACT W3 99 G6
Beechwood Ms ED N9 36 C4
Beechwood Pk SWFD E18 52 E6
Beechwood Ri CHST BR7 167 G6
Beechwood Rd
CEND/HSY/T N8 66 D1
HACK E8 86 B4
SAND/SEL CR2 212 A6
Beechworth Cl HAMP NW3 65 F6
Beecot La WOT/HER KT12 188 B6
Beecroft La BROCKY SE4 144 B6
Beecroft Ms BROCKY SE4 144 B6
Beecroft Rd BROCKY SE4 144 B6
Beehive Cl BORE WD6 29 K1
HACK E8 86 B5
Beehive La REDBR IG4 71 K2
Beehive Pl BRXN/ST SW9 142 B4
Beeken Dene ORP BR6 216 C2
Beeleigh Rd MRDN SM4 194 A1
Beeston Cl HACK E8 86 C3
OXHEY WD19 27 H6
Beeston Pl BGVA SW1W 15 K5
Beeston Rd EBAR EN4 33 H1
Beeston Wy
EBED/NFELT TW14 154 B1
Beethoven Rd BORE WD6 29 J2
Beethoven St NKENS W10 100 C2
Beeton Cl PIN HA5 42 A3
Begbie Rd BKHTH/KID SE3 146 B2
Beggar's Roost La SUT SM1 208 E4
Begonia Cl EHAM E6 107 J4
Begonia Pl HPTN TW12 173 F2
Beira St BAL SW12 161 G2
Bekesbourne St
POP/IOD E14 * 105 G5
Belcroft Cl BMLY BR1 183 J3
Beldham Gdns
E/WMO/HCT KT8 173 G6
Belfairs OXHEY WD19 41 H1
Belfairs Dr CHDH RM6 73 J4
Belfast Rd SNWD SE25 197 J1
STNW/STAM N16 68 B6
Belfield Rd HOR/WEW KT19 207 F6
Belford Gv WOOL/PLUM SE18 127 F4
Belford Rd PECK SE15 143 K3
Belfry Cl BERM/RHTH SE16 * 123 J5
Belgrade Rd HPTN TW12 173 G4
STNW/STAM N16 86 A2
Belgrave Cl ACT W3 117 K2
MLHL NW7 45 F1
STHGT/OAK N14 22 C6
STMC/STPC BR5 202 D1
Belgrave Crs SUN TW16 172 A4
Belgrave Gdns STAN HA7 43 J1
STHGT/OAK N14 22 D6
STJWD NW8 83 F6
Belgrave Ms South KTBR SW1X 15 H4
Belgrave Ms West KTBR SW1X 15 G4
Belgrave Pl KTBR SW1X 15 H5
Belgrave Rd BARN SW13 138 C1
HSLWW TW4 134 E4
IL IG1 71 K5
MTCM CR4 178 C6
PIM SW1V 16 A7
PLSTW E13 107 G3
SNWD SE25 197 G1
SUN TW16 172 A4
WALTH E17 69 J3
WAN E11 70 E5
Belgrave Sq KTBR SW1X 15 G4
Belgrave St WCHPL E1 105 F5
Belgrave Wk MTCM CR4 178 C6
Belgravia Cl BAR EN5 20 D4
Belgravia Gdns BMLY BR1 183 H2
Belgravia Ms KUT/HW KT1 190 E1
Belgrove St CAMTN NW1 4 E4
Belinda Rd BRXN/ST SW9 142 C4
Belitha Vls IS N1 85 G5
Bellamaine Cl THMD SE28 128 A2
Bellamy Cl EDGW HA8 30 E5
POP/IOD E14 124 D2
WKENS W14 119 J5
Bellamy Dr STAN HA7 43 H4
Bellamy Rd CHING E4 51 K2
ENC/FH EN2 * 23 K3
Bellamy St BAL SW12 161 G2
Bel La FELT TW13 154 D5
Bellasis Av BRXS/STRHM SW2 161 K3
Bell Av HARH RM3 57 K4
WDR/YW UB7 112 C3
Bell Cl PIN HA5 41 G6
Bellclose Rd WDR/YW UB7 112 B2
Bell Dr WAND/EARL SW18 159 H2
Bellefield Rd STMC/STPC BR5 202 C2
Bellefields Rd BRXN/ST SW9 142 A4
Bellegrove Cl WELL DA16 148 A3
Bellegrove Rd WELL DA16 147 K3
Bellenden Rd PECK SE15 143 G3
Belle Staines Pleasaunce
CHING E4 37 J4
Belleville Rd BTSEA SW11 140 E6
Belle Vue GFD/PVL UB6 78 D6
Belle Vue La BUSH WD23 28 D3
Bellevue Pk THHTH CR7 180 D6
Bellevue Pl WCHPL E1 * 104 E3
Belle Vue Rd CRW RM5 56 E2
WALTH E17 52 B5
Bellevue Rd BARN SW13 138 D3
BXLYHS DA6 149 G6
FBAR/BDGN N11 34 A6
KUT/HW KT1 175 F6
TOOT SW17 160 E2
WEA W13 97 H3
Bellew St TOOT SW17 160 B5
Bell Farm Av DAGE RM10 92 E1
Bellfield CROY/NA CR0 213 H6
Bellfield Av
KTN/HRWW/W HA3 42 D2
Bell Gdns LEY E10 * 69 J5
STMC/STPC BR5 202 D2
Bellgate Ms KTTN NW5 84 B2
Bell Gn CAT SE6 164 B6
Bell Green La SYD SE26 182 C1
Bell House Rd ROMW/RG RM7 74 E5
Bellina Ms KTTN NW5 84 B2
Bellingham Gn CAT SE6 164 D5
Bellingham Rd CAT SE6 165 F5
Bell La CAN/RD E16 125 K1
HDN NW4 64 B1
PEND EN3 25 F1
TWK TW1 156 B3
WBLY HA9 * 61 K6
WCHPL E1 13 J2
Bell Meadow NRWD SE19 163 F6
Bello Cl BRXS/STRHM SW2 162 C3
Bellot St GNWCH SE10 125 H5
Bell Pde HSLW TW3 * 135 G5
WWKM BR4 * 199 F6
Bellring Cl BELV DA17 129 H6
Bell Rd E/WMO/HCT KT8 189 J2
ENC/FH EN2 23 K2
HSLW TW3 135 G5
Bells Hl BAR EN5 20 B6
Bell St BAY/PAD W2 8 C1
WOOL/PLUM SE18 146 D2
Belltrees Gv
STRHM/NOR SW16 180 A1
Bell Water Ga
WOOL/PLUM SE18 127 F3
Bell Wharf La CANST EC4R 12 D6
Bellwood Rd PECK SE15 144 A5
Bell Yd LINN WC2A 11 J4
Bell Yard Ms STHWK SE1 19 H3
Belmont Av ALP/SUD HA0 80 B6
EBAR EN4 21 K6
ED N9 36 C3
NWDGN UB2 114 D3
NWMAL KT3 192 D2
PLMGR N13 48 E1
TOTM N17 49 J6
WELL DA16 147 K3
Belmont Cir
KTN/HRWW/W HA3 * 43 H4
Belmont Cl CHING E4 52 B1
CLAP SW4 141 H4
EBAR EN4 21 K5
TRDG/WHET N20 33 F3
WFD IG8 39 F6
Belmont Gv CHSWK W4 118 A4
LEW SE13 145 G4
Belmont Hl LEW SE13 145 G4
Belmont La CHST BR7 167 H6
STAN HA7 43 J3
Belmont Pde CHST BR7 * 185 G1
GLDGN NW11 * 64 D2
Belmont Pk LEW SE13 145 G5
Belmont Park Cl LEW SE13 145 H5
Belmont Park Rd LEY E10 69 K3
Belmont Ri BELMT SM2 208 D5
Belmont Rd BECK BR3 182 B5
CHST BR7 185 G1
CLAP SW4 141 H4
ERITH DA8 149 J1
IL IG1 90 C1
KTN/HRWW/W HA3 43 F6
SEVS/STOTM N15 67 J1
SNWD SE25 197 J2
WHTN TW2 155 J4
WLGTN SM6 210 C3
Belmont St CAMTN NW1 84 A5
Belmont Ter CHSWK W4 118 A4
Belmore Av YEAD UB4 94 E5
Belmore La HOLWY N7 * 84 D3
Belmore St VX/NE SW8 141 J2
Beloe Cl BARN SW13 138 D5
Belsham St HOM E9 86 E4
Belsize Av HAMP NW3 83 J3
PLMGR N13 49 F2
WEA W13 116 C3
Belsize Ct Garages HAMP NW3 83 H3
Belsize Crs HAMP NW3 83 H3
Belsize Gdns SUT SM1 209 F2
Belsize Gv HAMP NW3 83 J4

Belsize La HAMP NW3 * 83 H4
Belsize Ms HAMP NW3 * 83 H4
Belsize Pk HAMP NW3 ......83 H4
Belsize Park Gdns HAMP NW5 ......83 H4
Belsize Park Ms HAMP NW5 * 83 H4
Belsize Pl HAMP NW3 ......83 H5
Belsize Rd KIL/WHAMP NW6 ......82 A1
KTN/HRWW/W HA3 ......42 D5
Belsize Sq HAMP NW3 ......83 H5
Belsize Ter HAMP NW3 ......83 H5
Belson Dr WOOL/PLUM SE18 ......126 E4
Beltane Dr WIM/MER SW19 ......159 G5
Belthorn Crs BAL SW12 ......161 H2
Belton Rd FSTGT E7 ......89 F5
SCUP DA14 ......168 B6
TOTM N17 ......50 A6
WAN E11 ......88 C2
WLSDN NW10 ......81 J4
Belton Wy BOW E3 ......105 J4
Beltran Rd FUL/PGN SW6 ......140 A3
Beltwood Rd BELV DA17 ......129 K4
Belvedere Av CLAY IG5 ......54 B5
WIM/MER SW19 ......177 H1
Belvedere Blds
STHWK SE1 ......18 B3
Belvedere Cl ESH/CLAY KT10 ......204 B3
TEDD TW11 ......173 J1
Belvedere Ct BELV DA17 ......129 C3
Belvedere Dr WIM/MER SW19 ......177 H1
Belvedere Gdns
E/WMO/HCT KT8 ......188 E2
Belvedere Gv
WIM/MER SW19 ......177 H1
Belvedere Ms PECK SE15 ......143 K4
Belvedere Rd BXLYHN DA7 ......149 G4
HNWL W7 ......115 K3
LEY E10 ......69 G5
NRWD SE19 ......181 C3
STHWK SE1 ......17 G2
THMD SE28 ......128 E1
Belvedere Sq WIM/MER SW19 ......177 H1
Belvedere Strd
CDALE/KGS NW9 ......45 H5
The Belvedere
WBPTN SW10 * 140 B2
Belvedere Wy
KTN/HRWW/W HA3 ......62 A3
Belvoir Rd EDUL SE22 ......163 H2
Belvue Cl NTHLT UB5 ......78 A5
Belvue Rd NTHLT UB5 ......78 A5
Bembridge Cl
KIL/WHAMP NW6 ......82 C5
Bembridge Gdns RSLP HA4 ......58 B6
Bemerton Est IS N1 ......85 H5
Bemerton St IS N1 ......5 H1
Bemish Rd PUT/ROE SW15 ......139 G4
Bempton Dr RSLP HA4 ......59 F6
Bemsted Rd WALTH E17 ......51 H6
Benares Rd
WOOL/PLUM SE18 ......128 A4
Benbow Rd HMSMTH W6 ......118 E3
Benbow St DEPT SE8 ......124 D6
Benbury Cl BMLY BR1 ......183 F1
Bench Fld SAND/SEL CR2 ......212 B4
The Bench
RCHPK/HAM TW10 * 156 D5
Bencroft Rd
STRHM/NOR SW16 ......179 H3
Bencurtis Pk WWKM BR4 ......214 D1
Bendall Ms CAMTN NW1 ......8 D1
Bendemeer Rd
PUT/ROE SW15 ......139 G4
Bendmore Av ABYW SE2 ......128 B5
Bendon Va WAND/EARL SW18 ......160 A2
Benedict Cl ORP BR6 ......216 E1
Benedict Dr
EBED/NFELT TW14 ......153 G2
Benedict Rd BRXN/ST SW9 ......142 A4
MTCM CR4 ......178 C6
Benedict Wharf MTCM CR4 ......178 D6
Benenden Gn HAYES BR2 ......199 K2
Benett Gdns
STRHM/NOR SW16 ......179 K5
Benfleet Cl SUT SM1 ......209 G1
Benfleet Wy FBAR/BDGN N11 ......34 A4
Bengal Rd IL IG1 ......90 B2
Bengarth Dr
KTN/HRWW/W HA3 ......42 D5
Bengarth Rd NTHLT UB5 ......77 H6
Bengeworth Rd HRW HA1 ......61 G6
Ben Hale Cl STAN HA7 ......43 G1
Benham Cl BTSEA SW11 * 140 B4
CHSGTN KT9 ......205 J4
Benham Gdns HSLW TW5 ......134 E6
Benham Rd HNWL W7 ......96 E4
Benhill Av SUT SM1 ......209 G2
Benhill Rd CMBW SE5 ......142 E1
SUT SM1 ......209 H1
Benhill Wood Rd SUT SM1 ......209 G2
Benhilton Gdns SUT SM1 ......209 F1
Benhurst Av HCH RM12 ......93 K3
Benhurst La
STRHM/NOR SW16 ......180 B1
Benin St LEW SE13 ......165 G2
Benjafield Cl UED N18 ......36 D6
Benjamin Cl EMPK RM11 ......75 J3
HACK E8 ......86 C6
Benjamin St FARR EC1M 12 A1
Ben Jonson Rd WCHPL E1 ......105 G4
Benledi St POP/IOD E14 ......106 B5
Bennelong Cl SHB W12 ......99 K6
Bennerley Rd BTSEA SW11 ......140 E6
Bennet Cl KUT/HW KT1 ......174 D4
Bennetsfield Rd STKPK UB11 ......112 E1
Bennet's HI BLKFR EC4V 12 B5
Bennett Cl NTHWD HA6 ......40 A3
WELL DA16 ......148 B3
Bennett Gv LEW SE13 ......144 E2
Bennett Pk BKHTH/KID SE3 ......145 J4
Bennett Rd BRXN/ST SW9 ......142 B3
CHDH RM6 ......74 A3
PLSTW E13 ......107 G3
Bennetts Av CROY/NA CRO 198 B6

GFD/PVL UB6 ......78 E6
Bennett's Castle La BCTR RM8 ......91 J2
Bennetts Cl MTCM CR4 ......179 G4
TOTM N17 ......50 B2
Bennetts Copse CHST BR7 ......184 C2
Bennett St CHSWK W4 ......118 B6
WHALL SW1A 10 A7
Bennetts Wy CROY/NA CRO 198 B6
Benningholme Rd EDGW HA8 ......45 G2
Bennington Rd TOTM N17 ......50 A4
WFD IG8 ......52 C3
Benn St HOM E9 ......87 G4
Benrek Cl BARK/HLT IG6 ......54 C3
Bensbury Cl PUT/ROE SW15 ......158 E2
Bensham Cl THHTH CR7 ......196 D1
Bensham Gv THHTH CR7 ......180 D5
Bensham La THHTH CR7 ......196 C1
Bensham Manor Rd
THHTH CR7 ......196 D1
Ben Smith Wy
BERM/RHTH SE16 ......123 H5
Benson Av PLSTW E13 ......107 G1
Benson Cl HSLW TW3 ......135 F5
Benson Quay WAP E1W 104 E6
Benson Rd CROY/NA CRO 211 G1
FSTH SE23 ......163 K3
Benthal Rd STNW/STAM N16 ......68 B6
Bentham Rd HOM E9 ......87 F4
THMD SE28 ......128 C1
Ben Tillet Cl BARK IG11 ......91 G4
CAN/RD E16 * 126 E1
Bentinck Ms MHST W1U 9 H3
Bentinck Rd WDR/YW UB7 ......112 A1
Bentley Dr GNTH/NBYPK IG2 ......72 C5
Bentley Ms EN EN1 ......35 K1
Bentley Rd IS N1 ......86 A4
Bentley Wy STAN HA7 ......43 G1
WFD IG8 ......38 E5
Benton Rd IL IG1 ......72 D5
OXHEY WD19 ......41 H1
Benton's La WNWD SE27 ......162 D6
Benton's Ri WNWD SE27 ......180 E1
Bentry Cl BCTR RM8 ......74 A6
Bentry Rd BCTR RM8 ......74 A6
Bentworth Rd SHB W12 ......99 K5
Benwell Rd HOLWY N7 ......85 G2
Benwick Cl BERM/RHTH SE16 ......123 J4
Benwood Ct SUT SM1 ......209 G1
Benworth St BOW E3 ......105 H2
Benyon Rd IS N1 ......85 K6
Berberis Wk WDR/YW UB7 ......112 B4
Berber Rd BTSEA SW11 * 140 E6
Bercta Rd ELTH/MOT SE9 ......167 H4
Berenger Wk WBPTN SW10 * 140 C1
Berens Rd STMC/STPC BR5 ......202 D2
WLSDN NW10 ......100 B2
Berens Wy CHST BR7 ......202 A1
Beresford Av ALP/SUD HA0 ......80 C5
BRYLDS KT5 ......191 J5
HNWL W7 ......96 D4
TRDG/WHET N20 ......33 K4
TWK TW1 ......156 D1
Beresford Dr BMLY BR1 ......184 C6
WFD IG8 ......39 G6
Beresford Gdns CHDH RM6 ......74 A2
EN EN1 ......24 A5
HSLWW TW4 ......134 E6
Beresford Rd BELMT SM2 ......208 D5
CEND/HSY/T N8 ......67 G2
CHING E4 ......38 C3
EFNCH N2 ......47 J6
HBRY N5 ......85 K3
HRW HA1 ......60 D2
KUTN/CMB KT2 ......175 G4
NWMAL KT3 ......191 K1
STHL UB1 ......114 C1
WALTH E17 ......51 K4
Beresford Sq
WOOL/PLUM SE18 ......127 G4
Beresford St
WOOL/PLUM SE18 ......127 H3
Beresford Ter HBRY N5 ......85 J3
Berestede Rd HMSMTH W6 ......118 C5
Bere St WAP E1W 105 F6
Berger Cl STMC/STPC BR5 ......201 J3
Berger Rd HOM E9 ......87 F4
Bergholt Av GNTH/NBYPK IG2 ......71 K3
Bergholt Ms CAMTN NW1 ......84 C5
Bering Wk CAN/RD E16 ......107 H5
Berisford Ms
WAND/EARL SW18 ......160 B1
Berkeley Av BXLYHN DA7 ......148 E2
CLAY IG5 ......54 A5
CRW RM5 ......56 E3
GFD/PVL UB6 ......78 E4
HEST TW5 ......133 K2
Berkeley Cl KUTN/CMB KT2 ......175 F3
ORP BR6 ......201 K4
RSLP HA4 ......76 E1
Berkeley Ct WLGTN SM6 ......210 C1
EBAR EN4 ......21 H3
Berkeley Gdns
ESH/CLAY KT10 ......205 G5
KENS W8 * 119 K1
WCHMH N21 ......35 K2
Berkeley Ms MBLAR W1H 9 F3
Berkeley Pl WIM/MER SW19 ......177 G2
Berkeley Rd BARN SW13 ......138 D2
CDALE/KGS NW9 ......44 B4
CEND/HSY/T N8 ......66 D2
HGDN/ICK UB10 ......94 A3
MNPK E12 ......89 J3
SEVS/STOTM N15 ......67 K3
Berkeley Sq MYFR/PICC W1J 9 K6
The Berkeleys SNWD SE25 * 197 H1
Berkeley St MYFR/PICC W1J 9 K6
Berkeley Waye HEST TW5 ......134 D1
Berkhampstead Rd
BELV DA17 ......129 H5

Berkhamsted Av WBLY HA9 ......80 B4
Berkley Cl WHTN TW2 * 155 K5
Berkley Rd CAMTN NW1 ......83 K5
Berkshire Gdns PLMGR N13 ......49 G1
UED N18 ......50 D1
Berkshire Rd HOM E9 ......87 H4
Berkshire Wy MTCM CR4 ......195 K1
Bermans Wy WLSDN NW10 ......81 G2
Bermondsey Sq STHWK SE1 ......19 G1
Bermondsey Wall East
BERM/RHTH SE16 ......123 J2
Bermondsey Wall West
BERM/RHTH SE16 ......123 H2
Bernal Cl THMD SE28 ......109 K6
Bernard Av WEA W13 ......116 C3
Bernard Ashley Dr CHARL SE7 ......126 A5
Bernard Cassidy St
CAN/RD E16 * 106 D4
Bernard Gdns
WIM/MER SW19 ......177 J1
Bernard Rd ROMW/RG RM7 ......74 E4
SEVS/STOTM N15 ......68 B2
WLGTN SM6 ......210 B2
Bernards Cl BARK/HLT IG6 ......54 C3
Bernard St BMSBY WC1N 4 E7
Bernays Cl STAN HA7 ......43 J2
Bernay's Gv BRXN/ST SW9 ......142 A5
Bernel Dr CROY/NA CRO 213 H1
Berne Rd THHTH CR7 ......196 C2
Berners Dr WEA W13 ......97 G6
Berners Ms FITZ W1T 10 B2
Berners Pl FITZ W1T 10 B3
Berners Rd IS N1 ......6 A1
WDGN N22 ......49 G4
Berners St FITZ W1T 10 B2
Berner Ter WCHPL E1 * 104 C5
Berney Rd CROY/NA CRO 196 E4
Bernhardt Crs STJWD NW8 ......2 C6
Bernhart Cl EDGW HA8 ......44 E3
Bernwell Rd CHING E4 ......38 C5
Berridge Gn EDGW HA8 ......44 C3
Berridge Ms KIL/WHAMP NW6 ......82 E3
Berridge Rd NRWD SE19 ......180 E1
Berriman Rd HOLWY N7 ......85 F1
Berriton Rd RYLN/HDSTN HA2 ......59 K5
Berrybank Cl CHING E4 ......38 A4
Berry Cl DAGE RM10 ......92 C3
WCHMH N21 ......35 H3
WLSDN NW10 ......81 G5
Berrydale Rd YEAD UB4 ......95 J3
Berryfield Cl BMLY BR1 ......184 D4
Berry Field Cl WALTH E17 ......69 K1
Berryfield Rd WALW SE17 ......122 C5
Berryhill ELTH/MOT SE9 ......147 G5
Berryhill Gdns ELTH/MOT SE9 ......147 G5
Berrylands BRYLDS KT5 ......191 H2
ORP BR6 ......217 J1
RYNPK SW20 ......177 F6
Berrylands Rd BRYLDS KT5 ......191 G3
Berry La DUL SE21 ......162 E6
Berryman Cl BCTR RM8 ......91 J1
Berryman's La SYD SE26 ......164 A6
Berrymead Gdns ACT W3 ......117 K1
Berrymede Rd CHSWK W4 ......118 A3
Berry Pl FSBYE EC1V 6 B5
Berry St FSBYE EC1V 6 B6
Berry Wy EA W5 ......117 F3
Bertal Rd TOOT SW17 ......160 C6
Berthons Gdns WALTH E17 * 70 B2
Berthon St DEPT SE8 ......144 D1
Bertie Rd SYD SE26 ......182 A2
WLSDN NW10 ......81 J4
Bertram Rd EN EN1 ......24 B5
HDN NW4 ......63 J3
KUTN/CMB KT2 ......175 H3
Bertram St KTTN NW5 ......84 B1
Bertrand St LEW SE13 ......144 E4
Bertrand Wy THMD SE28 ......109 H6
Bert Rd THHTH CR7 ......196 D2
Bert Wy EN EN1 ......24 B5
Berwick Av YEAD UB4 ......95 H6
Berwick Cl STAN HA7 ......43 F2
WHTN TW2 ......155 F3
Berwick Crs BFN/LL DA15 ......167 K1
Berwick Rd CAN/RD E16 ......107 F5
WDGN N22 ......49 H4
WELL DA16 ......148 C2
Berwick St SOHO/CST W1F 10 B4
Berwyn Av HSLW TW3 ......135 G2
Berwyn Rd HNHL SE24 ......162 C3
RCHPK/HAM TW10 ......137 J6
Beryl Av EHAM E6 ......107 J4
Beryl Rd HMSMTH W6 ......119 G5
Berystede KUTN/CMB KT2 ......175 J3
Besant Cl CRICK NW2 * 82 C1
Besant Pl PECK SE15 ......143 G4
Besant Rd CRICK NW2 ......82 C2
Besant Wy WLSDN NW10 ......80 E3
Besley St STRHM/NOR SW16 ......179 H2
Bessant Dr RCH/KEW TW9 ......137 J2
Bessborough Pl PIM SW1V 121 J5
Bessborough Rd HRW HA1 ......60 D5
PUT/ROE SW15 ......158 D3
Bessborough St PIM SW1V 121 J5
Bessemer Rd CMBW SE5 ......142 D3
Bessie Lansbury Cl EHAM E6 ......108 A5
Bessingby Rd RSLP HA4 ......58 E6
Besson St NWCR SE14 ......143 K2
Bessy St BETH E2 * 104 E2
Best Ter SWLY BR8 * 203 K5
Bestwood St DEPT SE8 ......124 A4
Beswick Ms KIL/WHAMP NW6 ......83 F3
Betam Rd HYS/HAR UB3 ......113 G2
Betchworth Cl SUT SM1 ......209 H3
Betchworth Rd
GDMY/SEVK IG3 ......72 E6
Betham Rd GFD/PVL UB6 ......96 D2
Bethany Waye
EBED/NFELT TW14 ......153 H2
Bethecar Rd HRW HA1 ......60 E2
Bethel Av CAN/RD E16 ......106 D3
Bethell Av IL IG1 ......72 A4

Bethel Rd WELL DA16 ......148 D4
Bethersden Cl BECK BR3 ......182 C3
Bethnal Green Rd BETH E2 ......7 K6
Bethune Av FBAR/BDGN N11 ......33 K3
Bethune Rd STNW/STAM N16 ......67 K4
WLSDN NW10 ......99 F3
Bethwin Rd CMBW SE5 ......142 C1
Betjeman Cl RYLN/HDSTN HA2 ......60 E3
Betjeman Ct WDR/YW UB7 * 112 A1
Betony Cl CROY/NA CRO 198 A5
Betoyne Av CHING E4 ......38 C5
Betstyle Rd FBAR/BDGN N11 ......34 B3
Betterton Dr SCUP DA14 ......169 F4
Betterton Rd RAIN RM13 ......111 G1
Betterton St LSQ/SEVD WC2H 11 E4
Bettons Pk SRTFD E15 ......88 C6
Bettridge Rd FUL/PGN SW6 ......139 J3
Betts Cl BECK BR3 ......182 B5
Betts Ms WCHPL E1 ......104 D6
Betts Rd CAN/RD E16 ......107 F5
Betts St WCHPL E1 ......104 D6
Betts Wy PGE/AN SE20 ......181 J5
SURB KT6 ......190 C5
Beulah Av THHTH CR7 * 180 D5
Beulah Cl EDGW HA8 ......30 D5
Beulah Crs THHTH CR7 ......180 D5
Beulah Gv CROY/NA CRO 196 D3
Beulah Hl NRWD SE19 ......180 D2
Beulah Rd SUT SM1 ......208 E3
THHTH CR7 ......180 D6
WALTH E17 ......69 K2
WIM/MER SW19 ......177 J3
Beult Rd DART DA1 ......150 D4
Bevan Av BARK IG11 ......91 G5
Bevan Ct CROY/NA CRO 211 G3
Bevan Rd ABYW SE2 ......128 C5
EBAR EN4 ......21 K5
Bevan St IS N1 ......6 C2
Bev Callender Cl VX/NE SW8 ......141 G4
Bevenden St IS N1 ......7 F4
Beveridge Rd WLSDN NW10 ......81 G5
Beverley Av BFN/LL DA15 ......168 A2
HSLWW TW4 ......134 E5
RYNPK SW20 ......176 B4
Beverley Cl BARN SW13 ......138 D3
BTSEA SW11 ......140 C5
CHSGTN KT9 ......205 J2
WCHMH N21 ......35 J3
Beverley Crs WFD IG8 ......53 F4
Beverley Dr EDGW HA8 ......62 B1
Beverley Gdns BARN SW13 ......138 C4
GLDGN NW11 ......64 C4
HCH RM12 ......93 K1
STAN HA7 ......43 G4
WBLY HA9 ......62 B6
WPK KT4 ......192 D5
Beverley La KUTN/CMB KT2 ......176 B3
Beverley Rd BARN SW13 ......138 C4
BXLYHN DA7 ......149 K3
CHING E4 ......52 B2
CHSWK W4 ......118 C5
DAGW RM9 ......92 A3
EHAM E6 ......107 H2
HAYES BR2 ......200 D5
KUT/HW KT1 ......174 C5
MTCM CR4 ......195 J1
NWDGN UB2 ......114 C3
NWMAL KT3 ......192 D1
PGE/AN SE20 ......181 J5
RSLP HA4 ......58 E6
WHTN TW2 ......155 K2
WPK KT4 ......193 F6
Beverley Wy KUTN/CMB KT2 ......176 C4
Beverley Wy (Kingston By-Pass)
NWMAL KT3 ......176 C4
Beversbrook Rd ARCH N19 ......84 D1
Beverstone Rd
BRXS/STRHM SW2 ......142 A6
THHTH CR7 ......196 B1
Beverston Ms MBLAR W1H 8 E2
Bevill Cl SNWD SE25 ......181 H6
Bevin Cl BERM/RHTH SE16 ......124 B1
Bevington Rd BECK BR3 ......182 E5
NKENS W10 ......100 C4
Bevington St
BERM/RHTH SE16 ......123 H2
Bevin Rd YEAD UB4 ......94 E2
Bevin Sq TOOT SW17 ......160 E5
Bevin Wy IS N1 ......5 J3
Bevis Marks HDTCH EC3A 13 H3
Bewcastle Gdns ENC/FH EN2 ......22 E5
Bewdley St IS N1 ......85 G5
Bewick Ms PECK SE15 ......143 J1
Bewick St VX/NE SW8 ......141 G3
Bewley St WCHPL E1 ......104 D6
WIM/MER SW19 ......178 B2
Bewlys Rd WNWD SE27 ......180 C1
Bexhill Cl FELT TW13 ......154 D4
Bexhill Rd BROCKY SE4 ......164 C6
FBAR/BDGN N11 ......34 D4
MORT/ESHN SW14 ......137 K4
Bexley Cl DART DA1 ......150 B6
Bexley Gdns CHDH RM6 ......73 H2
ED N9 ......35 K5
Bexley High St BXLY DA5 ......169 H2
Bexley La DART DA1 ......150 B6
SCUP DA14 ......168 E6
Bexley Rd ELTH/MOT SE9 ......147 G6
ERITH DA8 ......150 A1
Beynon Rd CAR SM5 ......209 K3
Bianca Rd PECK SE15 ......123 G6
Bibsworth Rd FNCH N3 ......46 D5
Bibury Cl PECK SE15 ......123 F6
Bicester Rd RCH/KEW TW9 ......137 H4
Bickenhall St MHST W1U 9 F1
Bickersteth Rd TOOT SW17 ......178 E2
Bickerton Rd ARCH N19 ......84 C1
Bickley Crs BMLY BR1 ......184 D6
Bickley Park Rd BMLY BR1 ......184 E6
Bickley Rd BMLY BR1 ......184 C5
LEY E10 ......69 K4
Bickley St TOOT SW17 ......178 D1
Bicknell Rd CMBW SE5 ......142 D4
Bicknoller Rd EN EN1 ......24 B2
Bicknor Rd ORP BR6 ......201 K4

Bidborough Cl HAYES BR2 ......199 J2
Bidborough St STPAN WC1H 4 E5
Biddenden Wy
ELTH/MOT SE9 ......167 F6
Bidder St CAN/RD E16 ......106 C4
Biddestone Rd HOLWY N7 ......85 F2
Biddulph Rd MV/WKIL W9 ......101 F2
SAND/SEL CR2 ......211 J6
Bideford Av GFD/PVL UB6 ......97 H2
Bideford Cl EDGW HA8 ......44 C4
FELT TW13 ......154 E5
Bideford Gdns EN EN1 ......36 A2
Bideford Rd BMLY BR1 ......165 J5
PEND EN3 ......25 H1
RSLP HA4 ......58 E5
WELL DA16 ......148 C6
Bidwell Gdns FBAR/BDGN N11 ......48 C4
Bidwell St PECK SE15 ......143 J2
Biggerstaff Rd SRTFD E15 ......88 A6
Biggerstaff St FSBYPK N4 ......67 G6
Biggin Av MTCM CR4 ......178 E4
Biggin Hl NRWD SE19 ......180 C3
Biggin Wy NRWD SE19 ......180 C3
Bigginwood Rd
STRHM/NOR SW16 ......180 C3
Bigg's Rw PUT/ROE SW15 ......139 G4
Bigland St WCHPL E1 ......104 D5
Bignell Rd WOOL/PLUM SE18 ......127 G5
Bignold Rd FSTGT E7 ......88 E2
Bigwood Rd GLDGN NW11 ......65 F3
Billet Rd CHDH RM6 ......55 J6
WALTH E17 ......51 F4
Billets Hart Cl HNWL W7 ......115 K2
Bill Hamling Cl ELTH/MOT SE9 ......166 E4
Billingford Cl BROCKY SE4 ......144 A5
Billing Pl WBPTN SW10 ......140 A1
Billing Rd WBPTN SW10 ......140 A1
Billings Cl DAGW RM9 ......91 J5
Billing St WBPTN SW10 ......140 A1
Billington Rd NWCR SE14 ......144 A1
Billiter St FENCHST EC3M 13 H4
Billiter Sq FENCHST EC3M 13 H4
Billockby Cl CHSGTN KT9 ......206 B4
Billson St POP/IOD E14 ......125 F4
Bilton Rd ERITH DA8 ......150 D1
GFD/PVL UB6 ......79 H6
Bilton Wy HYS/HAR UB3 ......113 A2
PEND EN3 ......25 H2
Bina Gdns ECT SW5 ......120 B4
Bincote Rd ENC/FH EN2 ......23 F4
Binden Rd SHB W12 ......118 C3
Binfield Rd SAND/SEL CR2 ......212 B3
VX/NE SW8 ......141 K2
Bingfield St IS N1 ......84 E6
Bingham Pl MHST W1U 3 G1
Bingham Rd CROY/NA CRO 197 H5
IS N1 ......85 K4
Bingham St IS N1 ......85 K4
Bingley Rd CAN/RD E16 ......107 G5
GFD/PVL UB6 ......96 C3
Binney St MYFR/PKLN W1K 9 H5
Binns Rd CHSWK W4 ......118 B5
Binsey Wk ABYW SE2 ......128 D2
Binstead Cl YEAD UB4 ......95 J4
Binyon Crs STAN HA7 ......43 F1
Birbetts Rd ELTH/MOT SE9 ......166 E4
Birchanger Rd SNWD SE25 ......197 H2
Birch Av PLMGR N13 ......35 J5
Birch Cl BKHH IG9 ......39 H5
BTFD TW8 ......136 C1
CAN/RD E16 ......106 C4
HSLW TW3 ......135 J4
ROMW/RG RM7 ......56 D6
TEDD TW11 ......174 B1
Birch Ct WLGTN SM6 ......210 B2
Birchdale Gdns CHDH RM6 ......73 K4
Birchdale Rd FSTGT E7 ......89 G3
Birchdene Dr THMD SE28 ......128 B1
Birchen Cl CDALE/KGS NW9 ......63 F6
Birchend Cl SAND/SEL CR2 ......211 K4
Birchen Gv CDALE/KGS NW9 ......63 F6
Birchen La BANK EC3V 13 F4
Birches Cl MTCM CR4 ......178 E6
PIN HA5 ......59 J3
The Birches CHARL SE7 ......126 A6
CMBW SE5 * 143 F4
HSLWW TW4 * 154 E2
ORP BR6 ......216 A2
STHGT/OAK N14 ......35 F1
Birch Gdns DAGE RM10 ......92 E1
Birchgrove Cl BXLYHN DA7 ......213 F3
Birchington Cl BXLYHN DA7 ......149 K2
Birchington Rd BRYLDS KT5 ......191 G4
CEND/HSY/T N8 ......66 D3
KIL/WHAMP NW6 ......82 E6
Birchlands Av BAL SW12 ......160 E2
Birch Md HAYES BR2 ......201 F6
Birchmead Av PIN HA5 ......59 G1
Birchmere Rw BKHTH/KID SE3 ......145 J3
Birch Pk KTN/HRWW/W HA3 ......42 C3
Birch Rd FELT TW13 ......172 C1
ROMW/RG RM7 ......56 D6
Birch Rw HAYES BR2 ......201 F4
Birch Tree Av WWKM BR4 ......214 C3
Birch Tree Wy CROY/NA CRO 197 J6
Birch Wk MTCM CR4 ......179 G4
Birchway HYS/HAR UB3 ......113 K1
Birchwood Av BECK BR3 ......198 C1
MUSWH N10 ......48 A6
SCUP DA14 ......168 C5
WLGTN SM6 ......195 F6
Birchwood Cl MRDN SM4 ......194 A1
Birchwood Ct EDGW HA8 ......44 E5
Birchwood Dr HAMP NW3 ......83 F1
RDART DA2 ......170 B6
Birchwood Gv HPTN TW12 ......173 F2
Birchwood Pk BXLYHN DA7 ......169 K4
Birchwood Rd RDART DA2 ......187 K3
STMC/STPC BR5 ......201 J1
TOOT SW17 ......179 G1

Birchwood Ter SWLY BR8 * 187 K4
Birdbrook Cl DAGE RM10 92 E5
Birdbrook Rd BKHTH/KID SE3 146 B4
Birdcage Wk STJSPK SW1H 16 B3
Birdham Cl BMLY BR1 200 D2
Birdhurst Av SAND/SEL CR2 211 K2
Birdhurst Gdns SAND/SEL CR2 211 K2
Birdhurst Ri SAND/SEL CR2 212 A3
Birdhurst Rd SAND/SEL CR2 212 A3
WAND/EARL SW18 140 B5
WIM/MER SW19 178 D2
Bird In Bush Rd PECK SE15 143 H1
Bird-in-Hand La BMLY BR1 184 C5
Bird-in-Hand Ms FSTH SE23 163 K4
Bird-in-Hand Pas FSTH SE23 163 K4
Birds Farm Av ROMW/RG RM7 56 D4
Birdsfield La HOM E9 87 H6
Bird St MHST W1U 9 H4
Bird Wk WHTN TW2 154 E3
Birdwood Cl TEDD TW11 155 K6
Birkbeck Av ACT W3 98 E6
GFD/PVL UB6 78 C6
Birkbeck Gv ACT W3 118 A2
Birkbeck Hl DUL SE21 162 C4
Birkbeck Ms ACT W3 * 99 F6
HACK E8 86 B3
Birkbeck Pl DUL SE21 162 C3
Birkbeck Rd ACT W3 118 A1
BECK BR3 182 A5
CEND/HSY/T N8 66 E1
EA W5 116 D4
ENC/FH EN2 23 K2
GNTH/NBYPK IG2 72 D2
HACK E8 86 B3
MLHL NW7 45 H1
NFNCH/WDSP N12 47 G1
ROMW/RG RM7 75 F5
SCUP DA14 168 B5
TOTM N17 50 B4
WIM/MER SW19 178 A1
Birkbeck St BETH E2 104 D2
Birkbeck Wy GFD/PVL UB6 78 D6
Birkdale Av PIN HA5 42 A6
Birkdale Cl
BERM/RHTH SE16 * 123 J5
ORP BR6 201 J4
Birkdale Gdns CROY/NA CR0 213 F2
OXHEY WD19 27 H5
Birkdale Rd ABYW SE2 128 B4
EA W5 98 A3
Birkenhead Av
KUTN/CMB KT2 175 G5
Birkenhead St IS N1 5 F4
Birkhall Rd CAT SE6 165 G3
Birkwood Cl BAL SW12 161 J2
Birley Rd TRDG/WHET N20 33 G4
Birley St BTSEA SW11 141 F3
Birling Rd ERITH DA8 150 A1
Birnam Rd HOLWY N7 67 F6
Birse Crs WLSDN NW10 81 G2
Birstal Gn OXHEY WD19 27 H6
Birstall Rd SEVS/STOTM N15 68 A2
Biscay Rd HMSMTH W6 119 G5
Biscoe Cl HEST TW5 115 F6
Biscoe Wy LEW SE13 * 145 G5
Bisenden Rd CROY/NA CR0 197 F6
Bisham Cl MTCM CR4 194 E4
Bisham Gdns HGT N6 66 A5
Bishop Butt Cl ORP BR6 217 F1
Bishop Cl RCHPK/HAM TW10 156 E5
Bishop Fox Wy
E/WMO/HCT KT8 188 E1
Bishop Ken Rd
KTN/HRWW/W HA3 43 F5
Bishop Kings Rd WKENS W14 119 H4
Bishop Rd STHGT/OAK N14 34 B2
Bishops Av BMLY BR1 184 B6
CHDH RM6 73 J3
FUL/PGN SW6 139 G3
NTHWD HA6 26 C6
PLSTW E13 89 F6
The Bishops Av EFNCH N2 65 H3
Bishop's Bridge Rd
BAY/PAD W2 101 F5
Bishops Cl BAR EN5 32 B1
CHSWK W4 117 K5
ELTH/MOT SE9 167 H4
EN EN1 24 D3
SUT SM1 208 E1
WALTH E17 69 K1
Bishop's Ct STP EC4M 12 A3
Bishops Dr EBED/NFELT TW14 153 G1
NTHLT UB5 77 J6
Bishopsford Rd MRDN SM4 194 B4
Bishopsgate LVPST EC2M 13 H2
Bishopsgate Ar LVPST EC2M 13 H1
Bishops Gn BMLY BR1 * 184 B4
Bishops Gv EFNCH N2 65 H3
HPTN TW12 154 E6
Bishop's Hall KUT/HW KT1 174 E5
Bishops Md CMBW SE5 * 142 D1
Bishop's Park Rd
FUL/PGN SW6 139 G3
STRHM/NOR SW16 179 K4
Bishop's Pl SUT SM1 209 G3
Bishop's Rd CROY/NA CR0 196 C4
FUL/PGN SW6 139 J2
HGT N6 66 A3
HNWL W7 115 K2
HYS/HAR UB3 94 A5
Bishops Ter LBTH SE11 17 K6
Bishopsthorpe Rd SYD SE26 163 K6
Bishops Wk CHST BR7 185 H4
CROY/NA CR0 213 F3
Bishop's Wy BETH E2 104 E1
Bishopswood Rd HGT N6 65 K4
Bishop Wy WLSDN NW10 81 G5
Bisley Cl WPK KT4 193 F5
Bispham Rd WLSDN NW10 98 B2
Bisson Rd SRTFD E15 106 A1
Bistern Av WALTH E17 52 B6
Bittacy Cl MLHL NW7 46 B2
Bittacy Hl MLHL NW7 46 B2
Bittacy Park Av MLHL NW7 46 B2
Bittacy Ri MLHL NW7 46 B2
Bittacy Rd MLHL NW7 46 B2
Bittern Cl YEAD UB4 95 H4
Bittern Pl WDGN N22 * 49 F5
Bittern St STHWK SE1 18 C3
Bittoms Ct KUT/HW KT1 * 174 E6
The Bittoms KUT/HW KT1 174 E6
Bixley Cl NWDGN UB2 114 E4
Blackall St SDTCH EC2A 7 G6
Blackberry Farm Cl
HEST TW5 134 D1
Blackberry Fld
STMC/STPC BR5 186 B4
Blackbird Hl CDALE/KGS NW9 62 E6
Blackbird Yd BETH E2 7 K4
Blackborne Rd DAGE RM10 92 C4
Black Boy La SEVS/STOTM N15 67 J2
Blackbrook La HAYES BR2 201 F2
Blackburne's Ms
MYFR/PKLN W1K 9 G5
Blackburn Rd
KIL/WHAMP NW6 83 F4
Blackbush Av CHDH RM6 73 K2
Blackbush Cl BELMT SM2 209 F5
Blackdown Cl EFNCH N2 47 G5
Blackdown Ter
WOOL/PLUM SE18 * 146 E2
Blackenham Rd TOOT SW17 160 E6
Blackett St PUT/ROE SW15 139 G4
Black Fan Cl ENC/FH EN2 23 J2
Blackfen Pde BFN/LL DA15 * 168 B1
Blackfen Rd BFN/LL DA15 148 A6
Blackford Cl SAND/SEL CR2 211 H6
Blackford Rd OXHEY WD19 41 H1
Blackfriars Br STHWK SE1 12 A6
Black Friars La BLKFR EC4V 12 A4
Blackfriars Pas BLKFR EC4V 12 A5
Blackfriars Rd STHWK SE1 12 A7
Blackfriars U/P BLKFR EC4V 12 B5
Blackheath Av GNWCH SE10 145 H1
Blackheath Gv
BKHTH/KID SE3 145 J3
Blackheath Hl GNWCH SE10 145 F2
Blackheath Pk
BKHTH/KID SE3 145 K4
Blackheath Ri LEW SE13 145 F3
Blackheath Rd GNWCH SE10 144 E2
Blackheath V BKHTH/KID SE3 145 H3
Black Horse Ct STHWK SE1 * 19 F5
Blackhorse La CROY/NA CR0 197 H4
WALTH E17 51 F6
Black Horse Pde PIN HA5 * 59 F2
Black Horse Rd SCUP DA14 168 B6
Blackhorse Rd DEPT SE8 124 B6
WALTH E17 51 F6
Blacklands Dr YEAD UB4 94 A3
Blacklands Rd CAT SE6 165 F6
Blacklands Ter CHEL SW3 14 E7
Black Lion Ga BAY/PAD W2 101 F6
Black Lion La HMSMTH W6 118 D4
Blackmans Cl DART DA1 171 F3
Blackmans Yd BETH E2 * 7 K6
Blackmore Av STHL UB1 115 J1
Blackmore Dr WBLY HA9 80 D5
Blackmore Rd BKHH IG9 39 J2
Blackmore's Gv TEDD TW11 174 B2
Blackness La HAYES BR2 215 H6
Blackpool Gdns YEAD UB4 94 C3
Blackpool Rd PECK SE15 143 J3
Black Prince Rd LBTH SE11 17 G7
Black Rod Cl HYS/HAR UB3 113 J3
Blackshaw Rd TOOT SW17 178 C1
Blacksmith Cl CHDH RM6 73 J3
Blacksmith's La RAIN RM13 93 H6
STMC/STPC BR5 202 D2
Black's Rd HMSMTH W6 119 F5
Blackstock Rd FSBYPK N4 67 H6
Blackstone Est HACK E8 86 C5
Blackstone Rd CRICK NW2 82 A3
Black Swan Yd STHWK SE1 19 G2
Blackthorn Av WDR/YW UB7 112 D4
Blackthorn Ct HEST TW5 134 D1
Blackthorne Av CROY/NA CR0 197 K5
Blackthorne Dr CHING E4 38 B6
Blackthorn Gv BXLYHN DA7 149 F4
Blackthorn Rd IL IG1 90 D3
Blackthorn St BOW E3 105 J3
Blacktree Ms BRXN/ST SW9 * 142 B4
Blackwall La GNWCH SE10 125 H5
Blackwall Tunnel Ap
POP/IOD E14 106 A6
Blackwall Tunnel Northern Ap
BOW E3 105 K2
POP/IOD E14 106 A5
Blackwall Wy POP/IOD E14 106 B6
Blackwater Cl RAIN RM13 111 F4
Blackwater St EDUL SE22 143 G6
Blackwell Cl CLPT E5 87 G2
KTN/HRWW/W HA3 42 D3
Blackwell Dr OXHEY WD19 27 G1
Blackwell Gdns EDGW HA8 30 C6
Blackwood St WALW SE17 122 E5
Bladindon Dr BXLY DA5 168 E2
Bladon Gdns RYLN/HDSTN HA2 60 B3
Blagden's La STHGT/OAK N14 34 D4
Blagdon Rd LEW SE13 164 E1
NWMAL KT3 192 C1
Blagdon Wk TEDD TW11 174 D2
Blagrove Rd NKENS W10 100 C4
Blair Av CDALE/KGS NW9 63 G4
ESH/CLAY KT10 189 H6
Blair Cl BFN/LL DA15 147 K6
HYS/HAR UB3 113 K4
IS N1 85 J4
Blairderry Rd
BRXS/STRHM SW2 161 K4
Blairhead Dr OXHEY WD19 27 F5
Blair St POP/IOD E14 106 A5
Blake Av BARK IG11 90 E6
Blake Cl CAR SM5 194 D5
RAIN RM13 93 H6
WELL DA16 147 K2
Blakeden Dr ESH/CLAY KT10 205 F5
Blake Gdns DART DA1 151 J5
FUL/PGN SW6 139 K2
Blakehall Rd CAR SM5 209 K4
Blake Hall Rd WAN E11 70 E5
Blakemore Rd
STRHM/NOR SW16 161 K5
THHTH CR7 196 A2
Blakemore Wy BELV DA17 129 F3
Blakeney Av BECK BR3 182 C4
Blakeney Cl CAMTN NW1 4 C2
HACK E8 86 C3
TRDG/WHET N20 33 G3
Blakeney Rd BECK BR3 182 C4
Blaker Ct CHARL SE7 * 146 B1
Blake Rd CAN/RD E16 106 D3
CROY/NA CR0 197 F6
FBAR/BDGN N11 48 C3
MTCM CR4 178 D6
Blaker Rd SRTFD E15 88 A6
Blakes Av NWMAL KT3 192 C2
Blakes Cl WLSDN NW10 81 J4
Blake's Gn WWKM BR4 199 F4
Blakes La NWMAL KT3 192 C2
Blakesley Av EA W5 97 J5
Blakes Rd PECK SE15 143 F1
Blakes Ter NWMAL KT3 192 D2
Blakesware Gdns ED N9 35 K2
Blakewood Cl FELT TW13 154 B6
Blanchard Cl ELTH/MOT SE9 166 D5
Blanchard Gv PEND EN3 25 J1
Blanchard Wy HACK E8 * 86 C4
Blanch Cl PECK SE15 143 K1
Blanchedowne CMBW SE5 142 E5
Blanche St CAN/RD E16 106 D3
Blanchland Rd MRDN SM4 194 A2
Blandfield Rd BAL SW12 161 F1
Blandford Av BECK BR3 182 B5
WHTN TW2 155 G3
Blandford Cl CROY/NA CR0 210 E1
EFNCH N2 65 G2
ROMW/RG RM7 74 D1
Blandford Crs CHING E4 38 A2
Blandford Rd BECK BR3 182 A5
CHSWK W4 118 B3
EA W5 116 E2
NWDGN UB2 115 F4
TEDD TW11 173 J1
Blandford Sq CAMTN NW1 2 D7
Blandford St MHST W1U 9 F3
Blandford Waye YEAD UB4 95 G5
Bland St ELTH/MOT SE9 146 C5
Blaney Crs EHAM E6 108 B2
Blanmerle Rd ELTH/MOT SE9 167 G3
Blann Cl ELTH/MOT SE9 166 C1
Blantyre St WBPTN SW10 140 C1
Blantyre Wk WBPTN SW10 * 140 C1
Blashford St LEW SE13 165 G2
Blawith Rd HRW HA1 60 E1
Blaydon Cl RSLP HA4 58 C4
TOTM N17 * 50 D3
Blaydon Wk TOTM N17 50 D3
Bleak Hill La
WOOL/PLUM SE18 128 A6
Blean Gv PGE/AN SE20 181 K3
Bleasdale Av GFD/PVL UB6 97 G1
Blechynden St NTGHL W11 * 100 B6
Bledlow Cl THMD SE28 109 J6
Bledlow Ri GFD/PVL UB6 96 C1
Bleeding Heart Yd
HCIRC EC1N * 11 K2
Blegborough Rd
STRHM/NOR SW16 179 H2
Blendon Dr BXLY DA5 168 E1
Blendon Rd BXLY DA5 168 E1
Blendon Ter
WOOL/PLUM SE18 127 H5
Blendworth Wy PECK SE15 143 F1
Blenheim CDALE/KGS NW9 * 45 H5
Blenheim Av GNTH/NBYPK IG2 72 A3
Blenheim Cl DART DA1 171 F1
GFD/PVL UB6 * 96 D1
OXHEY WD19 27 G2
ROMW/RG RM7 74 E1
RYNPK SW20 177 F6
WCHMH N21 35 J3
WLGTN SM6 210 C5
Blenheim Ct BFN/LL DA15 167 J5
WFD IG8 53 F3
Blenheim Crs NTGHL W11 100 C6
RSLP HA4 58 B6
SAND/SEL CR2 211 J5
Blenheim Dr WELL DA16 148 A2
Blenheim Gdns
BRXS/STRHM SW2 162 A1
CRICK NW2 82 A3
KUTN/CMB KT2 175 J3
WBLY HA9 80 A1
WLGTN SM6 210 C4
Blenheim Gv PECK SE15 143 G3
Blenheim Park Rd
SAND/SEL CR2 211 J6
Blenheim Pas STJWD NW8 101 G1
Blenheim Pl TEDD TW11 174 A1
Blenheim Ri
SEVS/STOTM N15 * 68 B1
Blenheim Rd BAR EN5 20 B4
BFN/LL DA15 168 D3
CHSWK W4 118 B3
DART DA1 171 F1
EHAM E6 107 H2
HAYES BR2 200 D1
NTHLT UB5 78 B4
ORP BR6 202 D6
PGE/AN SE20 181 K3
RYLN/HDSTN HA2 60 B3
RYNPK SW20 177 F6
STJWD NW8 101 G1
SUT SM1 208 E1
WALTH E17 51 F6
WAN E11 88 C2
Blenheim St MYFR/PKLN W1K 9 J4
Blenheim Ter STJWD NW8 101 G1
Blenheim Wy ISLW TW7 136 B2
Blenkarne Rd BTSEA SW11 160 E1
Bleriot Rd HEST TW5 134 B1
Blessbury Rd EDGW HA8 44 E4
Blessington Rd LEW SE13 145 G5
Blessing Wy BARK IG11 109 J1
Bletchingly Cl THHTH CR7 196 C1
Bletchley St IS N1 6 D3
Bletchmore Cl HYS/HAR UB3 113 G5
Bletsoe Wk IS N1 6 D2
Blincoe Cl WIM/MER SW19 159 G4
Blissett St GNWCH SE10 145 F2
Bliss Ms NKENS W10 100 C2
Blisworth Cl YEAD UB4 95 J3
Blithbury Rd DAGW RM9 91 H4
Blithdale Rd ABYW SE2 128 B4
Blithfield St KENS W8 120 A3
Blockley Rd ALP/SUD HA0 61 H6
Bloemfontein Av SHB W12 118 E1
Bloemfontein Rd SHB W12 99 K6
Blomfield Rd MV/WKIL W9 101 F4
Blomfield St LVPST EC2M 13 F2
Blomfield Vls BAY/PAD W2 101 F4
Blomville Rd BCTR RM8 74 A6
Blondell Cl WDR/YW UB7 112 A6
Blondel St BTSEA SW11 141 F3
Blondin Av EA W5 116 D4
Blondin St BOW E3 105 J1
Bloomfield Crs
GNTH/NBYPK IG2 72 B3
Bloomfield Ct
LEY E10 * 87 K1
Bloomfield Pl MYFR/PKLN W1K 9 K5
Bloomfield Rd HAYES BR2 200 C2
HGT N6 66 A3
KUT/HW KT1 191 F1
WOOL/PLUM SE18 127 G5
Bloomfield Ter BGVA SW1W 121 F5
Bloom Gv WNWD SE27 162 C5
Bloomhall Rd NRWD SE19 180 E1
Bloom Park Rd FUL/PGN SW6 139 J1
Bloomsbury Cl EA W5 98 B6
Bloomsbury Pl
NOXST/BSQ WC1A 11 F2
Bloomsbury Sq
NOXST/BSQ WC1A 11 F2
Bloomsbury St GWRST WC1E 10 D1
Bloomsbury Wy
NOXST/BSQ WC1A 10 E2
Blore Cl VX/NE SW8 141 J2
Blossom Cl DAGW RM9 92 B6
EA W5 117 F2
SAND/SEL CR2 212 B3
Blossom La ENC/FH EN2 23 J2
Blossom St WCHPL E1 7 H7
Blossom Wy WDR/YW UB7 112 D4
Blossom Waye HEST TW5 114 D6
Blount St POP/IOD E14 105 G5
Bloxam Gdns ELTH/MOT SE9 146 D6
Bloxhall Rd LEY E10 69 H5
Bloxham Crs HPTN TW12 172 E4
Bloxworth Cl WLGTN SM6 210 C1
Blucher Rd CMBW SE5 142 D1
Blue Anchor La
BERM/RHTH SE16 123 H4
Blue Anchor Yd WCHPL E1 104 C6
Blue Ball Yd WHALL SW1A 16 A1
Bluebell Av FSTGT E7 89 H3
Bluebell Cl HOM E9 86 E6
ORP BR6 201 H6
ROMW/RG RM7 75 G6
SYD SE26 163 G6
WLGTN SM6 195 G5
Bluebell Wy IL IG1 90 B4
Blueberry Cl WFD IG8 52 E2
Bluebird La DAGE RM10 92 C5
Bluebird Wy THMD SE28 127 J2
Bluefield Cl HPTN TW12 173 F1
Bluegates EW KT17 207 J5
Bluehouse Rd CHING E4 38 C5
Blue Lion Pl STHWK SE1 19 G4
Blue Riband Est
CROY/NA CR0 * 196 C6
Blundell Rd EDGW HA8 45 G3
Blundell St HOLWY N7 84 E5
Blunden Cl BCTR RM8 73 J5
Blunt Rd CROY/NA CR0 211 K3
Blunts Av WDR/YW UB7 132 D1
Blunts Rd ELTH/MOT SE9 147 F6
Blurton Rd CLPT E5 87 F2
Blyth Cl TWK TW1 156 A1
Blythe Cl CAT SE6 164 C2
Blythe Hl CAT SE6 164 C2
STMC/STPC BR5 186 A4
Blythe Hill La CAT SE6 164 C2
Blythe Hill Pl FSTH SE23 * 164 B2
Blythe Ms WKENS W14 * 119 G3
Blythe Rd WKENS W14 119 G3
Blytheswood Pl
STRHM/NOR SW16 162 A6
Blythe V CAT SE6 164 C3
Blyth Rd BMLY BR1 183 J4
HYS/HAR UB3 113 H2
THMD SE28 109 J6
WALTH E17 69 H4
Blyth's Whf POP/IOD E14 * 105 G6
Blythswood Rd
GDMY/SEVK IG3 73 G5
Blythwood Rd FSBYPK N4 66 E4
PIN HA5 41 H4
Boadicea St IS N1 5 G1
Boakes Cl CDALE/KGS NW9 62 E1
Boardman Av CHING E4 25 K6
Boardman Cl BAR EN5 20 C6
Boardwalk Pl POP/IOD E14 125 F1
Boatemah Wk BRXN/ST SW9 142 B3
Boathouse Wk PECK SE15 143 G1
Boat Lifter Wy
BERM/RHTH SE16 124 B4
Boat Quay CAN/RD E16 107 G6
Bob Anker Cl PLSTW E13 106 E2
Bobbin Cl CLAP SW4 141 H4
Bob Marley Wy BRXN/ST SW9 142 B5
Bockhampton Rd
KUTN/CMB KT2 175 G3
Bocking St HACK E8 86 D6
Boddicott Cl WIM/MER SW19 159 H4
Bodiam Cl EN EN1 23 K3
Bodiam Rd
STRHM/NOR SW16 179 J4
Bodley Cl NWMAL KT3 192 B2
Bodley Rd NWMAL KT3 192 B3
Bodmin Cl RYLN/HDSTN HA2 77 K1
STMC/STPC BR5 202 D5
Bodmin Gv MRDN SM4 194 A1
Bodmin St WAND/EARL SW18 159 K3
Bodnant Gdns RYNPK SW20 176 D6
Bodney Rd CLPT E5 86 D3
Boeing Wy NWDGN UB2 114 A3
Bognor Gdns OXHEY WD19 * 41 G1
Bognor Rd WELL DA16 148 E2
Bohemia Pl HACK E8 86 E4
Bohn Rd WCHPL E1 105 G4
Bohun Gv EBAR EN4 33 J1
Boileau Rd BARN SW13 138 D1
EA W5 98 B5
Bolden St DEPT SE8 144 E3
Boldero Pl STJWD NW8 * 2 C7
Bolderwood Wy WWKM BR4 198 E6
Boldmere Rd PIN HA5 59 G4
Boleyn Av EN EN1 24 D2
Boleyn Cl LOU IG10 39 J1
Boleyn Ct BKHH IG9 38 E3
WALTH E17 69 J1
Boleyn Dr E/WMO/HCT KT8 172 E6
RSLP HA4 59 H6
Boleyn Gdns DAGE RM10 92 E5
WWKM BR4 198 E6
Boleyn Rd EHAM E6 107 H1
FSTGT E7 88 E5
STNW/STAM N16 86 A3
Boleyn Wy BAR EN5 21 G4
BARK/HLT IG6 54 C2
Bolina Rd BERM/RHTH SE16 123 K5
Bolingbroke Gv BTSEA SW11 140 D6
Bolingbroke Rd WKENS W14 119 G3
Bolingbroke Wk
BTSEA SW11 * 140 C1
Bolingbroke Wy
HYS/HAR UB3 113 G1
Bollo Bridge Rd ACT W3 117 K2
Bollo La ACT W3 117 J3
Bolney Ga SKENS SW7 14 C3
Bolney St VX/NE SW8 142 A1
Bolsover St GTPST W1W 3 K7
Bolstead Rd MTCM CR4 179 G4
Bolster Gv WDGN N22 * 48 D4
Bolt Ct FLST/FETLN EC4A * 11 K4
Bolton Cl CHSGTN KT9 205 K4
Bolton Crs CMBW SE5 122 B6
Bolton Dr MRDN SM4 194 B4
Bolton Gdns BMLY BR1 183 J2
ECT SW5 120 A5
TEDD TW11 174 B2
WLSDN NW10 100 B1
Bolton Gardens Ms
WBPTN SW10 120 A5
Bolton Pl IS N1 * 85 H5
Bolton Rd CHSGTN KT9 205 K4
CHSWK W4 137 K1
FSTGT E7 88 D4
HRW HA1 60 C1
KIL/WHAMP NW6 83 F6
UED N18 50 B1
WLSDN NW10 81 G6
Bolton's La WDR/YW UB7 133 F1
Boltons Pl WBPTN SW10 120 B5
The Boltons ALP/SUD HA0 79 F2
WBPTN SW10 * 120 B5
WFD IG8 * 38 E6
Bolton St MYFR/PICC W1J 9 K7
Bombay St BERM/RHTH SE16 123 J4
Bomer Cl WDR/YW UB7 132 D1
Bomore Rd NTGHL W11 100 B6
Bonar Pl CHST BR7 184 D3
Bonar Rd PECK SE15 143 H1
Bonchester Cl CHST BR7 185 F3
Bonchurch Cl BELMT SM2 209 F5
Bonchurch Rd NKENS W10 100 C4
WEA W13 116 C1
Bondfield Av YEAD UB4 94 E2
Bond Gdns WLGTN SM6 210 C2
Bond Rd MTCM CR4 178 E5
SURB KT6 191 G6
Bond St EA W5 97 K6
SRTFD E15 88 C3
Bondway VX/NE SW8 121 K6
Boneta Rd WOOL/PLUM SE18 126 E3
Bonfield Rd LEW SE13 145 F5
Bonham Gdns BCTR RM8 73 K6
Bonham Rd BCTR RM8 73 K6
BRXS/STRHM SW2 142 A6
Bonheur Rd CHSWK W4 118 A2
Bonhill St SDTCH EC2A 7 F7
Boniface Gdns
KTN/HRWW/W HA3 42 B3
Boniface Wk
KTN/HRWW/W HA3 42 B3
Bonita Ms BROCKY SE4 144 A4
Bonner Hill Rd KUT/HW KT1 175 G6
Bonner Rd BETH E2 104 E1
Bonnersfield Cl HRW HA1 61 G3
Bonnersfield La HRW HA1 61 G3
Bonner St BETH E2 * 104 E1
Bonneville Gdns CLAP SW4 161 H1
Bonnington Sq VX/NE SW8 122 A6
Bonny St CAMTN NW1 84 C5
Bonser Rd TWK TW1 156 A4
Bonsor St CMBW SE5 143 F1
Bonville Gdns HDN NW4 63 J1
Bonville Rd BMLY BR1 183 J1
Booker Rd UED N18 50 C1
Boones Rd LEW SE13 145 H5
Boone St LEW SE13 145 H5
Boord St GNWCH SE10 125 H3
Boothby Rd ARCH N19 66 D6
Booth Cl THMD SE28 128 C1
Booth La BLKFR EC4V 12 C5
Booth Rd CDALE/KGS NW9 45 F4
CROY/NA CR0 * 196 C6
Boot Pde EDGW HA8 * 44 C2
Boot St IS N1 7 G5
Bordars Rd HNWL W7 96 E4
Bordars Wk HNWL W7 96 E4
Borden Av WCHMH N21 35 K1
Border Crs SYD SE26 181 J1

Border Gdns CROY/NA CR0 ...213 K2
Borgard Ga MTCM CR4 ...178 D4
Border Rd SYD SE26 ...181 J1
Bordesley Rd MRDN SM4 ...194 A1
Bordon Wk WDGN N22 ...49 J4
Boreas Wk IS N1 ...6 E3
Boreham Av CAN/RD E16 ...106 E5
Boreham Rd WDGN N22 ...49 J4
Borgard House
  WOOL/PLUM SE18 ...146 D2
Borgard Rd
  WOOL/PLUM SE18 ...126 E4
Borkwood Pk ORP BR6 ...217 F2
Borkwood Wy ORP BR6 ...216 E2
Borland Rd PECK SE15 ...143 K5
  TEDD TW11 ...174 C2
Borneo St PUT/ROE SW15 ...139 F4
Borough High St STHWK SE1 ...18 D3
Borough HI CROY/NA CR0 ...211 H1
Borough Rd ISLW TW7 ...135 K2
  MTCM CR4 ...178 D6
  STHWK SE1 ...18 A4
Borough Sq STHWK SE1 ...18 C3
Borrett Cl WALW SE17 ...122 D5
Borrodaile Rd
  WAND/EARL SW18 ...160 A1
Borrowdale Av
  KTN/HRWW/W HA3 ...43 G5
Borrowdale Cl REDBR IG4 ...71 J1
Borthwick Ms WAN E11 * ...88 D2
Borthwick Rd CDALE/KGS NW9 ...63 H3
  SRTFD E15 ...88 C2
Borthwick St DEPT SE8 ...124 D5
Borwick Av WALTH E17 ...51 H6
Bosbury Rd CAT SE6 ...165 F5
Boscastle Rd KTTN NW5 ...84 B1
Boscobel Cl BMLY BR1 ...184 E5
Boscobel Pl BGVA SW1W ...15 H6
Boscobel St BAY/PAD W2 ...8 B1
Boscombe Av LEY E10 ...70 B5
Boscombe Cl CLPT E5 ...87 G3
Boscombe Rd SHB W12 ...118 D2
  TOOT SW17 ...179 F2
  WIM/MER SW19 ...177 K4
  WPK KT4 ...193 F5
Bosgrove CHING E4 ...38 A3
Boss St STHWK SE1 ...19 J2
Bostall Heath ABYW SE2 * ...128 D5
Bostall HI ABYW SE2 ...128 C5
Bostall La ABYW SE2 ...128 C5
Bostall Manorway ABYW SE2 * ...128 C4
Bostall Park Av BXLYHN DA7 ...149 F1
Bostall Rd STMC/STPC BR5 ...186 C5
Boston Cl CHSWK W4 ...116 B6
  CHSWK W4 ...118 B6
Boston Gv RSLP HA4 ...58 A3
Boston Manor Rd BTFD TW8 ...116 B4
Boston Pde HNWL W7 * ...116 B4
Boston Park Rd BTFD TW8 * ...116 D6
Boston Rd CROY/NA CR0 ...196 A3
  EDGW HA8 ...44 E5
  EHAM E6 ...107 J2
  HNWL W7 ...115 K1
Bostonthorpe Rd HNWL W7 * ...115 K2
Boston v HNWL W7 ...116 A4
Boswell Cl STMC/STPC BR5 ...202 B2
Boswell Ct BMSBY WC1N ...11 F1
Boswell Rd THHTH CR7 ...196 D1
Boswell St BMSBY WC1N * ...11 F1
Bosworth Cl WALTH E17 ...51 H4
Bosworth Rd BAR EN5 ...20 E4
  DAGE RM10 ...92 C2
  FBAR/BDGN N11 ...48 D2
  NKENS W10 ...100 C3
Botany Bay La CHST BR7 ...185 H5
Botany Cl EBAR EN4 ...21 J5
Botany Ter PUR RM19 * ...131 K5
Boteley Cl CHING E4 ...38 B4
Botham Cl EDGW HA8 ...44 E4
Botha Rd PLSTW E13 ...107 F4
Bothwell Cl CAN/RD E16 ...106 E4
Bothwell St HMSMTH W6 ...119 G6
Botolph Aly MON EC3R ...13 G6
Botolph La MON EC3R * ...13 G6
Botsford Rd RYNPK SW20 ...177 H5
Bott Rd RDART DA2 ...171 J6
Bott's Ms BAY/PAD W2 ...100 E5
Botwell Common Rd
  HYS/HAR UB3 ...94 B6
Botwell Crs HYS/HAR UB3 ...94 C6
Botwell La HYS/HAR UB3 ...94 C6
Boucher Cl TEDD TW11 ...174 A1
Boughton Av HAYES BR2 ...199 J4
Boughton Rd THMD SE28 ...127 K3
Boulcott St WCHPL E1 ...105 F5
The Boulevard WFD IG8 ...54 A3
Boulogne Rd CROY/NA CR0 ...196 D3
Boulter Gdns RAIN RG13 ...93 K5
Boulton Rd BCTR RM8 ...74 A6
Boultwood Rd EHAM E6 ...107 K5
Bounces La ED N9 ...36 D4
Bounces Rd ED N9 ...36 D4
Boundaries Rd BAL SW12 ...160 E4
  FELT TW13 ...154 B3
Boundary Av WALTH E17 ...69 H4
Boundary Cl BAR EN5 ...20 D2
  COMY/SEVK IG3 ...90 E2
  KUT/HW KT1 ...175 H6
  NWDGN UB2 ...115 F5
Boundary La PLSTW E13 ...107 H3
  WALW SE17 ...122 D6
Boundary Ms STJWD NW8 ...83 G6
Boundary Rd BARK IG11 ...108 C1
  BFN/LL DA15 ...147 K6
  ED N9 ...36 E1
  PIN HA5 ...59 H3
  PLSTW E13 ...107 G1
  ROM RM1 ...75 J3
  STJWD NW8 ...83 H6
  WALTH E17 ...69 J4
  WBLY HA9 ...80 A1
  WDGN N22 ...49 G2
  WIM/MER SW19 ...178 C2

WLGTN SM6 ...210 A6
Boundary Rw STHWK SE1 ...18 A2
Boundary St BETH E2 ...7 J4
  ERITH DA8 ...150 C1
Boundary Wy CROY/NA CR0 ...213 J5
Bounds Green Rd
  FBAR/BDGN N11 ...48 E3
Bourchier St SOHO/CST W1F ...10 C5
Bourdon Pl MYFR/PKLN W1K * ...9 K5
Bourdon Rd PGE/AN SE20 ...181 K5
Bourdon St MYFR/PKLN W1K * ...9 K6
Bourke Cl CLAP SW4 ...161 K1
  WLSDN NW10 ...81 G4
Bourlet Cl FITZ W1T ...10 A2
Bourn Av EBAR EN4 ...21 G6
  SEVS/STOTM N15 ...67 K1
Bournbrook Rd
  BKHTH/KID SE3 ...146 C4
Bourne Av HYS/HAR UB3 ...113 F3
  RSLP HA4 ...77 F3
Bourne Cl ESH/CLAY KT10 ...190 A6
Bourne Ct RSLP HA4 ...77 F3
Bourne Dr MTCM CR4 ...178 C5
Bourne End Rd NTHWD HA6 ...26 C6
Bourne Est HDCR EC1N * ...11 J1
Bourne Gdns CHING E4 ...37 K6
Bournehall Av BUSH WD23 ...28 A1
Bournehall La BUSH WD23 ...28 A1
Bournehall Rd BUSH WD23 ...28 A1
Bourne HI PLMGR N13 ...35 F4
Bourne Hill Cl PLMGR N13 * ...35 F4
Bourne Md BXLY DA5 ...149 K6
Bournemead Av NTHLT UB5 ...94 E1
Bournemead Cl NTHLT UB5 ...94 E2
Bournemouth Cl PECK SE15 ...143 H3
Bournemouth Rd PECK SE15 ...143 H3
  WIM/MER SW19 ...177 K4
Bourne Pde BXLY DA5 * ...169 J2
Bourne Rd BXLY DA5 ...169 K1
  CEND/HSY/T N8 ...66 E3
  FSTGT E7 ...88 D1
  HAYES BR2 ...200 C1
Bourneside Crs
  STHGT/OAK N14 ...34 D3
Bourneside Gdns CAT SE6 ...183 F1
Bourne St BGVA SW1W ...15 G7
  CROY/NA CR0 ...196 C6
Bourne Ter BAY/PAD W2 ...101 F4
Bourne Vw GFD/PVL UB6 ...79 F4
Bourne Wy HAYES BR2 ...199 K6
  HOR/WEW KT19 ...206 E2
  SUT SM1 ...208 D3
  YEAD UB4 * ...187 K6
Bournewood Rd
  STMC/STPC BR5 ...202 C4
  WOOL/PLUM SE18 ...148 B1
Bournville Rd CAT SE6 ...164 D2
Bournwell Cl EBAR EN4 ...21 K4
Bourton Cl HYS/HAR UB3 ...113 K1
Bousfield Rd NWCR SE14 ...144 A3
Boutflower Rd BTSEA SW11 ...140 D5
Boutique Hall LEW SE13 * ...145 F5
Bouverie Gdns
  KTN/HRWW/W HA3 ...61 K3
Bouverie Ms STNW/STAM N16 ...68 A1
Bouverie Pl BAY/PAD W2 ...8 B3
Bouverie Rd HRW HA1 ...60 C3
  STNW/STAM N16 ...68 A1
Bouverie St EMB EC4Y ...11 K4
Bouvier Rd PEND EN3 ...24 E1
Boveney Rd FSTH SE23 ...164 A2
Bovill Rd FSTH SE23 ...164 A2
Bovingdon Av WBLY HA9 ...80 C4
Bovingdon La
  CDALE/KGS NW9 ...45 G4
Bovingdon Rd FUL/PGN SW6 ...140 A2
Bow Arrow La DART DA1 ...171 K1
Bowater Cl BRXS/STRHM SW2 ...161 K1
  CDALE/KGS NW9 ...63 F2
Bowater Rd BKHTH/KID SE3 ...146 A1
  WOOL/PLUM SE18 ...126 C3
Bow Bridge Est BOW E3 ...105 K2
Bow Churchyard STP EC4M * ...12 D4
Bow Common La BOW E3 ...105 H4
Bowden Cl EBED/NFELT TW14 ...153 H3
Bowden St LBTH SE11 ...122 B5
Bowditch DEPT SE8 ...124 C5
Bowdon Rd LEY E10 ...69 J4
Bowen Dr DUL SE21 ...163 F5
Bowen Rd HRW HA1 ...60 C4
Bowen St POP/IOD E14 ...105 K5
Bowens Wd CROY/NA CR0 * ...213 H6
Bowenswood CROY/NA CR0 ...213 H6
Bower Av GNWCH SE10 ...145 H2
Bower Cl CRW RM5 ...57 F3
  NTHLT UB5 ...95 G1
Bowerdean St FUL/PGN SW6 ...140 A2
Bowerman Av NWCR SE14 ...124 B6
Bower St WCHPL E1 * ...105 F5
Bowes Rd ACT W3 ...99 G6

Bowling Green Cl
  PUT/ROE SW15 ...158 E2
Bradmore Rd WBLY DA5 ...169 H2
Bowling Green La CLKNW EC1R ...5 K7
Bowling Green Pl STHWK SE1 * ...18 E2
Bowling Green Rw
  WOOL/PLUM SE18 * ...126 E4
Bowling Green St LBTH SE11 ...122 B6
Bowling Green Wk IS N1 * ...7 G4
Bow Locks BOW E3 * ...106 A3
Bowls Cl STAN HA7 ...43 H1
Bowman Av CAN/RD E16 ...106 E6
Bowman Ms
  WAND/EARL SW18 ...159 J3
Bowmans Cl WEA W13 ...116 C1
Bowmans Lea FSTH SE23 ...163 K2
Bowman's Meadow
  WLGTN SM6 ...210 B1
Bowman's Pl HOLWY N7 ...84 E1
Bowmans Rd DART DA1 ...170 C2
Bowmead ELTH/MOT SE9 ...166 E4
Bowmore Wk CAMTN NW1 ...84 D5
Bowness Av HACK E8 * ...86 B4
Bowness Crs PUT/ROE SW15 ...176 B1
Bowness Dr HSLWW TW4 ...134 D5
Bowness Rd BXLYHN DA7 ...149 J3
  CAT SE6 ...164 E2
Bowness Wy HCH RM12 ...93 J3
Bowood Rd CLAP SW4 ...141 F6
  PEND EN3 ...25 F3
Bowring Gn OXHEY WD19 ...41 G1
Bow Rd BOW E3 ...105 J2
Bowrons Av ALP/SUD HA0 ...79 K5
Bowsley Ct FELT TW13 ...153 K4
Bow St COVGDN WC2E ...11 F4
  SRTFD E15 ...88 C3
Bowyer Cl EHAM E6 ...107 K4
Bowyer Pl CMBW SE5 ...142 D1
Bowyers Ct TWK TW1 ...136 C5
Bowyer St CMBW SE5 ...142 D1
Boxall Rd DUL SE21 ...163 F1
Boxelder Cl EDGW HA8 ...44 E1
Boxgrove Rd ABYW SE2 ...128 D3
Box La BARK IG11 ...109 J1
Boxley Rd MRDN SM4 ...194 B1
Boxley St CAN/RD E16 ...126 A1
Boxmoor Rd CRW RM5 ...56 E1
  KTN/HRWW/W HA3 ...61 H1
Boxoll Rd DAGW RM9 ...92 B2
Box Tree Cl BKHH IG9 ...39 J3
Boxtree La KTN/HRWW/W HA3 ...42 C4
Boxtree Rd
  KTN/HRWW/W HA3 ...42 D3
Boxwood Cl WDR/YW UB7 ...112 C2
Boxworth Gv IS N1 ...85 F6
Boyard Rd WOOL/PLUM SE18 ...127 G5
Boyce Wy PLSTW E13 ...106 E3
Boycroft Av CDALE/KGS NW9 ...62 E5
Boyd Av STHL UB1 ...114 E1
Boyd Cl KUTN/CMB KT2 ...175 H5
Boydell Ct STJWD NW8 ...2 E1
Boyd Rd WIM/MER SW19 ...178 C2
Boyfield St STHWK SE1 ...18 B3
Boyland Rd BMLY BR1 ...183 J1
Boyle Av STAN HA7 ...43 G2
Boyle Farm Rd THDIT KT7 ...190 B3
Boyne Av HDN NW4 ...64 B1
Boyne Rd DAGE RM10 ...92 C1
  LEW SE13 ...145 G4
Boyne Terrace Ms
  NTGHL W11 * ...119 J1
Boyson Rd WALW SE17 ...122 D6
Boyton Cl CEND/HSY/T N8 ...48 E6
  WCHPL E1 ...105 F3
Boyton Rd CEND/HSY/T N8 ...48 E6
Brabant Rd WDGN N22 ...49 F5
Brabazon Av WLGTN SM6 ...210 E5
Brabazon Rd HEST TW5 ...134 B1
  NTHLT UB5 ...96 A1
Brabazon St POP/IOD E14 ...105 K5
Brabourne Cl NRWD SE19 ...181 F1
Brabourne Crs BXLYHN DA7 ...129 G6
Brabourne Hs BRXN/ST SW9 ...142 B3
Brabourne Ri BECK BR3 ...199 G2
Brabourn Gv PECK SE15 ...143 K3
Bracewell Av GFD/PVL UB6 ...79 G3
Bracewell Rd NKENS W10 ...100 A4
Bracewood Gdns
  CROY/NA CR0 ...212 B1
Bracey Ms FSBYPK N4 * ...66 E6
Bracken Av BAL SW12 ...161 J1
  CROY/NA CR0 ...213 J1
Brackenbridge Dr RSLP HA4 ...77 H1
Brackenbury Gdns
  HMSMTH W6 ...118 E3
Brackenbury Rd EFNCH N2 ...47 G6
  HMSMTH W6 ...118 E3
Bracken Cl EHAM E6 ...107 K4
  WHTN TW2 ...155 F2
Brackendale WCHMH N21 ...35 F4
Brackendale Cl HEST TW5 ...135 G2
Brackendene BXLY DA5 ...170 B6
Bracken Dr CHIG IG7 ...54 B2
Bracken End ISLW TW7 ...135 J6
Brackenhill RSLP HA4 * ...77 J2
Bracken Hill Cl BMLY BR1 * ...183 J4
Bracken Hill La BMLY BR1 * ...183 J4
Bracken Ms ROMW/RG RM7 ...74 C3
The Brackens EN EN1 ...36 A2
  ORP BR6 ...217 G3
The Bracken CHING E4 ...38 A1
Brackley Cl WLGTN SM6 ...210 E5
Brackley Rd BECK BR3 ...182 C3
  CHSWK W4 ...118 B4
Brackley Sq WFD IG8 ...53 H3
Brackley St BARB EC2Y ...12 D1
Brackley Ter CHSWK W4 ...118 B5
Bracklyn Ct IS N1 ...6 E2
Bracknell Cl WDGN N22 ...49 G4
Bracknell Gdns HAMP NW3 ...83 F3
Bracknell Wy HAMP NW3 ...83 F3
Bracondale ESH/CLAY KT10 ...204 C3

Bracondale Rd ABYW SE2 ...128 B3
Bradbourne Rd BXLY DA5 ...169 H2
Bradbourne St FUL/PGN SW6 ...139 K3
Bradbury Cl NWDGN UB2 ...114 E4
Bradbury St STNW/STAM N16 ...86 A3
Braddock Cl CRW RM5 ...56 E2
Braddon Rd RCH/KEW TW9 ...137 G4
Braddyll St GNWCH SE10 ...125 H5
Bradenham Av WELL DA16 ...148 B5
Bradenham Cl WALW SE17 ...122 E6
Bradenham Rd
  KTN/HRWW/W HA3 ...61 H1
  YEAD UB4 ...94 E2
Braden St MV/WKIL W9 ...101 F3
Bradfield Dr BARK IG11 ...91 G3
Bradfield Rd CAN/RD E16 ...125 K2
  RSLP HA4 ...77 J3
Bradford Cl HAYES BR2 ...200 E3
  SYD SE26 ...163 J6
  UED N18 ...50 D2
Bradford Dr HOR/WEW KT19 ...207 H4
Bradford Rd ACT W3 ...118 C1
  IL IG1 ...72 D5
Bradgate Rd CAT SE6 ...164 E1
Brading Crs WAN E11 ...71 F6
Brading Rd BRXS/STRHM SW2 ...162 A2
  CROY/NA CR0 ...196 A3
Brading Ter SHB W12 ...118 D3
Bradiston Rd MV/WKIL W9 ...100 D2
Bradley Cl HOLWY N7 ...84 E5
Bradley Gdns WEA W13 ...97 H5
Bradley Rd NRWD SE19 ...180 D2
  PEND EN3 ...25 G1
  WDGN N22 ...49 G5
Bradley's Cl IS N1 ...5 J2
Bradley Stone Rd EHAM E6 ...107 K5
Bradman Rw EDGW HA8 ...44 E3
Bradmead VX/NE SW8 ...141 G1
Bradmore Park Rd
  HMSMTH W6 ...118 E3
Bradshaw Cl WIM/MER SW19 ...177 J2
Bradshaws Cl SNWD SE25 ...181 H6
Bradstock Rd EW KT17 ...207 K3
  HOM E9 ...87 F4
Brad St STHWK SE1 ...17 K1
Bradwell Av DAGE RM10 ...74 C1
Bradwell Cl HCH RM12 ...93 K4
  SWFD E18 ...70 D1
Bradwell Ms UED N18 ...36 C6
Bradwell Rd BKHH IG9 ...39 J3
Bradymead EHAM E6 ...108 A5
Brady St WCHPL E1 ...104 D3
Braemar Av ALP/SUD HA0 ...79 J5
  BXLYHN DA7 ...149 K5
  THHTH CR7 ...180 C6
  WAND/EARL SW18 ...159 K3
  WDGN N22 ...48 E4
  WLSDN NW10 ...81 F1
Braemar Gdns BFN/LL DA15 ...167 J3
  CDALE/KGS NW9 ...45 F4
  WWKM BR4 ...199 F5
Braemar Rd BTFD TW8 ...116 E6
  FSTGT E7 ...88 E5
  SEVS/STOTM N15 ...68 A2
  WPK KT4 ...207 K1
Braeside BECK BR3 ...182 D1
Braeside Av WIM/MER SW19 ...177 H4
Braeside Cl PIN HA5 ...42 A3
Braeside Crs BXLYHN DA7 ...150 A5
Braeside Rd
  STRHM/NOR SW16 ...179 H3
Braes St IS N1 ...85 H5
Braesyde Cl BELV DA17 ...129 G4
Brafferton Rd CROY/NA CR0 ...211 J2
Braganza St WALW SE17 ...122 B5
Bragg Rd TEDD TW11 ...173 K3
Braham St WCHPL E1 ...13 K3
Braid Av ACT W3 ...99 G5
Braid Cl FELT TW13 ...154 E4
Braidwood Rd CAT SE6 ...165 G3
Brailsford Cl WIM/MER SW19 ...178 C2
Brailsford Rd
  BRXS/STRHM SW2 ...162 B1
Brainton Av
  EBED/NFELT TW14 ...154 A2
Braintree Av REDBR IG4 ...71 J2
Braintree Rd DAGE RM10 ...74 B1
  RSLP HA4 ...77 F2
Braintree St BETH E2 * ...104 E2
Brair Bank CAR SM5 ...210 A6
Braithwaite Av
  ROMW/RG RM7 ...74 C4
Braithwaite Gdns STAN HA7 ...43 J4
Braithwaite Rd PEND EN3 ...25 J3
Bramall Cl SRTFD E15 ...88 D3
Bramber
  NFNCH/WDSP N12 ...47 J1
  WKENS W14 ...119 J6
Bramble Acres Cl BELMT SM2 ...208 E5
Bramble Banks CAR SM5 ...210 A6
Brambleberry Cl
  WOOL/PLUM SE18 ...127 J5
Bramble Cl BECK BR3 ...199 F2
  CROY/NA CR0 ...213 J2
  SEVS/STOTM N15 ...68 C1
  STAN HA7 ...43 K3
Bramble Cft ERITH DA8 ...129 K4
Brambledown Cl HAYES BR2 ...200 E5
Brambledown Rd CAR SM5 ...210 A5
  SAND/SEL CR2 ...212 A5
Bramble Gdns SHB W12 ...99 H6
Bramble La HPTN TW12 ...172 E2
Brambles Cl ISLW TW7 ...116 C6
The Brambles CHIG IG7 ...54 C2
  SUT SM1 ...194 B4
  WDR/YW UB7 ...112 A5
  WIM/MER SW19 * ...159 J6
Bramblewood Cl CAR SM5 ...194 D5
The Bramblings CHING E4 ...38 B6
Bramcote Av MTCM CR4 ...194 E1
Bramcote Gv
  BERM/RHTH SE16 ...123 K5
Bramcote Rd PUT/ROE SW15 ...138 E5

Bramdean Crs
  LEE/GVPK SE12 ...165 K3
Bramdean Gdns
  LEE/GVPK SE12 ...165 K3
Bramerton Rd BECK BR3 ...182 C6
Bramerton St CHEL SW3 ...120 D6
Bramfield Rd BTSEA SW11 ...160 D1
Bramford Rd
  WAND/EARL SW18 ...140 B5
Bramham Ct NTHWD HA6 * ...40 C1
Bramham Gdns CHSGTN KT9 * ...205 K3
  ECT SW5 ...120 A5
Bramhope La CHARL SE7 ...126 A6
Bramlands Cl BTSEA SW11 ...140 D4
Bramley Cl HYS/HAR UB3 ...96 B6
  ORP BR6 ...201 G5
  RSLP HA4 ...40 C6
  SAND/SEL CR2 ...211 H3
  STHGT/OAK N14 ...22 B6
  WALTH E17 ...51 G5
  WHTN TW2 ...155 H1
Bramley Crs GNTH/NBYPK IG2 ...72 A3
  VX/NE SW8 ...141 J1
Bramley Gdns OXHEY WD19 ...41 G2
Bramley Hl SAND/SEL CR2 ...211 J2
Bramley Hyrst
  SAND/SEL CR2 * ...211 J3
Bramley Ldg ALP/SUD HA0 ...79 K2
Bramley Pde STHGT/OAK N14 ...22 C5
Bramley Pl DART DA1 ...150 D5
Bramley Rd BELMT SM2 ...208 B6
  EA W5 ...116 D3
  NTGHL W11 ...100 B6
  STHGT/OAK N14 ...22 B6
  SUT SM1 ...209 H3
Bramley Wy HSLWW TW4 ...134 E6
  WWKM BR4 ...198 E6
Brampton Cl CLPT E5 ...68 D6
Brampton Gdns CEND/HSY/T N8 ...67 G1
Brampton Gv CDN N4 ...61 G1
  KTN/HRWW/W HA3 ...61 G1
  WBLY HA9 ...62 C5
Brampton La HDN NW4 ...46 A6
Brampton Park Rd WDGN N22 ...49 G6
Brampton Rd BXLYHN DA7 ...128 E6
  CAN/RD E16 ...107 G6
  CDALE/KGS NW9 ...44 C4
  CROY/NA CR0 ...197 G4
  EHAM E6 ...107 H3
  FSBYPK N4 ...67 J2
  OXHEY WD19 ...26 E5
Bramshaw Gdns OXHEY WD19 ...41 H1
Bramshaw Ri NWMAL KT3 ...192 B3
Bramshaw Rd HOM E9 ...87 F4
Bramshill Gdns ARCH N19 ...84 B1
Bramshill Rd WLSDN NW10 ...99 G1
Bramshot Av CHARL SE7 ...126 A6
Bramston Cl BARK/HLT IG6 ...55 F2
Bramston Rd TOOT SW17 ...178 E3
  WLSDN NW10 ...99 J1
Bramwell Cl SUN TW16 ...172 C5
Bramwell Ms IS N1 ...85 F6
Brancaster Dr MLHL NW7 ...45 J3
Brancaster Rd
  GNTH/NBYPK IG2 ...72 E3
  SRTFD E15 ...88 C3
  STRHM/NOR SW16 ...161 K5
Branceth Gdns BKHH IG9 ...38 E4
Branch HI HAMP NW3 ...83 G1
Branch Pl IS N1 ...85 K6
Branch Rd BARK/HLT IG6 ...55 H1
  POP/IOD E14 ...105 G6
Brancker Cl WLGTN SM6 ...210 E5
Brancker Rd
  KTN/HRWW/W HA3 ...43 K6
Brancroft Wy PEND EN3 ...25 G2
Brand Cl FSBYPK N4 ...67 H5
Brandesbury Sq WFD IG8 ...54 A2
Brandlehow Rd
  PUT/ROE SW15 ...139 J5
Brandon Est WALW SE17 ...122 C6
Brandon Ms BARB EC2Y * ...12 E1
Brandon Rd DART DA1 ...171 K2
  HOLWY N7 ...84 E5
  NWDGN UB2 ...115 F3
  SUT SM1 ...209 F2
  WALTH E17 ...70 A1
Brandon St WALW SE17 ...18 D7
Brandram Ms LEW SE13 * ...145 H5
Brandram Rd LEW SE13 ...145 H4
Brandreth Rd EHAM E6 ...107 K5
  TOOT SW17 ...161 G4
The Brandries WLGTN SM6 ...210 D1
Brand St GNWCH SE10 ...145 F1
Brandville Gdns BARK/HLT IG6 ...72 B1
Brandville Rd WDR/YW UB7 ...112 B2
Brandy Wy BELMT SM2 ...208 E5
Brangbourne Rd BMLY BR1 ...183 F1
Brangton Rd LBTH SE11 ...122 A5
Brangwyn Crs
  WIM/MER SW19 ...178 C5
Branksea St FUL/PGN SW6 ...139 H1
Branksome Av UED N18 ...50 B2
Branksome Cl WOT/HER KT12 ...188 C6
Branksome Rd
  BRXS/STRHM SW2 ...141 K6
  WIM/MER SW19 ...177 K4
Branksome Wy
  KTN/HRWW/W HA3 ...62 B3
  NWMAL KT3 ...175 K5
Bransby Rd CHSGTN KT9 ...206 A5
Branscombe Gdns
  WCHMH N21 ...35 G2
Branscombe St LEW SE13 ...144 E4
Bransdale Cl KIL/WHAMP NW6 ...82 E6
Bransell Cl SWLY BR8 ...203 K3
Bransgrove Rd EDGW HA8 ...44 B4
Branston Crs STMC/STPC BR5 ...201 J3
Branstone Rd RCH/KEW TW9 ...137 G2
Brants Wk HNWL W7 ...96 E3
Brantwood Cl WALTH E17 ...51 K6
Brantwood Gdns ENC/FH EN2 ...22 E4
  REDBR IG4 ...71 J2

Brantwood Rd *BXLYHN* DA7 ......149 J3
HNHL SE24 ....211 D6
SAND/SEL CR2 ....212 J6
TOTM N17 ....50 C2
Brantwood Wy
STMC/STPC BR5 ....186 D6
Brasenose Dr *BARN* SW13 ....119 F6
Brasher Cl *GFD/PVL* UB6 ....78 D3
Brassey Cl
EBED/NFELT TW14 * 153 K3
Brassey Rd *KIL/WHAMP* NW6 .....82 D4
Brassey Sq *BTSEA* SW11 ....141 F4
Brassie Av *ACT* W3 ....99 G5
Brasted Cl *BXLYHS* DA6 ....148 E6
SYD SE26 ....163 K6
Brasted Rd *ERITH* DA8 ....150 B1
Brathway Rd
WAND/EARL SW18 ....159 K2
Bratley St *WCHPL* E1 * 104 C3
Braund Av *GFD/PVL* UB6 ....96 B3
Braundton Av *BFN/LL* DA15 ......168 A3
Braunston Dr *YEAD* UB4 ....95 J3
Bravington Av *MV/WKIL* W9 ......100 D3
Bravington Rd *MV/WKIL* W9 ......100 D2
Bravingtons Wk *IS* N1 ....5 F3
Braxfield Rd *BROCKY* SE4 ....144 B5
Braxted Pk
STRHM/NOR SW16 ....180 A2
Brayard's Rd *PECK* SE15...........143 J3
Braybourne Dr *ISLW* TW7 ....136 A1
Braybrooke Gdns *NRWD* SE19 ..181 F3
Braybrook St *SHB* W12 ....99 H4
Brayburne Av *VX/NE* SW8 ....141 H3
Braycourt Av *WOT/HER* KT12 ....188 B4
Bray Crs *BERM/RHTH* SE16 ....124 A2
Braydon Rd *STNW/STAM* N16......68 B5
Bray Dr *CAN/RD* E16 ....106 D6
Brayfield Ter *IS* N1 ....85 G5
Brayford Sq *WCHPL* E1 * 104 E5
Bray Pl *CHEL* SW3 ....120 E5
Bray Rd *MLHL* NW7 ....46 B2
Brayton Gdns *ENC/FH* EN2 ....22 D5
Braywood Rd *ELTH/MOT* SE9 ....147 J5
Breach La *DAGW* RM9 ....110 C2
Bread St *ECAV* EC4V 12 D5
Breakspears Dr
STMC/STPC BR5 ....186 B4
Breakspears Ms *BROCKY* SE4 ...144 D3
Breakspears Rd *BROCKY* SE4 ...144 C4
Bream Cl *TOTM* N17 ....68 D1
Bream Gdns *EHAM* E6 ....108 A2
Breamore Cl *PUT/ROE* SW15 ....158 D3
Breamore Rd *GDMY/SEVK* IG3 ...73 F6
Bream's Bldgs *FLST/FETLN* EC4A ..11 J3
Bream St *BOW* E3 ....87 J5
Breamwater Gdns
RCHPK/HAM TW10 ....156 C5
Brearley Cl *EDGW* HA8 ....44 E3
Breasley Cl *PUT/ROE* SW15 ......138 E5
Breasy Pl *HDN* NW4 * 45 K3
Brecknock Rd *ARCH* N19 ....84 C2
Brecknock Road Est
ARCH N19 * 84 C2
Brecon Cl *MTCM* CR4 ....195 K1
WPK KT4 ....193 F6
Brecon Gn *CDALE/KGS* NW9 * ...63 G3
Brecon Ms *KTTN* NW5 ....84 D4
Brecon Rd *HMSMTH* W6 ....119 H6
PEND EN3 ....24 E5
Brede Cl *EHAM* E6 ....108 A2
Bredgar Rd *ARCH* N19 ....66 C6
Bredhurst Cl *PGE/AN* SE20 ......181 K2
Bredon Rd *CROY/NA* CR0 ....197 G4
ESH/CLAY KT10 ....204 C4
Breer St *FUL/PGN* SW6 ....140 A4
Breezer's HI *WAP* E1W * 104 C6
Brember Rd
RYLN/HDSTN HA2 ....60 C6
Bremer Ms *WALTH* E17 * 69 K1
Bremner Rd *SKENS* SW7 * 120 B3
Brenchley Cl *CHST* BR7 ....185 F4
HAYES BR2 ....199 J2
Brenchley Gdns *FSTH* SE23 ......163 K1
Brenchley Rd
STMC/STPC BR5 ....185 K4
Brenda Rd *TOOT* SW17 ....160 E4
Brende Gdns
E/WMO/HCT KT8 ....189 C1
Brendon Av *WLSDN* NW10 ....81 G2
Brendon Cl *ERITH* DA8 ....150 A2
ESH/CLAY KT10 ....204 C4
HYS/HAR UB3 ....133 F1
Brendon Dr *ESH/CLAY* KT10 .....204 C4
Brendon Gdns
RYLN/HDSTN HA2 ....78 B2
Brendon Rd *BCTR* RM8 ....74 B5
CHST BR7 ....167 J4
Brendon St *MBLAR* W1H 8 D3
Brendon Vis *WCHMH* N21 * 35 J3
Brendon Wy *EN* EN1 ....36 A2
Brenley Cl *MTCM* CR4 ....179 F6
Brenley Gdns *ELTH/MOT* SE9 ...146 C5
Brent Cl *BXLY* DA5 ....169 F3
Brentcot Cl *WEA* W13 ....97 H5
Brent Crs *WLSDN* NW10 ....98 B1
Brent Cross F/O *HDN* NW4 ....64 A3
Brentfield *WLSDN* NW10 ....80 D5
Brentfield Cl *WLSDN* NW10 * 81 F4
Brentfield Gdns *CRICK* NW2 * 64 B4
Brentfield Rd *DART* DA1 ....171 K1
WLSDN NW10 ....81 F4
Brentford End *YEAD* UB4 ....95 H3
Brent Gn *HDN* NW4 ....64 A2
Brentham Wy *EA* W5 ....97 K3
Brenthouse Rd *HACK* E8 ....86 D5
Brenthurst Rd *WLSDN* NW10 ....81 H4
Brentlands Dr *DART* DA1 ....171 K3
Brent La *DART* DA1 ....171 J2
Brent Lea *BTFD* TW8 ....136 D1
Brentmead Cl *HNWL* W7 ....96 E6
Brentmead Gdns
WLSDN NW10 ....98 B1
Brenton St *POP/IOD* E14 ....105 G5

Brent Park Rd
CDALE/KGS NW9 ....63 J5
Brent Pl *BAR* EN5 ....20 E6
Brent River Park Wk *WEA* W13 ...97 H2
Brent Rd *BTFD* TW8 ....116 D6
CAN/RD E16 ....106 E5
NWDGN UB2 ....114 B3
SAND/SEL CR2 ....212 D6
WOOL/PLUM SE18 ....147 G1
Brentside *BTFD* TW8 ....116 D6
Brentside Cl *WEA* W13 ....97 F3
Brent St *HDN* NW4 ....64 B2
Brent Ter *CRICK* NW2 ....64 A6
Brentvale Av *ALP/SUD* HA0 ....80 B6
STHL UB1 ....115 J1
Brent View Rd
CDALE/KGS NW9 ....63 J5
Brent Wy *BTFD* TW8 ....136 E1
FNCH N3 ....46 E2
WBLY HA9 ....80 D4
Brentwick Gdns *BTFD* TW8 ....117 F4
Brentwood Cl *ELTH/MOT* SE9 ...167 H3
Brentwood Rd *ROM* RM1 ....75 J3
WOOL/PLUM SE18 ....147 K1
Brereton Rd *TOTM* N17 ....50 B3
Bressenden Pl *WESTW* SW1E 15 K4
Bressey Av *EN* EN1 ....24 C2
Bressey Gv *SWFD* E18 ....52 D5
Brett Crs *WLSDN* NW10 ....81 F5
Brettell St *WALT* SE17 * 122 E5
Brettenham Av *WALTH* E17 ....51 J4
Brettenham Rd *UED* N18 ....36 C6
WALTH E17 ....51 J5
Brett Gdns *DAGW* RM9 ....92 A5
Brett Pas *HACK* E8 ....86 D3
Brett Rd *BAR* EN5 ....20 A6
HACK E8 ....86 D3
Brett Vls *ACT* W3 * 99 F4
Brewers Fld *RDART* DA2 ....171 F6
Brewer St *RECST* W1B 10 E5
Brewery Cl *ALP/SUD* HA0 ....79 G3
Brewery Rd *HAYES* BR2 ....200 D5
HOLWY N7 ....84 E5
WOOL/PLUM SE18 ....127 K5
Brewery Sq *FSBYE* EC1V * 6 B7
Brewhouse La *WAP* E1W 123 J1
Brewhouse Rd
WOOL/PLUM SE18 ....126 E4
Brewhouse St
PUT/ROE SW15 ....139 H5
Brewhouse Wk
BERM/RHTH SE16 ....124 B1
Brewhouse Yd *FSBYE* EC1V 6 A6
Brewood Rd *BCTR* RM8 ....91 H4
Brewster Gdns *NKENS* W10 ....100 A4
Brewster Rd *LEY* E10 ....69 K5
Brian Cl *HCH* RM12 ....93 K2
Brian Rd *CHDH* RM6 ....73 J2
Briants Cl *PIN* HA5 ....41 J4
Briant Av *STRHM/NOR* SW16 .....180 A3
Briant St *NWCR* SE14 ....144 A2
Briar Av *STRHM/NOR* SW16 ......180 A3
Briarbank Rd *WEA* W13 ....97 G5
Briar Cl *BKHH* IG9 ....39 H4
EFNCH N2 ....47 G5
HPTN TW12 ....172 E1
ISLW TW7 ....136 A6
PLMGR N13 ....35 J5
Briar Crs *NTHLT* UB5 ....78 B4
Briardale Gdns *CRICK* NW2 ....82 E1
Briarfield Av *EFNCH* N2 ....47 F6
Briarfield Cl *BXLYHN* DA7 ....149 H5
Briar Gdns *HAYES* BR2 ....199 J5
Briar La *CAR* SM5 ....210 A6
CROY/NA CR0 ....213 K2
Briar Rd *BXLY* DA5 ....170 A5
CRICK NW2 ....82 A2
KTN/HRWW/W HA3 ....42 E4
STRHM/NOR SW16 ....179 K6
WHTN TW2 ....155 K3
Briars Wy *ORP* BR6 ....217 F3
Briar Wk *EDGW* HA8 ....44 E3
NKENS W10 * 100 C3
PUT/ROE SW15 ....138 E5
Briar Wy *WDR/YW* UB7 ....112 D2
Briarwood Cl
CDALE/KGS NW9 ....62 E3
FELT TW13 ....153 H5
Briarwood Ct *WPK* KT4 * 192 D5
Briarwood Dr *NTHWD* HA6 ....40 E5
Briarwood Rd *CLAP* SW4 ....141 J6
EW KT17 ....207 J4
Briary Cl *EDGW* HA8 ....44 D5
HAMP NW3 * 83 J5
Briary Ct *SCUP* DA14 ....186 C1
Briary Gdns *BMLY* BR1 ....184 A1
Briary La *ED* N9 ....36 A5
Brickbarn Cl *WBPTN* SW10 * 140 B1
Brick Ct *EMB* EC4Y * 11 J4
Brickett Cl *RSLP* HA4 ....58 A2
Brick Farm Cl *RCH/KEW* TW9 ...137 J2
Brickfield Cl *BTFD* TW8 ....136 D1
Brickfield Cottages
WOOL/PLUM SE18 ....148 A1
Brickfield Farm Gdns
ORP BR6 ....216 C2
Brickfield La *BAR* EN5 ....31 H1
Brickfield Rd *BOW* E3 ....105 K3
THHTH CR7 ....180 C4
WIM/MER SW19 ....160 A6
Brickfields *RYLN/HDSTN* HA2 ......60 C6
Brickfields Wy *WDR/YW* UB7 .....112 C3
Brickfield Vis *SUT* SM1 * 209 J1
Brick La *BETH* E2 ....7 K5
Brick Kiln Cl *BUSH* WD23 ....28 E3
Brick La *BETH* E2 * 7 K5
EN EN1 ....24 D3
STAN HA7 ....43 K3
Brickwall La *RSLP* HA4 ....58 C5
Brickwood Cl *SYD* SE26 ....163 J5
Brickwood Rd *CROY/NA* CR0 .....197 F6
Brideale Cl *PECK* SE15 * 123 G6
Bride Cl *BLKFR* EC4V * 12 A4

Bride La *EMB* EC4Y 12 A4
Bridel Ms *FSBYE* EC1V 6 A3
Bridewain St *STHWK* SE1 ....19 J4
Bridewell Pl *BLKFR* EC4V 12 A4
WAP E1W 123 J1
Bridford Ms *REGST* W1B 9 K1
Bridge Av *HMSMTH* W6 ....119 F5
HNWL W7 ....96 D4
NKENS W10 ....100 B5
ROM RM1 ....75 G3
Bridge Dr *PLMGR* N13 ....35 F6
Bridge End *WALTH* E17 ....52 A4
Bridgefield Rd *SUT* SM1 ....208 E4
Bridge Gdns *E/WMO/HCT* KT8 ...189 J1
Bridge Ga *WCHMH* N21 ....35 J2
Bridge House Quay
POP/IOD E14 ....125 F1
Bridgeland Rd *CAN/RD* E16 ....106 E6
Bridgelands Cl *BECK* BR3 ....182 C5
Bridge La *BTSEA* SW11 ....140 D2
Bridge La *BTSEA* SW11 ....140 D2
GLDGN NW11 ....64 D3
Bridgeman Rd *IS* N1 ....85 F5
TEDD TW11 ....174 B2
Bridgeman St *STJWD* NW8 ....2 C3
Bridge Mdw *NWCR* SE14 ....124 A6
Bridgen Rd *EN* EN1 ....24 B2
Bridgen Rd *BXLY* DA5 ....169 F2
Bridge Pde
STRHM/NOR SW16 * 179 K1
WCHMH N21 * 35 J2
Bridge Pl *CROY/NA* CR0 ....196 E5
PIM SW1V 15 K6
Bridgepoint Pl *HGT* N6 ....66 C5
Bridgeport Pl *WAP* E1W * 123 H1
Bridge Rd *BECK* BR3 ....182 C3
BXLYHN DA7 ....149 F4
CHSGTN KT9 ....206 A3
E/WMO/HCT KT8 ....189 K1
ED N9 ....36 C5
EHAM E6 ....89 K6
ERITH DA8 ....150 D2
HSLW TW3 ....135 J4
NWDGN UB2 ....114 E2
RAIN RM13 ....111 J3
SRTFD E15 ....88 B6
STMC/STPC BR5 ....186 C4
SUT SM1 ....209 F4
TWK TW1 ....156 C1
WALTH E17 ....69 H4
WBLY HA9 ....80 C1
WEA W13 ....98 B5
WLSDN NW10 ....81 F5
Bridge Rw *CROY/NA* CR0 * 196 E5
Bridge Ter *LEW* SE13 * 145 G5
SRTFD E15 ....88 B5
The Bridge E4 *KTN/HRWW/W HA3* ...117 C1
Bridgetown Cl *NRWD* SE19 ....181 F1
Bridgeview *HMSMTH* W6 ....119 F5
Bridge Vls *WIM/MER* SW19 * 177 K1
Bridgewater Cl *CHST* BR7 ....185 K6
Bridgewater Gdns *EDGW* HA8 .....44 B5
Bridgewater Rd *ALP/SUD* HA0 ....79 J5
RSLP HA4 ....77 G5
Bridgewater Sq *BARB* EC2Y * 12 C1
Bridgewater St *BARB* EC2Y * 12 C1
Bridgewater Wy *BUSH* WD23 ....28 B1
Bridgeway *ALP/SUD* HA0 ....80 A5
BARK IG11 ....90 E6
Bridge Wy *GLDGN* NW11 ....64 D2
WHTN TW2 ....155 H2
Bridgeway St *CAMTN* NW1 ....4 B3
Bridgewood Cl *PGE/AN* SE20 ....181 J3
Bridgewood Rd
STRHM/NOR SW16 ....179 J3
WPK KT4 ....207 J2
Bridgford St
WAND/EARL SW18 ....160 B5
Bridgman Rd *CHSWK* W4 ....117 K3
Bridgwater Rd *RSLP* HA4 ....76 C2
Bridle Cl *HOR/WEW* KT19 ....206 E2
KUT/HW KT1 ....190 E1
Bridle La *SOHO/CST* W1F 10 B5
TWK TW1 ....156 C1
Bridle Pth *CROY/NA* CR0 ....210 E1
The Bridle Pth *WFD* IG8 ....52 C5
Bridlepath Wy
EBED/NFELT TW14 ....153 H2
Bridle Rd *CROY/NA* CR0 ....198 D6
ESH/CLAY KT10 ....205 H4
PIN HA5 ....59 G3
Bridle Wy *CROY/NA* CR0 ....213 J5
ORP BR6 ....216 C2
The Bridle Wy *WLGTN* SM6 .....210 C2
Bridlington Rd *ED* N9 ....36 D2
OXHEY WD19 ....27 H2
Bridport Av *ROMW/RG* RM7 ....74 D3
Bridport Pl *IS* N1 ....7 F2
Bridport Rd *NTHLT* UB5 ....78 B6
THHTH CR7 ....180 B6
UED N18 ....50 A1
Bridstow Pl *BAY/PAD* W2 ....100 E5
Brief St *CMBW* SE5 ....142 C2
Brierley *CROY/NA* CR0 ....213 K4
Brierley Av *ED* N9 ....36 E3
Brierley Cl *SNWD* SE25 ....197 H1
Brierley Rd *BAL* SW12 ....161 H4
LEY E10 ....87 J3
Brierly Gdns *BETH* E2 * 104 E1
Brigade Cl *RYLN/HDSTN* HA2 ......60 D6
Brigade St *BKHTH/KID* SE3 * 145 J3
Brigadier Av *ENC/FH* EN2 ....23 J2
Brigadier Hl *ENC/FH* EN2 ....23 J1
Briggeford Cl *CLPT* E5 ....68 C6
Briggs Cl *MTCM* CR4 ....179 G4
Bright Cl *BELV* DA17 ....128 E4

Brightfield Rd *LEW* SE13 ....145 H6
Brightling Rd *BROCKY* SE4 ....164 C1
Brightlingsea Pl *POP/IOD* E14 ...105 H6
Brightman Rd
WAND/EARL SW18 ....160 C3
Brighton Av *WALTH* E17 ....69 H2
Brighton Dr *NTHLT* UB5 * 78 A4
Brighton Rd *BELMT* SM2 ....209 G5
EFNCH N2 ....47 G5
EHAM E6 ....108 A2
SAND/SEL CR2 ....211 J6
STNW/STAM N16 ....86 A2
SURB KT6 ....190 D3
Brighton Ter *BRXN/ST* SW9 ......142 A5
Brights Av *RAIN* RM13 ....111 K3
Brightside Rd *LEW* SE13 ....165 G1
The Brightside *PEND* EN3 ....25 F2
Bright St *POP/IOD* E14 ....105 K5
Brightwell Cl *CROY/NA* CR0 ......196 B5
Brightwell Crs *TOOT* SW17 ....178 E1
Brig Ms *DEPT* SE8 ....124 D6
Brigstock Rd *BELV* DA17 ....129 J4
THHTH CR7 ....196 D1
Brill Pl *CAMTN* NW1 ....4 D3
Brim Hl *EFNCH* N2 ....65 G1
Brimpsfield Cl *ABYW* SE2 ....128 C3
Brimsdown Av *PEND* EN3 ....25 G2
Brimstone Cl *ORP* BR6 ....217 J5
Brindle Ga *BFN/LL* DA15 ....167 K3
Brindley Cl *BXLYHN* DA7 ....149 H4
GFD/PVL UB6 ....96 B6
Brindley St *NWCR* SE14 ....144 C2
Brindley Wy *BMLY* BR1 ....183 K1
STHL UB1 ....115 G1
Brindwood Rd *CHING* E4 ....37 J5
Brinkburn Cl *ABYW* SE2 ....128 B4
EDGW HA8 ....44 C6
Brinkburn Gdns *EDGW* HA8 ....44 C6
Brinkley Rd *WPK* KT4 ....192 E6
Brinklow Crs
WOOL/PLUM SE18 ....147 G1
Brinkworth Rd *CLAY* IG5 ....53 J6
Brinkworth Wy *HOM* E9 ....87 H4
Brinsdale Rd *HDN* NW4 ....46 B6
Brinsley Rd
KTN/HRWW/W HA3 ....42 D5
Brinsley St *WCHPL* E1 * 104 D5
Brinsworth Cl *WHTN* TW2 ....155 J3
Brinton Wk *STHWK* SE1 ....18 A1
Brion Pl *POP/IOD* E14 ....106 A4
Brisbane Av *WIM/MER* SW19 .....178 A4
Brisbane Rd *IL* IG1 ....72 C4
LEY E10 ....69 K6
Brisbane St *CMBW* SE5 ....142 E1
Briscoe Cl *WAN* E11 ....70 D6
Briscoe Rd *WIM/MER* SW19 ......178 C2
Briset Rd *ELTH/MOT* SE9 ....146 C4
Briset St *FARR* EC1M 12 A1
Briset Wy *HOLWY* N7 ....67 K2
Bristol Cl *STWL/WRAY* TW19 ....152 B1
WLGTN SM6 ....210 E6
Bristol Gdns *MV/WKIL* W9 ....101 F3
Bristol Ms *MV/WKIL* W9 ....101 F3
Bristol Park Rd *WALTH* E17 * 69 G1
Bristol Rd *EHAM* E6 ....90 A1
GFD/PVL UB6 ....78 B6
MRDN SM4 ....194 B2
Briston Gv *CEND/HSY/T* N8 ....66 E3
Bristow Rd *BXLYHN* DA7 ....149 F2
CROY/NA CR0 ....210 E2
HSLW TW3 ....135 G4
NRWD SE19 ....181 F1
Britannia Cl *CLAP* SW4 ....141 J5
ERITH DA8 ....130 C6
NTHLT UB5 ....95 H2
Britannia Ga *CAN/RD* E16 ....125 K1
Britannia La *WHTN* TW2 ....155 H2
Britannia Rd *BRYLDS* KT5 ....191 G5
FUL/PGN SW6 ....140 A1
IL IG1 ....90 B1
NFNCH/WDSP N12 ....33 G5
POP/IOD E14 ....124 D4
Britannia Rw *IS* N1 ....85 H6
Britannia St *FSBYW* WC1X 5 G4
Britannia Wy *FUL/PGN* SW6 ......140 A1
Britannia Wk *IS* N1 ....7 F4
British Est *BOW* E3 ....105 H2
British Gv *CHSWK* W4 ....118 C5
British Grove Pas
CHSWK W4 ....118 C5
British Legion Rd *CHING* E4 ....38 D4
British St *BOW* E3 ....105 H2
Brittain Rd *BCTR* RM8 ....92 A1
Britten Cl *BORE* WD6 ....29 K1
GLDGN NW11 ....65 F5
Brittenden Pde *ORP* BR6 * 217 F4
Britten Dr *STHL* UB1 ....96 A5
Britten St *CHEL* SW3 ....120 D5
Britton St *FARR* EC1M 6 A7
Brixham Crs *RSLP* HA4 ....58 D6
Brixham Gdns *GDMY/SEVK* IG3 ...90 E3
Brixham Rd *WELL* DA16 ....148 E2
Brixham St *CAN/RD* E16 ....126 E1
Brixton HI *BRXS/STRHM* SW2 ...162 A1
Brixton Hill Pl
BRXS/STRHM SW2 * 161 K2
Brixton Ov *BRXN/ST* SW9 ....142 B5
Brixton Rd *BRXN/ST* SW9 ....142 B5
LBTH SE11 ....122 B6
Brixton Station Rd
BRXN/ST SW9 ....142 B4
Brixton Water La
BRXS/STRHM SW2 ....142 B6

Broadcroft Rd
STMC/STPC BR5 ....201 J4
Broadeaves Cl *SAND/SEL* CR2 ...212 A3
Broadfield Cl *CRICK* NW2 ....82 A1
ROM RM1 ....75 G3
Broadfield Ct *BUSH* WD23 ....28 E4
Broadfield La *CAMTN* NW1 ....84 E5
Broadfield Pde *EDGW* HA8 * 30 D5
Broadfield Rd *CAT* SE6 ....165 H5
Broadfields *E/WMO/HCT* KT8 ....189 J3
PIN HA5 ....42 B5
Broadfields Av *EDGW* HA8 ....30 C2
WCHMH N21 ....35 G2
Broadfields Hts *EDGW* HA8 ....30 D2
Broadfields La *OXHEY* WD19 ....27 F3
Broadfield Sq *EN* EN1 ....24 D3
Broadfields Wy *WLSDN* NW10 .....81 H4
Broadgates Av *EBAR* EN4 ....21 F2
Broadgates Rd
WAND/EARL SW18 ....160 C3
Broad Green Av
CROY/NA CR0 ....196 C4
Broadhead Strd
CDALE/KGS NW9 ....45 H5
Broadheath Dr *CHST* BR7 ....184 E1
Broadhinton Rd *CLAP* SW4 ....141 G4
Broadhurst Av *EDGW* HA8 ....30 D5
GDMY/SEVK IG3 ....91 F2
Broadhurst Cl
KIL/WHAMP NW6 ....83 G4
RSLP HA4 * 59 G6
Broadhurst Gdns
KIL/WHAMP NW6 ....83 G4
RSLP HA4 ....59 G6
Broadlands *FELT* TW13 ....154 E5
Broadlands Av *PEND* EN3 ....24 D4
STRHM/NOR SW16 ....161 K4
PEND EN3 ....24 D4
Broadlands Cl *HGT* N6 ....66 A5
PEND EN3 ....24 D4
Broadlands Rd *BMLY* BR1 ....166 E6
HGT N6 ....65 K4
Broadlands Wy *NWMAL* KT3 ......192 C3
Broad La *HPTN* TW12 ....172 E3
RDART DA2 ....170 E6
SEVS/STOTM N15 ....68 C1
Broad Lawn *ELTH/MOT* SE9 .....167 F4
Broadlawns Ct
KTN/HRWW/W HA3 ....43 F4
Broadley St *STJWD* NW8 ....8 C1
Broadmead *CAT* SE6 ....164 D5
Broadmead Av *WPK* KT4 ....192 D4
Broadmead Cl *HPTN* TW12 ....173 F2
PIN HA5 * 41 J3
Broad Oak *WFD* IG8 ....53 F1
YEAD UB4 ....95 J3
Broad Oak Cl *STMC/STPC* BR5 ...186 B5
Broadoak Rd *ERITH* DA8 ....150 A1
Broad Oaks *SURB* KT6 ....191 J5
Broad Oaks Wy *HAYES* BR2 ....199 J2
Broadstone Pl *MHST* W1U 9 G2
Broadstone Rd *HCH* RM12 ....93 K4
Broad St *DAGE* RM10 ....92 C5
TEDD TW11 ....174 A2
Broad Street Av *LVPST* EC2M 13 G2
Broad Street Pl *LVPST* EC2M 13 F2
Broadview *CDALE/KGS* NW9 ....62 C3
Broadview Rd
STRHM/NOR SW16 ....179 J3
Broad Wk *BKHTH/KID* SE3 ....146 B3
HEST TW5 ....134 C2
ORP BR6 ....217 K1
RCH/KEW TW9 ....137 G1
WCHMH N21 ....35 F1
Broadwalk La *GLDGN* NW11 ....64 D4
The Broad Wk *KENS* W8 ....120 B2
NTHWD HA6 ....40 A5
Broadwall *STHWK* SE1 ....11 K7
Broadwater Gdns *ORP* BR6 ....216 C2
Broadwater Rd *TOOT* SW17 ......160 D6
TOTM N17 ....50 B5
WOOL/PLUM SE18 ....127 J3
Broadway *BARK* IG11 ....90 C6
BEXH DA6 ....149 F5
HCH RM12 ....75 H5
HNWL W7 ....115 K1
RAIN RM13 ....111 J3
SRTFD E15 ....88 B5
STJSPK SW1H 16 C4
SUT SM1 ....209 G2
Broadway Av *CROY/NA* CR0 ......196 E2
TWK TW1 ....156 C1
Broadway Cl *WFD* IG8 ....53 F2
Broadway Ct
WIM/MER SW19 * 177 K2
Broadway Gdns *MTCM* CR4 ....194 D1
Broadway Market *HACK* E8 ....86 D6
Broadway Market Ms
HACK E8 * 86 C6
Broadway Ms
STNW/STAM N16 ....68 B4
Broadway Pde *CHING* E4 * 52 A2
HYS/HAR UB3 * 113 J2
RYLN/HDSTN HA2 * 60 D6
WDR/YW UB7 * 112 B2
The Broadway *ACT* W3 * 117 H2
BCTR RM8 ....74 B6
CDALE/KGS NW9 ....63 H3
CEND/HSY/T N8 ....208 C4
CHEAM SM3 ....208 C4
EA W5 ....97 K6
ED N9 ....36 C5
FBAR/BDGN N11 * 47 K1
HCH RM12 ....93 K2
KTN/HRWW/W HA3 ....42 E5
MLHL NW7 ....45 H3
PIN HA5 ....41 J3
PLSTW E13 * 106 E1
RYLN/HDSTN HA2 * 60 D6
STAN HA7 ....43 J1

THDIT KT7 ....189 K5
WFD IG8 ....53 F2
WIM/MER SW19 ....177 J2

Broadwell Pde
KIL/WHAMP NW6 * 83 C4
Broadwick St SOHO/CST W1F 10 B4
Broadwood Av RSLP HA4 ....58 D3
Brockenhurst Ter
WKENS W14 * 119 J4
Broad Yd FARR EC1M 6 A7
Brocas Cl HAMP NW3 ....83 J5
Brockdene Dr HAYES BR2 ....215 H2
Brockdish Av BARK IG11.........91 F3
Brockenhurst
E/WMO/HCT KT8 ....45 J7
Brockenhurst Av WPK KT4 ....192 B5
Brockenhurst Gdns IL IG1 .....90 C3
MLHL NW7 ....45 G2
Brockenhurst Rd
CROY/NA CRO 197 J4
Brockenhurst Wy
STRHM/NOR SW16 ....179 J5
Brocket Wy CHIG IG7 ....54 E1
Brockham Cl
WIM/MER SW19 ....177 J1
Brockham Crs CROY/NA CRO....214 B5
Brockham Dr
BRXS/STRHM SW2 ....162 A2
GNTH/NBYPK IG2 ....72 C3
Brockhurst Cl STAN HA7 ....43 F2
Brockill Crs BROCKY SE4 ......144 B5
Brocklebank Rd CHARL SE7....126 A4
WAND/EARL SW18 ....160 D2
Brocklehurst St NWCR SE14...144 A1
Brocklesby Rd SNWD SE25 ....197 J1
Brockley Av EDGW HA8 ....30 E3
Brockley Cl STAN HA7 ....30 A6
Brockley Crs CRW RM5 ....56 E3
Brockley Cross BROCKY SE4...144 B4
Brockley Gv BROCKY SE4 ......144 C6
Brockley Hall Rd BROCKY SE4....164 B1
Brockley Hl STAN HA7 ....29 J4
Brockley Ms BROCKY SE4 ......144 B6
Brockley Pk FSTH SE23 ....164 B1
Brockley Ri FSTH SE23 ....164 B1
Brockley Rd BROCKY SE4 ......164 B1
Brockleyside STAN HA7 * 30 A6
Brockley Vw FSTH SE23 ....164 B2
Brockley Wy FSTH SE23 ....144 A6
Brockman Ri BMLY BR1 ....165 G6
Brock Pl BOW E3 ....105 K3
Brock Rd PLSTW E13 ....107 F4
Brocks Dr CHEAM SM3 ....208 C1
Brockshot Cl BTFD TW8 ....116 E6
Brock St PECK SE15 * 143 K4
Brockton Cl ROM RM1 ....75 H1
Brockway Cl WAN E11 ....70 C6
Brockwell Av BECK BR3 ....198 E2
Brockwell Cl STMC/STPC BR5....202 A2
Brockwell Park Gdns
HNHL SE24 ....162 C2
Brodia Rd STNW/STAM N16.....86 A1
Brodie Av CHING E4 ....38 A1
Brodie Rd CHING E4 ....38 A1
ENC/FH EN2 ....23 J1
Brodie St STHWK SE1 ....123 G5
Brodlove La WAP E1W 105 F6
Brodrick Gv ABYW SE2 ....128 C4
Brodrick Rd TOOT SW17 ....160 D4
Brograve Gdns BECK BR3 ......182 E5
Broke Farm Dr ORP BR6 ....217 J3
Broken Whf BLKFR EC4V 12 C5
Brokesley St BOW E3 ....105 H3
Broke Wk HACK E8 * 86 C6
Bromar Rd CMBW SE5 ....143 F4
Bromborough Gn
OXHEY WD19 ....41 G1
Bromefield STAN HA7 ....43 K3
Bromehead St WCHPL E1 ......104 E5
Brome House
WOOL/PLUM SE18 ....146 D1
Bromell's Rd CLAP SW4 ....141 H5
Brome Rd ELTH/MOT SE9 ......146 E4
Bromfelde Rd CLAP SW4 ....141 J4
Bromfield St IS N1 ....5 K2
Bromhall Rd DAGW RM9 ....91 H4
Bromhedge ELTH/MOT SE9....166 E5
Bromholm Rd ABYW SE2 ....128 C3
Bromley Av BMLY BR1 ....183 H1
Bromley Common
HAYES BR2 ....200 D4
Bromley Crs HAYES BR2 ....183 J6
RSLP HA4 ....76 D2
Bromley Gdns HAYES BR2 .....183 J5
Bromley Hall Rd POP/IOD E14....106 A4
Bromley High St BOW E3 ....106 A2
Bromley Hl BMLY BR1 ....183 H3
Bromley La CHST BR7 ....185 H5
Bromley Pk BECK BR3 * 182 E4
BECK BR3 ....183 F5
CAT SE6 ....184 E3
CHST BR7 ....185 H5
LEY E10 ....69 K5
TOTM N17 ....50 B4
WALTH E17 ....51 J6
Bromley St WCHPL E1 ....105 G4
Brompton Ar MYFR/SW1X *.....14 E4
Brompton Cl HSLWW TW4 ......134 E5
Brompton Dr ERITH DA8 ....150 E1
Brompton Gv EFNCH N2 ....65 J1
Brompton Park Crs
FUL/PGN SW6 ....120 A6
Brompton Pl CHEL SW3 ....14 C6
Brompton Rd CHEL SW3 ....14 C6
Brompton Sq CHEL SW3 ....14 C6
Brompton Ter
WOOL/PLUM SE18 * 147 F2
Bromwich Av HGT N6 ....66 A6
Bromyard Av ACT W3 ....118 B1
Brondesbury Ms
KIL/WHAMP NW6 * 82 E5
Brondesbury Pk CRICK NW2....82 A5

Brondesbury Rd
KIL/WHAMP NW6 ....100 D1
Brondesbury Vls
KIL/WHAMP NW6 ....100 D1
Bronhill Ter TOTM N17 * 50 C4
Bronsart Rd FUL/PGN SW6.....139 H1
Bronson Rd RYNPK SW20.......177 G5
Bronte Cl ERITH DA8 ....150 B1
FSTGT E7 ....88 E2
GNTH/NBYPK IG2 ....72 A2
Bronte Gv DART DA1 ....151 J5
Bronti Cl WALW SE17 ....122 D5
Bronze Age Wy BELV DA17....129 K3
Bronze St DEPT SE8 ....144 D1
Brook Av DAGE RM10 ....92 D5
EDGW HA8 ....44 D2
WBLY HA9 ....80 C1
Brookbank Av HNWL W7 ....96 D4
Brookbank Rd LEW SE13 ....144 E4
Brook Cl ACT W3 ....117 H1
GPK RM2 ....207 G6
HOR/WEW KT19 ....207 G6
RSLP HA4 ....58 C4
RYNPK SW20 ....176 E6
STWL/WRAY TW19 ....152 C2
TOOT SW17 ....161 F4
Brook Ct BECK BR3 * 182 C4
Brook Crs CHING E4 ....37 J6
ED N9 ....36 D6
Brookdale FBAR/BDGN N11.....34 C6
Brookdale Rd BXLY DA5 ....169 F1
CAT SE6 ....164 E2
LEY E10 ....51 J6
Brookdene Av OXHEY WD19....41 F1
Brookdene Dr NTHWD HA6.....40 D3
Brookdene Rd
WOOL/PLUM SE18 ....127 K4
Brook Dr HRW HA1 ....60 E3
RSLP HA4 ....58 C3
RYLN/HDSTN HA2 ....60 C1
STHWK SE1 ....17 K5
Brooke Av RYLN/HDSTN HA2....78 C1
Brooke Cl BUSH WD23 ....28 C2
Brookehowse Rd CAT SE6 .....164 E5
Brookend Rd BFN/LL DA15 ....167 K3
Brooke Rd CLPT E5 ....86 C1
WALTH E17 ....70 A1
Brooker Rd WAB EN9 ....9 J5
Brooke's Ct HCIRC EC1N 11 J2
Brooke Wy BUSH WD23 ....28 C2
Brookfield Av EA W5 ....97 K3
MLHL NW7 ....45 K2
SUT SM1 ....209 J1
WALTH E17 ....51 K6
Brookfield Cl MLHL NW7 ....45 K2
Brookfield Crs
KTN/HRWW/W HA3 ....62 A2
MLHL NW7 ....45 K2
Brookfield Gdns
ESH/CLAY KT10 ....205 F4
Brookfield Pk KTTN NW5 ....84 B1
Brookfield Pth CHING E4 ....52 B2
Brookfield Rd CHSWK W4 ......118 A2
ED N9 ....36 C5
HOM E9 ....87 G4
Brookfields PEND EN3 ....25 F5
Brookfields Av MTCM CR4 .....194 D2
Brook Gdns BARN SW13 ....138 C4
CHING E4 ....37 K6
KUTN/CMB KT2 ....175 K4
Brook Ga BAY/PAD W2 ....9 F6
Brook Gn HMSMTH W6 ....119 F3
Brookhill Cl EBAR EN4 ....21 J6
Brook Hill Cl
WOOL/PLUM SE18 ....127 G5
Brookhill Rd
WOOL/PLUM SE18 ....127 G5
Brookhouse Gdns CHING E4....38 C6
Brooking Cl BCTR RM8 ....91 J1
Brooking Rd FSTGT E7 ....88 E3
Brookland Garth GLDGN NW11....64 E1
Brookland Hl GLDGN NW11 .....64 E1
Brookland Ri GLDGN NW11 .....64 E1
Brooklands DART DA1 ....171 H5
Brooklands Ap ROM RM1 ....75 F1
Brooklands Av BFN/LL DA15....167 J4
WAND/EARL SW18 ....160 A4
Brooklands Cl
KIL/WHAMP NW6 * 82 D5
WCHMN N21 ....23 K6
Brooklands Dr GFD/PVL UB6....79 J6
Brooklands La ROMW/RG RM7....75 F1
Brooklands Pk
BKHTH/KID SE3 ....145 K4
Brooklands Pl HPTN TW12 .....173 G1
The Brooklands ISLW TW7 *....135 J2
Brook La BKHTH/KID SE3 ....146 A3
BMLY BR1 ....183 K2
Brook La North BTFD TW8.......116 E5
Brooklea Cl CDALE/KGS NW9....45 G4
Brooklyn Av SNWD SE25 ....197 J1
Brooklyn Cl CAR SM5 ....194 D6
Brooklyn Gv SNWD SE25 ......197 J1
Brooklyn Rd BMLY BR2 ....200 C2
SNWD SE25 ....197 J1
Brooklyn Wy WDR/YW UB7....112 A3
Brook Md HOR/WEW KT19 ....207 G4
Brookmead MTCM CR4 ....195 H3
Brook Meadow
NFNCH/WDSP N12 ....33 F6
Brook Meadow Cl WFD IG8.....52 C2
Brookmead Rd CROY/NA CRO....195 H3
Brook Ms North BAY/PAD W2....101 G6
Brookmill Cl OXHEY WD19 * 27 F2
Brook Park Cl WCHMN N21 .....35 H1
Brook Pl BAR EN5 ....20 E6
Brook Rd BKHH IG9 ....38 E4
CEND/HSY/T N8 ....66 E1
CRICK NW2 ....63 J6

GNTH/NBYPK IG2 ....72 E3
GPK RM2 ....57 H5
SURB KT6 ....191 F6
THHTH CR7 ....196 D1
TWK TW1 ....156 B1
WDGN N22 ....49 F5
Brook Rd South BTFD TW8 ....116 E6
Brooks Av EHAM E6 ....107 K3
Brooksbank St HOM E9 * 87 F4
Brooksby Ms IS N1 ....85 G5
Brooksby St IS N1 ....85 G5
Brooksby's Wk HOM E9 ....87 F3
Brookscroft CROY/NA CRO *....213 H6
Brookscroft Rd WALTH E17 .....51 K4
Brookshill KTN/HRWW/W HA3....42 E2
Brookshill Av
KTN/HRWW/W HA3 ....42 D1
Brookshill Dr
KTN/HRWW/W HA3 ....42 D1
Brookside BARK/HLT IG6 ....54 C2
CAR SM5 ....210 A3
EBAR EN4 ....33 J1
ORP BR6 ....202 A4
WCHMN N21 ....35 F1
Brookside Cl BAR EN5 ....32 B1
FELT TW13 ....153 K5
KTN/HRWW/W HA3 ....61 K2
RSLP HA4 ....77 J2
Brookside Crs WPK KT4 ....192 D5
Brookside Rd ARCH N19 ....66 C6
ED N9 ....36 D6
GLDGN NW11 ....64 C5
OXHEY WD19 ....27 F2
YEAD UB4 ....95 G6
Brookside South EBAR EN4 ....34 A2
Brookside Wy CROY/NA CRO....198 A3
Brooks La CHSWK W4 ....117 H6
Brook's Ms MYFR/PKLN W1K....9 K5
Brooks Rd CHSWK W4 ....117 H6
PLSTW E13 ....88 E6
Brook St BAY/PAD W2 ....9 J5
BELV DA17 ....129 J5
ERITH DA8 ....149 K1
KUT/HW KT1 ....175 F5
SEVS/STOTM N15 ....67 J2
TOTM N17 ....50 C5
Brookvale Av
KIL/WHAMP NW6 ....82 C6
Brookview Rd
STRHM/NOR SW16 ....179 H1
Brookville Rd FUL/PGN SW6....139 J1
Brook Wk EDGW HA8 ....45 F1
EFNCH N2 * 47 H4
Brook Water La HDN NW4 * 64 B2
Brookway BKHTH/KID SE3 .....145 K4
RAIN RM13 ....111 K4
Brookwood Av BARN SW13 ....138 C4
Brookwood Cl HAYES BR2 .....199 J5
Brookwood Rd HSLW TW3 .....135 G3
WAND/EARL SW18 ....159 J3
Broom Av STMC/STPC BR5 ....186 C5
Broom Cl ESH/CLAY KT10 .....204 B3
HAYES BR2 ....200 D3
TEDD TW11 ....174 E3
Broomcroft Av NTHLT UB5 ....95 G2
Broome Rd HPTN TW12 ....172 E4
Broome Wy CMBW SE5 ....142 E1
Broomfield WALTH E17 ....69 H4
Broomfield Av LOU IG10 ....39 K1
PLMGR N13 ....35 F6
Broomfield Cl CRW RM5 ....56 E2
Broomfield La PLMGR N13 ......34 E6
Broomfield Pl WEA W13 ....116 C1
Broomfield Rd BECK BR3 ......198 B1
BRYLDS KT5 ....191 J4
BXLYHS DA6 ....149 H6
DEN EN3 * 24 D6
PLMGR N13 ....34 E6
RCH/KEW TW9 ....137 G2
TEDD TW11 ....174 D1
WEA W13 ....116 C1
Broomfields ESH/CLAY KT10....204 C3
Broomfield St POP/IOD E14 ....105 J4
Broom Gdns CROY/NA CRO....213 J1
Broomgrove Rd
BRXN/ST SW9 ....142 A3
Broomhall Rd SAND/SEL CR2....211 K6
Broomhill Rd BXLYHS DA6 ....149 H6
Broomhill Rd DART DA1 ....170 E1
GDMY/SEVK IG3 ....73 G6
ORP BR6 ....202 B4
WAND/EARL SW18 ....139 K6
WFD IG8 ....52 E2
Broomhouse La
FUL/PGN SW6 ....139 K3
Broomhouse Rd
FUL/PGN SW6 ....139 K3
Broomloan La SUT SM1 ....194 E6
Broom Lock TEDD TW11 ....174 D1
Broom Md BXLYHS DA6 ....169 H1
Broom Pk KUT/HW KT1 ....174 E5
Broom Rd CROY/NA CRO 213 J1
TEDD TW11 ....174 D1
Broomsleigh St
KIL/WHAMP NW6 * 82 E3
Broom Water TEDD TW11 ....174 D1
Broom Water West
TEDD TW11 ....174 D1
Broomwood Cl BXLY DA5 ......170 A4
CROY/NA CRO 198 A2
Broomwood Rd BTSEA SW11....160 E1
STMC/STPC BR5 ....186 C5
Broseley Gv SYD SE26 ....182 B1
Broster Gdns SNWD SE25 ....181 G6
Brougham Rd ACT W3 ....98 E5
HACK E8 ....86 C6
Brougham St BTSEA SW11 ....140 E3
Brough Cl KUTN/CMB KT2 * ...174 E1
VX/NE SW8 ....141 K1
Broughton Av FNCH N3 ....46 C6
RCHPK/HAM TW10 ....156 D6
Broughton Dr BRXN/ST SW9....142 B5
Broughton Gdns HGT N6 ....66 C3
Broughton Rd FUL/PGN SW6....140 A3
ORP BR6 ....201 J6

THHTH CR7 ....196 B3
WEA W13 ....97 H6
Broughton Road Ap
FUL/PGN SW6 * 140 A3
Broughton St VX/NE SW8 ......141 H3
Brouncker Rd ACT W3 ....117 K2
Brow Cl STMC/STPC BR5 ......202 E4
Brow Crs STMC/STPC BR5 ....202 E4
Browells La FELT TW13 ....154 B4
Brown Cl WLGTN SM6 ....211 F6
Brownfield St POP/IOD E14 ....106 A5
Browngraves Rd
WDR/YW UB7 ....133 F1
Brown Hart Gdns
MYFR/PKLN W1K 9 K6
Brownhill Rd CAT SE6 ....165 F2
Browning Av HNWL W7 ....97 F5
SUT SM1 ....209 J2
WPK KT4 ....192 E5
Browning Cl HPTN TW12 ....154 E6
MV/WKIL W9 ....101 G3
WALTH E17 ....52 A3
WELL DA16 ....147 K2
Browning Ms CAVSQ/HST W1G *....9 J2
Browning Rd DART DA1 ....151 J5
ENC/FH EN2 ....23 K1
MNPK E12 ....89 K5
WAN E11 ....70 D4
Browning St WALW SE17 ....122 D5
Browning Wy HEST TW5 ....134 C2
Brownlea Gdns
GDMY/SEVK IG3 ....73 G6
Brownlow Ms FSBYW WC1X....5 H6
Brownlow Rd CROY/NA CRO....212 A2
FBAR/BDGN N11 ....48 E2
FNCH N3 ....47 F1
FSTGT E7 ....88 E2
HACK E8 ....86 B6
WEA W13 * 116 B1
WLSDN NW10 ....81 G6
Brownlow St GINN WC1R 11 H2
Brownrigg Rd ASHF TW15 .....152 D6
Brownspring Dr
ELTH/MOT SE9 ....167 G6
Brown St CB RYLDS KT5 *......191 C4
WALTH E17 ....51 J6
Brown's Rd MBLAR W1H 8 E5
Brownswell Rd EFNCH N2 ......47 H5
Brownswood Rd FSBYPK N4....67 H5
Broxash Rd BTSEA SW11 ......161 F1
Broxbourne Av WAN E11 ....71 F1
Broxbourne House BOW E3 *...105 K3
Broxbourne Rd FSTGT E7 ....88 E1
ORP BR6 ....202 A5
Broxholm Rd WNWD SE27 ....162 B5
Broxted Rd CAT SE6 ....164 C4
Broxwood Wy ST/WD NW8 ....2 D1
Bruce Castle Rd TOTM N17 .....50 B4
Bruce Cl NKENS W10 ....100 B4
WELL DA16 ....148 C2
Bruce Dr SAND/SEL CR2 ....213 F6
Bruce Gv ORP BR6 ....202 B5
Bruce Rd BAR EN5 * 20 C4
BOW E3 ....105 K2
KTN/HRWW/W HA3 ....42 E4
MTCM CR4 ....179 F3
SNWD SE25 ....196 E1
WLSDN NW10 ....81 F5
Bruckner St NKENS W10 ....100 C2
Brudenell Rd TOOT SW17 .....160 E5
Bruffs Meadow NTHLT UB5 .....77 J4
Bruford Ct DEPT SE8 ....124 D6
Bruges Pl CAMTN NW1 * 84 C5
Brumfield Rd HOR/WEW KT19....206 E3
Brumel Cl HEST TW5 ....133 J4
NRWD SE19 ....181 G2
NTHLT UB5 ....95 G3
ROM RM1 ....75 G1
Brunel Cl WLSDN NW10 ....99 J2
Brunel Est BAY/PAD W2 ....100 E4
Brunel Rd ACT W3 ....99 G4
BERM/RHTH SE16 ....123 K2
WALTH E17 ....69 G3
WFD IG8 ....53 K1
Brunel St CAN/RD E16 ....106 D5
Brunel Wk WHTN TW2 ....155 F2
Brunner Cl GLDGN NW11 ....65 F3
Brunner Rd EA W5 ....97 K3
WALTH E17 ....69 H2
Bruno Pl CDALE/KGS NW9 .....62 E6
Brunswick Av
FBAR/BDGN N11 ....34 A4
Brunswick Cl BXLYHS DA6 ....148 E5
PIN HA5 ....59 J3
THDIT KT7 ....190 A5
WHTN TW2 ....155 K4
WOT/HER KT12 ....188 B6
Brunswick Ct STHWK SE1 ......19 H3
Brunswick Gdns BARK/HLT IG6....54 C3
EA W5 ....98 A2
KENS W8 ....119 K1
Brunswick Gv FBAR/BDGN N11....34 A4
Brunswick Ms MBLAR W1H 9 F3
STRHM/NOR SW16 ....179 J2
Brunswick Park Gdns
FBAR/BDGN N11 ....34 A3
Brunswick Park Rd
FBAR/BDGN N11 ....34 A4
Brunswick Pl CAMTN NW1 ....3 H7
IS N1 ....7 F5
NRWD SE19 ....181 H3

SEVS/STOTM N15 ....68 A2
SUT SM1 ....209 F2
Brunswick Sq BMSBY WC1N....5 F6
TOTM N17 ....50 B2
Brunswick St WALTH E17 ....70 A2
Brunswick Vls CMBW SE5 .....143 F2
Brunswick Wy
FBAR/BDGN N11 ....34 B6
Brunton Pl POP/IOD E14 ....105 G5
Brushfield St WCHPL E1 ....13 H1
Brushwood Cl POP/IOD E14 ...105 K4
Brussels Rd BTSEA SW11 .....140 C5
Bruton Cl CHST BR7 ....184 E3
Bruton La MYFR/PICC W1J 9 K6
Bruton Pl MYFR/PKLN W1K 9 K6
Bruton Rd MRDN SM4 ....194 B1
Bruton St MYFR/PICC W1J 9 K6
Bruton Wy WEA W13 ....97 C4
Bryan Av WLSDN NW10 ....81 K5
Bryan Rd BERM/RHTH SE16...124 C2
Bryanston Av WHTN TW2 ......155 G3
Bryanston Cl NWDGN UB2 ....114 E4
Bryanstone Rd
CEND/HSY/T N8 ....66 C2
Bryanston Ms East
MBLAR W1H 8 E2
Bryanston Ms West
MBLAR W1H 8 E3
Bryanston Pl MBLAR W1H 8 E3
Bryanston Sq MBLAR W1H 8 E3
Bryanston St MBLAR W1H 8 E4
Bryant Cl BAR EN5 ....20 D6
Bryant Rd NTHLT UB5 ....95 G2
Bryant St SRTFD E15 ....88 B5
Bryantwood Rd HOLWY N7 .....85 G3
Brycedale Crs STHGT/OAK N14....34 D6
Bryce Rd BCTR RM8 ....91 J2
Bryden Cl SYD SE26 ....182 B1
Brydges Pl CHCR WC2N 10 E6
Brydges Rd SRTFD E15 ....88 B3
Brydon Wk IS N1 ....84 E6
Bryett Rd HOLWY N7 ....84 E1
Brymay Cl BOW E3 ....105 J1
Brynmaer Rd BTSEA SW11 ....140 E2
Bry-y-Mawr Rd EN EN1 ....24 B5
Bryony Rd SHB W12 ....99 J6
Buchanan Cl WCHMN N21 ....23 F6
Buchanan Gdns WLSDN NW10....99 J1
Buchan Rd PECK SE15 ....143 K4
Bucharest Rd
WAND/EARL SW18 ....160 B2
Buckden Cl LEE/GVPK SE12 ..165 J1
Buckfast Rd MRDN SM4 ....194 A1
Buckfast St BETH E2 ....104 C2
Buckhold Rd
WAND/EARL SW18 ....159 K1
Buckhurst Av CAR SM5 ....194 D5
Buckhurst St WCHPL E1 ....104 D3
Buckhurst Wy BKHH IG9 ....39 H5
Buckingham Av
E/WMO/HCT KT8 ....173 G5
EBED/NFELT TW14 ....154 A1
GFD/PVL UB6 ....79 G6
TRDG/WHET N20 ....33 G2
WELL DA16 ....147 K5
Buckingham Cl EA W5 ....97 J4
EN EN1 ....24 A3
HPTN TW12 ....172 E1
STMC/STPC BR5 ....201 K4
Buckingham Dr CHST BR7 .....185 G1
Buckingham Gdns
E/WMO/HCT KT8 ....173 G5
STAN HA7 ....44 A3
THHTH CR7 ....180 B5
Buckingham Ga WESTW SW1E....16 A4
Buckingham La FSTH SE23 ....164 B2
Buckingham Ms
WESTW SW1E * 16 A4
WLSDN NW10 ....99 H1
Buckingham Palace Rd
BGVA SW1W 15 J7
Buckingham Pde STAN HA7 *....43 J1
Buckingham Pl WESTW SW1E....16 A4
Buckingham Rd EDGW HA8 .....44 B3
FELT TW13 ....154 E6
HRW HA1 ....60 D2
IL IG1 ....90 D1
IS N1 ....86 A4
KUT/HW KT1 ....191 G1
LEY E10 ....87 K1
MTCM CR4 ....195 K2
RCHPK/HAM TW10 ....156 E4
SRTFD E15 ....88 D3
SWFD E18 ....52 D4
WAN E11 ....71 F1
WDGN N22 ....48 E4
WLSDN NW10 ....99 H1
Buckingham St CHCR WC2N....11 F6
Buckingham Wy WLGTN SM6....210 C6
Buckland Crs HAMP NW3 ....83 H5
Buckland Ri PIN HA5 ....41 G4
Buckland Rd CHSGTN KT9 ....206 B3
LEY E10 ....70 A6
ORP BR6 ....216 E2
Bucklands OXHEY WD19 * 27 H5
Bucklands Rd TEDD TW11 ....174 D2
Bucklands Wk MRDN SM4 ....194 B3
Buck La CDALE/KGS NW9 ....63 F2
Buck La CDALE/KGS NW9 ......177 J6
Buckleigh Av
RYNPK SW20 ....177 J6
Buckleigh Rd
STRHM/NOR SW16 ....179 J2
Buckleigh Wy NRWD SE19 ....181 G4
Bucklers' Wy CAR SM5 ....209 K1
Buckles Ct BELV DA17 * 128 E4
Buckle St WCHPL E1 ....13 K3
Buckley Cl DART DA1 ....150 E5
FSTH SE23 ....163 J2
Buckley Rd KIL/WHAMP NW6....82 D5
Bucknall St NOXST/BSQ WC1A....10 D3
Bucknall Wy BECK BR3 ....198 E1

Buckner Rd
 BRXS/STRHM SW2 ....142 A5
Buckrell Rd CHING E4 ....38 B4
Bucks Av OXHEY WD19...............27 J2
Buckstone Cl FSTH SE23..........163 K1
Buckstone Rd UED N18 ....50 C2
Buck St CAMTN NW1...................84 B6
Buckters Rents
 BERM/RHTH SE16 ....124 B1
Buckthorne Rd BROCKY SE4......144 B1
Budd Cl NFNCH/WDSP N12 ......35 F6
Buddings Cir WBLY HA9 ....80 E1
Bude Cl WALTH E17 ....69 H2
Budge La MTCM CR4 ....194 E4
Budge Rw MANHO EC4N 12 E5
Budleigh Crs WELL DA16 ....148 D2
Budoch Dr CDMY/SEVK IG3 ....73 G6
Buer Rd FUL/PGN SW6.............139 H5
Bugsbys Wy GNWCH SE10 ....125 H2
Bulganak Rd THHTH CR7 ....196 D1
Bulinca St WEST SW1P * 16 E7
Bullace Rw CMBW SE5...............142 E1
Bull Aly WELL DA16 ....148 C3
Bullard Cl PECK SE15.................143 H1
Bullard Rd TEDD TW11 *...........174 A2
Bullards Pl BETH E2 ....105 F2
Bullbanks Rd BELV DA17...........129 K4
Bulleid Wy PIM SW1V.................15 K7
Bullen St BTSEA SW11...............140 D3
Bull Bar BARK IG11 ....180 C6
Bullers Wood Dr CHST BR7 ......184 D4
Bullescroft Rd EDGW HA8 ....30 C5
Bullivant St POP/IOD E14 ....106 A6
Bull La CHST BR7 ....185 J3
 DAGE RM10 ....92 D1
 UED N18 ....50 A1
Bull Rd SRTFD E15....................106 C1
Bullrush Cl CAR SM5................194 D6
 CROY/NA CR0.........................197 F5
Bulls Aly MORT/ESHN SW14 * ..138 A4
Bulls Br HYS/HAR UB3 ....113 K3
Bulls Bridge Rd NWDGN UB2 ...114 A3
Bullsbrook Rd HYS/HAR UB3 ....114 B1
Bull Yd PECK SE15 ....143 H2
Bulmer Gdns
 KTN/HRWW/W HA3 ....61 K4
Bulstrode Av HSLW TW3 ....134 E4
Bulstrode Gdns HSLW TW3 ....135 F4
Bulstrode Pl MHST W1U 9 H2
Bulstrode Rd HSLW TW3 ....135 F4
Bulstrode St MHST W1U 9 H3
Bulwer Court Rd WAN E11 ....70 B5
Bulwer Rd BAR EN5 ....21 C5
 UED N18 ....36 A6
 WAN E11 ....70 B5
Bulwer St SHB W12 ....119 F1
Bunces La WFD IG8 ....52 D3
Bungalow Rd SNWD SE25 ....197 F1
The Bungalows
 RYLN/HDSTN HA2 * 77 K1
 STRHM/NOR SW16 ....179 C5
Bunhill Rw STLK EC1Y 6 E6
Bunhouse Pl BGVA SW1W 121 F5
Bunkers Hl SCUP DA14 ....169 G5
Bunning Wy HOLWY N7 * 84 E5
Bunn's La MLHL NW7 ....45 G2
Bunsen St BOW E3 ....105 C1
Buntingbridge Rd
 GNTH/NBYPK IG2 ....72 D2
Bunting Cl ED N9..........................37 F3
 MTCM CR4 ....194 E2
Bunting Ter SEDGW E6 ....108 A2
Bunton St WOOL/PLUM SE18 ...127 F3
Bunyan Rd WALTH E17 ....51 G6
Buonaparte Ms PIM SW1V 121 J5
Burbage Cl HYS/HAR UB3 ....94 B5
 STHWK SE1 ....18 E5
Burbage Rd HNHL SE24 ....162 E1
Burberry Cl NWMAL KT3............176 B5
Burbridge Wy TOTM N17.............50 C5
Burcham St POP/IOD E14 ....105 K5
Burcharbro Rd ABYW SE2 ....128 E6
Burchell Ct BUSH WD23 ....28 C2
Burchell Rd LEY E10 ....69 K5
 PECK SE15 ....143 J2
Burchwall Cl CRW RM5 ....56 E3
Burcote Rd
 WAND/EARL SW18 ....160 C3
Burden Cl BTFD TW8 ....116 D5
Burdenshott Av
 RCHPK/HAM TW10 ....137 J5
Burden Cl IS N1............................91 F6
Burder Rd IS N1............................86 A4
Burdett Av RYNPK SW20 ....176 D4
Burdett Cl HNWL W7 * 116 A1
 SCUP DA14 ....187 F1
Burdett Rd CROY/NA CR0 ....196 E3
 POP/IOD E14 ....105 G5
 RCH/KEW TW9 ....137 C5
Burdetts Rd DAGW RM9 ....92 B6
Burdock Cl CROY/NA CR0 ....198 A5
Burdock Rd TOTM N17 ....50 C6
Burdon La BELMT SM2 ....208 D6
Burdon Pk BELMT SM2 ....208 D6
Burfield Cl TOOT SW17..............160 B6
Burford Cl BARK/HLT IG6 ....72 C1
 BUSH WD23 ....91 J1
Burford Gdns PLMGR N13 ....35 F5
Burford Rd BMLY BR1................200 D1
 BTFD TW8 ....117 F5
 CAT SE6 ....164 E6
 EHAM E6 ....107 J2
 SRTFD E15 ....88 B5
 SUT SM1 ....193 K5
 WPK KT4 ....192 D4
Burford Wk FUL/PGN SW6 * 140 A1
Burford Wy CROY/NA CR0 ....214 A5
Burgate Cl DART DA1 ....150 C4

Burges Gv BARN SW13 ....138 E1
Burges Rd EHAM E6 ....90 A5
Burgess Av CDALE/KGS NW9 ....63 F3
Burgess Cl FELT TW13 ....154 D6
Burgess Hl CRICK NW2 ....82 E2
Burgess Rd SRTFD E15 ....88 C2
 SUT SM1 ....209 F2
Burgess St POP/IOD E14 ....105 J4
Burge St STHWK SE1 ....19 F5
Burghill Rd SYD SE26 ....164 A6
Burghley Av NWMAL KT3...........176 A4
Burghley Hall Cl
 WIM/MER SW19 * 159 H3
Burghley Pl MTCM CR4 ....194 E1
Burghley Rd CEND/HSY/T N8 .....49 G5
 KTTN NW5 ....84 B2
 SRTFD E15 ....88 C3
 WIM/MER SW19 ....159 H6
Burgh St IS N1..............................6 B2
Burgon Street Hl BLKFR EC4V....12 B4
Burgos Cl CROY/NA CR0............211 G4
Burgos Gv GNWCH SE10 ....144 E2
Burgoyne Rd BRXN/ST SW9 .....142 A5
 FSBYPK N4 ....67 H3
 SNWD SE25 ....197 G1
Burham Cl PGE/AN SE20 ....181 K3
Burhill Gv PIN HA5 ....41 J5
Burke Cl PUT/ROE SW15............138 B6
Burke St CAN/RD E16 ....106 D5
Burket Cl NWDGN UB2...............114 D4
Burland Rd BTSEA SW11............140 E6
 CRW RM5 ....56 E2
Burleigh Av BFN/LL DA15 ....148 A6
 WLGTN SM6 ....210 A1
Burleigh Gdns
 STHGT/OAK N14 ....34 C3
Burleigh Pde
 STHGT/OAK N14 * 34 D3
Burleigh Pl PUT/ROE SW15 ....139 G6
Burleigh Rd CHEAM SM3 ....193 H5
 EN EN1 ....24 A5
Burleigh St COVGDN WC2E 11 H4
Burleigh Wk CAT SE6 ....165 F3
Burleigh Wy ENC/FH EN2 ....23 K4
Burley Cl CHING E4 ....51 J1
 STRHM/NOR SW16 ....179 J4
Burley Rd CAN/RD E16 ....107 G5
Burlington Ar CONDST W1S 10 A6
Burlington Av RCH/KEW TW9 ....137 H2
 ROMW/RG RM7 ....74 D3
Burlington Cl
 EBED/NFELT TW14 ....153 G2
 EHAM E6 ....107 J5
 MV/WKIL W9 ....88 D3
 ORP BR6 ....201 G6
Burlington Gdns ACT W3 ....117 K1
 CHDH RM6 ....74 A4
 CHSWK W4 ....117 K5
 CONDST W1S 10 A6
Burlington La CHSWK W4 ....137 K1
Burlington Ms ACT W3 ....117 K1
Burlington Pde CRICK NW2 ....82 B2
Burlington Pl FUL/PGN SW6 ......139 H4
 PIN HA5 ....41 F6
 WFD IG8 ....38 E5
Burlington Ri EBAR EN4 ....33 J2
Burlington Rd CHSWK W4 * 117 K5
 ENC/FH EN1 ....139 H4
 FUL/PGN SW6 ....139 H4
 ISLW TW7 ....135 J2
 MUSWH N10 ....48 A6
 NWMAL KT3 ....192 C1
 THHTH CR7 ....180 D5
 TOTM N17 ....50 D4
Burma Rd STNW/STAM N16 ....85 K2
Burma Ter NRWD SE19 * 181 F1
Burmester Rd TOOT SW17 ....160 B5
Burnaby Crs CHSWK W4 ....117 J6
Burnaby Gdns CHSWK W4 ....117 J6
Burnaby St WBPTN SW10 ....140 B1
Burnbrae Cl FNCH N3 ....47 F2
Burnbury Rd BAL SW12 ....161 H3
Burncroft Av PEND EN3 ....25 F4
Burndell Wy YEAD UB4 ....95 H4
Burne Av RCHPK/HAM TW10 ....174 D1
 WELL DA16 ....148 B3
Burnell Gdns STAN HA7 ....43 K5
Burnell Rd SUT SM1 ....209 F2
Burnell Wk STHWK SE1 * 123 G5
Burnels Av EHAM E6 ....108 A2
Burness Cl HOLWY N7 ....85 F4
Burne St CAMTN NW1 * 8 C1
Burnet Cl HOM E9 ....86 E3
Burnett La WFD IG8 ....54 B3
Burnett Rd ERITH DA8 ....131 G6
Burney Av BRYLDS KT5 ....191 G2
Burney St GNWCH SE10 ....145 F1
Burnfoot Av FUL/PGN SW6 ....139 H2
Burnham Av HGDN/ICK UB10 .....76 A2
Burnham Cl ENC/FH EN1 ....24 A1
 KTN/HRWW/W HA3 ....61 K1
 MLHL NW7 ....45 J3
 STHWK SE1 ....19 K7
Burnham Crs DART DA1 ....151 F5
 WAN E11 ....71 G1
Burnham Dr WPK KT4.................193 G6
Burnham Gdns CROY/NA CR0 ...197 G4
 HEST TW5 ....134 A2
 HYS/HAR UB3 ....113 G3
Burnham Rd CHING E4 ....51 H1
 DAGW RM9 ....91 G6
 DART DA1 ....151 G6
 MRDN SM4 ....194 A2
 ROMW/RG RM7 ....56 E6
 SCUP DA14 ....169 F4
Burnham St BETH E2 ....104 E2
 KUTN/CMB KT2 ....175 H4
Burnham Wy SYD SE26 ....182 C1
 WEA W13 ....116 C3
Burnhill Rd BECK BR3 ....182 D5
Burnley Cl OXHEY WD19 ....19 C5
Burnley Rd BRXN/ST SW9 ....142 A3
 WLSDN NW10 ....81 H3

Burnsall St CHEL SW3 ....120 D5
Burns Av BFN/LL DA15 ....168 C1
 CHDH RM6 ....73 J4
 EBED/NFELT TW14 ....153 K1
 STHL UB1 ....96 A6
Burns Cl CAR SM5 ....210 A6
 ERITH DA8 ....150 C2
 WALTH E17 ....70 A1
 WELL DA16 ....148 A2
 WIM/MER SW19 ....178 C2
 YEAD UB4 ....94 E4
Burnside Av CHING E4 ....51 H2
Burnside Cl BAR EN5 ....20 E4
 BERM/RHTH SE16 ....124 A1
 TWK TW1 ....156 B1
Burnside Crs ALP/SUD HA0 ....79 K6
Burnside Rd BCTR RM8 ....73 J6
Burns Rd ALP/SUD HA0 ....98 A1
 BTSEA SW11 ....140 E3
 WEA W13 * 116 C2
 WLSDN NW10 ....81 H6
Burns Wy HEST TW5 ....134 C2
Burnt Ash HI LEE/GVPK SE12 ...165 K2
Burnt Ash La BMLY BR1 ....184 A1
Burnt Ash Rd LEE/GVPK SE12 ...145 J6
Burnt House La RDART DA2 ......171 H6
Burnthwaite Rd
 FUL/PGN SW6 ....139 J1
Burnt Oak Broadway
 EDGW HA8 ....44 D3
Burnt Oak Flds EDGW HA8 ....44 E4
Burnt Oak La BFN/LL DA15 ....168 B1
Burntwood Cl
 WAND/EARL SW18 * 160 C3
Burntwood Grange Rd
 WAND/EARL SW18 ....160 C3
Burntwood La TOOT SW17 ....160 B5
Burntwood Vw NRWD SE19 * 181 G1
Buross St WCHPL E1 ....104 D5
Burpham Cl YEAD UB4 ....95 H4
Burrage Gv
 WOOL/PLUM SE18 ....127 G4
Burrage Pl WOOL/PLUM SE18 ..127 G5
Burrage Rd
 WOOL/PLUM SE18 ....127 H4
Burrard Rd CAN/RD E16 ....106 E5
 KIL/WHAMP NW6 ....82 E3
Burr Bank Ter RDART DA2 * 171 H6
Burr Cl BXLYHN DA7 ....149 F4
 WAP E1W * 123 H1
Burrell Cl CROY/NA CR0 ....198 B3
 EDGW HA8 ....30 C4
Burrell Rw BECK BR3 ....182 D5
Burrell St STHWK SE1 ....12 A7
Burrells Whf POP/IOD E14 ....124 E5
Burrfield Dr STMC/STPC BR5 ....202 E2
Burritt Rd KUT/HW KT1 ....175 H5
Burroughs Gdns HDN NW4 ....63 K1
The Burroughs HDN NW4 ....63 K1
Burrow Gn CHIG IG7 ....55 F1
Burrow Rd DUL SE21 * 143 F5
 EDUL SE22 ....143 F5
Burrows Ms STHWK SE1 ....18 A2
Burrows Rd WLSDN NW10 ....100 A3
Burr Rd WAND/EARL SW18 ....159 K5
Bursar St STHWK SE1 * 19 G1
Bursdon Cl BFN/LL DA15 ....168 A4
Bursland Rd PEND EN3 ....25 F5
Burslem Av BARK/HLT IG6 ....55 G2
Burslem St WCHPL E1 * 104 C5
Burstock Rd PUT/ROE SW15 .....139 H5
Burstow Rd RYNPK SW20 ....177 H4
Burtenshaw Rd THDIT KT7 ....190 B4
Burtley Cl FSBYPK N4 ....67 J5
Burton Bank IS N1 * 85 K5
Burton Cl CHSGTN KT9 ....205 K5
 THHTH CR7 ....180 E6
Burton Gdns HEST TW5 ....134 E2
Burton Ms BGVA SW1W 15 H7
Burton Pl STPAN WC1H 4 E5
Burton Rd BRXN/ST SW9 ....142 C3
 KIL/WHAMP NW6 ....82 D5
 KUTN/CMB KT2 ....175 F3
 SWFD E18 ....53 F6
Burtons Ct SRTFD E15 ....88 B5
Burton's Rd HPTN TW12 ....155 G6
Burton St STPAN WC1H 4 D6
Burt Rd CAN/RD E16 ....126 B1
Burtwell La WNWD SE27 ....162 E6
Burwash Rd
 WOOL/PLUM SE18 ....127 J5
Burwell Av GFD/PVL UB6 ....78 E4
Burwell Cl WCHPL E1 ....104 D5
Burwell Rd LEY E10 ....69 G5
Burwood Av HAYES BR2 ....200 A6
 PIN HA5 ....59 G2
Burwood Cl SURB KT6 ....191 H5
Burwood Gdns RAIN RM13 ....111 H2
Burwood Pl BAY/PAD W2 ....8 C3
Bury Av RSLP HA4 ....58 A3
 YEAD UB4 ....94 C1
Bury Cl BERM/RHTH SE16 ....124 A1
Bury Pl NOXST/BSO WC1A 10 E2
Bury Rd DAGE RM10 ....92 E3
Bury St ED N9..............................36 C3
 HDTCH EC3A 13 H4
 RSLP HA4 ....58 B3
 STJS SW1Y 10 B7
Bury St West ED N9 ....36 A2
Bury Wk CHEL SW3 ....14 C7
Busby Pl KTTN NW5......................84 D4
Busch Cl ISLW TW7 ....136 C2
Bushbaby Cl STHWK SE1 ....19 G5
Bushberry Rd HOM E9 ....87 G4
Bush Cl GNTH/NBYPK IG2 ....72 D2

Bush Cottages
 WAND/EARL SW18 ....139 K6
Bushell Cl BRXS/STRHM SW2 ...162 A4
Bushell Gn BUSH WD23 ....28 D4
Bushell Wy CHST BR7 ....185 F1
Bush Elms Rd EMPK RM11 ....75 J4
Bushey Av STMC/STPC BR5 .....201 J4
 SWFD E18 ....52 D6
Bushey Cl CHING E4 ....38 A4
Bushey Hill Rd CMBW SE5 ....143 G2
Bushey Lees BFN/LL DA15 * 168 A1
Bushey Rd CROY/NA CR0 ....198 D6
 HYS/HAR UB3 ....113 G5
 PLSTW E13 ....107 G1
 RYNPK SW20 ....176 E6
 SUT SM1 ....208 E2
Bushey Wy BECK BR3 ....199 G3
Bushfield Cl EDGW HA8 ....30 D4
Bushfield Crs EDGW HA8 ....30 D4
Bush Gv CDALE/KGS NW9 ....62 E4
Bush Hl WCHMH N21 ....35 J2
Bush Hill Pde EN EN1 ....35 K2
Bush Hill Rd
 KTN/HRWW/W HA3 ....62 B3
 WCHMH N21 ....35 K1
Bush La CANST EC4R 12 E5
The Bush
 KTN/HRWW/W HA3 ....42 A4
Byfeild Gdns BARN SW13 ....138 D2
Byfield Cl BERM/RHTH SE16 ....124 B2
Byfield Rd ISLW TW7 ....136 B4
Byford Cl SRTFD E15 ....88 C5
Bygrove CROY/NA CR0...............213 K4
Bygrove Rd WIM/MER SW19 .....178 C2
Bygrove St POP/IOD E14 ....105 K5
Byland Cl ABYW SE2 ....128 C4
 CAR SM5 ....194 C4
 WCHMH N21 ....35 F2
Byne Rd CAR SM5 ....194 D6
 SYD SE26 ....181 K2
Bynes Rd SAND/SEL CR2 ....211 K5
Byng Pl GWRST WC1E 4 C7
Byng Rd BAR EN5 ....20 B4
Byng St POP/IOD E14 ....124 D2
Bynon Av BXLYHN DA7 ....149 F4
Byre Rd STHGT/OAK N14 ....34 A1
Byrne Rd BAL SW12 ....161 G3
Byron Av CDALE/KGS NW9 ....62 D1
 HSLWW TW4 ....134 A3
 MNPK E12 ....89 J4
 NWMAL KT3 ....192 D2
 SUT SM1 ....209 H2
 WLGTN SM6 ....210 E3
Byron Av East SUT SM1 ....209 H2
Byron Cl HACK E8 ....86 C6
 HPTN TW12 ....155 G4
 PGE/AN SE20 * 181 J6
 SYD SE26 * 164 B6
 THMD SE28 ....128 D1
 WOT/HER KT12 ....188 D5
Byron Ct ENC/FH EN2 ....23 H3
 ERITH DA8 ....149 J1
Byron Gdns SUT SM1 ....209 H2
Byron Hill Rd
 RYLN/HDSTN HA2 ....60 D5
Byron Ms HAMP NW3 ....83 J3
Byron Rd ALP/SUD HA0 ....61 J6
 EA W5 ....117 G1
 HRW HA1 ....60 E3
 KTN/HRWW/W HA3 ....61 K1
 LEY E10 ....69 K5
 MLHL NW7 ....45 J1
 WALTH E17 ....51 J4
Byron St POP/IOD E14 ....106 A5
Byron Ter ED N9 * 36 E2
Byron Wy NTHLT UB5 ....95 J2
 WDR/YW UB7 ....112 C4
 YEAD UB4 ....94 C3
Bysouth Cl CLAY IG5 ....54 B4
By the Wd OXHEY WD19 ....27 H1
Bythorn St BRXN/ST SW9 ....142 A4
Bytton Rd TOOT SW17 ....178 E2
Byward Av
 EBED/NFELT TW14 ....154 B1
Byward St MON EC3R 13 H6
Bywater Pl BERM/RHTH SE16 ...124 B1
Bywater St CHEL SW3 ....14 D7
The Byways HOR/WEW KT19 ....207 H2
The Byway BELMT SM2 ....209 H6
Bywell Pl GTPST W1W * 10 A2
Bywood Av CROY/NA CR0 ....197 K3

THHTH CR7 ....196 C2
 WALTH E17 ....69 G1
Buxton St WCHPL E1 ....7 K3
Byam St FUL/PGN SW6 ....140 B1
Byards Cft STRHM/NOR SW16 ...179 J4
Bychurch End TEDD TW11 * 174 A1
Bycroft Rd STHL UB1 ....96 A4
Bycroft St PGE/AN SE20 ....182 A3
Bycullah Av ENC/FH EN2 ....23 H4
Bycullah Rd ENC/FH EN2 ....23 H4
Byfield Cl BERM/RHTH SE16 ....124 B2
Byelands Cl BERM/RHTH SE16 ..124 A1
The Bye ACT W3 ....99 G5
Byewaters WATW WD18 ....26 A1
Bye Ways WHTN TW2 ....155 G5
The Byeway
 MORT/ESHN SW14 ....137 K4
The Byeways BRYLDS KT5 ....191 H2
The Bye Wy
 KTN/HRWW/W HA3 ....42 A4

C

Cabbell St CAMTN NW1 ....8 C2
Cabinet Wy CHING E4 ....51 H2
Cable Pl GNWCH SE10 ....145 F2
Cables Cl BELV DA17 ....129 K3
Cable St TWER EC3N 13 K5
 WCHPL E1 ....104 D6
Cabot Sq POP/IOD E14 ....124 D1
Cabot Wy EHAM E6 ....89 H6
Cabul Rd BTSEA SW11 ....140 D3
Cactus Cl CMBW SE5 * 143 F3
Cadbury Cl ISLW TW7 ....136 B2
Cadbury Wy BERM/RHTH SE16 ..19 K5
Caddington Cl EBAR EN4 ....21 J6
Caddington Rd CRICK NW2 ....82 C1
Caddis Cl STAN HA7 * 43 F3
Cadell Cl BETH E2 ....7 K3
Cade Rd GNWCH SE10 ....145 G1
Cader Rd WAND/EARL SW18 ....160 B1
Cadet Dr STHWK SE1 ....123 G5
Cadet Pl GNWCH SE10 ....125 H5
Cadiz Rd DAGE RM10 ....92 E5
Cadiz St WALW SE17 ....122 D5
Cadman Cl BRXN/ST SW9 ....142 C1
Cadmer Cl NWMAL KT3 ....192 B1
Cadmus Cl CLAP SW4 ....141 J3
Cadogan Cl BECK BR3 ....183 G5
 RYLN/HDSTN HA2 ....78 B2
 TEDD TW11 ....173 K1
Cadogan Ct BELMT SM2 ....209 F4
Cadogan Gdns CHEL SW3 ....15 F7
 FNCH N3 ....47 F4
 SWFD E18 ....53 F2

WCHMH N21 .....23 G6
Cadogan Ga KTBR SW1X 15 F6
Cadogan La KTBR SW1X 15 G5
Cadogan Pl KTBR SW1X 15 F6
Cadogan Rd SURB KT6 .....190 C2
WOOL/PLUM SE18 .....127 H5
Cadogan Sq KTBR SW1X 14 E5
Cadogan St CHEL SW3 .....14 E7
Cadogan Ter HOM E9 .....87 H4

Cadoxton Av
SEVS/STOTM N15 .....68 B3
Cadwallon Rd ELTH/MOT SE9 .....167 G4
Caedmon Rd HOLWY N7 .....85 F2
Caerleon Cl ESH/CLAY KT10 .....205 H5
SCUP DA14 .....186 D1
Caernarvon Cl MTCM CR4 .....179 K6
Caernarvon Dr CLAY IG5 .....54 A4
Caesars Wk MTCM CR4 .....194 E2
Cahill St STLK EC1Y * 6 D7
Cahir St POP/IOD E14 .....124 E4
Cain's La EBED/NFELT TW14 .....133 G6
Caird St NKENS W10 .....100 C2
Cairn Av EA W5 .....116 E1
Cairndale Cl BMLY BR1 .....183 J3
Cairnfield Av CRICK NW2 .....81 G1
Cairns Av WFD IG8 .....53 K2
Cairns Cl DART DA1 .....151 G6
Cairns Rd BTSEA SW11 .....140 D6
Cairn Wy STAN HA7 .....34 E6
Cairo New Rd CROY/NA CR0 .....196 C6
Cairo Rd WALTH E17 .....69 J1
Caistor Park Rd SRTFD E15 .....88 D6
Caistor Rd BAL SW12 .....161 G2
Caithness Gdns BFN/LL DA15 .....168 A1
Caithness Rd MTCM CR4 .....179 G3
WKENS W14 .....119 G3
Calabria Rd HBRY N5 .....85 H4
Calais St CMBW SE5 .....142 C2
Calbourne Av HCH RM12 .....93 K3
Calbourne Rd BAL SW12 .....160 E2
Caldbeck Av WPK KT4 .....192 E6
Caldecote Gdns BUSH WD23 .....28 E1
Caldecote La BUSH WD23 .....29 F2
Caldecot Rd CHDH NW5 .....142 D3
Caldecott Wy CLPT E5 .....87 F1
Calder Av GFD/PVL UB6 .....97 F1
Calder Gdns EDGW HA8 .....44 C6
Calderon Rd MANR E11 .....88 A2
Calder Rd MRDN SM4 .....194 B2
Caldervale Rd CLAP SW4 .....141 J6

Calderwood St
WOOL/PLUM SE18 .....127 F4
Caldicote Gn
CDALE/KGS NW9 * 63 G3
Caldwell Rd OXHEY WD19 .....27 H6
Caldwell St BRXN/ST SW9 .....142 A1
Caldy Rd BELV DA17 .....129 J3
Caldy St IS N1 * 85 J4
Caledonia Cl
GDMY/SEVK IG3 * 73 H5
Caledonian Rd IS N1 .....5 F3
Caledon Rd EHAM E6 .....89 K6
WLGTN SM6 .....210 A2
Cale St CHEL SW3 .....120 D5
Calidore Cl
BRXS/STRHM SW2 * 162 A1
California La BUSH WD23 .....28 D3
California Rd NWMAL KT3 .....191 K1
Callaby Ter IS N1 * 85 K4
Callander Rd CAT SE6 .....164 E4
The Callanders BUSH WD23 * 28 E3
Callard Av PLMGR N13 .....49 H1
Callcott Rd KIL/WHAMP NW6 .....82 D5
Callcott St KENS W8 .....119 K1
Callendar Rd SKENS SW7 .....14 A4
Callingham Cl POP/IOD E14 .....105 H4
Callis Farm Cl
STWL/WRAY TW19 .....152 B1
Callis Rd WALTH E17 .....69 H3
Callow St CHEL SW5 .....120 B6
Calmington Rd CMBW SE5 .....123 F6
Calmont Rd BMLY BR1 .....183 C2
Calne Av CLAY IG5 .....54 B4
Calonne Rd WIM/MER SW19 .....159 G6
Calshot St IS N1 .....5 C2
Calshot Wy ENC/FH EN2 .....23 H4
Calthorpe Gdns EDGW HA8 .....44 B1
SUT SM1 .....209 G1
Calthorpe St FSBYW WC1X 5 H6
Calton Av DUL SE21 .....163 F1
Calton Rd BAR EN5 .....33 G1
Calverley Cl BECK BR3 .....182 E2
Calverley Gdns DAGE RM10 .....74 C6
Calverley Gv ARCH N19 .....66 D5
Calverley Rd EW KT17 .....207 J4
Calvert Av BETH E2 .....7 H5
Calvert Cl BELV DA17 .....129 H4
SCUP DA14 .....187 F2
Calvert Dr BXLY DA5 .....169 H4
Calverton Rd EHAM E6 .....90 A6
Calvert Rd BAR EN5 .....20 B3
GNWCH SE10 .....125 J5
Calvert St CAMTN NW1 .....84 A6
Calvin Cl STMC/STPC BR5 .....186 E6
Calvin St WCHPL E1 .....7 J7
Calydon Rd CHARL SE7 .....126 A5
Calypso Crs PECK SE15 .....143 G1
Calypso Wy
BERM/RHTH SE16 .....124 C3
Camac Rd WHTN TW2 .....155 J3

Camarthen Gn
CDALE/KGS NW9 * 63 G3
Cambalt Rd PUT/ROE SW15 .....139 G6
Camberley Av EN EN1 .....24 A5
RYNPK SW20 .....176 E5
Camberley Cl CHEAM SM3 .....208 B1
Camberley Rd HTHAIR TW6 .....132 E5
Cambert Wy BKHTH/KID SE3 .....146 A5

Camberwell Church St
CMBW SE5 .....142 E2
Camberwell Glebe CMBW SE5 .....142 E2
Camberwell Gn CMBW SE5 .....142 E2
Camberwell Gv CMBW SE5 .....142 E2
Camberwell New Rd
CMBW SE5 .....142 C1
Camberwell Rd CMBW SE5 .....122 D6
Camberwell Station Rd
CMBW SE5 .....142 D2
Cambeys Rd DAGE RM10 .....92 E3
Camborne Av WEA W13 .....116 C2
Camborne Cl HTHAIR TW6 .....132 D4
Camborne Crs HTHAIR TW6 .....132 D4
Camborne Rd BELMT SM2 .....208 E5
CROY/NA CR0 .....197 H4
MRDN SM4 .....193 G3
SCUP DA14 .....168 D5
WAND/EARL SW18 .....159 K2
WELL DA16 .....147 K3
Camborne Wy HEST TW5 .....135 F2
Cambourne Av ED N9 .....37 F2
Cambourne Ms NTGHL W11 .....100 C5
Cambray Rd BAL SW12 .....161 H3
ORP BR6 .....202 A4
Cambria Cl BFN/LL DA15 .....167 H2
HSLW TW3 .....135 F5
Cambria Ct
EBED/NFELT TW14 .....154 A2
Cambria Gdns
STWL/WRAY TW19 .....152 B2
Cambrian Av GNTH/NBYPK IG2 .....72 E2
Cambrian Cl WNWD SE27 .....162 C5
Cambrian Gn
CDALE/KGS NW9 * 63 G2
Cambrian Rd LEY E10 .....69 J4
RCHPK/HAM TW10 .....157 G1
Cambria Rd CMBW SE5 .....142 D4
Cambria St FUL/PGN SW6 .....140 A1
Cambridge Av GFD/PVL UB6 .....79 F3
KIL/WHAMP NW6 .....100 E1
NWMAL KT3 .....176 C5
WELL DA16 .....148 A5
Cambridge Barracks Rd
WOOL/PLUM SE18 .....126 E4
Cambridge Circ
SOHO/SHAV W1D 10 D4
Cambridge Cl HSLWW TW4 .....134 D5
RYNPK SW20 .....176 E4
WALTH E17 .....69 H3
WDGN N22 .....49 G4
WDR/YW UB7 .....112 A6
WLSDN NW10 .....80 E1
Cambridge Crs BETH E2 .....104 D1
TEDD TW11 * 174 B1
Cambridge Dr LEE/GVPK SE12 .....145 K1
RSLP HA4 .....59 C6
Cambridge Gdns EN EN1 .....24 C3
KIL/WHAMP NW6 .....100 E1
MUSWH N10 .....48 A4
NKENS W10 .....100 C5
TOTM N17 .....49 K5
WCHMH N21 .....35 K2
Cambridge Ga CAMTN NW1 .....3 K5
Cambridge Gate Ms
CAMTN NW1 * 3 K5
Cambridge Gn ELTH/MOT SE9 .....167 G3
Cambridge Gv HMSMTH W6 .....118 E4
PGE/AN SE20 * 181 J4
Cambridge Grove Rd
KUT/HW KT1 .....175 H5
Cambridge Heath Rd
BETH E2 .....104 D2
Cambridge Pde EN EN1 * 24 C3
WAN E11 .....70 E3
Cambridge Park Rd WAN E11 .....70 E4
Cambridge Pas HOM E9 .....86 E5
Cambridge Pl KENS W8 * 120 A2
Cambridge Rd BARK IG11 .....90 C5
BARN SW13 .....138 C3
BMLY BR1 .....183 K3
BTSEA SW11 .....140 E2
CAR SM5 .....209 J4
CHING E4 .....38 B3
E/WMO/HCT KT8 .....188 E1
GDMY/SEVK IG3 .....72 E5
HNWL W7 .....116 A2
HPTN TW12 .....172 E5
HSLWW TW4 .....134 D5
KIL/WHAMP NW6 .....100 E2
KUT/HW KT1 * 175 H5
MTCM CR4 .....179 H6
NWMAL KT3 .....192 A1
PGE/AN SE20 .....181 H6
RCH/KEW TW9 .....137 H1
RYLN/HDSTN HA2 .....60 A2
RYNPK SW20 .....176 E4
SCUP DA14 .....168 A5
STHL UB1 * 114 E1
TEDD TW11 .....156 B6
TWK TW1 .....156 E1
WAN E11 .....70 E3
WDR/YW UB7 * 112 A3
Cambridge Rd North
CHSWK W4 .....117 J5
Cambridge Rd South
CHSWK W4 .....117 J5
Cambridge Rw
WOOL/PLUM SE18 .....127 G5
Cambridge Sq BAY/PAD W2 .....8 C3
Cambridge St PIM SW1V 121 G5
Cambridge Ter CAMTN NW1 * 3 J5
ED N9 * 36 B2
Cambridge Terrace Ms
CAMTN NW1 * 3 K5
Cambstow Yd HNWL W7 * 116 A2
Cambus Cl YEAD UB4 .....95 J4
Cambus Rd CAN/RD E16 .....106 E4
Camdale Rd
WOOL/PLUM SE18 .....148 A1
Camden Av FELT TW13 .....154 B4
YEAD UB4 .....95 G6
Camden Cl CHST BR7 .....185 H4

SUT SM1 .....209 F3
THHTH CR7 .....180 C6
Camden Gdns CAMTN NW1 * 84 B5
Camden Gv CHST BR7 .....185 G2
Camden High St CAMTN NW1 .....84 B5
Camden Hill Rd NRWD SE19 .....181 F2
Camdenhurst St
POP/IOD E14 .....105 G5
Camden La CAMTN NW1 .....84 C5
Camden Ms CAMTN NW1 .....84 C5
Camden Park Rd CAMTN NW1 .....84 D4
CHST BR7 .....184 E5
Camden Pas IS N1 .....6 A2
Camden Rd BXLY DA5 .....169 G3
CAMTN NW1 .....84 B6
SUT SM1 .....209 F3
WALTH E17 .....69 H3
WAN E11 .....71 F3
Camden Rw PermanentWy
CAMTN NW1 * 4 C1
Camden Rw BKHTH/KID SE3 .....145 H3
PIN HA5 * 41 G6
Camden Sq CAMTN NW1 .....84 D5
Camden St CAMTN NW1 .....84 B5
Camden Ter CAMTN NW1 * 84 D4
Camden Wk IS N1 .....6 A1
Camden Wy CHST BR7 .....184 E3
THHTH CR7 .....180 C6
Camelford Wk NTGHL W11 * 100 C5
Camel Gv KUTN/CMB KT2 .....174 E1
Camellia Pl WHTN TW2 .....155 G2
Camellia St VX/NE SW8 .....141 K1
Camelot Cl WIM/MER SW19 .....159 J6
WOOL/PLUM SE18 .....127 J2
Camel Rd CAN/RD E16 .....126 D1
Camera Pl WBPTN SW10 .....120 C6
Cameron Cl BXLY DA5 .....170 A5
TRDG/WHET N20 .....33 J4
UED N18 .....36 D6
Cameron Pl STRHM/NOR SW16 .....162 B5
Cameron Rd CAT SE6 * 164 C4
CROY/NA CR0 .....196 C3
GDMY/SEVK IG3 .....72 E5
HAYES BR2 .....199 K2
Cameron Ter
LEE/GVPK SE12 * 166 A5
Camerton Cl HACK E8 .....86 B4
Camilla Rd BERM/RHTH SE16 .....123 J4
Camille Cl SNWD SE25 .....181 H3
Camlan Rd BMLY BR1 .....165 J6
Camlet St BETH E2 .....7 J6
Camlet Wy BAR EN4 .....20 E3
Camley St CAMTN NW1 .....84 C4
Camm Gdns KUT/HW KT1 * 175 G5
THDIT KT7 .....189 K4
Camomile Av IL IG1 .....72 C1
Camomile St HDTCH EC3A 13 H3
Camomile Rd ROMW/RG RM7 .....75 G3
Campana Rd FUL/PGN SW6 .....139 K2
Campbell Av BARK/HLT IG6 .....72 C1
RSLP HA4 .....58 E3
STRHM/NOR SW16 * 179 J1
WHTN TW2 .....155 J3
WOOL/PLUM SE18 .....147 G2
Campbell Cft EDGW HA8 * 44 C1
Campbell Gordon Wy
CRICK NW2 .....81 K2
Campbell Pth BOW E3 * 105 J2
CROY/NA CR0 .....196 C4
EHAM E6 .....89 J6
HNWL W7 * 116 A2
SRTFD E15 * 88 C2
TOTM N17 .....50 B4
WALTH E17 .....69 G1
WHTN TW2 * 155 J4
Campbell Wk IS N1 .....84 E6
Campdale Rd ARCH N19 .....84 D1
Campden Crs ALP/SUD HA0 .....79 H1
BCTR RM8 .....91 J2
Campden Gv KENS W8 .....119 K2
Campden Hill KENS W8 .....119 K2
Campden Hill Gdns KENS W8 * 119 J1
Campden Hill Pl KENS W8 * 119 J1
Campden Hill Rd KENS W8 .....119 K2
Campden Hill Sq KENS W8 .....119 J1
Campden House Cl KENS W8 .....119 K2
Campden House Ter
KENS W8 * 119 K1
Campden St KENS W8 .....119 K1
Campden Ter CHSWK W4 * 118 B5
Campden Wy BCTR RM8 .....91 H2
Campen Cl WIM/MER SW19 .....159 H4
Camperdown St WCHPL E1 .....13 K4
Campfield Rd ELTH/MOT SE9 .....166 C2
Campion Cl EHAM E6 .....107 K6
KTN/HRWW/W HA3 .....62 B3
ROMW/RG RM7 .....75 F3
SAND/SEL CR2 .....212 A2
Campion Ct ALP/SUD HA0 * 98 A1
Campion Gdns WFD IG8 .....52 E1
Campion Pl THMD SE28 .....128 C1
Campion Rd ISLW TW7 .....136 A2
PUT/ROE SW15 .....139 F5
Campion Ter CRICK NW2 .....82 B1
Campion Wy EDGW HA8 .....30 E6
Camplin Rd
KTN/HRWW/W HA3 .....62 B1
Camplin St NWCR SE14 .....144 A1
Campsbourne Pde
CEND/HSY/T N8 * 66 E1
Campsbourne Rd
CEND/HSY/T N8 .....48 E6
The Campsbourne
CEND/HSY/T N8 .....66 E1
Campsey Gdns DAGE RM9 .....91 H5
Campshill Pl LEW SE13 .....145 F6
Campshill Rd LEW SE13 .....145 F6
Campus Rd WALTH E17 .....69 H3
Camp Vw WIM/MER SW19 .....176 E1
Cam Rd SRTFD E15 .....88 B6
Camrose Av ERITH DA8 .....129 K6

FELT TW13 .....154 A6
STAN HA7 .....44 A5
Camrose Cl CROY/NA CR0 .....198 A4
MRDN SM4 .....193 K1
Camrose St ABYW SE2 .....128 B5
Canada Av UED N18 .....49 J2
Canada Crs ACT W3 .....98 E4
Canada Pde EDGW HA8 * 44 E4
Canada Rd ACT W3 .....98 E4
ERITH DA8 .....150 E3
Canada Sqaure POP/IOD E14 .....124 E1
Canada St BERM/RHTH SE16 .....124 A2
Canada Wy SHB W12 .....99 K6
Canadian Av CAT SE6 .....164 E3
Canal Ap DEPT SE8 .....124 B6
Canal Cl NKENS W10 .....100 B3
WCHPL E1 .....105 G3
Canal Gv PECK SE15 .....123 H6
Canal Pth HACK E8 * 7 J1
Canal Rd WCPL E1 .....105 G3
Canal St CMBW SE5 .....122 E6
Canal Wk CROY/NA CR0 .....197 F3
IS N1 .....85 K6
WLSDN NW10 * 99 F1
Canal Wy NKENS W10 .....100 B3
Canal Whf GFD/PVL UB6 * 79 F4
Canal Yd NWDGN UB2 * 114 A4
Canberra Cl DAGE RM10 .....93 F5
HDN NW4 .....45 J2
Canberra Crs DAGE RM10 .....93 F5
Canberra Dr NTHLT UB5 .....95 C2
Canberra Pl HTHAIR TW6 .....133 F5
Canberra Rd ABYW SE2 * 128 E6
CHARL SE7 .....126 B6
EHAM E6 .....89 K6
HNWL W7 .....116 B1
WDR/YW NKENS W10 * 100 B3
Canbury Av KUTN/CMB KT2 .....175 G4
Canbury Ms SYD SE26 .....163 H5
Canbury Park Rd
KUTN/CMB KT2 .....175 F4
Canbury Pth STMC/STPC BR5 .....202 B1
Candahar Rd BTSEA SW11 .....140 D3
Candlelight Ct SRTFD E15 * 88 D4
Candlemas Ms MHST W1U * 9 G2
Candler St SEVS/STOTM N15 * 67 K3
Candover Rd EMPK RM11 .....75 K5
Candover St GTPST W1W * 10 A2
Candy St BOW E3 .....87 H6
Caney Ms CRICK NW2 .....64 B6
Canfield Dr RSLP HA4 .....77 F3
Canfield Gdns
KIL/WHAMP NW6 .....83 G4
Canfield Pl KIL/WHAMP NW6 * 83 G4
Canfield Rd RAIN RM13 .....93 H6
WFD IG8 .....53 J3
Canford Av NTHLT UB5 .....77 J6
Canford Cl ENC/FH EN2 .....23 C3
Canford Gdns NWMAL KT3 .....192 B3
Canford Pl TEDD TW11 .....174 D2
Canford Rd CLAP SW4 .....141 F5
Canham Rd CHSWK W4 .....118 B2
SNWD SE25 .....181 F6
Canmore Gdns
STRHM/NOR SW16 .....179 H3
Cann Hall Rd WAN E11 .....88 D2
Canning Crs WDGN N22 .....49 F4
Canning Pth HPTN TW12 .....173 G2
RYNPK SW20 .....177 F6
Canning Place Ms KENS W8 * 120 B3
Canning Rd CROY/NA CR0 .....197 G6
HBRY N5 .....85 H1
KTN/HRWW/W HA3 .....42 E6
SRTFD E15 .....106 C1
WALTH E17 .....69 G1
Cannington Rd DAGW RM9 .....91 J4
Cannizaro Rd
WIM/MER SW19 .....177 F2
Cannonbury Av PIN HA5 .....59 H5
Cannon Cl HPTN TW12 .....173 G2
RYNPK SW20 .....177 F6
Cannon Dr POP/IOD E14 .....124 D3
Cannon Hill KIL/WHAMP NW6 .....83 F3
STHGT/OAK N14 .....34 E5
Cannon Hill La MRDN SM4 .....193 G2
Cannon La HAMP NW3 .....83 H1
PIN HA5 .....59 J4
Cannon Pl CHARL SE7 .....126 D5
HAMP NW3 .....83 G1
Cannon Rd BXLYHN DA7 .....149 F2
STHGT/OAK N14 .....34 E5
Cannon Street Rd WCHPL E1 .....104 D5
Cannon Wy E/WMO/HCT KT8 .....189 F1
Canon Av CHDH RM6 .....73 J2
Canon Beck Rd
BERM/RHTH SE16 .....123 K2
Canonbie Rd FSTH SE23 .....163 K2
Canonbury Crs IS N1 .....85 J5
Canonbury Gv IS N1 .....85 J5
Canonbury La IS N1 .....85 H5
Canonbury Pk North IS N1 .....85 J4
Canonbury Pk South IS N1 .....85 J4
Canonbury Rd EN EN1 .....24 A2
IS N1 .....85 H5
Canonbury Sq IS N1 .....85 H5
Canonbury Vls IS N1 .....85 H5
Canon Mohan Cl EBAR EN4 .....20 B4
Canon Murnane Rd
BERM/RHTH SE16 .....19 J5
Canon Rd BMLY BR1 .....184 B6
Canon Rw WHALL SW1A 17 F3
Canons Cl EDGW HA8 .....44 B2
RDART DA2 .....170 D4
Canons Ct EDGW HA8 .....44 B2
EFNCH N2 .....65 H4
Canons Dr EDGW HA8 .....44 A2
Canon's Hill LAMRDN SM4 .....193 G2
Canon's Wk CROY/NA CR0 .....213 F1
Canopus Wy NTHWD HA6 .....40 E1
STWL/WRAY TW19 .....152 B2
Canrobert St BETH E2 .....104 D2
Cantelowes Rd CAMTN NW1 .....84 D5

Canterbury Av BFN/LL DA15 .....168 D4
IL IG1 .....71 J4
Canterbury Cl BECK BR3 .....182 E4
CMBW SE5 .....142 D3
DART DA1 .....171 K2
EHAM E6 .....107 K5
GFD/PVL UB6 .....96 B6
NTHWD HA6 .....40 D4
Canterbury Crs BRXN/ST SW9 .....142 B4
Canterbury Gv WNWD SE27 .....162 C5
Canterbury Pl WALW SE17 .....18 B7
Canterbury Rd CROY/NA CR0 .....196 A4
FELT TW13 .....154 D4
KIL/WHAMP NW6 .....100 E1
LEY E10 .....70 A4
MRDN SM4 .....194 B3
RYLN/HDSTN HA2 .....60 B2
Canterbury Ter
KIL/WHAMP NW6 .....100 E1
Cantley Gdns GNTH/NBYPK IG2 .....72 E3
NRWD SE19 .....181 G4
Cantley Rd HNWL W7 .....116 B3
Canton St POP/IOD E14 .....105 J5
Cantrell Rd BOW E3 .....105 J3
Cantwell Rd
WOOL/PLUM SE18 .....147 G1
Canvey St STHWK SE1 .....12 C7
Cape Cl BARK IG11 .....90 B5
Capel Av WLGTN SM6 .....211 F3
Capel Cl HAYES BR2 .....200 D5
TRDG/WHET N20 .....33 H3
Capel Gdns GDMY/SEVK IG3 .....91 F2
PIN HA5 .....59 K3
Capella Rd NTHWD HA6 .....40 D1
Capel Pl RDART DA2 .....171 F6
Capel Rd EBAR EN4 .....33 J1
FSTGT E7 .....89 F2
OXHEY WD19 .....27 H1
Capener's Cl KTBR SW1X * 15 G3
Capern Rd WAND/EARL SW18 .....160 B3
Cape Rd TOTM N17 * 50 C6
Cape Yd WAP E1W 123 H1
Capital Interchange Wy
CHSWK W4 .....117 H5
Capitol Wy CDALE/KGS NW9 * 44 E6
Capland St STJWD NW8 .....2 B6
Caple Pde WLSDN NW10 * 99 H1
Caple Rd WLSDN NW10 .....99 H1
Caprea Cl YEAD UB4 .....95 H4
Capri Rd CROY/NA CR0 .....197 G4
Capstan Cl CHDH RM6 .....73 H3
Capstan Ride ENC/FH EN2 .....23 G3
Capstan Rd DEPT SE8 .....124 C4
Capstan Sq POP/IOD E14 .....125 F2
Capstan Wy
BERM/RHTH SE16 .....124 B1
Capstone Rd BMLY BR1 .....165 J6
Capthorne Av
RYLN/HDSTN HA2 .....59 J5
Capuchin Cl STAN HA7 .....43 H2
Capulet Ms CAN/RD E16 .....125 K1
Capworth St LEY E10 .....69 J5
Caractacus Cottage Vw
WATW WD18 .....26 E2
Caractacus Gn WATW WD18 .....26 D1
Caradoc Evans Cl
FBAR/BDGN N11 * 48 B1
Caradoc St GNWCH SE10 .....125 H5
Caradon Cl WAN E11 .....70 C5
Caradon Wy SEVS/STOTM N15 .....67 K1
Caravel Ms DEPT SE8 * 124 D6
Caraway Cl PLSTW E15 .....107 F4
Caraway Pl WLGTN SM6 .....210 B1
Carberry Rd NRWD SE19 .....181 F2
Carbery Av ACT W3 .....117 G2
Carbis Cl CHING E4 .....38 C3
Carbis Rd POP/IOD E14 .....105 H5
Carburton St GTPST W1W 9 K1
Cardale St POP/IOD E14 .....125 F3
Carden Rd PECK SE15 .....143 J4
Cardiff Rd HNWL W7 .....116 B3
PEND EN3 .....24 D5
WATW WD18 .....26 C2
Cardiff St WOOL/PLUM SE18 .....147 K1
Cardigan Gdns GDMY/SEVK IG3 .....73 G6
Cardigan Pl BKHTH/KID SE3 * 145 J3
Cardigan Rd BARN SW13 .....138 D3
BOW E3 .....105 J1
RCH/PK/HAM TW10 .....157 F1
WIM/MER SW19 .....178 B2
Cardigan St LBTH SE11 .....122 B5
Cardigan Wk IS N1 * 85 J5
Cardinal Av KUTN/CMB KT2 .....175 F1
MRDN SM4 .....193 H3
Cardinal Bourne St
STHWK SE1 * 19 F5
Cardinal Cl CHST BR7 .....185 J4
EDGW HA8 .....44 E3
MRDN SM4 .....193 H3
WPK KT4 .....207 J2
Cardinal Crs NWMAL KT3 .....175 K5
Cardinal Dr BARK/HLT IG6 .....54 C2
WOT/HER KT12 .....188 C5
Cardinal Hinsey Cl
WLSDN NW10 .....99 J1
Cardinal Pl PUT/ROE SW15 .....139 G5
Cardinal Rd FELT TW13 .....153 K3
RSLP HA4 .....59 H5
Cardinals Wk HPTN TW12 .....173 H3
Cardinals Wy ARCH N19 .....66 D5
Cardinal Wy
KTN/HRWW/W HA3 .....42 E6
Cardine Ms PECK SE15 .....143 J1
Cardington Sq HSLWW TW4 .....134 B4
Cardington St CAMTN NW1 .....4 B4
Cardozo Rd HOLWY N7 .....84 E3
Cardrew Av NFNCH/WDSP N12 .....47 H1
Cardross St HMSMTH W6 .....118 E3
Cardwell Rd HOLWY N7 .....84 E2
Cardwell Ter HOLWY N7 * 84 E2
Carew Cl HOLWY N7 .....67 F6
Carew Rd MTCM CR4 .....179 F5
NTHWD HA6 .....40 C2
THHTH CR7 .....180 C6
TOTM N17 .....50 C5

WEA W13 ....116 D2
WLGTN SM6 ....210 C4
Carew St CHEL SW3 *..........................142 D5
Carew Wy OXHEY WD19........................27 K5
STMC/STPC BR5 ....202 D5
Carey Gdns VX/NE SW8 ....141 H2
Carey La CITYW EC2V 12 C3
Carey Pl WEST SW1P..............................16 C7
Carey Rd DAGW RM9 ....92 A2
Carey St LINN WC2A 11 H4
Carey Wy WBLY HA9...............................80 D2
Carfax Pl CLAP SW4 *...........................141 J5
Carfax Rd HCH RM12 ....93 H2
HYS/HAR UB3.....................................113 K5
The Carfax SYD SE26 *.........................163 K5
Carfree Cl IS N1......................................85 C5
Cargill Rd AW/EARL SW18 ....160 B3
Cargreen Rd SNWD SE25......................197 G3
Carholme Rd FSTH SE23.......................164 C3
Carisbrook Cl EN EN1 ....24 B2
Carisbrooke Av BXLY DA5.....................168 E4
Carisbrooke Cl FELT TW13 ....154 D3
STAN HA7 ....43 K5
Carisbrooke Cl NTHLT UB5 *...................77 K6
Carisbrooke Gdns PECK SE15 *............143 G1
Carisbrooke Rd HAYES BR2..................200 B1
MTCM CR4 ....179 J1
WALTH E17 *..69 C1
Carleton Av WLGTN SM6......................210 D6
Carleton Cl ESH/CLAY KT10 ....189 J5
Carleton Gdns ARCH N19 *.....................84 C3
Carleton Rd DART DA1..........................171 K2
HOLWY N7 ....84 D3
Carleton Vls KTTN NW5 *.......................84 C5
Carlile Cl BOW E3 ....105 H1
Carlina Gdns WFD IG8.............................53 F1
Carlingford Rd HAMP NW3 ....83 H2
MRDN SM4 ....193 G3
SEVS/STOTM N15.................................49 H6
Carlisle Av ACT W3..................................99 G5
TWRH EC3N..13 H4
Carlisle Cl KUTN/CMB KT2 ....175 H4
Carlisle Gdns IL IG1.................................71 J3
KTN/HRWW/W HA3..............................61 K4
Carlisle La STHWK SE1............................17 H4
Carlisle Pl FBAR/BDGN N11 ....34 B6
WEST SW1P...16 A5
Carlisle Rd CDALE/KGS NW9 ....44 E6
DART DA1...171 K1
FSBYPK N4...67 G5
HPTN TW12..173 G3
KIL/WHAMP NW6.................................82 C6
LEY E10...69 K4
ROM RM1...75 H2
SUT SM1..208 D4
Carlisle St SOHO/CST W1F.....................10 C4
Carlisle Wk HACK E8...............................86 B4
Carlisle Wy TOOT SW17 ....179 F1
Carlos Pl MYFR/PKLN W1K......................9 H6
Carlos St CAMTN NW1 *..........................22 C6
Carlton Av EBED/NFELT TW14...............154 B1
HYS/HAR UB3.....................................113 H4
KTN/HRWW/W HA3..............................61 H2
SAND/SEL CR2 ....211 K5
STHGT/OAK N14 ....22 C6
Carlton Av East WBLY HA9 ....62 A5
Carlton Av West ALP/SUD HA0 ....61 H6
EDGW HA8 ....44 C1
HAMP NW3 ....64 E6
Carlton Crs CHEAM SM3........................208 C2
Carlton Dene EW KT17 *.........................207 K3
Carlton Dr BARK/HLT IG6.........................54 D6
PUT/ROE SW15....................................139 G6
Carlton Gdns EA W5.................................97 J5
STJS SW1Y..16 C1
Carlton Gn SCUP DA14 *........................168 A6
Carlton Pk PECK SE15............................143 J3
Carlton Hl STJWD NW8 ....101 G1
Carlton House Ter STJS SW1Y.................16 C1
Carlton Ms KIL/WHAMP NW6 *...............82 E3
Carlton Pde WBLY HA9 *..........................62 A5
Carlton Park Av RYNPK SW20 ....177 F5
Carlton Rd CHSWK W4...........................118 A6
EA W5...97 J6
ERITH DA8...129 K6
FBAR/BDGN N11...................................48 A1
FSBYPK N4...67 G4
GPK RM2...75 J2
MNPK E12...89 J2
MORT/ESHN SW14...............................137 K4
NWMAL KT3..176 B5
SAND/SEL CR2 ....211 K5
SCUP DA14...186 A1
WALTH E17 *..51 G4
WAN E11..70 C5
WELL DA16...148 C4
WDT/HER KT12 ....188 A4
Carlton Sq WCHPL E1 *..........................105 F3
Carlton St STJS SW1Y.............................10 C6
Carlton Ter SYD SE26.............................163 K5
UED N18 *...35 K6
WAN E11 *...70 E5
Carlton Tower Pl KTBR SW1X..................15 F4
Carlton V KIL/WHAMP NW6....................100 E2
Carlwell St TOOT SW17..........................178 D1
Carlyle Av BMLY BR1..............................184 C6
STHL UB1..95 K6
Carlyle Cl E/WMO/HCT KT8....................173 C5
EFNCH N2...65 G3
WLSDN NW10..81 F6
Carlyle Gdns STHL UB1............................95 K6
Carlyle Rd CROY/NA CRO.......................197 H6
EA W5..97 J6
MNPK E12...89 J2
THMD SE28...109 H6
WLSDN NW10 *......................................81 F6
Carlyle Sq CHEL SW3 ....120 C5
Carlyon Av RYLN/HDSTN HA2 ....77 K2
Carlyon Cl ALP/SUD HA0 ....80 A4
Carlyon Rd ALP/SUD HA0........................98 A1
YEAD UB4 ....95 G5
Carlys Cl BECK BR3 ....182 A5
Carmalt Gdns PUT/ROE SW15...............139 F5

Carmel Ct KENS W8 *.............................120 A2
Carmelite Rd
KTN/HRWW/W HA3..............................42 C4
Carmelite St EMB EC4Y..........................11 K5
Carmen St POP/IOD E14.........................105 K5
Carmichael Cl BTSEA SW11 *................140 C4
RSLP HA4 ....76 E2
Carmichael Rd SNWD SE25...................197 H2
Carminia Rd BAL SW12..........................161 G4
Carnaby St REGST W1B.........................10 A5
Carnac St WNWD SE27..........................162 E6
Carnanton Rd WALTH E17 ....52 A4
Carnarvon Av EN EN1 ....24 B5
Carnarvon Dr HYS/HAR UB3..................113 F5
Carnarvon Rd BAR EN5............................20 C4
LEY E10...70 A3
SRTFD E15..88 D4
SWFD E18 ....52 D4
Carnation Cl ROMW/RG RM7...................75 G6
Carnation St ABYW SE2.........................128 C5
Carnbrook Rd BKHTH/KID SE3 ....146 C4
Carnecke Gdns
ELTH/MOT SE9 ....146 D6
Carnegie Cl PEND EN3 ....25 K1
SURB KT6...191 G6
Carnegie Pl WIM/MER SW19 ....159 G5
Carnforth Cl HOR/WEW KT19 ....206 E4
Carnforth Gdns HCH RM12 ....93 J5
Carnforth Rd
STRHM/NOR SW16 ....179 J5
Carnoustie Dr IS N1 ....85 F5
Carnoustie Cl THMD SE28 ....109 K5
Carnwath Rd FUL/PGN SW6 ....139 K4
Carolina Cl SRTFD E15.............................88 C3
Carolina Rd THHTH CR7.........................180 C5
Caroline Cl CROY/NA CRO.....................212 A2
STRHM/NOR SW16..............................162 A5
WDR/YW UB7..112 A2
Caroline Cl CR STAN HA7 *.....................43 G2
Caroline Gdns BETH E2 *..........................7 H4
PECK SE15 *..143 J1
Caroline Cl BAY/PAD W2 ....101 F6
HYS/HAR UB3..133 H1
OXHEY WD19..27 J1
VX/NE SW8...141 F3
Caroline Rd WIM/MER SW19 ....177 J3
Caroline St WCHPL E1...........................105 G5
Caroline Ter BGVA SW1W........................15 G7
Caroline Wk HMSMTH W6.......................119 H6
Carol St CAMTN NW1 ....84 C6
Carolyn Dr ORP BR6..............................217 G1
Carpenders Av OXHEY WD19 ....27 J5
Carpenter Gdns WCHMH N21..................35 H4
Carpenters Cl TRDG/WHET N20 ....33 F3
Carpenter's Pl CLAP SW4 ....141 J5
Carpenters Ms HOLWY N7 *....................84 E3
Carpenter's Rd SRTFD E15.......................87 K5
Carpenter St MYFR/PKLN W1K 9 J6
Carrara Ms HACK E8 ....68 C4
Carr Cl STAN HA7 ....43 G2
Carr Gv WOOL/PLUM SE18 ....126 D4
Carriage Dr East BTSEA SW11 ....121 F6
Carriage Dr North
BTSEA SW11 *......................................140 E1
Carriage Dr South
BTSEA SW11...140 E2
Carriage Dr West
BTSEA SW11...140 E1
Carriage Ms IL IG1 ....72 C6
Carrick Cl ISLW TW7...............................136 B4
Carrick Dr BARK/HLT IG6..........................54 C4
Carrick Gdns TOTM N17 ....50 A3
Carrick Ga ESH/CLAY KT10 ....204 C1
Carrick Ms DEPT SE8.............................124 D6
Carrill Wy BELV DA17.............................128 E4
Carrington Av HSLW TW3.......................135 G6
Carrington Cl CROY/NA CRO 198 B4
Carrington Gdns FSTGT E7......................88 E2
Carrington Pl
ESH/CLAY KT10 *.................................204 B2
Carrington Rd DART DA1.........................171 J1
RCHPK/HAM TW10..............................137 H5
Carrington Sq
KTN/HRWW/W HA3..............................42 C3
Carrol Cl KTTN NW5................................84 B2
Carroll Cl SRTFD E15...............................88 D3
Carronade Pl
WOOL/PLUM SE18 ....127 J5
Carron Cl POP/IOD E14...........................105 K5
Carroun Rd VX/NE SW8..........................142 A1
Carroway La FUL/PGN SW6 ....96 D2
Carrow Rd DAGW RM9 ....91 H5
Carr Rd NTHLT UB5.................................78 B5
WALTH E17..51 H5
Carrs La WCHMH N21 ....23 K6
Carr St POP/IOD E14 ....105 G5
Carshalton Gv SUT SM1.........................209 H2
Carshalton Park Rd CAR SM5 ....209 K4
Carshalton Pl CAR SM5..........................210 A2
Carshalton Rd MTCM CR4 ....195 F1
SUT SM1...209 G3
Carsington Gdns DART DA1....................171 G4
Carslake Rd PUT/ROE SW15 ....139 F1
Carson Rd CAN/RD E16..........................106 E4
DUL SE21...162 E4
EBAR EN4 ....21 K5
Carstairs Rd CAT SE6.............................165 F5
Carston Cl LEE/GVPK SE12 ....145 J6
Carswell Cl REDBR IG4.............................71 H1
Carswell Rd CAT SE6..............................165 F2
Carter Cl CDALE/KGS NW9......................63 F3
CRW RM5...56 D5
Carter Dr CRW RM5................................210 D5
Carteret St STJSPK SW1H........................16 C3
Carteret Wy DEPT SE8...........................124 B4
Carterhatch La EN EN1.............................24 C3
Carterhatch Rd PEND EN3 ....25 J1
Carter La BLKFR EC4V..............................12 B4
Carter Pl WALW SE17 ....122 D5
Carter Rd PLSTW E13...............................89 F6
WIM/MER SW19 ....178 C2
Carters Cl KTTN NW5 *.............................84 D4
WPK KT4 ....193 G6

Carters Hill Cl ELTH/MOT SE9 ....166 B3
Carter St WALW SE17.............................122 D6
Carter's Yd WAND/EARL SW18 ....159 H1
Carthew Rd HMSMTH W6.......................118 E3
Carthew Vls HMSMTH W6......................118 E3
Carthusian St FARR EC1M.......................12 C1
Cartier Cl POP/IOD E14.............................11 F6
Cart La CHING E4....................................38 C3
Cartmel Cl TOTM N17...............................50 D5
Cartmel Ct NTHLT UB5.............................77 J4
Cartmel Gdns MRDN SM4......................194 B2
Cartmel Rd BXLYHN DA7........................149 H2
Cartwright Gdns STPAN WC1H 4 E6
Cartwright St TWRH EC3N 13 K5
Cartwright Wy BARN SW13....................138 E1
Carver Rd HNHL SE24 ....162 D1
Carville Crs BTFD TW8...........................117 F5
Cary Rd WAN E11 ....88 C2
Carysfort Rd CEND/HSY/T N8...................66 D2
STNW/STAM N16..................................85 K1
Cascade Av MUSWH N10 ....65 C1
Cascade Cl STMC/STPC BR5..................186 D6
Cascade Rd BKHH IG9..............................39 H4
Casella Rd NWCR SE14..........................144 A1
Casewick Rd WNWD SE27.....................180 C1
Casey Cl STJWD NW8................................2 D7
Casimir Rd CLPT E5..................................86 D1
Casino Av HNHL SE24............................142 D6
Caspian St CMBW SE5............................142 E6
Caspian Wk CAN/RD E16........................107 H5
Cassandra Cl NTHLT UB5.........................78 D2
Casselden Rd WLSDN NW10....................81 F5
Cassidy Rd FUL/PGN SW6.....................139 K1
Cassilda Rd ABYW SE2...........................128 B4
Cassilis Rd TWK TW1..............................156 C1
Cassiobury Av
EBED/NFELT TW14 ....153 J2
Cassiobury Rd WALTH E17.......................69 F2
Cassland Rd HOM E9................................87 F4
THHTH CR7...196 E1
Cassocke Rd LEW SE13..........................164 C2
Casson St WCHPL E1 ....104 C4
Castalien Rd MV/WKIL W9.......................101 F5
Castellain Rd MV/WKIL W9 ....101 F5
Castell Av LEW SE13 *..............................43 F5
Castello Av PUT/ROE SW15 ....139 F6
Castelnau BARN SW13...........................138 E1
Casterbridge Rd
BKHTH/KID SE3 ....145 K4
Casterton St HACK E8...............................86 D4
Castile Rd WOOL/PLUM SE18 ....127 F4
Castillon Rd CAT SE6..............................165 H5
Castlands Rd CAT SE6............................164 C4
Castle Av CHING E4..................................52 B2
EW KT17 ....207 J6
RAIN RM13...93 G5
Castlebar Hl WEA W13..............................97 H4
Castlebar Ms EA W5..................................97 H4
Castlebar Pk EA W5..................................97 H4
Castlebar Rd WEA W13.............................97 J5
Castle Baynard St BLKFR EC4V 12 B5
Castlebrook Cl LBTH SE11 ....18 A6
Castle Cl ACT W3....................................117 J2
BUSH WD23...28 A1
HAYES BR2 ....183 G6
WIM/MER SW19 ....159 G5
Castlecombe Dr
WIM/MER SW19 ....159 G2
Castlecombe Rd
ELTH/MOT SE9 ....184 D1
Castle Ct BANK EC3V *............................13 F4
SYD SE26..164 B6
Castledine Rd PGE/AN SE20 ....181 J5
Castle Dr REDBR IG4................................71 J3
Castleford Av ELTH/MOT SE9 ....167 G3
Castleford Cl UED N18.............................50 B2
Castlehaven Rd CAMTN NW1...................84 B6
Castle Hill Av CROY/NA CRO 213 K6
Castle Hill Pde WEA W13 *........................97 H6
Castle La WESTW SW1E...........................16 A4
Castleleigh Ct ENC/FH EN2......................23 K6
Castlemaine Av EW KT17........................207 K6
SAND/SEL CR2 ....212 B5
Castlemaine St WCHPL E1 ....104 D4
Castle Md CMBW SE5 *..........................142 D1
Castle Ms CAMTN NW1............................84 B4
NFNCH/WDSP N12 ....47 G1
TOOT SW17...160 D6
Castle Pde EW KT17 *.............................207 J5
Castle Pl CAMTN NW1 ....84 B4
WEA W13...97 G4
WELL DA16...148 A4
WFD IG8...53 F5
Castle Rd CAMTN NW1.............................84 B4
NFNCH/WDSP N12 ....47 G1
STJWD NW8...2 B3
WEA W13...97 G4
Castleton Av BXLYHN DA7......................150 A2
WBLY HA9...80 A2
Castleton Cl CROY/NA CRO....................198 B3
Castleton Gdns WBLY HA9 ....80 A1
Castleton Rd ELTH/MOT SE9..................166 C6
CDMY/SEVK IG3....................................73 H5
MTCM CR4..195 J1
RSLP HA4 ....59 H5
WALTH E17..52 B5
Castletown Rd WKENS W14....................119 H5
Castleview Cl FSBYPK N4.........................67 J5
Castle View Gdns IL IG1............................71 J3
Castle Vw CRICK NW2 *............................81 J4
Castle Wk SUN TW16 *............................172 B6
Castle Wy FELT TW13.............................154 B6
WIM/MER SW19 ....159 G5
Castlewood Dr
ELTH/MOT SE9 ....146 E3
Castlewood Rd EBAR EN4.........................21 H4
STNW/STAM N16...................................68 C3
Castle Yd HGT N6 *...................................66 A4
RCHPK/HAM TW10 ....136 E6
STHWK SE1 *...12 B7

Castor La POP/IOD E14...........................105 K6
Catalina Rd HTHAIR TW6........................132 C4
Catalpa Ct LEW SE13 ....165 G1
Caterham Av CLAY IG5..............................54 A5
Caterham Rd LEW SE13..........................145 F4
Catesby St WALW SE17............................19 F7
Catford Broadway CAT SE6....................164 E2
Catford Hl CAT SE6.................................164 C3
Catford Island CAT SE6 *........................164 E2
Catford Rd CAT SE6................................164 D3
Cathall Rd WAN E11..................................70 B6
Cathay St BERM/RHTH SE16 ....123 J2
Cathcart Dr ORP BR6..............................201 K6
Cathcart Hl KTTN NW5..............................84 C1
Cathcart Rd WBPTN SW10 *...................120 A6
Cathcart St KTTN NW5.............................84 B4
Cathedral St STHWK SE1 ....12 E7
Catherall Rd HBRY N5...............................85 J1
Catherine Cl STHGT/OAK N14 ....22 C6
Catherine Dr RCH/KEW TW9 ....137 F5
Catherine Gdns HSLW TW3....................135 J5
Catherine Griffiths Ct
CLKNW EC1R...5 K6
Catherine Gv GNWCH SE10 ....144 E2
Catherine Pl HRW HA1..............................61 F2
WEST SW1E..16 A4
Catherine Rd GPK RM2.............................75 K2
SURB KT6..190 E2
Catherines Cl WDR/YW UB7 * 112 A2
Catherine St HOL/ALD WC2B *...............11 G5
Catherine Vls RYNPK SW20 *.................176 E3
Catherine Wheel Aly
LVPST EC2M..13 H2
Catherine Wheel Rd
BTFD TW8...136 E1
Catherine Wheel Yd
WHALL SW1A..16 A1
Cat Hl EBAR EN4 ....33 J1
Cathles Rd BAL SW12.............................161 G1
Cathnor Rd SHB W12..............................118 E2
Catling Cl FSTH SE23..............................163 K5
Catlin's La PIN HA5 ....41 F6
Catlin St BERM/RHTH SE16....................123 H5
Cator La BECK BR3.................................182 C5
Cator Rd CAR SM5..................................209 K3
Cator Rd PGE/AN SE20...........................182 A2
Cator St PECK SE15................................123 G6
Cato St MBLAR W1H..................................8 D2
Catsey La BUSH WD23..............................28 C2
Catsey Wd BUSH WD23 ....28 C2
Catterick Cl FBAR/BDGN N11 ....48 A2
Cattistock Rd ELTH/MOT SE9 ....184 D1
Cattley Cl BAR EN5...................................20 C5
Catton St RSQ WC1B................................11 G2
Caudwell Ter
WAND/EARL SW18 * 160 C1
Caulfield Rd EHAM E6...............................89 K5
PECK SE15 ....143 J3
Causeway EBED/NFELT TW14 ....134 A5
The Causeway BELMT SM2....................209 G6
CAR SM5...210 A1
CHSGTN KT9..206 A2
EFNCH N2...65 H1
ESH/CLAY KT10 ....205 F5
TEDD TW11...174 A2
WAND/EARL SW18 ....159 H1
WIM/MER SW19 ....177 F1
Cecil Wy HAYES BR2..............................199 K5
Cedar Av BFN/LL DA15...........................168 B2
CHDH RM6..74 A2
EBAR EN4 ....33 J2
HYS/HAR UB3...94 E5
PEND EN3...25 F1
RSLP HA4 ....77 G3
WDR/YW UB7 *.....................................112 A1
WHTN TW2...155 C1
Cedar Cl BKHH IG9 ....39 J4
BOW E3...105 K1
CAR SM5...209 K4
DUL SE21..162 D3
HAYES BR2 ....215 J1
IL IG1...90 D3
KUTN/CMB KT2 ....158 A6
ROMW/RG RM7......................................56 E4
SWLY BR8..187 K6
Cedar Copse BMLY BR1..........................184 E5
Cedar Ct CHARL SE7 *............................126 B6
ELTH/MOT SE9 *...................................166 D1
STJWD NW8 *...2 B3
Cedar Crs HAYES BR2 *..........................215 J1
Cedarcroft Rd CHSGTN KT9 ....206 B2
Cedar Dr EFNCH N2..................................65 J3
PIN HA5 ....42 A2
Cedar Gdns BELMT SM2........................209 G4
Cedar Gv BXLY DA5................................168 E1
EA W5..116 E3
STHL UB1..96 A5
Cedar Hts RCHPK/HAM TW10 ....157 F3
Cedarhurst BMLY BR1 *...........................183 H3
Cedarhurst Dr ELTH/MOT SE9................146 B6
Cedar Lawn Av BAR EN5...........................20 C6
Cedar Mt ELTH/MOT SE9 ....166 C3
Cedarne Rd FUL/PGN SW6....................139 K1
Cedar Park Gdns CHDH RM6...................73 K4
Cedar Park Rd ENC/FH EN2......................23 J1
Cedar Pl CHARL SE7...............................126 B5
Cedar Ri STHGT/OAK N14 ....34 A1
Cedar Rd BELMT SM2.............................209 G4
BMLY BR1...184 B5
CRICK NW2...82 A2
CROY/NA CRO.....................................197 F6
DART DA1...171 G3
E/WMO/HCT KT8..................................189 K1
EBED/NFELT TW14 ....153 G3
ENC/FH EN2..23 H1
ERITH DA8..150 B1
HEST TW5...134 B3
OXHEY WD19..27 F1
ROMW/RG RM7......................................74 E1
TEDD TW11...174 B1
TOTM N17...50 C4
Cedars Av MTCM CR4.............................195 F1
WALTH E17..51 J2
Cedars Cl HDN NW4..................................46 B6
LEW SE13..145 G4
Cedars Ct ED N9..36 A4

Cedars Ms CLAP SW4 * 141 G5
Cedars Rd BARN SW13 ....138 C3
  BECK BR3 ....182 B5
  CLAP SW4 ....141 G4
  CROY/NA CR0 ....210 E1
  E/WMO/HCT KT8 ....174 D4
  ED N9 ....36 C4
  MRDN SM4 ....193 K1
  SRTFD E15 ....88 C4
  WCHMH N21 ....35 H4
The Cedars BKHH IG9 ....38 E3
  HOM E9 * 87 F5
  SRTFD E15 * 88 D6
  TEDD TW11 ....174 A2
Cedar Ter RCH/KEW TW9 ....137 F5
Cedar Tree Gv WNWD SE27 ....180 C1
Cedarville Gdns
  STRHM/NOR SW16 ....180 A2
Cedar Wk ESH/CLAY KT10 ....205 F4
Cedric Av ROM RM1 ....57 G6
Cedric Rd ELTH/MOT SE9 ....167 H5
Celadon Cl PEND EN3 ....25 G4
Celandine Cl POP/IOD E14 * 105 J4
Celandine Dr E8
  THMD SE28 ....28 C7
Celandine Gv STHGT/OAK N14 .....22 C6
Celandine Wy SRTFD E15 ....106 C2
Celbridge Ms BAY/PAD W2 * 101 F5
Celestial Gdns LEE SE13 ....145 G5
Celia Rd ARCH N19 ....84 C2
Celtic Av HAYES BR2 ....183 H6
Celtic St POP/IOD E14 ....105 K4
Cemetery La CHARL SE7 ....126 D6
Cemetery Rd ABYW SE2 ....128 C6
  FSTGT E7 ....88 D3
  TOTM N17 ....50 A3
Cenacle Cl HAMP NW3 ....82 K4
Centaur Ct BTFD TW8 ....117 F5
Centaur St STHWK SE1 ....17 H4
Centenary St PEND EN5 ....25 H5
Centenary Wk LOU IG10 ....39 F1
  WAN E11 ....71 J1
  WFD IG8 ....52 C2
Centennial Av WDR6 ....29 J2
Centennial Pk BORE WD6 ....29 J2
Central Av ASHF TW15 ....152 C6
Central Av E/WMO/HCT KT8 ....188 E2
  ED N9 ....36 A5
  EFNCH N2 ....47 H5
  EN EN1 ....24 D5
  HSLW TW3 ....135 H5
  HYS/HAR UB3 ....113 J2
  PIN HA5 ....59 K3
  WAN E11 ....70 B6
  WELL DA16 ....148 B3
  WLGTN SM6 ....210 E3
Central Bldgs EA W5 * 97 K6
Central Circ HDN NW4 ....63 K2
Central Ct CHIG IG7 ....54 E1
Central Hall Bldgs ARCH N19 * 66 C6
Central HI NRWD SE19 ....180 D1
Central Pde ACT W3 * 117 H2
  E/WMO/HCT KT8 * 188 E1
  GFD/PVL UB6 * 97 C2
  HRW HA1 ....61 F2
  PEND EN3 * 24 E5
  PGE/AN SE20 * 182 A5
  SCUP DA14 * 168 B5
  STRHM/NOR SW16 ....161 K6
  SURB KT6 * 191 F3
  WALTH E17 * 69 J1
Central Park Av DAGE RM10 ....92 E1
Central Park Est
  HSLWW TW4 * 134 C5
Central Pk Rd EHAM E6 ....107 J1
Central Pl SNWD SE25 * 197 H1
Central Rd ALP/SUD HA0 ....79 H5
  DART DA1 ....151 H6
  MRDN SM4 ....193 K3
  WPK KT4 ....192 D6
Central Sq E/WMO/HCT KT8 ....188 E1
  GLDGN NW11 ....64 E3
Central Ter FSBYE EC1V 6 C5
Central Ter BECK BR3 ....182 A6
Centre Wy CAR SM5 ....209 J5
  EBED/NFELT TW14 ....134 A6
  NTHWD HA6 ....40 C5
  THMD SE28 ....109 H6
  WLSDN NW10 ....98 E2
Centre Av ACT W3 ....118 A1
  ED N9 ....36 E4
Centre Common Rd CHST BR7 ....185 H3
Centre Rd DAGE RM10 ....110 D1
  WAN E11 ....71 G4
The Centre FELT TW13 ....153 K4
Centre Wy ED N9 ....36 E4
Centric Cl CAMTN NW1 * 4 B2
Centurian Wy ERITHM DA18 ....129 G3
Centurion Cl HOLWY N7 ....85 F5
Centurion Ct WLGTN SM6 ....195 C6
Centurion La BOW E3 ....105 H1
Centurion Wy PUR RM19 ....131 J4
Century Cl HDN NW4 ....64 B2
Century Ct WATW WD18 * 26 A2
Century Ms CLPT E5 ....86 E2
Century Rd WALTH E17 ....51 G6
Cephas Av WCHPL E1 ....104 E3
Cephas St WCHPL E1 ....104 E3
Cerise Rd PECK SE15 ....143 H2
Ceres Rd WOOL/PLUM SE18 ......128 A4
Cerne Cl YEAD UB4 ....95 G6
Cerne Rd MRDN SM4 ....194 B3
Cervantes Ct BAY/PAD W2 * 101 F5
  NTHWD HA6 ....40 D3
Ceylon Rd WKENS W14 ....119 G3
Chadacre Av CLAY IG5 ....53 K6
Chadacre Rd EW KT17 ....207 K5
Chadbourn St POP/IOD E14 ....105 K4
Chadd Dr BMLY BR1 ....184 D6
Chadville Gdns CHDH RM6 ....73 K2
Chadway BCTR RM8 ....73 H5
Chadwell Av CHDH RM6 ....73 H4
Chadwell Heath La CHDH RM6 .....73 H1

Chadwell St CLKNW EC1R 5 K4
Chadwick Av CHING E4 ....38 B6
  WCHMH N21 * 23 F6
  WIM/MER SW19 ....177 K2
Chadwick Cl TEDD TW11 ....174 B2
Chadwick Pl SURB KT6 ....190 D5
  PECK SE15 * 90 B1
  WAN E11 ....70 C4
Chadwick Rd IL IG1 ....90 A1
  WLSDN NW10 ....81 H6
Chadwick St WEST SW1P 16 C5
Chadwick Wy THMD SE28 ....109 K6
Chadwin Rd PLSTW E13 ....107 F4
Chadworth Wy
  ESH/CLAY KT10 ....204 D3
Chaffinch Av CROY/NA CR0 ....198 A3
Chaffinch Cl CROY/NA CR0 ....198 A2
  ED N9 ....37 F3
  SURB KT6 ....206 C1
Chaffinch La WATW WD18 ....26 D2
Chaffinch Rd BECK BR3 ....182 B4
Chafford Wy CHDH RM6 ....73 J1
Chagford St CAMTN NW1 ....2 E7
Chailey Av EN EN1 ....24 B3
Chailey Cl HEST TW5 ....134 C2
Chailey St CLPT E5 ....86 E1
Chalbury Wk IS N1 ....5 K2
Chalcombe Rd ABYW SE2 ....128 C3
Chalcot Cl BELMT SM2 ....208 E5
Chalcot Crs CAMTN NW1 ....83 K6
Chalcot Gdns HAMP NW3 ....83 K4
Chalcot Ms
  STRHM/NOR SW16 ....161 K5
Chalcot Rd CAMTN NW1 ....84 A6
Chalcot Sq CAMTN NW1 ....84 A5
Chalcott Gdns SURB KT6 * 190 D5
Chalcroft Rd LEW SE13 ....145 H6
Chaldon Rd FUL/PGN SW6 ....139 H1
Chale Rd BRXS/STRHM SW2 ......161 K1
Chalet Est MLHL NW7 * 170 A6
Chalfont Av WBLY HA9 ....80 D4
Chalfont Ct CAMTN NW1 * 2 E5
  ED N9 ....36 A5
Chalfont Ms
  WAND/EARL SW18 ....159 J3
Chalfont Rd ED N9 ....36 A5
  HYS/HAR UB3 ....113 K2
  SNWD SE25 ....181 G6
Chalfont Wk PIN HA5 * 41 G5
Chalfont Wy WEA W13 ....116 C3
Chalford Cl E/WMO/HCT KT8 ......189 F1
Chalforde Gdns GPK RM2 ....75 K1
Chalford Rd DUL SE21 ....162 E6
Chalgrove Av MRDN SM4 ....193 K2
Chalgrove Crs CLAY IG5 ....53 J5
Chalgrove Gdns FNCH N3 ....46 C6
Chalgrove Rd BELMT SM2 ....209 H5
  HOM E9 ....86 A4
  TOTM N17 ....50 D4
Chalice Cl WLGTN SM6 ....210 D4
Chalkenden Cl PGE/AN SE20 ......181 J3
Chalk Farm Pde HAMP NW3 * 84 A5
Chalk HI OXHEY WD19 ....27 J1
Chalkhill Rd CDALE/KGS NW9 * 63 H2
Chalk Hill Rd HMSMTH W6 ....119 G4
Chalkhill Rd WBLY HA9 ....80 C1
Chalklands WBLY HA9 ....80 E1
Chalk La EBAR EN4 ....21 K4
Chalkley Cl MTCM CR4 ....178 E5
Chalk Pit Av STMC/STPC BR5 ....186 D6
Chalk Pit Rd SUT SM1 ....209 G5
Chalk Rd PLSTW E13 ....107 F4
Chalkstone Cl WELL DA16 ....148 B2
Chalkwell Park Av EN EN1 ....24 A5
Chalky La CHSGTN KT9 ....205 K6
Challenge Cl WLSDN NW10 ....81 G6
Challenge Rd FELT TW13 ....153 K5
Challice Wy
  BRXS/STRHM SW2 ....162 A3
Challin St PGE/AN SE20 ....181 K4
Challis Rd BTFD TW8 ....116 E5
Challoner Cl EFNCH N2 ....47 H5
Challoner Crs WKENS W14 ....119 J5
Challoners
  E/WMO/HCT KT8 ....189 J1
Challoner St WKENS W14 ....119 J5
Chalmers Rd ASHF TW15 ....152 E6
Chalmers Rd East ASHF TW15 ....152 E6
Chalmers Wk WALW SE17 * 122 C6
Chalmers Wy
  EBED/NFELT TW14 ....134 A4
  HSLW TW3 ....136 C5
  IL IG1 ....90 A1
  TWK TW1 ....156 C2
  WEA W13 ....116 B1
  WIM/MER SW19 * 178 A2
Chalsey Rd BROCKY SE4 ....144 C5
Chalton Dr EFNCH N2 ....65 G3
Chalton St CAMTN NW1 ....4 D4
Chamberlain Cl IL IG1 ....90 C1
  WOOL/PLUM SE18 ....127 J3
Chamberlain Crs WWKM BR4 ......198 E5
Chamberlain Gdns HSLW TW3 ....135 H2
Chamberlain La PIN HA5 ....58 E1
Chamberlain Pl WALTH E17 * 51 G6
Chamberlain Rd ED N9 ....36 C5
  EFNCH N2 ....47 G5
Chamberlain St HAMP NW3 ....83 K5
Chamberlain Wy PIN HA5 ....58 E1
  SURB KT6 ....191 F4
Chamberlayne Av WBLY HA9 ....80 A1
Chamberlayne Rd
  WLSDN NW10 ....82 A6
Chambers Gdns EFNCH N2 ....47 H4
Chambers La WLSDN NW10 ....81 K5
Chambers Rd HOLWY N7 ....84 E1
Chambers St
  BERM/RHTH SE16 ....123 H2
Chambers St WCHPL E1 ....13 K5
Chambers Wk STAN HA7 ....43 H2
Chambon Pl HMSMTH W6 ....118 D4
Chambord St BETH E2 ....7 K5
Champion Crs SYD SE26 ....164 B6
Champion Gv CMBW SE5 ....142 E4
Champion Hl CMBW SE5 ....142 E4
Champion Pk CMBW SE5 ....142 E4

Champion Rd SYD SE26 ....164 B6
Champness Cl WNWD SE27 ....162 E6
Champness Rd BARK IG11 ....91 F5
Champneys Cl BELMT SM2 ....208 D5
Champneys OXHEY WD19 * 27 J4
Chancellor Gdns
  SAND/SEL CR2 ....211 H6
Chancellor Gv DUL SE21 ....162 D4
Chancellor Pl CDALE/KGS NW9 .....45 H5
Chancellors Rd HMSMTH W6 ....119 F5
Chancellors St HMSMTH W6 ....119 F5
Chancellors Whf BARN SW13 ....119 F5
Chancelot Rd ABYW SE2 ....128 C4
Chancel Rd LEE SE13 ....145 F4
Chancel St STHWK SE1 ....12 A7
Chancery La BECK BR3 ....182 E5
  LINN WC2A 11 H2
Chancery Ms TOOT SW17 ....160 D4
Chance St BETH E2 ....7 J6
Chanctonbury Cl
  ELTH/MOT SE9 ....167 G5
Chanctonbury Gdns
  BELMT SM2 ....209 F5
Chanctonbury Wy
  NFNCH/WDSP N12 ....32 E6
Chandler Av CAN/RD E16 ....106 E4
Chandler Cl HPTN TW12 ....172 E4
Chandlers Cl
  EBED/NFELT TW14 ....153 J2
Chandlers Ct
  LEE/GVPK SE12 ....166 A4
Chandlers Dr ERITH DA8 ....130 A4
Chandlers Ms POP/IOD E14 ....124 D2
Chandler St WAP E1W 123 J1
Chandlers Wy ROM RM1 ....75 G2
Chandler Wy PECK SE15 ....143 G1
Chandos Av EA W5 ....116 D4
  STHGT/OAK N14 ....34 C5
  TRDG/WHET N20 ....33 H3
  WALTH E17 * 51 J5
Chandos Cl BKHH IG9 ....39 F4
Chandos Crs EDGW HA8 ....44 B3
Chandos Pl CHCR WC2N 10 E6
Chandos Rd CRICK NW2 ....82 A3
  EFNCH N2 ....47 H5
  HRW HA1 ....60 C2
  PIN HA5 ....59 G4
  SRTFD E15 ....88 B3
  TOTM N17 ....50 A5
  WLSDN NW10 ....99 G3
Chandos St CAVSO/HST W1G 9 K2
Chandos Wy GLDGN NW11 ....65 F5
Channel Cl HEST TW5 ....135 F2
Channel Gate Rd WLSDN NW10 ...100 A4
  WLSDN NW10 ....99 G2
Channelsea Rd SRTFD E15 ....88 B6
Chantress Cl DAGE RM10 ....92 E6
Chantrey Rd BRXN/ST SW9 ....142 A4
Chantry Cl ENC/FH EN2 ....23 J1
  KTN/HRWW/W HA3 ....42 B4
  MLHL NW7 ....31 H2
  MV/WKIL W9 ....100 D3
Chantry Crs WLSDN NW10 ....81 G3
Chantry La HAYES BR2 ....200 C2
Chantry Pl RYLN/HDSTN HA2 ....42 B4
Chantry Rd CHSGTN KT9 ....206 B3
  KTN/HRWW/W HA3 ....42 B4
Chantry Sq KENS W8 ....120 A3
Chantry St IS N1 ....6 B1
The Chantry CHING E4 * 38 A3
Chant Sq SRTFD E15 ....88 B5
Chant St SRTFD E15 ....88 B5
Chapel Cl DART DA1 ....150 B6
  WLSDN NW10 ....81 H3
Chapel Ct DART DA1 ....150 B6
  STHWK SE1 ....18 E2
  WOOL/PLUM SE18 ....128 A6
Chapel Farm Rd
  ELTH/MOT SE9 ....166 E5
Chapel Hl DART DA1 ....150 B5
  EFNCH N2 * 47 J5
Chapel House St
  POP/IOD E14 ....124 E5
Chapel La PIN HA5 ....41 H6
Chapel Market IS N1 ....5 J2
Chapel Mill Rd KUT/HW KT1 ....175 G6
Chapel Pl CAVSO/HST W1G 9 J3
  IS N1 * 5 K2
  TOTM N17 ....50 B3
Chapel Rd BXLYHN DA7 ....149 H5
  HSLW TW3 ....135 G4
  IL IG1 ....90 A1
  TWK TW1 ....156 C2
  WEA W13 ....116 C1
  WNWD SE27 ....162 C6
Chapel Side BAY/PAD W2 ....101 F6
Chapel St CAMTN NW1 ....8 C2
  ENC/FH EN2 ....23 J4
  KTBR SW1X 15 H4
Chapel Vw SAND/SEL CR2 ....212 D5
Chaplemount Rd WFD IG8 ....53 K2
Chaplin Cl ALP/SUD HA0 ....79 J4
  STHWK SE1 ....17 K2
Chaplin Rd ALP/SUD HA0 ....79 J4
  BCTR RM9 ....91 J4
  CRICK NW2 ....81 J4
  SRTFD E15 ....106 C1
  TOTM N17 ....50 B6
Chapman Av WDGN N22 * 49 G4
Chapman Crs
  KTN/HRWW/W HA3 ....62 A2
Chapman Rd BELV DA17 ....129 H5
  CROY/NA CR0 ....196 B5
  HOM E9 ....87 H4
Chapmans Gn WDGN N22 * 49 G4
Chapman's La
  STMC/STPC BR5 ....186 B5
  SWLY BR8 ....187 H5
Chapman Sq WIM/MER SW19 .....159 G4
Chapman St WCHPL E1 ....104 D6
Chapman St WDGN N22 * 104 D6
Chapter Rd CRICK NW2 ....81 J4
  WALW SE17 ....122 C5
Chapter St WEST SW1P 16 C7

Chapter Wy HPTN TW12 ....155 F6
Chara Pl CHSWK W4 ....118 A6
Charcroft Gdns PEND EN3 ....25 F5
Chardin Rd CHSWK W4 * 118 B4
Chardmore Rd
  STNW/STAM N16 ....68 C5
Chardwell Cl EHAM E6 ....107 J5
Charecroft Wy WKENS W14 ....119 G2
Charford Rd CAN/RD E16 ....106 E4
Chargeable La PLSTW E13 ....106 E3
Chargeable St CAN/RD E16 ....106 D3
Charing Cl ORP BR6 ....217 F2
Charing Cross CHCR WC2N 10 E7
Charing Cross Rd
  SOHO/SHAV W1D 10 D3
Chariot Cl BOW E3 ....87 J6
Charlbert St STJWD NW8 ....2 C2
Charlbury Av STAN HA7 ....43 K1
Charlbury Gdns
  GDMY/SEVK IG3 ....73 F6
Charlbury Gv EA W5 ....97 J5
Charldane Rd ELTH/MOT SE9 ......167 G5
Charlecote Gv SYD SE26 ....163 J5
Charlecote Rd BCTR RM8 ....92 A1
Charlemont Rd EHAM E6 ....107 K2
Charles Babbage Cl
  CHSGTN KT9 ....205 J5
Charles Barry Cl CLAP SW4 ....141 H4
Charles Cl SCUP DA14 ....168 C6
Charles Cobb Gdns
  CROY/NA CR0 ....211 G3
Charles Coveney Rd
  PECK SE15 ....143 G2
Charles Crs HRW HA1 ....60 D4
Charles Dickens Ter
  PGE/AN SE20 * 181 K3
Charlesfield ELTH/MOT SE9 ....166 B5
Charles Flemwell Ms
  CAN/RD E16 * 125 K1
Charles Grinling Wk
  WOOL/PLUM SE18 ....127 F4
Charles Haller St
  BRXS/STRHM SW2 ....162 B2
Charles II Pl CHEL SW3 * 120 E5
Charles II St STJS SW1Y 10 C7
Charles La STJWD NW8 ....2 C3
Charles Pl CAMTN NW1 ....4 B5
Charles Rd CHDH RM6 ....73 K4
  DAGE RM10 ....93 H4
  FSTGT E7 ....89 G5
  WEA W13 ....97 G5
  WIM/MER SW19 ....177 K4
Charles Sevright Dr
  MLHL NW7 ....46 B1
Charles Sq IS N1 ....7 F5
Charles Square Est IS N1 * 7 F5
Charles St BARN SW13 ....138 D4
  CAN/RD E16 ....126 A1
  CROY/NA CR0 ....211 J1
  EN EN1 ....24 B6
  HSLW TW3 ....134 E3
  MYFR/PICC W1J 9 J7
  WEA W13 ....97 G5
  WIM/MER SW19 ....177 K4
Charles Townsend Ho
  CLKNW EC1R * 6 A6
Charles Whincup Rd
  CAN/RD E16 * 126 A1
Charleston Cl FELT TW13 ....153 K5
Charleston St WALW SE17 ....18 D7
Charleville Circ SYD SE26 ....181 H1
Charleville Rd WKENS W14 ....119 H5
Charlie Chaplin Wk
  STHWK SE1 * 11 K7
Charlieville Rd ERITH DA8 ....149 K1
Charlmont Rd TOOT SW17 ....178 E2
Charlock Wy WATW WD18 ....26 D1
Charlotte Cl BXLYHN DA7 ....149 F6
Charlotte Despard Av
  BTSEA SW11 ....141 G2
Charlotte Gdns CRW RM5 ....56 E3
Charlotte Ms
  ESH/CLAY KT10 * 204 B2
  FITZ W1T 10 B1
  NKENS W10 ....100 B5
Charlotte Pde FSTH SE23 * 164 B4
Charlotte Park Av BMLY BR1 ....184 E6
Charlotte Pl FITZ W1T * 10 B1
Charlotte Rd BARN SW13 ....138 C2
  DAGE RM10 ....93 F4
  IS N1 ....7 G5
  WLGTN SM6 ....210 C4
Charlotte Rw CLAP SW4 ....141 H4
Charlotte St FITZ W1T 10 B1
Charlotte Ter IS N1 ....5 H1
Charlow Cl FUL/PGN SW6 ....140 B3
Charlton Church La
  CHARL SE7 ....126 B5
Charlton Crs BARK IG11 ....109 F1
Charlton Dene CHARL SE7 ....146 B1
Charlton King's Rd
  HOLWY N7 ....85 H2
Charlton La CHARL SE7 ....126 C5
Charlton Park La CHARL SE7 ....126 C5
Charlton Park Rd CHARL SE7 ......126 C6
Charlton Pl IS N1 ....6 A2
Charlton Rd BKHTH/KID SE3 ....145 K1
  ED N9 ....37 F3
  KTN/HRWW/W HA3 ....62 B5
  WBLY HA9 ....62 B5
  WLSDN NW10 ....81 G6
Charlton Wy BKHTH/KID SE3 ....145 J1
Charlwood CROY/NA CR0 ....213 H6
Charlwood Cl
  KTN/HRWW/W HA3 ....42 E2
Charlwood Pl PIM SW1V 16 B7
Charlwood Rd
  PUT/ROE SW15 ....139 G5
Charlwood St PIM SW1V 16 B7
Charlwood Ter
  PUT/ROE SW15 ....139 G5
Charminster Av
  WIM/MER SW19 ....177 K5
Charminster Rd
  ELTH/MOT SE9 ....166 C6
  WPK KT4 ....193 G5
Charmouth Rd WELL DA16 ....148 D2
Charnock Rd CLPT E5 ....86 D1
Charnwood Av
  WIM/MER SW19 ....177 K5
Charnwood Cl CHSWK W4 * 117 K6
  HDN NW4 ....45 K6
  WWKM BR4 ....199 J6

Charnwood Gdns
  POP/IOD E14 ....124 D4
Charnwood Pl
  TRDG/WHET N20 ....33 G5
Charnwood Rd SNWD SE25 ....196 E2
Charnwood St CLPT E5 ....68 C2
Charnwood Villas SWFD E18 * 53 F6
Charrington Rd CROY/NA CR0 ....4 C2
Charrington St CAMTN NW1 ....4 C2
Charsley Rd CAT SE6 ....164 E4
Chart Cl CROY/NA CR0 ....197 K3
  HAYES BR2 ....183 G5
  MTCM CR4 ....194 E1
Charter Av GNTH/NBYPK IG2 ....72 E3
Charter Crs HSLWW TW4 ....134 D5
Charter Dr BXLY DA5 ....169 F2
Charterhouse Av
  ALP/SUD HA0 ....79 J3
Charterhouse Bldgs FARR EC1M 6 C7
Charterhouse Ms FARR EC1M 6 C7
Charterhouse Rd HACK E8 ....86 C3
  ORP BR6 ....217 G1
Charterhouse St FARR EC1M 12 B1
  FARR EC1N 11 K2
The Charterhouse FARR EC1M * 6 B7
Charteris Rd FSBYPK N4 ....67 G5
  KIL/WHAMP NW6 ....82 D6
  WFD IG8 ....53 F2
Charter Rd KUT/HW KT1 ....175 J5
  WFD IG8 ....52 C2
The Charter Rd WFD IG8 ....52 C2
Charter Sq KUT/HW KT1 ....175 J5
Charter Sq KUT/HW KT1 ....181 F1
Charter Wy GLDGN NW11 ....64 C5
  STHGT/OAK N14 ....34 C5
Chartfield Av PUT/ROE SW15 ....138 E6
Chartfield Sq
  PUT/ROE SW15 ....139 G6
Chartham Gv WNWD SE27 ....162 B5
Chartham Rd SNWD SE25 ....181 J6
Chart Hills Cl THMD SE28 ....110 A5
Chartley Av CRICK NW2 ....81 F1
  STAN HA7 ....43 F2
Chartley Pde WLSDN NW10 * 81 G1
Charton Cl BELV DA17 * 129 G6
Chartridge Cl BUSH WD23 ....28 C1
Chart St IS N1 ....7 F4
Chartwell Cl CHST BR7 ....167 J4
  CROY/NA CR0 ....196 E5
  GFD/PVL UB6 * 78 B6
Chartwell Dr ORP BR6 ....216 D5
Chartwell Pl CHEAM SM3 ....208 C2
  RYLN/HDSTN HA2 ....60 C6
Chartwell Wy PGE/AN SE20 ....181 J4
Charville La HGDN/ICK UB10 ....94 A2
Charwood
  STRHM/NOR SW16 ....162 B6
Chase Ct RYNPK SW20 ....177 H5
Chase Court Gdns ENC/FH EN2 ....23 J3
Chase Cross Rd CRW RM5 ....56 E3
Chasefield Rd TOOT SW17 ....160 E6
Chase Gdns CHING E4 ....37 J6
  WHTN TW2 ....155 J1
Chase Gn ENC/FH EN2 ....23 J3
Chase Green Av ENC/FH EN2 ....23 H3
Chase Hl ENC/FH EN2 ....23 J4
Chase La BARK/HLT IG6 ....72 D2
Chaseley St POP/IOD E14 ....105 G5
Chasemore Cl MTCM CR4 ....194 E4
Chasemore Gdns
  CROY/NA CR0 ....211 G3
Chase Ridings ENC/FH EN2 ....23 G3
Chase Rd ENC/FH EN3 ....37 J5
  STHGT/OAK N14 ....22 C6
Chase Side EBAR EN4 ....22 A6
  ENC/FH EN2 ....23 J1
  STHGT/OAK N14 ....34 B2
Chase Side Av ENC/FH EN2 ....23 J2
Chaseside Av RYNPK SW20 ....177 H4
Chase Side Cl ROM RM1 * 57 G2
Chase Side Crs ENC/FH EN2 ....23 J2
The Chase BMLY BR1 ....184 A6
  BXLYHN DA7 ....149 J4
  CLAP SW4 ....141 G4
  DAGE RM10 ....93 F1
  EDGW HA8 ....44 D4
  LOU IG10 ....39 G2
  MNPK E12 ....89 G5
  PIN HA5 ....59 G5
  ROM RM1 ....57 G6
  STAN HA7 ....43 G2
  STRHM/NOR SW16 ....180 A3
  SUN TW16 ....172 A4
  WLGTN SM6 ....210 E3
Chaseville Pde WCHMH N21 * 23 F6
Chaseville Park Rd
  WCHMH N21 ....22 E6
Chase Wy STHGT/OAK N14 ....34 B3
Chasewood Av ENC/FH EN2 ....23 H3
Chasewood Pk HRW HA1 * 78 E1
Chastilian Rd DART DA1 ....170 D2
Chatfield Rd BTSEA SW11 ....140 B4
  CROY/NA CR0 ....196 C5
Chatham Av HAYES BR2 ....199 J5
Chatham Cl CHEAM SM3 ....193 J4
  GLDGN NW11 ....64 E2
Chatham Pl HOM E9 ....86 E4
Chatham Rd BTSEA SW11 ....160 E1
  KUTN/CMB KT2 ....175 H5
  SWFD E18 ....52 D5
  WALTH E17 ....51 H2
Chatham St WALW SE17 ....18 E6
  WOOL/PLUM SE18 ....127 G3
Chatsfield Pl EA W5 ....98 A5
Chatsworth Av BFN/LL DA15 ....168 B3
  BMLY BR1 ....166 A6
  HDN NW4 ....46 A5
  RYNPK SW20 ....177 H4
  WBLY HA9 ....80 C3
Chatsworth Cl CHSWK W4 * 117 K6
  HDN NW4 ....46 A5
  WWKM BR4 ....199 J6

Chatsworth Crs *HSLW* TW3 ... 135 J5
Chatsworth Dr *EN* EN1 ... 36 C2
Chatsworth Est *CLPT* E5 * ... 87 F2
Chatsworth Gdns *ACT* W3 ... 98 D6
  NWMAL KT3 * ... 192 C2
  RYLN/HDSTN HA2 ... 60 B5
Chatsworth Pl *MTCM* CR4 ... 178 E6
  TWK TW1 ... 158 B6
Chatsworth Ri *EA* W5 ... 98 B3
Chatsworth Rd *CHEAM* SM3 ... 208 B2
  CHSWK W4 ... 117 K6
  CLPT E5 ... 86 E1
  CRICK NW2 ... 82 B4
  CROY/NA CR0 ... 211 K2
  DART DA1 ... 151 F6
  EA W5 ... 98 B3
  SRTFD E15 ... 88 D3
  YEAD UB4 ... 95 F5
Chatsworth Wy *WNWD* SE27 ... 162 D4
Chattern Hl *ASHF* TW15 ... 152 C6
Chattern Rd *ASHF* TW15 ... 153 F6
Chatterton Ms *FSBYPK* N4 * ... 85 H1
Chatterton Rd *FSBYPK* N4 ... 85 H1
  HAYES BR2 ... 200 C2
Chatto Rd *BTSEA* SW11 ... 140 E6
Chaucer Av *HSLWW* TW4 ... 134 A5
  RCH/KEW TW9 ... 137 H5
  YEAD UB4 ... 94 E4
Chaucer Dr *STHWK* SE1 ... 19 K7
Chaucer Gdns *SUT* SM1 ... 208 E2
Chaucer Gn *CROY/NA* CR0 ... 197 J4
Chaucer Pk *DART* DA1 ... 171 J2
Chaucer Rd *ACT* W3 ... 117 K1
  ASHF TW15 ... 152 B6
  BFN/LL DA15 ... 168 D3
  FSTGT E7 ... 88 E4
  HARH RM3 ... 57 J1
  HNHL SE24 ... 142 C6
  SUT SM1 ... 208 E2
  WALTH E17 ... 52 A4
  WAN E11 ... 70 E3
  WELL DA16 ... 148 A2
Chaucer Wy *DART* DA1 ... 151 K5
Chauncey Cl *ED* N9 ... 36 C5
Chaundrye Cl *ELTH/MOT* SE9 ... 166 E1
Chauntler Rd *CAN/RD* E16 ... 107 F5
Chave Rd *DART* DA1 ... 171 H5
Cheam Common Rd *WPK* KT4 ... 192 E6
Cheam Man *CHEAM* SM3 * ... 208 C4
Cheam Park Wy *CHEAM* SM3 ... 208 B6
Cheam Rd *BELMT* SM2 ... 208 B6
Cheam St *PECK* SE15 * ... 143 J4
Cheapside *CITYW* EC2V ... 12 D4
  EFNCH N2 * ... 47 K6
  PLMGR N13 ... 35 J6
  WDGN N22 * ... 49 G6
Cheddar Cl *FBAR/BDGN* N11 ... 47 K2
Cheddar Wave *YEAD* UB4 ... 95 F5
Cheddington Rd *UED* N18 ... 36 A6
Cheeseman Cl *HPTN* TW12 ... 172 D2
Cheesemans Ter
  WKENS W14 * ... 119 J5
Cheldon Av *MLHL* NW7 ... 46 B3
Chelford Rd *BMLY* BR1 ... 183 C1
Chelmer Cl *BARK* IG11 ... 109 H1
Chelmer Rd *HOM* E9 ... 87 F3
Chelmsford Av *CRW* RM5 ... 57 F3
Chelmsford Cl *BELMT* SM2 ... 208 E6
  EHAM E6 ... 107 K5
  HMSMTH W6 ... 119 G6
Chelmsford Gdns *IL* IG1 ... 71 J4
Chelmsford Rd
  STHGT/OAK N14 ... 34 C2
  SWFD E18 ... 52 D4
  WALTH E17 ... 69 J3
  WAN E11 ... 70 B5
Chelmsford Sq *WLSDN* NW10 ... 82 A6
Chelsea Br *VX/NE* SW8 ... 121 G6
Chelsea Bridge Ga
  BTSEA SW11 * ... 121 F6
Chelsea Bridge Rd *CHEL* SW3 ... 121 F5
Chelsea Cl *EDGW* HA8 ... 44 C5
  HPTN TW12 ... 173 H2
  WLSDN NW10 ... 81 F6
  WPK KT4 ... 192 D4
Chelsea Crs *CRICK* NW2 * ... 82 D4
  WBPTN SW10 * ... 140 B2
Chelsea Emb *CHEL* SW3 ... 120 E6
Chelsea Gdns *CHEA* SW1W * ... 121 F5
  CHEAM SM3 ... 208 C2
Chelsea Harbour Dr
  WBPTN SW10 ... 140 B2
Chelsea Manor Gdns
  CHEL SW3 * ... 120 D6
Chelsea Manor St *CHEL* SW3 ... 120 D5
Chelsea Park Gdns
  WBPTN SW10 ... 120 C6
  CHEL SW5 ... 120 C5
Chelsea Sq *CAR* SM5 ... 209 K6
  CHEL SW3 ... 120 C5
Chelsea Towers *CHEL* SW3 * ... 120 D6
Chelsea Village
  FUL/PGN SW6 * ... 140 A1
Chelsfield Av *ED* N9 ... 37 F2
Chelsfield Gdns *SYD* SE26 ... 163 K5
Chelsfield La *ORP* BR6 ... 217 J6
Chelsfield Rd *STMC/STPC* BR5 ... 202 D2
Chelsfield Rd *STMC/STPC* BR5 ... 202 D3
Chelsham Rd *CLAP* SW4 ... 141 J4
  SAND/SEL CR2 ... 211 K5
Chelston Rd *RSLP* HA4 ... 58 E6
Chelsworth Dr
  WOOL/PLUM SE18 ... 127 J6
Cheltenham Av *TWK* TW1 ... 156 B2
Cheltenham Cl *NTHLT* UB5 ... 78 B4
  NWMAL KT3 ... 175 K6
Cheltenham Gdns *EHAM* E6 ... 107 J1
  LOU IG10 ... 39 J1
Cheltenham Pl *ACT* W3 ... 117 K2
  KTN/HRWW/W HA3 ... 62 A1
Cheltenham Rd *LEY* E10 ... 70 A3
  ORP BR6 ... 217 G1
  PECK SE15 ... 143 K5
Cheltenham Ter *CHEL* SW3 ... 120 E5

Chelverton Rd
  PUT/ROE SW15 ... 139 G5
Chelwood Cl *CHING* E4 ... 37 K1
  NTHWD HA6 ... 40 A3
Chelwood Gdns
  RCH/KEW TW9 ... 137 H5
Chenappa Ct *PLSTW* E13 ... 106 E2
Chenduit Wy *STAN* HA7 ... 43 F2
Cheney Rw *WALTH* E17 ... 51 H4
Cheney Rd *WAN* E11 ... 88 C1
Cheney St *PIN* HA5 ... 59 G1
Chenies Ms *GWRST* WC1E ... 4 C7
Chenies Pl *CAMTN* NW1 ... 4 E3
Chenies St *FITZ* W1T ... 10 C1
The Chenies *ORP* BR6 ... 201 K5
  RDART DA2 ... 170 B6
Chenies Wy *WATW* WD18 ... 26 C2
Cheniston Gdns *KENS* W8 * ... 120 A3
Chepstow Cl *PUT/ROE* SW15 ... 139 H6
Chepstow Cnr *BAY/PAD* W2 * ... 100 E5
Chepstow Crs *GDMY/SEVK* IG3 ... 72 E5
  NTGHL W11 ... 100 E6
Chepstow Gdns *STHL* UB1 ... 95 K5
Chepstow Pl *BAY/PAD* W2 ... 100 E6
Chepstow Ri *CROY/NA* CR0 ... 212 A1
Chepstow Rd *BAY/PAD* W2 ... 100 D5
  CROY/NA CR0 ... 212 A1
  HNWL W7 ... 116 B3
Chepstow Vls *NTGHL* W11 ... 100 D6
Chequer Rd *BKHH* IG9 ... 39 F3
Chequers Cl *CDALE/KGS* NW9 ... 45 G6
  STMC/STPC BR5 ... 202 A1
Chequers La *DAGW* RM9 ... 110 B3
Chequers Pde *PLMGR* N13 * ... 49 J1
  ELTH/MOT SE9 * ... 41 H6
Chequers St *STLK* EC1Y ... 6 E7
Chequers Wy *PLMGR* N13 ... 49 J1
Cherbury Ct *THMD* SE28 ... 109 K5
Cherbury St *IS* N1 ... 7 F3
Cherimoya Gdns
  E/WMO/HCT KT8 ... 173 G6
Cherington Rd *HNWL* W7 * ... 116 A1
Cheriton Av *CLAY* IG5 ... 54 A5
  HAYES BR2 ... 199 J2
Cheriton Cl *EA* W5 ... 97 J4
  EBAR EN4 ... 21 K4
Cheriton Ct *WOT/HER* KT12 ... 188 B5
Cheriton Dr
  WOOL/PLUM SE18 ... 147 J1
Cherry Av *STHL* UB1 ... 114 C1
Cherry Blossom Cl *PLMGR* N13 ... 49 H1
Cherry Cl *BRXS/STRHM* SW2 * ... 162 B2
  CAR SM5 ... 194 E6
  CDALE/KGS NW9 ... 45 G6
  EA W5 ... 116 E3
  MRDN SM4 ... 193 H1
  RSLP HA4 ... 76 C1
Cherrycot Ri *ORP* BR6 ... 216 C2
Cherry Ct *PIN* HA5 ... 41 H5
Cherry Crs *BTFD* TW8 ... 136 C1
Cherry Croft Gdns *PIN* HA5 * ... 41 K3
Cherrydown Av *CHING* E4 ... 37 H5
Cherrydown Cl *CHING* E4 ... 37 H5
Cherrydown Rd *SCUP* DA14 ... 168 E4
Cherrydown Wk
  ROMW/RG RM7 ... 56 D5
Cherry Gdns *DAGW* RM9 ... 92 B5
  NTHLT UB5 ... 78 B5
Cherry Garden St
  BERM/RHTH SE16 ... 123 J2
Cherry Garth *BTFD* TW8 ... 116 E4
Cherry Gv *HYS/HAR* UB3 ... 114 A1
  UX/CGN UB8 ... 94 A4
Cherry Hl *BAR* EN5 ... 33 F1
  KTN/HRWW/W HA3 ... 42 E2
Cherry Hill Gdns
  CROY/NA CR0 ... 211 F2
Cherry Hills *OXHEY* WD19 ... 41 J1
Cherrylands Cl
  CDALE/KGS NW9 * ... 62 E6
Cherry La *WDR/YW* UB7 ... 112 C4
Cherry Orch *CHARL* SE7 ... 126 B6
  WDR/YW UB7 ... 112 B2
Cherry Orchard Cl
  STMC/STPC BR5 ... 202 D2
Cherry Orchard Gdns
  CROY/NA CR0 ... 196 E5
  E/WMO/HCT KT8 ... 172 E6
Cherry Orchard Rd
  CROY/NA CR0 ... 196 E6
  E/WMO/HCT KT8 ... 173 F6
Cherry Rd *PEND* EN3 ... 24 E1
Cherry Rw *ROMW/RG* RM7 ... 75 F2
Cherry Tree Cl *ALP/SUD* HA0 ... 79 G2
  RAIN RM13 ... 111 J1
Cherry Tree Ct *CHARL* SE7 * ... 126 B6
Cherry Tree Dr
  STRHM/NOR SW16 * ... 161 K5
Cherry Tree Hl *EFNCH* N2 ... 65 J2
Cherry Tree La *RAIN* RM13 ... 111 H2
  RDART DA2 ... 170 C5
Cherry Tree Ri *BKHH* IG9 ... 39 G6
Cherry Tree Rd *EFNCH* N2 ... 65 K1
  ERITH DA8 ... 151 F1
  SRTFD E15 ... 88 C3
Cherry Tree Wk *BECK* BR3 ... 198 C1
  STLK EC1Y ... 6 D7
  WWKM BR4 ... 214 D2
Cherry Tree Wy *STAN* HA7 ... 43 H2
Cherry Wk *HAYES* BR2 ... 199 K5
  RAIN RM13 ... 111 H1
Cherry Wy *HOR/WEW* KT19 ... 207 F4
Cherrywood Cl *BOW* E3 ... 105 G2
  KUTN/CMB KT2 ... 175 H5
Cherrywood Dr
  PUT/ROE SW15 ... 139 G6
Cherrywood La *MRDN* SM4 ... 193 H1
Chertsey Dr *CHEAM* SM3 ... 193 H6
Chertsey Rd *FELT* TW13 ... 153 H6
  IL IG1 ... 90 D2
  TWK TW1 ... 156 B1
  WAN E11 ... 70 B6
  WHTN TW2 ... 155 K5

Chertsey St *TOOT* SW17 ... 179 F1
Chervil Cl *FELT* TW13 ... 153 K5
Chervil Ms *THMD* SE28 ... 128 C1
Cherwell Ct *HOR/WEW* KT19 ... 206 E2
Cherwell Wy *RSLP* HA4 ... 58 A3
Cheryls Cl *FUL/PGN* SW6 ... 140 A2
Cheseman St *SYD* SE26 ... 163 J5
Chesfield Rd *KUTN/CMB* KT2 ... 175 F3
Chesham Av *HAYES* BR2 ... 201 G3
Chesham Cl *KTBR* SW1X * ... 15 G5
  ROMW/RG RM7 ... 75 F1
Chesham Crs *PGE/AN* SE20 ... 181 K4
Chesham Ms *KTBR* SW1X ... 15 G4
Chesham Pl *KTBR* SW1X ... 15 G5
  KUTN/CMB KT2 * ... 175 H4
  PGE/AN SE20 ... 181 K5
Chesham St *KTBR* SW1X ... 15 G5
  WLSDN NW10 ... 81 G1
Chesham Ter *WEA* W13 ... 116 C2
Chesham Wy *WATW* WD18 ... 26 C1
Cheshire Cl *MTCM* CR4 ... 179 K6
  WALTH E17 ... 51 K4
Cheshire Gdns *CHSGTN* KT9 ... 205 K4
Cheshire Rd *WDGN* N22 ... 49 F3
Cheshire St *BETH* E2 ... 104 C3
Chesholm Rd *STNW/STAM* N16 ... 86 A1
Cheshunt Rd *BELV* DA17 ... 129 H5
  FSTGT E7 ... 89 F4
Chesilton Rd *FUL/PGN* SW6 ... 139 J2
Chesil Wy *YEAD* UB4 ... 94 D2
Chesley Gdns *EHAM* E6 ... 107 H1
Chesney Crs *CROY/NA* CR0 ... 214 A5
Chesney St *BTSEA* SW11 ... 141 F2
Chesnut Av North *WALTH* E17 ... 70 A1
  WCHPL E1 ... 104 C6
Chesnut Gv *TOTM* N17 ... 50 C6
Chesnut Rd *TOTM* N17 ... 50 C6
Chesnut Rw *FNCH* N3 * ... 46 E3
Chessington Av *BXLYHN* DA7 ... 149 F1
  FNCH N3 ... 46 C6
Chessington Cl
  HOR/WEW KT19 ... 206 E4
Chessington Ct *PIN* HA5 ... 59 K1
Chessington Hall Gdns
  CHSGTN KT9 ... 205 K5
Chessington Hill Pk
  CHSGTN KT9 ... 206 C4
Chessington Pde
  CHSGTN KT9 * ... 205 K5
Chesson Rd *WKENS* W14 ... 119 J6
Chessington Wy *WWKM* BR4 ... 198 E6
Chester Av *RCHPK/HAM* TW10 ... 157 G1
  WHTN TW2 ... 154 E3
Chester Cl *BARN* SW13 * ... 138 E4
  KTBR SW1X ... 15 H3
  SUT SM1 ... 193 K6
Chester Cl North *CAMTN* NW1 ... 3 K5
Chester Cl South *CAMTN* NW1 ... 3 K5
Chester Crs *HACK* E8 ... 86 B3
Chester Dr *RYLN/HDSTN* HA2 ... 60 A4
Chester Gdns
  STMC/STPC BR5 ... 202 C1
Chesterfield Dr *DART* DA1 ... 150 E6
  ESH/CLAY KT10 ... 190 B6
Chesterfield Gdns *FSBYPK* N4 ... 67 H2
  GNWCH SE10 ... 145 G1
  MYFR/PICC W1J * ... 9 J7
Chesterfield Gv *EDUL* SE22 ... 143 G6
Chesterfield Hl *MYFR/PICC* W1J ... 9 J6
Chesterfield Rd *BAR* EN5 ... 20 B6
  CHSWK W4 ... 117 K6
  FNCH N3 ... 46 E2
  HOR/WEW KT19 ... 207 F6
  LEY E10 ... 70 A4
Chesterfield St *MYFR/PICC* W1J ... 9 J7
Chesterfield Wy
  HYS/HAR UB3 * ... 113 K2
  PECK SE15 ... 143 K1
Chesterford Gdns *HAMP* NW3 ... 83 F2
Chesterford Rd *MNPK* E12 ... 89 K3
Chester Gdns *ED* N9 ... 36 D1
  MRDN SM4 ... 194 B2
  WEA W13 * ... 97 H5
Chester Ga *CAMTN* NW1 ... 3 J5
Chester Ms *KTBR* SW1X ... 15 J4
  NTHWD HA6 * ... 40 C5
Chester Pl *CAMTN* NW1 ... 3 J4
Chester Rd *ARCH* N19 ... 66 B6
  BFN/LL DA15 ... 147 K6
  CAMTN NW1 ... 3 J5
  CAN/RD E16 ... 106 C3
  ED N9 ... 36 D2
  FSTGT E7 ... 89 H5
  GDMY/SEVK IG3 ... 73 F5
  HSLWW TW4 ... 134 A4
  HTHAIR TW6 ... 132 D4
  NTHWD HA6 ... 40 C7
  TOTM N17 ... 49 K6
  WALTH E17 ... 69 F2
  WAN E11 ... 71 F3
  WIM/MER SW19 ... 177 F2
Chester Rw *BGVA* SW1W ... 15 G7
Chester Sq *BGVA* SW1W ... 15 H6
Chester Square Ms
  BGVA SW1W * ... 15 J5
The Chesters *NWMAL* KT3 ... 176 B4
Chester St *BETH* E2 ... 104 C3
  KTBR SW1X ... 15 H4
Chester Ter *CAMTN* NW1 ... 3 J4
Chesterton Cl *EW* KT17 * ... 207 H6
  STAN HA7 ... 44 A6
Chesterton Ct *EA* W5 * ... 97 K5
Chesterton Dr
  STWL/WRAY TW19 ... 152 C3
Chesterton Rd *NKENS* W10 ... 100 B4
  PLSTW E13 ... 106 E2
Chesterton Sq *WKENS* W14 ... 119 J4
Chesterton Ter *KUT/HW* KT1 ... 175 H5
  PLSTW E13 ... 106 E2
Chester Wy *LBTH* SE11 ... 121 H5
Chesthunte Rd *TOTM* N17 ... 49 J4
Chestnut Aly *FUL/PGN* SW6 * ... 119 J6
Chestnut Av *ALP/SUD* HA0 ... 79 H3

  BKHH IG9 ... 39 H5
  BTFD TW8 ... 116 E5
  CEND/HSY/T N8 ... 66 E2
  E/WMO/HCT KT8 ... 174 A6
  EDGW HA8 ... 43 K2
  ESH/CLAY KT10 ... 189 J4
  FSTGT E7 ... 89 F2
  HCH RM12 ... 75 H6
  HOR/WEW KT19 ... 207 G2
  HPTN TW12 ... 173 F3
  MORT/ESHN SW14 * ... 138 A4
  NTHWD HA6 ... 40 D5
  TEDD TW11 ... 174 A5
  WWKM BR4 ... 214 C3
Chestnut Av South *WALTH* E17 ... 70 A2
Chestnut Cl *ASHF* TW15 ... 152 E6
  BFN/LL DA15 ... 168 B4
  BKHH IG9 ... 39 H5
  CAR SM5 ... 194 E5
  CAT SE6 ... 165 F6
  HYS/HAR UB3 ... 94 C6
  NWCR SE14 ... 144 C2
  ORP BR6 ... 217 G3
  STHGT/OAK N14 ... 22 C6
  STRHM/NOR SW16 ... 162 B6
  WDR/YW UB7 ... 112 C1
Chestnut Dr *BXLYHN* DA7 ... 148 E4
  KTN/HRWW/W HA3 ... 43 F3
  PIN HA5 ... 59 H3
  WAN E11 ... 70 E1
Chestnut Gln *HCH* RM12 ... 75 H6
Chestnut Gv *ALP/SUD* HA0 ... 79 H5
  BAL SW12 ... 161 F2
  BARK/HLT IG6 ... 54 E2
  EA W5 ... 116 E3
  EBAR EN4 ... 21 K6
  ISLW TW7 ... 136 B5
  MTCM CR4 ... 195 J2
  RYNPK SW20 ... 177 G5
  WHTN TW2 ... 155 K4
  WNWD SE27 ... 162 C5
Chestnut La *TRDG/WHET* N20 ... 32 C3
Chestnut Ms *WFD* IG8 ... 52 E1
Chestnut Pl *SYD* SE26 ... 163 G6
Chestnut Ri *BUSH* WD23 ... 28 B2
  WOOL/PLUM SE18 ... 127 K5
Chestnut Rd *ASHF* TW15 ... 152 D6
  DART DA1 ... 171 G3
  KUTN/CMB KT2 ... 175 F2
  RYNPK SW20 ... 177 G5
  WHTN TW2 ... 155 K4
  WNWD SE27 ... 162 C5
The Chestnuts *BECK* BR3 * ... 182 A6
  PIN HA5 ... 41 K3
Chestnut Ter *SUT* SM1 * ... 209 F3
Chestnut Vw *FELT* TW13 ... 154 A5
Chestnut Wk *WFD* IG8 ... 52 E1
Cheston Av *CROY/NA* CR0 ... 198 B5
Cheswick Cl *DART* DA1 ... 150 C5
Chesworth Cl *ERITH* DA8 ... 150 B2
Chettle Cl *STHWK* SE1 ... 18 E4
Chetwode Rd *TOOT* SW17 ... 160 E5
Chetwood Wk *EHAM* E6 * ... 107 J4
Chetwynd Av *EBAR* EN4 ... 33 K5
Chetwynd Rd *KTTN* NW5 ... 84 B2
Chetwynd Vls *KTTN* NW5 * ... 84 B2
Chevalier Cl *STAN* HA7 ... 29 K5
Cheval Pl *SKENS* SW7 ... 14 D4
Cheval St *POP/IOD* E14 ... 124 D3
Cheveney Wk *HAYES* BR2 ... 183 K6
Chevening Rd *GNWCH* SE10 ... 125 J5
  KIL/WHAMP NW6 ... 100 B1
  NRWD SE19 ... 180 E2
The Chevenings *SCUP* DA14 ... 168 C5
Cheverton Rd *ARCH* N19 ... 66 D5
Chevet St *HOM* E9 ... 87 G3
Chevington *CRICK* NW2 * ... 82 D4
Cheviot Cl *BELMT* SM2 ... 209 H6
  BUSH WD23 ... 28 C1
  BXLYHN DA7 ... 150 B3
  ENC/FH EN2 ... 23 K3
  HYS/HAR UB3 ... 133 C1
Cheviot Gdns *CLDGN* NW11 ... 64 D6
  EMPK RM11 ... 75 J4
  WNWD SE27 ... 180 C1
Cheviot Wy *GNTH/NBYPK* IG2 ... 72 E2
Chevron Cl *CAN/RD* E16 ... 106 E5
Chevy Rd *NWDGN* UB2 ... 115 H2
Chewton Rd *WALTH* E17 ... 69 G1
Cheyne Av *SWFD* E18 ... 52 D6
  WHTN TW2 ... 154 E3
Cheyne Cl *HAYES* BR2 ... 215 J1
Cheyne Gdns *CHEL* SW3 ... 120 D6
Cheyne Hl *BRYLDS* KT5 ... 191 G1
Cheyne Ms *CHEL* SW3 ... 120 D6
Cheyne Pth *WEA* W13 ... 97 H4
Cheyne Pl *CHEL* SW3 * ... 120 E6
Cheyne Rw *CHEL* SW3 ... 120 D6
Cheyne Wk *CHEL* SW3 ... 120 D6
  CROY/NA CR0 ... 197 H6
  NFNCH/WDSP N4 ... 48 A1
  WBPTN SW10 ... 140 C1
  WCHMH N21 ... 23 G6
Cheyneys Av *EDGW* HA8 ... 43 K2
Chichele Gdns *CROY/NA* CR0 ... 212 A2
Chichele Rd *CRICK* NW2 ... 82 B3
Chicheley Rd
  KTN/HRWW/W HA3 ... 42 C3
Chicheley St *STHWK* SE1 ... 17 H2
Chichester Av *RSLP* HA4 ... 58 B6
Chichester Cl *BKHTH/KID* SE3 ... 146 B1
  EHAM E6 ... 107 J5
  HPTN TW12 ... 172 E2
Chichester Ct *EW* KT17 * ... 207 H6
  STAN HA7 ... 44 A6
Chichester Gdns *IL* IG1 ... 71 J4
Chichester Ms *LBTH* SE11 ... 17 J7
Chichester Rd *BAY/PAD* W2 * ... 101 F4
  CROY/NA CR0 ... 212 A1
  ED N9 ... 36 B3
  KIL/WHAMP NW6 ... 100 E1
  WAN E11 ... 88 C1
Chichester Wy
  EBED/NFELT TW14 ... 154 B2
  POP/IOD E14 ... 125 G4
Chicksand St *WCHPL* E1 ... 13 K2

Chiddingfold
  NFNCH/WDSP N12 ... 32 E5
Chiddingstone Av
  BXLYHN DA7 ... 129 G6
Chiddingstone St
  FUL/PGN SW6 ... 139 K3
Chieftan Dr *PUR* RM19 ... 131 K4
Chieveley Pde *BXLYHN* DA7 * ... 149 J4
Chieveley Rd *BXLYHN* DA7 ... 149 J5
Chignell Pl *WEA* W13 ... 116 B1
Chigwell La *WAP* E1W ... 104 D6
Chigwell Rd *WFD* IG8 ... 53 G4
Chilcott Cl *ALP/SUD* HA0 ... 79 J2
Childebert Rd *TOOT* SW17 ... 161 G4
Childeric Rd *NWCR* SE14 ... 144 B1
Childerley St *FUL/PGN* SW6 ... 139 H2
Childers St *DEPT* SE8 ... 124 B6
The Childers *WFD* IG8 ... 54 E1
Childs Ct *HYS/HAR* UB3 ... 94 E6
Childs La *NRWD* SE19 * ... 181 F2
Child's Pl *ECT* SW5 ... 119 K4
Child's St *ECT* SW5 ... 119 K4
Child's Wk *ECT* SW5 * ... 119 K4
Childs Wy *CLDGN* NW11 ... 64 D2
Chilham Cl *BXLY* DA5 ... 169 G2
  GFD/PVL UB6 ... 97 G1
Chilham Rd *ELTH/MOT* SE9 ... 166 D6
Chilham Wy *HAYES* BR2 ... 199 K4
Chillerton Rd *TOOT* SW17 ... 179 F1
Chillington Dr *BTSEA* SW11 ... 140 B5
Chillingworth Gdns
  TWK TW1 * ... 156 A5
Chillingworth Rd *HOLWY* N7 ... 85 G3
Chilmark Gdns *NWMAL* KT3 ... 192 C3
Chilmark Rd
  STRHM/NOR SW16 ... 179 J5
Chiltern Av *BUSH* WD23 ... 28 C1
  WHTN TW2 ... 155 F3
Chiltern Cl *BUSH* WD23 ... 28 B1
  BXLYHN DA7 ... 150 B2
  CROY/NA CR0 ... 212 A1
  WPK KT4 ... 193 F6
Chiltern Dene *ENC/FH* EN2 ... 23 F5
Chiltern Dr *BRYLDS* KT5 ... 191 J3
Chiltern Gdns *CRICK* NW2 ... 82 B1
  HAYES BR2 ... 199 J1
Chiltern Rd *BOW* E3 ... 105 J3
  GNTH/NBYPK IG2 ... 72 E1
  PIN HA5 ... 59 G2
The Chilterns *BELMT* SM2 * ... 209 F6
Chiltern St *MHST* W1U ... 9 G1
Chiltern Wy *WFD* IG8 ... 38 E5
Chilthorne Cl *CAT* SE6 ... 164 C2
Chilton Av *EA* W5 ... 116 E4
Chilton Gv *DEPT* SE8 ... 124 A4
Chilton Rd *EDGW* HA8 ... 44 C2
  RCH/KEW TW9 ... 137 H4
Chilton St *BETH* E2 ... 7 K6
Chilvers Cl *WHTN* TW2 ... 155 K4
Chilver St *GNWCH* SE10 ... 125 J5
Chilwell Gdns *OXHEY* WD19 ... 27 G6
Chilworth Gdns *SUT* SM1 ... 209 G1
Chilworth Ms *BAY/PAD* W2 ... 101 G5
Chilworth St *BAY/PAD* W2 ... 101 G5
Chimes Av *PLMGR* N13 ... 49 G1
China Hall Ms
  BERM/RHTH SE16 ... 123 K4
Chinbrook Crs *LEE/GVPK* SE12 ... 166 A5
Chinbrook Rd *ELTH/MOT* SE9 ... 166 B5
Chinchilla Dr *HSLWW* TW4 ... 134 A3
The Chine *ALP/SUD* HA0 ... 79 H3
  MUSWH N10 ... 66 C1
  WCHMH N21 ... 23 H6
Chingdale Rd *CHING* E4 ... 38 B1
Chingford Av *CHING* E4 ... 37 K5
Chingford La *WFD* IG8 ... 38 C6
Chingford Mount Rd *CHING* E4 ... 51 J3
Chingford Rd *CHING* E4 ... 51 J1
  WALTH E17 ... 38 A6
Chingley Cl *BMLY* BR1 ... 183 H2
Ching Vw *CHING* E4 ... 51 H2
Chinnery Cl *EN* EN1 ... 24 B1
Chinnor Crs *GFD/PVL* UB6 ... 96 C1
Chipka St *POP/IOD* E14 ... 125 F2
Chipley St *NWCR* SE14 ... 124 B6
Chippendale St *CLPT* E5 ... 87 F1
Chippenham Cl *RSLP* HA4 * ... 58 C1
Chippenham Gdns
  KIL/WHAMP NW6 ... 100 E2
Chippenham Ms
  MV/WKIL W9 ... 100 E3
Chippenham Rd *MV/WKIL* W9 ... 100 E3
Chipperfield Rd
  STMC/STPC BR5 ... 186 C6
Chipping Cl *BAR* EN5 ... 20 C4
Chipstead Av *THHTH* CR7 ... 196 C1
Chipstead Cl *BELMT* SM2 ... 209 F6
  NRWD SE19 ... 181 G3
Chipstead Gdns *CRICK* NW2 ... 63 K6
Chipstead Rd *ERITH* DA8 ... 150 B2
Chipstead St *FUL/PGN* SW6 ... 139 K2
Chirk Cl *YEAD* UB4 ... 95 J3
Chisenhale Rd *BOW* E3 ... 105 G1
Chisholm Rd *CROY/NA* CR0 ... 197 G6
  RCHPK/HAM TW10 ... 157 G1
Chisledon Wk *HOM* E9 * ... 87 H4
Chislehurst Av *NFNCH/WDSP* N12 ... 47 G3
Chislehurst High St *CHST* BR7 ... 185 G2
Chislehurst Rd *BMLY* BR1 ... 184 D5
  ORP BR6 ... 202 A6
  RCHPK/HAM TW10 ... 157 F1
  SCUP DA14 ... 186 B1
  STMC/STPC BR5 ... 201 K1
Chislet Cl *BECK* BR3 ... 182 D3
Chisley Rd *SEVS/STOTM* N15 ... 68 A3
Chiswell Sq *BKHTH/KID* SE3 ... 146 A3
Chiswell St *CMBW* SE5 * ... 142 E1
  STLK EC1Y ... 12 E1
Chiswick Br *MORT/ESHN* SW14 ... 137 K3
Chiswick Cl *CROY/NA* CR0 ... 211 F1
Chiswick Common Rd
  CHSWK W4 ... 118 A4
Chiswick High Rd *CHSWK* W4 ... 117 K4
Chiswick La *CHSWK* W4 ... 118 B5
Chiswick La South *CHSWK* W4 ... 118 C5
Chiswick Mall *CHSWK* W4 ... 118 C6
Chiswick Pk *CHSWK* W4 ... 117 J4

Chiswick Pier CHSWK W4 * 138 C1
Chiswick Quay CHSWK W4 ....137 K2
Chiswick Rd CHSWK W4 ....117 K4
ED N9 ....36 C4
Chiswick Sq CHSWK W4 ....137 J2
Chiswick Village CHSWK W4 ....117 H6
Chitterfield Ga WDR/YW UB7 ....132 D1
Chitty's La BCTR RM8 ....73 K6
Chitty St FITZ W1T 10 B1
Chivalry Rd BTSEA SW11 ....140 E6
Chivenor Gv KUTN/CMB KT2 ....174 E1
Chivers Rd CHING E4 ....37 K5
Choats Rd BARK IG11 ....109 J1
Chobham Gdns
  WIM/MER SW19 ....159 G4
Chobham Rd SRTFD E15 ....88 C3
Cholmeley CI HGT N6 * 66 B4
Cholmeley Crs HGT N6 ....66 B4
Cholmeley Pk HGT N6 ....66 B5
Cholmley Gdns
  KIL/WHAMP NW6 ....82 E3
Cholmley Rd THDIT KT7 ....190 C3
Cholmley Ter THDIT KT7 * 190 C4
Cholmley Vls THDIT KT7 * 190 C4
Cholmondeley Av
  WLSDN NW10 ....99 J1
Chopwell CI SRTFD E15 * 88 B5
Chorleywood Crs
  STMC/STPC BR5 ....186 A5
Choumert Gv PECK SE15 ....143 H3
Choumert Rd PECK SE15 ....143 G4
Chow Sq HACK E8 * 86 B3
Chrisaine CI
  STWL/WRAY TW19 ....152 A1
Chrisp St POP/IOD E14 ....105 K5
Christabel CI ISLW TW7 ....135 K4
Christ Church Av ERITH DA8 ....150 A6
Christchurch Av ALP/SUD HA0 ....80 A4
  KIL/WHAMP NW6 ....82 A5
  KTN/HRWW/W HA3 ....61 G1
  NFNCH/WDSP N12 ....47 G2
  RAIN RM13 ....111 H1
  TEDD TW11 ....174 B2
Christchurch CI ENC/FH EN2 ....23 J3
  NFNCH/WDSP N12 * 47 H5
  WIM/MER SW19 ....178 C3
Christchurch Gdns
  KTN/HRWW/W HA3 ....61 G1
Christchurch HI HAMP NW3 ....83 H1
Christ Church La BAR EN5 ....20 C3
Christchurch Ldg EBAR EN4 * 21 K5
Christchurch Pk BELMT SM2 ....209 G5
Christ Church Pas BRYLDS KT5 ....191 G4
  CEND/HSY/T N8 ....66 E3
Christchurch Rd BECK BR3 * 182 D5
  BFN/LL DA15 ....148 A6
  BRXS/STRHM SW2 ....162 A3
  DART DA1 ....171 F2
  IL IG1 ....72 B5
  MORT/ESHN SW14 ....137 J6
  WIM/MER SW19 ....178 C4
Christchurch Sq HOM E9 ....86 E6
Christchurch St CHEL SW3 ....120 E6
Christchurch Ter CHEL SW3 * 120 E6
Christchurch Wy GNWCH SE10 ....125 H5
Christian Flds
  STRHM/NOR SW16 ....180 B3
Christian St WCHPL E1 ....104 C5
Christie Dr SNWD SE25 ....197 H2
Christie Rd HOM E9 ....87 G4
Christina Sq FSBYPK N4 ....67 H5
Christina St SDTCH EC2A 7 F4
Christine Worsley CI
  WCHMH N21 * 35 H3
Christopher Av HNWL W7 ....116 B3
Christopher CI BFN/LL DA15 ....148 A6
Christopher Gdns DAGW RM9 ....91 K3
Christopher PI CAMTN NW1 * 4 D4
Christopher Rd NWDGN UB2 ....114 A4
Christophers Ms NTGHL W11 * 119 H1
Christopher St SDTCH EC2A 7 F7
Christy Ter WFD IG8 ....53 J5
Chryssell Rd BRXN/ST SW9 ....142 B1
Chubworthy St NWCR SE14 ....124 B6
Chudleigh Crs GDMY/SEVK IG3 ....90 E2
Chudleigh Gdns SUT SM1 ....209 G1
Chudleigh Rd BROCKY SE4 ....144 C6
  KIL/WHAMP NW6 ....82 A5
  WHTN TW2 ....155 K1
Chudleigh St WCHPL E1 ....105 F5
Chudleigh Wy RSLP HA4 ....58 E6
Chulsa Rd SYD SE26 ....181 J1
Chumleigh Gdns CMBW SE5 * 123 F6
Chumleigh St CMBW SE5 ....123 F6
Chumleigh Wk BRYLDS KT5 ....191 G1
Church Ap DUL SE21 ....162 E5
Church Av BECK BR3 ....182 D4
  CAMTN NW1 ....84 B4
  CHING E4 ....47 K5
  EFNCH N2 ....47 H5
  MORT/ESHN SW14 ....138 A5
  NTHLT UB5 ....77 K5
  NWDGN UB2 ....114 D3
  PIN HA5 ....59 J3
  RSLP HA4 ....58 A5
  SCUP DA14 ....186 E1
Church Crs FNCH N3 ....46 D4
  HOM E9 ....87 F5
  MUSWH N10 ....66 B1
  TRDG/WHET N20 ....33 J5
Churchcroft CI BAL SW12 * 161 F2
Churchdown BMLY BR1 ....165 H6

Church Dr CDALE/KGS NW9 ....63 F5
  RYLN/HDSTN HA2 ....60 A3
  WWKM BR4 ....214 C1
Church Elm La DAGE RM10 ....92 C4
Church End HDN NW4 ....45 K6
  WALTH E17 * 69 K1
Church Farm La EBAR EN4 * 33 K2
Church Farm La CHEAM SM3 ....208 C4
Church Fld DART DA1 ....171 G4
Churchfield Av
  NFNCH/WDSP N12 ....47 G2
Churchfield CI HYS/HAR UB3 ....94 D6
  RYLN/HDSTN HA2 ....60 C1
Churchfield Rd ACT W3 ....117 K1
  HNWL W7 ....115 K2
  WEA W13 ....116 C1
  WELL DA16 ....148 B4
Churchfields E/WMO/HCT KT8 ....173 F6
  GNWCH SE10 ....125 F6
  SWFD E18 ....52 E4
Churchfields Av FELT TW13 ....154 E5
Churchfields Rd BECK BR3 ....182 A5
Churchfield Wy
  NFNCH/WDSP N12 ....47 G2
Church Gdns ALP/SUD HA0 ....79 G2
  WEA W13 ....116 C1
Church Garth ARCH N19 * 66 D6
Church Gn BRXN/ST SW9 * 142 B3
  HYS/HAR UB3 ....94 D5
Church Gv KUT/HW KT1 ....174 D4
  LEW SE13 ....144 E5
Church HI CAR SM5 ....209 K3
  DART DA1 ....150 B5
  DART DA1 ....171 G3
  HRW HA1 ....60 E1
  ORP BR6 ....202 B4
  WALTH E17 ....69 J1
  WCHMH N21 ....35 F2
  WIM/MER SW19 ....177 J1
  WOOL/PLUM SE18 ....126 E3
Church Hill Rd CHEAM SM3 ....208 B2
  EBAR EN4 ....33 K2
  SURB KT6 ....191 F2
  WALTH E17 ....69 K1
Church Hill Wd
  STMC/STPC BR5 ....202 A2
Church Hollow PUR RM19 ....131 K5
Church Hyde
  WOOL/PLUM SE18 ....127 K6
Churchill Av
  KTN/HRWW/W HA3 ....61 H3
Churchill CI EBED/NFELT TW14 ....153 J3
Churchill Gdns ACT W3 ....98 C5
Churchill Gardens
  Rd PIM SW1V 121 G5
Churchill Pl POP/IOD E14 ....124 E1
Churchill Rd CAN/RD E16 ....107 G5
  CRICK NW2 ....81 K4
  EDGW HA8 ....44 B2
  KTTN NW5 ....84 B2
  SAND/SEL CR2 ....211 J6
Churchill Ter CHING E4 ....37 J6
Churchill Wk HOM E9 ....86 E5
Churchill Wy BMLY BR1 ....183 K5
Church La CDALE/KGS NW9 ....62 E5
  CDALE/KGS NW9 ....63 F4
  CEND/HSY/T N8 ....67 F1
  CHST BR7 ....185 H4
  DAGE RM10 ....92 E5
  ED N9 ....36 C4
  EFNCH N2 ....47 H6
  ENC/FH EN2 ....23 K4
  HAYES BR2 ....200 C5
  KTN/HRWW/W HA3 ....43 G4
  PIN HA5 ....41 J6
  PUR RM19 ....131 K5
  ROM RM1 ....75 G1
  TEDD TW11 ....174 A1
  THDIT KT7 ....190 A5
  TOOT SW17 ....178 C1
  TWK TW1 ....156 B3
  WALTH E17 ....69 K1
  WAN E11 ....70 C5
  WEA W13 ....116 D2
  WLGTN SM6 ....210 D1

GNTH/NBYPK IG2 ....72 E3
HAYES BR2 ....183 H6
HAYES BR2 ....215 H5
HDN NW4 ....63 K1
HEST TW5 ....114 A5
HEST TW5 ....135 F1
HNWL W7 ....96 E6
HOR/WEW KT19 ....207 F5
HYS/HAR UB3 ....113 J1
IS N1 ....85 J4
ISLW TW7 ....135 J2
KUT/HW KT1 ....175 G5
LEY E10 ....69 J5
MNPK E12 ....89 K5
MTCM CR4 ....178 D6
NRWD SE19 ....181 F3
NTHLT UB5 ....77 K6
NTHWD HA6 ....40 D3
NWDGN UB2 ....114 E3
ORP BR6 ....216 D4
ORP BR6 ....217 K4
PEND EN3 ....36 E1
RCHPK/HAM TW10 ....137 F6
RCHPK/HAM TW10 ....157 F6
SCUP DA14 ....168 B6
STAN HA7 ....43 H1
SURB KT6 ....190 D5
TEDD TW11 ....155 K6
TOTM N17 ....50 C5
WALTH E17 ....51 G5
WALTH E17 ....70 A1
WELL DA16 ....148 C5
WIM/MER SW19 ....159 H6
WLGTN SM6 ....210 C1
WLSDN NW10 ....99 J1
WPK KT4 ....192 C6
Church Rd South EFNCH N2 ....47 H5
Church Rw CHST BR7 ....185 H4
  FUL/PGN SW6 * 140 A1
  HAMP NW3 ....83 G2
  WAND/EARL SW18 ....139 K6
Church Row Ms CHST BR7 * 185 H5
Church St BAY/PAD W2 * 8 B1
  CHSWK W4 ....118 B6
  CROY/NA CRO 211 H1
  DAGE RM10 ....92 E5
  ED N9 ....35 K3
  ENC/FH EN2 ....23 J4
  ESH/CLAY KT10 ....204 B2
  EW KT17 ....207 J6
  HPTN TW12 ....173 H4
  HSLW TW3 ....135 H6
  ISLW TW7 ....136 C4
  KUT/HW KT1 ....174 E5
  SRTFD E15 ....88 C6
  TWK TW1 ....156 B3
Church Street Est STJWD NW8 * 2 B7
Church St North SRTFD E15 ....88 C5
Church Ter FUL/PGN SW6 * 140 A3
  HDN NW4 ....45 K3
  LEW SE13 ....145 H4
  RCHPK/HAM TW10 ....156 C6
Church V EFNCH N2 ....47 K6
  FSTH SE23 ....163 K4
Churchview Rd WHTN TW2 ....155 J3
Church Wk BTFD TW8 ....116 D6
  BUSH WD23 ....28 A1
  CDALE/KGS NW9 ....63 F4
  CRICK NW2 ....82 D1
  DART DA1 ....171 G5
  HYS/HAR UB3 ....94 C5
  RYNPK SW20 ....177 F6
  STNW/STAM N16 ....85 K3
  STRHM/NOR SW16 ....179 H5
  THDIT KT7 ....190 B4
Churchway CAMTN NW1 ....4 D4
Church Wy TRDG/WHET N20 ....33 J5
Churchyard Rw LBTH SE11 ....18 B6
Churston Av PLSTW E13 ....89 F6
Churston CI
  BRXS/STRHM SW2 ....162 C3
Churston Dr MRDN SM4 ....193 G2
Churston Gdns
  FBAR/BDGN N11 ....48 C2
Churton Pl CHSWK W4 * 117 J6
  PIM SW1V 16 B7
Churton St PIM SW1V 16 B7
Chyngton CI BFN/LL DA15 ....168 A5
Cibber Rd FSTH SE23 ....164 A4
Cicada Rd WAND/EARL SW18 ....160 B1
Cicely Rd PECK SE15 ....143 H2
Cinderford Wy BMLY BR1 ....165 H6
Cinema Pde EDGW HA8 * 44 E2
Cinnamon La CROY/NA CRO * 214 A4
  PECK SE15 ....143 G6
Cinnamon St WAP E1W 123 J1
Cintra Pk NRWD SE19 ....181 G3
Circle Gdns WIM/MER SW19 ....177 K4
Circle Rd EFNCH N2 ....47 H5
The Circle CRICK NW2 ....81 G1
  MLHL NW7 ....45 F2
The Circuits PIN HA5 ....59 G1
Circular Rd TOTM N17 * 50 B5
Circular Wy WOOL/PLUM SE18 ....126 E6
Circus Ms MBLAR W1H * 9 F1
Circus Pl LVPST EC2M * 13 F2
Circus Rd STJWD NW8 ....2 A4
Circus St GNWCH SE10 ....145 F1
Cirencester St BAY/PAD W2 ....101 F4
Cissbury Ring North
  NFNCH/WDSP N12 ....46 D1
Cissbury Ring South
  NFNCH/WDSP N12 ....46 D1
Cissbury Rd SEVS/STOTM N15 ....67 K2
Citadel Pl LBTH SE11 ....122 A5
Citizen Rd HOLWY N7 ....85 G1
Citron Ter PECK SE15 * 143 J4
City Barracks SHB W12 * 119 F1
City Garden Rw IS N1 ....6 B3
City Rd FSBYE EC1V 6 A3
  SDTCH EC2A 7 F1
  STLK EC1Y 6 D6
City Wk STHWK SE1 ....19 G4
Civic Wy BARK/HLT IG6 ....72 C1
  RSLP HA4 ....77 H3

Clabon Ms KTBR SW1X 14 E5
Clack St BERM/RHTH SE16 ....123 K2
Clacton Rd TOTM N17 * 50 B5
  WALTH E17 ....69 G3
Claire Ct NFNCH/WDSP N12 ....33 G5
Claire Gdns STAN HA7 ....43 J1
Claire Pl POP/IOD E14 ....124 D3
Clairvale Rd HEST TW5 ....134 C2
Clairville Gdns HNWL W7 ....116 A1
Clamp HI KTN/HRWW/W HA3 ....28 D6
Clancarty Rd FUL/PGN SW6 ....139 K3
Clandon CI ACT W3 ....117 J2
  EW KT17 ....207 H4
Clandon Gdns FNCH N3 ....46 E6
Clandon Rd GDMY/SEVK IG3 ....72 E6
Clandon St DEPT SE8 ....144 D3
Clandon Ter RYNPK SW20 * 177 G5
Clanricarde Gdns
  BAY/PAD W2 ....100 E6
Clapgate Rd BUSH WD23 ....28 B1
Clapham Common
  North Side CLAP SW4 ....141 G5
Clapham Common South Side
  CLAP SW4 ....161 G1
Clapham Common West Side
  CLAP SW4 ....140 E5
Clapham Court Ter
  BRXS/STRHM SW2 * 141 K6
Clapham Crs CLAP SW4 ....141 J5
Clapham High St CLAP SW4 ....141 J5
Clapham Manor St CLAP SW4 ....141 H4
Clapham Park Est CLAP SW4 * 161 J2
Clapham Park Rd CLAP SW4 ....141 J5
Clapham Park Ter
  BRXS/STRHM SW2 * 141 K6
Clapham Rd BRXN/ST SW9 ....141 K6
Clapton Common SN S N1 ....85 K4
  Claps Gate La EHAM E6 ....108 B3
Clapton Common
  STNW/STAM N16 ....68 C4
Clapton Sq CLPT E5 ....86 E3
Clapton Ter STNW/STAM N16 ....68 D4
Clapton Wy CLPT E5 ....86 C2
Clara Pl WOOL/PLUM SE18 ....127 F4
Clare Cl BORE WD6 ....30 B1
  EFNCH N2 ....47 G6
Clare Cnr ELTH/MOT SE9 ....167 G2
Clare Ct NTHWD HA6 ....40 C1
Claredale St BETH E2 ....104 C1
Clare Gdns BARK IG11 ....91 F4
  FSTGT E7 ....88 E2
  WALTH E17 * 69 J1
Clare Hl ESH/CLAY KT10 ....204 A4
Clare Hl (No 2) ESH/CLAY KT10 ....204 A4
Clare La IS N1 ....85 J5
Clare Lawn Av
  MORT/ESHN SW14 ....138 A6
Clare Ms FUL/PGN SW6 ....140 A1
Claremont Av
  KTN/HRWW/W HA3 ....62 A2
  NWMAL KT3 ....192 E2
  SUN TW16 ....172 A4
Claremont CI
  BRXS/STRHM SW2 ....162 A3
  CAN/RD E16 ....127 F1
  IS N1 ....5 K3
  ORP BR6 ....216 A2
Claremont Crs DART DA1 ....150 B5
Claremont Dr ESH/CLAY KT10 ....204 B5
Claremont End
  ESH/CLAY KT10 ....204 B4
Claremont Gdns
  GDMY/SEVK IG3 ....72 E6
  SURB KT6 ....191 F1
Claremont Gv WDR/YW UB7 * 112 B1
  WFD IG8 ....53 G2
Claremont House
  WATW WD18 * 26 B1
Claremont La ESH/CLAY KT10 ....204 A3
Claremont Pk FNCH N3 ....46 C4
Claremont Park Rd
  ESH/CLAY KT10 ....204 B4
Claremont Rd BMLY BR1 ....200 D1
  CRICK NW2 ....64 B5
  CROY/NA CRO 197 H5
  EBAR EN4 ....21 G5
  ESH/CLAY KT10 ....204 B5
  FSTGT E7 ....89 F3
  HGT N6 ....66 B4
  KIL/WHAMP NW6 ....100 C1
  KTN/HRWW/W HA3 ....42 E5
  ROM RM1 ....75 J3
  SURB KT6 ....191 F3
  TEDD TW11 ....174 A1
  TWK TW1 ....156 A1
  WAN E11 ....88 D1
  WEA W13 ....97 G4
Claremont St IS N1 ....5 J3
Claremont St GNWCH SE10 ....124 E6
  UED N18 ....50 C2
Claremont Ter THDIT KT7 * 190 C4
Claremont Vls CMBW SE5 * 142 E1
  KUT/HW KT1 * 175 G5
Claremount Wy CRICK NW2 ....81 G1
Clarence Av CLAP SW4 ....161 J2
  HAYES BR2 ....215 H5
  IL IG1 ....71 K3
  NWMAL KT3 ....175 K6

CAN/RD E16 ....106 C3
CHSWK W4 ....117 H5
CLPT E5 ....86 D2
CROY/NA CRO 196 E6
DEPT SE8 ....124 C6
ELTH/MOT SE9 ....166 D4
FSTGT E7 ....89 G2
KIL/WHAMP NW6 ....82 D5
PEND EN3 ....24 E6
SCUP DA14 ....168 C5
SEVS/STOTM N15 ....67 J2
SUT SM1 ....209 F2
TEDD TW11 ....174 A2
WALTH E17 ....51 F5
WDGN N22 ....48 E3
WIM/MER SW19 ....178 A2
WLGTN SM6 ....210 B3
Clarence St CAMTN NW1 * 3 H1
  HSLW TW3 ....135 G3
Clarence Vls KUT/HW KT1 * 175 G5
Clarence Wk CLAP SW4 ....141 K3
Clarence Wy CAMTN NW1 ....84 B5
Clarendon CI BAY/PAD W2 * 8 C5
  HOM E9 ....86 E5
  STMC/STPC BR5 ....186 B6
Clarendon Crs WHTN TW2 ....155 J5
Clarendon Cross NTGHL W11 ....100 B6
Clarendon Dr PUT/ROE SW15 ....139 F5
Clarendon Gdns HDN NW4 ....45 J6
  IL IG1 ....71 K5
  MV/WKIL W9 ....101 G3
  WBLY HA9 ....79 K1
Clarendon Ga BAY/PAD W2 ....8 B5
Clarendon Gn STMC/STPC BR5 ....186 B6
  Clarendon Gv MTCM CR4 ....178 E6
  STMC/STPC BR5 ....202 B1
Clarendon Ms BAY/PAD W2 ....8 C5
Clarendon Pth
  STMC/STPC BR5 ....202 B1
Clarendon PI BAY/PAD W2 ....8 C5
Clarendon RI LEW SE13 ....145 F4
Clarendon Rd ASHF TW15 ....152 C6
  CROY/NA CRO 196 C6
  EA W5 ....98 A2
  HRW HA1 ....60 E3
  HYS/HAR UB3 ....113 J1
  NTGHL W11 ....100 C6
  SEVS/STOTM N15 ....67 H1
  SWFD E18 ....52 E6
  UED N18 ....50 C2
  WALTH E17 ....69 K3
  WAN E11 ....70 B5
  WDGN N22 * 49 F5
  WIM/MER SW19 ....178 C3
  WLGTN SM6 ....210 C3
Clarendon St PIM SW1V 121 G5
Clarendon Ter MV/WKIL W9 ....101 G3
  Clarendon Wy CHST BR7 ....35 J2
  WCHMH N21 * 35 J2
Clarens St CAT SE6 ....164 C4
Clare Pde GFD/PVL UB6 * 78 D4
Clare Rd GFD/PVL UB6 ....78 D4
  HSLWW TW4 ....134 E4
  NWCR SE14 ....144 C5
  STWL/WRAY TW19 ....152 A1
  WAN E11 ....70 B3
  WLSDN NW10 ....81 J5
Clare St BETH E2 ....104 E1
Claret Gdns SNWD SE25 ....197 F1
Clareville Gv SKENS SW7 * 120 B4
Clareville Grove Ms
  SKENS SW7 * 120 B4
Clareville Rd SKENS SW7 ....120 B4
  STMC/STPC BR5 ....201 H6
Clareville St SKENS SW7 ....120 B4
Clarewood Dr CAMTN NW1 * 4 A3
Clarges Ms MYFR/PICC W1J 9 J7
Clarges St MYFR/PICC W1J 9 J7
Claribel Rd BRXN/ST SW9 ....142 C3
Clarice Wy WLGTN SM6 ....210 E6
Claridge Rd BCTR RM8 ....73 K5
Clarissa Rd CHDH RM6 ....73 K3
Clarissa St HACK E8 ....86 B6
Clark CI ERITH DA8 ....150 D2
Clarke Ms ED N9 ....36 D5
Clarkes Av WPK KT4 ....193 G5
Clarkes Ms CAVSQ/HST W1G 9 H1
Clarks Md BUSH WD23 ....28 C2
Clarkson Rd CAN/RD E16 ....106 D5
Clarkson Rw CAMTN NW1 * 4 A3
Clarkson St BETH E2 ....104 D2
Clark's Rd IL IG1 ....72 C6
Clark St WCHPL E1 ....104 E5
Clark Wy HEST TW5 ....134 C1
Classon CI WDR/YW UB7 * 112 B2
Claston CI DART DA1 ....150 A6
Claude Rd LEY E10 ....70 A5
  PECK SE15 ....143 J3
  PLSTW E13 ....89 F6
Claude St POP/IOD E14 ....124 D4
Claudia PI WIM/MER SW19 ....159 H3
Claudius CI STAN HA7 ....29 K5
Claughton Rd PLSTW E13 ....107 G1
Clauson Av NTHLT UB5 ....78 B3
Clavell St GNWCH SE10 ....125 F6
Claverdale Rd
  BRXS/STRHM SW2 ....162 A2
Clavering Av BARN SW13 ....118 E6
Clavering CI TWK TW1 ....156 B6
Clavering Rd MNPK E12 ....71 H5
Claverley Gv FNCH N3 ....46 E4
Claverley Vls FNCH N3 ....47 F5
Claverton St PIM SW1V 121 H5
Clave St WAP E1W 123 K1
Claxton Gv HMSMTH W6 ....119 G5
Claybank Gv LEW SE13 ....144 E4
Claybridge Rd
  LEE/GVPK SE12 ....166 B6
Claybrook CI EFNCH N2 ....47 H6
Claybrook Rd HMSMTH W6 ....119 G6
Claybury BUSH WD23 ....28 B2

Claybury Rd WFD IG8 ....53 J5
Claydon Dr CROY/NA CR0 ....210 E2
Claydown Ms
  WOOL/PLUM SE18 ....127 F5
Clayfarm Rd ELTH/MOT SE9 ...167 H4
Claygate Cl HCH RM12 ....93 J2
Claygate Crs CROY/NA 214 A4
Claygate La ESH/CLAY KT10...190 B6
Claygate Lodge Cl
  ESH/CLAY KT10 ....204 E5
Claygate Rd WEA W13 ....116 C3
Clayhall Av CLAY IG5 ....53 K5
Clayhill Crs ELTH/MOT SE9 ....166 C6
Claylands Pl BRXN/ST SW9 ....142 B1
Claylands Rd VX/NE SW8 ......122 A6
Clay La BUSH WD23 ....28 B1
  STWL/WRAY TW19 ....152 C2
Claymore Cl MRDN SM4 ....193 K4
Claypole Dr HEST TW5 ....134 D2
Claypole Rd SRTFD E15 * 106 A1
Clayponds Av BTFD TW8 ....117 F4
Clayponds Gdns EA W5 ....116 E4
Clayponds La BTFD TW8 ....117 G4
Clayside CHIG IG7 ....54 D2
Clays La SRTFD E15 ....87 K3
Clays Lane Cl SRTFD E15 ....87 K3
Clay St MHST W1U 9 F2
Clayton Cl EHAM E6 ....107 K5
Clayton Crs BTFD TW8 ....116 E5
  IS N1 ....5 L1
Clayton Croft Rd RDART DA2 ..170 D4
Clayton Dr DEPT SE8 ....124 B5
Clayton Fld CDALE/KGS NW9 ....45 G2
Clayton Ms GNWCH SE10 ....145 G1
Clayton Rd CHSGTN KT9 ....205 J2
  HYS/HAR UB3 ....113 H2
  ISLW TW7 ....135 K4
  PECK SE15 ....143 H2
  ROMW/RG RM7 ....74 E5
Clayton St LBTH SE11 ....122 B6
Clayton Ter YEAD UB4 * 95 H4
Claytonville Ter BELV DA17 *...129 K2
Clay Wood Cl ORP BR6 ....201 K4
Clayworth Cl BFN/LL DA15 ....168 C1
Cleanthus Cl
  WOOL/PLUM SE18 ....147 G2
Cleanthus Rd
  WOOL/PLUM SE18 ....147 G2
Clearbrook Wy WCHPL E1 ....104 E5
Clearwater Pl SURB KT6 ......190 D5
Clearwater Ter NTGHL W11 ...119 G2
Clearwell Dr MV/WKIL W9 ....113 H4
Cleave Av HYS/HAR UB3 ......113 H4
  ORP BR6 ....216 E4
Cleaveland Rd SURB KT6 .....190 E3
Cleaverholme Cl SNWD SE25...197 J3
Cleaver Sq LBTH SE11 ....122 B5
Cleaver St LBTH SE11 ....122 B5
Cleeve Hl FSTH SE23 ....163 J3
Cleeve Park Gdns SCUP DA14 ..168 C4
Cleeve Wy PUT/ROE SW15 ...158 C1
  SUT SM1 ....194 A5
Clegg St PLSTW E13 ....106 E1
  WAP E1W 123 J1
Clematis Gdns WFD IG8 ....52 E1
Clematis St SHB W12 ....99 H6
Clem Attlee Ct FUL/PGN SW6 ..119 J6
Clem Attlee Pde
  FUL/PGN SW6 * 119 J6
Clemence Rd DAGE RM10 ....92 E6
Clemence St POP/IOD E14 ...105 H4
Clement Av CLAP SW4 ....141 J5
Clement Cl CHSWK W4 ....118 A4
  KIL/WHAMP NW6 ....82 A5
Clement Gdns HYS/HAR UB3...113 H4
Clementhorpe Rd DAGW RM9 ...91 J4
Clementina Rd LEY E10 ....69 H5
Clementine Cl WEA W13 * 116 C2
Clement Rd BECK BR3 ....182 A5
  WIM/MER SW19 ....177 H1
Clements Av CAN/RD E16 ....106 E6
Clements Inn LINN WC2A 11 H4
Clements La IL IG1 ....90 B1
  MANHO EC4N 13 J5
Clements Pl BTFD TW8 ....116 E5
Clements Rd
  BERM/RHTH SE16 ....123 H3
  EHAM E6 ....89 K5
  IL IG1 ....90 B1
Clenston Ms MBLAR W1H 8 E3
Clennam St STHWK SE1 * 18 D2
Clensham La SUT SM1 ....193 K6
Clenston Ms MBLAR W1H 8 E3
Cleopatra Cl STAN HA7 ....35 J4
Clephane Rd IS N1 ....85 J4
Clere Pl SDTCH EC2A 7 F6
Clere St SDTCH EC2A 7 F6
Clerkenwell Cl CLKNW EC1R 5 K7
Clerkenwell Gn CLKNW EC1R ...6 A7
Clerkenwell Rd CLKNW EC1R...5 L7
Clermont Rd HOM E9 ....86 E6
Clevedon Gdns HEST TW5 ....134 A3
  HYS/HAR UB3 ....113 G3
Clevedon Rd KUT/HW KT1 ....175 H5
  PGE/AN SE20 ....182 A4
  TWK TW1 ....156 E1
Cleveland Av CHSWK W4 .....118 C4
  HPTN TW12 ....172 E3
Cleveland Gdns BARN SW13..138 C3
  BAY/PAD W2 ....101 G5
  CRICK NW2 ....64 B6
  FSBYPK N4 ....67 J3
  WPK KT4 ....192 B6
Cleveland Gv WCHPL E1 ....104 E3
Cleveland Ms FITZ W1T 10 A1
Cleveland Park Av WALTH E17 ..69 J1
Cleveland Park Crs WALTH E17 ..69 J1
Cleveland Pl STJS SW1Y 10 E7
Cleveland Ri MRDN SM4 ....193 G4
Cleveland Rd BARN SW13 .....138 C3
  CHSWK W4 ....117 K3
  ED N9 * 36 D2

IL IG1 ....90 B1
IS N1 ....85 K5
ISLW TW7 ....136 B5
NWMAL KT3 ....192 B1
SWFD E18 ....52 E6
WEA W13 ....97 G4
WELL DA16 ....148 A3
WPK KT4 ....192 B6
Cleveland Rw WHALL SW1A ...16 B1
Cleveland Sq BAY/PAD W2 ...101 G6
Cleveland St CAMTN NW1 ....3 K7
Cleveland Ter BAY/PAD W2 ...101 G5
Cleveland Wy WCHPL E1 ....104 E3
Cleveley Crs EA W5 ....98 A1
Cleveleys Rd CLPT E5 ....86 D1
Cleve Rd KIL/WHAMP NW6 ......82 E5
  SCUP DA14 ....168 E5
Cleves Av EW KT17 ....207 K6
Cleves Cl LOU IG10 ....39 J1
Cleves Rd EHAM E6 ....89 H6
  RCHPK/HAM TW10 ....156 D5
Cleves Wk BARK/HLT IG6 ....54 C3
Cleves Wy HPTN TW12 ....172 E2
  RSLP HA4 ....59 H5
Clewer Crs KTN/HRWW/W HA3...42 D4
Clifden Rd BTFD TW8 ....116 E6
  CLPT E5 ....86 E3
  TWK TW1 ....156 A3
Cliffe Rd SAND/SEL CR2 ....211 K5
Clifford Av CHST BR7 ....184 E2
  CLAY IG5 ....53 K6
  MORT/ESHN SW14 ....137 K5
  WLGTN SM6 ....210 C2
Clifford Cl NTHLT UB5 ....77 J6
Clifford Dr BRXN/ST SW9 ......142 C5
Clifford Gdns HYS/HAR UB3 ..113 G4
  WLSDN NW10 ....100 A1
Clifford Gv ASHF TW15 ....152 D6
Clifford Rd ALP/SUD HA0 ....79 K6
  BAR EN5 ....21 F4
  CAN/RD E16 ....106 D3
  EN EN1 ....36 E1
  HSLWW TW4 ....134 C4
  RCH/KEW TW9 ....156 E4
  SNWD SE25 ....197 H1
  WALTH E17 ....52 A5
Clifford St CONDST W1S 10 A6
Clifford Wy WLSDN NW10 ....81 H2
Cliff Rd HOLWY N7 ....84 D4
Cliff Ter DEPT SE8 ....144 D3
Cliffview Rd LEW SE13 ....144 D4
Cliff Vls HOLWY N7 ....84 D4
Cliff Wk CAN/RD E16 ....106 D4
Clifton Av ALP/SUD HA0 ....79 K3
  FELT TW13 ....154 B5
  FNCH N3 ....46 D4
  KTN/HRWW/W HA3 ....43 H5
  SHB W12 ....118 C2
  WALTH E17 ....69 F1
  WBLY HA9 ....80 B4
Clifton Cl ORP BR6 ....216 C5
Clifton Ct BECK BR3 * 182 E4
Clifton Crs PECK SE15 ....143 J1
Clifton Gdns CHSWK W4 ....118 A4
  ENC/FH EN2 ....22 E5
  GLDGN NW11 ....64 D5
  MV/WKIL W9 ....101 G3
  SEVS/STOTM N15 ....68 B3
Clifton Ga WBPTN SW10 * 120 B6
Clifton Gv HACK E8 ....86 C4
Clifton Hl STJWD NW8 ....101 G1
Clifton Ms SNWD SE25 ....197 F1
Clifton Pde FELT TW13 * 154 B6
Clifton Park Av RYNPK SW20...177 F5
Clifton Pl BAY/PAD W2 ....8 A5
  BERM/RHTH SE16 ....123 K2
  KUTN/CMB KT2 * 175 H4
  WBPTN SW10 * 120 B6
Clifton Ri NWCR SE14 ....144 B1
Clifton Rd ALP/SUD HA0 ....79 J5
  CEND/HSY/T N8 ....66 D3
  EMPK RM11 ....75 J5
  FNCH N3 ....47 G4
  FSTGT E7 ....89 H4
  GFD/PVL UB6 ....96 C3
  GNTH/NBYPK IG2 ....72 D5
  HTHAIR TW6 ....132 E5
  ISLW TW7 ....135 J3
  KTN/HRWW/W HA3 ....62 B2
  KUTN/CMB KT2 ....175 H4
  MV/WKIL W9 ....101 G3
  NWDGN UB2 ....114 D4
  SCUP DA14 ....167 K6
  SNWD SE25 ....197 F2
  TEDD TW11 ....155 K6
  WDGN N22 ....48 C4
  WELL DA16 ....148 D4
  WIM/MER SW19 ....177 G2
  WLGTN SM6 ....210 B3
  WLSDN NW10 ....99 J1
Clifton St SDTCH EC2A 7 J7
Clifton Ter FSBYPK N4 ....67 G6
Clifton Vls MV/WKIL W9 ....101 F4
Clifton Wy ALP/SUD HA0 ....80 A6
  PECK SE15 ....143 K1
Cline Rd FBAR/BDGN N11 ....48 C2
Clink St STHWK SE1 ....12 F8
Clinton Av E/WMO/HCT KT8...189 H1
  WELL DA16 ....148 A4
Clinton Crs BARK/HLT IG6 ....54 E2
Clinton Rd BOW E3 ....105 G2
  FSTGT E7 ....88 E2
  SEVS/STOTM N15 ....67 K1
Clinton Ter DEPT SE8 * 124 D6
  SUT SM1 * 209 G2
Clipper Cl BERM/RHTH SE16...124 A2
Clipper Wy LEW SE13 ....145 F5
Clippesby Cl CHSGTN KT9 ....206 B4
Clipstone Ms GTPST W1W 4 A7
Clipstone Rd HSLW TW3 ....135 F4
Clipstone St GTPST W1W 9 J1
Clissold Cl STNW/STAM N16....85 K2
Clissold Crs STNW/STAM N16..85 K1
Clissold Rd STNW/STAM N16...85 K1

Clitheroe Av RYLN/HDSTN HA2..60 A5
Clitheroe Gdns OXHEY WD19 ...27 H2
Clitheroe Rd BRXN/ST SW9 ..141 K3
  CRW RM5 ....56 C1
Clitherow Av HNWL W7 ....116 B3
Clitherow Rd BTFD TW8 ....116 C5
Clitterhouse Crs CRICK NW2 ...64 A5
Clitterhouse Rd CRICK NW2 ....64 A5
Clive Av DART DA1 ....150 C2
  UED N18 ....50 C2
Clive Cl WLSDN NW10 ....81 H5
Cliveden Cl NFNCH/WDSP N12...33 G3
Cliveden Pl BGVA SW1W 15 G6
Cliveden Rd WIM/MER SW19 ..177 H4
Clivedon Ct WEA W13 ....97 H4
Clivedon Rd CHING E4 ....52 C1
Clive Rd BELV DA17 ....129 H4
  DUL SE21 ....162 E5
  EBED/NFELT TW14 ....153 K1
  EN EN1 ....24 C5
  ESH/CLAY KT10 ....204 D2
  GPK RM2 ....75 K2
  TWK TW1 ....156 A6
  WIM/MER SW19 ....178 D2
Clivesdale Dr HYS/HAR UB3 ..113 K1
Clive Wy EN EN1 ....24 C5
Cloak La CANST EC4R 12 D5
Clockhouse Av BARK IG11 ....90 C6
Clockhouse Cl
  WIM/MER SW19 ....159 F5
Clockhouse La ASHF TW15 ....152 E5
Clock House Pde PLMGR N13 *...49 G1
Clockhouse Pl PUT/ROE SW15..139 H6
Clock House Rd BECK BR3 ....182 B6
Clock Pde EN EN1 * 23 K6
Clock Tower Ms IS N1 ....6 D2
  THMD SE28 ....109 H6
Clock Tower Pl HOLWY N7 * 84 E4
Clock Tower Rd ISLW TW7 .....136 A4
Cloister Cl RAIN RM13 ....111 K3
  TEDD TW11 ....174 C1
Cloister Gdns EDGW HA8 ....44 E1
  SNWD SE25 ....197 J3
Cloister Rd ACT W3 ....98 E4
  CRICK NW2 ....82 D1
Cloisters Av HAYS BR2 ....200 E2
Clonard Wy PIN HA5 ....42 A2
Clonbrock Rd STNW/STAM N16...86 A2
Cloncurry St FUL/PGN SW6 ...139 G3
Clonmel Cl RYLN/HDSTN HA2...60 D5
Clonmell Rd TOTM N17 ....49 K6
Clonmel Rd FUL/PGN SW6 ....139 J1
  HPTN TW12 ....155 J6
Clonmore St
  WAND/EARL SW18 ....159 J3
Cloonmore Av ORP BR6 ....217 F3
Clorane Gdns HAMP NW3 ....82 E1
Closemead Cl NTHWD HA6 ......40 A2
The Close ALP/SUD HA0 ....80 A4
  BECK BR3 ....198 B1
  BUSH WD23 ....28 A1
  BXLY DA5 ....169 G3
  CAR SM5 ....209 J6
  CHDH RM6 ....74 A3
  CHEAM SM3 ....193 J4
  CHING E4 ....52 A3
  EBAR EN4 ....33 K1
  GNTH/NBYPK IG2 ....72 E5
  ISLW TW7 ....135 J2
  MTCM CR4 ....194 E1
  NWMAL KT3 ....175 K5
  PIN HA5 ....59 G4
  PIN HA5 ....59 K4
  RCH/KEW TW9 ....137 J4
  RDART DA2 ....171 G5
  SCUP DA14 ....186 C1
  SNWD SE25 ....197 H3
  STHGT/OAK N14 ....34 D4
  STMC/STPC BR5 ....201 K3
  SURB KT6 ....191 F4
  TRDG/WHET N20 ....32 D4
  WBLY HA9 ....80 A2
  WLSDN NW10 ....81 H4
Cloth Ct STBT EC1A 12 B2
Cloth Fair STBT EC1A 12 B2
Clothier St HDTCH EC3A * 13 H3
Cloth St STBT EC1A 12 C1
Clothworkers Rd
  WOOL/PLUM SE18 ....147 J1
Cloudesdale Rd TOOT SW17..161 G4
Cloudesley Pl IS N1 ....5 K1
Cloudesley Rd BXLYHN DA7..149 G2
  ERITH DA8 ....150 C2
  IS N1 ....5 J1
Cloudesley Sq IS N1 ....5 K1
Cloudesley St IS N1 ....5 K1
Clouston Cl WLGTN SM6 ....210 E3
Clova Rd FSTGT E7 ....88 E4
Clove Crs POP/IOD E14 ....106 A6
Clovelly Av CDALE/KGS NW9 ...63 H1
  HGDN/ICK UB10 ....76 A2
Clovelly Cl HGDN/ICK UB10 ....76 A2
  PIN HA5 ....41 F6
Clovelly Gdns EN EN1 ....36 A2
  ROMW/RG RM7 ....56 D4
Clovelly Rd BXLYHN DA7 ......129 F6
  CEND/HSY/T N8 ....66 D1
  CHSWK W4 ....118 A2
  HSLW TW3 ....135 F3
  WEA W13 ....116 D2
Clovelly Wy ORP BR6 ....202 A3
  RYLN/HDSTN HA2 ....77 K1
  WCHPL E1 ....104 C5
Clover Cl WAN E11 * 70 B6
Cloverdale Gdns BFN/LL DA15..168 A1
The Clover Fld BUSH WD23 .....27 K1
Clover Ms CHEL SW3 ....120 F5
Clover Wy WLGTN SM6 ....195 F5
Clove St PLSTW E13 ....106 E3
Clowders Rd CAT SE6 ....164 C5
Clowser Cl SUT SM1 ....209 G3
Cloysters Gn WAP E1W * 123 H1
Cloyster Wd EDGW HA8 ....43 K3
Club Gardens Rd HAYES BR2..199 K4
Club Rw BETH E2 ....7 J6

The Clumps FELT TW13 ....153 G6
Clunbury Av NWDGN UB2 ....114 E5
Clunbury St IS N1 ....7 F5
Cluny Est STHWK SE1 ....19 G4
Cluny Ms ECT SW5 ....119 J4
Cluny Pl STHWK SE1 ....19 H4
Clutton St POP/IOD E14 ....105 K4
Clydach Rd EN EN1 ....24 B5
Clyde Circ SEVS/STOTM N15...68 A1
Clyde Pl LEY E10 ....69 K4
Clyde Rd CROY/NA CR0 ....197 G6
  SEVS/STOTM N15 ....68 A1
  STWL/WRAY TW19 ....152 A3
  SUT SM1 ....208 E3
  WDGN N22 ....48 D4
  WLGTN SM6 ....210 C3
Clydesdale PEND EN3 ....25 H5
Clydesdale Av
  KTN/HRWW/W HA3 ....43 K6
Clydesdale Cl ISLW TW7 ....136 A4
Clydesdale Gdns
  RCHPK/HAM TW10 ....137 J5
Clydesdale Rd EMPK RM11 .....75 H4
  NTGHL W11 ....100 D5
Clyde St DEPT SE8 ....124 C6
Clyde Ter FSTH SE23 ....163 K4
Clyde V FSTH SE23 ....163 K4
Clyde Vw ROM RM1 ....57 G4
Clymping Dene
  EBED/NFELT TW14 ....154 A2
Clyston Rd WATW WD18 ....26 D1
Clyston St VX/NE SW8 ....141 H3
Coach & Horses Yd
  CONDST W1S 9 K5
Coach House La HBRY N5 * 85 H2
  WIM/MER SW19 ....159 G6
Coach House Ms FSTH SE23..163 K1
  NWCR SE14 ....144 A2
Coach House Yd
  WAND/EARL SW18 * 140 A5
Coalecroft Rd PUT/ROE SW15..139 F5
Coal Post Cl ORP BR6 ....217 F5
Coates Av WAND/EARL SW18..160 D1
Coates Hill Rd BMLY BR1 .....185 F5
Coates Rd BORE WD6 ....29 K2
Coate St BETH E2 ....104 C1
Cobbett Rd ELTH/MOT SE9 ..146 D3
  WHTN TW2 ....155 F3
Cobbetts Av REDBR IG4 ....71 H2
Cobbett St VX/NE SW8 ....142 A1
Cobble La IS N1 ....85 H5
Cobble Ms FSBYPK N4 ....85 J1
Cobbler's Wk TEDD TW11 .....173 K3
Cobblestone Pl CROY/NA CR0..196 D5
Cobbold Ms SHB W12 * 118 C2
Cobbold Rd SHB W12 ....118 B2
  WAN E11 ....88 D1
  WLSDN NW10 ....81 H4
Cobb's Rd HSLWW TW4 ....134 E5
Cobb St WCHPL E1 ....13 J3
Cobden Ms SYD SE26 ....181 J1
Cobden Rd ORP BR6 ....216 D2
  SNWD SE25 ....197 H2
  WAN E11 ....88 C1
Cobham Av NWMAL KT3 ....192 D2
Cobham Cl BFN/LL DA15 ......168 C1
  BTSEA SW11 * 160 D1
  EDGW HA8 ....44 D5
  EN EN1 ....24 C4
  HAYES BR2 ....200 D4
  WLGTN SM6 ....210 E4
Cobham Ms CAMTN NW1 ....84 D5
Cobham Pl BXLYHS DA6 ....148 E6
Cobham Rd GDMY/SEVK IG3...72 E6
  HEST TW5 ....134 B1
  KUT/HW KT1 ....175 H5
  WALTH E17 ....52 A3
Cobland Rd LEE/GVPK SE12..166 B6
Coborn Rd BOW E3 ....105 H2
Coborn St BOW E3 ....105 H2
Cobourg Rd CMBW SE5 ....123 G6
Cobourg St CAMTN NW1 ....4 B5
Coburg Crs BRXS/STRHM SW2..162 A3
Coburg Gdns CLAY IG5 ....53 H5
Coburg Rd WDGN N22 ....49 F5
Cochrane Ms STJWD NW8 ....2 E3
Cochrane Rd WIM/MER SW19..177 H3
Cochrane St STJWD NW8 ....2 E3
Cockcrow Hl SURB KT6 * 190 E5
Cockerell Rd WALTH E17 ....69 G4
Cockfosters Pde EBAR EN4 * ...22 A5
Cockfosters Rd EBAR EN4 ....21 K1
Cock La STBT EC1A 12 A2
Cockmannings La
  STMC/STPC BR5 ....202 E4
Cockmannings Rd
  STMC/STPC BR5 ....202 E4
Cocks Crs NWMAL KT3 ....192 C1
Cocksett Av ORP BR6 ....216 E4
Cockspur Ct STJS SW1Y 10 D7
Cockspur St STJS SW1Y 10 D7
Cocksure La SCUP DA14 ....169 H6
Code St WCHPL E1 ....7 L9
Codling Cl WAP E1W * 123 H1
Codling Wy ALP/SUD HA0 ....79 K2
Codrington Hl FSTH SE23 ......164 B2
Codrington Ms NTGHL W11 ..100 C5
Cody Cl KTN/HRWW/W HA3 ....43 K6
  WLGTN SM6 ....210 D5
Cody Rd CAN/RD E16 ....106 B3
Coe Av SNWD SE25 ....197 H3
Coffey St DEPT SE8 ....144 D1
Cogan Av WALTH E17 ....51 G4
Coin St STHWK SE1 ....11 M8
Coity Rd KTTN NW5 ....84 A4
Cokers La DUL SE21 ....162 D3
Coke St WCHPL E1 ....104 C5
Colas Ms KIL/WHAMP NW6 .....82 E6
Colbeck Ms ECT SW5 ....120 A4
Colbeck Rd HRW HA1 ....60 D5
Colberg Pl STNW/STAM N16 ...68 A4
Colborne Wy WPK KT4 ....208 A1

Colbrook Av HYS/HAR UB3 ...113 G3
Colbrook Cl HYS/HAR UB3 ....113 G3
Colburn Av PIN HA5 ....41 K2
Colburn Wy SUT SM1 ....209 H1
Colby Rd NRWD SE19 ....181 F1
Colchester Dr PIN HA5 ....59 H2
Colchester Rd EDGW HA8 ....44 E3
  LEY E10 ....70 A4
  NTHWD HA6 ....40 E5
  WALTH E17 ....69 J5
Colchester St WCHPL E1 ....13 L4
Coldbath Sq CLKNW EC1R * 5 L7
Coldbath St LEW SE13 ....144 E3
Cold Blow Crs BXLY DA5 ......170 A3
Coldblow La NWCR SE14 ......144 A1
Coldershaw Rd HNWL W7 ......116 B2
Coldfall Av MUSWH N10 ....47 K5
Coldharbour Crest
  ELTH/MOT SE9 * 167 F5
Coldharbour La BRXN/ST SW9..142 B5
  BUSH WD23 ....28 B1
  HYS/HAR UB3 ....113 K1
  RAIN RM13 ....130 D1
Coldharbour Pl CMBW SE5 ..142 E3
Coldharbour Rd CROY/NA CR0..211 G3
Coldharbour Wy
  CROY/NA CR0 ....211 G3
Coldstream Gdns
  WAND/EARL SW18 ....159 J1
Colebert Av WCHPL E1 ....104 E3
Colebrook Cl
  WAND/EARL SW18 ....159 H1
Colebrooke Av WEA W13 ....97 H5
Colebrooke Dr WAN E11 ....71 F4
Colebrooke Pl IS N1 ....6 B1
Colebrooke Rw IS N1 ....6 A3
Colebrook Ri HAYES BR2 ......183 H5
Colebrook Rd
  STRHM/NOR SW16 ....179 K4
Colebrook St ERITH DA8 ....130 B6
Colebrook Wy FBAR/BDGN N11..48 B1
Coleby Pth CMBW SE5 * 142 E1
Coledale Dr STAN HA7 ....43 J4
Coleford Rd
  WAND/EARL SW18 ....140 B6
Cole Gdns HEST TW5 ....133 K1
Colegrave Rd SRTFD E15 ....88 B3
Colegrove Rd PECK SE15 ......123 H6
Coleherne Ms WBPTN SW10 ..120 A5
Coleherne Rd WBPTN SW10 ..120 A5
Colehill Gdns FUL/PGN SW6 *..139 H2
Colehill La FUL/PGN SW6 ......139 H2
Coleman Cl SNWD SE25 ....181 H5
Coleman Flds IS N1 ....85 J6
Coleman Rd BELV DA17 ....129 H3
  CMBW SE5 ....143 F1
Colemans Heath
  ELTH/MOT SE9 ....167 F5
Coleman St LOTH EC2R 12 E3
Colenso Dr MLHL NW7 ....45 J3
Colenso Rd CLPT E5 ....86 E2
  GNTH/NBYPK IG2 ....72 E5
Cole Park Gdns TWK TW1 ....156 B1
Cole Park Rd TWK TW1 ....156 B2
Colepits Wood Rd
  ELTH/MOT SE9 ....147 J6
Coleraine Rd BKHTH/KID SE3..125 K6
  CEND/HSY/T N8 ....48 D6
Coleridge Av MNPK E12 ....89 J4
  SUT SM1 ....209 J2
Coleridge Cl VX/NE SW8 ......141 G3
Coleridge Gdns
  KIL/WHAMP NW6 ....83 G5
  WBPTN SW10 ....140 B1
Coleridge Rd ASHF TW15 ......152 B6
  CEND/HSY/T N8 ....66 D5
  CROY/NA CR0 ....197 K4
  DART DA1 ....151 K5
  FSBYPK N4 ....67 G6
  FNCH N3 ....46 E4
  NFNCH/WDSP N12 ....47 G1
  WALTH E17 ....69 H1
Coleridge Sq WEA W13 * 97 G5
Coleridge Wk GLDGN NW11 ....64 E1
Coleridge Wy ORP BR6 ....202 B5
  WDR/YW UB7 ....112 C3
  YEAD UB4 ....94 E5
Cole Rd TWK TW1 ....156 B1
Colesburg Rd BECK BR3 ......182 C6
Coles Crs RYLN/HDSTN HA2 ..60 B6
Coles Gn BUSH WD23 ....28 C3
Coles Green Rd CRICK NW2 ...63 K5
Coleshill Rd TEDD TW11 ....173 K2
Colestown St BTSEA SW11 ...140 D3
Cole St STHWK SE1 ....18 E2
Colet Cl PLMGR N13 ....49 H2
Colet Gdns WKENS W14 ....119 G5
Coley St FSBYW WC1X * 5 L8
Colfe & Hatcliffe Glebe
  LEW SE13 * 144 E6
Colfe Rd FSTH SE23 ....164 B3
Colham Av WDR/YW UB7 ......112 B1
Colham Mill Rd WDR/YW UB7..112 A2
Colina Ms SEVS/STOTM N15 ..67 H1
Colina Rd CEND/HSY/T N8 ......67 H2
Colin Cl CDALE/KGS NW9 ....63 G1
  CROY/NA CR0 ....213 H1
  WWKM BR4 ....214 D1
Colin Crs CDALE/KGS NW9 ....63 H1
Colindale Av CDALE/KGS NW9..45 F5
Colindeep Gdns HDN NW4 .....45 J4
Colindeep La CDALE/KGS NW9..63 H1
Colin Dr CDALE/KGS NW9 ....63 H2
Colinette Rd PUT/ROE SW15..139 F5
Colin Gdns CDALE/KGS NW9 ..63 H1
Colin Park Rd CDALE/KGS NW9..45 G6
Colinton Rd GDMY/SEVK IG3 ..73 J6
Coliston Rd WAND/EARL SW18..159 K2
Collamore Av
  WAND/EARL SW18 ....160 D3
Collapit Cl RYLN/HDSTN HA2 ..60 B3
Collard Pl CAMTN NW1 * 4 A1
College Ap GNWCH SE10 ......125 F6
College Av KTN/HRWW/W HA3..42 E4

College Cl KTN/HRWW/W HA3....42 E3
 UED N18....50 B1
 WHTN TW2....155 J3
College Ct EA W5 *....98 A6
College Crs KIL/WHAMP NW6....83 C4
College Cross IS N1....155 C5
College Dr RSLP HA4....58 E4
 THDIT KT7....189 K4
College East WCHPL E1 *....13 K2
College Gdns CHING E4....37 K2
 ENC/FH EN2....23 J3
 NWMAL KT3....192 C2
 REDBR IG1....71 J2
 TOOT SW17....160 D4
 UED N18....50 B1
College Gn NRWD SE19....181 F3
College Gv CAMTN NW1....4 C1
College Hill CANST EC4R *....12 D5
College Hill Rd
  KTN/HRWW/W HA3....42 E3
College Ms IS N1....85 C5
 WEST SW1P....16 E4
College Pde KIL/WHAMP NW6 *....82 C6
College Park Cl LEW SE13....145 G5
College Pk CAN/RD E16 *....84 D6
 WALTH E17....70 C1
 WBPTN SW10 *....140 B1
College Rd BMLY BR1....183 K4
 CROY/NA CR0....196 E6
 DUL SE21....163 F2
 ENC/FH EN2....23 K3
 HRW HA1....60 E3
 ISLW TW7....136 A2
 KTN/HRWW/W HA3....42 E3
 NRWD SE19....181 G1
 TOTM N17....50 B2
 WALTH E17....70 A2
 WBLY HA9....61 K5
 WCHMH N21....35 G4
 WEA W13....97 H5
 WIM/MER SW19....178 C2
 WLSDN NW10....100 A1
College Ter FNCH N3....46 D4
College Vw ELTH/MOT SE9....166 C3
 HYS/HAR UB3....94 E6
College Wy ASHF TW15....152 C6
 NTHWD HA6....40 D2
College Yd KIL/WHAMP NW6 *....82 C6
 KTTN NW5 *....84 B3
Collent St HOM E9....86 E4
Colless Rd SEVS/STOTM N15....68 B2
Collett Rd BERM/RHTH SE16....123 H3
Collett Cl EHAM E6....108 B6
 HOR/WEW KT19....206 C4
Collier Dr EDGW HA8....44 C5
Collier Row La CRW RM5....56 C4
Collier Row Rd CRW RM5....56 C4
Colliers Water La THHTH CR7....196 C2
Colliers Wd HAYES BR2....215 H3
Collindale Av BFN/LL DA15....168 B3
 CDALE/KGS NW9....43 G6
 ERITH DA8....129 J6
Collingbourne Rd SHB W12....118 E1
Collingham Gdns ECT SW5....120 A4
Collingham Pl ECT SW5....120 A4
Collingham Rd ECT SW5....120 A4
Collings Cl WDGN N22....49 F2
Collington St GNWCH SE10 *....125 C5
Collingtree Rd SYD SE26....163 K6
Collingwood Av BRYLDS KT5....191 K5
 MUSWH N10....48 A6
Collingwood Cl HSLW TW3....155 F2
Collingwood Cl PGE/AN SE20....181 J4
 RAIN RM13....111 H1
 SEVS/STOTM N15....68 A1
 SUT SM1....193 J1
Collingwood Rd MTCM CR4....178 D5
 RAIN RM13....111 H1
 SEVS/STOTM N15....68 A1
 SUT SM1....193 J1
 WCHPL E1....104 D3
Collins Av STAN HA7....44 A5
Collins Dr RSLP HA4....59 C6
Collinson St STHWK SE1....18 C3
Collinson Wk STHWK SE1....18 C3
Collins Rd HBRY N5....85 J2
Collins Sq BKHTH/KID SE3....145 H3
Collinwood Av PEND EN3....24 E4
Collinwood Gdns
  GNTH/NBYPK IG2....71 K2
Coll's Rd PECK SE15....143 K2
Collyer Av CROY/NA CR0....210 E2
Collyer Pl PECK SE15....143 H2
Collyer Rd CROY/NA CR0....210 E2
Colman Pde EN EN1 *....24 A4
Colman Rd CAN/RD E16....107 G4
Colmar Cl WCHPL E1....105 F3
Colmer Pl KTN/HRWW/W HA3....42 D3
Colmer Rd STRHM/NOR SW16....179 K3
Colmore Ms PECK SE15....143 J2
Colmore Rd PEND EN3....24 E5
Colnbrook St STHWK SE1....18 A5
Coine Av OXHEY WD19....27 F1
Coine Ct HOR/WEW KT19....206 E2
Coine Rd CLPT E5....87 F2
 WCHMH N21....35 K3
 WHTN TW2....155 K3
Colne St PLSTW E13....106 E2
Colney Hatch La
  FBAR/BDGN N11....47 K2
 MUSWH N10....47 K6
Colney Rd DART DA1....171 J1
Cologne Rd BTSEA SW11....140 C5
Colombo Rd IL IG1....72 C5
Colombo St STHWK SE1....18 A1
Colonels Wk ENC/FH EN2....23 H5
Colonial Av WHTN TW2....155 H1
Colonial Dr CHSWK W4....117 K4
Colonial Rd EBED/NFELT TW14....153 H2
Colonnade BMSBY WC1N....4 E7
The Colonnade DEPT SE8 *....124 C4
Colosseum Ter CAMTN NW1 *....3 K6
Colson Rd CROY/NA CR0....197 C6
Colson Wy STRHM/NOR SW16....161 H6

Colsterworth Rd
  SEVS/STOTM N15....68 B1
Colston Av CAR SM5....209 J2
Colston Rd FSTGT E7....89 H4
 MORT/ESHN SW14....137 K5
Colthurst Crs FSBYPK N4....67 H6
Colthurst Dr ED N9....36 D5
Coltness Crs ABYW SE2....128 C5
Colton Rd HRW HA1....60 E2
Columbas Dr HAMP NW3....65 H5
Columbia Av EDGW HA8....44 D4
 RSLP HA4....59 F5
 WPK KT4....192 C4
Columbia Rd BETH E2....7 K4
 PLSTW E13 *....106 D3
Columbine Wy LEW SE13 *....145 F3
Columbus Gdns NTHWD HA6....40 E4
Colview Ct ELTH/MOT SE9....166 C3
Colvestone Crs HACK E8....86 B3
Colville Est IS N1....7 F1
Colville Gdns NTGHL W11....100 D5
Colville Houses NTGHL W11....100 D5
Colville Ms NTGHL W11....100 D5
Colville Pl FITZ W1T....10 B2
Colville Rd ACT W3....117 J3
 ED N9....36 D3
 NTGHL W11....100 D5
 WALTH E17....51 G5
 WAN E11....88 A1
Colville Sq NTGHL W11....100 D5
Colville Square Ms
  NTGHL W11 *....100 D5
Colville Ter NTGHL W11....100 D5
Colvin Cl SYD SE26....181 K1
Colvin Gdns BARK/HLT IG6....54 C3
 CHING E4....38 A5
 SWFD E18....53 F1
Colvin Rd EHAM E6....89 J5
 THHTH CR7....196 B2
Colwall Gdns WFD IG8....52 E1
Colwell Rd EDUL SE22....143 C6
Colwick Cl HGT N6....66 D4
Colwith Rd HMSMTH W6....119 F6
Colwood Gdns
  WIM/MER SW19....178 C3
Colworth Gv WALW SE17....18 D7
Colworth Rd CROY/NA CR0....197 H5
 WAN E11....70 C3
Colwyn Av GFD/PVL UB6....97 F1
Colwyn Cl STRHM/NOR SW16....179 H1
Colwyn Crs HSLW TW3....135 H2
Colwyn Gn CDALE/KGS NW9 *....63 G3
Colwyn Rd CRICK NW2....81 K1
Colyer Cl ELTH/MOT SE9....167 G4
Colyer Gdns ERITH DA8....150 A2
Colyers La ERITH DA8....149 K2
Colyton Cl ALP/SUD HA0....79 J4
 WELL DA16....148 E2
Colyton La STRHM/NOR SW16....180 B1
Colyton Rd EDUL SE22....143 J6
Colyton Wy UED N18....50 C1
Combe Av BKHTH/KID SE3....145 J1
Combedale Rd GNWCH SE10....125 K5
Combemartin Rd
  WAND/EARL SW18....159 H2
Comber Cl CRICK NW2....81 J1
Comber Gv CMBW SE5....142 D1
Combermere Rd
  BRXN/ST SW9....142 A4
 MRDN SM4....194 A3
Combe Rd WATW WD18....26 D1
Comberton Rd CLPT E5....68 D6
Combeside WOOL/PLUM SE18....148 A1
Combe Rd DAGW RM9....92 B6
Combwell Crs ABYW SE2....128 B5
Comely Bank Rd WALTH E17....70 A2
Comeragh Ms WKENS W14 *....119 H5
Comeragh Rd WKENS W14....119 H5
Comerford Rd BROCKY SE4....144 B5
Comet Cl MNPK E12....89 H1
 PUR RM19....131 K4
Comet Pl DEPT SE8....144 D1
Comet Rd STWL/WRAY TW19....152 A2
Comet St DEPT SE8....144 D1
Commerce Rd BTFD TW8....116 D6
 WDGN N22....49 F4
Commerce Wy CROY/NA CR0....211 F1
Commercial Rd POP/IOD E14....105 G5
 UED N18....50 A1
 WCHPL E1....13 K3
Commercial St WCHPL E1....7 J7
Commercial Wy PECK SE15....143 H1
 WLSDN NW10....98 D1
Commerell Pl GNWCH SE10 *....125 J5
Commerell St GNWCH SE10....125 H5
Commodore Pde
  STRHM/NOR SW16 *....180 A3
Commodore St WCHPL E1....105 C3
Commondale PUT/ROE SW15....139 F3
Common La ESH/CLAY KT10....205 C5
 RDART DA2....170 D4
Common Rd BARN SW13....138 D4
 ESH/CLAY KT10....205 G4
 STAN HA7....28 E4
Commonside HAYES BR2....215 H1
Commonside East MTCM CR4....179 F6
Commonside West MTCM CR4....179 F6
The Common EA W5....117 F1
 NWDGN UB2....114 C4
 SRTFD E15....88 C4
 STAN HA7....29 F4
Commonwealth Av
  HYS/HAR UB3....94 B5
 SHB W12....99 K6
Commonwealth Rd TOTM N17....50 C3
Commonwealth Wy
  ABYW SE2....128 C5
Community Cl HEST TW5....134 A2
Community Rd GFD/PVL UB6....78 B5
 SRTFD E15....88 B3
Como Rd FSTH SE23....164 B4

Como St ROMW/RG RM7....75 F2
Compass Hl
  RCHPK/HAM TW10....156 E1
Compayne Gdns
  KIL/WHAMP NW6....83 F5
Compton Av ALP/SUD HA0....79 H2
 EHAM E6....107 H1
 GPK RM2....75 J4
 HGT N6....65 J4
 IS N1....85 H4
 RYLN/HDSTN HA2....60 B1
Compton Cl CAMTN NW1....3 K5
 EDGW HA8....44 E3
 ESH/CLAY KT10....204 D4
Compton Crs CHSGTN KT9....206 A4
 CHSWK W4....117 K6
 NTHLT UB5....77 H6
 TOTM N17....49 J3
Compton Pas FSBYE EC1V....6 A6
Compton Pl ERITH DA8....130 C6
 HYS/HAR UB3 *....94 C6
 IS N1....85 H4
 WCHMH N21....35 H5
 WIM/MER SW19....177 J2
 WLSDN NW10....100 B2
Compton Ri PIN HA5....59 J2
Compton Rd CROY/NA CR0....197 J5
 HYS/HAR UB3....94 C6
 IS N1....85 H4
 WCHMH N21....35 H5
 WIM/MER SW19....177 J2
 WLSDN NW10....100 B2
Compton St FSBYE EC1V....6 A6
Compton Ter FSBYE EC1V....6 A6
 IS N1....85 H4
 WCHMH N21....35 G3
Comreddy Cl ENC/FH EN2....23 H2
Comus Pl WALW SE17....19 G7
Comyn Rd BTSEA SW11....140 D5
Comyns Cl CAN/RD E16....106 D4
Comyns Rd DAGW RM9....92 C5
The Comyns BUSH WD23....28 C3
Conant Ms WCHPL E1....104 C6
Concanon Rd
  BRXS/STRHM SW2....142 A5
Concert Hall Ap STHWK SE1....17 H1
Concord Cl NTHLT UB5....95 H2
Concorde Cl HSLW TW3....135 C3
Concorde Dr EHAM E6....107 K4
Concord Rd ACT W3....98 D4
 PEND EN3....24 E6
Condell Rd VX/NE SW8....141 H2
Conder St POP/IOD E14....105 G5
Condover Crs
  WOOL/PLUM SE18....147 G1
Condray Pl BTSEA SW11....140 D1
Conduit Av GNWCH SE10 *....145 G2
Conduit Ct LSQ/SEVD WC2E *....10 E5
Conduit La SAND/SEL CR2....212 C3
 UED N18....50 E1
Conduit Ms BAY/PAD W2....8 A4
 WOOL/PLUM SE18....127 G5
Conduit Pas BAY/PAD W2....8 A4
Conduit Pl BAY/PAD W2....8 A4
Conduit Rd WOOL/PLUM SE18....127 G5
 WDDT SL CONDST W1S....9 K5
Conduit Wy WLSDN NW10....80 E5
Conewood St HBRY N5....85 H1
Coney Burrows CHING E4....38 C4
Coney Hall Pde WWKM BR4 *....214 C1
Coney Hill Rd WWKM BR4....199 H6
Coney Wy VX/NE SW8....122 A6
Conference Cl CHING E4....38 A4
Conference Rd ABYW SE2....128 D4
Congleton Gv
  WOOL/PLUM SE18....127 H5
Congo Rd WOOL/PLUM SE18....127 J5
Congress Rd ABYW SE2....128 D4
Congreve Rd ELTH/MOT SE9....146 E4
Congreve St WALW SE17....19 G7
Conical Cnr ENC/FH EN2....23 J3
Conifer Av CRW RM5....56 D1
Conifer Cl ORP BR6....216 E3
Conifer Gdns EN EN1....35 K1
  STRHM/NOR SW16....162 A5
 SUT SM1....194 A6
Conifers Cl TEDD TW11....174 C3
Coningham Ms SHB W12....118 D1
Coningham Rd SHB W12....118 E2
Coningsby Cottages EA W5....116 E2
Coningsby Gdns CHING E4....51 K2
Coningsby Rd EA W5....116 D2
 FSBYPK N4....67 H4
 SAND/SEL CR2....211 J6
Conington Rd LEW SE13....144 E3
Conisbee Ct STHGT/OAK N14....22 C6
Conisborough Crs CAT SE6....165 F5
Coniscliffe Cl CHST BR7....185 F4
Coniscliffe Rd PLMGR N13....35 J5
Coniston Av BARK IG11....90 E5
 GFD/PVL UB6....97 H2
 WELL DA16....147 K4
Coniston Cl BARN SW13....138 C1
 BXLYHN DA7....150 A2
 CHSWK W4....137 K2
 DART DA1....170 B3
 ERITH DA8....150 B1
 MRDN SM4....193 G3
Coniston Ct BAY/PAD W2 *....8 D4
Conistone Wy HOLWY N7....84 E5
Coniston Gdns BELMT SM2....209 H4
 CDALE/KGS NW9....63 F2
 ED N9....36 E3
 PIN HA5....58 E1
 REDBR IG4....71 J1
 WBLY HA9....61 J2
Coniston Rd BMLY BR1....183 H2
 BXLYHN DA7....150 A1
 CROY/NA CR0....197 H4
 MUSWH N10....48 B5
 TOTM N17....50 C2
 WHTN TW2....155 G1
Colin Park Rd CDALE/KGS NW9 *....63 G1
Coolfin Rd CAN/RD E16....106 E5
Coolgardie Av CHING E4....52 B1
Coolhurst Rd CEND/HSY/T N8....66 D3
Cool Oak Br CDALE/KGS NW9....63 H4
Cool Oak La CDALE/KGS NW9....63 H4

Coomassie Rd MV/WKIL W9....100 D3
Coombe Av CROY/NA CR0....212 A2
Coombe Bank NWMAL KT3....176 B4
Coombe Cl EDGW HA8....44 B5
 HSLW TW3....135 F5
Coombe Cnr WCHMH N21....35 H3
Coombe Crs HPTN TW12....172 D3
Coombe Dr RSLP HA4....59 F5
Coombe End KUTN/CMB KT2....176 B2
Coombefield Cl NWMAL KT3....192 B2
Coombe Gdns NWMAL KT3....192 C1
 RYNPK SW20....176 D5
Coombe Hill Gld
  KUTN/CMB KT2....176 B3
Coombe Hill Rd
  KUTN/CMB KT2....176 B3
Coombe House Cha
  NWMAL KT3....176 A4
Coombehurst Cl EBAR EN4....21 K3
Coombe La CROY/NA CR0....212 D5
 NWMAL KT3....192 B1
 RYNPK SW20....176 D4
Coombe La West
  KUTN/CMB KT2....175 K4
Coombe Lea BMLY BR1....184 D6
Coombe Ldg CHARL SE7....126 B6
Coombe Neville
  KUTN/CMB KT2....175 K3
Coombe Pk KUTN/CMB KT2....175 K1
Coombe Ri KUTN/CMB KT2....175 K4
Coombe Ridings
  KUTN/CMB KT2....175 K1
Coombe Rd BUSH WD23....28 C2
 CHSWK W4....118 B5
 HPTN TW12....172 E2
 KUTN/CMB KT2....175 H5
 NWMAL KT3....176 B6
 SAND/SEL CR2....212 A2
 SYD SE26....163 J6
 WDGN N22....49 G4
 WEA W13....116 C3
 WLSDN NW10....81 F1
Coomber Wy CROY/NA CR0....195 K4
Coombe Vls
  WAND/EARL SW18 *....159 K2
Coombewood Dr CHDH RM6....74 B3
Coombe Wood Rd
  KUTN/CMB KT2....175 K1
Coombs St IS N1....6 B6
Coomer Ms FUL/PGN SW6 *....119 J6
Coomer Pl FUL/PGN SW6....119 J6
Cooms Wk EDGW HA8....44 E4
Cooperage Cl TOTM N17 *....50 B2
Cooper Av WALTH E17 *....51 F4
Cooper Cl STHWK SE1....17 K3
Cooperdale Cl WFD IG8....53 G3
Cooper Rd CRICK NW2....82 J3
 CROY/NA CR0....211 H2
 HDN NW4....64 B3
Coopersale Rd HOM E9....87 F3
Coopers Cl DAGE RM10....92 D4
 WCHPL E1....104 E3
Coopers Dr BXLY DA5....170 B4
Coopers La CAMTN NW1....4 E4
 LEE/GVPK SE12....166 A4
 LEY E10....69 K5
Coopers Ms BECK BR3....182 D5
Cooper's Rd STHWK SE1....123 C5
Cooper's Rw TWRH EC3N....13 J5
Coopers Rd STHWK SE1....123 G5
Coopers Yd IS N1 *....85 H5
 NRWD SE19....181 F2
Coote Gdns DAGE RM10....92 B1
 BXLYHN DA7....149 G2
Copeland Dr POP/IOD E14....124 D4
Copeland Rd PECK SE15....143 H3
 WALTH E17....69 K2
Copeman Cl SYD SE26....181 K1
Copenhagen Gdns CHEL SW3....120 C5
 CHSWK W4....118 A2
Copenhagen Pl POP/IOD E14....105 H5
Copenhagen St IS N1....5 F1
Cope Pl KENS W8....119 K3
Copers Cope Rd BECK BR3....182 C3
 SEV SE BERM/RHTH SE16....124 A4
Copford Wk IS N1 *....85 J5
Copgate Pth
  STRHM/NOR SW16....180 A2
Copland Av ALP/SUD HA0....79 K3
Copland Cl ALP/SUD HA0....80 A3
Copland Ms ALP/SUD HA0....80 A4
Copland Rd ALP/SUD HA0....80 A4
Copleston Rd PECK SE15....143 G4
Copley Cl HNWL W7....97 F4
  WALW SE17....122 C6
Copley Dene BMLY BR1....184 B4
Copley Pk STRHM/NOR SW16....180 A2
Copley Rd STAN HA7....43 J1
Copley St WCHPL E1....105 F4
Coppard Gdns CHSGTN KT9....205 J4
Coppelia Rd BKHTH/KID SE3....145 J5
Coppen Rd BCTR RM8....74 B4
Copperas St DEPT SE8....124 E6
Copper Beech Cl CLAY IG5....54 A4
  STMC/STPC BR5....202 D2
Copper Cl NRWD SE19....181 G3
Copperdale Rd HYS/HAR UB3....113 K2
Copperfield CHIG IG7....54 D2
Copperfield Dr
  SEVS/STOTM N15....68 B1
Copperfield Rd BOW E3....105 G3
  THMD SE28....109 J5
Copperfield St STHWK SE1....18 B2
Copperfield Wy CHST BR7....185 H2
  PIN HA5....41 K6
Coppergate Cl BMLY BR1....184 A4
Coppermead Cl CRICK NW2....82 A1
Copper Mill Dr ISLW TW7....136 A3
Copper Mill La TOOT SW17....160 B6
Coppermill La WALTH E17....68 E3
Copper Rw STHWK SE1....13 J8
Coppetts Cl NFNCH/WDSP N12....47 H3
Coppetts Rd MUSWH N10....47 K4
Coppice Cl BECK BR3....198 E1
 KTN/HRWW/W HA3....43 F2
 RSLP HA4....58 A3

RYNPK SW20 ...177 F6
Coppice Dr PUT/ROE SW15 ...158 D1
The Coppice BAR EN5 * ...33 F1
BXLY DA5 ...170 A5
ENC/FH EN2 ...23 H5
OXHEY WD19 ...27 G1
Coppice Wk TRDG/WHET N20...32 E5
Coppice Wy SWFD E18 ...70 D1
Copping Cl CROY/NA CRO ...212 A2
KTN/HRWW/W HA3 ...42 E2
Coppock Cl BTSEA SW11 ...140 D3
Coppsfield E/WMO/HCT KT8 ...173 F6
Copse Av WWKM BR4 ...213 K1
Copse Cl CHARL SE7...126 A6
NTHWD HA6 ...40 A4
WDR/YW UB7 ...112 A3
Copse Gld SURB KT6 ...190 E5
Copse Hl BELMT SM2 ...209 F5
RYNPK SW20 ...176 E3
Copsem Dr ESH/CLAY KT10 ...204 B4
Copsem La ESH/CLAY KT10 ...204 B4
Copsem Wy ESH/CLAY KT10 ...204 C4
The Copse CHING E4 ...38 D3
EFNCH N2 ...47 K6
Copse Vw SAND/SEL CR2...213 G6
Copsewood Cl BFN/LL DA15 ...167 K1
Copse Wood Wy NTHWD HA6....40 A4
Coptefield Dr BXLY DA17 ...128 E3
Copthall Av LOTH EC2R ...13 F3
Copthall Dr MLHL NW7 ...45 J3
Copthall Gdns MLHL NW7 ...45 J3
TWK TW1 ...156 B3
Copthorne Av BAL SW12 ...161 J2
BARK/HLT IG6 ...54 B2
HAYES BR2 ...200 E6
Copthorne Ms HYS/HAR UB3 ...113 H4
Coptic St NOXST/BSQ WC1A ...10 E2
Copton Cl BOW E3 ...105 J4
Coral Cl CHDH RM6 ...55 J6
Coraline Cl STHL UB1 ...95 K2
Coraline Wk ABYW SE2 ...128 D2
Coral St STHWK SE1 ...17 K3
Coram St STPAN WC1H...4 E7
Coran Cl ED N9 ...37 F2
Corban Rd HSLW TW3 ...135 F4
Corbar Cl EBAR EN4 ...21 H1
Corbet Cl WLGTN SM6 ...195 F5
Corbet Pl WCHPL E1 ...13 J1
Corbett Gv FBAR/BDGN N11 ...48 E5
Corbett Rd WALTH E17 ...52 B5
WAN E11 ...71 G5
Corbett's La BERM/RHTH SE16...123 K4
Corbicum WAN E11 ...70 C4
Corbin's La RYLN/HDSTN HA2...78 B1
Corbridge Crs BETH E2 ...104 D1
Corbridge Ms ROM RM1 ...75 H2
Corby Crs ENC/FH EN2 ...22 C3
Corbylands Rd BFN/LL DA15 ...167 K3
Corbyn St FSBYPK N4 ...66 E5
Corby Rd WLSDN NW10 ...98 E1
Cordelia Cl HNHL SE24 ...142 C5
Cordelia Gdns
STWL/WRAY TW19 ...152 B2
Cordelia Rd STWL/WRAY TW19 ...152 B2
Cordelia St POP/IOD E14 ...105 K5
Cording St POP/IOD E14 ...105 K4
Cordova Rd BOW E3 ...105 G2
Cordwell Rd LEW SE13 ...145 G6
Corelli Rd BKHTH/KID SE3 ...146 D2
Corfe Av RYLN/HDSTN HA2 ...78 A2
Corfe Cl HSLWW TW4 ...154 D3
YEAD UB4 ...95 G5
Corfield Rd WCHMH N21 ...23 F6
Corfield St BETH E2 ...104 D3
Corfton Rd EA W5...86 A6
Coriander Av POP/IOD E14 ...106 B5
Cories Cl BCTR RM8 ...73 K6
Corinium Cl WBLY HA9 ...80 B2
Corinne Rd HOLWY N7 ...84 C2
Corinthian Manorway
ERITH DA8 ...130 A4
Corinthian Rd ERITH DA8 ...130 A4
Corkran Rd SURB KT6 ...190 E4
Cork St Ms CONDST W1S ...10 A6
Corkscrew Hl WWKM BR4 ...199 F6
Cork Sq WAP E1W ...123 H1
Cork Tree Wy CHING E4 ...51 G1
Corlett St BAY/PAD W2 ...8 C1
Cormont Rd CMBW SE5 ...142 C2
Cormorant Rd FSTGT E7 ...88 D3
Cornbury Rd EDGW HA8 ...43 K3
Cornelia Dr YEAD UB4...95 G5
Cornelia St IS N1 ...85 F4
Cornell Cl SCUP DA14 ...187 F2
Cornell Wy CRW RM5 ...56 D1

Cornwall Cl BARK IG11 ...91 F4
Cornwall Crs NTGHL W11 ...100 C6
Cornwall Dr STMC/STPC BR5...186 D3
Cornwall Gdns SKENS SW7 ...120 A3
SNWD SE25 * ...197 G1
WLSDN NW10 ...81 K4
Cornwall Gardens Wk
SKENS SW7 ...120 A3
Cornwall Gv CHSWK W4 ...118 B5
Cornwallis Av BFN/LL DA15...167 J4
ED N9 ...36 D4
Cornwallis Cl ERITH DA8 ...130 C6
Cornwallis Gv ED N9 ...36 D4
Cornwallis Rd ARCH N19 ...66 E6
DAGW RM9 ...92 A2
ED N9 ...36 D4
WALTH E17 ...69 F1
WOOL/PLUM SE18 ...127 H4
Cornwallis Sq ARCH N19 ...66 E6
Cornwallis Wk ELTH/MOT SE9 ...146 E4
Cornwall Ms South
SKENS SW7 * ...120 B3
Cornwall Ms West
SKENS SW7 * ...120 A3
Cornwall Rd BELMT SM2 ...208 D5
CROY/NA CRO ...196 C6
DART DA1 ...151 J4
FSBYPK N4 ...67 G4
HRW HA1 ...60 C3
PIN HA5 ...41 K3
RSLP HA4 ...58 D6
STHWK SE1 ...11 J7
TWK TW1 ...156 B2
UED N18 ...50 C1
Cornwall Sq LBTH SE11 * ...122 B5
Cornwall St WCHPL E1 * ...104 D6
Cornwall Ter CAMTN NW1 ...3 F7
Cornwall Terrace Ms
CAMTN NW1 ...3 F7
Corn Wy WAN E11 ...88 B1
Cornwood Cl EFNCH N2 ...65 H2
Cornwood Dr WCHPL E1 ...104 E5
Cornworthy Rd BCTR RM8 ...91 J5
Corona Rd LEE/GVPK SE12 ...165 K2
Coronation Cl BARK/HLT IG6 ...72 C1
BXLY DA5 ...168 E1
Coronation Dr HCH RM12 ...93 K3
Coronation Rd HYS/HAR UB3 ...113 J4
PLSTW E13 ...107 G2
WLSDN NW10 ...98 B2
Coronation Vls WLSDN NW10 *...98 D3
Coronet Pde ALP/SUD HA0 *...80 A4
Coronet St IS N1 ...7 G3
Corporation Av HSLWW TW4 ...134 D5
Corporation Rw CLKNW EC1R ...5 K6
Corporation St HOLWY N7 ...84 E3
SRTFD E15 ...106 C1
Corrance Rd CLAP SW4 ...141 K5
Corri Av STHGT/OAK N14 ...34 D5
Corrib Dr SUT SM1 ...209 J3
Corrigan Cl HDN NW4 ...46 A6
Corringham Rd GLDGN NW11 ...64 E4
WBLY HA9 ...62 C6
Corringway EA W5 ...98 B4
GLDGN NW11 ...64 E4
Corris Gn CDALE/KGS NW9 * ...63 G3
Corsair Cl STWL/WRAY TW19 ...152 A2
Corsair Rd STWL/WRAY TW19 ...152 B2
Corscombe Cl KUTN/CMB KT2 ...175 K1
Corsehill St STRHM/NOR SW16 ...179 H2
Corsellis Sq TWK TW1 ...136 C5
Corsham St IS N1 ...7 F5
Corsica St HBRY N5...85 H4
Cortayne Rd FUL/PGN SW6 * ...139 J3
Cortina Dr DAGW RM9 ...110 E2
Cortis Rd PUT/ROE SW15 ...158 E1
Cortis Ter PUT/ROE SW15 ...138 E6
Corunna Rd VX/NE SW8 ...141 H2
Corunna Ter VX/NE SW8 ...141 H2
Corwell Gdns UX/CGN UB8 ...94 A5
Corwell La UX/CGN UB8 ...94 A5
Coryton Pth MV/WKIL W9 ...100 D3
Cosbycote Av HNHL SE24 ...142 D6
Cosdach Av WLGTN SM6 ...210 D5
Cosedge Crs CROY/NA CRO ...211 G3
Cosgrove Cl WCHMH N21 ...35 J4
YEAD UB4 ...95 J3
Cosmo Pl RSQ WC1B ...11 F1
Cosmur Cl SHB W12 ...118 C3
Cossall Wk PECK SE15 ...143 J2
Cosser St STHWK SE1 ...17 J4
Costa St PECK SE15 ...143 H3
Costons Av GFD/PVL UB6 ...96 D2
Costons La GFD/PVL UB6 ...96 D2
Cosway St CAMTN NW1 ...8 D1
Cotall St POP/IOD E14 ...105 J5
Coteford Cl PIN HA5 ...58 E2
Coteford St TOOT SW17 ...160 E6
Cotelands CROY/NA CRO ...212 A1
Cotesbach Rd CLPT E5 ...86 E1
Cotesmore Gdns BCTR RM8 ...91 J2
Cotford Rd THHTH CR7 ...196 D1
Cotham St WALW SE17 ...18 E7
Cotherstone Rd
BRXS/STRHM SW2 ...162 A3
Cotleigh Av BXLY DA5 ...168 E4
Cotleigh Rd KIL/WHAMP NW6...82 E5
ROMW/RG RM7 ...75 G3
Cotman Cl GLDGN NW11 ...65 G3
Cotman Ms BCTR RM8 ...91 H3
Cotmans Cl HYS/HAR UB3 ...113 K1
Coton Rd WELL DA16 ...148 B4
Cotsford Av NWMAL KT3 ...191 K2
Cotswold Av BUSH WD23 ...28 C1
Cotswold Cl BXLYHN DA7 ...150 B2
ESH/CLAY KT10 ...190 A6
KUTN/CMB KT2 ...175 K2
Cotswold Gdns CRICK NW2 ...64 B6
EHAM E6 ...107 H2
GNTH/NBYPK IG2 ...72 C3
Cotswold Ga CRICK NW2 ...64 C5
Cotswold Gn ENC/FH EN2 ...23 F5

Cotswold Ri ORP BR6 ...202 A3
Cotswold Rd HPTN TW12 ...173 F2
Cotswold St WNWD SE27 ...162 C6
Cotswold Wy ENC/FH EN2 ...23 F4
WPK KT4 ...193 F6
Cottage Av HAYES BR2 ...200 D5
Cottage Cl HRW HA1 ...60 E6
RSLP HA4 ...58 B5
Cottage Field Cl SCUP DA14 ...168 D3
Cottage Gn CMBW SE5 ...142 E1
Cottage Gv BRXN/ST SW9 ...141 K4
SURB KT6 ...190 E3
Cottage Rd HOR/WEW KT19 ...207 F5
Cottage St POP/IOD E14 ...105 K6
Cottenham Dr
CDALE/KGS NW9 ...45 H6
RYNPK SW20 ...176 E3
Cottenham Park Rd
RYNPK SW20 ...176 E3
Cottenham Pl RYNPK SW20...176 E3
Cottenham Rd WALTH E17 ...69 H1
Cotterill Rd SURB KT6 ...191 G6
Cottesbrook St NWCR SE14...144 B1
Cottesloe Ms STHWK SE1 ...17 K4
Cottesmore Av CLAY IG5 ...53 K5
Cottesmore Gdns KENS W8...120 A3
Cottimore Av WOT/HER KT12 ...188 A5
Cottimore Crs WOT/HER KT12 ...188 A4
Cottimore La WOT/HER KT12 ...188 A4
Cottimore Ter WOT/HER KT12 ...188 A4
Cottingham Cha RSLP HA4 ...76 E1
Cottingham Rd PGE/AN SE20 ...182 A3
VX/NE SW8 ...142 A1
Cottington Rd FELT TW13 ...154 C6
Cottington St LBTH SE11 ...122 B5
Cotton Av ACT W3 ...99 F5
Cotton Cl DAGW RM9 ...91 J5
Cotton Gardens Est LBTH SE11 ...18 A7
Cottongrass Cl CROY/NA CRO ...198 A5
Cotton Hl BMLY BR1 ...165 G6
Cotton Rw BTSEA SW11 ...140 B4
Cottons Ap ROMW/RG RM7 ...75 F2
Cottons Centre STHWK SE1 ...13 G7
Cotton's Gdns BETH E2 ...7 H4
Cotton St POP/IOD E14 ...106 A6
Couchmore Av CLAY IG5 ...53 K5
ESH/CLAY KT10 ...189 K6
Coulgate St BROCKY SE4 ...144 B4
Coulson Cl BCTR RM8 ...73 J5
Coulson St CHEL SW3 ...120 E5
Coulter Cl YEAD UB4 ...95 J3
Coulter Rd HMSMTH W6 ...118 E3
Councillor St CMBW SE5 ...142 D1
Counter St STHWK SE1 ...13 G7
Countess Rd KTTN NW5 ...84 C3
Countisbury Av EN EN1 ...36 B2
Country Wy FELT TW13 ...172 B1
County Ga BAR EN5 * ...33 H1
CHST BR7 ...167 H5
County Gv CMBW SE5 ...142 D2
County Pde BTFD TW8 * ...136 E1
County Rd EHAM E6 ...108 B4
THHTH CR7 ...180 C5
County St STHWK SE1 ...18 D5
Coupland Pl
WOOL/PLUM SE18 ...127 H5
Courcy Rd CEND/HSY/T N8 ...49 G6
Courier Rd DAGW RM9 ...110 E3
Courland Gv VX/NE SW8 ...141 J2
Courland St VX/NE SW8 ...141 J2
Course The ELTH/MOT SE9 ...167 F5
Courtauld Rd ARCH N19 ...66 D5
Courtaulds Cl THMD SE28 ...128 B1
Court Av BELV DA17 ...129 G5
Court Cl FELT TW13 ...155 G5
HAMP NW3 ...83 H5
KTN/HRWW/W HA3 ...43 K4
Court Close Av FELT TW13 ...155 G5
Court Crs CHSGTN KT9 ...205 K4
Court Downs Rd BECK BR3 ...182 E5
Court Dr CROY/NA CRO ...211 F2
SUT SM1 ...209 J2
Court Farm Av
HOR/WEW KT19 ...207 F3
Court Farm Rd ELTH/MOT SE9 ...166 C4
NTHLT UB5 ...78 A5
Courtfield Av HRW HA1 ...61 F2
Courtfield Crs HRW HA1 ...61 F2
Courtfield Gdns ECT SW5 ...120 A4
RSLP HA4 ...58 D6
WEA W13 ...97 G5
Courtfield Ms SKENS SW7 * ...120 B4
Courtfield Ri WWKM BR4 ...214 B1
Courtfield Rd ECT SW5 ...120 B5
Court Gdns HOLWY N7 ...85 G4
Courthill Rd LEW SE13 ...145 F6
Courthope Rd GFD/PVL UB6 ...96 D1
HAMP NW3 ...83 K2
WIM/MER SW19 ...177 H1
Courthope Vls
WIM/MER SW19 ...177 H3
Court House Rd FNCH N3 ...47 F2
Courtland Av CHING E4 ...38 C4
IL IG1 ...71 K6
MLHL NW7 ...31 F5
STRHM/NOR SW16 ...180 A3
Courtland Gv THMD SE28 ...109 K6
Courtland Rd EHAM E6 ...89 J6
Courtlands RCHPK/HAM TW10 ...137 H6

Courtlands Av HAYES BR2 ...199 H5
HPTN TW12 ...172 E2
LEE/GVPK SE12 ...146 A6
RCH/KEW TW9 ...137 J5
Courtlands Cl RSLP HA4 ...58 D5
Courtlands Dr HOR/WEW KT19 ...207 G4
Courtlands Rd BRYLDS KT5 ...191 H4
Court La DUL SE21 ...163 G2
Court Lane Gdns DUL SE21 ...163 F2
Courtleet Dr BXLYHN DA7 ...149 J2
Courtleigh Av EBAR EN4 ...21 H1
Courtleigh Gdns GLDGN NW11 ...64 C1
Courtman Rd TOTM N17 ...49 J5
Court Md NTHLT UB5 ...95 K2
Courtmead Cl HNHL SE24 ...162 D1
Courtnell St BAY/PAD W2 ...100 E5
Courtney Cl NRWD SE19 * ...181 F2
Courtney Crs CAR SM5 ...209 K5
Courtney Rd CROY/NA CRO ...211 G1
HOLWY N7 ...85 G3
HTHAIR TW6 ...132 D4
WIM/MER SW19 ...178 D3
Courtney Wy HTHAIR TW6...132 D4
Courtrai Rd BROCKY SE4 ...144 D3
Court Rd ELTH/MOT SE9 ...166 E3
NWDGN UB2...114 E4
SNWD SE25 ...181 G5
Court Rd (Orpington By-Pass)
ORP BR6 ...217 H1
Courtside CEND/HSY/T N8 ...66 D3
SYD SE26 * ...163 K5
Court St BMLY BR1 ...183 K5
WCHPL E1 ...104 D4
The Court MUSWH N10 * ...66 C1
RSLP HA4 ...77 J2
Court Wy ACT W3 ...98 E4
BARK/HLT IG6 ...54 C6
CDALE/KGS NW9 ...63 G1
WHTN TW2 ...156 A2
The Courtway OXHEY WD19 ...27 J4
Court Yd ELTH/MOT SE9 ...166 D1
The Courtyards WATW WD18 * ...26 B2
The Courtyard IS N1 ...85 F5
Cousin La CANST EC4R ...12 E6
Cousthurst Rd BKHTH/KID SE3...126 A6
Coutts Av CHSGTN KT9 ...206 A3
Coutts Crs KTTN NW5 * ...84 A1
Coval Gdns MORT/ESHN SW14 ...137 J5
Coval La MORT/ESHN SW14 ...137 J5
Coval Rd MORT/ESHN SW14 ...137 K5
Covelees Wall EHAM E6 ...108 A5
Covent Gdn COVGDN WC2E ...11 F5
Covent Gdn Piazza
COVGDN WC2E ...11 F5
Coventry Cl EHAM E6 ...107 K5
KIL/WHAMP NW6 ...100 E1
Coventry Cross Est BOW E3 ...106 A3
Coventry Rd IL IG1 ...72 B5
SNWD SE25 ...197 H1
WCHPL E1 ...104 D3
Coventry St MYFR/PICC W1J...10 C6
Coverack Cl CROY/NA CRO ...198 B4
STHGT/OAK N14 ...34 C1
Coverdale Gdns CROY/NA CRO ...212 B1
Coverdale Rd FBAR/BDGN N11 ...48 A2
KIL/WHAMP NW6 ...82 E6
SHB W12 ...118 E1
The Coverdales BARK IG11 ...108 D1
Coverley Cl WCHPL E1 * ...104 C4
Coverton Rd TOOT SW17 ...160 D6
Covert Rd BARK/HLT IG6 ...55 F2
Coverts Rd ESH/CLAY KT10 ...205 F5
The Covert NRWD SE19 * ...181 G5
NTHWD HA6 ...40 A4
ORP BR6 ...201 K3
Covert Wy EBAR EN4 ...21 G3
Covet Wood Cl
STMC/STPC BR5 ...186 D3
Covey Cl WIM/MER SW19 ...178 A5
Covington Gdns
STRHM/NOR SW16 ...180 C3
Covington Wy
STRHM/NOR SW16 ...180 C3
Cowbridge La BARK IG11 ...90 B5
Cowbridge Rd
KTN/HRWW/W HA3 ...62 B1
Cowcross St FARR EC1M ...12 A1
Cowdenbeath Pth IS N1 ...84 E6
Cowden Rd ORP BR6 ...202 A4
Cowden St CAT SE6 ...164 D6
Cowdray Rd HGDN/ICK UB10 ...76 A6
Cowdray Wy HCH RM12...93 J2
Cowdrey Cl EN EN1 ...24 A3
Cowdrey Ct DART DA1 ...170 E2
Cowdrey Rd WIM/MER SW19 ...178 A1
Cowen Av RYLN/HDSTN HA2 ...60 D6
Cowgate Rd GFD/PVL UB6 ...96 D2
Cowick Rd TOOT SW17 ...160 E6
Cowings Md NTHLT UB5 ...77 J5
Cowland Av PEND EN3 ...24 E5
Cow La BUSH WD23 * ...28 A1
Cow Leaze EHAM E6 ...108 A5
Cowleaze Rd KUTN/CMB KT2 ...175 F4
Cowley Cl SAND/SEL CR2 ...212 E6
Cowley La WAN E11 ...88 C1
Cowley Pl HDN NW4 ...64 A2
Cowley Rd ACT W3 ...118 C1
BRXN/ST SW9 ...142 B2
IL IG1 ...54 E5
MORT/ESHN SW14 ...138 B4
WAN E11 ...71 F2
Cowley St WEST SW1P ...16 E4
Cowling Cl NTGHL W11 ...100 C6
Cowper Av EHAM E6 ...89 J5
SUT SM1 ...209 H2
Cowper Cl HAYES BR2 ...200 C1
WELL DA16 ...148 B6
Cowper Gdns STHGT/OAK N14 ...34 C1
WLGTN SM6 ...210 C4
Cowper Rd ACT W3 ...118 A1
BELV DA17 ...129 G4
HAYES BR2 ...200 D1
HNWL W7 ...96 E6

RAIN RM13 ...111 J3
RCHPK/HAM TW10 ...175 G1
STHGT/OAK N14 ...34 B3
STNW/STAM N16...86 A2
UED N18 ...50 C1
WIM/MER SW19 ...178 B2
Cowper St STLK EC1Y ...7 F6
Cowper Ter NKENS W10 * ...100 B4
Cowslip Rd SWFD E18...53 F6
Cowthorne Rd VX/NE SW8 ...141 J2
Coxe Pl KTN/HRWW/W HA3...43 J1
Cox La CHSGTN KT9 ...206 B2
Coxmount Rd CHARL SE7 ...126 C5
Coxson Wy STHWK SE1 ...19 J3
Crabbs Croft Cl ORP BR6 * ...216 C3
Crab Hl BECK BR3 ...183 G3
Crabtree Av ALP/SUD HA0 ...98 A1
CHDH RM6 ...73 K1
Crabtree Cl BETH E2 ...7 J3
Crabtree La FUL/PGN SW6 ...139 G1
Crabtree Manorway North
BELV DA17 ...129 K2
Crabtree Manorway South
BELV DA17 ...129 K3
Craddock Rd EN EN1 ...24 B4
Craddock St CAMTN NW1 ...84 A4
Cradley Rd ELTH/MOT SE9 ...167 J3
Cragie La MUSWH N10 * ...66 B1
Craigdale Rd ROM RM1 ...75 H3
Craigen Av CROY/NA CRO ...197 J5
Craigerne Rd BKHTH/KID SE3 ...146 A1
Craig Gdns SWFD E18 ...52 D5
Craigholm WOOL/PLUM SE18 ...147 F3
Craigmuir Pk ALP/SUD HA0 ...80 B6
Craigmair Rd
BRXS/STRHM SW2 ...162 A2
Craignish Av
STRHM/NOR SW16 ...180 A5
Craig Park Rd UED N18 ...36 D6
Craig Rd RCHPK/HAM TW10 ...156 D6
Craig's Ct WHALL SW1A...10 E7
Craigton Rd ELTH/MOT SE9 ...146 E5
Craigweil Cl STAN HA7 ...43 K1
Craigweil Dr STAN HA7 ...43 K1
Craigwell Av FELT TW13 ...153 K5
Crail Rw WALW SE17 ...19 F7
Cramer St MHST W1U...9 H2
Crammond Cl HMSMTH W6 ...119 H6
Crampton Rd PGE/AN SE20 ...181 K2
Crampton St WALW SE17 ...122 C4
Cranberry Cl NTHLT UB5 ...95 H1
Cranberry La CAN/RD E16 ...106 C3
Cranbourne Av NWDGN UB2...115 F4
SURB KT6 ...206 C1
Cranbourne Cl
STRHM/NOR SW16 ...179 K6
Cranbourne Dr PIN HA5 ...59 H3
Cranbourne Gdns
BARK/HLT IG6 ...54 C6
GLDGN NW11 ...64 D2
Cranbourne Rd MNPK E12 ...89 J3
MUSWH N10 ...48 B5
NTHWD HA6 ...40 D6
SRTFD E15 ...88 A2
Cranbourn St LSQ/SEVD WC2H...10 D5
Cranbrook Cl HAYES BR2 ...199 K3
Cranbrook Dr ESH/CLAY KT10 ...189 K4
GPK RM2...75 K1
WHTN TW2 ...155 G3
Cranbrook La FBAR/BDGN N11 ...34 B6
Cranbrook Ms WALTH E17 ...69 H2
Cranbrook Pk WDGN N22 ...49 G4
Cranbrook Ri IL IG1 ...71 K3
Cranbrook Rd BXLYHN DA7 ...149 G2
CHSWK W4 ...118 B5
DEPT SE8 ...144 D3
EBAR EN4 ...33 H1
HSLWW TW4 ...134 E5
IL IG1 ...72 A4
THHTH CR7 ...180 D5
WIM/MER SW19 ...177 H3
Cranbrook St BETH E2 ...105 F1
Cranbury Rd FUL/PGN SW6 ...140 A3
Crane Av ACT W3 ...98 E6
ISLW TW7 ...136 B6
Cranebank Ms TWK TW1 * ...156 B4
Cranebrook WHTN TW2 ...155 H4
Crane Cl DAGE RM10...92 C4
Crane Ct FLST/FETLN EC4A...11 K4
MORT/ESHN SW14 * ...137 K5
Craneford Cl WHTN TW2 ...156 A2
Crane Gdns HYS/HAR UB3 ...113 J4
Crane Gv HOLWY N7 ...85 G4
Crane Lodge Rd HEST TW5 ...114 A6
Crane Md BERM/RHTH SE16 ...124 A5
Crane Park Rd WHTN TW2 ...155 G4
Crane Rd STWL/WRAY TW19 ...152 D1
WHTN TW2 ...155 K3
Cranesbill Cl CDALE/KGS NW9 ...45 G5
Cranes Dr BRYLDS KT5 ...191 F1
Cranes Pk SURB KT6 ...191 F1
Cranes Park Av SURB KT6 ...191 F1
Cranes Park Crs BRYLDS KT5 ...191 G1
Crane St PECK SE15 ...143 G2
Craneswater HYS/HAR UB3 ...133 J1
Craneswater Pk NWDGN UB2...114 E5
Crane Wy WHTN TW2 ...155 H2
Cranfield Dr CDALE/KGS NW9 ...45 G2
Cranfield Rd BROCKY SE4 ...144 C4
Cranfield Rd East CAR SM5 ...210 A6
Cranfield Rd West CAR SM5 * ...209 K6
Cranford Av PLMGR N13 ...48 E1
STWL/WRAY TW19 ...152 B2
Cranford Cl RYNPK SW20 * ...176 E4
STWL/WRAY TW19 ...152 B2
Cranford Dr HYS/HAR UB3 ...113 J4
Cranford La HEST TW5 ...134 C1
HTHAIR TW6 ...133 J2
HYS/HAR UB3 ...113 G6

Cranford Park Rd
 HYS/HAR UB5 ....113 J4
Cranford Rd ESH/CLAY KT10 ....204 C3
Cranford St WAP E1W 171 H3
Cranford Wy CEND/HSY/T N8 .....67 F2
Cranham Rd EMPK RM11 ....75 K5
Cranhurst Rd CRICK NW2 ....82 A5
Cranleigh CI BXLY DA5 ....169 J1
 ORP BR6 ....217 G1
 PGE/AN SE20 ....181 J5
Cranleigh Gdns BARK IG11 ....90 D5
 KTN/HRWW/W HA3 ....62 A2
 KUTN/CMB KT2 ....175 G3
 LOU IG10 ....39 K1
 SNWD SE25 ....181 F6
 STHL UB1 ....95 K5
 SUT SM1 ....194 A6
 WCHMH N21 ....23 G6
Cranleigh Ms BTSEA SW11 ......140 D3
Cranleigh Rd ESH/CLAY KT10 ...189 H5
 FELT TW13 ....153 J6
 SEVS/STOTM N15 ....67 J2
 WIM/MER SW19 ....177 K6
Cranleigh St CAMTN NW1 ....4 B5
Cranley Dr GNTH/NBYPK IG2 .....72 C4
 RSLP HA4 ....58 D6
Cranley Gdns MUSWH N10 ....66 B1
 PLMGR N13 ....35 F5
 SKENS SW7 ....120 B5
 WLGTN SM6 ....210 C5
Cranley Ms SKENS SW7 ....120 B5
Cranley PI SKENS SW7 ....14 A7
Cranley Rd GNTH/NBYPK IG2 .....72 C3
 PLSTW E13 ....107 F4
Cranley Ter HDN NW4 * 46 B5
Cranmer Av WEA W13 ....116 C3
Cranmer CI MRDN SM4 ....193 G3
 RSLP HA4 ....59 H4
 STAN HA7 ....43 J3
Cranmer Ct HPTN TW12 ....173 G1
Cranmer Farm CI MTCM CR4 .....194 E1
Cranmer Gdns DAGE RM10 ....92 E2
Cranmer Rd BRXN/ST SW9 ....142 B1
 CROY/NA CR0 ....211 H1
 EDGW HA8 ....30 D5
 FSTGT E7 ....89 F2
 HPTN TW12 ....173 G1
 HYS/HAR UB3 ....94 B5
 KUTN/CMB KT2 ....175 F1
 MTCM CR4 ....194 D1
Cranmer Ter TOOT SW17 ....178 C1
Cranmore Av ISLW TW7 ....135 H1
Cranmore Rd BMLY BR1 ....165 H5
 CHST BR7 ....184 E1
Cranmore Wy MUSWH N10 ....66 C1
Cranston CI HGDN/ICK UB10 ......58 B6
 HSLW TW3 ....134 D3
Cranston Est IS N1 ....7 F2
Cranston Gdns CHING E4 ....51 K2
Cranston Rd FSTH SE23 ....164 B3
Cranswick Rd
 BERM/RHTH SE16 ....123 J5
Crantock Rd CAT SE6 ....165 F4
Cranwell CI BOW E3 ....105 K3
Cranwich Av WCHMH N21 ....35 K1
Cranwich Rd STNW/STAM N16 ....68 A4
Cranwood St FSBYE EC1V 7 F5
Cranworth Crs CHING E4 ....38 B3
Cranworth Gdns
 BRXN/ST SW9 ....142 B2
Craster Rd BRXS/STRHM SW2 ...142 A2
Crathie Rd LEE/GVPK SE12 ......166 A1
Cravan Av FELT TW13 ....153 K4
Craven Av WEA W13 ....116 B1
Craven CI STNW/STAM N16 * 68 C4
 YEAD UB4 ....95 H3
Craven Gdns BARK IG11 ....108 E1
 BARK/HLT IG6 ....54 D5
 CRW RM5 ....56 C1
 WIM/MER SW19 ....178 A1
Craven Hill Gdns BAY/PAD W2 ...101 G6
Craven Ms BTSEA SW11 ....141 F4
Craven Pk WLSDN NW10 ....81 G6
Craven Park Ms WLSDN NW10 .....81 G5
Craven Park Rd
 STNW/STAM N16 ....68 B3
 WLSDN NW10 ....81 G6
Craven Pas CHCR WC2N 10 E7
Craven Rd BAY/PAD W2 ....101 G6
 CROY/NA CR0 ....197 J5
 KUTN/CMB KT2 ....175 G4
 WEA W13 ....97 J6
Craven St CHCR WC2N 10 E7
Craven Ter BAY/PAD W2 ....101 G6
Craven Wk STNW/STAM N16 ......68 C4
Crawford Av ALP/SUD HA0 ....79 K3
Crawford CI ISLW TW7 ....135 K3
Crawford Est CMBW SE5 ....142 D3
Crawford Gdns NTHLT UB5 ....95 K2
 PLMGR N13 ....35 H5
Crawford Pas CLKNW EC1R 5 J7
Crawford PI BAY/PAD W2 ....8 C3
Crawford Rd CMBW SE5 ....142 D3
Crawford St MBLAR W1H 8 E2
 WLSDN NW10 ....81 F5
Crawley Rd ED N9 ....36 B2
 LEY E10 ....69 K5
 WDGN N22 ....49 J5
Crawthew Gv EDUL SE22 ....143 G5
Cray Av STMC/STPC BR5 ....202 C2
Craybrooke Rd SCUP DA14 ......168 C6
Craybury End ELTH/MOT SE9 ....167 H4
Cray CI DART DA1 ....150 D6
Craydene Rd ERITH DA8 ....150 C2
Crayfield Rd KTTN NW5 ....4 A3
Crayford High St DART DA1 .....150 B6
Crayford Rd DART DA1 ....150 C6
 HOLWY N7 ....84 D2
Crayford Wy DART DA1 ....150 D5
Crayle Hi CHSGTN KT9 ....206 A5
Craylands STMC/STPC BR5 ......186 D6
Crayleigh Ter SCUP DA14 * 186 D2
Cray Rd BELV DA17 ....129 H6
 SCUP DA14 ....186 D2
 SWLY BR8 ....203 K3

Crays Pde STMC/STPC BR5 * 186 D5
Cray Valley Rd
 STMC/STPC BR5 ....202 B2
Crealock Gv WFD IG8 ....52 D1
Crealock St WAND/EARL SW18 ...160 A1
Creasey CI EMPK RM11 ....75 K5
Creasy St STEDUL SE22 ....15 G6
Credenhill St
 STRHM/NOR SW16 ....179 H2
Crediton HI KIL/WHAMP NW6 ......83 F3
Crediton Rd WLSDN NW10 ....82 B6
Crediton Wy ESH/CLAY KT10 ....205 G3
Credon Rd BERM/RHTH SE16 .....123 J5
 PLSTW E13 ....107 G1
Creechurch La HDTCH EC3A 13 H4
Creechurch PI HDTCH EC3A * 13 H4
Creed La BLKFR EC4V 12 B4
Creek Rd BARK IG11 ....109 F2
 DEPT SE8 ....124 D6
 E/WMO/HCT KT8 ....189 K1
Creekside DEPT SE8 ....124 E6
 RAIN RM13 ....111 H3
Creek Wy RAIN RM13 ....111 G4
Creeland Gv CAT SE6 ....164 C3
Cree Wy ROM RM1 ....57 G5
Crefeld CI FUL/PGN SW6 ....119 G6
Creffield Rd EA W5 ....98 C6
Creighton Av EFNCH N2 ....47 K5
 EHAM E6 ....107 H1
Creighton CI SHB W12 ....99 K6
Creighton Rd EA W5 ....116 E3
 KIL/WHAMP NW6 ....100 D1
 TOTM N17 ....50 A3
Creigton Av EFNCH N2 ....47 J6
Cremer St BETH E2 ....7 J3
Cremorne Est WBPTN SW10 * ...120 C6
Cremorne Gdns
 HOR/WEW KT19 ....207 F6
Cremorne Rd WBPTN SW10 ....140 B1
Crescent EW CG W13 * 116 A1
Crescent Av GNWCH SE10 ....125 F6
Crescent Av RAIN RM13 ....75 H6
Crescent Dr STMC/STPC BR5 ....201 H5
Crescent East EBAR EN4 ....21 G1
Crescent Gdns RSLP HA4 ....59 F4
 SWLY BR8 ....187 K5
 WIM/MER SW19 ....159 K5
Crescent Gv CLAP SW4 ....141 H5
Crescent La CLAP SW4 ....141 J6
Crescent PI CHEL SW3 ....14 C6
Crescent Ri EBAR EN4 ....21 J6
 FNCH N3 ....46 D4
 WDGN N22 ....48 D4
Crescent Rd BECK BR3 ....182 E5
 BFN/LL DA15 ....167 J3
 BMLY BR1 ....183 K3
 CEND/HSY/T N8 ....66 D3
 CHING E4 ....38 C2
 DAGE RM10 ....92 D2
 EBAR EN4 ....21 H5
 ED N9 ....36 C3
 ENC/FH EN2 ....23 H5
 ERITH DA8 ....130 C6
 FBAR/BDGN N11 ....33 K6
 FNCH N3 ....46 D4
 FSTGT E7 ....89 G5
 HNWL W7 ....96 C1
 HYS/HAR UB3 ....94 B5
 KUT/HW KT1 ....175 F4
 MUSWH N10 ....48 B3
 SKENS SW7 ....14 A6
 TEDD TW11 ....174 B2
 WALTH E17 ....51 J3
 WIM/MER SW19 ....177 K1
 WPK KT4 ....207 F1
Cresford Rd FUL/PGN SW6 ......140 A2
Crespigny Rd HDN NW4 ....63 K3
Cressage CI STHL UB1 ....96 A3
Cresset Rd HOM E9 ....86 E4
Cresset St CLAP SW4 ....141 J4
Cressfield CI KTTN NW5 ....84 A3
Cressida Rd ARCH N19 ....66 C5
Cressingham Gv SUT SM1 ....209 G2
Cressingham Rd EDGW HA8 ....45 F3
 LEW SE13 ....145 F4
Cressington CI
 STNW/STAM N16 ....86 A3
Cresswell Pk BKHTH/KID SE3 ...145 J4
Cresswell PI WBPTN SW10 ......120 B5
Cresswell Rd FELT TW13 ....154 D5
 SNWD SE25 ....197 H1
 TWK TW1 ....156 E1
Cresswell Wy WCHMH N21 ....35 G2

Cressy Ct HMSMTH W6 ....118 E3
Cressy Houses WCHPL E1 * 104 E4
Cressy PI WCHPL E1 ....104 E4
Cressy Rd HAMP NW3 ....83 K2
Cressys Cnr HSLW TW3 * 135 G4
Crestbrook Av PLMGR N13 ....35 H5
Crestbrook PI PLMGR N13 * 35 G5
Crestbrook PI PEND N15 ....24 E1
Crestfield St CAMTN NW1 ....5 F4
Crest Gdns RSLP HA4 ....77 G1
Creston Wy WPK KT4 ....193 G5
Crest Rd CRICK NW2 ....63 J6
 HAYES BR2 ....199 J4
 SAND/SEL CR2 ....212 D5
The Crest BRYLDS KT5 ....191 H2
 HDN NW4 ....64 A2
 HOLWY N7 * 84 D3
 PLMGR N13 ....35 G6
Crest Vw PIN HA5 ....59 H1
Crest Vw Dr STMC/STPC BR5 ...201 G2
Crestway PUT/ROE SW15 ....158 D1
Crestwood Wy HSLWW TW4 .....134 E6
Creswell Dr BECK BR3 ....198 E2
Creswick Rd ACT W3 ....98 D6
Creswick Wk GLDGN NW11 ....64 D1
Crewdson Rd BRXN/ST SW9 .....142 A1
Crewe PI WLSDN NW10 ....99 H2
Crews St POP/IOD E14 ....124 D4
Crewys Rd CRICK NW2 ....64 C6
 PECK SE15 ....143 J3
Crichton Av WLGTN SM6 ....210 D3
Crichton Rd CAR SM5 ....209 K5
Crichton St VX/NE SW8 ....141 H3
Cricketers Arms Rd
 ENC/FH EN2 * 23 J3
Cricketers CI CHSGTN KT9 .....205 K3
 ERITH DA8 ....130 B5
 WAND/EARL SW18 ....140 A6
Cricketers Ms BAL SW12 ....161 G2
 WAND/EARL SW18 ....140 A6
Cricketers Wk SYD SE26 ....181 K1
Cricketfield Rd CLPT E5 ....86 D2
Cricket Gn MTCM CR4 ....178 E6
Cricket Ground Rd CHST BR7 ...185 G4
Cricket La BECK BR3 ....182 B2
Cricket Rw EFNCH N2 * 47 H6
Cricklade Av
 BRXS/STRHM SW2 ....161 K4
Cricklewood Broadway
 CRICK NW2 ....82 A1
Cricklewood La CRICK NW2 ....82 C2
Cridland St SRTFD E15 ....88 D6
Crieff Rd WAND/EARL SW18 ....160 B1
Criffel Av BRXS/STRHM SW2 ...161 J4
Crimscott St STHWK SE1 ....19 H5
Crimsworth Rd VX/NE SW8 .....141 J1
Crinan St IS N1 ....5 F2
Cringle St VX/NE SW8 ....141 H1
Cripplegate St BARB EC2Y * 12 C1
Crispen Rd FELT TW13 ....154 D5
Crispian CI WLSDN NW10 ....81 G2
Crispin Crs CROY/NA CR0 ....210 D1
Crispin Rd EDGW HA8 ....44 E2
Crispin St WCHPL E1 ....13 J2
Crisp Rd HMSMTH W6 ....119 F5
Cristowe Rd FUL/PGN SW6 * ...139 J3
Criterion Ms ARCH N19 ....66 D6
Crockenhill HI
 STMC/STPC BR5 ....202 E5
Crockerton Rd TOOT SW17 .....160 E4
Crockham Wy ELTH/MOT SE9 ...167 F6
Crocus CI CROY/NA CR0 ....198 A5
Crocus Fld BAR EN5 ....32 D1
Croft Av WWKM BR4 ....199 F5
Croft CI BFN/LL DA15 ....167 K6
 CHST BR7 ....184 C1
 HYS/HAR UB3 ....133 F1
 MLHL NW7 ....31 G6
Croft Ct RSLP HA4 * 58 D5
 SUT SM1 * 194 C6
Croftdown Rd KTTN NW5 ....84 A1
Crofters CI ISLW TW7 ....135 J6
Crofters Ct DEPT SE8 ....124 B4
Crofters Rd NTHWD HA6 ....26 C6
Crofters Wy CAMTN NW1 ....5 F1
Croft Gdns DAGE RM10 ....92 C2
 HNWL W7 ....116 B2
Crofton Av BXLY DA5 ....168 E2
 CHSWK W4 ....137 K1
Crofton Gate Wy BROCKY SE4 ..144 B6
Crofton Gv CHING E4 ....38 B6
Crofton La STMC/STPC BR5 .....201 J5
Crofton Park Rd BROCKY SE4 ...144 C6
Crofton Rd CMBW SE5 ....143 F2
 EHAM E6 ....107 K2
 ORP BR6 ....216 A2
 PLSTW E13 ....107 F4
Crofton Ter RCH/KEW TW9 .....137 G5
Crofton Wy BAR EN5 * 23 J6
 ENC/FH EN2 ....23 H3
Croft Rd BMLY BR1 ....183 K2
 PEND EN3 ....25 G2
 STRHM/NOR SW16 ....180 B3
 SUT SM1 ....209 J3
 WIM/MER SW19 ....178 B3
Crofts La WCHMH N21 ....35 H1
Crofts Rd HRW HA1 ....61 G3
Crofts St WCHPL E1 ....104 C6
Croft St DEPT SE8 ....124 B4
The Croft ALP/SUD HA0 ....79 J5
 BAR EN5 ....20 C6
 CHING E4 ....38 C4
 EA W5 ....98 A4
 HEST TW5 ....135 G1
 PIN HA5 ....59 K4
 RSLP HA4 ....77 G2
 SWLY BR8 ....187 K6
 WLSDN NW10 ....81 H5
Croft Wy BFN/LL DA15 ....167 K5
 RCHPK/HAM TW10 ....156 C5
Crogsland Rd CAMTN NW1 ....84 A5

Croham CI SAND/SEL CR2 ....212 A4
Croham Manor Rd
 SAND/SEL CR2 ....212 A5
Croham Mt SAND/SEL CR2 ......212 A5
Croham Park Av
 SAND/SEL CR2 ....212 B3
Croham Rd SAND/SEL CR2 ......211 K3
Croham Valley Rd
 SAND/SEL CR2 ....212 C4
Croindene Rd
 STRHM/NOR SW16 ....179 K4
Cromartie Rd ARCH N19 ....66 D4
Cromartie Rd EDGW HA8 * 30 D4
Cromarty Vls BAY/PAD W2 * 101 G6
Crombie CI REDBR IG4 ....71 K2
Crombie Ms BTSEA SW11 * 140 D3
Crombie Rd BFN/LL DA15 ....167 J3
Cromer CI UX/CGN UB8 ....94 A5
Cromer Hyde MRDN SM4 * 194 A2
Cromer Rd BAR EN5 ....21 G5
 CHDH RM6 ....74 A2
 HTHAIR TW6 ....132 D4
 LEY E10 ....70 B4
 SNWD SE25 ....181 J6
 TOOT SW17 ....179 F2
 WDGN N22 ....49 G2
 WFD IG8 ....53 K2
 WIM/MER SW19 ....177 K3
Cross St BARN SW13 ....138 B3
 ERITH DA8 ....130 B6
 HPTN TW12 ....173 H1
 IS N1 ....85 H6
 UED N18 ....50 C1
Crossthwaite Av HNHL SE24 ....142 E5
Crosswall TWRH EC3N 13 J5
Cross Wy HYS/HAR UB3 ....113 G5
Crossway BCTR RM8 ....91 J1
 CDALE/KGS NW9 ....63 H1
 EN EN1 ....36 A2
 NFNCH/WDSP N12 ....47 H2
 NWMAL KT3 ....193 F1
 PIN HA5 ....40 E6
 RSLP HA4 ....77 G2
 STMC/STPC BR5 ....201 J1
 STNW/STAM N16 ....86 A3
 THMD SE28 ....109 J6
 WEA W13 ....97 F3
 WOT/HER KT12 ....188 A6
Crossway Pde WDGN N22 * 49 H3
Crossways BELMT SM2 ....209 H6
 GPK RM2 ....57 K6
 SAND/SEL CR2 ....213 H5
Crossways Rd BECK BR3 ....198 D1
 MTCM CR4 ....179 G6
Crossways Ter CLPT E5 * 86 E2
The Crossways BRYLDS KT5 * ...191 J5
 HEST TW5 ....134 E1
 WBLY HA9 ....62 C3
The Crossway ELTH/MOT SE9 ...166 C4
The Cross Wy
 KTN/HRWW/W HA3 ....42 E5
Crossways Rd WDGN N22 ....49 H3
Croston St HACK E8 ....86 C6
Crosts La WDGN N22 ....49 G3
Crothall CI PLMGR N13 ....35 F5
Crouch Av BARK IG11 ....109 H1
Crouch CI BECK BR3 ....182 D2
Crouch Cft ELTH/MOT SE9 .....167 F5
Crouch End HI ARCH N19 ....66 D4
Crouch Hall Rd CEND/HSY/T N8 ..66 D3
Crouch HI ARCH N19 ....66 E4
Crouchmans CI SYD SE26 ......163 G5
Crouch Rd WLSDN NW10 ....81 F5
Crowborough Pth
 OXHEY WD19 ....27 H6
Crowborough Rd TOOT SW17 ...179 F1
Crowden Wy THMD SE28 ....109 J6
Crowder St WCHPL E1 ....104 D6
Crowfoot CI HOM E9 ....87 H5
Crowfoot La THMD SE28 ....127 K1
Crowhurst CI BRXN/ST SW9 ....142 B3
Crowhurst Pth
 STMC/STPC BR5 ....202 D2
Crowland Av HYS/HAR UB3 .....113 H4
Crowland Gdns
 STHGT/OAK N14 ....34 E2
Crowland Rd SEVS/STOTM N15 ...68 B2
 THHTH CR7 ....196 E1
Crowlands Av ROMW/RG RM7 ....74 D3
Crowlands Ter ROMW/RG RM7 ....74 D3
Crowland Wk MRDN SM4 ....194 A3
Crow La ROMW/RG RM7 ....74 B4
Crowley Crs CROY/NA CR0 .....211 G3
Crowline Wk IS N1 * 85 J4
Crown Ar KUT/HW KT1 * 174 E6
Crownbourne Ct SUT SM1 * 209 F2
Crown Bldgs CHING E4 * 38 B3
Crown CI BOW E3 ....87 J6
 HYS/HAR UB3 ....113 J2
 KIL/WHAMP NW6 ....83 F4
 MLHL NW7 ....31 H4
 ORP BR6 ....217 G2
 WOT/HER KT12 ....188 B4
Crown Court Rd
 GNTH/NBYPK IG2 ....72 E2
Crownfield Av
 GNTH/NBYPK IG2 ....72 E2
Crownfield Rd SRTFD E15 ....88 B3
Crown Hi CROY/NA CR0 ....196 D6
Crownhill Rd WFD IG8 ....53 H3
 WLSDN NW10 ....81 H6
Crown La CHST BR7 ....185 H4
 HAYES BR2 ....200 C2
 STHGT/OAK N14 ....34 C3
 STRHM/NOR SW16 ....180 B1
 MRDN SM4 ....194 A1
Crown Lane Gdns
 WNWD SE27 * 180 B1
Crown Lane Sp WNWD SE27 ....180 B1
Crown Office Rw EMB EC4Y 11 J5
Crown Pde MRDN SM4 * 194 A1
 STHGT/OAK N14 * 34 C3
Crown Pas STJS SW1Y 16 B1
 KUT/HW KT1 * 174 E6
 SDTCH EC2A 7 G7
Crown Rd BARK/HLT IG6 ....72 D1
 EN EN1 ....24 D5
 MUSWH N10 ....48 A3
 NWMAL KT3 ....175 K4

ORP BR6 217 G3
RSLP HA4 77 H3
SUT SM1 208 E2
TWK TW1 156 C1
WIM/MER SW19 193 K1
Crownstone Rd
BRXS/STRHM SW2 142 B6
Crown St ACT W3 117 J1
CMBW SE5 142 D1
DAGE RM10 92 E4
RYLN/HDSTN HA2 60 D5
Crown Ter CRICK NW2 * 82 B2
RCH/KEW TW9 137 G5
STHGT/OAK N14 * 34 D3
Crowntree Cl ISLW TW7 116 A6
Crown Vls ACT W3 * 117 K2
Crown Wk WBLY HA9 80 B1
Crown Wy WDR/YW UB7 112 C1
Crown Woods Wy
ELTH/MOT SE9 147 J6
Crown Yd HSLW TW3 135 H4
Crowshott Av STAN HA7 43 J5
Crows Rd BARK IG11 90 B4
SRTFD E15 106 B2
Crowther Av BTFD TW8 117 F5
Crowther Rd SNWD SE25 197 H1
Crowthorne Cl
WAND/EARL SW18 159 J2
Crowthorne Rd NKENS W10 100 B5
Croxden Cl EDGW HA8 44 C6
Croxden Wk MRDN SM4 194 B3
Croxford Gdns WDGN N22 49 H3
Croxford Wy ROMW/RG RM7 75 F5
Croxley Cl STMC/STPC BR5 186 C5
Croxley Gn STMC/STPC BR5 186 C4
Croxley Rd MV/WKIL W9 100 D2
Croxley Vw WATW WD18 26 C1
Croxted Cl DUL SE21 162 D2
Croxted Rd DUL SE21 162 E4
Croyde Av GFD/PVL UB6 96 C2
HYS/HAR UB3 113 H4
Croyde Cl ELTH/MOT SE9 167 J2
The Croydon F/O
CROY/NA CR0 211 H2
Croydon Gv CROY/NA CR0 196 C5
Croydon Rd BECK BR3 182 B6
CROY/NA CR0 198 A2
MTCM CR4 195 G2
PGE/AN SE20 181 J5
PLSTW E13 106 D3
WLGTN SM6 210 B2
WWKM BR4 214 C1
Croyland Rd ED N9 36 C3
Croylands Dr SURB KT6 191 F4
Crozier Ter HOM E9 87 F3
Crucible Cl CHDH RM6 73 H3
Crucifix La STHWK SE1 19 G2
Cruden St IS N1 6 B1
Cruickshank St FSBYW WC1X 5 J4
Cruikshank Rd SRTFD E15 88 C2
Crummock Gdns
CDALE/KGS NW9 63 G2
Crumpsall St ABYW SE2 128 D4
Crundale Av CDALE/KGS NW9 62 C2
Crunden Rd SAND/SEL CR2 211 K5
Crusader Cl PUR RM19 131 K4
Crusader Gdns CROY/NA CR0 212 A1
Crusader Wy WATW WD18 26 D1
Crusoe Ms STNW/STAM N16 67 K6
Crusoe Rd ERITH DA8 130 A5
MTCM CR4 178 E3
Crutched Friars MON EC3R 13 H5
Crutchfield La WOT/HER KT12 188 A6
Crutchley Rd CAT SE6 165 J4
Crystal Palace NRWD SE19 * 181 H3
Crystal Palace Pde
NRWD SE19 181 G2
Crystal Palace Park Rd
SYD SE26 181 H1
Crystal Palace Rd EDUL SE22 163 G1
Crystal Ter NRWD SE19 180 E2
Crystal Wy BCTR RM8 73 J5
HRW HA1 61 F2
Cuba Dr PEND EN3 24 E3
Cuba St POP/IOD E14 124 D2
Cubitt Sq NWDGN UB2 * 115 H1
Cubitt St CROY/NA CR0 211 F3
FSBYW WC1X 5 H5
Cubitt Ter CLAP SW4 141 H4
Cuckoo Av HNWL W7 96 E3
Cuckoo Dene HNWL W7 96 D4
Cuckoo Hall La ED N9 36 E2
Cuckoo Hl PIN HA5 41 G6
Cuckoo Hill Dr PIN HA5 41 G6
Cuckoo Hill Rd PIN HA5 59 H1
Cuckoo La HNWL W7 96 E6
Cuda's Cl HOR/WEW KT19 207 H2
Cuddington Av WPK KT4 207 H1
Cudham St CAT SE6 164 E2
Cudworth St WCHPL E1 104 D3
Cuff Crs ELTH/MOT SE9 166 D1
Culford Gdns CHEL SW3 15 F7
Culford Gv IS N1 86 A4
Culford Ms IS N1 85 K4
Culford Rd IS N1 86 A6
Culgaith Gdns ENC/FH EN2 22 E5
Cullera Cl NTHWD HA6 40 D2
Culling Rd BERM/RHTH SE16 123 K3
Cullington Cl
KTN/HRWW/W HA3 61 G1
Cullingworth Rd WLSDN NW10 81 K3
Culloden Cl STHWK SE1 123 H5
Culloden Rd ENC/FH EN2 23 H3
Culloden St POP/IOD E14 106 A5
Cullum St FENCHST EC3M 13 G5
Culmington Pde WEA W13 * 97 J6
Culmington Rd SAND/SEL CR2 211 J5
WEA W13 116 D1
Culmore Rd PECK SE15 143 J1
Culmstock Rd BTSEA SW11 141 F6
Culpepper Cl CHIG IG7 54 B2
UED N18 50 D1
Culross Cl SEVS/STOTM N15 67 J1
Culross St MYFR/PKLN W1K 9 G6
Culsac Rd SURB KT6 191 F6
Culverden Rd BAL SW12 161 H5
OXHEY WD19 27 F5
Culver Gv STAN HA7 43 J5
Culverhouse Gdns
STRHM/NOR SW16 162 A6
Culverlands Cl STAN HA7 29 H6
Culverley Rd CAT SE6 164 E3
Culvers Av CAR SM5 194 E6
Culvers Retreat CAR SM5 194 E5
Culverstone Cl HAYES BR2 199 J3
Culvers Wy CAR SM5 194 E6
Culvert Pl BTSEA SW11 141 F3
Culvert Rd BTSEA SW11 140 E3
SEVS/STOTM N15 68 A2
Culworth St STJWD NW8 2 C3
Cumberland Av WELL DA16 147 K4
WLSDN NW10 98 D2
Cumberland Cl BARK/HLT IG6 * 54 C4
HACK E8 86 B4
RYNPK SW20 177 G3
TWK TW1 156 C1
Cumberland Dr BXLYHN DA7 149 F1
CHSGTN KT9 206 A1
DART DA1 171 J2
ESH/CLAY KT10 190 B6
Cumberland Gdns FSBYW WC1X 5 H4
HDN NW4 * 46 B5
Cumberland Ga BAY/PAD W2 8 E5
CAMTN NW1 3 J4
Cumberland Market
CAMTN NW1 3 K4
Cumberland Pk ACT W3 98 E6
Cumberland Pl CAMTN NW1 3 J4
CAT SE6 165 J3
Cumberland Rd ACT W3 98 E6
ASHF TW15 152 A5
BARN SW13 138 C2
ED N9 36 E3
HAYES BR2 199 H1
HNWL W7 116 A2
HRW HA1 60 B2
KTN/HRWW/W HA3 44 B6
MNPK E12 89 H2
PLSTW E13 107 F4
RCH/KEW TW9 137 H2
SNWD SE25 197 J3
WALTH E17 51 G5
WDGN N22 49 F5
Cumberland St PIM SW1V 121 G5
Cumberland Ter CAMTN NW1 3 J3
PGE/AN SE20 * 181 J3
Cumberland Terrace Ms
CAMTN NW1 3 J3
Cumberlow Av SNWD SE25 181 H6
Cumberton Rd TOTM N17 49 K4
Cumbrae Gdns SURB KT6 190 E6
Cumbrian Av BXLYHN DA7 150 B3
Cumbrian Gdns CRICK NW2 64 B6
Cumming St IS N1 5 H3
Cumnor Cl BRXN/ST SW9 * 142 A3
Cumnor Gdns EW KT17 207 J4
Cumnor Rd BELMT SM2 209 G4
Cunard Crs WCHMH N21 35 K1
Cunard Rd WLSDN NW10 99 F2
Cundy Rd CAN/RD E16 107 G5
Cundy St BGVA SW1W 15 H7
Cunliffe Rd HOR/WEW KT19 207 H2
Cunliffe St STRHM/NOR SW16 179 H2
Cunningham Cl CHDH RM6 73 J2
WWKM BR4 198 E6
Cunningham Ct LEY E10 * 87 K1
Cunningham Pk HRW HA1 60 D2
Cunningham Pl STJWD NW8 2 A6
Cunningham Rd
SEVS/STOTM N15 * 68 C1
Cunnington St CHSWK W4 117 K3
Cupar Rd BTSEA SW11 141 F2
Cupola Cl BMLY BR1 184 A1
Curates Wk DART DA1 171 G5
Cureton St WEST SW1P * 121 J5
Curlew Cl THMD SE28 109 K6
Curlew St STHWK SE1 19 J2
Curlew Wy YEAD UB4 95 H4
Curness St LEW SE13 145 F5
Curnick's La WNWD SE27 162 D6
Curran Av BFN/LL DA15 148 A6
WLGTN SM6 210 A1
Currey Rd GFD/PVL UB6 78 C4
Curricle St ACT W3 118 B1
Currie Hill Cl WIM/MER SW19 159 J6
Curry Ri MLHL NW7 46 B2
Cursitor St FLST/FETLN EC4A 11 J3
Curtain Pl SDTCH EC2A 7 H6
Curtain Rd SDTCH EC2A 7 G7
Curthwaite Gdns ENC/FH EN2 22 D5
Curtis Dr ACT W3 99 F5
Curtis Field Rd
STRHM/NOR SW16 162 A6
Curtis La ALP/SUD HA0 80 A4
Curtismill Cl STMC/STPC BR5 186 C6
Curtismill Wy STMC/STPC BR5 186 C6
Curtis Rd HOR/WEW KT19 206 E2
HSLWW TW4 154 E2
Curtis St STHWK SE1 19 J6
Curtis Wy STHWK SE1 19 J6
The Curve SHB W12 99 J6
Curwen Av FSTGT E7 89 F2
Curwen Rd SHB W12 118 D2
Curzon Av PEND EN3 25 F6
STAN HA7 43 G4
Curzon Cl ORP BR6 216 D2
Curzon Crs BARK IG11 109 F2
WLSDN NW10 81 G5
Curzon Pl MYFR/PKLN W1K 15 H1
PIN HA5 59 G2
Curzon Rd EA W5 97 H3
MUSWH N10 48 B5
THHTH CR7 196 B3
Curzon St MYFR/PICC W1J 9 K7
MYFR/PKLN W1K 15 H1
Cusack Cl TWK TW1 * 156 A6
Custom House Reach
BERM/RHTH SE16 * 124 C3
Cutcombe Rd CMBW SE5 142 D3
Cuthberga Cl BARK IG11 90 C5
Cuthbert Gdns SNWD SE25 181 F6
Cuthbert Rd CROY/NA CR0 196 C6
UED N18 50 C1
WALTH E17 52 A6
Cuthbert St BAY/PAD W2 2 A7
Cutlers Gardens Ar WCHPL E1 13 H3
Cutler St HDTCH EC3A 13 H3
The Cut STHWK SE1 17 K2
Cuxton Cl BXLYHS DA6 149 F6
Cyclamen Cl HPTN TW12 173 F2
Cyclamen Wy HOR/WEW KT19 206 E3
Cygnet Av EBED/NFELT TW14 154 C2
Cygnet Cl NTHWD HA6 40 A3
WLSDN NW10 81 F3
The Cygnets FELT TW13 154 D6
Cygnet St WCHPL E1 7 K6
Cygnet Wy YEAD UB4 95 H5
Cymbeline Ct HRW HA1 * 61 F3
Cynthia St IS N1 5 H3
Cypress Av WHTN TW2 155 H2
Cypress Gdns BROCKY SE4 144 B6
Cypress Gv BARK/HLT IG6 54 E2
Cypress Rd KTN/HRWW/W HA3 42 D5
SNWD SE25 181 F5
Cypress Tree Cl BFN/LL DA15 168 A3
Cyprus Av FNCH N3 46 C5
Cyprus Cl FSBYPK N4 67 G3
Cyprus Gdns FNCH N3 46 C5
Cyprus Pl BETH E2 104 E1
EHAM E6 108 A6
Cyprus Rd ED N9 36 B4
FNCH N3 46 D5
Cyprus St BETH E2 104 E1
Cyrena Rd EDUL SE22 163 G1
Cyril Rd BXLYHN DA7 149 F3
ORP BR6 202 B4
Cyrus St FSBYE EC1V 6 B6
Czar St DEPT SE8 124 D6

D

Dabbling Cl ERITH DA8 * 150 E1
Dabbs Hill La NTHLT UB5 77 K4
D'abernon Cl ESH/CLAY KT10 204 A2
Dabin Crs GNWCH SE10 145 F2
Dacca St DEPT SE8 124 C6
Dace Rd BOW E3 87 J6
Dacre Av CLAY IG5 54 A5
Dacre Cl GFD/PVL UB6 96 B1
Dacre Gdns LEW SE13 * 145 H5
Dacre Pk LEW SE13 145 H4
Dacre Pl LEW SE13 145 H4
Dacre Rd CROY/NA CR0 195 K4
PLSTW E13 89 F6
WAN E11 70 D5
Dacres Est FSTH SE23 * 164 A5
Dacres Rd FSTH SE23 164 A5
Dacre St STJSPK SW1H 16 C4
Dade Wy NWDGN UB2 114 E5
Daerwood Cl HAYES BR2 200 E5
Daffodil Cl CROY/NA CR0 198 A5
HPTN TW12 173 F2
Daffodil Gdns IL IG1 90 B3
Daffodil St SHB W12 99 H6
Dafforne Rd TOOT SW17 160 E5
Dagenham Av DAGW RM9 92 A6
Dagenham Rd DAGE RM10 92 E2
LEY E10 69 H5
RAIN RM13 93 F5
ROMW/RG RM7 75 F4
Dagger La BORE WD6 29 G1
Dagmar Av WBLY HA9 80 B2
Dagmar Gdns WLSDN NW10 100 B1
Dagmar Pas IS N1 85 H6
Dagmar Rd CMBW SE5 143 F2
DAGE RM10 92 E5
FSBYPK N4 67 G4
KUTN/CMB KT2 175 G4
NWDGN UB2 114 D3
SEVS/STOTM N15 67 K1
SNWD SE25 197 F1
WDGN N22 48 D4
Dagmar Ter IS N1 85 H6
Dagnall Pk SNWD SE25 197 F2
Dagnall Rd SNWD SE25 197 F2
Dagnall St BTSEA SW11 140 E3
Dagnan Rd BAL SW12 161 G2
Dagonet Rd BMLY BR1 165 K5
Dahlia Gdns IL IG1 90 B4
MTCM CR4 195 J1
Dahlia Rd ABYW SE2 128 C5
Dahomey Rd
STRHM/NOR SW16 179 H2
Daimler Wy WLGTN SM6 210 E5
Daines Cl MNPK E12 89 K1
Dainford Cl BMLY BR1 183 G1
Daintry Cl KTN/HRWW/W HA3 61 G1
Dairsie Rd ELTH/MOT SE9 147 F4
Dairy Cl BMLY BR1 * 184 A3
THHTH CR7 180 D5
Dairy La WOOL/PLUM SE18 126 E4
Dairyman Cl CRICK NW2 * 82 B2
Daisy Cl CROY/NA CR0 198 A5
Daisy La FUL/PGN SW6 139 K4
Daisy Rd SWFD E18 53 F5
Dakin Pl WCHPL E1 105 G4
Dakota Cl CROY/NA CR0 211 F5
Dakota Gdns EHAM E6 107 J3
Dalberg Rd BRXS/STRHM SW2 142 B6
Dalberg Wy ABYW SE2 128 E3
Dalby Rd WAND/EARL SW18 140 B5
Dalbys Crs TOTM N17 50 A2
Dalby St KTTN NW5 84 B4
Dalcross Rd HEST TW5 134 D3
Dale Av EDGW HA8 44 B4
HSLWW TW4 134 D4
Dalebury Rd TOOT SW17 160 E4
Dale Cl BAR EN5 33 F1
BKHTH/KID SE3 145 K4
DART DA1 170 C1
PIN HA5 41 F4
Dale Dr YEAD UB4 94 D3
Dale Gdns WFD IG8 39 F6
Dale Green Rd FBAR/BDGN N11 34 B5
Dale Gv NFNCH/WDSP N12 47 G1
Daleham Gdns HAMP NW3 83 H3
Daleham Ms HAMP NW3 * 83 H4
Dale Park Av CAR SM5 194 E6
Dale Park Rd NRWD SE19 180 D4
Dale Rd DART DA1 170 C1
GFD/PVL UB6 96 B4
KTTN NW5 84 A3
SUT SM1 208 D2
SWLY BR8 187 K6
WALW SE17 122 C6
Dale Rw NTGHL W11 100 C5
Daleside ORP BR6 217 G3
Daleside Cl ORP BR6 217 G4
Daleside Rd HOR/WEW KT19 207 F4
STRHM/NOR SW16 179 G1
Dale St CHSWK W4 118 B5
The Dale HAYES BR2 215 H2
Dale Vw BAR EN5 * 20 D4
ERITH DA8 150 D3
Dale View Av CHING E4 38 A4
Dale View Crs CHING E4 38 A5
Dale View Gdns CHING E4 38 B5
Daleview Rd SEVS/STOTM N15 68 A3
Dalewood Gdns WPK KT4 192 E6
Dale Wood Rd ORP BR6 201 K4
Daley St HOM E9 87 F4
Daley Thompson Wy
VX/NE SW8 141 G3
Dalgarno Gdns NKENS W10 100 A4
Dalgarno Wy NKENS W10 100 A3
Dalkeith Gv STAN HA7 43 K1
Dalkeith Rd DUL SE21 162 D3
IL IG1 90 C1
Dallas Rd CHEAM SM3 208 C4
EA W5 98 B4
HDN NW4 63 J4
SYD SE26 163 J6
Dallas Ter HYS/HAR UB3 113 J3
Dallega Cl HYS/HAR UB3 94 B6
Dallinger Rd LEE/GVPK SE12 165 J1
Dalling Rd HMSMTH W6 118 E4
Dallington Sq FSBYE EC1V 6 B6
Dallington St FSBYE EC1V 6 B7
Dallin Rd BXLYHS DA6 148 E5
WOOL/PLUM SE18 147 G1
Dalmain Rd FSTH SE23 164 A3
Dalmally Rd CROY/NA CR0 197 G4
Dalmeny Av HOLWY N7 84 D2
STRHM/NOR SW16 180 B5
Dalmeny Cl ALP/SUD HA0 79 J4
Dalmeny Crs HSLW TW3 135 J5
Dalmeny Rd BAR EN5 33 G1
CAR SM5 210 A5
ERITH DA8 149 J2
HOLWY N7 84 D2
WPK KT4 207 K1
Dalmeyer Rd WLSDN NW10 81 H4
Dalmore Av ESH/CLAY KT10 205 F4
Dalmore Rd DUL SE21 162 D4
Dalrymple Cl STHGT/OAK N14 34 D2
Dalrymple Rd BROCKY SE4 144 B5
Dalston Gdns STAN HA7 44 A4
Dalston La HACK E8 86 B4
Dalton Av MTCM CR4 178 D5
Dalton Cl ORP BR6 216 E1
YEAD UB4 94 B3
Daltons Rd SWLY BR8 203 K6
Dalton St WNWD SE27 162 C4
Dalwood St CMBW SE5 143 F2
Dalyell Rd BRXN/ST SW9 142 A4
Damask Crs CAN/RD E16 106 C3
Damer Ter WBPTN SW10 140 B1
Dames Rd FSTGT E7 88 E2
Dame St IS N1 6 C2
Damien St WCHPL E1 104 D4
Damon Cl SCUP DA14 168 C5
Damsel Ct BERM/RHTH SE16 * 123 H2
Damson Dr HYS/HAR UB3 94 E6
Damsonwood Rd NWDGN UB2 115 F3
Danbrook Rd
STRHM/NOR SW16 179 K4
Danbury Cl CHDH RM6 55 K6
Danbury Ms CAR SM5 210 B2
Danbury Rd LOU IG10 39 J1
RAIN RM13 93 H6
Danbury St IS N1 6 B2
Danbury Wy WFD IG8 53 G2
Danby St PECK SE15 143 G4
Dancer Rd FUL/PGN SW6 139 J2
RCH/KEW TW9 137 H4
Dandelion Cl ROMW/RG RM7 75 G6
Dando Crs BKHTH/KID SE3 146 A4
Dandridge Cl GNWCH SE10 125 J5
Danebury CROY/NA CR0 213 K4
Danebury Av PUT/ROE SW15 158 C2
Daneby Rd CAT SE6 165 F5
Dane Cl BXLY DA5 169 H2
ORP BR6 216 D3
Danecourt Gdns
CROY/NA CR0 212 B1
Danecroft Rd HNHL SE24 142 D6
Danehurst Gdns REDBR IG4 71 J2
Danehurst St FUL/PGN SW6 139 H2
Daneland EBAR EN4 21 K6
Danemead Gv NTHLT UB5 78 B3
Danemere St PUT/ROE SW15 139 F4
Dane Pl BOW E3 105 G1
Dane Rd IL IG1 90 C3
STHL UB1 95 J6
UED N18 36 E6
WEA W13 97 J6
WIM/MER SW19 178 B4
Danesbury Rd FELT TW13 154 A3
Danescombe LEE/GVPK SE12 165 K3
Danescourt Crs SUT SM1 194 B6
Danescroft Av HDN NW4 * 64 B2
Danescroft Gdns GLDGN NW11 64 B2
Danesdale Rd HOM E9 87 G4
Danes Ga HRW HA1 42 E6
Danes Rd ROMW/RG RM7 74 E4
Dane St GINN WC1R 11 G2
Daneswood Av CAT SE6 165 F5
Danethorpe Rd ALP/SUD HA0 79 K4
Danetree Cl HOR/WEW KT19 206 E5
Danetree Rd HOR/WEW KT19 206 E5
Danette Gdns DAGE RM10 74 B6
Daneville Rd CMBW SE5 142 E2
Dangan Rd WAN E11 70 E3
Daniel Bolt Cl POP/IOD E14 105 K4
Daniel Cl HSLWW TW4 154 E2
UED N18 36 E6
WIM/MER SW19 178 D2
Daniel Gdns PECK SE15 143 G1
Daniell Wy CROY/NA CR0 195 K5
Daniel Pl HDN NW4 63 K3
Daniel Rd EA W5 98 B6
Daniel's Rd PECK SE15 143 K4
Dan Leno Wk FUL/PGN SW6 * 140 A1
Dan Manson Dr CHSWK W4 138 A3
Dansey Pl SOHO/SHAV W1D 10 C5
Dansington Rd WELL DA16 148 B5
Danson Crs WELL DA16 148 C4
Danson La WELL DA16 148 C5
Danson Md WELL DA16 148 D4
Danson Rd BXLYHS DA6 148 E6
Danson U/P BFN/LL DA15 168 D1
Dante Rd LBTH SE11 18 A6
Danube St CHEL SW3 120 D5
Danvers Rd CEND/HSY/T N8 66 D1
Danvers St CHEL SW3 120 C6
Daphne Gdns CHING E4 38 A5
Daphne St WAND/EARL SW18 160 B1
Daplyn St WCHPL E1 104 C4
D'Arblay St SOHO/CST W1F 10 B4
Darby Crs SUN TW16 172 B5
Darby Gdns SUN TW16 172 B5
Darcy Av WLGTN SM6 210 C2
Darcy Cl TRDG/WHET N20 33 H4
D'Arcy Dr KTN/HRWW/W HA3 61 K1
D'Arcy Gdns DAGW RM9 92 B6
KTN/HRWW/W HA3 62 A1
D'Arcy Pl HAYES BR2 199 K1
D'Arcy Rd CHEAM SM3 208 B2
ISLW TW7 136 B2
STRHM/NOR SW16 179 K5
Darell Rd RCH/KEW TW9 137 H4
Darenth Rd DART DA1 171 K4
STNW/STAM N16 68 B4
WELL DA16 148 B2
Darent Valley Pth DART DA1 151 G2
Darfield Rd BROCKY SE4 144 C6
Darfield Wy NKENS W10 100 B6
Darfur St PUT/ROE SW15 139 G4
Dargate Cl NRWD SE19 181 G3
Darien Rd BTSEA SW11 140 C4
Darlands Dr BAR EN5 20 B6
Darlan Rd FUL/PGN SW6 139 J1
Darlaston Rd WIM/MER SW19 177 G3
Darley Cl CROY/NA CR0 198 A3
Darley Dr NWMAL KT3 176 A5
Darley Gdns MRDN SM4 194 A3
Darley Rd BTSEA SW11 160 E1
ED N9 36 B3
Darling Rd BROCKY SE4 144 D4
Darling Rw WCHPL E1 104 D3
Darlington Rd WNWD SE27 180 C1
Darlton Cl DART DA1 150 C4
Darmaine Cl SAND/SEL CR2 211 J5
Darndale Cl WALTH E17 51 H5
Darnley Rd HACK E8 86 D4
WFD IG8 52 E4
Darnley Ter NTGHL W11 119 G1
Darns Hl SWLY BR8 203 K4
Darrell Rd EDUL SE22 143 H6
Darren Cl FSBYPK N4 67 F4
Darrick Wood Rd ORP BR6 201 J6
Darris Cl NTHLT UB5 95 J3
Darsley Dr VX/NE SW8 141 J2
Dartford Av ED N9 36 E1
Dartford Rd BXLY DA5 169 K3
DART DA1 170 D1
Dartford St WALW SE17 122 D6
Dartmoor Wk POP/IOD E14 * 124 D4
Dartmouth Cl NTGHL W11 100 D5
Dartmouth Gv GNWCH SE10 145 F2
Dartmouth Hl GNWCH SE10 145 F2
Dartmouth Park Av KTTN NW5 84 B1
Dartmouth Park Hl ARCH N19 66 B5
KTTN NW5 84 B1
Dartmouth Park Rd KTTN NW5 84 B1
Dartmouth Pl CHSWK W4 118 B6
FSTH SE23 163 K4
Dartmouth Rd CRICK NW2 82 B4
HAYES BR2 199 K4
HDN NW4 63 J3
RSLP HA4 76 E1
SYD SE26 163 J5
Dartmouth Rw GNWCH SE10 145 F3
Dartmouth St STJSPK SW1H 16 C3
Dartmouth Ter GNWCH SE10 145 G2
Dartnell Rd CROY/NA CR0 197 G4
Dartrey Wk WBPTN SW10 * 140 B1
Dart St MV/WKIL W9 100 D2
Darville Rd STNW/STAM N16 86 B1
Darwell Cl EHAM E6 108 A1
Darwin Cl FBAR/BDGN N11 34 B5
ORP BR6 216 D3
Darwin Dr STHL UB1 96 B5
Darwin Gdns OXHEY WD19 41 G1
Darwin Rd EA W5 116 D5
WDGN N22 49 H4
WELL DA16 148 A4
Darwin St WALW SE17 19 F6
Daryngton Dr GFD/PVL UB6 96 D1
Dashwood Cl BXLYHS DA6 149 H6
Dashwood Rd CEND/HSY/T N8 67 F3
Dassett Rd WNWD SE27 180 C1
Datchelor Pl CMBW SE5 * 142 E2
Datchet Rd CAT SE6 164 C5
Date St WALW SE17 122 D5
Daubeney Gdns TOTM N17 49 J3
Daubeney Rd CLPT E5 87 G3
TOTM N17 49 J3
Dault Rd WAND/EARL SW18 160 B1
Davenant Rd ARCH N19 66 D6

Davenant St WCHPL E1 104 C4
Davenham Av NTHWD HA6 26 D6
Davenport Cl TEDD TW11 * 174 B2
Davenport Rd LEW SE13 164 E1
  SCUP DA14 168 E4
Davenport Dr STAN HA7 43 H4
Daventry Av WALTH E17 69 J3
Daventry St CAMTN NW1 2 C7
Davern Cl GNWCH SE10 125 J4
Davey Rd HOM E9 87 J5
Davey St PECK SE15 123 G6
David Av GFD/PVL UB6 96 E2
David Cl HYS/HAR UB3 133 G1
Davidge St STHWK SE1 18 A3
David Ms MHST W1U 9 F1
David Rd BCTR RM8 74 A6
Davidson Gdns VX/NE SW8 141 K1
Davidson Rd CROY/NA CRO 197 F5
David's Rd FSTH SE23 163 K3
David St SRTFD E15 88 B4
David Wy BARK/HLT IG6 54 E3
David Twigg Cl
  KUTN/CMB KT2 175 F4
Davies Cl SNWD SE25 197 G3
Davies La WAN E11 70 C6
Davies Ms MYFR/PKLN W1K 9 J5
Davies St MYFR/PKLN W1K 9 J5
Davington Gdns BCTR RM8 91 G1
Davington Rd BCTR RM8 91 H4
Davinia Cl WFD IG8 53 K2
Davis Rd ACT W3 118 C1
  CHSGTN KT9 206 C2
Davis St PLSTW E13 107 F1
Davisville Rd SHB W12 118 D2
Dawes Av HSLW TW3 136 B6
Dawes Ct ESH/CLAY KT10 204 B3
Dawes La FUL/PGN SW6 139 J1
Dawes Rd FUL/PGN SW6 139 H1
Dawes St WALW SE17 19 E5
Dawley Pde HYS/HAR UB3 94 A6
Dawley Rd HYS/HAR UB3 94 D6
Dawlish Av GFD/PVL UB6 97 G1
  PLMGR N13 34 E6
  WAND/EARL SW18 160 A4
Dawlish Dr GDMY/SEVK IG3 73 F1
  PIN HA5 59 J2
  RSLP HA4 58 E6
Dawlish Rd CRICK NW2 82 B4
  LEY E10 69 J6
  TOTM N17 50 C6
Dawnay Gdns
  WAND/EARL SW18 160 C4
Dawnay Rd WAND/EARL SW18 160 B4
Dawn Cl HSLWW TW4 134 D4
Dawn Crs SRTFD E15 88 B6
Dawpool Rd CRICK NW2 63 H6
Daws La MLHL NW7 45 H1
Dawson Av BARK IG11 91 F5
  STMC/STPC BR5 186 C5
Dawson Cl HYS/HAR UB3 133 H1
  WOOL/PLUM SE18 127 H4
Dawson Dr RAIN RM13 93 K5
Dawson Gdns BARK IG11 91 F5
Dawson Pl BAY/PAD W2 100 E6
Dawson Rd CRICK NW2 82 A3
  KUT/HW KT1 175 G6
Dawson St BETH E2 7 K3
Daybrook Rd WIM/MER SW19 178 A5
Daylesford Av PUT/ROE SW15 138 D5
Daymer Gdns PIN HA5 59 G1
Daysbrook Rd
  BRXS/STRHM SW2 162 A3
Days La BFN/LL DA15 167 K2
Dayton Dr ERITH DA8 131 G6
Dayton Gv PECK SE15 143 K2
Deacon Cl PUR/KEN CR8 210 E6
The Deacon Est CHING E4 * 51 H2
Deacon Ms IS N1 85 K5
Deacon Rd CRICK NW2 81 J4
  KUTN/CMB KT2 175 G4
Deacons Cl PIN HA5 41 F5
Deacons Hts BORE WD6 30 C1
Deacons Hl OXHEY WD19 27 J1
Deacons Leas ORP BR6 216 D2
Deacons Ri EFNCH N2 65 H2
Deacons Ter IS N1 * 85 J4
Deacons Wk HPTN TW12 155 F6
Deacon Wy WALW SE17 18 C5
  WFD IG8 53 K3
Deakin Cl WATW WD18 26 C2
Deakins Ter ORP BR6 202 B4
Deal Porters Wy
  BERM/RHTH SE16 123 K3
Deal Rd TOOT SW17 179 F2
Deals Gtwy DEPT SE8 144 E2
Deal St WCHPL E1 104 C4
Dealtry Rd PUT/ROE SW15 139 F5
Deal Wk BRXN/ST SW9 142 B1
Dean Bradley St WEST SW1P 16 E5
Dean Cl CLPT E5 86 E3
  ALP/SUD HA0 79 H1
Deancross St WCHPL E1 104 E5
Dean Dr STAN HA7 44 A5
Deane Av RSLP HA4 77 G3
Deane Croft Rd PIN HA5 59 G5
Deanery Ms MYFR/PKLN W1K * 9 H7
Deanery Rd SRTFD E15 88 C4
Deanery St MYFR/PKLN W1K 9 H7
Deane Wy RSLP HA4 41 G6
Dean Farrar St ST JSPK SW1H 16 D4
Deanfield Gdns
  CROY/NA CRO * 211 K2
Dean Gdns WALTH E17 70 B1
Deanhill Ct
  MORT/ESHN SW14 * 137 J5
Deanhill Rd MORT/ESHN SW14 137 J5
Dean Rd CRICK NW2 82 A4
  CROY/NA CRO 211 K2
  HPTN TW12 173 F1

HSLW TW3 135 G6
THMD SE28 109 G6
Dean Ryle St WEST SW1P 16 E6
Deansbrook Cl EDGW HA8 44 E5
Deansbrook Rd EDGW HA8 44 D6
Dean's Blds WALW SE17 19 F7
Dean's Ct CHSWK W4 117 J6
  CROY/NA CRO 212 B1
  EDGW HA8 44 E2
Dean's Ct BLKFR EC4V 12 B4
Deanscroft Av CDALE/KGS NW9 44 E7
Dean's Dr MLHL NW7 45 F1
  PLMGR N13 49 H2
Deans Gate Cl FSTH SE23 164 A5
Dean's La EDGW HA8 44 E2
Dean's Ms CAVSQ/HST W1G * 9 K3
Dean's Rd HNWL W7 116 A2
  SUT SM1 209 F1
Dean Stanley St WEST SW1P 16 E5
Deanston Rd FSTGT E7 88 E3
  SOHO/CST W1F 10 C3
Deans Wy EDGW HA8 44 E1
Deans Yd WEST SW1P 16 D4
Dean Trench St WEST SW1P 16 E5
Dean Wy NWDGN UB2 115 G2
Dearne Cl STAN HA7 43 G1
De'arn Gdns MTCM CR4 178 D6
Dearsley Rd EN EN1 24 C4
Deason St SRTFD E15 * 88 A6
De Barowe Ms HBRY N5 * 85 H2
Debden Cl KUTN/CMB KT2 174 E1
  WFD IG8 53 H5
De Beauvoir Crs IS N1 86 A6
De Beauvoir Est IS N1 * 86 A6
De Beauvoir Rd IS N1 86 A5
De Beauvoir Sq IS N1 86 A5
Debnams Rd
  BERM/RHTH SE16 123 K4
De Bohun Av STHGT/OAK N14 34 B1
Deborah Cl ISLW TW7 135 K2
De Broome Rd FELT TW13 154 B3
Deburgh Rd WIM/MER SW19 178 B3
Decima St STHWK SE1 19 G4
Decimus Cl SNWD SE25 196 E1
Deck Cl BERM/RHTH SE16 124 A1
Decoy Av GLDGN NW11 64 C2
De Crespigny Pk CMBW SE5 142 E3
Deeley Rd VX/NE SW8 141 J2
Deena Cl EA W5 98 B5
Deepdale WIM/MER SW19 159 G6
Deepdale Av HAYES BR2 199 J1
Deepdale Cl FBAR/BDGN N11 48 A2
Deepdene Av CROY/NA CRO 212 B1
Deepdene Cl WAN E11 70 E1
Deepdene Ct WCHMH N21 35 H1
Deepdene Gdns
  BRXS/STRHM SW2 162 A2
Deepdene Rd HNHL SE24 142 D5
Deere Av RAIN RM13 93 J5
Deerfield Cl CDALE/KGS NW9 63 H2
Deerhurst Cl FELT TW13 153 K6
Deerhurst Crs HPTN TW12 173 H1
Deerhurst Rd KIL/WHAMP NW6 82 E5
  STRHM/NOR SW16 180 A1
Deerings Dr PIN HA5 58 E5
Deerleap Gv CHING E4 25 K6
Deer Park Cl KUTN/CMB KT2 175 J3
Deer Park Gdns MTCM CR4 194 C1
Deer Park Rd WIM/MER SW19 178 A5
Deer Park Wy WWKM BR4 199 J6
Deeside Rd TOOT SW17 160 C5
Dee St POP/IOD E14 106 A5
Dee Wy ROM RM1 57 G4
Defiant Wy WLGTN SM6 210 E5
Defoe Av RCH/KEW TW9 137 H1
Defoe Cl WIM/MER SW19 178 C3
Defoe Pl TOOT SW17 * 160 D4
  STHWK SE1 * 12 D2
Defoe Rd BERM/RHTH SE16 124 C2
  STNW/STAM N16 68 A6
Defoe Wy CRW RM5 56 C2
De Frene Rd SYD SE26 164 A6
Degema Rd CHST BR7 185 G1
Dehar Crs CDALE/KGS NW9 63 H4
Dehavilland Cl NTHLT UB5 95 H2
De Havilland Dr
  WOOL/PLUM SE18 127 G6
De Havilland Rd EDGW HA8 44 D5
  HEST TW5 134 B1
De Havilland Wy
  STWL/WRAY TW19 152 A1
Dekker Rd DUL SE21 163 F1
Delacourt Rd BKHTH/KID SE3 146 A1
Delafield Rd CHARL SE7 126 A5
Delaford Rd BERM/RHTH SE16 123 J5
Delaford St FUL/PGN SW6 139 H1
Delamare Crs CROY/NA CRO 197 K3
Delamere Gdns MLHL NW7 45 F1
Delamere Rd EA W5 117 F2
  RYNPK SW20 177 G4
  YEAD UB4 95 H3
Delamere Ter BAY/PAD W2 101 G4
Delancey Pas CAMTN NW1 * 3 K1
Delancey St CAMTN NW1 3 K1
De Lapre Cl STMC/STPC BR5 202 E4
De Laune St WALW SE17 122 C6
Delaware Rd MV/WKIL W9 101 F3
Delawyk Crs HNHL SE24 162 E1
Delcombe Av WPK KT4 193 F5
Delft Wy ABYW SE2 * 128 B4
Delhi Rd EN EN1 36 B2
Delhi St IS N1 5 F1
Delia St WAND/EARL SW18 160 A2
Delisle Rd THMD SE28 127 K2
Delius Cl BORE WD6 29 G1
Dellbow Rd EBED/NFELT TW14 134 A6

Dell Cl SRTFD E15 88 B6
  WFD IG8 39 F5
  WLGTN SM6 210 C2
Dell Farm Rd RSLP HA4 58 B2
Dellfield Cl BECK BR3 183 F4
Dell La EW KT17 207 J3
Dellors Cl BAR EN5 20 B6
Dellow Cl GNTH/NBYPK IG2 72 D4
Dellow St WCHPL E1 104 D6
Dell Rd EW KT17 207 J4
  PEND EN3 25 G1
  WDR/YW UB7 112 C3
Dell's Ms PIM SW1V * 16 B7
The Dell ABYW SE2 128 B5
  ALP/SUD HA0 79 H3
  BECK BR3 * 182 D3
  BTFD TW8 116 D6
  BXLY DA5 170 B3
  EBED/NFELT TW14 154 A2
  NRWD SE19 181 G4
  NTHWD HA6 26 C4
  PIN HA5 41 H5
  WFD IG8 39 F5
Dell Wk NWMAL KT3 176 B5
Dell Wy WEA W13 97 J5
Dellwood Gdns CLAY IG5 54 A5
Delme Crs BKHTH/KID SE3 146 A3
Delmey Cl CROY/NA CRO 212 B1
Deloraine St DEPT SE8 144 D2
Delorme St HMSMTH W6 119 G6
Delta Cl WPK KT4 207 G1
Delta Gain OXHEY WD19 27 H4
Delta Gv NTHLT UB5 95 H2
Delta Rd WPK KT4 207 G1
Delta St BETH E2 * 104 C2
De Luci Rd ERITH DA8 129 K5
De Lucy St ABYW SE2 128 C4
Delvers Md DAGE RM10 92 E2
Delverton Rd WALW SE17 122 C5
Delvino Rd FUL/PGN SW6 139 K2
De Mandeville Ga EN EN1 24 C5
Demesne Rd WLGTN SM6 210 D2
Demeta Cl WBLY HA9 80 E1
De Montfort Pde
  STRHM/NOR SW16 * 161 K5
De Montfort Rd
  STRHM/NOR SW16 161 K5
De Morgan Rd FUL/PGN SW6 140 A4
Dempster Rd
  WAND/EARL SW18 140 B6
Denberry Dr SCUP DA14 168 C5
Denbigh Cl CHST BR7 184 E2
  NTGHL W11 100 D6
  STHL UB1 95 K6
  SUT SM1 208 D3
  WLSDN NW10 81 G5
Denbigh Gdns
  RCHPK/HAM TW10 137 G6
Denbigh Pl PIM SW1V 121 H5
Denbigh Rd EHAM E6 107 H2
  HSLW TW3 135 G3
  NTGHL W11 100 D6
  STHL UB1 95 K6
  WEA W13 97 H6
Denbigh St PIM SW1V * 16 A7
Denbigh Ter NTGHL W11 100 D6
Denbridge Rd BMLY BR1 184 E5
Den Cl BECK BR3 199 G1
Dendy St BAL SW12 161 F3
Dene Av BFN/LL DA15 168 C2
  HSLW TW3 134 E4
Dene Cl BROCKY SE4 144 B4
  HAYES BR2 199 J5
  RDART DA2 171 J2
  WPK KT4 192 C6
Dene Ct STAN HA7 43 J1
Dene Gdns STAN HA7 43 J1
  THDIT KT7 190 B6
Denehurst Gdns ACT W3 117 J1
  HDN NW4 64 A3
  RCHPK/HAM TW10 137 H5
  WFD IG8 39 J3
  WHTN TW2 155 J2
Dene Rd BKHH IG9 39 J3
  DART DA1 171 J2
  NTHWD HA6 40 A2
  TRDG/WHET N20 33 K3
The Dene CROY/NA CRO 213 F2
  E/WMO/HCT KT8 188 E2
  WBLY HA9 80 A2
  WEA W13 97 H4
Denewood BAR EN5 21 G6
Denewood Rd HGT N6 65 K3
Dengie Wk IS N1 * 85 A5
Denham Cl WELL DA16 148 D4
Denham Crs MTCM CR4 194 E1
Denham Dr GNTH/NBYPK IG2 72 D3
Denham Rd
  EBED/NFELT TW14 154 B2
  TRDG/WHET N20 33 K5
Denham Wy BARK IG11 90 E1
Denholme Rd MV/WKIL W9 100 D2
Denison Cl EFNCH N2 47 G6
Denison Rd EA W5 97 J3
  FELT TW13 153 J6
  WIM/MER SW19 178 C2
Deniston Av BXLY DA5 168 E3
Denleigh Gdns THDIT KT7 189 K3
  WCHMH N21 35 G2
Denman Dr ESH/CLAY KT10 205 G3
  GLDGN NW11 64 E2
Denman Dr North
  GLDGN NW11 64 E2
Denman Dr South
  GLDGN NW11 64 E2
Denman Rd PECK SE15 143 G2
Denman St REGST W1B 10 B6
Denmark Av WIM/MER SW19 177 H3
Denmark Ct MRDN SM4 193 K2
Denmark Gdns CAR SM5 209 K1
Denmark Gv IS N1 5 J2

Denmark Hl HNHL SE24 142 E5
Denmark Hill Dr
  CDALE/KGS NW9 45 J6
Denmark Rd BMLY BR1 184 A4
  CAR SM5 209 K1
  CEND/HSY/T N8 67 F1
  CMBW SE5 142 D2
  KIL/WHAMP NW6 100 D1
  KUT/HW KT1 175 F6
  LEW SE13 * 145 F5
  WEA W13 97 H6
  WHTN TW2 155 J5
Denmark St LSQ/SEVD WC2H 10 D4
  PLSTW E13 107 F4
  TOTM N17 50 D4
  WALTH E17 69 J1
  WAN E11 * 88 C1
Denmark Ter EFNCH N2 * 47 K6
Denmead Rd CROY/NA CRO 196 C5
Denmead Rd SURB KT6 191 G5
Denner Rd CHING E4 37 J4
Dennett Rd CROY/NA CRO 196 B4
Dennett's Gv NWCR SE14 144 A3
Dennett's Rd NWCR SE14 143 K2
Denning Av CROY/NA CRO 211 G3
Denning Cl HPTN TW12 172 E2
  STJWD NW8 101 G2
Denning Rd HAMP NW3 83 H2
Dennington Cl CLPT E5 * 68 D6
Dennington Park Rd
  KIL/WHAMP NW6 82 E4
The Denningtons WPK KT4 192 B6
Dennis Av WBLY HA9 80 B3
Dennis Gdns STAN HA7 43 J1
Dennis La STAN HA7 29 H5
Dennis Pde STHGT/OAK N14 * 34 D3
Dennis Park Crs RYNPK SW20 177 H4
Dennis Reeve Cl MTCM CR4 178 E4
Dennis Rd E/WMO/HCT KT8 189 H1
Dennis Wy CLAP SW4 141 J3
Den Rd HAYES BR2 199 G1
Densham Rd SRTFD E15 88 C6
Densole Cl BECK BR3 * 182 B4
Densworth Gv ED N9 36 E4
Denton Cl BAR EN5 20 A6
Denton Rd BXLY DA5 170 B3
  CEND/HSY/T N8 67 F2
  TWK TW1 156 E1
  UED N18 50 A1
  WELL DA16 148 D1
Denton St WAND/EARL SW18 160 A1
Denton Wy CLPT E5 87 F1
Dents Rd BTSEA SW11 160 E1
Denvale Trade Pk MTCM CR4 * 194 C1
Denver Cl ORP BR6 201 K5
Denver Rd DART DA1 170 D2
  STNW/STAM N16 68 A4
Denyer St CHEL SW3 14 D6
Denzil Rd WLSDN NW10 81 H3
Deodar Rd PUT/ROE SW15 139 H5
Deodora Cl TRDG/WHET N20 33 J5
Depot Rd HSLW TW3 135 H3
Depot St CMBW SE5 122 E6
Deptford Br DEPT SE8 144 D2
Deptford Broadway DEPT SE8 144 D2
Deptford Church St DEPT SE8 124 D6
Deptford Gn DEPT SE8 124 D6
Deptford High St DEPT SE8 124 D6
Deptford Whf DEPT SE8 124 C4
De Quincey Ms CAN/RD E16 125 K1
De Quincey Rd TOTM N17 49 K4
Derby Av KTN/HRWW/WS HA3 42 D4
  ROMW/RG RM7 74 E2
  UED N18 50 B1
Derby Ga WHALL SW1A 16 E2
Derby Hill FSTH SE23 163 K4
Derby Hill Crs FSTH SE23 163 K4
Derby Rd BRYLDS KT5 191 J6
  CROY/NA CRO 196 C6
  E/WMO/HCT KT8 189 H1
  GFD/PVL UB6 96 B1
  HOM E9 87 F6
  HSLW TW3 135 G5
  MORT/ESHN SW14 137 J5
  PEND EN3 24 D6
  SUT SM1 208 D4
  SWFD E18 52 D4
  UED N18 50 E1
  WIM/MER SW19 177 K3
Derbyshire St BETH E2 104 D2
Derby St MYFR/PICC W1J 15 H1
Dereham Pl SDTCH EC2A 7 H6
Dereham Rd BARK IG11 91 F4
Derek Av HOR/WEW KT19 206 C4
  WBLY HA9 80 D5
  WLGTN SM6 210 B3
Derek Cl HOR/WEW KT19 206 D3
Deri Av RAIN RM13 111 K3
Dericote St HACK E8 86 C6
Deri Dene Cl
  STWL/WRAY TW19 * 152 B1
Derifall Cl EHAM E6 107 K4
Dering Pl CROY/NA CRO 211 J3
Dering Rd CROY/NA CRO 211 J3
Dering St OXSTW W1C * 9 J4
Derinton Rd TOOT SW17 161 F6
Derley Rd NWDGN UB2 114 B3
Dermody Gdns LEW SE13 * 145 G6
Dermody Rd LEW SE13 145 G6
Deronda Rd
  BRXS/STRHM SW2 162 C3
Deroy Cl CAR SM5 209 K4
Derrick Gdns CHARL SE7 * 126 B3
Derrick Rd BECK BR3 198 C1
Derry Downs STMC/STPC BR5 202 E4
Derry Rd CROY/NA CRO 210 E1
Derry St KENS W8 120 A2

Dersingham Av MNPK E12 89 K2
Dersingham Rd CRICK NW2 82 C1
Derwent Av CDALE/KGS NW9 33 K3
  EBAR EN4 33 K3
  MLHL NW7 45 F1
  PIN HA5 41 J2
  PUT/ROE SW15 158 B6
  UED N18 49 K1
Derwent Cl DART DA1 170 E3
  EBED/NFELT TW14 153 J3
  ESH/CLAY KT10 204 E4
Derwent Crs BXLYHN DA7 149 H5
  NFNCH/WDSP N12 33 G5
  STAN HA7 43 J5
Derwent Dr STMC/STPC BR5 201 J4
  YEAD UB4 94 C4
Derwent Gdns REDBR IG4 71 J1
  WBLY HA9 61 J4
Derwent Gv EDUL SE22 143 G5
Derwent Ri CDALE/KGS NW9 63 G3
Derwent Rd EA W5 116 C3
  MRDN SM4 193 G3
  PGE/AN SE20 181 H5
  PLMGR N13 35 F6
  STHL UB1 95 K5
  WHTN TW2 155 F1
Derwent St GNWCH SE10 125 H5
Derwentwater Rd ACT W3 117 K1
Derwent Wy HCH RM12 93 K3
Derwent Yd EA W5 * 116 C3

De Salis Rd HGDN/ICK UB10 94 A3
Desborough Cl BAY/PAD W2 101 F4
Desenfans Rd DUL SE21 163 F1
Desford Rd CAN/RD E16 106 C3
Desford Wy ASHF TW15 152 C4
Desmond St NWCR SE14 124 B6
Desmond Tutu Dr FSTH SE23 164 B3
Despard Rd ARCH N19 66 C5
Detling Rd BMLY BR1 183 K1
  ERITH DA8 150 A1
  FELT TW13 153 K5
Detmold Rd CLPT E5 68 E6
Devalls Cl EHAM E6 108 A6
Devana End CAR SM5 209 K1
Devas Rd RYNPK SW20 177 F4
Devas St BOW E3 105 K3
Devema Cl CHST BR7 185 H5
Devenay Rd SRTFD E15 88 D5
Devenish Rd ABYW SE2 128 B2
De Vere Cl WLGTN SM6 210 E5
De Vere Gdns IL IG1 71 K5
  KENS W8 120 B2
Deverell St STHWK SE1 18 E5
De Vere Ms KENS W8 * 120 B3
Devereux Ct TPL/STR WC2R 11 J4
Devereux La BARN SW13 138 E1
Devereux Rd BTSEA SW11 160 E1
Deveron Wy ROM RM1 57 G4
Devey Cl KUTN/CMB KT2 176 C3
Devizes St IS N1 * 7 F1
Devoke Wy WOT/HER KT12 188 C6
Devon Av WHTN TW2 155 H3
Devon Cl BKHH IG9 39 F4
  GFD/PVL UB6 79 J6
  PLMGR N13 35 G5
Devoncroft Gdns TWK TW1 156 B2
Devon Gdns FSBYPK N4 67 H3
Devonhurst Pl CHSWK W4 * 118 A5
Devonia Gdns UED N18 49 J2
Devonia Rd IS N1 6 B2
Devon Man
  KTN/HRWW/WS HA3 * 61 J2
Devonport Gdns IL IG1 71 K3
Devonport Ms SHB W12 * 118 E1
Devonport Rd SHB W12 118 E2
Devonport St WCHPL E1 104 E5
Devon Ri EFNCH N2 65 H1
Devons Est BOW E3 105 K2
Devonshire Av BELMT SM2 209 G5
  DART DA1 171 G4
Devonshire Cl CAVSQ/HST W1G 9 J1
  SRTFD E15 88 C1
  SEVS/STOTM N15 68 A2
Devonshire Crs MLHL NW7 46 B3
Devonshire Dr GNWCH SE10 144 E1
  SURB KT6 190 D5
Devonshire Gdns CHSWK W4 137 K1
  TOTM N17 49 J3
  WCHMH N21 35 J2
Devonshire Hill La TOTM N17 49 K2
Devonshire Ms South
  CAVSQ/HST W1G 9 J1
Devonshire Ms West
  CAVSQ/HST W1G 3 H7
Devonshire Pl
  CAVSQ/HST W1G 3 H7
  CRICK NW2 * 82 E1
  KENS W8 120 A3
Devonshire Place Ms MHST W1U 3 H7
Devonshire Rd BELMT SM2 209 G5
  BXLYHN DA6 149 F5
  CAN/RD E16 107 F5
  CAR SM5 210 A2
  CHSWK W4 118 B5
  CROY/NA CRO 196 E4
  EA W5 116 E3
  ELTH/MOT SE9 166 D4
  FELT TW13 154 D5
  FSTH SE23 163 K3
  GNTH/NBYPK IG2 72 D4
  HCH RM12 93 J3
  MLHL NW7 46 B3
  ORP BR6 202 B4
  PIN HA5 41 K4
  PIN HA5 59 G3
  PLMGR N13 35 F6
  SEVS/STOTM N15 49 K5
  TOTM N17 49 J2
  WALTH E17 69 J3
  WIM/MER SW19 178 D3
Devonshire Rw LVPST EC2M 13 H2

Devonshire Sq *HAYES* BR2 .....200 A1
LVPST EC2M 13 H1
Devonshire St *CAVSO/HST* W1G 9 H1
CHSWK W4 .....118 B5
Devonshire Ter *BAY/PAD* W2 .....101 G5
EDUL SE22 * 143 H5
Devonshire Wy *CROY/NA* CRO 198 C6
YEAD UB4 .....95 F5
Devon Rd *BOW* E3 .....105 J4
Devon St *PECK* SE15 .....123 J6
Devon Wy *CHSGTN* KT9 .....205 J2
HOR/WEW KT19 .....206 D3
Devon Waye *HEST* TW5 .....134 E1
De Walden St *CAVSO/HST* W1G 9 H2
Dewar St *PECK* SE15 .....143 H4
Dewberry Gdns *EHAM* E6 .....107 K4
Dewberry St *POP/IOD* E14 .....106 A5
Dewey Rd *DAGE* RM10 .....92 E4
IS N1 .....5 J2
Dewey St *TOOT* SW17 .....178 E1
Dewhurst Rd *WKENS* W14 .....119 G3
Dewsbury Cl *PIN* HA5 .....59 J5
Dewsbury Gdns *WPK* KT4 .....207 J1
Dewsbury Rd *WLSDN* NW10 .....81 J3
Dexter Rd *BAR* EN5 .....32 B1
Deyncourt Rd *TOTM* N17 .....49 J4
Deyncourt Gdns *WAN* E11 .....71 G1
D'eynsford Rd *CMBW* SE5 .....142 E2
Diadem Ct *SOHO/SHAV* W1D * 10 C3
Diamedes Av
STWL/WRAY TW19 .....152 A2
Diameter Rd *STMC/STPC* BR5 .....201 G4
Diamond Rd *RSLP* HA4 .....77 G2
Diamond St *PECK* SE15 .....143 F1
WLSDN NW10 .....80 E5
Diana Cl *DEPT* SE8 .....124 C6
SCUP DA14 .....169 F4
SWFD E18 .....53 F2
Diana Gdns *SURB* KT6 .....191 G6
Diana Pl *CAMTN* NW1 .....3 K6
Diana Rd *WALTH* E17 .....51 H6
Dianne Wy *EBAR* EN4 .....21 J5
Dianthus Cl *ABYW* SE2 * 128 C5
Diban Av *HCH* RM12 .....93 K2
Dibden St *IS* N1 .....85 J5
Dibdin Cl *SUT* SM1 .....208 E1
Dibdin Rd *SUT* SM1 .....208 E1
Dicey Av *CRICK* NW2 .....82 A3
Dickens Av *DART* DA1 .....151 K5
FNCH N3 .....47 G4
Dickens Cl *ERITH* DA8 .....149 J1
HYS/HAR UB3 .....113 H4
RCHPK/HAM TW10 .....157 F4
Dickens Est
BERM/RHTH SE16 * 123 H5
Dickens La *UED* N18 .....50 A1
Dickens Ms *FARR* EC1M * 6 A7
Dickens Rd *ED* N9 .....36 C3
Dickenson Rd *CEND/HSY/T* N8 .....66 E4
FELT TW13 .....172 B1
Dickenson's La *SNWD* SE25 .....197 H3
Dickenson's Pl *SNWD* SE25 .....197 H3
Dickens Rd *EHAM* E6 .....107 H1
Dickens Sq *STHWK* SE1 .....18 D4
Dickens Wy *ROM* RM1 .....75 G1
Dickens St *VX/NE* SW8 .....141 G3
Dickens Wood Cl *NRWD* SE19 .....180 C3
Dickerage Hl *NWMAL* KT3 .....175 K5
Dickerage La *NWMAL* KT3 .....175 K6
Dickerage Rd *KUT/HW* KT1 .....175 K4
Dickson Fold *PIN* HA5 .....59 H1
Dickson House
WOOL/PLUM SE18 .....146 D2
Dickson Rd *ELTH/MOT* SE9 .....146 D4
Dick Turpin Wy
EBED/NFELT TW14 .....133 J3
Didsbury Cl *EHAM* E6 .....89 K6
Digby Crs *FSBYPK* N4 .....67 J6
Digby Gdns *DAGE* RM10 .....92 C6
Digby Pl *CROY/NA* CRO 212 B1
Digby Rd *BARK* IG11 .....91 F5
HOM E9 .....87 F4
Digby St *BETH* E2 .....104 E2
Diggon St *WCHPL* E1 .....105 F4
Dighton Rd *WAND/EARL* SW18 .....140 B6
Dignum St *IS* N1 * 5 J2
Digswell St *HOLWY* N7 * 85 G4
Dilhorne Cl *LEE/GVPK* SE12 .....166 A5
Dilke St *CHEL* SW3 .....120 F5
Dillwyn Cl *SYD* SE26 .....164 B6
Dilston Cl *NTHLT* UB5 .....95 G2
Dilton Gdns *PUT/ROE* SW15 .....158 D3
Dimes Pl *HMSMTH* W6 .....118 E4
Dimmock Dr *GFD/PVL* UB6 .....78 D3
Dimond Cl *FSTGT* E7 .....88 E2
Dimsdale Dr *CDALE/KGS* NW9 .....62 E5
EN EN1 .....36 C6
Dimson Crs *BOW* E3 .....105 J3
Dingle Cl *BAR* EN5 .....31 H1
Dingle Gdns *POP/IOD* E14 * 105 J6
Dingley La *STRHM/NOR* SW16 .....161 J4
Dingley Pl *FSBYE* EC1V 6 C5
Dingley Rd *FSBYE* EC1V 6 C5
Dingwall Av *CROY/NA* CRO 196 D6
Dingwall Gdns *GLDGN* NW11 .....64 E3
Dingwall Rd *CAR* SM5 .....209 K6
CROY/NA CRO 196 E6
WAND/EARL SW18 .....160 B2
Dinmont St *BETH* E2 * 104 D1
Dinsdale Gdns *BAR* EN5 .....21 F6
SNWD SE25 .....197 F1
Dinsdale Rd *BKHTH/KID* SE3 .....125 J6
Dinton Rd *KUTN/CMB* KT2 .....175 G3
WIM/MER SW19 .....178 C2
Diploma Av *EFNCH* N2 .....65 J1
Dirleton Rd *SRTFD* E15 .....88 D6
Disbrowe Rd *HMSMTH* W6 .....119 H6
Discovery Wk *WAP* E1W 104 D6
Dishforth La *CDALE/KGS* NW9 .....45 G4
Disney Pl *STHWK* SE1 .....18 D2
Disney St *STHWK* SE1 .....18 D2
Dison Cl *PEND* EN3 .....25 F1

Disraeli Cl *THMD* SE28 .....128 C1
Disraeli Rd *EA* W5 .....116 E1
FSTGT E7 * 88 E4
PUT/ROE SW15 .....139 H5
WLSDN NW10 .....98 E1
Diss St *BETH* E2 .....7 H4
Distaff La *BLKFR* EC4V 12 C5
Distillery La *HMSMTH* W6 .....119 F5
Distillery Rd *HMSMTH* W6 .....119 F5
Distin St *LBTH* SE11 .....17 J7
District Rd *ALP/SUD* HA0 .....79 H3
Ditchburn St *POP/IOD* E14 .....106 A6
Ditchfield Rd *YEAD* UB4 .....95 J3
Dittisham Rd *ELTH/MOT* SE9 .....166 D6
Ditton Cl *THDIT* KT7 .....190 B4
Dittoncroft Cl *SAND/SEL* CR2 .....212 A2
Ditton Grange Cl *SURB* KT6 .....190 E5
Ditton Grange Dr *SURB* KT6 .....190 E5
Ditton Hl *SURB* KT6 .....190 D5
Ditton Hill Rd *SURB* KT6 .....190 D5
Ditton Lawn *THDIT* KT7 .....190 B5
Ditton Pl *PGE/AN* SE20 * 181 J4
Ditton Reach *THDIT* KT7 .....190 C3
Ditton Rd *BXLYHS* DA6 .....148 E6
NWDGN UB2 .....114 E5
SURB KT6 .....191 F5
Dixon Cl *EHAM* E6 .....107 K5
Dixon Pl *WWKM* BR4 .....198 E5
Dixon Rd *NWCR* SE14 .....144 B2
SNWD SE25 .....181 F6
Dobbin Cl *KTN/HRWW/W* HA3 .....43 G5
Dobell Rd *ELTH/MOT* SE9 .....146 E6
Dobree Av *WLSDN* NW10 .....81 K5
Dobson Cl *KIL/WHAMP* NW6 .....83 H5
Dockers Tanner Rd
POP/IOD E14 .....124 D4
Dockhead *STHWK* SE1 .....19 K3
Dock Hill Av *BERM/RHTH* SE16 .....124 A2
Dockland St *CAN/RD* E16 .....127 F1
Dockley Rd *BERM/RHTH* SE16 .....123 H5
Dock Rd *BTFD* TW8 .....136 E1
CAN/RD E16 .....106 D6
Dockside Rd *CAN/RD* E16 .....107 H6
Dock St *WCHPL* E1 .....104 C6
Dockwell's La *EBED/NFELT* TW14 .....133 K5
Doctors Cl *SYD* SE26 .....181 K1
Dodbrooke Rd *WNWD* SE27 .....162 B5
Doddington Gv *WALW* SE17 .....122 C6
Doddington Pl *WALW* SE17 .....122 C6
Dodsley Pl *ED* N9 .....36 E5
Dodson St *STHWK* SE1 .....17 K3
Dod St *POP/IOD* E14 .....105 J5
Doebury Wk
WOOL/PLUM SE18 .....128 B6
Doel Cl *WIM/MER* SW19 .....178 B3
Doggett Rd *CAT* SE6 .....164 D2
Doggetts Ct *EBAR* EN4 .....21 J6
Doghurst Av *WDR/YW* UB7 .....132 L1
Doghurst Dr *WDR/YW* UB7 .....132 E1
Dog Kennel Hl *EDUL* SE22 .....143 F4
Dog La *WLSDN* NW10 .....81 G2
Dog Rose Ramble *NTHLT* UB5 .....76 E6
Dog Rose Ramble & Hillingdon
Trail *YEAD* UB4 .....76 D6
Doherty Rd *PLSTW* E13 .....106 E3
Dolben Ct *DEPT* SE8 * 124 C4
Dolben St *STHWK* SE1 * 18 B1
Dolby Rd *FUL/PGN* SW6 .....139 J3
Dolland St *LBTH* SE11 .....122 A5
Dollary Pde *KUT/HW* KT1 * 175 J6
Dollis Av *FNCH* N3 .....46 D4
Dollis Crs *RSLP* HA4 .....59 G5
Dollis Hill Av *CRICK* NW2 .....81 K1
Dollis Hill Est *CRICK* NW2 * 81 J1
Dollis Hill La *CRICK* NW2 .....81 G2
Dollis Pk *FNCH* N3 .....46 D4
Dollis Rd *FNCH* N3 .....46 C4
Dolls Valley Green Wk
GLDGN NW11 .....64 C1
TRDG/WHET N20 .....33 F1
EBAR EN4 .....21 H5
Dolman Cl *FNCH* N3 .....47 G5
Dolman Rd *CHSWK* W4 .....118 A4
Dolman St *BRXN/ST* SW9 .....142 A3
Dolphin Ap *ROM* RM1 .....75 H1
Dolphin Cl *SURB* KT6 .....190 E3
BERM/RHTH SE16 * 124 A2
THMD SE28 .....109 J5
Dolphin La *POP/IOD* E14 .....105 K6
Dolphin Rd *NTHLT* UB5 .....95 K1
Dolphin Sq *CHSWK* W4 * 138 A1
PIM SW1V 121 J5
Dolphin St *KUT/HW* KT1 .....175 F5
Dome Blds *RCHPK/HAM* TW10 * 136 E6
Dome Hill Pk *SYD* SE26 .....163 G6
Domett Cl *CMBW* SE5 .....142 E5
Domingo St *FSBYE* EC1V 6 C6
Dominica Cl *PLSTW* E13 .....107 H2
Dominion Pde *HSLW* TW3 .....135 J3
Dominion Dr *CRW* RM5 .....56 D2
Dominion Pde *HRW* HA1 * 61 F2
Dominion Rd *CROY/NA* CRO 197 G4
NWDGN UB2 .....114 D3
Dominion St *LVPST* EC2M 13 F1
Dominion Wy *RAIN* RM13 .....111 J2
Domonic Dr *ELTH/MOT* SE9 .....167 G5
Domville Cl *TRDG/WHET* N20 .....33 H4
Donald Dr *CHDH* RM6 .....73 J2
Donald Rd *CROY/NA* CRO 196 A3
PLSTW E13 .....89 F1
Donaldson Rd
KIL/WHAMP NW6 .....82 D6
WOOL/PLUM SE18 .....147 F2
Donald Woods Gdns
BRYLDS KT5 .....191 J6
Doncaster Dr *NTHLT* UB5 .....77 K3
Doncaster Gdns *FSBYPK* N4 * 67 J3
NTHLT UB5 .....77 K3
Doncaster Gn *OXHEY* WD19 .....41 G1
Doncaster Rd *ED* N9 .....36 D2
Doncaster Ter *ENC/FH* EN2 * 23 J6
Donegal St *IS* N1 .....5 H3
Doneraile St *FUL/PGN* SW6 .....139 G3
Dongola Rd *PLSTW* E13 .....107 F2
TOTM N17 .....50 A6

Dongola Rd West *PLSTW* E13 .....107 F2
Donington Av *BARK/HLT* IG6 .....72 C2
Donkey Aly *EDUL* SE22 .....163 H2
Donkey La *EN* EN1 .....24 C3
Donnefield Av *EDGW* HA8 .....44 A7
Donne Pl *CHEL* SW3 .....14 D6
MTCM CR4 .....195 G1
Donne Rd *BCTR* RM8 .....73 J6
Donnington Rd
KTN/HRWW/W HA3 .....61 K3
WLSDN NW10 .....81 K6
WPK KT4 .....192 D6
Donnybrook Rd
STRHM/NOR SW16 .....179 H3
Donovan Av *MUSWH* N10 .....48 B5
Don Phelan Cl *CMBW* SE5 .....142 E2
Don Wy *ROM* RM1 .....57 G3
Doone Cl *TEDD* TW11 .....174 B2
Doon St *STHWK* SE1 .....17 J1
Dorado Gdns *ORP* BR6 .....217 K1
Doral Wy *CAR* SM5 .....209 K3
Dorando Cl *SHB* W12 * 99 K6
Doran Gv *WOOL/PLUM* SE18 .....147 K1
Dora Rd *WIM/MER* SW19 .....177 K1
Dora St *POP/IOD* E14 .....105 H5
Dorchester Av *BXLY* DA5 .....168 E3
PLMGR N13 .....35 J6
RYLN/HDSTN HA2 .....60 C3
Dorchester Cl *DART* DA1 .....151 K3
NTHLT UB5 .....78 B3
STMC/STPC BR5 .....186 C5
Dorchester Ct *CRICK* NW2 .....82 A1
HNHL SE24 .....142 D6
STHGT/OAK N14 .....34 B2
Dorchester Dr
EBED/NFELT TW14 .....153 H1
HNHL SE24 .....142 D6
Dorchester Gv *CHSWK* W4 .....118 B6
Dorchester Ms *TWK* TW1 .....156 D1
Dorchester Pde
STRHM/NOR SW16 * 161 K4
Dorchester Rd *MRDN* SM4 .....194 A4
NTHLT UB5 .....78 B3
WPK KT4 .....193 F5
Dorchester Ter *HDN* NW4 * 46 B5
Dorchester Wy
KTN/HRWW/W HA3 .....62 B3
Dorchester Waye *YEAD* UB4 .....95 G5
Dorcis Av *BXLYHN* DA7 .....149 F3
Dordrecht Rd *ACT* W3 .....118 B1
Dore Av *MNPK* E12 .....90 A3
Doreen Av *CDALE/KGS* NW9 .....63 F5
Dore Gdns *MRDN* SM4 .....194 A4
Dorell Cl *STHL* UB1 .....95 K4
Dorian Rd *HCH* RM12 .....75 J5
Doria Rd *FUL/PGN* SW6 .....139 J3
Doric Wy *CAMTN* NW1 .....4 C4
Dorien Rd *RYNPK* SW20 .....177 G5
Doris Av *BXLYHN* DA7 .....149 F5
Doris Rd *FSTGT* E7 .....88 E5
Dorking Cl *DEPT* SE8 .....124 C6
WPK KT4 .....193 G6
Dorlcote Rd
WAND/EARL SW18 .....160 C2
Dorman Pl *ED* N9 .....36 C4
Dormans Cl *NTHWD* HA6 .....40 B3
Dorman Wy *STJWD* NW8 .....83 H6
Dormay St *WAND/EARL* SW18 .....140 A6
Dormer Cl *BAR* EN5 .....20 B6
SRTFD E15 .....88 D4
Dormers Av *STHL* UB1 .....96 A5
Dormers Ri *STHL* UB1 .....96 B6
Dormer's Wells La *STHL* UB1 .....96 A6
Dormywood *RSLP* HA4 .....58 D2
Dorney *BKHTH/KID* SE3 .....145 K1
Dornberg Rd *BKHTH/KID* SE3 * 146 A1
Dorncliffe Rd *FUL/PGN* SW6 .....139 H3
Dorney Ri *STMC/STPC* BR5 .....202 A1
Dorney Wy *HSLWW* TW4 .....134 D6
Dornfell St *KIL/WHAMP* NW6 .....82 D3
Dornton Rd *BAL* SW12 .....161 G4
SAND/SEL CR2 .....212 A3
Dorothy Av *ALP/SUD* HA0 .....80 A6
Dorothy Evans Cl *BXLYHN* DA7 .....149 J5
Dorothy Gdns *BCTR* RM8 .....91 H2
Dorothy Rd *BTSEA* SW11 .....140 E4
Dorrington Ct *HCIRC* EC1N 11 J1
Dorrington Wy *BECK* BR3 .....199 F2
Dorrit St *STHWK* SE1 * 18 E2
Dorrit Wy *CHST* BR7 .....185 H2
Dors Cl *CDALE/KGS* NW9 .....63 F5
Dorset Av *NWDGN* UB2 .....115 F4
RAIN RM13 .....111 J2
WELL DA16 .....148 A5
Dorset Blds *EMB* EC4Y * 12 A4
YEAD UB4 * 94 C2
Dorset Dr *EDGW* HA8 .....44 B2
Dorset Gdns
STRHM/NOR SW16 .....196 A1
Dorset Ms *FNCH* N3 .....46 E4
KTBR SW1X 15 J4
Dorset Pl *SRTFD* E15 .....88 B4
Dorset Ri *EMB* EC4Y 12 A4
Dorset Rd *ASHF* TW15 .....152 A5
BECK BR3 .....182 A6
EA W5 .....116 D3
ELTH/MOT SE9 .....166 D4
FSTGT E7 .....89 G5
HRW HA1 .....60 C3
MTCM CR4 .....178 D5
SEVS/STOTM N15 .....67 K1
VX/NE SW8 .....141 K1
WDGN N22 .....48 E4
WIM/MER SW19 .....177 K4
Dorset Sq *CAMTN* NW1 .....2 E7
Dorset St *MHST* W1U 9 G2
Dorset Wy *WHTN* TW2 .....155 H3
Dorset Waye *HEST* TW5 .....134 E1
Dorton Cl *PECK* SE15 .....143 F1
Dorville Crs *HMSMTH* W6 .....118 E3

Dorville Rd *LEE/GVPK* SE12 .....145 K6
Dothill Rd *WOOL/PLUM* SE18 .....147 H1
Douai Gv *HPTN* TW12 .....173 H4
Doughty Ms *BMSBY* WC1N 5 G7
Doughty St *BMSBY* WC1N 5 G6
Douglas Av *ALP/SUD* HA0 .....80 A5
NWMAL KT3 .....192 E1
WALTH E17 .....51 J4
Douglas Cl *STAN* HA7 .....43 G1
WLGTN SM6 .....210 E4
Douglas Crs *YEAD* UB4 .....95 G3
Douglas Dr *CROY/NA* CRO 213 J1
Douglas Est *IS* N1 .....85 J4
Douglas Ms *CRICK* NW2 .....82 C1
Douglas Pth *POP/IOD* E14 * 125 F5
Douglas Pl *POP/IOD* E14 * 125 F5
Douglas Rd *CAN/RD* E16 .....106 E4
CHING E4 .....38 C2
ESH/CLAY KT10 .....189 G6
GDMY/SEVK IG3 .....73 G4
HSLW TW3 .....135 G4
IS N1 .....85 J5
KIL/WHAMP NW6 .....82 D6
KUT/HW KT1 .....175 J5
ROM RM1 .....75 H5
STWL/WRAY TW19 .....152 A1
SURB KT6 .....191 G6
WDGN N22 .....49 G4
WELL DA16 .....148 C2
Douglas Rd North *IS* N1 .....85 J4
Douglas Rd South *IS* N1 * 85 J4
Douglas St *WEST* SW1P 16 C7
Douglas Ter *WALTH* E17 * 51 H4
Douglas Vls *KUT/HW* KT1 * 175 G5
Doulton Ms *KIL/WHAMP* NW6 * 83 F4
Dounesforth Gdns
WAND/EARL SW18 .....160 A3
Douro Pl *KENS* W8 .....120 A3
Douro St *BOW* E3 .....105 J1
Douthwaite Sq *WAP* E1W * 123 H1
Dove Ap *EHAM* E6 .....107 J4
Dove Cl *CROY/NA* CRO 180 D1
MLHL NW7 .....45 J3
NTHLT UB5 .....95 H3
Dovecot Cl *PIN* HA5 .....59 G2
Dove Ct *LOTH* EC2R * 12 E4
Dovedale Av *CLAY* IG5 .....54 A5
KTN/HRWW/W HA3 .....61 J3
Dovedale Cl *WELL* DA16 .....148 B2
Dovedale Ri *MTCM* CR4 .....178 E3
Dovedale Rd *EDUL* SE22 .....143 J6
Dovedon Cl *STHGT/OAK* N14 .....34 E4
Dove House Gdns *CHING* E4 .....37 J4
Dovehouse Md *BARK* IG11 .....108 D1
Dovehouse St *CHEL* SW3 .....120 D5
Dove Ms *ECT* SW5 .....120 D4
Doveney Cl *STMC/STPC* BR5 .....202 E1
Dove Pk *PIN* HA5 .....41 K3
Dover Cl *CRICK* NW2 .....64 B6
ROMW/RG RM7 .....56 E5
Dovercourt Av *THHTH* CR7 .....196 B1
Dovercourt Est *IS* N1 * 85 K4
Dovercourt Gdns *STAN* HA7 .....44 A1
Dovercourt La *SUT* SM1 .....209 G1
Dovercourt Rd *EDUL* SE22 .....163 F1
Doverfield Rd
BRXS/STRHM SW2 .....161 K1
Dover Gdns *CAR* SM5 .....209 K1
Dover House Rd
PUT/ROE SW15 .....138 D5
Dover Park Dr *PUT/ROE* SW15 .....158 E1
Dover Rd *ED* N9 .....36 E3
EHAM E6 .....108 A1
NRWD SE19 .....180 E2
WOOL/PLUM SE18 .....147 G3
Dover St *MYFR/PICC* W1J 10 A7
Dover Ter *RCH/KEW* TW9 * 137 H3
Doves Cl *HAYES* BR2 .....200 D6
Doves Yd *IS* N1 .....5 J1
Doveton Rd *SAND/SEL* CR2 .....211 K5
Doveton St *WCHPL* E1 .....104 E3
Dowanhill Rd *CAT* SE6 .....165 G3
Dowdeswell Cl *PUT/ROE* SW15 .....138 B5
Dowding Cl *HCH* RM12 .....93 K5
Dowding Pl *STAN* HA7 .....43 G2
Dowdney Cl *KTTN* NW5 .....84 C3
Dowgate Hl *CANST* EC4R 12 E5
Dowland St *NKENS* W10 .....100 C2
Dowlas St *CMBW* SE5 .....143 F1
Dowlerville Rd *ORP* BR6 .....217 F4
Dowman Cl *WIM/MER* SW19 .....178 A4
Downage *HDN* NW4 .....46 A6
Downalong *BUSH* WD23 .....28 D3
Downbank Av *BXLYHN* DA7 .....150 A2
Down Barns Rd *RSLP* HA4 .....77 H1
Down Cl *NTHLT* UB5 .....95 F2
Downderry Rd *BMLY* BR1 .....165 H6
Downe Cl *WELL* DA16 .....148 D1
Downend *WOOL/PLUM* SE18 * 147 G1
Downe Rd *HAYES* BR2 .....215 H6
MTCM CR4 .....178 E5
Downers Cottages *CLAP* SW4 * 141 H5
Downes Cl *TWK* TW1 .....156 C1
Downes Ct *WCHMH* N21 .....35 G3
Downfield Cl *MV/WKIL* W9 .....101 F3
Down Hall Rd *KUTN/CMB* KT2 .....174 E4
Downham La *BMLY* BR1 .....183 G5
Downham Rd *IS* N1 .....86 A5
Downham Wy *BMLY* BR1 .....183 H3
Downhills Park Rd *TOTM* N17 .....49 J6
Downhills Wy *TOTM* N17 .....49 J5
Downhurst Av *MLHL* NW7 .....45 F1
Downing Cl *RYLN/HDSTN* HA2 .....42 C6
Downing Dr *GFD/PVL* UB6 .....78 D6
Downing Rd *DAGW* RM9 .....92 B6
Downings *EHAM* E6 .....108 A5
Downing St *WHALL* SW1A 16 E2

Downland Cl *TRDG/WHET* N20 .....33 G3
Downleys Cl *ELTH/MOT* SE9 .....166 D4
Downman Rd *ELTH/MOT* SE9 .....146 D4
Down Pl *HMSMTH* W6 .....118 E4
Down Rd *TEDD* TW11 .....174 C2
Downs Av *CHST* BR7 .....166 E3
DART DA1 .....171 K2
PIN HA5 .....59 K3
Downs Bridge Rd *BECK* BR3 .....183 G4
Downs Court Pde *CLPT* E5 * 86 D1
Downsell Rd *WAN* E11 .....88 B2
Downshall Av *CDMY/SEVK* IG3 .....72 E5
Downs Hl *BECK* BR3 .....183 G4
Downshire Hl *HAMP* NW3 .....83 H2
Downside *BECK* BR3 * 182 D4
Downside Crs *HAMP* NW3 .....83 J3
WEA W13 .....97 G5
Downside Rd *BELMT* SM2 .....209 H4
Downs La *CLPT* E5 .....86 D2
Downs Park Rd *HACK* E8 .....86 C5
Downs Rd *BECK* BR3 .....182 E5
CLPT E5 .....86 C2
EN EN1 .....24 A5
THHTH CR7 .....180 D4
The Downs *RYNPK* SW20 .....177 G3
Down St *E/WMO/HCT* KT8 .....189 F2
MYFR/PICC W1J 15 J1
Down Street Ms
MYFR/PICC W1J 15 J2
Downs Vw *ISLW* TW7 .....136 A2
Downsview Gdns *NRWD* SE19 .....180 D3
Downsview Rd *NRWD* SE19 .....180 D3
Downsway *ORP* BR6 .....216 E3
The Downsway *BELMT* SM2 .....209 G6
Downton Av
BRXS/STRHM SW2 .....162 A4
Downtown Rd
BERM/RHTH SE16 .....124 B2
Downway *NFNCH/WDSP* N12 .....47 J3
Downs Wy *NTHLT* UB5 .....95 F2
Dowrey St *IS* N1 .....85 H6
Dowsett Rd *TOTM* N17 .....50 C5
Dowson Cl *CMBW* SE5 * 142 E5
Doyce St *STHWK* SE1 * 18 C2
Doyle Cl *ERITH* DA8 .....150 B2
Doyle Gdns *WLSDN* NW10 .....81 K6
Doyle Rd *SNWD* SE25 .....197 H1
D'Oyley St *KTBR* SW1X 15 G6
Doynton St *ARCH* N19 * 66 B6
Draco Ga *PUT/ROE* SW15 * 139 F4
Draco St *WALW* SE17 .....122 D6
Dragonfly Cl *PLSTW* E13 .....107 F2
Dragon Rd *LBTH* SE1 * 17 H7
PECK SE15 .....123 F6
Dragoon Rd *DEPT* SE8 .....124 C5
Dragor Rd *WLSDN* NW10 .....98 E3
Drake Cl *BERM/RHTH* SE16 .....124 A2
Drake Crs *THMD* SE28 .....109 J5
Drakefell Rd *NWCR* SE14 .....144 A3
Drakefield Rd *TOOT* SW17 .....161 F5
Drake Ms *HAYES* BR2 .....200 B1
HCH RM12 .....93 J5
Drake Rd *BROCKY* SE4 .....144 D4
CHSGTN KT9 .....206 C3
CROY/NA CRO 196 A4
MTCM CR4 .....195 F6
RYLN/HDSTN HA2 .....59 K6
Drake's Cl *ESH/CLAY* KT10 .....204 A3
Drakes Ctyd *KIL/WHAMP* NW6 * 82 D5
Drake St *BMSBY* WC1N 11 G2
ENC/FH EN2 .....23 K2
Drakewood Rd
STRHM/NOR SW16 .....179 J3
Draper Cl *BELV* DA17 .....129 G4
Draper Est *WALW* SE17 * 18 E6
Draper Pl *IS* N1 * 85 H6
Drapers Rd *ENC/FH* EN2 .....23 H3
SRTFD E15 .....88 B2
TOTM N17 .....50 B6
Drappers Wy
BERM/RHTH SE16 .....123 H4
Draven Cl *HAYES* BR2 .....199 J4
Draweil Cl *WOOL/PLUM* SE18 .....127 K5
Drax Av *RYNPK* SW20 .....176 D3
Draxmont *WIM/MER* SW19 .....177 H2
Draycot Rd *SURB* KT6 .....191 H5
WAN E11 .....71 F3
Draycott Av *CHEL* SW3 .....14 D7
KTN/HRWW/W HA3 .....61 H3
Draycott Cl *CMBW* SE5 .....142 E1
KTN/HRWW/W HA3 .....61 H3
Draycott Pl *CHEL* SW3 .....14 E6
Draycott Ter *CHEL* SW3 .....14 E6
Dray Ct *ALP/SUD* HA0 * 79 J4
Drayford Cl *MV/WKIL* W9 * 100 D3
Draymans Wy *ISLW* TW7 .....136 A4
Drayson Ms *KENS* W8 .....119 K2
Drayton Av *LOU* IG10 .....39 K1
ORP BR6 .....201 G5
WEA W13 .....97 G6
Drayton Bridge Rd *HNWL* W7 .....97 F6
Drayton Cl *HSLWW* TW4 .....134 E6
IL IG1 .....72 D5
Drayton Ct *WDR/YW* UB7 * 112 C4
Drayton Gdns
WBPTN SW10 .....120 B5
WCHMH N21 .....35 H2
WDR/YW UB7 .....112 A2
WEA W13 .....97 G6
Drayton Gn *WEA* W13 .....97 G6
Drayton Green Rd *WEA* W13 .....97 H6
Drayton Gv *WEA* W13 .....97 G6
Drayton Pk *HOLWY* N7 .....85 G3
Drayton Park Ms *HOLWY* N7 * 85 G3
Drayton Rd *CROY/NA* CRO 196 C6
TOTM N17 .....50 A5
WAN E11 .....70 B5
WEA W13 .....97 G6
WLSDN NW10 .....81 H6
Dreadnought St *GNWCH* SE10 .....125 H3

Drenon Sq HYS/HAR UB3 ......94 D6
Dresden Cl HAMP NW3 ......83 F4
Dresden Rd ARCH N19 ......66 C5
Dressington Av BROCKY SE4 ......164 D1
Drew Av MLHL NW7 ......38 D6
Drewery Ct BKHTH/KID SE3 * 145 H4
Drew Gdns GFD/PVL UB6 ......79 G3
Drew Rd CAN/RD E16 ......126 D1
Drewstead Rd
  STRHM/NOR SW16 ......161 J4
Driffield Rd BOW E3 ......105 G1
The Drift HAYES BR2 ......215 H1
The Driftway MTCM CR4 ......179 F4
Drinkwater Rd
  RYLN/HDSTN HA2 ......60 B6
Drive Ct EDGW HA8 * 44 C1
The Drive ACT W3 ......98 E5
  BAR EN5 ......20 C4
  BAR EN5 ......33 J1
  BARK IG11 ......91 F5
  BECK BR3 ......182 D5
  BKHH IG9 ......39 G2
  BXLY DA5 ......168 E2
  CHING E4 ......38 B2
  CHST BR7 ......186 A5
  CRW RM5 ......57 H4
  EBED/NFELT TW14 ......154 A2
  EDGW HA8 ......44 C1
  ENC/FH EN2 ......23 K2
  ERITH DA8 ......149 F1
  ESH/CLAY KT10 ......189 H5
  FBAR/BDGN N11 ......48 C2
  FNCH N3 ......46 E3
  GLDGN NW11 ......64 C4
  HGT N6 ......65 K2
  HOLWY N7 ......85 F4
  HOR/WEW KT19 ......207 J6
  HSLW TW5 ......135 J3
  IL IG1 ......71 J3
  KUTN/CMB KT2 ......175 K3
  MRDN SM4 ......194 B2
  NTHWD HA6 ......40 C4
  ORP BR6 ......202 A6
  RYLN/HDSTN HA2 ......60 B6
  RYNPK SW20 ......177 F3
  SCUP DA14 ......168 C5
  SURB KT6 ......191 F4
  SWFD E18 ......52 E6
  THHT CR7 ......196 C1
  WALTH E17 ......51 H6
  WBLY HA9 ......62 E6
  WWKM BR4 ......199 G4
Dr Johnson Av TOOT SW17 ......161 G1
Droitwich Cl SYD SE26 ......163 H5
Dromey Gdns
  KTN/HRWW/W HA3 ......43 F3
Dromore Rd PUT/ROE SW15 ......159 H1
Dronfield Gdns BCTR RM8 ......91 J3
Droop St NKENS W10 ......100 C3
Drovers Pl PECK SE15 ......143 J1
Drovers Rd SAND/SEL CR2 ......211 K3
Druce Rd DUL SE21 ......163 F1
Druid St STHWK SE1 ......19 J3
Druids Wy HAYES BR2 ......199 G1
Drumaline Rdg WPK KT4 ......192 C6
Drummond Cl ERITH DA8 ......150 B2
Drummond Crs CAMTN NW1 ......4 C4
Drummond Dr
  KTN/HRWW/W HA3 ......42 B6
Drummond Ga PIM SW1V 121 J5
Drummond Rd
  BERM/RHTH SE16 ......123 J3
  CROW/NA CRO 196 D6
  ROMW/RG RM7 ......74 E3
  WAN E11 ......71 F3
Drummonds Pl RCH/KEW TW9 ......137 F5
Drummond St CAMTN NW1 ......4 A6
Drum St WCHPL E1 ......13 K3
Drury Crs CROY/NA CRO 196 B6
Drury La HOL/ALD WC2B 11 F4
Drury Rd HRW HA1 ......60 C6
Drury Wy WLSDN NW10 ......81 F3
Dryad St PUT/ROE SW15 ......139 G4
Dryburgh Gdns
  CDALE/KGS NW9 ......44 C6
Dryburgh Rd PUT/ROE SW15 ......138 E4
Dryden Av HNWL W7 ......97 F5
Dryden Cl BARK/HLT IG6 ......55 F2
Dryden Rd EN EN1 ......36 A1
  KTN/HRWW/W HA3 ......43 F3
  WIM/MER SW19 ......178 B2
  WELL/PLUM SE18 ......148 A2
Dryden St COVGDN WC2E 11 F4
Dryden Wy ORP BR6 ......202 B5
Dryfield Cl WLSDN NW10 ......80 E4
Dryfield Rd EDGW HA8 ......44 E2
Dryhill Rd BELV DA17 ......129 G6
Dryland Av ORP BR6 ......217 F2
Drylands Rd CEND/HSY/T N8 ......66 E3
Drysdale Av CHING E4 ......37 N8
Drysdale Pl IS N1 ......7 J4
Drysdale St IS N1 ......7 H5
Dryslade Pl BETH E2 ......104 E2
Dryslade St IS N1 ......7 H5
Dublin Av HACK E8 ......86 C6
Du Burstow Ter HNWL W7 * 115 K2
Ducal St BETH E2 ......7 K5
Du Cane Cl SHB W12 ......100 A5
Du Cane Rd SHB W12 ......99 K5
Duchess Av BKHH IG9 * 39 F4
Duchess Ms CAVSQ/HST W1G 9 J2
Duchess of Bedfords Wk
  KENS W8 ......119 K2
Duchess St REGST W1B 9 J2
Duchy Rd EBAR EN4 ......21 H1
Duchy St STHWK SE1 ......17 K1
Ducie St BRXN/ST SW9 ......141 K3
Duckett Rd FSBYPK N4 ......67 H3
Duckett St WCHPL E1 ......105 F4
Ducking Stool Ct ROM RM1 ......75 G1
Duck Lees La PEND EN3 ......25 G5

Du Cros Dr STAN HA7 ......43 K2
Du Cros Rd ACT W3 ......118 B1
Dudden Hill La WLSDN NW10 ......81 H2
Dudden Hill Pde
  WLSDN NW10 * 81 H2
Duddington Cl ELTH/MOT SE9 ......166 C6
Dudley Av KTN/HRWW/W HA3 ......43 J6
Dudley Dr MRDN SM4 ......193 H5
  RSLP HA4 ......77 F3
Dudley Gdns RYLN/HDSTN HA2 ......60 D5
  WEA W13 ......116 C2
Dudley Pl HYS/HAR UB3 ......113 G4
Dudley Rd EBED/NFELT TW14 ......153 G3
  FNCH N3 ......47 F5
  IL IG1 ......90 B2
  KIL/WHAMP NW6 ......100 C1
  KUT/HW KT1 ......175 G6
  NWDGN UB2 ......114 C2
  RCH/KEW TW9 ......137 G3
  RYLN/HDSTN HA2 ......60 C6
  WALTH E17 ......51 J5
  WIM/MER SW19 ......177 K2
Dudley St BAY/PAD W2 * 8 A2
Dudlington Rd CLPT E5 ......68 E6
Dudmaston Ms CHEL SW3 ......120 C5
Dudrich Ms EDUL SE22 ......143 G6
Dudsbury Rd DART DA1 ......170 E1
Dudset La HEST TW5 ......133 K2
Dufferin Av STLK EC1Y 6 E7
Dufferin St STLK EC1Y 6 D7
Duffield Cl HRW HA1 ......61 F2
Duffield Dr SEVS/STOTM N15 ......68 B1
Duff St POP/IOD E14 ......105 K5
Dufour's Pl SOHO/CST W1F 10 B4
Dufrey Pl CMBW SE5 ......142 E1
Duggan Dr CHST BR7 ......184 D2
Duke Humphrey Rd
  BKHTH/KID SE3 ......145 H3
Duke of Cambridge Cl
  WHTN TW2 ......155 J1
Duke of Edinburgh Rd
  SUT SM1 ......209 H1
Duke of Wellington Pl
  MYFR/PICC W1J 15 H2
Duke of York Sq CHEL SW3 ......120 E5
Duke of York St STJS SW1Y 10 B7
Duke Rd BARK/HLT IG6 ......72 C1
  CHSWK W4 ......118 A5
Duke's Av CHSWK W4 ......118 A5
  EDGW HA8 ......44 B2
  FNCH N3 ......47 F4
  HRW HA1 ......60 E1
  HSLWW TW4 ......134 D5
  MUSWH N10 ......48 C6
  NTHLT UB5 ......78 B6
  PIN HA5 ......59 K3
  RCHPK/HAM TW10 ......156 D6
Dukes Cl ASHF TW15 ......153 F6
  HPTN TW12 ......172 E1
Dukes Ga CHSWK W4 * 117 K4
Dukes La KENS W8 ......119 K2
Dukes La Chambers
  KENS W8 * 120 A2
Dukes Lane Man KENS W8 * 120 A2
Duke's Ms MHST W1U 9 H3
Dukes Orch BXLY DA5 ......169 K3
Duke's Pl HDTCH EC3A 13 J4
Dukes Rd ACT W3 ......98 C3
  EHAM E6 ......90 A6
  STPAN WC1H 4 D5
Dukesthorpe Rd SYD SE26 ......164 A6
Duke St MBLAR W1H 9 H3
  RCH/KEW TW9 ......136 E5
  SUT SM1 ......209 H2
Duke Street Hl STHWK SE1 ......13 F7
Duke Street St James's
  MYFR/PICC W1J 10 B7
Dukes Wy WWKM BR4 ......214 C1
Duke's Yd MYFR/PKLN W1K 9 H5
Dulas Rd FSBYPK N4 ......67 F5
Dulford St NTGHL W11 ......100 C6
Dulka Rd BTSEA SW11 ......140 E6
Dulverton Rd ELTH/MOT SE9 ......167 H4
  RSLP HA4 ......58 E5
Dulwich Common DUL SE21 ......162 E3
The Dulwich Oaks DUL SE21 * 163 G5
Dulwich Ms EDUL SE22 ......143 G6
Dulwich Village DUL SE21 ......143 G5
Dulwich Wood Av NRWD SE19 ......181 F1
Dulwich Wood Pk NRWD SE19 ......163 F6
Dumbarton Rd
  BRXS/STRHM SW2 ......161 K1
Dumbleton Cl KUT/HW KT1 ......175 J4
Dumbreck Rd ELTH/MOT SE9 ......147 F5
Dumfries Cl OXHEY WD19 ......26 E5
Dumont Rd STNW/STAM N16 ......86 A1
Dumpton Pl CAMTN NW1 ......84 A5
Dunbar Av BECK BR3 ......198 B1
  DAGE RM10 ......92 C1
  STRHM/NOR SW16 ......180 B5
Dunbar Cl YEAD UB4 ......94 E4
Dunbar Ct WOT/HER KT12 ......188 B6
Dunbar Gdns DAGE RM10 ......92 C3
Dunbar Rd FSTGT E7 ......88 E4
  NWMAL KT3 ......191 K1
  WDGN N22 ......49 G4
Dunbar St WNWD SE27 ......162 D5
Dunblane Rd ELTH/MOT SE9 ......146 D3
Dunboyne Rd HAMP NW3 ......83 K3
Dunbridge St BETH E2 ......104 C3
Duncan Cl BAR EN5 ......21 G5
Duncan Gv ACT W3 ......99 G5
Duncannon St CHCR WC2N 10 E6
Duncan Rd HACK E8 ......86 D6
  RCH/KEW TW9 ......137 F5
Duncan St IS N1 ......5 K2
Duncan Ter IS N1 ......6 A2
Dunch St WCHPL E1 ......104 D5
Duncombe Hl FSTH SE23 ......164 B2
Duncombe Rd ARCH N19 ......66 D5
Duncrievie Rd LEW SE13 ......165 G1
Duncroft WOOL/PLUM SE18 ......147 K1

Dundalk Rd BROCKY SE4 ......144 B4
Dundas Gdns E/WMO/HCT KT8 ......173 G6
Dundas Rd PECK SE15 ......143 K3
Dundee Rd PLSTW E13 ......107 F1
  SNWD SE25 ......197 J2
Dundee St WAP E1W 123 J1
Dundee Wy PEND EN3 ......25 G4
Dundela Gdns WPK KT4 ......207 K2
Dundonald Cl EHAM E6 ......107 J5
Dundonald Rd
  WIM/MER SW19 ......177 J3
  WLSDN NW10 ......82 B6
Dunedin Rd IL IG1 ......72 C5
  LEY E10 ......87 K1
  RAIN RM13 ......111 H2
Dunedin Wy YEAD UB4 ......95 G3
Duneim Gv WNWD SE27 ......162 D6
Dunelm St WCHPL E1 ......105 F5
Dunfield Rd CAT SE6 ......182 E1
Dunford Rd HOLWY N7 ......85 F2
Dungarvan Av PUT/ROE SW15 ......138 D5
Dunheved Rd North
  THHTH CR7 ......196 A3
Dunheved Rd South
  THHTH CR7 ......196 A3
Dunheved Rd West
  THHTH CR7 ......196 A3
Dunholme Gn ED N9 ......36 B5
Dunholme La ED N9 ......36 B5
Dunholme Rd ED N9 ......36 B5
Dunkeld Rd BCTR RM8 ......73 H6
  SNWD SE25 ......196 E1
Dunkery Rd ELTH/MOT SE9 ......166 C6
Dunkin Rd DART DA1 ......151 K5
Dunkirk St WNWD SE27 * 162 D6
Dunlace Rd CLPT E5 ......86 E3
Dunleary Cl HSLWW TW4 ......154 E2
Dunley Dr CROY/NA CRO 214 A4
Dunloe Av TOTM N17 ......49 K6
Dunloe St BETH E2 ......7 K3
Dunlop Pl BERM/RHTH SE16 ......19 K5
Dunmore Rd KIL/WHAMP NW6 ......82 C6
  RYNPK SW20 ......177 F4
Dunmow Cl CHDH RM6 ......73 J2
  FELT TW13 * 154 C6
  LOU IG10 ......39 J1
Dunmow Rd SRTFD E15 ......88 B2
Dunmow Wk IS N1 * 85 J6
Dunningford Cl HCH RM12 ......93 H5
Dunn Md CDALE/KGS NW9 ......45 H3
Dunnock Cl ED N9 ......37 F4
Dunnock Rd EHAM E6 ......107 J5
Dunn St HACK E8 ......86 B3
Dunollie Pl KTTN NW5 ......84 C3
Dunollie Rd KTTN NW5 ......84 C3
Dunoon Gdns FSTH SE23 * 164 A2
Dunoon Rd FSTH SE23 ......163 K2
Dunraven Dr ENC/FH EN2 ......23 G3
Dunraven Rd SHB W12 ......118 D1
Dunraven St MYFR/PKLN W1K 9 F5
Dunsany Rd WKENS W14 ......119 G3
Dunsbury Cl BELMT SM2 ......209 F6
Dunsfold Wy CROY/NA CRO 213 K5
Dunsmore Cl BUSH WD23 ......28 D1
  YEAD UB4 ......95 H3
Dunsmore Rd WOT/HER KT12 ......188 A2
Dunsmure Wy BUSH WD23 ......28 C1
Dunsmure Rd STNW/STAM N16 ......68 A5
Dunspring La CLAY IG5 ......54 B5
Dunstable Ms CAVSQ/HST W1G 9 H1
Dunstable Rd
  E/WMO/HCT KT8 ......188 C1
  RCH/KEW TW9 ......137 F5
Dunstall Rd RYNPK SW20 ......176 E2
Dunstall Wy E/WMO/HCT KT8 ......173 G6
Dunstall Welling Est
  WELL DA16 * 148 C3
Dunstan Cl EFNCH N2 * 47 G6
Dunstan Gld STMC/STPC BR5 * 201 J3
Dunstan Houses WCHPL E1 * 104 E4
Dunstan Rd GLDGN NW11 ......64 D5
Dunstan's Gv EDUL SE22 ......163 J1
Dunster Av MRDN SM4 ......193 G5
Dunster Cl BAR EN5 ......20 B5
  ROMW/RG RM7 ......56 E5
Dunster Ct CDALE/KGS NW9 ......44 E5
Dunster Dr CDALE/KGS NW9 ......62 E5
Dunster Gdns KIL/WHAMP NW6 ......82 D5
Dunsterville Wy STHWK SE1 ......19 F3
Dunster Wy RYLN/HDSTN HA2 ......77 J1
Dunston Rd BTSEA SW11 ......141 F4
  HACK E8 ......7 J1
Dunston St HACK E8 ......86 B6
Dunton Cl SURB KT6 ......191 F5
Dunton Rd LEY E10 ......69 K4
  ROM RM1 ......75 G1
  STHWK SE1 ......19 J7
Dunstil Rd
  WAND/EARL SW18 ......160 A3
Dunvegan Cl
  E/WMO/HCT KT8 ......189 G1
Dunvegan Rd ELTH/MOT SE9 ......146 E5
Dunworth Ms NTGHL W11 ......100 D5
Duplex Ride KTBR SW1X 15 F3
Dupont Rd RYNPK SW20 ......177 G5
Duppas Av CROY/NA CRO 211 H2
Duppas Hill Rd CROY/NA CRO 211 G2
Duppas Hill Ter CROY/NA CRO 211 G2
Duppas Rd CROY/NA CRO 211 G1
Dupree Rd CHARL SE7 ......126 A5
Dura Den Cl BECK BR3 ......182 E3
Durand Cl CAR SM5 ......194 E6
Durand Gdns BRXN/ST SW9 ......142 A2
Durand Wy WLSDN NW10 ......80 E5
Durants Park Av PEND EN3 ......25 F5
Durants Rd PEND EN3 ......24 E5
Durant St BETH E2 ......104 C1
Durban Gdns DAGE RM10 ......92 E5
Durban Rd BECK BR3 ......182 C5
  GNTH/NBYPK IG2 ......72 E3
  SRTFD E15 ......106 C2

TOTM N17 ......50 A2
WALTH E17 ......51 H4
WNWD SE27 ......162 D6
Durbin Rd CHSGTN KT9 ......206 A2
Durdans Rd STHL UB1 ......95 K5
Durell Gdns DAGW RM9 ......91 K5
Durell Rd DAGW RM9 ......91 J5
Durfey Pl CMBW SE5 ......142 E1
Durford Crs PUT/ROE SW15 ......158 D3
Durham Av HAYES BR2 ......199 J1
  HEST TW5 ......114 E6
  WFD IG8 ......53 H1
Durham Hl BMLY BR1 ......165 J6
Durham House St
  CHCR WC2N * 11 F6
Durham Pl CHEL SW5 ......120 E5
Durham Ri WOOL/PLUM SE18 ......127 H5
Durham Rd CAN/RD E16 ......106 C3
  DAGE RM10 ......92 E3
  EA W5 ......116 E3
  EBED/NFELT TW14 ......154 B2
  ED N9 ......36 C4
  EFNCH N2 ......47 J6
  HAYES BR2 ......199 K1
  HOLWY N7 ......67 F1
  HRW HA1 ......60 B2
  MNPK E12 ......89 H2
  RYNPK SW20 ......176 E4
  SCUP DA14 ......186 C1
Durham Rw WCHPL E1 ......105 G4
Durham St LBTH SE11 ......122 A5
Durham Ter BAY/PAD W2 ......101 F5
  PGE/AN SE20 * 181 J3
Durham Yd BETH E2 * 104 D2
Durien Av HDN HA4 ......150 E1
Duriun Wy ERITH DA8 ......150 E1
Durley Av PIN HA5 ......59 J4
Durley Gdns ORP BR6 ......217 H2
Durley Rd STNW/STAM N16 ......68 A4
Durlston Rd CLPT E5 ......68 C6
  KUTN/CMB KT2 ......175 F2
Durnford St SEVS/STOTM N15 ......68 A2
Durning Rd NRWD SE19 ......180 E1
Durnsford Av
  WAND/EARL SW18 ......160 A4
Durnsford Rd FBAR/BDGN N11 ......48 D3
  WAND/EARL SW18 ......159 K4
Durrant Wy ORP BR6 ......216 D3
Durrell Rd FUL/PGN SW6 ......139 H2
Durrington Av RYNPK SW20 ......177 F4
Durrington Park Rd
  RYNPK SW20 ......177 F5
Durrington Rd CLPT E5 ......87 G2
Dursley Cl BKHTH/KID SE3 ......146 C2
Dursley Gdns BKHTH/KID SE3 ......146 C2
Dursley Rd BKHTH/KID SE3 ......146 B3
Durward St WCHPL E1 ......104 D4
Durweston Ms MHST W1U * 9 F1
Durweston St MBLAR W1H 9 F2
Dutch Barn Cl
  STWL/WRAY TW19 ......152 A1
Dutch Gdns KUTN/CMB KT2 ......175 J2
Dutch Yd WAND/EARL SW18 ......159 K1
Duthie St POP/IOD E14 ......106 A6
Dutton St GNWCH SE10 ......145 F2
Duxford Cl HCH RM12 ......93 K4
Dwight Rd WATW WD18 ......26 B2
Dye House La BOW E3 ......87 J6
Dyer's La PUT/ROE SW15 ......138 E5
Dyers Hall Rd WAN E11 ......70 C5
Dyer's Blds FLTT/FETLN EC4A 11 J2
Dyers Wy HARH RM3 ......57 J3
Dyke Dr STMC/STPC BR5 ......202 D4
Dykes Wy HAYES BR2 ......183 J6
Dykewood Cl BXLY DA5 ......170 A5
Dylan Cl BORE WD6 * 29 K1
Dylan Rd BELV DA17 ......129 H3
Dylways CMBW SE5 ......142 E5
Dymchurch Cl CLAY IG5 ......54 A6
  ORP BR6 ......216 E2
Dymock St FUL/PGN SW6 ......140 A4
Dymoke Rd ROM RM1 ......75 H4
Dyneley Rd LEE/GVPK SE12 ......166 B6
Dyne Rd KIL/WHAMP NW6 ......82 D5
Dynevor Rd
  RCHPK/HAM TW10 ......137 F6
  STNW/STAM N16 ......68 A1
Dynham Rd KIL/WHAMP NW6 ......82 E5
Dyott St RSQ WC1B 10 D2
Dysart Av KUTN/CMB KT2 ......174 D5
Dysart St SDTCH EC2A 7 F7
Dyson Ct ALP/SUD HA0 ......79 G2
Dyson Rd FSTGT E7 ......88 D4
  WAN E11 ......70 D3
Dyson's Rd UED N18 ......50 D2

E

Eade Rd FSBYPK N4 ......67 J4
Eagans Cl EFNCH N2 * 47 J5
Eagle Av CHDH RM6 ......74 A5
Eagle Cl BERM/RHTH SE16 ......123 J5
  HCH RM12 ......93 K4
  PEND EN3 ......25 F5
  WLGTN SM6 ......210 E4
Eagle Ct FARR EC1M 12 A1
Eagle Dr CDALE/KGS NW9 ......45 G5
Eagle Hl NRWD SE19 ......180 E2
Eagle La WAN E11 ......70 E1
Eagle Ms IS N1 ......86 A4
Eagle Pl WBPTN SW10 ......120 B6
Eagle Rd ALP/SUD HA0 ......79 K5
  HTHAIR TW6 ......133 J4
Eaglesfield Rd
  WOOL/PLUM SE18 ......147 G2
Eagle St GINN WC1R 11 G2
Eagle Ter WFD IG8 ......53 F3
Eagle Wharf Rd IS N1 ......6 D1
Ealdham Sq ELTH/MOT SE9 ......146 B5
Ealing Gn EA W5 ......116 E2
Ealing Park Gdns EA W5 ......116 D4

Ealing Rd ALP/SUD HA0 ......80 A4
  BOW E3 ......105 K2
  EA W5 ......116 E4
  NTHLT UB5 ......78 A6
Ealing Village EA W5 ......98 A5
Eamont St STJWD NW8 ......2 C2
Eardemont Cl DART DA1 ......150 C5
Eardley Crs ECT SW5 ......119 K5
Eardley Rd BELV DA17 ......129 H5
  STRHM/NOR SW16 ......179 H2
Earldom Rd PUT/ROE SW15 ......139 F5
Earle Gdns KUTN/CMB KT2 ......175 F3
Earlham Gv FSTGT E7 ......88 D3
  WDGN N22 ......49 F3
Earlham St LSQ/SEVD WC2H 10 D4
Earl Ri WOOL/PLUM SE18 ......127 J3
Earl Rd MORT/ESHN SW14 ......137 K5
Earls Court Gdns ECT SW5 ......120 A4
Earls Court Rd ECT SW5 ......119 K4
Earls Court Sq ECT SW5 ......120 A5
Earls Crs HRW HA1 ......60 E1
Earlsferry Wy IS N1 ......84 E5
Earlsfield Rd
  WAND/EARL SW18 ......160 B3
Earlshall Rd ELTH/MOT SE9 ......146 E5
Earlsmead RYLN/HDSTN HA2 ......77 K2
Earlsmead Rd
  SEVS/STOTM N15 ......68 B2
  WLSDN NW10 ......100 A2
Earls Ter KENS W8 ......119 K3
Earlsthorpe Ms BAL SW12 ......161 F1
Earlsthorpe Rd SYD SE26 ......164 A6
Earlstoke Est FSBYE EC1V 6 A4
Earlston Gv HOM E9 ......86 E5
Earl St SDTCH EC2A 13 G1
Earls Wk BCTR RM8 ......91 H2
  KENS W8 ......119 K3
Earlswood Av THHTH CR7 ......196 B2
Earlswood Gdns CLAY IG5 ......54 A6
Earlswood St GNWCH SE10 ......125 H5
Earnshaw St NOXST/BSQ WC1A 10 C3
Earsby St WKENS W14 ......119 H4
Easby Rd MRDN SM4 ......194 A3
Easebourne Rd BCTR RM8 ......91 J3
Easedale Dr HCH RM12 ......93 K3
East Acton Ar ACT W3 * 99 H6
East Acton La ACT W3 ......99 G6
East Arbour St WCHPL E1 ......105 F5
East Av CROY/NA CRO 211 F5
  HYS/HAR UB3 ......113 K1
  MNPK E12 ......89 J5
  STHL UB1 ......95 K6
  WALTH E17 ......69 K1
East Bank STNW/STAM N16 ......68 A2
Eastbank Rd HPTN TW12 ......173 H1
East Barnet Rd BAR EN5 ......21 G5
Eastbourne Av ACT W3 ......99 F5
Eastbourne Gdns
  MORT/ESHN SW14 ......137 K4
Eastbourne Ms BAY/PAD W2 ......101 G5
  CHSWK W4 ......117 K6
  EHAM E6 ......107 K6
  FELT TW13 ......154 C4
  SEVS/STOTM N15 ......68 C6
  SRTFD E15 ......179 J2
Eastbourne Ter BAY/PAD W2 ......101 G5
Eastbournia Av ED N9 ......36 D5
Eastbrook Av DAGE RM10 ......92 E2
  ED N9 ......24 A2
Eastbrook Rd DAGE RM10 ......92 E2
Eastbrook Rd BKHTH/KID SE3 ......146 A2
Eastbury Av BARK IG11 ......90 E6
  EN EN1 ......24 A2
  NTHWD HA6 ......40 C1
Eastbury Gv CHSWK W4 ......118 B5
Eastbury Rd EHAM E6 ......108 A3
  KUTN/CMB KT2 ......175 F3
  NTHWD HA6 ......40 C2
  OXHEY WD19 ......27 G2
  ROMW/RG RM7 ......75 F2
  STMC/STPC BR5 ......201 H5
Eastbury Sq BARK IG11 ......91 F6
Eastbury Ter WCHPL E1 ......105 F4
Eastcastle St GTPST W1W 10 A3
Eastcheap FENCHST EC3M 13 F5
East Churchfield Rd ACT W3 ......118 A1
Eastchurch Rd HTHAIR TW6 ......133 H4
East Cl EA W5 ......98 C3
  EBAR EN4 ......22 A5
  GFD/PVL UB6 ......96 C1
  RAIN RM13 ......111 K3
Eastcote ORP BR6 ......202 A5
Eastcote Av E/WMO/HCT KT8 ......188 C2
  GFD/PVL UB6 ......79 G3
  RYLN/HDSTN HA2 ......60 B6
Eastcote La NTHLT UB5 ......78 A5
  RYLN/HDSTN HA2 ......77 K2
Eastcote La North NTHLT UB5 ......78 A4
Eastcote Rd PIN HA5 ......59 H2
  RSLP HA4 ......58 C4
  RYLN/HDSTN HA2 ......78 B1
  WELL DA16 ......147 J3
Eastcote St BRXN/ST SW9 ......141 K3
Eastcote Vw PIN HA5 ......59 G1
East Ct ALP/SUD HA0 ......61 J6
East Crs EN EN1 ......24 A6
  TRDG/WHET N20 ......33 K6
Eastcroft Rd HOR/WEW KT19 ......207 G5
East Cross Route HOM E9 ......87 H4
Eastdown Pk LEW SE13 ......145 G5
East Dr CAR SM5 ......209 J6
  NTHWD HA6 ......26 C4
  STMC/STPC BR5 ......202 C3
East Duck Lees La PEND EN3 ......25 G5
East Dulwich Gv EDUL SE22 ......143 F6
East Dulwich Rd EDUL SE22 ......143 H5
East End Rd EFNCH N2 ......47 G6
  FNCH N3 ......46 E5

East End Wy *PIN* HA5 .....41 J6
East Entrance *DAGE* RM10 .....110 D1
Eastern Av *GNTH/NBYPK* IG2 .....72 C3
  PIN HA5 .....59 H4
  REDBR IG4 .....71 H5
Eastern Av East *CHDH* RM6 .....74 A1
Eastern Av West *CHDH* RM6 .....57 F6
Eastern Gtwy *CAN/RD* E16 .....107 G6
Eastern Perimeter Rd
  HTHAIR TW6 .....133 H5
Easternville Gdns
  GNTH/NBYPK IG2 .....72 C3
Eastern Wy *ERITHM* DA18 .....129 F1
  THMD SE28 .....128 L1
East Ferry Rd *POP/IOD* E14 .....124 E4
Eastfield Gdns *DAGW* RM10 .....92 C2
  DAGE RM10 .....92 C2
  PEND EN3 .....25 F1
  WALTH E17 .....69 J1
Eastfields *PIN* HA5 .....59 G2
Eastfields Rd *ACT* W3 .....98 E4
  MTCM CR4 .....179 F5
Eastfield St *POP/IOD* E14 .....105 G4
East Gdns *WIM/MER* SW19 .....178 D2
Eastgate Cl *THMD* SE28 .....109 K5
Eastglade *NTHWD* HA6 .....40 C1
  PIN HA5 .....41 K6
East Hall Rd *STMC/STPC* BR5 .....203 F4
Eastham Cl *BAR* EN5 .....20 C5
East Ham Manor Wy *EHAM* E6 .....108 A5
East Harding St
  FLST/FETLN EC4A 11 K3
East Heath Rd *HAMP* NW3 .....83 H1
East Hl *DART* DA1 .....171 J2
  WAND/EARL SW18 .....140 B6
  WBLY HA9 .....62 C6
East Hill Dr *DART* DA1 .....171 J2
Eastholm *GLDGN* NW11 .....65 F1
Eastholme *ERITH* DA8 .....150 A2
Eastholme *HYS/HAR* UB3 .....113 K1
East India Dock Rd
  POP/IOD E14 .....105 J5
East India Wy *CROY/NA* CR0 .....197 G5
Eastlake Rd *CMBW* SE5 .....142 C3
Eastlands Crs *EDUL* SE22 .....163 G1
East La *ALP/SUD* HA0 .....79 J1
  BERM/RHTH SE16 .....123 H2
  KUT/HW KT1 .....174 E6
Eastlea Ms *CAN/RD* E16 .....106 C5
Eastleigh Av *KUT/HW/HDSTN* HA2 .....60 B6
Eastleigh Cl *BELMT* SM2 .....209 F5
  CRICK NW2 .....81 G1
Eastleigh Rd *BXLYHN* DA7 .....149 K3
  WALTH E17 .....51 H5
Eastleigh Wy
  EBED/NFELT TW14 .....153 K3
Eastman Rd *ACT* W3 .....118 A2
East Md *RSLP* HA4 .....77 H1
Eastmead Av *GFD/PVL* UB6 .....96 B2
Eastmead Cl *BMLY* BR1 .....184 D5
Eastmearn Rd *DUL* SE21 .....162 D4
Eastmoor Pl
  WOOL/PLUM SE18 .....126 C3
Eastmoor St *CHARL* SE7 .....126 C4
East Mount St *WCHPL* E1 * 104 D4
Eastney Rd *CROY/NA* CR0 .....196 C5
Eastney St *GNWCH* SE10 .....125 J5
Eastnor Rd *ELTH/MOT* SE9 .....167 H5
Easton St *FSBYW* WC1X 5 J6
East Park Cl *CHDH* RM6 .....73 K2
East Pl *WNWD* SE27 .....162 D6
East Poultry Av *FARR* EC1M 12 A2
East Rd *BRYLDS* KT5 .....191 G5
East Rd *CHDH* RM6 .....74 A2
  EBAR EN4 .....34 A3
  EBED/NFELT TW14 .....153 G2
  EDGW HA8 .....44 E4
  EFNCH N2 .....47 J4
  IS N1 .....7 F4
  KUTN/CMB KT2 .....175 F4
  PEND EN3 .....24 E1
  ROMW/RG RM7 .....75 F4
  SRTFD E15 .....88 E6
  WDR/YW UB7 .....112 C4
  WELL DA16 .....148 C3
  WIM/MER SW19 .....178 B2
East Rochester Wy
  BFN/LL DA15 .....146 F6
  DART DA1 .....170 A2
East Rw *NKENS* W10 .....100 C3
  WAN E11 .....70 E3
East Sheen Av
  MORT/ESHN SW14 .....138 A6
Eastside Rd *GLDGN* NW11 .....64 D1
East Smithfield *WAP* E1W 13 K6
East St *BARK* IG11 .....90 C6
  BMLY BR1 .....183 K5
  BTFD TW8 .....136 D1
  BXLYHN DA7 .....149 H5
  WALW SE17 .....122 D5
East Surrey Gv *PECK* SE15 .....143 G1
East Tenter St *WCHPL* E1 .....13 K4
East Ter *BFN/LL* DA15 * 167 K3
East Towers *PIN* HA5 .....59 H5
East V *ACT* W3 * 118 C1
East Vw *BAR* EN5 .....20 D4
  CHING E4 .....52 A1
Eastview Av
  WOOL/PLUM SE18 .....147 K1
Eastville Av *GLDGN* NW11 .....64 D4
East Wk *EBAR* EN4 .....34 A3
  HYS/HAR UB3 .....113 K1
East Wy *CROY/NA* CR0 .....198 B6
  HYS/HAR UB3 .....113 K1
  RSLP HA4 .....58 E5

Eastway *HAYES* BR2 .....199 K4
  HOM E9 .....87 G6
  LEY E10 .....87 J2
  MRDN SM4 .....193 G2
  WAN E11 .....71 F2
  WLGTN SM6 .....210 C2
Eastway Crs *RYLN/HDSTN* HA2 .....60 B6
Eastwell Cl *BECK* BR3 .....182 B4
Eastwood Cl *SWFD* E18 .....52 E5
  TOTM N17 * 50 D3
Eastwood Dr *RAIN* RM13 .....111 K5
Eastwood Rd *GDMY/SEVK* IG3 .....73 G4
  MUSWH N10 .....48 A5
  SWFD E18 .....52 E5
Eastwood St
  STRHM/NOR SW16 .....179 H2
Eatington Rd *LEY* E10 .....70 B2
Eaton Cl *BGVA* SW1W 15 G6
  STAN HA7 .....29 H6
Eaton Dr *BRXN/ST* SW9 .....142 C5
  CRW RM5 .....56 D3
  KUTN/CMB KT2 .....175 H5
Eaton Gdns *DAGW* RM9 .....92 A5
Eaton Ga *BGVA* SW1W 15 G6
Eaton La *BGVA* SW1W 15 K5
Eaton Ms North *KTBR* SW1X 15 H6
Eaton Ms South *BGVA* SW1W 15 H6
Eaton Ms West *BGVA* SW1W 15 H6
Eaton Park Rd *PLMGR* N13 .....35 G4
Eaton Pl *KTBR* SW1X 15 G6
Eaton Ri *EA* W5 .....98 A5
  WAN E11 .....71 G2
Eaton Rd *BELMT* SM2 .....209 H4
  EN EN1 .....24 A4
  HDN NW4 .....64 A2
  ISLW TW7 .....135 J5
  SCUP DA14 .....168 E4
Eaton Rw *BGVA* SW1W 15 J4
Eatons Md *CHING* E4 .....37 J4
Eaton Sq *BGVA* SW1W 15 H6
Eaton Ter *BOW* E3 * 105 G2
  KTBR SW1X 15 G6
Eaton Terrace Ms *KTBR* SW1X 15 G6
Eatonville Rd *TOOT* SW17 .....160 E4
Eatonville Vls *TOOT* SW17 .....160 E4
Ebbisham Dr *VX/NE* SW8 .....122 A6
Ebbisham Rd *WPK* KT4 .....193 F6
Ebbsfleet Rd *CRICK* NW2 .....82 C3
Ebdon Wy *BKHTH/KID* SE3 .....146 A4
Ebenezer St *IS* N1 .....6 E4
Ebenezer Wk *MTCM* CR4 .....179 H4
Ebley Cl *PECK* SE15 .....123 G6
Ebner St *WAND/EARL* SW18 .....140 A6
Ebor St *BETH* E2 .....7 J6
Ebrington Rd
  KTN/HRWW/W HA3 .....61 J3
Ebsworth St *FSTH* SE23 .....164 A2
Eburne Rd *HOLWY* N7 .....84 E1
Ebury Br *BGVA* SW1W 121 G5
Ebury Bridge Rd *BGVA* SW1W 121 F5
Ebury Cl *HAYES* BR2 .....215 J1
  NTHWD HA6 .....40 A1
Ebury Ms *BGVA* SW1W 15 J5
Ebury Ms East *BGVA* SW1W 15 J5
Ebury Sq *BGVA* SW1W 15 J7
Ebury St *BGVA* SW1W 15 J5
Ecclesbourne Cl *PLMGR* N13 .....49 G1
Ecclesbourne Gdns *PLMGR* N13 .....49 G1
Ecclesbourne Rd *IS* N1 .....85 J5
  THHTH CR7 .....196 D2
Eccles Rd *BTSEA* SW11 .....140 E5
Eccleston Cl *EBAR* EN4 .....21 J6
  ORP BR6 * 201 J5
Eccleston Crs *CDNH* RM6 .....73 H4
Eccleston Ct *WBLY* HA9 .....80 A3
Ecclestone Ms *WBLY* HA9 .....80 A3
Ecclestone Pl *WBLY* HA9 .....80 B3
Eccleston Ms *KTBR* SW1X 15 H5
Eccleston Pl *BGVA* SW1W 15 J7
Eccleston Rd *HNWL* W7 .....97 G6
Eccleston Sq *PIM* SW1V 15 K7
Eccleston Square Ms *PIM* SW1V 15 K7
Eccleston St *BGVA* SW1W 15 H5
Echelforde Dr *ASHF* TW15 .....152 D6
Echo Hts *CHING* E4 * 37 K3
Eckford St *IS* N1 .....6 A1
Eckstein Rd *BTSEA* SW11 .....140 D5
Eclipse Rd *PLSTW* E13 .....107 F4
Ector Rd *CAT* SE6 .....165 H4
Edans Ct *SHB* W12 .....118 C2
Edbrooke Rd *MV/WKIL* W9 .....100 E3
Eddiscombe Rd *FUL/PGN* SW6 .....139 J3
Eddy Cl *ROMW/RG* RM7 .....74 D3
Eddystone Rd *BROCKY* SE4 .....144 B6
Ede Cl *HSLW* TW5 .....134 E4
Edenbridge Cl
  BERM/RHTH SE16 * 123 J5
  STMC/STPC BR5 .....202 E1
Eden Cl *ALP/SUD* HA0 .....79 K6
  BXLY DA5 .....170 A6
  HAMP NW3 .....64 E6
  KENS W8 .....119 K3
  PEND EN3 .....25 J1
Edencourt Rd
  STRHM/NOR SW16 .....179 G2
Edendale Rd *BXLYHN* DA7 .....150 A2
Edenfield Gdns *WPK* KT4 .....207 H1
Eden Gv *HOLWY* N7 .....85 F3
  WALTH E17 .....69 K1
Edenham Wy *NKENS* W10 .....100 D3
Edenhurst Av *FUL/PGN* SW6 .....139 J4
Eden Pde *BECK* BR3 * 198 B1
Eden Park Av *BECK* BR3 .....198 B1
Eden Rd *BECK* BR3 .....198 A1
  BXLY DA5 .....169 K6
  CROY/NA CR0 .....211 K2
  WALTH E17 .....69 K1
  WNWD SE27 .....180 C1
Edensor Rd *CHSWK* W4 .....138 B1
Eden St *KUT/HW* KT1 .....174 E5
Edenvale Rd *MTCM* CR4 .....179 F3
Edenvale St *FUL/PGN* SW6 .....140 A3
Eden Wk *KUT/HW* KT1 * 175 F5

Eden Wy *BECK* BR3 .....198 D2
Ederline Av *STRHM/NOR* SW16 .....180 A6
Edgar Kail Wy *CMBW* SE5 .....143 F4
Edgarley Ter *FUL/PGN* SW6 * 139 H2
Edgar Rd *BOW* E3 .....105 K2
  HSLWW TW4 .....154 E2
Edgeborough Wy *BMLY* BR1 .....184 C4
Edgebury *CHST* BR7 .....167 G6
Edgecombe Cl *KUTN/CMB* KT2 .....176 A3
Edgecombe *SAND/SEL* CR2 .....213 F6
Edgecote Cl *ACT* W3 .....117 K1
Edgefield Av *BARK* IG11 .....91 F5
Edge Hl *WIM/MER* SW19 .....177 G5
  WOOL/PLUM SE18 .....127 G6
Edge Hill Av *GLDGN* NW11 .....64 E1
Edgehill Ct *WOT/HER* KT12 * 188 B5
Edgehill Gdns *DAGE* RM10 .....92 C2
Edgehill Rd *CHST* BR7 .....167 H5
  MTCM CR4 .....179 G5
  WEA W13 .....97 J5
Edgeley La *CLAP* SW4 .....141 J4
Edgeley Rd *CLAP* SW4 .....141 H4
Edgel St *WAND/EARL* SW18 .....140 A5
Edgepoint Cl *WNWD* SE27 * 180 C1
Edge St *KENS* W8 .....119 K1
Edgewood Dr *ORP* BR6 .....217 F3
Edgewood Gn *CROY/NA* CR0 .....198 A5
Edgeworth Av *HDN* NW4 .....63 J2
Edgeworth Cl *HDN* NW4 .....63 J2
Edgeworth Rd *EBAR* EN4 .....21 J5
  ELTH/MOT SE9 .....146 B5
Edgington Rd
  STRHM/NOR SW16 .....179 J2
Edgington Wy *SCUP* DA14 .....186 D3
Edgware Ct *EDGW* HA8 * 44 C1
Edgwarebury Gdns *EDGW* HA8 .....44 C1
Edgwarebury La *EDGW* HA8 .....30 B2
Edgware Rd *BAY/PAD* W2 .....2 A7
  MTCM CR4 .....179 G5
Edgware Rd Burnt Oak
  Broadway *EDGW* HA8 .....44 D3
Edgware Rd High St *EDGW* HA8 .....44 C2
Edgware Rd The Hyde
  CDALE/KGS NW9 .....63 H2
Edgware Wy (Watford By-Pass)
  EDGW HA8 .....30 A4
Edinburgh Cl *BETH* E2 .....104 E1
  PIN HA5 .....59 J4
Edinburgh Ct *KUT/HW* KT1 * 175 F6
Edinburgh Ga *BAY/PAD* W2 .....14 E2
Edinburgh Rd *HNWL* W7 .....116 A2
  PLSTW E13 .....107 F1
  SUT SM1 .....194 B6
  UED N18 * 50 C1
  WALTH E17 .....69 J2
Edinburgh's Dr *ROMW/RG* RM7 .....74 E1
Edington Rd *ABYW* SE2 .....128 C3
  PEND EN3 .....24 E3
Edison Av *HCH* RM12 .....75 H5
Edison Cl *HCH* RM12 .....75 H5
Edison Dr *STHL* UB1 .....96 B5
  WBLY HA9 .....62 A6
Edison Gv *WOOL/PLUM* SE18 .....148 A1
Edison Rd *CEND/HSY/T* N8 .....66 D3
  HAYES BR2 .....183 K5
  PEND EN3 .....25 H3
  WELL DA16 .....148 A2
Edis St *CAMTN* NW1 .....84 A6
Edith Cavell Wy
  WOOL/PLUM SE18 .....146 D2
Edith Gv *WBPTN* SW10 .....120 B6
Edithna St *BRXN/ST* SW9 .....141 K4
Edith Nesbit Wk
  ELTH/MOT SE9 .....146 D5
Edith Rd *CHDH* RM6 .....73 K4
  EHAM E6 .....89 H1
  FBAR/BDGN N11 .....48 D3
  ORP BR6 .....217 G3
  SNWD SE25 .....196 E2
  SRTFD E15 .....88 B4
  WIM/MER SW19 .....178 A2
  WKENS W14 .....119 H4
Edith Rw *FUL/PGN* SW6 .....140 A2
Edith St *BETH* E2 .....7 K2
Edith Ter *WBPTN* SW10 * 140 B1
Edith Vls *WKENS* W14 .....119 J4
Edison Cl *WALTH* E17 .....69 K2
Edmeston Cl *HOM* E9 .....87 G4
Edmund Halley Wy
  GNWCH SE10 .....125 H2
Edmund Hurst Dr *EHAM* E6 .....108 B4
Edmund Rd *MTCM* CR4 .....178 E6
  RAIN RM13 .....111 G2
  STMC/STPC BR5 .....202 D3
  WELL DA16 .....148 B4
Edmunds Av *STMC/STPC* BR5 .....186 E6
Edmunds Cl *YEAD* UB4 .....95 G4
Edmund St *CMBW* SE5 .....142 E1
Edmunds Wk *EFNCH* N2 .....65 J1
Edna Rd *RYNPK* SW20 .....177 G5
Edna St *BTSEA* SW11 .....140 D2
Edrick Rd *EDGW* HA8 .....44 E2
Edrick Wk *EDGW* HA8 .....44 E2
Edridge Rd *CROY/NA* CR0 .....211 J1
Edward Av *CHING* E4 .....51 K1
  MRDN SM4 .....194 C2
Edward Cl *ED* N9 .....36 B2
  HPTN TW12 .....173 H1
Edward Ct *CAN/RD* E16 .....106 E4
Edwardes Pl *WKENS* W14 .....119 J3
Edwardes Sq *KENS* W8 .....119 J3
Edward Gv *EBAR* EN4 .....21 H6
Edward Mann Cl East
  WCHPL E1 * 105 F5
Edward Mann Cl West
  WCHPL E1 * 105 F5
Edward Ms *CAMTN* NW1 * 3 K4
Edward Pl *DEPT* SE8 .....124 C6
Edward Rd *BMLY* BR1 .....184 A3
  CHDH RM6 .....74 A3
  CHST BR7 .....185 G1
  CROY/NA CR0 .....197 F4

EBAR EN4 .....21 H6
EBED/NFELT TW14 .....133 G6
HPTN TW12 .....173 H1
NTHLT UB5 .....95 G1
PGE/AN SE20 .....182 A3
RYLN/HDSTN HA2 .....42 C6
WALTH E17 .....69 F1
Edwards Av *RSLP* HA4 .....77 G3
Edwards Cl *WPK* KT4 .....193 G6
Edward's La *STNW/STAM* N16 .....67 K6
  .....85 H5
Edward Sq *IS* N1 .....5 G1
Edwards Rd *BELV* DA17 .....129 H4
Edward St *CAN/RD* E16 .....106 E3
  DEPT SE8 .....144 C1
  NWCR SE14 .....144 C1
Edward's Wy *LEW* SE13 .....146 B2
Edward Temme Av *SRTFD* E15 .....88 D5
Edward Tyler Rd
  LEE/GVPK SE12 .....166 A4
Edward Wy *ASHF* TW15 .....152 C4
Edwina Gdns *REDBR* IG4 .....71 J2
Edwin Av *EHAM* E6 .....108 A1
Edwin Cl *BXLYHN* DA7 .....149 G6
Edwin Hall Pl *LEW* SE13 .....165 G1
  RDART DA2 .....170 E5
Edwin Pl *CROY/NA* CR0 * 196 E6
Edwin Rd *EDGW* HA8 .....45 F2
  WHTN TW2 .....155 K3
Edwin's Md *HOM* E9 .....87 G2
Edwin St *CAN/RD* E16 .....106 E4
  WCHPL E1 .....104 E3
Edwin Ware Ct *PIN* HA5 * 41 G5
Edwyn Cl *BAR* EN5 .....31 K1
Effie Pl *FUL/PGN* SW6 .....139 K1
Effie Rd *FUL/PGN* SW6 .....139 K1
Effingham Cl *BELMT* SM2 .....209 F5
Effingham Rd *CEND/HSY/T* N8 .....67 G2
  CROY/NA CR0 .....196 A4
  LEW SE13 .....145 H6
  SURB KT6 .....190 C4
Effort St *TOOT* SW17 .....178 E1
Effra Pde *BRXS/STRHM* SW2 .....142 B6
Effra Rd *BRXS/STRHM* SW2 .....142 B6
  WIM/MER SW19 .....178 A2
Egan Wy *HYS/HAR* UB3 .....94 C6
Egbert St *CAMTN* NW1 .....84 A6
Egerton Cl *DART* DA1 .....170 C6
  PIN HA5 .....58 E1
Egerton Crs *CHEL* SW3 .....14 D6
Egerton Dr *GNWCH* SE10 .....144 E2
Egerton Gdns *CHEL* SW3 .....14 C6
  GDMY/SEVK IG3 .....91 F1
  HDN NW4 .....45 K3
  WEA W13 .....97 H5
  WLSDN NW10 .....82 A6
Egerton Gardens Ms *CHEL* SW3 .....14 D5
Egerton Pl *CHEL* SW3 * 14 D6
Egerton Rd *ALP/SUD* HA0 .....80 D5
  NWMAL KT3 .....192 C1
  SNWD SE25 .....181 F6
  STNW/STAM N16 * 68 B4
  WHTN TW2 .....155 K2
Egerton Ter *CHEL* SW3 .....14 D5
Egham Cl *CHEAM* SM3 .....193 H6
Egham Crs *CHEAM* SM3 .....208 B1
Egham Rd *PLSTW* E13 .....107 F4
Eglantine Rd
  WAND/EARL SW18 .....140 B6
Egleston Rd *MRDN* SM4 .....194 A3
Eglington Rd *CHING* E4 .....38 B2
Eglinton Hl *WOOL/PLUM* SE18 .....127 G6
Eglinton Rd *WOOL/PLUM* SE18 .....127 F6
Egliston Ms *PUT/ROE* SW15 .....139 F4
Egliston Rd *PUT/ROE* SW15 .....139 F4
Eglon Ms *CAMTN* NW1 .....83 K6
Egmont Av *SURB* KT6 .....191 H5
Egmont Rd *BELMT* SM2 .....209 G5
  NWMAL KT3 .....192 C1
  SURB KT6 .....191 H5
  WOT/HER KT12 .....188 A4
Egmont St *NWCR* SE14 .....144 A1
Egremont Rd *WNWD* SE27 .....162 B5
Egret Wy *YEAD* UB4 .....95 H4
Eider Cl *EBED/NFELT* TW14 * 153 H2
  YEAD UB4 * 95 H4
Eighteenth Rd *MTCM* CR4 .....195 K1
Eighth Av *HYS/HAR* UB3 .....113 K1
  MNPK E12 .....89 K2
Eileen Rd *SNWD* SE25 .....196 E2
Eindhoven Cl *MTCM* CR4 .....195 F5
Eisenhower Dr *EHAM* E6 .....107 J4
Elaine Gv *KTTN* NW5 .....84 A3
Elam Cl *CMBW* SE5 .....142 C3
Elam St *CMBW* SE5 .....142 C3
Eland Rd *BTSEA* SW11 .....140 E4
  CROY/NA CR0 .....211 H1
Elba Pl *WALW* SE17 * 18 D6
Elberon Av *CROY/NA* CR0 .....195 H5
Elbe St *FUL/PGN* SW6 .....140 B3
Elborough Rd *SNWD* SE25 .....197 H2
Elborough St
  WAND/EARL SW18 .....159 K3
Elbury Dr *CAN/RD* E16 .....106 E5
Elcho St *BTSEA* SW11 .....140 D1
Elcot Av *PECK* SE15 .....143 J1
Elderberry Gv *WNWD* SE27 * 162 D6
Elderberry Rd *EA* W5 .....117 F2
Elderberry Wy *EHAM* E6 .....107 K2
Elder Cl *BFN/LL* DA15 .....168 A3
  WCHMH N21 .....35 F2
Elderfield Pl *TOOT* SW17 .....161 H1
Elderfield Rd *CLPT* E5 .....87 F2
Elderfield Wk *WAN* E11 .....71 F2
Elderflower Wy *SRTFD* E15 .....88 C6
Elder Oak Cl *PGE/AN* SE20 .....181 J4
Elder Rd *WNWD* SE27 .....180 D1
Elderslie Cl *BECK* BR3 .....198 D3
Elderslie Rd *ELTH/MOT* SE9 .....147 F6
Elder St *WCHPL* E1 .....13 J1
Elderton Rd *SYD* SE26 .....164 B6
Eldertree Wy *MTCM* CR4 .....179 G4

Elder Wk *IS* N1 .....85 H6
Eldon Av *CROY/NA* CR0 .....197 K6
  HEST TW5 .....135 F1
Eldon Gv *HAMP* NW3 .....83 H3
Eldon Pde *SNWD* SE25 * 197 J1
Eldon Pk *SNWD* SE25 .....197 J1
Eldon Rd *ED* N9 .....36 E4
  KENS W8 .....120 A3
  WALTH E17 .....69 H1
  WDGN N22 .....49 H4
Eldon St *LVPST* EC2M 13 F2
Eldon Wy *WLSDN* NW10 .....98 D1
Eldred Dr *STMC/STPC* BR5 .....202 E6
Eldridge Cl *EBED/NFELT* TW14 .....153 J2
Eleanora Ter *SUT* SM1 * 209 G3
Eleanor Cl *TOTM* N17 .....50 B6
Eleanor Crs *MLHL* NW7 .....32 B6
Eleanor Gdns *BAR* EN5 .....20 B6
  DAGW RM9 .....92 B1
Eleanor Gv *BARN* SW13 .....138 D4
Eleanor Rd *FBAR/BDGN* N11 .....48 E2
  HACK E8 .....86 D5
  SRTFD E15 .....88 D4
Eleanor St *BOW* E3 .....105 J2
Electra Av *HTHAIR* TW6 .....133 J4
Electric Av *BRXN/ST* SW9 .....142 B5
Electric La *BRXN/ST* SW9 * 142 B5
Electric Pde *SURB* KT6 .....190 E3
Elephant & Castle *STHWK* SE1 .....18 B6
Elephant La *BERM/RHTH* SE16 .....123 K2
Elephant Rd *WALW* SE17 .....18 C5
Elers Rd *HYS/HAR* UB3 .....113 F4
  WEA W13 .....116 D2
Eley Rd *UED* N18 .....51 F1
Elfindale Rd *HNHL* SE24 .....142 D6
Elfin Gv *TEDD* TW11 .....174 A1
Elford Cl *BKHTH/KID* SE3 .....146 B5
Elfort Rd *HBRY* N5 .....85 G2
Elfrida Crs *CAT* SE6 .....164 D6
Elf Rw *WAP* E1W 104 E6
Elfwine Rd *HNWL* W7 .....96 E4
Elgal Cl *ORP* BR6 .....216 B3
Elgar Av *BRYLDS* KT5 .....191 J5
  EA W5 .....117 F2
  STRHM/NOR SW16 .....179 K6
  WLSDN NW10 .....81 F4
Elgar Cl *BKHH* IG9 .....39 H4
  BORE WD6 .....29 J2
  DEPT SE8 .....144 D1
  PLSTW E13 .....107 G1
Elgar St *BERM/RHTH* SE16 .....124 B2
Elgin Av *KTN/HRWW/W* HA3 .....43 H5
  MV/WKIL W9 .....100 E3
  WAE W12 .....118 E3
Elgin Cl *SHB* W12 .....118 E2
Elgin Crs *HTHAIR* TW6 .....133 H5
  NTGHL W11 .....100 D5
Elgin Dr *NTHWD* HA6 .....40 C3
Elginmeads South
  MV/WKIL W9 * 101 F2
Elgin Ms *NTGHL* W11 .....100 C5
Elgin Ms North *MV/WKIL* W9 * 101 F2
Elgin Ms South
  MV/WKIL W9 * 101 F2
Elgin Rd *CROY/NA* CR0 .....197 G6
  GDMY/SEVK IG3 .....72 E5
  SUT SM1 .....209 G1
  WDGN N22 .....48 C5
  WLGTN SM6 .....210 C4
Elgood Av *NTHWD* HA6 .....40 E3
Elgood Cl *NTGHL* W11 .....100 C6
Elham Cl *BMLY* BR1 .....184 C3
Elia Ms *IS* N1 .....6 A2
Elias Pl *LBTH* SE11 .....122 B6
Elia St *IS* N1 .....6 A3
Elibank Rd *ELTH/MOT* SE9 .....147 F5
Elim St *STHWK* SE1 .....19 G4
Elim Wy *PLSTW* E13 .....106 D2
Eliot Bank *FSTH* SE23 .....163 J4
Eliot Dr *RYLN/HDSTN* HA2 .....60 B6
Eliot Gdns *PUT/ROE* SW15 .....138 D5
Eliot Hl *LEW* SE13 .....145 F3
Eliot Pk *LEW* SE13 .....145 F3
Eliot Pl *BKHTH/KID* SE3 .....145 H5
Eliot Rd *DAGW* RM9 .....91 K2
Eliot V *BKHTH/KID* SE3 .....145 G5
Elizabethan Wy
  STWL/WRAY TW19 .....152 A2
Elizabeth Av *ENC/FH* EN2 .....23 H4
  IL IG1 .....72 D6
  IS N1 .....85 J5
Elizabeth Barnes Ct
  FUL/PGN SW6 * 140 A3
Elizabeth Br *BGVA* SW1W 15 J7
Elizabeth Cl *BAR* EN5 .....20 B4
  MV/WKIL W9 .....101 G3
  ROMW/RG RM7 .....56 D4
  SUT SM1 .....208 D2
Elizabeth Clyde Cl
  SEVS/STOTM N15 .....68 A1
Elizabeth Cottages
  RCH/KEW TW9 .....137 G2
Elizabeth Gdns *ACT* W3 .....118 C1
  ISLW TW7 .....136 B5
  STAN HA7 .....43 J2
  SUN TW16 .....172 B6
Elizabeth Ms *HAMP* NW3 .....83 J4
Elizabeth Pl *SEVS/STOTM* N15 * 67 K1
Elizabeth Ride *ED* N9 .....36 D2
Elizabeth Rd *EHAM* E6 .....89 H4
  RAIN RM13 .....111 K4
  SEVS/STOTM N15 .....68 A2
Elizabeth Sq
  BERM/RHTH SE16 .....105 G6
Elizabeth St *BGVA* SW1W 15 H6
Elizabeth Wy *FELT* TW13 .....154 B6
  NTGHL W11 * 180 E3
  STMC/STPC BR5 .....202 D2
Elkington Rd *PLSTW* E13 .....107 F3
The Elkins *ROM* RM1 .....57 G5
Elkstone Rd *NKENS* W10 .....100 D4
Ella Cl *BECK* BR3 .....182 D5
Ellaline Rd *HMSMTH* W6 .....119 G6
Ellanby Crs *UED* N18 .....50 D1
Elland Rd *PECK* SE15 .....143 K5
  WOT/HER KT12 .....188 C6
Ella Rd *CEND/HSY/T* N8 .....66 E4
Ellement Cl *PIN* HA5 .....59 H2

Ellenborough Pl
  PUT/ROE SW15 ...138 D5
Ellenborough Rd SCUP DA14 ...186 E2
  WDGN N22 ...49 J4
Ellenbridge Wy SAND/SEL CR2 ...212 A6
Ellen Ct ED N9 ...36 E4
Ellen St WCHPL E1 ...104 C5
Ellen Webb Dr
  KTN/HRWW/W HA3 ...42 E6
Elleray Rd TEDD TW11 ...174 A2
Ellerby St FUL/PGN SW6 ...139 G2
Ellerdale Rd HAMP NW3 ...83 G3
Ellerdale St LEW SE13 ...144 E5
Ellerdine Rd HSLW TW3 ...135 H5
Ellerker Gdns
  RCHPK/HAM TW10 ...157 F1
Ellerman Av WHTN TW2 ...154 E5
Ellerslie Rd SHB W12 ...118 E1
Ellerton Gdns DAGW RM9 ...91 J5
Ellerton Rd BARN SW13 ...138 D2
  DAGW RM9 ...91 J5
  RYNPK SW20 ...176 D3
  SURB KT6 ...191 G6
  WAND/EARL SW18 ...160 C3
Ellery Rd NRWD SE19 ...180 E2
Ellery St PECK SE15 ...143 J3
Ellesborough Cl OXHEY WD19 ...41 G1
Ellesmere Av BECK BR3 ...182 E5
  MLHL NW7 ...31 F5
Ellesmere Cl RSLP HA4 ...58 A4
  WAN E11 ...70 D2
Ellesmere Gdns REDBR IG4 ...71 J2
Ellesmere Gv BAR EN5 ...20 D6
Ellesmere Rd BOW E3 ...105 C1
  GFD/PVL UB6 ...96 C3
  TWK TW1 ...156 D1
  WLSDN NW10 ...81 H3
Ellesmere St POP/IOD E14 ...105 K5
Ellies Ms ASHF TW15 ...152 B4
Ellingfort Rd HACK E8 ...86 D5
Ellingham Rd CHSGTN KT9 ...205 K4
  SHB W12 ...118 D2
  WAN E11 ...88 B2
Ellington Rd FELT TW13 ...153 J6
  HSLW TW3 ...135 G3
  MUSWH N10 ...66 B1
Ellington St HOLWY N7 ...85 G4
Elliot Cl WLSDN NW10 ...81 J5
Elliot Rd BRXN/ST SW9 ...142 C1
  CHSWK W4 ...118 B4
  HAYES BR2 ...200 C1
  STAN HA7 ...43 G5
  THHTH CR7 ...196 C1
Elliott's Pl IS N1 ...6 B1
Elliott Sq HAMP NW3 ...83 J5
Elliott's Row LBTH SE11 ...18 B6
Elliott Av RAIN RM13 ...111 J4
Ellis Cl CRICK NW2 ...82 A4
  EDGW HA8 ...45 G2
  ELTH/MOT SE9 ...167 H4
Elliscombe Mt CHARL SE7 * ...126 B6
Elliscombe Rd CHARL SE7 ...126 B5
Ellisfield Dr PUT/ROE SW15 ...158 C2
Ellison Gdns NWDGN UB2 ...114 E4
Ellison Rd BARN SW13 ...138 C3
  BFN/LL DA15 ...167 J3
  STRHM/NOR SW16 ...179 J3
Ellis Rd MTCM CR4 ...194 E3
  NWDGN UB2 ...115 H1
Ellis St KTBR SW1X ...15 F6
Ellis Wy DART DA1 * ...171 J4
Ellmore Cl HARH RM3 ...57 K4
Ellora Rd STRHM/NOR SW16 ...179 J1
Ellsworth St BETH E2 * ...104 D2
Elmar Rd SEVS/STOTM N15 ...67 K1
Elm Av EA W5 ...117 F1
  OXHEY WD19 ...27 J2
  RSLP HA4 ...58 E5

RYLN/HDSTN HA2 ...42 A6
Elmcroft Dr CHSGTN KT9 ...206 A1
Elmcroft Gdns CDALE/KGS NW9 ...62 C2
Elmcroft Rd ORP BR6 ...202 B4
Elmcroft St CLPT E5 ...86 E2
Elmdale Rd PLMGR N13 ...49 F1
Elmdene BRYLDS KT5 ...191 K5
Elmdene Cl BECK BR3 ...198 C2
Elmdene Rd
  WOOL/PLUM SE18 ...127 G5
Elmdon Rd HEST TW5 ...134 C3
  HTHAIR TW6 ...133 J4
Elm Dr RYLN/HDSTN HA2 ...60 B5
  SUN TW16 ...172 B5
Elmer Cl ENC/FH EN2 ...23 F4
Elmer Gdns EDGW HA8 ...44 D3
  ISLW TW7 ...135 J4
  RAIN RM13 ...93 J5
Elmer Rd CAT SE6 ...165 F2
Elmer's Dr TEDD TW11 ...174 C2
Elmers End Rd BECK BR3 ...181 K6
Elmerside Rd BECK BR3 ...198 B1
Elmers Rd CROY/NA CR0 ...197 H4
Elmfield Av CEND/HSY/T N8 ...66 E2
  TEDD TW11 ...174 A1
Elmfield Cl HRW HA1 ...60 E6
Elmfield Pk BMLY BR1 ...183 K6
Elmfield Rd BAL SW12 ...161 G4
  BMLY BR1 ...183 K6
  CHING E4 ...38 A4
  EFNCH N2 ...47 H6
  NWDGN UB2 ...114 D3
  WALTH E17 ...69 F3
Elmfield Wy MV/WKIL W9 ...100 E4
  SAND/SEL CR2 ...212 B6
Elm Friars Wk CAMTN NW1 ...84 D5
Elm Gdns EFNCH N2 ...47 G6
  ENC/FH EN2 ...23 K1
  ESH/CLAY KT10 ...205 F4
  MTCM CR4 ...195 J1
Elmgate Av FELT TW13 ...154 A5
Elmgate Gdns EDGW HA8 ...44 E1
Elm Gn ACT W3 ...99 G5
Elmgreen Cl SRTFD E15 ...88 C6
Elm Gv CEND/HSY/T N8 ...66 E3
  CRICK NW2 ...82 B2
  ERITH DA8 ...150 A1
  KUTN/CMB KT2 ...175 F4
  ORP BR6 ...202 A5
  PECK SE15 ...143 H5
  RYLN/HDSTN HA2 ...60 A4
  SUT SM1 ...209 F2
  WIM/MER SW19 ...177 H5
Elmgrove Crs HRW HA1 ...61 F2
Elmgrove Gdns HRW HA1 ...61 G2
Elm Grove Pde WLGTN SM6 ...210 A1
Elm Grove Rd BARN SW13 ...138 D3
  EA W5 ...117 F2
Elmgrove Rd CROY/NA CR0 ...197 J4
  KTN/HRWW/W HA3 ...61 G2
  PLMGR N13 ...48 E1
Elm Hall Gdns WAN E11 ...71 F3
Elm Hatch PIN HA5 ...41 K3
Elmhurst BELV DA17 ...129 F6
Elmhurst Av EFNCH N2 * ...47 H6
  MTCM CR4 ...179 F3
Elmhurst Crs EFNCH N2 ...47 H6
Elmhurst Dr SWFD E18 ...52 E5
Elmhurst Rd ELTH/MOT SE9 ...166 D4
  FSTGT E7 ...89 F5
  TOTM N17 ...50 A5
Elmhurst St CLAP SW4 ...141 J4
Elmhurst Wy LOU IG10 ...39 K2
Elmington Cl BXLY DA5 ...169 J2
Elmington Est CMBW SE5 ...142 E1
Elmington Rd CMBW SE5 ...142 E2
Elmira St LEW SE13 ...144 E4
Elm La CAT SE6 ...164 C4
Elmlee Cl CHST BR7 ...184 E2
Elmley St WOOL/PLUM SE18 ...127 J4
Elmore Cl ALP/SUD HA0 ...98 B1
Elmore Rd PEND EN3 ...25 F2
  WAN E11 ...88 A1
Elmore St IS N1 ...85 K5
Elm Pde SCUP DA14 * ...168 B6
Elm Pk BRXS/STRHM SW2 ...162 A1
  STAN HA7 ...43 H1
Elm Park Av HCH RM12 ...93 K2
  SEVS/STOTM N15 ...68 B2
Elm Park Gdns HDN NW4 ...64 B2
  WBPTN SW10 ...120 C5
Elm Park La CHEL SW3 ...120 C6
Elm Park Rd CHEL SW3 ...120 C6
  FNCH N3 ...46 D5
  LEY E10 ...69 G5
  PIN HA5 ...41 H6
  SNWD SE25 ...181 G6
  WCHMH N21 ...35 J2
Elm Pd SKENS SW7 ...120 D5
Elm Pl SKENS SW7 ...120 C5

Elmscott Gdns WCHMH N21 ...35 J1
Elmscott Rd BMLY BR1 ...183 H1
Elms Cl ALP/SUD HA0 ...79 F2
Elms Crs CLAP SW4 ...161 H1
Elmsdale Rd WALTH E17 ...69 H1
Elms Gdns ALP/SUD HA0 ...79 G2
  DAGW RM9 ...92 B2
Elmshaw Rd PUT/ROE SW15 ...138 D6
Elmshurst Crs EFNCH N2 ...65 G1
Elmside CROY/NA CR0 ...213 K4
Elmside Rd WBLY HA9 ...80 C1
Elms La ALP/SUD HA0 ...79 G2
Elmsleigh Av
  KTN/HRWW/W HA3 ...61 H1
Elmsleigh Rd WHTN TW2 ...155 J4
Elmslie Cl WFD IG8 ...53 K2
Elms Ms BAY/PAD W2 ...8 A5
Elms Park Av ALP/SUD HA0 ...79 G2
Elms Rd CLAP SW4 ...141 H6
  KTN/HRWW/W HA3 ...42 E3
Elmstead Av CHST BR7 ...184 E1
  WBLY HA9 ...62 A5
Elmstead Cl HOR/WEW KT19 ...207 J1
  TRDG/WHET N20 ...32 E4
Elmstead Gdns WPK KT4 ...207 J1
Elmstead Gld CHST BR7 ...184 E2
Elmstead La CHST BR7 ...184 D3
Elmstead Rd ERITH DA8 ...150 B2
  GDMY/SEVK IG3 ...72 E6
Elmsted Crs WELL DA16 ...128 D6
The Elms BARN SW13 ...138 C4
  ESH/CLAY KT10 * ...205 F5
  NFNCH/WDSP N12 * ...47 J1
  TOOT SW17 * ...161 F5
  WLGTN SM6 * ...210 C2
Elmstone Rd FUL/PGN SW6 ...139 K2
Elmstone Ter
  STMC/STPC BR5 * ...202 D1
Elms Wt FSBYW WC1X ...5 H7
Elmsworth Av HSLW TW3 ...135 G3
Elm Ter CRICK NW2 ...82 E1
  ELTH/MOT SE9 ...167 F1
  KTN/HRWW/W HA3 ...42 D3
Elm Tree Av ESH/CLAY KT10 ...189 J4
Elm Tree Cl NTHLT UB5 ...95 K2
  STJWD NW8 ...2 A4
Elm Tree Rd STJWD NW8 ...2 A4
Elmtree Rd TEDD TW11 ...173 K1
Elm Vis HNWL W7 * ...96 E6
Elm Wk GPK RM2 ...57 J6
  HAMP NW3 ...64 E6
  ORP BR6 ...215 K1
  RYNPK SW20 ...193 F1
Elm Wy FBAR/BDGN N11 ...48 A2
  HOR/WEW KT19 ...207 F3
  WLSDN NW10 ...81 G2
  WPK KT4 ...208 A1
Elmwood Av FELT TW13 ...153 K5
  KTN/HRWW/W HA3 ...61 G2
  PLMGR N13 ...48 E1
  WLGTN SM6 ...195 G6
Elmwood Crs CDALE/KGS NW9 ...62 E1
Elmwood Dr BXLY DA5 ...169 F2
  EW KT17 ...207 J5
Elmwood Gdns HNWL W7 ...96 E5
Elmwood Rd CHSWK W4 ...117 K6
  HNHL SE24 ...142 E6
  MTCM CR4 ...178 E6
Elmworth Gv DUL SE21 ...162 E4
Elnathan Ms MV/WKIL W9 ...101 F3
Elphinstone Rd WALTH E17 ...51 H5
Elphinstone St HBRY N5 ...85 H2
Elrick Cl ERITH DA8 ...130 B6
Elrington Rd HACK E8 ...86 C4
  WFD IG8 ...52 E1
Elruge Cl WDR/YW UB7 ...112 A3
Elsa Rd WELL DA16 ...148 D5
Elsa St WCHPL E1 * ...105 G4
Elsdale St HOM E9 ...86 E4
Elsden Ms BETH E2 * ...104 E1
Elsden Rd TOTM N17 ...50 B4
Elsenham Rd MNPK E12 ...89 K3
Elsenham St
  WAND/EARL SW18 ...159 J3
Elsham Rd WAN E11 ...88 C2
  WKENS W14 ...119 H2
Elsham Ter WKENS W14 * ...119 H2
Elsiedene Rd WCHMH N21 ...35 J2
Elsie Lane Ct BAY/PAD W2 ...100 E4
Elsiemaud Rd BROCKY SE4 ...144 C6
Elsie Rd EDUL SE22 ...143 G5
Elsinore Av
  STWL/WRAY TW19 ...152 B2
Elsinore Gdns CRICK NW2 * ...82 C1
Elsinore Rd FSTH SE23 ...164 B3
Elsinore Wy RCH/KEW TW9 ...137 J4
Elsley Rd BTSEA SW11 ...140 E4
Elspeth Rd ALP/SUD HA0 ...80 A3
  BTSEA SW11 ...140 E5
Elsrick Av MRDN SM4 ...193 K2
Elstan Wy CROY/NA CR0 ...198 B4
Elsted St WALW SE17 ...19 F7
Elstow Cl ELTH/MOT SE9 ...146 E6
  RSLP HA4 ...59 H4
Elstow Gdns DAGW RM9 ...92 A6
Elstow Rd DAGW RM9 ...92 A5
Elstree Gdns BELV DA17 ...129 F4
  ED N9 ...36 D3
  IL IG1 ...90 C3
Elstree HI BMLY BR1 ...183 H3
Elstree HI North BORE WD6 ...29 K2
Elstree Pk MLHL NW7 * ...31 F1
Elstree Rd BUSH WD23 ...28 B1
  STAN HA7 ...43 F1
Elswick Rd LEW SE13 ...144 E4
Elswick St FUL/PGN SW6 ...140 B3
Elsworth Cl EBED/NFELT TW14 ...153 H5
Elsworthy THDIT KT7 ...189 K3
Elsworthy Ri HAMP NW3 ...83 J5
Elsworthy Rd HAMP NW3 ...83 J6
Elsworthy Ter HAMP NW3 ...83 J5

Elsynge Rd WAND/EARL SW18 ...140 C6
Eltham Gn ELTH/MOT SE9 ...146 B6
Eltham Green Rd
  ELTH/MOT SE9 ...146 B6
Eltham High St ELTH/MOT SE9 ...166 E1
Eltham HI ELTH/MOT SE9 ...146 C6
Eltham Palace Rd
  ELTH/MOT SE9 ...166 C1
Eltham Park Gdns
  ELTH/MOT SE9 ...147 F5
Eltham Rd ELTH/MOT SE9 ...146 B6
Elthiron Rd FUL/PGN SW6 ...139 K2
Elthorne Av HNWL W7 ...116 A2
Elthorne Ct FELT TW13 ...154 B3
Elthorne Park Rd HNWL W7 ...116 A3
Elthorne Rd ARCH N19 ...66 D6
  CDALE/KGS NW9 ...63 F4
Elthorne Wy CDALE/KGS NW9 ...63 F3
Elthruda Rd LEW SE13 ...165 G1
Eltisley Rd IL IG1 ...90 B3
Elton Av BAR EN5 ...20 D6
  GFD/PVL UB6 ...79 F4
Elton Cl E/WMO/HCT KT8 ...174 D5
Elton Pl STNW/STAM N16 ...86 A3
Elton Rd KUTN/CMB KT2 ...175 G4
Eltringham St
  WAND/EARL SW18 ...140 B5
Elvaston Ms SKENS SW7 ...120 B3
Elvaston Pl SKENS SW7 ...120 B3
Elveden Pl WLSDN NW10 ...98 C1
Elveden Rd FBAR/BDGN N11 ...48 E2
Elver Gdns BETH E2 ...104 C2
Elverson Rd DEPT SE8 ...144 C1
Elverton St WEST SW1P ...16 C6
Elvington Gn HAYES BR2 ...199 J2
Elvington La CDALE/KGS NW9 ...45 G4
Elvino Rd SYD SE26 ...182 A1
Elvis Rd CRICK NW2 ...82 A4
Elwill Wy BECK BR3 ...199 G1
Elwin St BETH E2 ...104 C2
Elwood St HBRY N5 ...85 H1
Elwyn Gdns LEE/GVPK SE12 ...165 K2
Ely Cl ERITH DA8 ...150 C3
  NWMAL KT3 ...176 C5
Ely Gdns DAGE RM10 ...92 E1
Elyne Rd FSBYPK N4 ...67 G3
Ely Pl HCIRC EC1N ...11 J3
Ely Rd CROY/NA CR0 ...196 E2
  HSLWW TW4 ...134 B4
  HTHAIR TW6 ...133 J3
  LEY E10 ...70 A3
Elysian Av STMC/STPC BR5 ...201 K3
Elysium Pl FUL/PGN SW6 ...139 J3
Elysium St FUL/PGN SW6 ...139 J3
Elystan Cl WLGTN SM6 ...210 C6
Elystan Pl CHEL SW3 ...120 D5
Elystan St CHEL SW3 ...14 C7
Elystan Wk IS N1 ...5 J1
Emanuel Av ACT W3 ...98 E5
Embankment PUT/ROE SW15 ...139 G4
Embankment Gdns CHEL SW3 ...120 E6
Embankment La CHCR WC2N ...11 F7
  WHALL SW1A ...17 F1
The Embankment TWK TW1 ...156 B3
Embassy Ct SCUP DA14 ...168 C5
  WLGTN SM6 * ...210 B4
Emba St BERM/RHTH SE16 ...123 H2
Ember Cl FUL/PGN SW6 ...140 A2
Emberton CMBW SE5 ...123 F6
Embercourt Rd THDIT KT7 ...189 K3
Ember Farm Av
  E/WMO/HCT KT8 ...189 J3
Ember Farm Wy
  E/WMO/HCT KT8 ...189 J3
Ember Gdns ESH/CLAY KT10 ...189 K4
Ember La ESH/CLAY KT10 ...189 J5
Embleton Rd LEW SE13 ...144 E5
  OXHEY WD19 ...26 E5
Embry Cl STAN HA7 ...29 G6
Embry Dr STAN HA7 ...43 G2
Embry Wy STAN HA7 ...43 G1
Emden Cl WDR/YW UB7 ...112 D2
Emden St FUL/PGN SW6 ...140 A2
Emerald Cl CAN/RD E16 ...107 J5
Emerald Gdns BCTR RM8 ...74 C5
Emerald Rd WLSDN NW10 ...81 F6
Emerald Sq NWDGN UB2 ...114 C3
Emerald St BMSBY WC1N ...11 G1
Emerson Rd
  KTN/HRWW/W HA5 ...62 B3
Emerson Rd IL IG1 ...72 C7
Emerson St STHWK SE1 ...12 C7
Emerton Cl BXLYHS DA6 ...149 F5
Emery Hill St WEST SW1P ...16 A5
Emery St STHWK SE1 ...17 K4
Emes Rd ERITH DA8 ...149 K1
Emilia Cl PEND EN3 ...24 D6
Emily Pl HOLWY N7 ...85 G2
Emily St CAN/RD E16 ...106 D5
Emlyn Rd SHB W12 ...118 B2
Emmanuel Rd BAL SW12 ...161 H3
  NTHWD HA6 ...40 D3
Emma Rd PLSTW E13 ...106 D1
Emma St BETH E2 ...104 D1
Emma Ter RYNPK SW20 * ...177 F5
Emmaus Wy CHIG IG7 ...54 A1
Emmott Av BARK/HLT IG6 ...72 C2
Emmott Cl EFNCH N2 ...65 J1
  WCHPL E1 ...105 G3
Emperor's Ga SKENS SW7 ...120 A3
Empire Av UED N18 * ...49 J2
Empire Pde UED N18 * ...49 K2
  WBLY HA9 ...80 C1
Empire Rd GFD/PVL UB6 ...79 J6
Empire Wy WBLY HA9 ...80 B2
Empire Wharf Rd
  POP/IOD E14 ...125 G4
Empress Av CHING E4 ...51 J3
  IL IG1 ...72 A6
  MNPK E12 ...71 G6
  WFD IG8 ...52 D3
Empress Dr CHST BR7 ...185 G2
Empress Pde CHING E4 * ...51 J3

Empress Pl ECT SW5 ...119 K5
Empress St WALW SE17 ...122 D6
Empson St BOW E3 ...105 K3
Emsworth Cl ED N9 ...36 E3
Emsworth Rd BARK/HLT IG6 ...54 B5
Emsworth St
  BRXS/STRHM SW2 ...162 A4
Emu Rd VX/NE SW8 ...141 G3
Ena Rd STRHM/NOR SW16 ...179 K6
Enbrook St NKENS W10 ...100 C2
Enclave Ct FSBYE EC1V ...6 B6
Endale Cl CAR SM5 ...194 E6
Endeavour Wy BARK IG11 ...109 G1
  CROY/NA CR0 ...195 K4
  WIM/MER SW19 ...160 A6
Endell St LSQ/SEVD WC2H ...10 E3
Enderby St GNWCH SE10 ...125 H5
Enderley Rd
  KTN/HRWW/W HA3 ...42 D4
Endersby Rd BAR EN5 ...20 A6
Endersleigh Gdns HDN NW4 ...63 J1
Endlebury Rd CHING E4 ...38 A4
Endlesham Rd BAL SW12 ...161 F2
Endsleigh Gdns IL IG1 ...71 K5
  STPAN WC1H ...4 C6
  SURB KT6 ...190 C5
Endsleigh Pl STPAN WC1H ...4 D6
Endsleigh Rd HNWL W7 ...116 B1
  NWDGN UB2 ...114 D4
Endsleigh St STPAN WC1H ...4 D6
Endway BRYLDS KT5 ...191 H4
Endwell Rd BROCKY SE4 ...144 B3
Endymion Rd
  BRXS/STRHM SW2 ...162 A2
  FSBYPK N4 ...67 H4
Energen Cl WLSDN NW10 ...81 G4
Enfield Rd ACT W3 ...117 J2
  BTFD TW8 ...116 E5
  EBAR EN4 ...22 D5
  HTHAIR TW6 ...133 H3
  IS N1 ...86 A5
Enford St MBLAR W1H ...8 E1
Engadine Cl CROY/NA CR0 ...212 B1
Engadine St
  WAND/EARL SW18 ...159 J3
Engate St LEW SE13 ...145 F5
Engel Pk MLHL NW7 ...46 A2
Engineer Cl WOOL/PLUM SE18 ...127 F6
Engineers Wy WBLY HA9 ...80 C2
England's La HAMP NW3 ...83 K4
England Wy NWMAL KT3 ...191 J1
Englefield Cl CROY/NA CR0 ...196 D3
  ENC/FH EN2 ...23 H3
  STMC/STPC BR5 ...202 A1
Englefield Crs STMC/STPC BR5 ...202 B2
Englefield Pth S
  TMC/STPC BR5 ...202 B1
Englefield Rd IS N1 ...85 K5
Engleheart Dr
  EBED/NFELT TW14 ...153 J1
Engleheart Rd CAT SE6 ...164 E2
Englewood Rd BAL SW12 ...161 G1
English St BOW E3 ...105 H3
Enid St STHWK SE1 ...19 K4
Enmore Av SNWD SE25 ...197 H2
Enmore Gdns
  MORT/ESHN SW14 ...138 A6
Enmore Rd PUT/ROE SW15 ...139 F5
  SNWD SE25 ...197 H2
  STHL UB1 ...96 A5
Ennerdale Av HCH RM12 ...93 J3
  STAN HA7 ...43 J6
Ennerdale Cl
  EBED/NFELT TW14 ...153 J5
  SUT SM1 ...208 D2
Ennerdale Dr CDALE/KGS NW9 ...63 G2
Ennerdale Gdns WBLY HA9 ...61 J5
Ennerdale Rd BXLYHN DA7 ...149 H2
  RCH/KEW TW9 ...137 G3
Ennersdale Rd LEW SE13 ...145 G6
Ennis Rd FSBYPK N4 ...67 G5
  WOOL/PLUM SE18 ...127 J6
Ensign Cl STWL/WRAY TW19 ...152 A3
Ensign Dr PLMGR N13 ...35 J5
Ensign Wy STWL/WRAY TW19 ...152 A3
Enslin Rd ELTH/MOT SE9 ...167 F1
Ensor Ms SKENS SW7 ...120 C5
Enstone Rd PEND EN3 ...25 G4
Enterprise Cl CROY/NA CR0 ...196 B5
Enterprise Rw
  SEVS/STOTM N15 ...68 B2
Enterprise Wy TEDD TW11 ...174 A1
  WAND/EARL SW18 ...139 K5
  WLSDN NW10 ...99 H2
Enterprize Wy DEPT SE8 ...124 C4
Epcot Ms NKENS W10 * ...100 D2
Epirus Ms FUL/PGN SW6 ...119 K6
Epirus Rd FUL/PGN SW6 ...139 J1
Epping Cl POP/IOD E14 ...124 D4
  ROMW/RG RM7 ...56 D6
Epping Gld CHING E4 ...38 A1
Epping New Rd BKHH IG9 ...39 F5
Epping Pl HOLWY N7 ...85 C4
Epping Wy CHING E4 ...37 K4
Epple Rd FUL/PGN SW6 ...139 J2
Epsom Cl BXLYHN DA7 ...149 J4
  NTHLT UB5 ...77 K3
Epsom Rd CROY/NA CR0 ...211 G2
  GDMY/SEVK IG3 ...73 F5
  LEY E10 ...70 A3
  MRDN SM4 ...193 J4
Epsom Sq HTHAIR TW6 * ...133 J3
Epstein Rd THMD SE28 ...128 C1
Epworth Rd ISLW TW7 ...136 C1
Epworth St SDTCH EC2A ...7 F7
Equity Sq BETH E2 * ...7 K5
Erasmus St WEST SW1P ...16 D7

Erconwald St *ACT* W3 ....99 H5
Erebus Dr *WOOL/PLUM* SE18 .....127 H3
Eresby Dr *BECK* BR3 ....198 D5
Eresby Pl *KIL/WHAMP* NW6 ....82 E5
Erica Gdns *CROY/NA* CR0 ....213 K2
Erica St *SHB* W12 ....99 J6
Eric Clarke La *BARK* IG11 ....108 E5
Ericcson Cl *WAND/EARL* SW18 ...139 K6
Eric Est *BOW* E3 ....105 H3
Eric High St *ERITH* DA8 ....130 C6
Eric Rd *BELV* DA17 ....129 J5
   BXLYHN DA7 ....149 J4
Erlanger Rd *NWCR* SE14 ....144 A2
Eriesmere Gdns *HNWL* W7 ....116 B3
Ermine Rd *LEW* SE13 ....134 B3
   SEVS/STOTM N15 ....68 B5
Ermine Side *EN* EN1 ....24 C6
Ermington Rd *ELTH/MOT* SE9 ....167 H4
Ernald Av *EHAM* E6 ....107 J1
Erncroft Wy *TWK* TW1 ....156 A1
Ernest Av *WNWD* SE27 ....162 C6
Ernest Cl *BECK* BR3 ....198 D2
Ernest Gdns *CHSWK* W4 ....117 J6
Ernest Gv *BECK* BR3 ....198 C2
Ernest Rd *KUT/HW* KT1 ....175 J5
Ernest St *WCHPL* E1 ....105 F3
Ernle Rd *RYNPK* SW20 ....176 F3
Ernshaw Pl *PUT/ROE* SW15 ....139 H6
Erpingham Rd *PUT/ROE* SW15 ...139 F4
Erridge Rd *WIM/MER* SW19 ......177 K5
Errington Rd *MV/WKIL* W9 ....100 D3
Errol Gdns *NWMAL* KT3 ....192 D1
   YEAD UB4 ....95 F5
Erroll Rd *ROM* RM1 ....75 H1
Errol St *STLK* EC1Y 6 D7
Erskine Cl *SUT* SM1 ....209 J1
Erskine Crs *TOTM* N17 ....68 D1
Erskine Hl *GLDGN* NW11 ....64 E1
Erskine Ms *HAMP* NW3 * 83 K5
Erskine Rd *HAMP* NW3 ....83 K5
   SUT SM1 ....209 H2
   WALTH E17 ....69 H1
Erwood Rd *CHARL* SE7 ....126 D5
Esam Wy *STRHM/NOR* SW16 .....180 B1
Escot Wy *BAR* EN5 ....20 A6
Escreet Gv *WOOL/PLUM* SE18 ...127 F4
Esher Av *CHEAM* SM3 ....208 B1
   ROMW/RG RM7 ....74 E3
   WOT/HER KT12 ....188 A5
Esher Cl *BXLY* DA5 ....169 F3
   ESH/CLAY KT10 ....204 B3
Esher Crs *HTHAIR* TW6 ....133 J3
Esher Gn *ESH/CLAY* KT10 ....204 B2
Esher Green Dr
   ESH/CLAY KT10 ....204 A1
Esher Ms *MTCM* CR4 ....179 F6
Esher Park Av *ESH/CLAY* KT10 ...204 C3
Esher Place Av
   ESH/CLAY KT10 ....204 B2
Esher Rd *E/WMO/HCT* KT8 ....189 J3
   GDMY/SEVK IG3 ....90 E1
Eskdale Av *NTHLT* UB5 ....77 K6
Eskdale Cl *WBLY* HA9 ....61 K6
Eskdale Rd *BXLYHN* DA7 ....149 H5
Eskmont Rdg *NRWD* SE19 ....181 F3
Esk Rd *PLSTW* E13 ....107 F3
Esk Wy *ROM* RM1 ....57 G3
Esmar Crs *CDALE/KGS* NW9 ....63 J4
Esmeralda Rd *STHWK* SE1 ....123 H4
Esmond Cl *RAIN* RM13 * 93 K5
Esmond Gdns *CHSWK* W4 * 118 A4
Esmond Rd *CHSWK* W4 ....118 A5
   KIL/WHAMP NW6 ....82 D6
Esmond St *PUT/ROE* SW15 ....139 H5
Esparto St *WAND/EARL* SW18 ....160 A2
Essenden Rd *BELV* DA17 ....129 H5
   SAND/SEL CR2 ....212 A5
Essendine Rd *MV/WKIL* W9 ....100 E2
Essex Av *ISLW* TW7 ....135 K4
Essex Cl *MRDN* SM4 ....193 G4
   ROMW/RG RM7 ....75 H1
   RSLP HA4 ....59 H5
   WALTH E17 ....69 G1
Essex Ct *BARN* SW13 ....138 C5
   TPL/STR WC2R * 11 J4
Essex Gdns *FSBYPK* N4 ....67 H3
Essex Gv *NRWD* SE19 ....180 E2
Essex Pk *FNCH* N3 ....47 F2
Essex Park Ms *ACT* W3 ....118 B1
Essex Pl *CHSWK* W4 ....117 K4
Essex Place Sq *CHSWK* W4 * 118 A4
Essex Rd *ACT* W3 ....98 E6
   BARK IG11 ....90 D5
   CHDH RM6 ....73 J5
   CHING E4 ....38 C3
   CHSWK W4 ....118 A4
   DAGE RM10 ....92 D1
   DART DA1 ....171 G1
   ENC/FH EN2 ....23 K5
   IS N1 ....6 C2
   LEY E10 ....70 A3
   MNPK E12 ....89 J3
   ROMW/RG RM7 ....74 D3
   SWFD E18 ....53 F5
   WALTH E17 ....69 G3
   WLSDN NW10 ....81 G5
Essex Rd South *LEY* E10 ....70 B4
Essex St *FSTGT* E7 ....88 E3
   TPL/STR WC2R 11 J4
Essex Vls *KENS* W8 ....119 K2

Essex Whf *CLPT* E5 * 69 F6
Essian St *WCHPL* E1 ....105 G4
Essoldo Wy *EDGW* HA8 ....44 B6
Estate Wy *LEY* E10 ....69 H5
Estcourt Rd *FUL/PGN* SW6 ....139 J1
   SNWD SE25 ....197 J1
Estella Av *NWMAL* KT3 ....192 E1
Estelle Rd *HAMP* NW3 ....83 K2
Esterbrooke St *WEST* SW1P 16 C7
Este Rd *BTSEA* SW11 ....140 D4
Esther Cl *WCHMH* N21 ....35 G2
Esther Rd *WAN* E11 ....70 C4
Estoria Cl *BRXS/STRHM* SW2 .....162 B2
Estreham Rd
   STRHM/NOR SW16 ....179 J2
Estridge Cl *HSLW* TW3 ....135 F5
Estuary Cl *BARK* IG11 ....109 H2
Eswyn Rd *TOOT* SW17 ....160 E6
Etchingham Park Rd *FNCH* N3 ...47 F3
Etchingham Rd *SRTFD* E15 ....88 A2
Etfield Gv *SCUP* DA14 ....186 C1
Ethelbert Cl *HAYES* BR2 ....183 K5
Ethelbert Gdns
   GNTH/NBYPK IG2 ....71 K2
Ethelbert Rd *BMLY* BR1 ....183 K6
   ERITH DA8 ....149 K1
   RDART DA2 ....171 H6
   RYNPK SW20 ....177 G4
   STMC/STPC BR5 ....186 E6
Ethelbert St *BAL* SW12 ....161 G3
Ethelburga St *BTSEA* SW11 * 140 D2
Etheldene Av *MUSWH* N10 ....66 C1
Ethelden Rd *SHB* W12 ....118 E1
Ethelred Est *LBTH* SE11 ....17 J7
Ethel Rd *CAN/RD* E16 ....107 F6
Ethel St *WALW* SE17 * 18 D7
Ethel Ter *ORP* BR6 ....217 J6
Etheridge Rd *CRICK* NW2 ....64 A4
Etherley Rd *SEVS/STOTM* N15 ....67 J2
Etherow St *EDUL* SE22 ....163 H1
Etherstone Rd
   STRHM/NOR SW16 ....162 A6
Ethnard Rd *PECK* SE15 ....123 J6
Ethronvi Rd *BXLYHN* DA7 ....149 G4
Etloe Rd *LEY* E10 ....69 J6
Eton Av *ALP/SUD* HA0 ....79 J2
   EBAR EN4 ....33 J1
   HAMP NW3 ....83 J5
   HEST TW5 ....114 E6
   NFNCH/WDSP N12 ....47 G3
   NWMAL KT3 ....192 A2
Eton Cl *WAND/EARL* SW18 ....160 A2
Eton College Rd *HAMP* NW3 ......83 K4
Eton Garages *HAMP* NW3 * 83 J4
Eton Gv *CDALE/KGS* NW9 ....44 C6
   LEW SE13 ....145 H4
Eton Hl *HAMP* NW3 * 83 J4
Eton Ri *HAMP* NW3 * 83 K4
Eton Rd *HAMP* NW3 ....83 K5
   HYS/HAR UB3 ....133 J1
   IL IG1 ....90 C2
   ORP BR6 ....217 H2
Eton St *RCHPK/HAM* TW10 ....136 E6
Eton Vls *HAMP* NW3 ....83 K4
Eton Wy *DART* DA1 ....151 F5
Etta St *DEPT* SE8 ....124 B6
Ettrick St *POP/IOD* E14 ....106 A5
Etwell Pl *BRYLDS* KT5 ....191 G3
Euesden Cl *ED* N9 ....36 D5
Eugenia Rd *BERM/RHTH* SE16 ...123 K5
Eureka Rd *KUT/HW* KT1 ....175 H5
Europa Pl *FSBYE* EC1V 6 C5
Europe Rd *WOOL/PLUM* SE18 ...126 E3
Eustace Pl *WOOL/PLUM* SE18 ...126 E4
Eustace Rd *CHDH* RM6 ....73 K4
   EHAM E6 ....107 J2
   FUL/PGN SW6 ....139 K1
Euston Centre *CAMTN* NW1 ....4 A6
Euston Rd *CAMTN* NW1 ....4 A6
   CAMTN NW1 ....4 E5
   CROY/NA CR0 ....196 B5
Euston Sq *CAMTN* NW1 ....4 C5
Euston St *CAMTN* NW1 ....4 B5
Evandale Rd *BRXN/ST* SW9 ....142 B3
Evangelist Rd *KTTN* NW5 ....84 B2
Evans Cl *HACK* E8 ....86 B4
Evansdale *RAIN* RM13 ....111 H2
Evans Gv *FELT* TW13 ....155 F4
Evans Rd *CAT* SE6 ....165 H4
Evanston Av *CHING* E4 ....52 A5
Evanston Gdns *REDBR* IG4 ....71 J3
Eva Rd *CHDH* RM6 ....73 J4
Evelina Rd *PECK* SE15 ....143 K4
   PGE/AN SE20 ....181 K5
Eveline Louse Est
   BERM/RHTH SE16 ....123 H3
Eveline Rd *MTCM* CR4 ....178 E4
Evelyn Av *CDALE/KGS* NW9 ....63 F1
   RSLP HA4 ....58 E3
Evelyn Cl *WHTN* TW2 ....155 G2
Evelyn Denington Rd
   EHAM E6 ....107 J3
Evelyn Dr *PIN* HA5 ....41 H3
Evelyn Est *DEPT* SE8 ....124 B6
Evelyn Gdns *RCH/KEW* TW9 ......137 G5
   WBPTN SW10 ....120 B5
Evelyn Gv *EA* W5 ....117 G1
   STHL UB1 ....95 K5
Evelyn Rd *CAN/RD* E16 ....125 K1
   EBAR EN4 ....21 K5
   FSTGT E7 ....89 F3
   RCH/KEW TW9 ....137 F5
   RCHPK/HAM TW10 ....156 D5
   WALTH E17 ....70 A1
   WIM/MER SW19 ....178 A1
Evelyn St *DEPT* SE8 ....124 B5
Evelyn Ter *RCH/KEW* TW9 ....137 F4
Evelyn Wy *WLGTN* SM6 ....210 D2
Evensyde *WATW* WD18 ....26 A5
Evenwood Cl *PUT/ROE* SW15 * ...139 H6
Everard Av *HAYES* BR2 ....199 K5
Everard Wy *WBLY* HA9 ....80 A1
Everatt Cl *WAND/EARL* SW18 * ...159 J1
Everdon Rd *BARN* SW13 ....118 D6

Everest Pl *POP/IOD* E14 ....106 A4
Everest Rd *ELTH/MOT* SE9 ....146 D6
   STWL/WRAY TW19 ....152 A2
Everett Cl *BUSH* WD23 ....28 E3
   PIN HA5 ....40 D6
The Everglades *HSLW* TW3 * 135 H4
Evergreen Cl *PGE/AN* SE20 ....181 K3
Evergreen Ct
   STWL/WRAY TW19 * 152 A2
Evergreen Sq *HACK* E8 ....86 B5
Evergreen Wy *HYS/HAR* UB3 .....113 J1
   STWL/WRAY TW19 ....152 A2
Everilda St *IS* N1 ....5 H1
Evering Rd *CLPT* E5 ....86 C1
Everington Rd *MUSWH* N10 ......47 K5
Everington St *HMSMTH* W6 ....119 G6
Everitt Rd *WLSDN* NW10 ....99 F2
Everleigh St *FSBYPK* N4 ....67 F5
Eve Rd *ISLW* TW7 ....136 B5
   SRTFD E15 ....106 C1
   TOTM N17 ....50 A6
   WAN E11 ....88 C2
Everseld Gdns *EDGW* HA8 ....45 C5
Eversfield Rd *RCH/KEW* TW9 .....137 G3
Evershed Wk *CHSWK* W4 ....117 K3
Eversholt St *CAMTN* NW1 ....4 B3
Evershot Rd *FSBYPK* N4 ....67 F5
Eversleigh Rd *BAR* EN5 ....21 G6
   BTSEA SW11 ....140 E4
   EHAM E6 ....89 H6
   FNCH N3 ....46 D5
Eversley Av *BXLYHN* DA7 ....150 B3
   WBLY HA9 ....62 C6
Eversley Cl *WCHMH* N21 ....35 F1
Eversley Crs *ISLW* TW7 ....135 J2
   RSLP HA4 ....58 D6
   WCHMH N21 ....35 F1
Eversley Mt *WCHMH* N21 ....35 F1
Eversley Pk *WIM/MER* SW19 .....176 E1
Eversley Park Rd *WCHMH* N21 ...35 F1
Eversley Rd *BRYLDS* KT5 ....191 G3
   CHARL SE7 ....126 A6
   NRWD SE19 ....180 E3
Eversley Wy *CROY/NA* CR0 ....213 J1
Everthorpe Rd *PECK* SE15 ....143 G4
Everton Blds *CAMTN* NW1 ....4 A5
Everton Dr *STAN* HA7 ....44 B6
Everton Rd *CROY/NA* CR0 ....197 H5
Evesham Av *WALTH* E17 ....51 J5
Evesham Cl *BELMT* SM2 ....208 E5
   GFD/PVL UB6 ....96 B1
Evesham Gn *MRDN* SM4 ....194 A3
Evesham Rd *FBAR/BDGN* N11 ....48 C1
   MRDN SM4 ....194 A3
   SRTFD E15 ....88 D5
Evesham Wy *BTSEA* SW11 ....141 F4
   CLAY IG5 ....54 A6
Evry Rd *SCUP* DA14 ....186 D2
Ewald Rd *FUL/PGN* SW6 ....139 J3
Ewanrigg Ter *WFD* IG8 ....53 G1
Ewart Gv *WDGN* N22 ....49 G4
Ewart Pl *BOW* E3 * 105 H1
Ewart Rd *FSTH* SE23 ....164 A2
Ewe Cl *HOLWY* N7 ....84 E4
Ewell By-Pass *EW* KT17 ....207 J5
Ewell Court Av
   HOR/WEW KT19 ....207 G3
Ewellhurst Rd *CLAY* IG5 ....53 J5
Ewell Park Gdns *EW* KT17 ....207 J5
Ewell Park Wy *EW* KT17 ....207 J4
Ewell Rd *CHEAM* SM3 ....208 B4
   SURB KT6 ....191 G3
   THDIT KT7 ....190 C4
Ewelme Rd *FSTH* SE23 ....163 K3
Ewen Crs *BRXS/STRHM* SW2 .....162 B2
Ewer St *STHWK* SE1 ....18 C1
Ewhurst Av *SAND/SEL* CR2 ....212 B6
Ewhurst Cl *BELMT* SM2 ....208 A6
   WCHPL E1 ....104 E4
Ewhurst Rd *BROCKY* SE4 ....164 D1
Exbury Rd *CAT* SE6 ....164 D4
Excel Ct *LSQ/SEVD* WC2H 10 D6
Excel Marina *CAN/RD* E16 ....106 E6
Excelsior Cl *KUT/HW* KT1 ....175 H5
Excel Waterfront *CAN/RD* E16 ....107 F6
Exchange Ar *LVPST* EC2M 13 G2
Exchange Ct *COVGDN* WC2E * 11 F6
Exchange Sq *SDTCH* EC2A 13 H1
Exeter Cl *EHAM* E6 ....107 K5
Exeter Gdns *IL* IG1 ....71 K5
Exeter Ms *FUL/PGN* SW6 * 139 K1
Exeter Pde *CRICK* NW2 * 82 C4
Exeter Rd *CAN/RD* E16 ....106 E4
   CRICK NW2 ....82 C4
   CROY/NA CR0 ....197 F4
   DAGE RM10 ....92 D4
   ED N9 ....36 E4
   FELT TW13 ....154 E5
   HTHAIR TW6 ....133 H4
   PEND EN3 ....25 F4
   RYLN/HDSTN HA2 ....59 J6
   STHGT/OAK N14 ....34 B3
   WALTH E17 ....69 J2
   WELL DA16 ....148 A3
Exeter St *COVGDN* WC2E 11 F5
Exeter Wy *HTHAIR* TW6 ....133 H5
   NWCR SE14 ....144 C1
Exford Gdns *LEE/GVPK* SE12 .....166 A3
Exford Rd *LEE/GVPK* SE12 ....166 A4
Exhibition Rd *SKENS* SW7 ....14 B5
Exit Rd *EFNCH* N2 ....47 H5
Exmoor Cl *BARK/HLT* IG6 ....54 C4
Exmoor St *NKENS* W10 ....100 B3
Exmouth Market *CLKNW* EC1R 5 J6
Exmouth Ms *CAMTN* NW1 * 4 B5
Exmouth Pl *HACK* E8 ....86 D6

Exmouth Rd *RSLP* HA4 ....77 G1
   WALTH E17 ....69 H2
   WELL DA16 ....148 C2
   YEAD UB4 ....94 C2
Exmouth St *WCHPL* E1 ....104 E5
Exning Rd *CAN/RD* E16 ....106 D3
Exon St *WALW* SE17 ....19 G7
Explorer Av *STWL/WRAY* TW19 ..152 B3
Explorer Dr *WATW* WD18 ....26 D1
Express Dr *GDMY/SEVK* IG3 ....73 H5
Exton Crs *WLSDN* NW10 ....80 E5
Exton Gdns *BCTR* RM8 ....91 K3
Exton St *STHWK* SE1 ....17 J1
Eynham Rd *WFD* RM12 ....93 J1
Eynhurst Cl *CRICK* NW2 ....63 J6
Eylewood Rd *WNWD* SE27 ....180 D1
Eynella Rd *DUL* SE21 ....163 G2
Eynham Rd *SHB* W12 ....100 A5
Eynsford Cl *STMC/STPC* BR5 .....201 H4
Eynsford Crs *BXLY* DA5 ....168 D3
Eynsford Rd *GDMY/SEVK* IG3 ....72 E6
Eynsham Dr *ABYW* SE2 ....128 B3
Eynswood Dr *SCUP* DA14 ....186 C1
Eyot Gdns *HMSMTH* W6 ....118 C5
Eyre Cl *GPK* RM2 * 75 J2
Eyre Street HI *CLKNW* EC1R 5 J7
Eythorne Rd *BRXN/ST* SW9 ....142 B2
Ezra St *BETH* E2 ....7 K4

Faber Gdns *HDN* NW4 ....63 J2
Fabian Rd *FUL/PGN* SW6 ....139 J1
Fabian St *EHAM* E6 ....107 K3
The Facade *FSTH* SE23 * 163 K4
Factory La *CROY/NA* CR0 ....196 A6
   TOTM N17 ....50 B5
Factory Pl *POP/IOD* E14 ....125 F5
Factory Rd *CAN/RD* E16 ....126 C1
Factory Yd *HNWL* W7 * 115 K1
Faesten Wy *BXLY* DA5 ....170 B5
Fagg's Rd *EBED/NFELT* TW14 ....133 K6
Faircharm *ISLW* TW7 * 135 J2
   NWMAL KT3 ....176 B6
Fair Acres *HAYES* BR2 ....200 A1
Faircrees *CROY/NA* CR0 ....213 H6
   RSLP HA4 ....58 D4
Fairbank Av *ORP* BR6 ....201 G6
Fairbank Est *IS* N1 ....6 E3
Fairbanks Rd *TOTM* N17 ....50 C6
Fairbourne Rd *TOTM* N17 ....50 A6
Fairbridge Rd *ARCH* N19 ....66 D6
Fairbrook Cl *PLMGR* N13 ....49 G1
Fairby Rd *LEE/GVPK* SE12 ....146 A6
Fairchild Cl *BTSEA* SW11 ....140 C3
Fairchild Pl *SDTCH* EC2A * 7 H7
Fairchild St *SDTCH* EC2A 7 H7
Fair Cl *BUSH* WD23 ....28 B2
Fairclough St *WCHPL* E1 ....104 C5
Fircross Av *BARK* IG11 ....91 F5
   CRW RM5 ....57 F3
Fairdale Gdns *HYS/HAR* UB3 .....113 K2
   PUT/ROE SW15 ....138 E5
Fairey Av *HYS/HAR* UB3 ....45 H5
Fairey Av *HYS/HAR* UB3 ....113 J3
Fairfax Cl *WOT/HER* KT12 ....188 A5
Fairfax Gdns *BKHTH/KID* SE3 ....146 B2
Fairfax Ms *CAN/RD* E16 ....126 A1
   CEND/HSY/T N8 * 67 F2
   PUT/ROE SW15 ....139 F5
Fairfax Pl *KIL/WHAMP* NW6 ....83 F4
   WKENS W14 ....119 H3
Fairfax Rd *CEND/HSY/T* N8 ....67 G2
   CHSWK W4 ....118 B3
   KIL/WHAMP NW6 ....83 F4
   TEDD TW11 ....174 B2
Fairfax Wy *MUSWH* N10 ....48 A3
Faircield Av *EDGW* HA8 ....44 D3
   HDN NW4 ....63 K3
   OXHEY WD19 ....27 F1
   RSLP HA4 ....58 A4
   WHTN TW2 ....155 G3
Fairfield Cl *BFN/LL* DA15 ....168 A1
   HCH RM12 ....75 J5
   HOR/WEW KT19 ....207 G3
   NFNCH/WDSP N12 ....33 G6
   * PEND* EN3 ....25 H3
   WIM/MER SW19 * 178 D5
Fairfield Cnr *KUT/HW* KT1 * 175 G5
Fairfield Ct *RSLP* HA4 ....58 E6
Fairfield Dr *GFD/PVL* UB6 ....79 H4
   RYLN/HDSTN HA2 ....42 C6
   WAND/EARL SW18 ....140 A6
Fairfield East *KUT/HW* KT1 ....175 F5
Fairfield Gdns *CEND/HSY/T* N8 ..66 E2
Fairfield Gv *CHARL* SE7 ....126 B6
Fairfield North *KUT/HW* KT1 ......175 F5
Fairfield Pth *CROY/NA* CR0 ....211 K1
   CROY/NA CR0 ....175 H1
Fairfield Rd *BECK* BR3 ....182 D5
   BMLY BR1 ....183 K3
   BOW E3 ....105 J1
   BXLYHN DA7 ....149 G4
   CEND/HSY/T N8 * 66 E2
   CROY/NA CR0 ....197 H5
   IL IG1 ....90 B4
   KUT/HW KT1 ....175 F5
   STHL UB1 ....95 K4
   STMC/STPC BR5 ....201 H4
   UED N18 ....36 D6
   WALTH E17 ....51 G5
   WDR/YW UB7 ....112 B1
   WFD IG8 ....52 E2
Fairfields *CAT* SE6 ....164 E4
Fairfields Cl *CDALE/KGS* NW9 ....62 E2
Fairfields Crs *CDALE/KGS* NW9 ..62 E1
Fairfield South *KUT/HW* KT1 ......175 F6
Fairfield St *WAND/EARL* SW18 ...140 A6

Fairfield Wy *BAR* EN5 ....20 E6
   HOR/WEW KT19 ....207 G3
Fairfield West *KUT/HW* KT1 ....175 F5
Fairfoot Rd *BOW* E3 * 105 J3
Fairford Av *BXLYHN* DA7 ....149 K2
   CROY/NA CR0 ....198 A2
Fairford Cl *CROY/NA* CR0 ....198 A2
Fairford Ct *BELMT* SM2 * 209 F5
Fairford Gdns *WPK* KT4 ....192 C1
Fairgreen *EBAR* EN4 ....21 K4
Fairgreen Ct *EBAR* EN4 * 21 K4
Fairgreen Rd *THHTH* CR7 ....196 C2
Fairhaven Av *CROY/NA* CR0 ....198 A3
Fairhaven Crs *OXHEY* WD19 ......26 E5
Fairhazel Gdns
   KIL/WHAMP NW6 ....83 F4
Fairholme *EBED/NFELT* TW14 ....153 G2
Fairholme Av *GPK* RM2 ....75 J2
Fairholme Cl *FNCH* N3 ....64 C1
Fairholme Ct *PIN* HA5 * 42 A2
Fairholme Crs *YEAD* UB4 ....94 D3
Fairholme Gdns *FNCH* N3 ....46 C6
Fairholme Rd *CROY/NA* CR0 ......196 B4
   HRW HA1 ....61 F3
   IL IG1 ....71 K4
   SUT SM1 ....208 D4
   WKENS W14 ....119 H5
Fairholt Rd *STNW/STAM* N16 .....67 K5
Fairholt St *SKENS* SW7 ....14 D4
Fairland Rd *SRTFD* E15 ....88 D4
Fairlands Av *BKHH* IG9 ....38 E4
   SUT SM1 ....195 K6
   THHTH CR7 ....196 A2
Fairlawn *CHARL* SE7 ....126 B1
Fairlawn Av *BXLYHN* DA7 ....148 E3
   CHSWK W4 ....117 K4
   EFNCH N2 ....65 J1
Fairlawn Cl *ESH/CLAY* KT10 ....205 F4
   FELT TW13 ....154 E6
   KUTN/CMB KT2 ....175 K2
   STHGT/OAK N14 ....34 C1
Fairlawn Ct *CHARL* SE7 * 146 B1
Fairlawn Dr *WFD* IG8 ....52 E3
Fairlawn Gdns *STHL* UB1 * 95 K6
Fairlawn Gv *CHSWK* W4 ....117 K4
Fairlawn Pk *SYD* SE26 ....182 B1
Fairlawn Rd *WIM/MER* SW19 .....177 J3
Fairlawns *TWK* TW1 ....156 D1
Fairlea Pl *EA* W5 ....97 J4
Fairlie Gdns *FSTH* SE23 ....163 K2
Fairlight Av *CHING* E4 ....38 B3
   WFD IG8 ....52 E2
   WLSDN NW10 ....99 G1
Fairlight Cl *CHING* E4 ....38 B4
   WPK KT4 ....208 A2
Fairlight Rd *TOOT* SW17 ....160 C6
Fairlop Cl *HCH* RM12 ....93 K4
Fairlop Gdns *BARK/HLT* IG6 ......54 C5
Fairlop Rd *BARK/HLT* IG6 ....54 C5
   WAN E11 ....70 B4
Fairmead *BMLY* BR1 ....200 E1
   SURB KT6 ....191 J5
Fairmead Cl *BMLY* BR1 ....200 E1
   HEST TW5 ....134 C1
   NWMAL KT3 ....176 A6
Fairmead Crs *EDGW* HA8 ....30 E4
Fairmead Gdns *REDBR* IG4 ....71 H2
Fairmead Rd *CROY/NA* CR0 ......196 B4
   HOLWY N7 ....85 G1
Fairmile Av *STRHM/NOR* SW16 ..179 J1
Fairmont Cl *BELV* DA17 ....129 G5
Fairmount Rd
   BRXS/STRHM SW2 ....162 A1
Fairoak Cl *STMC/STPC* BR5 ....201 G4
Fairoak Dr *ELTH/MOT* SE9 ....147 K6
Fair Oak Pl *BARK/HLT* IG6 ....54 C5
Fairseat Cl *BUSH* WD23 ....29 F3
Fairstead Wk *IS* N1 * 85 J6
Fair St *HSLW* TW3 ....135 H4
   STHWK SE1 ....19 H2
Fairthorn Rd *CHARL* SE7 ....125 H5
Fairview *ERITH* DA8 ....150 C1
Fairview Av *ALP/SUD* HA0 ....79 K4
Fair View Cl *WALTH* E17 ....51 G4
Fairview Ct *HDN* NW4 ....46 B5
Fairview Crs *RYLN/HDSTN* HA2 ..60 A5
Fairview Dr *CHIG* IG7 ....54 D1
   ORP BR6 ....216 D2
Fairview Gdns *WFD* IG8 ....53 F4
Fairview Pl *BRXS/STRHM* SW2 ...162 A2
Fairview Rd *ENC/FH* EN2 ....23 G2
   SEVS/STOTM N15 ....68 B3
   SUT SM1 ....209 H4
   STRHM/NOR SW16 ....180 A3
Fairview Vls *CHING* E4 * 51 J3
Fairview Wy *EDGW* HA8 ....30 C5
Fairwater Av *WELL* DA16 ....148 B5
Fairway *BXLYHS* DA6 ....149 F6
   RYNPK SW20 ....177 H6
   STMC/STPC BR5 ....201 J3
   WFD IG8 ....39 G6
Fairway Av *CDALE/KGS* NW9 ......44 D6
Fairway Cl *CROY/NA* CR0 ....198 B2
   GLDGN NW11 ....65 G4
   HOR/WEW KT19 ....206 E2
Fairway Dr *GFD/PVL* UB6 ....78 B5
   THMD SE28 ....109 K5
Fairway Gdns *BECK* BR3 ....199 G3
   IL IG1 ....90 C3
Fairways *ISLW* TW7 ....135 K2
   STAN HA7 ....44 B5
   TEDD TW11 ....174 E3
   WALTH E17 * 70 A1
The Fairway *ACT* W3 ....99 G5
   ALP/SUD HA0 ....61 H6
   BAR EN5 ....33 F1
   BELMT SM2 * 208 E1
   E/WMO/HCT KT8 ....173 G6
   HNWL W7 ....96 B6
   MLHL NW7 ....31 F5
   NTHLT UB5 ....78 C4
   NTHWD HA6 ....26 C6

NWMAL KT3 ....176 A4
PLMGR N13 ....35 J5
RSLP HA4 ....77 C2
STHGT/OAK N14 ....34 B1
Fairweather Cl
SEVS/STOTM N15 ....68 A1
Fairweather Rd
STNW/STAM N16 ....68 C3
Faithfield BUSH WD25 * 27 J1
Fakenham Cl MLHL NW7 ....45 J5
NTHLT UB5 ....78 A4
Fakruddin St WCHPL E/1 ....104 C5
Falaize Av IL IG1 ....90 B2
Falcon Av BMLY BR1 ....184 D6
Falconberg Ct
SOHO/SHAV W1D * 10 C3
Falcon Cl CHSWK W4 ....117 J6
DART DA1 ....151 J6
NTHWD HA6 ....40 C3
STHWK SE1 ....12 B7
Falcon Ct IS N1 ....6 B3
Falcon Crs PEND EN3 ....25 F6
Falcon Dr STWL/WRAY TW19 ....152 A1
Falconer Rd BARK/HLT IG6 ....55 J1
BUSH WD23 ....28 A1
Falcon Gv BTSEA SW11 ....140 D4
Falcon La BTSEA SW11 ....140 D4
Falcon Pk PLSTW E15 ....106 C5
Falcon Rd BTSEA SW11 ....140 D4
HPTN TW12 ....172 E3
PEND EN3 ....25 F6
Falcon Ter BTSEA SW11 * 140 D4
Falcon Wy CDALE/KGS NW9 ....45 G5
KTN/HRWW/W HA3 ....62 A2
WAN E11 ....70 E1
Falconwood Av WELL DA16 ....147 J3
Falconwood Pde WELL DA16 ....147 K5
Falconwood Rd
CROY/NA CRO 213 J5
Falcourt Cl SUT SM1 ....209 F3
Falkirk Gdns OXHEY WD19 ....41 H1
Falkirk St IS N1 ....7 H4
Falkland Av FBAR/BDGN N11 ....34 A6
FNCH N3 ....46 E3
Falkland Park Av SNWD SE25 ....181 F5
Falkland Pl KTTN NW5 ....84 C3
Falkland Rd BAR EN5 ....20 C3
CEND/HSY/T N8 ....67 G1
KTTN NW5 ....84 C3
Fallodon Wy GLDGN NW11 ....64 E3
Fallow Cl CHIG IG7 ....55 F1
Fallow Ct STHWK SE1 * 123 H5
Fallow Court Av
NFNCD/WDSP N12 ....47 G3
Fallowfield STAN HA7 ....29 G5
Fallowfield Ct STAN HA7 ....29 G5
Fallow Flds LOU IG10 ....39 G2
Fallowfields Dr
NFNCH/WDSP N12 ....47 J2
Fallows Cl EFNCH N2 ....47 G5
Falisbrook Rd
STRHM/NOR SW16 ....179 G2
Falman Cl ED N9 ....36 C3
Falmer Rd EN EN1 ....24 A5
SEVS/STOTM N15 ....67 J2
WALTH E17 ....51 K1
Falmouth Av CHING E4 ....52 B1
Falmouth Cl LEE/GVPK SE12 ....145 J6
Falmouth Gdns REDBR IG4 ....71 H1
Falmouth Rd STHWK SE1 ....18 C5
Falmouth St SRTFD E15 ....88 B3
Falstaff Cl DART DA1 ....171 J4
Fambridge Cl SYD SE26 ....164 C6
Fambridge Rd BCTR RM8 ....74 C5
Fane St WKENS W14 ....119 J6
Fanns Ri PUR RM19 ....131 K4
Fann St FARR EC1M 6 C7
Fanshawe Av BARK IG11 ....90 C4
Fanshawe Crs DAGW RM9 ....92 A3
Fanshawe Rd
RCHPK/HAM TW10 ....156 C6
Fanshaw St IS N1 ....7 G4
Fantail Cl THMD SE28 ....109 J5
Fanthorpe St PUT/ROE SW15 ....139 F4
Faraday Av SCUP DA14 ....168 C5
Faraday Cl HOLWY N7 ....85 F4
WATW WD18 ....26 B1
Faraday Rd ACT W3 ....98 E6
E/WMO/HCT KT8 ....189 F1
NKENS W10 ....100 C4
SRTFD E15 ....88 D5
STHL UB1 ....96 B6
WELL DA16 ....148 B4
WIM/MER SW19 ....178 A2
Faraday Wy STMC/STPC BR5 ....202 C1
WOOL/PLUM SE18 ....114 B3
Fareham Rd
EBED/NFELT TW14 ....154 A1
Fareham St SOHO/CST W1F * 10 C3
Farewell Pl MTCM CR4 ....178 C4
Faringdon Av HAYES BR2 ....201 J3
Faringford Rd SRTFD E15 ....88 C5
Farjeon Rd BKHTH/KID SE3 ....146 C2
Farleigh Av HAYES BR2 ....199 J4
Farleigh Court Rd
CROY/NA CRO 196 A6
Farleigh Pl STNW/STAM N16 ....86 B2
Farleigh Rd STNW/STAM N16 ....86 B2
Farley Dr GDMY/SEVK IG3 ....72 E5
Farley Pl SNWD SE25 ....181 H6
Farley Rd CAT SE6 ....165 F2
SAND/SEL CR2 ....212 A5
Farlington Pl PUT/ROE SW15 ....158 E2
Farlow Rd PUT/ROE SW15 ....139 G4
Farlton Rd WAND/EARL SW18 ....160 A2
Farman Ter
KTN/HRWW/W HA3 * 61 K1
Farm Av ALP/SUD HA0 ....79 J4
CRICK NW2 ....82 C1
RYLN/HDSTN HA2 ....60 A4
STRHM/NOR SW16 ....161 K6
SWLY BR8 ....187 K6
Farmborough Cl HRW HA1 ....60 D4
Farm Cl BELMT SM2 ....209 H6

BKHH IG9 ....39 G5
DAGE RM10 ....92 E5
FUL/PGN SW6 * 139 K1
STHL UB1 ....96 B6
Farncote Rd LEE/GVPK SE12 ....165 K5
Farmdale Rd CAR SM5 ....209 J5
GNWCH SE10 ....125 K5
Farm Dr CROY/NA CRO 198 C6
Farmer Rd LEY E10 ....69 K5
Farmers Rd CMBW SE5 ....142 C1
Farmer St KENS W8 * 119 K1
Farmfield Rd BMLY BR1 ....183 H1
Farmhouse Rd
STRHM/NOR SW16 ....179 H5
Farmilo Rd WALTH E17 ....69 J4
Farmington Av SUT SM1 ....209 H1
Farmlands ENC/FH EN2 ....23 G2
PIN HA5 ....58 E1
The Farmlands NTHLT UB5 ....77 K4
Farmland Wk CHST BR7 ....185 G1
Farm La CROY/NA CRO 198 C6
FUL/PGN SW6 ....119 K6
Farmleigh STHGT/OAK N14 ....34 C2
KENS W8 ....119 K1
Farm Pl DART DA1 ....150 D5
KENS W8 ....119 K1
Farm Rd BELMT SM2 ....209 H5
EDGW HA8 ....44 E1
ESH/CLAY KT10 ....189 F5
HSLWW TW4 ....154 D5
MRDN SM4 ....194 A2
NTHWD HA6 ....40 A1
WCHMH N21 ....35 J3
WLSDN NW10 ....81 F6
Farmstead Rd CAT SE6 ....164 E6
KTN/HRWW/W HA3 ....42 D4
Farm St MYFR/PICC W1J 9 J6
Farm V BXLY DA5 ....169 J1
Farmway BCTR RM8 ....91 J2
Farm Wy BKHH IG9 ....39 G6
HCH RM12 ....93 J1
NTHWD HA6 ....26 C6
WPK KT4 ....208 A1
Farnaby Rd BMLY BR1 ....183 H4
ELTH/MOT SE9 ....146 B5
Farnan Av WALTH E17 ....51 J5
Farnan Rd STRHM/NOR SW16 ....179 K1
Farnborough Av
SAND/SEL CR2 ....213 G5
WALTH E17 * 51 G6
Farnborough Cl WBLY HA9 ....62 D6
Farnborough Common
ORP BR6 ....216 B3
Farnborough Crs HAYES BR2 ....199 J5
SAND/SEL CR2 ....213 G6
Farnborough Wy ORP BR6 ....216 E5
PECK SE15 * 143 F1
Farncombe St
BERM/RHTH SE16 ....123 H2
Farndale Av PLMGR N13 ....35 H5
Farndale Crs GFD/PVL UB6 ....96 C2
Farnell Ms ECT SW5 ....120 A5
Farnell Rd ISLW TW7 ....135 J4
Farnham Cl TRDG/WHET N20 ....33 G2
Farnham Gdns RYNPK SW20 ....176 E5
Farnham Pl STHWK SE1 ....18 B1
Farnham Rd GDMY/SEVK IG3 ....73 F5
WELL DA16 ....148 D3
Farnham Royal LBTH SE11 ....122 A5
Farningham Rd TOTM N17 ....50 C3
Farnley Rd CHING E4 ....38 C2
SNWD SE25 ....180 E6
Farnol Rd DART DA1 ....151 K6
Faro Cl BMLY BR1 ....185 F5
Faroe Rd WKENS W14 ....119 G3
Faroma Wk ENC/FH EN2 ....23 G2
Farquhar Rd NRWD SE19 ....181 G1
WIM/MER SW19 ....159 K5
Farquharson Rd
CROY/NA CRO 196 D4
Farrance Rd CHDH RM6 ....74 A3
Farrance St POP/IOD E14 ....105 J5
Farrant Av WDGN N22 ....49 G5
Farrant Cl ORP BR6 ....217 G5
Farr Av BARK IG11 ....109 G1
Farren Rd FSTH SE23 ....164 B4
Farrer Ms CEND/HSY/T N8 ....66 C1
Farrer Rd CEND/HSY/T N8 ....66 C1
KTN/HRWW/W HA3 ....62 B2
Farrier Cl BMLY BR1 ....184 C6
Farrier Rd NTHLT UB5 ....96 A1
Farrier St CAMTN NW1 ....84 B5
Farriers Wy BORE WD6 ....31 F1
Farrier Wk WBPTN SW10 * 120 B6
Farringdon La CLKNW EC1R 5 K7
Farringdon Rd FSBYW WC1X 5 J6
HCRC EC1N 6 A5
Farringdon St STBT EC1A 12 A3
Farrington Av
STMC/STPC BR5 ....186 C6
Farrington Pl CHST BR7 ....185 J3
Farrins Rents
BERM/RHTH SE16 ....124 B1
Farrow La NWCR SE14 ....143 K1
Farrow Pl BERM/RHTH SE16 ....124 B3
Farr Rd ENC/FH EN2 ....23 K2
Farthingale Wk SRTFD E15 ....88 B5
Farthing Flds WAP E1W * 123 J1
Farthing Flds WAP E1W 123 J1
Farthings Cl CHING E4 ....38 C5
PIN HA5 ....59 F3
The Farthings KUTN/CMB KT2 ....175 H4
Farthing St ORP BR6 ....215 K5
Farwell Rd SCUP DA14 ....168 C6
Farwig La BMLY BR1 ....183 K4
Fashion St WCHPL E1 ....13 J2
Fashoda Rd HAYES BR2 ....200 C1
Fassett Rd HACK E8 ....86 C4
KUT/HW KT1 ....191 F1
Fassett Sq HACK E8 ....86 C4
Fauconberg Rd CHSWK W4 ....117 K6
Faulkner Cl BCTR RM8 ....73 K4

Faulkner St NWCR SE14 ....143 K2
Fauna Cl CHDH RM6 ....73 J3
STAN HA7 ....29 K5
Faunce St WALW SE17 ....122 C5
Favart Rd FUL/PGN SW6 ....139 K2
Faversham Av CHING E4 ....38 C3
EN EN1 ....35 K1
Faversham Rd BECK BR3 ....164 C2
CAT SE6 ....164 C2
MRDN SM4 ....194 A3
Fawcett Cl BTSEA SW11 ....140 C3
STRHM/NOR SW16 ....162 B6
Fawcett Est CLPT E///5 * 68 C5
Fawcett Rd CROY/NA CRO 211 H1
WLSDN NW10 ....81 H6
Fawcett St WBPTN SW10 ....120 B6
Fawe Park Rd PUT/ROE SW15 ....139 J5
Fawe St POP/IOD E14 ....105 K4
Fawkes Av DART DA1 ....171 J4
Fawley Rd KIL/WHAMP NW6 ....83 F3
Fawnbrake Av HNHL SE24 ....142 C6
Fawn Rd CHIG IG7 ....55 F1
PLSTW E13 ....107 G1
Fawns Manor Rd
EBED/NFELT TW14 ....153 G3
Fawood Av WLSDN NW10 ....81 F5
Faygate Crs BXLYHS DA6 ....149 H6
Faygate Rd BRXS/STRHM SW2 ....162 A4
Fayland Av STRHM/NOR SW16 ....179 H1
Fearnley Crs HPTN TW12 ....172 E2
Fearon St GNWCH SE10 ....125 K5
Featherbed La CROY/NA CRO 213 H5
Feathers Pl GNWCH SE10 ....125 H6
Featherstone Av FSTH SE23 ....163 J4
Featherstone Rd MLHL NW7 ....45 K2
NWDGN UB2 ....114 D3
Featherstone St STLK EC1Y 6 E6
Featherstone Ter
NWDGN UB2 ....114 D3
Featley Rd BRXN/ST SW9 ....142 C4
Federal Rd GFD/PVL UB6 ....97 J1
Federation Rd ABYW SE2 ....128 C4
Fee Farm Rd ESH/CLAY KT10 ....205 F5
Felbridge Av STAN HA7 ....43 G4
Felbridge Cl BELMT SM2 ....209 G6
STRHM/NOR SW16 ....162 B6
Felbrigge Rd GDMY/SEVK IG3 ....73 F6
Felday Rd LEW SE13 ....164 E1
Felden Cl PIN HA5 ....41 J3
Felden St FUL/PGN SW6 ....139 J2
Feldman Cl STNW/STAM N16 ....68 C5
Felgate Ms HMSMTH W6 ....118 E4
Felhampton Rd
ELTH/MOT SE9 ....167 G5
Felix Av CEND/HSY/T N8 ....66 E3
Felix Pl BRXS/STRHM SW2 ....142 B6
Felixstowe Rd ABYW SE2 ....128 C3
ED N9 ....36 C6
TOTM N17 ....50 C6
WLSDN NW10 ....99 K2
Felix St BETH E2 * 104 D1
Feilbrigg Rd EDUL SE22 ....143 G6
Feilbrigg St WCHPL E1 ....104 D3
Fellbrook RCHPK/HAM TW10 ....156 C5
Fellmongers Yd CROY/NA CRO * 211 J3
Fellowes Cl YEAD UB4 ....95 H3
Fellowes Rd CAR SM5 ....209 J1
Fellows Rd HAMP NW3 ....83 H5
Fell Rd CROY/NA CRO 211 J1
Felltram Wy CHARL SE7 ....125 K5
Felmersham Cl CLAP SW4 ....141 K5
Felmingham Rd PGE/AN SE20 ....181 K5
Felsberg Rd
BRXS/STRHM SW2 ....161 K1
Fels Cl DAGE RM10 ....92 D1
Fels Farm Av DAGE RM10 ....92 E1
Felsham Rd PUT/ROE SW15 ....139 G4
Felspar Cl WOOL/PLUM SE18 ....128 A5
Felstead Av CLAY IG5 ....54 A4
Felstead Rd CRW RM5 ....56 E2
HOM E9 ....87 J4
LOU IG10 ....39 J2
ORP BR6 ....202 B6
WAN E11 ....70 E6
Felstead St HOM E9 ....87 H4
Felsted Rd CAN/RD E16 ....107 H5
Feltham Av E/WMO/HCT KT8 ....189 K1
Felthambrook Wy FELT TW13 ....154 A5
Feltham Rd ASHF TW15 ....152 E6
MTCM CR4 ....178 E5
Felton St IS N1 ....7 F1
Fenchurch Av FENCHST EC3M 13 G4
Fenchurch Bldgs FENCHST EC3M * 13 H4
Fenchurch Pl FENCHST EC3M 13 H4
Fenchurch St FENCHST EC3M 13 G5
Fendall Rd HOR/WEW KT19 ....206 E3
Fendall St STHWK SE1 ....19 H5
Fendt Cl CAN/RD E16 ....106 D5
Fendyke Rd ABYW SE2 ....128 A3
Fenelon Pl WKENS W14 ....119 J4
Fen Gv BFN/LL DA15 ....168 A1
Fenham Rd PECK SE15 ....143 H1
Fenman Ct TOTM N17 ....50 D4
Fenman Gdns GDMY/SEVK IG3 ....73 H1
Fenn Cl BMLY BR1 ....183 K2
Fennel Cl CAN/RD E16 ....106 C3
CROY/NA CRO 198 A5
Fennells Md HOR/WEW KT19 ....207 H6
Fennel St WOOL/PLUM SE18 ....127 F6
Fenner Cl BERM/RHTH SE16 ....123 J4
Fenner Sq BTSEA SW11 * 140 C4
Fenning St STHWK SE1 ....19 G2
Fenn St HOM E9 ....87 F3
Fenstanton Av
NFNCH/WDSP N12 ....47 H1
Fen St CAN/RD E16 ....106 D6
Fentiman Rd VX/NE SW8 ....121 K6
Fenton Cl BRXN/ST SW9 ....142 A3

CHST BR7 ....184 E1
HACK E8 ....86 B4
Fenton Rd TOTM N17 ....49 J5
Fenwick Cv PECK SE15 ....143 H4
Fenwick Pl BRXN/ST SW9 ....141 K4
SAND/SEL CR2 ....211 H5
Fenwick Rd PECK SE15 ....143 H4
Ferdinand Pl CAMTN NW1 ....84 A5
Ferdinand St CAMTN NW1 ....84 A4
Ferguson Av BRYLDS KT5 ....191 G2
Ferguson Cl BECK BR3 ....183 F6
Ferguson Dr ACT W3 ....99 F5
Ferguson's Cl POP/IOD E14 ....124 D4
Fergus Rd HBRY N5 ....85 H5
Ferme Park Rd CEND/HSY/T N8 ....66 E2
Fermor Rd FSTH SE23 ....164 B3
Fermoy Rd GFD/PVL UB6 ....96 B3
MV/WKIL W9 ....100 D3
Fern Av MTCM CR4 ....195 J1
Fernbank BKHH IG9 ....39 F3
Fernbank Av ALP/SUD HA0 ....79 F2
WOT/HER KT12 ....188 D4
Fernbank Ms BAL SW12 ....161 G1
Fernbrook Dr
RYLN/HDSTN HA2 ....60 B4
Fernbrook Rd LEW SE13 ....165 H1
Ferncliff Rd HACK E8 ....86 C3
Fern Cl ERITH DA8 ....150 C2
IS N1 * 7 G1
Ferncroft Av HAMP NW3 ....82 E1
NFNCH/WDSP N12 ....47 J2
RSLP HA4 ....59 G6
Ferndale BMLY BR1 ....184 B5
Ferndale Av HSLWW TW4 ....134 D4
WALTH E17 ....70 B2
Ferndale Cl BXLYHN DA7 ....149 F2
Ferndale Rd CLAP SW4 ....141 K5
CRW RM5 ....57 E7
FSTGT E7 ....89 F5
SEVS/STOTM N15 ....68 B3
SNWD SE25 ....197 J2
WAN E11 ....70 D6
Ferndale St EHAM E6 ....108 B6
Ferndale Ter HRW HA1 ....61 F1
Ferndale Wy ORP BR6 ....216 D4
Ferndell Av BXLY DA5 ....170 A5
Ferndene HNHL SE24 ....142 D5
Ferndene Wy KONM/RG RM7 ....74 D3
Ferndown NTHWD HA6 ....40 E5
Ferndown Av ORP BR6 ....201 J5
Ferndown Cl BELMT SM2 ....209 H4
PIN HA5 ....41 J4
Ferndown Rd ELTH/MOT SE9 ....166 C2
OXHEY WD19 ....41 G4
Ferney Meade Wy ISLW TW7 ....136 B3
Ferney Rd EBAR EN4 ....34 A2
Fern Gv EBED/NFELT TW14 ....154 A2
Fernhall Dr REDBR IG4 ....71 H2
Fernham Rd THHTH CR7 ....196 D1
Fern Hl EBAR EN4 ....21 K1
Fernhead Rd MV/WKIL W9 ....100 D3
Fernhill Ct WALTH E17 ....52 E5
Fernhill Gdns KUTN/CMB KT2 ....174 E1
Fernhill St CAN/RD E16 ....126 E1
Fernholme Rd PECK SE15 ....144 A6
Fernhurst Gdns EDGW HA8 ....44 C2
Fernhurst Rd ASHF TW15 ....153 F6
CROY/NA CRO 197 H4
FUL/PGN SW6 ....139 H2
Fern La NWDGN UB2 ....114 C5
Fernlea Rd BAL SW12 ....161 G3
MTCM CR4 ....179 F5
Fernleigh Cl CROY/NA CRO 211 G2
MV/WKIL W9 ....100 D7
Fernleigh Ct RYLN/HDSTN HA2 ....42 B5
WBLY HA9 ....62 A5
Fernley Cl PIN HA5 ....58 E1
Fernsbury St FSBYW WC1X 5 J5
Fernshaw Rd WBPTN SW10 ....120 B6
Fernside AV FELT TW13 ....154 A6
MLHL NW7 ....31 F5
Fernside Rd BAL SW12 ....160 E3
Fern St BOW E3 ....105 J3
Fernthorpe Rd
STRHM/NOR SW16 ....179 H2
Ferntower Rd HBRY N5 ....85 K3
Fern Wk STHWK SE1 ....123 H5
Fernways IL IG1 ....90 B2
Fernwood Av ALP/SUD HA0 ....79 J4
STRHM/NOR SW16 ....161 J6
Fernwood Cl BMLY BR1 ....184 B5
Fernwood Crs TRDG/WHET N20 ....33 K3
Ferraro Cl HEST TW5 ....115 F6
Ferrers Av WDR/YW UB7 ....112 A2
WLGTN SM6 ....210 D2
Ferrers Rd STRHM/NOR SW16 ....179 J1
Ferrestone Rd CEND/HSY/T N8 ....67 F1
Ferrey Ms BRXN/ST SW9 ....142 B3
Ferriby Cl IS N1 ....85 G5
Ferrier St WAND/EARL SW18 ....140 A5
Ferring Cl RYLN/HDSTN HA2 ....60 C5
Ferrings DUL SE21 ....163 F4
Ferris Av CROY/NA CRO 213 H1
Ferris Rd EDUL SE22 ....143 H5
Ferron Rd CLPT E5 ....86 D1
Ferro Rd RAIN RM13 ....111 J3
Ferryhills Cl OXHEY WD19 ....27 G5
Ferry La BARN SW13 ....118 C6
BTFD TW8 ....117 F6
RAIN RM13 ....111 H4
STNW/STAM N16 ....68 A4

TWK TW1 ....156 C3
Ferry Sq BTFD TW8 * 117 F6
Ferry St POP/IOD E14 ....125 F5
Festing Rd PUT/ROE SW15 ....139 G4
Festival Cl BXLY DA5 ....168 E3
ERITH DA8 ....150 C1
Festoon Wy CAN/RD E16 ....107 H6
Fetter La FLST/FETLN EC4A 11 K4
Ffinch St DEPT SE8 ....144 D1
Fidler Pl BUSH WD23 ....28 B1
Field Cl BKHH IG9 ....39 G5
BMLY BR1 ....184 B5
CHING E4 ....51 K2
CHSGTN KT9 ....205 J3
E/WMO/HCT KT8 ....189 G2
HSLWW TW4 ....134 A2
HYS/HAR UB3 ....133 F1
RSLP HA4 ....58 A5
Fieldcommon La
WOT/HER KT12 ....188 D5
Field Ct GINN WC1R 11 H2
Field End RSLP HA4 ....77 H4
RYLN/HDSTN HA2 ....60 D3
Field End Cl OXHEY WD19 ....27 J2
Field End Rd PIN HA5 ....59 F2
RSLP HA4 ....77 H1
Fieldend Rd
STRHM/NOR SW16 ....179 H4
Fielders Cl EN EN1 ....24 A5
RYLN/HDSTN HA2 ....60 C5
Fieldfare Rd THMD SE28 ....109 J6
Fieldgate St WCHPL E1 ....104 C4
Fieldhouse Cl SWFD E18 ....53 F4
Fieldhouse Rd BAL SW12 ....161 H3
Fielding Av WHTN TW2 ....155 H5
Fielding Rd CHSWK W4 ....118 A3
WKENS W14 ....119 G3
The Fieldings FSTH SE23 ....163 K3
Fielding St WALW SE17 ....122 D6
Fielding Ter EA W5 * 98 B6
Field La BTFD TW8 ....136 D1
TEDD TW11 ....174 B1
Field Md CDALE/KGS NW9 ....45 G3
Field Pl NWMAL KT3 ....192 C3
Field Rd EBED/NFELT TW14 ....154 A1
FSTGT E7 ....88 E2
HMSMTH W6 ....119 H6
OXHEY WD19 ....27 H1
Fieldsend Rd CHEAM SM3 ....208 C3
Fields Est HACK E8 * 86 C5
Fieldside Cl ORP BR6 ....216 C2
Fields Park Crs CHDH RM6 ....73 K2
Field St FSBYW WC1X 5 G4
Fieldview WAND/EARL SW18 ....160 C3
Fieldway BCRP HA4 ....77 F2
Field Wy CROY/NA CRO 213 K5
GFD/PVL UB6 ....78 B6
RSLP HA4 ....58 A5
WLSDN NW10 ....80 E5
Fieldway BCTR RM8 ....73 J2
STMC/STPC BR5 ....201 J3
Fieldway Crs HBRY N5 ....85 G3
Fiennes Cl BCTR RM8 ....73 J5
Fiesta Dr DAGW RM9 ....110 E3
Fife Rd CAN/RD E16 ....106 E4
KUT/HW KT1 ....175 F6
MORT/ESHN SW14 ....137 K6
WDGN N22 ....49 H5
Fife Ter IS N1 ....5 H2
Fifield Pth FSTH SE23 ....164 K5
Fifth Av MNPK E12 ....89 K2
NKENS W10 ....100 C3
Fifth Cross Rd WHTN TW2 ....155 J4
Fifth Wy WBLY HA9 ....80 D2
Figge's Rd MTCM CR4 ....179 F3
Filby Rd CHSGTN KT9 ....206 B4
Filey Av STNW/STAM N16 ....68 C5
Filey Cl BELMT SM2 ....209 G5
Filey Waye RSLP HA4 ....58 E6
Fillebrook Av EN EN1 ....24 A5
Fillebrook Rd WAN E11 ....70 B5
Filmer Chambers
FUL/PGN SW6 * 139 J2
Filmer Rd FUL/PGN SW6 ....139 J2
Finborough Rd TOOT SW17 ....178 E3
WBPTN SW10 ....120 A6
Finchale Rd ABYW SE2 ....128 C3
Fincham Cl HGDN/ICK UB10 ....76 A1
Finch Cl BAR EN5 ....20 E6
Finch Ct DEPT/NFELT TW14 ....154 C1
Finch Gdns CHING E4 ....51 J1
Finchingfield Av WFD IG8 ....53 G3
Finch La BANK EC3V 13 F4
Finchley La HDN NW4 ....64 B1
Finchley Pk NFNCH/WDSP N12 ....33 G6
Finchley Pl STJWD NW8 ....2 A1
Finchley Rd GLDGN NW11 ....64 D2
HAMP NW3 ....83 H2
STJWD NW8 ....2 A1
Finchley Vls
NFNCH/WDSP N12 * 33 H6
Finch Ms PECK SE15 * 143 G2
Finch Rd RSLP HA4 ....59 F6
Finden Rd FSTGT E7 ....89 F3
Findhorn Av YEAD UB4 ....95 H4
Findhorn St POP/IOD E14 ....106 A5
Findon Cl RYLN/HDSTN HA2 * 78 B1
WAND/EARL SW18 ....159 K1
Findon Gdns RAIN RM13 ....111 J4
Findon Rd ED N9 ....36 D3
SHB W12 ....118 D2
Fingal St GNWCH SE10 ....125 K5
Finglesham Cl
STMC/STPC BR5 ....202 E5
Finland Rd BROCKY SE4 ....144 B4
Finland St BERM/RHTH SE16 ....124 B3
Finlays Cl CHSGTN KT9 ....206 C3
Finlay St FUL/PGN SW6 ....139 G2
Finnis St BETH E2 ....104 D2
Finnymore Rd DAGW RM9 ....92 A5
Finsbury Av LVPST EC2M * 13 F2
Finsbury Circ LVPST EC2M 13 F2

Finsbury Cottages WDGN N22 .....48 E3
Finsbury Est CLKNW EC1R 5 K5
  FSBYE EC1V * 6 A5
Finsbury Market SDTCH EC2A 7 G7
Finsbury Park Av FSBYPK N4 ...67 J3
Finsbury Park Rd FSBYPK N4 ...67 H5
Finsbury Pavement
  SDTCH EC2A 13 F1
Finsbury Rd WDGN N22 ....49 F4
Finsbury Sq STLK EC2Y 7 F7
Finsbury Wy BXLY DA5 ....169 G1
Finsen Rd HNHL SE24 ....142 D5
Finstock Rd NKENS W10 ....100 B5
Finucane Dr STHC/STPC BR5 ....202 D4
Finucane Gdns RAIN RM13 ....93 J4
Finucane Rd BUSH WD23 ....28 C4
Fiona Ct ENC/FH EN2 * 23 J5
Firbank Cl CAN/RD E16 ....107 H4
  ENC/FH EN2 ....23 J5
Firbank Dr OXHEY WD19 ....27 J2
Firbank Rd CRW RM5 ....56 D1
  PECK SE15 ....143 J3
Fircroft Gdns HRW HA1 * 48 A2
Fircroft Rd CHSGTN KT9 ....206 B2
  TOOT SW17 ....160 E5
Firdene BRYLDS KT5 ....191 K5
Fire Bell Aly SURB KT6 ....191 F3
Firebell Ms SURB KT6 ....191 F3
Firecrest Dr HAMP NW3 ....83 F1
Firefly Cl WLGTN SM6 ....210 E5
Firefly Gdns EHAM E6 ....107 J3
Firethorn Cl EDGW HA8 ....30 E6
Fir Gv NWMAL KT3 ....192 C3
Firhill Rd CAT SE6 ....164 D5
Fir Rd FELT TW13 ....172 C1

Firbank Cl CAN/RD E16 ....107 H4
Firs Av FBAR/BDGN N11 ....48 A2
  BXLYHN DA7 ....148 D1
  CHDH RM6 ....73 J2
  DAGE RM10 ....110 D1
  E/WMO/HCT KT8 ....188 E1
  EN EN1 ....24 B6
  HDN NW4 ....63 K1
  HOR/WEW KT19 ....207 G6
  HYS/HAR UB3 ....113 J1
  MNPK E12 ....89 J2
  MORT/ESHN SW14 ....138 B3
  MV/WKIL W9 ....100 D3
  PLSTW E13 ....106 E2
  UED N18 ....50 C3
  WALTH E17 ....69 K2
  WBLY HA9 ....61 K6
  WOT/HER KT12 ....188 A3
First Cl E/WMO/HCT KT8 ....189 H1
First Cross Rd WHTN TW2 ....155 K4
First Dr WLSDN NW10 ....80 E5
Firs Dr CDALE/KGS NW9 ....44 B4
  HEST TW5 ....134 A1
Firside Gv BFN/LL DA15 ....168 A3
Firs La WCHMH N21 ....35 J2
Firs Park Av WCHMH N21 ....35 K3
Firs Park Gdns WCHMH N21 ....35 K3
First Av ACT W3 ....99 H6
  BXLYHN DA7 ....148 D1
  CHDH RM6 ....73 J2
  DAGE RM10 ....110 D1
  E/WMO/HCT KT8 ....188 E1
  EN EN1 ....24 B6
  HDN NW4 ....63 K1
  HOR/WEW KT19 ....207 G6
  HYS/HAR UB3 ....113 J1
  MNPK E12 ....89 J2
  MORT/ESHN SW14 ....138 B3
  MV/WKIL W9 ....100 D3
  PLSTW E13 ....106 E2
  UED N18 ....50 C3
  WALTH E17 ....69 K2
  WBLY HA9 ....61 K6
  WOT/HER KT12 ....188 A3
First Cl E/WMO/HCT KT8 ....189 H1
First Cross Rd WHTN TW2 ....155 K4
First Dr WLSDN NW10 ....80 E5
First St CHEL SW3 ....14 D6
Firstway RYNPK SW20 ....177 F5
First Wy WBLY HA9 ....80 E2
Firs Wk NTHWD HA6 ....40 B2
  WFD IG8 ....52 E1
Firswood Av HOR/WEW KT19 .....207 G3
Firth Gdns FUL/PGN SW6 ....139 H2
Firtree Av MTCM CR4 ....179 F5
Fir Tree Av WDR/YW UB7 ....112 D3
Fir Tree Cl EA W5 ....98 A5
  ESH/CLAY KT10 ....204 C3
  HOR/WEW KT19 ....207 H2
  ORP BR6 ....217 F3
  ROM RM1 ....57 F5
  STRHM/NOR SW16 ....179 H1
Fir Tree Gdns CROY/NA CRO 213 J2
Fir Tree Gv CAR SM5 ....209 K6
Fir Tree Pl ASHF TW15 * 152 D6
Fir Tree Rd HSLWW TW4 ....134 D5
Fir Trees Cl BERM/RHTH SE16 ..124 B1
Fir Tree Wk EN EN1 ....24 C3
Fir Wk HAW KT17 ....208 B4
Fisher Cl CROY/NA CRO 197 G5
  GFD/PVL UB6 ....96 A2
Fisherdene ESH/CLAY KT10 .....205 G5
Fisherman Cl
  RCHPK/HAM TW10 ....156 D6
Fishermans Dr
  BERM/RHTH SE16 ....124 A2
Fisher Rd KTN/HRWW/WS HA3 ...43 F5
Fishers Ct NWCR SE14 ....144 A2
Fisher's La CHSWK W4 ....118 A4
Fisher St CAN/RD E16 ....106 E4
  RSQ WC1B 11 G2
Fisher's Wy BELV DA17 ....129 K1
Fisherton St STJWD NW8 ....2 A7
Fishguard Wy CAN/RD E16 ......127 G1
Fishponds Rd HAYES BR2 ....215 H3
  TOOT SW17 ....160 D6
Fish Street HI MON EC3R 13 F6
Fisons Rd CAN/RD E16 ....125 K1
Fitzalan Rd ESH/CLAY KT10 ....204 E5
  FNCH N3 ....46 C6
Fitzalan St LBTH SE11 ....17 H6
Fitzgeorge Av WKENS W14 .....119 H4
Fitzgerald Av
  MORT/ESHN SW14 ....138 B4
Fitzgerald Rd
  MORT/ESHN SW14 ....138 A4
  LEY E10 ....70 A6
  WAN E11 ....70 E2
Fitzhardinge St MBLAR W1H 9 G3
Fitzhugh Gv
  WAND/EARL SW18 ....160 C1
Fitzjames Av CROY/NA CRO 197 H6
  WKENS W14 ....119 H4
Fitzjohn Av BAR EN5 ....20 C6
Fitzjohn's Av HAMP NW3 ....83 H5
Fitzneal St ACT W3 ....99 H5
Fitzroy Cl HGT N6 ....65 K5
Fitzroy Crs CHSWK W4 * 138 A1
Fitzroy Gdns NRWD SE19 ....181 F3
Fitzroy Ms GTPST W1W 4 A7
Fitzroy Pk HGT N6 ....65 K5
Fitzroy Rd CAMTN NW1 ....84 A6
Fitzroy Sq FITZ W1T * 4 A7
Fitzroy St CAMTN NW1 ....4 A7
  FITZ W1T 10 A1
Fitzstephen Rd BCTR RM8 ....91 H3
Fitzwarren Gdns ARCH N19 ......66 C5
Fitzwilliam Av RCH/KEW TW9 ...137 G3
Fitzwilliam Ms CAN/RD E16 ....125 K1
Fitzwilliam Rd CLAP SW4 ......141 H4
Fitz Wygram Cl HPTN TW12 .....173 H5
Five Acre CDALE/KGS NW9 ....45 H5
Fiveacre Cl THHTH CR7 ....196 B3
Five Elms Rd DAGW RM9 ....92 B1
  HAYES BR2 ....215 G1
Five Fields Cl OXHEY WD19 .....27 K4
Five Oak Ms BML1Y BR1 * 165 K5
Five Oaks La CHIG IG7 ....56 A2
Fiveways Cnr ELTH/MOT SE9 ...167 G4
Five Ways Jct HDN NW4 ....45 J4
Fiveways Rd BRXN/ST SW9 ......142 B3
Fladbury Rd SEVS/STOTM N15 ...67 K3
Fladgate Rd WAN E11 ....70 C3
Flag Cl CROY/NA CRO 198 A5
Flag Wk PIN HA5 ....58 E3
Flambard Rd HRW HA1 ....61 G3
Flamborough Rd RSLP HA4 ....76 E1
Flamborough St POP/IOD E14 ...105 G5
Flamborough Wk
  POP/IOD E14 * 105 G5
Flamingo Wk HCH RM12 ....93 J5
Flamstead Gdns DAGW RM9 ....91 J5
Flamstead Rd DAGW RM9 ....91 J5
Flamsted Av WBLY HA9 ....80 C4
Flamsteed Rd CHARL SE7 ....126 D5
Flanchford Rd SHB W12 ....118 C3
Flanders Crs TOOT SW17 ....178 E3
Flanders Rd CHSWK W4 ....118 B4
  EHAM E6 ....107 K1
Flanders Wy HOM E9 ....87 F4
Flandrian Cl EN EN3 ....25 J1
Flank St WCHPL E1 ....104 C6
Flask Wk HAMP NW3 ....83 G2
Flavell Ms GNWCH SE10 ....125 H5
Flaxen Cl CHING E4 ....37 K5
Flaxen Rd CHING E4 ....37 K5
Flaxley Rd MRDN SM4 ....194 A4
Flaxman Rd CMBW SE5 ....142 C3
Flaxman Ter STPAN WC1H 4 E6
Flaxton Rd WOOL/PLUM SE18 ...147 J2
Flecker Cl STAN HA7 ....43 F1
Fleece Dr ED N9 ....36 C6
Fleece Rd SURB KT6 ....190 D5
Fleece Wk HOLWY N7 * 84 E4
Fleeming Cl WALTH E17 ....51 H5
Fleeming Rd WALTH E17 ....51 H5
Fleet Cl E/WMO/HCT KT8 ....188 E2
  RSLP HA4 ....58 A3
Fleet Pl STP EC4M * 12 A3
Fleet Rd HAMP NW3 ....83 J3
Fleetside E/WMO/HCT KT8 ....189 F2
Fleet Sq FSBYW WC1X 5 G5
Fleet St FLST/FETLN EC4A 11 K4
Fleet Street HI BETH E2 * 104 C3
Fleet Ter CAT SE6 * 165 F2
Fleetwood Cl CAN/RD E16 ......107 H4
  CHSGTN KT9 ....205 K5
  CROY/NA CRO 212 B1
Fleetwood Rd NWMAL KT3 ......175 J6
  WLSDN NW10 ....81 J5
Fleetwood Sq NWMAL KT3 ....175 J6
Fleetwood St STNW/STAM N16 ...68 A6
Fleetwood Wy OXHEY WD19 ....27 G6
Fleming Cl MV/WKIL W9 ....100 E3
  WBPTN SW10 * 120 A6
Fleming Ct CROY/NA CRO 211 G3
Fleming Md MTCM CR4 ....178 D3
Fleming Rd STHL UB1 ....96 B5
  WALW SE17 ....122 C6
Fleming Wy ISLW TW7 ....136 A4
  THMD SE28 ....109 K6
Flemming Av RSLP HA4 ....59 F5
Flempton Rd WALTH E17 ....51 F6
Fletcher Cl EHAM E6 ....108 B6
Fletcher La LEY E10 ....70 A4
Fletcher Rd CHIG IG7 ....55 F1
  CHSWK W4 ....117 K3
Fletchers Cl HAYES BR2 ....200 A1
Fletcher St WCHPL E1 ....104 C6
Fletching Rd CHARL SE7 ....126 C6
  CLPT E5 ....86 E1
Fletton Rd FBAR/BDGN N11 ......48 E3
Fleur De Lis St WCHPL E1 ....7 H7
Flexmere Rd TOTM N17 ....49 K4
Flight Ap CDALE/KGS NW9 * 45 H4
Flimwell Cl BMLY BR1 ....183 H1
Flint Cl ORP BR6 ....217 F6
  SRTFD E15 ....88 D4
Flint Down Cl
  STMC/STPC BR5 * 186 C6
Flintmill Crs BKHTH/KID SE3 ..146 D3
Flinton St WALW SE17 ....123 H5
Flint St WALW SE17 ....19 F7
Flitcroft St LSQ/SEVD WC2H 10 D4
Floathaven Cl THMD SE28 ......128 B1

Flock Mill Pl WAND/EARL SW18 .160 A3
Flockton St BERM/RHTH SE16 ...123 H2
Flodden Rd CMBW SE5 ....142 D2
Flood La TWK TW1 * 156 B3
Flood St CHEL SW3 ....120 D5
Flood Wk CHEL SW3 ....120 D6
Flora Cl POP/IOD E14 ....105 K5
  STAN HA7 ....29 K5
Flora Gdns CHDH RM6 ....73 J3
  HMSMTH W6 * 118 E4
Floral St COVGDN WC2E 11 F5
Flora St BELV DA17 ....129 G5
Florence Av ENC/FH EN2 ....23 J4
  MRDN SM4 ....194 B2
Florence Cl WOT/HER KT12 ....188 A4
Florence Ct WAN E11 ....71 F1
Florence Dr ENC/FH EN2 ....23 J4
Florence Gdns CHSWK W4 ......117 K6
Florence Rd ABYW SE2 ....128 C3
  BECK BR3 ....182 A5
  BMLY BR1 ....183 K4
  CHSWK W4 ....118 A3
  EA W5 ....98 A6
  EHAM E6 ....89 G6
  FELT TW13 ....154 A3
  FSBYPK N4 ....67 H4
  KUTN/CMB KT2 ....175 G3
  NWCR SE14 ....144 C2
  NWDGN UB2 ....114 C4
  PLSTW E13 ....89 K6
  SAND/SEL CR2 ....211 K6
  WIM/MER SW19 ....178 A2
  WOT/HER KT12 ....188 A4
Florence St CAN/RD E16 ....106 D3
  HDN NW4 ....64 A1
  IS N1 ....85 H5
Florence Ter NWCR SE14 ......144 C2
Florence Vls HGT N6 * 66 B4
Florence Wy BAL SW12 ....160 E3
Florfield Rd HACK E8 ....86 D4
Florian Av SUT SM1 ....209 H2
Florian Rd PUT/ROE SW15 .....139 H5
Florida Cl BUSH WD23 ....28 D4
Florida Rd THHTH CR7 ....180 C4
Florida St BETH E2 ....104 C2
Florin Ct UED N18 ....36 A6
Floriston Av HGDN/ICK UB10 ....76 A5
Floriston Cl STAN HA7 ....43 H4
Floriston Gdns STAN HA7 ....43 H4
Floss St PUT/ROE SW15 ....139 F3
Flower & Dean Wk WCHPL E1 ...13 K2
Flower La MLHL NW7 ....45 H1
Flowers Cl CRICK NW2 ....81 J1
Flowers Ms ARCH N19 ....66 C6
Floyd Rd CHARL SE7 ....126 B5
Floyer Cl RCHPK/HAM TW10 ....137 G6
Fludyer St LEW SE13 ....145 H5
Foley Ms ESH/CLAY KT10 ......204 E4
Foley Rd ESH/CLAY KT10 ......204 E5
Foley St GTPST W1W 10 A2
Folgate St WCHPL E1 ....13 H1
Foliot St SHB W12 ....99 H5
Folkestone Rd EHAM E6 ....108 A1
  UED N18 ....36 C6
  WALTH E17 ....69 K1
Folkingham La
  CDALE/KGS NW9 ....45 F4
Folkington Cnr
  NFNCH/WDSP N12 ....46 D1
Follett St POP/IOD E14 ....106 A5
Folly La WALTH E17 ....51 G4
Folly Wall POP/IOD E14 ......125 F2
Fontaine Rd STRHM/NOR SW16 .180 A2
Fontarabia Rd BTSEA SW11 ....141 F5
Fontayne Av RAIN RM15 ....93 J4
  ROM RM1 ....57 G5
Fontenoy Rd BAL SW12 ....161 G4
Fonteyne Gdns WFD IG8 ....53 H5
Fonthill Ms FSBYPK N4 ....67 F6
Fonthill Rd FSBYPK N4 ....67 F5
Font Hills EFNCH N2 ....47 G5
Fontley Wy PUT/ROE SW15 .....158 D3
Fontwell Cl KTN/HRWW/WS HA3 .42 E3
  NTHLT UB5 ....78 A4
Fontwell Dr HAYES BR2 ....201 F2
Football La HRW HA1 * 61 F5
Footbury Hill Rd ORP BR6 ....202 B4
The Footpath
  PUT/ROE SW15 * 138 D6
Foots Cray High St SCUP DA14 .186 D2
Foots Cray La SCUP DA14 .....168 D5
Footscray Rd ELTH/MOT SE9 ...167 F1
Forbes Cl CRICK NW2 ....81 J1
  EMPK RM11 ....75 J5
Forbes St WCHPL E1 ....104 C5
Forbes Wy RSLP HA4 ....58 E6
Forburg Rd STNW/STAM N16 .....68 C5
Ford Cl HRW HA1 ....60 D4
  RAIN RM13 ....111 G2
  THHTH CR7 ....196 C3
Fordcroft Rd STMC/STPC BR5 ..202 C2
Ford Dr BMLY BR1 ....184 B6
Fordel Rd CAT SE6 ....165 G3
Ford End WFD IG8 ....53 F2
Fordham STMC/STPC BR5 ....186 C5
Fordham Rd EBAR EN4 ....21 H4
Fordham St WCHPL E1 ....104 C5
Fordhook Av EA W5 ....98 B6
Fordingley Rd MV/WKIL W9 ......100 D2
Fordington Rd HGT N6 ....65 K1
Ford La RAIN RM13 ....93 H5
Fordmill Rd CAT SE6 ....164 D4
Ford Rd ASHF TW15 ....152 C6
  BOW E3 ....105 G1
  DAGE RM10 ....92 C5
Ford's Gv WCHMH N21 ....35 J3
Fords Park Rd CAN/RD E16 ....106 E5
Ford Sq WCHPL E1 ....104 D4
Ford St BOW E3 ....105 G1
  CAN/RD E16 ....106 D5
Fordwich Cl ORP BR6 ....202 A4
Fordwych Rd CRICK NW2 ....82 C3
Fordyce Rd LEW SE13 ....165 F1
Fordyke Rd BCTR RM8 ....74 A6
Foreland Ct HDN NW4 ....46 C4
Foreland St WOOL/PLUM SE18 ..127 J4
Foreman Ct HMSMTH W6 * ......118 E4...

Foremark Cl BARK/HLT IG6 ......55 F2
Forest Ap CHING E4 ....38 C2
  WFD IG8 ....52 E3
Forest Av CHIG IG7 ....54 A1
  CHING E4 ....38 C2
Forest Cl CHST BR7 ....185 F4
  WAN E11 ....70 D2
  WFD IG8 ....39 F6
Forest Ct CHING E4 ....38 D3
  WAN E11 ....70 C1
Forestdale STHGT/OAK N14 .....34 D6
Forest Dr HAYES BR2 ....215 J2
  MNPK E12 ....89 H1
  WFD IG8 ....52 B3
Forest Dr East WAN E11 ....70 B4
Forest Dr West WAN E11 ....70 A4
Forest Edge BKHH IG9 ....39 G1
Forester Rd PECK SE15 ....143 J5
Foresters Cl WLGTN SM6 ......210 D5
Foresters Crs BXLYHN DA7 ....149 J5
Foresters Dr WALTH E17 ....70 B1
  WLGTN SM6 ....210 D5
Forest Gdns TOTM N17 ....50 B5
Forest Gld CHING E4 ....52 C1
Forest Gld CHING E4 ....70 C3...

Forest Hill Rd EDUL SE22 .....163 J1
Forestholme Cl FSTH SE23 ....163 K4
Forest La CHIG IG7 ....54 A1
  FSTGT E7 ....88 C3
Forest Mount Rd WFD IG8 ....52 B3
Fore St BARB EC2Y 12 E2
  ED N9 ....36 C6
  PIN HA5 ....58 E1
Forest Rdg BECK BR3 ....182 D6
  HAYES BR2 ....215 J2
Forest Ri WALTH E17 ....52 B6
Forest Rd BARK/HLT IG6 ....54 E4
  BARK/HLT IG6 ....55 H2
  CHEAM SM3 ....193 J5
  ED N9 ....36 D5
  ERITH DA8 ....150 D2
  FELT TW13 ....154 B5
  FSTGT E7 ....88 C2
  HACK E8 ....86 B4
  RCH/KEW TW9 ....137 H1
  WALTH E17 ....51 G5
  WALTH E17 ....52 C5
  WAN E11 ....68 E1
  WAN E11 ....70 B4
  WFD IG8 ....38 C5
Forest Side FSTGT E7 ....71 F4
  CHING E4 ....38 E3
  FSTGT E7 ....89 F2
  WPK KT4 ....192 C5
Forest St FSTGT E7 ....88 E3
The Forest WALTH E17 ....70 C1
Forest Vw CHING E4 ....38 B2
  WAN E11 ....70 D1
Forest View Av WAN E11 ....70 E2
Forest View Rd MNPK E12 ....89 J2
  WALTH E17 ....52 A4
Forest Wy BFN/LL DA15 ....167 J2
  STMC/STPC BR5 ....202 B2
  WFD IG8 ....39 F6
Forfar Rd BTSEA SW11 ....141 F2
  WDGN N22 ....49 H4
Forge Cl HAYES BR2 ....199 K5
Forge Dr ESH/CLAY KT10 ......205 G5
Forge La BELMT SM2 ....208 C5
  FELT TW13 ....172 D1
  WFD IG8 ....40 A1...

Forge Ms CROY/NA CRO 213 J3
Forman Pl STNW/STAM N16 * 86 B2
Formby Av STAN HA7 ....43 J6
Formosa St MV/WKIL W9 ....101 F3
Formunt Cl CAN/RD E16 ....106 D4
Forres Gdns GLDGN NW11 ....64 E3
Forrester Ptin SYD SE26 ......163 K6
Forrest Gdns
  STRHM/NOR SW16 ....180 A6
Forris Av HYS/HAR UB3 ....113 J1
Forset St MBLAR W1H 8 D3
Forstal Cl HAYES BR2 ....183 K6
Forster Cl CHING E4 ....52 B5
Forster Rd BECK BR3 ....182 B6
  BRXS/STRHM SW2 * 161 K2
  TOTM N17 ....50 B6
  WALTH E17 ....69 G3
Forsters Cl CHDH RM6 ....74 B3
Forston St IS N1 ....6 D2
Forsyte Crs NRWD SE19 ....181 F4
Forsyth Gdns WALW SE17 ....122 C6
Forsythia Cl IL IG1 ....90 B3
Forsyth Pl EN EN1 ....24 A6
Fortescue Rd WIM/MER SW19 ..178 C2
  EDGW HA8 ....45 F4
Fortess Gv KTTN NW5 ....84 C3
Fortess Rd KTTN NW5 ....84 C3
Forthbridge Rd BTSEA SW11 ...141 F5
Fortis Cl CAN/RD E16 ....107 G5
Fortis Gn EFNCH N2 ....47 K6
Fortis Green Av EFNCH N2 ......48 A6
Fortis Green Rd MUSWH N10 ....48 A6
Fortismere Av MUSWH N10 ......48 A6
Fortnam Rd ARCH N19 ....66 D6
Fortnums Acre STAN HA7 ....43 F2
Fort Rd NTHLT UB5 ....78 A5
  STHWK SE1 ....19 K7
Fortrose Cl POP/IOD E14 .....106 B5
Fortrose Gdns
  BRXS/STRHM SW2 ....161 K3
Fort St CAN/RD E16 ....126 A1
  WCHPL E1 ....13 H2
Fortuna Cl HOLWY N7 * 85 F4
Fortunegate Rd WLSDN NW10 ....81 G6
Fortune Green Rd
  KIL/WHAMP NW6 ....82 E2
Fortune La BORE WD6 ....29 K1

Fortune Pl STHWK SE1 ....123 G5
Fortunes Md NTHLT UB5 ....77 J4
Fortune St STLK EC1Y 6 E7
Fortune Wy WLSDN NW10 ....99 J2
Forty Acre La CAN/RD E16 ....106 E4
Forty Av WBLY HA9 ....80 B1
Forty La WBLY HA9 ....62 E6
Forum Cl BOW E3 ....87 J6
Forum Magnum Sq STHWK SE1 ...17 G2
Forumside EDGW HA8 ....44 C2
The Forum E/WMO/HCT KT8 .....189 G1
Forum Wy EDGW HA8 ....44 C2
Forval Cl MTCM CR4 ....194 E2
Forward Dr KTN/HRWW/WS HA3 ..61 F1
Fosbury Ms BAY/PAD W2 * 101 F6
Foscote Ms MV/WKIL W9 ....100 E3
Foscote Rd HDN NW4 ....63 K3
Foskett Rd FUL/PGN SW6 ....139 J3
Foss Av CROY/NA CRO 211 G4
Fossdene Rd CHARL SE7 ....126 A5
Fossdyke Cl YEAD UB4 ....95 J4
Fosse Wy WEA W13 ....97 G4
Foss Rd LEW SE13 * 145 J3
Fossington Rd BELV DA17 .....128 E4
Foss Rd TOOT SW17 ....160 C6
Fossway BCTR RM8 ....73 J5
Foster La CITYW EC2V 12 C3
Foster Rd ACT W3 ....99 G6
  CHSWK W4 ....118 A5
  PLSTW E13 ....106 E3
Fosters Cl CHST BR7 ....184 E1
  SWFD E18 ....53 F3
Foster St HDN NW4 ....64 A1
Fothergill Cl PLSTW E13 ....106 E1
Fothergill Dr WCHMH N21 ....22 E6
Fotheringham Rd EN EN1 ....24 D5
Foubert's Pl SOHO/CST W1F 10 A4
Foulden Rd STNW/STAM N16 .....86 B2
Foulden Ter STNW/STAM N16 ....86 B2
Foulis Ter SKENS SW7 ....14 A7
Foulser Rd TOOT SW17 ....160 E5
Foulsham Rd THHTH CR7 ....180 D6
Founders Gdns NRWD SE19 ....180 D3
Foundry Cl BERM/RHTH SE16 ..124 B1
Foundry Ms CAMTN NW1 * 4 B6
  THHTH CR7 ....197 F1...

Foundry Pl
  WAND/EARL SW18 * 160 A2
Fountain Cl CAN/RD E16 * 106 C6
Fountain Dr CAR SM5 ....209 K6
  NRWD SE19 ....163 G6
Fountain Green Sq
  BERM/RHTH SE16 ....123 H2
Fountain Ms HAMP NW3 * 83 K4
  IS N1 ....85 K5
Fountain Pl BRXN/ST SW9 .....142 B2
  TOOT SW17 ....178 C4
Fountains Av FELT TW13 ....154 E5
Fountains Cl FELT TW13 ......154 E4
Fountains Crs STHGT/OAK N14 ..34 E2
Fountayne Rd
  SEVS/STOTM N15 ....68 C1
  STNW/STAM N16 ....68 C5
Fount St VX/NE SW8 ....141 J1
Fouracres PEND EN3 ....25 G2
Fourland Wk EDGW HA8 ....44 E2
Fournier St WCHPL E1 ....13 J1
Four Seasons Cl BOW E3 * 105 J1
Four Seasons Crs CHEAM SM3 ..193 J6
Fourth Av HYS/HAR UB3 ....113 J1
  MNPK E12 ....89 K2
  NKENS W10 ....100 C3
  ROMW/RG RM7 ....75 F5
Fourth Cross Rd WHTN TW2 ....155 J4
Fourth Wy WBLY HA9 ....80 E2
The Four Tubs BUSH WD23 ......28 D3
The Four Wents CHING E4 ....38 B4
Fowey Av REDBR IG4 ....71 H2
Fowey Cl WAP E1W * 123 J1
Fowler Cl BTSEA SW11 ....140 C4
  SCUP DA14 ....187 F1
Fowler Rd BARK/HLT IG6 ....55 F2
  FSTGT E7 ....88 E2
  IS N1 ....85 H6
Fowler's Wk EA W5 ....97 K3
Fownes St BTSEA SW11 ....140 D4
Fox and Knot St FARR EC1M * ...12 B1
Foxberry Rd BROCKY SE4 ......144 B5
Foxborough Gdns
  BROCKY SE4 ....164 D1
Foxbourne Rd TOOT SW17 ......161 F4
Fox Burrow Rd CHIG IG7 ....55 J1
Foxbury Cl BMLY BR1 ....184 A2
  ORP BR6 ....217 G4
Foxbury Dr ORP BR6 ....217 G5
Foxbury Rd BMLY BR1 ....184 A2
Fox Cl BORE WD6 ....29 K1
  CAN/RD E16 ....106 E4
  CRW RM5 ....56 D1
  ORP BR6 ....217 G3
  WCHPL E1 ....104 E3
Foxcombe CROY/NA CRO 213 K6
Foxcroft Rd
  WOOL/PLUM SE18 ....147 G2
Foxdell NTHWD HA6 ....40 B2
Foxearth Sp SAND/SEL CR2 ....212 E6
Foxes Dl BKHTH/KID SE3 ......145 K4
  HAYES BR2 ....183 G6
Foxfield Rd ORP BR6 ....201 J6
Foxglove Cl BFN/LL DA15 .....168 B1
  ED N9 ....36 E3
  STHL UB1 ....95 J6
  STWL/WRAY TW19 ....152 A2
Foxglove Dr WAN E11 ....71 J3
Foxglove La CHSGTN KT9 ......206 C2
Foxglove Rd ROMW/RG RM7 .....75 G6
Foxglove St SHB W12 ....118 C1
Foxglove Wy MTCM CR4 ....195 F4
Foxgrove STHGT/OAK N14 ....34 E5
Fox Gv WOT/HER KT12 ....188 A4

Foxgrove Av BECK BR3 ....182 E3
Foxgrove Pth OXHEY WD19 .....41 H1
Foxgrove Rd BECK BR3 ....182 E3
Foxham Rd ARCH N19 ....84 D1
Fox Hl NRWD SE19 ....181 G3
Fox Hill Gdns NRWD SE19 ....181 G3
Foxhole Rd ELTH/MOT SE9 ......146 D6
Fox Hollow Cl
    WOOL/PLUM SE18 ....127 K5
Fox Hollow Dr BXLYHN DA7 .....148 E4
Foxholt Gdns WLSDN NW10 ....80 E5
Foxhome Cl CHST BR7 ....185 F2
Fox House Rd BELV DA17 ....129 J4
Foxlands Crs DAGE RM10 ....92 E5
Foxlands Rd DAGE RM10 ....92 E3
Fox La EA W5 ....98 A4
    HAYES BR2 ....215 F3
    PLMGR N13 ....35 G2
Foxlees ALP/SUD HA0 ....79 G2
Foxley Cl HACK E8 ....86 C3
Foxley Rd CMBW SE5 ....142 B1
    THHTH CR7 ....196 C1
Foxleys OXHEY WD19 ....27 J5
Foxley Sq BRXN/ST SW9 *........142 C1
Foxmead Cl ENC/FH EN2 ....23 F4
Foxmore St BTSEA SW11 ....140 E2
Fox Rd CAN/RD E16 ....106 D4
Foxton Gv MTCM CR4 ....178 C5
Foxwarren ESH/CLAY KT10 ......205 F5
Foxwell Rd BROCKY SE4 ....144 B4
Foxwood Cl FELT TW13 ....154 A5
    MLHL NW7 ....31 G6
Foxwood Green Cl EN EN1 ....36 A1
Foxwood Rd BKHTH/KID SE3 ...145 J5
Foyle Rd BKHTH/KID SE3 ....125 J6
    TOTM N17 ....50 C4
Framfield Cl NFNCH/WDSP N12 ..32 E6
Framfield Rd HBRY N5 ....85 H3
    HNWL W7 ....97 J5
    MTCM CR4 ....179 F3
Framlingham Crs
    ELTH/MOT SE9 ....166 D6
Frampton Cl BELMT SM2 ....208 E6
Frampton Park Rd HOM E9 ....86 E4
Frampton Rd HSLWW TW4 ....134 D6
Frampton St STJWD NW8 ....2 B7
Francemary Rd LEW SE13 ....144 D6
Frances Rd CHING E4 ....51 J2
Frances Ct WOOL/PLUM SE18 ..126 E4
Frances Court Rd TOOT SW17 ...205 F5
Francis Av BXLYHN DA7 ....149 H3
    FELT TW13 ....153 K5
    IL IG1 ....72 D2
Francis Barber Cl
    STRHM/NOR SW16 * 162 A6
Franciscan Rd TOOT SW17 ....161 F6
Francis Chichester Wy
    BTSEA SW11 * 141 F2
Francis Cl HOR/WEW KT19 ....207 F2
Francis Gv WIM/MER SW19 ......177 J2
Francis Ms LEE/GVPK SE12 * ...165 J1
Francis Rd CROY/NA CRO 196 C4
    DART DA1 ....151 G6
    ERITH N2 * 85 H3
    GFD/PVL UB6 ....97 G1
    HRW HA1 ....61 G2
    HSLWW TW4 ....134 C3
    LEY E10 ....70 A6
    PIN HA5 ....59 G2
    STMC/STPC BR5 ....186 E6
    WLGTN SM6 ....210 C4
Francis St SRTFD E15 ....88 C3
    WEST SW1P 16 B6
Francis Ter ARCH N19 ....84 C1
Francis Wk IS N1 ....85 F6
Francklyn Gdns EDGW HA8 ....30 C5
Francombe Gdns ROM RM1 ....75 J3
Franconia Rd CLAP SW4 ....141 H6
Frank Burton Cl CHARL SE7 .....126 A5
Frank Dixon Cl DUL SE21 ....163 F2
Frank Dixon Wy DUL SE21 ....163 F3
Frankfurt Rd HNHL SE24 ....142 D6
Frankham St DEPT SE8 ....144 D1
Frankland Cl
    BERM/RHTH SE16 ....123 J3
    WFD IG8 ....53 G1
Frankland Rd CHING E4 ....51 J1
    SKENS SW7 ....14 A5
Franklin Cl KUT/HW KT1 ....175 H6
    LEW SE13 ....144 E2
    TRDG/WHET N20 ....33 G2
    WNWD SE27 ....162 C5
Franklin Crs MTCM CR4 ....195 H1
Franklin Rd BXLY DA5 ....170 B4
    BXLYHN DA7 ....149 F2
    PGE/AN SE20 ....181 K3
Franklins Ms RYLN/HDSTN HA2 ..60 C6
Franklin Sq WKENS W14 ....119 J5
Franklins Rw CHEL SW3 ....120 E5
Franklin St BOW E3 ....105 K2
    SEVS/STOTM N15 * 67 K2
Franklin Wy CROY/NA CRO 195 K5
Franklyn Gdns BARK/HLT IG6 ...54 D2
Franklyn Rd WLSDN NW10 ....81 H5
    WOT/HER KT12 ....188 A3
Franks Av NWMAL KT3 ....191 K1
Franks Wood Av
    STMC/STPC BR5 ....201 G2
Franlaw Crs PLMGR N13 ....35 J6
Franmil Rd EMPK RM11 ....75 H4
Fransfield Gv SYD SE26 ....163 J5
Fransmans BUSH WD23 * 28 E4
Frant Cl PGE/AN SE20 ....181 K5
Frant Rd THHTH CR7 ....196 C2
Fraser Cl BXLY DA5 ....169 K3
Fraser Rd ED N9 ....36 D5
    ERITH DA8 ....129 K5
    GFD/PVL UB6 ....79 G2
    WALTH E17 ....69 K2
Fraser St CHSWK W4 ....118 B5
Frating Crs WFD IG8 ....52 E2
Frays Av WDR/YW UB7 ....112 A2
Frays Cl WDR/YW UB7 ....112 A3
Frazer Av RSLP HA4 ....77 G3
Frazer Cl ROMW/RG RM7 ....75 H4

Frazier St STHWK SE1 ....17 J3
Frean St BERM/RHTH SE16 ......123 H3
Freda Corbett Cl PECK SE15 .....143 H1
Frederica Rd CHING E4 ....38 B2
Frederica St HOLWY N7 ....85 F5
Frederick Cl BAY/PAD W2 ....8 D5
    SUT SM1 ....208 D2
Frederick Crs BRXN/ST SW9 ....142 C1
    PEND EN3 ....24 E3
Frederick Gdns CROY/NA CRO ..196 C3
    SUT SM1 ....208 D3
Frederick Pl
    WOOL/PLUM SE18 ....127 G5
Frederick Rd RAIN RM13 ....111 F1
    SUT SM1 ....208 D3
    WALW SE17 ....122 C6
Frederick's Pl LOTH EC2R * 12 E4
    NFNCH/WDSP N12 ....33 G6
Frederick Sq
    BERM/RHTH SE16 ....105 G6
Frederick's Rw FSBYE EC1V 6 A4
Frederick St FSBYW WC1X 5 G5
Frederick St WALTH E17 * 86 B5
Frederic Ms KTBR SW1X * 15 G3
Frederic St WALTH E17 * 86 B5
Fredora Av YEAD UB4 ....94 D5
Freeborne Gdns RAIN RM13 ....93 J4
Freedom Cl WALTH E17 ....69 F1
Freedom St BTSEA SW11 ....140 E3
Freegrove Rd HOLWY N7 ....84 E3
Freeland Pk HDN NW4 ....46 C1
Freeland Rd EA W5 ....98 B6
Freelands Av SAND/SEL CR2 ....213 F6
Freelands Gv BMLY BR1 ....184 A4
Freelands Rd BMLY BR1 ....184 A4
Freeland Wy ERITH DA8 ....150 D2
Freeling St IS N1 ....85 F5
Freeman Cl NTHLT UB5 ....77 J5
Freeman Dr
    E/WMO/HCT KT8 ....188 D1
Freeman Rd MRDN SM4 ....194 C2
Freemans La HYS/HAR UB3 ....94 C6
Freemantle Av PEND EN3 ....25 G5
Freemantle St WALW SE17 ....123 F5
Freemasons Rd CAN/RD E16 .....107 F5
    CROY/NA CRO 197 F5
Freesia Cl ORP BR6 ....217 F3
Freethorpe Cl NRWD SE19 ....181 H4
Freightmaster Est
    RAIN RM13 * 130 D4
Freke Rd BTSEA SW11 ....141 F4
Fremantle Rd BARK/HLT IG6 ......54 B5
    BELV DA17 ....129 H4
Fremont St HOM E9 ....86 E6
French Pl SDTCH EC2A 7 H5
French St SUN TW16 ....172 B5
Frendsbury Rd BROCKY SE4 .....144 B5
Frensham Cl STHL UB1 ....95 K3
Frensham Dr CROY/NA CRO 214 A6
    PUT/ROE SW15 ....158 D5
Frensham Rd BFN/LL DA15 ....167 J4
    CHARL SE7 ....126 D6
Frere St BTSEA SW11 ....140 D3
Freshfield Av HACK E8 ....86 B5
Freshfield Dr STHGT/OAK N14 ...34 B2
Freshfields CROY/NA CRO 198 C4
Freshford St TOOT SW17 ....160 B5
Freshwater Cl TOOT SW17 ....179 F2
Freshwater Rd BCTR RM8 ....73 K5
    TOOT SW17 ....179 F2
Freshwell Av CHDH RM6 ....73 J1
Fresh Wharf Rd BARK IG11 ....90 B6
Freshwood Cl BECK BR3 ....182 E4
Freshwood Wy WLGTN SM6 ......210 C6
Freston Gdns EBAR EN4 ....34 A2
Freston Pk FNCH N3 ....46 D5
Freston Rd NKENS W10 ....100 B6
Freta Rd BXLYHS DA6 ....149 G6
Frewin Rd WAND/EARL SW18 ...160 C3
Friar Ms WNWD SE27 * 162 C5
Friar St STMC/STPC BR5 ....202 B2
    YEAD UB4 ....95 H3
Friars Av PUT/ROE SW15 ....158 C5
    TRDG/WHET N20 ....33 J5
Friars Cl CHING E4 ....38 A5
    IL IG1 ....72 C5
    NTHLT UB5 ....95 H2
    STHWK SE1 * 12 B7
Friars Gdns ACT W3 ....99 F5
Friars Ga WFD IG8 ....38 E6
Friars La RCH/KEW TW9 ....136 E6
Friars Md POP/IOD E14 ....125 F3
Friars Ms ELTH/MOT SE9 ....147 F6
Friars Place La ACT W3 ....99 F6
Friars Rd EHAM E6 ....89 H6
Friars Stile Rd
    RCHPK/HAM TW10 ....157 F1
Friars Wk ABYW SE2 ....128 E5
    STHGT/OAK N14 ....34 B3
Friars Wy ACT W3 ....99 F5
Friars Wd CROY/NA CRO * 213 G6
Friary Cl NFNCH/WDSP N12 ......47 J1
Friary Est PECK SE15 ....143 H1
Friary La WFD IG8 ....38 E6
Friary Pk TRDG/WHET N20 * 33 H6
Friary Park Ct ACT W3 * 98 E5
Friary Rd ACT W3 ....98 E5
    NFNCH/WDSP N12 ....33 H6
    PECK SE15 ....143 H1
Friary Wy NFNCH/WDSP N12 .....33 J6
Friday Hl CHING E4 ....38 C5
Friday Hl East CHING E4 ....38 D5
Friday Hl West CHING E4 ....38 C4
Friday Rd ERITH DA8 ....130 A5
    MTCM CR4 ....178 E3
Friday St BLKFR EC4V 12 C5
Frideswide Pl KTTN NW5 ....84 C3
Friendly Pl LEWSH SE10 ....144 E2
Friendly St DEPT SE8 ....144 D2
Friendly Street Ms DEPT SE8 .....144 D3
Friendship Wy SRTFD E15 * 88 A6
Friends' Rd CROY/NA CRO 211 K1
Friern Barnet La
    FBAR/BDGN N11 ....47 K1
    TRDG/WHET N20 ....33 H5
Friern Barnet Rd
    FBAR/BDGN N11 ....48 A1
Friern Mount Dr
    TRDG/WHET N20 ....33 G2
Friern Pk
    NFNCH/WDSP N12 ....47 H1
Friern Rd EDUL SE22 ....163 H1
Frigate Ms DEPT SE8 ....124 D6
Frimley Av WLGTN SM6 ....210 E3
Frimley Cl CROY/NA CRO 214 A5
    WIM/MER SW19 ....159 H4
Frimley Ct SCUP DA14 ....186 D1
Frimley Crs CROY/NA CRO 214 A5
Frimley Gdns MTCM CR4 ....178 D6
Frimley Rd CHSGTN KT9 ....205 K3
    GDMY/SEVK IG3 ....90 E1
Frimley Wy WCHPL E1 * 105 F3
Frinstead Gv STMC/STPC BR5 ...202 E1
Frinsted Rd ERITH DA8 ....150 A1
Frinton Cl OXHEY WD19 ....27 F4
Frinton Dr WFD IG8 ....52 E3
Frinton Ms IL IG1 ....72 A3
Frinton Rd CRW RM5 ....56 C5
    EHAM E6 ....107 H2
    SCUP DA14 ....169 F4
    SEVS/STOTM N15 ....68 A3
    TOOT SW17 ....179 F2
Friston St FUL/PGN SW6 ....140 A3
Friswell Pl BXLYHN DA7 ....149 H5
Fritham Cl NWMAL KT3 ....192 B3
Frith Cl MLHL NW7 ....46 C2
Frith La MLHL NW7 ....46 C2
Frith Rd CROY/NA CRO 196 D6
    WAN E11 ....88 A2
Frith St SOHO/SHAV W1D 10 C4
Frithville Gdns SHB W12 ....119 F1
Frithwood Av NTHWD HA6 ....40 D2
Frizlands La DAGE RM10 ....92 D1
Frobisher Cl BUSH WD23 ....28 A1
    PIN HA5 ....59 H4
Frobisher Crs BARB EC2Y * 12 D1
    STWL/WRAY TW19 ....152 B2
Frobisher Gdns LEY E10 * 69 K3
Frobisher Rd CEND/HSY/T N8 .....67 G1
    EHAM E6 ....108 A5
    ERITH DA8 ....150 D1
Frog La DAGW RM9 ....111 F4
Frogley Rd EDUL SE22 ....143 G5
Frogmore WAND/EARL SW18 ....139 K6
Frogmore Av YEAD UB4 ....94 C3
Frogmore Cl CHEAM SM3 ....208 B1
Frogmore Est HBRY N5 * 85 J2
Frogmore Gdns CHEAM SM3 .....208 C2
    YEAD UB4 ....94 C3
Frognal HAMP NW3 ....83 G3
Frognal Cl HAMP NW3 ....83 G3
Frognal Gdns HAMP NW3 ....83 G2
Frognal La HAMP NW3 ....82 E3
Frognal Man HAMP NW3 * 83 G2
Frognal Pde HAMP NW3 * 83 G3
Frognal Pl SCUP DA14 ....186 C1
Frognal Ri HAMP NW3 ....83 G1
Frognal Wy HAMP NW3 ....83 G2
Froissart Rd ELTH/MOT SE9 ......146 D6
Frome Rd SEVS/STOTM N15 ....49 H6
Frome St IS N1 ....6 C2
Fromondes Rd CHEAM SM3 ....208 B2
Fromows Cnr CHSWK W4 * 117 K5
Frostic Wk WCHPL E1 ....13 K2
Froude St VX/NE SW8 ....141 G3
Fruen Rd EBED/NFELT TW14 .....153 J2
Fryatt Rd TOTM N17 ....49 K5
Fry Cl CRW RM5 ....56 C1
Fryday Grove Ms BAL SW12 ....161 H2
Fryent Cl KTN/HRWW/W HA3 ......62 C3
Fryent Crs CDALE/KGS NW9 ....63 G3
Fryent Flds CDALE/KGS NW9 .....63 G3
Fryent Gv CDALE/KGS NW9 ....63 G3
Fryent Wy CDALE/KGS NW9 ....62 C3
Fry Rd EHAM E6 ....89 H5
    WLSDN NW10 ....81 H6
Fryston Av CROY/NA CRO 197 H6
Fuchsia St ABYW SE2 ....128 C5
Fulbeck Dr CDALE/KGS NW9 ......45 G4
Fulbeck Wy RYLN/HDSTN HA2 ...42 C3
Fulbourne Rd WALTH E17 ....52 A5
Fulbourne St WCHPL E1 ....104 D4
Fulbrook Rd ARCH N19 ....84 C2
Fulford Gv OXHEY WD19 ....27 F2
Fulford Rd HOR/WEW KT19 ....207 F5
Fulford St BERM/RHTH SE16 .....123 J2
Fulham Broadway
    FUL/PGN SW6 ....139 K1
Fulham Cl HGDN/ICK UB10 ....94 A3
Fulham High St FUL/PGN SW6 ...139 H4
Fulham Palace Rd
    FUL/PGN SW6 ....139 G1
Fulham Park Gdns
    FUL/PGN SW6 ....139 J3
Fulham Park Rd FUL/PGN SW6 ..139 J3
Fulham Rd FUL/PGN SW6 ....139 H5
Fullbrooks Av WPK KT4 ....192 C5
Fuller Cl BETH E2 * 13 K5
    ORP BR6 ....217 F3
Fuller Rd BCTR RM8 ....91 H1
Fullers Av SURB KT6 ....191 G6
Fullers Cl CRW RM5 ....56 E3
Fuller's Rd SWFD E18 ....52 D4
Fuller St HDN NW4 ....64 A1
Fullers Wy North SURB KT6 ....206 B1
Fuller's Wd CROY/NA CRO 213 J3
Fullerton Rd CAR SM5 ....209 J6
    CROY/NA CRO 197 G4

Galata Rd BARN SW13 ....138 D1
Galatea Sq PECK SE15 ....143 J4
Galbraith St POP/IOD E14 ....125 F3
Galdana Av BAR EN5 ....21 G4
Galeborough Av WFD IG8 ....52 B3
Gale Cl HPTN TW12 ....172 D2
    MTCM CR4 ....178 C6
Galena Rd HMSMTH W6 ....118 E4
Galen Pl NOXST/BSQ WC1A 10 E2
Galesbury Rd
    WAND/EARL SW18 ....160 B1
Gales Gdns BETH E2 ....104 D2
Gale St BOW E3 ....105 J4
    DAGW RM9 ....91 K4
Gales Wy WFD IG8 ....53 J3
Galgate Cl WIM/MER SW19 ....159 H5
Galiants Farm Rd EBAR EN4 ....33 J2
Galleon Cl BERM/RHTH SE16 ....124 A1
    ERITH DA8 ....130 A4
Galleons Dr BARK IG11 ....109 G2
The Galleries IS N1 * 6 A2
Gallery Gdns NTHLT UB5 ....95 H1
Gallery Rd DUL SE21 ....162 E3
Gallerywall Rd
    BERM/RHTH SE16 ....123 J4
Galley La BAR EN5 ....19 K2
Gallia Rd HBRY N5 ....85 H3
Galliard Cl ED N9 ....36 E2
Galliard Rd ED N9 ....36 C2
Gallia Rd HBRY N5 ....85 H3
Gallions Cl BARK IG11 ....109 G2
Gallions Rd CHARL SE7 ....126 A4
    CHARL SE7 ....126 A4
Gallions View Rd THMD SE28 ....127 K2
Gallon Cl CHARL SE7 ....126 B4
The Gallop BELMT SM2 ....209 H6
Gallosson Rd
    WOOL/PLUM SE18 ....127 K4
Galloway Dr DART DA1 ....170 B2
Galloway Pth CROY/NA CRO 211 K2
Galloway Rd SHB W12 ....118 D1
Gallus Cl WCHMH N21 ....35 F1
Gallus Sq BKHTH/KID SE3 ....146 A4
Galpin's Rd THHTH CR7 ....195 K1
Galsworthy Av CHDH RM6 ....73 H4
    POP/IOD E14 ....105 G5
Galsworthy Cl THMD SE28 ....128 C1
Galsworthy Crs
    BKHTH/KID SE3 * 146 B2
Galsworthy Rd CRICK NW2 ....82 C2
    KUTN/CMB KT2 ....175 J4
Galton St NKENS W10 ....100 C3
Galva Cl EBAR EN4 ....22 A5
Galveston Rd PUT/ROE SW15 ...139 J6
Galway Cl BERM/RHTH SE16 * ..123 J5
Galway St FSBYE EC1V 6 D5
Gambetta St VX/NE SW8 ....141 G3
Gambia St STHWK SE1 ....18 B1
Gambole Rd TOOT SW17 ....160 D6
Games Rd EBAR EN4 ....21 J4
Gamlen Rd PUT/ROE SW15 ....139 G5
Gander Green Crs HPTN TW12 ...173 F4
Gander Green La CHEAM SM3 ....193 H6
    SUT SM1 ....208 D4
Gandhi Cl WALTH E17 ....69 J3
Gandolfi St PECK SE15 * 123 F6
Ganton St SOHO/CST W1F * 10 C4
Ganton Wk OXHEY WD19 * 27 J6
Gantshill Crs GNTH/NBYPK IG2 ...72 A4
Gap Rd WIM/MER SW19 ....177 K1
Garage Rd ACT W3 ....98 C5
Garbrand Wk EW KT17 ....207 H6
Garbutt Pl MHST W1U * 9 H1
Garden Av BXLYHN DA7 ....149 G4
    MTCM CR4 ....179 G3
Garden City EDGW HA8 ....44 C2
Garden Cl BAR EN5 ....20 A5
    CHING E4 ....51 J1
    HPTN TW12 ....172 E1
    LEE/GVPK SE12 ....166 A5
    NTHLT UB5 ....77 J6
    PUT/ROE SW15 ....158 E2
    RSLP HA4 ....58 C6
    WLGTN SM6 ....210 E3
Garden Ct TPL/STR WC2R * 11 J5
Gardeners Rd CROY/NA CRO 196 C5
Gardenia Rd EN EN1 ....36 A1
Gardenia Wy WFD IG8 ....52 E2
Garden La BMLY BR1 ....184 A2
    BRXS/STRHM SW2 ....162 A3
Garden Lodge Ct EFNCH N2 * 47 H6
Garden Pl HACK E8 ....86 B6
    RDART DA2 ....171 G5
Garden Rd BMLY BR1 ....184 A3
    PGE/AN SE20 ....181 K4
    RCH/KEW TW9 ....137 H4
    STJWD NW8 ....2 A3
    WOT/HER KT12 ....188 A3
Garden Rw STHWK SE1 ....18 A5
The Gardens BECK BR3 ....183 F5
    CEND/HSY/T N8 * 66 E1
    EBED/NFELT TW14 ....153 G1
    EDUL SE22 ....143 H5
    ESH/CLAY KT10 ....204 A2
    HRW HA1 ....59 K3
    PIN HA5 * 59 K3
    STNW/STAM N16 * 68 B4
Garden Ter PIM SW1V * 121 J5
Garden Vis ESH/CLAY KT10 * 205 F5
Gardiner Av CRICK NW2 * 82 A3
Gardiner Cl BCTR RM8 ....91 K2
    PEND EN3 ....37 F1
    STMC/STPC BR5 ....186 D5
Gardiner House
    WOOL/PLUM SE18 ....146 D1
Gardner Cl WAN E11 ....71 F3
Gardner Pl EBED/NFELT TW14 ...154 A1
Gardner Rd PLSTW E13 ....107 F3
Gardners Cl FNCH N3 ....46 D6
Gardners La BLKFR EC4V 12 C5

Gardnor Rd HAMP NW3 .....83 H2
Gard St FSBYE EC1V 6 B4
Garendon Gdns MRDN SM4.....194 A4
Garendon Rd MRDN SM4.....194 A4
Gareth Cl WPK KT4 .....193 G6
Gareth Gv BMLY BR1 .....165 K6
Garfield Rd BTSEA SW11.....141 F4
   CHING E4 .....38 B3
   PEND EN3 .....24 E5
   PLSTW E13 .....106 D3
   TWK TW1 .....156 B3
   WIM/MER SW19 .....178 B2
Garford St POP/IOD E14 .....105 J6
Garganey Wk THMD SE28 .....109 J6
Garibaldi St WOOL/PLUM SE18 ..127 K4
Garland Rd STAN HA7 .....44 A4
   WOOL/PLUM SE18 .....147 J1
Garlick Hl BLKFR EC4V 12 D5
Garlies Rd FSTH SE23.....164 B5
Garlinge Rd CRICK NW2 .....82 D4
Garman Cl UED N18 .....49 K1
Garman Rd TOTM N17.....50 E3
Garnault Ms CLKNW EC1R 5 K5
Garnault Pl CLKNW EC1R 5 K5
Garnault Rd EN EN1 .....24 B1
Garner Cl BCTR RM8.....73 K5
Garner Rd WALTH E17.....52 A4
Garnet Rd BETH E2.....104 C1
Garnet Rd THHTH CR7 .....196 D1
   WLSDN NW10.....81 G4
Garnet St WAP E1W.....104 E6
Garnett Cl ELTH/MOT SE9.....146 E4
Garnett Rd HAMP NW3 .....83 K3
Garnham St STNW/STAM N16 .....68 B6
Garnies Cl PECK SE15 .....143 G1

Garrad's Rd
   STRHM/NOR SW16 .....161 J5
Garrard Cl BXLYHN DA7 .....149 H4
   CHST BR7.....185 G1
Garratt La WAND/EARL SW18 ..160 A2
Garratt Rd EDGW HA8 .....44 C3
Garratt Rd BUSH WD23.....28 C2
Garratt Ter TOOT SW17 .....160 D6
Garrett Cl ACT W3 .....99 F4
Garrett St STLK EC1Y 6 C6
Garrick Av GLDGN NW11.....64 C3
Garrick Cl BTSEA SW11.....140 B5
   RICH/KEW TW9 .....136 D6
Garrick Crs CROY/NA CRO.....197 F6
Garrick Dr HDN NW4.....46 A5
   WOOL/PLUM SE18 .....127 J3
Garrick Gdns E/WMO/HCT KT8 ..173 F1
Garrick Pk HDN NW4 .....46 B5
Garrick Rd CDALE/KGS NW9 ..63 H3
   GFD/PVL UB6.....96 B3
   RCH/KEW TW9 .....137 H3
Garrick St WCGVDN WC2E 10 E5
Garrick Wy HDN NW4.....64 B1
Garrick Yd CHCR WC2N.....10 E5
Garrison Cl HSLWW TW4.....134 E6
   WOOL/PLUM SE18 .....147 F1
Garrison La CHSGTN KT9.....206 A5
Garrison Rd BOW E3.....87 J6
Garry Cl ROM RM1 .....57 G3
Garry Wy ROM RM1 .....57 G3
Garsdale Cl FBAR/BDGN N11.....48 A2
Garsdale Ter WKENS W14 * 119 J5
Garside Cl HPTN TW12 .....173 G5
   WOOL/PLUM SE18 .....127 J3
Garsington Ms BROCKY SE4 ....144 C4
Garth Cl KUTN/CMB KT2 .....175 C1
   MRDN SM4.....193 F3
   RSLP HA4 .....59 H5
Garth Ms EA W5 * 98 A3
Garthorne Rd FSTH SE23.....164 A2
Garth Rd CRICK NW2 .....64 D6
   KUTN/CMB KT2 .....175 F1
   MRDN SM4.....193 G5
Garthside KUTN/CMB KT2 .....175 F1
The Garth HPTN TW12 .....173 G2
   KTN/HRWW/W HA3.....62 B3
   NFNCH/WDSP N12 * 47 F1
Garthway NFNCH/WDSP N12 ..47 J2
Gartmoor Gdns
   WIM/MER SW19 .....159 J3
Gartmore Rd GDMY/SEVK IG3 ..73 F5
Garton Pl WAND/EARL SW18 ..160 B1
Gartons Wy BTSEA SW11 .....140 B4
Garvary Rd CAN/RD E16 .....107 F5
Garway Rd BAY/PAD W2.....101 F5
Gascoigne Gdns WFD IG8.....52 C3
Gascoigne Pl BETH E2 .....7 J4
Gascoigne Rd BARK IG11.....90 C6
Gascony Av KIL/WHAMP NW6 ..82 E5
Gascoyne Dr DART DA1.....150 C4
Gascoyne Rd HOM E9.....87 F5
Gaselee St POP/IOD E14.....106 A6
Gasholder Pl LBTH SE11.....122 A5
Gaskarth Rd BAL SW12.....161 G1
   EDGW HA8.....44 E4
Gaskell Rd HGT N6.....65 K3
Gaskell St CLAP SW4.....141 K3
Gaskin St IS N1.....85 H6
Gaspar Ms ECT SW5.....120 A4
Gassiot Rd TOOT SW17.....160 E6
Gassiot Wy SUT SM1.....209 H1
Gaston Bell Cl RCH/KEW TW9 ..137 G4
Gaston Rd MTCM CR4.....179 F6
Gataker St BERM/RHTH SE16 ..123 J3
Gatcombe Ms EA W5.....98 B6
Gatcombe Rd ARCH N19.....84 D1
   CAN/RD E16.....21 K4
Gate End NTHWD HA6.....40 E3
Gateforth St STJWD NW8.....2 C7
Gatehill Rd NTHWD HA6.....40 D1
Gatehouse Cl KUTN/CMB KT2 ..175 K3
Gateley Rd BRXN/ST SW9.....142 A4
Gate Ms SKENS SW7.....14 D5

Gater Dr ENC/FH EN2 .....23 K2
Gates Cl WALW SE17 * 122 D5
Gates Green Rd WWKM BR4 ....214 E2
Gateside Rd TOOT SW17.....160 E5
Gatestone Rd NRWD SE19.....181 F3
Gate St HHOL WC1V.....11 G3
Gateway WALW SE17.....122 D6
Gateway Ar IS N1 * 6 A2
Gateway Cl NTHWD HA6.....40 A2
Gateway Ms HACK E8 * 86 B5
The Gateways
   RCH/KEW TW9 * 136 E5
Gatfield Gv FELT TW13.....155 F4
Gathorne Rd WDGN N22.....49 G5
Gathorne St BETH E2 * 105 F1
Gatley Av HOR/WEW KT19.....206 D3
Gatliff Cl BGVA SW1W * 121 F5
Gatliff Rd BGVA SW1W.....121 G5
Gatonby St PECK SE15.....143 G2
Gatton Cl BELMT SM2 * 209 F6
Gatton Rd TOOT SW17.....160 D6
Gattons Wy SCUP DA14.....169 G6
Gatward Cl WCHMH N21.....35 H1
Gatward Gn ED N9.....36 A4
Gatwick Rd WAND/EARL SW18 ..159 J2
Gauden Cl CLAP SW4.....141 J3
Gauden Rd CLAP SW4.....141 J4
Gaumont Ter SHB W12 * 119 F2
Gauntlet Cl NTHLT UB5.....77 J5
Gauntlett Cl ALP/SUD HA0.....79 G3
Gauntlett Rd SUT SM1.....209 H3
Gaunt St STHWK SE1.....18 B4
Gautrey Rd PECK SE15.....143 K3
Gavel St WALW SE17 *.....19 F6
Gaverick Ms POP/IOD E14.....124 D4
Gavestone Crs LEE/GVPK SE12 ..166 A3
Gavestone Rd LEE/GVPK SE12 ..166 A2
Gavina Cl MRDN SM4.....194 D2
Gawain Wk ED N9.....36 C5
Gawber St BETH E2.....104 E2
Gawsworth Cl SRTFD E15.....88 D3
Gawthorne Av MLHL NW7.....46 C1
Gay Cl CRICK NW2.....81 K3
Gaydon La CDALE/KGS NW9.....45 G4
Gayfere Rd CLAY IG5.....53 K6
   EW KT17 .....207 J3
Gayfere St WEST SW1P.....16 E5
Gayford Rd SHB W12.....118 C2
Gay Gdns DAGE RM10.....92 E2
Gayhurst Rd HACK E8.....86 C5
Gaylor Rd NTHLT UB5.....77 K3
Gaynesford Rd CAR SM5.....209 K5
   FSTH SE23.....164 A4
Gaynes Hill Rd WFD IG8.....53 K2
Gay Rd SRTFD E15.....106 B1
Gaysham Av GNTH/NBYPK IG2 ..72 A2
Gayton Crs HAMP NW3.....83 H2
Gayton Rd HAMP NW3.....83 H2
   HRW HA1.....61 F2
Gayville Rd BTSEA SW11.....160 E1
Gaywood Cl
   BRXS/STRHM SW2.....162 A3
Gaywood Rd WALTH E17.....51 J6
Gaywood St STHWK SE1.....18 B5
Gaza St WALW SE17.....122 C5
Gearriesville Gdns BARK/HLT IG6 ..54 B6
Gearing Cl TOOT SW17.....161 G6
Geary Rd WLSDN NW10.....81 J3
Geary St HOLWY N7.....85 F3
Geddes Pl BXLYHN DA7.....149 H5
Gedeney Rd TOTM N17.....49 J4
Gedling Pl STHWK SE1.....19 J4
Geere Rd SRTFD E15.....88 D6
Gees Ct MHST W1U.....9 H4
Gee St FSBYE EC1V.....6 C6
Geffrye Est IS N1.....7 H3
Geffrye St BETH E2.....7 J2
Geldart Rd PECK SE15.....143 J1
Geldeston Rd CLPT E5.....68 C6
Gellatly Rd PECK SE15.....143 K3
Geisthorpe Rd CRW RM5.....56 D5
General Wolfe Rd
   GNWCH SE10.....145 G2
Genesis Cl STWL/WRAY TW19 ..152 C3
Genesta Rd WOOL/PLUM SE18 ..127 G6
Geneva Dr BRXN/ST SW9.....142 B5
Geneva Gdns CHDH RM6.....74 A2
Geneva Rd KUT/HW KT1.....175 F6
   THHTH CR7.....196 D2
Genever Cl CHING E4.....51 J1
Genista Rd UED N18.....50 D1
Genoa Av PUT/ROE SW15.....139 F6
Genoa Rd PGE/AN SE20.....181 K4
Genotin Rd EN EN1.....23 K4
Gentleman's Rw ENC/FH EN2 ..23 J4
Geoffrey Cl CMBW SE5.....142 D3
Geoffrey Gdns EHAM E6.....107 J1
Geoffrey Rd BROCKY SE4.....144 C4
George Beard Rd DEPT SE8 ....124 C4
George Crs MUSWH N10.....48 A3
George Downing Est
   STNW/STAM N16.....68 B6
George Gange Wy
   KTN/HRWW/W HA3.....42 E6
George Groves Rd
   PGE/AN SE20.....181 H4
George La HAYES BR2.....200 A5
   LEW SE13.....165 F1
   SWFD E18.....53 F1
George Lowe Ct
   BAY/PAD W2 *.....101 F4
George Mathers Rd
   LBTH SE11 *.....18 A6
George Ms CAMTN NW1.....4 A5
   CHING E4.....51 J2
   KUTN/CMB KT2.....175 F6
   NWMAL KT3.....192 C1
George Rw BERM/RHTH SE16 ..123 H2
Georges Md BORE WD6.....30 A1
Georges Rd HOLWY N7.....85 F4
George St BARK IG11.....90 C6
   CAN/RD E16.....106 D5
   CROY/NA CRO.....196 D1
   HNWL W7.....115 K1

HSLW TW3.....134 E3
MBLAR W1H.....9 F3
NWDGN UB2.....114 D4
RCHPK/HAM TW10.....136 E6
ROM RM1.....75 H5
Georgetown Cl NRWD SE19 ....180 E1
Georgette Pl GNWCH SE10 ....145 F1
George V Av PIN HA5.....41 K5
Georgeville Gdns BARK/HLT IG6 ..72 B1
George V Wy GFD/PVL UB6.....79 H5
George Wyver Cl
   WAND/EARL SW18.....159 H2
George Yd BANK EC3V.....13 F4
   MYFR/PKLN W1K.....9 H5
Georgiana St CAMTN NW1.....84 C6
Georgian Cl HAYES BR2.....200 A5
   STAN HA7.....43 G3
Georgian Ct WBLY HA9.....80 C4
Georgian Wy HRW HA1.....60 D6
Georgia Rd NWMAL KT3.....191 K1
   THHTH CR7.....180 C4
Georgina Gdns BETH E2 *.....7 K4
Geraint Rd BMLY BR1.....165 K5
Geraldine Rd CHSWK W4.....117 H6
   WAND/EARL SW18.....140 B6
Geraldine St LBTH SE11.....18 A5
Gerald Rd BCTR RM8.....74 B6
   BGVA SW1W.....15 H6
   CAN/RD E16.....106 D3
Gerard Av HSLWW TW4.....155 F2
Gerard Gdns RAIN RM13.....111 G1
Gerard Rd BARN SW13.....138 C2
   HRW HA1.....61 G3
Gerards Cl BERM/RHTH SE16 ..123 K6
Gerda Rd ELTH/MOT SE9.....167 G4
Gerdview Dr RDART DA2.....171 F6
Germander Wy SRTFD E15 ....106 C2
Gernon Rd BOW E3.....105 G1
Geron Wy CRICK NW2.....64 A6
Gerrard Gdns PIN HA5.....58 E2
Gerrard Pl SOHO/SHAV W1D *..10 D5
Gerrard Rd IS N1.....6 B2
Gerrards Cl STHGT/OAK N14 ..22 C6
Gerrard St SOHO/SHAV W1D ..10 C5
Gerridge St STHWK SE1.....17 K3
Gertrude Rd BELV DA17.....129 H4
Gertrude St WBPTN SW10.....120 B6
Gervase Cl WBLY HA9.....80 E1
Gervase Rd EDGW HA8.....44 E4
Gervase St PECK SE15.....143 J1
Ghent St CAT SE6.....164 D4
Ghent Wy HACK E8.....86 B4
Giant Arches Rd HNHL SE24 ..162 D2
Giant Tree Hl BUSH WD23.....28 D4
Gibbfield Cl CHDH RM6.....56 A6
Gibbings Rd SRTFD E15.....88 A5
Gibbon Rd ACT W3.....99 G6
   KUTN/CMB KT2.....175 F4
   PECK SE15.....143 K3
Gibbons Rd WLSDN NW10.....81 F4
Gibbon Wk PUT/ROE SW15 *..138 D5
Gibbs Av NRWD SE19.....180 E2
Gibbs Cl NRWD SE19 *.....180 E1
Gibbs Couch OXHEY WD19.....27 H1
Gibbs Gn EDGW HA8.....30 E6
   WKENS W14 *.....119 J5
Gibbs Rd UED N18.....36 E6
Gibbs Sq NRWD SE19 *.....180 E1
Gibraltar Wk BETH E2 *.....7 J5
Gibson Cl CHSGTN KT9 *.....205 J3
   ISLW TW7.....135 J4
   WCHPL E1.....104 E3
   WHTN TW2.....155 F2
Gibson Gdns STNW/STAM N16 ..68 B1
Gibson Rd BCTR RM8.....73 J5
   LBTH SE11.....17 H7
   SUT SM1.....209 F3
Gibson's Hl STRHM/NOR SW16 ..180 B3
Gibson Sq IS N1.....85 G6
Gibson St GNWCH SE10.....125 H5
Gidea Av GPK RM2.....57 J6
Gidea Cl GPK RM2.....57 J6
Gideon Cl BELV DA17.....129 J4
Gideon Ms EA W5 *.....116 E2
Gideon Rd BTSEA SW11.....141 F4
Giesbach Rd ARCH N19.....66 D6
Giffard Rd UED N18.....50 A1
Giffin St DEPT SE8.....144 D1
Gifford Gdns HNWL W7.....96 D4
Gifford St IS N1.....84 E5
Gift La SRTFD E15.....88 C6
Giggs Hill STMC/STPC BR5 ....186 B5
Giggs Hill Gdns THDIT KT7 ....190 B4
Giggs Hill Rd THDIT KT7.....190 B4
Gilbert Cl WIM/MER SW19 * ..178 A4
   WOOL/PLUM SE18.....146 E2
Gilbert Gv EDGW HA8.....44 E4
Gilbert Pl NOXST/BSQ WC1A ..10 E2
Gilbert Rd BELV DA17.....129 H3
   BMLY BR1.....183 K5
   LBTH SE11.....17 K6
   PIN HA5.....59 H1
   ROM RM1.....75 H1
   WIM/MER SW19.....178 B3
Gilbert St HSLW TW3.....135 H4
   MYFR/PKLN W1K.....9 H4
   SRTFD E15.....88 C2

Gill Cl WATW WD18.....26 A1
Gillender St BOW E3.....106 A3
Gillespie Rd HBRY N5.....85 G1
Gillett Av EHAM E6.....107 J1
Gillett Pl HACK E8.....86 B3
Gillett Rd THHTH CR7.....196 E1
Gillfoot CAMTN NW1.....86 A3
Gillham Ter TOTM N17.....50 C2
Gillian Park Rd CHEAM SM3 ..193 J5
Gillian St LEW SE13.....144 E6
Gillian Ter BRYLDS KT5 *.....191 G3
Gillingham Ms PIM SW1V.....15 K6
Gillingham Rd CRICK NW2.....82 C1
Gillingham Rw PIM SW1V.....16 A6
Gillingham St PIM SW1V.....15 K7
Gillison Wk
   BERM/RHTH SE16 *.....123 H3
Gillman Dr SRTFD E15.....88 D6
Gillmans Rd STMC/STPC BR5 ..202 C5
Gill St POP/IOD E14.....105 H5
Gilmore Rd LEW SE13.....145 G5
Gilpin Av MORT/ESHN SW14 ..138 A5
Gilpin Cl MTCM CR4.....178 D5
Gilpin Crs HSLW TW3.....155 G2
   UED N18.....50 A4
Gilpin Rd CLPT E5.....87 G2
Gilpin Wy HYS/HAR UB3.....133 G1
Gilroy Cl RAIN RM13.....93 H4
Gilroy Wy STMC/STPC BR5 ....202 D5
Gilsland Rd THHTH CR7.....196 E1
Gilstead Rd FUL/PGN SW6.....140 A3
Gilston Rd WBPTN SW10.....120 B5
Gilton Rd CAT SE6.....165 H5
Giltspur St STBT EC1A.....12 B3
Gilwell Cl CHING E4.....25 K5
Gippeswyck Cl PIN HA5.....41 H4
Gipsy Hi NRWD SE19.....181 F1
Gipsy La BARN SW13.....138 D4
Gipsy Rd WELL DA16.....148 E3
   WNWD SE27.....162 E6
Gipsy Road Gdns WNWD SE27 ..162 D6
Giralda Cl CAN/RD E16.....107 H4
Giraldia Cl CAN/RD E16.....107 H4
Giraud St POP/IOD E14.....105 K5
Girdlers Rd WKENS W14.....119 G4
Girdwood Rd
   WAND/EARL SW18.....159 H2
Girling Wy EBED/NFELT TW14 ..133 K4
Gironde Rd FUL/PGN SW6.....139 J1
Girton Av CDALE/KGS NW9.....44 C6
Girton Cl NTHLT UB5.....78 C4
Girton Gdns CROY/NA CRO.....213 J1
Girton Rd NTHLT UB5.....78 C4
   SYD SE26.....182 A1
Gisbourne Cl WLGTN SM6.....210 D1
Gisburn Rd CEND/HSY/T N8 ..67 F1
Gissing Wk IS N1 *.....85 G5
Gittens Cl BMLY BR1.....165 J6
Glacier Wy ALP/SUD HA0.....97 K1
Gladbeck Wy ENC/FH EN2.....23 J5
Gladding Rd MNPK E12.....89 H2
Glade Cl SURB KT6 *.....190 E6
Glade Gdns CROY/NA CRO.....198 B4
Glade La NWDGN UB2.....115 G2
Gladeside CROY/NA CRO.....198 A4
   WCHMH N21.....35 F2
Gladesmore Rd
   SEVS/STOTM N15.....68 B3
The Glade BELMT SM2.....208 C6
   BMLY BR1.....183 K4
   CAR SM5.....209 K4
   CEND/HSY/T N8.....67 F1
   CHDH RM6.....73 K2
   CROY/NA CRO.....198 A2
   ENC/FH EN2.....23 G4
   EW KT17.....207 J4
   HACK E8 *.....86 B5
   RAIN RM13.....111 H1
   STAN HA7.....43 J1
   WFD IG8.....38 E6
Gladeswood Rd BELV DA17 ....129 J4
Gladiator St FSTH SE23.....164 B1
Glading Ter STNW/STAM N16 ..68 B1
Gladioli Cl HPTN TW12 *.....173 F2
Gladsdale Dr PIN HA5.....58 E1
Gladsmuir Rd ARCH N19.....66 C5
   BAR EN5.....20 C3
Gladstone Av
   EBED/NFELT TW14.....153 K1
   MNPK E12.....89 J5
   WDGN N22.....49 H5
   WHTN TW2.....155 J2
Gladstone Gdns HSLW TW3 ....135 H2
Gladstone Ms KIL/WHAMP NW6 ..82 D5
   PGE/AN SE20.....181 K3
   WDGN N22.....49 G5
Gladstone Pde CRICK NW2 *..82 A1
Gladstone Park Gdns
   CRICK NW2.....81 K1
Gladstone Pl BAR EN5 *.....20 B5
   E/WMO/HCT KT8.....189 K2
Gladstone Rd BKHH IG9.....39 G3
   CHSWK W4.....118 A3
   CROY/NA CRO.....196 E4
   DART DA1.....171 J1
   KUT/HW KT1.....175 H6
   NWDGN UB2.....114 D2
   ORP BR6.....216 C3
   SURB KT6.....190 E6
   WIM/MER SW19.....177 K3
Gladstone St VX/NE SW8 *.....141 G2
   WNWD SE27 *.....162 D6
Gladstone Ter VX/NE SW8 *..141 G2
Gladwell Rd BMLY BR1.....183 K2
   CEND/HSY/T N8.....67 F3
Gladys Rd KIL/WHAMP NW6 ..82 E5
Glaisher St DEPT SE8.....124 E6
Glamis Crs HYS/HAR UB3.....113 F3
Glamis Pl WAP E1W.....104 E6
Glamis Rd WAP E1W.....104 E6
Glamis Wy NTHLT UB5.....78 C4

Glamorgan Cl MTCM CR4.....179 K6
Glamorgan Rd KUT/HW KT1 ..174 D5
Glandford Wy CHDH RM6.....73 H3
Glanfield Rd BECK BR3.....198 C1
Glanleam Rd STAN HA7.....29 K5
Glanville Rd BRXS/STRHM SW2 ..141 K6
   HAYES BR2.....184 A6
Glasbrook Av WHTN TW2.....154 E3
Glasbrook Rd ELTH/MOT SE9 ..166 C2
Claserton Rd STNW/STAM N16 ..68 A4
Glasford St TOOT SW17.....178 E2
Glasgow Rd PLSTW E13 *.....107 F1
   UED N18.....50 D1
Glasgow Ter PIM SW1V.....121 H5
Glasse Cl WEA W13.....97 G6
Glasshill St STHWK SE1.....18 B2
Glasshouse Flds WAP E1W 105 F6
Glasshouse St REGST W1B 10 B6
Glasshouse Wk LBTH SE11 ....121 K5
Glasshouse Yd STBT EC1A.....6 C7
Glasslyn Rd CEND/HSY/T N8 ..66 D2
Glassmill La HAYES BR2.....183 J5
Glass St BETH E2 *.....104 D3
Glass Yd WOOL/PLUM SE18 ..127 F3
Glastonbury Av WFD IG8.....53 H3
Glastonbury Pl WCHPL E1 ....104 E5
Glastonbury Rd ED N9.....36 C3
   MRDN SM4.....193 K4
Glastonbury St
   KIL/WHAMP NW6.....82 D3
Glaston Ct EA W5 *.....116 E1
Glaucus St BOW E3.....105 K4
Clazbury Rd WKENS W14.....119 H4
Glazebrook Cl DUL SE21.....162 E4
Glazebrook Rd TEDD TW11 ....174 A3
Glebe Av ENC/FH EN2.....23 H4
   HGDN/ICK UB10.....76 A2
   KTN/HRWW/W HA3.....44 A6
   MTCM CR4.....178 D6
   RSLP HA4.....77 F4
   WFD IG8.....52 E2
Glebe Cl CHSWK W4 *.....118 B5
   HGDN/ICK UB10.....76 A2
Glebe Ct BKHTH/KID SE3 *.....145 H4
   EA W5.....116 E1
   STAN HA7 *.....43 J1
Glebe Crs HDN NW4.....64 A1
   KTN/HRWW/W HA3.....44 A6
Glebe House Dr HAYES BR2 ....200 A5
Glebelands DART DA1.....150 C5
   E/WMO/HCT KT8.....189 G2
   ESH/CLAY KT10.....205 F6
Glebelands Av
   GNTH/NBYPK IG2.....72 D4
   SWFD E18.....52 E5
Glebelands Cl CMBW SE5 *.....143 F4
   NFNCH/WDSP N12.....47 H3
Glebelands Rd
   EBED/NFELT TW14.....153 K2
Glebe La BAR EN5.....31 J1
   KTN/HRWW/W HA3.....62 A1
Glebe Pl CHEL SW3.....120 D6
Glebe Rd BARN SW13.....138 D3
   BELMT SM2.....208 C5
   BMLY BR1.....183 K4
   CAR SM5.....209 K4
   CEND/HSY/T N8.....67 F1
   DAGE RM10.....92 D4
   FNCH N3.....47 F4
   HACK E8.....86 B5
   RAIN RM13.....111 H1
   STAN HA7.....43 J1
   WLSDN NW10.....81 H4
Glebe Side TWK TW1.....156 A1
Glebe Sq MTCM CR4 *.....178 E6
Glebe St CHSWK W4.....118 A5
Glebe Ter BOW E3.....105 K2
The Glebe BKHTH/KID SE3 ....145 H4
   CHST BR7.....185 H4
   STRHM/NOR SW16 *.....161 J6
   WDR/YW UB7.....112 A2
   WPK KT4.....192 C5
Glebe Wy ERITH DA8.....130 B6
   FELT TW13.....155 F5
   WWKM BR4.....199 G6
Glebeway WFD IG8.....53 G2
Gledhow Gdns ECT SW5.....120 B4
Gledstanes Rd WKENS W14 ....119 H5
Gledwood Av YEAD UB4.....94 E4
Gledwood Crs YEAD UB4.....94 D4
Gledwood Dr YEAD UB4.....94 D4
Gleed Av BUSH WD23.....28 D4
Gleeson Dr ORP BR6.....217 F3
Clegg Pl PUT/ROE SW15 *.....139 G5
Glenaffric Av POP/IOD E14 ....125 F4
Glen Albyn Rd
   WIM/MER SW19.....159 G4
Glenalla Rd RSLP HA4.....58 D4
Glenalmond Rd
   KTN/HRWW/W HA3.....62 A1
Glenavon Cl ESH/CLAY KT10 ..205 G5
Glenavon Rd SRTFD E15.....88 C5
Glenbarr Cl ELTH/MOT SE9 ....147 G4
Glenbow Rd BMLY BR1.....183 H2
Glenbrook North ENC/FH EN2 ..23 F5
Glenbrook Rd KIL/WHAMP NW6 ..82 E3
Glenbrook South ENC/FH EN2 ..23 F5
Glenbuck Rd SURB KT6.....190 E3
Glenburnie Rd TOOT SW17 ....160 E5
Glencairn Dr EA W5.....97 H3
Glencairne Cl CAN/RD E16 ....107 H4
Glencairn Rd
   STRHM/NOR SW16.....179 K3
Glencoe Av GNTH/NBYPK IG2 ..72 E4
Glencoe Rd BUSH WD23.....28 A1
   DAGE RM10.....92 C2

YEAD UB4 ....95 J4
Glencorse Gn *OXHEY* WD19 * 27 H6
Glen Crs *WFD* IG8 ....53 F2
Glendale Av *CHDH* RM6 ....73 J4
EDGW HA8 ....30 B6
WDGN N22 ....49 G3
Glendale Cl *ELTH/MOT* SE9 ....147 F4
Glendale Dr *WIM/MER* SW19 ....177 J1
Glendale Gdns *WBLY* HA9 ....61 K5
Glen Dale Ms *BECK* BR3 ....182 E4
Glendale Rd *ERITH* DA8 ....129 K4
Glendale Wy *THMD* SE28 ....128 D1
Glendall St *BRXN/ST* SW9 ....142 A4
Glendarvon St
PUT/ROE SW15 ....139 G4
Glendevon Cl *EDGW* HA8 ....30 D5
Glendish Rd *TOTM* N17 ....50 C4
Glendor Gdns *MLHL* NW7 ....31 F6
Glendower Crs *ORP* BR6 ....202 B3
Glendower Gdns
MORT/ESHN SW14 ....138 A4
Glendower Pl *SKENS* SW7 ....14 A6
Glendower Rd *CHING* E4 ....38 B3
MORT/ESHN SW14 ....138 A4
Glendown Rd *ABYW* SE2 ....128 B5
Glendun Rd *ACT* W3 ....99 G6
Gleneagle Ms
STRHM/NOR SW16 ....179 J1
Gleneagle Rd
STRHM/NOR SW16 ....179 J1
Gleneagles *STAN* HA7 ....43 H2
Gleneagles Cl
BERM/RHTH SE16 * 123 J5
ORP BR6 ....201 J5
OXHEY WD19 * 41 H1
Gleneldon Ms
STRHM/NOR SW16 ....179 K1
Gleneldon Rd
STRHM/NOR SW16 ....161 K6
Glenelg Rd *BRXS/STRHM* SW2 ....141 K6
Glenesk Rd *ELTH/MOT* SE9 ....147 F5
Glenfarg Rd *CAT* SE6 ....165 G3
Glenfield Crs *RSLP* HA4 ....58 B4
Glenfield Rd *BAL* SW12 ....161 H3
WEA W13 ....116 C2
Glenfinlas Wy *CMBW* SE5 ....142 C1
Glenforth St *GNWCH* SE10 ....125 J4
Glengall Br *POP/IOD* E14 ....124 E3
Glengall Gv *POP/IOD* E14 ....124 E3
Glengall Rd *BXLYHN* DA7 ....149 F4
EDGW HA8 ....30 D5
KIL/WHAMP NW6 ....82 D6
PECK SE15 ....123 G6
WFD IG8 ....52 E2
Glengall Ter *PECK* SE15 ....123 G6
Glen Gdns *CROY/NA* CR0 ....211 G1
Glengarnock Av *POP/IOD* E14 ....125 F4
Glengarry Rd *EDUL* SE22 ....143 F5
Glenham Dr *GNTH/NBYPK* IG2 ....72 B2
Glenhead Cl *ELTH/MOT* SE9 ....147 G4
Glenhill Cl *FNCH* N3 ....46 E5
Glenhouse Rd *ELTH/MOT* SE9 ....147 F6
Glenhurst Av *BXLY* DA5 ....169 G3
KTTN NW5 ....84 A2
RSLP HA4 ....58 A4
Glenhurst Ri *NRWD* SE19 ....180 D3
Glenhurst Rd *BTFD* TW8 ....116 D6
NFNCH/WDSP N12 ....33 H6
Glenilla Rd *HAMP* NW3 ....83 J4
Glenister Park Rd
STRHM/NOR SW16 ....179 J3
Glenister Rd *GNWCH* SE10 ....125 J5
Glenlea Rd *ELTH/MOT* SE9 ....147 F6
Glenloch Rd *HAMP* NW3 ....83 J4
PEND EN3 ....24 E3
Glenluce Rd *BKHTH/KID* SE3 ....146 A4
Glenluge Rd *BKHTH/KID* SE3 ....125 K6
Glenlyon Rd *ELTH/MOT* SE9 ....147 F6
Glenmere Av *MLHL* NW7 ....45 J3
Glenmore Lawns *WEA* W13 * 97 G5
Glenmore Pde *ALP/SUD* HA0 * 80 A6
Glenmore Rd *HAMP* NW3 ....83 J4
WELL DA16 ....148 A2
Glenmore Wy *BARK* IG11 ....109 G2
Glennie Rd *WNWD* SE27 ....162 B5
Glenny Rd *BARK* IG11 ....90 C4
Glenorchy Cl *YEAD* UB4 ....95 J4
Glenparke Rd *FSTGT* E7 ....89 F4
Glen Ri *WFD* IG8 ....53 F2
Glen Rd *CHSGTN* KT9 ....206 A1
PLSTW E13 ....107 G3
WALTH E17 ....69 H2
Glen Road End *WLGTN* SM6 ....210 B6
Glenrosa St *FUL/PGN* SW6 ....140 B3
Glenroy St *SHB* W12 ....100 A5
Glensdale Rd *BROCKY* SE4 ....144 C4
Glenshiel Rd *ELTH/MOT* SE9 ....147 F6
Glenside *CHIG* IG7 ....54 B2
Glentanner Wy *TOOT* SW17 ....160 C5
Glen Ter *POP/IOD* E14 ....125 F2
Glentham Gdns *BARN* SW13 ....118 E5
Glentham Rd *BARN* SW13 ....118 D6
The Glen *BELMT* SM2 * 209 G4
CROY/NA CR0 ....213 F1
ENC/FH EN2 ....23 H5
HAYES BR2 ....183 H5
NTHWD HA6 ....40 B3
NWDGN UB2 ....114 E5
ORP BR6 ....215 K1
PIN HA5 ....59 F2
PIN HA5 ....59 J4
WBLY HA9 ....79 K2
Glenthorne Av *CROY/NA* CR0 ....197 K5
Glenthorne Cl *CHEAM* SM3 ....193 K5
Glenthorne Gdns *BARK/HLT* IG6 ....54 A6
CHEAM SM3 ....193 K5
Glenthorne Rd
FBAR/BDGN N11 ....47 K1
HMSMTH W6 ....118 E4
KUT/HW KT1 ....191 G1
WALTH E17 ....69 G2
Glenthorpe Rd *MRDN* SM4 ....193 G2
Glenton Cl *ROM* RM1 ....57 G3
Glenton Rd *LEW* SE13 ....145 H5
Glenton Wy *ROM* RM1 ....57 G3
Glentrammon Av *ORP* BR6 ....217 F4
Glentrammon Cl *ORP* BR6 ....217 F4
Glentrammon Gdns *ORP* BR6 ....217 F4
Glentrammon Rd *ORP* BR6 ....217 F4
Glentworth St *CAMTN* NW1 ....3 F7
Glenure Rd *ELTH/MOT* SE9 ....147 F6
Glenview *ABYW* SE2 ....128 E6
Glen View Rd *BMLY* BR1 ....184 C5
Glenville Av *ENC/FH* EN2 ....23 J1
Glenville Gv *DEPT* SE8 ....144 C1
Glenville Rd *KUTN/CMB* KT2 ....175 H4
Glenwood Av *CDALE/KGS* NW9 ....63 G5
RAIN RM13 ....111 J3
Glenwood Cl *HRW* HA1 ....61 F2
Glenwood Dr *GPK* RM2 ....75 J2
Glenwood Gdns
GNTH/NBYPK IG2 ....72 A2
Glenwood Gv *CDALE/KGS* NW9 ....62 E5
Glenwood Rd *CAT* SE6 ....164 C3
EW KT17 ....207 J4
HSLW TW3 ....135 J4
MLHL NW7 ....31 G5
SEVS/STOTM N15 ....67 H2
Glenwood Rw *NRWD* SE19 * 181 G4
Glenwood Wy *CROY/NA* CR0 ....198 A3
Glenworth Av *POP/IOD* E14 ....125 G4
Gliddon Dr *CLPT* E5 ....86 D2
Gliddon Rd *WKENS* W14 ....119 H4
Glimpsing Gn *ERITHM* DA18 ....129 F3
Gload Crs *STMC/STPC* BR5 ....202 E6
Globe Pond Rd
BERM/RHTH SE16 ....124 B1
Globe Rd *BETH* E2 ....104 E2
EMPK RM11 ....75 J3
SRTFD E15 ....88 D3
WFD IG8 ....53 G2
Globe St *STHWK* SE1 ....18 E3
Globe Ter *BETH* E2 ....104 E2
Glossop Rd *SAND/SEL* CR2 ....211 K6
Gloster Rd *NWMAL* KT3 ....192 B1
Gloucester Av *BFN/LL* DA15 ....167 K4
CAMTN NW1 ....84 A5
WELL DA16 ....148 A6
Gloucester Circ *GNWCH* SE10 ....145 F1
Gloucester Cl *THDIT* KT7 * 190 B5
WLSDN NW10 ....81 F5
Gloucester Ct *MON* EC3R 13 H6
MTCM CR4 * 195 K2
RCH/KEW TW9 * 137 H1
Gloucester Crs *CAMTN* NW1 ....84 B6
Gloucester Dr *FSBYPK* N4 ....67 H6
GLDGN NW11 ....64 E1
Gloucester Gdns
BAY/PAD W2 * 101 G5
EBAR EN4 ....22 A5
GLDGN NW11 ....64 D4
IL IG1 ....71 J4
SUT SM1 ....194 A6
Gloucester Ga *CAMTN* NW1 ....3 J2
Gloucester Gate Ms *CAMTN* NW1 ....3 J2
Gloucester Gv *EDGW* HA8 ....45 F4
Gloucester Ms *BAY/PAD* W2 ....101 G5
Gloucester Ms West
BAY/PAD W2 ....101 G5
Gloucester Pde *BFN/LL* DA15 * 148 B6
HYS/HAR UB3 * 113 F3
Gloucester Pl *CAMTN* NW1 ....2 E6
MHST W1U 9 F2
Gloucester Place Ms
MBLAR W1H 9 F2
Gloucester Rd *ACT* W3 ....117 K2
BAR EN5 ....21 F6
BELV DA17 ....129 G5
CROY/NA CR0 ....196 E4
DART DA1 ....170 E1
EA W5 ....116 D2
ENC/FH EN2 ....23 J1
FELT TW13 ....154 B3
HPTN TW12 ....173 G3
HSLWW TW4 ....134 D5
KUT/HW KT1 ....175 H5
LEY E10 ....69 J4
MNPK E12 ....89 K1
RCH/KEW TW9 ....137 H1
ROM RM1 ....75 G3
RYLN/HDSTN HA2 ....60 B2
SKENS SW7 ....120 B4
TEDD TW11 ....173 K1
TOTM N17 ....49 K6
UED N18 ....50 B1
WALTH E17 ....51 F5
WAN E11 ....71 F2
WHTN TW2 ....155 H3
Gloucester Sq *BAY/PAD* W2 ....8 B5
BETH E2 ....86 C6
Gloucester St *PIM* SW1V 121 H5
Gloucester Ter *BAY/PAD* W2 ....101 G5
STHGT/OAK N14 * 34 D3
Gloucester Wk *KENS* W8 * 119 K2
Gloucester Wy *CLKNW* EC1R 5 K5
Glover Cl *ABYW* SE2 ....128 D4
Glover Dr *UED* N18 ....50 E2
Glover Rd *PIN* HA5 ....59 H3
Glycena Rd *BTSEA* SW11 ....140 E4
Glyn Av *EBAR* EN4 ....21 H5
Glyn Cl *EW* KT17 ....207 J6
SNWD SE25 ....181 F5
Glyndebourne Pk *ORP* BR6 ....216 B1
Glynde Ms *CHEL* SW3 ....14 D5
Glynde Rd *BXLYHN* DA7 ....148 E4
Glynde St *BROCKY* SE4 ....164 C1
Glyndon Rd *WOOL/PLUM* SE18 ....127 H4
Glyn Dr *SCUP* DA14 ....168 C6
Glynfield Rd *WLSDN* NW10 ....81 G5
Glynne Rd *WDGN* N22 ....49 G5
Glyn Rd *CLPT* E5 ....87 F2
PEND EN3 ....24 E5
WPK KT4 ....193 G6
Glyn St *LBTH* SE11 ....122 A5
Goat La *EN* EN1 ....24 B1
Goat Rd *MTCM* CR4 ....195 F4
Goat Whf *BTFD* TW8 ....117 F6
Gobions Av *CRW* RM5 ....57 F3
Godalming Av *WLGTN* SM6 ....210 E3
Godalming Rd *POP/IOD* E14 ....105 K4
Godbold Rd *SRTFD* E15 ....106 C3
Goddard Pl *ARCH* N19 ....84 C1
Goddard Rd *BECK* BR3 ....198 A1
Goddards Wy *IL* IG1 ....72 D5
Goddington Cha *ORP* BR6 ....217 H2
Goddington La *ORP* BR6 ....217 G1
Godfrey Av *NTHLT* UB5 ....77 J6
WHTN TW2 ....155 J2
Godfrey Hl *WOOL/PLUM* SE18 ....126 D4
Godfrey Rd *WOOL/PLUM* SE18 ....126 E4
Godfrey St *CHEL* SW3 ....120 D5
SRTFD E15 ....106 A1
Godfrey Wy *HSLWW* TW4 ....154 D2
Goding St *LBTH* SE11 ....121 K5
Godley Rd *WAND/EARL* SW18 ....160 C3
Godliman St *BLKFR* EC4V * 12 B4
Godman Rd *PECK* SE15 * 143 J3
Godolphin Cl *PLMGR* N13 ....49 H2
Godolphin Pl *ACT* W3 ....99 F6
Godolphin Rd *SHB* W12 ....118 E2
Godric Crs *CROY/NA* CR0 ....214 B6
Godson Rd *CROY/NA* CR0 ....211 G1
Godson St *IS* N1 ....5 J2
Godstone Rd *SUT* SM1 ....209 G2
TWK TW1 ....156 B1
Godstow Rd *ABYW* SE2 ....128 D2
Godwin Cl *HOR/WEW* KT19 ....206 E4
IS N1 ....6 D2
Godwin Rd *FSTGT* E7 ....89 F2
HAYES BR2 ....184 B6
Goffers Rd *BKHTH/KID* SE3 ....145 H3
Goidel Cl *WLGTN* SM6 ....210 D2
Golborne Gdns *NKENS* W10 * 100 C3
Golborne Ms *NKENS* W10 ....100 C4
Golborne Rd *NKENS* W10 ....100 C4
Golda Cl *BAR* EN5 ....32 B1
Goldbeaters Gv *EDGW* HA8 ....45 G3
Goldcliff Cl *MRDN* SM4 ....193 K4
Goldcrest Cl *CAN/RD* E16 ....107 H4
THMD SE28 ....109 J6
Goldcrest Ms *EA* W5 * 97 K4
Goldcrest Wy *BUSH* WD23 ....28 C3
CROY/NA CR0 ....214 B6
Golden Ct *ISLW* TW7 ....135 J3
Golden Crs *HYS/HAR* UB3 ....113 H1
Golden Cross Ms *NTGHL* W11 * 100 D5
Golden Hind Pl *DEPT* SE8 * 124 C4
Golden La *STLK* EC1Y 6 C6
Golden Lane Est *STLK* EC1Y 6 C7
Golden Mnr *HNWL* W7 ....96 E6
Golden Pde *WALTH* E17 * 52 A6
Golden Plover Cl *CAN/RD* E16 ....106 E5
Golden Sq *SOHO/CST* W1F 10 B5
Golden Yd *HAMP* NW3 * 83 G2
Golders Cl *EDGW* HA8 ....44 D1
Golders Gdns *GLDGN* NW11 ....64 C4
Golders Green Crs
GLDGN NW11 ....64 D4
Golders Green Rd
GLDGN NW11 ....64 C3
Golders Hl *HAMP* NW3 * 65 F6
Goldersiea *GLDGN* NW11 * 65 E5
Golders Manor Dr *GLDGN* NW11 ....64 B3
Golders Park Cl *GLDGN* NW11 ....64 E6
Golders Ri *HDN* NW4 ....64 B2
Golders Wy *GLDGN* NW11 ....64 D4
Goldfinch Cl *ORP* BR6 ....217 G3
Goldfinch Rd *THMD* SE28 ....127 J3
Goldhawk Ms *SHB* W12 ....118 E2
Goldhawk Rd *HMSMTH* W6 ....118 C4
Goldhaze Cl *WFD* IG8 ....53 H3
Gold Hl *EDGW* HA8 ....45 F2
Goldhurst Ter *KIL/WHAMP* NW6 ....83 G4
Golding St *WCHPL* E1 ....104 C5
Goldington Crs *CAMTN* NW1 ....4 C2
Goldington St *CAMTN* NW1 ....4 C2
Gold La *EDGW* HA8 ....45 F2
Goldman Cl *BETH* E2 ....104 C3
Goldney Rd *MV/WKIL* W9 ....100 E3
Goldrill Dr *FBAR/BDGN* N11 ....34 A4
Goldsboro Rd *VX/NE* SW8 ....141 J2
Goldsborough Crs *CHING* E4 ....37 K4
Goldsdown Cl *PEND* EN3 ....25 G3
Goldsdown Rd *PEND* EN3 ....25 F3
Goldsmid St
WOOL/PLUM SE18 ....127 K5
Goldsmith Av *ACT* W3 ....99 F6
CDALE/KGS NW9 ....63 G2
MNPK E12 ....89 J4
ROMW/RG RM7 ....74 C4
Goldsmith Cl *RYLN/HDSTN* HA2 ....60 A5
Goldsmith La *CDALE/KGS* NW9 ....62 E1
Goldsmith Pl
KIL/WHAMP NW6 * 83 F6
Goldsmith Rd *ACT* W3 ....118 A1
FBAR/BDGN N11 ....47 K1
LEY E10 ....69 K5
PECK SE15 ....143 H2
WALTH E17 ....51 F5
Goldsmiths Cl *ACT* W3 * 118 A1
Goldsmith's Rw *BETH* E2 ....86 C6
Goldsmith St *CITYW* EC2V 12 D3
Goldsworthy Gdns
BERM/RHTH SE16 ....123 K4
Goldwell Rd *THHTH* CR7 ....196 A1
Goldwing Cl *CAN/RD* E16 ....106 E5
Golf Cl *STAN* HA7 ....43 J3
STRHM/NOR SW16 ....180 B4
Golf Club Dr *KUTN/CMB* KT2 ....176 A3
Golfe Rd *IL* IG1 ....90 D1
Golf Rd *BMLY* BR1 ....185 F6
EA W5 * 98 B5
Golf Side *WHTN* TW2 ....155 J5
Golf Side Cl *NWMAL* KT3 ....176 B5
Golfside Cl *TRDG/WHET* N20 ....33 J5
Gollogly Ter *CHARL* SE7 ....126 B5
Gomer Gdns *TEDD* TW11 ....174 B2
Gomer Pl *TEDD* TW11 ....174 B2
Gomm Rd *BERM/RHTH* SE16 ....123 K3
Gomshall Av *WLGTN* SM6 ....210 E3
Gondar Gdns *KIL/WHAMP* NW6 ....82 D3
Gonson St *DEPT* SE8 ....124 E6
Gonston Cl *WIM/MER* SW19 ....159 H4
Gonville Crs *NTHLT* UB5 ....78 B4
Gonville Rd *THHTH* CR7 ....196 A2
Gonville St *FUL/PGN* SW6 ....139 H4
Goodall Rd *WAN* E11 ....88 A1
Gooden Ct *HRW* HA1 ....78 E1
Goodenough Rd
WIM/MER SW19 ....177 J3
Goodey Rd *BARK* IG11 ....91 F5
Goodge Pl *FITZ* W1T 10 B2
Goodge St *FITZ* W1T 10 B2
Goodhall Cl *STAN* HA7 ....43 G2
Goodhall St *WLSDN* NW10 ....99 H2
Goodhart Wy *WWKM* BR4 ....199 H3
Goodhew Rd *SNWD* SE25 ....197 H3
Gooding Cl *NWMAL* KT3 ....191 K1
Goodinge Cl *HOLWY* N7 ....84 E4
Goodinge Rd *HOLWY* N7 ....84 E4
Goodman Ct *ALP/SUD* HA0 * 79 K2
Goodman Crs
BRXS/STRHM SW2 ....161 K4
Goodman Rd *LEY* E10 ....70 A4
Goodmans Ct *ALP/SUD* HA0 ....79 K2
Goodman's Stile *WCHPL* E1 ....104 C5
Goodman's Yd *TWRH* EC3N 13 J5
Goodmayes Av *GDMY/SEVK* IG3 ....73 G5
Goodmayes La *GDMY/SEVK* IG3 ....91 G2
Goodmayes Rd *GDMY/SEVK* IG3 ....73 G5
Goodmead Rd *ORP* BR6 ....202 B4
Goodrich Rd *EDUL* SE22 ....163 G1
Goodson Rd *WLSDN* NW10 ....81 G5
Goods Wy *CAMTN* NW1 ....4 E2
Goodsway *CAMTN* NW1 ....4 E2
Goodway Gdns *POP/IOD* E14 ....106 B5
Goodwin Cl *BERM/RHTH* SE16 ....19 K5
MTCM CR4 ....178 C6
Goodwin Dr *SCUP* DA14 ....168 E4
Goodwin Gdns *CROY/NA* CR0 ....211 H4
Goodwin Rd *CROY/NA* CR0 ....211 H3
ED N9 ....36 E3
SHB W12 ....118 D2
Goodwins Ct *CHCR* WC2N 10 E5
Goodwin St *FSBYPK* N4 ....67 G6
Goodwood Cl *MRDN* SM4 ....193 K1
Goodwood Dr *NTHLT* UB5 ....78 A4
Goodwood Pde *BECK* BR3 * 198 B1
Goodwood Rd *NWCR* SE14 ....144 B1
Goodwyn Av *MLHL* NW7 ....45 G1
Goodwyn's V *MUSWH* N10 ....48 A4
Goodyers Gdns *HDN* NW4 ....64 B2
Goosander Wy
WOOL/PLUM SE18 ....127 J3
Gooseacre La
KTN/HRWW/W HA3 ....61 K2
Goose Green Cl
STMC/STPC BR5 ....186 B5
Gooseley La *EHAM* E6 ....108 A2
Goossens Cl *SUT* SM1 ....209 G3
Gophir La *CANST* EC4R * 12 E5
Gopsall St *IS* N1 ....7 F1
Gordon Av *CHING* E4 ....52 C2
HCH RM12 ....75 H6
MORT/ESHN SW14 ....138 B5
STAN HA7 ....43 F2
TWK TW1 ....136 B6
Gordonbrock Rd *BROCKY* SE4 ....144 D6
Gordon Cl *WALTH* E17 ....69 J3
Gordon Crs *CROY/NA* CR0 ....197 F5
HYS/HAR UB3 ....113 K4
Gordondale Rd
WIM/MER SW19 ....159 K4
Gordon Gdns *EDGW* HA8 ....44 D5
Gordon Gv *CMBW* SE5 ....142 C3
Gordon Hl *ENC/FH* EN2 ....23 J2
Gordon House Rd *KTTN* NW5 ....84 A2
Gordon Pl *KENS* W8 ....119 K2
Gordon Rd *ASHF* TW15 ....152 B5
BARK IG11 ....90 E6
BECK BR3 ....182 C6
BELV DA17 ....129 K4
BFN/LL DA15 ....147 K6
BRYLDS KT5 ....191 G4
CAR SM5 ....209 K4
CHDH RM6 ....74 B3
CHING E4 ....38 C2
CHSWK W4 ....117 J6
DART DA1 ....171 G2
EA W5 ....97 J6
ED N9 ....36 D4
ENC/FH EN2 ....23 K2
ESH/CLAY KT10 ....204 E5
FBAR/BDGN N11 ....48 D3
FNCH N3 ....46 D3
HSLW TW3 ....135 H5
IL IG1 ....90 D1
KTN/HRWW/W HA3 ....42 E6
KUTN/CMB KT2 ....175 G4
NWDGN UB2 ....114 D4
PECK SE15 ....143 J3
RCH/KEW TW9 ....137 G3
SRTFD E15 ....88 A2
SWFD E18 ....53 F4
WAN E11 ....70 E3
Gordon Sq *STPAN* WC1H 4 D6
Gordon St *PLSTW* E13 ....106 E2
STPAN WC1H 4 C6
Gordon Wy *BAR* EN5 ....20 D5
BMLY BR1 ....183 K4
Gorefield Pl *KIL/WHAMP* NW6 ....100 E1
Gore Rd *HOM* E9 ....86 E6
RYNPK SW20 ....177 F5
Goresbrook Rd *DAGW* RM9 ....91 J6
Gore St *SKENS* SW7 ....120 B3
Gorham Pl *NTGHL* W11 ....100 C6
Goring Cl *CRW* RM5 ....56 E4
Goring Gdns *BCTR* RM8 ....91 J2
Goring Rd *DAGE* RM10 ....93 F4
FBAR/BDGN N11 * 48 E2
Goring St *HDTCH* EC3A 13 H3
Goring Wy *GFD/PVL* UB6 ....96 C1
Gorleston Rd *SEVS/STOTM* N15 ....67 K2
Gorleston St *WKENS* W14 ....119 H4
Gorman Rd *WOOL/PLUM* SE18 ....126 E4
Gorringe Park Av *MTCM* CR4 ....178 E3
Gorse Cl *CAN/RD* E16 ....106 E5
Gorse Ri *TOOT* SW17 ....179 F1
Gorse Rd *CROY/NA* CR0 ....213 J1
STMC/STPC BR5 ....203 H6
Gorseway *ROMW/RG* RM7 ....75 G6
Gorst Rd *BTSEA* SW11 ....160 E1
WLSDN NW10 ....98 E3
Gorsuch Pl *BETH* E2 ....7 J4
Gorsuch St *BETH* E2 ....7 J4
Gosberton Rd *BAL* SW12 ....160 E3
Gosbury Hl *CHSGTN* KT9 ....206 A2
Gosfield Rd *BCTR* RM8 ....74 C5
Gosfield St *GTPST* W1W 9 K1
Gosford Gdns *REDBR* IG4 ....71 K2
Gosforth La *OXHEY* WD19 ....26 E5
Gosforth Pth *OXHEY* WD19 ....26 E5
Goshawk Gdns *YEAD* UB4 ....94 C2
Goslett Yd *SOHO/SHAV* W1D 10 D3
Gosling Cl *GFD/PVL* UB6 ....96 A2
Gosling Wy *BRXN/ST* SW9 ....142 B2
Gospatrick Rd *TOTM* N17 ....49 J4
Gosport Rd *WALTH* E17 ....69 H2
Gosport Wy *PECK* SE15 ....143 G1
Gossage Rd *WOOL/PLUM* SE18 ....127 J5
Gosset St *BETH* E2 ....104 C2
Gosshill Rd *CHST* BR7 ....185 F5
Gossington Cl *CHST* BR7 ....167 G6
Gosterwood St *DEPT* SE8 ....124 B6
Gostling Rd *WHTN* TW2 ....155 F3
Goston Gdns *THHTH* CR7 ....180 B6
Goswell Pl *FSBYE* EC1V 6 B5
Goswell Rd *FSBYE* EC1V 6 B4
Gothic Cl *DART* DA1 ....171 G5
Gothic Ct *HYS/HAR* UB3 ....113 G6
Gothic Rd *WHTN* TW2 ....155 J4
Gottfried Ms *KTTN* NW5 ....84 C2
Goudhurst Rd *BMLY* BR1 ....183 H1
Gough Rd *EN* EN1 ....24 D3
FSTGT E7 ....88 D2
Gough Sq *FLST/FETLN* EC4A 11 K3
Gough St *FSBYW* WC1X 5 H6
Goulding Gdns *THHTH* CR7 ....180 D5
Gould Rd *EBED/NFELT* TW14 ....153 H2
WHTN TW2 ....155 K3
Gould Ter *HACK* E8 ....86 D3
Goulston St *WCHPL* E1 ....13 J3
Goulton Rd *CLPT* E5 ....86 D3
Gourley Pl *SEVS/STOTM* N15 ....68 A2
Gourley St *SEVS/STOTM* N15 ....68 A2
Gourock Rd *ELTH/MOT* SE9 ....147 F6
Govan St *BETH* E2 ....86 C6
Govier Cl *SRTFD* E15 ....88 C5
Gowan Av *FUL/PGN* SW6 ....139 H2
Gowan Rd *WLSDN* NW10 ....81 K5
Gower Cl *CLAP* SW4 ....161 H1
Gower Ms *GWRST* WC1E 10 D2
Gower Pl *STPAN* WC1H 4 B6
Gower Rd *FSTGT* E7 ....88 E4
ISLW TW7 ....116 A6
Gower St *GWRST* WC1E 4 C7
Gower's Wk *WCHPL* E1 ....104 C5
Gowland Pl *BECK* BR3 ....182 C5
Gowlett Rd *PECK* SE15 ....143 H4
Gowlland Cl *CROY/NA* CR0 ....197 H4
Gowrie Rd *BTSEA* SW11 ....141 F4
Graburn Wy *E/WMO/HCT* KT8 ....173 J6
Grace Av *BXLYHN* DA7 ....149 G3
Gracechurch St *BANK* EC3V 13 F5
Grace Cl *BARK/HLT* IG6 ....55 F2
EDGW HA8 ....44 E3
ELTH/MOT SE9 ....166 C5
Gracedale Rd
STRHM/NOR SW16 ....179 G1
Gracefield Gdns
STRHM/NOR SW16 ....161 K5
Grace Jones Cl *HACK* E8 * 86 B4
Grace Pl *BOW* E3 ....105 K2
Grace Rd *CROY/NA* CR0 ....196 D3
Graces Aly *WCHPL* E1 * 104 C6
Grace's Ms *CMBW* SE5 ....142 E3
STJWD NW8 * 101 G1
Grace's Rd *CMBW* SE5 ....143 F3
Grace St *BOW* E3 ....105 K2
The Gradient *SYD* SE26 ....163 H6
Graduate Pl *STHWK* SE1 ....19 G4
Graeme Rd *EN* EN1 ....24 A3
Graemesdyke Av
MORT/ESHN SW14 ....137 J4
Grafton Cl *HSLWW* TW4 ....154 D3
WEA W13 ....97 G5
WPK KT4 ....207 G1
Grafton Crs *CAMTN* NW1 ....84 B4
Grafton Gdns *BCTR* RM8 ....74 A6
FSBYPK N4 ....67 J3
Grafton Ms *FITZ* W1T 4 A7
Grafton Park Rd *WPK* KT4 ....192 B6
Grafton Pl *CAMTN* NW1 ....4 C5
Grafton Rd *ACT* W3 ....98 E6
BCTR RM8 ....74 A6
CROY/NA CR0 ....196 B5
ENC/FH EN2 ....23 F4
HRW HA1 ....60 C2
KTTN NW5 ....84 A3
NWMAL KT3 ....192 B1
WPK KT4 ....207 F1
Grafton Sq *CLAP* SW4 ....141 H5
Grafton St *MYFR/PICC* W1J 9 K6
Grafton Ter *KTTN* NW5 ....83 K3
Grafton Wy *E/WMO/HCT* KT8 ....188 E1
FITZ W1T 4 B7
GTPST W1W 10 A1
Grafton Yd *KTTN* NW5 ....84 B4
Graham Av *MTCM* CR4 ....179 F4
WEA W13 ....116 C2
Graham Cl *CROY/NA* CR0 ....198 D6
Grahame Park Wy *MLHL* NW7 ....45 H3
Graham Gdns *SURB* KT6 ....191 F5
Graham Rd *BXLYHN* DA7 ....149 G5
CHSWK W4 ....118 A3
HACK E8 ....86 C4
HDN NW4 ....63 K3
HPTN TW12 ....155 F6
KTN/HRWW/W HA3 ....42 E6
MTCM CR4 ....179 F4
PLSTW E13 ....106 E3
SEVS/STOTM N15 ....49 H6
WIM/MER SW19 ....177 J3
Graham St *IS* N1 ....6 B3
Graham Ter *BFN/LL* DA15 * 168 C1

BGVA SW1W 15 H7
Grainger CI NTHLT UB5 ....78 C3
Grainger Rd ISLW TW7 ....136 A5
WDGN N22 ....49 J4
Gramer CI WAN E11 ....70 B6
Grampian CI BELMT SM2 ....209 G5
HYS/HAR UB3 ....133 G1
ORP BR6 ....202 A3
Granada CI CRICK NW2 ....64 C5
Gramsci Wy CAT SE6 ....164 E5
Granada St TOOT SW17 ....178 E1
Granard Av PUT/ROE SW15 ....138 E6
Granard Rd BAL SW12 ....160 E2
Granary CI ED N9 ....36 E2
Granary Rd WCHPL E1 ....104 D3
Granary Sq IS N1 ....85 G4
Granary St CAMTN NW1 ....4 C1
Granby Rd ELTH/MOT SE9 ......146 E3
WOOL/PLUM SE18 ....127 G3
Granby St BETH E2 ....7 K6
Granby Ter CAMTN NW1 ....4 A5
Grand Av BRYLDS KT5 ....191 J5
FARR EC1M 12 B1
MUSWH N10 ....66 A1
WBLY HA9 ....80 C3
Grand Av East WBLY HA9 ....80 D3
Grand Depot Rd
WOOL/PLUM SE18 ....127 F5
Grand Dr WNDGN UB2 ....115 H2
RYNPK SW20 ....177 F6
Granden Rd
STRHM/NOR SW16 ....179 K5
Grandison Rd CLAP SW4 ....141 J6
WPK KT4 ....193 H6
Grand Junction Whf IS N1 * 6 C3
Grand Pde FSBYPK N4 * 67 H3
MORT/ESHN SW14 * 137 K5
SURB KT6 * 191 H5
WBLY HA9 * 62 D6
Grand Union Canal Wk
HNWL W7 ....115 K3
MV/WKIL W9 * 100 E4
NWDGN UB2 ....114 A3
STHL UB1 ....95 K3
STKPK UB11 ....93 J6
WLSDN NW10 ....98 D1
Grand Union CI MV/WKIL W9 ....100 D4
Grand Union Crs HACK E8 * 86 C6
Grand Union Wk CAMTN NW1 * ...84 B5
Grand Wk WCHPL E1 * 105 G3
Granfield St BTSEA SW11 * 140 C4
Grange Av EBAR EN4 ....33 J3
KTN/HRWW/W HA3 ....43 H5
NFNCH/WDSP N12 ....47 G1
SNWD SE25 ....181 F5
TRDG/WHET N20 ....32 C2
WFD IG8 ....52 E2
WHTN TW2 ....155 K4
Grangecliffe Gdns SNWD SE25 ..181 F5
Grange CI BFN/LL DA15 ....168 B5
E/WMO/HCT KT8 ....189 G1
HYS/HAR UB3 ....94 C4
NWDGN UB2 ....114 E5
WFD IG8 ....52 E2
Grange Ct ALP/SUD HA0 * 79 J3
BELMT SM2 * 209 F5
HRW HA1 * 79 F1
NTHLT UB5 ....95 G1
PIN HA5 * 41 J6
WLGTN SM6 * 210 B1
Grangecourt Rd
STNW/STAM N16 ....68 A5
Grange Crs CHIG IG7 ....54 D1
THMD SE28 ....109 J5
Grangedale CI NTHWD HA6 ....40 C4
Grange Dr CHST BR7 ....184 D2
ORP BR6 ....217 J6
Grange Farm CI
RYLN/HDSTN HA2 ....60 C6
Grange Gdns HAMP NW3 ....83 F1
PIN HA5 ....41 J6
SNWD SE25 ....181 F5
STHGT/OAK N14 ....34 D3
Grangehill PI ELTH/MOT SE9 ...146 E4
Grangehill Rd ELTH/MOT SE9 ...146 E5
Grange Houses HBRY N5 * 85 J2
Grange La DUL SE21 ....163 G4
Grange Ms FELT TW13 ....155 G5
Grangemill Rd CAT SE6 ....164 D5
Grangemill Wy CAT SE6 ....164 D4
Grange Pk EA W5 ....117 F1
Grange Park Av WCHMH N21 ....35 H1
Grange Park PI RYNPK SW20 ...176 E3
Grange Park Rd LEY E10 ....69 K5
THHTH CR7 ....180 E6
Grange PI KIL/WHAMP NW6 ......82 E5
Grange Rd BARN SW13 ....138 D2
BELMT SM2 ....208 E5
CHSGTN KT9 ....206 A2
CHSWK W4 ....117 J5
E/WMO/HCT KT8 ....189 G1
EA W5 ....116 E1
EDGW HA8 ....45 F2
HARH RM3 ....58 A3
HGT N6 ....66 A3
HRW HA1 ....61 G3
HYS/HAR UB3 ....94 C5
IL IG1 ....90 C2
KUT/HW KT1 ....175 H5
ORP BR6 ....201 H6
PLSTW E13 ....106 D3
RYLN/HDSTN HA2 ....60 D6
SNWD SE25 ....180 E6
STHL UB1 ....114 D2
STHWK SE1 ....19 H5
TOTM N17 ....50 C4
WALTH E17 ....69 G2
WLSDN NW10 ....98 E2
Granger Wy ROM RM1 ....75 J3
Grange St IS N1 * 7 F1
The Grange ALP/SUD HA0 * 80 C5
CROY/NA CR0 ....198 C6

HOR/WEW KT19 ....207 F2
NWMAL KT3 * 192 D2
WIM/MER SW19 ....177 G2
WKENS W14 * 119 J4
WOT/HER KT12 ....188 A6
Grange V BELMT SM2 ....209 F5
Grangeview Rd
TRDG/WHET N20 ....33 G3
Grange Wk STHWK SE1 ....19 H5
Grange Walk Ms STHWK SE1 ....19 H5
Grange Wy ERITH DA8 ....150 C1
Grangeway KIL/WHAMP NW6 ....82 E5
NFNCH/WDSP N12 ....47 J3
WFD IG8 ....39 G6
Grangeway Gdns REDBR IG4 ....71 J2
The Grangeway WCHMH N21 ....35 H1
Grangewood BXLY DA5 ....169 G3
Grangewood CI PIN HA5 ....58 E2
Grangewood La BECK BR3 ......182 C2
Grangewood St EHAM E6 ....89 H6
Grange Yd STHWK SE1 ....19 K4
Granham Gdns ED N9 ....36 B4
Granite St WOOL/PLUM SE18 ...128 A5
Granleigh Rd WAN E11 ....70 C6
Gransden Av HACK E8 ....86 D5
Gransden Rd SHB W12 ....118 C2
Grantbridge St IS N1 ....6 B2
Grantchester KUT/HW KT1 * 175 H5
Grantchester CI HRW HA1 ....79 F1
Grant CI STHGT/OAK N14 ....34 C2
TOTM N17 ....50 A5
Grantham CI EDGW HA8 ....30 A5
Grantham Gdns CHDH RM6 ......74 B5
Grantham PI MYFR/PICC W1J ...15 J1
Grantham Rd BRXN/ST SW9 * ..142 A4
CHSWK W4 ....138 B1
MNPK E12 ....90 A1
Grantley PI ESH/CLAY KT10 ....204 B3
Grantley Rd HSLWW TW4 ....134 B3
Grantley St WCHPL E1 ....105 F3
Grantock Rd WALTH E17 ....52 B4
Granton Rd GDMY/SEVK IG3 ....73 G5
SCUP DA14 ....186 C2
STRHM/NOR SW16 ....179 H4
Grant Rd BTSEA SW11 ....140 D4
CROY/NA CR0 ....197 G5
KTN/HRWW/W HA3 ....43 F2
Grants CI MLHL NW7 ....46 A5
Grant St IS N1 ....5 J1
PLSTW E13 ....106 E2
Grant Ter STNW/STAM N16 * 68 C4
Grantully Rd MV/WKIL W9 ....101 F2
Grant Wy ISLW TW7 ....116 A6
Granville Av BRXN/ST SW9 * 142 B5
Granville Av ED N9 ....36 E5
FELT TW13 ....153 K4
HSLW TW3 ....135 F6
Granville CI CROY/NA CR0 ......197 F6
Granville Gdns EA W5 * 117 J1
STRHM/NOR SW16 ....180 A4
Granville Gv LEW SE13 ....145 F4
Granville Ms SCUP DA14 ....168 B6
Granville Pk LEW SE13 ....145 F4
Granville PI FUL/PGN SW6 * 140 A1
MBLAR W1H 9 G1
NFNCH/WDSP N12 * 47 G3
PIN HA5 ....41 H6
Granville Rd BAR EN5 ....20 A5
CRICK NW2 ....64 D6
FSBYPK N4 ....67 F3
HAYS/HAR UB3 ....113 J4
IL IG1 ....90 C2
KIL/WHAMP NW6 ....100 E1
NFNCH/WDSP N12 ....47 G3
PLMGR N13 ....49 F2
SCUP DA14 ....168 B6
SWFD E18 ....53 F5
WAND/EARL SW18 ....159 K2
WDGN N22 ....49 H4
WELL DA16 ....148 D4
WIM/MER SW19 ....177 K3
Granville Sq PECK SE15 * 143 F1
Granville St FSBYW WC1X * 5 J5
Grape St LSQ/SEVD WC2H * 10 E5
Graphite Sq LBTH SE11 * 122 A5
Grapsome CI CHSGTN KT9 ......205 J5
Grasdene Rd
WOOL/PLUM SE18 ....148 B1
Grasgarth CI ACT W3 ....98 E6
HSLW TW3 ....155 G1
ORP BR6 ....216 B1
PUT/ROE SW15 ....158 A6
RSLP HA4 ....58 A4
WBLY HA9 ....61 K4
WIM/MER SW19 ....177 K6
Grasmere Av ACT W3 ....98 E6
HSLW TW3 ....155 G1
ORP BR6 ....216 B1
PUT/ROE SW15 ....158 A6
RSLP HA4 ....58 A4
STRHM/NOR SW16 ....50 D2
TOTM N17 ....50 D2
Grasshaven Wy THMD SE28 ....128 A1
Grassington CI FBAR/BDGN N11 ..48 A1
Grassington Rd SCUP DA14 ....168 B6
Grassmount FSTH SE23 ....163 J4
Grass Pk FNCH N3 ....46 D4
Grassway WLGTN SM6 ....210 C2
Grasvenor Av BAR EN5 ....32 E1
Grately Wy PECK SE15 * 143 F1
Gratton Rd WKENS W14 ....119 H3
Gratton Ter CRICK NW2 ....82 B1
Gravel HI BXLYHS DA6 ....149 J6
CROY/NA CR0 ....213 F4
FNCH N3 ....46 D5

Gravel Hill CI BXLY DA5 ....169 J1
BXLYHS DA6 ....149 J6
Gravel La WCHPL E1 ....13 J3
Gravel Pit Wy ORP BR6 ....202 B6
Gravel Rd HAYS/HAR UB3 ....200 D6
WHTN TW2 ....155 K3
Gravelwood CI CHST BR7 ....167 H5
Gravenel Gdns TOOT SW17 * ...178 D1
Graveney Gv PGE/AN SE20 ......181 K3
Graveney Rd TOOT SW17 ....160 D6
Gravesend Rd SHB W12 ....99 J6
Gray Av BCTR RM8 ....74 B5
Gray Gdns HCH RM12 ....93 J4
Grayham Crs NWMAL KT3 ......192 A1
Grayham Rd NWMAL KT3 ....192 A1
Grayland CI BMLY BR1 ....184 B4
Grayling CI CAN/RD E16 ....106 C3
Grayling Ct EA W5 * 116 E1
Grayling Rd STNW/STAM N16 ...67 K6
Grayling Sq BETH E2 * 104 C2
Grayscroft Rd
STRHM/NOR SW16 ....179 J3
Grays Farm Rd
STMC/STPC BR5 ....186 C4
Grayshott Rd BTSEA SW11 ......141 F4
Gray's Inn Rd IS N1 ....5 F4
Gray's Inn Sq GINN WC1R 11 J1
Grays La ASHF TW15 ....152 E6
Gray St STHWK SE1 ....18 A2
Grayswood Gdns RYNPK SW20 ..176 E5
Gray's Yd MHST W1U * 9 H4
Graywood Ct
NFNCH/WDSP N12 ....47 G3
Grazebrook Rd
STNW/STAM N16 ....67 K6
Grazeley CI BXLYHS DA6 ....149 K6
Great Benty WDR/YW UB7 ....112 B4
Great Brownings SYD SE26 .....163 G6
Great Cambridge
Jct PLMGR N13 ....49 J1
Great Cambridge Rd UED N18 ...49 K1
Great Castle St REGST W1B 10 A3
Great Central Av RSLP HA4 ....77 G3
Great Central St CAMTN NW1 .....8 E1
Great Central Wy WBLY HA9 .....63 G3
WLSDN NW10 ....80 D1
Great Chapel St SOHO/CST W1F ...10 C3
Great Chart St BTSEA SW11 ....140 B4
Great Chertsey Rd CHSWK W4 ..138 A2
FELT TW13 ....154 E5
Great Church La HMSMTH W6 ...119 G5
Great College St WEST SW1P 16 E4
Great Cross Av GNWCH SE10 ...145 H1
Great Cullings ROMW/RG RM7 ...75 G6
Great Cumberland Ms
MBLAR W1H 8 E4
Great Cumberland PI
MBLAR W1H 8 E3
Great Dover St STHWK SE1 ......18 E4
Greatdown Rd HNWL W7 ....97 F4
Great Eastern Rd SRTFD E15 ....88 B5
Great Eastern St SDTCH EC2A 7 H4
Great Eastern Whf
BTSEA SW11 * 140 D1
Great Elms Rd HAYES BR2 .....200 B1
Great Fld CDALE/KGS NW9 ....45 G4
Greatfield Av EHAM E6 ....107 K3
Greatfield CI LEW SE13 ....144 D5
Greatfields Rd BARK IG11 ....90 D6
Great Galley CI BARK IG11 ....109 H2
Great Gardens Rd EMPK RM11 ...75 K3
Great Gatton CI CROY/NA CR0 ..198 B4
Great George St STJSPK SW1H ...16 D3
Great Guildford St STHWK SE1 ...18 C1
Great Harry Dr ELTH/MOT SE9 ...167 F5
Great James St BMSBY WC1N ...11 G1
Great Marlborough St
SOHO/CST W1F 10 A4
Great Maze Pond STHWK SE1 ...19 F1
Great New St
FLST/FETLN EC4A * 11 K3
Great North Rd BAR EN5 ....33 F1
BAR EN5 ....20 D4
Great North Wy (Barnet By-Pass)
HDN NW4 ....45 K4
Greatorex St WCHPL E1 ....104 C4
Great Ormond St BMSBY WC1N ..11 F1
Great Percy St FSBYW WC1X 5 H4
Great Peter St WEST SW1P 16 C5
Great Portland St GTPST W1W ...9 K1
Great Pulteney St
SOHO/CST W1F 10 B5
Great Queen St DART DA1 ....171 J1
HOL/ALD WC2B 11 G3
Great Russell St FITZ W1T 10 D3
Great St Helen's HDTCH EC3A ...13 G4
Great Scotland Yd
WHALL SW1A 16 E1
Great Smith St WEST SW1P 16 D4
Great South-West Rd
EBED/NFELT TW14 ....153 F2
Great Spilmans EDUL SE22 .....143 F6
Great Strd CDALE/KGS NW9 .....45 H5
Great Suffolk St STHWK SE1 .....18 B1
Great Sutton St FSBYE EC1V 6 B7
Great Swan Aly LOTH EC2R 12 E3
Great Thrift STMC/STPC BR5 ...201 H1
Great Titchfield St GTPST W1W ...9 K1
Great Tower St MON EC3R 13 G5
Great Trinity La BLKFR EC4V 12 D5
Great Turnstile HHOL WC1V * 11 H2
Great Western Rd
BAY/PAD W2 ....100 D4
Great West Rd BTFD TW8 ....116 D5
HEST TW5 ....134 D3
HMSMTH W6 ....118 C5
Great West Rd Chiswick
CHSWK W4 ....118 C6
Great West Rd Ellesmere Rd
CHSWK W4 ....117 K6

Great West Rd Hogarth La
CHSWK W4 ....118 A6
Great Winchester St
OBST EC2N 13 F3
Great Windmill St
SOHO/CST W1F 10 C5
Greatwood CHST BR7 ....185 F3
Greaves CI BARK IG11 ....90 E5
Greaves PI TOOT SW17 ....160 D6
Grebe Av HYS/HAR UB3 ....133 G1
Grebe CI BARK IG11 ....109 J1
FSTGT E7 ....88 D3
WALTH E17 ....51 G3
Grebe Ct SUT SM1 ....208 D2
Grebe PI WLGTN SM6 ....180 C2
Grebe Ter KUT/HW KT1 * 175 F5
Grecian Crs NRWD SE19 ....180 C6
Greek St SOHO/SHAV W1D 10 D4
Greenacre CI BAR EN5 ....20 D1
NTHLT UB5 ....77 K3
Greenacre Gdns WALTH E17 .....51 G3
Greenacre PI WLGTN SM6 ....195 G6
Greenacres BUSH WD23 ....28 C4
ELTH/MOT SE9 ....167 F1
Green Acres CROY/NA CR0 .....212 B1
Greenacres CI ORP BR6 ....216 C2
Greenacres Dr STAN HA7 ....43 H5
Greenacre Sq
BERM/RHTH SE16 ....124 A2
Greenacre Wk STHGT/OAK N14 ..34 D5
Green Arbour Ct STP EC4M * 12 A3
Green Av MLHL NW7 ....31 F6
WEA W13 ....116 C3
Greenaway Av UED N18 * 51 F1
Greenaway Gdns HAMP NW3 ....83 F2
Green Bank NFNCH/WDSP N12 ...33 F6
WAP E1W 123 J1
Greenbank Av ALP/SUD HA0 .....79 G3
Greenbank CI CHING E4 ....38 A4
Greenbank Crs FNCH N3 ....64 C1
Greenbanks DART DA1 ....171 H4
Greenbay Rd CHARL SE7 ....146 C1
Greenberry St STJWD NW8 ....2 C3
Greenbrook Av EBAR EN4 ....21 G2
Green Chain Wk BECK BR3 .....183 F1
CHARL SE7 ....126 C4
ELTH/MOT SE9 ....147 G6
SYD SE26 ....182 A2
THMD SE28 ....128 E1
Green CI CAR SM5 ....194 E6
CDALE/KGS NW9 ....62 E3
EFNCH N2 ....65 H3
FELT TW13 ....172 D1
HAYES BR2 ....183 G1
WCHMH N21 ....35 H4
Greencoat PI WEST SW1P 16 B6
Greencoat Rw WEST SW1P 16 A5
Green Court Av CROY/NA CR0 ...197 G6
Greencourt Av EDGW HA8 ....44 C4
Green Court Gdns
CROY/NA CR0 ....197 J5
Greencourt Rd
STMC/STPC BR5 ....201 K2
Greencrest PI CRICK NW2 * 81 G1
Greencroft EDGW HA8 ....44 E1
Greencroft Av RSLP HA4 ....59 G2
Greencroft Gdns EN EN1 ....24 A4
KIL/WHAMP NW6 ....83 F5
Greencroft Rd HEST TW5 ....134 E2
Green Dr EDUL SE22 * 143 F6
STHL UB1 ....115 F1
Green Dragon La BTFD TW8 .....117 F5
WCHMH N21 ....35 F6
Green Dragon Yd WCHPL E1 ....104 C4
Green Dr STHL UB1 ....115 F1
Green End CHSGTN KT9 ....205 K2
WCHMH N21 ....35 H4
Greenend Rd CHSWK W4 ....118 B2
Green Farm CI ORP BR6 ....217 F3
Greenfell Man DEPT SE8 * 124 C5
Greenfield Av BRYLDS KT5 .....191 J4
OXHEY WD19 ....27 J4
Greenfield Dr BMLY BR1 ....184 B5
EFNCH N2 ....65 K1
Greenfield Gdns CRICK NW2 .....64 C6
DAGW RM9 ....91 J6
STMC/STPC BR5 ....201 H4
WCHPL E1 ....13 K1
Greenfields STHL UB1 ....96 A6
Greenfield Wy
RYLN/HDSTN HA2 ....42 B4
Greenford Av HNWL W7 ....96 E3
STHL UB1 ....95 K6
Greenford Gdns GFD/PVL UB6 ...96 B2
Greenford Rd GFD/PVL UB6 ......78 E3
STHL UB1 ....115 F2
SUT SM1 ....209 F2
Green Gdns ORP BR6 ....216 C3
Greengate GFD/PVL UB6 ....79 H4
Greengate St PLSTW E13 ....107 F1
Greenhalgh Wk EFNCH N2 ....65 G1
Greenham CI STHWK SE1 ....17 J3
Greenham Crs CHING E4 ....51 H2
Greenham Rd MUSWH N10 ....48 A5
Greenhaven Dr THMD SE28 ....109 H5
Greenheys CI NTHWD HA6 ....40 C4
Greenheys Dr SWFD E18 ....52 D6
Greenhill BKHH IG9 ....39 H5
HAMP NW3 ....83 H2
SUT SM1 ....209 G1
WBLY HA9 ....62 D5
Greenhill Gv MNPK E12 ....89 J2
Greenhill Pde BAR EN5 * 21 F6
Greenhill Pk BAR EN5 * 21 F6
WLSDN NW10 ....81 G6
Greenhill Rd HRW HA1 ....60 D3
WLSDN NW10 ....81 G6
Greenhill's Rents FARR EC1M * ...12 A1
Greenhill Ter NTHLT UB5 * 95 K1
Greenhill Wy HRW HA1 ....60 D3
WBLY HA9 ....62 D5

Greenhithe CI ELTH/MOT SE9 ...167 K2
Greenholm Rd ELTH/MOT SE9 ...147 G6
Green Hundred Rd PECK SE15 ...123 H6
Greenhurst Rd WNWD SE27 ....180 B1
Greening St ABYW SE2 ....128 D4
Greenland Crs NWDGN UB2 .....114 B3
Greenland Ms DEPT SE8 ....124 A5
Greenland Quay
BERM/RHTH SE16 ....124 A4
Greenland Rd BAR EN5 ....32 A1
CAMTN NW1 ....84 B5
Greenlands HOR/WEW KT19 ...206 D3
Greenland St CAMTN NW1 * 84 B6
Greenland Wy CROY/NA CR0 ...195 J4
Green La BCTR RM8 ....74 B6
ELTH/MOT SE9 ....167 F4
FELT TW13 ....172 D1
HDN NW4 ....64 B2
HNWL W7 ....115 K2
HSLWW TW4 ....134 D5
IL IG1 ....72 B6
MRDN SM4 ....194 A4
NTHWD HA6 ....40 B3
NWMAL KT3 ....191 K2
OXHEY WD19 ....27 G3
PGE/AN SE20 ....182 A3
STAN HA7 ....29 H6
THHTH CR7 ....180 C4
UX/CGN UB8 ....64 A3
WPK KT4 ....192 E4
Green Lane Gdns THHTH CR7 ...180 D5
Green Lanes CEND/HSY/T N8 ....48 F1
FSBYPK N4 ....67 H5
HOR/WEW KT19 ....207 G6
PLMGR N13 ....49 F1
WCHMH N21 ....35 G4
Greenlaw Ct EA W5 * 97 K5
Greenlaw Gdns NWMAL KT3 ...192 C4
Greenlawn La BTFD TW8 ....116 E5
Green Lawns
NFNCH/WDSP N12 ....47 F2
RSLP HA4 * 59 G5
Greenlaw St
WOOL/PLUM SE18 ....127 F3
Green Leaf Av WLGTN SM6 .....210 D2
Greenleaf CI
BRXS/STRHM SW2 * 162 B2
Greenleafe Dr BARK/HLT IG6 ....54 B6
Greenleaf Rd EHAM E6 ....89 G6
WALTH E17 ....51 H6
Greenleigh Av
STMC/STPC BR5 ....202 C1
Greenlink Wk RCH/KEW TW9 ...137 J2
Greenleigh Av
EBED/NFELT TW14 ....153 K5
RSLP HA4 * 59 G5
Greenlaw St
Greenman St IS N1 ....85 J5
Greenmead CI SNWD SE25 .....197 H2
Green Moor Link WCHMH N21 ...35 H2
Greenmoor Rd PEND EN3 ....24 E3
Greenoak PI EBAR EN4 ....21 K3
Green Oaks NWDGN UB2 * 114 C4
Greenoak Wy WIM/MER SW19 ..159 G6
Greenock Rd ACT W3 ....117 J3
STRHM/NOR SW16 ....179 J4
Greenock Wy ROM RM1 ....57 G3
Green Pde HSLW TW3 * 155 G1
Green Park Wy GFD/PVL UB6 ....78 E6
Green Pond CI WALTH E17 ....51 G6
Green Pond Rd WALTH E17 ....51 G6
Green Ride LOU IG10 ....38 E1
Green Rd STHGT/OAK N14 ....34 B1
TRDG/WHET N20 ....33 G5
Greens Ct NTGHL W11 * 119 J1
Greens End WOOL/PLUM SE18 ...127 G4
Greenshank CI WALTH E17 * 51 H3
Greenside BCTR RM8 ....73 J6
BXLY DA5 ....169 F3
Greenside CI CAT SE6 ....165 G4
Greenside Rd CROY/NA CR0 ....196 B4
SHB W12 ....118 D3
Greenslade Rd BARK IG11 ....90 D5
Greenstead Av WFD IG8 ....53 G2
Greenstead Gdns
PUT/ROE SW15 ....138 D6
WFD IG8 ....53 G2
Greensted Rd LOU IG10 ....39 J2
Greenstone Ms WAN E11 ....71 E3
Green St FSTGT E7 ....89 F3
MYFR/PKLN W1K 9 F5
Green St EN EN1 ....25 F4
Greenstreet Green Rd
DART DA1 ....171 K3
Greenstreet HI NWCR SE14 * ...144 A4
Greensward BUSH WD23 ....28 B1
Green Ter CLKNW EC1R 5 K5
The Green ACT W3 ....99 G5
BKHH IG9 ....39 F3
BXLYHN DA7 ....149 H2
CAR SM5 * 210 A2
CROY/NA CR0 ....213 H6
ED N9 ....36 C4
FELT TW13 ....154 A4
HAYES BR2 ....199 J4
HEST TW5 ....134 E1
HGDN/ICK UB10 ....58 A6
HRW HA1 ....61 J4
MRDN SM4 ....193 H1
NWDGN UB2 ....114 C2
NWMAL KT3 ....175 K6
RCH/KEW TW9 ....136 E6
SCUP DA14 ....186 B3
SRTFD E15 ....88 D4
STHGT/OAK N14 ....34 D5
STMC/STPC BR5 ....186 C3
SUT SM1 ....209 F1
TOTM N17 ....49 J2
WAN E11 ....71 F3

WCHMH N21 .....35 G2
WDR/YW UB7 .....112 A3
WEA IG8 .....147 K5
WHTN TW2 .....155 K3
Green V BXLYHS DA6 .....148 E6
EA W5 .....98 B5
Greenvale Rd ELTH/MOT SE9 .....146 E5
Green Vw CHSGTN KT9 .....206 B5
Green Verges STAN HA7 .....43 K3
Greenview Av BECK BR3 .....198 E3
Greenview CI ACT W3 .....118 B1
Green Wk DART DA1 .....150 C5
HDN NW4 .....64 B2
NWDGN UB2 .....115 F5
RSLP HA4 .....58 D5
STHWK SE1 .....19 G5
WAN E11 .....53 J2
The Green Wk CHING E4 .....38 A3
Green Wy ELTH/MOT SE9 .....146 C6
HAYES BR2 .....200 D3
Greenway BCTR RM8 .....73 J6
CHST BR7 .....185 F1
KTN/HRWW/W HA3 .....62 A2
PIN HA5 .....41 F5
RYNPK SW20 .....193 F1
STHGT/OAK N14 .....34 E4
TRDG/WHET N20 .....32 E4
WLGTN SM6 .....210 C2
YEAD UB4 .....95 F3
Greenway Av WALTH E17 .....70 B1
Greenway CI CDALE/KGS NW9 .....45 F5
FBAR/BDGN N11 .....48 A2
FSBYPK N4 .....67 J6
TRDG/WHET N20 .....32 E4
Greenway Ct IL IG1 .....72 A5
SRTFD E15 .....106 C1
Greenway Gdns
CDALE/KGS NW9 .....44 E5
CROY/NA CRO 213 H1
GFD/PVL UB6 .....96 A2
Green Way Gdns
KTN/HRWW/W HA3 .....42 E5
Greenways BECK BR3 .....182 D5
ESH/CLAY KT10 .....204 E2
NFNCH/WDSP N12 * 47 F1
The Greenways TWK TW1 * 156 B1
The Green Wy
KTN/HRWW/W HA3 .....42 E5
The Greenway CDALE/KGS NW9 .....45 F5
HSLWW TW4 .....134 C5
PIN HA5 .....59 K3
Greenwell St GTPST W1W 3 K7
Greenwich Church St
GNWCH SE10 .....125 F6
Greenwich Crs EHAM E6 .....107 J4
Greenwich Foot Tnl
GNWCH SE10 .....125 G5
Greenwich Hts
WOOL/PLUM SE18 .....146 D1
Greenwich High Rd
GNWCH SE10 .....144 E1
Greenwich Park St
GNWCH SE10 * 125 G6
Greenwich Quay DEPT SE8 .....124 E6
Greenwich South St
GNWCH SE10 .....144 E2
Greenwich Vw CI POP/IOD E14 .....124 E3
Greenwood Av DAGE RM10 .....92 D2
PEND EN3 .....25 F3
Greenwood CI BFN/LL DA15 .....168 B4
MRDN SM4 .....193 H1
STMC/STPC BR5 .....201 K3
THDIT KT7 .....190 D5
Greenwood Dr CHING E4 .....52 A1
Greenwood Gdns
BARK/HLT IG6 .....54 C3
PLMGR N13 .....35 H5
Greenwood La HPTN TW12 .....173 G1
Greenwood Pk
KUTN/CMB KT2 .....176 B3
Greenwood PI KTTN NW5 * 84 B3
Greenwood Rd BXLY DA5 .....170 A6
CROY/NA CRO 196 C4
HACK E8 .....86 C4
ISLW TW7 .....135 K4
MTCM CR4 .....179 J6
PLSTW E13 .....106 D1
THDIT KT7 .....190 B5
Greenwood Ter WLSDN NW10 * 81 F6
Green Wrythe Crs CAR SM5 .....194 D5
Green Wrythe La MRDN SM4 .....194 C3
Green Yd FSBYW WC1X 5 H6
Greer Rd KTN/HRWW/W HA3 .....42 C4
Greet St STHWK SE1 .....17 K1
Greg CI LEY E10 .....70 A3
Gregor Ms BKHTH/KID SE3 .....145 K1
Gregory Crs ELTH/MOT SE9 .....166 C2
Gregory PI KENS W8 .....120 A2
Gregory Rd CHDH RM6 .....73 K1
NWDGN UB2 .....115 F3
Greig CI EDGW HA8 .....44 B3
Greig Ter WALW SE17 .....122 C6
Grenaby Av CROY/NA CRO 196 E4
Grenaby Rd CROY/NA CRO 196 E4
Grenada Rd CHARL SE7 .....146 B1
Grenade St POP/IOD E14 .....105 H6
Grenadier CI CAN/RD E16 .....127 F1
Grena Gdns RCH/KEW TW9 .....137 G5
Grenard CI PECK SE15 * 143 H1
Grena Rd RCH/KEW TW9 .....137 G5
Grendon Gdns WBLY HA9 .....62 C6
Grendon St STJWD NW8 .....2 C6
Grenfell Av HCH RM12 .....75 H5
Grenfell CI BORE WD6 * 24 E1
Grenfell Gdns
KTN/HRWW/W HA3 .....62 A4
Grenfell Rd NTGHL W11 .....100 B6
TOOT SW17 .....178 E2
Grenfell Wk NTGHL W11 .....100 B6
Grennell CI SUT SM1 .....194 C6
Grennell Rd SUT SM1 .....194 B6
Grenoble Gdns PLMGR N13 .....49 G2
Grenville CI BRYLDS KT5 .....191 K5
FNCH N3 .....46 D4
Grenville Gdns WFD IG8 .....53 G3

Grenville Ms ARCH N19 .....66 E5
HPTN TW12 .....173 G1
Grenville PI MLHL NW7 .....45 F1
SKENS SW7 * 120 B3
Grenville Rd ARCH N19 .....66 E5
SRTFD E15 * 5 F7
Gresham Av TRDG/WHET N20 .....33 K6
Gresham CI BXLY DA5 .....169 F1
ENC/FH EN2 .....23 J3
Gresham Dr CHDH RM6 .....73 H2
Gresham Gdns CRICK NW2 .....64 C5
Gresham Rd BECK BR3 .....182 B5
BRXN/ST SW9 .....142 B4
CAN/RD E16 .....107 F5
EDGW HA8 .....44 B2
EHAM E6 .....107 K1
HEST TW5 .....135 H2
HPTN TW12 .....173 F2
SNWD SE25 * 197 H1
WLSDN NW10 .....81 F3
Gresham St CITYW EC2V 12 C5
Gresham Wy WIM/MER SW19 .....159 K5
Cresley CI SEVS/STOTM N15 * 67 K1
WALTH E17 * 69 G3
Gresley Rd ARCH N19 .....66 C5
Gressenhall Rd
WAND/EARL SW18 .....159 J1
Gresse St FITZ W1T 10 C2
Cresswell CI SCUP DA14 .....168 B5
Cresswell Rd FUL/PGN SW6 .....139 G2
Gretton Rd TOTM N17 .....49 K3
Greville CI TWK TW1 .....156 C2
Greville Ms KIL/WHAMP NW6 .....83 F6
Greville PI KIL/WHAMP NW6 .....101 F1
Greville Rd KIL/WHAMP NW6 .....101 F1
RCHPK/HAM TW10 .....157 G1
WALTH E17 .....70 A1
Greville St HCIRC EC1N 11 K2
Grey CI EFNCH N2 .....65 K1
Greycoat PI WEST SW1P 16 C5
Greycoat St WEST SW1P 16 C5
Greycot Rd BECK BR3 .....182 D1
Grey Eagle St WCHPL E1 .....13 K1
Greyfell CI STAN HA7 * 43 H1
Greyhound Hill HDN NW4 .....45 J6
Greyhound La
STRHM/NOR SW16 .....179 K2
Greyhound Rd HMSMTH W6 .....119 J6
SUT SM1 .....209 G3
TOTM N17 .....50 A6
WLSDN NW10 .....99 K2
Greyhound Ter
STRHM/NOR SW16 .....179 H4
Greyhound Wy DART DA1 .....150 B6
Greys Park CI HAYES BR2 .....215 G3
Greystead Rd FSTH SE23 .....163 K2
Greystoke Av PIN HA5 .....42 A6
Greystoke Gdns EA W5 .....98 A3
ENC/FH EN2 .....22 E5
Greystone Gdns BARK/HLT IG6 .....54 C5
KTN/HRWW/W HA3 .....61 J3
Greyswood Av UED N18 * 51 F1
Greyswood St
STRHM/NOR SW16 .....179 G2
Grierson Rd FSTH SE23 .....164 B1
Griffin CI WLSDN NW10 .....81 K3
Griffin Manor Wy THMD 127 J3
Griffin Rd TOTM N17 .....50 A5
WOOL/PLUM SE18 .....127 J5
Griffith CI CHDH RM6 .....73 J4
Griffiths Rd WIM/MER SW19 .....177 K3
Griggs Ap IL IG1 .....72 C6
Grigg's PI STHWK SE1 .....19 H5
Griggs Rd LEY E10 .....70 A3
Grimsby Gv CAN/RD E16 .....127 G2
Grimsby St WCHPL E1 .....7 K7
Grimsdyke Rd PIN HA5 .....41 K3
Grimsel Pth CMBW SE5 .....142 C1
Grimshaw CI HGT N6 * 66 A4
Grimshaw Wy ROM RM1 .....75 G2
Grimston Rd FUL/PGN SW6 .....139 J3
Grimwade Av CROY/NA CRO 212 C1
Grimwood Rd TWK TW1 .....156 A2
Grindall CI CROY/NA CRO 211 H2
Grindal St STHWK SE1 .....17 J3
Grindleford Av
FBAR/BDGN N11 .....34 A4
Grindley Gdns CROY/NA CRO * 197 G3
Grinling PI DEPT SE8 .....124 D6
Grinstead Rd DEPT SE8 .....124 B5
Grisle CI ED N9 .....36 D5
Grittleton Av WBLY HA9 .....80 D4
Grittleton Rd MV/WKIL W9 .....100 E3
Grocers' Hall Ct LOTH EC2R * 12 E4
Groombridge CI WELL DA16 .....148 B6
Groombridge Rd HOM E9 .....87 F5
Groom CI HAYES BR2 .....200 A1
Groom Crs WAND/EARL SW18 .....160 C2
Groomfield CI TOOT SW17 .....161 F6
Groom PI KTBR SW1X 15 H4
Grooms Dr PIN HA5 .....58 E2
Grosmont Rd
WOOL/PLUM SE18 .....128 A5
Grosse Wy PUT/ROE SW15 .....158 E1
Grosvenor Av CAR SM5 .....209 K4
HBRY N5 .....85 J3
MRDN SM4 .....193 K5
RYLN/HDSTN HA2 .....60 A6
YEAD UB4 .....94 D1
Grosvenor Br VX/NE SW8 .....141 J5
Grosvenor Cottages
KTBR SW1X 15 G6
Grosvenor Crs CDALE/KGS NW9 .....62 C1
DART DA1 .....151 G6
KTBR SW1X 15 H3
Grosvenor Crescent Ms
KTBR SW1X 15 G3
Grosvenor Gdns BGVA SW1W 15 K5
CRICK NW2 .....82 A3
GLDGN NW11 .....64 D3
KUTN/CMB KT2 .....174 E2
MORT/ESHN SW14 .....138 B4
MUSWH N10 .....48 C6

STHGT/OAK N14 .....22 D6
WFD IG8 .....52 E2
WLGTN SM6 .....210 C5
Grosvenor Gardens Ms East
BGVA SW1W * 15 K4
Grosvenor Gardens Ms North
BGVA SW1W * 15 J5
Grosvenor Ga BAY/PAD W2 .....9 F6
Grosvenor HI MYFR/PKLN W1K 9 J5
WIM/MER SW19 .....177 H2
Grosvenor Pde EA W5 * 117 H1
Grosvenor Pk CMBW SE5 .....142 D1
Grosvenor Park Rd WALTH E17 .....69 J2
Grosvenor PI KTBR SW1X 15 J3
Grosvenor Ri East WALTH E17 .....69 K2
Grosvenor Rd BCTR RM8 .....74 B5
BELV DA17 .....129 G6
BTFD TW8 .....116 E6
BXLYHS DA6 .....148 E6
CHSWK W4 .....117 K5
ED N9 .....36 D5
FNCH N3 .....46 D3
FSTGT E7 .....89 F4
HNWL W7 .....116 A1
HSLW TW3 .....134 E4
IL IG1 .....90 C1
LEY E10 .....70 A5
MUSWH N10 .....48 B4
NTHWD HA6 .....40 D1
NWDGN UB2 .....114 E3
PIM SW1V 121 H6
RCHPK/HAM TW10 .....75 F4
SNWD SE25 .....197 H1
STMC/STPC BR5 .....201 K3
TWK TW1 .....156 B2
WAN E11 .....71 F2
WLGTN SM6 .....210 C4
WWKM BR4 .....199 F6
Grosvenor Sq MYFR/PKLN W1K 9 H5
Grosvenor St MYFR/PKLN W1K 9 J5
Grosvenor Ter CMBW SE5 .....142 D1
Grosvenor V RSLP HA4 .....58 D6
Grosvenor Wy CLPT E5 .....68 E6
Grosvenor Wharf Rd
POP/IOD E14 .....125 G4
Grote's Bldgs BKHTH/KID SE3 .....145 H3
Grote's PI BKHTH/KID SE3 .....145 H3
Groton Rd WAND/EARL SW18 .....160 A4
Grotto Ct STHWK SE1 * 18 C2
Grotto Pas MHST W1U 9 G1
Grotto Rd TWK TW1 .....156 A4
Grove Av HNWL W7 .....96 E5
MUSWH N10 .....48 C5
PIN HA5 .....59 J1
SUT SM1 .....208 E4
TWK TW1 .....156 A3
Grove Bank OXHEY WD19 * 27 H1
Grovebury CI ERITH DA8 .....130 A6
Grovebury Ct STHGT/OAK N14 .....34 C2
Grovebury Rd THMD SE28 .....128 C2
Grove CI FSTH SE23 .....164 A3
HAYES BR2 .....199 K6
KUT/HW KT1 .....175 G6
STHGT/OAK N14 .....34 B2
Grove Cottages CHEL SW3 .....120 D6
Grove Ct E/WMO/HCT KT8 .....189 J2
EA W5 * 117 F1
Grove Crs CDALE/KGS NW9 .....62 E1
FELT TW13 .....154 D6
KUT/HW KT1 .....175 F6
SWFD E18 .....52 D5
WOT/HER KT12 .....188 A4
Grove Crescent Rd SRTFD E15 .....88 B4
Grovedale Rd ARCH N19 .....66 D6
Grove End KTTN NW5 .....84 B2
SWFD E18 .....52 D5
Grove End La ESH/CLAY KT10 .....189 J5
Grove End Rd STJWD NW8 .....2 A4
Grove Farm Pk NTHWD HA6 .....40 B1
Grove Footpath SURB KT6 .....191 F1
Grove Gdns HDN NW4 .....63 J2
PEND EN3 .....25 F2
STJWD NW8 .....2 D4
TEDD TW11 .....156 B6
Grove Green Rd LEY E10 .....88 A1
Grove Hall Ct STJWD NW8 * 2 A4
Grove Hill HRW HA1 .....60 E4
SWFD E18 .....52 D5
Grove Hill Rd CMBW SE5 .....143 F4
HRW HA1 .....61 F4
Grove House Rd
CEND/HSY/T N8 .....66 E1
Groveland Av
STRHM/NOR SW16 .....180 A3
Groveland Ct STP EC4M 12 D4
Groveland Rd BECK BR3 .....182 C6
Grovelands E/WMO/HCT KT8 .....189 F1
Grovelands CI CMBW SE5 .....143 F3
RYLN/HDSTN HA2 .....60 A6
Grovelands Ct STHGT/OAK N14 .....34 D2
Grovelands Rd PLMGR N13 .....35 F6
SEVS/STOTM N15 .....68 C3
STMC/STPC BR5 .....186 B5
Groveland Wy NWMAL KT3 .....191 K2
Grove La CMBW SE5 .....142 E2
KUT/HW KT1 .....191 F1
Grove Market PI
ELTH/MOT SE9 * 166 E1
Grove Ms HMSMTH W6 .....119 F3
Grove Pk CDALE/KGS NW9 .....62 E1
CMBW SE5 .....143 F3
WAN E11 .....71 F2
Grove Park Av CHING E4 .....51 K3
Grove Park Br CHSWK W4 .....137 K1
Grove Park Gdns CHSWK W4 .....137 K2
ELTH/MOT SE9 .....166 D4
RAIN RM13 .....93 J6
SEVS/STOTM N15 .....68 A3
Grove Park Rd CHSWK W4 .....137 J1
Grove PI ACT W3 .....117 K1
BAL SW12 .....161 G1
HAMP NW3 .....83 H1

Grove Rd ACT W3 .....117 K1
BARN SW13 .....138 C3
BELV DA17 .....129 G6
BOW E3 .....105 G1
BTFD TW8 .....116 D5
BXLYHN DA7 .....149 K5
CHDH RM6 .....73 J4
CHING E4 .....52 A3
CRICK NW2 .....82 A4
E/WMO/HCT KT8 .....189 J2
EA W5 .....97 K6
EBAR EN4 .....21 J4
EDGW HA8 .....44 C2
FBAR/BDGN N11 .....48 E1
HOM E9 .....87 F5
HSLW TW3 .....135 G5
ISLW TW7 .....135 K2
MTCM CR4 .....179 G5
NFNCH/WDSP N12 .....47 H2
PIN HA5 .....59 K2
RCHPK/HAM TW10 .....157 G1
SEVS/STOTM N15 .....68 A2
SURB KT6 .....190 E2
SUT SM1 .....208 E4
SWFD E18 .....52 D5
THHTH CR7 .....196 B1
WALTH E17 .....69 K2
WAN E11 .....70 D4
WHTN TW2 .....155 J5
WIM/MER SW19 .....178 B3
Grover Rd OXHEY WD19 .....27 H1
Groveside CI ACT W3 .....98 C5
CAR SM5 .....194 D6
Groveside Rd CHING E4 .....38 C5
Grovestile Waye
EBED/NFELT TW14 .....153 G2
Grove St BERM/RHTH SE16 .....124 C4
UED N18 .....50 B2
Grove Ter KTTN NW5 .....84 A1
STHL UB1 * 96 A4
TEDD TW11 .....156 B6
The Grove BXLYHS DA6 .....148 E5
CDALE/KGS NW9 .....62 E3
CEND/HSY/T N8 .....66 D2
EA W5 .....116 E1
EDGW HA8 .....30 D6
ENC/FH EN2 .....23 J4
FNCH N3 .....46 E3
FSBYPK N4 .....67 F4
GFD/PVL UB6 .....96 C5
GLDGN NW11 .....64 C4
HGT N6 .....66 A6
ISLW TW7 .....135 K2
PLMGR N13 .....35 G6
SCUP DA14 .....187 F1
STHL UB1 .....95 K6
TEDD TW11 .....156 B5
WOT/HER KT12 .....188 A4
WWKM BR4 .....199 F6
Grove V CHST BR7 .....185 F2
EDUL SE22 .....143 F5
Groveway BCTR RM8 .....91 K2
BRXN/ST SW9 .....142 A2
Grove Wy ESH/CLAY KT10 .....189 H5
WBLY HA9 .....80 E3
Grovewood PI WFD IG8 .....53 K2
Grummant Rd PECK SE15 .....143 G2
Grundy St POP/IOD E14 .....105 K5
Gruneisen Rd FNCH N3 .....47 F3
Guardian CI EMPK RM11 .....75 K6
Gubyon Av HNHL SE24 .....142 D6
Guernsey CI HEST TW5 .....135 F2
Guernsey Gv HNHL SE24 .....162 D2
Guernsey Rd IS N1 .....70 B5
LEY E10 .....70 A6
WALTH E17 .....52 D5
Guibal Rd LEE/GVPK SE12 .....166 A3
Guildersfield Rd
STRHM/NOR SW16 .....179 K3
Guildford Av FELT TW13 .....153 K4
Guildford Gv GNWCH SE10 .....144 E2
Guildford Rd CROY/NA CRO 196 E3
EHAM E6 .....107 J5
GDMY/SEVK IG3 .....72 E6
VX/NE SW8 .....141 K2
WALTH E17 .....52 A4
Guildford Wy WLGTN SM6 .....210 E3
Guildhall Blds CITYW EC2V * 12 C3
Guildhall Yd CITYW EC2V * 12 D3
Guildhouse St PIM SW1V 16 A7
Guildown Av
NFNCH/WDSP N12 .....33 F6
Guild Rd CHARL SE7 .....126 C5
ERITH DA8 .....150 D1
Guildsway WALTH E17 .....51 H4
Guilford Av BRYLDS KT5 .....191 G2
Guilford PI BMSBY WC1N 5 G7
Guilford St BMSBY WC1N 5 F7
Guilsborough CI WLSDN NW10 .....81 G5
Guinness CI HOM E9 .....87 G5
HYS/HAR UB3 .....113 G3
Guinness Ct CROY/NA CRO * 197 G6
STHWK SE1 .....19 G3
Guinness Sq STHWK SE1 .....19 G5
Guinness Trust Est CHEL SW3 .....14 F7
SRTFD E15 * 88 D6
STNW/STAM N16 .....68 A5
Guion Rd FUL/PGN SW6 .....139 J3
Gulland Wk IS N1 * 85 J4
Gulliver CI NTHLT UB5 .....77 K6
Gulliver Rd BFN/LL DA15 .....167 K4
Gulliver St BERM/RHTH SE16 .....124 C3
Gumleigh Rd EA W5 .....116 D4
Gumley Gdns ISLW TW7 .....136 B4
Gumping Rd STMC/STPC BR5 .....201 H6
Gundulph Rd HAYES BR2 .....184 B6
Gunmakers La HOM E9 .....86 E3
Gunnell CI SNWD SE25 * 197 G3
CROY/NA CRO 197 G3
Gunner La WOOL/PLUM SE18 .....127 F5
Gunnersbury Av ACT W3 .....98 B6
Gunnersbury Av
(North Circular Rd) EA W5 .....98 B6
Gunnersbury CI CHSWK W4 * 117 J5
Gunnersbury Crs ACT W3 .....117 H2

Gunnersbury Dr EA W5 .....117 H2
Gunnersbury Gdns ACT W3 .....117 H2
Gunnersbury La ACT W3 .....117 J1
Gunners Gv CHING E4 .....38 A5
Gunners Rd WAND/EARL SW18 .....160 C4
Gunning St WOOL/PLUM SE18 .....127 K4
Gunstor Rd STNW/STAM N16 .....86 A2
Gun St WCHPL E1 .....13 J2
Gunter Gv EDGW HA8 .....45 F4
WBRPTN SW10 .....120 B6
Gunterstone Rd WKENS W14 .....119 H5
Gunthorpe St WCHPL E1 .....13 K2
Gunton Rd CLPT E5 .....86 D1
TOOT SW17 .....179 F2
Gunwhale CI
BERM/RHTH SE16 .....124 A1
Gurdon Rd CHARL SE7 .....125 K5
Gurnell Gv WEA W13 .....97 F3
Gurney CI BARK IG11 .....90 B4
SRTFD E15 .....88 C3
WALTH E17 .....51 F4
Gurney Crs CROY/NA CRO 196 A5
Gurney Dr EFNCH N2 .....65 H1
Gurney Rd CAR SM5 .....140 B4
FUL/PGN SW6 .....140 B4
NTHLT UB5 .....95 F2
SRTFD E15 .....88 C3
Guthrie St CHEL SW3 .....120 D5
Gutter La CITYW EC2V 12 C3
Guyatt Gdns MTCM CR4 .....179 F5
Guy Barnett Gv
BKHTH/KID SE3 .....145 K4
Guy Rd CROY/NA CRO 210 E1
Guyscliff Rd LEW SE13 .....145 F6
Guysfield CI RAIN RM13 .....93 J6
Guysfield Dr RAIN RM13 .....93 J6
Guy St STHWK SE1 .....19 F2
Gwalior Rd PUT/ROE SW15 .....139 G5
Gwendolen Av PUT/ROE SW15 .....139 G6
Gwendoline Av PLSTW E13 .....89 F6
Gwendwr Rd WKENS W14 .....119 H5
Gwillim CI BFN/LL DA15 .....168 B1
Gwydor Rd BECK BR3 .....198 A2
Gwydyr Rd HAYES BR2 .....183 J6
Gwyn CI FUL/PGN SW6 .....140 B1
Gwynne Av CROY/NA CRO 198 A4
Gwynne Park Av WFD IG8 .....53 K2
Gwynne Rd BTSEA SW11 .....140 C3
Gwynne Whf CHSWK W4 .....118 C6
Gyles Pk STAN HA7 .....43 J4
Gyllyngdune Gdns
GDMY/SEVK IG3 .....91 F1

H

Haarlem Rd WKENS W14 .....119 G3
Haberdasher PI IS N1 .....7 F4
Haberdasher St IS N1 .....7 F4
Habington CI CMBW SE5 * 142 E1
Habitat CI PECK SE15 .....143 J3
Haccombe Rd
WIM/MER SW19 .....178 B2
Hackbridge Park Gdns
CAR SM5 .....194 E6
Hackbridge Rd CAR SM5 .....195 F6
Hackford Rd BRXN/ST SW9 .....142 A2
Hackford Wk BRXN/ST SW9 .....142 A3
Hackington Crs BECK BR3 .....182 D2
Hackney Gv HACK E8 * 86 D4
Hackney Rd BETH E2 .....7 J4
Haddenham Ct OXHEY WD19 * 27 H5
Hadden Rd THMD SE28 .....127 K3
Hadden Wy GFD/PVL UB6 .....78 D4
Haddington Rd BMLY BR1 .....165 G5
Haddo Gdns CHARL SE7 * 146 D1
NWMAL KT3 .....192 C2
Haddon CI BFN/LL DA15 .....168 B3
STMC/STPC BR5 .....202 D2
SUT SM1 .....209 F2
Haddo St GNWCH SE10 .....124 E6
Hadfield CI STHL UB1 .....96 A3
Hadfield Rd STWL/WRAY TW19 .....152 A1
Hadleigh CI RYNPK SW20 .....177 J5
WCHPL E1 .....104 E3
Hadleigh Dr BELMT SM2 .....208 E6
Hadleigh Rd ED N9 .....36 D2
Hadleigh St BETH E2 .....104 E3
Hadley CI WCHMH N21 .....35 G1
Hadley Common BAR EN5 .....21 G3
Hadley Gdns CHSWK W4 .....118 A5
NWDGN UB2 .....114 E5
Hadley Gn BAR EN5 .....20 D3
Hadley Green Rd BAR EN5 .....20 D3
Hadley Gn West BAR EN5 .....20 D3
Hadley Gv BAR EN5 .....20 C3
Hadley Highstone BAR EN5 * 20 D2
Hadley Pde BAR EN5 * 20 D4
Hadley Rdg BAR EN5 .....20 D4
Hadley Rd BAR EN5 .....21 F3
BELV DA17 .....129 C4
EBAR EN4 .....22 A1
ENC/FH EN2 .....22 D1
MTCM CR4 .....195 J1
Hadley Wy WCHMH N21 .....35 G1
Hadlow PI NRWD SE19 .....181 H3
Hadlow Rd BFN/LL DA15 .....168 B5
WELL DA16 .....148 D1
Hadrian CI BOW E3 .....87 J6
STWL/WRAY TW19 .....152 B2
Hadrian Est BETH E2 * 104 C1
Hadrian Ms HOLWY N7 * 85 F5
Hadrian Ride EN EN1 .....24 B6
Hadrian St GNWCH SE10 .....125 H5
Hadrian Wy STWL/WRAY TW19 .....152 B2
Hadyn Park Rd SHB W12 .....118 D2
Hafer Rd BTSEA SW11 .....140 E5
Hafton Rd CAT SE6 .....165 H3
Haggard Rd TWK TW1 .....156 C2
Hagger Ct WALTH E17 * 52 B6

Haggerston Rd HACK E8 86 B5
Hague St BETH E2 104 C2
Ha-Ha Rd WOOL/PLUM SE18 126 E6
Haig Rd STAN HA7 43 J1
Haig Rd East PLSTW E13 107 G2
Haig Rd West PLSTW E13 107 G2
Haigville Gdns BARK/HLT IG6 72 B1
Hailes Cl WIM/MER SW19 178 B2
Haileybury Av EN EN1 36 B1
Haileybury Rd ORP BR6 217 G2
Hailey Rd ERITHM DA18 129 H2
Hailsham Av
BRXS/STRHM SW2 162 A4
Hailsham Cl SURB KT6 190 E4
Hailsham Dr HRW HA1 42 D6
Hailsham Rd TOOT SW17 179 F2
Hailsham Ter PLMGR N13 * 49 K1
Haimo Rd ELTH/MOT SE9 146 C6
Hainault Blds LEY E10 * 70 A5
Hainault Gore CHDH RM6 74 A2
Hainault Rd CHDH RM6 55 H3
CHDH RM6 74 B3
ROM RM1 57 F6
ROMW/RG RM7 56 E6
WAN E11 70 A5
Hainault St ELTH/MOT SE9 167 G3
IL IG1 72 B6
Haines Wk MRDN SM4 194 A4
Hainford Cl BROCKY SE4 144 A5
Haining Cl CHSWK W4 117 H5
Hainthorpe Rd WNWD SE27 162 C5
Hainton Cl WCHPL E1 104 D5
Halbutt St DAGW RM9 92 B2
Halcomb St IS N1 7 G1
Halcot Av BXLYHS DA6 149 J6
Halcrow St WCHPL E1 * 104 D4
Haldane Cl MUSWH N10 48 B3
PEND EN3 25 K1
Haldane Pl WAND/EARL SW18 160 A3
Haldane Rd EHAM E6 107 H2
FUL/PGN SW6 139 J1
STHL UB1 96 C6
THMD SE28 109 K6
Haldan Rd CHING E4 52 A2
Haldon Rd WAND/EARL SW18 159 J1
Hale Cl CHING E4 38 A5
EDGW HA8 44 E1
ORP BR6 216 C2
Hale Dr MLHL NW7 44 E2
Hale End HARH RM3 57 K2
Hale End Cl RSLP HA4 58 E3
Hale End Rd CHING E4 52 B2
Halefield Rd TOTM N17 50 C4
Hale Gdns ACT W3 117 H1
TOTM N17 50 C6
Hale Grove Gdns MLHL NW7 45 F1
Hale La EDGW HA8 44 E1
MLHL NW7 45 F1
Hale Rd EHAM E6 107 J3
TOTM N17 50 C6
Halesowen Rd MRDN SM4 194 A4
Hales St DEPT SE8 144 D1
Hale St POP/IOD E14 105 K6
Halesworth Rd LEW SE13 144 E4
The Hale CHING E4 52 B3
TOTM N17 50 C6
Haley Rd HDN NW4 64 A3
Half Acre BTFD TW8 116 E6
Half Acre Ms BTFD TW8 136 E1
Half Acre Rd HNWL W7 115 K1
Half Moon Crs IS N1 5 H2
Half Moon La HNHL SE24 162 E1
Half Moon Pas WCHPL E1 13 K4
Halfmoon Pas WCHPL E1 * 13 K4
Half Moon St MYFR/PICC W1J 9 K7
Halford Cl EDGW HA8 44 D5
Halford Rd FUL/PGN SW6 119 K6
RCHPK/HAM TW10 137 F6
WALTH E17 70 B2
Halfway Ct PUR RM19 131 K4
Halfway St BFN/LL DA15 167 K3
Haliburton Rd TWK TW1 136 B6
Haliday Wk IS N1 85 K4
Halifax Cl TEDD TW11 173 K2
Halifax Rd ENC/FH EN2 23 J3
GFD/PVL UB6 78 B6
Halifax St SYD SE26 163 J5
Halifield Dr BELV DA17 129 F3
Haling Gv SAND/SEL CR2 211 J5
Haling Park Gdns
SAND/SEL CR2 211 H4
Haling Park Rd SAND/SEL CR2 211 H4
Haling Rd SAND/SEL CR2 211 K4
Halkin Ar KTBR SW1X 15 G4
Halkin Ms KTBR SW1X * 15 G4
Halkin Pl KTBR SW1X 15 G4
Halkin St KTBR SW1X 15 H3
Hallam Cl CHST BR7 184 E1
Hallam Gdns PIN HA5 41 J3
Hallam Ms REGST W1B 9 K1
Hallam Rd SEVS/STOTM N15 67 H1
Hallam St GTPST W1W 9 K1
Halland Wy NTHWD HA6 40 B2
Hall Cl EA W5 98 A4
Hall Ct TEDD TW11 174 A1
Hall Dr SYD SE26 181 K1
Halley Rd FSTGT E7 89 G4
Halley St POP/IOD E14 105 G4
Hall Farm Cl STAN HA7 29 H6
Hall Farm Dr WHTN TW2 155 J2
Hallfield Est BAY/PAD W2 * 101 G5
Halliford Wy DART DA1 171 F1
Hall Gdns CHING E4 37 H6
Halliday Sq NWDGN UB2 115 J1
Halliford St IS N1 85 J5
Halliwell Rd BRXS/STRHM SW2 162 A1
Halliwick Court Pde
FBAR/BDGN N11 * 47 K1
Halliwick Rd MUSWH N10 48 A4
Hall La CHING E4 51 H1
HDN NW4 45 J5
HYS/HAR UB3 133 G1
Hallmead Rd SUT SM1 209 F1
Hall Oak Wk KIL/WHAMP NW6 82 D4
Hallowell Av CROY/NA CR0 210 E2
Hallowell Cl MTCM CR4 179 F6
Hallowell Rd NTHWD HA6 40 C3
Hallowes Crs OXHEY WD19 26 E5
Hallowfield Wy MTCM CR4 178 C6
Hall Pl BAY/PAD W2 2 A7
Hall Place Crs BXLY DA5 149 K6
Hall Rd CHDH RM6 73 J3
DART DA1 151 J5
EHAM E6 89 K6
GPK RM2 57 K6
ISLW TW7 135 J6
STJWD NW8 101 G2
WAN E11 88 B2
WLGTN SM6 210 B6
Hallside Rd EN EN1 24 B1
Hall St FSBYE EC1V 6 B4
NFNCH/WDSP N12 47 G1
Hallsville Rd CAN/RD E16 106 D5
Hallswelle Pde GLDGN NW11 * 64 D2
Hallswelle Rd GLDGN NW11 64 D2
The Hall BKHTH/KID SE3 145 K4
Hall Vw ELTH/MOT SE9 166 C4
Hallywell Crs EHAM E6 107 K4
Halons Rd ELTH/MOT SE9 167 F2
Halpin Pl WALW SE17 19 F7
Halsbrook Rd BKHTH/KID SE3 146 B4
Halsbury Cl STAN HA7 43 H1
Halsbury Rd SHB W12 118 E1
Halsbury Rd East NTHLT UB5 78 C2
Halsbury Rd West NTHLT UB5 78 B3
Halsend HYS/HAR UB3 * 114 A1
Halsey St CHEL SW3 14 E6
Halsham Crs BARK IG11 91 F4
Halsmere Rd CMBW SE5 142 C2
Halstead Cl CROY/NA CR0 211 J1
Halstead Gdns WCHMH N21 35 K3
Halstead Rd EN EN1 24 A5
ERITH DA8 150 B2
WAN E11 71 F2
WCHMH N21 35 K3
Halstow Rd GNWCH SE10 125 K5
WLSDN NW10 100 B2
Halsway HYS/HAR UB3 113 K1
Halton Cl FBAR/BDGN N11 47 K2
Halton Cross St IS N1 * 85 H6
Halton Rd IS N1 85 H5
Halt Pde CDALE/KGS NW9 * 63 F1
Halt Robin Rd BELV DA17 129 J4
Hambalt Rd CLAP SW4 141 H6
Hamble Cl RSLP HA4 58 C6
Hambledon WALW SE17 * 122 E6
Hambledon Ct EA W5 * 98 A6
Hambledon Gdns SNWD SE25 181 G6
Hambledon Pl DUL SE21 163 G3
Hambledon Rd
WAND/EARL SW18 159 J2
Hambledown Rd
ELTH/MOT SE9 * 167 J2
Hamble St FUL/PGN SW6 140 A4
Hambleton Cl WPK KT4 193 F6
Hambro Av HAYES BR2 199 K5
Hambrook Rd SNWD SE25 181 J6
Hambro Rd
STRHM/NOR SW16 179 J2
Hambrough Rd STHL UB1 114 D1
Ham Common
RCHPK/HAM TW10 156 E5
Ham Croft Cl FELT TW13 153 K5
Hamden Crs DAGE RM10 92 D1
Hamel Cl KTN/HRWW/W HA3 61 K1
Hameway EHAM E6 108 A3
Ham Farm Rd
RCHPK/HAM TW10 156 E6
Hamfrith Rd SRTFD E15 88 D4
Ham Gate Av
RCHPK/HAM TW10 157 G6
Hamilton Av BARK/HLT IG6 72 B1
CHEAM SM3 193 H6
ED N9 36 C2
ROM RM1 57 F5
SURB KT6 191 H6
Hamilton Cl BERM/RHTH SE16 124 B2
EBAR EN4 21 J5
STJWD NW8 2 A5
TOTM N17 50 B6
Hamilton Ct EA W5 98 B6
Hamilton Crs HSLW TW3 135 G6
PLMGR N13 35 G6
RYLN/HDSTN HA2 77 K1
Hamilton Gdns STJWD NW8 101 G2
Hamilton Pde FELT TW13 * 153 K6
Hamilton Pk HBRY N5 85 H2
Hamilton Pk West HBRY N5 85 H2
Hamilton Pl MYFR/PKLN W1K 15 H1
SUN TW16 172 A3
Hamilton Rd BFN/LL DA15 168 B6
BTFD TW8 116 E6
BXLYHN DA7 149 F3
CHSWK W4 118 B3
EA W5 98 A6
EBAR EN4 21 J5
ED N9 36 C2
EFNCH N2 47 G6
GLDGN NW11 64 B4
GPK RM2 75 K2
HRW HA1 60 E2
HYS/HAR UB3 95 F6
IL IG1 90 B2
OXHEY WD19 27 F5
SRTFD E15 106 C2
STHL UB1 114 E1
THHTH CR7 180 E6
WALTH E17 51 G5
WHTN TW2 155 K3
WIM/MER SW19 178 A3
WLSDN NW10 81 J3
WNWD SE27 162 E6
Hamilton Road Ms
WIM/MER SW19 178 A3
Hamilton Sq
NFNCH/WDSP N12 * 47 G2
Hamilton St DEPT SE8 124 D6
Hamilton Ter STJWD NW8 101 G2
Hamilton Wy FNCH N3 46 E2
PLMGR N13 35 H6
WLGTN SM6 210 D6
Hamlea Cl BKHTH/KID SE3 145 K6
Hamlet Cl CRW RM5 56 C3
LEW SE13 145 H5
Hamlet Gdns HMSMTH W6 118 D4
Hamlet Rd CRW RM5 56 C3
NRWD SE19 181 G3
Hamlet Sq CRICK NW2 82 C1
Hamlets Wy BOW E3 105 H3
The Hamlet CMBW SE5 142 E4
Hamlet Wy STHWK SE1 19 F3
Hamlin Crs PIN HA5 59 G2
Hamlyn Cl EDGW HA8 30 A5
Hamlyn Gdns NRWD SE19 181 F3
Hammelton Rd BMLY BR1 183 K4
Hammers La MLHL NW7 31 J6
Hammersmith Br
HMSMTH W6 118 E5
Hammersmith Bridge Rd
BARN SW13 118 E6
HMSMTH W6 119 F5
Hammersmith Broadway
HMSMTH W6 119 F4
Hammersmith Emb
BARN SW13 * 119 F6
Hammersmith F/O
HMSMTH W6 119 F5
Hammersmith Gv
HMSMTH W6 119 F4
Hammersmith Rd
HMSMTH W6 119 F4
Hammersmith Ter
HMSMTH W6 * 118 D5
Hammet Cl YEAD UB4 95 H4
Hammett St TWRH EC3N 13 J5
Hammond Av MTCM CR4 179 G5
Hammond Cl GFD/PVL UB6 78 D3
HPTN TW12 173 F4
Hammond Rd EN EN1 24 D4
NWDGN UB2 114 D3
Hammonds Cl BCTR RM8 91 J1
Hammond St KTTN NW5 84 C4
Hamond Cl SAND/SEL CR2 211 H6
Hamonde Cl EDGW HA8 30 D4
Hamond Sq IS N1 7 G2
Ham Park Rd FSTGT E7 88 E5
Hampden Av BECK BR3 182 B5
Hampden Cl CAMTN NW1 4 D3
Hampden Gurney St
MBLAR W1H 8 E4
Hampden La TOTM N17 50 B4
Hampden Rd ARCH N19 66 D6
BECK BR3 182 B5
CEND/HSY/T N8 67 G1
KTN/HRWW/W HA3 42 C4
KUT/HW KT1 175 H6
MUSWH N10 48 A3
TOTM N17 50 C4
Hampden Wy STHGT/OAK N14 34 B3
Hampermill La OXHEY WD19 26 E3
Hampshire Cl UED N18 50 D1
Hampshire Hog La
HMSMTH W6 * 118 E4
Hampshire Rd WDGN N22 49 F3
Hampshire St KTTN NW5 * 84 D4
Hampson Wy VX/NE SW8 142 A2
Hampstead Av WFD IG8 54 A3
Hampstead Cl THMD SE28 128 C1
Hampstead Gdns GLDGN NW11 64 E3
Hampstead Ga HAMP NW3 83 G3
Hampstead Gn HAMP NW3 83 J3
Hampstead Gv HAMP NW3 83 G2
Hampstead Hill Gdns
HAMP NW3 83 J2
Hampstead La HGT N6 65 K4
Hampstead Rd CAMTN NW1 4 A5
Hampstead Sq HAMP NW3 83 G1
Hampstead Wy GLDGN NW11 64 E2
Hampton Cl FBAR/BDGN N11 48 A1
KIL/WHAMP NW6 100 E2
RYNPK SW20 * 177 F3
Hampton Ct IS N1 85 H4
Hampton Court Av
E/WMO/HCT KT8 189 J3
Hampton Court Crs
E/WMO/HCT KT8 * 173 J6
Hampton Court Est
THDIT KT7 * 189 K2
Hampton Court Rd
E/WMO/HCT KT8 174 B6
HPTN TW12 173 J5
Hampton Court Wy
E/WMO/HCT KT8 189 K1
Hampton La FELT TW13 154 D6
Hampton Ri
KTN/HRWW/W HA3 62 A3
Hampton Rd CHING E4 51 H1
CROY/NA CR0 196 D3
FSTGT E7 89 F3
HPTN TW12 173 J1
IL IG1 90 C2
WAN E11 70 B5
WHTN TW2 155 J5
WPK KT4 192 D6
Hampton Rd East FELT TW13 154 E6
Hampton Rd West FELT TW13 154 D4
Hampton St WALW SE17 18 B7
Ham Ridings
RCHPK/HAM TW10 175 G1
Ham Shades Cl BFN/LL DA15 168 A5
Ham St RCHPK/HAM TW10 156 D4
The Ham BTFD TW8 136 D1
Ham Vw CROY/NA CR0 198 B3
Ham Yd SOHO/SHAV W1D * 10 C5
Hanameel St CAN/RD E16 125 K1
Hanbury Cl HDN NW4 46 A6
Hanbury Ct HRW HA1 * 61 F3
Hanbury Dr WCHMH N21 23 F5
Hanbury Rd ACT W3 117 J2
TOTM N17 50 D5
Hanbury St WCHPL E1 13 K1
Hancock Rd BOW E3 106 A2
NRWD SE19 180 E2
Handa Wk IS N1 85 J4
Hand Ct HHOL WC1V 11 H2
Handcroft Rd CROY/NA CR0 196 C5
Handel Cl EDGW HA8 44 B2
Handel Pde EDGW HA8 * 44 C2
Handel Pl WLSDN NW10 81 F4
Handel St BMSBY WC1N 5 F6
Handel Wy EDGW HA8 44 C3
Handen Rd LEW SE13 145 H6
Handforth Rd BRXN/ST SW9 142 B1
IL IG1 90 B1
Handley Gv CRICK NW2 82 B1
Handley Page Rd WLGTN SM6 211 F5
Handley Rd HOM E9 86 E5
Handowe Cl HDN NW4 63 J1
Handside Cl WPK KT4 193 G5
Handsworth Av CHING E4 52 B2
Handsworth Cl OXHEY WD19 26 E5
Handsworth Rd TOTM N17 49 K6
Handtrough Wy BARK IG11 108 B1
Hanford Cl WAND/EARL SW18 159 K3
Hangar Ruding OXHEY WD19 27 K5
Hangar View Wy ACT W3 98 C5
Hanger Gn EA W5 98 C3
Hanger La (North Circular Rd)
EA W5 98 A2
Hanger Vale La EA W5 98 B5
Hankey Pl STHWK SE1 19 F3
Hankins La MLHL NW7 31 G4
Hanley Gdns ARCH N19 67 F5
Hanley Pl BECK BR3 182 D3
Hanley Rd FSBYPK N4 66 E5
Hanmer Wk HOLWY N7 67 F6
Hannah Cl BECK BR3 182 E6
WBLY HA9 80 E2
Hannah Mary Wy
STHWK SE1 * 123 H4
Hannards Wy CHIG IG7 55 H1
Hannay La ARCH N19 66 D4
Hannell Rd FUL/PGN SW6 139 H1
Hannen Rd WNWD SE27 * 162 C5
Hannibal Rd
STWL/WRAY TW19 152 B2
WCHPL E1 104 E4
Hannibal Wy CROY/NA CR0 211 F3
Hannington Rd CLAP SW4 141 G4
Hanover Av CAN/RD E16 125 K1
FELT TW13 153 K3
Hanover Cir HYS/HAR UB3 94 A5
Hanover Cl CHEAM SM3 208 C2
RCH/KEW TW9 137 H1
Hanover Dr CHST BR7 167 H6
Hanover Gdns BARK/HLT IG6 54 C3
LBTH SE11 122 B6
Hanover Pk PECK SE15 143 H2
Hanover Pl COVGDN WC2E 11 F4
Hanover Rd SEVS/STOTM N15 68 B1
WIM/MER SW19 178 B3
WLSDN NW10 82 A5
Hanover Sq CONDST W1S 9 K4
Hanover Steps BAY/PAD W2 * 8 D4
Hanover St CONDST W1S 9 K4
CROY/NA CR0 211 H1
Hanover Ter CAMTN NW1 2 E5
Hanover Terrace Ms
CAMTN NW1 2 D5
Hanover Wy BXLYHN DA7 148 E4
Hanover Yd IS N1 * 6 B2
Hansard Ms NTGHL W11 119 G2
Hansart Wy ENC/FH EN2 23 G2
Hans Crs CHEL SW3 14 E4
Hanselin Cl STAN HA7 43 F1
Hansen Dr WCHMH N21 23 F6
Hanshaw Dr EDGW HA8 45 F4
Hansler Gv E/WMO/HCT KT8 189 J2
Hansler Rd EDUL SE22 143 G6
Hansol Rd BXLYHS DA6 149 F6
Hansom Ter BMLY BR1 * 184 A4
Hanson Cl BAL SW12 161 G2
BECK BR3 * 182 E2
MORT/ESHN SW14 137 K4
WDR/YW UB7 112 C3
Hanson Gdns STHL UB1 114 D2
Hanson St GTPST W1W 10 A1
Hans Pl KTBR SW1X 14 E4
Hans Rd CHEL SW3 14 E4
Hans St KTBR SW1X 15 F5
Hanway Pl FITZ W1T 10 C3
Hanway Rd HNWL W7 96 D5
Hanway St FITZ W1T 10 C3
Hanworth Rd FELT TW13 154 A3
HPTN TW12 154 E6
HSLW TW3 135 G5
HSLWW TW4 154 E2
Hanworth Ter HSLW TW3 135 G5
Hapgood Cl GFD/PVL UB6 78 D3
Harben Pde HAMP NW3 * 83 H5
Harben Rd KIL/WHAMP NW6 83 G5
Harberson Rd BAL SW12 161 G3
SRTFD E15 88 D6
Harberton Rd ARCH N19 66 C5
Harbet Rd BAY/PAD W2 8 B2
UED N18 51 F1
Harbex Cl BXLY DA5 169 J2
Harbinger Rd POP/IOD E14 124 E4
Harbledown Pl
STMC/STPC BR5 202 D1
Harbledown Rd FUL/PGN SW6 139 K2
Harbord Cl CMBW SE5 142 E3
Harbord St FUL/PGN SW6 139 G2
Harborne Cl OXHEY WD19 41 G1
Harborough Av BFN/LL DA15 167 K2
Harborough Rd
STRHM/NOR SW16 162 A6
Harbour Av WBPTN SW10 140 B2
Harbourer Rd BARK/HLT IG6 55 H1
Harbour Rd CMBW SE5 142 D4
Harbour Yd WBPTN SW10 * 140 B2
Harbridge Av PUT/ROE SW15 158 C2
Harbury Rd CAR SM5 209 J6
Harbut Rd BTSEA SW11 140 C5
Harcastle Cl NTHLT UB5 95 J3
Harcombe Rd STNW/STAM N16 86 A1
Harcourt Av BFN/LL DA15 168 D1
EDGW HA8 30 E5
MNPK E12 89 K2
WLGTN SM6 210 B2
Harcourt Blds EMB EC4Y * 11 J5
Harcourt Cl ISLW TW7 136 B4
Harcourt Fld WLGTN SM6 210 B2
Harcourt Ms ROM RM1 75 H2
Harcourt Rd BROCKY SE4 144 C5
BXLYHS DA6 149 F5
SRTFD E15 106 D1
THHTH CR7 196 A3
WDGN N22 48 D4
WIM/MER SW19 177 K3
WLGTN SM6 210 B2
Harcourt St CAMTN NW1 8 D2
Harcourt Ter WBPTN SW10 120 A5
Hardcastle Cl SNWD SE25 197 H3
Hardcourts Cl WWKM BR4 213 K2
Hardel Wk BRXS/STRHM SW2 162 B2
Hardens Manorway
WOOL/PLUM SE18 126 C3
Harders Rd PECK SE15 143 J3
Hardess St HNHL SE24 142 D4
Hardie Cl WLSDN NW10 81 F3
Hardie Rd DAGE RM10 92 E1
Harding Cl CROY/NA CR0 212 B1
KUTN/CMB KT2 175 G4
WALW SE17 122 D6
Hardinge Rd UED N18 50 A1
WLSDN NW10 82 A6
Hardinge St WCHPL E1 104 E5
WOOL/PLUM SE18 127 G3
Harding Rd BXLYHN DA7 149 G3
Hardings La PGE/AN SE20 182 A2
Hardman Rd CHARL SE7 126 A5
KUTN/CMB KT2 175 F5
Hardres Ter STMC/STPC BR5 * 202 E6
Hardwick Cl STAN HA7 43 J1
Hardwicke Av HEST TW5 * 135 F2
Hardwicke Ms FSBYW WC1X * 5 H5
Hardwicke Rd CHSWK W4 117 K4
PLMGR N13 48 E1
RCHPK/HAM TW10 156 D6
Hardwicke St BARK IG11 90 C6
Hardwick Gn WEA W13 97 H4
Hardwick St CLKNW EC1R 5 K5
Hardwick's Wy
WAND/EARL SW18 139 K6
Hardwidge St STHWK SE1 19 G2
Hardy Av CAN/RD E16 125 K1
RSLP HA4 77 F3
Hardy Cl BAR EN5 20 C6
BERM/RHTH SE16 124 A2
PIN HA5 59 H4
Hardy Gv DART DA1 151 K5
Hardy Pas WDGN N22 49 F4
Hardy Rd BKHTH/KID SE3 125 J6
CHING E4 51 H2
WIM/MER SW19 178 A3
Hardy Wy ENC/FH EN2 23 G2
Harebell Dr EHAM E6 108 A4
Hare & Billet Rd
BKHTH/KID SE3 145 G2
Hare Ct EMB EC4Y * 11 J4
Harecourt Rd IS N1 85 J4
Haredale Rd HNHL SE24 142 D5
Haredon Cl FSTH SE23 163 K2
Harefield ESH/CLAY KT10 204 E1
Harefield Av BELMT SM2 208 C6
Harefield Cl ENC/FH EN2 23 G2
Harefield Ms BROCKY SE4 144 C4
Harefield Rd BROCKY SE4 144 C4
CEND/HSY/T N8 66 D2
SCUP DA14 168 E4
STRHM/NOR SW16 180 A3
Hare Hall La GPK RM2 75 K1
Hare La ESH/CLAY KT10 204 E4
Hare Marsh BETH E2 104 C3
Hare Rw BETH E2 104 D1
Haresfield Rd DAGE RM10 92 C4
Hare St WOOL/PLUM SE18 127 F3
Hare Wk IS N1 7 H3
Harewood Av NTHLT UB5 77 J5
STJWD NW8 2 D6
Harewood Cl NTHLT UB5 77 K5
Harewood Dr CLAY IG5 53 K5
Harewood Pl CONDST W1S 9 K4
Harewood Rd ISLW TW7 136 A1
OXHEY WD19 27 F4
SAND/SEL CR2 212 A4
WIM/MER SW19 178 D2
Harewood Rw CAMTN NW1 8 D1
Harewood Ter NWDGN UB2 114 E4
Harfield Gdns CMBW SE5 * 143 F4
Harfield Rd SUN TW16 172 C5
Harford Cl CHING E4 37 K2
Harford Rd CHING E4 37 K2
Harford St WCHPL E1 105 G3
Harford Wk EFNCH N2 65 H1
Harfst Wy SWLY BR8 187 K4
Harglaze Ter CDALE/KGS NW9 * 45 G6
Hargood Cl KTN/HRWW/W HA3 62 A3
Hargood Rd BKHTH/KID SE3 146 B2
Hargrave Pk ARCH N19 66 C6
Hargrave Pl KTTN NW5 84 D3
Hargrave Rd ARCH N19 66 C6
Hargwyne St BRXN/ST SW9 142 A4
Haringey Pk CEND/HSY/T N8 66 E3
Haringey Rd CEND/HSY/T N8 66 E1
Harington Ter UED N18 * 35 K6
Harkett Cl KTN/HRWW/W HA3 43 F5
Harland Av BFN/LL DA15 167 J5
CROY/NA CR0 212 B1
Harland Cl WIM/MER SW19 178 A6
Harland Rd LEE/GVPK SE12 165 K3
Harlands Gv ORP BR6 216 B2
Harlech Gdns HEST TW5 114 B6
RSLP HA4 59 H4
Harlech Rd STHGT/OAK N14 34 E5
Harlequin Av BTFD TW8 116 B6
Harlequin Cl ISLW TW7 135 K6
YEAD UB4 95 H4
Harlequin Ct WEA W13 * 97 J6
Harlequin Rd TEDD TW11 * 174 C3
Harlescott Rd PECK SE15 144 A5
Harlesden Gdns WLSDN NW10 81 H6
Harlesden Rd WLSDN NW10 81 J6
Harley Cl ALP/SUD HA0 * 79 K4

Harley Crs HRW HA1 60 D1
Harleyford BMLY BR1 184 A4
Harleyford Rd LBTH SE11 122 A6
Harley Gdns ORP BR6 216 E2
WBPTN SW10 120 B5
Harley Gv BOW E3 105 H2
Harley Pl CAVSQ/HST W1G 9 J2
Harley Rd HAMP NW3 83 H5
HRW HA1 60 D1
WLSDN NW10 99 G1
Harley St CAVSQ/HST W1G 3 J7
Harley Vls WLSDN NW10 * 99 G1
Harlinger St
WOOL/PLUM SE18 126 D3
Harlington Cl HYS/HAR UB3 133 F1
Harlington Rd BXLYHN DA7 149 F4
Harlington Rd East
EBED/NFELT TW14 154 A2
Harlington Rd West
EBED/NFELT TW14 154 A1
Harlow Gdns CRW RM5 56 E2
Harlow Rd PLMGR N13 35 K5
RAIN RM13 93 H6
Harlyn Dr PIN HA5 41 F6
Harman Av WFD IG8 52 D3
Harman Cl CHING E4 38 B6
CRICK NW2 82 C1
STHWK SE1 * 123 H5
Harman Dr BFN/LL DA15 168 A1
CRICK NW2 82 C1
Harman Rd EN EN1 24 B6
Harmondsworth La
WDR/YW UB7 112 B6
Harmondsworth Rd
WDR/YW UB7 112 B3
Harmony Cl GLDGN NW11 64 C2
WLGTN SM6 210 E6
Harmony Wy HAYES BR2 183 K5
HDN NW4 64 A1
Harmood Gv CAMTN NW1 84 B5
Harmood St CAMTN NW1 84 B4
Harmsworth Ms STHWK SE1 17 K5
Harmsworth St WALW SE17 122 C5
Harmsworth Wy
TRDG/WHET N20 32 D3
Harness Rd THMD SE28 128 B2
Harold Av BELV DA17 129 G5
HYS/HAR UB3 113 J3
Harold Rd CEND/HSY/T N8 67 F2
CHING E4 38 A5
NRWD SE19 180 E3
PLSTW E13 89 F6
RDART DA2 171 J6
SEVS/STOTM N15 68 B2
SUT SM1 209 H2
WAN E11 70 C5
WFD IG8 52 E4
WLSDN NW10 99 F2
Haroldstone Rd WALTH E17 69 F2
Harp Cross La MON EC3R 13 G6
Harpenden Rd MNPK E12 71 G6
WNWD SE27 162 C4
Harper Cl STHGT/OAK N14 22 C6
Harper Rd EHAM E6 107 K5
STHWK SE1 18 D4
Harpers Yd ISLW TW7 * 136 A3
Harp Island Cl WLSDN NW10 63 F6
Harpley Sq WCHPL E1 104 E3
Harpour Rd BARK IG11 90 C4
Harp Rd HNWL W7 97 F3
Harpsden St BTSEA SW11 141 F2
Harpur St BMSBY WC1N 11 G1
Harraden Rd BKHTH/KID SE3 146 B2
Harrier Cl HCH RM12 93 K4
Harrier Ms THMD SE28 127 J2
Harriers Cl EA W5 98 A6
Harrier Wy EHAM E6 107 K4
Harries Rd YEAD UB4 95 G3
Harriet Cl BRXS/STRHM SW2 162 B2
HACK E8 86 C6
Harriet Gdns CROY/NA CR0 197 H6
Harriet St KTBR SW1X 15 F3
Harriet Wk KTBR SW1X 15 F3
Harriet Wy BUSH WD23 28 D2
Harringay Gdns
CEND/HSY/T N8 67 H1
Harringay Rd CEND/HSY/T N8 67 H2
Harrington Cl CROY/NA CR0 195 K6
WLSDN NW10 81 F1
Harrington Ct MV/WKIL W9 * 100 D2
Harrington Gdns ECT SW5 120 A4
Harrington Hl CLPT E5 68 D5
Harrington Rd SKENS SW7 14 A6
SNWD SE25 197 H1
WAN E11 70 C5
Harrington Sq CAMTN NW1 4 A2
Harrington St CAMTN NW1 4 A4
Harrington Wy
WOOL/PLUM SE18 126 C3
Harriott Cl GNWCH SE10 125 J4
Harris Cl ENC/FH EN2 23 H2
HEST TW5 135 F2
Harrison Cl NTHWD HA6 40 A2
TRDG/WHET N20 33 J3
Harrison Rd DAGE RM10 92 D4
WLSDN NW10 81 F6
Harrison's Ri CROY/NA CR0 211 H1
Harrison St STPAN WC1H 5 F5
Harrisons Whf PUR RM19 131 K5
Harris Rd BXLYHN DA7 149 F2
DAGW RM9 92 B3
Harris St CMBW SE5 142 E1
WALTH E17 69 H4
Harrods Gn EDGW HA8 * 44 C1
Harrogate Rd OXHEY WD19 27 G5
Harrold Rd BCTR RM8 91 H3
Harrow Av EN EN1 36 B1
Harroway Rd BTSEA SW11 140 C3
Harrowby St MBLAR W1H 8 D3
Harrow Cl CHSGTN KT9 205 K5
Harrow Crs HARH RM3 57 K3
Harrowdene Cl ALP/SUD HA0 79 K2
Harrowdene Gdns TEDD TW11 174 B3
Harrowdene Rd ALP/SUD HA0 79 K2
Harrow Dr ED N9 36 B3
Harrowes Meade EDGW HA8 30 C5
Harrow Fields Gdns HRW HA1 78 E1
Harrow Gdns ORP BR6 217 H2
Harrowgate Rd HOM E9 87 G5
Harrow Gn WAN E11 88 C1
Harrow La POP/IOD E14 106 A6
Harrow Manor Wy
THMD SE28 128 D1
Harrow Pk HRW HA1 60 E6
Harrow Pl WCHPL E1 13 H3
Harrow Rd ALP/SUD HA0 79 G2
ASHF TW15 152 D3
BARK IG11 90 E6
BAY/PAD W2 101 G4
CAR SM5 209 J4
IL IG1 90 C2
MV/WKIL W9 100 E3
WAN E11 88 D1
WBLY HA9 80 B3
WLSDN NW10 99 K2
Harrow Rd F/O BAY/PAD W2 8 B2
Harrow St CAMTN NW1 * 8 D1
Harrow Vw HGDN/ICK UB10 94 A2
HYS/HAR UB3 94 E6
RYLN/HDSTN HA2 42 D6
Harrow View Rd EA W5 97 H3
Harrow Wy OXHEY WD19 27 J5
Harrow Weald Pk
KTN/HRWW/W HA3 42 D2
Harston Dr PEND EN3 25 J1
Hartcliff Ct HNWL W7 * 116 A2
Hart Crs CHIG IG7 55 F1
Hart Dyke Rd STMC/STPC BR5 202 D6
Harte Rd HSLW TW3 134 E3
Hartfield Av NTHLT UB5 95 F1
Hartfield Crs WIM/MER SW19 177 J3
WWKM BR4 214 E1
Hartfield Gv PGE/AN SE20 181 J4
Hartfield Rd CHSGTN KT9 205 K3
WIM/MER SW19 177 J3
WWKM BR4 214 E2
Hartfield Ter BOW E3 105 J1
Hartford Av
KTN/HRWW/W HA3 43 G6
Hartford Rd BXLY DA5 169 H1
HOR/WEW KT19 206 C4
Hart Gv ACT W3 117 H1
STHL UB1 96 A4
Hartham Cl HOLWY N7 84 E3
ISLW TW7 136 B2
Hartham Rd HOLWY N7 84 E3
ISLW TW7 136 A2
TOTM N17 50 B5
Harting Rd ELTH/MOT SE9 166 D6
Hartington Cl HRW HA1 78 E2
ORP BR6 216 C3
Hartington Rd CAN/RD E16 107 F5
CHSWK W4 137 K2
NWDGN UB2 * 114 D3
TWK TW1 156 C2
VX/NE SW8 141 K2
WALTH E17 69 G3
WEA W13 97 H6
Hartismere Rd FUL/PGN SW6 139 J1
Hartlake Rd HOM E9 87 F4
Hartland Cl EDGW HA8 30 C4
WCHMH N21 35 J1
Hartland Dr EDGW HA8 30 C4
RSLP HA4 77 F1
Hartland Rd CAMTN NW1 * 84 B5
FBAR/BDGN N11 47 K1
HCH RM12 75 J6
HPTN TW12 155 G6
ISLW TW7 136 B4
KIL/WHAMP NW6 100 D1
MRDN SM4 193 K4
SRTFD E15 88 D5
Hartland Rd Arches
CAMTN NW1 * 84 A5
Hartlands Cl BXLY DA5 169 G1
The Hartlands HEST TW5 114 A6
Hartland Wy CROY/NA CR0 198 B6
MRDN SM4 193 J4
Hartley Av EHAM E6 89 J6
MLHL NW7 45 H1
Hartley Cl BMLY BR1 184 E5
MLHL NW7 45 H1
Hartley Rd CROY/NA CR0 196 D4
WAN E11 70 D5
WELL DA16 148 D1
Hartley St BETH E2 104 E2
Hartmann Rd CAN/RD E16 126 D1
Hartnoll St HOLWY N7 85 F3
Harton Cl BMLY BR1 184 C4
Harton Rd ED N9 36 D4
Harton St DEPT SE8 144 D2
Hartsbourne Av BUSH WD23 28 C4
Hartsbourne Cl BUSH WD23 28 D4
Hartsbourne Rd BUSH WD23 28 D4
Hartscroft CROY/NA CR0 213 G6
Harts Gv WFD IG8 52 E1
Hartshorn Gdns EHAM E6 108 A3
Harts La BARK IG11 90 B5
NWCR SE14 144 B1
Hartslock Dr ABYW SE2 128 E2
Hartsmead Rd ELTH/MOT SE9 166 E4
Hart Sq MRDN SM4 * 194 A2
Hart St MON EC3R 13 H5
Hartsway PEND EN3 24 D5
Hartswood Gdns SHB W12 * 118 C3
Hartswood Gn BUSH WD23 28 D4
Hartswood Rd SHB W12 118 C2
Hartsworth Cl PLSTW E13 106 D1
Hartville Rd WOOL/PLUM SE18 127 K4
Hartwell Dr CHING E4 52 A2
Hartwell St HACK E8 86 B4
Harvard Hl CHSWK W4 117 J5
Harvard Rd CHSWK W4 117 J5
ISLW TW7 135 K2
LEW SE13 145 F6
Harvel Cl CHST BR7 186 B6
Harvel Crs ABYW SE2 128 E5
Harvest Bank Rd WWKM BR4 214 E1
Harvesters Cl ISLW TW7 135 J6
Harvest La LOU IG10 39 H2
THDIT KT7 190 B3
Harvest Rd FELT TW13 153 K6
Harvest Wy SWLY BR8 203 K4
Harvey Dr HPTN TW12 173 G4
Harvey Gdns CHARL SE7 126 C5
Harvey Rd CEND/HSY/T N8 67 F2
CMBW SE5 142 E2
HSLWW TW4 154 E2
IL IG1 90 B3
NTHLT UB5 77 G5
WAN E11 70 C5
Harvey's La ROMW/RG RM7 75 F6
Harvey St IS N1 7 F1
Harvill Rd SCUP DA14 186 E1
Harvington Wk HACK E8 * 86 C5
Harvist Rd KIL/WHAMP NW6 100 C1
Harwell Cl RSLP HA4 58 B5
Harwood Av BMLY BR1 184 A5
MTCM CR4 178 D6
Harwood Cl ALP/SUD HA0 79 K2
NFNCH/WDSP N12 47 J2
Harwood Ms FUL/PGN SW6 * 140 A1
Harwood Rd FUL/PGN SW6 139 K1
Harwood Ter FUL/PGN SW6 140 A2
Hascombe Ter CMBW SE5 * 142 E3
Haselbury Rd ED N9 36 A5
Haseley End FSTH SE23 * 163 K2
Haselrigge Rd CLAP SW4 141 J5
Haseltine Rd SYD SE26 164 C6
Haselwood Dr ENC/FH EN2 23 H5
Haskard Rd DAGW RM9 91 K2
Hasker St CHEL SW3 14 D6
Haslam Av CHEAM SM3 193 H5
Haslam Cl HGDN/ICK UB10 58 A6
IS N1 85 G5
Haslam St PECK SE15 143 G2
Haslemere Av EBAR EN4 33 K3
HDN NW4 64 B3
HEST TW5 134 B3
HNWL W7 116 B3
MTCM CR4 178 C5
WAND/EARL SW18 160 A4
Haslemere Cl HPTN TW12 172 E1
WLGTN SM6 210 E3
Haslemere Gdns FNCH N3 46 D6
Haslemere Heathrow Est
HSLWW TW4 * 134 A3
Haslemere Rd BXLYHN DA7 149 G3
CEND/HSY/T N8 66 E4
GDMY/SEVK IG3 73 F6
THHTH CR7 196 C2
WCHMH N21 35 H4
Hasler Cl THMD SE28 109 H6
Hasluck Gdns BAR EN5 33 G1
Hassard St BETH E2 7 K3
Hassendean Rd
BKHTH/KID SE3 126 A6
Hassett Rd HOM E9 87 F4
Hassocks Cl SYD SE26 163 J5
Hassocks Rd
STRHM/NOR SW16 179 J4
Hassock Wd HAYES BR2 215 H2
Hassop Rd CRICK NW2 82 B2
Hasted Rd CHARL SE7 126 C5
Hastings Av BARK/HLT IG6 72 C1
Hastings Cl ALP/SUD HA0 79 J2
BAR EN5 21 G5
PECK SE15 * 143 H1
Hastings Dr SURB KT6 190 D3
Hastings Rd CROY/NA CR0 197 G5
FBAR/BDGN N11 48 C1
GPK RM2 75 K2
HAYES BR2 200 D5
TOTM N17 * 49 K6
WEA W13 97 H6
Hastings St STPAN WC1H 4 E5
Hastings Ter
SEVS/STOTM N15 * 67 J2
Hastings St WOOL/PLUM SE18 127 H3
Hastoe Cl YEAD UB4 95 J3
Hatcham Park Ms NWCR SE14 144 A2
Hatcham Park Rd NWCR SE14 144 A2
Hatcham Rd PECK SE15 123 K6
Hatchard Rd ARCH N19 66 D6
Hatchcroft HDN NW4 45 K6
Hatchers Ms STHWK SE1 19 H3
Hatchett Rd
EBED/NFELT TW14 153 F3
Hatch Gv CHDH RM6 74 A1
Hatch La CHING E4 38 B6
WDR/YW UB7 132 A1
Hatch Pl RCHPK/HAM TW10 175 G1
Hatch Rd STRHM/NOR SW16 179 K5
Hatch Side CHIG IG7 54 A1
The Hatch PEND EN3 25 F2
Hatchwoods WFD IG8 38 D6
Hatcliffe Cl BKHTH/KID SE3 145 J4
Hatcliffe St GNWCH SE10 125 J5
Hatfield Cl BARK/HLT IG6 54 B6
BELMT SM2 208 E6
MTCM CR4 * 194 C1
Hatfield Ct BKHTH/KID SE3 * 145 K1
Hatfield Rd CHSWK W4 118 A2
HNWL W7 116 B1
SRTFD E15 88 C3
Hatfields STHWK SE1 11 K7
Hathaway Cl CHIG IG7 54 B2
HAYES BR2 200 E5
RSLP HA4 76 D2
STAN HA7 43 G1
Hathaway Crs MNPK E12 89 K4
Hathaway Gdns CHDH RM6 73 K2
WEA W13 97 F4
Hathaway Rd CROY/NA CR0 196 C4
Hatherleigh Cl CHSGTN KT9 205 K3
MRDN SM4 193 K1
Hatherleigh Rd RSLP HA4 58 E6
Hatherley Crs SCUP DA14 168 B4
Hatherley Gdns
CEND/HSY/T N8 66 E3
EHAM E6 107 H2
Hatherley Gv BAY/PAD W2 101 F5
Hatherley Rd RCH/KEW TW9 137 G2
SCUP DA14 168 B5
WALTH E17 69 H1
Hatherley St WEST SW1P 16 B7
Hathern Gdns ELTH/MOT SE9 167 F6
Hatherop Rd HPTN TW12 172 E3
Hathorne Cl PECK SE15 143 J3
Hathorne Ter ARCH N19 * 66 D5
Hathway St PECK SE15 143 K3
Hatley Av BARK/HLT IG6 72 C1
Hatley Cl FBAR/BDGN N11 47 K1
Hatley Rd HOLWY N7 67 F6
Hat & Mitre Ct FARR EC1M 6 B7
Hatteraick St
BERM/RHTH SE16 123 K2
Hattersfield Cl BELV DA17 129 G4
Hatters La WATW WD18 26 B1
Hatton Cl WOOL/PLUM SE18 147 J1
Hatton Cross Est
HTHAIR TW6 * 133 J5
Hatton Gdn CLKNW EC1R 5 K7
HCIRC EC1N 11 K1
Hatton Gdns MTCM CR4 194 E2
Hatton Gn EBED/NFELT TW14 133 K5
Hatton Gv WDR/YW UB7 * 112 A2
Hatton Pl HCIRC EC1N 5 K7
Hatton Rd CROY/NA CR0 196 B5
EBED/NFELT TW14 153 F2
HTHAIR TW6 133 J5
Hatton Rd North HTHAIR TW6 133 G2
Hatton Rw STJWD NW8 * 2 B7
Hatton St STJWD NW8 2 B7
Hatton Wall HCIRC EC1N 11 J1
Haunch of Venison Yd
MYFR/PKLN W1K 9 J4
Havana Cl ROM RM1 75 G2
Havana Rd WIM/MER SW19 159 K4
Havannah St POP/IOD E14 124 D2
Havant Rd WALTH E17 52 A6
Havelock Cl SHB W12 * 99 K6
Havelock Pl HRW HA1 60 E3
Havelock Rd BELV DA17 * 129 G4
CROY/NA CR0 197 G6
DART DA1 170 E2
HAYES BR2 200 B1
KTN/HRWW/W HA3 42 E6
NWDGN UB2 114 D3
TOTM N17 50 C5
WIM/MER SW19 178 B1
Havelock St IL IG1 72 B6
IS N1 84 E6
Havelock Ter VX/NE SW8 141 G1
Havelock Wk FSTH SE23 163 K3
Haven Cl ELTH/MOT SE9 166 E5
SCUP DA14 186 D2
WIM/MER SW19 159 G5
YEAD UB4 94 C4
Haven Ct BRYLDS KT5 * 191 G3
Haven Gn EA W5 97 K6
Havenhurst Ri ENC/FH EN2 23 G3
Haven La EA W5 98 A5
Haven Rd ASHF TW15 152 E6
Havens Ms BOW E3 105 H4
Haven St CAMTN NW1 84 B5
The Haven RCH/KEW TW9 137 H4
Havenwood WBLY HA9 80 D1
Haverfield Est BTFD TW8 117 F6
Haverfield Gdns
RCH/KEW TW9 137 H1
Haverfield Rd BOW E3 105 F2
Haverford Wy EDGW HA8 44 B4
Havergal Vls CEND/HSY/T N8 * 67 H1
Haverhill Rd BAL SW12 161 H3
CHING E4 38 A3
Havering Dr ROM RM1 75 G1
Havering Gdns CHDH RM6 73 J2
Havering Rd ROM RM1 57 F1
Havering St WCHPL E1 105 F5
Havering Wy BARK IG11 109 H2
Haversham Cl TWK TW1 156 E2
Haverstock Hl HAMP NW3 83 J4
Haverstock Pl IS N1 * 5 K3
Haverstock Rd KTTN NW5 84 A3
Haverstock St IS N1 6 B3
Haverthwaite Rd ORP BR6 216 D1
Havil St CMBW SE5 143 F2
Havisham Pl NRWD SE19 180 C2
Hawarden Gv HNHL SE24 162 D2
Hawarden Hl CRICK NW2 81 J1
Hawarden Rd WALTH E17 69 F1
Hawbridge Rd WAN E11 70 B5
Hawes Cl NTHWD HA6 40 D3
Hawes La WWKM BR4 199 F5
Hawes Rd BMLY BR1 184 A4
UED N18 50 D2
Hawes St IS N1 85 H5
Hawfield Bank ORP BR6 217 K1
Hawgood St BOW E3 105 J4
Hawkdene CHING E4 37 K1
Hawke Park Rd WDGN N22 49 H6
Hawke Pl BERM/RHTH SE16 * 124 A2
Hawke Rd NRWD SE19 180 E2
Hawkesbury Rd
PUT/ROE SW15 138 E6
Hawkesfield Rd FSTH SE23 164 B4
Hawkesley Cl TWK TW1 156 B6
Hawkes Rd EBED/NFELT TW14 153 K2
MTCM CR4 178 D4
Hawkesworth Cl NTHWD HA6 40 C3
Hawkhurst Gdns CRW RM5 57 F2
Hawkhurst Rd
STRHM/NOR SW16 179 J4
Hawkhurst Wy NWMAL KT3 192 A2
WWKM BR4 198 E6
Hawkins Cl EDGW HA8 45 F1
HRW HA1 60 D4
Hawkins Rd TEDD TW11 174 C2
Hawkins Ter CHARL SE7 126 D5
Hawkins Wy CAT SE6 182 D1
Hawkley Gdns WNWD SE27 162 C4
Hawkridge Cl CHDH RM6 73 J3
Hawksbrook La BECK BR3 198 E3
Hawkshead Cl BMLY BR1 183 H3
Hawkshead Rd CHSWK W4 118 B3
WLSDN NW10 * 81 H5
Hawkshill Cl ESH/CLAY KT10 204 A4
Hawkshill Pl ESH/CLAY KT10 * 204 A4
Hawkslade Rd PECK SE15 144 A6
Hawksley Rd
STNW/STAM N16 85 K1
Hawks Ms GNWCH SE10 * 145 F1
Hawksmoor Cl EHAM E6 107 J5
WOOL/PLUM SE18 127 K5
Hawksmoor Ms WCHPL E1 104 D6
Hawksmoor St HMSMTH W6 119 G6
Hawksmouth CHING E4 37 K2
Hawks Rd KUT/HW KT1 175 G5
Hawkstone Est
BERM/RHTH SE16 123 K4
Hawkstone Rd
BERM/RHTH SE16 123 K4
Hawkwell Wk IS N1 * 85 J6
Hawkwood Crs CHING E4 37 K1
Hawkwood La CHST BR7 185 H4
Hawkwood Mt CLPT E5 68 D5
Hawlands Dr PIN HA5 59 J4
Hawley Cl HPTN TW12 172 E2
Hawley Crs CAMTN NW1 84 B5
Hawley Ms CAMTN NW1 84 B5
Hawley Rd CAMTN NW1 84 B5
DART DA1 171 H4
UED N18 51 F1
Hawley Ter RDART DA2 * 171 K6
Hawstead Rd LEW SE13 164 E1
Hawsted BKHH IG9 39 F2
Hawthorn Av PLMGR N13 48 E1
RAIN RM13 111 K3
THHTH CR7 180 C4
Hawthorn Centre HRW HA1 61 F1
Hawthorn Cl HEST TW5 134 A1
HPTN TW12 173 F1
STMC/STPC BR5 201 J3
Hawthornden Cl
NFNCH/WDSP N12 47 J2
Hawthorndene Cl
HAYES BR2 * 199 J6
Hawthorndene Rd HAYES BR2 199 K6
Hawthorn Dr RYLN/HDSTN HA2 60 A3
WWKM BR4 214 C2
Hawthorne Av CAR SM5 210 A5
HOM E9 87 H6
HRW HA1 61 G3
MTCM CR4 178 C5
RSLP HA4 59 F3
Hawthorne Cl BMLY BR1 184 E6
IS N1 86 A4
Hawthorne Ct
STWL/WRAY TW19 * 152 A2
Hawthorne Crs WDR/YW UB7 112 C2
Hawthorne Gv CDALE/KGS NW9 62 E4
Hawthorne Rd BMLY BR1 184 E6
UED N18 50 B2
WALTH E17 51 J6
Hawthorne Wy ED N9 36 B4
Hawthorn Farm Av NTHLT UB5 77 J6
Hawthorn Gdns EA W5 116 E3
Hawthorn Gv ENC/FH EN2 23 K1
PGE/AN SE20 181 J4
Hawthorn Hatch BTFD TW8 136 C1
Hawthorn Ms HDN NW4 46 C4
Hawthorn Pl ERITH DA8 129 K5
HYS/HAR UB3 * 94 D6
Hawthorn Rd BKHH IG9 39 G6
BTFD TW8 136 C1
BXLYHS DA6 * 149 G5
CEND/HSY/T N8 48 D6
DART DA1 171 G4
FELT TW13 153 K3
SUT SM1 209 H3
WLGTN SM6 210 B5
WLSDN NW10 81 J5
Hawthorns WFD IG8 38 E5
The Hawthorns EW KT17 207 H4
Hawthorn Ter BFN/LL DA15 168 A1
Hawthorn Wk NKENS W10 100 C3
Hawtrey Av NTHLT UB5 95 H1
Hawtrey Dr RSLP HA4 58 E4
Hawtrey Rd HAMP NW3 83 J5
Haxted Rd BMLY BR1 184 A4
Hayburn Wy HCH RM12 75 H5
Hay Cl SRTFD E15 88 C5
Haycroft Gdns WLSDN NW10 81 J6
Haycroft Rd BRXS/STRHM SW2 141 K6
SURB KT6 190 E6
Hay Currie St POP/IOD E14 105 K5
Hayday Rd CAN/RD E16 106 E4
Hayden Dell BUSH WD23 27 K1
Haydens Cl STMC/STPC BR5 202 D4
Hayden's Pl NTGHL W11 100 D5
Hayden Wy CRW RM5 56 E5
Haydock Av NTHLT UB5 78 A4
Haydock Gn NTHLT UB5 78 A4
Haydon Cl CDALE/KGS NW9 62 E1
EN EN1 36 A1
HARH RM3 57 K3
Haydon Dell Farm
BUSH WD23 * 27 K2
Haydon Dr PIN HA5 58 E1
Haydon Park Rd
WIM/MER SW19 177 K1
Haydon Rd BCTR RM8 73 J6
OXHEY WD19 27 J1
Haydon's Rd WIM/MER SW19 178 B2
Haydon St TWRH EC3N 13 J5
Haydon Wk WCHPL E1 13 J4
Haydon Wy BTSEA SW11 140 B5
Hayes Cha WWKM BR4 199 G3
Hayes Cl HAYES BR2 199 K6
Hayes Crs CHEAM SM3 208 B2
GLDGN NW11 64 D2
Hayes Dr RAIN RM13 93 K5
Hayes End Dr YEAD UB4 94 B4
Hayes End Rd YEAD UB4 94 B3
Hayesford Park Dr HAYES BR2 199 J2
Hayes Gdn HAYES BR2 199 K6
Hayes Gv EDUL SE22 143 G4
Hayes Hl HAYES BR2 199 H5
Hayes Hill Rd HAYES BR2 199 J5
Hayes La BECK BR3 183 G6
HAYES BR2 199 K3
Hayes Mead Rd HAYES BR2 199 H5
Hayes Pl CAMTN NW1 2 D7
Hayes Rd HAYES BR2 199 K1

NWDGN UB2 ....114 A4
Hayes St HAYES BR3 ....200 A5
Hayes Wy BECK BR3 ....199 F1
Hayes Wood Av HAYES BR2 ......200 A5
Hayfield Pas WCHPL E1 ....104 E3
Hayfield Rd STRM/STPC BR5 ....202 B2
Haygarth PI WIM/MER SW19 ....177 C1
Haygreen CI KUTN/CMB KT2 ....175 J2
Hay Hi MYFR/PICC W1J 9 K6
Hayland CI CDALE/KGS NW9 ......63 F1
Hay La CDALE/KGS NW9 ....63 F1
Hayles St LBTH SE11 ....18 A6
Hayling Gdns KUT/HW KT1 * 190 C1
Hayling Av FELT TW13 ....153 K5
Hayling CI STNW/STAM N16 ......86 A3
Hayling Rd OXHEY WD19 ....26 D5
Hayman Crs YEAD UB4 ....94 B1
Haymarket STJS SW1Y 10 C6
Haymeads Dr ESH/CLAY KT10 ...204 C4
Haymer Gdns WAR E4 ....207 J1
Haymerle Rd PECK SE15 ....123 H6
Haymill CI GFD/PVL UB6 ....97 F2
Hayne Rd BECK BR3 ....182 C5
Haynes CI ED N9 ....36 D5
Haynes La NRWD SE19 ....181 F2
Haynes Rd ALP/SUD HA0 ....80 A5
Hayne St STBT EC1A 12 B1
Haynt Wk RYNPK SW20 ....177 H6
Hay PI SWLY BR8 * 203 K5
Hays La STHWK SE1 ....13 G7
Haysleigh Gdns PGE/AN SE20 ....181 H5
Hay's Ms MYFR/PICC W1J 9 J7
Haysoms CI ROM RM1 ....75 G1
Haystall CI YEAD UB4 ....94 C1
Hay St BETH E2 ....6 C1
Hayter Rd BRXS/STRHM SW2 ...141 K6
Hayton CI HACK E8 ....86 B4
Hayward CI DART DA1 ....150 A6
WIM/MER SW19 ....178 A3
Hayward Dr DART DA1 ....171 J5
Haywards CI CHDH RM6 ....73 J2
Hayward's PI CLKNW EC1R * 6 A7
Haywood CI PIN HA5 ....41 H5
Haywood Rd ORP BR6 ....216 E3
Haywood Ri HAYES BR2 ....200 C1
Hazel Av WDR/YW UB7 ....112 D3
Hazel Bank BRYLDS KT5 ....191 K5
Hazelbank Rd CAT SE6 ....165 G4
Hazelbourne Rd BAL SW12 ....161 G1
Hazelbrouck Gdns
BARK/HLT IG6 ....54 D3
Hazelbury CI WIM/MER SW19 ...177 K5
Hazelbury Gn ED N9 ....36 A5
Hazelbury La ED N9 ....36 A5
Hazel CI BTFD TW8 * 136 C1
CDALE/KGS NW9 ....45 H5
CROY/NA CRO 198 A4
HCH HM12 ....93 K1
MTCM CR4 ....195 J1
PLMGR N13 ....35 K5
WHTN TW2 ....155 H2
Hazelcroft PIN HA5 ....42 A2
Hazeldean Rd WLSDN NW10 ......81 F5
Hazeldene Dr PIN HA5 ....47 G2
Hazeldene Gdns
HGDN/ICK UB10 ....76 A6
Hazeldon Rd BCTR RM8 ....73 H6
Hazel Dr ERITH DA8 ....150 D2
Hazeleigh Gdns WFD IG8 ....53 J1
Hazel Gdns EDGW HA8 ....30 D6
Hazelgreen CI WCHMH N21 ......35 H3
Hazel Gv ALP/SUD HA0 ....80 A6
CHDH RM6 ....56 A6
EN EN1 * 36 C1
ORP BR6 ....201 G6
SYD SE26 ....164 A6
Hazelhurst BECK BR3 ....183 C4
Hazelhurst Rd TOOT SW17 .....160 B6
Hazel La WFD IG8 ....54 B5
Hazell Crs ROMW/RG RM7 ......56 D4
Hazellville Rd ARCH N19 ....66 D4
Hazelmere CI
EBED/NFELT TW14 ....153 G1
NTHLT UB5 ....95 K1
Hazelmere Dr NTHLT UB5 ....95 K1
Hazelmere Gdns EMPK RM11 ...75 K2
Hazelmere Rd
KIL/WHAMP NW6 ....82 E6
NTHLT UB5 ....95 K1
STMC/STPC BR5 ....201 H1
Hazelmere Wk NTHLT UB5 ......95 K1
Hazelmere Wy HAYES BR2 ......199 K5
Hazel Rd DART DA1 ....171 G4
ERITH DA8 ....150 D2
SRTFD E15 * 88 C3
WLSDN NW10 ....99 K2
Hazel Rw NFNCH/WDSP N12 * ...47 H1
Hazeltree La NTHLT UB5 ....95 J2
Hazel Wk HAYES BR2 ....201 F3
Hazel Wy CHING E4 ....51 H2
STHWK SE1 ....19 K6
Hazelwood Av MRDN SM4 ....194 A1
Hazelwood CI CLPT E5 ....69 F2
EA W5 ....117 F2
RYLN/HDSTN HA2 ....60 A5
Hazelwood Ct SURB KT6 ....191 F3
Hazelwood Crs PLMGR N13 ....35 G6
Hazelwood Dr PIN HA5 ....41 F5
Hazelwood La PLMGR N13 ....35 G6
Hazelwood Park CI
BARK/HLT IG6 ....54 E1
Hazelwood Rd EN EN1 ....36 B1
RKW/CH/CXG WD3 ....26 A1
WALTH E17 ....69 G2
Hazlebury Rd FUL/PGN SW6 ....140 A3
Hazledean Rd CROY/NA CR0 ....196 D6
Hazledene Rd CHSWK W4 ....117 K6

Hazlemere Gdns WPK KT4 ......192 D5
Hazlewell Rd PUT/ROE SW15 ..139 F6
Hazlewood Crs NKENS W10 .....100 C5
Hazlitt CI FELT TW13 ....154 B6
Hazlitt Ms WKENS W14 * 119 H3
Hazlitt Rd WKENS W14 ....119 H3
Heacham Av HGDN/ICK UB10 ...76 A1
Headcorn Rd BMLY BR1 ....183 J1
THHTH CR7 ....196 C1
TOTM N17 ....50 B3
Headfort PI KTBR SW1X 15 H5
Headington Rd
WAND/EARL SW18 ....160 B3
Headlam Rd CLAP SW4 ....161 J2
Headlam St WCHPL E1 ....104 D5
Headley Ap IL IG1 ....72 A2
Headley Av WLGTN SM6 ....211 F3
Headley CI CHSGTN KT9 ....206 C4
Headley Dr CROY/NA CR0 ....214 A5
CNTH/NBYPK IG2 ....72 B5
Headstone Dr HRW HA1 ....60 D1
Headstone Gdns
RYLN/HDSTN HA2 ....60 C1
Headstone La
KTN/HRWW/W HA3 ....42 B4
Headstone Pde HRW HA1 * 60 D1
Headstone Rd HRW HA1 ....60 E3
Head St WCHPL E1 ....105 F5
Headway Cl
RCHPK/HAM TW10 ....156 D6
The Headway EW KT17 ....207 H6
Heald St NWCR SE14 ....144 C2
Healey Rd WATW WD18 ....26 D1
Healey St CAMTN NW1 ....84 B4
Healy Dr ORP BR6 ....217 F2
Hearne Rd CHSWK W4 ....117 H5
Hearn Ri NTHLT UB5 ....77 H6
Hearn Rd ROM RM1 ....75 H3
Hearn's Bldgs WALW SE17 ....19 F7
Hearns CI STMC/STPC BR5 .....202 D1
Hearns Rd STMC/STPC BR5 ....202 D1
Hearn St SDTCH EC2A 7 H7
Hearnville Rd BAL SW12 ....161 F3
Heatham Pk WHTN TW2 ....156 A2
Heath Av BXLYHN DA7 ....128 E6
Heathbourne Rd BUSH WD23 ...29 F3
STAN HA7 ....29 F3
Heath Brow HAMP NW3 ....83 G1
Heath CI EA W5 ....98 B3
GLDGN NW11 ....65 F4
GPK RM2 ....57 J6
HYS/HAR UB3 ....133 G1
SAND/SEL CR2 ....211 H4
STMC/STPC BR5 ....202 D5
Heathclose Av DART DA1 ....170 E2
Heathclose Rd DART DA1 ....170 D3
Heathcote Av CLAY IG5 ....53 K5
Heathcote Gv CHING E4 ....38 A5
Heathcote Rd TWK TW1 ....156 C1
Heathcote St BMSBY WC1N 5 G6
Heathcote Wy WDR/YW UB7 ...112 A1
Heathcroft EA W5 ....98 B3
Heathcroft Gdns WALTH E17 ....52 B4
Heathdene Dr BELV DA17 ....129 J4
Heathdene Rd
STRHM/NOR SW16 ....180 A3
WLGTN SM6 ....210 B5
Heath Dr BELMT SM2 ....209 G6
GPK RM2 ....57 J4
HAMP NW3 ....83 F2
RYNPK SW20 ....193 F1
Heathedge SYD SE26 ....163 J4
Heathend Rd BXLY DA5 ....170 B3
Heather Av ROM RM1 ....57 F5
Heatherbank CHST BR7 ....185 F5
ELTH/MOT SE9 ....146 E3
Heatherbank CI DART DA1 ......170 B1
Heather CI EHAM E6 ....108 A5
HPTN TW12 ....172 E4
ISLW TW7 ....135 J6
LEW SE13 ....165 G2
ROM RM1 ....57 F4
VX/NE SW8 ....141 G4
Heatherdale CI
KUTN/CMB KT2 ....175 H2
Heatherdene CI FNCH N3 ....47 G3
MTCM CR4 ....194 C1
Heather Dr DART DA1 ....170 D2
ENC/FH EN2 ....23 H3
ROM RM1 ....57 F5
Heatherfold Wy PIN HA5 ....40 D6
Heather Gdns BELMT SM2 ......208 E4
GLDGN NW11 ....64 C3
ROM RM1 ....57 F5
Heather Gln ROM RM1 ....57 F5
Heatherley Dr CLAY IG5 ....53 H3
Heather Park Dr ALP/SUD HA0 ...80 C5
Heather Park Pde
ALP/SUD HA0 * 80 B5
Heather Pl ESH/CLAY KT10 ....204 B2
Heather Rd CHING E4 ....51 H2
CRICK NW2 ....63 H6
LEE/GVPK SE12 ....165 K4
Heatherset Cl ESH/CLAY KT10 ..204 C3
Heatherset Gdns
STRHM/NOR SW16 ....180 A3
Heatherside Rd
HOR/WEW KT19 ....207 F5
SCUP DA14 ....168 D5
The Heathers
STWL/WRAY TW19 ....152 C2
Heather Wk EDGW HA8 ....44 D1
NKENS W10 ....100 C3
Heather Wy ROM RM1 ....57 F4
SAND/SEL CR2 ....213 F6
STAN HA7 ....43 F2
Heatherwood CI MNPK E12 ....71 F6
Heatherwood Dr YEAD UB4 ......94 B3
Heathfield CHING E4 ....38 A5
CHST BR7 ....185 H2
HRW HA1 ....61 G4
Heathfield Av
WAND/EARL SW18 ....160 C2
Heathfield CI CAN/RD E16 ....107 H4

HAYES BR2 ....215 G3
OXHEY WD19 ....27 G2
Heathfield Dr MTCM CR4 ....178 D4
Heathfield Gdns CHSWK W4 ....117 K5
CROY/NA CR0 * 211 J7
GLDGN NW11 ....64 B5
WAND/EARL SW18 ....160 C1
Heathfield La CHST BR7 ....185 H2
Heathfield North WHTN TW2 ...155 K2
Heathfield Pk CRICK NW2 ....82 A4
Heathfield Park Dr CHDH RM6 ..73 H2
Heathfield Ri RSLP HA4 ....58 A4
Heathfield Rd ACT W3 ....117 J2
BMLY BR1 ....183 J3
BXLYHS DA6 ....149 G5
CROY/NA CR0 ....211 J7
HAYES BR2 ....215 G3
WAND/EARL SW18 ....160 B1
Heathfield South WHTN TW2 ...156 A2
Heathfield Sq
WAND/EARL SW18 ....160 C2
Heathfield Ter CHSWK W4 ....117 K5
WOOL/PLUM SE18 ....127 K6
Heathfield V SAND/SEL CR2 ....213 F6
Heath Gdns DART DA1 ....171 F3
TWK TW1 ....156 A3
Heathgate GLDGN NW11 ....65 F3
Heathgate PI HAMP NW3 ....83 K3
Heath Gv PGE/AN SE20 ....181 K3
Heathhurst Rd SAND/SEL CR2 ..212 A6
Heathland Rd STNW/STAM N16 ..68 A5
Heathlands CI TWK TW1 ....156 A4
Heathlands Ct HSLWW TW4 ....154 D6
Heathlands Ri DART DA1 ....170 E2
Heathlands Wy HSLWW TW4 ...134 D6
Heath La BKHTH/KID SE3 ....145 G3
DART DA1 ....170 D3
Heathlee Rd BKHTH/KID SE3 ...145 J5
DART DA1 ....170 D1
Heathley End CHST BR7 ....185 H2
Heath Ldg BUSH WD23 ....28 D3
Heathman's Rd
FUL/PGN SW6 ....139 J2
Heath Md WIM/MER SW19 .....159 G5
Heathpool Ct BMLY BR1 ....184 D6
Heath Park Rd GPK RM2 ....75 J2
Heath Ri HAYES BR2 ....199 K5
PUT/ROE SW15 ....159 G1
Heath Rd BXLY DA5 ....169 K3
CHDH RM6 ....73 K4
DART DA1 ....170 C1
HGDN/ICK UB10 ....94 A1
HRW HA1 ....60 C4
OXHEY WD19 ....27 H2
THHTH CR7 ....180 D6
TWK TW1 ....156 A3
VX/NE SW8 ....141 J3
Heath's CI EN EN1 ....23 K5
Heathside ESH/CLAY KT10 .....204 E1
HAMP NW3 ....83 H2
HSLWW TW4 ....154 E2
Heath Side STMC/STPC BR5 ...201 H5
Heathside Av BXLYHN DA7 .....149 F5
Heathside CI ESH/CLAY KT10 ...204 E1
GNTH/NBYPK IG2 ....72 D2
NTHWD HA6 ....40 B1
Heathstan Rd SHB W12 ....99 J5
Heathstan Rd WLGTN SM6 ....99 J5
Heath Vw EFNCH N2 ....65 G1
Heath View CI EFNCH N2 ....65 G1
Heath View Crs DART DA1 ....170 D2
Heath View Dr ABYW SE2 ......128 E6
Heathview Gdns
PUT/ROE SW15 ....159 F2
Heath View Rd THHTH CR7 .....196 B1
Heath Vis WAND/EARL SW18 * ..160 B3
WOOL/PLUM SE18 ....128 A5
Heathville Rd ARCH N19 ....66 E4
Heathwall St BTSEA SW11 ......140 E4
Heathway BKHTH/KID SE3 .....145 K1
CROY/NA CR0 ....213 H1
DAGW RM9 ....92 B2
NWDGN UB2 * 114 C4
WFD IG8 ....39 G6
Heathwood Gdns CHARL SE7 ..126 D4
SWLY BR8 ....187 K5
Heathwood Pde SWLY BR8 * ...187 K5
Heathwood Wk BXLY DA5 ....170 B3
Heaton Av ROM RM3 ....57 K3
Heaton CI CHING E4 ....38 A5
Heaton Grange Rd GPK RM2 ....57 H4
Heaton Rd MTCM CR4 ....179 F3
PECK SE15 ....143 J4
Heaven Tree CI IS N1 ....85 J3
Heaver Rd BTSEA SW11 * 140 C4
Heavitree CI
WOOL/PLUM SE18 ....127 J5
Heavitree Rd
WOOL/PLUM SE18 ....127 J5
Hebden Ter N17 ....50 A2
Hebdon Rd TOOT SW17 ....160 D5
Heber Rd CRICK NW2 ....82 B3
EDUL SE22 ....163 G1
Hebron Rd HMSMTH W6 ....118 E3
Hecham CI WALTH E17 ....51 G5
Heckfield PI FUL/PGN SW6 .....139 K1
Heckford St WAP E1W 105 F6
Hector St WOOL/PLUM SE18 * ..127 K4
Heddington Gv HOLWY N7 ....85 F3
Heddon CI ISLW TW7 ....136 B5
Heddon Court Av EBAR EN4 ......21 K6
Heddon Court Pde EBAR EN4 * ..22 A6
Heddon Rd EBAR EN4 ....21 K6
Heddon St CONDST W1S 10 A5
Hedge HI ENC/FH EN2 ....23 H2
Hedge La PLMGR N13 ....35 J6
Hedgeley REDBR IG4 ....71 K1
Hedgemans Rd DAGW RM9 ......91 K5

Hedgemans Wy DAGW RM9 .....92 A4
Hedgerley Gdns GFD/PVL UB6 ..96 C1
Hedger's Gv HOM E9 * 87 G4
Hedger St LBTH SE11 ....18 A6
Hedgewood Gdns CLAY IG5 ......72 A1
Hedingham CI IS N1 ....85 J5
Hedingham Rd BCTR RM8 ....91 H3
Hedley Rd WHTN TW2 ....155 F2
Hedley Rw HBRY N5 ....85 K3
Heenan CI BARK IG11 ....90 C4
Heene Rd ENC/FH EN2 ....23 K3
Heidegger Crs BARN SW13 .....138 E1
Heigham Rd EHAM E6 ....89 J5
Heighton Gdns CROY/NA CR0 ..211 H3
Heights CI RYNPK SW20 ....176 E3
The Heights BECK BR3 * 183 F5
CHARL SE7 ....126 B5
NTHLT UB5 ....78 A3
Heiron St WALW SE17 ....122 C6
Helby Rd CLAP SW4 ....161 J1
Helder Gv LEE/GVPK SE12 .....165 J2
Helder St SAND/SEL CR2 ....211 K4
Heldmann CI ISLW TW7 ....135 J5
Helena CI EBAR EN4 ....21 J1
Helena PI HACK E8 ....86 D5
Helena Rd EA W5 ....97 K4
PLSTW E13 ....106 D1
WALTH E17 ....69 J2
WLSDN NW10 ....81 K3
Helena Sq BERM/RHTH SE16 ..105 G6
Helen Av EBED/NFELT TW14 ...154 A2
Helen CI DART DA1 ....170 E1
E/WMO/HCT KT8 ....189 G1
EFNCH N2 ....65 G1
Helenslea Av GLDGN NW11 ......64 D5
Helen's PI BETH E2 ....6 E2
Helen St WOOL/PLUM SE18 * ..127 G4
Helford CI RSLP HA4 ....58 C6
Heligan CI ORP BR6 ....217 F2
Helios Rd WLGTN SM6 ....195 F5
Helix Gdns BRXS/STRHM SW2 ..162 A1
Helix Rd BRXS/STRHM SW2 ....162 A1
Hellings St WAP E1W 123 H1
Helme CI WIM/MER SW19 ......177 J1
Helmet Rw FSBYE EC1V 6 D6
Helmore Rd BARK IG11 ....91 F6
Helmsdale CI ROM RM1 ....57 G3
YEAD UB4 * 95 J3
Helmsdale Rd ROM RM1 ....57 G3
STRHM/NOR SW16 ....179 H4
Helmsley St HACK E8 ....86 D5
Helmsley St HACK E8 ....86 D5
Helperby Rd WLSDN NW10 ......81 G5
Helsinki Sq BERM/RHTH SE16 ..124 C5
Helston CI PIN HA5 ....41 K3
Helvetia St CAT SE6 ....164 A4
Hemans St VX/NE SW8 ....141 J1
Hemery Rd GFD/PVL UB6 ....78 D3
Hemingford Rd CHEAM SM3 ....208 A2
IS N1 ....85 F1
Heming Rd EDGW HA8 ....44 D3
Hemington Av FBAR/BDGN N11 ..47 K1
Hemlock Rd SHB W12 ....99 H6
Hemmen La HYS/HAR UB3 ....94 D6
Hemming CI HPTN TW12 ....173 F4
Hemmings CI SCUP DA14 ....168 C2
Hemming St WCHPL E1 ....104 C3
Hemmingway CI KTTN NW5 ......84 A2
Hempstead CI BKHH IG9 ....38 E4
Hempstead Rd WALTH E17 ....52 B6
Hemp Wk WALW SE17 ....19 F6
Hemsby Rd CHSGTN KT9 ....206 B4
Hemstal Rd KIL/WHAMP NW6 ...82 E5
Hemsted Rd ERITH DA8 ....150 B2
Hemswell Dr CDALE/KGS NW9 ..45 G4
Hemsworth St IS N1 ....7 G2
Henbury Wy OXHEY WD19 ....27 H5
Henchman St SHB W12 ....99 H5
Hendale Av HDN NW4 ....45 J6
Henderson CI EMPK RM11 ....75 K6
WLSDN NW10 ....80 E5
Henderson Dr DART DA1 ....151 K5
STJWD NW8 ....2 A6
Henderson Rd CROY/NA CR0 ..196 E3
ED N9 ....36 D3
FSTGT E7 ....89 G4
WAND/EARL SW18 ....160 D2
YEAD UB4 ....94 D2
Hendham Rd TOOT SW17 ......160 D4
Hendon Av FNCH N3 ....46 C4
Hendon Gdns CRW RM5 ....56 E2
Hendon Gv HOR/WEW KT19 ...206 C6
Hendon Hall Ct HDN NW4 * 46 B3
Hendon La FNCH N3 ....46 C5
Hendon Park Rw
GLDGN NW11 * 64 D3
Hendon Rd ED N9 ....36 C4
Hendon Wy HDN NW4 ....64 A3
STWL/WRAY TW19 ....152 A1
Hendon Wood La MLHL NW7 ....31 J2
Hendren CI GFD/PVL UB6 ....78 D3
Hendre Rd STHWK SE1 ....19 H7
Hendrick Av BAL SW12 ....160 E1
Heneage La HDTCH EC3A 13 H4
Heneage St WCHPL E1 ....13 K1
Henfield CI ARCH N19 ....66 C5
BXLY DA5 ....169 H1
Henfield Rd WIM/MER SW19 ..177 H4
Hengelo Gdns MTCM CR4 ....194 C1
Hengist Rd ERITH DA8 ....149 K1
LEE/GVPK SE12 ....165 K3
Hengrave Rd FSTH SE23 ....163 K2
Hengrove Ct BXLY DA5 ....169 F3
Hengrove Crs ASHF TW15 ....152 A4
Henley Av CHEAM SM3 ....208 C2
Henley CI BERM/RHTH SE16 * ..123 K2
GFD/PVL UB6 * 96 C2
ISLW TW7 ....136 A2
Henley Dr BERM/RHTH SE16 ...19 M6
KUTN/CMB KT2 ....176 E3
Henley Gdns CHDH RM6 ....74 A2
PIN HA5 ....58 E1
Henley Rd CAN/RD E16 ....126 E2
IL IG1 ....90 C2

UED N18 ....36 A6
WLSDN NW10 ....82 A6
Henley St BTSEA SW11 ....141 F3
Henly Wy FELT TW13 ....172 C1
Hennel CI FSTH SE23 ....163 K5
Hennessy Rd ED N9 ....36 E4
Henniker Gdns EHAM E6 ....107 H2
Henniker Ms CHEL SW3 ....120 E5
Henniker Rd SRTFD E15 ....88 B3
Henningham Rd TOTM N17 ......49 K4
Henning St BTSEA SW11 ....140 D2
Henrietta CI DEPT SE8 ....124 D6
Henrietta Ms BMSBY WC1N 5 F6
Henrietta PI CAVSQ/HST W1G ...9 J3
Henrietta St CAVSQ/HST W2E ...11 F5
SRTFD E15 ....88 A3
Henriques St WCHPL E1 ....104 C5
Henry Addington CI EHAM E6 ..108 A4
Henry CI ENC/FH EN2 ....24 A1
Henry Cooper Wy
ELTH/MOT SE9 ....166 C5
Henry Darlot Dr MLHL NW7 ......46 C1
Henry Dickens Ct NTGHL W11 ..100 B6
Henry Doulton Dr TOOT SW17 ..161 H3
Henry Jackson Rd
PUT/ROE SW15 ....139 G4
Henry Macaulay Av
KUTN/CMB KT2 ....175 F4
Henry Peters Dr TEDD TW11 ...173 K1
Henry Rd EBAR EN4 ....21 H6
EHAM E6 ....107 J1
FSBYPK N4 ....67 J5
Henry's Av WFD IG8 ....52 D1
Henryson Rd BROCKY SE4 .....144 D6
Henry St BMLY BR1 ....184 A4
Hensford Gdns SYD SE26 ......163 J6
Henshall St IS N1 ....85 K4
Henshawe Rd BCTR RM8 ....91 K1
Henshaw St WALW SE17 ....18 E6
Henslowe Rd EDUL SE22 ....143 H6
Henson Av CRICK NW2 ....82 A3
Henson PI NTHLT UB5 ....77 G6
Henstridge PI STJWD NW8 ....2 C2
Henty CI BTSEA SW11 ....140 D1
Henty Wk PUT/ROE SW15 ......138 E6
Henville Rd BMLY BR1 ....184 A4
Henwick Rd ELTH/MOT SE9 ....146 C4
Henwood Side WFD IG8 ....53 K2
Hepburn Gdns HAYES BR2 .....199 J5
Hepple CI ISLW TW7 ....136 C3
Hepscott Rd HOM E9 ....87 J4
Hepworth Gdns BARK IG11 ......91 G3
Hepworth Rd
STRHM/NOR SW16 ....179 K3
Herald Gdns WLGTN SM6 ......210 B1
Heralds PI LBTH SE11 ....18 A6
Herald St BETH E2 ....104 D3
Herbert Crs KTBR SW1X 15 F4
Herbert Gdns CHDH RM6 ....73 K4
CHSWK W4 ....117 J6
WLSDN NW10 ....99 K1
Herbert PI WOOL/PLUM SE18 ..127 G6
Herbert Rd BXLYHN DA7 ....149 F3
CAN/RD E16 ....107 G6
EBAR EN4 ....21 J5
FBAR/BDGN N11 ....48 E3
GDMY/SEVK IG3 ....72 E6
HAYES BR2 ....200 C2
KUT/HW KT1 ....175 G6
MNPK E12 ....89 J2
SEVS/STOTM N15 ....68 B2
STHL UB1 ....95 J7
WALTH E17 ....69 H4
WIM/MER SW19 ....177 J3
WOOL/PLUM SE18 ....147 G1
Herbert St KTTN NW5 ....84 A4
PLSTW E13 ....106 E1
Herbrand St BMSBY WC1N 4 E7
Hercules PI HOLWY N7 ....84 E1
Hercules Rd STHWK SE1 ....17 H5
Hercules St HOLWY N7 ....84 E1
Hereford Av EBAR EN4 ....33 K5
Hereford Gdns IL IG1 ....71 J4
PIN HA5 ....59 J2
WHTN TW2 * 155 H5
Hereford Ms BAY/PAD W2 * 100 E5
Hereford PI NWCR SE14 ....144 C1
Hereford Retreat PECK SE15 ..143 H1
Hereford Rd ACT W3 ....98 E6
BAY/PAD W2 ....100 E5
EA W5 ....116 D3
FELT TW13 ....154 B3
WAN E11 ....71 F2
Hereford Sq SKENS SW7 ....120 B4
Hereford St BETH E2 ....104 C3
Hereford Wy CHSGTN KT9 .....205 J3
Hereward Gdns PLMGR N13 ....49 G1
Hereward Rd TOOT SW17 ......160 D6
Herga Rd KTN/HRWW/W HA3 ...43 F4
Heriot Av CHING E4 ....37 J4
Heriot Rd HDN NW4 ....64 A2
Heriots CI STAN HA7 ....29 G6
Heritage HI HAYES BR2 ....215 G3
Heritage PI
WAND/EARL SW18 * 160 C1
Heritage Vw HRW HA1 ....79 F1
Herkomer CI BUSH WD23 ....28 B1
Herkomer Rd BUSH WD23 ....28 A1
Herlwyn Av RSLP HA4 ....58 B1
Herlwyn Gdns TOOT SW17 .....160 E6
Herm CI ISLW TW7 ....135 H1
Hermes CI MV/WKIL W9 ....100 C3
Hermes St IS N1 ....5 J3
Hermes Wy WLGTN SM6 ....210 D5
Hermiston Av CEND/HSY/T N8 ..66 E2
Hermitage CI ENC/FH EN2 ....23 H5
ESH/CLAY KT10 ....205 G4
RCHPK/HAM TW10 ....136 E6
SWFD E18 ....70 D1
Hermitage Gdns HAMP NW3 ....82 E1
NRWD SE19 ....180 D3
Hermitage La CRICK NW2 ....82 E1
CROY/NA CR0 ....197 G4
STRHM/NOR SW16 ....180 A3

Hermitage Rd FSBYPK N4 67 J4
NRWD SE19 180 E2
Hermitage Rw HACK E8 * 86 C3
Hermitage St BAY/PAD W2 8 A2
The Hermitage BARN SW13 * 138 C2
FELT TW13 * 153 J5
FSTH SE23 163 K3
KUT/HW KT1 * 190 E1
LEW SE13 * 145 F3
RCHPK/HAM TW10 137 F6
Hermitage Wk SWFD E18 70 D1
Hermitage Wall WAP E1W 123 H1
Hermitage Wy STAN HA7 43 G4
Hermit Rd CAN/RD E16 106 D4
Hermit St FSBYE EC1V 6 A4
Hermon Gv HYS/HAR UB3 113 K1
Hermon Hl WAN E11 70 E1
Herndon Rd
WAND/EARL SW18 140 B6
Herne Cl WLSDN NW10 81 F3
Herne Ct BUSH WD23 * 28 C3
Herne Hl HNHL SE24 142 D6
Herne Hill Rd HNHL SE24 142 D4
Herne Ms UED N18 36 C6
Herne Pl HNHL SE24 162 C1
Herne Rd BUSH WD23 28 B1
SURB KT6 190 E6
Heron Cl BKHH IG9 38 E3
WALTH E17 51 H5
WLSDN NW10 81 G4
Heron Ct HAYES BR2 200 B1
KUT/HW KT1 * 175 F6
Heron Crs SCUP DA14 167 K6
Herondale SAND/SEL CR2 213 F6
Herondale Av
WAND/EARL SW18 160 C3
Heron Dr FSBYPK N4 67 J6
Heron Flight Av HCH RM12 93 J5
Herongate Rd MNPK E12 71 G6
Heron Hl BELV DA17 129 G4
Heron Md PEND EN3 25 J1
Heron Ms IL IG1 72 B6
Heron Quays POP/IOD E14 124 D1
Heron Rd CROY/NA CR0 * 197 F5
HNHL SE24 142 D5
TWK TW1 136 B5
Heronsforde WEA W13 97 J5
Heronsgate EDGW HA8 44 C1
Herons Lea HGT N6 * 65 K3
Heronslea Dr STAN HA7 44 A1
Herons Pl ISLW TW7 136 C4
Herons Ri EBAR EN4 21 J5
Heron Wk NTHWD HA6 26 C6
Heron Wy EBED/NFELT TW14 133 K5
Herrick Rd HBRY N5 85 J1
Herrick St WEST SW1P 16 D7
Herries St NKENS W10 100 C1
Herringham Rd CHARL SE7 126 B3
Herrongate Cl EN EN1 24 A3
Hersant Cl WLSDN NW10 81 J6
Herschell Rd FSTH SE23 164 A2
Hersham Cl PUT/ROE SW15 158 D2
Hersham Rd WOT/HER KT12 188 A6
Hershell Ct
MORT/ESHN SW14 * 137 J5
Hertford Av
MORT/ESHN SW14 138 A6
Hertford Cl EBAR EN4 21 H4
Hertford Ct STAN HA7 * 43 K3
Hertford End Ct NTHWD HA6 * 40 C1
Hertford Rd BARK IG11 90 A5
EBAR EN4 21 G4
ED N9 36 D3
EFNCH N2 47 J6
GNTH/NBYPK IG2 72 E3
IS N1 86 A6
PEND EN3 24 E2
Hertford Road High St
PEND EN3 36 E1
Hertford St MYFR/PICC W1J 9 J7
MYFR/PKLN W1K 15 J1
Hertford Wy MTCM CR4 195 K1
Hertslet Rd HOLWY N7 85 F1
Hertsmere Rd POP/IOD E14 105 J6
Hertswood Ct BAR EN5 * 20 C5
Hervey Cl FNCH N3 46 E4
Hervey Park Rd WALTH E17 69 G1
Hesa Rd HYS/HAR UB3 94 E5
Hesewall Cl VX/NE SW8 141 H3
Hesketh Pl NTGHL W11 100 C6
Hesketh Rd FSTGT E7 88 E1
Heslop Rd BAL SW12 160 E3
Hesper Ms ECT SW5 120 A5
Hesperus Crs POP/IOD E14 124 E4
Hessel Rd WEA W13 116 B2
Hessel St WCHPL E1 104 D5
Hesselyn Dr RAIN RM13 93 K5
Hestercombe Av
FUL/PGN SW6 139 H3
Hesterman Wy CROY/NA CR0 195 K5
Hester Rd BTSEA SW11 140 D1
UED N18 50 C1
Hester Ter RCH/KEW TW9 137 H4
Heston Av HEST TW5 134 D1
Heston Grange La HEST TW5 114 E6
Heston Rd HEST TW5 135 F1
Heston St DEPT SE8 144 C2
Heswell Gn OXHEY WD19 * 26 E5
Hetherington Rd CLAP SW4 141 K5
Hetley Rd SHB W12 118 E1
Heton Gdns HDN NW4 63 J1
Hevelius Cl GNWCH SE10 125 J5
Hever Cft ELTH/MOT SE9 167 F6
Hever Gdns BMLY BR1 185 F5
Heverham Rd
WOOL/PLUM SE18 127 K4
Heversham Rd BXLYHN DA7 149 H3
Hevingham Dr CHDH RM6 73 H2
Hewens Rd HGDN/ICK UB10 94 A2
Hewer St NKENS W10 100 B4
Hewett Cl STAN HA7 29 H6
Hewett St SDTCH EC2A 7 H7
Hewish Rd UED N18 36 A6
Hewison St BOW E3 105 H1
Hewitt Av WDGN N22 49 H5
Hewitt Cl CROY/NA CR0 213 J1
Hewitt Rd CEND/HSY/T N8 67 G2
Hewlett Rd BOW E3 105 G1
The Hexagon HGT N6 65 K5
Hexal Rd CAT SE6 165 H5
Hexham Gdns ISLW TW7 136 B1
Hexham Rd BAR EN5 21 F5
MRDN SM4 194 A5
WNWD SE27 162 D4
Heybourne Rd TOTM N17 50 D3
Heybridge Av
STRHM/NOR SW16 180 A2
Heybridge Dr BARK/HLT IG6 54 D6
Heybridge Wy WALTH E17 69 G4
Heyford Av RYNPK SW20 177 J6
VX/NE SW8 141 K1
Heyford Rd MTCM CR4 178 D5
Heyford Ter VX/NE SW8 141 K1
Heygate Est WALW SE17 18 D6
Heygate St WALW SE17 18 C7
Heynes Rd BCTR RM8 91 J2
Heysham Dr OXHEY WD19 41 G1
Heysham La HAMP NW3 83 G1
Heysham Rd SEVS/STOTM N15 67 K3
Heythorp St
WAND/EARL SW18 159 J4
Heywood Av CDALE/KGS NW9 45 G4
Heyworth Rd CLPT E5 86 D2
SRTFD E15 88 D3
Hibbert Rd KTN/HRWW/W HA3 43 F5
WALTH E17 69 H4
Hibbert St BTSEA SW11 140 B4
Hibernia Gdns HSLW TW3 135 F6
Hibernia Rd HSLW TW3 135 F5
Hichisson Rd PECK SE15 143 K6
Hickin Cl CHARL SE7 126 C4
Hickin St POP/IOD E14 125 F3
Hickling Rd IL IG1 90 B3
Hickman Av CHING E4 52 A2
Hickman Cl CAN/RD E16 107 H4
Hickman Rd CHDH RM6 73 J4
Hicks Av GFD/PVL UB6 96 D2
Hicks Cl BTSEA SW11 140 D4
Hicks St DEPT SE8 124 B5
Hidcote Gdns RYNPK SW20 176 E6
Hide Pl WEST SW1P 16 C7
Hide Rd HRW HA1 60 D1
Higham Hill Rd WALTH E17 51 G4
Higham Pl WALTH E17 51 G6
Higham Rd TOTM N17 49 K6
WFD IG8 52 E2
Higham Station Av CHING E4 51 K2
The Highams WALTH E17 * 52 A4
Higham St WALTH E17 51 G6
Highbank Pl
WAND/EARL SW18 * 160 A3
Highbanks Cl WELL DA16 148 B1
Highbanks Rd PIN HA5 42 B2
Highbank Wy CEND/HSY/T N8 67 G3
Highbarrow Rd CROY/NA CR0 197 G5
High Beech SAND/SEL CR2 212 A5
High Beeches ORP BR6 217 G4
SCUP DA14 187 F1
Highbridge Rd BARK IG11 90 B6
Highbrook Rd BKHTH/KID SE3 146 C4
High Broom Crs WWKM BR4 198 E4
Highbury Av THHTH CR7 180 B5
Highbury Cl NWMAL KT3 191 K1
WWKM BR4 198 E6
Highbury Cnr HBRY N5 85 H4
Highbury Crs HBRY N5 85 H3
Highbury Est HBRY N5 85 J3
Highbury Gdns GDMY/SEVK IG3 72 E6
Highbury Gra HBRY N5 85 H2
Highbury Gv HBRY N5 85 H3
Highbury Hl HBRY N5 85 H2
Highbury New Pk HBRY N5 85 J3
Highbury Pk HBRY N5 85 H2
Highbury Pl HBRY N5 85 H4
Highbury Qd HBRY N5 85 J1
Highbury Rd WIM/MER SW19 177 H1
Highbury Station Pde IS N1 * 85 H4
Highbury Station Rd IS N1 * 85 G4
Highbury Ter HBRY N5 85 H3
Highbury Terrace Ms HBRY N5 85 H3
High Cedar Dr RYNPK SW20 176 E3
Highclere Rd NWMAL KT3 176 A6
Highclere St SYD SE26 164 B6
Highcliffe Dr PUT/ROE SW15 158 C1
Highcliffe Gdns REDBR IG4 71 J2
Highcombe CHARL SE7 126 A6
Highcombe Cl ELTH/MOT SE9 166 C3
High Coombe Pl
KUTN/CMB KT2 176 A3
Highcroft CDALE/KGS NW9 63 G2
Highcroft Av ALP/SUD HA0 80 B5
Highcroft Gdns GLDGN NW11 64 D3
Highcroft Rd ARCH N19 66 E4
High Cross Rd TOTM N17 50 C6
Highdaun Dr
STRHM/NOR SW16 196 A1
Highdown WPK KT4 192 B6
Highdown Rd PUT/ROE SW15 158 E1
High Dr NWMAL KT3 175 K4
High Elms WFD IG8 52 E1
High Elms Cl NTHWD HA6 40 A2
High Elms Rd ORP BR6 216 C6
Highfield OXHEY WD19 27 K5
Highfield Av CDALE/KGS NW9 62 E2
ERITH DA8 129 K6
GFD/PVL UB6 78 E3
GLDGN NW11 64 B4
ORP BR6 217 F4
PIN HA5 59 K2
WBLY HA9 80 A1
Highfield Cl CDALE/KGS NW9 62 E2
CRW RM5 56 E2
LEW SE13 165 G1
NTHWD HA6 40 C4
SURB KT6 190 D5
WDGN N22 49 G4
Highfield Ct STHGT/OAK N14 34 C1
Highfield Crs NTHWD HA6 40 C4
Highfield Dr HAYES BR2 199 H1
HOR/WEW KT19 207 H5
WWKM BR4 213 K1
Highfield Gdns GLDGN NW11 64 C3
Highfield Hl NRWD SE19 180 E3
Highfield Link CRW RM5 56 E2
Highfield Rd ACT W3 98 E4
BMLY BR1 200 E1
BRYLDS KT5 191 K4
BXLYHS DA6 149 G6
CRW RM5 56 E2
DART DA1 171 G2
FELT TW13 153 K3
GLDGN NW11 * 64 C3
ISLW TW7 136 A2
NTHWD HA6 40 C4
STMC/STPC BR5 186 A6
SUT SM1 209 J3
WCHMH N21 35 H4
WFD IG8 53 J3
Highfield Rd North DART DA1 171 G1
Highfield Rd South DART DA1 171 G2
Highfields Gv HGT N6 66 A5
High Foleys ESH/CLAY KT10 205 H5
High Garth ESH/CLAY KT10 204 C4
Highgate Av HGT N6 66 B4
Highgate Cl HGT N6 66 A4
Highgate Edge EFNCH N2 * 65 J2
Highgate High St HGT N6 66 A5
Highgate Hl ARCH N19 66 B5
Highgate Rd KTTN NW5 84 B2
Highgate Spinney
CEND/HSY/T N8 * 66 D3
Highgate West Hl HGT N6 66 A6
High Gv BMLY BR1 184 B4
WOOL/PLUM SE18 147 J1
Highgrove Cl CHST BR7 184 D4
FBAR/BDGN N11 48 A1
Highgrove Ms CAR SM5 209 J1
Highgrove Rd BCTR RM8 91 J3
Highgrove Wy RSLP HA4 58 E3
High Hill Ferry CLPT E5 68 D5
High Holborn HHOL WC1V 11 F3
Highland Av DAGE RM10 92 E1
HNWL W7 96 E5
LOU IG10 39 K1
Highland Cft BECK BR3 182 E1
Highland Dr BUSH WD23 28 B2
Highland Pk FELT TW13 153 J6
Highland Rd BMLY BR1 183 J4
BXLYHS DA6 149 H6
NRWD SE19 181 F2
NTHWD HA6 40 E5
Highlands OXHEY WD19 27 G3
Highlands Av ACT W3 98 E6
WCHMH N21 23 F6
Highlands Cl HSLW TW3 135 G2
Highlands Gdns IL IG1 71 K5
Highlands Rd BAR EN5 20 E6
STMC/STPC BR5 202 C4
The Highlands BAR EN5 * 21 F5
EDGW HA8 44 D5
Highland Ter LEW SE13 * 144 E4
High La HNWL W7 96 D5
Highlea Cl CDALE/KGS NW9 45 G4
High Level Dr SYD SE26 163 H6
Highlever Rd NKENS W10 100 A4
High Limes NRWD SE19 * 181 F2
High Md HRW HA1 60 E2
WWKM BR4 199 G6
Highmead WOOL/PLUM SE18 148 A1
Highmead Crs ALP/SUD HA0 80 B5
High Meadow Cl PIN HA5 59 F1
High Meadow Crs
CDALE/KGS NW9 63 F2
High Mdw CHIG IG7 54 D1
High Meads Rd CAN/RD E16 107 H5
Highmore Rd BKHTH/KID SE3 145 H1
High Mt HDN NW4 * 63 J3
High Oaks ENC/FH EN2 23 F1
The High Pde
STRHM/NOR SW16 * 161 K5
High Park Rd RCH/KEW TW9 137 H2
High Pth WIM/MER SW19 178 A4
High Point ELTH/MOT SE9 167 G5
High Rdg MUSWH N10 * 48 B4
Highridge Pl ENC/FH EN2 * 23 F1
High Rd BKHH IG9 39 F4
BUSH WD23 28 D3
CHDH RM6 74 B3
EFNCH N2 47 H5
FBAR/BDGN N11 48 B1
GDMY/SEVK IG3 73 G5
IL IG1 90 B1
KTN/HRWW/W HA3 42 E4
LEY E10 69 K3
NFNCH/WDSP N12 47 G3
RDART DA2 170 E5
SEVS/STOTM N15 68 B2
TOTM N17 50 B6
TRDG/WHET N20 33 G2
WBLY HA9 80 A3
WDGN N22 49 F3
WLSDN NW10 81 J4
High Rd Eastcote PIN HA5 59 G1
High Rd Great North Rd
EFNCH N2 47 H5
High Rd Ickenham
HGDN/ICK UB10 58 A6
High Rd Leyton LEY E10 69 K6
High Rd Leytonstone WAN E11 88 C1
High Rd Woodford Gn WFD IG8 38 E6
Highshore Rd PECK SE15 143 H3
Highstead Crs ERITH DA8 150 B2
Highstone Av WAN E11 70 E3
High St ACT W3 117 K1
BAR EN5 20 D5
BARK/HLT IG6 54 C6
BECK BR3 182 D5
BELMT SM2 209 G5
BMLY BR1 183 K6
BORE WD6 29 K1
BTFD TW8 116 E6
BTFD TW8 136 D1
BUSH WD23 28 A1
CAR SM5 209 K3
CEND/HSY/T N8 66 E1
CHEAM SM3 208 C4
CROY/NA CR0 211 J1
DART DA1 171 H1
E/WMO/HCT KT8 189 F1
EA W5 97 K6
ESH/CLAY KT10 204 B3
EW KT17 207 H6
FBAR/BDGN N11 48 B1
FELT TW13 154 A3
HEST TW5 134 A1
HPTN TW12 173 G4
HRW HA1 60 E6
HSLW TW3 135 H4
HYS/HAR UB3 113 G6
KTN/HRWW/W HA3 42 E6
KUT/HW KT1 174 D4
MLHL NW7 45 K1
NTHWD HA6 40 D4
NWMAL KT3 192 B1
ORP BR6 202 C4
ORP BR6 216 C3
PGE/AN SE20 181 K3
PIN HA5 41 J6
PLSTW E13 106 E1
PUR RM19 131 J5
ROM RM1 75 G2
RSLP HA4 58 C5
SCUP DA14 168 B6
SNWD SE25 197 G1
SRTFD E15 106 A1
STHGT/OAK N14 34 D3
STMC/STPC BR5 202 D1
STWL/WRAY TW19 152 A1
SUT SM1 209 F2
TEDD TW11 174 B1
THDIT KT7 190 B4
THHTH CR7 196 D1
WALTH E17 69 H1
WAN E11 71 F3
WBLY HA9 80 B2
WDR/YW UB7 112 A6
WDR/YW UB7 112 B4
WHTN TW2 155 H2
WIM/MER SW19 177 G1
WWKM BR4 198 E5
High St Collier's Wd
WIM/MER SW19 178 C3
High St Harlesden
WLSDN NW10 99 H1
High St Harlington
HYS/HAR UB3 113 G6
High Street Ms
WIM/MER SW19 177 H1
High St North MNPK E12 89 J4
High St South EHAM E6 107 K1
High Timber St BLKFR EC4V 12 C5
High Tor Cl BMLY BR1 184 A3
High Trees BRXS/STRHM SW2 162 B3
CROY/NA CR0 198 B5
EBAR EN4 21 J6
High Vw PIN HA5 59 G1
WATW WD18 26 D1
Highview Av EDGW HA8 30 E6
High View Av WLGTN SM6 211 F3
High View Cl NRWD SE19 181 G5
Highview Gdns EDGW HA8 44 E1
FBAR/BDGN N11 48 C1
FNCH N3 46 C6
High View Rd NRWD SE19 180 E2
SWFD E18 52 D5
Highview Rd SCUP DA14 168 C6
WEA W13 97 G5
Highview Ter DART DA1 * 151 G6
The Highway BELMT SM2 209 G6
ORP BR6 217 H3
STAN HA7 43 F4
WAP E1W 104 C6
Highwood Av
NFNCH/WDSP N12 33 G6
Highwood Cl ORP BR6 201 H6
Highwood Dr ORP BR6 201 H6
Highwood Gdns CLAY IG5 71 K2
Highwood Gv MLHL NW7 45 F1
Highwood Hl MLHL NW7 31 H5
Highwood Rd ARCH N19 84 E1
High Worple RYLN/HDSTN HA2 59 J4
Highworth Rd FBAR/BDGN N11 48 D2
Highworth St CAMTN NW1 * 8 D1
Hilary Av MTCM CR4 179 F6
Hilary Cl BXLYHN DA7 149 J2
FUL/PGN SW6 * 140 A1
Hilary Rd ACT W3 99 H6
Hilberry Ct BUSH WD23 * 28 B2
Hilbert Rd CHEAM SM3 208 B2
Hilborough Cl WIM/MER SW19 178 B3
Hilborough Rd HACK E8 86 B5
Hilborough Wy ORP BR6 216 D3
Hilda Lockert Wk
BRXN/ST SW9 142 C3
Hilda Rd CAN/RD E16 106 C3
EHAM E6 89 H5
Hilda Ter BRXN/ST SW9 * 142 B3
Hilda Vale Rd ORP BR6 216 A2
Hildenborough Gdns
BMLY BR1 183 H2
Hilden Dr ERITH DA8 150 E1
Hildenlea Pl HAYES BR2 183 H5
Hildreth St BAL SW12 161 G3
Hildyard Rd FUL/PGN SW6 119 K6
Hiley Rd WLSDN NW10 100 A2
Hilgrove Rd KIL/WHAMP NW6 83 G5
Hiliary Gdns STAN HA7 43 J5
Hillary Crs WOT/HER KT12 188 B5
Hillary Dr ISLW TW7 136 A5
Hillary Ri BAR EN5 20 E5
Hillary Rd NWDGN UB2 115 F3
Hillbeck Cl PECK SE15 143 K1
Hillbeck Wy GFD/PVL UB6 78 D6
Hillborne Cl HYS/HAR UB3 113 K5
Hillborough Cl
WIM/MER SW19 * 178 B3
Hillbrook Rd TOOT SW17 160 E5
Hill Brow BMLY BR1 184 C4
DART DA1 170 C1
Hillbrow NWMAL KT3 176 C6
Hillbrow Cl BXLY DA5 170 A6
Hillbrow Rd BMLY BR1 183 H3
ESH/CLAY KT10 204 C2
Hill Bunker's BELV DA17 129 H4
Hillbury Av KTN/HRWW/W HA3 61 H2
Hillbury Rd TOOT SW17 161 G5
Hill Cl BAR EN5 20 A6
CHST BR7 185 G1
CRICK NW2 81 K1
GLDGN NW11 64 E3
HRW HA1 78 E1
STAN HA7 29 H6
Hillcote Av STRHM/NOR SW16 180 B3
Hillcourt Av NFNCH/WDSP N12 47 F2
Hillcourt Rd EDUL SE22 163 J1
Hill Crs BRYLDS KT5 191 G2
BXLY DA5 169 K3
HRW HA1 61 G2
TRDG/WHET N20 33 F4
WPK KT4 193 F6
Hill Crest BFN/LL DA15 168 B2
SURB KT6 * 191 F4
Hillcrest CMBW SE5 * 142 E5
HGT N6 66 A4
WCHMH N21 35 H2
Hillcrest Av EDGW HA8 30 D6
GLDGN NW11 64 C2
PIN HA5 59 H1
Hillcrest Cl BECK BR3 198 C3
SYD SE26 163 H6
Hill Crest Gdns CRICK NW2 81 J1
Hillcrest Gdns ESH/CLAY KT10 205 F2
FNCH N3 64 C1
Hillcrest Rd ACT W3 117 H1
BMLY BR1 165 K6
DART DA1 170 B2
EA W5 98 A4
EMPK RM11 75 J4
LOU IG10 39 H1
ORP BR6 202 B6
WALTH E17 52 B5
Hillcrest Vw BECK BR3 198 C3
Hillcroft Av PIN HA5 59 K3
Hillcroft Crs EA W5 97 K5
OXHEY WD19 27 F3
RSLP HA4 77 H1
WBLY HA9 80 B2
Hillcroft Rd EHAM E6 108 B4
Hillcroome Rd BELMT SM2 209 H4
Hillcross Av MRDN SM4 193 H3
Hilldale Rd SUT SM1 208 D2
Hilldown Rd HAYES BR2 199 H5
STRHM/NOR SW16 179 K3
Hill Dr CDALE/KGS NW9 62 E5
STRHM/NOR SW16 180 A6
Hilldrop Crs HOLWY N7 84 D3
Hilldrop Est HOLWY N7 84 E2
Hilldrop La HOLWY N7 84 D3
Hilldrop Rd BMLY BR1 184 A2
HOLWY N7 84 D3
Hill End ORP BR6 202 A6
WOOL/PLUM SE18 147 F2
Hillersdon Av BARN SW13 138 D3
EDGW HA8 44 B1
Hillery Cl WALW SE17 19 F7
Hill Farm Rd NKENS W10 100 A4
Hillfield Av ALP/SUD HA0 80 A5
CDALE/KGS NW9 63 G2
CEND/HSY/T N8 67 F1
MRDN SM4 194 D3
Hillfield Cl RYLN/HDSTN HA2 60 C1
Hillfield La South BUSH WD23 28 E1
Hillfield Ms CEND/HSY/T N8 67 F1
Hillfield Pde MRDN SM4 * 194 C3
Hillfield Pk MUSWH N10 48 B6
WCHMH N21 35 G4
Hillfield Park Ms MUSWH N10 66 B1
Hill Field Rd HPTN TW12 172 E3
Hillfield Rd KIL/WHAMP NW6 82 D3
Hillfoot Av CRW RM5 56 E4
Hillfoot Rd CRW RM5 56 E4
Hillgate Pl BAL SW12 161 G1
KENS W8 119 K1
Hillgate St KENS W8 * 119 K1
Hill Gv FELT TW13 154 E4
ROM RM1 57 G6
Hill House Av STAN HA7 43 F3
Hill House Cl WCHMH N21 35 G2
Hill House Dr HPTN TW12 173 F4
Hill House Rd
STRHM/NOR SW16 180 A1
Hilliard Rd NTHWD HA6 40 D4
Hilliard's Ct WAP E1W * 123 K1
Hillier Cl BAR EN5 33 F1
Hillier Gdns CROY/NA CR0 211 G3
Hillier Pl CHSGTN KT9 205 K4
Hillier Rd BTSEA SW11 160 E1
Hillier's La CROY/NA CR0 210 E1
Hillingdon Av
STWL/WRAY TW19 152 B3
Hillingdon Rd BXLYHN DA7 149 K4
Hillingdon St WALW SE17 122 C6
Hillingdon Trail HYS/HAR UB3 113 K5
Hill La RSLP HA4 58 A5
Hillman Dr NKENS W10 100 A3
Hillman St HACK E8 86 D4
Hillmarton Rd HOLWY N7 84 E3
Hillmarton Ter HOLWY N7 * 84 E3
Hillmead Dr BRXN/ST SW9 142 C5
Hillmont Rd ESH/CLAY KT10 204 E1
Hillmore Gv SYD SE26 182 A1
Hillreach WOOL/PLUM SE18 126 E5
Hill Ri ED N9 36 D1
ESH/CLAY KT10 190 C6
GFD/PVL UB6 78 C6
GLDGN NW11 65 F1
RCHPK/HAM TW10 136 E6
RSLP HA4 58 A5
Hillrise Rd ARCH N19 66 E4
CRW RM5 56 E2
Hill Rd ALP/SUD HA0 79 H1
CAR SM5 209 J4
DART DA1 171 H4
HRW HA1 61 G2
MTCM CR4 179 G4

MUSWH N10 ....47 K4
NTHWD HA6 ....40 B2
PIN HA5 ....59 J3
STJWD NW8 ....101 G1
SUT SM1 ....209 F3
Hillsboro Rd EDUL SE22 ....143 H6
Hillsborough Gn OXHEY WD19 * 26 E5
Hillsgrove CI WELL DA16 ....148 D1
Hill Side BAR EN5 ....21 G6
Hillside CDALE/KGS NW9 ....63 F1
 ESH/CLAY KT10 * 204 B3
 WIM/MER SW19 ....177 G2
 WLSDN NW10 ....81 F6
Hillside Av FBAR/BDGN N11 ....47 K2
 WBLY HA9 ....80 B2
 WFD IG8 ....53 C1
Hillside CI KIL/WHAMP NW6 ....101 F1
 MLHL NW7 ....193 H1
 WFD IG8 ....53 G1
Hillside Crs ENC/FH EN2 ....23 K1
 NTHWD HA6 ....40 E4
 OXHEY WD19 ....27 H1
 RYLN/HDSTN HA2 ....60 C6
Hillside Dr EDGW HA8 ....44 C2
Hillside Gdns BAR EN5 ....20 C5
 BRXS/STRHM SW2 * 162 B4
 EDGW HA8 ....30 B6
 FBAR/BDGN N11 * 48 B2
 HGT N6 ....66 A3
 KTN/HRWW/W HA3 ....62 A4
 NTHWD HA6 ....40 E5
 WALTH E17 ....52 B6
 WLGTN SM6 ....210 C5
The Hillside ORP BR6 ....217 H6
Hills La NTHWD HA6 ....40 C4
Hillsleigh Rd KENS W8 ....119 J1
Hills Ms EA W5 * 98 A6
Hills PI SOHO/CST W1F 10 A4
Hill's Rd BKHH IG9 ....39 F3
Hillstowe St CLPT E5 ....68 E6
Hill St MYFR/PICC W1J 9 J7
 RCHPK/HAM TW10 ....136 E6
Hilltop GLDGN NW11 ....65 F1
 MRDN SM4 ....193 J4
Hilltop WALTH E17 * 51 K6
Hill Top Vw WLSDN NW10 ....80 E5
Hilltop Gdns DART DA1 ....151 J4
 ORP BR6 ....201 K6
Hilltop Rd KIL/WHAMP NW6 ....82 E5
Hill Top Vw WFD IG8 * 53 K2
Hilltop Wy STAN HA7 ....29 G5
Hillview RYNPK SW20 ....176 E4
Hillview Av KTN/HRWW/W HA3 ....62 A2
Hillview CI PIN HA5 ....41 K2
Hill View Crs IL IG1 ....71 K3
Hillview Dr THMD SE28 ....127 K1
 WELL DA16 ....147 K3
Hillview Gdns CDALE/KGS NW9 ....63 F2
Hill View Gdns HDN NW4 ....64 B1
 PIN HA5 ....42 A6
Hill View Rd ESH/CLAY KT10 ....205 G5
 ORP BR6 ....202 A5
 TWK TW1 ....156 B1
Hillway CDALE/KGS NW9 ....63 G5
 HGT N6 ....66 A6
Hillworth BECK BR3 * 182 E5
Hillworth Rd BRXS/STRHM SW2 ....162 B2
Hillyard Rd HNWL W7 ....96 E4
Hillyard St BRXN/ST SW9 ....142 B2
Hillyfield CI HOM E9 ....87 G3
Hilly Flds BROCKY SE4 * 144 D5
Hilly Fields Crs BROCKY SE4 ....144 D5
Hilsea St CLPT E5 ....86 E2
Hilton Av NFNCH/WDSP N12 ....47 H1
Himalayan Wy WATW WD18 ....26 D1
Himley Rd TOOT SW17 ....178 D1
Hinchley CI ESH/CLAY KT10 ....205 F3
Hinchley Dr ESH/CLAY KT10 ....205 G3
Hinchley Wy ESH/CLAY KT10 ....205 G3
Hinckley Rd EDUL SE22 ....143 H5
Hind CI CHIG IG7 ....55 F1
Hind Ct FLST/FETLN EC4A * 11 K4
Hind Crs ERITH DA8 ....149 K1
Hinde Ms MHST W1U * 9 H3
Hinde St MHST W1U 9 H3
Hind Gv POP/IOD E14 ....105 J5
Hindhead Gdns NTHLT UB5 ....77 K6
Hindhead CI OXHEY WD19 ....41 G1
Hindhead Wy WLGTN SM6 ....210 E3
Hindmans Rd EDUL SE22 ....143 H6
Hindmarsh CI WCHPL E1 * 104 C6
Hindrey Rd CLPT E5 ....86 D3
Hindsley's PI FSTH SE23 ....163 K4
Hinkler Rd KTN/HRWW/W HA3 ....43 K6
Hinksey Pth ABYW SE2 ....128 E3
Hinstock Rd WOOL/PLUM SE18 ....147 H1
Hinton Av HSLWW TW4 ....134 C5
Hinton CI ELTH/MOT SE9 ....166 D3
Hinton Rd BRXN/ST SW9 ....142 C4
 UED N18 ....36 A6
 WLGTN SM6 ....210 C4

Hippodrome PI NTGHL W11 ....100 C6
Hirst Crs WBLY HA9 ....80 A1
Hitcham Rd WALTH E17 ....69 H4
Hitherbroom Rd HYS/HAR UB3 ....113 K1
Hither Farm Rd BKHTH/KID SE3 ....146 B4
Hitherfield Rd BCTR RM8 ....74 A6
 STRHM/NOR SW16 ....162 A4
Hither Green La LEW SE13 ....145 H6
Hitherwell Dr KTN/HRWW/W HA3 ....42 D4
Hitherwood Dr DUL SE21 ....163 G6
Hive Rd BUSH WD23 ....28 D4
Hoadly Rd STRHM/NOR SW16 ....161 J5
Hobart CI TRDG/WHET N20 ....33 J4
 YEAD UB4 ....95 H4
Hobart Dr YEAD UB4 ....95 H3
Hobart Gdns THHTH CR7 ....180 E6
Hobart La YEAD UB4 ....95 H3
Hobart PI BGVA SW1W 15 J5
 RCHPK/HAM TW10 ....157 G2
Hobart Rd BARK/HLT IG6 ....54 C5
 DAGW RM9 ....91 K2
 WPK KT4 ....207 K1
 YEAD UB4 ....95 H3
Hobbayne Rd HNWL W7 ....96 D5
Hobbes Wk PUT/ROE SW15 ....138 E6
Hobbs Gn EFNCH N2 ....47 G6
Hobbs PI IS N1 ....7 G1
Hobbs Place Est IS N1 * 7 G2
Hobbs Rd WNWD SE27 ....162 D6
Hobday St POP/IOD E14 ....105 K5
Hoblands End CHST BR7 ....185 K2
Hobsons PI WCHPL E1 * 104 C4
Hobury St WBPTN SW10 ....120 B6
Hockenden La SWLY BR8 ....187 H6
Hocker St BETH E2 * 7 J5
Hockley Av EHAM E6 ....107 J1
Hockley Dr GPK RM2 * 57 K5
Hockley Ms BARK IG11 ....108 E1
Hocroft Av CRICK NW2 ....82 D1
Hocroft Rd CRICK NW2 ....82 D2
Hocroft Wk CRICK NW2 ....82 D1
Hodder Dr GFD/PVL UB6 ....97 F1
Hoddesdon Rd BELV DA17 ....129 H5
Hodford Rd GLDGN NW11 ....64 D5
Hodges Wy WATW WD18 ....26 E1
Hodgkins CI THMD SE28 ....109 K6
Hodister CI CMBW SE5 ....142 D1
Hodnet Gv BERM/RHTH SE16 * 124 A4
Hodson CI RYLN/HDSTN HA2 ....77 K1
Hodson Crs STMC/STPC BR5 ....202 E3
Hodson PI PEND EN3 * 25 J1
Hoe La EN EN1 ....24 D1
Hoe St WALTH E17 ....69 J2
The Hoe OXHEY WD19 ....27 H4
Hoffman Gdns SAND/SEL CR2 ....212 D5
Hoffman Sq IS N1 * 7 F4
Hofland Rd WKENS W14 ....119 H3
Hogan Ms BAY/PAD W2 ....8 A1
Hogarth CI CAN/RD E16 ....107 H4
 EA W5 ....98 A4
Hogarth Gdns HEST TW5 ....135 F1
 WIM/MER SW19 ....178 C4
Hogarth HI GLDGN NW11 ....64 D1
Hogarth PI ECT SW5 * 120 A4
Hogarth Rd BCTR RM8 ....91 H5
 ECT SW5 ....120 A4
 EDGW HA8 ....44 C5
Hogarth Ter CHSWK W4 * 118 B6
Hogarth Wy HPTN TW12 ....173 H4
Hog Hill Rd CRW RM5 ....56 B3
Hogshead Pas WAP E1W * 104 D6
Hogsmill Wy HOR/WEW KT19 ....206 E3
Holbeach Gdns BFN/LL DA15 ....167 K1
Holbeach Rd CAT SE6 ....164 D2
Holbeck Rw PECK SE15 ....143 H1
Holbein Ga NTHWD HA6 ....40 C1
Holbein Ms BGVA SW1W 121 F5
Holbein PI BGVA SW1W 15 G7
Holberton Gdns WLSDN NW10 ....99 K2
Holborn HCIRC EC1N 11 J2
Holborn Circ HCIRC EC1N 11 K2
Holborn PI HHOL WC1V 11 G2
Holborn Rd PLSTW E13 ....107 F4
Holborn Viad HCIRC EC1N 11 K2
 STBT EC1A 11 J2
Holborn Wy MTCM CR4 ....178 E5
Holbrook CI EN EN1 ....24 B2
Holbrooke Ct HOLWY N7 ....84 E1
Holbrook La CHST BR7 ....185 J3
Holbrook Rd SRTFD E15 ....106 D1
Holbrook Wy HAYES BR2 ....200 E3
Holburne CI BKHTH/KID SE3 ....146 B2
Holburne Gdns BKHTH/KID SE3 ....146 C2
Holburne Rd BKHTH/KID SE3 ....146 B2
Holcombe HI MLHL NW7 ....31 J5
Holcombe Rd IL IG1 ....72 A6
 TOTM N17 ....50 B6
Holcombe St HMSMTH W6 ....118 E5
Holcote CI BELV DA17 ....129 F3
Holcroft Rd HOM E9 ....86 E5
Holden Av CDALE/KGS NW9 ....62 E5
 NFNCH/WDSP N12 ....47 F1
Holdenby Rd BROCKY SE4 ....144 B6
Holden CI BCTR RM8 ....91 H1
Holdenhurst Av FNCH N3 ....47 F3
Holden Rd NFNCH/WDSP N12 ....33 F6
Holden St BTSEA SW11 ....141 F3
Holdernesse Rd ISLW TW7 ....136 A1
 TOOT SW17 ....160 E5
Holderness Wy WNWD SE27 ....180 C1
Holders Hill Av HDN NW4 ....46 B5
Holders Hill Crs HDN NW4 ....46 B5
Holders Hill Dr HDN NW4 ....46 B6
Holders Hill Gdns HDN NW4 ....46 C5
Holders Hill Pde HDN NW4 * 46 C4
Holders Hill Rd HDN NW4 ....46 B5
Holford Ms FSBYW WC1X * 5 G4
Holford Rd HAMP NW3 ....83 G1
Holford St FSBYW WC1X 5 J4
Holford Yd IS N1 * 5 J3

Holgate Av BTSEA SW11 ....140 C4
Holgate Rd DAGE RM10 ....92 C3
Holgate St CHARL SE7 ....126 C3
Holland Av BELMT SM2 ....208 E5
 RYNPK SW20 ....176 C4
Holland CI BAR EN5 ....33 H2
 HAYES BR2 ....199 J6
 ROMW/RG RM7 ....74 E2
 STAN HA7 ....43 H1
Holland Dr FSTH SE23 ....164 B5
Holland Gdns BTFD TW8 ....117 G5
 WKENS W14 ....119 H3
Holland Gv BRXN/ST SW9 ....142 B1
Holland Pk KENS W8 ....119 J2
Holland Park Av GDMY/SEVK IG3 ....72 E3
 NTGHL W11 ....119 H1
Holland Park Gdns NTGHL W11 ....119 H1
Holland Park Ms NTCHL W11 ....119 J1
Holland Park Rd WKENS W14 ....119 J3
Holland Park Ter NTGHL W11 * 119 H1
Holland Pas IS N1 * 85 J6
Holland Rd KENS W8 ....120 A2
Holland Rd Chambers KENS W8 * 120 A2
Holland Rd ALP/SUD HA0 ....79 K4
 EHAM E6 ....89 K1
 SNWD SE25 ....197 H2
 SRTFD E15 ....106 C2
 WKENS W14 ....119 G2
 WLSDN NW10 ....81 J6
The Hollands WPK KT4 ....192 C5
Holland St KENS W8 ....119 K2
 STHWK SE1 ....12 B7
Holland Villas Rd WKENS W14 ....119 H2
Holland Wk STAN HA7 ....43 G1
Holland Wy HAYES BR2 ....199 J6
Hollar Rd STNW/STAM N16 ....86 B1
Hollen St SOHO/CST W1F 10 B3
Holles CI HPTN TW12 ....173 F2
Holles St CAVSQ/HST W1G 9 K3
Holley Rd ACT W3 ....118 B2
Hollickwood Av NFNCH/WDSP N12 ....47 K2
Holliday Sq BTSEA SW11 * 140 C4
Hollidge Wy DAGE RM10 ....92 D5
Hollies Av BFN/LL DA15 ....168 A4
Hollies CI STRHM/NOR SW16 ....180 B2
 TWK TW1 ....156 A4
Hollies End MLHL NW7 ....45 K1
Hollies Rd EA W5 ....116 D4
The Hollies KTN/HRWW/W HA3 * 61 G1
Hollies Wy BAL SW12 * 161 F2
Holligrave Rd BMLY BR1 ....183 K4
Hollingbourne Av BXLYHN DA7 ....149 G2
Hollingbourne Gdns WEA W13 ....97 H4
Hollingbourne Rd HNHL SE24 ....142 D6
Hollingsworth Rd SAND/SEL CR2 ....212 D4
Hollington Crs NWMAL KT3 ....192 C3
Hollington Rd EHAM E6 ....107 K2
 TOTM N17 ....50 D5
Hollingworth CI E/WMO/HCT KT8 ....188 E1
Hollingworth Rd STMC/STPC BR5 ....201 G4
Hollman Gdns STRHM/NOR SW16 ....180 C2
Holloway CI WDR/YW UB7 ....112 B5
Holloway La WDR/YW UB7 ....112 B6
Holloway Rd ARCH N19 ....66 D6
 EHAM E6 ....107 K2
 HOLWY N7 ....85 F2
 WAN E11 ....88 B1
Holloway St HSLW TW3 ....135 G4
The Hollow WFD IG8 ....38 D6
Holly Av STAN HA7 ....44 A5
 WOT/HER KT12 ....188 C5
Holly Bank MUSWH N10 * 66 C1
Hollybank CI HPTN TW12 ....173 F1
Hollybrake CI CHST BR7 ....185 J3
Hollybush CI HAMP NW3 ....83 G1
 WAN E11 ....70 E2
Hollybush Gdns BETH E2 ....104 D2
Hollybush HI WAN E11 ....70 D4
Holly Bush La HPTN TW12 ....172 E3
Hollybush PI BETH E2 ....104 D2
Hollybush Rd KUTN/CMB KT2 ....175 F1
Hollybush Ter NRWD SE19 * 181 F2
Holly Bush V HAMP NW3 ....83 G2
Holly CI BECK BR3 ....199 F1
 BKHH IG9 ....39 H5
 FELT TW13 ....172 E1
 WLSDN NW10 ....81 G5
Holly Crs BECK BR3 ....198 C2
 WFD IG8 ....52 B3
Hollycroft Av HAMP NW3 ....82 E1
 WBLY HA9 ....62 A6
Hollycroft CI SAND/SEL CR2 ....212 A3
 WDR/YW UB7 ....112 D6
Hollycroft Gdns WDR/YW UB7 ....112 D6
Hollydale CI NTHLT UB5 ....78 B3
Hollydale Dr HAYES BR2 ....215 K1
Hollydale Rd PECK SE15 ....143 K3
Hollydene HAYES BR2 * 88 B1
Holly Dr CHING E4 ....37 K2
Holly Farm Rd NWDGN UB2 ....114 D5
Hollyfield Av FBAR/BDGN N11 ....47 K1
Hollyfield Rd BRYLDS KT5 ....191 G4
Holly Gdns BXLYHN DA7 ....149 K5
 WDR/YW UB7 ....112 C2
Hollygrove BUSH WD23 ....28 D2
Holly Gv CDALE/KGS NW9 ....62 E4
 PECK SE15 ....143 G3
 PIN HA5 ....41 J4
Hollygrove CI HSLW TW3 ....134 E5
Holly Hedge Ter LEW SE13 ....145 H6
Holly HI HAMP NW3 ....83 G2
 WCHMH N21 ....35 F1
Holly Hill Rd BELV DA17 ....129 J5
Holly Lodge Gdns HGT N6 ....66 A6

Holly Ms WBPTN SW10 * 120 B5
Holly Mt HAMP NW3 * 83 G2
Hollymount CI GNWCH SE10 ....145 F2
Holly Pk FNCH N3 ....46 E6
 FSBYPK N4 ....66 E4
Holly Park Gdns FNCH N3 ....46 E6
Holly Park Rd FBAR/BDGN N11 ....48 A1
 HNWL W7 ....116 A1
Holly Rd CHSWK W4 * 118 A4
 DART DA1 ....171 G3
 HPTN TW12 ....173 H2
 HSLW TW3 ....135 G5
 ORP BR6 ....217 G5
 TWK TW1 ....156 B3
Holly St HACK E8 ....86 B5
Hollytree CI WIM/MER SW19 ....159 G3
Hollytree Pde SCUP DA14 * 186 D1
Hollyview CI HDN NW4 ....63 J3
Holly Vis HMSMTH W6 ....118 E3
Holly Wk HAMP NW3 ....83 G2
Holly Wy MTCM CR4 ....195 J1
Hollywood Gdns YEAD UB4 ....95 F5
Hollywood Ms WBPTN SW10 * 120 B6
Hollywood Rd CHING E4 ....51 G1
 WBPTN SW10 ....120 B6
Hollywoods CROY/NA CR0 ....213 H6
Hollywood Wy ERITH DA8 ....150 E2
 WFD IG8 ....52 B3
Holman Ct EW KT17 * 207 J6
Holman Rd BTSEA SW11 ....140 C3
 HOR/WEW KT19 ....206 E3
Holmbridge Gdns PEND EN3 ....25 F5
Holmbrook Dr HDN NW4 ....64 B2
Holmbury Ct TOOT SW17 ....160 E5
Holmbury Gv CROY/NA CR0 ....213 H5
Holmbury Mnr SCUP DA14 * 168 B6
Holmbury Pk CHST BR7 ....184 D3
Holmbury Vw CLPT E5 ....68 D5
Holmbush Rd PUT/ROE SW15 ....159 H1
Holmcote Gdns HBRY N5 ....85 J3
Holmcroft Wy HAYES BR2 ....200 E2
Holmdale Gdns HDN NW4 ....64 B2
Holmdale Rd CHST BR7 ....185 H1
 KIL/WHAMP NW6 ....82 E4
Holmdale Ter SEVS/STOTM N15 ....68 A3
Holmdene Av HNHL SE24 ....142 D6
 MLHL NW7 ....45 J2
 RYLN/HDSTN HA2 ....42 B6
Holmdene CI BECK BR3 ....183 F5
Holmdene Ct BMLY BR1 ....184 D6
Holmead Rd FUL/PGN SW6 ....140 A1
Holmebury CI BUSH WD23 * 28 E4
Holme Lacey Rd LEE/GVPK SE12 ....165 J1
Holme Rd EHAM E6 ....89 J6
Holmes Av MLHL NW7 ....46 C1
 WALTH E17 ....51 H6
Holmes CI EDUL SE22 ....143 H5
Holmesdale Av MORT/ESHN SW14 ....137 J4
 CROY/NA CR0 ....196 E2
 HGT N6 ....66 A4
 RCH/KEW TW9 ....137 G2
 SNWD SE25 ....197 F1
 TEDD TW11 ....174 D3
Holmesley Rd BROCKY SE4 ....164 B1
Holmes Rd KTTN NW5 ....84 B4
 TWK TW1 ....156 B3
 WIM/MER SW19 ....178 B3
Holmes Ter STHWK SE1 ....17 J2
Holme Wy STAN HA7 ....43 F2
Holmewood Gdns BRXS/STRHM SW2 ....162 A2
Holmewood Rd BRXS/STRHM SW2 ....161 K2
 SNWD SE25 ....181 F6
Holmfield Av HDN NW4 ....64 B2
Holmhurst Rd BELV DA17 ....129 J5
Holmleigh Av DART DA1 ....151 F5
Holmleigh Rd STNW/STAM N16 ....68 A5
Holm Oak CI PUT/ROE SW15 ....159 J1
Holmsdale CI BXLYHN DA7 ....150 B3
Holmshaw CI SYD SE26 ....164 B6
Holmside Rd BAL SW12 ....161 F1
Holmsley CI NWMAL KT3 ....192 C3
Holmstall Av EDGW HA8 ....44 E5
Holmstall Pde EDGW HA8 * 44 E5
Holmwood CI BELMT SM2 ....208 B6
 NTHLT UB5 ....78 B4
 RYLN/HDSTN HA2 ....42 C6
Holmwood Gdns FNCH N3 ....46 E5
 WLGTN SM6 ....210 B4
Holmwood Gv MLHL NW7 ....45 F1
Holmwood Rd BELMT SM2 ....208 A6
 CHSGTN KT9 ....206 A3
 GDMY/SEVK IG3 ....73 G1
Holne Cha EFNCH N2 ....65 G3
 MRDN SM4 ....193 K3
Holness Rd SRTFD E15 ....88 D4
Holroyd Rd ESH/CLAY KT10 ....205 G6
 PUT/ROE SW15 ....139 F5
Holstein Wy ERITH DA18 ....128 E3
Holstock Rd IL IG1 ....72 C6
Holsworth CI RYLN/HDSTN HA2 ....60 C2
Holsworthy Sq FSBYW WC1X 5 H7
Holsworthy Wy CHSGTN KT9 ....205 J3
Holt CI CHIG IG7 ....55 F1
 MUSWH N10 ....66 A2
 THMD SE28 ....109 H6
Holton St WCHPL E1 ....105 F3
Holt Rd ALP/SUD HA0 ....79 H1
 CAN/RD E16 ....126 D1
The Holt BARK/HLT IG6 ....54 C2
 MRDN SM4 * 193 K1
 WLGTN SM6 ....210 C2
Holt Wy CHIG IG7 ....55 F1
Holtwhite Av ENC/FH EN2 ....23 J3
Holtwhite's HI ENC/FH EN2 ....23 H2
Holwell PI PIN HA5 ....59 J1
Holwood CI WOT/HER KT12 * 188 B6

Holwood Park Av ORP BR6 ....215 K2
Holwood PI CLAP SW4 ....141 J5
Holybourne Av PUT/ROE SW15 ....158 D2
Holyhead CI BOW E3 ....105 J2
Holyoake Ct BERM/RHTH SE16 ....124 B2
Holyoake Wk EA W5 ....97 J3
 EFNCH N2 ....47 G6
Holyoak Rd LBTH SE11 ....18 A6
Holyport Rd FUL/PGN SW6 ....139 F1
Holyrood Av RYLN/HDSTN HA2 ....77 J2
Holyrood Gdns EDGW HA8 ....44 D5
Holyrood Rd BAR EN5 ....33 F1
Holyrood St STHWK SE1 ....19 G1
Holywell CI BERM/RHTH SE16 * 123 J5
 BKHTH/KID SE3 ....125 K6
 ORP BR6 ....217 G2
 STWL/WRAY TW19 ....152 B3
Holywell La SDTCH EC2A 7 H5
Holywell Rw SDTCH EC2A 7 G7
Holywell Wy STWL/WRAY TW19 ....152 B3
Home CI CAR SM5 ....194 E6
 NTHLT UB5 ....95 K2
Home Ct FELT TW13 * 153 K3
 SURB KT6 * 190 E2
Homecroft Rd SYD SE26 ....181 K1
Home Farm CI ESH/CLAY KT10 ....204 B4
 THDIT KT7 ....190 A4
Home Farm Gdns WOT/HER KT12 ....188 B6
Homefarm Rd HNWL W7 ....96 E5
Homefield Av GNTH/NBYPK IG2 ....72 E2
Homefield CI STMC/STPC BR5 ....202 C1
 WLSDN NW10 ....80 E4
 YEAD UB4 ....95 H3
Homefield Gdns EFNCH N2 ....47 H6
 WIM/MER SW19 ....178 B5
Homefield Ms BECK BR3 ....182 D4
Homefield Pk SUT SM1 ....209 F4
Homefield Ri ORP BR6 ....202 B5
Homefield Rd ALP/SUD HA0 ....79 G2
 BMLY BR1 ....184 B4
 CHSWK W4 ....118 C4
 EDGW HA8 ....45 F2
 WIM/MER SW19 ....177 H2
 WOT/HER KT12 ....188 E4
Homefield St IS N1 * 7 G3
The Homefield MRDN SM4 * 193 K1
Home Gdns DAGE RM10 ....92 E1
 DART DA1 ....171 H1
Homeland Dr BELMT SM2 ....209 F6
Homelands Dr NRWD SE19 ....181 F3
Home Lea ORP BR6 ....217 F3
Homeleigh Rd PECK SE15 ....144 A6
Home Md STAN HA7 ....43 J4
Homemead CROY/NA CR0 ....195 H3
 BAL SW12 ....161 G4
Home Park Ct KUT/HW KT1 * 190 E1
Home Park Rd WIM/MER SW19 ....159 J6
Home Park Ter KUT/HW KT1 ....174 E5
Home Park Wk SURB KT6 ....190 E1
Homer CI BXLYHN DA7 ....149 K2
Homer Dr POP/IOD E14 ....124 D4
Home Rd BTSEA SW11 ....140 D3
Homer Rd CROY/NA CR0 ....198 A3
 HOM E9 ....87 G4
Homer Rw CAMTN NW1 ....8 D2
Homersham Rd KUT/HW KT1 ....175 H5
Homerton High St HOM E9 ....87 F3
Homerton Rd HOM E9 ....87 H3
Homerton Rw HOM E9 ....86 E3
Homerton Ter HOM E9 ....86 E4
Homesdale CI WAN E11 ....70 E2
Homesdale Rd HAYES BR2 ....200 B1
 ORP BR6 ....201 K4
Homesfield GLDGN NW11 ....64 E2
Homestall Rd EDUL SE22 ....143 K6
Homestead Gdns ESH/CLAY KT10 ....204 E3
Homestead Paddock STHGT/OAK N14 ....22 B6
Homestead Pk CRICK NW2 ....81 H1
Homestead Rd BCTR RM8 ....74 B6
 FUL/PGN SW6 ....139 J1
 ORP BR6 ....217 H5
The Homestead DART DA1 ....150 D6
Homewillow CI WCHMH N21 ....35 H1
Homewood CI HPTN TW12 ....172 E2
Homewood Crs CHST BR7 ....185 K2
Homewood Gdns SNWD SE25 * 197 F2
Honduras St FSBYE EC1V 6 C6
Honeybourne Rd KIL/WHAMP NW6 ....83 F3
Honeybourne Wy STMC/STPC BR5 ....201 H5
Honeybrook Rd BAL SW12 ....161 H2
Honey CI DAGE RM10 ....92 E4
Honeycroft HI CROY/NA CR0 ....198 A4
Honeyden Rd SCUP DA14 ....187 F2
Honeyman CI CRICK NW2 ....82 B5
Honeypot CI KTN/HRWW/W HA3 ....62 B1
Honeypot La CDALE/KGS NW9 ....62 B1
 STAN HA7 ....43 K4
Honeysett Rd TOTM N17 * 50 B5
Honeysuckle CI STHL UB1 ....95 J6
Honeysuckle Gdns CROY/NA CR0 ....198 A4
Honeywell Rd BTSEA SW11 ....160 D1
Honeywood Rd ISLW TW7 ....136 B5
 WLSDN NW10 ....99 H1
Honeywood Wk CAR SM5 ....209 K2
Honister CI STAN HA7 ....43 H4
Honister Gdns STAN HA7 ....43 H3
Honister PI STAN HA7 ....43 H4
Honiton Gdns PECK SE15 * 143 K3
Honiton Rd KIL/WHAMP NW6 ....100 D1
 ROMW/RG RM7 ....75 F3
 WELL DA16 ....148 A3

Honley Rd CAT SE6 ....164 E2
Honnor Gdns ISLW TW7 ....135 J3
Honor Oak Pk FSTH SE23 ....163 K2
Honor Oak Rd FSTH SE23 ....163 K3
Honor Oak Rd FSTH SE23 ....163 K5
Hood Av MORT/ESHN SW14 ...137 K6
  STHGT/OAK N14 ....34 B1
  STMC/STPC BR5 ....202 C2
Hoodcote Gdns WCHMH N21 ...35 H2
Hood Rd RAIN RM13 ....93 G6
  RYNPK SW20 ....176 C3
Hood Wk ROMW/RG RM7 ....56 D4
Hooker's Rd WALTH E17 ....51 F6
Hook Farm Rd HAYES BR2 ....200 C2
Hook Green La RDART DA2 ....190 D5
Hooking Gn RYLN/HDSTN HA2 ...60 A3
Hook La WELL DA16 ....148 A6
Hook Ri North SURB KT6 ....206 C1
Hook Ri South CHSGTN KT9 ...206 B1
Hook Rd CHSGTN KT9 ....205 K3
  HOR/WEW KT19 ....206 E6
  SURB KT6 ....191 F6
Hooks Hall Dr DAGE RM10 ...92 E1
Hookstone Wy WFD IG8 ....53 H3
The Hook BAR EN5 ....33 H1
Hook Underpass (Kingston
  By-Pass) SURB KT6 ...205 K1
Hooper Rd CAN/RD E16 ....106 E5
Hooper's Ms ACT W3 ....117 K1
  BUSH WD23 ....28 B3
Hooper St WCHPL E1 ....104 C6
Hope La GLDGN NW11 ....64 D4
Hope Cl BTFD TW8 ....117 F5
  CHDH RM6 ....73 K1
  IS N1 ....85 J4
  LEE/GVPK SE12 ....166 A5
  SUT SM1 ....209 G3
Hopedale Rd CHARL SE7 ....126 A6
Hopefield Av
  KIL/WHAMP NW6 ....100 C1
Hope Gdns ACT W3 ....117 J2
Hope Pk BMLY BR1 ....183 J3
Hope Cl HEST TW5 ....115 F6
Hope St BTSEA SW11 ....140 C4
Hopetown St WCHPL E1 * ...13 K2
Hopewell St CMBW SE5 ...142 E1
Hopewell Yd CMBW SE5 ...142 E1
Hop Gdns CHCR WC2N 10 E6
Hopgood St SHB W12 ....119 F1
Hopkins Cl MUSWH N10 ...48 B3
Hopkins Ms SRTFD E15 ....88 D6
Hopkinsons Pl CAMTN NW1 * ...83 K6
Hoppers Rd WCHMH N21 ...35 G4
Hoppett Rd CHING E4 ....38 C5
Hopping La IS N1 * 85 H4
Hoppingwood Av NWMAL KT3 ...176 B6
Hoppner Rd YEAD UB4 ....94 B1
Hopton Gdns NWMAL KT3 ...192 D5
Hopton Pde
  STRHM/NOR SW16 * ...179 K1
Hopton Rd STRHM/NOR SW16 ...179 K1
  WOOL/PLUM SE18 ....127 G3
Hoptons Gdns STHWK SE1 * ...12 B7
Hopton St STHWK SE1 ....12 B7
Hopwood Cl TOOT SW17 ....160 B5
Hopwood Rd WALW SE17 ....122 E6
Hopwood Wk HACK E8 * 86 C5
Horace Av ROMW/RG RM7 ...75 F5
Horace Rd BARK/HLT IG6 ...54 C6
  FSTGT E7 ....89 F2
  KUT/HW KT1 ....175 G6
Horatio Pl POP/IOD E14 ....125 F2
  POP/IOD E14 ....7 K3
Horatius Wy CROY/NA CRO ...211 F4
Horbury Crs NTGHL W11 ....100 E6
Horbury Ms NTGHL W11 ....100 D6
Horder Rd FUL/PGN SW6 ...139 H2
Hordle Prom East PECK SE15 ...143 G1
Hordle Prom North PECK SE15 ...143 F1
Hordle Prom West PECK SE15 ...143 G1
Horley Cl BXLYHS DA6 ....149 H6
Horley Rd ELTH/MOT SE9 ...166 D6
Hormead Rd MV/WKIL W9 ...100 D3
Hornbeam Cl BIL IG1 ....90 D3
  LBTH SE11 ....17 J6
  MLHL NW7 ....31 H5
Hornbeam Crs BTFD TW8 ....136 C1
Hornbeam Gv CHING E4 ....38 C5
Hornbeam La BKHH IG9 ....39 H5
  YEAD UB4 ....95 G3
Hornbeam Sq BOW E3 * ...87 H6
Hornbeams Ri FBAR/BDGN N11 ...48 A2
Hornbeam Wy HAYES BR2 ...201 F3
Hornbuckle Cl
  RYLN/HDSTN HA2 ....60 D6
Hornby Cl HAMP NW3 ....83 H5
Horncastle Cl LEE/GVPK SE12 ...165 K1
Horncastle Rd LEE/GVPK SE12 ...165 K1
Hornchurch Cl KUTN/CMB KT2 ...174 E1
Hornchurch Rd EMPK RM11 ...75 K5
Horndean Cl PUT/ROE SW15 ...158 D3
Horndon Cl CRW RM5 ....56 E4
Horndon Gn CRW RM5 ....56 E4
Horndon Rd CRW RM5 ....56 E4
Horne House
  WOOL/PLUM SE18 ....146 D2
Horner La MTCM CR4 ....178 C5
Horne Wy PUT/ROE SW15 ...139 F3
Hornfair Rd CHARL SE7 ....126 C6
Hornford Wy ROMW/RG RM7 ...75 F4
Horniman Dr FSTH SE23 ...163 J3
Horning Cl ELTH/MOT SE9 ...166 D6
Horn La ACT W3 ....98 E5
  GNWCH SE10 ....125 K4
  WFD IG8 ....52 E2
Horn Link Wy GNWCH SE10 ...125 K4
Horn Park Cl LEE/GVPK SE12 ...146 A6
Horn Park La LEE/GVPK SE12 ...146 A6

Horns End Pl PIN HA5 ....59 G1
Hornsey Chambers CLPT E5 * ...68 D6
Hornsey La HGT N6 ....66 C4
Hornsey La East ARCH N19 ...66 D4
Hornsey Lane Gdns HGT N6 ...66 C4
Hornsey Park Rd
  CEND/HSY/T N8 ....49 F6
Hornsey Ri ARCH N19 ....66 D4
Hornsey Rd ARCH N19 ....66 C3
Hornsey Rise Gdns ARCH N19 ...66 D4
Hornsey St HOLWY N7 ....85 F3
Hornshay St PECK SE15 ...123 K6
Horns Rd BARK/HLT IG6 ...72 C2
Hornton Pl KENS W8 ....119 K2
Hornton St KENS W8 ....119 K2
Horsa Rd ERITH DA8 ....149 K1
  LEE/GVPK SE12 ....166 B2
Horsebridges Cl DAGW RM9 ...92 A6
Horsecroft Cl ORP BR6 ....202 C5
Horsecroft Rd EDGW HA8 ...45 F3
Horse Fair KUT/HW KT1 ....174 E5
Horseferry Pl GNWCH SE10 ...125 F6
Horseferry Rd POP/IOD E14 ...105 G6
  WEST SW1P 16 C5
Horse Guards Av WHALL SW1A ...16 E1
Horse Guards Rd WHALL SW1A ...16 D1
Horse Leaze EHAM E6 ....108 B5
Horsell Rd HBRY N5 ....85 G3
  STMC/STPC BR5 ....186 B4
Horselydown La STHWK SE1 ...19 J2
Horsenden Av GFD/PVL UB6 ...78 E3
Horsenden Crs GFD/PVL UB6 ...79 F3
Horsenden La North
  GFD/PVL UB6 ....78 E4
Horsenden La South
  GFD/PVL UB6 ....79 G6
Horseshoe Cl CRICK NW2 ...63 K6
  POP/IOD E14 ....125 F5
Horse Shoe Crs NTHLT UB5 ...96 A1
Horseshoe La ENC/FH EN2 ...23 J4
  TRDG/WHET N20 ....32 B3
Horseshoe Ms
  BRXS/STRHM SW2 ....141 K5
Horse Yd IS N1 * 85 H6
Horsfeld Gdns ELTH/MOT SE9 ...146 D6
Horsfeld Rd ELTH/MOT SE9 ...146 C6
Horsford Rd
  BRXS/STRHM SW2 ....142 A6
Horsham Av NFNCH/WDSP N12 ...47 J1
Horsham Rd BXLYHS DA6 ...149 H6
  EBED/NFELT TW14 ....153 F1
Horsley Dr CROY/NA CRO ...214 A5
  KUTN/CMB KT2 ....174 E1
Horsley Rd BMLY BR1 ....184 A4
  CHING E4 ....38 A4
Horsley St WALW SE17 ....122 E6
Horsmans Pl DART DA1 * ...171 H2
Horsman St CMBW SE5 ....122 D6
Horsmonden Cl ORP BR6 ....201 K4
Horsmonden Rd BROCKY SE4 ...144 C6
Hortensia Rd WBPTN SW10 ...120 B6
Horticultural Pl CHSWK W4 ...118 A5
Horton Av CRICK NW2 ....82 C2
Horton Bridge Rd
  WDR/YW UB7 ....112 C1
Horton La HOR/WEW KT19 ...206 E6
Horton Pde WDR/YW UB7 * ...112 B1
Horton Rd HACK E8 ....86 D4
  WDR/YW UB7 ....112 B1
Horton St LEW SE13 ....144 E4
Horton Wy CROY/NA CRO ...198 A2
Hortus Rd NWDGN UB2 ....114 E2
Hosack Rd BAL SW12 ....160 C4
Hoser Av LEE/GVPK SE12 ...165 K4
Hosier La STBT EC1A 12 A2
Hoskins Cl CAN/RD E16 ....107 G5
  HYS/HAR UB3 ....113 J5
Hoskins St GNWCH SE10 ...125 G5
Hospital Bridge Rd WHTN TW2 ...155 G4
Hospital Rd HEST TW5 ....135 F4
Hospital Wy LEW SE13 ....165 G1
Hotham Cl E/WMO/HCT KT8 ...173 F6
Hotham Rd PUT/ROE SW15 ...139 F4
  WIM/MER SW19 ....178 B3
Hotham St SRTFD E15 ....88 C6
Hothfield Pl BERM/RHTH SE16 ...123 K3
Hotspur Rd NTHLT UB5 ....96 A1
Hotspur St LBTH SE11 ....17 J7
Houblon Rd
  RCHPK/HAM TW10 ....137 F6
Houghton Cl HACK E8 * ...86 B4
Houghton Rd SEVS/STOTM N15 ...68 B1
Houghton St HOL/ALD WC2B * ...11 H4
Houlder Crs CROY/NA CRO ...211 H4
Hounsden Rd WCHMH N21 ...35 F1
Houndsfield Rd ED N9 ....36 D2
Hounslow Av HSLW TW3 ...135 G6
Hounslow Gdns HSLW TW3 ...135 G6
Hounslow Rd
  EBED/NFELT TW14 ....154 A2
  FELT TW13 ....154 C4
  HSLW TW3 ....135 G6
Houseman Wy CMBW SE5 ...142 E1
Houston Rd FSTH SE23 ....164 B4
  SURB KT6 ....190 C4
Hove Av WALTH E17 ....69 H2
Hoveden Rd CRICK NW2 ....82 C3
Hovenden Wy BARK/HLT IG6 ...54 B3
Hoveton Rd THMD SE28 ....109 J5
Hoveton Wy WFD IG8 ....53 H3
Howard Av BXLY DA5 ....168 E3
Howard Cl ACT W3 ....98 D5
  BUSH WD23 ....28 E2
  CRICK NW2 * 82 C2
  FBAR/BDGN N11 ....34 A4
  HPTN TW12 ....173 H1
  LOU IG10 ....39 J1
Howard Rd BARK IG11 ....90 D6
  BMLY BR1 ....183 K3
  BRYLDS KT5 ....191 G3
  CRICK NW2 ....82 B2
  DART DA1 ....171 K1
  EHAM E6 ....107 K1

IL IG1 ....90 B2
  ISLW TW7 ....136 A4
  NWMAL KT3 ....176 B6
  PGE/AN SE20 ....181 K4
  SEVS/STOTM N15 ....68 A3
  SNWD SE25 ....197 H2
  STHL UB1 ....96 B5
  STNW/STAM N16 ....85 K2
  WALTH E17 ....51 J6
Howards Cl PIN HA5 * 41 F5
Howards Crest Cl BECK BR3 ...183 F5
Howard's La PUT/ROE SW15 ...139 F5
Howard's Rd PLSTW E13 ....106 E2
Howard St THDIT KT7 ....190 C4
Howards Yd
  WAND/EARL SW18 ....160 A2
Howard Wk EFNCH N2 ....65 G1
Howarth Rd ABYW SE2 ....128 B5
Howberry Cl EDGW HA8 ....43 K2
Howberry Rd EDGW HA8 ....43 K3
  THHTH CR7 ....180 E4
Howbury La ERITH DA8 ....150 D3
Howbury Rd PECK SE15 ...143 K4
Howcroft Crs FNCH N3 ....46 E3
Howcroft La GFD/PVL UB6 ...96 D2
Howden Cl THMD SE28 ....109 J6
Howden Rd SNWD SE25 ....181 G5
Howden St PECK SE15 ....143 H4
Howe Cl ROMW/RG RM7 ....56 C4
Howell Cl CHDH RM6 ....73 K2
Howell Wk WALW SE17 ....18 B7
Howerd Wy WOOL/PLUM SE18 ...146 D2
Howfield Pl TOTM N17 * 50 B6
Howgate Rd
  MORT/ESHN SW14 ....138 A4
Howick Pl WEST SW1P 16 B5
Howie St BTSEA SW11 ....140 D1
Howitt Cl HAMP NW3 * 83 J4
  STNW/STAM N16 ....86 A1
Howitt Rd HAMP NW3 ....83 J4
Howland Ct PIN HA5 * 42 A2
Howland Ms East FITZ W1T ...10 B1
Howland St FITZ W1T 10 B1
Howland Wy
  BERM/RHTH SE16 ....124 B2
Howletts La RSLP HA4 ....58 A3
Howletts Rd HNHL SE24 ....162 D1
Howley Pl BAY/PAD W2 ....101 G4
Howley Rd CROY/NA CRO ...211 H1
Howsman Rd BARN SW13 ...118 D6
Howson Rd BROCKY SE4 ...144 B5
Howson Ter
  RCHPK/HAM TW10 ....157 F1
How's St BETH E2 ....7 J2
Howton Pl BUSH WD23 ....28 D3
Hoxton Market IS N1 ....7 G5
Hoxton Sq IS N1 ....7 G5
Hoxton St IS N1 ....7 G4
Hoylake Gdns MTCM CR4 ...179 H6
  OXHEY WD19 ....27 H6
  RSLP HA4 ....59 H1
Hoylake Rd ACT W3 ....99 G5
Hoyland Cl PECK SE15 ....143 J1
Hoyle Rd TOOT SW17 ....178 D1
Hoy St CAN/RD E16 ....106 D5
Hubbard Dr CHSGTN KT9 ...205 J4
Hubbard Rd WNWD SE27 ...162 D6
Hubbard St SRTFD E15 ....88 C6
Hubert Cl WIM/MER SW19 * ...178 B4
Hubert Gv BRXN/ST SW9 ...141 K4
Hubert Rd EHAM E6 ....107 H2
  RAIN RM13 ....111 H2
Huddart St BOW E3 ....105 H4
Huddleston Cl BETH E2 * ...104 E1
Huddlestone Rd CRICK NW2 ...81 K4
  FSTGT E7 ....88 D2
Huddleston Rd ARCH N19 ...84 C1
Hudson Cl SHB W12 * 99 K6
Hudson Pl WOOL/PLUM SE18 ...127 H5
Hudson Rd BXLYHN DA7 ...149 G3
  HYS/HAR UB3 ....113 G6
Huggin Hl BLKFR EC4V 12 D5
Huggins Pl BRXS/STRHM SW2 ...162 A3
Hughan Rd SRTFD E15 ....88 B3
Hugh Dalton Av FUL/PGN SW6 ...119 J6
Hughenden Av
  KTN/HRWW/W HA3 ....61 H2
Hughenden Gdns NTHLT UB5 ...95 G3
Hughenden Rd WPK KT4 ...192 D4
Hughes Rd HYS/HAR UB3 ...95 F6
Hughes Ter CAN/RD E16 * ...106 D4
Hughes Wk CROY/NA CRO ...196 D4
Hugh Gaitskell Cl
  FUL/PGN SW6 ....119 J6
Hugh Ms PIM SW1V 15 K7
Hugh Pl WEST SW1P 16 C6
Hugh St PIM SW1V 15 K7
Hugo Gdns RAIN RM13 ....93 H4
Hugo Rd ARCH N19 ....84 C2
Huguenot Pl
  WAND/EARL SW18 ....140 B6
  WCHPL E1 ....13 K1
Hullbridge Ms IS N1 * 85 K5
Hull Cl BERM/RHTH SE16 ...124 A1
Hull St FSBYE EC1V 6 C5
Hulme Pl STHWK SE1 ....18 D3
Hulse Av BARK IG11 ....90 D4
  ROMW/RG RM7 ....56 D1
Hulsewood Cl RDART DA2 ...170 C5
Humber Dr NKENS W10 ....100 B3
Humber Rd BKHTH/KID SE3 ...125 H6
  CRICK NW2 ....63 K6
  DART DA1 ....171 H6
Humberstone Rd PLSTW E13 ...107 G2
Humbolt Rd HMSMTH W6 ...119 H6
Humes Av HNWL W7 ....116 A3
Hume Wy RSLP HA4 ....58 E3
Humphrey Cl CLAY IG5 * 53 K4
Humphries Cl DAGW RM9 ...92 B2
Hundred Acre CDALE/KGS NW9 ...45 H5
Hungerdown CHING E4 ....38 A3

Hungerford Br STHWK SE1 ...11 G7
Hungerford Rd HOLWY N7 ...84 E3
Hungerford St WCHPL E1 * ...104 D5
Hunsdon Cl DAGW RM9 ....92 A4
Hunsdon Rd NWCR SE14 ...144 A1
Hunslett St BETH E2 * 104 E1
Hunston Rd MRDN SM4 ...194 A5
Hunt Cl BKHTH/KID SE3 * ...145 K3
  NTGHL W11 ....119 G1
Hunter Cl BAL SW12 ....161 F3
  STHWK SE1 ....19 F5
  WLGTN SM6 ....210 E6
Hunter Ct CMBW SE5 * ...142 E5
Huntercombe Gdns
  OXHEY WD19 ....41 G1
Hunter Rd RYNPK SW20 ...177 F4
  THHTH CR7 ....180 E6
  IL IG1 ....90 B5
Hunters Cl RCH/KEW TW9 ...136 E6
Hunter's Gv CRW RM5 ....56 D1
  HYS/HAR UB3 ....113 K1
  KTN/HRWW/W HA3 ....61 J1
Hunters Hall Rd DAGE RM10 ...92 C2
Hunters Hl RSLP HA4 ....77 G1
Hunters Meadow NRWD SE19 ...163 F6
Hunters Rd CHSGTN KT9 ...206 A1
  IL IG1 ....90 B5
Hunters Sq DAGE RM10 ...92 C2
Hunter St BMSBY WC1N 5 F6
Hunters Wy CROY/NA CRO ...212 A2
  ENC/FH EN2 ....23 G2
Huntingdon Cl ESH/CLAY KT10 ...204 A2
Huntingdon Ct
  MORT/ESHN SW14 ....137 K1
Huntingdon Gdns
  CHSWK W4 ....137 K1
  WPK KT4 ....208 A1
Huntingdon Rd ED N9 ....36 E3
  EFNCH N2 ....47 J6
Huntingdon St CAN/RD E16 ...106 D5
  IS N1 ....85 F5
Huntingfield CROY/NA CRO ...213 H5
Huntingfield Rd
  PUT/ROE SW15 ....138 D5
Hunting Gate Cl ENC/FH EN2 ...23 G4
Hunting Gate Dr CHSGTN KT9 ...206 A5
Hunting Gate Ms WHTN TW2 * ...155 K3
Huntings Rd DAGE RM10 ...92 C4
Huntley Cl STWL/WRAY TW19 ...152 B2
Huntley St GWRST WC1E 4 B7
Huntley Wy RYNPK SW20 ...176 D5
Huntly Dr FNCH N3 ....46 E2
Huntly Rd SNWD SE25 ....197 F1
Hunton St WCHPL E1 ....104 C4
Hunt's Cl BKHTH/KID SE3 ...145 K3
Hunt's La SRTFD E15 ....106 A1
Huntsman Cl FELT TW13 ...154 A6
Huntsman Rd BARK/HLT IG6 ...55 H2
Huntsman St WALW SE17 ...19 G7
Hunts Md PEND EN3 ....25 F4
Hunts Mede Cl CHST BR7 ...184 E3
Huntsmoor Rd
  HOR/WEW KT19 ....207 F3
Huntspill St TOOT SW17 ...160 B5
Hunts Slip Rd DUL SE21 ...163 F5
Huntsworth Ms CAMTN NW1 * ...2 E6
Hurdwick Pl CAMTN NW1 * ...4 A2
Hurley Cl WOT/HER KT12 ...188 A6
Hurley Rd GFD/PVL UB6 ....96 B3
Hurlfield RDART DA2 ....171 F5
Hurlingham Gdns
  FUL/PGN SW6 ....139 J4
Hurlingham Pk
  FUL/PGN SW6 ....139 J3
Hurlingham Rd BXLYHN DA7 ...149 G1
  FUL/PGN SW6 ....139 J3
Hurlingham Sq
  FUL/PGN SW6 ....139 K4
Hurlock St HBRY N5 ....85 H1
Hurlstone Rd SNWD SE25 ...196 E2
Hurn Court Rd HEST TW5 ...134 C3
Huron Cl ORP BR6 ....216 E4
Huron Rd TOOT SW17 ....161 F4
Hurren Cl BKHTH/KID SE3 ...145 H4
Hurricane Rd WLGTN SM6 ...211 F5
Hurry Cl SRTFD E15 ....88 C5
Hursley Rd CHIG IG7 ....55 F1
Hurst Av CHING E4 ....37 J5
  HGT N6 ....66 C3
Hurstbourne Gdns BARK IG11 ...90 E4
Hurstbourne Rd FSTH SE23 ...164 B3
Hurst Cl CHING E4 ....37 J5
  CHSGTN KT9 ....206 C3
  GLDGN NW11 ....65 F3
  HAYES BR2 ....199 J5
  NTHLT UB5 ....77 K4
Hurstcourt Rd SUT SM1 ...194 A5
Hurstdene Av HAYES BR2 ...199 J5
Hurstdene Gdns
  SEVS/STOTM N15 ....68 A4
Hurstfield HAYES BR2 ....199 K2
Hurstfield Crs YEAD UB4 ....94 C4
Hurstfield Rd
  E/WMO/HCT KT8 ....173 F6
Hurst La ABYW SE2 ....128 E5
  E/WMO/HCT KT8 ....189 H1
Hurstleigh Gdns CLAY IG5 ...53 K4
Hurst Pl ABYW SE2 ....128 D5
Hurst Ri BAR EN5 ....20 E4
Hurst Rd BFN/LL DA15 ....168 C4
  BXLY DA5 ....169 F3
  CROY/NA CRO 211 K3
  E/WMO/HCT KT8 ....173 K6
  EBAR EN4 ....21 K6
  ERITH DA8 ....150 A1
  SUT SM1 ....209 G1
  WALTH E17 ....52 B2
Hurst Springs BXLY DA5 ...169 F3
Hurst St HNHL SE24 ....162 C1
Hurst View Rd SAND/SEL CR2 ...212 A5
Hurst Wy SAND/SEL CR2 ...212 A4
Hurstway Rd NTGHL W11 * ...100 B6

Hurstwood Av BXLY DA5 ...169 F3
  ERITH DA8 ....150 B2
  SWFD E18 ....71 F1
Hurstwood Dr BMLY BR1 ...184 E1
Hurstwood Rd GLDGN NW11 ...64 C1
Hurtwood Rd WOT/HER KT12 ...188 D4
Huson Cl HAMP NW3 ....83 J5
Hussain Cl HRW HA1 ....79 F2
Hussars Cl HSLWW TW4 ...134 D4
Husseywell Crs HAYES BR2 ...199 K5
Hutchings St POP/IOD E14 ...124 D2
Hutchings Wk GLDGN NW11 ...65 F1
Hutchins Cl SRTFD E15 ....88 A5
Hutchinson Ter WBLY HA9 ...79 K3
Hutchins Rd THMD SE28 ...109 G6
Hutton Cl GFD/PVL UB6 ....78 D3
  WFD IG8 ....53 F2
Hutton Gv NFNCH/WDSP N12 ...47 F1
Hutton La KTN/HRWW/W HA3 ...42 C3
Hutton Rw EDGW HA8 ....44 E3
Hutton St EMB EC4Y 11 K4
Hutton Wk KTN/HRWW/W HA3 ...42 C3
Huxbear St BROCKY SE4 ...164 C1
Huxley Cl NTHLT UB5 * 49 K1
Huxley Dr CHDH RM6 ....73 H4
Huxley Gdns WLSDN NW10 ...98 A2
Huxley Pde UED N18 * 49 K1
Huxley Pl PLMGR N13 ....35 H5
Huxley Rd LEY E10 ....70 A6
  UED N18 ....49 J1
  WELL DA16 ....148 A4
Huxley Sayze UED N18 * ...49 K1
Huxley St NKENS W10 ....100 C3
Hyacinth Cl HPTN TW12 * ...173 F2
Hyacinth Dr PUT/ROE SW15 ...158 D3
Hyde Cl BAR EN5 ....20 D4
  PLSTW E13 ....106 E1
Hyde Crs CDALE/KGS NW9 ...63 G2
Hyde Dr STMC/STPC BR5 ...202 C1
Hyde Estate Rd
  CDALE/KGS NW9 ....63 H2
Hyde Farm Ms BAL SW12 ...161 J3
Hydefield Cl ED N9 ....36 E4
Hydefield Ct ED N9 ....36 B4
Hyde La BTSEA SW11 ....140 D2
Hyde Park Av WCHMH N21 ...35 J4
Hyde Park Cnr MYFR/PICC W1J ...15 H7
Hyde Park Crs BAY/PAD W2 ...8 C4
Hyde Park Gdns BAY/PAD W2 ...8 B5
  WCHMH N21 ....35 J3
Hyde Park Gardens Ms
  BAY/PAD W2 ....8 B5
Hyde Park Ga SKENS SW7 ...120 B3
Hyde Park Gate Ms
  SKENS SW7 * 120 B2
Hyde Park Pl BAY/PAD W2 ...8 D5
Hyde Park Sq BAY/PAD W2 ...8 C4
Hyde Park St BAY/PAD W2 ...8 C4
Hyde Rd BXLYHN DA7 ....149 G3
  IS N1 ....7 F1
  RCHPK/HAM TW10 ....137 G6
Hydeside Gdns ED N9 ....36 B4
Hyde's Pl IS N1 ....85 H5
The Hyde CDALE/KGS NW9 ...45 H6
Hydethorpe Av ED N9 ....36 B4
Hydethorpe Rd BAL SW12 ...161 H3
Hyde V GNWCH SE10 ....145 F1
Hyde Wk MRDN SM4 ....193 K4
Hyde Wy ED N9 ....36 B4
  HYS/HAR UB3 ....113 J4
Hyland Cl EMPK RM11 ....75 K4
Hylands Rd WALTH E17 ....52 B5
Hyland Wy EMPK RM11 ....75 K4
Hylton St WOOL/PLUM SE18 ...128 A4
Hyndewood FSTH SE23 ....164 A5
Hyndman St PECK SE15 ....123 J6
Hynton Rd BCTR RM8 ....73 J6
Hyperion Pl HOR/WEW KT19 ...207 F6
Hyson Rd BERM/RHTH SE16 ...123 J5
Hythe Av BXLYHN DA7 ....149 G2
Hythe Cl STMC/STPC BR5 ...202 C1
  UED N18 ....36 C6
Hythe Rd THHTH CR7 ....180 E5
  WLSDN NW10 ....99 J3
Hythe St DART DA1 ....151 H6
Hyver HI MLHL NW7 ....31 F1

I

Ibbotson Av CAN/RD E16 ...106 D5
Ibbott St WCHPL E1 ....104 E3
Iberian Av WLGTN SM6 ...210 D2
Ibis La CHSWK W4 ....137 K2
Ibis Wy YEAD UB4 ....95 H5
Ibscott Cl DAGE RM10 ...92 E4
Ibsley Gdns PUT/ROE SW15 ...158 C3
Ibsley Wy EBAR EN4 ....21 J6
Iceland Rd BOW E3 ....87 J6
Ickburgh Est CLPT E5 * ...68 D6
Ickburgh Rd CLPT E5 ....68 D1
Ickenham Cl RSLP HA4 ....58 A5
Ickenham Rd RSLP HA4 ...58 B5
Ickleton Rd ELTH/MOT SE9 ...166 D6
Icknield Dr CNTH/NBYPK IG2 ...72 B2
Ickworth Park Rd WALTH E17 ...69 G1
Ida Rd SEVS/STOTM N15 ....67 K2
Ida St POP/IOD E14 ....106 A5
Iden Cl HAYES BR2 ....183 H6
Idlecombe Rd TOOT SW17 ...179 F2
Idmiston Rd SRTFD E15 ....88 D3
  WNWD SE27 ....162 D5
  WPK KT4 ....192 C4
Idmiston Sq WPK KT4 ....192 C4
Idol La MON EC3R 13 G6
Idonia St DEPT SE8 ....144 C1
Iffley Rd HMSMTH W6 ....118 E3

Ifield Rd WBPTN SW10 ....120 A6
ightham Rd ERITH DA8 ......149 H1
Ilbert St NKENS W10 ....100 C2
Ilchester Gdns W14 ....119 J3
Ilchester Rd BCTR RM8........91 H5
Ildersly Gv DUL SE21..........162 E4
Ilderton Rd
  BERM/RHTH SE16........123 K6
Ilex Cl SUN TW16..............172 B5
Ilex Rd WLSDN NW10 ....81 H4
Ilex Wy STRHM/NOR SW16 ...180 B1
Ilford Hi IL IG1.....................90 A1
Ilford La IL IG1..................90 B2
Ilfracombe Gdns CHDH RM6.....73 H4
Ilfracombe Rd BMLY BR1 .....165 J5
Iliffe St WALW SE17.............122 C5
Iliffe Yd WALW SE17 ....122 C5
Ilkley Cl WNWD SE19 * 180 E2
Ilkley Rd CAN/RD E16 ....107 G4
  OXHEY WD19......................41 H1
Illingworth Cl MTCM CR4......178 C6
Illingworth Wy EN EN1.........24 A6
Ilmington Rd
  KTN/HRWW/W HA3............61 K3
Ilminster Gdns BTSEA SW11 ..140 D5
Imber Cl ESH/CLAY KT10 ......34 C2
Imber Cross THDIT KT7 *.......190 A4
Imber Gv ESH/CLAY KT10 .....189 J3
Imber Park Rd ESH/CLAY KT10 ...189 J5
Imber St IS N1.......................6 E1
Imperial Av STNW/STAM N16 *...86 A2
Imperial Cl RYLN/HDSTN HA2 ...60 A3
Imperial College Rd SKENS SW7 ..14 B4
Imperial Dr RYLN/HDSTN HA2 ...60 A5
Imperial Gdns MTCM CR4......179 G6
Imperial Ms EHAM E6 *.........89 G1
Imperial Rd EBED/NFELT TW14...153 H2
  FUL/PGN SW6....................140 A2
Imperial Sq FUL/PGN SW6 ....140 A2
Imperial St BOW E3.............106 A2
Imperial Wy CHST BR7 ....167 G6
  CROY/NA CRO...................211 G4
  KTN/HRWW/W HA3 ....62 A3
Imre Cl SHB W12................118 E1
Inca Dr ELTH/MOT SE9........167 G2
Inchmery Rd CAT SE6..........164 E4
Inchwood CROY/NA CRO.......213 K2
Independent Pl HACK E8........86 B5
Independents Rd
  BKHTH/KID SE3................145 J4
Inderwick Rd CEND/HSY/T N8...67 F3
Indescon Ct POP/IOD E14 .....124 E2
India St TWRH EC3N..............13 J4
India Wy SHB W12..............118 E3
Indigo Ms POP/IOD E14 *......106 A6
  STNW/STAM N16..............85 K1
Indus Rd CHARL SE7...........146 B1
Ingal Rd PLSTW E13...........106 E3
Ingate Pl VX/NE SW8..........141 G2
Ingatestone Rd MNPK E12.....71 G5
  SNWD SE25......................197 J2
  WFD IG8...........................53 F3
Ingelow Rd VX/NE SW8........141 G3
Ingersoll Rd PEND EN3..........24 E1
  SHB W12.........................118 E1
Ingestre Pl SOHO/CST W1F....10 B4
Ingestre Rd FSTGT E7..........88 E3
  KTTN NW5........................84 B2
Ingham Cl SAND/SEL CR2......215 H6
Ingham Rd KIL/WHAMP NW6...82 E2
  SAND/SEL CR2..................212 E6
Inglebert St CLKNW EC1R........5 J4
Ingleborough St
  BRXN/ST SW9..................142 B3
Ingleby Dr HRW HA1..............78 D1
Ingleby Rd DAGE RM10..........92 D4
  HOLWY N7.........................84 E1
  IL IG1..............................72 B5
Ingleby Wy CHST BR7..........185 F1
  WLGTN SM6.....................210 D6
Ingle Cl PIN HA5..................41 K6
Ingledew Rd
  WOOL/PLUM SE18...........127 J5
Inglefield Sq WAP E1W *......123 J1
Inglehurst Gdns REDBR IG4 ...71 K2
Inglemere Rd FSTH SE23 .....164 A5
  TOOT SW17.....................178 E3
Ingleside Cl BECK BR3.........182 D3
Ingleside Gv BKHTH/KID SE3...125 J5
Inglethorpe St FUL/PGN SW6...139 G2
Ingleton Av WELL DA16........148 B6
Ingleton Rd CAR SM5..........209 J6
  UED N18..........................50 C1
Ingleton St BRXN/ST SW9 ....142 B3
Ingleway NFNCH/WDSP N12...47 H2
Inglewood CL BARK/HLT IG6 ...55 F2
  POP/IOD E14...................124 D4
Inglewood Copse BMLY BR1...184 D5
Inglewood Rd BXLYHN DA7 ...150 A5
  KIL/WHAMP NW6..............82 E3
Inglis Rd CROY/NA CRO........197 G5
  EA W5..............................98 B6
Inglis St CMBW SE5............142 C2
Ingram Av EFNCH N2.............65 K3
Ingram Cl LBTH SE11............17 H6
  STAN HA7.........................43 J1
Ingram Rd DART DA1..........171 H3
  EFNCH N2..........................65 J1
  THHTH CR7......................180 D2
Ingrave Rd ROM RM1............75 F1
Ingrave St BTSEA SW11.......140 C4
Ingrebourne Rd RAIN RM13...111 K3
Ingress St CHSWK W4..........118 B5
Inigo Jones Rd CHARL SE7....146 C1
Inkerman Rd KTTN NW5........84 B4
Inks Gn CHING E4...................52 A1
Inkwell Cl NFNCH/WDSP N12...33 G5
Inman Rd WAND/EARL SW18...160 B2
  WLSDN NW10....................81 G6
Inmans Rw WFD IG8.............38 E6
Inner Cir CAMTN NW1............3 H6
Inner Park Rd WIM/MER SW19...159 G4

Inner Ring East HTHAIR TW6...132 E4
Innes Cl RYNPK SW20.........177 H5
Innes Gdns PUT/ROE SW15...158 E1
Innes St PECK SE15............143 F1
Innes Yd CROY/NA CRO........211 J1
Inniskilling Rd PLSTW E13 ...107 G1
Inskip Cl LEY E10.................69 K6
Inskip Rd BCTR RM8............73 K5
Institute Pl HACK E8.............86 D5
Instone Rd DART DA1..........171 G2
Integer Gdns WAN E11 *.......70 B4
International Av HEST TW5....134 A5
Inver Ct BAY/PAD W2 *.......101 F5
Inveresk Gdns WPK KT4......207 H1
Inverforth Cl HAMP NW3........65 G6
Inverforth Rd FBAR/BDGN N11...48 B1
Inverine Rd CHARL SE7........126 A5
Invermore Pl
  WOOL/PLUM SE18...........127 H4
Inverness Av EN EN1............24 A2
Inverness Dr BARK/HLT IG6....54 E2
Inverness Gdns KENS W8.....120 A1
Inverness Pl BAY/PAD W2 *...101 F6
Inverness Rd HSLW TW3......134 E5
  NWDGN UB2.....................114 D4
  UED N18...........................50 D1
  WPK KT4..........................193 G5
Inverness St CAMTN NW1......84 B6
Inverness Ter BAY/PAD W2...101 F6
  WDGN N22........................49 H4
Invicta Cl CHST BR7............185 F1
  EBED/NFELT TW14............153 J5
Invicta Gv NTHLT UB5...........95 K2
Invicta Pde SCUP DA14 *.....168 C6
Invicta Plaza STHWK SE1.......12 A7
Invicta Rd BKHTH/KID SE3 ...145 K1
  DART DA1........................151 K5
Inville Rd WALW SE17.........122 E5
Inwood Av HSLW TW3.........135 H4
Inwood Cl CROY/NA CRO......198 B6
Inwood Rd HSLW TW3.........135 H5
Inworth St BTSEA SW11.......140 D3
Inworth Wk IS N1 *..............85 J6
Iona Cl CAT SE6..................164 D2
  MRDN SM4.......................194 A4
Ion Sq BETH E2 *................104 C1
Ipswich Rd TOOT SW17.......179 F3
Ireland Cl EHAM E6.............107 K4
Ireland Pl WDGN N22............48 E3
Irene Ms HNWL W7 *...........116 A1
Irene Rd FUL/PGN SW6........139 K2
  ORP BR6..........................202 A4
Ireton Cl MUSWH N10............48 A5
Ireton St BOW E3................105 J3
Iris Av BXLY DA5................169 F1
Iris Cl CROY/NA CRO...........198 A5
  EHAM E6............................89 H5
  SURB KT6........................191 G4
Iris Crs BXLYHN DA7...........129 G6
Iris Rd HOR/WEW KT19........206 E5
Iris Wy CHING E4..................51 H2
Irkdale Av EN EN1.................24 B2
Iron Bridge Cl NWDGN UB2...115 H1
Iron Bridge Rd North
  WDR/YW UB7....................112 D1
Iron Bridge Rd South
  WDR/YW UB7....................112 D2
Iron Mill La DART DA1.........150 C5
Iron Mill Pl DART DA1.........150 D5
  WAND/EARL SW18 *.........160 A1
Iron Mill Rd WAND/EARL SW18...160 A1
Ironmonger La CITYW EC2V...12 E4
Ironmonger Rw FSBYE EC1V....6 D5
Ironside Cl BERM/RHTH SE16...124 A2
Irons Wy CRW RM5................56 E3
Irvine Av KTN/HRWW/W HA3...43 G6
Irvine Cl TRDG/WHET N20.....33 J4
Irvine Wy ORP BR6.............202 A4
Irving Av NTHLT UB5.............77 H6
Irving Gv BRXN/ST SW9......142 A3
Irving Ms IS N1 *..................85 J4
Irving Rd WKENS W14.........119 G3
Irving St LSQ/SEVD WC2H 10 D6
Irwell Est BERM/RHTH SE16 *...123 K2
Irwin Av WOOL/PLUM SE18...147 K1
Irwin Gdns WLSDN NW10......81 K6
Isaac Wy STHWK SE1............18 D2
Isabella Cl STHGT/OAK N14...34 C2
Isabella Ct RCHPK/HAM TW10...157 G1
Isabella Dr ORP BR6............216 C2
Isabella Rd HOM E9 *............86 E3
Isabella St STHWK SE1..........18 A1
Isabel St BRXN/ST SW9........142 A2
Isambard Ms POP/IOD E14 ...125 F3
Isambard Pl BERM/RHTH SE16...123 K1
Isham Rd STRHM/NOR SW16...179 K5
Isis Cl RSLP HA4....................58 A3
Isis St WAND/EARL SW18.....160 B4
Island Farm Av
  E/WMO/HCT KT8..............188 E2
Island Farm Rd
  E/WMO/HCT KT8..............188 E2
Island Rd BERM/RHTH SE16...124 A4
  MTCM CR4........................178 E3
Island Rw POP/IOD E14........105 H5
Isla Rd WOOL/PLUM SE18 ...127 H6
Islay Gdns HSLW TW4.........134 C5
Islay Wk IS N1 *....................85 J4
Islay Whf POP/IOD E14 *......106 A4
Isledon Rd HOLWY N7...........85 G1
Islehurst Cl CHST BR7.........185 F4
Island Gn IS N1......................6 A1
Islington Gn IS N1...................6 A1
Islington High St IS N1............6 A2
Islington Park Ms IS N1..........85 H5
Islington Park St IS N1...........85 G5
Islip Gdns EDGW HA8............45 F2
  NTHLT UB5.......................77 J5
Islip Manor Rd NTHLT UB5....77 J5
Islip St KTTN NW5.................84 C3
Ismailia Rd FSTGT E7............89 F5
Isom Cl PLSTW E13.............107 F2

Ivanhoe Dr KTN/HRWW/W HA3...43 H5
Ivanhoe Rd CMBW SE5........143 G4
  HSLW TW4.......................134 C4
Ivatt Pl WKENS W14.............119 J5
Ivatt Wy SEVS/STOTM N15....49 H6
Iveagh Av WLSDN NW10........98 C1
Iveagh Cl HOM E9..................87 F6
  WLSDN NW10....................98 C1
Ivedon Rd WELL DA16.........148 D3
Ive Farm Cl LEY E10.............69 J6
Ive Farm La LEY E10.............69 J6
Iveley Rd CLAP SW4............141 H5
Ivere Dr BAR EN5..................33 F1
Iverhurst Cl BXLYHS DA6.....148 E6
Iverna Ct KENS W8..............119 K3
Iverna Gdns
  EBED/NFELT TW14...........133 G6
  KENS W8..........................119 K3
Iverson Rd KIL/WHAMP NW6...82 D4
Ives Rd CAN/RD E16.............106 C4
Ives St CHEL SW3................14 D6
Ivimey St BETH E2 *............104 C2
Ivinghoe Cl EN EN1...............24 A3
Ivinghoe Rd BCTR RM8..........91 H5
  BUSH WD23.......................28 D2
Ivor Gv ELTH/MOT SE9........167 G3
Ivor Pl CAMTN NW1...............2 E7
Ivor St CAMTN NW1..............84 C5
Ivory Ct FELT TW13.............153 K3
Ivorydown BMLY BR1...........165 K6
Ivybridge Cl TWK TW1.........156 B1
Ivychurch Cl PGE/AN SE20...181 J3
Ivy Church La STHWK SE1 *...123 G5
Ivy Cl DART DA1..................171 K1
  PIN HA5.............................59 G4
  RYLN/HDSTN HA2..............77 K2
  SUN TW16.......................172 B5
Ivy Ct STHWK SE1 *............123 H5
Ivy Crs CHSWK W4..............117 K4
Ivydale Rd BROCKY SE4.......144 D6
  CAR SM5.........................194 E6
Ivyday Gv STRHM/NOR SW16...162 A5
Ivydene E/WMO/HCT KT8....188 E2
Ivydene Cl SUT SM1............209 G2
Ivy Gdns CEND/HSY/T N8......66 E3
  MTCM CR4.......................179 J6
Ivyhouse Rd DAGW RM9......91 K4
Ivy La HSLW TW4................134 E5
Ivymount Rd WNWD SE27....162 B5
Ivy Rd BROCKY SE4.............144 C5
  CAN/RD E16....................106 E5
  CRICK NW2........................82 A3
  HSLW TW3.......................135 G5
  STNGT/OAK N14................34 D2
  SURB KT6........................191 H6
  TOOT SW17.....................178 D1
  WALTH E17........................69 J3
Ivy St IS N1...........................7 G3
Ivy Wk DAGW RM9...............92 A4
  NTHWD HA6......................40 C4
Ixworth Pl CHEL SW3............15 J7
Izane Rd BXLYHS DA6..........149 G5

J

Jacaranda Cl NWMAL KT3.....176 B3
Jacaranda Gv HACK E8...........86 B5
Jackass La HAYES BR2.........215 F4
Jack Clow Rd SRTFD E15.....106 C1
Jack Cornwell St MNPK E12 ...90 A2
Jackman Ms WLSDN NW10.....81 G1
Jackman St HACK E8.............86 D6
Jackson Cl HOM E9................87 F5
Jackson Rd BARK IG11..........90 D6
  EBAR EN4..........................33 J1
  HAYES BR2.....................200 E5
  HOLWY N7..........................85 F2
Jackson's La HGT N6..............66 A4
Jackson's Pl CROY/NA CRO...196 E5
Jackson St WOOL/PLUM SE18...127 F6
Jackson's Wy CROY/NA CRO...213 J1
Jack Walker Ct HBRY N5........85 H2
Jacobs Cl DAGE RM10...........92 D2
Jacob St STHWK SE1..............19 J2
Jacob's Well Ms MHST W1U.....9 H3
Jacqueline Creft Ter HGT N6 *...66 A3
Jacqueline Vis WALTH E17 *...70 A2
Jade Cl BCTR RM8..................73 J5
  CAN/RD E16....................107 H5
Jade Ter KIL/WHAMP NW6 *...83 G5
Jaffe Rd IL IG1.....................72 C5
Jaffray Rd HAYES BR2.........200 C1
Jaggard Wy BAL SW12.........160 E2
Jago Cl WOOL/PLUM SE18...127 H6
Jago Wk CMBW SE5.............142 E1
Jamaica Rd BERM/RHTH SE16...123 J3
  THHTH CR7......................196 C5
Jamaica St WCHPL E1..........104 E4
James Av BCTR RM8..............74 B1
  CRICK NW2........................82 A3
James Cl GLDGN NW11 *.......64 C3
  GPK RM2............................75 J2
  PLSTW E13......................106 E1
James Collins Cl MV/WKIL W9...100 D3
James Dudson Ct WLSDN NW10...80 E5
James Joyce Wk HNHL SE24 *...142 C5
James La LEY E10..................70 A4
James Lee Sq PEND EN3........25 F1
Jameson St KENS W8...........119 K1
James Pl TOTM N17................50 B5
James Rd DART DA1.............170 D2
James St BARK IG11..............90 C5
  COVGDN WC2E...................11 F5
  EN EN1.............................24 B6
  HSLW TW3......................135 J4
  MHST W1U..........................9 H4

Jamestown Rd CAMTN NW1...84 B6
Jamestown Wy POP/IOD E14...106 B6
James Watt Wy ERITH DA8...130 C6
James Wy OXHEY WD19.........27 H1
James Yd CHING E4 *.............52 B2
Jamuna Cl POP/IOD E14........105 G4
Jane St WCHPL E1...............104 D5
Janet St POP/IOD E14..........124 D3
Janeway Pl BERM/RHTH SE16...123 J2
Janeway St BERM/RHTH SE16...123 H2
Janson Cl SRTFD E15............88 C3
  WLSDN NW10.....................81 F1
Janson Rd SRTFD E15...........88 C3
Jansons Rd SEVS/STOTM N15...50 A6
Japan Crs FSBYPK N4.............67 F5
Japan Rd CHDH RM6..............73 K3
Jardine Rd WAP E1W............105 F6
Jarrett Cl BRXS/STRHM SW2...162 C3
Jarrow Cl MRDN SM4...........194 A2
Jarrow Rd BERM/RHTH SE16...123 K4
  CHDH RM6.........................73 J3
  TOTM N17..........................68 D1
Jarrow Wy HOM E9................87 H3
Jarvis Cl BAR EN5..................20 B6
Jarvis Rd EDUL SE22...........143 F5
  SAND/SEL CR2................211 K4
Jasmin Cl NTHWD HA6...........40 D4
Jasmine Cl IL IG1..................90 B5
  STHL UB1..........................95 J6
Jasmine Gdns CROY/NA CRO...213 K1
  RYLN/HDSTN HA2..............60 A6
Jasmine Gv PGE/AN SE20....181 J4
Jasmine Rd HOR/WEW KT19...206 D4
  ROMW/RG RM7...................75 G6
Jasmine Ter WDR/YW UB7 *...112 D2
Jasmin Rd HOR/WEW KT19...206 D4
Jason Wk ELTH/MOT SE9.....167 F6
Jasper Cl PEND EN3...............24 E1
Jasper Rd CAN/RD E16.........107 H5
  NRWD SE19......................181 G2
Javelin Wy NTHLT UB5...........95 H2
Jaycroft ENC/FH EN2.............23 G2
Jay Gdns CHST BR7.............166 E6
Jebb Av BRXS/STRHM SW2...161 K1
Jebb St BOW E3...................105 J1
Jedburgh Rd PLSTW E13.......107 G2
Jedburgh St BTSEA SW11.....141 F5
Jeddo Ms SHB W12..............118 C2
Jeddo Rd SHB W12..............118 C2
Jefferson Cl GNTH/NBYPK IG2...72 C3
  WEA W13.........................116 C3
Jeffrey's Pl CAMTN NW1........84 C5
Jeffrey's Rd CLAP SW4........141 K3
  PEND EN3..........................25 H5
Jeffrey's St CAMTN NW1........84 B5
Jeffs Cl HPTN TW12.............173 G2
Jeffs Rd SUT SM1...............208 D2
Jeger Av BETH E2 *..................7 J1
Jeken Rd ELTH/MOT SE9......146 B5
Jelf Rd BRXS/STRHM SW2....142 B6
Jellicoe Gdns STAN HA7.........43 G2
Jellicoe Rd TOTM N17............49 K3
  WATW WD18......................26 E1
Jemmett Cl KUTN/CMB KT2...175 J4
Jem Paterson Ct HRW HA1 *...78 E2
Jengar Cl SUT SM1...............209 F2
Jenkins Cl BARK IG11...........108 C2
Jenkins Rd PLSTW E13.........107 F3
Jenner Av ACT W3..................99 F4
Jenner Cl SCUP DA14...........168 B6
Jenner Rd STNW/STAM N16....68 B6
Jenner Wy HOR/WEW KT19...206 D6
Jennett Rd CROY/NA CRO......211 G1
Jennifer Rd BMLY BR1.........165 J5
Jennings Cl SURB KT6..........190 D4
Jennings Rd EDUL SE22.......163 G1
Jennings Wy BAR EN5............20 A3
Jenningtree Rd ERITH DA8...150 E1
Jenningtree Wy BELV DA17...129 K2
Jenny Hammond Cl WAN E11...88 D1
Jenson Wy NRWD SE19........181 G3
Jenton Av BXLYHN DA7........149 F2
Jephson Rd FSTGT E7............89 G5
Jephson St CMBW SE5.........142 E2
Jephtha Rd WAND/EARL SW18...159 K1
Jeppo's La MTCM CR4..........194 E1
Jerdan Pl FUL/PGN SW6.......139 K1
Jeremiah St POP/IOD E14.....105 K5
Jeremys Gn UED N18.............50 D6
Jermyn St STJS SW1Y...........10 A7
Jerningham Av CLAY IG5........54 B5
Jerningham Rd NWCR SE14...144 B3
Jerome Crs STJWD NW8..........2 C6
Jerome St WCHPL E1..............13 J1
Jerrard St LEW SE13.............144 E4
Jerrold St IS N1 *....................7 H3
Jersey Av KTN/HRWW/W HA3...43 H5
Jersey Dr STMC/STPC BR5...201 J3
Jersey Rd CAN/RD E16.........107 G4
  HEST TW5.......................135 G2
  HNWL W7........................116 B2
  IL IG1...............................90 B2
  LEY E10............................70 B5
  RAIN RM13........................93 J5
Jersey St BETH E2................104 D2
Jersey Vis HNWL W7 *.........115 K2
Jerusalem Pas CLKNW EC1R....6 A7
Jerviston Gdns
  STRHM/NOR SW16...........180 B2
Jesmond Av WBLY HA9..........80 B4
Jesmond Cl MTCM CR4.........179 G6
Jesmond Dene HAMP NW3 *...83 G4
Jesmond Rd CROY/NA CRO...197 G4
Jesmond Wy STAN HA7.........44 A1
Jessam Av CLPT E5................68 D5
Jessamine Rd HNWL W7......115 K1
Jessamine Ter SWLY BR8 *...187 K4
Jesse Rd LEY E10..................70 A5
Jessett Cl ERITH DA8...........130 A4

Jessica Rd WAND/EARL SW18...160 B1
Jessop Av NWDGN UB2........114 E4
Jessops Wy MTCM CR4.........195 H3
Jessup Cl WOOL/PLUM SE18...127 H4
Jetstar Wy NTHLT UB5............95 J2
Jevington Wy LEE/GVPK SE12...166 A3
Jewel Rd WALTH E17.............51 J6
Jewry St TWRH EC3N.............13 J4
Jews Rw WAND/EARL SW18...140 A5
Jews Wk SYD SE26...............163 J6
Jeymer Av CRICK NW2...........81 K5
Jeymer Dr GFD/PVL UB6.........78 C6
Jeypore Rd WAND/EARL SW18...160 B2
Jillian Cl HPTN TW12...........173 F3
Jim Bradley Cl
  WOOL/PLUM SE18...........127 F4
Joan Crs ELTH/MOT SE9......166 C2
Joan Gdns BCTR RM8............74 A6
Joan Rd BCTR RM8................74 A6
Joan St STHWK SE1...............18 A1
Jocelyn Rd RCH/KEW TW9...137 F4
Jocelyn St PECK SE15...........143 H2
Jockey's Flds FSBYW WC1X...11 H1
Jodane St DEPT SE8.............124 C4
Jodrell Cl ISLW TW7.............136 B2
Jodrell Rd HOM E9.................87 H6
Joel St NTHWD HA6................40 C5
Johanna St STHWK SE1 *.......17 J3
John Adam St CHCR WC2N....11 F7
John Aird Ct BAY/PAD W2....101 G4
John Archer Wy
  WAND/EARL SW18...........160 C1
John Ashby Cl
  BRXS/STRHM SW2...........161 K1
John Austin Cl KUTN/CMB KT2...175 G4
John Bradshaw Rd S
  THGT/OAK N14..................34 D3
John Burns Dr BARK IG11......90 E6
John Campbell Rd
  STNW/STAM N16................86 A3
John Carpenter St EMB EC4Y...12 A5
John Felton Rd
  BERM/RHTH SE16............123 H2
John Fisher St WCHPL E1.....104 C6
John Gooch Dr ENC/FH EN2....23 H2
John Goodchild Wy KUT/HW KT1...175 J6
John Harrison Wy
  BERM/RHTH SE16............124 A3
  GNWCH SE10....................125 J3
John Islip St WEST SW1P.......16 E7
John Lamb Ct
  KTN/HRWW/W HA3............42 E4
John Maurice Cl WALW SE17...18 E6
John McKenna Wk
  BERM/RHTH SE16............123 H3
John Parker Sq BTSEA SW11 *...140 C4
John Penn St LEW SE13.......144 E2
John Perrin Pl
  KTN/HRWW/W HA3............62 A4
John Prince's St
  CAVSO/HST W1G................9 K5
John Rennie Wk WAP E1W...104 D6
John Roll Wy
  BERM/RHTH SE16............123 H5
John Ruskin St CMBW SE5...142 C1
John Silkin La DEPT SE8......124 A5
John's Cl ASHF TW15...........153 F6
John's Ct SUT SM1 *............209 F4
Johns La MRDN SM4............194 B2
John's Ms BMSBY WC1N........5 H7
John Smith Av FUL/PGN SW6...139 J1
Johnson Cl HACK E8...............86 C6
Johnson Rd CROY/NA CRO...196 E4
  HAYES BR2.....................200 C2
  HEST TW5.......................134 B1
  WLSDN NW10....................81 F6
Johnson's Cl CAR SM5.........209 K1
Johnsons Dr HPTN TW12.....173 H4
Johnson's Pl PIM SW1V.......121 H5
Johnson St NWDGN UB2.....114 B3
  WCHPL E1........................104 E5
Johnsons Wy WLSDN NW10...98 D3
John Spencer Sq IS N1 *.......85 H4
Johns Pl WCHPL E1..............104 D5
John's Ter CROY/NA CRO.....197 F5
Johnston Cl BRXN/ST SW9...142 A2
Johnston Ct LEY E10 *............87 K1
Johnstone Rd EHAM E6.......107 K2
Johnstone Ter CRICK NW2......82 B1
Johnston Rd WFD IG8............52 E1
John St BMSBY WC1N............5 H7
  EN EN1.............................24 B6
  HSLW TW3......................134 D3
  SNWD SE25.....................197 H1
  SRTFD E15......................107 F1
John Trundle Highwalk
  BARB EC2Y *.....................12 C1
John Williams Cl NWCR SE14...124 A6
John Wilson St
  WOOL/PLUM SE18...........127 F4
John Wooley Cl LEW SE13 *...145 H5
Joiners Arms Yd CMBW SE5 *...142 E2
Joiner St STHWK SE1............19 F1
Joint Rd EFNCH N2..................47 J3
Jollys La YEAD UB4...............95 J4
Jonathan St LBTH SE11........122 A5
Jones Rd PLSTW E13...........107 F3
Jonson Cl MTCM CR4...........195 G2
  YEAD UB4.........................94 C4
Jordan Cl RYLN/HDSTN HA2...77 H3
Jordan Rd GFD/PVL UB6........79 H6
Jordans Cl DAGE RM10..........92 D2
  ISLW TW7........................135 K2
Jordans Ms WHTN TW2.......155 K4
Joseph Av ACT W3..................99 F5
Joseph Hardcastle Cl
  NWCR SE14.....................144 A1
Josephine Av
  BRXS/STRHM SW2...........142 A6
Joseph Locke Wy
  ESH/CLAY KT10................189 J4
Joseph Powell Cl BAL SW12...161 H1
Joseph Ray Rd WAN E11.......70 C6
Joseph St BOW E3................105 H3
Joseph Trotter Cl CLKNW EC1R...5 K4
Joshua Cl MUSWH N10...........48 B3

SAND/SEL CR2 ....211 H5
Joshua St POP/IOD E14 ....106 A5
Joslings CI SHB W12 ....99 J6
Joslyn Ct PEND EN3................25 J1
Joubert St BTSEA SW11 ....140 E5
Jowett St PECK SE15 ....143 G1
Joyce Av UED N18..................50 B1
Joyce Green La DART DA1 ....151 G2
Joyden Ct CHDH RM6.............73 H3
Joyners CI DAGW RM9 ....92 A2
Jubilee Av CHING E4 ....52 A2
ROMW/RG RM7........................74 E2
WHTN TW2 ....155 H5
Jubilee CI CDALE/KGS NW9 ...63 F5
KUT/HW KT1 ....174 D4
PIN HA5 ....41 G5
ROMW/RG RM7........................74 D2
Jubilee Crs ED N9 ....36 C3
Jubilee Dr RSLP HA4 ....77 H2
Jubilee Gdns STHL UB1..........96 A4
STHWK SE1 *........................17 H1
Jubilee Pl CHEL SW3 ....120 D5
GFD/PVL UB6.........................79 H6
Jubilee St WCHPL E1 ....104 E5
Jubilee Ter FUL/PGN SW6 *..139 H5
The Jubilee GNWCH SE10 *...144 E1
Jubilee Wy ESH/CLAY KT10 *.189 K5
Jubilee Wy CHSGTN KT9 ......206 D1
EBED/NFELT TW14 ....153 K5
SCUP DA14 ....168 B4
WIM/MER SW19 ....178 A4
Judd St STPAN WC1H 4 D5
Jude St CAN/RD E16 ....106 D5
Judge Heath La HYS/HAR UB3 ..94 A5
Judges' Wk HAMP NW3 ....83 G1
Judge Wk ESH/CLAY KT10 ....204 E4
Judith Av CRW RM5.................56 D2
Juer St BTSEA SW11 ....140 D1
Juglans Rd ORP BR6..............202 B5
Jules Thorn Av EN EN1..........25 J4
Julia Gdns BARK IG11 ....109 K1
Juliana CI EFNCH N2 ....47 G6
Julian Av ACT W3....................98 C6
Julian CI BAR EN5...................21 F4
Julian HI HRW HA1 ....60 E6
Julian Pl POP/IOD E14 ....124 E5
Julian Rd ORP BR6................217 G4
Julian Tayler Pth FSTH SE23 *.163 J4
Julien Rd EA W5....................116 D3
Juliette Rd PLSTW E13 ....106 E1
Juliette Wy RAIN RM13...........111 J2
Julius Caesar Wy STAN HA7 ....29 J5
Julius Nyerere CI IS N1............5 K4
Junction Ap BTSEA SW11 .....140 D4
LEW SE13 ....145 F4
Junction Ms BAY/PAD W2 ....8 B3
Junction Pl BAY/PAD W2 *........8 A3
Junction Rd ARCH N19...........84 C1
DART DA1 ....171 H1
EA W5 ....116 D4
ED N9 ....36 C3
HRW HA1 ....60 E3
PLSTW E15 ....89 F6
ROM RM1 ....75 H1
SAND/SEL CR2 ....211 K6
TOTM N17 ....50 B5
Junction Rd East CHDH RM6...74 A4
Junction Rd West CHDH RM6 ...73 K4
Juniper CI BAR EN5...............206 B3
CHSGTN KT9 ....206 B3
Juniper Ct CHDH RM6.............74 A4
KTN/HRWW/W HA3 *..............43 F4
NTHWD HA6 *........................40 E4
Juniper Crs CAMTN NW1 ....84 A5
Juniper Gdns MTCM CR4 ......179 H4
Juniper La EHAM E6 ....107 J4
Juniper Rd IL IG1....................90 A2
Juniper St WCHPL E1 *..........104 E6
Juno Wy NWCR SE14............124 A6
Jupiter Wy HOLWY N7.............85 F4
Jupp Rd SRTFD E15.................88 B5
Jupp Rd West SRTFD E15........88 B6
Justice Wk CHEL SW3 ....120 D6
Justin CI BTFD TW8...............136 E1
Justin Rd CHING E4 ....51 H2
Jute La PEND EN3...................25 G3
Jutland Rd CAT SE6...............165 F2
PLSTW E13 ....106 E3
Jutsums Av ROMW/RG RM7 ....74 D3
Jutsums La ROMW/RG RM7 ....74 D5
Juxon CI RYLN/HDSTN HA2 ....42 B5
Juxon St LBTH SE11 ....17 H6

K

Kaduna CI PIN HA5 ....59 F2
Kale Rd ERITHM DA18...........128 E2
Kambala Rd BTSEA SW11 .....140 C5
Kangley Bridge Rd SYD SE26 .182 C1
Kaplan Dr WCHMH N21..........23 F6
Kara Wy CRICK NW2................82 B2
Karen Ct BARN RM13 ....111 G1
Karen Ct BMLY SR1................183 J4
ELTH/MOT SE9......................146 E6
Karenza Ct WBLY HA9 *..........61 J4
Kariba CI ED N9 ....36 E5
Karina CI CHIG IG7...................55 A6
Kashgar Rd WOOL/PLUM SE18.128 A5
Kashmir Rd CHARL SE7..........146 C1
Kassala Rd BTSEA SW11 ....140 E2
Katharine St CROY/NA CR0....211 J1
Katherine CI
BERM/RHTH SE16.................124 A1
Katherine Gdns BARK/HLT IG6 ..54 B3
ELTH/MOT SE9......................146 C5
Katherine Rd EHAM E6 ....89 K4
Katherine Sq NTGHL W11 *....119 H1

Kathleen Av ACT W3...............98 E4
ALP/SUD HA0..........................80 A5
Kathleen Rd BTSEA SW11 .....140 E4
Kayemoor Rd BELMT SM2.....209 J5
Kay Rd BRXN/ST SW9 ....141 K3
Kays Ter SWFD E18 *..............52 D5
Kay St BETH E2 ....104 C1
SRTFD E15 ....88 B5
WELL DA16 ....148 C2
Kean St HOL/ALD WC2B..........11 G4
Keatley Gn CHING E4 ....51 H1
Keats Av CAN/RD E16............126 A1
HARH RM3.............................57 K3
Keats CI CHIC IG7...................54 C2
PEND EN3..............................25 F6
STHWK SE1...........................19 J7
WAN E11................................71 F2
WIM/MER SW19 ....178 C2
YEAD UB4 ....94 A4
Keats Est STNW/STAM N16 *...68 B6
Keats Gv HAMP NW3...............83 J2
Keats Pde ED N9.....................36 C4
Keats Rd BELV DA17 ....129 K3
WELL DA16 ....147 K2
Keats Wy CROY/NA CR0 ....197 K3
GFD/PVL UB6.........................96 B4
WDR/YW UB7 ....112 C4
Keble CI NTHLT UB5................78 C5
Keble St TOOT SW17 ....160 B6
Kechill Gdns HAYES BR2 ......199 K4
Kedleston Dr STMC/STPC BR5 .202 A3
Kedleston Wk BETH E2 ....104 D2
Keedle CI WOOL/PLUM SE18 *.127 G6
Keedonwood Rd BMLY BR1 ...165 H6
Keel CI BARK IG11..................109 J1
BERM/RHTH SE16.................124 A1
Keeley Rd CROY/NA CR0 ......196 D6
Keeley St HOL/ALD WC2B 11 G4
Keeling Rd ELTH/MOT SE9 ....146 C6
Keely CI EBAR EN4 ....21 J6
Keemor CI WOOL/PLUM SE18 *.147 F1
Keens CI STRHM/NOR SW16 ..179 J1
Keen's Rd CROY/NA CR0 ....211 J2
Keen's Yd IS N1 ....85 H4
Keepers Ms TEDD TW11 ....174 D2
The Keep BKHTH/KID SE3 .....145 K5
KUTN/CMB KT2 *..................175 G2
Keesey St WALW SE17 ....122 E6
Keetons Rd BERM/RHTH SE16 .123 J3
Keevil Dr WIM/MER SW19 .....159 G2
Keighley CI HOLWY N7 ....84 E2
Keightley Dr ELTH/MOT SE9 ..167 H5
Keildon Rd BTSEA SW11 ....140 E5
Keir Hardie Est CLPT E5 ....68 D5
Keir Hardie Wy BARK IG11 ......91 G5
YEAD UB4 *............................94 E2
Keith Connor CI VX/NE SW8 ..141 G4
Keith Gv SHB W12 ....118 D2
Keith Rd BARK IG11 ....108 D1
HYS/HAR UB3.......................113 H5
WALTH E17 ....51 H4
Kelbrook Rd BKHTH/KID SE3 ...146 E3
Kelburn Wy RAIN RM13 ....111 J2
Kelceda CI CRICK NW2 ....63 J6
Kelf Gv HYS/HAR UB3............113 J5
Kelfield Gdns NKENS W10 .....100 B5
Kelfield Ms NKENS W10 ....100 B4
Kelland CI CEND/HSY/T N8 *...66 D2
Kelland Rd PLSTW E13 ....106 E3
Kellaway Rd BKHTH/KID SE3 .146 C2
Keller Crs MNPK E12 ....71 H2
Kellerton Rd LEW SE13 ....145 H6
Kellett Rd BRXS/STRHM SW2 .142 B5
Kelling Gdns CROY/NA CR0 ...196 C4
Kellino St TOOT SW17............160 E6
Kellner Rd THMD SE28 ....128 A1
Kell St STHWK SE1...................18 B4
Kelly Av PECK SE15 ....143 G1
Kelly CI WLSDN NW10 ....81 F1
Kelly Ms MV/WKIL W9 *.........100 D4
Kelly St CAMTN NW1 ....84 B4
Kelly Wy CHDH RM6 ....74 A2
Kelmore Gv EDUL SE22.........143 H5
Kelmscott CI WALTH E17 ....51 H4
WATW WD18 ....26 E1
Kelmscott Gdns SHB W12 .....118 D3
Kelmscott Rd BTSEA SW11 ...140 E6
Kelross Rd HBRY N5 ....85 H2
Kelsall CI BKHTH/KID SE3 .....146 A3
Kelsall Ms RCH/KEW TW9 .....137 J2
Kelsey Park Av BECK BR3 .....182 E5
Kelsey Park Rd BECK BR3 .....182 D5
Kelsey Rd STMC/STPC BR5 ...185 J5
Kelsey Sq BECK BR3 ....182 D5
Kelsey St BETH E2 ....104 C3
Kelsey Wy BECK BR3 ....182 D6
Kelsie Wy BARK/HLT IG6 ....54 E2
Kelso PI KENS W8 ....120 A3
Kelso Rd CAR SM5.................194 B4
Kelston Rd BARK/HLT IG6........54 B5
Kelton Vls KUT/HW KT1 ....175 G5
Kelvedon CI KUTN/CMB KT2 ..175 H2
Kelvedon Rd FUL/PGN SW6 ..139 J1
Kelvedon Wy WFD IG8 ....53 K2
Kelvin Av PLMGR N13 ....49 F2
Kelvinbrook E/WMO/HCT KT8 .173 G6
Kelvin CI HOR/WEW KT19 .....206 C4
Kelvin Crs KTN/HRWW/W HA3 .42 E3
ELTH/MOT SE9......................146 E6
Kelvin Dr TWK TW1................156 C1
Kelvin Gdns CROY/NA CR0 ....195 K4
STHL UB1...............................96 A5
Kelvin Gv SURB KT6...............205 K6
SYD SE26.............................163 J5
Kelvington CI CROY/NA CR0 ..198 B4
Kelvington Rd PECK SE15 .....144 B6
Kelvin Pde ORP BR6...............201 K5
Kelvin Rd HBRY N5 ....85 H2
WELL DA16 ....148 B4
Kember St IS N1.........................5 J1
Kemble Dr HAYES BR2 ....215 J1

Kemble Rd CROY/NA CR0 .....211 H1
FSTH SE23 ....164 A3
TOTM N17 ....50 C4
Kemble St HOL/ALD WC2B 11 G4
Kemerton Rd BECK BR3.........182 E5
CMBW SE5...........................142 D4
CROY/NA CR0 ....197 G4
Kemey's St HOM E9 ....87 H1
Kemnal Rd CHST BR7 ....185 H2
Kempe Rd KIL/WHAMP NW6 ..100 B1
Kempis Wy EDUL SE22 *........143 F6
Kemplay Rd HAMP NW3...........83 H2
Kemp PI BUSH WD23 ....28 A1
Kemps Dr NTHWD HA6 ....40 D3
POP/IOD E14 ....105 J6
Kempsford Gdns ECT SW5 ....119 K5
Kempsford Rd LBTH SE11 ....17 K7
Kempshott Rd
STRHM/NOR SW16 ....179 K3
Kempson Rd FUL/PGN SW6 ..139 K2
Kempthorne Rd DEPT SE8 ....124 B4
Kempton Av NTHLT UB5 ....78 A4
SUN TW16.............................172 A4
Kempton CI ERITH DA8..........129 K6
HGDN/ICK UB10 ....76 D2
Kempton Ct SUN TW16..........172 A4
Kempton Pk SUN TW16...........172 A4
Kempton Wk CROY/NA CR0 ...198 B3
Kemsing St WAP E1W 123 H1
Kemsing Rd GNWCH SE10 ....126 A5
Kenbury CI CMBW SE5 ....142 D3
Kenchester CI VX/NE SW8 ....141 K1
Kencot Wy ERITH DA8...........129 K6
Kendal Av ACT W3....................98 D4
BARK IG11..............................90 E6
UED N18.................................35 K6
Kendal CI CMBW SE5.............142 C1
EBED/NFELT TW14 ....153 J3
WFD IG8 *..............................38 D4
YEAD UB4 ....94 C1
Kendal Ct ACT W3....................98 D4
Kendal Cft HCH RM12 ....93 J3
Kendale Rd BMLY BR1 ....183 H1
Kendale Gdns SUT SM1..........194 B6
Kendal Gv BFN/LL DA15 ....168 B3
SAND/SEL CR2 *...................211 K6
Kendall PI MHST W1U 9 G2
Kendall Rd BECK BR3 ....182 B5
ISLW TW7 ....136 B3
WOOL/PLUM SE18 ....146 D2
Kendalmere CI MUSWH N10 ...48 B4
Kendal Pde UED N18 *.............35 K5
Kendal PI PUT/ROE SW15 .....139 J6
Kendal Rd WLSDN NW10 ....81 J2
Kendal Steps BAY/PAD W2 *.....8 D4
Kendal St BAY/PAD W2 ....8 D4
Kender St NWCR SE14 ....143 K1
Kendoa Rd CLAP SW4 ....141 J5
Kendon CI WAN E11..................71 F2
Kendra Hall Rd SAND/SEL CR2 .211 H5
Kendrey Gdns WHTN TW2 .....155 K1
Kendrick Ms SKENS SW7 *......14 A6
Kendrick PI SKENS SW7 * 14 A7
Kenelm CI HRW HA1 ....79 G6
Kenerne Dr BAR EN5 ....20 C6
Kenilford Rd BAL SW12 ....161 G2
Kenilworth Av
RYLN/HDSTN HA2 ....77 K2
WALTH E17 ....51 J5
WIM/MER SW19 ....177 K1
Kenilworth Crs EN EN1 ....24 A2
Kenilworth Gdns
GDMY/SEVK IG3.....................73 F6
LOU IG10 ....39 K1
OXHEY WD19 ....41 G1
STHL UB1...............................95 K2
WOOL/PLUM SE18 ....147 G5
YEAD UB4 ....94 D3
Kenilworth Rd ASHF TW15 ....152 A5
BOW E3.................................105 G1
EDGW HA8 ....30 D5
EW KT17 ....207 J4
KIL/WHAMP NW6 ....82 D6
PGE/AN SE20 ....182 A4
STMC/STPC BR5 ....201 H3
Kenilworth Ter BELMT SM2 ....208 E5
Kenley Av CDALE/KGS NW9 ...45 G3
Kenley CI BXLY DA5 ....169 H2
CHST BR7 ....185 K6
EBAR EN4 ....21 J5
Kenley Rd KUT/HW KT1 ....175 J5
TWK TW1 ....156 B2
WIM/MER SW19 ....177 K6
Kenley Wk CHEAM SM3.........208 B2
NTGHL W11 *........................119 H1
Kenlor Rd TOOT SW17...........178 C1
Kenmare Dr MTCM CR4 ....178 E3
TOTM N17 ....50 A3
Kenmare Gdns PLMGR N13.....35 J6
Kenmare Rd THHTH CR7 ....196 B3
Kenmere Gdns ALP/SUD HA0 ..98 C2
Kenmere Rd WELL DA16 ....148 D3
Kenmont Gdns WLSDN NW10 ..99 K2
Kenmore Av
KTN/HRWW/W HA3 ....61 J2
Kenmore CI RCH/KEW TW9 ...137 H1
Kenmore Gdns EDGW HA8 .....44 D5
Kenmore Rd
KTN/HRWW/W HA3 ....43 K6
HAYES BR2 ....200 B6
Kenmure Rd HACK E8 * 86 D3
Kenmure Yd HACK E8 *............86 D3
Kennard Rd FBAR/BDGN N11 ..47 K1
SRTFD E15 ....88 B5
Kennard St BTSEA SW11 ....141 F2
CAN/RD E16 ....126 E1
Kennedy Av PEND EN3 ....36 E1
Kennedy CI MTCM CR4 ....179 F5
PIN HA5 ....41 J2
PLSTW E13 ....106 E1

STMC/STPC BR5 ....201 J5
Kennedy Rd BARK IG11 ....90 E6
HNWL W7 ....96 E4
Kennedy Wk WALW SE17 *......19 F7
Kenneth Av IL IG1....................90 B2
Kenneth Crs CRICK NW2..........81 K3
Kenneth Gdns STAN HA7 ....43 G2
Kenneth Moor Rd IL IG1 *........90 B1
Kenneth Rd CHDH RM6...........74 A4
Kenneth Rd DART DA1 ....150 D4
ISLW TW7 ....136 A4
MV/WKIL W9 ....100 D3
Kenneth St WAP E1W 123 H1
Kennet CI BTSEA SW11 ....140 C5
Kenning St BERM/RHTH SE16 .123 K2
Kennings Wy LBTH SE11 ....122 B6
Kennington Gv LBTH SE11 ....122 A6
Kennington La LBTH SE11 .....122 A6
Kennington Ov LBTH SE11 ....122 A6
Kennington Park Gdns
LBTH SE11 ....122 C6
Kennington Park Pl
WALW SE17 ....122 B6
Kennington Park Rd
LBTH SE11 ....122 B6
Kennington Rd LBTH SE11 ......17 J5
Kennylands Rd BARK/HLT IG6 ..55 G3
Kenny Rd MLHL NW7 ....46 C2
Kenrick PI MHST W1U 9 G1
Kensal Rd NKENS W10 ....100 C3
Kensal Wy NKENS W10 *.........100 B3
Kensington Av MNPK E12 ....89 K4
THHTH CR7 ....180 A4
Kensington Church Ct
KENS W8...............................120 A2
Kensington Church St
KENS W8...............................119 K2
Kensington Church Wk
KENS W8...............................120 A2
Kensington CI
FBAR/BDGN N11 ....48 A1
Kensington Ct KENS W8 ....120 A3
Kensington Court Gdns
KENS W8 *.............................120 A3
Kensington Court Ms
KENS W8 *.............................120 A3
Kensington Court PI KENS W8 .120 A3
Kensington Dr WFD IG8 ....53 H5
Kensington Gdns IL IG1 ....71 K5
Kensington Gardens Sq
BAY/PAD W2 *.......................101 F5
Kensington Gate KENS W8 ....120 B3
Kensington Gore SKENS SW7 .120 B2
Kensington Hall Gdns
WKENS W14 *........................119 J5
Kensington High St
WKENS W14 ....119 H4
Kensington MI KENS W8 ....119 K1
Kensington Palace KENS W8 *.120 A1
Kensington Park Gdns
NTGHL W11 ....100 D6
Kensington Park Ms
NTGHL W11 *........................100 D5
Kensington Park Rd
NTGHL W11 ....100 D6
Kensington PI KENS W8 ....119 K1
Kensington Rd KENS W8........120 A2
NTHLT UB5.............................96 A1
ROMW/RG RM7.......................74 E2
SKENS SW7...........................14 C5
Kensington Sq KENS W8 ....120 A2
Kent Av DAGW RM9 ....110 D1
WEA W13 ....97 H4
WELL DA16 ....148 A6
Kent CI MTCM CR4 ....195 K1
Kent Dr EBAR EN4 ....21 K5
TEDD TW11 ....173 K1
Kentford Wy NTHLT UB5 ....77 J6
Kent Gdns RSLP HA4...............58 E3
WEA W13 ....97 H4
Kent Gate Wy CROY/NA CR0 .213 H4
Kent House La BECK BR3 ......182 B2
Kent House Rd BECK BR3 .....182 A5
Kentish Rd BELV DA17 ....129 H4
Kentish Town Rd CAMTN NW1 .84 B4
Kentish Wy BMLY BR1 ....184 A5
Kentlea Rd THMD SE28 ....127 K2
Kentmere Rd
WOOL/PLUM SE18 ....127 K4
Kenton Av HRW HA1................61 F4
STHL UB1...............................96 A6
SUN TW16.............................172 C5
Kenton Gdns
KTN/HRWW/W HA3 ....61 J2
Kenton La KTN/HRWW/W HA3 .43 G4
Kenton Park Av
KTN/HRWW/W HA3 ....61 J1
Kenton Park CI
KTN/HRWW/W HA3 ....61 J1
Kenton Park Pde
KTN/HRWW/W HA3 ....61 J2
Kenton Park Rd
KTN/HRWW/W HA3 ....61 J1
Kenton Rd HOM E9 ....87 F4
HRW HA1 ....61 H4
KTN/HRWW/W HA3 ....61 J2
Kenton St STPAN WC1H 4 D6
Kenton Wy YEAD UB4 *............94 C2
Kents Pas HAM TW10 *...........156 D3
Kent St BETH E2 ....7 K2
PLSTW E13 ....107 F2
Kent Ter CAMTN NW1 ....2 D5
Kent View Gdns
GDMY/SEVK IG3......................72 E6
Kent Wy SURB KT6 ....206 A1
Kentwell CI BROCKY SE4 *.....144 B5
Kentwode Gn BARN SW13 .....138 D1
Kent Yd SKENS SW7 ....14 D3
Kenver Av NFNCH/WDSP N12 ..47 H2
Kenward Rd ELTH/MOT SE9 ...146 B6
Kenway ROMW/RG RM7..........56 E5
Ken Wy WBLY HA9 ....62 E6
Kenway Rd ECT SW5..............120 A4
Kenwood CI HAMP NW3...........65 H3
WDR/YW UB7 ....112 D6
Kenwood Dr BECK BR3 ....199 G1
Kenwood Gdns CLAY IG5 ....72 A1
SWFD E18..............................53 F6
Kenwood Rd ED N9 ....36 C4
HGT N6 ....65 K3
Kenworthy Rd HOM E9 ....87 G3
Kenwyn Dr CRICK NW2 ....62 B4
Kenwyn Rd CLAP SW4 ....141 J5
DART DA1 ....151 G6
RYNPK SW20 ....177 F5
Kenya Rd CHARL SE7.............146 C1
Kenyngton PI
KTN/HRWW/W HA3 ....61 J2
Kenyon St FUL/PGN SW6 ......139 G2
Keogh Rd SRTFD E15 ....88 C4
Kepler Rd CLAP SW4 ....141 K5
Keppel Rd DAGW RM9 ....92 A2
EHAM E6.................................89 K5
Keppel St GWRST WC1E 10 D1
Kerbey St POP/IOD E14 ....105 K5
Kerfield Crs CMBW SE5 ....142 E2
Kerfield PI CMBW SE5 ....142 E2
Kerri CI BAR EN5 ....19 K5
Kerrison PI EA W5 ....116 E1
Kerrison Rd BTSEA SW11 .....140 D4
EA W5 ....116 E1
SRTFD E15 ....88 B6
Kerry Av PUR RM19 ....131 J2
STAN HA7..............................29 J6
Kerry CI CAN/RD E16..............107 F5
PLMGR N13 ....35 H5
Kerry Pth NWCR SE14 ....124 C6
Kerry Rd NWCR SE14 ....124 C6
Kersey Gdns ELTH/MOT SE9 .166 D1
Kersfield Rd PUT/ROE SW15 .159 G1
Kershaw CI WAND/EARL SW18 *.160 C1
Kersley Ms BTSEA SW11 ....140 E3
Kersley Rd STNW/STAM N16 ..68 A1
Kersley St BTSEA SW11 ....140 E3
Kerstin CI HYS/HAR UB3 ....94 D6
Kerswell CI SEVS/STOTM N15 ..68 A2
Kerwick CI HOLWY N7 ....85 F5
Keslake Rd KIL/WHAMP NW6 .100 B1
Kessock CI TOTM N17 ....68 B2
Kesteven CI BARK/HLT IG6 .....55 F2
Keston Av HAYES BR2 ....215 G5
WELL DA16 ....148 D3
Keston CI UED N18 ....35 K6
WELL DA16 ....148 D1
Keston Gdns HAYES BR2 ....215 G2
Keston Park CI HAYES BR2 ....215 K2
Keston Rd PECK SE15 ....143 H4
THHTH CR7 ....196 A5
TOTM N17 ....49 K6
Kestrel Av HERNE SE24 ....142 C6
HNHL SE24 ....142 C6
Kestrel CI CDALE/KGS NW9 ....45 G5
HCH RM12 ....93 K5
KUTN/CMB KT2 *..................156 E6
WLSDN NW10.........................81 F3
Kestrel PI NWCR SE14 *.........124 B6
Kestrel Wy CROY/NA CR0 .....214 B6
HYS/HAR UB3.......................113 G2
Keswick Av PUT/ROE SW15 ..176 B2
RYNPK SW20 ....177 K5
Keswick CI SUT SM1 ....209 G2
Keswick Gdns REDBR IG4 ....71 K2
RSLP HA4 ....58 B3
WBLY HA9 ....80 A2
Keswick Ms EA W5 ....117 F1
Keswick Rd BXLYHN DA7 ......149 H2
ORP BR6 ....217 F1
PUT/ROE SW15 ....139 H6
WHTN TW2 ....155 H1
WWKM BR4 ....199 H1
Kettering St
STRHM/NOR SW16 ....179 G2
Kettlebaston Rd LEY E10 ....69 H5
Kettlewell CI FBAR/BDGN N11 ..48 A2
Kevelioc Rd TOTM N17 ....49 J4
Kevin CI HSLWW TW4 ....134 B3
Kevington CI STMC/STPC BR5 .202 A1
Kevington Dr CHST BR7 ....202 A1
Kew Br RCH/KEW TW9 ....117 H6
Kew Bridge Rd BTFD TW8 .....117 H6
Kew Crs CHEAM SM3..............208 D1
Kewferry Rd NTHWD HA6 ....40 A2
Kew Foot Rd RCH/KEW TW9 ..137 F5
Kew Gardens Rd
RCH/KEW TW9 ....137 G1
Kew Gn RCH/KEW TW9 ....117 G6
Kew Meadow Pth
RCH/KEW TW9 ....137 J2
Kew Riverside Pk
RCH/KEW TW9 ....137 J1
Kew Rd RCH/KEW TW9 ....117 G6
Keyes Rd CRICK NW2 ....82 B3
DART DA1 ....151 K5
Key CI WCHPL E1 ....104 D3
Keymer CI BRXS/STRHM SW2 *.162 A4
Keynes CI EFNCH N2 ....47 K6

Keynsham Av WFD IG8.....38 C6
Keynsham Gdns
  ELTH/MOT SE9.....146 D6
Keynsham Rd ELTH/MOT SE9.....146 C6
  MRDN SM4.....194 A5
Keyse Rd STHWK SE1.....19 J5
Keyse Rd WEST TW5.....133 K2

Keystone Crs IS N1.....5 F5
Keyworth Cl CLPT E5.....87 G2
Keyworth St STHWK SE1.....18 B4
Kezia St DEPT SE8.....124 B5
Khama Rd TOOT SW17.....160 D6
Khartoum Rd IL IG1.....90 E2
  PLSTW E13.....107 F2
  TOOT SW17.....160 C6
Khyber Rd BTSEA SW11.....140 D5
Kibworth St VX/NE SW8.....142 A1
Kidbrooke Gdns
  BKHTH/KID SE3.....145 K3
Kidbrooke Gv
  BKHTH/KID SE3.....145 K2
Kidbrooke La ELTH/MOT SE9.....146 D5
Kidbrooke Park Cl
  BKHTH/KID SE3.....146 A2
Kidbrooke Park Rd
  BKHTH/KID SE3.....146 A2
Kidbrooke Wy BKHTH/KID SE3.....146 A3
Kidderminster Pl
  CROY/NA CRO.....196 C5
Kidderminster Rd
  CROY/NA CRO.....196 C5
Kidderpore Av HAMP NW3.....82 E2
Kidderpore Gdns HAMP NW3.....82 E2
Kidd Pl CHARL SE7.....126 D5
Kidlington Wy CDALE/KGS NW9.....45 G5
Kielder Cl BARK/HLT IG6.....55 F2
Kilberry Cl ISLW TW7.....135 J2
Kilburn Br KIL/WHAMP NW6.....82 E6
Kilburn High Rd
  KIL/WHAMP NW6.....82 E5
Kilburn La NKENS W10.....100 B2
Kilburn Park Rd
  KIL/WHAMP NW6.....100 E2
Kilburn Pl KIL/WHAMP NW6.....82 E6
Kilburn Priory
  KIL/WHAMP NW6.....83 F6
Kilburn Sq KIL/WHAMP NW6.....82 E6
Kilburn V KIL/WHAMP NW6.....82 E6
Kildare Cl RSLP HA4.....59 G5
Kildare Gdns BAY/PAD W2.....100 E6
Kildare Rd BAY/PAD W2.....100 E5
Kildoran Rd BRXS/STRHM SW2.....141 K6
Kildowan Rd GDMY/SEVK IG3.....73 G5
Kilgour Rd FSTH SE23.....164 B1
Kilkie St FUL/PGN SW6.....140 B3
Killarney Rd
  WAND/EARL SW18.....160 B1
Kilburns Mill Cl WLGTN SM6.....195 G6
Killearn Rd CAT SE6.....165 G3
Killester Gdns EW KT17.....207 K2
Killewarren Wy
  STMC/STPC BR5.....202 D4
Killick St IS N1.....5 G2
Killieser Av BRXS/STRHM SW2.....161 K4
Killip Cl CAN/RD E16.....106 D5
Killowen Cl NTHLT UB5.....78 C3
Killowen Rd HOM E9.....87 F4
Killyon Rd VX/NE SW8.....141 H3
Kilmaine Rd FUL/PGN SW6.....139 H1
Kilmarnock Gdns BCTR RM8.....91 J1
Kilmarnock Rd OXHEY WD19.....27 H1
Kilmarsh Rd HMSMTH W6.....119 F4
Kilmartin Av
  STRHM/NOR SW16.....180 B6
Kilmartin Rd GDMY/SEVK IG3.....73 G6
Kilmartin Wy HCH RM12.....93 K3
Kilmington Rd BARN SW13.....118 D6
Kilmorey Gdns TWK TW1.....136 C6
Kilmorey Rd TWK TW1.....136 C5
Kilmorie Rd FSTH SE23.....164 B3
Kiln Cl HYS/HAR UB3.....113 G6
Kilner St POP/IOD E14.....105 J4
Kiln Ms TOOT SW17.....178 C1
Kiln Pl KTTN NW5.....84 A2
Kilnside ESH/CLAY KT10.....205 G5
Kiln Wy NTHWD HA6.....40 C2
Kiln Wood La CRW RM5.....57 F1
Kilpatrick Wy YEAD UB4.....95 J4
Kilravock St NKENS W10.....100 C2
Kilross Rd EBED/NFELT TW14.....153 G3
Kilsha Rd FUL/PGN SW6.....139 K1
Kilvinton Dr ENC/FH EN2.....23 K1
Kimbell Gdns FUL/PGN SW6.....139 H2
Kimbell Pl ELTH/MOT SE9.....146 E5
Kimberley Av EHAM E6.....107 J1
  GNTH/NBYPK IG2.....72 D2
  PECK SE15.....143 K4
  ROMW/RG RM7.....74 D5
Kimberley Ct KIL/WHAMP NW6.....82 C5
Kimberley Dr SCUP DA14.....168 E4
Kimberley Gdns EN EN1.....24 B4
  FSBYPK N4.....67 H2
Kimberley Rd BECK BR3.....182 A5
  BRXN/ST SW9.....141 K3
  CAN/RD E16.....106 D3
  CHING E4.....38 C3
  CROY/NA CRO.....196 C3
  KIL/WHAMP NW6.....82 C6
  TOTM N17.....50 C5
  UED N18.....50 D2
  WALTH E17.....51 G4
Kimberley Wy CHING E4.....38 C3
Kimber Rd WAND/EARL SW18.....159 K2
Kimble Cl WATW WD18.....26 C2
Kimble Crs BUSH WD23.....28 C2
Kimble Rd WIM/MER SW19.....178 C2
Kimbolton Cl LEE/GVPK SE12.....165 J1
Kimmeridge Gdns
  ELTH/MOT SE9.....166 D6
Kimmeridge Rd
  ELTH/MOT SE9.....166 D6
Kimpton Rd CHEAM SM3.....208 D1
  CMBW SE5.....142 E2
Kinburn St BERM/RHTH SE16 *.....124 A2

Kincaid Rd PECK SE15.....143 J1
Kincardine Gdns
  MV/WKIL W9 *.....100 E3
Kinch Gv WBLY HA9.....62 B4
Kinder Cl THMD SE28.....109 J6
Kinder St WCHPL E1.....104 D5
Kinfauns Rd
  BRXS/STRHM SW2.....162 B4
  GDMY/SEVK IG3.....73 H5
Kingaby Gdns RAIN RM13.....93 J5
King Alfred Av CAT SE6.....164 D6
King Arthur Cl PECK SE15.....143 K1
Kingfishers Crs BRYLDS KT5.....191 G4
King Charles I Island
  CHCR WC2N.....10 E7
King Charles' Rd BRYLDS KT5.....191 G5
King Charles St WHALL SW1A.....16 D2
King Charles Ter WAP E1W *.....104 D6
King Charles Wk
  WIM/MER SW19 *.....159 H5
Kingcup Cl CROY/NA CRO.....198 A5
King David La WCHPL E1.....104 E6
Kingdon Rd KIL/WHAMP NW6.....82 E4
King Edward Av DART DA1.....171 G1
King Edward Dr SURB KT6.....206 A1
King Edward Rd BAR EN5.....20 E5
  LEY E10.....70 A5
  OXHEY WD19.....27 J1
  ROM RM1.....75 G3
  WALTH E17.....51 G6
King Edward's Gdns ACT W3.....117 H1
King Edward's Gv TEDD TW11.....174 C2
King Edward's Rd BARK IG11.....90 D6
  ED N9.....36 D2
  HACK E8.....86 D6
  PEND EN3.....25 F4
  RSLP HA4.....58 B5
King Edward St STBT EC1A.....12 C3
King Edward the Third Ms
  BERM/RHTH SE16 *.....123 J2
King Edward Wk STHWK SE1.....17 K4
Kingfield Rd EA W5.....97 K3
Kingfield St POP/IOD E14.....125 F4
Kingfisher Cl
  KTN/HRWW/W HA3.....43 F3
  STMC/STPC BR5.....202 E1
  THMD SE28.....109 J6
Kingfisher Dr
  RCHPK/HAM TW10.....156 D6
Kingfisher Ms LEW SE13.....144 E6
Kingfisher Pl WDGN N22 *.....49 F5
Kingfisher St EHAM E6.....107 J4
Kingfisher Wy CROY/NA CRO.....198 A2
  WLSDN NW10 *.....81 F4
King Gdns CROY/NA CRO.....211 H3
King Garth Ms FSTH SE23.....163 K4
King George Av BUSH WD23.....28 B1
  CAN/RD E16.....107 H5
  GNTH/NBYPK IG2.....72 C5
  WOT/HER KT12.....188 C5
King George Cl ROMW/RG RM7.....56 E6
King George Sq
  RCHPK/HAM TW10.....157 G1
King George St GNWCH SE10.....145 F1
King George VI Av MTCM CR4.....194 E1
Kingham Cl NTGHL W11.....119 H2
  WAND/EARL SW18.....160 B2
King Harolds Wy BXLYHN DA7.....148 E1
King Henry Ms ORP BR6.....217 F3
King Henry's Dr CROY/NA CRO.....214 A6
King Henry's Reach
  HMSMTH W6.....119 F6
King Henry's Rd HAMP NW3.....83 J5
  KUT/HW KT1.....175 J6
King Henry St
  STNW/STAM N16.....86 A3
King Henry's Wk IS N1.....86 A4
King Henry Ter WAP E1W *.....104 D6
Kinghorn St STBT EC1A.....12 C2
King James St STHWK SE1.....18 B3
King John Ct SDTCH EC2A.....7 H6
King John St WCHPL E1.....105 F4
King John's Wk
  ELTH/MOT SE9.....166 D2
Kinglake Est WALW SE17 *.....123 F5
Kinglake St WALW SE17.....123 F5
Kinglet Cl FSTGT E7.....88 E4
Kingly Ct REGST W1B *.....10 B5
Kingly St REGST W1B.....10 A4
King & Queen Cl
  ELTH/MOT SE9.....166 D6
King & Queen St WALW SE17.....122 D5
King & Queen Whf
  BERM/RHTH SE16 *.....124 A1
Kingsand Rd LEE/GVPK SE12.....165 K4
Kings Arbour NWDGN UB2.....114 D5
King's Arms Yd LOTH EC2R.....12 E3
Kingsash Dr YEAD UB4.....95 J3
Kings Av BAL SW12.....161 J3
  BMLY BR1.....183 J2
  CAR SM5.....209 J5
  CHDH RM6.....74 B3
  EA W5.....97 K5
  GFD/PVL UB6.....96 B5
  HEST TW5.....135 G2
  MUSWH N10.....48 C5
  NWMAL KT3.....192 C1
  WCHMH N21.....35 H3
  WFD IG8.....53 G1
King's Bench St STHWK SE1.....18 B2
King's Bench Wk EMB EC4Y *.....11 K5
Kingsbridge Av ACT W3.....117 G2
Kingsbridge Ct POP/IOD E14.....124 D4
Kingsbridge Rd BARK IG11.....90 D1
  MRDN SM4.....193 G4
  NKENS W10.....100 A5
  NWDGN UB2.....114 E4
  WOT/HER KT12.....188 A4
Kingsbury Gn
  CDALE/KGS NW9 *.....62 E2
Kingsbury Rd CDALE/KGS NW9.....62 C2
  IS N1.....86 A4
Kingsbury Ter IS N1.....86 A4
Kings Cha E/WMO/HCT KT8.....173 H6
Kingsclere Cl PUT/ROE SW15.....158 D2
Kingsclere Pl ENC/FH EN2.....23 J3

Kingscliffe Gdns
  WIM/MER SW19.....159 J5
Kings Cl DART DA1.....150 B5
  HDN NW4.....64 B1
  LEY E10.....69 K4
  NTHWD HA6.....40 D3
  THDT KT7.....190 B5
  WOT/HER KT12 *.....188 A4
King's College Rd HAMP NW3 *.....83 H5
  RSLP HA4.....58 C4
Kingscote Rd CHSWK W4.....118 A3
  CROY/NA CRO.....197 J4
  NWMAL KT3.....176 A6
Kingscote St EMB EC4Y.....12 A5
Kings Ct PLSTW E13.....89 F6
  STHWK SE1 *.....18 B2
Kingscourt Rd
  STRHM/NOR SW16.....161 J5
King's Crs HBRY N5.....85 J1
King's Crs Est FSBYW WC1X.....5 F4
King's Cross Br FSBYW WC1X.....5 F4
King's Cross Rd FSBYW WC1X.....5 H4
Kingsdale Gdns NTGHL W11.....119 G1
Kingsdale Rd PGE/AN SE20.....182 A4
  WOOL/PLUM SE18.....128 A6
Kingsdown Av ACT W3.....99 G6
  SAND/SEL CR2.....211 J6
  WEA W13.....116 C2
Kingsdown Cl
  BERM/RHTH SE16 *.....123 J5
  NTGHL W11.....100 B5
Kingsdowne Ct EA W5 *.....98 A6
Kingsdowne Rd SURB KT6.....191 F4
Kingsdown Rd ARCH N19.....84 E1
  CHEAM SM5.....208 C3
  WAN E11.....88 C1
Kingsdown Wy HAYES BR2.....199 K3
Kings Dr BRYLDS KT5.....191 H4
  EDGW HA8.....30 B5
  THDT KT7.....190 C3
  WBLY HA9.....62 D6
Kingsend RSLP HA4.....58 C5
Kingsend Ct RSLP HA4 *.....58 C5
Kings Farm WALTH E17 *.....51 K4
Kings Farm Av
  RCHPK/HAM TW10.....137 H5
Kingsfield Av RYLN/HDSTN HA2.....60 B2
Kingsfield Ct OXHEY WD19.....27 H1
Kingsfield Rd HRW HA1 *.....60 D5
  OXHEY WD19.....27 H2
Kingsfield Ter DART DA1 *.....171 G1
Kingsford St KTTN NW5.....83 K3
Kingsford Wy EHAM E6.....107 K4
Kings Gdns IL IG1.....72 D5
  KIL/WHAMP NW6.....82 E5
Kingsgate WBLY HA9.....80 E1
Kingsgate Av FNCH N3.....46 E6
Kingsgate Cl BXLYHN DA7.....149 F2
  STMC/STPC BR5.....186 D6
Kingsgate Pl KIL/WHAMP NW6.....82 E5
Kingsgate Rd KIL/WHAMP NW6.....82 E5
  KUT/HW KT1.....175 F4
Kingsground ELTH/MOT SE9.....146 C5
King's Gv PECK SE15.....143 J2
  ROM RM1.....75 J2
Kings Hall Ms LEW SE13 *.....145 F4
Kings Hall Rd BECK BR3.....182 A3
Kings Head Hi CHING E4.....37 K2
King's Hwy WOOL/PLUM SE18.....127 K6
Kingshill Av CRWF RM5.....56 D2
  KTN/HRWW/W HA3.....43 H5
  NTHLT UB5.....95 H1
  WPK KT4.....192 D4
  YEAD UB4.....94 C2
Kingshill Ct BAR EN5 *.....20 C5
Kingshill Dr KTN/HRWW/W HA3.....43 H6
Kingshold Rd HOM E9.....86 E5
Kingsholm Gdns
  ELTH/MOT SE9.....146 C5
Kingshurst Rd LEE/GVPK SE12.....165 K2
Kings Keep HAYES BR2 *.....183 H6
  SURB KT6 *.....191 F1
Kingsland Gdn STNW/STAM N16.....86 A4
Kingsland High St HACK E8.....86 B4
Kingsland Pas HACK E8.....86 A4
Kingsland Rd BETH E2.....7 G3
  HACK E8.....86 B5
  PLSTW E13.....107 G2
King's La SUT SM1.....209 H3
Kingslawn Cl PUT/ROE SW15.....138 E6
Kingsleigh Cl BTFD TW8.....116 E6
Kingsleigh Pl MTCM CR4.....178 E6
Kingsleigh Wk HAYES BR2.....199 J2
Kingsley Av DART DA1.....151 K6
  EA W5.....97 K5
  HSLW TW3.....135 H3
  SUT SM1.....209 H2
  WEA W13.....97 G5
Kingsley Cl DAGE RM10.....92 D2
  GLDGN NW11.....64 C4
Kingsley Ct EDGW HA8.....30 D4
  GPK RM2.....57 K6
Kingsley Dr WPK KT4.....192 C6
Kingsley Gdns CHING E4.....51 J1
Kingsley Ms CHST BR7.....185 G2
  IL IG1.....72 A6
  KENS W8 *.....120 A5
  WAP E1W *.....104 D6
Kingsley Pl HGT N6.....66 A5
Kingsley Rd BARK/HLT IG6.....54 C4
  CROY/NA CRO.....196 B5
  FSTGT E7.....89 F5
  HSLW TW3.....135 H3
  KIL/WHAMP NW6.....82 D6
  ORP BR6.....217 H6
  PIN HA5.....59 K2
  PLMGR N13.....35 G6
  RYLN/HDSTN HA2.....60 A3
  WALTH E17.....52 A1
  WIM/MER SW19.....178 A1
Kingsley St BTSEA SW11.....140 E4
Kingsley Wy EFNCH N2.....65 G3
Kingsley Wood Dr
  ELTH/MOT SE9.....166 E5

Kingslyn Crs NRWD SE19.....181 F4
Kings MI HMSMTH W6 *.....119 F4
Kingsman St
  WOOL/PLUM SE18.....126 E4
Kingsmead BAR EN5.....20 E5
  RCHPK/HAM TW10.....157 G1
Kingsmead Av CDALE/KGS NW9.....63 F4
  ED N9.....36 D3
  MTCM CR4.....179 H6
  ROM RM1.....75 G3
  SUN TW16.....172 B6
  SURB KT6.....191 H6
  WPK KT4.....207 K1
Kingsmead Cl BFN/LL DA15.....168 B4
  HOR/WEW KT19.....207 F5
  TEDD TW11.....174 C2
Kingsmead Dr NTHLT UB5.....77 K5
Kingsmead Pde NTHLT UB5 *.....77 K5
Kings Mead Pk
  ESH/CLAY KT10.....204 E5
Kingsmead Rd
  BRXS/STRHM SW2.....162 B4
Kingsmere Cl PUT/ROE SW15.....139 G4
Kingsmere Pk CDALE/KGS NW9.....62 E5
Kingsmere Pl
  STNW/STAM N16 *.....67 K5
Kingsmere Rd
  WIM/MER SW19.....159 G4
King's Ms BMSBY WC1N.....5 H7
Kingsmill Gdns DAGW RM9.....92 B5
Kingsmill Rd DAGW RM9.....92 B5
Kingsmill Ter STJWD NW8.....2 B2
Kingsnympton Pk
  KUTN/CMB KT2.....175 J3
Kings Oak ROMW/RG RM7.....56 C6
King's Orch ELTH/MOT SE9.....166 D1
King's Paddock HPTN TW12.....173 H4
Kings Pde CAR SM5 *.....209 J1
  SHB W12 *.....118 D3
  TOTM N17 *.....50 B6
  WLSDN NW10.....82 A6
Kingspark Ct SWFD E18.....52 E6
Kings Pas KUTN/CMB KT2.....174 E5
Kings Pl BKHH IG9.....39 H4
  CHSWK W4.....117 K5
  LOU IG10.....39 H2
  STHWK SE1.....18 C3
King's Quay WBPTN SW10 *.....140 B2
Kings Reach EMB EC4Y *.....11 K5
Kingsridge Gdns DART DA1.....171 G1
Kings Rd BAR EN5.....90 C5
  BARK IG11.....90 C5
  BGVA SW1W.....15 G6
  CHEL SW3.....120 C6
  EA W5.....98 B8
  EA W5.....97 K4
  EHAM E6.....89 G6
  FELT TW13.....154 B3
  FUL/PGN SW6.....140 B1
  KUTN/CMB KT2.....175 G3
  MORT/ESHN SW14.....138 A4
  MTCM CR4.....179 F6
  ORP BR6.....217 F2
  RCHPK/HAM TW10.....137 G6
  ROM RM1.....75 J2
  RYLN/HDSTN HA2.....59 K6
  SNWD SE25.....181 H6
  SURB KT6.....190 D5
  TEDD TW11.....173 J1
  TOTM N17.....50 B6
  TWK TW1.....156 C1
  UED N18.....50 C1
  WALTH E17.....69 H1
  WDGN N22.....49 G4
  WIM/MER SW19.....177 J2
  WLSDN NW10.....81 H5
  WOT/HER KT12.....188 A6
King's Scholars' Pas
  WEST SW1P.....16 A5
King Stairs Cl
  BERM/RHTH SE16.....123 J2
Kingsthorpe Rd SYD SE26.....164 A6
Kingston Av CHEAM SM3.....208 C1
  EBED/NFELT TW14.....153 G6
  HOR/WEW KT19.....207 H3
Kingston By-Pass BRYLDS KT5.....191 G6
  CHSGTN KT9.....206 B3
  ESH/CLAY KT10.....204 E1
Kingston Cl CHDH RM6.....56 A6
  NTHLT UB5.....77 K5
  TEDD TW11.....174 C2
Kingston Crs BECK BR3.....182 C4
Kingston Gdns CROY/NA CRO.....210 E1
Kingston Hall Rd KUT/HW KT1.....174 E6
Kingston Hi KUTN/CMB KT2.....175 H4
Kingston Hill Av CHDH RM6.....56 A6
Kingston Hill Pl
  KUTN/CMB KT2 *.....157 K6
Kingston La TEDD TW11.....174 C2
  WDR/YW UB7.....112 C2
Kingston Ldg NWMAL KT3.....192 B1
Kingston Pl
  KTN/HRWW/W HA3.....43 J2
Kingston Rd BRYLDS KT5.....191 J6
  EW KT19.....207 G3
  IL IG1.....90 B2
  KUT/HW KT1.....175 J6
  NWMAL KT3.....192 A1
  PUT/ROE SW15.....158 D4
  RYNPK SW20.....177 H5
  TEDD TW11.....174 C2
  WIM/MER SW19.....177 K5
Kingston Sq NRWD SE19.....180 E1
Kingston V PUT/ROE SW15.....158 A6
Kingstown St CAMTN NW1.....3 J1
King St CITYW EC2V.....12 D4
  COVGDN WC2E.....10 E5
  EFNCH N2.....47 H6

  HMSMTH W6.....118 C4
  NWDGN UB2.....114 D3
  PLSTW E13.....106 E1
  RCH/KEW TW9.....136 E6
  STJS SW1Y.....16 B1
  TOTM N17.....50 B4
  TWK TW1.....156 B3
King St Cloisters
  HMSMTH W6 *.....118 E4
King Street Pde TWK TW1 *.....156 B3
Kingswater Pl BTSEA SW11 *.....140 D1
Kings Wy CROY/NA CRO.....211 F3
Kingsway HOL/ALD WC2B.....11 G4
  HYS/HAR UB3.....94 A5
  MORT/ESHN SW14.....137 J4
  NWMAL KT3.....193 F1
  PEND EN3.....24 D6
  STMC/STPC BR5.....201 J2
  STWL/WRAY TW19.....152 A3
  WBLY HA9.....80 A2
  WWKM BR4.....214 D1
Kingsway Av SAND/SEL CR2.....212 E6
Kingsway Crs
  RYLN/HDSTN HA2.....60 C1
Kingsway Pde
  TNW/STAM N16 *.....85 K1
Kingsway Pl CLKNW EC1R *.....5 K6
Kingsway Rd CHEAM SM3.....208 C5
Kingswear Rd KTTN NW5.....84 B1
  RSLP HA4.....58 E3
Kingswood Av BELV DA17.....129 G4
  HAYES BR2.....183 H6
  HEST TW5.....134 D3
  HPTN TW12.....173 G2
  KIL/WHAMP NW6.....81 K6
  THHTH CR7.....196 B2
Kingswood Cl DART DA1.....171 F1
  EN EN1.....24 B5
  NWMAL KT3.....192 C3
  ORP BR6.....201 J4
  SURB KT6.....191 F4
  TRDG/WHET N20.....33 H2
  VX/NE SW8.....141 K1
Kingswood Ct LEW SE13.....165 G1
Kingswood Dr BELMT SM2.....209 F6
  CAR SM5.....194 E5
  NRWD SE19.....163 F6
Kingswood Pk FNCH N3.....46 D5
Kingswood Pl LEW SE13.....165 H5
Kingswood Rd
  BRXS/STRHM SW2.....161 K1
  CHSWK W4.....117 K3
  GDMY/SEVK IG3.....73 G5
  HAYES BR2.....183 G5
  PGE/AN SE20.....163 K6
  WAN E11.....70 C4
  WBLY HA9.....80 D1
  WIM/MER SW19.....177 J4
Kingswood Ter CHSWK W4.....117 K3
Kingswood Wy WLGTN SM6.....210 E3
Kingsworth Cl BECK BR3.....198 B2
Kingsworthy Cl KUT/HW KT1.....175 G5
Kings Yd PUT/ROE SW15 *.....139 G5
  SRTFD E15 *.....87 J4
Kingthorpe Rd WLSDN NW10.....81 F5
Kingthorpe Ter WLSDN NW10.....81 F5
Kingwell Rd EBAR EN4.....21 H1
Kingweston Cl CRICK NW2.....125 H5
King William La GNWCH SE10.....125 H5
King William St CANST EC4R.....13 F6
King William Wk GNWCH SE10.....125 F6
Kingwood Rd FUL/PGN SW6.....139 G1
Kinlet Rd WOOL/PLUM SE18.....147 H1
Kinloch Dr CDALE/KGS NW9.....63 G4
Kinloch St HOLWY N7.....85 F1
Kinloss Gdns FNCH N3.....46 D6
Kinloss Rd CAR SM5.....194 B4
Kinnaird Av BMLY BR1.....183 J2
  CHSWK W4.....137 K1
Kinnaird Cl BMLY BR1.....183 J2
Kinnaird Wy WFD IG8.....53 K2
Kinnear Rd SHB W12.....118 C2
Kinnerton Pl North
  KTBR SW1X *.....15 F3
Kinnerton Pl South
  KTBR SW1X *.....15 F3
Kinnerton St KTBR SW1X.....15 G3
Kinnerton Yd KTBR SW1X *.....15 G3
Kinnoul Rd HMSMTH W6.....119 H6
Kinross Av WPK KT4.....192 D6
Kinross Cl KTN/HRWW/W HA3.....62 B2
Kinross Ter WALTH E17.....51 H5
Kinsale Rd PECK SE15.....143 H4
Kintyre Cl STRHM/NOR SW16.....180 A6
Kinveachy Gdns CHARL SE7.....126 D5
Kinver Rd SYD SE26.....163 K6
Kipling Dr WIM/MER SW19.....178 C2
Kipling Est STHWK SE1.....19 F3
Kipling Rd BXLYHN DA7.....149 F2
Kipling St STHWK SE1.....19 F3
Kipling Ter ED N9 *.....35 K5
Kippington Dr ELTH/MOT SE9.....166 C3
Kirby Cl BARK/HLT IG6.....54 C2
  HOR/WEW KT19.....207 H3
  LOU IG10.....39 J2
  NTHWD HA6.....40 D2
Kirby Est BERM/RHTH SE16 *.....123 J3
Kirby Gv STHWK SE1.....19 G2
Kirby St HCIRC EC1N.....11 K1
Kirchen Rd WEA W13.....97 H6
Kirkcaldy Gn OXHEY WD19.....27 G5
Kirkdale SYD SE26.....163 J4
Kirkdale Cnr SYD SE26.....163 K6
Kirkdale Rd LEY E10.....70 C5
Kirkfield Cl WEA W13.....116 C1
Kirkham Rd EHAM E6.....107 J5
Kirkham St WOOL/PLUM SE18.....128 A6
Kirkland Av CLAY IG5.....54 A3
Kirkland Cl BFN/LL DA15.....147 K5
Kirkland Dr ENC/FH EN2.....23 J2
Kirkland Ter BECK BR3.....182 D2
Kirk La WOOL/PLUM SE18.....127 H6
Kirkleas Rd SURB KT6.....191 F5
Kirklees Rd BCTR RM8.....91 J3

THHTH CR7 ....196 B2
Kirkley Rd WIM/MER SW19 .....177 K4
Kirkly Cl SAND/SEL CR2 ....212 A6
Kirkmichael Rd POP/IOD E14 ...106 A5
Kirk Rd WALTH E17 ....69 H3
Kirkside Rd BKHTH/KID SE3 .....125 K6
Kirkstall Av TOTM N17 ....67 K1
Kirkstall Gdns
    BRXS/STRHM SW2 ....161 G3
Kirkstall Rd BRXS/STRHM SW2 ..161 H1
Kirksted Rd MRDN SM4 ....194 A5
Kirkstone Wy BMLY BR1 ....183 H5
Kirkton Rd SEVS/STOTM N15 ......68 A1
Kirkwall Pl BETH E2 * 104 E2
Kirkwood Rd PECK SE15 ....143 J3
Kirkwall Rd WEA W13 ....85 J5
Kirrane Cl NWMAL KT3 ....192 C2
Kirtley Rd SYD SE26 ....164 B6
Kirtling St VX/NE SW8 ....141 H1
Kirton Cl CHSWK W4 ....118 A4
Kirton Ldg
    WAND/EARL SW18 * 160 A1
Kirton Rd PLSTW E13 ....107 G1
Kirton Wk EDGW HA8 ....44 E3
Kirwyn Wy CMBW SE5 ....142 D1
Kitchener Cl FSTGT E7 ....105 J2
Kitchen Ct LEY E10 * 7 K6
Kitchener Rd EFNCH N2 ....47 J6
    FSTGT E7 ....89 F4
    THHTH CR7 ....180 E6
    TOTM N17 ....50 A6
Kite Pl BETH E2 * 104 C2
Kite Yd BTSEA SW11 * 140 E2
Kitley Gdns NRWD SE19 ....181 G4
Kitson Rd BARN SW13 ....138 D2
    CMBW SE5 ....142 D1
Kittiwake Rd NTHLT UB5 ....95 H2
Kittiwake Wy YEAD UB4 ....95 H4
Kiver Rd ARCH N19 ....66 D6
Kiwi Ter EHAM E6 ....108 A2
Klea Av CLAP SW4 ....161 H1
Knapdale Cl FSTH SE23 ....163 J4
Knapmill Rd CAT SE6 ....164 D4
Knapmill Wy CAT SE6 ....164 D4
Knapp Cl WLSDN NW10 ....81 G4
Knapp Rd ASHF TW15 ....152 C6
    BOW E3 ....105 J3
Knapton Ms TOOT SW17 ....179 F2
Knaresborough Dr
    WAND/EARL SW18 ....160 A3
Knaresborough Pl ECT SW5 ....120 A4
Knatchbull Rd CMBW SE5 ....142 D2
    WLSDN NW10 ....81 F6
Knebworth Av WALTH E17 ....51 J4
Knebworth Rd
    STNW/STAM N16 * 86 A2
Knee Hl ABYW SE2 ....128 D5
Knee Hill Crs ABYW SE2 ....128 D5
Kneller Gdns ISLW TW7 ....155 J1
Kneller Rd BROCKY SE4 ....144 B5
    NWMAL KT3 ....192 A5
    WHTN TW2 ....155 H1
Knevett Ter HSLW TW3 ....135 F5
Knight Cl BCTR RM8 ....73 J6
Knighten St WAP E1W 123 J1
Knighthead Point
    POP/IOD E14 * 124 D2
Knighton Cl ROMW/RG RM7 ....75 F3
Knighton Cl ROMW/RG RM7 ....75 F3
    SAND/SEL CR2 ....211 H6
    WFD IG8 ....39 F6
Knighton Dr WFD IG8 ....39 F6
Knighton La BKHH IG9 ....39 F4
Knighton Park Rd SYD SE26 ....182 A1
Knighton Rd FSTGT E7 ....88 E1
    ROMW/RG RM7 ....74 E3
Knightrider Ct BLKFR EC4V 12 B5
Knightrider St BLKFR EC4V 12 C5
Knight's Av EA W5 ....117 F2
Knightsbridge KTBR SW1X 15 F3
    SKENS SW7 ....14 D3
Knightsbridge Gdns
    ROMW/RG RM7 ....75 F2
Knightsbridge Gn KTBR SW1X * ...14 E3
Knights Chambers ED N9 * 36 C5
Knights Hill WNWD SE27 ....180 C1
Knight's Hill Sq WNWD SE27 ......180 C1
Knights's La ED N9 ....36 C5
Knights Manor Wy DART DA1 ......171 J1
Knight's Pk KUT/HW KT1 ....175 F6
Knights Rdg ORP BR6 ....217 H3
Knightswood Rd RAIN RM13 ....111 H1
Knobs Hill Rd SRTFD E15 ....87 K6
Knockholt Rd ELTH/MOT SE9 ......146 C6
Knole Cl CROY/NA CRO * 197 K3
Knole Rd DART DA1 ....170 D2
The Knole ELTH/MOT SE9 ....167 F6
Knoll Crs NTHWD HA6 ....40 D5
Knoll Dr STHGT/OAK N14 ....34 A2
Knoll Rd BXLY DA5 ....169 H2
    SCUP DA14 ....186 C1
Knolls Cl WPK KT4 ....207 K1
The Knoll BECK BR3 ....182 E4
    HAYES BR2 ....199 K6
    PIN HA5 * 41 H5
    WEA W13 ....97 J4
Knolly's Cl STRHM/NOR SW16 ...162 B5
Knolly's Rd STRHM/NOR SW16 ..162 B5
Knottisford St BETH E2 ....92 E2
Knotts Green Rd LEY E10 ....69 K3
Knowle Av BXLYHN DA7 ....149 F1
Knowle Cl BRXN/ST SW9 ....142 B4

Knowle Rd HAYES BR2 ....200 D6
    WHTN TW2 ....155 K3
Knowles Cl WDR/YW UB7 ....112 B1
Knowles Ct HRW HA1 ....61 F3
Knowles Hill Crs LEW SE13 ....145 G6
Knowlton Gn HAYES BR2 ....199 J2
Knowsley Av STHL UB1 ....115 G1
Knowsley Rd BTSEA SW11 ....140 E3
Knox Rd FSTGT E7 ....88 E4
Knox St MBLAR W1H 8 E2
Knoyle St NWCR SE14 ....124 B6
Kohat Rd WIM/MER SW19 ....178 A1
Koh-i-noor Av BUSH WD23 ....28 A1
Kossuth St GNWCH SE10 ....125 H5
Kramer Ms ECT SW5 * 119 K5
Kreedman Wk HACK E8 * 86 C5
Kuala Gdns STRHM/NOR SW16 ..180 A4
Kydbrook Cl STMC/STPC BR5 ....201 H4
Kylemore Cl EHAM E6 ....107 H1
Kylemore Rd
    KIL/WHAMP NW6 ....82 E5
Kymberley Rd HRW HA1 * 60 E3
Kyme Rd ROM RM1 ....75 H5
Kynance Ms KENS W8 ....14 A4
Kynance Ms STAN HA7 ....43 J4
Kynance Pl KENS W8 ....120 A3
Kynance Pl SKENS SW7 ....120 B3
Kynaston Cl
    KTN/HRWW/W HA3 ....42 D3
Kynaston Crs THHTH CR7 ....196 D2
Kynaston Rd BMLY BR1 ....183 K1
    ENC/FH EN2 ....23 K2
    STNW/STAM N16 ....86 A1
    THHTH CR7 ....196 D2
Kynaston Wd
    KTN/HRWW/W HA3 ....42 D3
Kynersley Cl CAR SM5 ....209 K1
Kynoch Rd UED N18 ....37 F6
Kyrle Rd BTSEA SW11 ....161 F1
Kyverdale Rd STNW/STAM N16 ....68 B4

Laburnum Av DART DA1 ....171 F3
    ED N9 ....36 A4
    HCH RM12 ....93 K4
    SUT SM1 ....209 J1
    TOTM N17 ....49 K3
Laburnum Cl ALP/SUD HA0 ....80 C6
    CHING E4 ....51 H2
Laburnum Ct STAN HA7 ....29 J6
Laburnum Crs SUN TW16 ....172 A4
Laburnum Gdns CROY/NA CRO ...198 A4
    HSLW TW3 ....134 E5
    NWMAL KT3 ....176 A5
    STHL UB1 ....95 K5
Laburnum Gv CDALE/KGS NW9 ...62 E4
    HSLW TW3 ....134 E5
    NWMAL KT3 ....176 A5
    STHL UB1 ....95 K5
Laburnum Pl ELTH/MOT SE9 * 147 F6
Laburnum Rd HYS/HAR UB3 ......113 J4
    MTCM CR4 ....179 F5
    WIM/MER SW19 ....178 B3
Laburnum St BETH E2 ....7 J1
Lacebark Cl BFN/LL DA15 ....168 A2
Lacewing Cl PLSTW E13 ....106 E2
Lacey Cl ED N9 ....36 C4
Lacey Dr BCTR RM8 ....73 J1
    HPTN TW12 ....172 E4
Lackington St SDTCH EC2A 13 F1
Lacock Cl WIM/MER SW19 ....178 B2
Lacon Rd EDUL SE22 ....143 H5
Lacrosse Wy
    STRHM/NOR SW16 ....179 J4
Lacy Rd PUT/ROE SW15 ....139 G5
Ladas Rd WNWD SE27 ....180 D1
Ladbroke Crs NTGHL W11 ....100 C5
Ladbroke Gdns NTGHL W11 ....100 D6
Ladbroke Gv NKENS W10 ....100 C4
Ladbroke Ms NTGHL W11 ....119 H1
Ladbroke Rd EN EN1 ....36 B1
    NTGHL W11 ....119 J1
Ladbroke Sq NTGHL W11 ....100 D6
Ladbroke Ter NTGHL W11 ....100 D6
Ladbroke Wk NTGHL W11 ....119 J1
Ladbrook Cl PIN HA5 ....59 K2
Ladbrook Rd SNWD SE25 ....180 E6
Ladderstile Ride
    RCHPK/HAM TW10 ....175 J1
Laddersworld Wy
    FBAR/BDGN N11 ....48 C1
Lady Alesford Av STAN HA7 ....43 H1
Lady Booth Rd KUT/HW KT1 ....175 F5
Ladycroft Gdns ORP BR6 ....216 C3
Ladycroft Rd LEW SE13 ....144 E4
Ladycroft Wk STAN HA7 ....43 K3
Ladycroft Wy ORP BR6 ....216 C3
Lady Forsdyke Wy
    HOR/WEW KT19 ....206 C6
Ladygate La RSLP HA4 ....58 A3
Ladygrove CROY/NA CRO 213 G6
Lady Harewood Wy
    HOR/WEW KT19 ....206 C6
Lady Hay WPK KT4 ....192 C6
Lady Margaret Rd ARCH N19 ....84 C2
    STHL UB1 ....95 K5
Ladymount WLGTN SM6 ....210 D2
Ladyship Ter EDUL SE22 * 163 H2
Ladysmith Av EHAM E6 ....107 J1
    GNTH/NBYPK IG2 ....72 C2
Ladysmith Rd CAN/RD E16 ....106 D2
    ELTH/MOT SE9 ....167 F1
    EN EN1 ....24 B3
    KTN/HRWW/W HA3 ....42 E5
    TOTM N17 ....50 C5
    UED N18 ....50 D1

Lady Somerset Rd KTTN NW5 ......84 B2
Lamb La HACK E8 ....86 D5
Lambeth Bridge LBTH SE11 ....17 H5
Lambeth High St STHWK SE1 ....17 K6
Lambeth Hill BLKFR EC4V 12 C5
Lambeth Palace Rd STHWK SE1 ...17 H6
Lambeth Rd STHWK SE1 ....17 J5
    STHWK SE1 ....18 A5
Lambeth Wk LBTH SE11 ....17 H6
    PECK SE15 ....143 H3
Lamb La HACK E8 ....86 D5
Lamble St KTTN NW5 ....84 A3
Lambley Rd DAGW RM9 ....91 H5
Lamble Pl HAMP NW3 ....83 H4
Lambolle Rd HAMP NW3 ....83 J4
Lambourn Cl HNWL W7 ....116 A2
    KTTN NW5 * 84 C3
Lambourne Av
    WIM/MER SW19 ....159 J6
Lambourne Gdns BARK IG11 ....91 F5
    CHING E4 ....37 J4
    EN EN1 ....24 C2
Lambourne Gv
    BERM/RHTH SE16 ....124 A4
    KUT/HW KT1 ....175 J5
Lambourne Pl
    BKHTH/KID SE3 ....146 A2
    GDMY/SEVK IG3 ....72 E5
    WAN E11 ....71 F3
Lambourne Rd CLAP SW4 ....141 G4
    CHIG IG7 ....55 F1
    GNTH/NBYPK IG2 ....72 D5
    ORP BR6 ....202 D4
    WEA W13 ....97 H6
Lambourn Rd CLAP SW4 ....141 G4
Lambrook Ter FUL/PGN SW6 ......139 H2
Lamb's Buildings STLK EC1Y 6 E7
Lamb's Conduit Pas
    FSBYW WC1X 11 G1
Lamb's Conduit St
    BMSBY WC1N 5 G7
Lambscroft Av ELTH/MOT SE9 ....166 B5
Lambs Meadow WFD IG8 ....53 H4
Lamb's Ms IS N1 * 6 A1
Lamb's Pas STLK EC1Y 6 E7
Lambs Ter ED N9 * 35 K4
Lamb St WCHPL E1 ....13 H1

Lambton Pl NTGHL W11 * 100 D6
Lambton Rd ARCH N19 ....66 E5
    RYNPK SW20 ....177 F5
Lamb Wk STHWK SE1 ....19 G3
Lamerton Rd BARK/HLT IG6 ....54 B5
Lamerton St DEPT SE8 ....124 D6
Lamford Cl TOTM N17 ....49 K6
Lamington St HMSMTH W6 ....118 E4
Lamlash St LBTH SE11 ....18 A6
Lammas Av MTCM CR4 ....179 F5
Lammas Park Gdns EA W5 ....116 D1
Lammas La ESH/CLAY KT10 ....204 A2
Lammas Rd HOM E9 ....87 F5
    LEY E10 ....69 G6
    RCHPK/HAM TW10 ....156 D6
Lammermoor Rd BAL SW12 * 161 G2
Lamont Rd WBPTN SW10 ....120 C6
Lamont Road Pas
    WBPTN SW10 * 120 C6
Lamorbey Cl BFN/LL DA15 ....168 A4
Lamorbey Pk BFN/LL DA15 * 168 C3
Lamorna Cl ORP BR6 ....202 B4
    WALTH E17 ....52 A5
Lamorna Gv STAN HA7 ....43 K4
Lampard Gv STNW/STAM N16 ......68 B5
Lampeter Sq HMSMTH W6 ....119 H6
Lamplighter Cl WCHPL E1 ....104 E3
Lamplighters Cl DART DA1 ....171 J1
Lampmead Rd LEW SE13 ....145 H6
Lamport Cl WOOL/PLUM SE18 ...126 E4
Lampton Av HEST TW5 ....135 F2
Lampton House Cl
    WIM/MER SW19 ....159 G6
Lampton Park Rd HSLW TW3 ......135 G3
Lampton Rd HSLW TW3 ....135 G3
Lamson Rd RAIN RM13 ....111 H4
Lanacre Av CDALE/KGS NW9 ....45 G4
Lanark Cl EA W5 ....97 J4
Lanark Pl MV/WKIL W9 ....101 G3
Lanark Rd MV/WKIL W9 ....101 G2
Lanbury Rd PECK SE15 ....144 A5
Lancashire Ct MYFR/PKLN W1K 9 J5
Lancaster Av BARK IG11 ....90 E5
    MTCM CR4 ....195 K4
    WAN E11 ....71 F1
    WIM/MER SW19 ....177 G1
    WNWD SE27 ....162 C4
Lancaster Cl ASHF TW15 ....152 B6
    CDALE/KGS NW9 ....45 G4
    HAYES BR2 ....199 J3
    IS N1 * 86 A5
    STNW/STAM N16 * 86 A3
    STWL/WRAY TW19 ....152 B1
    TOTM N17 ....50 C3
Lancaster Dr HAMP NW3 ....83 J4
    HCH RM12 ....93 K3
    POP/IOD E14 ....125 F1
Lancaster Gdns
    WIM/MER SW19 ....177 H1
Lancaster Ga BAY/PAD W2 ....101 G6
Lancaster Gv HAMP NW3 ....83 H4
Lancaster Ms BAY/PAD W2 * 101 G6
    RCHPK/HAM TW10 ....157 F1
    WAND/EARL SW18 * 140 A3
Lancaster Pk
    RCHPK/HAM TW10 ....137 F6
Lancaster Pl COVGDN WC2E 11 G5
    TWK TW1 ....156 B2
    WIM/MER SW19 ....177 G1
Lancaster Rd EBAR EN4 ....21 K5
    ENC/FH EN2 ....23 K2
    FBAR/BDGN N11 ....48 D2
    FSTGT E7 ....89 F6
    NTGHL W11 ....100 C5
    NTHLT UB5 ....78 C4
    RYLN/HDSTN HA2 ....60 A2
    SNWD SE25 ....181 H6
    STHL UB1 ....95 J6
    UED N18 ....50 B1
    WALTH E17 ....51 F5
    WAN E11 ....70 C6
    WIM/MER SW19 ....177 G1
    WLSDN NW10 ....81 H3
Lancaster Stables HAMP NW3 * ...83 J4
Lancaster St STHWK SE1 ....18 B3
Lancaster Ter BAY/PAD W2 ....8 A5
Lancaster Wk HYS/HAR UB3 ....94 A5
Lancaster Wy WPK KT4 ....192 D5
Lancastrian Rd WLGTN SM6 ....210 E5
Lancefield St NKENS W10 ....100 D2
Lancell St STNW/STAM N16 ....68 A1
Lancelot Av ALP/SUD HA0 ....79 K2
Lancelot Crs ALP/SUD HA0 ....79 K2
Lancelot Gdns EBAR EN4 ....34 A2
Lancelot Pde ALP/SUD HA0 * 80 A3
Lancelot Pl SKENS SW7 ....14 E3
Lancelot Rd ALP/SUD HA0 ....79 K3
    BARK/HLT IG6 ....54 E2
    WELL DA16 ....148 B5
Lance Rd HRW HA1 ....60 C4
Lancer Sq KENS W8 * 120 A2
Lancey Cl CHARL SE7 * 126 C4
Lanchester Rd HGT N6 ....65 K3
Lancing Gdns ED N9 ....36 B3
Lancing Rd CROY/NA CRO 196 A3
    FELT TW13 ....153 J4
    GNTH/NBYPK IG2 ....72 E5
    ORP BR6 ....202 D4
    WEA W13 ....97 H6
Lancing St CAMTN NW1 ....4 C5
Landale Gdns DART DA1 ....171 F3
Landau Wy ERITH DA8 ....131 G5
Landcroft Rd EDUL SE22 ....163 G1
Landells Rd EDUL SE22 ....163 G1
Lander Rd PUT/ROE SW15 ....139 F4
Landgrove Rd
    WIM/MER SW19 ....177 K1
Landleys Flds HOLWY N7 * 84 D3

Landmann Wy NWCR SE14 ....124 A6
Landmark Pl WSWTH SW1 ....144 A4
Landons Cl POP/IOD E14 ....125 F1
Landor Rd BRXN/ST SW9 ....141 K4
Landor Wk SHB W12 ....118 D2
Landra Gdns WCHMH N21 ....35 H1
Landridge Dr EN EN1 ....24 D1
Landridge Rd FUL/PGN SW6 ......139 H3
Landrock Rd CEND/HSY/T N8 ....66 E3
Landscape Rd WFD IG8 ....53 F3
Landseer Av MNPK E12 ....90 A3
Landseer Cl EDGW HA8 ....44 C5
    EMPK RM11 ....75 K5
    WIM/MER SW19 ....178 B4
Landseer Rd ARCH N19 ....84 E1
    EN EN1 ....24 C6
    NWMAL KT3 ....192 A4
    SUT SM1 ....208 E4
Lands' End BORE WD6 ....29 K1
Landstead Rd
    WOOL/PLUM SE18 ....147 J1
The Landway STMC/STPC BR5 ...186 D6
Lane Ap MLHL NW7 * 46 C1
Lane Cl CRICK NW2 ....81 K1
Lane End BXLYHN DA7 ....149 J4
Lane Gdns BUSH WD23 ....28 E1
    ESH/CLAY KT10 ....205 F5
Lanercost Gdns
    STHGT/OAK N14 ....34 E1
Lanercost Rd
    BRXS/STRHM SW2 ....162 B4
    EDGW HA8 ....44 E1
Laneside CHST BR7 ....185 G1
    EDGW HA8 ....44 E1
Laneside Av BCTR RM8 ....56 A5
The Lane BKHTH/KID SE3 ....145 K4
    STJWD NW8 ....101 H1
Laneway PUT/ROE SW15 ....138 E6
Lanfranc Rd BOW E3 ....105 G1
Lanfrey Pl WKENS W14 ....119 J5
Langbourne Av HGT N6 ....66 A6
Langbrook Rd BKHTH/KID SE3 ...146 C4
Langcroft Cl CAR SM5 ....209 K1
Langdale Av MTCM CR4 ....194 E1
Langdale Cl BCTR RM8 ....73 J5
    MORT/ESHN SW14 ....137 J5
    ORP BR6 ....201 G6
Langdale Crs BXLYHN DA7 ....149 H2
Langdale Dr YEAD UB4 ....94 C1
Langdale Gdns HCH RM12 ....93 J5
    PERIVALE UB6 ....97 J3
Langdale Pde MTCM CR4 * 178 E6
Langdale Rd DEPT SE8 ....144 C1
    THHTH CR7 ....196 B1
Langdale St WCHPL E1 * 104 D5
Langdon Crs EHAM E6 ....108 A1
Langdon Dr CDALE/KGS NW9 ......62 E5
Langdon Pk TEDD TW11 ....174 C3
Langdon Park Rd HGT N6 ....66 C4
Langdon Pl MORT/ESHN SW14 ...137 K4
Langdon Rd EHAM E6 ....108 A6
    HAYES BR2 ....184 A6
    MRDN SM4 ....194 B2
Langdon Shaw SCUP DA14 ....186 A1
Langdon Wk MRDN SM4 ....194 B2
Langdon Wy STHWK SE1 * 123 H4
Langford Cl HACK E8 ....86 C3
    SEVS/STOTM N15 ....68 A3
Langford Crs EBAR EN4 ....21 K5
Langford Gn CMBW SE5 ....143 F4
Langford Pl SCUP DA14 ....168 B5
    STJWD NW8 ....101 H1
Langford Rd EBAR EN4 ....21 K5
    FUL/PGN SW6 ....140 A3
    WFD IG8 ....53 G2
Langfords BKHH IG9 ....39 J3
Langham Dr GDMY/SEVK IG3 ....73 H3
Langham Gdns ALP/SUD HA0 ....61 J6
    EDGW HA8 ....44 E3
    RCHPK/HAM TW10 ....156 D6
    WCHMH N21 ....23 G6
    WEA W13 ....97 H6
Langham House Cl
    RCHPK/HAM TW10 ....156 D6
Langham Pde
    SEVS/STOTM N15 * 49 H6
Langham Park Pl HAYES BR2 ......199 J3
Langham Pl CAVSQ/HST W1G 9 K3
    CHSWK W4 ....118 B6
    SEVS/STOTM N15 ....49 H6
Langham Rd EDGW HA8 ....44 E2
    RYNPK SW20 ....177 F4
    SEVS/STOTM N15 ....67 G1
    TEDD TW11 ....174 C1
Langham St REGST W1B 9 K2
Langhedge Cl UED N18 ....50 B2
Langhedge La UED N18 ....50 B1
Langholm Cl BAL SW12 ....161 J2
Langhorn Dr WHTN TW2 ....155 K2
Langhorne Rd DAGE RM10 ....92 C5
Langland Ct NTHWD HA6 ....40 A3
Langland Crs STAN HA7 ....43 K6
Langland Dr PIN HA5 ....41 J3
Langland Gdns CROY/NA CRO 198 C6
    HAMP NW3 ....83 F3
Langler Rd WLSDN NW10 ....100 A1
Langley Av RSLP HA4 ....58 E6
    SURB KT6 ....190 E5
    WPK KT4 ....193 J6
Langley Ct BECK BR3 ....198 E1
    COVGDN WC2E 10 E5
Langley Crs DAGW RM9 ....91 J5
    EDGW HA8 ....30 E5
    HYS/HAR UB3 ....133 J1
    WAN E11 ....71 F4
Langley Dr ACT W3 ....117 J2
    WAN E11 ....71 F4
Langley Gdns DAGW RM9 ....91 K5
    STMC/STPC BR5 ....201 G3
Langley Gv NWMAL KT3 ....176 A5
Langley La VX/NE SW8 ....121 K6
Langley Pk EDGW HA8 ....45 G2

Langley Park Rd BELMT SM2 ....209 G4
Langley Rd BECK BR3 ....198 A1
  ISLW TW7 ....136 A3
  SAND/SEL CR2 ....213 F6
  SURB KT6 ....191 F4
  WELL DA16 ....128 C6
  WIM/MER SW19 ....177 J4
Langley Rw BAR EN5 ....20 D2
Langley St LSQ/SEVD WC2H......10 E4
Langley Wy BECK BR3 * 199 G5
Langmead Dr BUSH WD23........28 C3
Langmead St WNWD SE27.......162 C6
Langport Ct WOT/HER KT12.....188 B5
Langridge Ms HPTN TW12..........172 E2
Langroyd Rd TOOT SW17...........160 E4
Langside Av PUT/ROE SW15......138 D5
Langside Crs STHGT/OAK N14...34 D5
Langston Hughes Cl
  HNHL SE24 * 142 C5
Lang St WCHPL E1 ....104 E3
Langthorn Ct LOTH EC2R *........13 F3
Langthorne Rd WAN E11...............88 B1
Langthorne St FUL/PGN SW6.....139 G2
Langton Av EHAM E6 ....108 A2
  TRDG/WHET N20....................33 J2
Langton Cl FSBYW WC1X............5 H5
Langton Gv NTHWD HA6...............40 A1
Langton Ri FSTH SE23.................163 J2
Langton Rd BRXN/ST SW9.........142 C1
  CRICK NW2 ....82 A1
  E/WMO/HCT KT8.....................189 H2
  KTN/HRWW/W HA3...................42 C3
Langton St WBPTN SW10..........120 B6
Langton Vis TOTM N17 * 50 C4
Langton Wy BKHTH/KID SE3.....145 K2
  CROY/NA CR0.........................212 A2
Langtry Pl FUL/PGN SW6...........119 K2
  NTHLT UB5 ....95 H1
Langtry Rd STJWD NW8 ....83 F6
Langtry Wk KIL/WHAMP NW6......83 G6
Langwood Cha TEDD TW11.......174 D2
Langworth Cl RDART DA2...........171 G5
Langworth Dr HAYE UB3...............95 F5
Lanhill Rd MV/WKIL W9 ....100 E3
Lanier Rd LEW SE13 ....165 F1
Lanigan Dr HSLW TW3 ....135 G6
Lankaster Gdns EFNCH N2 ....47 H4
Lankers Dr RYLN/HDSTN HA2....59 K3
Lankton Cl BECK BR3 ....183 F4
Lannock Rd HYS/HAR UB3.........113 J1
Lannoy Rd ELTH/MOT SE9.........167 H3
Lanrick Rd POP/IOD E14............106 B5
Lanridge Rd ABYW SE2 ....128 E3
Lansbury Av BARK IG11................91 G5
  CHDH RM6 ....74 A2
  EBED/NFELT TW14 ....154 A1
  UED N18 ....49 K1
Lansbury Cl WLSDN NW10...........80 E3
Lansbury Crs DART DA1 ....151 K6
Lansbury Dr YEAD UB4 ....94 D2
Lansbury Gdns POP/IOD E14 * ..106 B5
Lansbury Rd PEND EN3 ....25 F2
Lansbury Wy UED N18...................50 A1
Lanscombe Wk VX/NE SW8 * 141 K1
Lansdell Rd MTCM CR4 ....179 F5
Lansdowne Av BXLYHN DA7......148 D1
  ORP BR6 ....201 G5
Lansdowne Cl BRYLDS KT5 ....191 J6
  RYNPK SW20............................177 G3
  TWK TW1 ....156 A3
Lansdowne Copse WPK KT4 * ...192 D6
Lansdowne Ct WPK KT4.............192 D6
Lansdowne Crs NTGHL W11.......100 C6
Lansdowne Dr HACK E8................86 C4
Lansdowne Gdns VX/NE SW8 * ..141 K2
Lansdowne Gn VX/NE SW8 *......141 K1
Lansdowne Gv WLSDN NW10.......81 G2
Lansdowne Hl WNWD SE27.......162 C5
Lansdowne La CHARL SE7 ....126 C5
Lansdowne Ms CHARL SE7 ....126 C5
  NTGHL W11 * 119 J1
Lansdowne Pl NRWD SE19.........181 G3
  STHWK SE1 ....19 F4
Lansdowne Rd BMLY BR1...........183 K3
  CHING E4 ....37 J4
  CROY/NA CR0.........................196 E6
  FNCH N3 ....46 C6
  GDMY/SEVK IG3.......................73 F5
  HOR/WEW KT19......................206 E5
  HSLW TW3 ....135 G4
  MUSWH N10 ....48 B2
  NTHLT UB5 ....78 B6
  NTGHL W11 ....100 C6
  RYNPK SW20............................177 F3
  STAN HA7..................................43 J2
  SWFD E18...................................52 E6
  TOTM N17..................................50 C4
  WALTH E17.................................52 A6
  WAN E11 ....70 D6
Lansdowne Ter BMSBY WC1N 5 F7
Lansdowne Wk NTGHL W11.......119 H1
Lansdowne Wy VX/NE SW8.......141 K2
Lansdowne Wood Cl
  WNWD SE27............................162 C5
Lansdown Rd FSTGT E7...............89 G3
  SCUP DA14...............................168 C5
Lansfield Av UED N18 ....36 C6
Lantern Cl ALP/SUD HA0.............79 K3
  PUT/ROE SW15.......................138 D5
Lanterns Ct POP/IOD E14...........124 D3
Lant St STHWK SE1 ....17 J3
Lanvanor Rd PECK SE15.............143 K3
Lapford Cl MV/WKIL W9 ....100 D3
Lapse Wood Wk FSTH SE23.......163 J3
Lapstone Gdns
  KTN/HRWW/W HA3...................61 J3
Lapwing Cl ERITH DA8 *.............150 E1
Lapwing Ter FSTGT E7 ....89 H3
Lapwing Wy YEAD UB4 ....95 H5
Lapworth Cl ORP BR6................202 D6
Lapworth Ct BAY/PAD W2..........101 F4
Lara Cl CHSGTN KT9..................206 A5

LEW SE13 ....165 F1
Larbert Rd STRHM/NOR SW16 ..179 H4
Larch Av ACT W3 ....118 B1
Larch Cl BAL SW12....................161 G4
  DEPT SE8.................................124 C6
  DEPT SE8 *..............................124 C6
Larch Crs HOR/WEW KT19........206 D4
  YEAD UB4.................................95 G4
Larch Dene ORP BR6.................201 F6
Larch Dr CHSWK W4 * 117 H5
Larches Av MORT/ESHN SW14 ..138 A5
The Larches PLMGR N13 ....35 J5
Larch Gv BFN/LL DA15 ....168 A5
Larch Rd CRICK NW2 ....82 A2
  DART DA1 ....171 G3
  LEY E10 ....69 J6
Larch Tree Wy CROY/NA CR0.....213 J1
Larch Wy HAYES BR2 ....201 F4
Larchwood Av CRW RM5............56 D2
Larchwood Cl CRW RM5............56 E2
Larchwood Rd ELTH/MOT SE9 ..167 G4
Larcombe Cl CROY/NA CR0 ......212 B2
Larcom St WALW SE17 ....18 D7
Larden Rd ACT W3 ....118 B2
Largewood Av SURB KT6...........191 H6
Larissa St WALW SE17 * 19 F7
Larkbere Rd SYD SE26 ....164 B6
Larken Cl BUSH WD23.................28 C3
Larken Dr BUSH WD23.................28 C3
Larkfield Av
  KTN/HRWW/W HA3...................43 H6
Larkfield Rd RCH/KEW TW9......137 F5
  SCUP DA14 ....168 A5
Larkhall La CLAP SW4 ....141 K3
Larkhall Ri CLAP SW4 ....141 H4
Larkham Cl FELT TW13...............153 H5
Larkhill Ter
  WOOL/PLUM SE18 * 147 F1
Lark Rw BETH E2 ....86 E6
Larksfield Gv EN EN1 ....24 D2
Larkshall Crs CHING E4................38 A6
Larkshall Rd CHING E4.................52 C2
Larkspur Cl CDALE/KGS NW9 .....62 D2
  ERP BR6 ....202 D6
  TOTM N17..................................49 K5
Larkspur Gv EDGW HA8 ....30 E6
Larkspur Wy HOR/WEW KT19 ...206 D4
Larkswood Cl ERITH DA8...........150 D2
Larkswood Ri PIN HA5 ....59 G1
Larkswood Rd CHING E4.............37 J6
Lark Wy CAR SM5.......................194 D4
Larkway Cl CDALE/KGS NW9 *....63 F1
Larnach Rd HMSMTH W6...........119 G6
Larne Rd RSLP HA4......................58 D4
Larner Rd ERITH DA8 ....150 B1
Larpent Av PUT/ROE SW15........139 F6
Larwood Cl GFD/PVL UB6 ....78 D3
Lascelles Av HRW HA1 ....60 D4
Lascelles Cl WAN E11...................70 B6
Lascott's Rd WDGN N22...............49 F2
Lassa Rd ELTH/MOT SE9...........146 D6
Lassell St CNWCH SE10.............125 G5
Latchett Rd SWFD E18 ....53 F5
Latchingdon Gdns WFD IG8 ....53 J2
Latchmere Cl
  RCHPK/HAM TW10 ....156 E5
Latchmere La KUTN/CMB KT2...175 G2
Latchmere Rd BTSEA SW11 ......140 E3
  KUTN/CMB KT2 ....175 F2
Latchmere St BTSEA SW11 ....140 E3
Lateward Rd BTFD TW8 ....116 E6
Latham Cl EHAM E6 ....107 J5
Latham Rd BXLYHS DA6............149 J6
  TWK TW1..................................156 A2
Latham's Wy CROY/NA CR0......196 A5
Lathkill Cl EN EN1 ....36 C2
Lathom Rd EHAM E6 ....89 K5
Latimer Av EHAM E6 ....89 K6
Latimer Cl PIN HA5........................41 G4
  WATW WD18 ....26 C2
  WPK KT4...................................207 K2
Latimer Gdns PIN HA5 ....41 G4
Latimer Pl NKENS W10...............100 A5
Latimer Rd BAR EN5 ....21 F4
  CROY/NA CR0 *......................211 H1
  FSTGT E7...................................89 F2
  NKENS W10..............................100 A4
  SEVS/STOTM N15 ....68 A3
  TEDD TW11 ....174 A1
  WIM/MER SW19 ....178 A2
Latona Rd PECK SE15 ....123 H6
La Tourne Gdns ORP BR6..........216 C1
Lattimer Pl CHSWK W4...............138 B1
Latymer Cl WALTH E17 * 51 J3
Latymer Ct HMSMTH W6 * 119 H4
Latymer Rd ED N9 ....36 B4
Lauder Cl NTHLT UB5 ....95 H1
Lauderdale Dr
  RCHPK/HAM TW10 ....156 E5
Lauderdale Pde
  MV/WKIL W9 * 101 F2
Lauderdale Pl BARB EC2Y * 12 D2
Lauderdale Rd MV/WKIL W9......101 F2
Laud St CROY/NA CR0................211 J1
  LBTH SE11................................122 A5
Laughton Rd NTHLT UB5 ....95 H1
Launcelot Rd BMLY BR1.............165 K6
Launcelot St STHWK SE1 ....17 J3
Launceston Gdns GFD/PVL UB6 ..79 J6
Launceston Pl KENS W8.............120 B3
Launceston Rd GFD/PVL UB6 .....79 J6
Launch St POP/IOD E14..............125 F3
Launders Ga ACT W3 *...............117 J2
Laundress La STNW/STAM N16 ...86 C1
Laundry Rd HMSMTH W6 ....119 H6
Laura Cl EN EN1...........................24 A6
  WAN E11 ....70 B2
Lauradale Rd EFNCH N2...............65 K1
Laura Pl CLPT E5 ....86 E2
Laura Ter FSBYPK N4 * 67 H6
Laurel Av TWK TW1 ....156 A3
Laurel Bank
  NFNCH/WDSP N12 * 33 G6

Laurel Bank Gdns
  FUL/PGN SW6 ....139 J3
Laurel Bank Rd ENC/FH EN2 ....23 J2
Laurel Cl BARK/HLT IG6................54 C2
  DART DA1 ....171 F3
  CROY/NA CR0 * 196 A3
  SUT SM1 ....208 D3
  TOOT SW17..............................178 D1
Laurel Crs CROY/NA CR0...........213 J1
  ROMW/RG RM7..........................75 G5
Laurel Dr WCHMH N21................35 G2
Laurel Gdns CHING E4..................37 K2
  HNWL W7 ....115 K1
  HSLWW TW4............................134 C5
  MLHL NW7..................................31 F5
Laurel Gv PGE/AN SE20.............181 J3
  SYD SE26 ....182 A1
Laurel La WDR/YW UB7..............112 B4
Laurel Pk KTN/HRWW/W HA3.....43 F3
Laurel Rd BARN SW13................138 D3
  HPTN TW12..............................173 J1
  RYNPK SW20...........................177 F4
The Laurels BUSH WD23 * 28 C4
  CMBW SE5 * 142 C1
  RDART DA2.............................171 J3
Laurel St HACK E8 ....86 B4
Laurel Vw NFNCH/WDSP N12 .....33 F5
Laurel Vis HNWL W7 * 115 K2
Laurel Wy NFNCH/WDSP N12 .....32 E5
  SWFD E18...................................70 D1
Laurence Ms SHB W12 ....118 D2
Laurence Pountney Hl
  CANST EC4R..............................12 E5
Laurence Pountney La
  CANST EC4R..............................12 E5
Laurie Gv NWCR SE14 ....144 B2
Laurie Rd HNWL W7 ....96 E4
Laurier Rd CROY/NA CR0...........197 G4
  KTTN NW5 ....84 B1
Laurimel Cl STAN HA7 ....43 H2
Laurino Pl BUSH WD23.................28 C4
Lauriston Rd HOM E9 ....87 F6
  WIM/MER SW19 ....177 F2
Lauriston Rd CEND/HSY/T N8......67 G1
  PECK SE15...............................143 K2
Lavender Av CDALE/KGS NW9.....62 E5
  MTCM CR4 ....178 D4
  WPK KT4..................................208 A1
Lavender Cl CAR SM5 ....210 A2
  CHEL SW3...............................120 C6
  HAYES BR2...............................200 D3
Lavender Ct E/WMO/HCT KT8 ...173 G6
Lavender Gdns BTSEA SW11......140 E5
  ENC/FH EN2..............................23 H1
  KTN/HRWW/W HA3...................42 E2
Lavender Gv HACK E8...................86 C5
  MTCM CR4 ....178 D4
Lavender Hl BTSEA SW11...........140 E4
  ENC/FH EN2 ....23 J2
Lavender Pl IL IG1.........................90 B3
Lavender Ri WDR/YW UB7..........112 D2
Lavender Rd
  BERM/RHTH SE16....................124 B1
  BTSEA SW11 ....140 C4
  CAR SM5 ....210 A2
  CROY/NA CR0 ....196 A3
  ENC/FH EN2 ....23 J2
  HOR/WEW KT19 ....206 D5
  SUT SM1 ....209 H2
Lavender St SRTFD E15 ....88 C4
Lavender Sweep BTSEA SW11...140 E5
Lavender Ter BTSEA SW11 * 140 D4
Lavender V WLGTN SM6.............210 D4
Lavender Wy CROY/NA CR0.......198 A3
Lavengro Rd WNWD SE27..........162 D4
Lavenham Rd
  WAND/EARL SW18...................159 J3
Lavernock Rd BXLYHN DA7.......149 H3
Lavers Rd STNW/STAM N16 ....86 A1
Laverstoke Gdns
  PUT/ROE SW15 ....158 C2
Laverton Ms ECT SW5 ....120 A4
Laverton Pl ECT SW5 ....120 A4
Lavidge Rd ELTH/MOT SE9 ....166 D4
Lavina Gv IS N1 ....5 G2
Lavington Cl HOM E9....................87 H4
Lavington Rd CROY/NA CR0.......211 F1
  WEA W13..................................116 C1
Lavington St STHWK SE1............18 B1
Lavinia Rd DART DA1 ....171 J1
Lawdon Gdns CROY/NA CR0......211 H2
Lawford Gdns DART DA1.............151 F6
Lawford Rd CHSWK W4...............137 K1
  IS N1..86 A5
  KTTN NW5 ....84 C4
Lawless St POP/IOD E14 * 105 K6
Lawley Rd STHGT/OAK N14 ....34 B2
Lawley St CLPT E5 ....86 E2
Lawn Cl BMLY BR1......................184 A3
  EN EN1 ....36 B2
  NWMAL KT3.............................176 A6
  RSLP HA4 ....76 D1
  SWLY BR8.................................187 K5
Lawn Crs RCH/KEW TW9 ....137 H3
Lawn Farm Gv CHDH RM6............74 A1
Lawn Gdns HNWL W7 ....115 K1
Lawn House Cl POP/IOD E14......125 F2
Lawn La VX/NE SW8 ....141 K1
Lawn Rd BECK BR3.....................182 D3
  HAMP NW3.................................83 K3
Lawns Ct WBLY HA9 *..................62 C6
The Lawns BELMT SM2 ....208 C5
  BKHTH/KID SE3 * 145 J4
  CHING E4 ....37 H4
  NRWD SE19 ....180 E4
  PIN HA5 ....42 B3
  SCUP DA14..............................168 C6
Lawns Wy CRW RM5....................56 E3
Lawnswood BAR EN5 * 20 C6
Lawn Ter BKHTH/KID SE3..........145 H4
The Lawn NWDGN UB2 ....115 F5
Lawn VI PIN HA5 ....41 H5
Lawrence Av MLHL NW7...............31 G4
  MNPK E12..................................90 A1
  NWMAL KT3.............................192 A3
  PLSTW E13.................................89 F1

WALTH E17 ....51 F4
  WLSDN NW10 ....81 F6
Lawrence Blds STNW/STAM N16 ..86 B1
Lawrence Cl SEVS/STOTM N15 ...68 A1
  SHB W12 * 99 K6
Lawrence Ct MLHL NW7...............45 G5
  OXHEY WD19 * 27 H5
Lawrence Crs DAGE RM10 ....92 D1
  EDGW HA8.................................44 C5
Lawrence Dr HGDN/ICK UB10......76 A2
Lawrence Gdns MLHL NW7 ....31 H5
Lawrence La CHING E4..................37 J4
Lawrence Pde ISLW TW7 * 136 C4
Lawrence Rd EA W5 ....116 D4
  ERITH DA8................................149 J1
  GPK RM2....................................75 K2
  HPTN TW12..............................172 E3
  HSLWW TW4............................134 B5
  PIN HA5 ....59 H2
  PLSTW E13.................................89 F6
  RCHPK/HAM TW10 ....156 D6
  SEVS/STOTM N15 ....50 A6
  SNWD SE25..............................197 G1
  UED N18 ....36 D6
  WWKM BR4 ....214 E2
  YEAD UB4 ....94 A1
Lawrence St CAN/RD E16...........106 D4
  CHEL SW3 ....120 C6
  MLHL NW7..................................31 H6
Lawrence Wy WLSDN NW10 ....80 E1
Lawrence Yd SEVS/STOTM N15...68 A1
Lawrie Park Av SYD SE26...........181 J1
Lawrie Park Crs SYD SE26 ....181 J1
Lawrie Park Gdns SYD SE26 ......181 J1
Lawrie Park Rd SYD SE26 ....181 K2
Laws Cl THHTH CR7....................196 E1
Lawson Cl CAN/RD E16...............107 G5
  IL IG1 ....90 D3
  WIM/MER SW19 ....159 G3
Lawson Gdns DART DA1.............151 G6
  PIN HA5 ....41 F6
Lawson Rd DART DA1.................151 G5
  PEND EN3...................................24 E2
  STHL UB1 ....95 K3
Law St STHWK SE1 ....19 F4
Lawton Rd BOW E3.....................105 G2
  EBAR EN4 ....21 H4
  LEY E10 ....70 A5
Laxcon Cl WLSDN NW10 ....81 F3
Laxey Rd ORP BR6.....................217 F4
Laxley Cl CMBW SE5 ....142 C1
Laxton Pl CAMTN NW1.................4 A7
Layard Rd BERM/RHTH SE16.....123 J4
  EN EN1.......................................24 B2
  THHTH CR7..............................180 E5
Laycock St IS N1 ....85 G4
Layer Gdns ACT W3 * 98 C6
Layfield Cl HDN NW4 ....63 K4
Layfield Crs HDN NW4 ....63 K4
Layhams Rd WWKM BR4 ....214 C2
Laymarsh Cl BELV DA17.............129 G3
Laymead Cl NTHLT UB5 ....77 J4
Laystall St FSBYW WC1X 5 J7
Layton Crs CROY/NA CR0 ....211 G3
Layton Pl RCH/KEW TW9 * 137 H2
Layton Rd BTFD TW8 ....116 E5
  HSLW TW3 ....135 G5
Layzell Wk ELTH/MOT SE9.........166 C5
Lazenby Ct COVGDN WC2E * 10 E5
Leabank Cl HRW HA1 * 78 E1
Leabank Sq HOM E9.....................87 J4
Leabank Vw SEVS/STOTM N15 ...68 C3
Leabourne Rd STNW/STAM N16 ..68 C3
Lea Bridge Rd CLPT E5.................69 F6
  WALTH E17.................................51 F1
Lea Cl WHTN TW2 ....154 E2
Lea Crs RSLP HA4 ....76 D2
Leacroft Av BAL SW12................160 E2
Leacroft Cl WCHMH N21 ....35 H4
Leadale Av CHING E4 ....37 J4
Leadale Rd SEVS/STOTM N15 ....68 C3
Leadbeaters Cl
  FBAR/BDGN N11 * 47 K1
Leadenhall Pl FENCHST EC3M 13 G4
Leadenhall St BANK EC3V 13 G4
Leader Av MNPK E12 ....90 A3
The Leadings WBLY HA9...............80 E1
Leaf Cl NTHWD HA6 ....40 B3
  THDIT KT7 ....189 K2
Leaf Gv STRHM/NOR SW16 ....180 B1
Leafield Cl STRHM/NOR SW16 ...180 C2
Leafield La SCUP DA14...............169 G6
Leafield Rd RYNPK SW20...........177 J6
  SUT SM1 ....193 K6
Leafy Gv HAYES BR2 ....215 G5
Leafy Oak Rd LEE/GVPK SE12...166 B6
Leafy Wy CROY/NA CR0 ....197 G6
Lea Gdns WBLY HA9.....................80 A2
Leagrave St CLPT E5 ....86 E1
Lea Hall Gdns LEY E10 * 69 J5
Lea Hall Rd LEY E10......................69 J5
Leahurst Rd LEW SE13 ....145 G6
Leake St STHWK SE1 ....17 H2
Lealand Rd SEVS/STOTM N15 .....68 B3
Leamington Av BMLY BR1...........184 B1
  MRDN SM4.................................193 J1
  ORP BR6 ....216 E2
  WALTH E17.................................69 J2
Leamington Cl BMLY BR1............166 B6
  HSLW TW3 ....135 H6
Leamington Crs
  RYLN/HDSTN HA2......................77 J1
Leamington Gdns
  GDMY/SEVK IG3.......................73 F6
Leamington Pk ACT W3 ....99 F4
Leamington Rd NWDGN UB2 ......114 C4
Leamington Road Vis
  NTGHL W11..............................100 D4

Leamore St HMSMTH W6............118 E4
Leamouth Rd EHAM E6 ....107 J5
  POP/IOD E14 ....106 B5
Leander Rd BRXS/STRHM SW2 ..162 A1
  NTHLT UB5 ....96 A1
  THHTH CR7..............................196 A1
Learner Dr RYLN/HDSTN HA2 .....60 A6
Lea Rd BECK BR3 ....182 D5
  ENC/FH EN2 ....23 K2
  NWDGN UB2............................114 D4
Learoyd Gdns EHAM E6 ....108 A6
Leas Cl CHSGTN KT9..................206 B5
Leas Gn ELTH/MOT SE9 ....167 F5
Leas Gn CHST BR7......................186 A2
Leaside Av MUSWH N10 ....66 A1
Leaside Rd CLPT E5 ....68 E5
Leasowes Rd LEY E10 ....69 J5
Leathart Cl HCH RM12..................93 K5
Leatherbottle Gn
  ERITH DA18.............................129 G3
Leather Cl MTCM CR4 ....179 F5
Leatherdale St WCHPL E1 *.........105 F2
Leather Gdns SRTFD E15 ....88 C6
Leatherhead Cl
  STNW/STAM N16 ....68 A5
Leather La CLKNW EC1R 11 J1
  HCIRC EC1N...............................11 J3
Leathermarket Ct STHWK SE1 .....19 G3
Leathermarket St STHWK SE1 .....19 G3
Leather Rd BERM/RHTH SE16.....124 A4
Leathersellers Cl BAR EN5 *.........20 C4
Leather St WAP E1W 105 F6
Leathsale Rd RYLN/HDSTN HA2 ..78 B1
Leathwaite Rd BTSEA SW11 ......140 E5
Leathwell Rd DEPT SE8 ....144 E3
Lea V DART DA1 ....150 A5
Lea Valley Rd CHING E4................37 J2
Lea Valley Wk TOTM N17..............50 D5
Leaveland Cl BECK BR3...............198 D1
Leaver Gdns GFD/PVL UB6 ....96 D1
Leavesden Rd STAN HA7 ....43 G2
Leaway CLPT E5 ....68 C6
Leaway Av FELT TW13.................172 C1
Lebanon Gdns
  WAND/EARL SW18...................159 K1
Lebanon Pk TWK TW1 ....156 C2
Lebanon Rd CROY/NA CR0.........197 F5
  WAND/EARL SW18...................139 K6
Lebrun Sq BKHTH/KID SE3.........146 A5
Lechmere Ap WFD IG8..................53 G5
Lechmere Av CHIG IG7.................54 C1
Lechmere Rd CRICK NW2 ....81 K4
Leckford Rd
  WAND/EARL SW18...................160 B3
Leckwith Av ABYW SE2.................129 F6
Lecky St SKENS SW7 ....120 B5
Leconfield Av BARN SW13 ....138 C4
Leconfield Rd HBRY N5.................85 K2
Leda Av PEND EN3.......................25 F2
Leda Rd WOOL/PLUM SE18........126 E3
Ledbury Ms North NTGHL W11 ...100 E6
Ledbury Ms West NTGHL W11 ....100 E6
Ledbury Rd CROY/NA CR0 ....211 J2
  NTGHL W11..............................100 E5
Ledbury St PECK SE15................143 H1
Ledrington Rd NRWD SE19.........181 G2
Ledway Dr WBLY HA9...................62 B2
Lee Av CHDH RM6........................74 A3
Leechcroft Av BFN/LL DA15 ....148 A6
Leechcroft Rd WLGTN SM6 ....210 A1
Lee Church St LEW SE13 ....145 H5
Lee Cl BAR EN5.............................21 J5
Lee Conservancy Rd HOM E9 ......87 H3
Leecroft Rd BAR EN5 ....20 C6
Leeds Cl ORP BR6......................202 E6
Leeds Rd IL IG1.............................72 D5
Leeds St UED N18.........................50 C1
Lee Gn STMC/STPC BR5 ....202 B2
Lee High Rd LEW SE13 ....145 G5
Lee Rd BFN/LL DA15 * 168 B3
Lee Gn STMC/STPC BR5 ....202 B2
Leeland Rd WEA W13..................116 B1
Leeland Ter WEA W13 ....116 B1
Leeland Wy WLSDN NW10 ....81 G1
Leemount Cl HDN NW4 * 64 B1
Lee Pk BKHTH/KID SE3...............145 J5
Lee Rd BKHTH/KID SE3 ....145 J4
  EN EN1.......................................36 B1
  GFD/PVL UB6.............................96 B3
  MLHL NW7..................................46 B3
  WIM/MER SW19 ....178 A5
Lees Av NTHWD HA6 ....40 D1
The Lees CROY/NA CR0 ....198 C6
Lee St HACK E8.............................86 A5
Lee Ter BKHTH/KID SE3..............145 H4
The Lee NTHWD HA6 ....40 D1
Leeward Gdns
  WIM/MER SW19 ....177 H2
Leeway DEPT SE8 ....124 C5
The Leeways CHEAM SM3 * 208 C5
Leewood Cl LEE/GVPK SE12 * 165 J1
Lefevre Wk BOW E3 ....87 H6
Leffern Rd SHB W12 ....118 D2
Lefroy Rd SHB W12 ....118 C2
Left Side STHGT/OAK N14 * 34 D3
Legard Rd HBRY N5 ....85 H1
Legatt Rd ELTH/MOT SE9 ....146 C5
Leggatt Rd SRTFD E15 ....106 A1
Legge St LEW SE13.....................145 F6
Leghorn Rd WLSDN NW10...........99 H1
  WOOL/PLUM SE18...................127 J5
Legion Cl IS N1..............................85 G5
Legion Ter BOW E3 ....87 J6
Legion Wy NFNCH/WDSP N12 .....47 J3
Legon Av ROMW/RG RM7 ....74 E5
Legrace Av HSLWW TW4.............134 C3

eicester Av MTCM CR4 ....195 K1
eicester CI WPK KT4 ....208 A2
eicester Gdns GDMY/SEVK IG3 ..72 E4
eicester PI LSO/SEVD WC2H *...10 C5
eicester Rd BAR EN5 ....10 C5
CROY/NA CR0 ....197 F4
EFNCH N2 ....47 J6
WAN E11 ....71 F2
WLSDN NW10 ....81 F5
eicester Sq LSO/SEVD WC2H *...10 D6
eicester St SOHO/SHAV W1D ...10 D5
eigham Av
STRHM/NOR SW16 ....161 K5
eigham CI
STRHM/NOR SW16 ....125 K5
eigham Court Rd
STRHM/NOR SW16 ....162 A5
eigham Dr ISLW TW7 ....135 K1
eigham Hall Pde
STRHM/NOR SW16 ....161 K5
eigham V STRHM/NOR SW16 ...162 B5
eigh Av REDBR IG4 ....71 H1
eigh CI NWMAL KT3 ....192 A1
eigh Ct RYLN/HDSTN HA2 *.......90 A3
eigh Gdns CROY/NA CR0 ....213 K5
eigh Hunt Dr STHGT/OAK N14 ...34 C4
eigh Orchard CI
STRHM/NOR SW16 ....162 A5
eigh PI FELT TW15 ....154 B3
WELL DA16 ....148 B3
eigh Rd EHAM E6 ....90 A5
HBRY N5 ....85 H2
HSLW TW3 ....135 J5
LEY E10 ....70 A4
eigh Rodd OXHEY WD19 ....27 J5
eigh St STAN WC1H 4 L6
eigh Ter STMC/STPC BR5 *.....186 C6
he Leigh KUTN/CMB KT2 ....176 B2
eighton Av MNPK E12 ....90 A3
PIN HA5 ....41 J6
eighton CI EDGW HA8 ....44 C5
eighton Crs KTTN NW5 ....84 C3
eighton Gdns WLSDN NW10 .....100 A1
eighton PI KTTN NW5 ....84 C3
eighton Rd EN EN1 ....24 B6
KTN/HRWW/W HA3 ....42 D5
KTTN NW5 ....84 C3
WEA W13 ....116 B2
eighton St CROY/NA CR0 ....196 C5
eila Parnell PI CHARL SE7 ....126 A4
eila Rd MORT/ESHN SW14 ......137 K4
einster Av MORT/ESHN SW14 ...137 K4
einster Gdns BAY/PAD W2 .....101 G5
einster PI BAY/PAD W2 ....101 G5
einster Rd MUSWH N10 ....66 B1
einster Ter BAY/PAD W2 ....100 E6
eisure Wy NFNCH/WDSP N12 ...47 F1
eith CI CDALE/KGS NW9 ....63 F5
eithcote Gdns
STRHM/NOR SW16 ....162 A6
eithcote Pth
STRHM/NOR SW16 ....162 A5
eith HI STMC/STPC BR5 ....186 B4
eith Rd WDGN N22 ....49 G5
eith Towers BELMT SM2 *.......209 F5
eith Yd KIL/WHAMP NW6 *.......2 E6
ela Av HSLW TW4 ....134 D3
eletia CI HACK E8 ....86 C6
eman St WCHPL E1 ....13 K4
emark CI STAN HA7 ....43 J2
e May Av LEE/GVPK SE12 ....166 A5
emmon Rd GNWCH SE10 ....125 H5
emna Rd WAN E11 ....70 C4
emonwell Dr ELTH/MOT SE9 ...147 G6
emsford CI SEVS/STOTM N15 ...68 C3
ena Crs ED N9 ....36 E4
ena Gdns HMSMTH W6 ....119 F3
ena Kennedy CI CHING E4 ....52 A2
endal Ter CLAP SW4 ....141 J4
enelby Rd SURB KT6 ....191 H5
en Freeman PI FUL/PGN SW6 ..119 J3
enham Rd BXLYHN DA7 ....129 G6
LEW SE13 ....145 J5
SUT SM1 ....209 J2
THHTH CR7 ....180 E5
ennard Av WWKM BR4 ....199 H6
ennard Rd CRICK NW2 ....82 A3
ennard Rd CROY/NA CR0 ....196 C5
HAYES BR2 ....200 E3
PGE/AN SE20 ....182 A2
SYD SE26 ....181 K2
ennard Ter SYD SE26 * 182 A2
ennon Rd CRICK NW2 ....82 A3
ennox Gdns CROY/NA CR0 ....211 H2
IL IG1 ....71 K5
KTBR SW1X 14 E5
WLSDN NW10 ....81 H1
ennox Gardens Ms CHEL SW3 ..14 E6
ennox Rd FSBYPK N4 ....67 F6
WALTH E17 ....69 J3
enthall Rd HACK E8 ....86 B5
enthorp Rd GNWCH SE10 ....125 J3
entmead Rd BMLY BR1 ....165 J5
enton R RCH/KEW TW9 ....137 F4
enton St WOOL/PLUM SE18 ....127 J4
enton Ter FSBYPK N4 * 67 G2
eof Crs CAT SE6 ....182 E1
eominster Rd MRDN SM4 ....194 B3
eominster Wk MRDN SM4 ....194 B2
eonard Av MRDN SM4 ....194 B2
ROMW/RG RM7 ....75 F6
eonard Ct KENS W8 ....119 K3
eonard PI HAYES BR2 * 215 J1
STNW/STAM N16 * 86 A2
eonard Rd CHING E4 ....51 J2
ED N9 ....36 B5
MTCM CR4 ....179 H4
SWFD E18 ....53 F1
WDGN N22 ....114 C3
Leonard St CAN/RD E16 ....126 D1
SDTCH EC2A 7 H7
Leontine CI PECK SE15 ....143 H1
Leopold Av WIM/MER SW19 ....177 J1
Leopold Ms HOM E9 ....86 E6
Leopold Rd EA W5 ....117 G1
EFNCH N2 ....47 H6
UED N18 ....50 D1
WALTH E17 ....69 J2
WIM/MER SW19 ....159 J6
WLSDN NW10 ....81 G5
Leopold St BOW E3 ....105 H4
Leo St PECK SE15 ....143 J1
Leppoc Rd CLAP SW4 ....141 J6
Leroy St STHWK SE1 ....19 G6
Lerry CI WKENS W14 ....119 J6
Lescombe CI FSTH SE23 ....164 B5
Lescombe Rd FSTH SE23 ....164 B5
Lesley CI BXLY DA5 ....169 J2
Leslie Gdns BELMT SM2 ....208 E5
Leslie Gv CROY/NA CR0 ....196 E5
Leslie Grove PI CROY/NA CR0 *.197 F5
Leslie Rd CAN/RD E16 ....107 F5
EFNCH N2 ....47 H6
WAN E11 ....88 C1
Lesney Pk ERITH DA8 ....130 A6
Lesney Park Rd ERITH DA8 ......130 A6
Lessar Av CLAP SW4 ....141 H6
Lessingham Av TOOT SW17 .....160 E6
Lessing St FSTH SE23 ....164 B2
Lessington Av ROMW/RG RM7 ..74 E3
Lessness Av BXLYHN DA7 ......108 E7
Lessness Pk BELV DA17 ....129 G5
Lessness Rd MRDN SM4 ....194 B3
Lessar Av SRTFD E15 ....106 C3
Lestock CI SNWD SE25 ....181 H6
Leston CI RAIN RM13 ....111 K2
Leswin Pl STNW/STAM N16 ....86 B1
Leswin Rd STNW/STAM N16 ......86 B1
Letchford Gdns WLSDN NW10 ...99 J2
Letchford Ms WLSDN NW10 * 99 J2
Letchford Ter
KTN/HRWW/W HA3 * 42 B4
Letchworth Av
EBED/NFELT TW14 ....153 J2
Letchworth CI HAYES BR2 ....199 K2
OXHEY WD19 ....41 H1
Letchworth Dr HAYES BR2 ......199 K2
Letchworth St TOOT SW17 ......160 E6
Letterstone Rd FUL/PGN SW6 ..139 J1
Lettice St FUL/PGN SW6 ....139 J3
Lett Rd SRTFD E15 ....88 B5
Leucha Rd WALTH E17 ....57 G4
Levana CI WIM/MER SW19 ......159 H5
Levehurst Wy CLAP SW4 ....141 K3
Leven CI OXHEY WD19 * 41 H1
Levendale Rd FSTH SE23 ....164 B4
Leven Rd POP/IOD E14 ....106 A4
Leven Wy HYS/HAR UB3 ....94 C5
Leverett St CHEL SW3 * 14 D6
Leverholme Gdns
ELTH/MOT SE9 ....167 F6
Leverson St
STRHM/NOR SW16 ....179 H2
Lever St FSBYE EC1V 6 C5
Leverton PI KTTN NW5 ....84 C3
Leverton St KTTN NW5 ....84 C3
Levett Gdns BARK IG11 ....91 F2
Levett Rd BARK IG11 ....90 E4
Levine Gdns BARK IG11 ....109 K1
Lewesdon CI WIM/MER SW19 ..159 G3
Lewes Rd BMLY BR1 ....184 C5
NFNCH/WDSP N12 ....47 J1
Leweston Pl STNW/STAM N16 ...68 B4
Lewgars Av CDALE/KGS NW9 ...62 E3
Lewing CI ORP BR6 ....201 K5
Lewin Rd BXLYHS DA6 ....148 E6
MORT/ESHN SW14 ....138 A4
STRHM/NOR SW16 ....179 J2
Lewis Av WALTH E17 ....51 J4
Lewis CI STHGT/OAK N14 ....34 C2
Lewis Crs WLSDN NW10 ....80 E3
Lewisham High St LEW SE13 ...144 E4
Lewisham Hl LEW SE13 ....145 F3
Lewisham Pk LEW SE13 ....164 E1
Lewisham Rd LEW SE13 ....144 E2
Lewisham Wy BROCKY SE4 ....144 C3
Lewis Rd HACK E8 * 86 C3
Lewis Rd MTCM CR4 ....178 D5
RCHPK/HAM TW10 * 136 E6
SCUP DA14 ....168 D5
STHL UB1 ....114 D2
SUT SM1 ....209 F2
WELL DA16 ....148 D4
Lewis St CAMTN NW1 ....84 B5
Lewiston CI WPK KT4 ....192 E4
Lewis Wy DAGE RM10 ....92 D4
Lexden CI CHDH RM6 ....73 K3
Lexden Dr ACT W3 ....98 D6
MTCM CR4 ....195 J1
Lexham Gdns ECT SW5 ....120 A4
KENS W8 ....119 K4
Lexham Ms KENS W8 ....119 K4
Lexington St SOHO/CST W1F 10 B4
Lexington Wy BAR EN5 ....20 A5
Lexton Gdns BAL SW12 ....161 J3
Leyborne Av WEA W13 ....116 C2
Leyborne Pk RCH/KEW TW9 ....137 H2
Leybourne CI HAYES BR2 ....199 K2
Leybourne Rd CAMTN NW1 * 84 B5
CDALE/KGS NW9 ....62 C2
HGDN/ICK UB10 ....76 A6
WAN E11 ....70 D5
Leybourne St CAMTN NW1 ....84 B5
Leyburn CI WALTH E17 ....70 A1
Leyburn Gdns CROY/NA CR0 ...197 F6
Leyburn Gv UED N18 ....50 C2
Leyburn House
WOOL/PLUM SE18 ....146 D1
Leyburn Rd UED N18 ....50 C2
Leycroft Gdns ERITH DA8 ....150 E2
Leyden St WCHPL E1 ....13 J2
Leyes Rd CAN/RD E16 ....107 H6
Leyfield WPK KT4 ....192 B6
Leyland Av PEND EN3 ....25 G3
Leyland Gdns WFD IG8 ....53 G1
Leyland Rd LEE/GVPK SE12 ....145 K6
Leyland Rd NWCR SE14 ....144 A1
Leys Av DAGE RM10 ....92 E6
Leys CI DAGE RM10 ....92 E5
HRW HA1 ....60 E3
Leysdown Av BXLYHN DA7 ......149 K5
Leysdown Rd ELTH/MOT SE9 ...166 D4
Leysfield Rd SHB W12 ....118 D2
Leys Gdns EBAR EN4 ....22 A6
Leyspring Rd WAN E11 ....70 D5
Leys Rd East PEND EN3 ....25 G2
Leys The EFNCH N2 ....65 G1
The Leys KTN/HRWW/W HA3 ...62 B3
Ley St IL IG1 ....72 B6
Leyswood Dr GNTH/NBYPK IG2 ..72 E2
Leythe Rd ACT W3 ....117 J2
Leyton Cora LEY E10 ....69 J6
Leyton Cross Rd RDART DA2 ...170 C5
Leyton Gra LEY E10 ....69 J5
Leyton Green Rd LEY E10 ....70 A3
Leyton Park Rd LEY E10 ....70 A6
Leyton Rd SRTFD E15 ....88 B3
WIM/MER SW19 ....178 A3
Leytonstone Rd SRTFD E15 ......88 C4
Leywick St SRTFD E15 ....106 C1
Leyton Av ORP BR6 ....217 F4
Liardet St NWCR SE14 ....124 B6
Liberia Rd HBRY N5 ....85 H4
Liberty Av WIM/MER SW19 .....178 C4
Liberty Ms BRXN/ST SW9 ....142 A2
Libra Rd BOW E3 ....105 H1
PLSTW E13 ....106 E1
Library Pde WLSDN NW10 * 81 G6
Library St STHWK SE1 ....18 B3
Lichfield CI EBAR EN4 ....21 K4
Lichfield Gdns
RCHPK/HAM TW10 * 137 F6
Lichfield Gv FNCH N3 ....46 E5
Lichfield Rd BCTR RM8 ....91 H2
BOW E3 ....105 G2
CRICK NW2 ....82 C2
ED N9 ....36 C4
EHAM E6 ....107 H2
HSLW TW4 ....134 B3
NTHWD HA6 ....40 E6
RCH/KEW TW9 ....137 G2
WFD IG8 ....52 C1
Lichfield Ter
RCHPK/HAM TW10 * 137 F6
Lidbury Rd MLHL NW7 ....46 C2
Lidcote Gdns BRXN/ST SW9 *...142 B3
Liddall Wy WDR/YW UB7 ....112 C1
Liddell CI KTN/HRWW/W HA3 ....43 K6
Liddell Gdns WLSDN NW10 ......100 A1
Liddell Rd KIL/WHAMP NW6 ......83 F4
Lidding Rd KTN/HRWW/W HA3 ...61 K2
Liddington Rd SRTFD E15 ....88 D6
Liddon Rd BMLY BR1 ....184 B6
PLSTW E13 ....107 F2
Liden CI WALTH E17 ....69 H4
Lidfield Rd STNW/STAM N16 .....85 K2
Lidgate Rd PECK SE15 * 143 G1
Lidiard Rd WAND/EARL SW18 ..160 B4
Lido Sq TOTM N17 ....49 K5
Lidyard Rd ARCH N19 ....66 C5
Liffler Rd WOOL/PLUM SE18 ....127 K5
Lifford St PUT/ROE SW15 ....139 G5
Lightcliffe Rd PLMGR N13 ....35 G6
Lighterman Ms WCHPL E1 ....105 F5
Lighterman's Rd POP/IOD E14 ..124 D2
Lightfoot Rd CEND/HSY/T N8 ....66 E2
Ligonier St BETH E2 ....7 J6
Lilac CI CHING E4 ....51 J2
Lilac Gdns CROY/NA CR0 ....213 J1
EA W5 ....116 E3
HYS/HAR UB3 ....94 D4
Lilac PI LBTH SE11 ....17 G7
Lilac Rd EN EN1 ....24 B3
Lilah Ms HAYES BR2 ....183 H5
Lilburne Gdns ELTH/MOT SE9 ..146 D6
Lilburne Rd ELTH/MOT SE9 .....146 D6
Lile Crs HNWL W7 ....96 E4
Lilestone Rd STJWD NW8 ....2 D6
Lilestone St STJWD NW8 ....2 E7
Lilian Av PLSTW E13 ....117 H2
Lilian Board Wy GFD/PVL UB6 ...78 D2
Lilian CI STNW/STAM N16 ....86 A1
Lilian Gdns WFD IG8 ....53 F4
Lilian Rd MTCM CR4 ....179 H4
Lillechurch Rd BCTR RM8 ....91 H4
Lilleshall Rd MRDN SM4 ....194 C3
Lilley CI WAP E1W * 123 H1
Lilley La MLHL NW7 ....45 F1
Lillian Av ACT W3 ....117 H2
Lillian Rd BARN SW13 ....118 E6
Lillie Rd FUL/PGN SW6 ....119 G6
Lillieshall Rd CLAP SW4 ....141 G4
Lillie Yd FUL/PGN SW6 ....119 K6
Lillington Gardens Est
PIM SW1V 16 A7
Lilliput Av NTHLT UB5 ....77 J1
Lilliput Rd ROMW/RG RM7 ....75 F4
Lily CI WKENS W14 ....119 G4
Lily Dale Rd SYD SE26 * 181 K3
Lily Gdns ALP/SUD HA0 ....97 J1
Lily PI HCIRC EC1N 11 K1
Lily Rd LEY E10 ....70 A6
Lilyville Rd FUL/PGN SW6 ....139 J2
Limburg Rd BTSEA SW11 ....140 D5
Limeburner La STP EC4M 12 A3
Lime CI BKHH IG9 ....39 H6
BMLY BR1 ....200 D1
KTN/HRWW/W HA3 ....43 J6
OXHEY WD19 ....27 H2
ROMW/RG RM7 ....74 E2
WAP E1W 123 H1
Lime Crs SUN TW16 ....172 B5
Limecroft CI HOR/WEW KT19 ...207 F5
Limedene CI PIN HA5 ....41 H4
Lime Gv BARK/HLT IG6 ....55 F2
BFN/LL DA15 ....168 A1
HYS/HAR UB3 ....94 B6
NWMAL KT3 ....176 A6
ORP BR6 ....201 G6
RSLP HA4 ....59 F3
SHB W12 ....119 F2
TRDG/WHET N20 ....33 K4
TWK TW1 ....156 A1
Limeharbour POP/IOD E14 ....124 E3
Limehouse POP/IOD E14 ....105 H6
Limehouse Cswy POP/IOD E14 .105 H6
Limehouse Link POP/IOD E14 ...105 G6
Limehouse Link (Tunnel)
POP/IOD E14 ....105 H6
Lime Kiln Dr CHARL SE7 ....126 A6
Limerick CI BAL SW12 ....161 H2
Limerston St WBPTN SW10 .....120 B6
Limes Av BARN SW13 ....138 C3
CAR SM5 ....194 E6
CHIG IG7 ....54 C1
CROY/NA CR0 ....211 F1
GLDGN NW11 ....64 C4
MLHL NW7 ....45 G2
NFNCH/WDSP N12 ....33 G6
PGE/AN SE20 ....181 J4
WAN E11 ....71 F1
The Limes Av FBAR/BDGN N11 ..48 B1
FBAR/BDGN N11 * 48 C1
Limes CI CAR SM5 ....194 E6
FBAR/BDGN N11 * 48 C1
Limesdale Gdns EDGW HA8 ......44 E5
Limes Field Rd BARN SW13 * ...138 C2
Limesford Rd PECK SE15 ....144 B5
Limes Gdns WAND/EARL SW18 .159 K1
Limes Gv LEW SE13 ....145 F5
Limes Rd BECK BR3 ....182 E5
CROY/NA CR0 ....196 E3
Limes Rw ORP BR6 ....216 B5
The Limes CMBW SE5 ....142 E1
PUM SW13 ....131 K5
WAND/EARL SW18 ....159 K1
Limestone Wk ERITH DA8 ....128 E2
Lime St FENCHST EC3M 13 G5
WALTH E17 ....69 G1
Lime Street Pas BANK EC3V * ...13 G5
Limes Wk EA W5 * 116 E2
PECK SE15 ....143 K5
Lime Tree Av THDIT KT7 ....189 K5
Limetree CI BRXS/STRHM SW2 .162 A3
Lime Tree Gv CROY/NA CR0 ....214 A6
Lime Tree PI MTCM CR4 ....179 G4
Lime Tree Rd HEST TW5 ....135 G2
Lime Tree Ter CAT SE6 ....164 C3
Lime Tree Wk BUSH WD23 ....28 E3
ENC/FH EN2 ....23 J1
WWKM BR4 ....214 D2
Limewood CI BECK BR3 ....199 F2
WALTH E17 ....69 H1
WEA W13 ....97 H5
Limewood Rd ERITH DA8 ....149 K1
Limpsfield Av THHTH CR7 ....196 A2
WIM/MER SW19 ....159 G4
Linacre CI PECK SE15 ....143 J4
Linacre Rd CRICK NW2 ....81 J4
Linchmere Rd LEE/GVPK SE12 .165 J2
Lincoln Av ROMW/RG RM7 ....75 G5
STHGT/OAK N14 ....34 C5
TWK TW2 ....155 H4
WIM/MER SW19 ....159 G3
Lincoln CI ERITH DA8 ....150 C3
GFD/PVL UB6 ....78 C6
RYLN/HDSTN HA2 ....59 K2
Lincoln Crs EN EN1 ....24 A5
Lincoln Dr OXHEY WD19 ....27 G5
Lincoln Est BOW E3 ....105 J3
Lincoln Gdns IL IG1 ....71 J4
Lincoln Green Rd
STMC/STPC BR5 ....202 A2
Lincoln Ms KIL/WHAMP NW6 .....82 D6
Lincoln Pde EFNCH N2 * 47 J6
Lincoln Rd ALP/SUD HA0 ....79 J6
EN EN1 ....24 A5
ERITH DA8 ....150 C3
FELT TW13 ....154 E5
FSTGT E7 ....89 H4
MTCM CR4 ....195 K3
NFNCH/WDSP N12 ....47 G2
NWMAL KT3 ....175 K6
PLSTW E13 ....107 F3
RYLN/HDSTN HA2 ....59 K2
SCUP DA14 ....186 C1
SNWD SE25 ....181 J6
SWFD E18 ....52 E3
WPK KT4 ....192 E6
Lincoln's Inn Flds LINN WC2A 11 L3
The Lincolns MLHL NW7 ....31 H5
Lincoln St CHEL SW3 ....14 E7
WAN E11 ....70 C6
Lincoln Ter BELMT SM2 * 208 E5
Lincombe Rd BMLY BR1 ....165 J5
Lindal Crs STHGT/OAK N14 ....22 C6
The Lindales TOTM N17 ....50 C2
Lindal Rd BROCKY SE4 ....144 C6
Lindberg Wy ERITH DA8 ....130 D6
Linden Av DART DA1 ....171 J5
EN EN1 ....24 D1
HSLW TW3 ....135 G6
NTHWD HA6 ....40 D6
THHTH CR7 ....196 C1
THHTH CR7 ....196 C1
WBLY HA9 ....80 B5
Linden CI ORP BR6 ....217 G3
RSLP HA4 ....58 E5
STAN HA7 ....43 H1
STHGT/OAK N14 ....34 C1
THDIT KT7 ....190 A4
TEDD TW11 ....174 A1
Linden Crs GFD/PVL UB6 ....79 F4
KUT/HW KT1 ....175 G5
WFD IG8 ....53 F2

FSBYPK N4 .....67 J4
PIN HA5 .....41 H4
RYNPK SW20 .....176 G6
The Linkway BAR EN5 *
BELMT SM2 .....209 G6
Linkwood Wk CAMTN NW1 .....84 D5
Linley Crs ROMW/RG RM7 .....56 D6
Linley Rd TOTM N17 .....50 A5
Linnell Cl GLDGN NW11 .....65 F3
Linnell Dr GLDGN NW11 .....65 F3
Linnell Rd CMBW SE5 .....143 F5
UED N18 .....50 C1
Linnet Cl BUSH WD23 .....28 C3
ED N9 .....37 F3
THMD SE28 .....109 J6
Linnet Ms BAL SW12 .....161 F2
Linnett Cl CHING E4 .....36 A1
Linom Rd CLAP SW4 .....141 K5
Linscott Rd CLPT E5 .....86 E2
Linsdell Rd BARK IG11 .....90 C6
Linsey St BERM/RHTH SE16 .....123 H4
Linslade Cl HSLWW TW4 .....134 D6
PIN HA5 .....46 E1
Linslade Rd POP/IOD BR6 .....217 G4
Linstead St KIL/WHAMP NW6 .....82 E5
Linstead Wy
WAND/EARL SW18 .....159 H2
Lintaine Cl FUL/PCN SW6 * 119 H6
Linthorpe Av ALP/SUD HA0 .....79 J4
Linthorpe Rd EBAR EN4 .....33 J1
STNW/STAM N16 .....68 A4
Linton Cl CAR SM5 .....194 E4
CHARL SE7 .....126 B5
WELL DA16 .....148 B2
Linton Ct ROM RM1 .....57 G5
Linton Gdns EHAM E6 .....107 J5
Linton Rd BARK IG11 .....90 C5
Linton St IS N1 .....6 D1
Lintott Ct STWL/WRAY TW19 .....152 A1
Linver Rd FUL/PCN SW6 .....139 J3
Linwood Cl CMBW SE5 .....143 G3
Linwood Crs EN EN1 .....24 C2
Linzee Rd CEND/HSY/T N8 .....66 E1
Lion Av TWK TW1 .....156 A3
Lion Cl BROCKY SE4 .....164 D1
Lionel Gdns ELTH/MOT SE9 .....146 C6
Lionel Ms NKENS W10 * 100 C4
Lionel Rd ELTH/MOT SE9 .....146 C6
Lionel Rd North BTFD TW8 .....117 F3
Lionel Rd South BTFD TW8 .....117 G5
Lion Gate Gdns RCH/KEW TW9 .....137 G4
Lion Mills BETH E2 * 104 C1
Lion Park Av CHSGTN KT9 .....206 C2
CROY/NA CRO 196 D2
ED N9 .....36 C4
EHAM E6 .....107 K4
WHTN TW2 .....156 A3
Lions Cl ELTH/MOT SE9 .....166 B5
Lion Wy BTFD TW8 .....136 E1
Lion Wharf Rd ISLW TW7 .....136 C4
Liphook Cl HCH RM12 .....93 H2
Liphook Crs FSTH SE23 .....163 K2
Liphook Rd OXHEY WD19 .....27 H6
Lisbon Av WHTN TW2 .....155 H4
Lisburne Rd HAMP NW3 .....83 K2
Lisford St PECK SE15 .....143 G2
Lisgar Ter WKENS W14 .....119 J4
Liskeard Gdns BKHTH/KID SE3 .....145 K2
Lisle Cl TOOT SW17 .....161 G6
Lisle St SOHO/SHAV W1D 10 D5
Lismore Wlk IS N1 * 177 J1
Lismore Circ HAMP NW3 .....83 K3
Lismore Cl ISLW TW7 .....136 B3
Lismore Rd SAND/SEL CR2 .....212 A4
TOTM N17 .....49 K6
Lismore Wlk IS N1 .....85 J4
Lissant Cl SURB KT6 .....190 D4
Lissenden Gdns KTTN NW5 .....84 A2
Lisson Gv STJWD NW8 .....2 C7
Lisson St STJWD NW8 .....8 C1
Lister Cl ACT W3 .....99 F4
MTCM CR4 .....178 D4
Lister Gdns UED N18 .....49 J1
Lister Ms HOLWY N7 .....85 F2
Lister Rd WAN E11 .....70 C5
Liston Rd CLAP SW4 .....141 H4
TOTM N17 .....50 C4
Liston Wy WFD IG8 .....53 G5
Listowel Cl BRXN/ST SW9 .....142 B1
Listowel Rd DAGE RM10 .....92 C1
Listria Pk STNW/STAM N16 .....68 A1
Litchfield Av MRDN SM4 .....193 J4
SRTFD E15 * 88 C4
Litchfield Gdns WLSDN NW10 .....81 J4
Litchfield Rd SUT SM1 .....209 G2
Lithgow's Rd HTHAIR TW6 .....133 H5
Lithos Rd HAMP NW3 .....83 F4
Little Acre BECK BR3 .....182 D6
Little Albany St CAMTN NW1 .....3 K4
Little Argyll St CONDST W1S * 10 A4
Little Benty WDR/YW UB7 .....112 A5
Little Birches BFN/LL DA15 .....167 K4
The Little Boltons
WBPTN SW10 .....120 A5
Little Bornes DUL SE21 .....163 F6
Little Britain STBT EC1A 12 C2
Littlebrook Cl CROY/NA CRO 198 A3
Littlebrook Manor Wy
DART DA1 .....151 K6
Little Brownings FSTH SE23 .....163 J4
Littlebury Rd CLAP SW4 * 141 J4
Little Bury St ED N9 .....36 A2
Little Cedars
NFNCH/WDSP N12 * 33 G6
Little Chester St KTBR SW1X 15 J4
Little Cloisters WEST SW1P * 16 E4
Littlecombe Cl
PUT/ROE SW15 * 159 G1
Littlecote Cl WIM/MER SW19 .....159 G2
Littlecote Pl PIN HA5 .....41 K4
Little Ct WWKM BR4 .....199 H6

Littlecroft ELTH/MOT SE9 .....147 F4
Littledale ABYW SE2 .....128 B6
Little Deans Yd WEST SW1P * 16 E4
Little Dimocks BAL SW12 .....161 G4
Little Dorrit Ct STHWK SE1 .....18 D2
Little Ealing La WEA W13 .....116 D4
Little Edward St CAMTN NW1 * 3 K4
Little Elms HYS/HAR UB5 .....133 G1
Little Essex St TPL/STR WC2R * 11 J5
Little Ferry Rd TWK TW1 * 156 C5
Littlefield Cl ARCH N19 .....84 C2
KUT/HW KT1 .....175 F5
Littlefield Rd EDGW HA8 .....44 E3
Little Friday Rd CHING E4 .....38 C4
Little Gearies BARK/HLT IG6 .....72 B1
Little George St WEST SW1P * 16 E3
Little Green St KTTN NW5 * 84 B2
Littlegrove EBAR EN4 .....33 J1
Little Heath CHARL SE7 .....126 D6
CHDH RM6 .....73 H1
Little Heath Rd BXLYHN DA7 .....149 G2
Littleheath Rd SAND/SEL CR2 .....212 D6
Little Ilford La MNPK E12 .....89 K2
Littlejohn Rd HNWL W7 .....97 F5
STMC/STPC BR5 .....202 B3
Little Marlborough St
REGST W1B * 10 A4
Littlemead ESH/CLAY KT10 .....204 D2
Littlemede ELTH/MOT SE9 .....166 E5
Littlemoor Rd IL IG1 .....90 D1
Littlemore Rd ABYW SE2 .....128 B2
Little Moss La PIN HA5 .....41 J5
Little Newport St
LSQ/SEVD WC2H 10 D5
Little New St FLST/FETLN EC4A 11 K3
Little Orchard Cl PIN HA5 * 41 J5
Little Oxhey La OXHEY WD19 .....41 J1
Little Park Dr FELT TW13 .....154 C4
Little Park Gdns ENC/FH EN2 .....23 K4
Little Pluckett's Wy BKHH IG9 .....39 H5
Little Portland St REGST W1B 9 K3
Little Potters BUSH WD23 .....28 D2
Little Queens Rd TEDD TW11 .....174 A2
Little Queen St DART DA1 .....171 J2
Little Redlands BMLY BR1 .....184 D5
Little Rd HYS/HAR UB3 .....113 J2
Litters Cl WIM/MER SW19 .....178 C4
Little Russell St
NOXST/BSQ WC1A 10 E2
Little St James's St
WHALL SW1A 16 A1
Little St Leonards
MORT/ESHN SW14 .....137 K4
Little Smith St WEST SW1P 16 D4
Littlestone Cl BECK BR3 .....182 D2
Little Strd CDALE/KGS NW9 .....45 H5
Little Stream Cl NTHWD HA6 .....26 C6
Little Thrift STMC/STPC BR5 .....201 H1
Little Titchfield St GTPST W1W 10 A2
Littleton Av CHING E4 .....38 D5
Littleton Crs HRW HA1 .....61 F6
Littleton Rd HRW HA1 .....61 F6
Littleton St WAND/EARL SW18 .....160 B4
Little Trinity La BLKFR EC4V 12 D5
Little Turnstile HHOL WC1V 11 G2
Littlewood LEW SE13 .....165 F1
Little Wood Cl STMC/STPC BR5 .....186 B4
Littlewood Cl WEA W13 .....116 C3
Littleworth Av ESH/CLAY KT10 .....204 D3
Littleworth Common Rd
ESH/CLAY KT10 .....204 D1
Littleworth La ESH/CLAY KT10 .....204 D2
Littleworth Pl ESH/CLAY KT10 .....204 D2
Littleworth Rd ESH/CLAY KT10 .....204 D2
Livermere Rd HACK E8 .....86 B6
Liverpool Gv WALW SE17 .....122 E5
Liverpool Rd CAN/RD E16 .....106 C4
EA W5 .....116 E2
IS N1 .....85 G5
KUTN/CMB KT2 .....175 H5
LEY E10 .....70 A3
THHTH CR7 .....180 D6
Liverpool St LVPST EC2M 13 G2
Livesey Cl KUT/HW KT1 .....175 G6
Livesey Pl PECK SE15 .....123 H6
Livingstone Rd BTSEA SW11 .....140 C4
HSLW TW3 .....135 H5
PLMGR N13 .....48 E2
SRTFD E15 .....88 A6
STHL UB1 .....95 H6
THHTH CR7 .....180 E5
Lizard St FSBYE EC1V 6 D5
Lizban St BKHTH/KID SE3 .....146 A1
Llanelly Rd CRICK NW2 .....64 D6
Llanover Rd ABYW SE2 .....128 C5
WBLY HA9 .....62 A2
Llanthony Rd MRDN SM4 .....194 C3
Llanvanor Rd CRICK NW2 .....64 D6
Llewellyn St BERM/RHTH SE16 .....123 H2
Lloyd Av STRHM/NOR SW16 .....179 K4
Lloyd Baker St FSBYW WC1X 5 J5
Lloyd Ct PIN HA5 .....59 H2
Lloyd Ms PEND EN3 .....25 J1
Lloyd Park Av CROY/NA CRO 212 B2
Lloyd Rd DAGW RM9 .....92 B4
EHAM E6 .....89 K6
WALTH E17 .....69 F1
WPK KT4 .....208 A1
Lloyd's Av FENCHST EC3M 13 H4
Lloyd's Pl BKHTH/KID SE3 * 145 H3
Lloyd's Rw CLKNW EC1R 5 K5
Lloyd Sq FSBYW WC1X 5 J4
Lloyd St FSBYW WC1X 5 J4
Lloyd Thomas Ct WDGN N22 * 49 F3
Lloyd Vls BROCKY SE4 .....144 D3
Loampit Hi LEW SE13 .....144 D4
Loampit V LEW SE13 .....144 D4
Loanda Cl HACK E8 .....86 B6
Loats Rd BRXS/STRHM SW2 .....161 K1
Locarno Rd ACT W3 .....117 K1
GFD/PVL UB6 .....96 C3
Lochaber Rd LEW SE13 .....145 H5

Lochaline St HMSMTH W6 .....119 F6
Lochan Cl YEAD UB4 .....95 J3
Lochinvar St BAL SW12 .....161 G2
Lochleven Cl DART DA1 * 171 F5
Lochmere Cl ERITH DA8 .....129 J6
Lochnagar St POP/IOD E14 .....106 A4
Lock Cha LEW SE13 .....145 H4
Locke Cl RAIN RM13 .....93 H4
Locke Cl NWDGN UB2 * 115 H2
Lockesley Dr STMC/STPC BR5 .....202 A3
Lockesley Sq SURB KT6 * 190 E3
Locket Rd KTN/HRWW/W HA3 .....43 F5
Locket Road Ms
KTN/HRWW/W HA3 .....42 E5
Lockfield Dr PEND EN3 .....25 G3
Lockgate Cl HOM E9 .....87 H3
Lockhart Cl HOLWY N7 .....85 F4
Lockhart St BOW E3 .....105 H3
Lockhurst St CLPT E5 .....87 F2
Lockington Rd VX/NE SW8 .....141 G2
Lockmead Rd LEW SE13 .....145 F4
SEVS/STOTM N15 .....68 C3
Lock Rd RCH/KEW TW9 .....156 D6
Lock's La MTCM CR4 .....179 F4
Locksley Est POP/IOD E14 .....105 H5
Locksley St POP/IOD E14 .....105 H4
Locksmeade Rd
RCHPK/HAM TW10 .....156 C6
Lockton St NTGHL W11 * 100 B6
Lockwood Cl SYD SE26 .....164 A6
Lockwood Pl CHING E4 .....51 J2
Lockwood Sq
BERM/RHTH SE16 .....123 J3
Lockwood Wy CHSGTN KT9 .....206 C3
WALTH E17 .....51 F5
Lockyer St STHWK SE1 .....19 F3
Locomotive Dr
EBED/NFELT TW14 .....153 K3
Locton Gn BOW E3 * 87 H6
Loddiges Rd HOM E9 .....86 E5
Loder St PECK SE15 .....143 K1
Lodge Av CROY/NA CRO 211 F1
DAGW RM9 .....91 F6
DART DA1 .....171 F1
GPK RM2 .....75 J2
KTN/HRWW/W HA3 .....62 A1
Lodge Cl EDGW HA8 * 44 B2
ISLW TW7 .....136 C2
ORP BR6 .....202 C5
UED N18 .....49 J1
WLGTN SM6 .....195 F5
Lodge Ct ALP/SUD HA0 .....80 A3
Lodge Crs ORP BR6 .....202 C5
Lodge Gdns BECK BR3 .....198 C2
Lodge Hi REDBR IG4 .....71 K2
WELL DA16 .....148 C1
Lodgehill Park Cl
RYLN/HDSTN HA2 .....60 B3
Lodge La BXLY DA5 .....168 E1
CROY/NA CRO 213 K5
ED N9 .....36 C4
NFNCH/WDSP N12 .....47 G1
Lodge Mansions Pde
PLMGR N13 * 35 G6
Lodge Ms HBRY N5 * 85 J2
Lodge Pl SUT SM1 .....209 F3
Lodge Rd BMLY BR1 .....184 A3
CROY/NA CRO 196 C3
HDN NW4 .....64 A1
STJWD NW8 .....2 B5
SUT SM1 .....209 F3
WLGTN SM6 .....210 B3
Lodge Vis SHB W12 .....118 C1
Lodge Wy ASHF TW15 .....152 B4
Lodore Gdns CDALE/KGS NW9 .....63 G2
Lodore St POP/IOD E14 .....106 A5
Lofthouse Pl CHSGTN KT9 .....205 J4
Loftie St BERM/RHTH SE16 .....123 H2
Lofting Rd IS N1 .....85 G5
Loftus Rd SHB W12 .....118 E1
Loftus Vls SHB W12 * 118 E1
Logan Cl HSLWW TW4 .....134 E4
PEND EN3 .....25 J1
Logan Ms KENS W8 .....119 K4
ROM RM1 .....75 G2
Logan Pl KENS W8 .....119 K4
Logan Rd ED N9 .....36 D4
WBLY HA9 .....62 A6
The Logans BAR EN5 * 20 B4
Logs Hill CHST BR7 .....184 D4
Logs Hill Cl CHST BR7 .....184 C5
Lolesworth Cl WCHPL E1 .....13 K2
Lollard St LBTH SE11 .....17 J7
Loman St STHWK SE1 .....18 B2
Lomas Cl CROY/NA CRO 214 A5
Lombard Av CROY/NA CRO 197 G4
Lombard La EMB/SEVK IG3 .....72 E5
PEND EN3 * 25 J1
Lombard Rd BTSEA SW11 .....140 C3
FBAR/BDGN N11 * 48 B1
WIM/MER SW19 .....178 A5
Lombard St BANK EC3V 13 F4
Lombard Wall CHARL SE7 .....126 A3
Lombardy Pl BAY/PAD W2 .....101 F6
Lomond Cl ALP/SUD HA0 .....80 B5
SEVS/STOTM N15 .....68 A1
Lomond Gdns SAND/SEL CR2 .....213 G5
Lomond Gv CMBW SE5 .....142 E1
Loncroft Rd CMBW SE5 .....123 F6
Londesborough Rd
STNW/STAM N16 .....86 A2
London Br CANST EC4R 13 F6
London Bridge St STHWK SE1 .....19 F1
London Flds HACK E8 * 86 D5
London Flds East Side HACK E8 .....86 D5
London Flds West Side
HACK E8 .....86 C5
London La BMLY BR1 .....183 K3
HACK E8 .....86 D5
London Loop BORE WD6 .....30 D1
CROY/NA CRO 213 F1

ENC/FH EN2 .....23 J1
WWKM BR4 .....214 B1
London Ms BAY/PAD W2 .....8 C4
London Rd BARK IG11 .....90 B5
BMLY BR1 .....183 J3
BUSH WD23 .....27 J1
CHDH RM6 .....74 C5
CHEAM SM5 .....208 B1
DART DA1 .....150 A6
EN EN1 .....23 K5
EW KT17 .....207 H6
HRW HA1 .....60 E6
ISLW TW7 .....135 K3
KUTN/CMB KT2 .....175 G5
MRDN SM4 .....193 K2
MTCM CR4 .....178 E4
MTCM CR4 .....194 D1
PLSTW E13 .....106 E1
SOCK/AV RM15 .....131 J1
STAN HA7 .....43 J1
STHWK SE1 .....18 A4
STRHM/NOR SW16 .....180 A5
STWL/WRAY TW19 .....152 A4
SWLY BR8 .....187 K5
THHTH CR7 .....196 B3
TWK TW1 .....156 B3
WLGTN SM6 .....210 B2
London Stile CHSWK W4 * 117 H5
London Ter BETH E2 * 7 J4
London Wall BARB EC2Y 12 E2
London Wall Blds LVPST EC2M 13 G2
Lonesome Wy MTCM CR4 .....179 G4
Long Acre COVGDN WC2E 10 E4
STMC/STPC BR5 .....202 E6
Long Acre Ct WEA W13 * 97 G4
Longacre Pl CAR SM5 * 210 A4
Longacre Rd WALTH E17 .....52 B4
Longbeach Rd BTSEA SW11 .....140 E4
Longboat Rw STHL UB1 * 95 K5
Longbridge Rd BARK IG11 .....90 D4
BCTR RM8 .....91 G2
Longbridge Wy LEW SE13 .....145 F6
Longbury Cl STMC/STPC BR5 .....186 C6
Longbury Dr STMC/STPC BR5 .....186 C6
Longcliffe Pth OXHEY WD19 .....26 E5
Long Ct PUR RM19 .....131 K4
Longcroft ELTH/MOT SE9 .....167 F5
Longcroft Dr BARK IG11 .....108 E1
Longcrofte Rd EDGW HA8 .....43 K3
Long Deacon Rd CHING E4 .....38 C3
Longdon Wd HAYES BR2 .....215 J2
Longdown Rd CAT SE6 .....164 D6
Long Dr ACT W3 .....99 G5
GFD/PVL UB6 .....78 B6
RSLP HA4 .....77 J2
Long Elmes KTN/HRWW/W HA3 .....42 C4
Longfellow Rd BOW E3 * 105 J2
WALTH E17 .....69 H3
WPK KT4 .....192 D5
Longfellow Wy STHWK SE1 * 19 K7
Longfield BMLY BR1 .....183 J4
Long Fld CDALE/KGS NW9 .....45 G3
Longfield Av EA W5 .....97 J6
EMPK RM11 .....75 H4
MLHL NW7 .....45 J3
WALTH E17 .....69 G1
WLGTN SM6 .....195 F5
Longfield Crs SYD SE26 .....163 K5
Longfield Dr
MORT/ESHN SW14 .....137 J6
WIM/MER SW19 .....178 D4
Longfield Est STHWK SE1 .....19 K6
Longfield Rd EA W5 .....97 J5
Longfield St
WAND/EARL SW18 .....159 K2
Longford Av
EBED/NFELT TW14 .....153 H1
STHL UB1 .....96 A6
STWL/WRAY TW19 .....152 A1
Longford Cl FELT TW15 .....154 D5
HPTN TW12 .....155 F6
YEAD UB4 .....95 H6
Longford Ct HOR/WEW KT19 .....206 E2
STWL/WRAY TW19 * 152 A1
Longford Gdns SUT SM1 .....209 G1
YEAD UB4 .....95 H6
Longford Rd WHTN TW2 .....155 F3
Longford St CAMTN NW1 .....3 K6
Longford Wy
STWL/WRAY TW19 .....152 B3
Longhayes Av CHDH RM6 .....55 K6
Longheath Gdns
CROY/NA CRO 197 K2
Longhedge St BTSEA SW11 .....141 F3
Longhill Rd CAT SE6 .....165 G4
Longhook Gdns NTHLT UB5 .....94 E1
Longhurst Rd CROY/NA CRO 197 K3
LEW SE13 .....145 H5
Longland Dr TRDG/WHET N20 .....33 F5
Longlands Ct
BFN/LL DA15 .....167 K5
WIM/MER SW19 .....178 A1
Longlands Park Crs
BFN/LL DA15 .....167 K5
Longlands Rd BFN/LL DA15 .....167 K5
Long La BXLYHN DA7 .....148 E3
CROY/NA CRO 197 K3
FNCH N3 .....47 F4
STBT EC1A 12 B1
STHWK SE1 .....19 G4
STWL/WRAY TW19 .....152 C3
Longleat Rd EN EN1 .....24 A6
Longleat Wy
EBED/NFELT TW14 .....153 F2
Longleigh La ABYW SE2 .....128 D6
Longley Av ALP/SUD HA0 .....80 B6
Longley Rd CROY/NA CRO 196 C4
HRW HA1 .....60 D2
TOOT SW17 .....178 D2
Longley St STHWK SE1 .....123 H4
Longley Wy CRICK NW2 .....82 A1

Long Mark Rd CAN/RD E16 .....107 H5
Longmarsh La THMD SE28 .....127 K1
Long Md CDALE/KGS NW9 .....45 H4
Longmead CHST BR7 .....185 F5
Longmead Dr SCUP DA14 .....168 E4
Long Meadow HOLWY N7 * 84 D4
Longmeadow Rd
BFN/LL DA15 .....167 K3
Longmead Rd HYS/HAR UB3 .....94 E6
THDIT KT7 .....189 K4
TOOT SW17 .....178 E1
Longmoore St PIM SW1V 16 A7
Longmore Av BAR EN5 .....33 G1
Longnor Rd WCHPL E1 .....105 F2
Long Pond Rd
BKHTH/KID SE3 .....145 H2
Longport Cl BARK/HLT IG6 .....55 G2
Long Reach Rd BARK IG11 .....109 F3
Longreach Rd ERITH DA8 .....150 E1
Longridge La STHL UB1 .....96 B6
Longridge Rd ECT SW5 .....119 K4
Long Rd CLAP SW4 .....141 H5
Longshaw Rd CHING E4 .....38 C5
Longshore DEPT SE8 .....124 C4
Longstaff Crs
WAND/EARL SW18 .....159 K1
Longstaff Rd
WAND/EARL SW18 .....159 K1
Longstone Av WLSDN NW10 .....81 H5
Longstone Rd
STRHM/NOR SW16 .....179 G1
Long St BETH E2 .....7 J4
Longthornton Rd
STRHM/NOR SW16 .....179 H5
Longton Av SYD SE26 .....163 H6
Longton Gv SYD SE26 .....163 J6
Longview Wy CRW RM5 .....57 F4
Longville Rd LBTH SE11 .....18 A6
Long Wk NWMAL KT3 .....175 K6
Longwalk Rd STKPK UB11 .....112 E2
Longwood Cl WPK KT4 .....192 E6
Longwood Dr PUT/ROE SW15 .....158 D1
Longwood Gdns CLAY IG5 .....71 J3
Longworth Cl THMD SE28 .....109 K5
The Loning CDALE/KGS NW9 .....63 H1
PEND EN3 .....24 E1
Lonsdale Av EHAM E6 .....107 H3
ROMW/RG RM7 .....74 E3
WBLY HA9 .....80 A3
Lonsdale Cl EHAM E6 .....107 J3
ELTH/MOT SE9 .....166 C5
UX/CGN UB8 .....94 A5
Lonsdale Crs GNTH/NBYPK IG2 .....72 B3
Lonsdale Dr ENC/FH EN2 .....22 D5
Lonsdale Dr North ENC/FH EN2 .....22 E6
Lonsdale Gdns
STRHM/NOR SW16 .....196 A1
Lonsdale Ms RCH/KEW TW9 * 137 H2
Lonsdale Pl IS N1 .....85 G5
Lonsdale Rd BARN SW13 .....138 C1
BXLYHN DA7 .....149 G3
CHSWK W4 .....118 C4
KIL/WHAMP NW6 .....100 D1
NWDGN UB2 .....114 D4
SNWD SE25 .....197 J1
WAN E11 .....71 D4
Lonsdale Sq IS N1 * 85 G5
Loobert Rd SEVS/STOTM N15 .....50 A6
Looe Gdns BARK/HLT IG6 .....54 A6
Loop Rd CHST BR7 .....185 H2
Lopen Rd UED N18 .....36 A6
Loraine Cl PEND EN3 .....24 E6
Loraine Rd CHSWK W4 .....117 J6
HOLWY N7 .....85 F2
Lord Av CLAY IG5 .....71 J1
Lord Chancellor Wk
KUTN/CMB KT2 .....175 K4
Lord Gdns CLAY IG5 .....71 J1
Lord Hills Rd BAY/PAD W2 .....101 F4
Lord Holland La
BRXN/ST SW9 * 142 B3
Lord Knyvett Cl
STWL/WRAY TW19 .....152 A1
Lord Knyvetts Ct
STWL/WRAY TW19 * 152 A1
Lord Napier Pl HMSMTH W6 .....118 D5
Lord North St WEST SW1P * 16 E5
Lord Roberts Ms
FUL/PCN SW6 * 140 A1
Lorden Wk BETH E2 .....104 C2
Lords Cl DUL SE21 .....162 D4
FELT TW13 .....154 D4
Lordship Gv STNW/STAM N16 .....67 K6
Lordship La EDUL SE22 .....163 G1
WDGN N22 .....49 H4
Lordship Pk STNW/STAM N16 .....67 H6
Lordship Park Ms
STNW/STAM N16 .....67 J6
Lordship Pl CHEL SW3 .....120 D6
Lordship Rd NTHLT UB5 .....77 J5
STNW/STAM N16 .....67 K6
Lordship Ter STNW/STAM N16 .....67 K6
Lordsmead Rd TOTM N17 .....50 A4
Lord St CAN/RD E16 .....126 D1
Lords Vw STJWD NW8 .....2 C3
Lord Warwick St
WOOL/PLUM SE18 .....126 E3
Lorenzo St FSBYW WC1X 5 G4
Loretto Gdns
KTN/HRWW/W HA3 .....62 A1
Lorian Cl NFNCH/WDSP N12 .....33 F6
Loring Rd ISLW TW7 .....136 A3
TRDG/WHET N20 .....33 J4
Loris Rd HMSMTH W6 .....119 F3
Lorn Ct BRXN/ST SW9 .....142 B3
Lorne Av CROY/NA CRO 198 A4
Lorne Cl STJWD NW8 .....2 D4
Lorne Gdns CROY/NA CRO 198 B4
NTGHL W11 .....119 G1
WAN E11 .....71 G1
Lorne Rd FSBYPK N4 .....67 F5
FSTGT E7 .....89 F2

KTN/HRWW/W HA3 ....43 F5
RCHPK/HAM TW10 ...137 G6
Lorne Ter FNCH N3 * 46 D5
Lorn Rd BRXN/ST SW9 ....69 J2
Lorraine Pk KTN/HRWW/W HA3 ....42 E3
Lorrimore Rd WALW SE17 ....122 C6
Lorrimore Sq WALW SE17 ....122 C6
Loseberry Rd ESH/CLAY KT10 ..204 D3
Lothair Rd EA W5 ....116 E2
Lothair Rd North FSBYPK N4 ....67 H5
Lothair Rd South FSBYPK N4 ....67 G4
Lothbury LOTH EC2R 12 E5
Lothian Av YEAD UB4 ....95 H4
Lothian Cl ALP/SUD HA0 ....79 C2
Lothian Rd BRXN/ST SW9 ....142 C2
Lothrop St NKENS W10 ....100 C2
Lots Rd WBPTN SW10 ....140 C1
Loubet St TOOT SW17 ....178 E2
Loudoun Av CNTH/NBYPK IG2 ...72 B3
Loudoun Rd STJWD NW8 ....83 G6
Loughborough Pk BRXN/ST SW9 ....142 C5
Loughborough Rd BRXN/ST SW9 ....142 C5
Loughborough St LBTH SE11 ..122 K5
Lough Rd HOLWY N7 ....85 F4
Loughton Av BKHH IG9 ....39 H3
Louisa Cl HOM E9 ....86 E5
Louisa St WCHPL E1 ....105 F4
Louis Ct CHST BR7 ....166 E6
Louise Bennett Cl HNHL SE24 *...142 C5
Louise Gdns RAIN RM13 ....111 G2
Louise Rd SRTFD E15 ....88 C4
Louisville Rd TOOT SW17 ....161 F5
Louvaine Rd BTSEA SW11 ....140 C5
Lovage Ap EHAM E6 ....107 J4
Lovat Cl CRICK NW2 ....81 H1
Lovat La FENCHST EC3M 13 G5
Lovatt Cl EDGW HA8 ....44 D2
Loveday Rd WEA W13 ....116 C1
Lovegrove St STHWK SE1 ....123 H5
Lovegrove Wk POP/IOD E14 ....125 F1
Lovekyn Cl KUTN/CMB KT2 ....175 F5
Lovelace Av HAYES BR2 ....201 F5
SURB KT6 ....190 E6
Lovelace Gdns BARK IG11 ....91 G2
SURB KT6 ....190 E6
Lovelace Gn ELTH/MOT SE9 ....146 E4
Lovelace Rd DUL SE21 ....162 D4
EBAR EN4 ....33 J2
SURB KT6 ....190 E6
Lovelace Vls THDIT KT7 * 190 C4
Love La BXLY DA5 ....169 H1
CHEAM SM3 ....208 C4
CITYW EC2V 12 D3
MRDN SM4 ....193 J5
MTCM CR4 ....178 D6
PIN HA5 ....59 J1
SNWD SE25 ....181 J6
SURB KT6 ....190 E6
TOTM N17 ....50 B3
WFD IG8 ....53 K2
WOOL/PLUM SE18 ...127 H4
Lovel Av WELL DA16 ....148 B3
Lovelinch Cl DEPT SE8 ....123 K6
Lovell Pl BERM/RHTH SE16 ....124 B3
Lovell Rd RCHPK/HAM TW10 ...156 D5
STHL UB1 ....96 B5
Lovell Wk RAIN RM13 ....93 J4
Loveridge Ms KIL/WHAMP NW6 ..82 D4
Loveridge Rd KIL/WHAMP NW6 ..82 D4
Lovett Dr CAR SM5 ....194 B4
Lovett Wy WLSDN NW10 ....80 E5
Love Wk CMBW SE5 ....142 E3
Lowbonds Av ORP BR6 ....216 B1
Lowbrook Rd IL IG1 ....90 B3
Lowden Rd ED N9 ....36 D3
HNHL SE24 ....142 C5
STHL UB1 ....95 J6
Lowe Av CAN/RD E16 ....106 E4
Lowell St POP/IOD E14 ....105 G5
Lower Addiscombe Rd CROY/NA CR0 ....196 E5
Lower Addison Gdns WKENS W14 ....119 H1
Lower Bedfords Rd ROM RM1 ...57 J2
Lower Belgrave St BGVA SW1W 15 J5
Lower Boston Rd HNWL W7 ....115 K1
Lower Broad St DAGE RM10 ...92 C6
Lower Camden CHST BR7 ....184 E4
Lower Church St CROY/NA CR0 ....196 C6
Lower Clapton Rd CLPT E5 ....86 D2
Lower Clarendon Wk NTGHL W11 ....100 C5
Lower Common South PUT/ROE SW15 ....138 E4
Lower Coombe St CROY/NA CR0 ....211 J2
Lower Downs Rd RYNPK SW20 ....177 G4
Lower Gravel Rd HAYES BR2 ..200 D5
Lower Green Gdns WPK KT4 ..192 D5
Lower Green Rd ESH/CLAY KT10 ....189 G6
Lower Gn West MTCM CR4 ....178 D6
Lower Grosvenor Pl KTBR SW1X 15 J4
Lower Grove Rd RCHPK/HAM TW10 ..157 G1
Lower Hall La CHING E4 ....51 G1
Lower Hampton Rd SUN TW16 ....172 C5
Lower Ham Rd KUTN/CMB KT2 ....174 E2
Lower James St SOHO/CST W1F ...10 C5
Lower John St SOHO/CST W1F ..10 C5
Lower Kenwood Av STHGT/OAK N14 ....22 E6
Lower Kings Rd KUTN/CMB KT2 ....175 F4

Lower Lea Crossing POP/IOD E14 ....106 C6
Lower Maidstone Rd FBAR/BDGN N11 ....48 C2
Lower Mardyke Av RAIN RM13...110 E1
Lower Marsh STHWK SE1 ....17 J3
Lower Marsh La KUT/HW KT1 ..191 G1
Lower Merton Ri HAMP NW3 ....83 J5
Lower Morden La MRDN SM4..193 F5
Lower Mortlake Rd RCH/KEW TW9 ....137 G4
Lower Paddock Rd OXHEY WD19 ....27 J1
Lower Park Rd BELV DA17....129 H3
FBAR/BDGN N11 ....48 C1
Lower Queen's Rd BKHH IG9 ....39 J4
Lower Richmond Rd PUT/ROE SW15 ....139 F4
RCH/KEW TW9 ....137 H4
Lower Rd BELV DA17 ....129 K3
BERM/RHTH SE16 ....123 K3
ERITH DA8 ....130 A4
RYLN/HDSTN HA2 ....60 D6
STMC/STPC BR5 ....202 C3
SUT SM1 ....209 H3
Lower Sand Hills SURB KT6 ....190 D4
Lower Sloane St BGVA SW1W ...15 F7
Lower Station Rd DART DA1...170 B1
Lower Strd CDALE/KGS NW9 ....45 H5
Lower Sunbury Rd HPTN TW12 ....172 E5
Lower Tail OXHEY WD19 ....27 J5
Lower Teddington Rd KUT/HW KT1 ....174 E4
Lower Ter HAMP NW3 ....83 G1
Lower Thames St MON EC3R ..13 H6
Lower Tub BUSH WD23 ....28 D2
Lower Wood Rd ESH/CLAY KT10 ....205 H4
Loweswater Cl WBLY HA9 ....61 K6
The Lowe CHIG IG7 ....55 G1
Lowfield Rd ACT W3 ....98 E5
KIL/WHAMP NW6 ....82 E5
Lowfield St DART DA1 ....171 H2
Low Hall Cl CHING E4 ....37 J2
Low Hall La WALTH E17 ....69 G3
Lowick Rd HRW HA1 ....60 E1
Lowland Gdns ROMW/RG RM7...74 D3
Lowlands Rd HRW HA1 ....60 E4
PIN HA5 ....59 G4
STWL/WRAY TW19 ....132 A6
Lowman Rd HOLWY N7 ....85 F2
Lowndes Cl KTBR SW1X 15 H5
Lowndes Ct REGST W1B 10 A4
Lowndes Pl KTBR SW1X * 15 G5
Lowndes Sq KTBR SW1X 15 F3
Lowndes St KTBR SW1X 15 F4
Lowood St WCHPL E1 ....104 D6
Lowry Crs MTCM CR4 ....178 D5
Lowry Rd BCTR RM8 ....91 H3
Lowson Gv ROMW/RG RM7 ...56 D4
Lowswood Cl NTHWD HA6 ....40 A4
Lowther Dr ENC/FH EN2 ....22 E5
Lowther Hl FSTH SE23 ....164 B2
Lowther Rd BARN SW13 * 138 C2
Lowther Rd BARN SW13 * 138 C2
HOLWY N7 * 85 G3
KUTN/CMB KT2 ....175 G4
STAN HA7 ....44 B6
WALTH E17 ....51 G5
Lowth Rd CMBW SE5 ....142 D3
Loxford Av EHAM E6 ....107 H1
Loxford La IL IG1 ....90 C3
Loxford Rd BARK IG11 ....90 B4
Loxham Rd CHING E4 ....51 K3
Loxham St STPAN WC1H * 5 F1
Loxley Cl SYD SE26 ....182 A1
Loxley Rd HPTN TW12 ....154 E6
Loxley Rd BARN SW18 ....160 C3
Loxton Rd FSTH SE23 ....164 A3
Loxwood Cl EBED/NFELT TW14 ....153 C3
STMC/STPC BR5 ....202 E6
Loxwood Rd TOTM N17 ....50 A6
Lubbock Rd CHST BR7 ....184 E4
Lubbock St NWCR SE14 ....143 K1
Lucan Pl CHEL SW5 ....14 C7
Lucan Rd BAR EN5 ....20 C4
Lucas Av PLSTW E13 ....89 F6
RYLN/HDSTN HA2 ....60 A6
Lucas Gdns EFNCH N2 ....47 G5
Lucas Rd PGE/AN SE20 ....181 K2
Lucas Sq GLDGN NW11 ....64 E3
Lucas St DEPT SE8 ....144 D3
Lucerne Cl PLMGR N13 ....34 E5
Lucerne Cv WALTH E17 ....70 B1
Lucerne Ms KENS W8 ....119 K1
Lucerne Rd HBRY N5 ....85 H2
ORP BR6 ....202 A5
THHTH CR7 ....196 C2
Lucey Rd BERM/RHTH SE16 ..123 H3
Lucey Wy BERM/RHTH SE16 ..123 H3
Lucien Rd TOOT SW17 ....161 F6
Lucien Rd WAND/EARL SW18 ..160 A4
Lucknow St WOOL/PLUM SE18 ....147 K1
Lucorn Cl LEE/GVPK SE12 ....165 J1
Luctons Av BKHH IG9 ....39 G3
Luddesdon Rd ERITH DA8 ....149 H1
Ludford Cl CDALE/KGS NW9 ....45 G5
CROY/NA CR0 ....211 H2
Ludgate Broadway BLKFR EC4V * 12 B4
Ludgate Circ STP EC4M * 12 A4
Ludgate Hl STP EC4M 12 A4
Ludgate Sq BLKFR EC4V * 12 B4
Ludham Cl THMD SE28 ....109 J5
WFD IG8 ....54 C4
Ludlow Cl HAYES BR2 ....183 K6
RYLN/HDSTN HA2 ....77 K2
Ludlow Md OXHEY WD19 ....27 F5
Ludlow Rd EA W5 ....97 J3
FELT TW13 ....153 K5

Ludlow St FSBYE EC1V * 6 C6
Ludlow Wy EFNCH N2 ....65 G1
Ludovick Wk PUT/ROE SW15 ..138 B5
Luffield Rd ABYW SE2 ....128 C3
Luffman Rd LEE/GVPK SE12 ..166 A5
Lugard Rd PECK SE15 ....143 J3
Lugg Ap MNPK E12 ....90 A1
Luke St SDTCH EC2A 7 G6
Lukin Crs CHING E4 ....38 B5
Lukin St WCHPL E1 ....104 E6
Lullingstone Cl STMC/STPC BR5 ....186 C3
Lullingstone Crs STMC/STPC BR5 ....186 B3
Lullingstone La LEW SE13 ....165 G1
Lullingstone Rd BELV DA17 ..129 G6
Lullington Garth BMLY BR1 * ...183 H5
MLHL NW7 ....46 D1
Lullington Rd DAGW RM9 ....92 A5
PGE/AN SE20 ....181 H3
Lulot Gdns ARCH N19 ....66 B6
Lulworth Av HEST TW5 ....135 G1
WBLY HA9 ....61 J4
Lulworth Cl RYLN/HDSTN HA2 ...77 K1
Lulworth Crs MTCM CR4 ....178 D5
Lulworth Dr CRW RM5 ....56 D1
PIN HA5 ....59 H4
Lulworth Gdns RYLN/HDSTN HA2 ....59 J6
Lulworth Rd ELTH/MOT SE9 ..166 D4
WELL DA16 ....148 A3
Lulworth Wave YEAD UB4 ....95 H5
Lumen Rd WBLY HA9 ....61 J6
Lumley Cl BELV DA17 ....129 H6
Lumley Flats BGVA SW1W * ..121 F5
Lumley Gdns CHEAM SM3 ....208 C3
Lumley Rd CHEAM SM3 ....208 D4
Lumley St MYFR/PKLN W1K 9 H4
Luna Rd THHTH CR7 ....180 D6
Lundin Wk OXHEY WD19 * 27 H6
Lundy Dr HYS/HAR UB3 ....113 H4
Lundy Wk IS N1 * 85 J4
Lunham Rd NRWD SE19 ....181 F2
Lupin Cl BRXS/STRHM SW2 ..162 C4
CROY/NA CR0 ....198 A5
ROMW/RG RM7 ....75 F6
WDR/YW UB7 ....112 A5
Lupton Cl LEE/GVPK SE12 ....166 A6
Lupton St KTTN NW5 ....84 C2
Lupus St PIM SW1V 121 C5
Lurgan Av HMSMTH W6 ....119 G6
Lurline Gdns BTSEA SW11 ....141 F2
Luscombe Wy VX/NE SW8 ....141 K1
Lushington Rd CAT SE6 ....182 E1
WLSDN NW10 ....99 K1
Lushington Ter HACK E8 ....86 C3
Luther Cl EDGW HA8 ....30 E4
Luther King Cl WALTH E17 ....69 G3
Luther Ms TEDD TW11 ....174 A1
Luther Rd TEDD TW11 ....174 A1
Luton Pl GNWCH SE10 ....145 F1
Luton Rd PLSTW E13 ....106 E3
SCUP DA14 ....168 D5
WALTH E17 ....51 H5
Luton St STJWD NW8 ....2 B7
Luttrell Av PUT/ROE SW15 ..138 E6
Lutwyche Rd FSTH SE23 ....164 C4
Luxborough La CHIG IG7 ....53 H6
Luxborough St MHST W1U 3 G7
Luxemburg Ms SRTFD E15 ....88 C3
Luxemburg Gdns HMSMTH W6 ....119 G4
Luxfield Rd ELTH/MOT SE9 ..166 D3
Luxford St BERM/RHTH SE16 ..124 A4
Luxmore St BROCKY SE4 ....144 C2
Luxor St CMBW SE5 ....142 D4
Lyall Av DUL SE21 ....163 F6
Lyall Ms KTBR SW1X 15 G5
Lyall Ms West KTBR SW1X * ...15 G5
Lyall St KTBR SW1X 15 G5
Lyal Rd BOW E3 ....105 G1
Lycett Pl SHB W12 ....118 D2
Lych Gate Rd ORP BR6 ....202 B5
Lych Gate Wk HYS/HAR UB3 ...94 D6
Lyconby Gdns CROY/NA CR0 ...198 B4
Lydd Cl BFN/LL DA15 ....167 K3
Lydden Gv WAND/EARL SW18 ..160 A2
Lydden Rd WAND/EARL SW18 ..160 A2
Lydd Rd BXLYHN DA7 ....149 G1
Lydeard Rd EHAM E6 ....89 K5
Lydford Cl STNW/STAM N16 ...86 A3
Lydford Rd CRICK NW2 ....82 A4
MV/WKIL W9 ....100 D3
SEVS/STOTM N15 ....67 K2
Lydhurst Av BRXS/STRHM SW2 ....162 A4
Lydia Rd ERITH DA8 ....130 C6
Lydney Cl WIM/MER SW19 ..159 H4
Lydon Rd CLAP SW4 ....141 H4
Lydstep Rd CHST BR7 ....167 F6
Lyford Rd WAND/EARL SW18 ..160 C2
Lyford St WOOL/PLUM SE18 ..126 D4
Lygon Pl BGVA SW1W * 15 J5
Lyham Cl BRXS/STRHM SW2 ..141 K6
Lyham Rd BRXS/STRHM SW2 ..141 K6
Lyle Cl MTCM CR4 ....195 F4
Lyme Farm Rd LEE/GVPK SE12..145 K5
Lyme Gv HOM E9 ....86 E5
Lymer Av NRWD SE19 ....181 G1
Lyme Rd WELL DA16 ....148 C2
Lymescote Gdns SUT SM1 ..193 K6
Lyme St CAMTN NW1 ....84 C5
Lyme Ter CAMTN NW1 ....84 C5
Lyminge Cl SCUP DA14 ....168 A6
Lyminge Gdns WAND/EARL SW18 ....160 D3
Lymington Av WDGN N22 ....49 G5
Lymington Cl STRHM/NOR SW16 ....179 J5
Lymington Dr RSLP HA4 ....58 B7
Lymington Gdns HOR/WEW KT19 ....207 H3
Lymington Rd BCTR RM8 ....73 K5
KIL/WHAMP NW6 ....83 F4

Lyminster Cl YEAD UB4 ....95 J4
Lympstone Gdns PECK SE15..143 H1
Lynbridge Gdns PLMGR N13...35 H6
Lynbrook Cl RAIN RM13 ....111 F1
Lynchen Cl HEST TW5 ....133 K2
Lyncourt BKHTH/KID SE3 * ..145 G3
Lyncroft Av PIN HA5 ....59 J2
Lyncroft Gdns EW KT17 ....207 H6
HSLW TW3 ....135 H6
KIL/WHAMP NW6 ....82 E3
WEA W13 ....116 D2
Lyndale CRICK NW2 ....82 D2
ESH/CLAY KT10 ....204 D2
Lyndale Av CRICK NW2 ....82 D1
ESH/CLAY KT10 ....189 K4
Lyndale Cl BKHTH/KID SE3 ..125 J6
Lyndale Hampton Court Wy ESH/CLAY KT10 ....189 K4
Lynden Wy SWLY BR8 ....187 K6
Lyndhurst Av BRYLDS KT5 ..191 J5
MLHL NW7 ....45 G2
NFNCH/WDSP N12 ....47 K2
PIN HA5 ....41 F4
STHL UB1 ....115 G1
STRHM/NOR SW16 ....179 J5
WHTN TW2 ....155 F3
Lyndhurst Cl BELMT SM2 * ..208 E5
BXLYHN DA7 ....149 J4
CROY/NA CR0 ....212 B1
ORP BR6 ....216 B2
WLSDN NW10 ....81 F1
Lyndhurst Ct BELMT SM2 * ..208 E5
Lyndhurst Dr LEY E10 ....70 A4
NWMAL KT3 ....192 B3
Lyndhurst Gdns BARK IG11 ...90 E5
EN EN1 ....24 A5
FNCH N3 ....46 C4
GNTH/NBYPK IG2 ....72 E3
HAMP NW3 ....83 H3
PIN HA5 ....41 F4
Lyndhurst Gv CMBW SE5 ....143 F3
Lyndhurst Leys HAYES BR2 *..183 G5
Lyndhurst Prior SNWD SE25 *..181 F6
Lyndhurst Rd BXLYHN DA7 ..149 J4
CEND/HSY/T N8 ....48 D5
CHING E4 ....52 A5
CFD/PVL UB6 ....96 B3
HAMP NW3 ....83 H3
THHTH CR7 ....196 B1
UED N18 ....36 C5
WDGN N22 ....49 F1
Lyndhurst Sq PECK SE15 ....143 G2
Lyndhurst Ter HAMP NW3 ....83 H3
Lyndhurst Wy BELMT SM2 ..208 E6
PECK SE15 ....143 G2
Lyndon Av BFN/LL DA15 ....148 A6
PIN HA5 ....41 J3
WLGTN SM6 ....210 A1
Lyndon Rd BELV DA17 ....129 H4
Lyne Cv WALTH E17 ....38 C6
Lyne Crs WALTH E17 * 51 H4
Lyneham Wk CLPT E5 * 87 G3
Lynette Av CLAP SW4 ....161 G1
Lynford Cl EDGW HA8 ....44 E4
Lynford Gdns EDGW HA8 ....30 D6
GDMY/SEVK IG3 ....73 F5
Lynford Ter ED N9 * 36 B3
Lynmere Rd WELL DA16 ....148 C3
Lyn Ms STNW/STAM N16 * 86 B2
Lyn Ms BOW E3 * 105 H2
MRDN SM4 ....193 G4
Lynmouth Av EN EN1 ....24 C6
MRDN SM4 ....193 F4
Lynmouth Dr RSLP HA4 ....58 F6
Lynmouth Gdns CFD/PVL UB6 ....97 H6
HEST TW5 ....134 C2
Lynmouth Ri STMC/STPC BR5..202 C1
Lynmouth Rd EFNCH N2 ....47 K6
GFD/PVL UB6 ....97 H6
STNW/STAM N16 ....68 B5
WALTH E17 ....69 G3
Lynn Cl KTN/HRWW/W HA3 ...42 D5
Lynne Cl ORP BR6 ....217 F4
Lynne Rd BCTR RM8 ....73 K6
Lynne Wk ESH/CLAY KT10 ..204 C3
Lynne Wy NTHLT UB5 ....95 H1
WLSDN NW10 ....81 G4
Lynn Ms WAN E11 ....70 C5
Lynn Rd BAL SW12 ....161 G2
GNTH/NBYPK IG2 ....72 E3
WAN E11 ....70 C5
Lyn St EN EC/FH EN2 ....23 K2
Lynscott Wy SAND/SEL CR2 ..211 H6
Lynsted Cl BMLY BR1 ....184 B5
Lynsted Cl BXLYHS DA6 ....149 J6
Lynsted Ct BECK BR3 * 182 B5
Lynsted Gdns ELTH/MOT SE9..146 C1
Lynton Av ACT W3 ....98 E5
CDALE/KGS NW9 ....63 H1
NFNCH/WDSP N12 ....33 H6
ROMW/RG RM7 ....56 D4
STMC/STPC BR5 ....202 C1
WDGN N22 ....49 K2
Lynton Cl CHSGTN KT9 ....206 A2
ISLW TW7 ....136 A5
WLSDN NW10 ....81 H2
Lynton Crs GNTH/NBYPK IG2...72 B3
Lynton Gdns EN EN1 ....36 B1
FBAR/BDGN N11 ....48 D2
Lynton Md TRDG/WHET N20 ..32 E2
Lynton Rd ACT W3 ....98 C6
CEND/HSY/T N8 ....66 D3
CHING E4 ....51 K1
CROY/NA CR0 ....196 B3
KIL/WHAMP NW6 ....100 D1
NWMAL KT3 ....192 A2
RYLN/HDSTN HA2 ....59 J6
STHWK SE1 ....19 K7
Lynton Ter ACT W3 ....98 E5
Lynwood Cl CRW RM5 ....56 D2
RYLN/HDSTN HA2 ....77 H1
WFD IG8 ....53 G1
Lynwood Dr CRW RM5 ....56 D2
NTHWD HA6 ....40 C4
WPK KT4 ....192 D6
Lynwood Gdns CROY/NA CR0..211 F2
STHL UB1 ....95 K5

Lynwood Gv ORP BR6 ....201 K4
WCHMH N21 ....35 G3
Lynwood Rd EA W5 ....97 K2
ESH/CLAY KT10 ....190 A6
TOOT SW17 ....160 E5
Lynwood Ter WIM/MER SW19 * 177 J4
Lyon Meade STAN HA7 ....43 J4
Lyon Park Av ALP/SUD HA0...80 A4
Lyon Rd HRW HA1 ....61 F3
ROM RM1 ....75 H4
WIM/MER SW19 ....178 B4
WOT/HER KT12 ....188 B6
Lyonsdown Av BAR EN5 ....33 G1
Lyonsdown Rd BAR EN5 ....21 G6
Lyons Pl STJWD NW8 ....2 A7
Lyon St IS N1 ....85 G5
Lyons Wk WKENS W14 ....119 H4
Lyon Wy GFD/PVL UB6 ....78 B6
Lyoth Rd STMC/STPC BR5 ..201 H6
Lyric Dr GFD/PVL UB6 ....96 B3
Lyric Ms SYD SE26 ....163 K6
Lyric Rd BARN SW13 ....138 C2
Lysander CDALE/KGS NW9 * ...45 H4
Lysander Gdns SURB KT6 ....191 G3
Lysander Gv ARCH N19 ....66 D5
Lysander Ms ARCH N19 * 66 C5
Lysander Rd CROY/NA CR0 ..211 F4
RSLP HA4 ....58 B6
Lysander Wy ORP BR6 ....216 C1
Lysias Rd BAL SW12 ....161 G1
Lysia St FUL/PGN SW6 ....139 G1
Lysons Wk PUT/ROE SW15 * ..138 D6
Lytchet Rd BMLY BR1 ....183 K3
Lytchet Wy PEND EN3 ....24 E2
Lytchgate Cl SAND/SEL CR2..212 A5
Lytcott Gv EDUL SE22 ....143 G5
Lytham Av OXHEY WD19 ....41 H1
Lytham Cl THMD SE28 ....110 A5
Lytham Gv EA W5 ....98 A2
Lytham St WALW SE17 ....122 E5
Lyttelton Rd EFNCH N2 ....65 G2
LEY E10 ....87 K3
Lyttelton Cl HAMP NW3 ....83 J5
Lyttelton Rd CEND/HSY/T N8 * ..49 G6
PLMGR N13 ....35 G4
Lyttleton Cl EFNCH N2 ....65 H2
NTHLT UB5 ....95 K1
Lyton Av BFN/LL DA15 ....168 C5
Lytton Av PEND EN3 ....25 G1
Lytton Cl EFNCH N2 ....65 H2
NTHLT UB5 ....77 K5
Lytton Gdns WLGTN SM6 ....210 D3
Lytton Gv PUT/ROE SW15 ..139 G6
Lytton Rd BAR EN5 ....21 G5
GPK RM2 ....75 K2
PIN HA5 ....41 J3
WAN E11 ....70 C4
Lyveden Rd BKHTH/KID SE3..146 A1
WIM/MER SW19 ....178 A2

Maberley Crs NRWD SE19 ....181 H3
Maberley Rd BECK BR3 ....182 A6
NRWD SE19 ....181 G4
Mabledon Pl CAMTN NW1 ......4 D5
Mablethorpe Rd FUL/PGN SW6 ....139 H1
Mabley St HOM E9 ....87 G3
Macaret Cl TRDG/WHET N20 ...33 F2
Macarthur Cl FSTGT E7 ....88 E4
Macarthur Ter CHARL SE7 * ..126 C6
Macaulay Av ESH/CLAY KT10..189 K6
Macaulay Rd CLAP SW4 ....141 G4
EHAM E6 ....107 H1
Macbean St WOOL/PLUM SE18...127 F3
Macbeth St HMSMTH W6 ....118 E5
Macclesfield Br STJWD NW8 ...2 D2
Macclesfield Rd FSBYE EC1V ...6 C4
SNWD SE25 ....197 J2
Macclesfield St SOHO/SHAV W1D * 10 D5
Macdonald Av DAGE RM10 ....92 D1
Macdonald Rd ARCH N19 ....66 C6
FBAR/BDGN N11 ....47 K1
FSTGT E7 ....88 E2
WALTH E17 ....52 A5
Macduff Rd BTSEA SW11 ....141 F2
Mace Cl WAP E1W 123 J1
Mace St BETH E2 ....105 F1
Macfarlane La ISLW TW7 ....116 A6
Macfarlane Rd SHB W12 ....119 F1
Mac Farren Pl CAMTN NW1 * ...3 H7
Macgregor Rd CAN/RD E16...107 G4
Machell Rd PECK SE15 ....143 K4
Mackay Rd CLAP SW4 ....141 G4
Mackennal St STJWD NW8 * 2 D3
Mackenzie Cl SHB W12 * 99 K6
Mackenzie Rd BECK BR3 ....181 B4
HOLWY N7 ....85 F4
Mackeson Rd HAMP NW3 * 83 K2
Mackie Rd BRXS/STRHM SW2 ..162 B2
Mackintosh La HOM E9 ....87 F3
Macklin St HOL/ALD WC2B * ..11 F3
Macks Rd BERM/RHTH SE16 ..123 H4
Mackworth St CAMTN NW1 ......4 A4
Maclean Rd FSTH SE23 ....164 B1
Macleod House WOOL/PLUM SE18 ....146 D1
Macleod Rd STHGT/OAK N14...22 E6
Macleod St WALW SE17 ....122 D5
Maclise Rd WKENS W14 ....119 H3
Macmillan Wy TOOT SW17 ..161 G6
Maconochie Rd WOOL/PLUM SE18...127 J6
Macoma Ter WOOL/PLUM SE18 ....127 J6
Maconochie's Rd POP/IOD E14 * 124 E5
Macquarie Wy POP/IOD E14..124 E4
Macroom Rd MV/WKIL W9 ..100 D2
Mada Rd ORP BR6 ....216 B1

Maddams St *BOW* E3 ....105 K3
Maddison Cl *TEDD* TW11 ....174 A2
Maddocks Cl *SCUP* DA14 ....186 E2
Maddock Wy *WALW* SE17 ....129 C6
Maddox St *MYFR/PKLN* W1K 9 K5
Madeira Av *BMLY* BR1 ....183 H4
Madeira Gv *WFD* IG8 ....53 G2
Madeira Rd *MTCM* CR4 ....194 E1
PLMCR N13 ....35 H6
STRHM/NOR SW16 ....179 K1
WAN E11 ....70 B5
Madeley Rd *EA* W5 ....97 K6
Madeline Gv *IL* IG1 ....90 D3
Madeline Rd *PGE/AN* SE20 ....181 H3
Madge Gill Wy *EHAM* E6 ....89 J6
Madge Hl *HNWL* W7 * 96 E6
Madinah Rd *HACK* E8 ....86 C4
Madison Crs *WELL* DA16 ....148 D1
Madison Gdns *BXLYHN* DA7 ....148 D1
Madras Rd *IL* IG1 ....90 B2
Madrid Rd *BARN* SW13 ....138 D2
Madron St *STHWK* SE1 ....123 F5
Mafeking Av *BTFD* TW8 ....117 F6
EHAM E6 ....107 H1
GNTH/NBYPK IG2 ....72 D4
Mafeking Rd *CAN/RD* E16 ....106 D3
EN EN1 ....24 B4
TOTM N17 ....50 C5
Magazine Ga *BAY/PAD* W2 * 8 D7
Magdala Av *ARCH* N19 ....66 C6
Magdala Rd *ISLW* TW7 ....136 B4
SAND/SEL CR2 ....211 K5
Magdalene Gdns *EHAM* E6 ....108 A3
Magdalen Rd
WAND/EARL SW18 ....160 B3
Magdalen St *STHWK* SE1 ....19 G1
Magdelan Gv *ORP* BR6 ....217 H2
Magee St *LBTH* SE11 ....122 B6
Magnaville Rd *BUSH* WD23 ....28 E2
Magnet Rd *WBLY* HA9 ....61 K6
Magnin Cl *HACK* E8 ....86 C6
Magnolia Cl *KUTN/CMB* KT2 ....175 J2
LEY E10 ....69 J6
Magnolia Ct
KTN/HRWW/W HA3 ....62 B4
Magnolia Gdns *EDGW* HA8 ....30 E6
Magnolia Pl *CLAP* SW4 * 141 K6
EA W5 ....97 K4
Magnolia Rd *CHSWK* W4 ....117 J6
Magnolia Wy *HOR/WEW* KT19 .....206 E3
Magnolia Whf *CHSWK* W4 * 117 J6
Magpie Cl *CDALE/KGS* NW9 ....45 G1
EN EN1 ....24 C2
FSTGT E7 ....88 D3
Magpie Hall Cl *HAYES* BR2 ....200 D3
Magpie Hall La *HAYES* BR2 ....200 D4
Magpie Hall Rd *BUSH* WD23 ....28 E4
Magpie Pl *NWCR* SE14 * 124 B6
Magri Wk *WCHPL* E1 ....104 E4
Maguire Dr *RCHPK/HAM* TW10 ....156 D6
Maguire St *STHWK* SE1 ....19 K2
Mahlon Av *RSLP* HA4 ....77 F5
Mahogany Cl
BERM/RHTH SE16 ....124 B1
Mahon Cl *EN* EN1 ....24 B2
CHING E4 ....37 K2
Maida Av *BAY/PAD* W2 ....101 G4
Maida Rd *BELV* DA17 ....129 H5
Maida V *MV/WKIL* W9 ....101 G2
STJWD NW8 ....2 C3
Maida Vale Rd *DART* DA1 ....170 D1
Maida Wy *CHING* E4 ....37 K2
Maiden Erlegh Av *BXLY* DA5 ....169 F3
Maiden La *CAMTN* NW1 ....84 D5
COVGDN WC2E 11 F6
DART DA1 ....150 D5
STHWK SE1 ....18 D1
Maiden Rd *SRTFD* E15 ....88 C5
Maidenstone Hl *GNWCH* SE10 .....145 F2
Maidstone Av *CRW* RM5 ....56 E5
Maidstone Buildings Ms
STHWK SE1 ....18 D1
Maidstone Rd *FBAR/BDGN* N11 ....48 D2
SCUP DA14 ....186 E2
Main Av *EN* EN1 ....24 B6
NTHWD HA6 ....26 B4
Main Barracks
WOOL/PLUM SE18 * 126 E5
Main Dr *GFD/PVL* UB6 * 97 C2
WBLY HA9 ....79 K1
Mainridge Rd *CHST* BR7 ....167 F6
Main St *BFN/LL* DA15 ....167 K5
GPK RM2 ....75 H1
ORP BR6 * 217 J6
STMC/STPC BR5 ....202 C5
SWLY BR8 ....203 K3
Main St *FELT* TW13 ....172 C1
Maise Webster Cl
STWL/WRAY TW19 * 152 A2
Maismore St *PECK* SE15 ....123 H6
Maitland Cl *GNWCH* SE10 ....144 E1
HSLWW TW4 ....134 E4
WOT/HER KT12 ....188 D6
Maitland Park Rd *HAMP* NW3 ....83 K4
Maitland Park Vls *HAMP* NW3 ....83 K4
Maitland Rd *SRTFD* E15 ....88 D4
SYD SE26 ....182 A2
Majendie Rd
WOOL/PLUM SE18 ....127 J5
Major Cl *BRXN/ST* SW9 ....142 C4
Major Rd *BERM/RHTH* SE16 * 123 H3
SRTFD E15 ....88 B3
Makepeace Av *HGT* N6 ....66 A6
Makepeace Rd *NTHLT* UB5 ....95 J1
WAN E11 ....70 E1
Makins St *CHEL* SW3 ....14 D7
Malabar St *POP/IOD* E14 ....124 D2
Malam Gdns *POP/IOD* E14 ....105 K6
Malan Sq *RAIN* RM13 ....93 K4
Malcolm Cl *PGE/AN* SE20 * 181 K3
Malcolm Ct *STAN* HA7 ....43 J1
Malcolm Crs *HDN* NW4 ....63 J2

Malcolm Dr *SURB* KT6 ....190 E5
Malcolm Pl *BETH* E2 ....104 E3
Malcolm Rd *PGE/AN* SE20 ....181 K3
SNWD SE25 ....197 H5
WCHPL E1 ....104 E3
WIM/MER SW19 ....177 H2
Malcolms Wy *STHGT/OAK* N14 ....22 C6
Malcolm Wy *WAN* E11 ....70 E2
Malden Av *GFD/PVL* UB6 ....78 E4
SNWD SE25 ....197 J1
Malden Green Av *WPK* KT4 ....192 C5
Malden Hl *NWMAL* KT3 ....192 C1
Malden Hill Gdns *NWMAL* KT3 .....176 C6
Malden Pk *NWMAL* KT3 ....192 C3
Malden Pl *KTTN* NW5 ....84 A3
Malden Rd *CHEAM* SM3 ....208 B2
KTTN NW5 ....83 K3
NWMAL KT3 ....192 C4
Malden Wy *NWMAL* KT3 ....192 C4
Malden Wy (Kingston By-Pass)
NWMAL KT3 ....192 B3
Maldon Cl *CMBW* SE5 * 143 F4
IS N1 ....6 J6
Maldon Rd *ACT* W3 ....98 E6
ED N9 ....36 B5
ROMW/RG RM7 ....74 E4
WLGTN SM6 ....210 B3
Maldon Wk *WFD* IG8 ....53 G2
Malet St *GWRST* WC1E 4 C7
Maley Av *WNWD* SE27 ....162 C4
Malford Gv *GNTH/NBYPK* IG2 * 72 B2
Malfort Rd *CMBW* SE5 ....143 F4
Malham Cl *FBAR/BDGN* N11 ....48 A2
Malham Rd *FSTH* SE23 ....164 A3
Malham Ter *UED* N18 * 50 D2
Malliams Ms *BRXN/ST* SW9 ....142 B4
Mallard Cl *BAR* EN5 * 33 H1
DART DA1 ....151 J6
KIL/WHAMP NW6 ....100 E1
WHTN TW2 ....155 F2
Mallard Ct *WALTH* E17 * 52 B6
Mallard Pl *TWK* TW1 ....156 B5
WDGN N22 ....49 F5
Mallards Ct *OXHEY* WD19 * 27 K5
Mallards Rd *BARK* IG11 ....109 G2
WFD IG8 ....53 F3
Mallard Wk *CROY/NA* CR0 ....198 A2
Mallard Wy *CDALE/KGS* NW9 ....62 E4
NTHWD HA6 ....40 A3
WLGTN SM6 ....210 C6
Mall Chambers *KENS* W8 * 119 K1
Mallet Dr *NTHLT* UB5 ....77 K3
Mallet Rd *LEW* SE13 ....165 G1
Malling Cl *CROY/NA* CR0 * 197 K3
Malling Gdns *MRDN* SM4 ....194 B3
Malling Wy *HAYES* BR2 ....199 J4
Mallinson Rd *BTSEA* SW11 ....140 D6
CROY/NA CR0 ....210 D1
Mallord St *CHEL* SW3 ....120 C6
Mallory Cl *BECK* BR3 ....182 B5
BROCKY SE4 ....144 B5
Mallory Gdns *EBAR* EN4 ....34 A2
STJWD NW8 * 2 D7
Mallow Cl *CROY/NA* CR0 ....198 A5
Mallow Md *MLHL* NW7 ....46 C1
Mallow St *FSBYE* EC1V 6 E6
Mall Rd *HMSMTH* W6 ....118 E5
The Mall *BTFD* TW8 * 116 E6
EA W5 ....98 A6
EMPK RM11 ....75 K5
KTN/HRWW/W HA3 ....62 B5
MORT/ESHN SW14 ....137 K6
STHGT/OAK N14 ....34 E5
SURB KT6 ....190 E4
WHALL SW1A 16 C2
Mall Vis *HMSMTH* W6 * 118 E5
Malmains Cl *BECK* BR3 ....199 G2
Malmains Wy *BECK* BR3 ....198 E2
Malmesbury Cl *PIN* HA5 ....58 E1
Malmesbury Rd *BOW* E3 ....105 H2
CAN/RD E16 ....106 C4
MRDN SM4 ....194 B4
SRTFD E15 ....88 D4
Malmesbury Ter *CAN/RD* E16 ....106 D4
Malmesbury West Est
BOW E3 ....105 H2
Malpas Dr *PIN* HA5 ....59 H2
Malpas Rd *BROCKY* SE4 ....144 C3
DAGW RM9 ....91 K4
HACK E8 ....86 D4
Malta Rd *LEY* E10 ....69 J5
Malta St *FSBYE* EC1V 6 A6
Maltby Cl *ORP* BR6 ....202 B5
Maltby Dr *EN* EN1 ....24 D1
Maltby Rd *CHSGTN* KT9 ....206 C5
Maltby St *STHWK* SE1 ....19 J4
Malthouse Dr *FELT* TW13 ....172 C1
Maltings Pl *FUL/PGN* SW6 ....140 A2
STHWK SE1 ....19 H2
The Maltings *ORP* BR6 ....202 A5
ROM RM1 ....75 H4
SNWD SE25 * 181 F6
Malting Wy *ISLW* TW7 ....136 A4
Malton Ms *NKENS* W10 * 100 C5
WOOL/PLUM SE18 ....127 K6
Malton Rd *WOOL/PLUM* SE18 ......127 K6
Maltravers St *TPL/STR* WC2R 11 H5
Malt St *STHWK* SE1 ....123 H6
Malva Cl *WAND/EARL* SW18 ....140 A6
Malvern Av *BXLYHN* DA7 ....149 F1
CHING E4 ....52 B3
RYLN/HDSTN HA2 ....77 J1
Malvern Cl *BUSH* WD23 ....28 C2
MTCM CR4 ....179 H6
NKENS W10 ....100 D4
SURB KT6 ....191 F5
Malvern Dr *FELT* TW13 ....172 C1
GDMY/SEVK IG3 ....91 F2
WFD IG8 ....53 G1
Malvern Gdns *CRICK* NW2 ....64 C6
KTN/HRWW/W HA3 ....62 B5
LOU IG10 ....39 K1
Malvern Ms *KIL/WHAMP* NW6 ......100 E2
Malvern Pl *MV/WKIL* W9 * 100 D2

Malvern Rd *CEND/HSY/T* N8 ....49 F6
EHAM E6 ....89 J6
EMPK RM11 ....75 J5
HACK E8 ....86 C5
HPTN TW12 ....173 F4
HYS/HAR UB3 ....133 H1
KIL/WHAMP NW6 ....100 E2
ORP BR6 ....217 H2
SURB KT6 ....191 F6
THHTH CR7 ....196 B1
TOTM N17 ....50 C6
WAN E11 ....70 C6
Malvern Ter *ED* N9 ....36 B3
IS N1 ....85 G6
Malvern Wy *WEA* W13 * 97 H4
Malwood Rd *BAL* SW12 ....161 G1
Malyons Rd *LEW* SE13 ....144 E6
Malyons Ter *LEW* SE13 ....144 E6
Managers St *POP/IOD* E14 * 125 F1
Manaton Cl *PECK* SE15 ....143 J4
Manaton Crs *STHL* UB1 ....96 A5
Manbey Gv *SRTFD* E15 ....88 C4
Manbey Park Rd *SRTFD* E15 ....88 C4
Manbey Rd *SRTFD* E15 * 88 C4
Manbey St *SRTFD* E15 ....88 C4
Manbre Rd *HMSMTH* W6 ....119 F6
Manbrough Av *EHAM* E6 ....108 A2
Manchester Dr *NKENS* W10 * 100 C3
Manchester Gv *POP/IOD* E14 ....125 F5
Manchester Ms *MHST* W1U 9 G2
Manchester Rd *POP/IOD* E14 ....125 F5
SEVS/STOTM N15 ....67 K3
THHTH CR7 ....180 D6
Manchester Sq *MBLAR* W1H 9 G3
Manchester St *MHST* W1U 9 G2
Manchuria Rd *BTSEA* SW11 ....161 F1
Manciple St *STHWK* SE1 ....19 F3
Mandalay Rd *CLAP* SW4 ....141 H6
Mandarin Wy *YEAD* UB4 ....95 H5
Mandela Cl *WLSDN* NW10 ....81 F5
Mandela Rd *CAN/RD* E16 ....106 E5
Mandela St *BRXN/ST* SW9 ....142 B1
CAMTN NW1 ....84 C6
Mandela Wy *STHWK* SE1 ....19 J7
Mandeville Cl *WIM/MER* SW19 * ...177 H3
Mandeville Dr *SURB* KT6 ....190 E5
Mandeville Pl *MHST* W1U 9 H3
Mandeville Rd *ISLW* TW7 ....136 B3
NTHLT UB5 ....78 A4
STHGT/OAK N14 ....34 B4
Mandrake Rd *TOOT* SW17 ....160 E5
Mandrake Wy *SRTFD* E15 * 88 C5
Mandrell Rd
BRXS/STRHM SW2 ....141 K6
Manette St *SOHO/SHAV* W1D 10 D4
Manford Cross *CHIG* IG7 ....55 G1
Manford Wy *CHIG* IG7 ....54 E1
Manfred Rd *PUT/ROE* SW15 ....139 J6
Manger Rd *HOLWY* N7 ....84 E4
Mangold Wy *ERITHM* DA18 ....128 E3
Manilla St *POP/IOD* E14 ....124 D2
Manister Rd *ABYW* SE2 ....128 B3
Manley Ct *STNW/STAM* N16 ....86 B1
Manley St *CAMTN* NW1 ....84 A6
Mann Cl *CROY/NA* CR0 ....211 J1
Manningford Cl *FSBYE* EC1V * 6 A4
Manning Gdns
KTN/HRWW/W HA3 ....61 K4
Manning Pl *RCHPK/HAM* TW10 ....157 G1
Manning Rd *DAGE* RM10 ....92 C5
STMC/STPC BR5 ....202 E2
WALTH E17 ....69 G2
Manningtree Cl
WIM/MER SW19 ....159 H3
Manningtree Rd *RSLP* HA4 ....77 F2
Manningtree St *WCHPL* E1 * 104 C5
Mannin Rd *CHDH* RM6 ....73 H4
Mannock Rd *DART* DA1 ....151 J4
WDGN N22 ....49 H6
Mann's Cl *ISLW* TW7 ....136 A6
Manns Rd *EDGW* HA8 ....44 C2
Manoel Rd *WHTN* TW2 ....155 H4
Manor Av *BROCKY* SE4 ....144 C3
HSLWW TW4 ....134 C4
NTHLT UB5 ....77 K5
Manorbrook *BKHTH/KID* SE3 ....145 K5
Manor Cl *BAR* EN5 ....20 C5
CDALE/KGS NW9 ....62 D1
DAGE RM10 ....93 F4
DART DA1 ....150 A5
MLHL NW7 * 45 F1
RDART DA2 ....150 A4
ROM RM1 ....75 J2
RSLP HA4 ....58 D5
WPK KT4 ....192 B6
Manor Cottages *NTHWD* HA6 ....40 D4
Manor Cottages App *EFNCH* N2 .....47 G5
Manor Ct *ACT* W3 * 117 H4
E/WMO/HCT KT8 * 189 F1
HRW HA1 * 61 F3
KUTN/CMB KT2 * 175 H4
WBLY HA9 ....80 B2
Manor Court Rd *HNWL* W7 ....96 E6
Manor Crs *BRYLDS* KT5 ....191 H5
Manor Cft *EDGW* HA8 * 44 E5
Manor Farm Dr *CHING* E4 ....38 C4
Manor Farm Rd *ALP/SUD* HA0 ....97 K1
STRHM/NOR SW16 ....180 B5
Manor Flds *PUT/ROE* SW15 ....159 G1
Manorfields Cl *CHST* BR7 ....186 A6
Manor Gdns *ACT* W3 * 117 H4

HOLWY N7 ....84 E1
HPTN TW12 ....173 G5
RCH/KEW TW9 ....137 G4
RSLP HA4 ....77 G3
RYNPK SW20 ....177 J5
SAND/SEL CR2 ....212 B4
VX/NE SW8 * 141 H3
Manor Ga *NTHLT* UB5 ....77 J5
Manorgate Rd *KUTN/CMB* KT2 ....175 H4
Manor Gv *BECK* BR3 ....182 E5
PECK SE15 ....123 K6
RCH/KEW TW9 ....137 H5
Manor Hall Av *HDN* NW4 ....46 A5
Manor Hall Dr *HDN* NW4 ....46 B5
Manor Hall Gdns *LEY* E10 ....69 J5
Manor House Dr
KIL/WHAMP NW6 ....82 B5
Manor House Wy *ISLW* TW7 ....136 C4
Manor La *FELT* TW13 ....153 K4
HYS/HAR UB3 ....113 C6
LEW SE13 ....145 H6
SUN TW16 ....172 A5
SUT SM1 ....209 G3
Manor Lane Ter *LEW* SE13 ....145 H5
Manor Ms *KIL/WHAMP* NW6 ....100 E1
NWCR SE14 ....124 B6
Manor Mt *FSTH* SE23 ....163 K3
Manor Pde *HRW* HA1 * 61 F3
STNW/STAM N16 * 68 A5
Manor Pk *CHST* BR7 ....185 J5
LEW SE13 ....145 G6
RCH/KEW TW9 ....137 G5
Manor Park Cl *WWKM* BR4 ....198 E5
Manor Park Crs *EDGW* HA8 ....44 C2
Manor Park Dr
RYLN/HDSTN HA2 ....42 B6
Manor Park Gdns *EDGW* HA8 ....44 C1
MNPK E12 ....89 H2
Manor Park Pde *LEW* SE13 * 145 H5
SUT SM1 ....209 G4
WLSDN NW10 ....81 H6
WWKM BR4 ....198 E5
Manor Pl *CHST* BR7 * 185 J5
EBED/NFELT TW14 ....153 K3
MTCM CR4 ....179 H6
SUT SM1 ....209 F3
WALW SE17 ....122 C5
Manor Rd *BARK* EN5 ....20 C5
BARK IG11 ....91 F4
BECK BR3 ....182 D5
BELMT SM2 ....208 D5
BFN/LL DA15 ....168 A5
BXLY DA5 ....169 J3
CAN/RD E16 ....106 C4
CHDH RM6 ....73 K3
CHIG IG7 ....54 A2
DAGE RM10 ....92 E4
DART DA1 ....150 B5
E/WMO/HCT KT8 * 189 J1
ENC/FH EN2 ....23 K3
ERITH DA8 ....130 C6
HRW HA1 ....61 G3
HYS/HAR UB3 ....94 E5
LEY E10 ....69 J4
LOU IG10 ....39 J3
MTCM CR4 ....179 H6
RCH/KEW TW9 ....137 G4
ROM RM1 ....75 J2
RSLP HA4 ....58 B5
RYNPK SW20 ....177 H5
SNWD SE25 ....197 H1
STNW/STAM N16 ....68 A5
TEDD TW11 ....174 B1
TOTM N17 ....50 C4
WALTH E17 ....51 G5
WDGN N22 ....48 E2
WEA W13 * 97 G6
WFD IG8 ....53 K2
WLGTN SM6 ....210 B2
WWKM BR4 ....198 E6
Manor Rd North
ESH/CLAY KT10 ....205 F1
HSLW TW4 ....134 D4
WLGTN SM6 ....210 B2
Manor Rd South
ESH/CLAY KT10 ....204 E2
Manorside *BAR* EN5 ....20 C5
Manor Sq *BCTR* RM8 ....73 J6
Manor St *BTFD* TW8 ....116 D5
FNCH N3 ....47 F5
Manor Vw *FNCH* N3 ....47 F5
Manor Wy *BECK* BR3 ....182 D5
BKHTH/KID SE3 ....145 K5
BXLY DA5 ....169 H3
BXLYHN DA7 ....150 A4
CDALE/KGS NW9 ....63 G1
CHING E4 ....38 B6
HAYES BR2 ....200 D3
MTCM CR4 ....195 H1
NWDGN UB2 ....114 C4
RAIN RM13 ....111 G3
RSLP HA4 ....58 A4
RYLN/HDSTN HA2 ....60 B1
SAND/SEL CR2 ....212 A4
STMC/STPC BR5 ....201 J1
WPK KT4 ....192 B5
Manorway *EN* EN1 ....36 A2
WFD IG8 ....53 G3
The Manor Wy *WLGTN* SM6 ....210 B2
Manresa Rd *CHEL* SW3 ....120 C5
Mansard Beeches
TOOT SW17 ....179 F1
Mansard Cl *HCH* RM12 ....75 J6
PIN HA5 ....41 H6
Manse Cl *HYS/HAR* UB3 ....113 G6
Mansel Gv *WALTH* E17 ....51 J4
Mansell Rd *ACT* W3 ....118 A1
GFD/PVL UB6 ....96 B4
Mansell St *WCHPL* E1 ....13 K4
Mansel Rd *WIM/MER* SW19 ....177 H2
Mansergh Cl
WOOL/PLUM SE18 ....146 D1
Manse Rd *STNW/STAM* N16 ....86 B1
Manser Rd *RAIN* RM13 ....111 G3
Mansfield Av *EBAR* EN4 ....33 K1
RSLP HA4 ....59 G1
SEVS/STOTM N15 ....67 K1

Mansfield Cl *ED* N9 ....36 C1
STMC/STPC BR5 ....202 E4
Mansfield Dr *YEAD* UB4 ....94 C3
Mansfield Hl *CHING* E4 ....37 K3
Mansfield Ms *CAVSQ/HST* W1G 9 J2
Mansfield Rd *ACT* W3 ....98 D3
CHSGTN KT9 ....205 J5
HAMP NW3 ....83 K3
IL IG1 ....71 K6
SAND/SEL CR2 ....211 K4
WALTH E17 ....69 H1
WAN E11 ....71 F3
Mansfield St *CAVSQ/HST* W1G 9 J2
Mansford St *BETH* E2 ....104 D2
Manship Rd *MTCM* CR4 ....179 F4
Mansion House Pl
MANHO EC4N * 12 E4
The Mansions *ECT* SW5 * 120 A5
Manson Ms *SKENS* SW7 * 120 B4
Manson Pl *SKENS* SW7 ....14 A7
Manstead Gdns *CHDH* RM6 ....73 J4
RAIN RM13 ....111 J5
Manston Av *NWDGN* UB2 ....115 F4
Manston Cl *PGE/AN* SE20 ....181 K4
Manstone Rd *CRICK* NW2 ....82 C3
Manston Gv *KUTN/CMB* KT2 ....174 E1
Manston Wy *HCH* RM12 ....93 K4
Manthorp Rd
WOOL/PLUM SE18 ....127 H5
Mantilla Rd *TOOT* SW17 ....161 F6
Mantle Rd *BROCKY* SE4 ....144 B4
Mantlet Cl *STRHM/NOR* SW16 ......179 H3
Mantle Wy *SRTFD* E15 ....88 C5
Manton Av *HNWL* W7 ....116 A2
Manton Cl *HYS/HAR* UB3 ....94 C6
Manton Rd *ABYW* SE2 ....128 B4
CHING E4 ....25 K1
Mantua St *BTSEA* SW11 ....140 C4
Mantus Cl *WCHPL* E1 ....104 E3
Mantus Rd *WCHPL* E1 ....104 E3
Manus Wy *TRDG/WHET* N20 ....33 G4
Manville Gdns *TOOT* SW17 ....161 G5
Manville Rd *TOOT* SW17 ....161 F5
Manwood Rd *BROCKY* SE4 ....164 C3
Manwood St *CAN/RD* E16 ....126 C1
Many Gates *BAL* SW12 ....161 G4
Mapesbury Rd *CRICK* NW2 ....82 C4
Mapeshill Pl *CRICK* NW2 ....82 A4
Mape St *BETH* E2 ....104 D3
Maple Av *ACT* W3 ....118 B1
CHING E4 ....51 H2
RYLN/HDSTN HA2 ....60 B6
Maple Cl *BARK/HLT* IG6 ....55 G2
BKHH IG9 ....39 H5
CLAP SW4 ....161 J1
FNCH N3 ....46 E2
HCH RM12 ....75 K6
HPTN TW12 ....172 E2
MTCM CR4 ....179 H4
RSLP HA4 ....59 F5
STMC/STPC BR5 ....201 J2
STNW/STAM N16 ....68 C3
YEAD UB4 ....95 H2
Maple Ct *NWMAL* KT3 ....176 A6
Maplecroft Cl *EHAM* E6 ....107 H5
Mapledale Av *CROY/NA* CR0 ....212 D1
Mapledene Est *HACK* E8 * 86 C5
Mapledene Rd *HACK* E8 ....86 C5
Maple Gdns *ASHF* TW15 ....152 B4
EDGW HA8 ....45 G4
Maple Gv *BTFD* TW8 ....136 C1
CDALE/KGS NW9 ....62 E4
EA W5 ....116 E3
STHL UB1 ....96 A5
Maplehurst Cl *KUT/HW* KT1 ....191 F1
Maple Leaf Dr *BFN/LL* DA15 ....168 A3
Mapleleafe Gdns *BARK/HLT* IG6 ....54 B6
Maple Leaf Sq
BERM/RHTH SE16 * 124 A2
Maple Ms *KIL/WHAMP* NW6 * 101 F1
STRHM/NOR SW16 ....180 A1
Maple Pl *FITZ* W1T 10 B1
WDGN N22 * 112 B1
Maple Rd *DART* DA1 ....171 F3
PGE/AN SE20 ....181 J4
SURB KT6 ....190 E2
WAN E11 ....70 C4
YEAD UB4 ....95 G2
Maples Pl *WCHPL* E1 * 104 D4
Maplestead Rd
BRXS/STRHM SW2 ....162 A2
DAGW RM9 ....109 H6
The Maples *E/WMO/HCT* KT8 * 174 D3
ESH/CLAY KT10 ....205 G5
Maple St *ROMW/RG* RM7 ....74 E1
FITZ W1T 10 A1
Maplethorpe Rd *THHTH* CR7 ....196 B1
Mapleton Cl *HAYES* BR2 ....199 K2
Mapleton Crs *PEND* EN3 ....25 F1
WAND/EARL SW18 ....160 A1
Mapleton Rd *CHING* E4 ....38 A4
EN EN1 ....24 C3
WAND/EARL SW18 ....159 K1
Maple Tree Pl *BKHTH/KID* SE3 ......146 D3
Maple Wk *NKENS* W10 * 100 C3
Maple Wy *FELT* TW13 ....153 K5
Maplin Cl *WCHMH* N21 ....35 F1
Maplin Gdns *BARK/HLT* IG6 ....54 B5
Maplin Rd *CAN/RD* E16 ....106 E5
Maplin St *BOW* E3 ....105 H2
Mapperley Dr *WFD* IG8 ....52 C3
Marabou Cl *MNPK* E12 ....89 J3
Maran Wy *ERITHM* DA18 ....128 E3
Marathon Wy *THMD* SE28 ....128 A2
Marban Rd *MV/WKIL* W9 ....100 D2
Marble Cl *ACT* W3 ....117 J1
Marble Dr *CRICK* NW2 ....64 B3
Marble Hill Cl *TWK* TW1 ....156 C2
Marble Hill Gdns *TWK* TW1 ....156 C2
Marble Quay *WAP* E1W 13 K7
Marbrook Ct *LEE/GVPK* SE12 ....166 B5
Marcella Rd *BRXN/ST* SW9 ....142 B3
Marcellina Wy *ORP* BR6 ....216 E1
Marcet Rd *DART* DA1 ....151 F6
Marchant Rd *WAN* E11 ....70 B6

Marchant St NWCR SE14 * 124 B6
Marchbank Rd WKENS W14 ...119 J6
Marchmont Rd
  RCHPK/HAM TW10 ....137 C6
Marchmont St BMSBY WC1N ...A E6
Marchside Cl HEST TW5 ....134 C2
Marchwood Cl CMBW SE5 .....143 F1
Marchwood Crs EA W5 ....97 J5
Marcia Rd STHWK SE1 ....19 H7
Marcilly Rd WAND/EARL SW18 ..100 C6
Marconi Rd FBAR/BDGN N11 ...34 B6
Marconi Rd LEY E10 ....69 J5
Marconi Pl HACK E8 ....86 D4
Marco Rd HMSMTH W6 ....118 E5
Marcus Garvey Wy
  BRXN/ST SW9 ....142 B5
Marcus Rd DART DA1 ....170 D2
  WAND/EARL SW18 ....160 A1
Marcus Ter WAND/EARL SW18 160 A1
Mardale Dr CDALE/KGS NW9 ..63 F2
Mardell Rd CROY/NA CRO 198 A2
Marden Av HAYES BR2 ....199 K3
  CROY/NA CRO 196 A3
Marden Crs BXLY DA5 ....149 K6
  CROY/NA CRO 196 A3
  ROM RM1 ....75 G3
  TOTM N17 ....50 D6
Marden Sq BERM/RHTH SE16 123 J3
Marder Rd WEA W13 ....116 B2
Mardyke Cl DAGE RM10 ....110 E1
Marechal Niel Av BFN/LL DA15 167 J3
Marechal Niel Pde
  BFN/LL DA15 * 167 J3
Maresfield CROY/NA CRO 212 A1
Maresfield Gdns HAMP NW3 ...83 G3
Mare St HACK E8 ....86 D3
Marfleet Cl WPK KT4 ....192 D5
Marfleet Ct CAR SM5 ....194 D6
Margaret Av CHING E4 ....37 K1
Margaret Bondfield Av
  BARK IG11 ....91 G5
Margaret Cl GPK RM2 ....75 K2
Margaret Gardner Dr
  ELTH/MOT SE9 ....166 E4
Margaret Ingram Cl
  FUL/PGN SW6 * 119 J6
Margaret Lockwood Cl
  KUT/HW KT1 * 191 G1
Margaret Rd BXLY DA5 ....168 E1
  EBAR EN4 ....21 K5
  GPK RM2 ....75 K2
  STNW/STAM N16 * 68 B5
Margaret St GTPST W1W 10 A3
Margaretta Ter CHEL SW3 ....120 D6
Margaretting Rd MNPK E12 ......71 G6
Margaret Wy REDBR IG4 ....71 J1
Margate Rd BRXS/STRHM SW2 141 K6
Margeholes OXHEY WD19 ....27 J4
Margery Pk BCTR RM8 ....91 K1
Margery St FSBYW WC1X 5 J5
Margin Dr WIM/MER SW19 .....177 G1
Margravine Gdns
  HMSMTH W6 ....119 G5
Margravine Rd HMSMTH W6 ...119 G6
Marguerite Vls RYNPK SW20 * ..176 E5
Marham Gdns MRDN SM4 ....194 B3
  WAND/EARL SW18 ....160 D3
Maria Cl BERM/RHTH SE16 .....123 H4
Maria Ct YEAD UB4 ....95 H3
Marian Pl BETH E2 ....104 D1
Marian Rd STRHM/NOR SW16 179 H4
Marian Sq BETH E2 * 104 D1
Marian Wy WLSDN NW10 ....81 H5
Maria Ter WCHPL E1 ....105 F4
Maria Theresa Cl NWMAL KT3 192 A2
Maricas Av KTN/HRWW/W HA3 42 D3
Marie Curie CMBW SE5 * 143 F2
Marie Lloyd Wk HACK E8 * 86 C4
Mariette Wy WLGTN SM6 ....210 E6
Marigold Aly STHWK SE1 ....12 A6
Marigold Cl STHL UB1 * 95 J6
Marigold St
  BERM/RHTH SE16 ....123 J2
Marigold Wy CROY/NA CRO 198 A5
Marina Av NWMAL KT3 ....192 E3
Marina Dr DART DA1 ....171 K3
  WELL DA16 ....147 K2
Marina Gdns ROMW/RG RM7 ...74 D2
Marina Wy TEDD TW11 ....174 E3
Marine Ct PUR RM19 ....131 J4
Marine Dr BARK IG11 ....109 H2
  WOOL/PLUM SE18 ....126 E4
Marinefield Rd FUL/PGN SW6 ..140 A3
Mariner Gdns
  RCHPK/HAM TW10 ....156 C5
Mariner Rd MNPK E12 ....90 A1
Mariners Ms POP/IOD E14 ......125 G3
Marion Cl BUSH WD23 ....28 B1
Marion Cl BARK/HLT IG6 ....54 D3
Marion Gv WFD IG8 ....52 C1
Marion Rd CROY/NA CRO 196 D2
  MLHL NW7 ....45 J1
Marischal Rd LEW SE13 ....145 G4
Maritime Quay POP/IOD E14 ..124 D5
Maritime St BOW E3 ....105 H4
Marius Rd TOOT SW17 ....161 F4
Marjorie Gv BTSEA SW11 ....140 E5
Mark Av CHING E4 ....37 K1
Mark Cl BXLYHN DA7 ....149 F2
  HAYES BR2 ....215 J2
  STHL UB1 ....115 F1
Markeston Gn OXHEY WD19 ....27 H6
Market Chambers
  ENC/FH EN2 * 23 K4
Market Est HOLWY N7 ....84 E4
Market La EDGW HA8 ....44 E4
Market Link ROM RM1 ....75 G1

Market Meadow
  STMC/STPC BR5 ....202 D1
Market Ms MYFR/PICC W1J 15 J1
Market Pde BMLY BR1 * 183 K4
  ED N9 ....36 C4
  EW KT17 * 207 H6
  FELT TW13 * 154 D4
  LEY E10 * 69 K3
  SCUP DA14 * 168 B6
  SNWD SE25 * 197 H1
  STNW/STAM N16 * 68 C5
  WALTH E17 * 51 H6
Market Pl ACT W3 ....117 K1
  BERM/RHTH SE16 * 123 H4
  BTFD TW8 ....136 D1
  BXLYHN DA7 ....149 H5
  DART DA1 ....171 H2
  EFNCH N2 ....47 J6
  KUT/HW KT1 * 174 E5
  ROM RM1 ....75 G2
  SOHO/SHAV W1D 10 A3
Market Rd HOLWY N7 ....84 E4
  RCH/KEW TW9 ....137 H4
Market Sq BMLY BR1 * 183 K5
  ED N9 ....36 D4
Market St DART DA1 ....171 H2
  EHAM E6 ....108 A1
  WOOL/PLUM SE18 ....127 F4
Market Ter BTFD TW8 * 117 F6
Market Yard Ms STHWK SE1 .....19 G4
Markfield Gdns CHING E4 ....37 K2
Markfield Rd SEVS/STOTM N15 68 C1
Markham Pl CHEL SW3 ....120 E5
Markham Sq CHEL SW3 ....120 E5
Markham St CHEL SW3 ....120 D5
Markhole Cl HPTN TW12 ....172 E3
Markhouse Av WALTH E17 ....69 G1
Markhouse Rd WALTH E17 ....69 H3
Mark La MON EC3R 13 H5
Markmanor Av WALTH E17 ....69 G4
Mark Rd WDGN N22 ....49 H5
Marksbury Av RCH/KEW TW9 ..137 H4
Marks Rd ROMW/RG RM7 ....74 E1
Markstone Rd SDTCH EC2A 7 G6
  SRTFD E15 ....88 C5
Mark Ter RYNPK SW20 ....177 F3
The Markway SUN TW16 ....172 E5
Markwell Cl SYD SE26 ....163 J6
Markyate Rd BCTR RM8 ....91 H3
Marlands Rd CLAY IG5 ....53 K5
Marlborough Av EDGW HA8 ......30 D5
  HACK E8 * 86 C6
  RSLP HA4 ....58 D5
  STHGT/OAK N14 ....34 C5
Marlborough Cl ORP BR6 ....202 A4
  TRDG/WHET N20 ....33 K5
  WALW SE17 ....18 B7
  WIM/MER SW19 ....178 C2
Marlborough Ct REGST W1B 10 A5
Marlborough Crs CHSWK W4 ...118 A3
  HYS/HAR UB3 ....133 G1
Marlborough Dr CLAY IG5 ....53 K5
Marlborough Gdns
  TRDG/WHET N20 ....33 K5
Marlborough Ga BAY/PAD W2 ....8 A4
Marlborough Gv STHWK SE1 ....123 H6
Marlborough Hl HRW HA1 ....60 E1
  STJWD NW8 ....83 G6
Marlborough La CHARL SE7 .....126 B6
Marlborough Ms
  BRXN/ST SW9 ....142 A5
Marlborough Pde FSBYPK N4 * ..67 J3
Marlborough Park Av
  BFN/LL DA15 ....168 B3
Marlborough Pl STJWD NW8 ....100 G1
Marlborough Rd ARCH N19 ......66 E6
  BCTR RM8 ....91 J2
  BXLYHN DA7 ....148 E4
  CHING E4 ....51 K2
  CHSWK W4 ....117 K5
  DART DA1 ....171 F1
  EA W5 ....116 E2
  ED N9 ....36 C3
  FELT TW13 ....154 C4
  FSTGT E7 * 89 G5
  HAYES BR2 ....200 B1
  HPTN TW12 ....173 F2
  HYS/HAR UB3 ....133 G1
  NWDGN UB2 ....114 B3
  RCHPK/HAM TW10 ....157 F1
  ROMW/RG RM7 ....74 C1
  SAND/SEL CR2 ....211 J5
  SRTFD E15 * 88 C2
  SUT SM1 ....208 E1
  SWFD E18 ....52 E6
  WAN E11 ....70 E5
  WHALL SW1A 16 B1
  WIM/MER SW19 ....178 D2
  WOOL/PLUM SE18 ....127 G5
Marlborough St CHEL SW3 ....14 C7
Marlborough Yd ARCH N19 ....66 D6
Marler Rd FSTH SE23 ....164 C3
Marley Av BXLYHN DA7 ....128 E6
Marley Cl GFD/PVL UB6 ....96 A2
  SEVS/STOTM N15 ....67 H1
Marley Rd BERM/RHTH SE16 * 124 A4
Marlingdene Cl HPTN TW12 .....173 F2
Marlings Cl CHST BR7 ....201 K1
Marlings Park Av CHST BR7 .....201 K1
Marlins Cl SUT SM1 * 209 G3
The Marlins NTHWD HA6 ....40 D3
Marloes Cl ALP/SUD HA0 ....79 K2
Marloes Rd KENS W8 ....120 A3
Marlow Av PUR RM19 ....131 H4
Marlow Cl PGE/AN SE20 ....181 J6
Marlow Ct CDALE/KGS NW9 .....45 H6
Marlow Crs TWK TW1 ....156 A1
Marlow Dr CHEAM SM3 ....208 B1
Marlowe Cl BARK/HLT IG6 ....54 D6
  CHST BR7 ....185 J2
Marlowe Rd WALTH E17 ....70 A1
The Marlowes DART DA1 ....150 A5

STJWD NW8 ....2 A1
Marlowe Wy CROY/NA CRO 195 K6
Marlow Gdns HYS/HAR UB3 ....113 G3
Marlow Rd EHAM E6 ....107 K2
  PGE/AN SE20 ....181 J6
Marlton St GNWCH SE10 ....125 J5
Marl Rd WAND/EARL SW18 .....140 A4
Marlton St GNWCH SE10 ....125 J5
Marmadon Rd
  WOOL/PLUM SE18 ....128 A4
Marmion Av CHING E4 ....37 J6
Marmion Av CHING E4 ....37 J6
Marmion Cl CHING E4 ....37 H6
Marmion Ms BTSEA SW11 * 141 F4
Marmion Rd BTSEA SW11 ....141 F5
Marmont Rd PECK SE15 ....143 H2
Marmora Rd EDUL SE22 ....163 K1
Marmot Rd HSLWW TW4 ....134 C4
Marne Av FBAR/BDGN N11 ......34 A6
  WELL DA16 ....148 B4
Marnell Wy HSLWW TW4 ....134 C4
Marne St NKENS W10 ....88 C2
Marney Rd BTSEA SW11 ....141 F5
Marnfield Crs
  BRXS/STRHM SW2 ....162 A3
Marnham Av CRICK NW2 ....82 C2
Marnham Crs GFD/PVL UB6 .....96 B3
Mamock Rd BROCKY SE4 ....144 C6
Maroon St POP/IOD E14 ....105 G4
Maroons Wy CAT SE6 ....182 D1
Marquess Rd IS N1 ....85 K4
Marquess Rd North IS N1 * 85 J4
Marquess Rd South IS N1 ....85 J4
Marquis Cl ALP/SUD HA0 ....80 B5
Marquis Rd CAMTN NW1 ....84 B4
  FSBYPK N4 ....67 F5
  WDGN N22 ....49 F2
Marrabon Cl BFN/LL DA15 ....168 A1
Marrick Cl PUT/ROE SW15 ......138 D5
Marrilyne Av PEND EN3 ....25 H1
Mariner Ct HYS/HAR UB3 * 113 J6
Marriot Rd MUSWH N10 ....47 K4
Marriott Cl EBED/NFELT TW14 153 G1
Marriott Rd BAR EN5 ....20 B4
  DART DA1 ....171 J1
  FSBYPK N4 ....67 F5
  SRTFD E15 ....88 C6
Marriotts Cl CDALE/KGS NW9 ...63 H3
Marriotts Yd BAR EN5 * 20 D5
Marryat Cl HSLW TW3 ....135 F5
Marryat Pl WIM/MER SW19 .....159 H6
Marsala Rd LEW SE13 ....144 E5
Marsden Rd ED N9 ....36 D4
  PECK SE15 ....143 G4
Marsden St KTTN NW5 ....84 A4
Marsden Wy ORP BR6 ....217 F2
Marshall Cl FBAR/BDGN N11 ....34 B6
  HRW HA1 ....60 D4
  HSLWW TW4 ....134 E5
  WAND/EARL SW18 ....160 B1
Marshall Dr YEAD UB4 ....95 F3
Marshall Est MLHL NW7 * 31 J6
Marshall Rd LEYE10 * 69 H6
  TOTM N17 ....49 K4
Marshalls Dr ROM RM1 ....57 G6
Marshalls Gv
  WOOL/PLUM SE18 ....126 D4
Marshall's Pl BERM/RHTH SE16 19 K5
Marshalls Rd ROMW/RG RM7 ....75 F1
  SUT SM1 ....209 F2
Marshall St SOHO/CST W1F 10 B4
Marshalsea Rd STHWK SE1 ....18 D2
Marsham Cl CHST BR7 ....185 G1
Marsham St WEST SW1P 16 D5
Marshbrook Cl
  BKHTH/KID SE3 ....146 C4
Marsh Cl MLHL NW7 ....31 H5
Marsh Dr CDALE/KGS NW9 ....63 H3
Marsh Farm Rd WHTN TW2 .....156 A3
Marshfield St POP/IOD E14 ......125 F3
Marshgate La SRTFD E15 ....87 K6
Marsh Green Rd DAGE RM10 .....92 C6
Marsh Hl HOM E9 ....87 G3
Marsh La LEY E10 ....69 H6
  MLHL NW7 ....31 F4
  STAN HA7 ....43 J1
  TOTM N17 ....50 D3
Marsh Rd ALP/SUD HA0 ....97 K2
  PIN HA5 ....59 J1
Marshside Cl ED N9 ....36 E4
Marsh St DART DA1 ....150 E4
  POP/IOD E14 * 124 E4
Marsh Wall POP/IOD E14 ....124 D2
Marsh Wy DAGE RM9 ....111 F3
Marsland Cl WALW SE17 ....122 C5
Marston Av CHSGTN KT9 ....206 A4
  DAGE RM10 ....92 C1
Marston Cl DAGE RM10 ....92 C1
  KIL/WHAMP NW6 ....83 G5
Marston Rd CLAY IG5 ....53 J5
  TEDD TW11 ....156 C5
Marston Wy NRWD SE19 ....180 C3
Marsworth Av PIN HA5 ....41 H4
Marsworth Cl WATW WD18 * 26 C1
  YEAD UB4 ....95 J4
Martaban Rd STNW/STAM N16 68 A1
Martara Ms WALW SE17 ....122 D5
Martello St HACK E8 ....86 D5
Martello Ter HACK E8 * 86 D5
Marten Rd DUL SE21 ....162 E5
Martens Av BXLYHN DA7 ....149 K5
Martens Cl BXLYHN DA7 ....149 K5
Martham Cl BARK/HLT IG6 ....55 G1
Martha Rd SRTFD E15 * 88 C4
Martha St WCHPL E1 ....104 D5
Martin Bds FSBYE EC1V * 6 E6
Martha St WCHPL E1 ....104 E5

Marthorne Crs
  KTN/HRWW/W HA3 ....42 D5
Martin Bowes Rd
  ELTH/MOT SE9 ....146 E4
Martin Cl ED N9 ....37 F3
Martin Crs CROY/NA CRO 196 A5
Martindale MORT/ESHN SW14 137 K6
Martindale Av CAN/RD E16 .....106 E6
  ORP BR6 ....217 G3
Martindale Rd BAL SW12 ....161 G2
  HSLWW TW4 ....134 D5
Martin Dene BXLYHS DA6 ....149 G6
Martin Dr NTHLT UB5 ....78 A3
  RAIN RM13 ....111 K3
Martineau Cl ESH/CLAY KT10 ..204 D2
Martineau Dr TWK TW1 ....136 C5
Martineau Ms HBRY N5 ....85 H2
Martineau St WCHPL E1 ....104 E6
Martingales Cl
  RCHPK/HAM TW10 ....156 E5
Martin Gdns BCTR RM8 ....91 J2
Martin Gv MRDN SM4 ....177 K6
Martin La CANST EC4R 13 G5
Martin Ri BXLYHS DA6 ....149 G6
Martin Rd BCTR RM8 ....91 J2
  DART DA1 ....171 J5
Martins Cl STMC/STPC BR5 ....186 E6
Martin St THMD SE28 ....128 A1
Martins Mt BAR EN5 ....20 D5
Martins Pl THMD SE28 ....128 A1
Martin's Rd HAYES BR2 ....183 H5
The Martins SYD SE26 ....181 J1
  WBLY HA9 ....80 B1
Martin St THMD SE28 ....127 K1
Martin Wk MLSWH N10 * 48 A4
Martin Wy RYNPK SW20 ....177 H6
  THMD SE28 ....127 K1
Martlet Gv NTHLT UB5 ....95 H2
Martlett Ct HOL/ALD WC2B 11 F4
Martley Dr IL IG1 ....72 B2
Martock Cl KTN/HRWW/W HA3 ..61 G1
Martock Gdns FBAR/BDGN N11 47 J1
Marton Cl CAT SE6 ....164 D5
Marton Rd STNW/STAM N16 * ...68 A5
Martys Yd HAMP NW3 * 83 H2
Marvell Av YEAD UB4 ....94 E4
Marvels Cl LEE/GVPK SE12 ......166 A4
Marvels La LEE/GVPK SE12 ......166 A3
Marville Rd FUL/PGN SW6 ....139 J1
Marvin St HACK E8 ....86 D4
Marwell Cl ROM RM1 * 75 H2
  WWKM BR4 ....199 J6
Marwood Cl WELL DA16 ....148 C4
Marwood Dr MLHL NW7 ....46 B3
Mary Adelaide Cl
  PUT/ROE SW15 ....158 B5
Mary Ann Bldgs DEPT SE8 * 124 D6
Maryat Sq FUL/PGN SW6 ....139 G2
Mary Datchelor Cl CMBW SE5 .142 E2
Maryfield Cl BXLY DA5 ....170 B5
Maryland Pk SRTFD E15 ....88 C3
Maryland Rd MV/WKIL W9 ....100 E3
  SRTFD E15 ....88 B3
  WDGN N22 ....49 G2
Maryland Sq SRTFD E15 ....88 C3
Maryland St SRTFD E15 ....88 B3
Maryland Wk IS N1 * 85 J6
Mary Lawrenson Pl
  BKHTH/KID SE3 ....145 J1
Marylebone High St MHST W1U ..9 H2
Marylebone La MHST W1U 9 H4
Marylebone Ms CAVSQ/HST W1G ..9 H2
Marylebone Rd CAMTN NW1 ......8 D1
Marylebone St MHST W1U 9 H3
Marylee Wy LBTH SE11 ....17 H7
Maryon Gv WOOL/PLUM SE18 126 D4
Maryon Ms HAMP NW3 * 83 J2
Maryon Rd CHARL SE7 ....126 D4
  WOOL/PLUM SE18 ....126 D4
Mary Peters Dr GFD/PVL UB6 .....78 D3
Mary Rose Cl HPTN TW12 ....173 F4
Maryrose Wy TRDG/WHET N20 ..33 H3
Mary Seacole Cl HACK E8 * 86 B6
Mary Secole Cl HACK E8 ....86 B6
Mary's Ter TWK TW1 ....156 B2
Mary St CAN/RD E16 ....106 D4
  IS N1 ....6 D1
Masbro' Rd WKENS W14 ....119 G3
Mascalls Ct CHARL SE7 ....146 B6
Mascalls Rd CHARL SE7 ....146 B6
Mascotte Rd PUT/ROE SW15 ...139 G5
Mascotts Cl CRICK NW2 ....81 K1
Masefield Av STAN HA7 ....29 F4
  STHL UB1 ....96 A6
Masefield Cl ERITH DA8 ....150 B1
Masefield Crs STHGT/OAK N14 22 C6
Masefield Gdns EHAM E6 ....108 A3
Masefield La YEAD UB4 ....95 F3
Masefield Rd HPTN TW12 ....154 E6
Masefield Vw ORP BR6 ....216 C1
Masefield Wy
  STWL/WRAY TW19 ....152 C3
Mashie Rd ACT W3 ....99 G5
Mashiters HI ROM RM1 ....57 F3
Mashiters Wk ROM RM1 ....57 G6
Maskall Cl BRXS/STRHM SW2 * 162 B3
Maskell Rd TOOT SW17 ....160 B5
Maskelyne Cl BTSEA SW11 ......140 D2
Mason Cl BERM/RHTH SE16 ...123 H5
  BXLYHN DA7 ....149 J4
  HPTN TW12 ....172 E4
  RYNPK SW20 ....177 G4
Mason Ct WFD IG8 ....38 C6
Mason's Arms Ms CONDST W1S * ..9 K4
Mason's Av CITYW EC2V 12 E3
  CROY/NA CRO 211 J1
  KTN/HRWW/W HA3 ....42 E6

Masons Ct EW KT17 * 207 J6
Masons HI HAYES BR2 ....183 K6
  WOOL/PLUM SE18 ....127 G4
  MTCM CR4 ....178 E4
Mason St WALW SE17 ....19 F7
Masons Yd FSBYE EC1V 6 C6
  STJS SW1Y 10 B7
Massey Cl FBAR/BDGN N11 ......48 B1
Massie Rd HACK E8 ....86 C4
Massingberd Wy TOOT SW17 ..161 G6
Massinger St WALW SE17 ....19 G7
Massingham St WCHPL E1 ....105 F3
Masson Av RSLP HA4 ....77 G4
Master Gunners Pl
  WOOL/PLUM SE18 ....146 D2
Masterman Rd EHAM E6 ....107 J2
Masters Cl STRHM/NOR SW16 179 H2
Masters Dr BERM/RHTH SE16 .123 J5
Master's St WCHPL E1 ....105 F4
Mast House Ter
  POP/IOD E14 * 124 D4
Masthouse Ter POP/IOD E14 ...124 D4
Mastmaker Rd POP/IOD E14 ...124 D2
Maswell Park Crs HSLW TW3 ...135 H6
Maswell Park Rd HSLW TW5 ....135 G6
Matcham Rd WAN E11 ....88 C1
Matchless Dr
  WOOL/PLUM SE18 ....147 F1
Matfield Cl HAYES BR2 ....199 K2
Matfield Rd BELV DA17 ....129 H6
Matham Gv EDUL SE22 ....143 G5
Matham Rd E/WMO/HCT KT8 ..189 J2
Matheson Rd WKENS W14 ....119 J4
Mathews Av EHAM E6 ....108 A1
Mathews Park Av SRTFD E15 .....88 D4
Mathews Yd LSQ/SEVD WC2H * .10 E4
Mathieson Ct STHWK SE1 * 18 B3
Matilda Cl NRWD SE19 ....180 L5
Matilda St IS N1 ....5 H1
Matlock Cl BAR EN5 ....20 B6
Matlock Crs CHEAM SM3 ....208 C2
  OXHEY WD19 ....27 G5
Matlock Gdns CHEAM SM3 ......208 C2
Matlock Pl CHEAM SM3 ....208 C2
Matlock Rd LEY E10 ....70 A3
Matlock St POP/IOD E14 ....105 G5
Matlock Wy NWMAL KT3 ....176 A4
Matthew Cl NKENS W10 * 100 B3
Matthew Ct MTCM CR4 ....195 J2
Matthews Rd GFD/PVL UB6 ....78 D3
Matthews St BTSEA SW11 * 140 E3
Matthias Rd STNW/STAM N16 ...85 K5
Mattingly Wy PECK SE15 ....143 G1
Mattock La WEA W13 ....116 D1
Maud Cashmore Wy
  WOOL/PLUM SE18 ....126 E3
Maude Rd CMBW SE5 ....143 F3
  WALTH E17 ....69 G2
Maudesville Cottages
  HNWL W7 * 115 K1
Maude Ter WALTH E17 ....69 G1
  PLSTW E13 ....106 E1
Maudlins Gn WAP E1W * 13 K1
Maud Rd LEY E10 ....88 A1
  PLSTW E13 ....106 D1
Maudslay Rd ELTH/MOT SE9 ...146 E4
Maud St CAN/RD E16 ....106 D4
Maud Wilkes Cl KTTN NW5 ....84 C3
Mauleverer Rd
  BRXS/STRHM SW2 ....141 K6
Maundeby Wk WLSDN NW10 * ..81 G3
Maunder Rd HNWL W7 ....115 K1
Maunsel St WEST SW1P 16 C6
Maurice Av WDGN N22 ....49 H5
Maurice Brown Cl MLHL NW7 * ..46 B1
Maurice St SHB W12 ....99 K5
Maurice Wk GLDGN NW11 ....65 G1
Maurier Cl NTHLT UB5 ....77 G6
Mauritius Rd GNWCH SE10 .....125 H4
Maury Rd STNW/STAM N16 ....68 C1
Mavelstone Cl BMLY BR1 ....184 D4
Maverton Rd BOW E3 ....87 J5
Mavis Av HOR/WEW KT19 ....207 G4
Mavis Cl HOR/WEW KT19 ....207 G4
Mawbey Pl STHWK SE1 ....123 G5
Mawbey Rd STHWK SE1 ....123 G5
Mawbey St VX/NE SW8 ....141 K1
Mawney Cl ROMW/RG RM7 ....56 D6
Mawney Rd ROMW/RG RM7 .....74 E3
Mawson Cl RYNPK SW20 ....177 H5
Mawson La CHSWK W4 ....118 C6
Maxey Gdns DAGW RM9 ....92 A2
Maxey Rd DAGW RM9 ....92 A2
  WOOL/PLUM SE18 ....127 H4
Maxfield Cl TRDG/WHET N20 ....33 G2
Maximfeldt Rd ERITH DA8 ....130 B5
Maxim Rd DART DA1 ....150 B6
  ERITH DA8 ....130 A5
  WCHMH N21 ....35 G1
Maxted Pk HRW HA1 ....60 E3
Maxted Rd PECK SE15 ....143 G4
Maxwell Cl CROY/NA CRO 195 K5
  HYS/HAR UB3 ....94 E6
Maxwell Gdns ORP BR6 ....217 F1
Maxwell Rd BORE WD6 ....27 J2
Maxwell Rd FUL/PGN SW6 ......140 A1
  NTHWD HA6 ....40 C4
  WDR/YW UB7 ....112 B4
  WELL DA16 ....148 B5
Maxwelton Av MLHL NW7 ....45 F1
Maxwelton Cl MLHL NW7 ....45 F1
Maya Cl PECK SE15 ....143 J3
Mayall Cl CHING E4 ....25 J1
Mayall Rd HNHL SE24 ....142 C6
  STHWK SE1 ....18 D1
Mayall Rd BRXS/STRHM SW2 .142 C6
Maya Pl FBAR/BDGN N11 ....48 D3
Maya Rd EFNCH N2 ....65 G1
Mayav STMC/STPC BR5 ....202 C2
Maybank Av ALP/SUD HA0 ....79 K3
  HCH RM12 ....93 K3
  SWFD E18 ....53 F5
Maybank Gdns PIN HA5 ....58 E2

Maybank Rd *SWFD* E18 ....53 G4
May Bate Av *KUTN/CMB* KT2....174 E4
Mayberry Pl *BRYLDS* KT5 ....191 C4
Maybourne Cl *SYD* SE26 * 181 J2
Maybury Cl *EN* EN1....................24 D1
STMC/STPC BR5 ....201 G2
Maybury Rd *BARK* IG11 ....109 G1
PLSTW E13 ....107 G3
Maybury St *TOOT* SW17 ....178 D1
Maychurch Cl *STAN* HA7.............43 K4
May Cl *CHSGTN* KT9 ....206 B4
Maycock Gv *NTHWD* HA6............40 D2
Maycroft *PIN* HA5 ....41 F5
Maycross Av *MRDN* SM4 ....193 J1
Mayday Gdns *BKHTH/KID* SE3..146 C5
Mayday Rd *THHTH* CR7 ....196 C5
Mayfield Rd *THHTH* CR7 ....196 A1
Mayerne Rd *ELTH/MOT* SE9 ......146 C6
Mayesbrook Rd *BARK* IG11 ....91 F6
Mayesford Rd *CHDH* RM6 ....73 J4
Mayes Rd *WDGN* N22 ....49 F5
Mayeswood Rd *LEE/GVPK* SE12.166 B6
Mayfair Av *BXLYHN* DA7 ....148 E2
CHDH RM6 ....73 K3
IL IG1 ....71 K6
WHTN TW2 ....155 H2
WPK KT4 ....192 C5
Mayfair Ct *BECK* BR3 ....182 C6
SURB KT6 ....191 F5
Mayfair Ct *EDGW* HA8................44 B1
Mayfair Gdns *TOTM* N17 ....49 J2
WFD IG8 ....52 E3
Mayfair Ms *HAMP* NW3 * 83 K5
Mayfair Pl *MYFR/PICC* W1J 9 K7
Mayfair Rd *DART* DA1 ....151 G6
Mayfair Ter *STHGT/OAK* N14 ......34 D2
Mayfield *BXLYHN* DA7 ....149 G4
Mayfield Av *CHSWK* W4 ....118 B4
KTN/HRWW/W HA3 ....61 H2
NFNCH/WDSP N12 ....33 G6
ORP BR6 ....202 A5
STHGT/OAK N14 ....34 C4
WEA W13 ....116 C5
WFD IG8 ....52 E2
Mayfield Cl *CLAP* SW4 ....141 J6
HACK E8 ....86 E5
PGE/AN SE20 * 181 J4
THDIT KT7 ....190 C5
Mayfield Crs *ED* N9 ....36 D1
THHTH CR7 ....196 A1
Mayfield Dr *PIN* HA5 ....59 K1
Mayfield Gdns *HDN* NW4.............64 B5
HNWL W7 ....96 D6
Mayfield Rd *ACT* W3 ....98 D6
BCTR RM8 ....73 J5
BELMT SM2 ....209 H4
BELV DA17 ....129 K4
BMLY BR1.................................200 D2
CEND/HSY/T N8 ....66 E2
CHING E4 ....38 B4
HACK E8 ....86 B5
PEND EN3 ....25 F3
PLSTW E13 ....106 D3
SAND/SEL CR2 ....211 K6
SHB W12 ....118 C2
WALTH E17 ....51 G5
WIM/MER SW19 ....177 J4
Mayfields *WBLY* HA9 ....62 C6
Mayfields Cl *WBLY* HA9...............62 C6
Mayfield Vis *SCUP* DA14 * 186 D2
Mayflower Cl
BERM/RHTH SE16.....................124 A4
RSLP HA4 ....58 A3
Mayflower Rd *BRXN/ST* SW9 .....141 K4
Mayflower St
BERM/RHTH SE16.....................123 K2
Mayfly Cl *PIN* HA5 ....59 C4
STMC/STPC BR5 ....202 E1
Mayford Cl *BAL* SW12 ....160 E2
BECK BR3 ....182 A6
Mayford Rd *BAL* SW12 ....160 E2
May Gdns *BORE* WD6 ....29 K1
GFD/PVL UB6 ....97 J2
Maygood St *IS* N1 ....5 H2
Maygreen Crs *EMPK* RM11 ....75 J4
Maygrove Rd *KIL/WHAMP* NW6 ...82 D4
Mayhew Cl *CHING* E4 ....37 J5
Mayhill Rd *BARN* EN5 ....20 C6
CHARL SE7 ....126 A6
Maylands Av *HCH* RM12 ....93 K2
Maylands Dr *SCUP* DA14 ....168 E5
Maylands Rd *OXHEY* WD19 ....27 G6
Maynard Cl *ERITH* DA8 ....150 C1
FUL/PGN SW6 ....140 A1
SEVS/STOTM N15 ....68 A2
Maynard Rd *WALTH* E17 ....70 A5
Maynards Quay *WAP* E1W * 104 E6
Maynooth Gdns *MTCM* CR4 ....194 E4
Mayola Rd *CLPT* E5 ....86 E2
Mayo Rd *CROY/NA* CR0 ....196 E2
WLSDN NW10..............................81 G4
Mayow Rd *SYD* SE26 ....164 A6
Mayplace Av *DART* DA1 ....150 D5
Mayplace Cl *BXLYHN* DA7 ....149 J4
Mayplace La
WOOL/PLUM SE18 ....127 G6
Mayplace Rd East
BXLYHN DA7..............................149 K4
Mayplace Rd West
BXLYHN DA7 ....149 H5
Maypole Crs *BARK/HLT* IG6 ....54 D3
ERITH DA8 ....131 G6
May Rd *CHING* E4 ....51 J2
PLSTW E13 ....106 E1
RDART DA2 ....171 J6
WHTN TW2 ....155 H3
Mayroyd Av *SURB* KT6 ....191 H6
May's Buildings Ms
GNWCH SE10 ....145 G1
Mays Ct *CHCR* WC2N...................10 E6
May's Hill Rd *HAYES* BR2 ....183 H5
Mays La *BAR* EN5.........................31 K2
Maysoule Rd *BTSEA* SW11 ....140 C5
Mays Rd *HPTN* TW12..................173 J1
May St *WKENS* W14.....................119 J5
Mayswood Gdns *DAGE* RM10 ......92 E4
Maythorne Cottages
LEW SE13 ....165 G1
Mayton St *HOLWY* N7...................85 F1
Maytree Cl *EDGW* HA8................30 E5
RAIN RM13 ....111 G1
Maytree Ct *MTCM* CR4 ....179 F6
Maytree La *STAN* HA7..................43 F4
Maytree Wk
BRXS/STRHM SW2 * 162 B4
Mayville Est *STNW/STAM* N16 * ...86 A3
Mayville Rd *IL* IG1 ....90 B3
WAN E11 ....70 C6
Maywood Cl *BECK* BR3 ....182 E3
Maze Hi *BKHTH/KID* SE3 ....145 J1
GNWCH SE10 ....125 H6
Mazenod Av *KIL/WHAMP* NW6 ....82 E5
Maze Rd *RCH/KEW* TW9 ....137 H1
McAdam Dr *ENC/FH* EN2 ....23 H3
McAuley Cl *ELTH/MOT* SE9........147 F6
STHWK SE1 ....17 J4
McCall Cl *CLAP* SW4 ....141 K3
Mc Call Crs *CHARL* SE7 ....126 D5
McCarthy Rd *FELT* TW13 ....172 C1
McCoid Wy *STHWK* SE1 ....18 C3
McCrone Ms *HAMP* NW3 ....83 J5
McCudden Rd *DART* DA1 * 151 J4
McCullum Rd *BOW* E3 ....87 H6
McDermott Cl *BTSEA* SW11 ......140 D5
McDermott Rd *PECK* SE15 ....143 H4
McDonough Cl *CHSGTN* KT9 .....206 A2
McDougall Ct *RCH/KEW* TW9 .....137 H2
McDowall Ct *CAN/RD* E16...........106 E4
McEntee Av *WALTH* E17...............51 G4
McEwan Wy *SRTFD* E15 * 88 B6
McGrath Rd *FSTGT* E7 ....88 D4
McGregor Rd *NTGHL* W11 ....100 D5
McIntosh Cl *ROM* RM1 ....57 G6
McIntosh Rd *ROM* RM1 ....57 G6
McKay Rd *RYNPK* SW20 ....176 E5
Mc Kellar Cl *BUSH* WD23 ....28 C4
McKerrell Rd *PECK* SE15 ....143 H2
McKillop Wy *SCUP* DA14............186 D3
McLeod Rd *ABYW* SE2 ....128 D4
McLeod's Ms *SKENS* SW7 ....120 A3
McMillan St *DEPT* SE8 * 124 D6
McNair Rd *NWDGN* UB2 ....115 F3
McNeil Rd *CMBW* SE5 ....143 F3
McNicol Dr *WLSDN* NW10............98 E1
McRae La *MTCM* CR4 ....194 E4
Mead Cl *CAMTN* NW1 * 84 A5
GPK RM2 ....57 J5
KTN/HRWW/W HA3......................42 E3
Meadcroft Rd *LBTH* SE11 ....122 B6
Meade Cl *CHSWK* W4 ....117 H6
Meadfield *EDGW* HA8 ....30 D4
Mead Fld *RYLN/HDSTN* HA2 * 77 K1
Meadfoot Rd
STRHM/NOR SW16 ....179 H4
Meadgate Av *WFD* IG8 ....53 J1
Mead Gv *CHDH* RM6 ....55 K6
Mead House La *YEAD* UB4............94 B3
Meadlands Dr
RCHPK/HAM TW10 ....156 E4
Meadow Av *CROY/NA* CR0.........198 A3
Meadowbank *BKHTH/KID* SE3...145 J4
BRYLDS KT5 ....191 G3
HAMP NW3 ....84 A5
OXHEY WD19 ....27 G2
WCHMH N21 ....35 F1
Meadowbank Cl
FUL/PGN SW6 ....139 F1
Meadowbank Gdns *HEST* TW5 ...133 K2
Meadowbank Rd
CDALE/KGS NW9 ....63 F4
Meadow Cl *BAR* EN5.....................32 D1
BXLYHN DA6.............................149 G6
CAT SE6 ....182 D1
CHING E4 ....37 K3
CHST BR7 ....185 H1
ESH/CLAY KT10 ....205 F1
HOM E9 ....87 H3
HSLWW TW4 ....155 F1
NTHLT UB5 ....96 A1
PEND EN3 ....25 G2
RCHPK/HAM TW10....................157 F3
RSLP HA4 ....58 D3
RYNPK SW20 ....193 G1
Meadowcourt Rd
BKHTH/KID SE3 ....145 J5
Meadow Cft *BMLY* BR1 ....184 E6
Meadowcroft *BUSH* WD23 * 28 B1
Meadowcroft Rd *PLMGR* N13 * 35 H4
Meadowcroft Rd *PLMGR* N13 .....35 G4
Meadow Dr *HDN* NW4 ....46 A5
MUSWH N10 ....48 B3
Meadowford Cl *THMD* SE28 ......109 G6
Meadow Gdns *EDGW* HA8 ....44 D2
Meadow Garth *WLSDN* NW10......80 E4
Meadow Hi *NWMAL* KT3 ....192 B5
Meadow La *LEE/GVPK* SE12 ......166 B5
Meadowlea Cl *WDR/YW* UB7 .....112 A6
Meadow Ms *VX/NE* SW8..............122 A6
Meadow Pl *CHSWK* W4 * 138 B1
VX/NE SW8................................141 K1
Meadow Rd *BARK* IG11 ....91 F5
DAGW RM9 ....92 B4
ESH/CLAY KT10 ....204 E3
FELT TW15 ....154 D4
HAYES BR2 ....183 H4
PIN HA5 ....41 H5
ROMW/RG RM7..........................74 E5
STHL UB1 ....95 K6
SUT SM1 ....209 J2
VX/NE SW8................................122 A6
WIM/MER SW19 ....178 A3
Meadow Rw *STHWK* SE1 ....18 C5
Meadows Cl *LEY* E10.....................69 J6
Meadowside *DART* DA1 ....171 H3
ELTH/MOT SE9..........................146 B5
TWK TW1 ....156 C3
WOT/HER KT12 ....188 B6
Meadowside Rd *BELMT* SM2 .....208 C6
The Meadows *ORP* BR6 ....217 J4
Meadow Stile *CROY/NA* CR0 .....211 J1
Meadowsweet Cl *CAN/RD* E16 ...107 H4
NWMAL KT3 ....193 F2
The Meadow *CHST* BR7 ....185 H2
Meadow Vw *BFN/LL* DA15..........168 C1
HRW HA1 ....60 E5
Meadowview Rd *BXLY* DA5 ....169 F1
CAT SE6 ....164 D6
HOR/WEW KT19 ....207 G6
Meadow View Rd *THHTH* CR7 ...196 C6
YEAD UB4 ....94 B3
Meadow Wk *DAGW* RM9 ....92 B4
EW KT17 ....207 H5
RDART DA2 ....171 F6
SWFD E18 ....70 E1
WLGTN SM6 ....210 B1
Meadow Wy *CDALE/KGS* NW9 ....63 F2
CHSGTN KT9 ....206 A3
ORP BR6 ....216 A1
RSLP HA4 ....59 F3
WBLY HA9 ....79 K2
Meadow Waye *HEST* TW5 ....134 D1
The Meadow Wy
KTN/HRWW/W HA3......................42 E4
Mead Pth *WIM/MER* SW19 ....178 C2
Mead Pl *CROY/NA* CR0 ....196 C5
HOM E9 ....86 E4
Mead Plat *WLSDN* NW10.............80 E4
Mead Rd *CHST* BR7 ....185 H2
DART DA1 ....171 G5
EDGW HA8 ....44 B2
RCHPK/HAM TW10 ....156 D5
Mead Rw *STHWK* SE1 ....17 J4
Meads La *GDMY/SEVK* IG3 ....73 F4
Meads Rd *PEND* EN3 ....25 G2
WDGN N22 ....49 H5
The Meads *CHEAM* SM3 ....208 B1
EDGW HA8 ....45 F2
MTCM CR4 * 194 D2
The Mead *BECK* BR3 ....183 F5
EFNCH N2 ....47 H5
OXHEY WD19 ....27 J5
WEA W13 ....97 H4
WLGTN SM6 ....210 D4
WWKM BR4...............................199 G5
Meadvale Rd *CROY/NA* CR0 ......197 G4
EA W5 ....98 B4
Mead Wy *CROY/NA* CR0 ....198 B6
HAYES BR2 ....199 K3
RSLP HA4 ....58 B3
Meadway *ASHF* TW15 ....152 D6
BAR EN5 ....20 E5
BECK BR3 ....183 F4
BRYLDS KT5 ....191 J5
ESH/CLAY KT10 ....204 B6
GDMY/SEVK IG3 ....90 E2
GLDGN NW11 ....65 F3
GPK RM2 ....57 J5
RYNPK SW20 ....193 F1
STHGT/OAK N14 ....34 D3
WFD IG8 ....53 G1
WHTN TW2 ....155 J3
Meadway Cl *BAR* EN5 ....20 E4
GLDGN NW11 ....65 F3
PIN HA5 ....42 B2
Meadway Ct *EA* W5 * 98 B4
Meadway Gdns *RSLP* HA4 ....58 B3
The Meadway *BKHH* IG9 ....39 H5
BKHTH/KID SE3 ....145 G3
ORP BR6 ....217 H5
Meaford Wy *PGE/AN* SE20 ....181 J3
Meanley Rd *MNPK* E12 ....89 J3
Meard St *SOHO/CST* W1F 10 C4
Meath Cl *STMC/STPC* BR5 ....202 C2
Meath Rd *IL* IG1 ....90 C1
SRTFD E15 ....106 D1
Meath St *BTSEA* SW11 ....141 G2
Mecklenburgh Pl *BMSBY* WC1N ...5 G6
Mecklenburgh Sq *BMSBY* WC1N ..5 G6
Mecklenburgh St *BMSBY* WC1N...5 G6
Medburn St *CAMTN* NW1 ....4 C2
Medcroft Gdns
MORT/ESHN SW14 ....137 K5
Medebourne Cl
BKHTH/KID SE3 ....145 K4
Medesenge Wy *PLMGR* N13 ....49 H2
Medfield St *PUT/ROE* SW15 ......158 D2
Medhurst Cl *BOW* E3 ....105 G1
Median Rd *CLPT* E5 ....86 E5
Medina Av *ESH/CLAY* KT10.......204 E1
Medina Rd *HOLWY* N7 ....85 G1
Medland Cl *WLGTN* SM6 ....195 F5
Medlar Cl *NTHLT* UB5 ....95 H1
Medlar St *CMBW* SE5 ....142 D2
Medley Rd *KIL/WHAMP* NW6 ....82 E4
Medora Rd *BRXS/STRHM* SW2 ..162 A1
ROMW/RG RM7..........................75 F2
Medusa Rd *LEW* SE13 ....164 E1
Medway Cl *CROY/NA* CR0..........197 K3
IL IG1 ....90 C3
Medway Dr *GFD/PVL* UB6 ....97 F1
Medway Gdns *ALP/SUD* HA0 ....79 G2
Medway Pde *GFD/PVL* UB6 * 97 F1
Medway Rd *BOW* E3....................105 G1
DART DA1 ....150 D4
Medway St *WEST* SW1P 16 C5
Medwin St *BRXN/ST* SW9 ....142 C3
Meerbrook Rd *BKHTH/KID* SE3 .146 B4
Meeson Rd *SRTFD* E15 ....88 D6
Meeson St *CLPT* E5 ....87 G2
Meesons Whf *SRTFD* E15 * 88 A1
Meeting Field Pth *HOM* E9 * 86 E4
Meeting House Aly
WAP E1W * 123 J1
Meeting House La *PECK* SE15 ...143 J2
Mehetabel Rd *HOM* E9 ....86 E4
Meister Cl *IL* IG1 ....72 D5
Melanda Cl *CHST* BR7 ....184 E1
Melanie Cl *BXLYHN* DA7 ....149 F2
Melaris Ms *KIL/WHAMP* NW6......82 E5
Melbourne Av *PLMGR* N13 ....49 F2
RYLN/HDSTN HA2 ....42 B5
WEA W13 ....116 C1
Melbourne Cl *ORP* BR6..............201 K4
WLGTN SM6 ....210 C3
Melbourne Gdns *CHDH* RM6 ....74 A2
Melbourne Gv *EDUL* SE22 ....143 G5
Melbourne Ms *BRXN/ST* SW9 ....142 B2
CAT SE6 ....165 F2
Melbourne Pl *HOL/ALD* WC2B 11 H4
Melbourne Rd *EHAM* E6..............107 K1
IL IG1 ....72 B5
LEY E10 ....69 K4
TEDD TW11 ....174 D2
WALTH E17 ....51 G4
WIM/MER SW19 ....177 K4
WLGTN SM6 ....210 B3
Melbourne Sq *BRXN/ST* SW9 ....142 B2
Melbourne Ter *EDUL* SE22 * 143 F5
FUL/PGN SW6 * 140 A1
Melbury Av *NWDGN* UB2 ....115 G3
Melbury Cl *CHST* BR7 ....184 E2
ESH/CLAY KT10 ....205 H4
Melbury Ct *WKENS* W14 ....119 J3
Melbury Dr *CMBW* SE5 ....143 F1
Melbury Gdns *RYNPK* SW20 .....176 E4
Melbury Rd *KTN/HRWW/W* HA3...62 B2
WKENS W14 ....119 J3
Melbury Ter *CAMTN* NW1............2 D7
Melcombe Gdns
KTN/HRWW/W HA3......................62 B3
Melcombe Pl *CAMTN* NW1 ....8 E1
Melcombe St *CAMTN* NW1 * 3 F7
Meldon Cl *FUL/PGN* SW6 * 140 A2
Meldone Cl *BRYLDS* KT5 ....191 J3
Meldrum Cl *STMC/STPC* BR5 ....202 D3
Meldrum Rd *GDMY/SEVK* IG3 .....73 G6
Melfield Gdns *CAT* SE6 ....164 E6
Melford Av *BARK* IG11 ....90 E4
Melford Rd *BARK* IG11 ....90 E4
EDUL SE22 ....163 H3
EHAM E6 ....107 K3
IL IG1 ....72 D6
WALTH E17 ....69 G1
WAN E11 ....70 C6
Melfort Rd *THHTH* CR7 ....180 C6
Meigund Rd *HBRY* N5 ....85 G3
Melina Cl *HYS/HAR* UB3 ....94 B4
Melina Pl *STJWD* NW8...................2 A5
Melina Rd *SHB* W12 ....118 E2
Melior Pl *STHWK* SE1 * 19 G2
Melior St *STHWK* SE1 ....19 F2
Meliot Rd *CAT* SE6 ....165 G4
Meller Cl *CROY/NA* CR0 ....210 E1
Melling Dr *EN* EN1 ....24 C2
Melling St *WOOL/PLUM* SE18 ....127 K6
Mellish Gdns *WFD* IG8 ....52 E1
Mellish St *POP/IOD* E14 ....124 D3
Mellison Rd *TOOT* SW17 ....178 D1
Melliss Av *RCH/KEW* TW9 ....137 J2
Mellitus St *SHB* W12 ....99 H5
Mellor Cl *WOT/HER* KT12 ....188 E4
Mellow La East *YEAD* UB4 ....94 A5
Mellows Rd *CLAY* IG5 ....53 K6
WLGTN SM6 ....210 D3
Mells Crs *ELTH/MOT* SE9...........166 E6
Mell St *GNWCH* SE10 ....125 H5
Melody Rd *WAND/EARL* SW18 ...140 B6
Melon Pl *KENS* W8......................119 K2
Melon Rd *PECK* SE15 ....143 H2
WAN E11 ....88 C1
Melrose Av *CRICK* NW2................82 A3
DART DA1 ....170 B2
GFD/PVL UB6 ....96 B1
MTCM CR4 ....179 G5
STRHM/NOR SW16 ....180 A6
WDGN N22 ....49 H4
WHTN TW2 ....155 G2
WIM/MER SW19 ....159 J4
Melrose Cl *GFD/PVL* UB6.............96 B1
LEE/GVPK SE12 ....165 K3
YEAD UB4 ....94 C4
Melrose Crs *ORP* BR6 ....216 D2
Melrose Dr *STHL* UB1 ....115 F1
Melrose Gdns *EDGW* HA8............44 D5
NWMAL KT3 ....176 A6
Melrose Rd *BARN* SW13 ....138 C3
MORT/ESHN SW14 ....137 J4
PIN HA5 ....59 K1
WAND/EARL SW18 ....159 J1
WIM/MER SW19 ....177 K5
Melrose Ter *HMSMTH* W6 ....119 F2
Melsa Rd *MRDN* SM4 ....194 B3
Melthorne Dr *RSLP* HA4 ....77 G1
Melthorpe Gdns
BKHTH/KID SE3 ....146 C2
Melton Cl *RSLP* HA4 ....59 G5
Melton Flds *HOR/WEW* KT19 ....207 F6
Melton Gdns *ROM* RM1 ....75 H4
Melton Pl *HOR/WEW* KT19 ....207 F6
Melton St *CAMTN* NW1 ....4 B5
Melville Av *GFD/PVL* UB6 ....79 F3
RYNPK SW20 ....176 D5
SAND/SEL CR2 ....212 B5
Melville Cl *HGDN/ICK* UB10 ....76 A1
Melville Ct *DEPT* SE8 ....124 A4
Melville Gdns *PLMGR* N13 ....49 G1
Melville Pl *IS* N1 * 5 J5
Melville Rd *BARN* SW13 ....138 D2
RAIN RM13 ....111 J3
ROMW/RG RM7..........................56 D3
SCUP DA14 ....168 D4
WALTH E17 ....51 H1
WLSDN NW10..............................81 F5
Melville Villas Rd *ACT* W3 * 118 A1
Melvin Rd *PGE/AN* SE20 ....181 K4
Memel St *STLK* EC1Y * 12 D1
Memorial Av *SRTFD* E15 ....106 C2
Memorial Cl *HEST* TW5 ....134 E6
Memorial Sq *KUT/HW* KT1 ....174 E5
Mendip Cl *HYS/HAR* UB3 ....133 G3
SYD SE26 ....163 K6
WPK KT4 ....193 F6
Mendip Dr *GLDGN* NW11.............64 C6
Mendip Houses *BETH* E2 * 104 E2
Mendip Rd *BTSEA* SW11 ....140 B4
BUSH WD23 ....28 C1
BXLYHN DA7.............................150 A3
EMPK RM11 ....75 J4
GNTH/NBYPK IG2 ....72 D3
Mendora Rd *FUL/PGN* SW6 ....139 H1
Menelik Rd *CRICK* NW2 ....82 C2
Menlo Gdns *NRWD* SE19 ....180 E3
Menon Dr *ED* N9 ....36 D5
Menotti St *BETH* E2 * 104 C3
Mentmore Cl
KTN/HRWW/W HA3......................61 J3
Mentmore Ter *HACK* E8 ....86 D5
Meon Rd *ACT* W3 ....117 K2
Meopham Rd *MTCM* CR4 ....179 H4
Mepham Crs
KTN/HRWW/W HA3......................42 C3
Mepham Gdns
KTN/HRWW/W HA3......................42 C3
Mepham St *STHWK* SE1 * 17 H1
Mera Dr *BXLYHN* DA7 ....149 H5
Merantum Wy
WIM/MER SW19 ....178 B4
Merbury Cl *LEW* SE13 ....145 G5
Merbury Rd *THMD* SE28 ....127 K1
Merbury St *WOOL/PLUM* SE18 ..127 G3
Mercator Pl *POP/IOD* E14 ....124 D5
Mercator Rd *LEW* SE13 ....145 G5
Mercer Cl *THDIT* KT7..................190 A4
Merceron Houses *BETH* E2 * 104 E2
Merceron St *WCHPL* E1 ....104 D5
Mercer Pl *PIN* HA5........................41 G5
Mercers Cl *GNWCH* SE10 ....125 J4
Mercers Ms *ARCH* N19 ....84 D2
Mercers Pl *HMSMTH* W6 ....119 F4
Mercers Rd *ARCH* N19 ....84 D3
Mercer St *LSQ/SEVD* WC2H 10 E4
Merchants Cl *SNWD* SE25 ....197 H1
Merchant St *BOW* E3 * 105 H2
Merchiston Rd *CAT* SE6 ....165 G4
Merchland Rd *ELTH/MOT* SE9 ...167 H3
Mercia Gv *LEW* SE13 ....145 F4
Mercier Rd *PUT/ROE* SW15 ....139 H6
Mercury Gdns *ROM* RM1 ....75 H2
Mercury House
HYS/HAR UB3 * 113 J2
Mercury Rd *BTFD* TW8 ....116 D5
Mercury Wy *NWCR* SE14 ....124 A6
Merebank La *CROY/NA* CR0.......211 F3
Mere Cl *ORP* BR6 ....201 G6
WIM/MER SW19 ....159 G2
Meredith Av *CRICK* NW2..............82 A3
Meredith Cl *PIN* HA5.....................41 H3
Meredith Ms *BROCKY* SE4 * 144 C5
Meredith St *CLKNW* EC1R 6 A5
PLSTW E13 ....106 E2
Meredyth Rd *BARN* SW13 ....138 D3
Mere End *CROY/NA* CR0............198 A4
Mereside *ORP* BR6 ....201 F6
Mereside Pk *ASHF* TW15 * 153 F6
Merewood Cl *BROCKY* SE4 ....166 A5
Merevale Crs *MRDN* SM4 ....194 B3
Mereway Rd *WHTN* TW2 ....155 J3
Merewood Cl *BMLY* BR1 ....185 J3
Merewood Gdns
CROY/NA CR0 ....198 A4
Merewood Rd *BXLYHN* DA7 ......149 K3
Mereworth Cl *HAYES* BR2 ....199 J2
Mereworth Dr
WOOL/PLUM SE18 ....147 G1
Meriden Cl *BARK/HLT* IG6 ....54 C4
BMLY BR1 ....184 C5
Meridian Rd *CHARL* SE7 ....146 C1
Meridian Sq *SRTFD* E15 ....88 B5
Meridian Wy *ED* N9 ....37 F4
Merifield Rd *ELTH/MOT* SE9 ......146 B5
Merino Cl *WAN* E11.......................71 G1
Merivale Rd *HRW* HA1 ....60 C4
PUT/ROE SW15 ....139 H5
Merlewood Dr *CHST* BR7 ....184 E4
Merley Ct *CDALE/KGS* NW9 ....62 E6
Merlin Cl *BARK/HLT* IG6 ....55 H1
CROY/NA CR0 ....211 K4
CRW RM5 ....57 F2
MTCM CR4 ....178 D6
NTHLT UB5 ....95 G2
Merlin Crs *EDGW* HA8 ....44 B4
Merlin Gdns *ROM* RM1 ....57 F2
Merlin Gv *BARK/HLT* IG6 ....54 B3
BECK BR3 ....198 C1
Merlin Rd *CAN/RD* E16 * 106 D3
MNPK E12 ....71 G6
WELL DA16 ....148 B5
Merlin Rd North *WELL* DA16 ......148 B5
Merlins Av *RYLN/HDSTN* HA2 .....77 K1
Merlin St *FSBYW* WC1X 5 J5
Mermagen Dr *RAIN* RM13 ....93 K5
Mermaid Ct *STHWK* SE1 ....18 E2
Merredene St
BRXS/STRHM SW2 ....162 A1
Merriam Av *HOM* E9 ....87 H4
Merriam Cl *CHING* E4 ....52 A1
Merrick Rd *NWDGN* UB2 ....114 E4
Merrick Sq *STHWK* SE1 ....18 E4
Merridene *WCHMH* N21 ....35 H1
Merrielands Crs *DAGW* RM9 ......110 B1
Merrilands Rd *WPK* KT4 ....193 F5
Merrilees Rd *BFN/LL* DA15 ....167 K2
Merrilyn Cl *ESH/CLAY* KT10 ......205 G4
Merriman Rd *BKHTH/KID* SE3 ...146 B2
Merrington Rd *FUL/PGN* SW6 ....119 K6
Merrion Av *STAN* HA7 ....43 K1
Merritt Gdns *CHSGTN* KT9 ....205 J4
Merritt Rd *BROCKY* SE4 ....144 C6
Merrivale *STHGT/OAK* N14...........22 D6
Merrivale Av *REDBR* IG4 ....71 H1
Merrivale Ms *WDR/YW* UB7 * 112 A1
Merrow Rd *BELMT* SM2 ....208 B6

Merrows Cl NTHWD HA6 ....40 A2
Merrow St WALW SE17 ....122 E5
Merrow Wk WALW SE17 * 122 E5
Merrow Wy CROY/NA CR0 ....214 A4
Merrydown Wy CHST BR7 ....184 D4
Merryfield BKHTH/KID SE3 ....145 J3
Merryfield Gdns STAN HA7 ....43 J1
Merryfield Wy CAT SE6 ....164 E2
Merryhill Cl CHING E4 ....31 K4
Merry Hill Mt BUSH WD23 ....28 B3
Merry Hill Rd BUSH WD23 ....28 A2
Merryhills Dr ENC/FH EN2 ....22 E5
Merryweather Cl DART DA1 ....171 J1
Merryweather Ct NWMAL KT3 ....192 B2
Mersey Rd WALTH E17 ....51 H6
Mersham Dr CDALE/KGS NW9 ....62 C2
Mersham Pl PGE/AN SE20 ....181 J4
THHTH CR7 ....180 E5
Mersham Rd THHTH CR7 ....180 E6
Merten Rd CHDH RM6 ....74 A4
Merton Av CHSWK W4 ....118 C4
NTHLT UB5 ....78 D3
Merton Gdns STMC/STPC BR5 ....201 G2
Merton Hall Gdns
RYNPK SW20 ....177 H4
Merton Hall Rd
WIM/MER SW19 ....177 H5
Merton High St
WIM/MER SW19 ....178 B3
Merton La HGT N6 ....65 K6
Merton Pl WIM/MER SW19 * 178 B4
Merton Rd BARK IG11 ....91 H5
ENC/FH EN2 ....23 K3
GDMY/SEVK IG5 ....73 F4
RYLN/HDSTN HA2 ....60 C5
SNWD SE25 ....197 G2
WALTH E17 ....70 A2
WAND/EARL SW18 ....159 K3
WIM/MER SW19 ....178 A3
Merton Wy E/WMO/HCT KT8 ....189 H1
Mertoun Ter MBLAR W1H * 8 C3
Merttins Rd PECK SE15 ....144 A5
Meru Cl KTTN NW5 ....84 A3
Mervan Rd BRXS/STRHM SW2 ....142 B4
Mervyn Av ELTH/MOT SE9 ....167 H5
Mervyn Rd WEA W13 ....116 B3
Messaline Av ACT W3 ....98 E5
Messent Rd ELTH/MOT SE9 ....146 B6
Messeter Pl ELTH/MOT SE9 ....167 F1
Messina Av KIL/WHAMP NW6 ....82 E6
Meteor St BTSEA SW11 ....141 F5
Meteor Wy WLGTN SM6 ....210 E5
Metford Crs PEND EN3 ....25 J1
Metheringham Wy
CDALE/KGS NW9 ....45 G5
Methley St LBTH SE11 ....122 B5
Methuen Cl EDGW HA8 ....44 C3
Methuen Pk MUSWH N10 ....48 B5
Methuen Rd BELV DA17 ....129 J4
BXLYHS DA6 ....149 G5
EDGW HA8 ....44 C3
Methwold Rd NKENS W10 ....100 B4
Metropolitan Cl POP/IOD E14 ....105 J4
Metropolitan Whf E1W * 125 K1
Mews North BGVA SW1W 15 J5
Mews Pl WFD IG8 ....38 E6
Mews South PIM SW1V 121 H5
Mews St WAP E1W 13 K7
The Mews BECK BR3 * 182 D4
CEND/HSY/T N8 * 47 F1
NFNCH/WDSP N12 * 47 H1
REDBR IG4 ....71 H2
ROM RM1 ....75 G1
STRHM/NOR SW16 ....180 A4
TWK TW1 * 156 C5
Mexfield Rd PUT/ROE SW15 ....139 J6
Meyer Gn EN EN1 ....24 C1
Meyer Rd ERITH DA8 ....129 K6
Meymott St STHWK SE1 ....18 A1
Meynell Crs HOM E9 ....87 F5
Meynell Gdns HOM E9 ....87 F5
Meynell Rd HARH RM3 ....57 K2
HOM E9 ....87 F5
Meyrick Rd BTSEA SW11 ....140 C4
WLSDN NW10 ....81 J4
Mezen Cl NTHWD HA6 ....40 B1
Miah Ter WAP E1W * 123 H1
Micawber St IS N1 ....6 D4
Michael Gaynor Cl HNWL W7 ....116 A1
Michaelmas Cl RYNPK SW20 ....177 F6
Michael Rd FUL/PGN SW6 ....140 A2
SNWD SE25 ....181 F6
WAN E11 ....70 C5
Michaels Cl LEW SE13 ....145 H4
Micheldever Rd LEW SE13 ....165 H1
Michelham Gdns TWK TW1 ....156 A5
Michel Wk WOOL/PLUM SE18 ....127 G5
Michigan Av MNPK E12 ....89 J2
Michleham Down
NFNCH/WDSP N12 ....32 D6
Mickleham Cl STMC/STPC BR5 ....186 A4
Mickleham Gdns CHEAM SM3 ....208 C4
Mickleham Rd STMC/STPC BR5 ....186 A4
Mickleham Wy CROY/NA CR0 ....214 B6
Micklethwaite Rd FUL/PGN SW6 ....119 K6
Midcroft RSLP HA4 ....58 C5
Middle Dartrey Wk
WBPTN SW10 * 140 B1
Middle Dene MLHL NW7 ....31 F5
Middlefield STJWD NW8 ....2 C3
Middlefields CROY/NA CR0 ....213 G6
WEA W13 ....97 H4
Middle Green Cl SURB KT5 ....191 G4
Middleham Gdns UED N18 ....50 C2
Middleham Rd UED N18 ....50 C2
Middle La CEND/HSY/T N8 ....66 E2
TEDD TW11 ....174 A2
Middle Lane Ms
CEND/HSY/T N8 ....66 E2
Middle Park Av ELTH/MOT SE9 ....146 C6
Middle Rd EBAR EN4 ....33 J1

PLSTW E13 ....106 E1
RYLN/HDSTN HA2 ....60 D6
STRHM/NOR SW16 ....179 H5
Middle Rw NKENS W10 ....100 C3
Middlesborough Rd UED N18 ....50 C2
Middlesex Pl HOM E9 * 86 E4
Middlesex Rd MTCM CR4 ....195 K4
Middlesex St WCHPL E1 ....13 H2
Middle St CROY/NA CR0 ....196 D6
STBT EC1A 12 C1
Middle Temple La TPL/STR WC2R 11 J4
Middleton Av CHING E4 ....37 H6
GFD/PVL UB6 ....96 D1
SCUP DA14 ....186 D2
Middleton Blds GTPST W1W 10 A2
Middleton Cl CHING E4 ....37 H5
Middleton Dr
BERM/RHTH SE16 ....124 A2
PIN HA5 ....40 E6
Middleton Gdns
GNTH/NBYPK IG2 ....72 B5
Middleton Gv HOLWY N7 ....84 E3
Middleton La GTPST W1W 10 A2
Middleton Rd GLDGN NW11 ....64 E4
HACK E8 ....86 B5
HYS/HAR UB3 ....113 H2
MRDN SM4 ....194 B3
NWMAL KT3 ....175 K6
Middleton St BETH E2 ....104 D2
Middleton Wy LEW SE13 ....145 G5
Middleway GLDGN NW11 ....65 F2
Middle Wy STRHM/NOR SW16 ....179 J5
The Middle Wy
KTN/HRWW/W HA3 ....43 F5
Midfield Av BXLYHN DA7 ....149 K4
Midfield Wy STMC/STPC BR5 ....186 C4
Midford Pl FITZ W1T * 4 B7
Midholm GLDGN NW11 ....65 F1
Midholm Cl GLDGN NW11 * 65 F1
Midholm Rd CROY/NA CR0 ....213 G6
Midhope St STPAN WC1H 5 F5
Midhurst Av CROY/NA CR0 ....196 B4
MUSWH N10 ....48 A6
Midhurst Cl HCH RM12 ....93 J2
Midhurst Gdns HGDN/ICK UB10 ....76 A5
Midhurst Hl BXLYHS DA6 ....149 H6
Midhurst Pde MUSWH N10 * 48 A6
Midhurst Rd WEA W13 ....116 B3
Midhurst Wy CLPT E5 ....86 C2
Midland Arches CRICK NW2 * 63 K6
Midland Crs HAMP NW3 ....83 G4
Midland Pl POP/IOD E14 ....125 F5
Midland Rd CAMTN NW1 ....4 D3
LEY E10 ....70 A4
Midland Ter CRICK NW2 ....63 A2
WLSDN NW10 ....99 G3
Midlothian Rd BOW E3 ....105 H4
Midmoor Rd BAL SW12 ....161 H3
WIM/MER SW19 ....177 G4
Midship Cl BERM/RHTH SE16 * 124 A1
Midship Point POP/IOD E14 * 124 D2
Midstrath Rd WLSDN NW10 ....81 G2
Midsummer Av HSLWW TW4 ....134 E5
Midway CHEAM SM3 ....193 J4
WOT/HER KT12 ....188 A6
Midwinter Cl WELL DA16 ....148 B4
Mighell Av REDBR IG4 ....71 H2
Milan Rd STHL UB1 ....114 E2
Milborne Gv WBPTN SW10 ....120 E5
Milborne St HOM E9 ....86 E4
Milborough Crs LEE/GVPK SE12 ....165 H1
Milbourne La ESH/CLAY KT10 ....204 C4
Milbrook ESH/CLAY KT10 ....204 C4
Milcote St STHWK SE1 ....18 A3
Mildenhall Rd CLPT E5 ....86 E2
Mildmay Av IS N1 ....85 K4
Mildmay Gv North IS N1 ....85 K3
Mildmay Gv South IS N1 ....85 K3
Mildmay Pk IS N1 ....85 K3
Mildmay Pl STNW/STAM N16 * 85 K3
Mildmay Rd IL IG1 ....90 B1
IS N1 ....85 K3
ROMW/RG RM7 ....74 E2
Mildmay St IS N1 ....85 K4
Mildred Av HYS/HAR UB3 ....113 G4
NTHLT UB5 ....78 B3
Mildred Cl DART DA1 ....171 K1
Mildred Rd ERITH DA8 ....130 B5
Mile End Pl WCHPL E1 ....105 F3
Mile End Rd BOW E3 ....105 H2
WCHPL E1 ....104 E4
The Mile End WALW SE17 * 122 E6
Mile Rd WLGTN SM6 ....195 F5
Miles Dr THMD SE28 ....127 K1
Milespit Hl MLHL NW7 ....45 K1
Miles Pl BRYLDS KT5 ....191 G1
Miles Rd CEND/HSY/T N8 ....48 E6
MTCM CR4 ....178 D6
Miles St VX/NE SW8 ....121 K6
Milestone Cl BELMT SM2 ....209 H4
ED N9 ....36 C4
Milestone Rd NRWD SE19 ....181 G2
Miles Wy TRDG/WHET N20 ....33 J4
Milford Cl ABYW SE2 ....129 F6
Milford Gdns ALP/SUD HA0 ....79 K5
EDGW HA8 ....44 C3
Milford Gv SUT SM1 ....209 G2
Milford La TPL/STR WC2R 11 J5
Milford Ms STRHM/NOR SW16 ....162 A5
Milford Rd STHL UB1 ....96 A6
WEA W13 ....116 C1
Milk St BMLY BR1 ....184 A2
CAN/RD E16 ....127 G1
CITYW EC2V 12 D3
Milkwell Gdns WFD IG8 ....53 F3
Milkwell Yd CMBW SE5 ....142 D2
Milkwood Rd HNHL SE24 ....142 C6
Milk Yd WAP E1W 104 E6
Millais Av MNPK E12 ....90 A3
Millais Crs HOR/WEW KT19 ....207 G3

Millais Gdns EDGW HA8 ....44 C5
Millais Rd EN EN1 ....24 B6
NWMAL KT3 ....192 B4
WAN E11 ....88 A2
Millais Wy HOR/WEW KT19 ....206 E2
Milliard Cl STNW/STAM N16 ....86 A3
Millars Meadow
LEE/GVPK SE12 *
Millbank WEST SW1P 16 E6
Millbank Est WEST SW1P 16 E6
Millbank Wy LEE/GVPK SE12 ....145 K6
Millbourne Rd FELT TW13 ....154 D6
Mill Br BAR EN5 ....20 D6
Millbrook Av WELL DA16 ....147 J5
Millbrook Gdns CHDH RM6 ....74 A3
GPK RM2 ....57 G5
Millbrook Rd BRXN/ST SW9 ....142 B4
ED N9 ....36 D3
Mill Brook Rd STMC/STPC BR5 ....202 D1
Mill Cl CAR SM5 ....195 F6
Miller Cl BMLY BR1 ....183 K1
MTCM CR4 ....194 E4
PIN HA5 ....41 G6
Miller Rd CROY/NA CR0 ....196 A5
WIM/MER SW19 ....178 C2
Miller's Av HACK E8 ....86 B3
Millers Cl MLHL NW7 ....31 J6
Millers Green Cl ENC/FH EN2 ....23 H3
Miller's Ter HACK E8 ....86 B3
Miller's Wy HMSMTH W6 ....119 F2
Millers Yd FNCH N3 ....46 E4
Miller Wk STHWK SE1 ....17 K1
Millfield PIN HA5 ....59 G3
Millfield Av WALTH E17 ....51 H4
Millfield La HGT N6 ....65 K6
Millfield Rd EDGW HA8 ....44 E5
HSLWW TW4 ....134 C6
Millfields Cl STMC/STPC BR5 ....202 C1
Millfields Rd CLPT E5 ....86 E2
Mill Gdns SYD SE26 ....163 J6
Mill Gn MTCM CR4 ....195 F6
Mill Green Rd MTCM CR4 ....195 F4
Millgrove St BTSEA SW11 ....141 F2
Millharbour POP/IOD E14 ....124 E3
Millhaven Cl CHDH RM6 ....73 H3
Mill HI BARN SW13 ....138 D3
Mill Hill Gv ACT W3 * 117 J1
Mill Hill Rd ACT W3 ....117 J1
BARN SW13 ....138 D3
Mill Hill Ter ACT W3 * 117 J1
Millhouse Pl WNWD SE27 ....162 C6
Millicent Rd LEY E10 * 69 G5
Milligan St POP/IOD E14 ....105 H6
Milling Rd EDGW HA8 ....45 F3
Millington Rd HYS/HAR UB3 ....113 H3
Mill La CAR SM5 ....210 A2
CHDH RM6 ....74 A3
CHING E4 ....25 C5
CRICK NW2 ....82 C1
CROY/NA CR0 ....211 G1
EW KT17 ....207 H6
WFD IG8 ....52 D1
WOOL/PLUM SE18 ....127 G4
Millman Ms BMSBY WC1N * 5 G7
Millman Pl BMSBY WC1N 5 G7
Millman St BMSBY WC1N 5 G7
Millmark Gv NWCR SE14 ....144 B3
Millmarsh La PEND EN3 ....25 G2
Mill Mead Rd TOTM N17 ....50 D6
Mill Pl CHST BR7 ....185 G4
DART DA1 ....150 D5
KUT/HW KT1 ....175 G6
POP/IOD E14 ....105 G5
Mill Plat ISLW TW7 ....136 B4
Mill Plat Av ISLW TW7 ....136 B3
Mill Pond Cl VX/NE SW8 ....141 H1
Millpond Est BERM/RHTH SE16 * 123 J2
Mill Pond Rd DART DA1 ....171 H1
Mill Rdg EDGW HA8 ....44 B1
Mill Rw BXLY DA5 * 169 J2
Mills Ct SDTCH EC2A 7 H5
Mills Gv HDN NW4 ....46 B6
POP/IOD E14 ....106 A4
Millshott Cl FUL/PGN SW6 ....139 F2
Millside CAR SM5 ....194 E6
Millside Pl ISLW TW7 ....136 C3
Millson Cl TRDG/WHET N20 ....33 H1
Mills Rw CHSWK W4 ....118 A4
Millstream Cl PLMGR N13 ....49 G1
Millstream Rd STHWK SE1 ....19 J3
Mill St CONDST W1S 9 K5
KUT/HW KT1 ....175 F6
STHWK SE1 ....19 K3
Mill V BMLY BR1 ....184 A4
Mill View Cl EW KT17 ....207 H6
Mill View Gdns CROY/NA CR0 ....213 F1
Millwall Dock Rd POP/IOD E14 ....124 D3
Millwall EBED/NFELT TW14 ....134 A6
Millway Gdns NTHLT UB5 ....78 A4
Millwell Crs CHIG IG7 ....54 C1
Millwood Rd HSLW TW3 ....135 H6
STMC/STPC BR5 ....186 D6

Millwood St NKENS W10 * 100 C4
Mill Yd WCHPL E1 * 13 K5
Milman Cl PIN HA5 ....41 H6
Milman Rd KIL/WHAMP NW6 ....100 B1
Milmans St WBPTN SW10 ....120 E6
Milne Fld PIN HA5 ....42 A3
Milne Gdns ELTH/MOT SE9 ....146 D6
Milner Ct BUSH WD23 ....28 B1
Milner Dr WHTN TW2 ....155 J2
Milner Pl IS N1 ....85 G6
Milner Rd DGDN RM8 ....75 J6
KUT/HW KT1 ....174 E6
MRDN SM4 ....194 C2
SRTFD E15 ....106 C2
THHTH CR7 ....180 D6
WIM/MER SW19 ....178 A4
Milner Sq IS N1 * 85 H5
Milner St CHEL SW3 ....14 E6
Milnthorpe Rd CHSWK W4 ....118 A6
Milo Rd EDUL SE22 ....163 G1
Milroy Wk STHWK SE1 ....11 K7
Milson Rd WKENS W14 ....119 H3
Milton Av BAR EN5 ....20 C6
CDALE/KGS NW9 ....44 D6
CROY/NA CR0 ....196 E4
EHAM E6 ....89 H5
HCH RM12 ....93 H2
HGT N6 ....66 C4
SUT SM1 ....209 H1
WLSDN NW10 ....80 E6
Milton Cl EFNCH N2 ....65 G3
STHWK SE1 ....19 J7
SUT SM1 ....209 H1
Milton Ct BARB EC2Y 12 E1
Milton Court Rd NWCR SE14 ....124 B6
Milton Crs GNTH/NBYPK IG2 ....72 C4
Milton Gdns STWL/WRAY TW19 ....152 C5
Milton Gv FBAR/BDGN N11 ....48 C1
STNW/STAM N16 ....85 K2
Milton Pk HGT N6 ....66 C4
Milton Rd ACT W3 ....118 A1
BELV DA17 ....129 H4
CDALE/KGS NW9 ....63 J1
CROY/NA CR0 ....196 E4
EHAM E6 ....89 H5
HCH RM12 ....93 J2
HNHL SE24 ....142 C6
HNWL W7 ....97 F6
HPTN TW12 ....173 F3
HRW HA1 ....60 E3
MLHL NW7 ....45 J1
MORT/ESHN SW14 ....138 A4
MTCM CR4 ....179 F3
ROM RM1 ....75 J3
SEVS/STOTM N15 ....49 H6
SUT SM1 ....208 E1
WALTH E17 ....69 J1
WELL DA16 ....148 A2
WIM/MER SW19 ....178 A4
Milton St BARB EC2Y 12 E1
Milton Wy WDR/YW UB7 ....112 C4
Milverton Dr HGDN/ICK UB10 ....76 A2
Milverton Gdns GDMY/SEVK IG3 ....73 F6
Milverton Rd KIL/WHAMP NW6 ....82 A5
Milverton St LBTH SE11 ....122 B5
Milverton Wy ELTH/MOT SE9 ....167 F6
Milward St WCHPL E1 ....104 D4
Mimosa Cl GPK RM2 ....57 K5
Mimosa Rd YEAD UB4 ....95 G4
Mimosa St FUL/PGN SW6 ....139 J2
Minard Rd CAT SE6 ....165 H3
Mina Rd WALW SE17 ....122 E5
WIM/MER SW19 ....177 K4
Minchenden Crs
STHGT/OAK N14 ....34 C5
Mincing La MON EC3R 13 G5
Minden Rd CHEAM SM3 ....193 H6
PGE/AN SE20 ....181 J4
Minehead Rd RYLN/HDSTN HA2 ....78 A1
STRHM/NOR SW16 ....180 A1
Mineral St WOOL/PLUM SE18 ....127 K4
Minera Cl BECK BR3 ....166 B3
Minera Ms BGVA SW1W 15 H6
Minerva Cl BRXN/ST SW9 ....142 B1
SCUP DA14 ....168 E5
Minerva Rd CAN/RD E16 ....107 H5
KUT/HW KT1 ....175 G5
WLSDN NW10 ....98 E2
Minerva St BETH E2 ....104 D1
Minet Av WLSDN NW10 ....99 G1
Minet Dr HYS/HAR UB3 ....113 K1
Minet Gdns HYS/HAR UB3 ....113 K1
WLSDN NW10 ....99 G1
Minet Rd CMBW SE5 ....142 C3
Minford Gdns WKENS W14 ....119 G2
Ming St POP/IOD E14 ....105 J6
Ministry Av ELTH/MOT SE9 ....166 E4
Ministry Wy ELTH/MOT SE9 ....166 E4
Mink Ct HSLWW TW4 ....134 B3
Minniedale BRYLDS KT5 ....191 G2
Minnow St WALW SE17 ....19 H7
Minshull Pl BECK BR3 * 182 D3
Minshull St VX/NE SW8 * 141 J2
Minson Rd HOM E9 ....87 F6
Minstead Gdns PUT/ROE SW15 ....158 C2
Minstead Wy NWMAL KT3 ....192 B3
Minster Av SUT SM1 ....193 K6
Minster Ct FENCHST EC3M * 13 G5
Minster Dr CROY/NA CR0 ....212 A2
Minster Gdns E/WMO/HCT KT8 * 188 E2
Minster Rd BMLY BR1 ....184 A3
CRICK NW2 ....82 C3
Minstrel Gdns BRYLDS KT5 ....191 G1
Mintern Cl PLMGR N13 ....35 H6
Minterne Av NWDGN UB2 ....115 F4
Minterne Rd KTN/HRWW/W HA3 ....62 B2
Minterne Waye YEAD UB4 ....95 G5
Mintern St IS N1 ....7 F2
Minton Ms KIL/WHAMP NW6 ....83 F4
Mint Rd WLGTN SM6 ....210 B3
Mint St STHWK SE1 ....18 C2
Mint Wk CROY/NA CR0 ....211 J1

Mirabel Rd FUL/PGN SW6 ....139 J1
Miranda Cl WCHPL E1 ....104 E4
Miranda Rd ARCH N19 ....66 C5
Mirfield St CHARL SE7 ....126 C3
Miriam Rd WOOL/PLUM SE18 ....128 A5
Mirren Cl RYLN/HDSTN HA2 ....77 K2
Miskin Rd DART DA1 ....171 F2
Missenden Cl
EBED/NFELT TW14 ....153 J3
Missenden Gdns MRDN SM4 ....194 B3
Mission Gv WALTH E17 ....69 H2
Mission Pl PECK SE15 ....143 H2
Mistletoe Cl CROY/NA CR0 ....198 A5
Misty's Fld WOT/HER KT12 ....188 B5
Mitali Pas WCHPL E1 ....104 C5
Mitcham La STRHM/NOR SW16 ....179 H1
Mitcham Pk MTCM CR4 ....194 E1
Mitcham Rd CROY/NA CR0 ....195 K3
EHAM E6 ....107 J2
GDMY/SEVK IG3 ....73 F4
TOOT SW17 ....178 E2
Mitchellbrook Wy WLSDN NW10 ....81 F4
Mitchell Cl ABYW SE2 ....128 D5
BELV DA17 ....129 K3
DART DA1 ....171 H4
Mitchell Rd ORP BR6 ....217 F3
PLMGR N13 ....49 H1
Mitchell St FSBYE EC1V 6 C6
Mitchell Wy BMLY BR1 ....183 K4
WLSDN NW10 ....80 E4
Mitchison Rd IS N1 ....85 K4
Mitchley Rd TOTM N17 ....50 C6
Mitford Rd ARCH N19 ....66 E6
Mitre Cl BELMT SM2 ....209 G5
HAYES BR2 ....183 J6
Mitre Rd SRTFD E15 ....106 C1
STHWK SE1 ....17 K2
Mitre Sq HDTCH EC3A 13 H4
Mitre St HDTCH EC3A 13 H4
The Mitre POP/IOD E14 ....105 H6
Mitre Wy WLSDN NW10 ....99 K4
Moat Cl ORP BR6 ....217 F4
Moat Crs EFNCH N2 ....47 F6 (?)
Moat Dr HRW HA1 ....60 C1
RSLP HA4 ....58 C4
Moat Farm Rd NTHLT UB5 ....77 K4
Moat La ERITH DA8 ....150 D2
Moat Pl ACT W3 ....98 D5
BRXN/ST SW9 ....142 A4
Moat Side FELT TW13 ....154 B6
PEND EN3 ....24 E5
The Moat NWMAL KT3 ....176 B6
Moberly Rd CLAP SW4 ....161 J2
Modbury Gdns HAMP NW5 ....84 A4
Model Farm Cl ELTH/MOT SE9 ....166 C5
Moelyn Ms HRW HA1 ....61 G2
Moffat Rd PLMGR N13 ....48 E2
THHTH CR7 ....180 D5
TOOT SW17 ....160 E6
Mogden La ISLW TW7 ....136 A6
Mohmmad Khan Rd WAN E11 * 70 D5
Moiety Rd POP/IOD E14 ....124 D2
Moira Cl TOTM N17 ....50 A5
Moira Rd ELTH/MOT SE9 ....146 E5
Moir Cl SAND/SEL CR2 ....212 C6
Molash Rd STMC/STPC BR5 ....202 E1
Mole Abbey Gdns
E/WMO/HCT KT8 ....173 F6
Mole Ct HOR/WEW KT19 ....206 E2
Molember Rd
E/WMO/HCT KT8 ....189 K2
Molescroft ELTH/MOT SE9 ....167 H4
Molesey Av E/WMO/HCT KT8 ....188 E2
Molesey Dr CHEAM SM3 ....193 H6
Molesey Park Av
E/WMO/HCT KT8 ....189 G2
Molesey Park Cl
E/WMO/HCT KT8 ....188 E2
Molesey Park Rd
E/WMO/HCT KT8 ....189 G2
Molesford Rd FUL/PGN SW6 ....139 K2
Molesham Cl E/WMO/HCT KT8 ....173 F6
Molesham Wy
E/WMO/HCT KT8 ....173 F6
Molesworth St LEW SE13 ....145 F4
Mollison Av PEND EN3 ....25 F4
Mollison Dr WLGTN SM6 ....210 E5
Mollison Wy EDGW HA8 ....44 C5
Molly Huggins Cl BAL SW12 ....161 H2
Molyneux Dr TOOT SW17 ....161 G6
Molyneux St MBLAR W1H 8 D2
Monarch Cl EBED/NFELT TW14 ....153 H2
RAIN RM13 ....111 J1
WWKM BR4 ....214 D2
Monarch Dr CAN/RD E16 ....107 H4
Monarch Ms WNWD SE27 ....162 E6
Monarch Pde MTCM CR4 ....178 E5
Monarch Rd BELV DA17 ....129 H3
Monarch Wy GNTH/NBYPK IG2 ....72 D3
Monarch's Wy RSLP HA4 ....58 B5
Mona Rd PECK SE15 ....143 K3
Monastery Gdns ENC/FH EN2 ....23 K3
Mona St CAN/RD E16 ....106 D4
Monaveen Gdns
E/WMO/HCT KT8 ....173 G6
Monck St WEST SW1P 16 D5
Monclar Rd CMBW SE5 ....142 E5
Moncorvo Cl SKENS SW7 ....14 C3
Moncrieff Pl PECK SE15 ....143 H3
Mondial Wy WDR/YW UB7 ....133 F1
Monega Rd FSTGT E7 ....89 G4
Money La WDR/YW UB7 ....112 A3
Monier Rd BOW E3 ....87 J6
Monivea Rd BECK BR3 ....182 C3
Monk Dr CAN/RD E16 ....106 E6
Monkfrith Av STHGT/OAK N14 ....34 B1
Monkfrith Wy STHGT/OAK N14 ....34 A2
Monkham's Av WFD IG8 ....53 F1
Monkham's Dr WFD IG8 ....53 F1

274 Mon - Mou

Monkham's La WFD IG8 39 F6
Monkleigh Rd MRDN SM4 177 H6
Monks Av BAR EN5 33 G1
E/WMO/HCT KT8 188 E2
Monks Cl ABYW SE2 128 E4
ENC/FH EN2 23 J3
RSLP HA4 77 H2
RYLN/HDSTN HA2 * 60 A6
Monks Crs WOT/HER KT12 188 A5
Monksdene Gdns SUT SM1 209 F1
Monks Dr ACT W3 98 C4
Monks Orch DART DA1 171 F4
Monks Orchard Rd BECK BR3 198 D5
Monks Pk WBLY HA9 80 E4
Monks Park Gdns WBLY HA9 80 D4
Monks Rd ENC/FH EN2 23 H3
Monk St WOOL/PLUM SE18 127 F4
Monks Wy BECK BR3 198 D3
GLDGN NW11 64 D1
STMC/STPC BR5 201 H5
Monkswood Gdns CLAY IG5 54 A6
Monk Ter FSTH SE23 164 C4
Monkton Rd WELL DA16 148 A3
Monkton St LBTH SE11 17 K6
Monkville Av GLDGN NW11 64 D1
Monkville Pde GLDGN NW11 * 64 D1
Monkwell Sq BARB EC2Y 12 D2
Monkwood Cl ROM RM1 75 J2
Monmouth Av KUT/HW KT1 174 D3
SWFD E18 71 F1
Monmouth Cl CHSWK W4 118 A3
MTCM CR4 195 K1
WELL DA16 148 B5
Monmouth Gv BTFD TW8 117 F4
Monmouth Pl BAY/PAD W2 100 E5
Monmouth Rd BAY/PAD W2 100 E5
DAGW RM9 92 B3
ED N9 36 D4
EHAM E6 107 K2
HYS/HAR UB3 113 H4
Monmouth St LSQ/SEVD WC2H 10 E4
Monnery Rd ARCH N19 84 C1
Monnow Rd STHWK SE1 123 H5
Monoux Gv WALTH E17 51 J4
Monroe Crs EN EN1 24 D2
Monroe Dr MORT/ESHN SW14 137 J6
Monro Gdns
KTN/HRWW/W HA3 42 E3
Monro Pl HOR/WEW KT19 206 C6
Monsell Rd FSBYPK N4 85 H1
Monson Rd NWCR SE14 144 A1
WLSDN NW10 99 J1
Mons Wy HAYES BR2 200 D3
Montacute Rd BUSH WD23 28 E2
CAT SE6 164 C2
CROY/NA CR0 214 A6
MRDN SM4 194 C3
Montagu Crs UED N18 36 D6
Montague Av BROCKY SE4 144 C5
HNWL W7 116 A1
Montague Cl STHWK SE1 12 E7
Montague Gdns EA W5 98 C6
Montague Hall Pl BUSH WD23 28 A1
Montague Pl GWRST WC1E 10 D1
Montague Rd CEND/HSY/T N8 67 F2
CROY/NA CR0 196 C5
HACK E8 86 C3
HNWL W7 116 A2
HSLW TW3 135 G4
NWDGN UB2 114 D4
RCHPK/HAM TW10 157 F1
TOTM N17 * 68 C1
WAN E11 70 D6
WEA W13 97 H5
WIM/MER SW19 178 A3
Montague Sq NWCR SE14 143 K1
Montague St RSQ WC1B 10 E1
STBT EC1A 12 C2
Montague Ter HAYES BR2 199 K1
Montagu Gdns UED N18 36 D6
WLGTN SM6 210 C2
Montagu Man MHST W1U 9 F2
Montagu Ms North MBLAR W1H 9 F2
Montagu Ms South MBLAR W1H 9 F3
Montagu Ms West MBLAR W1H 9 F3
Montagu Pl MBLAR W1H 8 E2
Montagu Rd HDN NW4 63 J3
UED N18 50 D1
Montagu Rw MHST W1U 9 F2
Montagu Sq MBLAR W1H 9 F2
Montagu St MBLAR W1H 9 F3
Montalt Rd WFD IG8 52 D1
Montana Gdns CAT SE6 182 C1
SUT SM1 209 G3
Montana Rd RYNPK SW20 177 F4
TOOT SW17 161 F5
Montbelle Rd ELTH/MOT SE9 167 G5
Montbretia Cl STMC/STPC BR5 202 D1
Montcalm Cl HAYES BR2 199 K3
YEAD UB4 95 F2
Montcalm Rd CHARL SE7 146 C1
Montclare St BETH E2 7 J5
Monteagle Av BARK IG11 90 C4
Monteagle Wy PECK SE15 143 J4
Montefiore St VX/NE SW8 141 G3
Montem Rd FSTH SE23 164 C2
NWMAL KT3 192 B1
Montem St FSBYPK N4 67 F5
Montenotte Rd
CEND/HSY/T N8 66 C2
Monterey Cl BXLY DA5 169 K4
Montesquieu Ter
CAN/RD E16 * 106 D5
Montford Pl LBTH SE11 122 B6
Montfort Gdns BARK/HLT IG6 54 C2
Montfort Pl WIM/MER SW19 159 G3
Montgomerie Ms FSTH SE23 163 K2
Montgomery Av
ESH/CLAY KT10 189 K6
Montgomery Cl BFN/LL DA15 147 K6
MTCM CR4 * 195 K1
Montgomery Gdns
BELMT SM2 209 H5
Montgomery Rd CHSWK W4 117 K4
EDGW HA8 44 B2
Montholme Rd BTSEA SW11 160 E1
Monthorpe Rd WCHPL E1 104 C4
Montolieu Gdns PUT/ROE SW15 138 E6
Montpelier Av BXLY DA5 168 E2
EA W5 97 J4
Montpelier Gdns CHDH RM6 73 J4
EHAM E6 107 H2
Montpelier Gv KTTN NW5 84 C3
Montpelier Ms SKENS SW7 14 D4
Montpelier Pl SKENS SW7 14 D4
WCHPL E1 104 E5
Montpelier Ri GLDGN NW11 64 C4
WBLY HA9 61 K5
Montpelier Rd EA W5 97 K4
FNCH N3 47 G4
PECK SE15 143 J2
SUT SM1 209 G2
Montpelier Rw
BKHTH/KID SE3 145 J3
TWK TW1 156 C2
Montpelier Sq SKENS SW7 14 D4
Montpelier St SKENS SW7 14 D3
Montpelier Ter SKENS SW7 14 D3
Montpelier V BKHTH/KID SE3 * 145 J3
Montpelier Wk SKENS SW7 14 D3
Montpelier Wy GLDGN NW11 64 C4
Montrave Rd PGE/AN SE20 181 K2
Montreal Pl HOL/ALD WC2B 11 G5
Montreal Rd IL IG1 72 C4
Montrell Rd BRXS/STRHM SW2 161 K3
Montrose Av BFN/LL DA15 168 B2
EDGW HA8 45 F5
KIL/WHAMP NW6 100 C1
WELL DA16 147 J4
WHTN TW2 155 G2
Montrose Cl WELL DA16 148 A4
WFD IG8 38 E6
Montrose Crs ALP/SUD HA0 80 A4
NFNCH/WDSP N12 47 F2
Montrose Gdns MTCM CR4 178 E6
SUT SM1 194 A6
Montrose Pl KTBR SW1X 15 H3
Montrose Rd
EBED/NFELT TW14 153 G1
KTN/HRWW/W HA3 42 E5
Montrose Vls HMSMTH W6 * 118 D5
Montrose Wy FSTH SE23 164 A3
Montserrat Av WFD IG8 52 B3
Montserrat Cl NRWD SE19 180 E1
Montserrat Rd PUT/ROE SW15 139 H5
Monument St MON EC3R 13 F6
Monument Wy TOTM N17 50 B6
Monza St WAP E1W 104 E6
Moodkee St BERM/RHTH SE16 123 K3
Moody St WCHPL E1 105 F2
Moon Ct LEE/GVPK SE12 * 145 K5
Moon La BAR EN5 20 D4
Moon St IS N1 85 H6
Moorcroft EDGW HA8 * 44 D4
Moorcroft Gdns HAYES BR2 200 D2
Moorcroft Rd
STRHM/NOR SW16 161 K5
Moorcroft Wy PIN HA5 59 J2
Moordown WOOL/PLUM SE18 147 G2
Moore Cl MORT/ESHN SW14 137 K4
MTCM CR4 * 179 G5
Moore Crs DAGW RM9 91 H6
Moorefield Rd TOTM N17 50 B6
Mooreland Rd BMLY BR1 183 J3
Moore Park Rd FUL/PGN SW6 140 A1
Moore Rd NRWD SE19 180 D2
Moore St CHEL SW3 14 E6
Moore Wy BELMT SM2 208 E6
Moorey Cl SRTFD E15 88 D6
Moorfield Av EA W5 97 K3
Moorfield Rd CHSGTN KT9 206 A3
ORP BR6 202 B4
PEND EN3 24 E2
Moorfields LVPST EC2M 12 E2
Moorfields Highwalk
BARB EC2Y 12 E2
Moorgate LOTH EC2R 12 E3
Moorgate Pl LOTH EC2R * 12 E3
Moorhead Wy BKHTH/KID SE3 146 A5
Moorhen Cl ERITH DA8 150 E1
Moorhouse Rd BAY/PAD W2 100 E5
KTN/HRWW/W HA3 43 K6
The Moorings CHSWK W4 * 117 H6
Moorland Cl HSLWW TW4 155 F2
ROMW/RG RM7 56 D4
Moorland Rd BRXN/ST SW9 142 C5
Moorlands Av MLHL NW7 45 K2
Moor La BARB EC2Y 12 E2
CHSGTN KT9 206 B3
Moor La Crossing WATW WD18 26 A2
Moormead Dr HOR/WEW KT19 207 G3
Moor Mead Rd TWK TW1 156 B1
Moor Park Gdns
KUTN/CMB KT2 176 B3
NTHWD HA6 * 26 A4
Moor Park Rd NTHWD HA6 40 B2
Moorside Rd BMLY BR1 165 H6
Moor St SOHO/SHAV W1D 10 D4
Moortown Rd OXHEY WD19 27 G6
Moor Vw WATW WD18 26 E2
Morant Gdns CRW RM5 56 D1
Morant St POP/IOD E14 105 J6
Mora Rd CRICK NW2 82 A2
Mora St FSBYE EC1V 6 D5
Morat St BRXN/ST SW9 142 A2
Moravian Pl WBPTN SW10 120 C6
Moravian St BETH E2 104 E1
Moray Av HYS/HAR UB3 113 J1
Moray Cl EDGW HA8 * 30 D4
ROM RM1 57 G3
Moray Ms HOLWY N7 67 F6
Moray Rd HOLWY N7 67 F6
Moray Wy ROM RM1 57 F3
Mordaunt Gdns DAGW RM9 92 A5
Mordaunt Rd WLSDN NW10 81 F6
Mordaunt St BRXN/ST SW9 142 A4
Morden Ct MRDN SM4 194 A1
Morden Court Pde
WIM/MER SW19 * 178 A6
Morden Gdns GFD/PVL UB6 79 F3
MTCM CR4 194 C1
Morden Hall Rd MRDN SM4 178 A6
Morden Hl LEW SE13 145 F3
Morden La LEW SE13 145 F3
Morden Rd BKHTH/KID SE3 145 K3
CHDH RM6 74 A4
WIM/MER SW19 178 A5
Morden Road Ms
BKHTH/KID SE3 145 K3
Morden St LEW SE13 144 E2
Morden Wy CHEAM SM3 193 K4
Morden Wharf Rd
GNWCH SE10 125 H3
Mordon Rd GDMY/SEVK IG3 73 F4
Mordred Rd CAT SE6 165 H4
Morecambe Cl HCH RM12 93 K3
WCHPL E1 * 105 F4
Morecambe Gdns STAN HA7 29 K6
Morecambe St POP/IOD E14 124 E5
WALW SE17 18 D7
Morecambe Ter UED N18 * 35 K6
More Cl CAN/RD E16 106 D5
WKENS W14 119 G4
Morecoombe Cl
KUTN/CMB KT2 175 J3
Moree Wy UED N18 36 C6
Moreland St FSBYE EC1V 6 B4
Moreland Wy CHING E4 37 K5
More La ESH/CLAY KT10 204 B1
Morella Rd BAL SW12 160 E2
More London Pl STHWK SE1 19 G1
More London Riverside
STHWK SE1 19 H1
Moremead Rd CAT SE6 164 C6
Morena St CAT SE6 164 E2
Moresby Av BRYLDS KT5 191 J4
Moresby Rd CLPT E5 68 D5
Mores Gdn CHEL SW3 * 120 C6
Moretaine Rd ASHF TW15 152 A5
Moreton Av ISLW TW7 135 J2
Moreton Cl CLPT E5 68 E6
MLHL NW7 46 A2
SEVS/STOTM N15 67 K3
Moreton Ct DART DA1 150 B4
Moreton Gdns WFD IG8 53 J1
Moreton Pl PIM SW1V 121 H5
Moreton Rd SAND/SEL CR2 211 K3
SEVS/STOTM N15 67 K3
WPK KT4 192 D6
Moreton St PIM SW1V 121 H5
Moreton Ter PIM SW1V 121 H5
Moreton Terrace Ms North
PIM SW1V 121 H5
Moreton Terrace Ms South
PIM SW1V * 121 H5
Morford Cl RSLP HA4 59 F4
Morford Wy RSLP HA4 59 F4
Morgan Av WALTH E17 70 B1
Morgan Cl DAGE RM10 92 C5
NTHWD HA6 40 D1
Morgan Rd BMLY BR1 183 K3
HOLWY N7 85 G3
NKENS W10 100 D4
Morgan's La HYS/HAR UB3 94 B4
STHWK SE1 19 G1
Morgan St BOW E3 105 G2
CAN/RD E16 106 E4
Morgan Wy WFD IG8 53 J2
Moriatry Cl HOLWY N7 84 E2
Morie St WAND/EARL SW18 140 A5
Morieux Rd LEY E10 69 H5
Moring Rd TOOT SW17 161 F6
Morkyns Wk DUL SE21 * 163 F5
Morland Av CROY/NA CR0 197 F5
DART DA1 150 E6
Morland Cl GLDGN NW11 65 F5
HPTN TW12 172 E1
MTCM CR4 178 D6
Morland Est HACK E8 * 86 C5
Morland Gdns STHL UB1 115 G1
WLSDN NW10 81 F5
Morland Ms IS N1 85 G5
Morland Rd CROY/NA CR0 197 G4
DAGE RM10 92 C5
IL IG1 72 B6
KTN/HRWW/W HA3 62 A2
PGE/AN SE20 182 A3
SUT SM1 209 G3
WALTH E17 69 F2
Morley Av CHING E4 52 B3
UED N18 36 C6
WDGN N22 49 H4
Morley Cl ORP BR6 201 G6
Morley Crs EDGW HA8 30 E4
RSLP HA4 59 G6
Morley Crs East STAN HA7 43 J6
Morley Crs West STAN HA7 43 J6
Morley Hl ENC/FH EN2 23 K1
Morley Rd BARK IG11 90 D6
CHDH RM6 74 A2
CHEAM SM3 193 J5
CHST BR7 185 H4
LEW SE13 145 F5
LEY E10 70 A5
SRTFD E15 106 D1
TWK TW1 156 E1
Morley St STHWK SE1 17 K3
Morna Rd CMBW SE5 142 D3
Morning La HOM E9 86 E4
Morningside Rd WPK KT4 192 E6
Mornington Av BMLY BR1 184 B6
IL IG1 72 A4
WKENS W14 119 J4
Mornington Ct BXLY DA5 170 A3
Mornington Crs CAMTN NW1 4 A2
HEST TW5 134 A2
Mornington Gv BOW E3 105 J2
Mornington Ms CMBW SE5 142 D2
Mornington Pl CAMTN NW1 3 K2
Mornington Rd CHING E4 38 B2
DEPT SE8 144 C1
GFD/PVL UB6 96 B4
WAN E11 70 D5
WFD IG8 38 E6
Mornington St CAMTN NW1 3 K2
Mornington Ter CAMTN NW1 3 K1
Mornington Wk
RCHPK/HAM TW10 156 D6
Morocco St STHWK SE1 19 G3
Morpeth Gv HOM E9 87 F6
Morpeth Rd HOM E9 86 E6
Morpeth St BETH E2 105 F2
Morpeth Ter WEST SW1P 16 A5
Morpeth Wk TOTM N17 * 50 D3
Morrab Gdns GDMY/SEVK IG3 91 F1
Morrel Cl BAR EN5 21 G4
Morris Av MNPK E12 89 K3
Morris Bishop Ter HGT N6 * 66 A3
Morris Cl CROY/NA CR0 198 B3
ORP BR6 216 E1
Morris Ct CHING E4 37 K5
Morris Gdns DART DA1 151 K6
WAND/EARL SW18 159 K2
Morrish Rd BRXS/STRHM SW2 161 K2
Morrison Av CHING E4 51 J2
TOTM N17 50 A6
Morrison Rd BARK IG11 110 A1
DAGW RM9 92 A6
YEAD UB4 95 F2
Morrison St BTSEA SW11 141 F4
Morris Pl FSBYPK N4 67 G6
Morris Rd BCTR RM8 74 B6
HARH RM3 57 K3
ISLW TW7 136 A4
POP/IOD E14 105 K4
WAN E11 88 C2
Morris St WCHPL E1 104 D5
Morriston Cl OXHEY WD19 41 G1
Morse Cl PLSTW E13 106 E2
Morshead Rd MV/WKIL W9 100 E2
Morson Rd PEND EN3 37 G1
Morteyne Rd TOTM N17 49 K4
Mortham St SRTFD E15 88 C6
Mortimer Cl BAL SW12 161 J4
BUSH WD23 28 B1
CRICK NW2 82 D1
Mortimer Crs
KIL/WHAMP NW6 83 F6
WPK KT4 207 F1
Mortimer Dr EN EN1 23 K6
Mortimer Pl KIL/WHAMP NW6 83 F6
Mortimer Rd EHAM E6 107 K2
ERITH DA8 130 A6
IS N1 86 A5
MTCM CR4 178 E4
ORP BR6 202 B6
WEA W13 97 J5
WLSDN NW10 100 A2
Mortimer Sq NTGHL W11 100 B6
Mortimer St REGST W1B 9 K3
Mortimer Ter KTTN NW5 * 84 B2
Mortlake Cl CROY/NA CR0 211 F1
Mortlake Dr MTCM CR4 178 D4
Mortlake High St
MORT/ESHN SW14 138 A4
Mortlake Rd CAN/RD E16 107 F5
IL IG1 90 C2
RCH/KEW TW9 137 H1
Morton Cl CROY/NA CR0 211 F5
Morton Crs FBAR/BDGN N11 34 D6
Morton Gdns WLGTN SM6 210 C3
Morton Ms ECT SW5 * 120 A4
Morton Pl STHWK SE1 17 J5
Morton Rd IS N1 85 J5
MRDN SM4 194 C2
SRTFD E15 88 D5
Morton Wy STHGT/OAK N14 34 D6
Morvale Cl BELV DA17 129 G4
Morval Rd BRXS/STRHM SW2 142 B6
Morven Rd TOOT SW17 160 E5
Morville St BOW E3 105 J1
Morwell St FITZ W1T 10 C2
Moscow Pl BAY/PAD W2 * 101 F6
Moscow Rd BAY/PAD W2 100 E6
Moselle Av WDGN N22 49 G5
Moselle Cl CEND/HSY/T N8 49 F6
Moselle St TOTM N17 50 B3
Mossborough Cl
NFNCH/WDSP N12 47 F2
Mossbury Rd BTSEA SW11 140 D4
Moss Cl PIN HA5 41 K5
WCHPL E1 104 C4
Mossdown Cl BELV DA17 129 H4
Mossford Gn BARK/HLT IG6 54 B6
Mossford La BARK/HLT IG6 54 C5
Mossford St BOW E3 105 H3
Moss Gdns FELT TW13 153 K4
SAND/SEL CR2 213 F5
Moss Hall Crs
NFNCH/WDSP N12 47 F2
Moss Hall Gv FNCH N3 47 F2
Moss La PIN HA5 41 K6
ROM RM1 75 H3
Mosslea Rd HAYES BR2 200 C2
ORP BR6 216 C1
PGE/AN SE20 181 K3
Mossop St CHEL SW3 14 D6
Moss Rd DAGE RM10 92 C5
Mossville Gdns MRDN SM4 177 J6
Moston Cl HYS/HAR UB3 113 J5
Mostyn Av WBLY HA9 80 B3
Mostyn Gdns WLSDN NW10 100 B2
Mostyn Gv BOW E3 105 H1
Mostyn Rd BRXN/ST SW9 142 B2
EDGW HA8 45 G3
WIM/MER SW19 177 J5
Mosul Wy HAYES BR2 200 D3
Mosyer Dr STMC/STPC BR5 202 E6
Motcomb St KTBR SW1X 15 G4
Moth Cl WLGTN SM6 210 E5
The Mothers Sq CLPT E5 * 86 D2
Motley St VX/NE SW8 141 H3
Motspur Pk NWMAL KT3 192 C3
Mottingham Gdns
ELTH/MOT SE9 166 C3
Mottingham La
ELTH/MOT SE9 166 B3
Mottingham Rd ED N9 37 F1
ELTH/MOT SE9 166 E5
Mottisfont Rd ABYW SE2 128 B3
Moulins Rd HOM E9 86 E5
Moulton Av HEST TW5 134 D3
Moundfield Rd
STNW/STAM N16 68 C3
Mountacre Cl SYD SE26 163 G6
Mount Adon Pk EDUL SE22 163 H2
Mountague Pl POP/IOD E14 106 A6
Mount Angelus Rd
PUT/ROE SW15 158 C2
Mount Ararat Rd
RCHPK/HAM TW10 137 F6
Mount Ash Rd SYD SE26 163 J5
Mount Av CHING E4 37 J5
EA W5 97 K4
STHL UB1 96 A5
Mountbatten Cl NRWD SE19 181 F1
WOOL/PLUM SE18 127 K6
Mountbatten Ct BKHH IG9 39 H4
Mountbel Rd
KTN/HRWW/W HA3 * 43 G5
Mount Cl BMLY BR1 184 D4
CAR SM5 210 A6
EA W5 * 97 J4
EBAR EN4 22 A5
Mountcombe Cl SURB KT6 191 F4
Mount Ct WWKM BR4 199 H6
Mount Culver Av SCUP DA14 186 E2
Mount Dr CDALE/KGS NW9 62 E6
RYLN/HDSTN HA2 59 K2
Mountearl Gdns
STRHM/NOR SW16 162 A5
Mount Echo Av CHING E4 37 K3
Mount Echo Dr CHING E4 37 K3
Mount Ephraim La
STRHM/NOR SW16 161 J5
Mount Ephraim Rd
STRHM/NOR SW16 161 J5
Mountfield Cl LEW SE13 165 G2
Mountfield Rd EA W5 97 K5
EHAM E6 108 A1
FNCH N3 46 E6
Mountfield Ter CAT SE6 165 G2
Mountfield Wy
STMC/STPC BR5 202 D1
Mountfort Crs IS N1 85 G5
Mountfort Ter IS N1 85 G5
Mount Gdns SYD SE26 163 J5
Mount Gv EDGW HA8 30 E5
Mountgrove Rd HBRY N5 85 J1
Mounthurst Rd HAYES BR2 199 K4
Mountington Park Cl
KTN/HRWW/W HA3 61 K3
Mountjoy Cl THMD SE28 128 C2
Mount Mills FSBYE EC1V 6 B5
Mount Nod Rd
STRHM/NOR SW16 162 A5
Mount Pde EBAR EN4 * 21 J5
Mount Pk CAR SM5 210 A6
Mount Park Av HRW HA1 60 D6
SAND/SEL CR2 211 H6
Mount Park Crs EA W5 97 K5
Mount Park Rd EA W5 97 K4
HRW HA1 60 D6
PIN HA5 58 E2
Mount Pl ACT W3 117 J1
Mount Pleasant ALP/SUD HA0 80 A6
EBAR EN4 21 K5
FSBYW WC1X 5 J7
HRW HA1 * 60 E6
RSLP HA4 77 G1
WNWD SE27 162 D6
Mount Pleasant Crs
FSBYPK N4 * 67 F4
Mount Pleasant Hl CLPT E5 68 D6
Mount Pleasant La CLPT E5 68 D5
Mount Pleasant Pl
WOOL/PLUM SE18 127 J4
Mount Pleasant Rd CRW RM5 57 F2
DART DA1 171 J1
EA W5 97 J3
LEW SE13 165 F1
NWMAL KT3 175 K6
TOTM N17 50 A6
WALTH E17 51 G5
WLSDN NW10 82 A5
Mount Pleasant Vls FSBYPK N4 67 F4
Mount Ri FSTH SE23 163 K4
Mount Rd BCTR RM8 74 B5
BXLYHS DA6 149 F6
CHSGTN KT9 206 B3
CRICK NW2 81 K1
DART DA1 170 C1
EBAR EN4 21 J6
FELT TW13 154 D5
HDN NW4 63 J3
HYS/HAR UB3 113 K2
IL IG1 90 B3
MTCM CR4 178 C5
NRWD SE19 * 180 E2
NWMAL KT3 176 A6
WAND/EARL SW18 159 K4
Mount Rw MYFR/PKLN W1K 9 J6
Mountside KTN/HRWW/W HA3 43 F4
Mounts Pond Rd
BKHTH/KID SE3 145 G3
The Mount Sq HAMP NW3 * 83 G1
Mount Stewart Av
KTN/HRWW/W HA3 61 K3
Mount St MYFR/PKLN W1K 9 G6
Mount Ter WCHPL E1 104 D4
The Mount BMLY BR1 * 184 D4
BXLYHS DA6 * 149 J6
CLPT E5 68 D6
ESH/CLAY KT10 204 A4
HAMP NW3 83 G2
NTHLT UB5 * 78 B3
NWMAL KT3 176 C6
TRDG/WHET N20 33 G4
WBLY HA9 62 D6
WPK KT4 207 K2
Mount Vw ENC/FH EN2 23 F1
NWDGN UB2 * 114 C4
Mountview MLHL NW7 31 F5
NTHWD HA6 40 E2
Mountview Cl GLDGN NW11 65 G5

Mount View Rd
CDALE/KGS NW9 63 F1
CHING E4 38 A2
ESH/CLAY KT10 205 H5
FSBYPK N4 67 F4
Mountview Rd ORP BR6 202 B4
Mount Vls WNWD SE27 162 C5
Mount Wy CAR SM5 210 A6
Mountwood E/WMO/HCT KT8 173 G6
Movers La BARK IG11 90 D6
Mowatt Cl ARCH N19 66 D6
Mowbray Gdns NTHLT UB5 * 78 A6
Mowbray Rd BAR EN5 21 G5
EDGW HA8 30 C6
KIL/WHAMP NW6 82 C5
NRWD SE19 181 G4
RCHPK/HAM TW10 156 D5
Mowbrays Cl CRW RM5 56 E4
Mowbrays Rd CRW RM5 56 E5
Mowlem St BETH E2 104 D1
Mowll St BRXN/ST SW9 142 B1
Moxon Cl PLSTW E13 106 D1
Moxon St BAR EN5 20 D4
MHST W1U 9 G2
Moye Cl BETH E2 * 104 C1
Moyers Rd LEY E10 70 A5
Moylan Rd HMSMTH W6 119 H6
Moyne Pl WLSDN NW10 98 C2
Moynihan Dr STHGT/OAK N14 22 E6
Moys Cl CROY/NA CR0 195 K3
Moyser Rd STRHM/NOR SW16 179 G1
Mozart St NKENS W10 100 D2
Muchelney Rd MRDN SM4 194 B3
Muggeridge Cl
SAND/SEL CR2 211 K3
Muggeridge Rd DAGE RM10 92 D2
Muirdown Av
MORT/ESHN SW14 137 K5
Muir Dr WAND/EARL SW18 160 D1
Muirfield ACT W3 99 G5
Muirfield Cl
BERM/RHTH SE16 * 123 J5
OXHEY WD19 41 G1
Muirfield Crs POP/IOD E14 124 E3
Muirfield Gn OXHEY WD19 27 G6
Muirfield Rd OXHEY WD19 27 G6
Muirkirk Rd CAT SE6 165 F3
Muir Rd CLPT E5 86 C1
Muir St CAN/RD E16 126 E1
Mulberry Av
STWL/WRAY TW19 152 B3
Mulberry Cl CHEL SW3 * 120 C6
CHING E4 37 J4
EBAR EN4 21 H5
GPK RM2 75 K1
HDN NW4 46 A6
NTHLT UB5 95 J1
STRHM/NOR SW16 161 H6
Mulberry Crs BTFD TW8 136 C1
WDR/YW UB7 112 D2
Mulberry Dr PUR RM19 131 J4
Mulberry La CROY/NA CR0 197 G5
Mulberry Ms NWCR SE14 144 C2
Mulberry Pde WDR/YW UB7 112 D3
Mulberry Pl ELTH/MOT SE9 146 C5
HMSMTH W6 118 D5
Mulberry Rd HACK E8 86 B5
Mulberry St WCHPL E1 104 C5
Mulberry Wk CHEL SW3 120 C6
Mulberry Wy BARK/HLT IG6 72 C1
BELV DA17 129 K2
SWFD E18 53 F5
Mulgrave Rd BELMT SM2 208 D5
CROY/NA CR0 211 K1
EA W5 97 K2
HRW HA1 61 G6
WKENS W14 119 J6
WLSDN NW10 81 H2
WOOL/PLUM SE18 126 E4
Mulholland Cl MTCM CR4 179 G5
Mulkern Rd ARCH N19 66 D5
Mullards Cl MTCM CR4 194 E5
Mullet Gdns BETH E2 104 C2
Mullins Pth MORT/ESHN SW14 138 A4
Mullion Cl KTN/HRWW/W HA3 42 B4
Mullion Wk OXHEY WD19 27 H6
Mull Wk IS N1 85 J4
Mulready St STJWD NW8 2 C7
Multi Wy ACT W3 118 B2
Multon Rd WAND/EARL SW18 160 C2
Mumford Ct CITYW EC2V 12 D3
Mumford Rd HNHL SE24 142 C6
Mumford Mills LEW SE13 144 E2
Muncaster Cl ASHF TW15 152 D6
Muncaster Rd CLAP SW4 140 E5
Muncies Ms CAT SE6 165 F4
Mundania Rd EDUL SE22 163 J1
Munday Rd CAN/RD E16 106 E5
Munden St WKENS W14 119 H4
Mundesly Cl OXHEY WD19 27 G6
Mundford Rd CLPT E5 68 E6
Mundon Gdns IL IG1 72 D5
Mund St WKENS W14 119 J5
Mundy St IS N1 7 G4
Mungo-Park Cl BUSH WD23 * 28 C4
Mungo Park Rd RAIN RM13 93 J4
Mungo Park Wy
STMC/STPC BR5 202 D4
Munnery Wy ORP BR6 216 A1
Munnings Gdns ISLW TW7 135 J6
Munro Dr FBAR/BDGN N11 * 48 C2
Munro Ms NKENS W10 100 C4
Munro Wy CLPT E5 86 C2
Munslow Gdns SUT SM1 209 G2
Munster Av HSLWW TW4 134 D5
Munster Gdns PLMGR N13 35 J6
Munster Ms FUL/PGN SW6 * 139 J1
Munster Rd FUL/PGN SW6 139 J2
TEDD TW11 174 D2
Munster Sq CAMTN NW1 3 K5
Munton Rd WALW SE17 18 D6
Murchison Av BXLY DA5 168 E3
Murchison Rd LEY E10 70 A6
Murdock Cl CAN/RD E16 106 D5
Murdock St PECK SE15 123 J6
Murfett Cl WIM/MER SW19 159 H4
Muriel St IS N1 5 H2
Murillo Rd LEW SE13 145 G5
Murphy St STHWK SE1 17 J3
Murray Av BMLY BR1 184 A6
HSLW TW3 135 G6
Murray Crs PIN HA5 41 H4
Murray Gv IS N1 6 E3
Murray Ms CAMTN NW1 84 D5
Murray Rd EA W5 116 D4
NTHWD HA6 40 C4
RCHPK/HAM TW10 156 C4
STMC/STPC BR5 186 C6
WIM/MER SW19 177 G2
Murray Sq CAN/RD E16 106 E5
Murray St CAMTN NW1 84 D5
Murray Ter HAMP NW3 83 G2
Murtwell Dr CHIG IG7 54 C2
Musard Rd WKENS W14 119 H6
Musbury St WCHPL E1 104 E5
Muscatel Pl CMBW SE5 143 F2
Muschamp Rd CAR SM5 194 D6
PECK SE15 143 G4
Muscovy St TWRH EC3N 13 H6
Museum St NOXST/BSQ WC1A 10 E3
Musgrave Cl EBAR EN4 21 G2
Musgrave Crs FUL/PGN SW6 139 K1
Musgrave Rd ISLW TW7 136 A2
Musgrove Rd NWCR SE14 144 A2
Musjid Rd BTSEA SW11 140 C3
Musquash Wy HSLWW TW4 134 B3
Muston Rd CLPT E5 68 D6
Muswell Av MUSWH N10 48 B5
Muswell Hl MUSWH N10 48 B6
Muswell Hl Broadway
MUSWH N10 48 B6
Muswell Hill Pl MUSWH N10 66 B1
Muswell Hill Rd MUSWH N10 66 A1
Muswell Ms MUSWH N10 48 B6
Muswell Rd MUSWH N10 48 B5
Mutrix Rd KIL/WHAMP NW6 82 E6
Mutton Pl CAMTN NW1 84 A4
Muybridge Rd NWMAL KT3 175 K5
Myatt Rd BRXN/ST SW9 142 C2
Mycenae Rd BKHTH/KID SE3 125 K6
Myddelton Av EN EN1 24 A1
Myddelton Gdns WCHMH N21 35 J2
Myddelton Pk TRDG/WHET N20 33 H5
Myddelton Pas CLKNW EC1R 5 K4
Myddelton Rd CEND/HSY/T N8 48 E6
Myddelton Sq CLKNW EC1R 5 K4
Myddelton St CLKNW EC1R 5 K5
Myddleton Av FSBYPK N4 67 H6
Myddleton Rd WDGN N22 48 E3
Myers La NWCR SE14 124 A6
Mylis Cl SYD SE26 163 J6
Mylne Cl HMSMTH W6 * 118 D5
Mylne St CLKNW EC1R 5 J3
Myra St ABYW SE2 128 B5
Myrdle St WCHPL E1 104 C4
Myrna Cl WIM/MER SW19 178 D3
Myron Pl LEW SE13 145 F4
Myrtle Aly WOOL/PLUM SE18 127 F3
Myrtle Av EBED/NFELT TW14 133 H5
RSLP HA4 58 E4
Myrtleberry Cl HACK E8 * 86 B4
Myrtle Cl EBAR EN4 33 K3
ERITH DA8 150 B1
WDR/YW UB7 112 C4
Myrtledene Rd ABYW SE2 128 B5
Myrtle Gdns HNWL W7 115 K1
Myrtle Gv ENC/FH EN2 23 K1
NWMAL KT3 175 K5
Myrtle Rd ACT W3 117 K1
CROY/NA CR0 213 J1
DART DA1 171 G4
EHAM E6 89 J6
HPTN TW12 173 H2
HSLW TW3 135 H3
IL IG1 72 B6
PLMGR N13 35 J5
SUT SM1 209 G3
WALTH E17 69 G3
Myrtleside Cl NTHWD HA6 40 B3
Myrtle St IS N1 7 G3
Myrtle Wk IS N1 7 G3
Mysore Rd BTSEA SW11 140 E5
Myton Rd DUL SE21 162 E5

N

Nadine St CHARL SE7 126 B5
Nagle Cl WALTH E17 52 B5
Nag's Head La WELL DA16 148 C4
Nags Head Rd PEND EN3 24 E5
Nairne Gv EDUL SE22 142 E6
Nairn Gn OXHEY WD19 26 E5
Nairn Rd RSLP HA4 77 G4
Nairn St POP/IOD E14 106 A4
Nallhead Rd FELT TW13 172 B1
Namba Roy Cl
STRHM/NOR SW16 162 A6
Namton Dr STRHM/NOR SW16 196 A1
Nan Clark's La MLHL NW7 31 H4
Nancy Downs OXHEY WD19 27 G2
Nankin St POP/IOD E14 105 J5
Nansen Rd BTSEA SW11 141 F5
Nansen Village
NFNCH/WDSP N12 * 33 F6
Nantes Cl WAND/EARL SW18 140 B5
Nant Rd CRICK NW2 64 D6
Nant St BETH E2 104 D2
Naoroji St FSBYW WC1X 5 J5
Napier Av FUL/PGN SW6 139 J4
POP/IOD E14 124 D5
Napier Cl DEPT SE8 144 C1
EMPK RM11 75 K5
WDR/YW UB7 112 C3
Napier Ct LEE/GVPK SE12 166 A4
Napier Gv IS N1 6 D3
Napier Pl WKENS W14 119 J3
Napier Rd ALP/SUD HA0 79 K3
BELV DA17 129 G4
EHAM E6 90 A6
HAYES BR2 184 A6
ISLW TW7 136 B5
PEND EN3 25 F6
SAND/SEL CR2 211 K5
SNWD SE25 197 J1
SRTFD E15 106 C1
TOTM N17 50 A6
WAN E11 88 C1
WDR/YW UB7 132 A2
WKENS W14 119 J3
WLSDN NW10 99 K2
Napier Ter IS N1 85 H5
Napoleon Rd CLPT E5 86 D1
TWK TW1 * 156 C2
Napton Cl YEAD UB4 95 J3
Narbonne Av CLAP SW4 161 H1
Narboro Ct ROM RM1 75 J3
Narborough Cl HGDN/ICK UB10 58 A6
Narborough St FUL/PGN SW6 140 A3
Narcissus Rd KIL/WHAMP NW6 82 E3
Narford Rd CLPT E5 86 C1
Narrow Boat Cl THMD SE28 127 J2
Narrow St ACT W3 117 J1
POP/IOD E14 105 G6
Narrow Wy HAYES BR2 200 D3
Nascot St SHB W12 100 A5
Naseby Cl ISLW TW7 135 K2
KIL/WHAMP NW6 * 83 G5
Naseby Ct WOT/HER KT12 * 188 B6
Naseby Rd CLAY IG5 53 K4
DAGE RM10 92 C1
NRWD SE19 180 E2
Nash Cl SUT SM1 209 H1
Nash Gn BMLY BR1 183 K3
Nash La HAYES BR2 214 E4
Nash Rd BROCKY SE4 144 B5
CHDH RM6 73 K1
ED N9 36 E4
Nash St CAMTN NW1 3 K4
Nash Wy KTN/HRWW/W HA3 61 H3
Nasmyth St HMSMTH W6 118 E3
Nassau Rd BARN SW13 138 C2
Nassau St GTPST W1W 10 A2
Nassington Rd HAMP NW3 83 J2
Natalie Cl EBED/NFELT TW14 153 G2
Natal Rd FBAR/BDGN N11 48 E1
IL IG1 90 B2
STRHM/NOR SW16 179 J2
THHTH CR7 180 E6
Nathaniel Cl WCHPL E1 13 K2
Nathans Rd ALP/SUD HA0 61 J6
Nathan Wy THMD SE28 128 B2
National Ter
BERM/RHTH SE16 * 123 J2
Nation Wy CHING E4 38 A3
Naval Rw POP/IOD E14 106 A6
Navarino Gv HACK E8 86 C4
Navarino Rd HACK E8 86 C4
Navarre Gdns CRW RM5 56 D2
Navarre Rd EHAM E6 107 J1
Navarre St BETH E2 7 J6
Navestock Cl CHING E4 * 38 A5
Navestock Crs WFD IG8 53 G4
Navestock Ter WFD IG8 53 G3
Navigator Dr NWDGN UB2 115 H2
Navy St CLAP SW4 141 J4
Nayim Pl HACK E8 86 D4
Naylor Gv PEND EN3 25 F6
Naylor Rd PECK SE15 143 J1
TRDG/WHET N20 33 G4
Nazareth Cl PECK SE15 143 J3
Nazrul St BETH E2 7 J4
Neal Av STHL UB1 95 K3
Neal Cl NTHWD HA6 40 E4
Nealden St BRXN/ST SW9 142 A4
Neale Cl EFNCH N2 47 G6
Neal St LSQ/SEVD WC2H 10 E4
Neal Ter FSTH SE23 * 164 A3
Neal Yd LSQ/SEVD WC2H 10 E4
Near Acre CDALE/KGS NW9 45 H4
Neasden Cl WLSDN NW10 81 G3
Neasden La WLSDN NW10 81 G1
Neasden La North
WLSDN NW10 81 G1
Neasham Rd BCTR RM8 91 H3
Neate St CMBW SE5 123 F6
Neath Gdns MRDN SM4 194 B3
Neathouse Pl PIM SW1V 16 A6
Neats Acre RSLP HA4 58 B4
Neatscourt Rd EHAM E6 107 H4
Neckinger STHWK SE1 19 K4
Neckinger Est
BERM/RHTH SE16 19 K4
Neckinger St STHWK SE1 19 K3
Nectarine Wy LEW SE13 144 E3
Needham Rd BAY/PAD W2 100 E5
Needleman St
BERM/RHTH SE16 124 A2
Neeld Crs HDN NW4 63 K2
WBLY HA9 80 C3
Neils Yd LSQ/SEVD WC2H * 10 E4
Nelgarde Rd CAT SE6 164 D2
Nella Rd HMSMTH W6 119 G6
Nelldale Rd BERM/RHTH SE16 123 J4
Nello James Gdns WNWD SE27 162 E6
Nelson Cl CROY/NA CR0 196 C5
EBED/NFELT TW14 * 153 J3
KIL/WHAMP NW6 100 E2
ROMW/RG RM7 56 D4
WOT/HER KT12 188 A5
Nelson Gdns BETH E2 104 C2
HSLW TW3 155 F1
Nelson Grove Rd
WIM/MER SW19 178 A4
Nelson Mandela Cl
MUSWH N10 47 K5
Nelson Mandela Rd
BKHTH/KID SE3 146 B4
Nelson Pl IS N1 6 B3
SCUP DA14 168 B6
Nelson Rd BELV DA17 129 G5
CEND/HSY/T N8 67 F2
CHING E4 51 K2
DART DA1 171 F1
ED N9 36 D5
GNWCH SE10 125 F6
HAYES BR2 200 B1
HRW HA1 60 D5
HSLW TW3 155 F1
NWMAL KT3 192 A2
PEND EN3 37 F1
RAIN RM13 111 H1
SCUP DA14 168 B6
SEVS/STOTM N15 68 A1
STAN HA7 43 J2
WAN E11 70 E1
WDR/YW UB7 132 C2
WIM/MER SW19 178 A3
Nelson Sq STHWK SE1 18 A2
Nelsons Rw CLAP SW4 141 J5
Nelson St CAN/RD E16 106 D6
EHAM E6 90 A6
WCHPL E1 104 D5
Nelsons Yd CAMTN NW1 4 A2
Nelson Ter FSBYE EC1V 6 B3
Nelson Wk HOR/WEW KT19 206 C6
Nemoure Rd ACT W3 98 E6
Nene Gdns FELT TW13 154 E4
Nene Rd HTHAIR TW6 132 E2
Nepaul Rd BTSEA SW11 140 D3
Nepean St PUT/ROE SW15 158 D1
Neptune Cl RAIN RM13 111 H1
Neptune Rd HRW HA1 60 D3
HTHAIR TW6 * 133 F2
Neptune St BERM/RHTH SE16 123 K3
Nesbit Cl BKHTH/KID SE3 145 H4
Nesbit Rd ELTH/MOT SE9 146 C5
Nesbitts Aly BAR EN5 * 20 D4
Nesbitt Sq NRWD SE19 * 181 F3
Nesham St WAP E1W 123 H1
Ness Rd ERITH DA8 131 G6
Ness St BERM/RHTH SE16 123 H3
Nesta Rd WFD IG8 52 D2
Nestle's Av HYS/HAR UB3 113 J3
Nestor Av WCHMH N21 35 H1
Netheravon Rd CHSWK W4 118 C4
HNWL W7 116 A1
Netheravon Rd South
CHSWK W4 118 C6
Netherbury Rd EA W5 116 E3
Netherby Gdns ENC/FH EN2 22 E5
Netherby Rd FSTH SE23 163 K2
Nether Cl FNCH N3 46 E3
Nether Ct MLHL NW7 * 46 D2
Nethercourt Av FNCH N3 46 E2
Netherfield Gdns BARK IG11 90 D4
Netherfield Rd
NFNCH/WDSP N12 47 F1
TOOT SW17 161 F5
Netherford Rd CLAP SW4 141 H3
Netherhall Gdns HAMP NW3 83 G3
Netherhall Wy HAMP NW3 83 G3
Netherlands Rd BAR EN5 33 H1
Netherleigh Cl ARCH N19 66 B5
Netherpark Dr GPK RM2 57 H5
Nether St FNCH N3 46 E4
FNCH N3 47 F2
Netherton Gv WBPTN SW10 120 B6
Netherton Rd SEVS/STOTM N15 67 K3
TWK TW1 136 B6
Netherwood Pl WKENS W14 * 119 G3
Netherwood Rd WKENS W14 119 G3
Netherwood St
KIL/WHAMP NW6 82 D5
Netley Cl CHEAM SM3 208 B3
CROY/NA CR0 214 A5
Netley Dr WOT/HER KT12 188 E4
Netley Gdns MRDN SM4 194 B4
Netley Rd BTFD TW8 117 F6
GNTH/NBYPK IG2 72 D2
MRDN SM4 194 B4
WALTH E17 69 H2
Netley St CAMTN NW1 4 A5
Nettlecombe Cl BELMT SM2 209 F6
Nettleden Av WBLY HA9 80 C4
Nettlefold Pl WNWD SE27 162 C5
Nettlestead Cl BECK BR3 182 C3
Nettleton Rd HTHAIR TW6 132 E2
NWCR SE14 144 A1
Nettlewood Rd
STRHM/NOR SW16 179 J3
Neuchatel Rd CAT SE6 164 C4
Nevada Cl NWMAL KT3 191 K1
Nevada St GNWCH SE10 145 F1
Nevern Pl ECT SW5 119 K4
Nevern Rd ECT SW5 119 K4
Nevern Sq ECT SW5 119 K4
Nevil Cl NTHWD HA6 40 B1
Neville Av NWMAL KT3 176 A4
Neville Cl ACT W3 117 K2
BFN/LL DA15 168 A6
HSLW TW3 135 F3
KIL/WHAMP NW6 100 D1
PECK SE15 143 H1
WAN E11 88 D1
Neville Dr EFNCH N2 65 G3
Neville Gdns BCTR RM8 91 K1
Neville Gill Cl
WAND/EARL SW18 159 K1
Neville Pl WDGN N22 49 F4
Neville Rd BARK/HLT IG6 54 C4
BCTR RM8 73 K6
CROY/NA CR0 196 E4
EA W5 97 K3
FSTGT E7 88 E5
KIL/WHAMP NW6 * 100 D1
KUT/HW KT1 175 H5
RCHPK/HAM TW10 156 D5
Neville St SKENS SW7 120 C5
Neville Ter SKENS SW7 * 120 C5
Neville Wk CAR SM5 194 D4
Nevill Rd STNW/STAM N16 86 A2
Nevill Wy LOU IG10 39 J1
Nevil Wk CAR SM5 * 194 D4
Nevin Dr CHING E4 37 K3
Nevinson Cl WAND/EARL SW18 160 C1
Nevis Cl ROM RM1 57 G2
Nevis Rd TOOT SW17 161 F4
New Acres Rd THMD SE28 127 K2
Newall Rd HTHAIR TW6 133 F2
Newark Ct WOT/HER KT12 188 B5
Newark Crs WLSDN NW10 99 F2
Newark Knok EHAM E6 108 A5
Newark Rd SAND/SEL CR2 211 K4
Newark St WCHPL E1 104 D4
Newark Wy HDN NW4 63 J1
New Ash Cl EFNCH N2 47 H6
New Barn Cl CROY/NA CR0 211 F4
New Barns Av MTCM CR4 195 J1
New Barn St PLSTW E13 106 E3
Newbery Rd ERITH DA8 150 C2
Newbiggin Pth OXHEY WD19 27 G6
Newbolt Av CHEAM SM3 208 A3
Newbolt Rd STAN HA7 43 F2
New Bond St MYFR/PICC W1J 9 K5
Newborough Gn NWMAL KT3 192 A1
New Brent St HDN NW4 64 A2
New Bridge St STP EC4M 12 A4
New Broad St LVPST EC2M 13 F2
New Broadway EA W5 97 K6
Newburgh Rd ACT W3 117 K1
Newburgh St SOHO/CST W1F 10 A4
New Burlington Ms
CONDST W1S 10 A5
New Burlington Pl
CONDST W1S 10 A5
New Burlington St
CONDST W1S 10 A5
Newburn St LBTH SE11 122 A5
Newbury Cl NTHLT UB5 77 K4
Newbury Gdns
HOR/WEW KT19 207 H2
Newbury Ms KTTN NW5 84 A4
Newbury Rd CHING E4 52 A2
GNTH/NBYPK IG2 72 D3
HAYES BR2 183 K6
WDR/YW UB7 132 C2
Newbury St STBT EC1A 12 C2
Newbury Wy NTHLT UB5 77 J4
New Butt La DEPT SE8 * 144 D1
Newby Cl EN EN1 24 A3
Newby Pl POP/IOD E14 106 A6
Newby St VX/NE SW8 141 G4
Newcastle Av BARK/HLT IG6 55 G2
Newcastle Cl STP EC4M 12 A3
Newcastle Pl BAY/PAD W2 8 B2
Newcastle Rw CLKNW EC1R 5 K7
New Cavendish St MHST W1U 9 H2
New Change STP EC4M 12 C4
New Charles St FSBYE EC1V 6 B4
New Church Rd CMBW SE5 142 E1
New City Rd PLSTW E13 107 G2
New Cl FELT TW13 172 D1
WIM/MER SW19 178 B6
New College Ms IS N1 * 85 G5
New College Pde
HAMP NW3 * 83 G4
Newcombe Gdns HSLW TW3 134 E5
Newcombe Pk ALP/SUD HA0 80 B6
MLHL NW7 45 G1
Newcombe St KENS W8 * 119 K1
Newcome Gdns
STRHM/NOR SW16 161 K6
Newcomen Rd BTSEA SW11 140 C4
WAN E11 * 88 D1
Newcomen St STHWK SE1 18 E2
New Compton St
LSQ/SEVD WC2H * 10 D4
New Ct NTHLT UB5 78 B3
TPL/STR WC2R * 11 J5
Newcourt St STJWD NW8 2 C3
New Crane Pl WAP E1W * 123 K1
New Crescent Yd
WLSDN NW10 * 99 H1
New Cross Rd NWCR SE14 144 C1
Newdales Cl ED N9 36 C4
Newdene Av NTHLT UB5 95 H1
Newdigate
STRHM/NOR SW16 * 162 B6
Newell St POP/IOD E14 105 H6
New End HAMP NW3 83 G2
New End Sq HAMP NW3 83 H2
Newent Cl CAR SM5 194 E5
New Era Est IS N1 7 G1
New Farm Av HAYES BR2 199 K1
New Farm La NTHWD HA6 40 C4
New Ferry Ap
WOOL/PLUM SE18 127 F3
New Fetter La
FLST/FETLN EC4A 11 K3
Newfield Cl HPTN TW12 173 F4
Newfield Ri CRICK NW2 81 J1
New Forest La CHIG IG7 54 A2
Newgale Gdns EDGW HA8 44 B4
New Garden Dr
WDR/YW UB7 112 B2
Newgate CROY/NA CR0 196 D5
Newgate Cl FELT TW13 154 D4
Newgate St CHING E4 38 C5
STBT EC1A 12 B3
New Globe Wk STHWK SE1 12 C7
New Goulston St WCHPL E1 13 J3
New Green Pl
BRXS/STRHM SW2 162 B2
NRWD SE19 181 F2
Newhall Gdns WOT/HER KT12 188 B6
Newham's Rw STHWK SE1 19 H3
Newham Wy CAN/RD E16 106 D4
EHAM E6 107 J3
Newhaven Cl HYS/HAR UB3 113 J4
Newhaven Gdns
ELTH/MOT SE9 146 C5
Newhaven La CAN/RD E16 106 E4
Newhaven Rd SNWD SE25 196 E2
New Heston Rd HEST TW5 134 E1
Newhouse Av CHDH RM6 55 K6
Newhouse Cl NWMAL KT3 192 B4
Newhouse Wk MRDN SM4 194 B4
Newick Cl BXLY DA5 169 J1
Newick Rd CLPT E5 86 D1
Newing Gn BMLY BR1 184 C3

Newington Barrow Wy
HOLWY N7 ....85 F1
Newington Butts LBTH SE11 ...18 B7
Newington Cswy STHWK SE1 ...18 C4
Newington Dr
STNW/STAM N16.......85 K5
New Inn Broadway
SDTCH EC2A * 7 H6
New Inn Sq SDTCH EC2A * 7 H6
New Inn St SDTCH EC2A * 7 H6
New Inn Yd SDTCH EC2A * 7 H6
New Kelvin Av TEDD TW11 ...173 K2
New King's Rd FUL/PGN SW6 ...139 K2
New King St DEPT SE8 ....124 D6
Newland Cl PIN HA5 ....41 J2
Newland Dr EN EN1 ....24 D2
Newland Gdns HNWL W7 ....116 B2
Newland Rd CEND/HSY/T N8 ...48 E6
Newlands Av THDIT KT7 ....189 K5
Newlands Cl ALP/SUD HA0 ....79 J4
  EDGW HA8 ....30 A5
  NWDGN UB2 ....114 D5
Newlands Ct WBLY HA9 ....62 C6
Newlands Pk SYD SE26 ....181 K2
Newlands Pl BAR EN5 ....20 B6
Newlands Quay WAP E1W 104 E6
Newlands Rd
  STRHM/NOR SW16 ....179 K5
  WFD IG8 ....38 C4
The Newlands WLGTN SM6 ...210 C5
Newland St CAN/RD E16 ....126 D1
Newlands Wy CHSGTN KT9 ...205 J3
Newlands Wd CROY/NA CRO ...213 H6
Newlands Woods
  CROY/NA CRO * 213 H6
Newling Cl EHAM E6 ....107 K5
Newling Est BETH E2 * 7 K5
New London St MON EC3R * ...13 H5
New Lydenburg St CHARL SE7 ...126 B5
Newlyn Cl ORP BR6 ....217 F2
Newlyn Gdns RYLN/HDSTN HA2 ...59 K4
  TOTM N17 ....50 B4
  WELL DA16 ....148 A5
Newman Rd BMLY BR1 ....183 K4
  CROY/NA CRO 196 A4
  HYS/HAR UB3 ....95 F6
  PLSTW E13 ....107 F2
  WALTH E17 * 57 F5
Newman's Rw LINN WC2A 11 H2
Newman St FITZ W1T 10 B2
Newman's Wy EBAR EN4 ....21 G3
Newmarket Av NTHLT UB5 ...78 A3
Newmarsh Rd THMD SE28 ...128 A1
New Mill Rd STMC/STPC BR5 ...186 D4
Newminster Ct ENC/FH EN2 * ...23 H5
Newminster Rd MRDN SM4 ...194 B3
New Mount St SRTFD E15 ....88 B5
Newnham Av RSLP HA4 ....59 G5
Newnham Cl LOU IG10 ....39 H1
  NTHLT UB5 ....78 D3
  THHTH CR7 ....180 D5
Newnham Gdns NTHLT UB5 ...78 D4
Newnham Ms WDGN N22 * ...49 G4
Newnham Rd WDGN N22 ....49 F4
Newnhams Cl BMLY BR1 ....184 E6
Newnham Ter STHWK SE1 ....17 J4
Newnham Wy
  KTN/HRWW/W HA3 ....62 A2
New North Pl SDTCH EC2A * ...7 G6
New North Rd BARK/HLT IG6 ...54 D3
  IS N1 ....7 F3
New North St BMSBY WC1N ...11 G1
New Oak Rd EFNCH N2 ....47 G5
New Oxford St
  NOXST/BSQ WC1A 10 E3
  WDR/YW UB7 * 112 B1
New Park Av PLMGR N13 ....35 J5
New Park Cl NTHLT UB5 ....77 J4
New Park Ct STRHM/NOR SW2 * ...161 K3
New Park Rd
  BRXS/STRHM SW2 ....161 K3
New Place Sq
  BERM/RHTH SE16 * 123 J3
New Plaistow Rd SRTFD E15 ...88 C6
New Pond Pde RSLP HA4 * ...76 E1
Newport Av POP/IOD E14 ...106 B6
Newport Cl SOHO/SHAV W1D ...10 C5
Newport Md OXHEY WD19 * ...27 H6
Newport Pl SOHO/SHAV W1D * ...10 D5
Newport Rd BARN SW13 ....138 D2
  HTHAIR TW6 ....132 D2
  LEY E10 ....70 B6
  WALTH E17 * 69 G1
  YEAD UB4 ....94 B4
Newport St LBTH SE11 ....17 G7
Newquay Crs RYLN/HDSTN HA2 ...59 J6
Newquay Gdns OXHEY WD19 ...27 F4
Newquay Rd CAT SE6 ....164 E4
New Quebec St MBLAR W1H ...9 F4
New River Av CEND/HSY/T N8 ...49 F3
New River Crs PLMGR N13 ...35 H6
New River Wy STNW/STAM N16 ...67 K4
New Rd ABYW SE2 ....128 E4
  BTFD TW8 * 116 E6
  CEND/HSY/T N8 ....66 D2
  CHING E4 ....37 K6
  DAGW RM9 ....92 C6
  E/WMO/HCT KT8 * 173 F6
  EBED/NFELT TW14 ....153 G1
  EBED/NFELT TW14 ....153 J3
  ED N9 ....36 D4
  ESH/CLAY KT10 ....204 C2
  FELT TW13 ....172 D1
  GDMY/SEVK IG3 ....72 E6
  HGDN/ICK UB10 ....94 A3
  HRW HA1 ....79 F2
  HSLW TW3 ....135 G5
  HYS/HAR UB3 ....133 J5
  KUTN/CMB KT2 ....175 H3
  MLHL NW7 ....46 C3

  MTCM CR4 ....195 F5
  ORP BR6 ....202 B4
  RAIN RM13 ....111 J2
  RAIN RM13 ....131 J1
  RCHPK/HAM TW10 ....156 D6
  WCHPL E1 ....104 D4
  WDGN N22 ....49 J4
  WELL DA16 ....148 C3
New Road Hl HAYES BR2 ....215 J6
New Rw CHCR WC2N 10 E5
Newry Rd TWK TW1 ....136 B5
Newsam Av SEVS/STOTM N15 ...67 K2
Newsholme Dr WCHMH N21 ...23 F6
New Spring Gardens Wk
  LBTH SE11 * 121 K5
New Sq LINN WC2A 11 H3
Newstead Av ORP BR6 ....216 D1
Newstead Cl NFNCH/WDSP N12 ...47 J2
Newstead Ct NTHLT UB5 * ...95 J3
Newstead Rd LEE/GVPK SE12 ...165 J2
Newstead Wk MRDN SM4 ...194 B4
Newstead Wy
  WIM/MER SW19 ....159 G6
New St LVPST EC2M 13 H2
  STBT EC1A 11 K3
New Street HI BMLY BR1 ....184 A1
New Street Sq
  FLST/FETLN EC4A 11 K3
Newton Av ACT W3 ....117 K2
  MUSWH N10 ....48 A4
Newton Cl RYLN/HDSTN HA2 ...60 A6
  WALTH E17 ....69 G3
Newton Gv CHSWK W4 ....118 B3
Newton Rd POP/IOD E14 ....124 D4
Newton Rd ACT W3 ....117 K2
  ALP/SUD HA0 ....80 B5
  BAY/PAD W2 ....101 F5
  CRICK NW2 ....82 A2
  ISLW TW7 ....136 A3
  KTN/HRWW/W HA3 ....42 E4
  SEVS/STOTM N15 ....68 B3
  SRTFD E15 * 88 B3
  WDR/YW UB7 ....132 B2
  WELL DA16 ....148 B4
  WIM/MER SW19 ....177 H3
Newtons Cl RAIN RM13 ....93 G5
Newton St HOL/ALD WC2B 11 F3
Newton's Yd
  WAND/EARL SW18 ....139 K6
Newton Ter HAYES BR2 ....200 C3
Newton Wk EDGW HA8 ....44 E4
Newton Wy UED N18 ....49 J1
New Tower Blds WAP E1W * ...123 J1
Newtown St BTSEA SW11 ....141 G2
New Trinity Rd EFNCH N2 ....47 H6
New Union Cl POP/IOD E14 ....125 F3
New Union St BARB EC2Y 12 E2
New Wanstead WAN E11 ....70 D3
New Way Rd CDALE/KGS NW9 ...63 G1
New Wharf Rd IS N1 ....5 F2
New Zealand Av RAIN RM13 ...111 H2
Niagara Av EA W5 ....116 D4
Niagara Cl IS N1 ....6 D2
Nibthwaite Rd HRW HA1 ....60 E2
Nicholas Cl GFD/PVL UB6 ....96 B1
Nicholas Gdns EA W5 ....116 E3
Nicholas La MANHO EC4N 13 F5
Nicholas Rd BCTR RM8 ....74 B6
  BORE WD6 ....30 B1
  CROY/NA CRO 210 E2
  WCHPL E1 * 104 E3
Nicholas Wy NTHWD HA6 ....40 A4
Nicholay Rd ARCH N19 ....66 D5
Nichol Cl STHGT/OAK N14 ....34 D3
Nicholes Rd HSLW TW3 ....135 F5
Nichol La BMLY BR1 ....183 K5
Nicholl St BETH E2 ....86 C6
Nichols Cl FSBYPK N4 * 67 G5
Nichols Gn EA W5 ....98 A4
Nicholson Cl ISLW TW7 ....50 B6
Nicholson Dr BUSH WD23 ....28 C3
Nicholson Ms KUT/HW KT1 * ...191 F1
Nicholson Rd CROY/NA CRO ...197 G5
Nicholson St STHWK SE1 ....11 K6
Nickelby Cl THMD SE28 ....109 J5
Nickols Wk WAND/EARL SW18 ...140 A5
Nicola Cl KTN/HRWW/W HA3 ...42 D5
  SAND/SEL CR2 ....211 J5
Nicola Ms BARK/HLT IG6 ....54 B3
Nicoll Pl HDN NW4 ....63 K5
Nicoll Rd WLSDN NW10 ....81 G6
Nicolson Rd STMC/STPC BR5 ...202 E4
Nicosia Rd WAND/EARL SW18 ...160 D2
Niederwald Rd SYD SE26 ...164 B6
Nield Rd HYS/HAR UB3 ....113 J2
Nigel Cl NTHLT UB5 ....77 J6
Nigel Fisher Wy CHSGTN KT9 ...205 J5
Nigel Ms IL IG1 ....90 B2
Nigel Playfair Av HMSMTH W6 ...118 E5
Nigel Rd FSTGT E7 ....89 G3
  PECK SE15 ....143 H4
Nigeria Rd CHARL SE7 ....146 B1
Nightingale Av CHING E4 ....52 C1
Nightingale Cl CAR SM5 ....195 F6
  CHING E4 ....38 C6
  CHSWK W4 ....117 K6
  FBAR/BDGN N11 * 59 J2
Nightingale Cnr
  STMC/STPC BR5 * 202 E1
Nightingale Dr
  HOR/WEW KT19 ....206 D4
Nightingale Gv LEW SE13 ...145 G6
Nightingale La BAL SW12 ....161 F1
  BMLY BR1 ....184 B5
  CEND/HSY/T N8 ....66 E1
  RCHPK/HAM TW10 ....157 F2
  WAN E11 ....71 F2
Nightingale Ms KUT/HW KT1 * ...174 E6
  LEY E10 * 69 J4
  STHWK SE1 ....17 K6
Nightingale Pl WBPTN SW10 ...120 B6
  WOOL/PLUM SE18 ....127 F6
Nightingale Rd CAR SM5 ....209 K1
  CLPT E5 ....86 D1

  E/WMO/HCT KT8 ....189 G2
  ED N9 ....36 E2
  HNWL W7 ....116 A1
  HPTN TW12 ....173 F2
  STMC/STPC BR5 ....201 H5
  WDGN N22 ....48 E4
  WOT/HER KT12 * 188 B4
Nightingale Sq BAL SW12 ....161 F2
The Nightingales
  STWL/WRAY TW19 ....152 C3
Nightingale V
  WOOL/PLUM SE18 ....127 F6
Nightingale Wk BAL SW12 ....161 G1
Nightingale Wy EHAM E6 ....107 J4
Nile Cl STNW/STAM N16 ....86 B1
Nile Dr ED N9 ....36 E4
Nile Pth PLSTW E13 ....107 G1
Nile St IS N1 ....6 E4
Nile Ter PECK SE15 ....123 G5
Nimmo Dr BUSH WD23 ....28 D2
Nimrod Cl NTHLT UB5 ....95 H2
Nimrod Pas IS N1 * 86 A4
Nimrod Rd STRHM/NOR SW16 ...179 G2
Nina Mackay Cl SRTFD E15 * ...88 C3
Nine Acres Cl MNPK E12 ....89 J3
Nine Elms Cl
  EBED/NFELT TW14 ....153 J3
Nine Elms La VX/NE SW8 ....141 H1
Nineteenth Rd MTCM CR4 ....195 K1
Ninhams Wd ORP BR6 ....216 A2
Ninth Av HYS/HAR UB3 ....94 E6
Nisbet Av UED N18 ....168 B6
Nithdale Rd WOOL/PLUM SE18 ...147 G1
Niton Cl BAR EN5 ....32 B1
Niton Rd RCH/KEW TW9 ....137 H4
Niton St FUL/PGN SW6 ....139 G1
No1 St WOOL/PLUM SE18 ....127 G3
No2 St WOOL/PLUM SE18 ....127 G3
Noak Hill Rd HARH RM3 ....57 J1
Nobel Dr HYS/HAR UB3 ....133 H1
Nobel Rd UED N18 ....36 E6
Noble Cnr HEST TW5 * 135 F2
Noble St CITYW EC2V 12 C3
Noel Rd ACT W3 ....98 C5
  EHAM E6 ....107 J5
  IS N1 ....6 B2
Noel St SOHO/CST W1F * 10 B4
Nolan Wy CLPT E5 ....86 C2
Nolton Pl EDGW HA8 ....44 B4
Nonsuch Cl BARK/HLT IG6 ....54 B2
Nonsuch Pl CHEAM SM3 * ...208 B5
Norbiton Av KUT/HW KT1 ....175 H5
Norbiton Common Rd
  NWMAL KT3 ....175 J6
Norbiton Rd POP/IOD E14 ....105 H5
Norbroke St ACT W3 ....99 H6
Norbury Av HSLW TW3 ....135 J6
  STRHM/NOR SW16 ....180 A4
Norbury Cl
  STRHM/NOR SW16 ....180 B4
Norbury Court Rd
  STRHM/NOR SW16 ....179 K5
Norbury Crs
  STRHM/NOR SW16 ....180 B5
Norbury Cross
  STRHM/NOR SW16 ....179 K6
Norbury Gdns CHDH RM6 ....73 K2
Norbury Hl STRHM/NOR SW16 ...180 B3
Norbury Ri STRHM/NOR SW16 ...179 K6
Norbury Rd CHING E4 ....51 J1
  FELT TW13 ....153 H5
  THHTH CR7 ....180 D5
Norbury Vis KUT/HW KT1 * ...175 G5
Norcombe Gdns
  KTN/HRWW/W HA3 ....61 J3
Norcott Cl YEAD UB4 ....95 G3
Norcott Rd STNW/STAM N16 ...68 C6
Norcroft Gdns EDUL SE22 ...163 H2
Norcutt Rd WHTN TW2 ....155 K3
Nordenfeldt Rd ERITH DA8 ...130 A5
Norfield Rd RDART DA2 ....169 K6
Norfolk Av PLMGR N13 ....49 H2
  SEVS/STOTM N15 ....68 B3
Norfolk Cl DART DA1 ....171 K1
  EBAR EN4 ....22 A5
  RCH/KEW TW9 ....137 H2
  RYLN/HDSTN HA2 ....60 B3
  STHL UB1 ....95 J6
  UED N18 ....36 C6
  WEA W13 ....97 H5
Norfolk Ct BAR EN5 * 20 C5
Norfolk Crs BAY/PAD W2 ....8 C3
  BFN/LL DA15 ....167 K2
Norfolk Gdns BXLYHN DA7 ...149 G2
Norfolk House Rd
  STRHM/NOR SW16 ....161 J5
Norfolk Ms NKENS W10 ....100 C4
Norfolk Pl BAY/PAD W2 ....8 B3
  WELL DA16 ....148 B3
Norfolk Rd BAR EN5 ....20 C4
  BARK IG11 ....90 E5
  DAGE RM10 ....92 D5
  EHAM E6 ....89 K6
  ESH/CLAY KT10 ....204 E3
  FELT TW13 ....154 B3
  GDMY/SEVK IG3 ....72 E5
  HRW HA1 ....60 B3
  PEND EN3 ....24 D6
  ROMW/RG RM7 ....74 E3
  STJWD NW8 ....2 B1
  THHTH CR7 ....180 D6
  WALTH E17 ....51 G4
  WIM/MER SW19 ....178 E2
  WLSDN NW10 ....81 G5
Norfolk Rw STHWK SE1 ....17 G6
Norfolk Sq BAY/PAD W2 ....8 B4
Norfolk Square Ms BAY/PAD W2 ...8 B4
Norfolk St FSTGT E7 ....88 E3
Norgrove St BAL SW12 ....161 F2
Norhyrst Av SNWD SE25 ....181 G6
Norland Pl NTGHL W11 ....119 H1
Norland Rd NTGHL W11 ....119 G1

Norlands Crs CHST BR7 ....185 G4
Norlands Ga CHST BR7 * 185 G4
Norland Sq NTGHL W11 ....119 H1
Norley V PUT/ROE SW15 ....158 D5
Norlington Rd WAN E11 ....70 A5
Norman Av FELT TW13 ....154 D4
  STHL UB1 ....95 J6
  TWK TW1 ....156 C2
  WDGN N22 ....49 J4
Normanby Cl PUT/ROE SW15 ...139 J6
Normanby Rd WLSDN NW10 ...81 H1
Norman Cl ORP BR6 ....216 C1
  ROMW/RG RM7 ....56 D5
Norman Crs HEST TW5 ....134 C1
  PIN HA5 ....41 G4
Normand Gdns WKENS W14 * ...119 H6
Normand Ms WKENS W14 ....119 H6
Normand Rd WKENS W14 ....119 J6
Normandy Av BAR EN5 ....20 D6
Normandy Cl SYD SE26 ....164 B5
Normandy Dr HYS/HAR UB3 ...94 A5
Normandy Rd BRXN/ST SW9 ...142 B2
Normandy Ter CAN/RD E16 ...107 F5
Normandy Wy ERITH DA8 ....150 B2
Norman Gv BOW E3 ....105 G1
Normanhurst Av WELL DA16 ...148 E2
Normanhurst Dr TWK TW1 ....136 C6
Normanhurst Rd
  BRXS/STRHM SW2 ....162 A4
  STMC/STPC BR5 ....186 C5
  WOT/HER KT12 ....188 C6
Norman Pde SCUP DA14 * ...169 F5
Norman Rd BELV DA17 ....129 J3
  DART DA1 ....171 H6
  EHAM E6 ....107 K3
  EMPK RM11 ....75 J4
  GNWCH SE10 ....144 E1
  IL IG1 ....90 B3
  SEVS/STOTM N15 ....68 B2
  SUT SM1 ....208 E3
  THHTH CR7 ....196 C2
  WAN E11 ....70 C6
  WIM/MER SW19 ....178 B3
Normans Cl WDGN N22 * ...49 J4
  WLSDN NW10 ....81 F4
Normansfield Av
  E/WMO/HCT KT8 ....174 D3
Normansfield Cl BUSH WD23 ...28 B2
Normanshire Dr CHING E4 ....37 J6
Normans Md WLSDN NW10 ....81 F4
Norman St FSBYE EC1V 6 C5
Norman Ter KIL/WHAMP NW6 * ...82 D5
Normanton Av
  WIM/MER SW19 ....159 K4
Normanton Pk CHING E4 ....38 C5
Normanton Rd SAND/SEL CR2 ...212 A4
Normanton St FSTH SE23 ....164 A4
Norman Wy ACT W3 ....98 D4
  STHGT/OAK N14 ....34 E4
Normington Cl
  STRHM/NOR SW16 ....180 B1
Norrice Lea EFNCH N2 ....65 H2
Norris St STJS SW1Y 10 C6
Norris Wy DART DA1 ....150 C4
Norroy Rd PUT/ROE SW15 ....139 G5
Norrys Cl EBAR EN4 ....21 K6
Norrys Rd EBAR EN4 ....21 K5
Norseman Cl GDMY/SEVK IG3 ...73 H5
Norseman Wy GFD/PVL UB6 * ...78 B6
Norstead Pl PUT/ROE SW15 ....158 D4
North Access Rd WALTH E17 ...69 F3
North Acre CDALE/KGS NW9 ...45 G4
North Acton Rd WLSDN NW10 ...99 F1
Northall Rd BXLYHN DA7 ....149 K3
Northampton Gv IS N1 ....85 K3
Northampton Pk IS N1 ....85 J4
Northampton Rd CLKNW EC1R ...5 K6
  CROY/NA CRO 197 H2
  PEND EN3 ....25 G5
Northampton Rw CLKNW EC1R * ...5 K6
Northampton Sq FSBYE EC1V ...6 A5
Northampton St IS N1 ....85 J5
Northanger Rd
  STRHM/NOR SW16 ....179 K2
North Ap RKW/CH/CXG WD3 ...26 A4
North Audley St
  MYFR/PKLN W1K 9 G4
North Av CAR SM5 ....210 A5
  HYS/HAR UB3 ....94 E6
  RCH/KEW TW9 ....137 H2
  RYLN/HDSTN HA2 ....60 B3
  STHL UB1 ....95 J5
  UED N18 ....36 C6
  WEA W13 ....97 H5
North Bank STJWD NW8 ....2 C5
Northbank Rd WALTH E17 ....52 A5
North Birkbeck Rd WAN E11 ...88 B1
Northborough Rd
  STRHM/NOR SW16 ....179 K6
Northbourne HAYES BR2 ....199 K4
Northbourne Rd CLAP SW4 ....141 J5
Northbrook Rd BAR EN5 ....32 C1
  CROY/NA CRO * 196 E4
  IL IG1 ....72 A6
  LEW SE13 ....145 G6
  WDGN N22 ....48 E2
Northburgh St FSBYE EC1V ...6 B7
North Carriage Dr BAY/PAD W2 ...8 D5
Northchurch Rd IS N1 ....85 K5
  WBLY HA9 ....80 C4
Northchurch Ter IS N1 ....86 A5
North Circular PLMGR N13 ....49 G1
North Circular Rd BARK IG11 ...90 A5
  CRICK NW2 ....63 K5
  EFNCH N2 ....47 G5
  GLDGN NW11 ....64 D4
  SWFD E18 ....53 G4
  WLSDN NW10 ....98 B1
Northcliffe Cl WPK KT4 ....207 G1
Northcliffe Dr TRDG/WHET N20 ...32 D2
North Cl BAR EN5 ....20 A6
  BXLYHS DA6 ....148 E5

  CHIG IG7 ....55 G1
  DAGE RM10 ....92 C6
  EBED/NFELT TW14 ....153 G1
  MRDN SM4 ....193 H1
North Colonnade
  POP/IOD E14 ....124 E1
North Common Rd EA W5 ....98 A6
  ISLW TW7 ....136 B6
Northcote Av BRYLDS KT5 ...191 H4
  EA W5 ....98 A6
  ISLW TW7 ....156 B6
  STHL UB1 ....95 J6
Northcote Rd BTSEA SW11 ....140 D5
  CROY/NA CRO 196 E4
  NWMAL KT3 ....175 K6
  SCUP DA14 ....167 K6
  TWK TW1 ....136 B6
  WALTH E17 ....69 G1
  WLSDN NW10 ....81 G5
Northcott Av WDGN N22 ....48 E4
North Countess Rd
  WALTH E17 ....51 H5
North Cray Rd BXLY DA5 ....169 H4
  SCUP DA14 ....187 F2
North Crs CAN/RD E16 ....106 B5
  FITZ W1T 10 C1
  FNCH N3 ....46 D5
Northcroft Rd
  HOR/WEW KT19 ....207 G5
  WEA W13 ....116 C2
North Cross Rd BARK/HLT IG6 ...72 C1
  EDUL SE22 ....143 G6
Northdene CHIG IG7 ....54 D1
North Dene HEST TW5 ....135 G2
  MLHL NW7 * 31 F5
Northdene Gdns
  SEVS/STOTM N15 ....68 B3
Northdown Cl RSLP HA4 ....76 D1
Northdown Gdns
  GNTH/NBYPK IG2 ....72 E2
Northdown Rd EMPK RM11 ...75 K4
  WELL DA16 ....148 C3
Northdown St IS N1 ....5 G3
North Dr BECK BR3 ....198 E1
  HSLW TW3 ....135 H5
  ORP BR6 ....216 E2
  RSLP HA4 ....58 C4
  STRHM/NOR SW16 ....161 H6
North End BKHH IG9 ....39 G2
  CROY/NA CRO 196 D6
  HAMP NW3 ....65 G6
North End Av HAMP NW3 ....65 G6
  WEA W13 ....116 C2
North End Crs WKENS W14 ...119 J4
North End La ORP BR6 ....216 B6
North End Rd ERITH DA8 ....150 C2
  FUL/PGN SW6 ....139 K1
  GLDGN NW11 ....65 G5
  WBLY HA9 ....80 C1
  WKENS W14 ....119 H4
North End Wy HAMP NW3 ....65 G6
Northern Av ED N9 ....36 B4
Northernhay Wk MRDN SM4 ...193 H1
Northern Perimeter Rd
  HTHAIR TW6 ....133 F2
Northern Perimeter Rd (West)
  HTHAIR TW6 ....132 C7
Northern Relief Rd BARK IG11 ...90 C5
North Eyot Gdns
  HMSMTH W6 * 118 C5
North Farm LOU IG10 ....39 G1
Northfield Av PIN HA5 ....59 H1
  STMC/STPC BR5 ....202 D3
  WEA W13 ....116 C2
Northfield Cl BMLY BR1 ....184 D4
  HYS/HAR UB3 ....113 J3
Northfield Crs CHEAM SM3 ...208 C2
Northfield Pde
  HYS/HAR UB3 * 113 J3
Northfield Pk HYS/HAR UB3 ...113 H3
Northfield Rd DAGW RM9 ....92 B2
  EBAR EN4 ....21 J4
  EHAM E6 ....89 K4
  PEND EN3 ....24 D6
  STNW/STAM N16 ....68 A4
  WEA W13 ....116 C2
Northfields WAND/EARL SW18 ...139 K5
Northfields Rd ACT W3 ....98 E4
North Gdns WIM/MER SW19 ...178 C3
Northgate Dr CDALE/KGS NW9 ...63 G3
North Gower St CAMTN NW1 ...4 A5
North Gv HGT N6 ....66 A4
  SEVS/STOTM N15 ....67 K2
North Hill HGT N6 ....65 K3
North Hl Av HGT N6 ....65 K3
North Hyde Gdns HYS/HAR UB3 ...113 K3
North Hyde La NWDGN UB2 ...114 D5
North Hyde Rd HYS/HAR UB3 ...113 H5
North Hyde Whf
  NWDGN UB2 * 114 B4
Northiam NFNCH/WDSP N12 ...32 E5
Northiam St HACK E8 ....86 D6
Northington St BMSBY WC1N ...11 G1
Northlands Av ORP BR6 ....216 E2
Northlands St CMBW SE5 ...142 D3
North La TEDD TW11 ....174 A2
North Lodge Cl
  PUT/ROE SW15 * 139 G2
North Ms BMSBY WC1N 5 H7
North Mt TRDG/WHET N20 * ...33 G4
Northolm EDGW HA8 ....31 F5
Northolme Gdns EDGW HA8 ...44 C4
Northolme Ri ORP BR6 ....201 K6
Northolme Rd HBRY N5 ....85 J2
Northolt Av RSLP HA4 ....77 F3
Northolt Gdns GFD/PVL UB6 ...79 F3
Northolt Rd RYLN/HDSTN HA2 ...78 B1
  WDR/YW UB7 * 132 A2
Northover BMLY BR1 ....165 J6
North Pde CHSGTN KT9 ....206 B3
  EDGW HA8 * 44 C5
  STHL UB1 * 96 A5
North Pas WAND/EARL SW18 ...139 K6

North Peckham Est
 PECK SE15 .....143 G1
North Pl TEDD TW11 .....174 A2
 WIM/MER SW19 .....209 C1
North Pole La HAYES BR2 .....214 G4
North Pole Rd SHB W12 .....100 A5
Northport St IS N1 .....7 F1
North Ri BAY/PAD W2 * 8 D4
North Rd BELV DA17 .....129 J5
 BMLY BR1 .....184 A4
 BTFD TW8 .....117 F6
 CHDH RM6 .....74 A2
 DART DA1 .....170 C1
 EA W5 .....116 E3
 EBED/NFELT TW14 .....153 G1
 ED N9 .....36 D5
 EDGW HA8 .....44 D4
 EFNCH N2 .....47 J4
 GDMY/SEVK IG3 .....72 E6
 HEST TW5 .....114 B6
 HGT N6 .....66 A4
 HOLWY N7 .....84 E3
 HYS/HAR UB3 .....94 B4
 RCH/KEW TW9 .....137 H5
 STHL UB1 .....96 A6
 SURB KT6 .....190 E3
 WDR/YW UB7 .....112 C3
 WIM/MER SW19 .....178 C2
 WOOL/PLUM SE18 .....127 K4
 WWKM BR4 .....198 E5
Northrop Rd HTHAIR TW6 .....133 H2
North Rw MYFR/PKLN W1K 9 K5
North Several
 BKHTH/KID SE3 * 145 G3
Northside Rd BMLY BR1 .....183 K1
North Side Wandsworth
 Common
 WAND/EARL SW18 .....140 B6
Northspur Rd SUT SM1 .....208 E1
North Sq ED N9 .....36 D4
 GLDGN NW11 .....64 E5
Northstead Rd
 BRXS/STRHM SW2 .....162 B4
North St BARK IG11 .....90 C5
 BMLY BR1 .....183 K4
 BXLYHN DA7 .....149 H5
 CAR SM5 .....209 K2
 DART DA1 .....171 J1
 HDN NW4 .....64 A2
 ISLW TW7 .....136 B4
 PLSTW E13 .....107 F1
 ROM RM1 .....75 F1
 VX/NE SW8 .....141 J1
North Tenter St WCHPL E1 .....13 K4
North Ter CHEL SW3 .....14 C6
Northumberland Aly
 TWRH EC3N * 13 H4
Northumberland Av
 CHCR WC2N 10 E7
 EN EN1 .....24 D1
 ISLW TW7 .....136 A2
 MNPK E12 .....71 G5
 WELL DA16 .....147 K5
Northumberland Cl
 ERITH DA8 .....149 K1
 STWL/WRAY TW19 .....152 B1
Northumberland Crs
 EBED/NFELT TW14 .....153 H1
Northumberland Gdns
 BMLY BR1 .....201 F1
 ED N9 .....36 B5
 MTCM CR4 .....195 K2
Northumberland Gv
 TOTM N17 .....50 D3
Northumberland Pk
 ERITH DA8 .....149 K1
 TOTM N17 .....50 D3
Northumberland Pl
 BAY/PAD W2 .....100 E5
Northumberland Rd
 BAR EN5 .....33 G1
 EHAM E6 .....107 J5
 RYLN/HDSTN HA2 .....59 K2
 WALTH E17 .....69 J4
Northumberland St
 CHCR WC2N 10 E7
Northumberland Wy
 ERITH DA8 .....149 K1
Northumbria St POP/IOD E14 .....105 J5
North Verbena Gdns
 HMSMTH W6 * 118 D5
North Vw W5 .....97 J3
 PIN HA5 .....59 C4
 WIM/MER SW19 .....176 E1
Northview Crs WLSDN NW10 .....81 H2
Northview Dr WFD IG8 .....53 H3
Northview Pde HOLWY N7 * 84 E1
North View Rd
 CEND/HSY/T N8 .....48 D6
North Vls CAMTN NW1 .....84 D4
North Wk CROY/NA CRO 213 K3
North Wy CDALE/KGS NW9 .....44 D6
 ED N9 .....36 E4
 FBAR/BDGN N11 .....34 B2
 PIN HA5 .....41 G6
Northway GLDGN NW11 .....65 F2
 RYNPK SW20 .....177 H6
 WLGTN SM6 .....210 D2
Northway Crs MLHL NW7 .....31 G6
Northway Rd CMBW SE5 .....142 D4
 CROY/NA CRO 197 G3
Northways Pde HAMP NW3 * 83 H5
North Weald La
 KUTN/CMB KT2 .....174 D1
North Wharf Rd BAY/PAD W2 .....8 A2
Northway Av HRW HA1 .....61 G1
Northwick Cir
 KTN/HRWW/W HA3 .....61 J3
Northwick Cl STJWD NW8 .....2 A4
Northwick Park Rd HRW HA1 .....61 F3
Northwick Rd ALP/SUD HA0 .....79 K6
 OXHEY WD19 .....27 G1
Northwick Ter STJWD NW8 .....2 A6
Northwold Dr PIN HA5 .....41 G6

Northwold Rd
 STNW/STAM N16 .....68 C6
Northwood Av HCH RM12 .....93 J2
Northwood Gdns CLAY IG5 .....72 A1
 GFD/PVL UB6 .....79 H1
 NFNCH/WDSP N12 .....47 H1
Northwood Pl ERITH DA18 .....129 C3
Northwood Rd CAR SM5 .....210 A4
 FSTH SE23 .....164 C3
 HGT N6 .....66 B4
 HTHAIR TW6 .....132 A2
 THHTH CR7 .....180 D5
Northwood Wy NTHWD HA6 .....40 E4
North Woolwich Rd
 CAN/RD E16 .....126 A1
North Worple Wy
 MORT/ESHN SW14 .....138 A4
Norton Av BRYLDS KT5 .....191 J4
Norton Cl CHING E4 .....51 J1
Norton Folgate WCHPL E1 .....7 H7
Norton Gdns
 STRHM/NOR SW16 .....179 K5
Norton Rd ALP/SUD HA0 .....79 G4
 DAGE RM10 .....92 D4
 LEY E10 .....69 H5
Norval Gn BRXN/ST SW9 * 142 B3
Norval Rd ALP/SUD HA0 .....61 H6
Norway Ga BERM/RHTH SE16 .....124 B3
Norway Pl POP/IOD E14 .....105 H5
Norway St GNWCH SE10 .....124 E6
Norwich Crs CHDH RM6 .....73 H3
Norwich Rd BXLYHS DA6 .....149 H5
 GFD/PVL UB6 .....78 B6
 PIN HA5 .....40 C6
 THHTH CR7 .....180 D6
Norwich St FLST/FETLN EC4A 11 J3
Norwich Wk EDGW HA8 .....44 E3
Norwood Av ALP/SUD HA0 .....80 B6
 ROMW/RG RM7 .....75 F4
Norwood Cl NWDGN UB2 .....115 F4
 WHTN TW2 .....155 J3
Norwood Crs HTHAIR TW6 .....133 F2
Norwood Dr
 RYLN/HDSTN HA2 .....59 K3
Norwood Gdns NWDGN UB2 .....114 E4
 YEAD UB4 .....95 G3
Norwood Green Rd
 NWDGN UB2 .....115 F4
Norwood High St WNWD SE27 .....162 D6
Norwood Park Rd
 WNWD SE27 .....180 D1
Norwood Rd HNHL SE24 .....162 C3
 NWDGN UB2 .....114 D3
Notley St CMBW SE5 .....142 E1
Notson Rd SNWD SE25 .....197 J1
Notting Barn Rd NKENS W10 .....100 B3
Nottingdale Sq NTGHL W11 * 119 H1
Nottingham Av CAN/RD E16 .....107 C4
Nottingham Cl
 LSO/SEVD WC2H * 10 E4
Nottingham Pl MHST W1U 3 G7
Nottingham Rd ISLW TW7 .....136 A3
 LEY E10 .....70 A3
 SAND/SEL CR2 .....211 J3
 TOOT SW17 .....160 E5
Nottingham St MHST W1U 9 G1
Nottingham Ter CAMTN NW1 * 3 G7
Notting Hill Ga NTGHL W11 .....119 K1
Nova Ms MRDN SM4 .....193 H4
Novar Cl ORP BR6 .....202 A4
Nova Rd CROY/NA CRO 196 C5
Novar Rd ELTH/MOT SE9 .....167 H3
Novello St FUL/PGN SW6 .....139 K2
Nowell Rd BARN SW13 .....118 D6
Nower Hi PIN HA5 .....59 K1
Noyna Rd TOOT SW17 .....160 E5
Nubia Wy BMLY BR1 .....165 H6
Nuding Cl LEW SE13 .....144 E4
Nugent Rd ARCH N19 .....66 E5
 SNWD SE25 .....181 G6
Nugents Ct PIN HA5 * 41 J4
Nugent's Pk PIN HA5 .....41 K4
Nugent Ter STJWD NW8 .....101 G1
Nuneaton Rd DAGW RM9 .....91 K5
Nunhead Crs PECK SE15 .....143 J4
Nunhead Gn PECK SE15 .....143 J4
Nunhead La PECK SE15 .....143 J4
Nunnington Cl
 ELTH/MOT SE9 .....166 D5
Nunn's Rd ENC/FH EN2 .....23 J3
Nupton Dr BAR EN5 .....32 A1
Nurse Cl EDGW HA8 .....44 E4
Nursery Av BXLYHN DA7 .....149 G4
 CROY/NA CRO 198 A6
 FNCH N3 .....47 F5
Nursery Cl BROCKY SE4 .....144 C3
 CHDH RM6 .....73 K3
 CROY/NA CRO 198 A6
 EBED/NFELT TW14 .....154 A2
 ORP BR6 .....202 A4
 PEND EN3 .....25 F2
 SWLY BR8 .....187 K5
 WFD IG8 .....53 F1
Nursery Gdns CHST BR7 .....185 G3
 HSLWW TW4 .....134 E6
 PEND EN3 .....25 F2
Nurserymans Rd
 FBAR/BDGN N11 .....34 A4
Nursery La BETH E2 .....7 J1
 FSTGT E7 .....88 E4
 NKENS W10 .....100 A4
Nursery Rd BRXN/ST SW9 .....142 A5
 EFNCH N2 .....47 H4
 HOM E9 .....86 E4
 MTCM CR4 .....178 D6
 PIN HA5 .....41 G6
 STHGT/OAK N14 .....34 C2
 THHTH CR7 .....196 E1
 WIM/MER SW19 .....177 H3
 WIM/MER SW19 .....178 A5
Nursery Rw BAR EN5 * 20 C4
 WALW SE17 .....18 E7
Nursery St TOTM N17 .....50 B3
The Nursery ERITH DA8 .....150 C1

Nursery Wk HDN NW4 .....45 K6
Nurstead Rd ERITH DA8 .....149 H1
Nutbourne St NKENS W10 .....100 C2
Nutbrook St PECK SE15 .....143 G4
Nutbrowne Rd DAGW RM9 .....92 B6
Nutcroft Rd PECK SE15 .....143 J1
Nutfield Cl CAR SM5 .....209 J1
 UED N18 .....50 C2
Nutfield Gdns GDMY/SEVK IG3 .....73 F6
 NTHLT UB5 .....95 C1
Nutfield Rd CRICK NW2 .....63 J6
 EDUL SE22 .....143 G6
 SRTFD E15 .....88 A2
 THHTH CR7 .....196 C5
Nutfield Wy ORP BR6 .....201 F6
Nutford Pl BAY/PAD W2 .....8 D3
Nuthatch Gdns THMD SE28 .....127 J2
Nuthurst Av
 BRXS/STRHM SW2 .....162 A4
Nutley Ter HAMP NW3 .....83 H4
Nutmead Cl BXLY DA5 .....169 K3
Nutmeg Cl CAN/RD E16 .....106 C3
Nutmeg La POP/IOD E14 .....106 B5
Nuttall St IS N1 .....7 H2
Nutter La WAN E11 .....71 G2
Nutt Gv EDGW HA8 .....29 K4
Nut Tree Cl ORP BR6 .....217 K1
Nutt St PECK SE15 .....143 G1
Nutwell St TOOT SW17 .....178 D1
Nuxley Rd BELV DA17 .....129 G6
Nyanza St WOOL/PLUM SE18 .....127 J6
Nylands Av RCH/KEW TW9 .....137 H3
Nymans Gdns RYNPK SW20 .....176 E6
Nynehead St NWCR SE14 .....144 B1
Nyon Gv FSTH SE23 .....164 C4
Nyssa Cl WFD IG8 .....53 K2

O

Oak Av CEND/HSY/T N8 .....66 E1
 CROY/NA CRO 198 D6
 ENC/FH EN2 .....23 F2
 HEST TW5 .....134 C1
 HPTN TW12 .....156 C1
 MUSWH N10 .....48 B3
 TOTM N17 .....49 K3
 WDR/YW UB7 .....112 D3
Oakbank CROY/NA CRO 214 A4
Oakbank Av WOT/HER KT12 .....188 E4
Oakbank Gv HNHL SE24 .....142 D5
Oakbrook Cl BMLY BR1 .....166 A6
Oak Cl DART DA1 .....150 A6
 STHGT/OAK N14 .....34 B2
Oakcombe Cl NWMAL KT3 .....176 B4
Oak Cottage Cl CAT SE6 .....165 H5
Oak Crs CAN/RD E16 .....106 C4
Oakcroft Cl PIN HA5 .....41 F5
Oakcroft Rd CHSGTN KT9 .....206 B2
 LEW SE13 .....145 G3
Oakcroft Vls CHSGTN KT9 .....206 B2
Oakdale STHGT/OAK N14 .....34 B3
Oakdale Av KTN/HRWW/W HA3 .....62 A2
 NTHWD HA6 .....40 E5
Oakdale Cl OXHEY WD19 .....27 G2
Oakdale Gdns CHING E4 .....52 A1
Oakdale Rd FSBYPK N4 .....67 J3
 FSTGT E7 .....89 F5
 NR/HE/WE KT19 .....207 F6
 OXHEY WD19 .....27 G2
 PECK SE15 .....143 K4
 STRHM/NOR SW16 .....179 K1
 SWFD E18 .....53 F5
 WAN E11 .....70 B6
Oakdale Wy MTCM CR4 .....195 F4
Oakdene Av CHST BR7 .....185 F1
 ERITH DA8 .....129 K6
 THDIT KT7 .....190 B5
Oakdene Cl PIN HA5 .....41 K5
Oak Dene Cl KNM RM1 * 75 K3
Oakdene Dr BRYLDS KT5 .....191 K5
Oakdene Ms CHEAM SM3 .....193 J5
Oakdene Pk FNCH N3 .....46 D3
Oakdene Rd STMC/STPC BR5 .....202 B3
Oakden St LBTH SE11 .....17 K6
Oaken Dr ESH/CLAY KT10 .....205 F4
Oaken La ESH/CLAY KT10 .....204 E2
Oakenshaw Cl SURB KT6 .....191 F4
Oakeshott Av HGT N6 .....66 A6
Oakey La STHWK SE1 .....17 J4
Oakfield CHING E4 .....51 K1
Oakfield Av KTN/HRWW/W HA3 .....43 H6
Oakfield Cl NWMAL KT3 .....192 C2
Oakfield Gdns BECK BR3 .....198 E2
 CAR SM5 .....194 D5
 GFD/PVL UB6 .....96 D3
 UED N18 .....36 A6
Oakfield La HAYES BR2 .....215 F6
 RDART DA2 .....170 D4
Oakfield Park Rd DART DA1 .....171 G4
Oakfield Pl DART DA1 .....171 G4
Oakfield Rd ASHF TW15 .....152 E6
 CROY/NA CRO 196 D6
 EHAM E6 .....89 J6
 FNCH N3 .....47 F4
 FSBYPK N4 .....67 G3
 IL IG1 .....90 B1
 PGE/AN SE20 .....181 J4
 STHGT/OAK N14 .....34 E4
 WALTH E17 .....51 G5
 WIM/MER SW19 .....159 G5
Oakfield St WBPTN SW10 .....120 B6
Oakford Rd KTTN NW5 .....84 C2
Oak Gdns CROY/NA CRO 198 D6
 EDGW HA8 .....44 E5
Oak Gv CRICK NW2 .....82 B2
 RSLP HA4 .....59 F5
 SUN TW16 .....172 A3
 WWKM BR4 .....199 F6
Oak Lodge Av CHIG IG7 .....54 D1

Oak Grove Rd PGE/AN SE20 .....181 K4
Oak Hall Rd WAN E11 .....71 F3
Oakham Cl CAT SE6 * 164 C4
Oakham Dr HAYES BR2 .....199 K1
Oakhampton Rd MLHL NW7 .....46 B4
Oakhill ESH/CLAY KT10 .....205 G4
Oak Hl SURB KT6 .....191 F4
 WFD IG8 .....52 B5
Oakhill Av HAMP NW3 .....83 F2
 PIN HA5 .....41 J5
Oak Hill Crs SURB KT6 .....191 F4
 WFD IG8 .....52 C5
Oak Hill Gdns WALTH E17 .....52 C4
Oak Hill Gv SURB KT6 .....191 F3
Oak Hill Pk HAMP NW3 .....83 F2
Oak Hill Park Ms HAMP NW3 .....83 G2
Oakhill Pl WAND/EARL SW18 .....139 K6
Oak Hill Rd SURB KT6 .....191 F3
Oakhill Rd BECK BR3 .....183 F5
 ORP BR6 .....202 A6
 PUT/ROE SW15 .....139 J6
 STRHM/NOR SW16 .....179 K4
 SUT SM1 .....209 F1
Oak Hill Wy HAMP NW3 .....83 G2
Oakhouse Rd BXLYHS DA6 .....149 H6
Oakhurst Av BXLYHN DA7 .....149 F1
 EBAR EN4 .....33 J2
Oakhurst Cl BARK/HLT IG6 .....54 C4
 CHST BR7 .....184 E4
 TEDD TW11 .....173 K1
 WALTH E17 .....70 C1
Oakhurst Gdns BXLYHN DA7 .....149 F1
 CHING E4 .....38 D5
 WALTH E17 .....70 C1
Oakhurst Gv EDUL SE22 .....143 H5
Oakhurst Rd HOR/WEW KT19 .....206 E4
Oakington Av HYS/HAR UB3 .....113 G4
 RYLN/HDSTN HA2 .....60 A1
 WBLY HA9 .....80 B1
Oakington Dr SUN TW16 .....172 B5
Oakington Manor Dr WBLY HA9 .....80 C3
Oakington Rd MV/WKIL W9 .....100 E3
Oakington Wy CEND/HSY/T N8 .....66 E3
Oakland Rd SRTFD E15 .....88 C2
Oaklands PLMGR N13 .....35 H4
Oaklands Av BFN/LL DA15 .....168 A2
 ED N9 .....36 D1
 ESH/CLAY KT10 .....189 J5
 ISLW TW7 .....116 A6
 OXHEY WD19 .....27 F3
 ROM RM1 .....57 G6
 THHTH CR7 .....196 B1
 WWKM BR4 .....213 K4
Oaklands Cl ALP/SUD HA0 .....80 A6
 BXLYHS DA6 .....149 G6
 CHSGTN KT9 .....205 J2
 STMC/STPC BR5 .....201 K3
Oaklands Ct NWMAL KT3 .....176 A6
Oaklands Gv SHB W12 .....118 D1
Oaklands Ms CRICK NW2 .....82 B2
Oaklands Park Av IL IG1 .....72 D6
Oaklands Pl CLAP SW4 .....141 J5
Oaklands Rd BMLY BR1 .....183 H3
 BXLYHS DA6 .....149 G5
 CRICK NW2 .....82 B2
 HNWL W7 .....116 A2
 MORT/ESHN SW14 .....138 A4
 TRDG/WHET N20 .....32 D2
Oakland Wy HOR/WEW KT19 .....207 F4
Oak La BFDCN N11 .....48 E1
 ISLW TW7 .....135 K5
 POP/IOD E14 .....105 H6
 TWK TW1 .....156 B2
 WFD IG8 .....38 D6
Oakleafe Gdns BARK/HLT IG6 .....54 B1
Oakleigh Av EDGW HA8 .....44 D5
 SURB KT6 .....191 H5
 TRDG/WHET N20 .....33 H3
Oakleigh Cl TRDG/WHET N20 .....33 J3
Oakleigh Crs EDGW HA8 * 44 E5
Oakleigh Crs TRDG/WHET N20 .....33 J4
Oakleigh Dr RKW/CH/CXG WD3 .....26 A4
Oakleigh Gdns EDGW HA8 .....44 B1
 ORP BR6 .....216 E2
 TRDG/WHET N20 .....33 G3
Oakleigh Ms TRDG/WHET N20 * 33 G3
Oakleigh Park Av CHST BR7 .....185 F5
Oakleigh Pk North
 TRDG/WHET N20 .....33 H3
Oakleigh Pk South
 TRDG/WHET N20 .....33 J3
Oakleigh Rd HGDN/ICK UB10 .....76 A3
 PIN HA5 .....41 K2
Oakleigh Rd North
 STHGT/OAK N14 .....34 B3
Oakleigh Rd South
 FBAR/BDGN N11 .....34 A6
Oakleigh Wy MTCM CR4 .....179 G4
 SURB KT6 .....191 H5
Oakley Av BARK IG11 .....91 F5
 CROY/NA CRO 210 E2
 EA W5 .....98 C6
Oakley Cl CHING E4 .....38 A5
 HNWL W7 .....96 E6
 ISLW TW7 .....135 J2
Oakley Ct MTCM CR4 * 195 F4
Oakley Crs FSBYE EC1V * 6 B3
Oakley Dr BFN/LL DA15 .....167 J4
 HAYES BR2 .....215 J1
 LEW SE13 .....165 G1
Oakley Gdns CEND/HSY/T N8 .....67 F2
 CHEL SW3 .....120 D6
Oakley Pk BFN/LL DA15 .....167 J3
Oakley Pl STHWK SE1 .....19 K8
Oakley Rd HAYES BR2 .....200 C3
 HRW HA1 .....60 E3
 IS N1 .....85 K5
 SNWD SE25 .....197 J2
Oakley Sq CAMTN NW1 .....4 B2
Oakley St CHEL SW3 .....120 D6
Oakley Yd BETH E2 * 7 K5

Oak Lodge Cl STAN HA7 .....43 J1
Oak Lodge Dr WWKM BR4 .....198 E4
Oakmead Av BMLY BR2 .....199 K3
Oakmeade PIN HA5 .....42 A2
Oakmead Gdns EDGW HA8 .....31 F4
Oakmead Pl MTCM CR4 .....178 D4
Oakmead Rd BAL SW12 .....161 G3
 CROY/NA CRO 195 J3
Oakmere Rd ABYW SE2 .....128 B6
Oakmoor Wy CHIG IG7 .....54 E1
Oakmore Gdns STMC/STPC BR5 .....202 D1
Oak Park Gdns WIM/MER SW19 .....159 G3
Oakridge Dr EFNCH N2 .....47 H6
Oakridge Rd BMLY BR1 .....165 H6
Oak Ri BKHH IG9 .....39 H5
Oak Rd EA W5 .....97 K6
 ERITH DA8 .....130 D2
 NWMAL KT3 .....176 A5
 ORP BR6 .....217 G5
Oak Rw MTCM CR4 .....179 H5
Oaks Av CRW RM5 .....56 E5
 FELT TW13 .....154 D1
 NRWD SE19 .....181 F1
 WPK KT4 .....207 K2
Oaksford Av SYD SE26 .....163 J5
Oaks Gv CHING E4 .....38 C4
Oakshade Rd BMLY BR1 .....165 G6
Oakshaw Rd
 WAND/EARL SW18 .....160 A2
Oaks La CROY/NA CRO 212 E1
 GNTH/NBYPK IG2 .....72 E2
Oaks Rd CROY/NA CRO 212 D3
 STWL/WRAY TW19 .....132 A6
The Oaks FELT TW13 .....154 D4
 HAYES BR2 * 199 H1
 MRDN SM4 .....193 H1
 NFNCH/WDSP N12 .....33 F6
 OXHEY WD19 .....27 G3
 RSLP HA4 .....58 B4
 SURB KT6 .....205 J1
 WFD IG8 .....52 B2
 WOOL/PLUM SE18 .....127 H5
 YEAD UB4 .....94 A1
Oak St ROMW/RG RM7 .....74 E2
Oaks Wy CAR SM5 .....209 K6
 SURB KT6 .....190 E6
Oakthorpe Rd PLMGR N13 .....49 G1
Oaktree Av PALMGR N13 .....35 C5
Oak Tree Cl STAN HA7 .....43 J3
 WEA W15 * 97 J5
Oak Tree Dell CDALE/KGS NW9 .....62 E2
Oak Tree Dr TRDG/WHET N20 .....33 F1
Oak Tree Gdns BMLY BR1 .....184 A1
Oaktree Gv IL IG1 .....90 D3
Oak Tree Rd STJWD NW8 .....2 B5
Oakview Gdns EFNCH N2 .....65 H1
Oakview Gv CROY/NA CRO 198 B5
Oakview Rd CAT SE6 .....182 E1
Oak Village HAMP NW3 .....84 A2
Oak Vls GLDGN NW11 * 64 D3
Oak Wy ACT W3 .....118 B1
 CROY/NA CRO 198 A3
 EBED/NFELT TW14 .....153 H3
 STHGT/OAK N14 .....34 B2
Oakway BMLY BR1 .....183 G1
 RYNPK SW20 .....193 F1
Oakway Cl BXLY DA5 .....169 F1
Oakways ELTH/MOT SE9 .....167 G1
Oakwood WLGTN SM6 .....210 B6
Oakwood Av BECK BR3 .....183 F5
 HAYES BR2 .....200 C1
 HOR/WEW KT19 .....206 C6
 MTCM CR4 .....178 C5
 STHGT/OAK N14 .....34 D2
 STHL UB1 .....96 A6
Oakwood Cl CHST BR7 .....184 E2
 STHGT/OAK N14 .....34 C1
 WFD IG8 .....53 J2
Oakwood Ct WKENS W14 .....119 J3
Oakwood Crs GFD/PVL UB6 .....79 G4
 WCHMH N21 .....34 E1
Oakwood Dr BXLYHN DA7 .....149 K5
 EDGW HA8 .....44 E3
 NRWD SE19 .....180 E2
Oakwood Gdns GDMY/SEVK IG3 .....73 F6
 ORP BR6 .....201 H6
 SUT SM1 .....193 K6
Oakwood La WKENS W14 .....119 J3
Oakwood Pk North * 34 E1
Oakwood Pl CROY/NA CRO 196 B3
Oakwood Rd CROY/NA CRO 196 B3
 GLDGN NW11 .....64 E2
 PIN HA5 .....41 F5
 RYNPK SW20 .....176 D4
Oakworth Rd NKENS W10 .....100 A4
Oarsman Pl E/WMO/HCT KT8 .....189 K1
Oast House Wy
 STMC/STPC BR5 .....202 C1
Oates Cl HAYES BR2 * 183 G6
Oates Rd CRW RM5 .....56 D1
Oatfield Rd ORP BR6 .....202 A5
Oatland Ri WALTH E17 .....51 G5
Oatlands Rd PEND EN3 .....24 E2
Oat La CITYW EC2V 12 C3
Oban Cl PLSTW E13 .....107 G3
Oban Rd PLSTW E13 .....107 G2
 SNWD SE25 .....196 E1
Oban St POP/IOD E14 .....106 B5
Oberstein Rd BTSEA SW11 .....140 C5
Oborne Cl HNHL SE24 .....162 C6
Observatory Rd
 MORT/ESHN SW14 .....137 K5
 SKENS SW7 .....14 B4
Occupation La EA W5 .....116 E4
 WOOL/PLUM SE18 .....147 G2
Occupation Rd WALW SE17 .....122 D5
 WEA W13 .....116 C2
Ocean Est WCHPL E1 .....105 F3

Ocean St WCHPL E1 ....105 F4
Ockendon Ms IS N1 * 85 K4
Ockendon Rd IS N1 ....85 K4
Ockham Dr STMC/STPC BR5 ....186 E5
Ockley Rd CROY/NA CR0 ....196 A4
STRHM/NOR SW16 ....161 K6
Octagon Ar LVPST EC2M * 13 G2
Octavia CR MTCM CR4 ....194 D2
Octavia Ms CRICK NW2 ....81 K4
Octavia Rd IS N1 * 81 K4
Octavia St BTSEA SW11 ....140 D2
Octavius St DEPT SE8 ....144 D1
October PI HDN NW4 * 46 B6
Odard Rd E/WMO/HCT KT8 ....189 F1
Odeon Pde ELTH/MOT SE9 * 146 D5
GFD/PVL UB6 ....79 H4
HOLWY N7 * 84 E1
ISLW TW7 * 135 K3
Odessa Rd FSTGT E7 ....88 D2
WLSDN NW10 ....99 J1
Odessa St BERM/RHTH SE16 ....124 C3
Odger St BTSEA SW11 ....140 E3
Odhams Wk LSO/SEVD WC2H * 10 E4
Odsey Vls FSBYPK N4 * 67 G5
Offa's Md HOM E9 ....87 G2
Offenham Rd ELTH/MOT SE9 ....166 E6
Offerton Rd CLAP SW4 ....141 H4
Offham Slope
NFNCH/WDSP N12 ....46 D1
Offley Rd BRXN/ST SW9 ....142 B1
Offord CI TOTM N17 ....50 C3
Offord Rd IS N1 ....85 G5
Offord St IS N1 ....85 F5
Ogilby St WOOL/PLUM SE18 ....126 E4
Oglander Rd PECK SE15 ....143 G5
Ogle St GTPST W1W 10 A1
Oglethorpe Rd DAGE RM10 ....92 B1
Ohio Rd PLSTW E13 ....106 D3
Oil Mill La HMSMTH W6 ....118 D5
Okeburn Rd TOOT SW17 ....179 F1
Okehampton Crs WELL DA16 ....148 C2
Okehampton Rd WLSDN NW10 ....82 A6
Olaf St NTGHL W11 ....100 B6
Old Bailey STP EC4M 12 B4
Old Barn CI BELMT SM2 ....208 C5
Old Barn Wy BXLYHN DA7 ....150 A5
Old Barrack Yd KTBR SW1X 15 G2
Oldberry Rd EDGW HA8 ....45 F2
Old Bethnal Green Rd
BETH E2 ....104 D2
Old Bexley La BXLY DA5 ....170 B4
Old Bond St CONDST W1S 10 A6
Oldborough Rd ALP/SUD HA0 ....61 J6
Old Brewery Ms HAMP NW3 ....83 H2
Old Bridge CI NTHLT UB5 ....96 A1
Old Bridge St KUT/HW KT1 ....174 E5
Old Broad St LVPST EC2M 13 G3
Old Bromley Rd BMLY BR1 ....183 G1
Old Brompton Rd ECT SW5 ....119 K5
Old Bldg LINN WC2A 11 J5
Old Burlington St CONDST W1S 10 A6
Oldbury CI STMC/STPC BR5 ....202 E1
Oldbury PI MHST W1U 9 H1
Oldbury Rd EN EN1 ....24 C3
Old Castle St WCHPL E1 ....13 J3
Old Cavendish St
CAVSQ/HST W1G 9 J3
Old Chapel Rd SWLY BR8 ....203 K4
Old Chestnut Av
ESH/CLAY KT10 ....204 A4
Old Church La
CDALE/KGS NW9 ....62 E6
GFD/PVL UB6 ....97 G2
STAN HA7 ....43 J2
Old Church Pth
ESH/CLAY KT10 ....204 B2
Oldchurch Ri ROMW/RG RM7 ....75 G3
Old Church La CHING E4 ....37 J5
WCHPL E1 * 105 F5
Oldchurch Rd ROMW/RG RM7 ....75 G5
Old Church St CHEL SW3 ....120 C6
Old Claygate La
ESH/CLAY KT10 ....205 G4
Old Compton St
SOHO/SHAV W1D 10 C5
Old Cote Dr HEST TW5 ....115 F6
Old Court PI KENS W8 ....120 A2
The Old Ctyd BMLY BR1 ....184 A4
Old Dairy Ms BAL SW12 ....161 F3
KTTN NW5 * 84 B4
Old Deer Pk RCH/KEW TW9 ....137 G4
Old Deer Park Gdns
RCH/KEW TW9 ....137 F4
Old Devonshire Rd BAL SW12 ....161 G2
Old Dock CI RCH/KEW TW9 ....117 H6
Old Dover Rd BKHTH/KID SE3 ....145 K1
Old Farm Av BFN/LL DA15 ....167 J3
STHGT/OAK N14 ....34 C4
Old Farm CI HSLW TW3 ....134 E5
Old Farm Rd EFNCH N2 ....47 H4
HPTN TW12 ....172 E2
WDR/YW UB7 ....112 A2
Old Farm Rd East
BFN/LL DA15 ....168 B4
Old Farm Rd West
BFN/LL DA15 ....168 A4
Oldfield Farm Gdns
GFD/PVL UB6 ....78 D6
Oldfield Gv DEPT SE8 ....124 A4
Oldfield La North GFD/PVL UB6 ....78 D1
Oldfield La South GFD/PVL UB6 ....96 C2
Oldfield Ms HGT N6 ....66 C4
Oldfield Rd ACT W3 ....118 C2
BMLY BR1 ....200 E1
BXLYHN DA7 ....149 F3
HPTN TW12 ....173 F4
STNW/STAM N16 ....86 A1
WIM/MER SW19 ....177 H2
WLSDN NW10 ....81 H5
Oldfields Circ NTHLT UB5 ....78 E4
Oldfields Rd SUT SM1 ....193 K6
Old Fish Street HI BLKFR EC4V * 12 C5

Old Fleet La STP EC4M 12 A3
Old Fold CI BAR EN5 * 20 D2
Old Fold La BAR EN5 ....20 D2
Old Fold Rd BAR EN5 ....20 A4
Old Ford Lock SRTFD E15 * 87 F3
Old Ford Rd BETH E2 ....104 E1
BOW E3 ....87 H6
Old Forge CI STAN HA7 ....29 G6
Old Forge Rd ARCH N19 ....66 D6
EN EN1 ....24 B1
Old Forge Wy SCUP DA14 ....168 C6
Old Gannon CI NTHWD HA6 ....26 A6
Old Gloucester St BMSBY WC1N 11 F1
Old Hall CI PIN HA5 ....41 J4
Old Hall Dr PIN HA5 ....41 J4
Oldham Ter ACT W3 ....117 K1
Old Hill CHST BR7 ....185 F4
ORP BR6 ....216 D4
Oldhill St STNW/STAM N16 ....68 C5
Old Homesdale Rd HAYES BR2 ....200 B1
Old Hospital CI TOOT SW17 ....160 E3
Old House CI WIM/MER SW19 ....177 H1
Old House Gdns TWK TW1 * 156 D1
Old Howlett's La RSLP HA4 * 58 B5
Old Jamaica Rd STHWK SE1 ....123 H3
Old James St PECK SE15 ....143 J4
Old Jewry LOTH EC2R * 12 E4
Old Kenton La CDALE/KGS NW9 ....62 D2
Old Kent Rd STHWK SE1 ....123 F5
Old Kingston Rd WPK KT4 ....206 E1
Old Lodge Wy STAN HA7 ....43 G1
Old London Rd KUT/HW KT1 ....175 F5
Old Maidstone Rd SCUP DA14 ....187 G3
Old Malden La WPK KT4 ....192 B6
Old Manor Dr ISLW TW7 ....155 H1
Old Manor Wy BXLYHN DA7 ....150 A3
ELTH/MOT SE9 ....146 A6
Old Manor Yd ECT SW5 * 120 A4
Old Market Sq BETH E2 * 7 J4
Old Marylebone Rd CAMTN NW1 * 8 D2
Old Mill Ct SWFD E18 ....53 G6
Old Mill Rd WOOL/PLUM SE18 ....127 J6
Old Mitre Ct EMB EC4Y * 11 K4
Old Montague St WCHPL E1 ....104 C4
Old Nichol St BETH E2 ....7 J6
Old North St FSBYW WC1X * 11 G1
Old Oak Common La
ACTN W3 ....99 G3
Old Oak La WLSDN NW10 ....99 H2
Old Oak Rd ACT W3 ....99 H6
Old Orch SUN TW16 ....172 B5
The Old Orch HAMP NW3 * 83 K2
Old Palace Rd CROY/NA CR0 ....211 J1
Old Palace Yd RCH/KEW TW9 ....136 D6
Old Paradise St LBTH SE11 ....17 G6
Old Park Av BAL SW12 ....161 F1
ENC/FH EN2 ....23 J5
Old Park Gv WCHMH N21 ....35 H3
Old Park La MYFR/PICC W1J 15 H1
Old Park Ms HEST TW5 ....114 E6
Old Park Ridings WCHMH N21 ....35 H1
Old Park Rd ABYW SE2 ....128 B5
ENC/FH EN2 ....23 G5
PLMGR N13 ....35 F5
Old Park Road South ENC/FH EN2 ....23 H5
Old Park Vw ENC/FH EN2 ....23 G4
Old Perry St CHST BR7 ....185 K3
Old Post Office La
BKHTH/KID SE3 ....146 A4
Old Pound CI ISLW TW7 ....136 B2
Old Pye St WEST SW1P 16 C4
Old Quebec St MBLAR W1H 9 F4
Old Queen St STJSPK SW1H 16 D3
Old Rectory Gdns EDGW HA8 ....44 C2
Old Redding
KTN/HRWW/W HA3 ....42 B1
Oldridge Rd BAL SW12 ....161 F2
Old Rd DART DA1 ....150 A5
LEW SE13 ....145 H5
PEND EN3 ....24 E2
Old Royal Free Sq IS N1 * 95 H1
Old Ruislip Rd NTHLT UB5 ....95 H1
Old's App WATW WD18 ....26 A3
Old School CI BECK BR3 ....182 A5
Old School Crs FSTGT E7 ....88 E4
Old School PI CROY/NA CR0 ....211 G2
Old Schools La EW KT17 ....207 H6
Old School Sq THDIT KT7 ....190 A3
Old School Ter CHEAM SM3 * 208 B5
Old Seacoal La STP EC4M * 12 A4
Old South CI PIN HA5 ....41 H4
Old South Lambeth Rd
VX/NE SW8 * 141 K1
Old Sq LINN WC2A 11 H3
Old Stable Ms HBRY N5 * 85 J1
Old Station Gdns TEDD TW11 * 174 B2
Old Station Rd HYS/HAR UB3 ....113 J3
Old Stockley Rd WDR/YW UB7 ....112 E2
Old St FSBYE EC1V 6 C6
PLSTW E13 ....107 F1
STLK EC1Y 6 E7
Old Swan Yd CAR SM5 ....209 K2
Old Town CLAP SW4 ....141 H5
CROY/NA CR0 ....211 H1
Old Tramyard
WOOL/PLUM SE18 ....127 K4
Old Woolwich Rd
GNWCH SE10 ....125 G6
Old York Rd WAND/EARL SW18 ....140 A6
Oleander CI ORP BR6 ....216 D3
O'Leary sq WCHPL E1 ....104 E4
Olga St BOW E3 ....105 G1
Olinda Rd STNW/STAM N16 ....68 B3
Oliphant St NKENS W10 ....100 C3
Olive Gv SEVS/STOTM N15 ....67 J1
Oliver Av SNWD SE25 ....181 G6
Oliver CI CHSWK W4 ....117 J6
Oliver Gdns EHAM E6 ....107 J5
Oliver Gv SNWD SE25 ....197 G1
Oliver Ms PECK SE15 ....143 H3
Olive Rd CRICK NW2 ....82 A2
DART DA1 ....171 G3
EA W5 ....116 E3
PLSTW E13 ....107 G2
WIM/MER SW19 * 178 B3

Oliver Rd LEY E10 ....69 K6
NWMAL KT3 ....175 K5
RAIN RM13 ....93 H6
SWLY BR8 ....187 J3
WALTH E17 ....209 H2
Oliver's Yd STLK EC1Y 70 A2
Olive St ROMW/RG RM7 ....75 F2
Ollerton Gn BOW E3 ....87 H6
Ollerton Rd FBAR/BDGN N11 ....48 D1
Olley CI WLGTN SM6 ....210 E5
Oligar CI ACT W3 ....98 B2
Oliffe St POP/IOD E14 ....125 F3
Olmar St STHWK SE1 ....123 H6
Olney Rd WALW SE17 ....122 D6
Olron Crs BXLYHS DA6 ....148 E6
Olven Rd WOOL/PLUM SE18 ....147 H1
Olveston Wk BRXN/ST SW9 ....194 C3
Olwen Ms PIN HA5 ....41 H5
Olyffe Av WELL DA16 ....148 B3
Olyffe Dr BECK BR3 ....183 F4
Olympia Wy WKENS W14 ....119 H3
Olympic Wy GFD/PVL UB6 ....78 B6
WBLY HA9 ....80 C2
Olympus Sq CLPT E5 ....86 C1
Oman Av CRICK NW2 ....82 A3
O'Meara St STHWK SE1 ....18 D1
Omega PI IS N1 ....5 F3
Omega St NWCR SE14 ....144 C2
Ommaney Rd NWCR SE14 ....144 A2
Omnibus Wy WALTH E17 ....51 J5
Ondine Rd EDUL SE22 ....143 G5
Onega Ga BERM/RHTH SE16 ....124 B3
One Tree CI FSTH SE23 ....163 K1
Ongar CI CHDH RM6 ....73 J2
Ongar Rd FUL/PGN SW6 ....119 K6
Ongar Wy RAIN RM13 ....93 G6
Onra Rd WALTH E17 ....69 J4
Onslow Av RCHPK/HAM TW10 ....137 F6
Onslow Av CI CHING E4 ....38 B4
MV/WKIL W9 ....100 D2
Onslow Ct DART DA1 * 151 J5
SKENS SW7 * 14 B7
Onslow Dr SCUP DA14 ....168 E5
Onslow Gdns MUSWH N10 ....66 B2
SWFD E18 ....53 F3
THDIT KT7 ....189 K5
WCHMH N21 ....23 G6
WLGTN SM6 ....210 C5
Onslow Ms East SKENS SW7 ....14 A7
Onslow Ms West SKENS SW7 ....14 A7
Onslow Pde STHGT/OAK N14 * 34 B3
NWMAL KT3 ....192 D1
RCHPK/HAM TW10 ....157 F1
Onslow Rd CROY/NA CR0 ....196 B4
NWMAL KT3 ....192 D1
Onslow Sq SKENS SW7 ....14 B7
Onslow St FARR EC1M 5 K7
Onslow Wy THDIT KT7 ....189 K5
Ontario St STHWK SE1 ....18 B5
Ontario Wy POP/IOD E14 ....105 J6
On the HI OXHEY WD19 ....27 J3
Onyx Ms SRTFD E15 * 88 C4
Opal CI CAN/RD E16 ....107 H5
Opal St LBTH SE11 ....18 A7
Openshaw Rd ABYW SE2 ....128 C5
Openview WAND/EARL SW18 ....160 B3
Ophir Ter PECK SE15 ....143 H2
Opossum Wy HSLWW TW4 ....134 B4
Oppenheim Rd LEW SE13 ....145 F3
Oppidans Rd HAMP NW3 ....83 K5
Optima Pk DART DA1 * 150 D4
Orange Court La ORP BR6 ....216 A6
Orange Gv CHIG IG7 ....54 C2
WAN E11 ....88 C1
Orange Hill Rd EDGW HA8 ....44 E3
Orange PI BERM/RHTH SE16 ....123 K3
Orangery La ELTH/MOT SE9 ....146 E6
The Orangery
RCHPK/HAM TW10 ....156 D4
Orange St LSQ/SEVD WC2H 10 D6
WAP E1W * 123 H1
Orange Tree HI ROM RM1 ....57 F1
Oransay Rd IS N1 ....85 J4
Oratory La CHEL SW3 * 120 C5
Orbain Rd FUL/PGN SW6 ....139 H1
Orb St WALW SE17 ....18 E7
Orchard Av BELV DA17 ....129 G6
CROY/NA CR0 ....198 B6
DART DA1 ....170 E2
EBED/NFELT TW14 ....133 H6
FNCH N3 ....46 E6
HEST TW5 ....134 D1
MTCM CR4 ....195 F5
NWMAL KT3 ....176 B5
RSLP HA4 ....58 A4
STHGT/OAK N14 ....34 C1
STHL UB1 ....114 E1
THDIT KT7 ....190 B5
TRDG/WHET N20 ....33 H4
Orchard CI ALP/SUD HA0 ....80 A6
BXLYHN DA7 ....149 F2
CHING E4 ....37 J6
CRICK NW2 ....81 J1
EDGW HA8 ....44 A2
FSTH SE23 ....163 K1
HOR/WEW KT19 ....206 D4
NKENS W10 ....100 C4
RSLP HA4 ....58 A4
RYNPK SW20 ....193 H2
WOT/HER KT12 ....188 A4
Orchard Crs EDGW HA8 ....44 E1
EN EN1 ....24 B2
Orchard Dr BKHTH/KID SE3 ....145 H3
EDGW HA8 ....44 A1
KTN/HRWW/W HA3 ....42 B2

ORP BR6 ....202 A6
PGE/AN SE20 ....181 H3
Orchard HI DART DA1 ....150 B6
LEW SE13 ....144 E3
Orchard La E/WMO/HCT KT8 ....189 J1
RYNPK SW20 ....176 E4
WFD IG8 ....39 G6
Orchardleigh Av PEND EN3 ....24 E3
Orchardmede EN 35 K1
Orchard Ms IS N1 ....85 K5
Orchard PI POP/IOD E14 ....106 C6
STMC/STPC BR5 ....186 D6
TOTM N17 ....50 B3
Orchard Ri CROY/NA CR0 ....198 B5
KUTN/CMB KT2 ....175 K4
RCHPK/HAM TW10 ....137 J5
RSLP HA4 ....40 D6
Orchard Ri East BFN/LL DA15 ....147 K6
Orchard Ri West BFN/LL DA15 ....147 K6
Orchard Rd BAR EN5 ....20 C5
BELV DA17 ....129 H4
BMLY BR1 ....184 B4
BTFD TW8 ....116 C6
CHSGTN KT9 ....206 A2
DAGE RM10 ....92 C6
HGT N6 ....66 B4
HPTN TW12 ....172 E3
HSLWW TW4 ....134 E6
HYS/HAR UB3 ....94 E5
KUT/HW KT1 ....175 F5
ORP BR6 ....216 B3
ORP BR6 ....217 J6
PEND EN3 ....24 E6
RCH/KEW TW9 ....137 H4
ROMW/RG RM7 ....56 D5
SCUP DA14 ....168 A5
SUN TW16 ....172 A5
SUT SM1 ....208 E3
TWK TW1 ....156 C4
WELL DA16 ....148 C4
Orchardson St STJWD NW8 ....2 B7
Orchard Sq WDGN N22 ....49 H5
Orchard St DART DA1 ....171 H1
MBLAR W1H 9 G4
WALTH E17 ....51 F6
Orchard Ter EN EN1 * 36 C1
The Orchard BKHTH/KID SE3 ....145 G3
CHSWK W4 ....118 A4
EW KT17 ....207 H5
GLDGN NW11 ....64 E2
WCHMH N21 ....35 K1
Orchard Vls SCUP DA14 * 186 E2
Orchard Wy ASHF TW15 ....152 C4
CROY/NA CR0 ....198 B4
EN EN1 ....24 A4
ESH/CLAY KT10 ....204 C4
RDART DA2 ....171 G5
SUT SM1 ....209 G2
Orchid CI CHSGTN KT9 ....205 J5
STHL UB1 ....95 J5
Orchid Gdns HSLW TW3 ....134 E5
Orchid Rd STHGT/OAK N14 ....34 C2
Orchid St SHB W12 ....99 J6
Orde Hall St BMSBY WC1N * 11 F1
Ordell Rd BOW E3 ....105 H1
Ordnance CI FELT TW13 ....153 K4
Ordnance Crs GNWCH SE10 ....125 H2
Ordnance Ms STJWD NW8 ....2 B2
Ordnance Rd CAN/RD E16 ....106 D4
WOOL/PLUM SE18 ....127 F6
Oregon Av MNPK E12 ....89 K2
Oregon CI NWMAL KT3 ....191 K1
Oregon Sq ORP BR6 ....201 J5
Orestes Ms KIL/WHAMP NW6 * 82 E3
Orford Gdns TWK TW1 ....156 A4
Orford Rd CAT SE6 ....164 E5
SWFD E18 ....53 F6
WALTH E17 ....69 J2
Oriel CI MTCM CR4 ....195 J1
Oriel Ct HAMP NW3 ....83 G2
Oriel Dr BARN SW13 ....119 F6
Oriel Gdns CLAY IG5 ....53 K6
Oriel Rd HOM E9 ....87 F4
Oriel Wy NTHLT UB5 ....78 B5
Oriental Rd CAN/RD E16 ....126 C1
Orient St LBTH SE11 ....18 A6
Orient Wy CLPT E5 ....87 F1
LEY E10 ....69 G6
Oriole Wy THMD SE28 ....109 H6
Orion Rd MUSWH N10 ....48 A2
Orion Wy NTHWD HA6 ....26 D6
Orissa Rd WOOL/PLUM SE18 ....127 K5
Orkney St BTSEA SW11 ....141 F3
Orlando Rd CLAP SW4 ....141 H4
Orleans CI ESH/CLAY KT10 ....189 K6
Orleans Rd NRWD SE19 ....180 E2
TWK TW1 ....156 C2
Orleston Ms HOLWY N7 ....85 G4
Orleston Rd HOLWY N7 ....85 G4
Orley Farm Rd HRW HA1 ....78 E1
Ormanton Rd SYD SE26 ....163 H6
Orme Ct BAY/PAD W2 ....101 F6
Ormeley Rd BAL SW12 ....161 G2
Orme Rd KUT/HW KT1 ....175 J5
SUT SM1 ....209 F4
Ormerod Gdns MTCM CR4 ....179 F5
Ormesby CI THMD SE28 ....109 K6

Ormonde Rd
MORT/ESHN SW14 ....137 J4
NTHWD HA6 ....26 B6
Ormonde Ter STJWD NW8 ....2 E1
Ormond Av HPTN TW12 ....173 F4
RCHPK/HAM TW10 ....156 E6
Ormond CI BMSBY WC1N * 11 F2
Ormond Yd STJS SW1Y 10 B7
Ormsby BELMT SM2 * 209 F5
Ormsby Gdns GFD/PVL UB6 ....96 C1
Ormsby PI STNW/STAM N16 ....68 B2
Ormsby St BETH E2 ....7 J2
Ormside St PECK SE15 ....123 K6
Ormskirk Rd OXHEY WD19 ....27 H5
Ornan Rd HAMP NW3 ....83 J3
Oronsay Wk IS N1 * 85 J4
Orpheus St CMBW SE5 ....142 E2
Orpington Gdns ED N9 ....36 A5
Orpington Rd CHST BR7 ....185 K6
WCHMH N21 ....35 G3
Orpwood CI HPTN TW12 ....172 E2
Orsett Ms BAY/PAD W2 * 101 G5
Orsett St LBTH SE11 ....122 A5
Orsett Ter BAY/PAD W2 ....101 G5
WFD IG8 ....53 G4
Orsman Rd IS N1 * 7 H1
Orton St WAP E1W * 123 H1
Orville Rd BTSEA SW11 ....140 C3
Orwell CI HYS/HAR UB3 ....94 C6
Orwell Rd PLSTW E13 ....107 G1
Osbaldeston Rd
STNW/STAM N16 ....68 C6
Osberton Rd LEE/GVPK SE12 ....145 K6
Osbert St WEST SW1P 16 C7
Osborn CI HACK E8 ....86 C6
Osborne Av STWL/WRAY TW19 ....152 B3
Osborne CI BECK BR3 ....198 B1
EBAR EN4 ....21 K4
EMPK RM11 ....75 K3
FELT TW13 ....172 C1
Osborne Ct EA W5 * 98 A4
Osborne Gdns THHTH CR7 ....180 D5
Osborne Gv WALTH E17 ....69 J1
Osborne Rd ACT W3 ....117 J2
BELV DA17 ....129 G5
BKHH IG9 ....39 F3
CRICK NW2 ....81 K4
EMPK RM11 ....75 K3
FSBYPK N4 ....67 G5
FSTGT E7 ....89 F3
HOM E9 ....87 H4
HSLW TW3 ....134 E4
KUTN/CMB KT2 ....175 F3
LEY E10 ....87 K1
PEND EN3 ....25 F2
PLMGR N13 ....35 G5
STHL UB1 ....96 D6
THHTH CR7 ....180 D5
Osborne Ter TOOT SW17 * 179 F1
Osborn Gdns MLHL NW7 ....46 B3
Osborn La FSTH SE23 ....164 B2
Osborn St WCHPL E1 ....13 K2
Osborn Ter BKHTH/KID SE3 ....145 J5
Osbourne Ct
RYLN/HDSTN HA2 * 60 B1
Oscar Faber PI IS N1 * 86 A5
Oscar St DEPT SE8 ....144 D3
Oseney Crs KTTN NW5 ....84 C4
Osgood Av ORP BR6 ....217 F3
Osgood Gdns ORP BR6 ....217 F3
O'shea Gv BOW E3 ....87 H6
Osier La STHGT/OAK N14 ....34 A3
Osier Crs MUSWH N10 ....47 K4
Osiers Rd WAND/EARL SW18 ....139 K5
Osier St WCHPL E1 ....104 E3
Osier Wy LEY E10 ....87 K1
MTCM CR4 ....194 D2
Oslac Rd CAT SE6 ....182 E1
Osman Rd ED N9 ....36 C5
HMSMTH W6 * 119 F3
Osmond CI RYLN/HDSTN HA2 ....60 C6
Osmond Gdns WLGTN SM6 ....210 C3
Osmund St SHB W12 ....99 H5
Osnaburgh St CAMTN NW1 ....3 K6
Osnaburgh Ter CAMTN NW1 ....3 K7
Osney Wk MRDN SM4 ....194 C5
Osprey CI EHAM E6 ....107 J4
HAYES BR2 ....200 D5
SWFD E18 ....70 E1
WALTH E17 ....51 G4
WDR/YW UB7 ....112 B1
Osprey Est BERM/RHTH SE16 ....124 A4
Osprey Ms PEND EN3 ....24 D6
Ospringe CI PGE/AN SE20 ....181 K3
Ospringe Rd KTTN NW5 ....84 C2
Osram Rd WBLY HA9 ....79 K1
Ossian Rd FSBYPK N4 ....67 F4
Ossington Bldgs MHST W1U * 9 G1
Ossington CI BAY/PAD W2 * 100 E6
Ossington St BAY/PAD W2 ....101 F6
Ossory Rd STHWK SE1 ....123 H6
Ossulston St CAMTN NW1 ....4 C3
Ossulton PI EFNCH N2 * 47 G6
Ossulton Wy EFNCH N2 ....65 G1
Ostade Rd BRXS/STRHM SW2 ....162 A2
Ostell Crs PEND EN3 ....24 E1
Osten Ms SKENS SW7 * 120 A3
Osterberg Rd DART DA1 ....151 J5
Osterley Av ISLW TW7 ....135 J1
Osterley CI STMC/STPC BR5 ....186 C4
Osterley Crs ISLW TW7 ....135 K2
Osterley Gdns THHTH CR7 ....180 D5
Osterley La ISLW TW7 ....115 K6
Osterley Park Rd NWDGN UB2 ....114 E3
Osterley Park Vw Rd
HNWL W7 ....115 K2
Osterley Rd ISLW TW7 ....135 K1
STNW/STAM N16 ....86 A2
Oster Ter WALTH E17 * 69 F1
Ostliffe Rd PLMGR N13 ....49 H1
Oswald Rd STHL UB1 ....114 D1
Oswald's Md CLPT E5 ....87 G2
Oswald St CLPT E5 ....87 F1
Oswald Ter CRICK NW2 * 82 A1
Oswald CROY/NA CR0 * 213 H6
Osward PI ED N9 ....36 D4

Osward Rd BAL SW12 ...160 E4
Oswin St LBTH SE11 ...18 B6
Oswyth Rd CMBW SE5 ...143 F5
Otford Cl BMLY BR1 ...185 F6
  BXLY DA5 ...169 J1
  PGE/AN SE20 ...181 K4
Otford Crs BROCKY SE4 ...164 C1
Othello Cl LBTH SE11 ...122 C5
Otis St BOW E3 ...106 A2
Otley Dr GNTH/NBYPK IG2 ...72 B3
Otley Rd CAN/RD E16 ...107 G5
Otley Ter CLPT E5 ...68 E6
Otley Wy OXHEY WD19 ...27 G5
Otlinge Rd STMC/STPC BR5 ...202 E1
Ottawa Gdns DAGE RM10 ...93 F5
Ottaway St CLPT E5 ...86 C1
Otterbourne Rd CHING E4 ...38 B5
  CROY/NA CRO ...196 D6
Otterburn Gdns ISLW TW7 ...136 B1
Otterburn St TOOT SW17 ...178 E2
Otterden Cl ORP BR6 ...216 C2
Otterden St CAT SE6 ...164 D6
Otter Rd GFD/PVL UB6 ...96 C3
Oulton Cl THMD SE28 ...109 J5
Oulton Crs BARK IG11 ...91 F4
Oulton Wy OXHEY WD19 ...27 K2
Oundle Av BUSH WD23 ...28 C1
Ouseley Rd BAL SW12 ...160 E3
Outer Cir CAMTN NW1 ...3 J2
Outgate Rd WLSDN NW10 ...81 H5
Outram Pl IS N1 ...84 E6
Outram Rd CROY/NA CRO ...197 G6
  EHAM E6 ...89 J6
  WDGN N22 ...48 D4
Outwich St HDTCH EC3A * ...13 H3
Oval Cl EDGW HA8 * ...44 E3
Oval Pl VX/NE SW8 ...142 A1
Oval Rd CAMTN NW1 ...84 B6
  CROY/NA CRO ...196 E6
Oval Rd North DAGE RM10 ...92 E6
Oval Rd South DAGE RM10 ...110 E1
The Oval BETH E2 ...104 D1
  BFN/LL DA15 ...168 B2
Oval Wy LBTH SE11 ...122 A5
Overbrae BECK BR3 ...182 D2
Overbrook Wk EDGW HA8 ...44 C3
Overbury Av BECK BR3 ...182 E6
Overbury Rd SEVS/STOTM N15 ...67 K3
Overbury St CLPT E5 ...87 F2
Overcliff Rd LEW SE13 ...144 D4
Overcourt Cl BFN/LL DA15 ...168 C1
Overdale Av NWMAL KT3 ...175 K5
Overdale Rd EA W5 ...116 D3
Overdown Rd CAT SE6 ...164 D6
Overhill Rd EDUL SE22 ...163 H2
  PUR/KEN CR8 ...211 G6
Overhill Wy BECK BR3 ...199 G2
Overlea Rd CLPT E5 ...68 C4
Overstand Cl BECK BR3 ...182 D1
Overstone Gdns CROY/NA CRO ...198 C4
Overstone Rd HMSMTH W6 ...119 F4
Overton Cl ISLW TW7 ...136 A2
  WLSDN NW10 ...80 E4
Overton Dr CHDH RM6 ...73 J4
  WAN E11 ...71 F4
Overton Rd ABYW SE2 ...128 D3
  BELMT SM2 ...208 E5
  BRXN/ST SW9 ...142 B3
  LEY E10 ...69 G5
  STHGT/OAK N14 ...22 D4
Overton's Yd CROY/NA CRO ...211 J1
Overy Liberty DART DA1 ...171 H2
Overy St DART DA1 ...171 J1
Ovesdon Av RYLN/HDSTN HA2 ...59 K5
Ovett Cl NRWD SE19 ...181 F2
Ovex Cl POP/IOD E14 ...125 F3
Ovington Gdns CHEL SW3 ...14 D5
Ovington Ms CHEL SW3 ...14 D5
Ovington Sq CHEL SW3 ...14 D5
Ovington St CHEL SW3 ...14 D5
Owen Cl CROY/NA CRO ...196 E5
  CRW RM5 ...56 C2
  HYS/HAR UB3 ...94 D6
  NTHLT UB5 * ...78 A4
  THMD SE28 ...128 D1
Owen Gdns WFD IG8 ...53 J2
Owenite St ABYW SE2 ...128 C4
Owen Rd HAYES BR2 ...200 C1
  PLMGR N13 ...49 J1
Owens Ms WAN E11 ...70 C6
Owen's Rw FSBYE EC1V ...6 A4
Owen St FSBYE EC1V ...5 K3
Owens Wy FSTH SE23 ...164 B2
Owen Wk PGE/AN SE20 ...181 H3
Owen Wy WLSDN NW10 ...80 E4
Owgan Cl CMBW SE5 ...142 E1
Oxberry Av FUL/PGN SW6 ...139 H3
Oxendon Wood Rd ORP BR6 ...217 H4
Oxendon St SOHO/SHAV W1D * ...10 C6
Oxenford St PECK SE15 ...143 G4
Oxenpark Av WBLY HA9 ...62 A4
Oxestalls Rd DEPT SE8 ...124 B5
Oxford Av HEST TW5 ...115 F5
  HYS/HAR UB3 ...133 J1
  RYNPK SW20 ...177 H5
  STHGT/OAK N14 ...34 C2
Oxford Cl ED N9 ...36 D4
  MTCM CR4 ...179 H6
  NTHWD HA6 ...26 A6
Oxford Ct MANHO EC4N ...12 E5
Oxford Crs NWMAL KT3 ...192 A3
Oxford Dr RSLP HA4 ...59 C6
Oxford Gdns CHSWK W4 ...117 H5
  NKENS W10 ...100 B5
  TRDG/WHET N20 ...33 H4
  WCHMH N21 ...35 J2
Oxford Ga HMSMTH W6 ...119 G4
Oxford Ms BXLY DA5 ...169 H3
Oxford Rd CAR SM5 ...209 J4
  EA W5 ...97 K6
  ED N9 ...36 D4

FSBYPK N4 ...67 G5
HPTN TW12 ...173 J1
HRW HA1 ...60 C3
IL IG1 ...90 C2
KIL/WHAMP NW6 ...100 E1
KTN/HRWW/W HA3 ...43 F6
NRWD SE19 ...180 E2
PEND EN3 ...24 D6
PUT/ROE SW15 ...139 H5
SCUP DA14 ...186 C1
SRTFD E15 ...88 B4
WFD IG8 ...53 H1
WLGTN SM6 * ...210 C3
Oxford Rd North CHSWK W4 ...117 J5
Oxford Rd South CHSWK W4 ...117 J5
Oxford Sq BAY/PAD W2 ...8 D4
Oxford Rw SUN TW16 * ...172 B6
Oxford Sq MYFR/PKLN W1K ...9 G4
  SOHO/CST W1F ...10 C5
Oxford Wk STHL UB1 ...114 E1
Oxford Wy FELT TW13 ...154 C6
Oxgate Court Pde CRICK NW2 * ...63 K6
Oxgate Gdns CRICK NW2 ...81 K1
Oxgate La CRICK NW2 ...63 K6
Oxhawth Crs HAYES BR2 ...201 C5
Oxhey Av OXHEY WD19 ...27 H3
Oxhey Dr OXHEY WD19 ...27 F6
Oxhey Dr South OXHEY WD19 ...41 F1
Oxhey La OXHEY WD19 ...27 H2
  PIN HA5 ...42 B2
Oxhey Ridge Cl OXHEY WD19 ...40 E1
Oxhey Rd OXHEY WD19 ...27 G2
Oxleas EHAM E6 ...108 B5
Oxleas Cl WELL DA16 ...147 J3
Oxleay Rd RYLN/HDSTN HA2 ...60 A5
Oxleigh Cl NWMAL KT3 ...192 B2
Oxley Cl STHWK SE1 ...123 C5
Oxleys Rd CRICK NW2 ...81 K1
Oxlow La DAGE RM10 ...92 B3
Oxonian St EDUL SE22 ...143 G5
Oxted Cl MTCM CR4 ...178 C6
Oxtoby Wy STRHM/NOR SW16 ...179 J4
Oyster Catchers Cl
  CAN/RD E16 ...107 F5
Oyster Rw WCHPL E1 ...104 E5
Ozolins Wy CAN/RD E16 ...106 D5

P

Paceheath Cl CRW RM5 ...57 F2
Pace Pl WCHPL E1 ...104 D5
Pacific Cl EBED/NFELT TW14 ...153 J3
Pacific Rd CAN/RD E16 ...106 E5
Packington Sq IS N1 ...6 C1
Packington St IS N1 ...85 H6
Packmores Rd ELTH/MOT SE9 ...147 K6
Padbury Cl EBED/NFELT TW14 ...153 G3
Padbury Ct BETH E2 ...7 J5
Padcroft Rd WDR/YW UB7 ...112 A1
Paddenswick Rd HMSMTH W6 ...118 D3
Paddington Cn NTHLT UB5 ...95 H5
Paddington Gn BAY/PAD W2 ...8 A1
Paddington St MHST W1U ...9 G1
Paddock Cl BKHTH/KID SE3 ...145 K4
  NTHLT UB5 ...95 H2
  ORP BR6 ...216 B2
  OXHEY WD19 ...27 J1
  SYD SE26 ...164 A6
  WPK KT4 ...192 B5
Paddock Gdns NRWD SE19 ...181 F2
Paddock Rd BXLYHS DA6 ...148 E5
  CRICK NW2 ...81 J1
  RSLP HA4 ...77 H1
Paddocks Cl RYLN/HDSTN HA2 ...78 B2
  STMC/STPC BR5 ...202 E6
The Paddocks EA W5 * ...116 E3
  KUTN/CMB KT2 ...175 H3
  MLHL NW7 * ...46 D2
  WBLY HA9 ...62 D6
Paddock Wy CHST BR7 ...185 J3
Padfield Rd CMBW SE5 ...142 D4
Padley Cl CHSGTN KT9 ...206 B3
Padnall Rd CHDH RM6 ...73 K1
Padstow Cl ORP BR6 ...217 F2
Padstow Rd ENC/FH EN2 ...23 H3
Padstow Wk
  EBED/NFELT TW14 ...153 J4
Padua Rd PGE/AN SE20 ...181 K4
Pagden St VX/NE SW8 ...141 G2
Pageant Crs BERM/RHTH SE16 ...124 C1
Pageant Wk CROY/NA CRO ...212 A1
Page Cl DAGW RM9 ...92 A3
  FELT TW13 ...172 D2
  KTN/HRWW/W HA3 ...62 B3
Page Crs CROY/NA CRO ...211 H3
  ERITH DA8 ...150 C1
Page Green Rd
  SEVS/STOTM N15 * ...68 C2
Page Heath La BMLY BR1 ...184 C6
Page Heath Vls BMLY BR1 ...184 C6
Pagehurst Rd CROY/NA CRO ...197 H4
Page Meadow MLHL NW7 ...45 J3
Page Rd EBED/NFELT TW14 ...153 G1
Page's Hl MUSWH N10 ...48 A5
Page's La MUSWH N10 ...48 A5
  WEST SW1P ...16 D6
Pages Wk STHWK SE1 ...19 H5
Pages Yd CHSWK W4 * ...118 B6
Paget Av SUT SM1 ...209 H1
Paget Cl HPTN TW12 ...155 K6
Paget Gdns CHST BR7 ...185 G4
Paget La ISLW TW7 ...135 J4
Paget Pl KUTN/CMB KT2 * ...175 K2
  THDIT KT7 ...190 C5
Paget Ri WOOL/PLUM SE18 ...147 F1
Paget Rd HDGN/ICK UB10 ...94 A3
  IL IG1 ...90 B2
  STNW/STAM N16 ...67 J4
Paget St FSBYE EC1V ...6 A4

Paget Ter WOOL/PLUM SE18 ...127 G6
Pagitts Gv EBAR EN4 ...21 F2
Pagnell St NWCR SE14 ...144 C1
Pagoda Av RCH/KEW TW9 ...137 G4
Pagoda Gdns BKHTH/KID SE3 ...145 G3
Paignton Rd RSLP HA4 ...76 E1
  SEVS/STOTM N15 ...68 A3
Paines Cl PIN HA5 ...41 J6
Paine's La PIN HA5 ...41 J5
Pain's Cl MTCM CR4 ...179 G5
Painsthorpe Rd
  STNW/STAM N16 ...86 A1
Painters Rd GNTH/NBYPK IG2 ...55 H2
Paisley Rd CAR SM5 ...194 C5
  WDGN N22 ...49 H4
Pakeman St HOLWY N7 ...85 F1
Pakenham Cl BAL SW12 ...161 F3
Pakenham St FSBYW WC1X ...5 H5
Palace Av KENS W8 ...120 A2
Palace Ct BAY/PAD W2 ...101 F6
  KTN/HRWW/W HA3 ...62 A3
Palace Court Gdns
  MUSWH N10 ...48 C6
Palace Garden Ms KENS W8 ...120 A1
Palace Gdns BKHH IG9 ...39 H5
Palace Gardens Ter KENS W8 ...120 A1
Palace Ga KENS W8 ...120 B2
Palace Gates Rd WDGN N22 ...48 E4
Palace Gn CROY/NA CRO ...213 H5
  KENS W8 ...120 A2
Palace Gv BMLY BR1 ...184 A4
  NRWD SE19 ...181 G3
Palace Ms FUL/PGN SW6 * ...139 J1
Palace Pde WALTH E17 * ...69 H1
Palace Pl WESTW SW1E ...16 A4
Palace Rd BMLY BR1 ...184 A4
  BRXS/STRHM SW2 ...162 A5
  CEND/HSY/T N8 ...66 D2
  E/WMO/HCT KT8 ...173 J6
  FBAR/BDGN N11 ...48 E3
  KUT/HW KT1 ...174 E3
  NRWD SE19 ...181 G3
  RSLP HA4 ...77 J2
Palace Sq NRWD SE19 ...181 G3
Palace St WESTW SW1E ...16 A4
Palace Vw BMLY BR1 ...184 A6
  CROY/NA CRO ...213 H2
  LEE/GVPK SE12 ...165 K4
Palace View Rd CHING E4 ...51 K1
Palamos Rd LEY E10 ...69 J5
Palatine Av STNW/STAM N16 ...86 A2
Palatine Rd STNW/STAM N16 ...86 A2
Palemead Cl FUL/PGN SW6 ...139 G2
Palermo Rd WLSDN NW10 ...99 J1
Palestine Gv WIM/MER SW19 ...178 C4
Palewell Cl STMC/STPC BR5 ...186 C5
Palewell Common Dr
  MORT/ESHN SW14 ...138 A6
Palewell Pk MORT/ESHN SW14 ...138 A6
Palfrey Pl BRXN/ST SW9 ...142 A1
Palgrave Av STHL UB1 ...96 A6
Palgrave Gdns CAMTN NW1 ...2 C6
Palgrave Rd SHB W12 ...118 C3
Palissy St BETH E2 ...7 J5
Pallant Wy ORP BR6 ...216 A1
Pallet Wy WOOL/PLUM SE18 ...146 D2
Palliser Dr RAIN RM13 ...111 J4
Palliser Rd WKENS W14 ...119 H5
Pall Mall STJS SW1Y ...16 B1
Pall Mall East STJS SW1Y ...10 C7
Pall Mall Pl STJS SW1Y ...16 B1
Palmar Crs BXLYHN DA7 ...149 H4
Palmar Rd BXLYHN DA7 ...149 H3
Palmarsh Rd STMC/STPC BR5 ...202 E1
Palm Av SCUP DA14 ...186 E5
Palm Cl LEY E10 ...87 K1
Palmeira Rd BXLYHN DA7 ...148 E4
Palmer Av BUSH WD23 ...28 B1
  CHEAM SM3 ...208 A2
Palmer Cl HEST TW5 ...135 F2
  WWKM BR4 ...199 G6
Palmer Crs KUT/HW KT1 ...175 F6
Palmer Gdns EBAR EN4 ...20 E6
Palmer Pl HOLWY N7 ...85 G3
Palmer Rd BCTR RM8 ...73 K5
  PLSTW E13 ...107 F3
Palmers Gv E/WMO/HCT KT8 ...189 H1
Palmers La PEND EN3 ...24 E2
Palmers Rd BETH E2 ...105 F1
  FBAR/BDGN N11 ...48 C1
  MORT/ESHN SW14 ...137 K4
  STRHM/NOR SW16 ...180 A5
Palmerston Crs PLMGR N13 ...49 F1
  WOOL/PLUM SE18 ...127 H6
Palmerston Gv
  WIM/MER SW19 ...177 K3
Palmerston Rd ACT W3 ...117 K3
  BKHH IG9 ...39 F4
  CROY/NA CRO ...196 C2
  FSTGT E7 ...89 F3
  HSLW TW3 ...135 H2
  KIL/WHAMP NW6 ...82 D5
  KTN/HRWW/W HA3 ...43 F6
  MORT/ESHN SW14 ...137 K5
  ORP BR6 ...216 C2
  SUT SM1 ...209 G3
  WALTH E17 ...69 H1
  WDGN N22 ...49 F3
  WHTN TW2 ...155 K1
  WIM/MER SW19 ...177 K3
Palmerston Wy VX/NE SW8 * ...141 G1
Palmer St STJSPK SW1H ...16 C4
Palmers Wy KUT/HW KT1 * ...174 E5
Palm Gv EA W5 ...117 F3
Palm Rd ROMW/RG RM7 ...74 E2
Pamela Ct FNCH N3 ...47 F2
Pamela Gdns PIN HA5 ...59 F2
Pams Wy HOR/WEW KT19 ...207 F3
Pancras La MANHO EC4N ...12 D4
Pancras Rd CAMTN NW1 ...4 C3
Pandora Rd KIL/WHAMP NW6 ...82 E4
Panfield Ms GNTH/NBYPK IG2 ...72 A3
Panfield Rd ABYW SE2 ...128 B3
Pangbourne Av NKENS W10 * ...100 A4
Pangbourne Dr STAN HA7 ...43 K1

Panhard Pl STHL UB1 ...96 B6
Pank Av BAR EN5 ...21 H6
Pankhurst Av CAN/RD E16 ...126 A1
Pankhurst Cl ISLW TW7 ...136 A4
Pankhurst Rd WOT/HER KT12 ...188 B4
Pankridge OXHEY WD19 * ...27 H1
Panmuir Rd RYNPK SW20 ...176 E4
Panmure Cl HBRY N5 ...85 H2
Panmure Rd SYD SE26 ...163 J5
Pansy Gdns SHB W12 ...99 J6
Panther Dr WLSDN NW10 ...81 F3
Pantiles Cl PLMGR N13 ...49 H1
The Pantiles BMLY BR1 ...184 D6
  BUSH WD23 ...28 D5
  BXLYHN DA7 ...149 G1
Panton Cl CROY/NA CRO ...196 C5
Panton St STJS SW1Y ...10 C6
Paper Bldgs EMB EC4Y * ...11 K5
Papermill Cl CAR SM5 ...210 A2
Papillons Wk BKHTH/KID SE3 ...145 K4
Papworth Gdns HOLWY N7 ...85 F3
Papworth Wy
  BRXS/STRHM SW2 ...162 B2
Parade Ms BRXS/STRHM SW2 ...162 A3
Parade Ter CDALE/KGS NW9 * ...63 F3
The Parade ALP/SUD HA0 * ...79 H4
  BROCKY SE4 * ...144 C2
  BTSEA SW11 * ...140 E5
  CAR SM5 * ...209 K3
  CROY/NA CRO * ...211 F3
  DART DA1 * ...150 C6
  EA W5 * ...97 K5
  EDUL SE22 * ...143 F4
  ESH/CLAY KT10 ...204 E4
  KUT/HW KT1 * ...175 F5
  OXHEY WD19 ...27 J5
  PGE/AN SE20 * ...181 K4
  RCH/KEW TW9 * ...137 H4
  SUT SM1 * ...208 D1
  SYD SE26 * ...163 J6
Paradise Pas HOLWY N7 ...85 G3
Paradise Rd CLAP SW4 ...141 K3
  RCHPK/HAM TW10 ...137 F6
Paradise Rw BETH E2 * ...104 D2
Paradise Wk CHEL SW3 ...120 E6
Paragon Cl CAN/RD E16 ...106 E5
Paragon Gv BRYLDS KT5 ...191 G3
Paragon Ms STHWK SE1 * ...19 F5
Paragon Pl BKHTH/KID SE3 ...145 J3
  BRYLDS KT5 * ...191 G3
Paragon Rd HACK E8 ...86 B4
The Paragon BKHTH/KID SE3 ...145 K3
Parbury Ri CHSGTN KT9 ...206 A4
Parbury Rd FSTH SE23 ...164 B1
Parchmore Rd THHTH CR7 ...180 C5
Parchmore Wy THHTH CR7 ...180 C4
Pardoner St STHWK SE1 ...19 F4
Pardon St FSBYE EC1V ...6 A6
Parfett St WCHPL E1 ...104 C4
Parfrey St HMSMTH W6 ...119 F6
Parham Dr GNTH/NBYPK IG2 ...72 A3
Paris Gdn STHWK SE1 ...12 A7
Parish Cl EMPK RM11 ...75 K6
Parish Gate Dr BFN/LL DA15 ...167 K1
Parish La PGE/AN SE20 ...182 A3
Parish Whf WOOL/PLUM SE18 ...126 D4
Park Ap BERM/RHTH SE16 * ...123 K3
  WELL DA16 ...148 B4
Park Av BARK IG11 ...90 C4
  BMLY BR1 ...183 K2
  CAR SM5 ...210 A3
  CRICK NW2 ...82 A4
  EHAM E6 ...90 A6
  EN EN1 ...24 A6
  FNCH N3 ...47 F5
  GLDGN NW11 ...65 F5
  HSLW TW3 ...155 G5
  IL IG1 ...90 B1
  MORT/ESHN SW14 ...138 A5
  MTCM CR4 ...179 G3
  ORP BR6 ...200 E6
  ORP BR6 ...217 H2
  PLMGR N13 ...35 G5
  RSLP HA4 ...58 D4
  SRTFD E15 ...88 C4
  STHL UB1 ...114 D2
  UED N18 ...36 C6
  WDGN N22 ...48 E5
  WFD IG8 ...53 G2
  WLSDN NW10 ...98 B2
Park Av North CEND/HSY/T N8 ...48 D6
Park Av South CEND/HSY/T N8 ...66 D1
Park Av West EW KT17 ...207 J4
Park Bvd GPK RM2 ...57 H4
Park Cha WBLY HA9 ...80 B2
Park Cha WBLY HA9 ...209 K4
Park Cl CAR SM5 ...86 E1
  CRICK NW2 ...86 E6
  HOM E9 * ...173 H4
  HPTN TW12 ...135 H6
  HSLW TW3 ...42 E4
  KTN/HRWW/W HA3 ...175 G1
  KUTN/CMB KT2 ...14 E3
  SKENS SW7 * ...33 H4
  TRDG/WHET N20 * ...69 G1
  WALTH E17 * ...48 E5
  WDGN N22 ...162 E5
Park Cl DUL SE21 * ...192 A1
  NWMAL KT3 ...181 J1
  SYD SE26 * ...80 B1
  WBLY HA9 ...124 A2
Park Crs BERM/RHTH SE16 ...23 K5
  ENC/FH EN2 ...129 K6
  ERITH DA8 ...47 F3
  FNCH N3 ...42 E4
  KTN/HRWW/W HA3 ...3 J7
  REGST W1B ...155 J3
  WHTN TW2 ...3 K7
Park Crescent Ms East
  REGST W1B ...3 K7

Park Crescent Ms West
  CAVSO/HST W1G ...3 J7
Park Cft EDGW HA8 ...44 E4
Parkcroft Rd LEE/GVPK SE12 ...165 J3
Parkdale Crs WPK KT4 ...207 F1
Parkdale Rd
  WOOL/PLUM SE18 ...127 K5
Park Dr ACT W3 ...117 H3
  CHARL SE7 ...126 D6
  DAGE RM10 ...92 E1
  GLDGN NW11 ...65 F5
  KTN/HRWW/W HA3 ...42 D2
  MORT/ESHN SW14 ...138 A6
  ROM RM1 ...75 F1
  RYLN/HDSTN HA2 ...60 A4
  WCHMH N21 ...35 J1
Park End BMLY BR1 ...183 J2
  HAMP NW3 ...83 J2
Park End Rd ROM RM1 ...75 G1
Parker Cl CAN/RD E16 ...126 D1
  CAR SM5 ...209 K4
Parker Ms HOL/ALD WC2B * ...11 F3
Parke Rd BARN SW13 ...138 D2
  SUN TW16 ...172 A6
Parker Rd CROY/NA CRO ...211 J2
Parker's Rw STHWK SE1 ...19 K3
Parker St CAN/RD E16 ...126 D1
  HOL/ALD WC2B ...11 F3
Parker Ter FSTH SE23 ...164 C4
Parkes Rd CHIG IG7 ...55 F1
Park Farm Cl EFNCH N2 ...47 G6
Park Farm Rd BMLY BR1 ...184 C4
  KUTN/CMB KT2 ...175 F3
Parkfield Av FELT TW13 ...153 K5
  MORT/ESHN SW14 ...138 B5
  NTHLT UB5 ...95 H1
  RYLN/HDSTN HA2 ...42 C5
Parkfield Cl EDGW HA8 ...44 D2
  NTHLT UB5 ...95 J1
Parkfield Crs FELT TW13 ...153 K5
  RSLP HA4 ...59 J6
  RYLN/HDSTN HA2 ...42 C5
Parkfield Dr NTHLT UB5 ...95 H1
Parkfield Gdns
  RYLN/HDSTN HA2 ...42 B6
Parkfield Pde FELT TW13 * ...153 K5
Parkfield Rd FELT TW13 ...153 K5
  NTHLT UB5 ...95 J1
  NWCR SE14 ...144 C1
  RYLN/HDSTN HA2 ...60 B6
  WLSDN NW10 ...81 J5
Parkfields CROY/NA CRO ...198 C5
  PUT/ROE SW15 ...139 F5
Parkfields Av CDALE/KGS NW9 ...44 D4
  RYNPK SW20 ...176 E4
Parkfields Cl CAR SM5 ...210 A2
Parkfields Rd KUTN/CMB KT2 ...175 G1
Parkfield St IS N1 ...5 K2
Parkgate BKHTH/KID SE3 ...145 J4
  CAR SM5 ...209 K4
Park Ga EA W5 ...97 K4
  EFNCH N2 ...47 H6
Park Gdns CDALE/KGS NW9 ...44 D4
  ERITH DA8 ...130 A4
  KUTN/CMB KT2 ...175 H1
Parkgate Av EBAR EN4 ...21 G2
Parkgate Cl KUTN/CMB KT2 ...175 J2
Park Gate Ct HPTN TW12 * ...173 H1
Parkgate Crs EBAR EN4 ...21 G2
Parkgate Gdns
  MORT/ESHN SW14 ...138 A6
Parkgate Rd BTSEA SW11 ...140 D1
  CAR SM5 ...210 A3
  WLGTN SM6 ...210 A3
Park Gv BMLY BR1 ...184 A4
  BXLYHN DA7 ...149 K5
  EDGW HA8 ...44 B1
  FBAR/BDGN N11 ...48 D3
  SRTFD E15 ...88 E6
Park Grove Rd WAN E11 ...70 C6
Park Hall Rd DUL SE21 ...162 E5
  EFNCH N2 ...65 J1
Parkham St BTSEA SW11 ...140 D2
Park HI BMLY BR1 ...200 D1
  CAR SM5 ...209 K4
  CLAP SW4 ...141 J6
  EA W5 ...97 K4
  FSTH SE23 ...163 J4
  RCHPK/HAM TW10 ...157 G1
Park Hill Ri CROY/NA CRO ...197 H6
Park Hill Rd CROY/NA CRO ...197 H6
  HAYES BR2 ...183 H6
  SCUP DA14 ...186 B1
  WLGTN SM6 ...210 B5
Parkhill Rd BFN/LL DA15 ...167 K3
  BXLY DA5 ...169 G2
  CHING E4 ...38 A2
  HAMP NW3 ...83 K3
Parkholme Rd HACK E8 ...86 C4
Park House Gdns TWK TW1 ...136 D6
Parkhouse St CMBW SE5 ...142 E1
Parkhurst Gdns BXLY DA5 ...169 H2
Parkhurst Rd BXLY DA5 ...169 H2
  FBAR/BDGN N11 ...48 A1
  HOLWY N7 ...84 E2
  MNPK E12 ...90 A2
  SUT SM1 ...209 H2
  TOTM N17 ...50 C5
  WALTH E17 ...69 G1
  WDGN N22 ...49 F2
Parkland Av ROM RM1 ...57 G5
Parkland Gdns
  WIM/MER SW19 * ...159 G3
Parkland Gv ASHF TW15 ...152 D6
Parkland Rd ASHF TW15 ...152 D6
  WDGN N22 ...49 F5
  WFD IG8 ...53 F5
Parklands BRYLDS KT5 ...191 G2
  BUSH WD23 * ...27 K1
  HGT N6 ...66 B4
Parklands Cl EBAR EN4 ...21 H1
  GNTH/NBYPK IG2 ...72 E4
  MORT/ESHN SW14 ...137 K6
Parklands Dr FNCH N3 ...46 C2
Parklands Pde HEST TW5 * ...134 E1
Parklands Rd TOOT SW17 ...179 H1

Parklands Wy WPK KT4 ......192 B6
Park La CAR SM5 ......210 A3
　CHDH RM6 ......73 K5
　CHEAM SM5 ......208 C4
　CRO/NA CR0 ......196 E6
　ED N9 ......36 B5
　EMPK RM11 ......75 J4
　HCH RM12 ......93 K4
　HYS/HAR UB3 ......133 K1
　MBLAR W1H 9 F5
　MYFR/PICC W1J 15 H2
　RCH/KEW TW9 ......13 J6
　RYLN/HDSTN HA2 ......78 B1
　SRTFD E15 * 88 A6
　STAN HA7 ......29 G5
　TEDD TW11 ......174 A2
　TOTM N17 ......50 C3
　WBLY HA9 ......80 A2
　YEAD UB4 ......94 C4
Park Lane CI TOTM N17 ......50 C3
Parklea CI CDALE/KGS NW9 ......45 K4
Parkleigh Rd WIM/MER SW19 ......178 A5
Parkleys RUTN/CMB KT2 * 156 E6
Parkleys Pde KUTN/CMB KT2 * 156 E6
Park Me BFN/LL DA15......148 B6
　RYLN/HDSTN HA2 ......78 B1
Parkmead FSTH SE23......158 E1
Parkmead Gdns MLHL NW7 ......45 H2
Park Ms CHST BR7 ......185 G2
　GNWCH SE10 ......125 J5
　NKENS W10 ......100 C1
　STWL/WRAY TW19 ......152 C2
Park Pde ACT W3 * 117 H3
　HYS/HAR UB3 * 94 C5
　WLSDN NW10 ......99 H1
Park Piazza LEW SE13 ......165 G1
Park PI ACT W3 ......117 H4
　BMLY BR1 * 184 A4
　EA W5 ......116 E1
　HPTN TW12 ......173 H2
　IS N1 ......85 K6
　POP/IOD E14 ......124 D1
　WBLY HA9 ......80 A2
　WHALL SW1A 16 A1
Park Place VIs BAY/PAD W2 ......101 G4
Park Ridings CEND/HSY/T N8 ......49 G6
Park Ri KTN/HRWW/W HA3 ......42 E4
Park Rise Rd FSTH SE23 ......164 D3
Park Rd ALP/SUD HA0 ......80 A4
　BAR EN5 ......20 D5
　BECK BR3 ......182 C3
　BMLY BR1 ......184 A4
　BRYLDS KT5 ......191 G3
　BUSH WD23 ......28 A1
　CDALE/KGS NW9 ......63 F4
　CEND/HSY/T N8 ......66 D2
　CEND/HSY/T N8 ......49 G6
　CHEAM SM3 ......208 C4
　CHST BR7 ......185 G2
　CHSWK W4 ......118 A6
　DART DA1 ......171 H5
　E/WMO/HCT KT8 ......189 H1
　EBAR EN4 ......21 H5
　ED N9 ......36 B6
　EFNCH N2 ......47 H6
　EHAM E6 ......89 G6
　ESH/CLAY KT10 ......204 B2
　FBAR/BDGN N11 ......48 D3
　FELT TW13 ......154 C6
　HNWL W7 ......97 F6
　HPTN TW12 ......173 H1
　HSLW TW3 ......135 H6
　IL IG1 ......90 D1
　ISLW TW7 ......136 C2
　KUT/HW KT1 ......174 D4
　KUTN/CMB KT2 ......175 G1
　KUTN/CMB KT2 ......175 H4
　LEY E10 ......69 J5
　MNPK E12 ......71 F6
　NWMAL KT3 ......192 A1
　RCHPK/HAM TW10 ......157 G1
　SNWD SE25 ......197 F1
　SRTFD E15 ......88 E6
　STHGT/OAK N14 ......34 D2
　STJWD NW8 ......2 D5
　STMC/STPC BR5 ......202 D3
　SUN TW16 ......172 A3
　TEDD TW11 ......174 A3
　TWK TW1 ......156 D1
　WALTH E17 ......69 H2
　WIM/MER SW19 ......178 C3
　WLGTN SM6 ......195 G6
　WLSDN NW10 * 81 G6
　YEAD UB4 ......94 C3
Park Rd East ACT W3 ......117 J2
Park Rd North ACT W3 ......117 J2
　CHSWK W4 ......118 A6
Park Rw GNWCH SE10 ......125 G6
Park Royal Rd WLSDN NW10......98 E2
Parkshot RCH/KEW TW9 ......136 E5
Park Side BKHH IG9......39 J3
　CRICK NW2 ......81 J1
　HYS/HAR UB3 * 94 C6
Parkside BECK BR3 * 182 E5
　BKHTH/KID SE3 * 145 J1
　CHEAM SM3 ......208 C4
　FNCH N3 ......47 F4
　HPTN TW12 ......173 J1
　MLHL NW7 ......45 J2
　OXHEY WD19 * 27 G2
　SCUP DA14 ......168 C4
　WIM/MER SW19 ......159 G6
Parkside Av BMLY BR1 ......200 D1
　BXLYHN DA7 ......150 A3
　ROM/RMR SW17 ......177 G1
Parkside CI PGE/AN SE20 ......181 K3
Parkside Crs BRYLDS KT5 ......191 K3
　HOLWY N7 ......85 G1
Parkside Cross BXLYHN DA7 ......150 B3
Parkside Dr EDGW HA8 ......30 C5
Parkside Est HOM E9 * 87 F6
Parkside Gdns EBAR EN4 ......33 K3

WIM/MER SW19 ......159 G6
Parkside Pde ERITH DA8 * 150 C3
Parkside Rd BELV DA17 ......129 J4
　HSLW TW3 ......135 G6
　NTHWD HA6 ......40 D1
Parkside St BTSEA SW11 ......141 F2
Parkside Ter ORP BR6 * 202 B5
　UED N18 * 35 K6
Parkside Wy RYLN/HDSTN HA2 ......60 B1
Park Sq East CAMTN NW1 ......3 J6
Park Square Ms CAMTN NW1 * 3 J7
Park Sq West CAMTN NW1 ......3 J6
Parkstead Rd PUT/ROE SW15 ......138 D6
Park Steps BAY/PAD W2 * 8 D5
Parkstone Av UED N18 ......50 B1
Parkstone Rd PECK SE15 * 143 H3
Park St CROY/NA CR0 ......211 J1
　MYFR/PKLN W1K 9 G6
　STHWK SE1 * 12 C7
　TEDD TW11 ......173 K2
Park Ter CAR SM5 * 209 J1
　PEND EN3 * 25 G1
　WPK KT4 ......192 D5
The Park CAR SM5 ......209 K3
　EA W5 ......116 E1
　GLDGN NW11 ......64 D5
　HGT N6 ......66 B3
　SCUP DA14 ......186 A1
Parkthorne CI
　RYLN/HDSTN HA2 * 60 B3
Parkthorne Dr
　RYLN/HDSTN HA2 * 60 A3
Parkthorne Rd BAL SW12 ......161 J2
Park Vw ACT W5 ......98 E4
　NWMAL KT3 ......176 C6
　PIN HA5 ......41 K4
　WBLY HA9 ......80 D3
　WCHMH N21 ......35 F2
Park View Ct
　NFNCH/WDSP N12 * 33 J6
Park View Crs
　FBAR/BDGN N11 ......34 B6
Park View Dr MTCM CR4 ......178 C5
Park View Est HBRY N5 * 85 J2
Parkview Gdns CLAY IG5 ......71 K1
Park View Gdns HDN NW4 ......64 A2
　WDGN N22 * 49 G4
Park View Rd CRICK NW2 ......81 H2
　EA W5 ......98 A4
　ELTH/MOT SE9 ......167 G3
　FNCH N3 ......47 F3
　PIN HA5 ......41 F2
　STHL UB1 ......115 F1
　TOTM N17 ......50 D5
　WELL DA16 ......148 B4
Parkview Rd CROY/NA CR0 ......197 H5
Park Village East CAMTN NW1 ......3 J2
Park Village West CAMTN NW1 ......3 J2
Parkville Rd FUL/PGN SW6 ......139 J1
Park VIs GNWCH SE10 ......125 G6
Park Vista Apartments
　CAN/RD E16 ......106 D2
Park Wk WBPTN SW10 ......120 B6
Park Wy BXLY DA5 ......170 C5
　E/WMO/HCT KT8 ......173 H6
　EBED/NFELT TW14 ......154 A2
　EDGW HA8 ......44 D4
　ENC/FH EN2 ......23 G3
　GLDGN NW11 ......64 C2
　RSLP HA4 ......58 E5
　TRDG/WHET N20 ......33 K6
Parkway CROY/NA CR0 ......214 A6
　ERITH DA8 ......129 F5
　GDMY/SEVK IG3 ......91 F1
　GPK RM2 ......57 K5
　RAIN RM13 ......111 J5
　RYNPK SW20 ......193 G1
　STHGT/OAK N14 ......34 C4
　WFD IG8 ......53 G1
The Parkway HEST TW5 ......113 K6
　NTHLT UB5 ......95 H2
Park West BAY/PAD W2 ......8 D3
Park West PI BAY/PAD W2 ......8 D3
Parkwood BECK BR3 ......182 D3
Parkwood Av ESH/CLAY KT10 ......189 F6
Parkwood Ms HGT N6 ......66 B3
Parkwood Rd BXLY DA5 ......169 G2
　ISLW TW7 ......136 A2
　WIM/MER SW19 ......177 J1
Parliament Ct WCHPL E1 * 13 H2
Parliament HI HAMP NW3 ......83 J2
Parliament Hill Flds
　KTTN NW5 ......84 A1
Parliament Sq WEST SW1P 16 E3
Parliament St WHALL SW1A 16 E2
Parma Crs BTSEA SW11 ......140 E5
Parmiter St BETH E2 ......104 D1
Parnell CI EDGW HA8 ......30 D6
　SHB W12 ......118 E3
Parnell Rd BOW E3 ......87 H6
Parnham St POP/IOD E14 * 105 G5
Parolles Rd ARCH N19 ......66 C5
Paroma Rd BELV DA17 ......129 H3
Parr Av EW KT17 ......207 K6
Parr CI ED N9 ......36 D6
Parr Rd EHAM E6 ......89 H4
　STAN HA7 ......43 K5
Parrs CI SAND/SEL CR2 ......211 K6
Parr's PI HPTN TW12 ......173 F3
Parr St IS N1 ......6 E2
Parry Av EHAM E6 ......107 K5
Parry CI EW KT17 ......207 K5
Parry Rd NKENS W10 ......100 C2
　SNWD SE25 ......181 F6
Parry St VX/NE SW8 ......121 K6
Parsifal Rd KIL/WHAMP NW6 ......82 E3
Parsloes Av DAGW RM9 ......92 A3
Parsonage Gdns ENC/FH EN2 ......23 K3
Parsonage La ENC/FH EN2 ......23 K3
　SCUP DA14 ......169 G2
Parsonage Manorway
　ERITH DA8 ......129 H6

Parsonage St POP/IOD E14 ......125 F4
Parsons Crs EDGW HA8 ......30 C5
Parsons Gn FUL/PGN SW6 ......139 K2
Parsons Green La
　FUL/PGN SW6 ......139 K2
Parsons Gv EDGW HA8 ......30 C5
Parsons La RDART DA2 ......170 D5
Parsons Md CRO/NA CR0 ......196 C5
　E/WMO/HCT KT8 ......173 H6
Parsons Rd PLSTW E13 ......107 G1
Parson St HDN NW4 ......46 A6
Parthenia Rd FUL/PGN SW6 ......139 K2
Partingdale La MLHL NW7 ......46 B1
Partridge CI BAR EN5 ......32 A1
　BUSH WD23 * 28 C5
　CAN/RD E16 ......107 H4
　STAN HA7 ......30 A6
Partridge Dr ORP BR6 ......216 C1
Partridge Gn ELTH/MOT SE9 ......167 F5
Partridge Rd HPTN TW12 ......172 E2
　SCUP DA14 ......167 K5
Partridge Sq EHAM E6 ......107 J4
Pasadena CI HYS/HAR UB3 ......113 K2
Pascal St VX/NE SW8 ......141 J1
Pascoe Rd LEW SE13 ......165 G4
Pasley CI WALW SE17 ......122 C5
Pasquier Rd WALTH E17 ......51 G6
Passey PI ELTH/MOT SE9 ......166 E1
Passfield Dr POP/IOD E14 ......105 K4
Passmore Gdns
　FBAR/BDGN N11 ......48 D2
Passmore St BCVA SW1W 15 G7
Pasteur CI CDALE/KGS NW9 ......45 G5
Pasteur Gdns UED N18 ......49 J1
Paston CI WLGTN SM6 ......210 C1
Paston Crs LEE/GVPK SE12 ......166 A2
Paston St LBTH SE11 ......18 E6
Pasture CI ALP/SUD HA0 ......79 F3
　BUSH WD23 ......28 C2
Pasture Rd ALP/SUD HA0 ......61 H6
　CAT SE6 ......165 H5
　DAGW RM9 ......92 B3
The Pastures OXHEY WD19 ......27 F2
　TRDG/WHET N20 ......32 C5
Patcham Ter VX/NE SW8 ......141 G2
Patching Wy YEAD UB4 ......95 J4
Paternoster Rw STP EC4M 12 C4
Paternoster Sq STP EC4M 12 B4
Pater St KENS W8 ......119 K3
Pates Manor Dr
　EBED/NFELT TW14 ......153 G2
Pathfield Rd
　STRHM/NOR SW16 ......179 J2
The Path WIM/MER SW19 ......178 A4
The Pathway OXHEY WD19 ......27 H5
Patience Rd BTSEA SW11 ......140 D3
Patio CI CLAP SW4 ......161 J1
Patmore St VX/NE SW8 ......141 H2
Patmore Wy CRW RM5 ......56 D1
Patmos Rd BRXN/ST SW9 ......142 C1
Paton CI BOW E3 ......105 J2
Patricia CI WELL DA16 ......148 C1
Patricia VIs TOTM N17 ......50 D5
Patrick Rd PLSTW E13 ......107 G2
Patriot Sq BETH E2 ......104 D1
Patrol PI CAT SE6 ......164 E1
Patshull PI KTTN NW5 ......84 C4
Patshull Rd KTTN NW5 ......84 C4
Pattenden Rd CAT SE6 ......164 C3
Patten Rd WAND/EARL SW18 ......160 D2
Patterdale CI BMLY BR1 ......183 H2
Patterdale Rd PECK SE15 ......143 K1
Patterson Rd NRWD SE19 ......181 G2
Pattina Wk BERM/RHTH SE16 ......124 B1
Pattison Rd CRICK NW2 ......82 E1
Paul CI SRTFD E15 ......88 C5
Paulet Rd CMBW SE5 ......142 C3
Paul Gdns CROY/NA CR0 ......197 G6
Paulhan Rd
　KTN/HRWW/W HA3 ......61 K1
Paulin Dr WCHMH N21 ......35 G2
Pauline Crs WHTN TW2 ......155 H3
Paulinus CI STMC/STPC BR5 ......186 D5
Paul Julius CI POP/IOD E14 ......106 B6
Paul Robeson CI EHAM E6 ......108 A2
Paul St SDTCH EC2A 7 G6
　SRTFD E15 ......88 B6
Paultons Sq CHEL SW3 ......120 C6
Paultons St CHEL SW3 ......120 C6
Pauntley St ARCH N19 ......66 C5
Paveley Dr BTSEA SW11 ......140 D1
Paveley St STJWD NW8 ......2 D6
The Pavement CLAP SW4 ......141 H5
　EA W5 * 117 F3
　TEDD TW11 * 174 C5
　WAN E11 * 70 A5
　WIM/MER SW19 * 177 J2
　WNWD SE27 * 162 D6
Pavet CI DAGE RM10 ......92 D4
Pavilion Ldg
　RYLN/HDSTN HA2 * 60 D5
Pavilion Pde SHB W12 * 100 A5
Pavilion Rd IL IG1 ......71 K4
　KTBR SW1X 15 F3
Pavilion St KTBR SW1X 15 F5
Pavilion Wy EDGW HA8 ......44 E4
　RSLP HA4 ......59 G6
Pavillion Sq TOOT SW17 ......160 D5
Pavillion Ter SHB W12 * 100 A5
Pawleyne CI PGE/AN SE20 ......181 K3
Pawsey CI PLSTW E13 ......88 E6
Pawsons Rd CROY/NA CR0 ......196 D3
Paxford Rd ALP/SUD HA0 ......61 H6
Paxton CI RCH/KEW TW9 ......137 G3
　WOT/HER KT12 * 188 B4
Paxton PI WNWD SE27 ......163 H6
Paxton Rd BMLY BR1 ......183 K5
　CHSWK W4 ......118 B6
　FSTH SE23 ......164 B5
　TOTM N17 ......50 C3
Paxton Ter PIM SW1V 121 G6
Payne CI BARK IG11 ......90 E5
Paynell Ct BKHTH/KID SE3 ......145 H4
Payne Rd BOW E3 ......105 K1

Paynesfield Av
　MORT/ESHN SW14 ......138 A4
Paynesfield Rd BUSH WD23 ......29 F2
Payne St DEPT SE8 ......124 C6
Paynes Wk HMSMTH W6 ......119 H6
Payzes Gdns WFD IG8 * 52 D2
Peabody Av PIM SW1V 121 G5
Peabody CI CROY/NA CR0 ......197 K5
　GNWCH SE10 * 144 E2
　PIM SW1V 121 G6
Peabody Est BTSEA SW11 ......140 D5
　CHEL SW3 ......120 D6
　CLKNW EC1R * 5 K7
　CMBW SE5 * 142 E2
　FUL/PGN SW6 ......119 K6
　HMSMTH W6 ......119 F5
　HNHL SE24 ......162 C2
　NKENS W10 ......100 A4
　STHWK SE1 * 11 K2
　STLK EC1Y * 6 D7
　TOTM N17 * 50 A4
Peabody HI DUL SE21 ......162 C3
Peabody Sq IS N1 * 85 J6
Peabody Ter CLKNW EC1R * 5 K7
Peace CI GFD/PVL UB6 ......78 D6
　SNWD SE25 ......197 F1
　STHGT/OAK N14 ......22 B6
Peace Gv WBLY HA9 ......80 D1
Peace St WOOL/PLUM SE18 ......127 F6
Peaches CI BELMT SM2 ......208 C5
Peach Rd FELT TW13 ......153 K5
Peachum Rd BKHTH/KID SE3 ......125 J6
Peacock Av
　EBED/NFELT TW14 ......153 G3
Peacock St WALW SE17 ......18 B7
Peacock Yd WALW SE17 ......18 B7
Peaketon Av REDBR IG4 ......71 H1
Peak HI SYD SE26 ......163 K6
Peak Hill Av SYD SE26 ......163 K6
Peak Hill Gdns SYD SE26 ......163 K6
The Peak SYD SE26 ......163 K6
Peal Gdns WEA W13 ......97 G2
Peall Rd CROY/NA CR0 ......196 A3
Pearce CI MTCM CR4 ......179 F5
Pearcefield Av FSTH SE23 ......163 K3
Pear CI CDALE/KGS NW9 ......45 G3
　NWCR SE14 ......144 B1
Pearcroft Rd WAN E11 ......70 B6
Peardon St VX/NE SW8 ......141 G3
Peareswood Gdns STAN HA7 ......43 K4
Peareswood Rd ERITH DA8 ......150 C2
Pearfield Rd FSTH SE23 ......164 B5
Pear Gv WAN E11 ......88 B1
Pearl CI CRICK NW2 ......64 B4
　EHAM E6 ......108 A5
Pearl Rd WALTH E17 ......51 J6
Pearl St WAP E1W 123 J1
Pearman St STHWK SE1 ......17 J4
Pear PI STHWK SE1 ......17 J2
Pearscroft Ct FUL/PGN SW6 ......140 A3
Pearscroft Rd FUL/PGN SW6 ......140 A3
Pearse St PECK SE15 ......123 F6
Pearson's Av NWCR SE14 ......144 D2
Pearson's Rd NWCR SE14 ......144 D2
Pearson St BETH E2 ......7 J1
Pearson Wy DART DA1 ......171 J4
Pears Rd HSLW TW3 ......135 J4
Peartree Av TOOT SW17 ......160 B5
Pear Tree CI BETH E2 ......7 J1
　ERITH DA8 * 150 A2
　MTCM CR4 ......178 D5
Peartree CI HAYES BR2 ......200 C2
Pear Tree Ct CLKNW EC1R * 5 K7
Peartree Gdns BCTR RM8 ......91 H3
　ROMW/RG RM7 ......56 D5
Peartree La WAP E1W * 104 E6
Peartree Rd EN EN1 ......24 A4
Peartree St FSBYE EC1V 6 B6
Peartree Wy GNWCH SE10 ......125 K4
Peary PI BETH E2 * 104 E2
Pease CI HCH RM12 ......93 K5
Peasmead Ter CHING E4 * 38 A6
Peatfield CI BFN/LL DA15 ......167 K5
Pebworth Rd HRW HA1 ......61 G6
Peckarmans Wd SYD SE26 ......163 H5
Peckett Sq HBRY N5 * 85 J2
Peckford PI BRXN/ST SW9 ......142 B3
Peckham Gv PECK SE15 ......143 F1
Peckham High St PECK SE15 ......143 H2
Peckham Hill St PECK SE15 ......143 H1
Peckham Park Rd PECK SE15 ......143 H1
Peckham Rye EDUL SE22 ......143 J5
Pecks Yd WCHPL E1 * 13 J1
Peckwater St KTTN NW5 ......84 C3
Pedlars Wk HOLWY N7 ......84 E4
Pedley Rd BCTR RM8 ......73 J5
Pedley St WCHPL E1 ......7 K7
Pedro St CLPT E5 ......87 F1
Peek Crs WIM/MER SW19 ......177 G1
Peel CI CHING E4 ......37 K4
　ED N9 ......36 C5
Peel Dr CDALE/KGS NW9 ......45 J3
　CLAY IG5 ......53 J6
Peel Gv BETH E2 ......104 E1
Peel Pas KENS W8 ......119 K1
Peel PI CLAY IG5 ......53 J5
Peel Prec KIL/WHAMP NW6 ......100 E1
Peel Rd ALP/SUD HA0 ......79 J1
　KIL/WHAMP NW6 ......100 D2
　KTN/HRWW/W HA3 ......42 E6
　ORP BR6 ......216 C2
　SWFD E18 ......52 D4
Peel St KENS W8 ......119 K1
Peerage Wy EMPK RM11 ......75 K5
Peerless St FSBYE EC1V 6 E5
Pegamoid Rd UED N18 ......37 F5
Pegasus CI STNW/STAM N16 * 85 K2
Pegasus PI FUL/PGN SW6 * 139 K3
　LBTH SE11 * 122 B6
Pegasus Rd CROY/NA CR0 ......211 G4
Pegasus Wy FBAR/BDGN N11 ......48 B2

Pegg Rd HEST TW5 ......134 C1
Pegley Gdns LEE/GVPK SE12 ......165 K4
Pegwell St WOOL/PLUM SE18 ......147 K1
Pekin St POP/IOD E14 ......105 J5
Peldon Wk IS N1 * 85 H6
Pelham Av BARK IG11 ......91 F6
Pelham CI CMBW SE5 ......143 F4
Pelham Crs SKENS SW7 ......14 C7
Pelham PI SKENS SW7 ......14 C7
Pelham Rd BXLYHN DA7 ......149 H4
　IL IG1 ......72 D6
　PGE/AN SE20 ......181 K5
　SEVS/STOTM N15 ......68 B1
　SWFD E18 ......53 F6
　WDGN N22 ......49 G5
　WIM/MER SW19 ......177 K3
Pelhams CI ESH/CLAY KT10 ......204 A3
Pelham St SKENS SW7 ......14 B6
Pelhams Wk ESH/CLAY KT10 ......204 A2
Pelier St WALW SE17 ......122 D6
Pelinore Rd CAT SE6 ......165 H4
Pellant Rd FUL/PGN SW6 ......139 H1
Pellatt Gv WDGN N22 ......49 G4
Pellatt Rd EDUL SE22 ......143 G6
　WBLY HA9 ......62 A6
Pellerin Rd STNW/STAM N16 ......86 A3
Pellings CI HAYES BR2 ......183 H6
Pelling St POP/IOD E14 ......105 J5
Pellipar CI PLMGR N13 ......35 G5
Pellipar Rd WOOL/PLUM SE18 ......126 E5
Pelly Rd PLSTW E13 ......88 E6
Pelter St BETH E2 ......7 J4
Pelton Rd GNWCH SE10 ......125 H5
Pembar Av WALTH E17 * 51 G2
Pemberley Cha
　HOR/WEW KT19 ......206 D3
Pemberley CI HOR/WEW KT19 ......206 D3
Pember Rd WLSDN NW10 ......100 D2
Pemberton Av GPK RM2 ......57 K6
Pemberton Gdns ARCH N19 ......84 C1
　CHDH RM6 ......74 A2
Pemberton PI ESH/CLAY KT10 ......204 C1
　HACK E8 * 86 D5
Pemberton Rd
　E/WMO/HCT KT8 ......189 H1
　FSBYPK N4 ......67 H2
Pemberton Rw
　FLST/FETLN EC4A 11 K3
Pemberton Ter ARCH N19 ......84 C1
Pembridge Crs NTGHL W11 ......100 D6
Pembridge Gdns
　BAY/PAD W2 * 100 E6
Pembridge Ms NTGHL W11 ......100 E6
Pembridge PI BAY/PAD W2 ......100 E6
　WAND/EARL SW18 ......160 E1
Pembridge Rd NTGHL W11 ......100 E6
Pembridge Sq BAY/PAD W2 ......100 E6
Pembridge VIs BAY/PAD W2 ......100 E6
Pembroke Av BRYLDS KT5 ......191 J2
　EN EN1 ......24 C1
　KTN/HRWW/W HA3 ......43 G2
　PIN HA5 ......59 H3
　RSLP HA4 ......59 H5
Pembroke CI ERITH DA8 * 129 K4
　KTBR SW1X 15 H3
Pembroke Gdns DAGE RM10 ......92 D1
　KENS W8 ......119 J3
Pembroke Gardens CI
　KENS W8 ......119 J3
Pembroke Ms KENS W8 ......119 K3
　MUSWH N10 ......48 A4
Pembroke Pde ERITH DA8 * 129 K5
Pembroke PI EDGW HA8 ......44 C3
　ISLW TW7 ......135 K3
　KENS W8 ......119 K3
Pembroke Rd BMLY BR1 ......184 B5
　CEND/HSY/T N8 ......66 E1
　EHAM E6 ......107 K4
　ERITH DA8 ......129 K5
　GDMY/SEVK IG3 ......73 F5
　GFD/PVL UB6 ......96 B5
　KENS W8 ......119 K4
　MTCM CR4 ......178 E5
　MUSWH N10 ......48 A4
　NTHWD HA6 ......26 A5
　PLMGR N13 ......35 J5
　RSLP HA4 ......58 C5
　SEVS/STOTM N15 ......68 B2
　SNWD SE25 ......197 F1
　WALTH E17 ......69 K1
　WBLY HA9 ......80 A2
Pembroke Sq KENS W8 ......119 K3
Pembroke St IS N1 ......84 E5
Pembroke Ter STJWD NW8 * 2 A1
Pembroke VIs KENS W8 ......119 K4
　RCH/KEW TW9 ......136 E5
Pembroke Wk KENS W8 ......119 K4
Pembry CI BRXN/ST SW9 ......142 B2
Pembury Av WPK KT4 ......192 D5
Pembury CI CLPT E5 ......86 D3
　HAYES BR2 ......199 J4
Pembury Crs SCUP DA14 ......169 F4
Pembury PI CLPT E5 ......86 D3
Pembury Rd BXLYHN DA7 ......149 F1
　CLPT E5 ......86 D3
　SNWD SE25 ......197 H1
　TOTM N17 ......50 B5
Pemdevon Rd CROY/NA CR0 ......196 B4
Pemell CI WCHPL E1 ......104 E3
Pemerich CI HYS/HAR UB3 ......113 J5
Pempath PI WBLY HA9 ......61 K6
Penally PI IS N1 ......85 K6
Penang St WAP E1W 123 J1
Penard Rd NWDGN UB2 ......115 F3
Penarth St PECK SE15 ......123 K6
Penates ESH/CLAY KT10 ......204 D2
Penberth Rd CAT SE6 ......165 F4
Penbury Rd NWDGN UB2 ......114 C5
Pencombe Ms NTGHL W11 ......100 D6
Pencraig Wy PECK SE15 ......123 J6
Pencroft DART DA1 ......
Pendall CI EBAR EN4 ......21 J5
Pendarves Rd RYNPK SW20 ......177 F4
Penda's Md HOM E9 ......87 G2

Pendell Av HYS/HAR UB3 133 J1
Pendennis Rd ORP BR6 202 D6
STRHM/NOR SW16 161 K6
TOTM N17 49 K6
Penderel Rd HSLW TW3 135 F6
Penderry Ri CAT SE6 165 G4
Penderyn Wy HOLWY N7 84 D2
Pendlebury House
WOOL/PLUM SE18 146 D2
Pendle Rd STRHM/NOR SW16 179 G2
Pendlestone Rd WALTH E17 69 K2
Pendragon Rd BMLY BR1 165 K5
Pendrell Rd BROCKY SE4 144 B4
Pendrell St WOOL/PLUM SE18 127 J6
Pendula Dr YEAD UB4 95 H3
Pendulum Ms HACK E8 * 86 B3
Penerley Rd CAT SE6 164 E3
RAIN RM13 111 K4
Penfold Cl CROY/NA CR0 211 G1
Penfold Pl BAY/PAD W2 8 C1
Penfold Rd ED N9 37 F3
Penfold St STJWD NW8 2 B7
Penford Gdns ELTH/MOT SE9 146 C5
Penford St CMBW SE5 142 C3
Pengarth Rd BXLY DA5 148 E6
Penge La PGE/AN SE20 181 K3
Penge Rd PLSTW E13 89 G5
SNWD SE25 181 H6
Penhale Cl ORP BR6 217 G2
Penhall Rd CHARL SE7 126 C4
Penhill Rd BXLY DA5 168 D2
Penhurst Rd BARK/HLT IG6 54 B3
Penifather La GFD/PVL UB6 96 D2
Peninsular Cl
EBED/NFELT TW14 153 G1
Peninsular Park Rd CHARL SE7 125 K5
Penistone Rd
STRHM/NOR SW16 179 K3
Penmon Rd ABYW SE2 128 B3
Pennack Rd PECK SE15 123 G6
Pennant Ms KENS W8 120 A4
Pennant Ter WALTH E17 51 H5
Pennard Rd SHB W12 119 F2
The Pennards SUN TW16 172 B6
Penn Cl GFD/PVL UB6 96 B1
KTN/HRWW/W HA3 61 J1
Penner Cl WIM/MER SW19 159 H4
Penners Gdns SURB KT6 191 F4
Pennethorne Cl HOM E9 86 E6
Pennethorne Rd PECK SE15 143 J1
Penney Cl DART DA1 171 G2
Penn Gdns CHST BR7 185 G5
CRW RM5 56 C3
Pennine Dr CRICK NW2 64 C6
Pennine La CRICK NW2 64 C6
Pennine Pde CRICK NW2 * 64 C6
Pennine Wy BXLYHN DA7 150 B2
HYS/HAR UB3 133 G1
Pennington Cl CRW RM5 56 C2
Pennington Dr STHGT/OAK N14 22 E6
Pennington St WAP E1W 104 D6
Pennington Wy
LEE/GVPK SE12 166 A4
Penniston Cl WDGN N22 49 J5
Penn La BXLY DA5 168 E1
Penn Rd HOLWY N7 84 E3
Penn St IS N1 7 F1
Penny Cl RAIN RM13 111 K2
Pennycroft SAND/SEL CR2 213 G6
Pennyfields POP/IOD E14 105 J6
Penny Ms WAND/EARL SW18 139 K6
Pennymoor Wk MV/WKIL W9 100 D3
Pennyroyal Av EHAM E6 108 A5
Penpoll Rd HACK E8 86 D4
Penpool La WELL DA16 148 C4
Penrhyn Av WALTH E17 51 J4
Penrhyn Crs
MORT/ESHN SW14 137 K5
WALTH E17 51 J4
Penrhyn Gdns KUT/HW KT1 190 E1
Penrhyn Gv WALTH E17 51 J4
Penrhyn Rd KUT/HW KT1 175 F6
Penrith Cl BECK BR3 182 E4
PUT/ROE SW15 139 H6
Penrith Crs HCH RM12 93 J3
Penrith Pl STRHM/NOR SW16 162 C4
Penrith Rd BARK/HLT IG6 55 F2
NWMAL KT3 192 A1
SEVS/STOTM N15 67 K2
THHTH CR7 180 D5
Penrith St STRHM/NOR SW16 179 H2
Penrose Av OXHEY WD19 27 J4
Penrose Gv WALW SE17 122 D5
Penrose St WALW SE17 122 D5
Penryn St CAMTN NW1 4 C2
Penry St STHWK SE1 19 H7
Pensbury Pl VX/NE SW8 141 H3
Pensbury St VX/NE SW8 141 H3
Pensford Av RCH/KEW TW9 137 H3
Penshurst Av BFN/LL DA15 168 B1
Penshurst Gdns EDGW HA8 44 D1
Penshurst Gn HAYES BR2 199 J2
Penshurst Rd BXLYHN DA7 149 G2
HOM E9 87 F5
THHTH CR7 196 C2
TOTM N17 50 B3
Penshurst Wy BELMT SM2 208 E5
STMC/STPC BR5 202 D1
Pensilver Cl EBAR EN4 * 21 J5
Penstemon Cl FNCH N3 46 E2
Pentelow Gdns
EBED/NFELT TW14 153 K1
Pentire Rd WALTH E17 52 B4
Pentland Av EDGW HA8 30 D4
Pentland Cl CRICK NW2 64 C6
ED N9 36 E4
Pentland Pl NTHLT UB5 77 J6
Pentland Rd BUSH WD23 28 C1
Pentlands Cl MTCM CR4 179 G6
Pentland St WAND/EARL SW18 160 B1
Pentland Wy HGDN/ICK UB10 76 A1
Pentlow St PUT/ROE SW15 139 F3
Pentlow Wy BKHH IG9 39 J2
Pentney Rd BAL SW12 161 H3
CHING E4 38 B3
WIM/MER SW19 177 H4
Penton Gv IS N1 5 J3
Penton Pl WALW SE17 18 B7
Penton Ri FSBYW WC1X 5 H4
Penton St IS N1 5 J2
Pentonville Rd IS N1 5 H3
Pentrich Av EN EN1 24 C1
Pentridge St PECK SE15 143 G1
Pentyre Av UED N18 49 K1
Penwerris Av ISLW TW7 135 H1
Penwith Rd WAND/EARL SW18 160 A4
Penwortham Rd
STRHM/NOR SW16 179 G2
Penylan Pl EDGW HA8 * 44 C4
Penywern Rd ECT SW5 119 K5
Penzance Pl NTGHL W11 119 H1
Penzance St NTGHL W11 119 H1
Peony Gdns SHB W12 99 J6
Peploe Rd KIL/WHAMP NW6 100 B1
Peplow Cl WDR/YW UB7 112 A1
Pepper Cl EHAM E6 107 K4
Peppercorn Cl THHTH CR7 180 E5
Peppermead Sq LEW SE13 * 144 D6
Peppermint Cl CROY/NA CR0 195 K4
Peppermint Pl WAN E11 88 C1
Pepper St POP/IOD E14 124 E3
STHWK SE1 18 C2
Peppie Cl STNW/STAM N16 68 A6
Pepys Crs BAR EN5 20 A6
Pepys Est DEPT SE8 124 C5
Pepys Park Est DEPT SE8 124 C4
Pepys Ri ORP BR6 202 A5
Pepys Rd NWCR SE14 144 A3
RYNPK SW20 177 F5
Pepys St TWRH EC3N 13 H5
Perceval Av HAMP NW3 83 J3
Percheron Rd BORE WD6 31 F1
Perch St HACK E8 86 B2
Percival Ct TOTM N17 50 B3
Percival Gdns CHDH RM6 73 J3
Percival Rd EN EN1 24 B5
FELT TW13 153 J4
MORT/ESHN SW14 137 K6
ORP BR6 201 G6
Percival St FSBYE EC1V 6 B5
Percival Wy HOR/WEW KT19 206 E2
Percy Bush Rd WDR/YW UB7 112 C3
Percy Gdns PEND EN3 25 F6
WPK KT4 192 A5
YEAD UB4 94 C2
Percy Ms FITZ W1T 10 C2
Percy Rd BXLYHN DA7 149 F3
CAN/RD E16 106 C4
GDMY/SEVK IG3 73 G4
HPTN TW12 173 F3
ISLW TW7 136 B5
MTCM CR4 195 F4
NFNCH/WDSP N12 47 G1
PGE/AN SE20 182 A4
ROMW/RG RM7 56 E6
SHB W12 118 D2
SNWD SE25 197 G2
WAN E11 70 C4
WCHMH N21 35 J2
WHTN TW2 155 G3
Percy St FITZ W1T 10 C2
Percy Wy WHTN TW2 155 H3
Peregrine Cl WLSDN NW10 81 F3
Peregrine Ct WELL DA16 148 A2
Peregrine Gdns CROY/NA CR0 198 B6
Peregrine Rd BARK/HLT IG6 55 H1
Peregrine Wy WIM/MER SW19 177 F3
Perham Rd WKENS W14 119 H5
Peridot St EHAM E6 107 J4
Perifield DUL SE21 162 D3
Perimeade Rd GFD/PVL UB6 97 J1
Periton Rd ELTH/MOT SE9 146 C5
Perivale Gdns WEA W13 97 H3
Perivale La GFD/PVL UB6 97 G2
Perivale Village GFD/PVL UB6 * 97 J2
Perkin Cl ALP/SUD HA0 79 H3
HSLW TW3 135 G5
Perkin's Rents WEST SW1P 16 C4
Perkins Rd BARK/HLT IG6 72 D2
Perkins Sq STHWK SE1 12 D7
Perks Cl BKHTH/KID SE3 145 H3
Perpins Rd ELTH/MOT SE9 167 K1
Perran Rd BRXS/STRHM SW2 162 C4
Perrers Rd HMSMTH W6 118 E3
Perrin Rd ALP/SUD HA0 79 G2
Perrin's Ct HAMP NW3 * 83 G2
Perrin's Wk HAMP NW3 83 G2
Perry Av ACT W3 99 F5
Perry Cl RAIN RM13 111 F1
Perry Ct SEVS/STOTM N15 * 68 A3
Perryfield Wy CDALE/KGS NW9 63 H3
RCHPK/HAM TW10 156 C4
Perry Gdns ED N9 36 A5
Perry Garth NTHLT UB5 77 G6
Perry Gv DART DA1 151 K5
Perry Hall Cl ORP BR6 202 B4
Perry Hall Rd ORP BR6 202 A3
Perry Hl CAT SE6 164 C4
Perry How WPK KT4 192 C5
Perry Mnr CHST BR7 185 K2
Perrymans Farm Rd
GNTH/NBYPK IG2 72 D3
Perry Md BUSH WD23 28 C1
ENC/FH EN2 23 H3
Perrymead St FUL/PGN SW6 139 K2
Perryn Rd ACT W3 99 F6
BERM/RHTH SE16 123 J3
Perry Ri FSTH SE23 164 B5
Perry St CHST BR7 185 K2
DART DA1 150 B4
Perry V FSTH SE23 163 K4
Persant Rd CAT SE6 165 H5
Perseverance Pl
BRXN/ST SW9 * 142 B1
Pershore Cl GNTH/NBYPK IG2 72 B2
Pershore Gv CAR SM5 194 C3
Pert Cl MUSWH N10 48 B3
Perth Av CDALE/KGS NW9 63 F4
YEAD UB4 95 G3
Perth Cl RYNPK SW20 176 D5
Perth Rd BARK IG11 108 D1
BECK BR3 183 F5
FSBYPK N4 67 G5
GNTH/NBYPK IG2 72 B3
LEY E10 69 G5
PLSTW E13 107 F1
WDGN N22 49 H4
Perth Ter GNTH/NBYPK IG2 72 C4
Perwell Av RYLN/HDSTN HA2 59 K5
Petauel Rd TEDD TW11 173 K1
Petavel Rd TEDD TW11 173 K2
Peter Av WLSDN NW10 81 K5
Peterboat Cl GNWCH SE10 125 H4
Peterborough Ms
FUL/PGN SW6 139 K3
Peterborough Rd CAR SM5 194 D3
FUL/PGN SW6 139 K3
HRW HA1 60 E5
LEY E10 70 A2
Peterborough Vls
FUL/PGN SW6 140 A2
Petergate BTSEA SW11 140 B5
Peters Cl BCTR RM8 73 K5
EDGW HA8 43 K2
WELL DA16 147 K3
Petersfield Cl UED N18 49 J1
Petersfield Ri PUT/ROE SW15 158 E3
Petersfield Rd ACT W3 117 K2
Petersham Cl
RCHPK/HAM TW10 156 E4
SUT SM1 208 D3
Petersham Dr STMC/STPC BR5 186 A5
Petersham Gdns
STMC/STPC BR5 186 B5
Petersham La SKENS SW7 * 120 B3
Petersham Ms SKENS SW7 120 B3
Petersham Pl SKENS SW7 120 B3
Petersham Rd
RCHPK/HAM TW10 156 E5
RCHPK/HAM TW10 157 F1
Petersham Ter
CROY/NA CR0 * 210 E1
Peter's Hl BLKFR EC4V 12 C5
Peterstone Rd ABYW SE2 128 C2
Peterstow Cl WIM/MER SW19 159 H4
Peter St SOHO/CST W1F 10 C5
Peterwood Wy CROY/NA CR0 196 A6
Petherton Rd HBRY N5 85 J3
Petiver Cl HOM E9 * 86 E5
Petley Rd HMSMTH W6 119 F6
Peto Pl CAMTN NW1 3 K6
Peto St North CAN/RD E16 106 D5
Petrie Cl CRICK NW2 * 82 C4
Petros Gdns HAMP NW3 * 83 F3
Petro St South CAN/RD E16 106 D6
Pett Cl EMPK RM11 75 K6
Petten Cl STMC/STPC BR5 202 E5
Petten Gv STMC/STPC BR5 202 D5
Petticoat La WCHPL E1 13 H2
Petticoat Sq WCHPL E1 13 J3
Petticoat Tower WCHPL E1 * 13 J3
Pettits Bvd ROM RM1 57 G5
Pettits Cl ROM RM1 57 G5
Pettits La ROM RM1 57 G6
Pettits La North ROM RM1 57 F4
Pettit's Pl DAGE RM10 92 C3
Pettit's Rd DAGE RM10 92 C3
Pettiward Cl PUT/ROE SW15 139 F5
Pettley Gdns ROMW/RG RM7 75 F2
Pettman Crs THMD SE28 127 J4
Pettsgrove Av ALP/SUD HA0 79 J3
Pett's Hl RYLN/HDSTN HA2 78 B2
Pett St WOOL/PLUM SE18 126 D4
Petts Wood Rd
STMC/STPC BR5 201 J2
Petty France STJSPK SW1H 16 B4
Petty Wales MON EC3R 13 H6
Petworth Cl NTHLT UB5 77 K5
Petworth Gdns
HGDN/ICK UB10 76 A6
RYNPK SW20 176 E6
Petworth Rd BXLYHS DA6 149 H6
NFNCH/WDSP N12 47 J1
Petworth St BTSEA SW11 140 D2
Petworth Wy HCH RM12 93 H2
Petyt Pl CHEL SW3 * 120 D6
Petyward CHEL SW3 14 D7
Pevensey Av EN EN1 23 K3
FBAR/BDGN N11 48 D1
Pevensey Cl ISLW TW7 135 H1
Pevensey Rd FELT TW13 154 D3
FSTGT E7 88 E2
TOOT SW17 160 C6
Peveret Cl FBAR/BDGN N11 * 48 B1
Peveril Dr TEDD TW11 173 J1
Pewsey Cl CHING E4 51 J1
Peyton Pl GNWCH SE10 145 F1
Pharaoh Cl MTCM CR4 194 E4
Pheasant Cl CAN/RD E16 107 F5
Phelp St WALW SE17 122 E6
Phelps Wy HYS/HAR UB3 113 J4
Phene St CHEL SW3 120 D6
Philan Wy CRW RM5 57 F2
Philbeach Gdns ECT SW5 119 K5
Philchurch Pl WCHPL E1 104 C5
Philimore Cl
WOOL/PLUM SE18 127 K5
Philip Av ROMW/RG RM7 75 F5
Philip Gdns CROY/NA CR0 198 C6
Philip La SEVS/STOTM N15 67 K1
Philippa Gdns ELTH/MOT SE9 146 C6
Philip Rd PECK SE15 143 H4
RAIN RM13 111 G2
Philips Cl MTCM CR4 195 F5
Philip St PLSTW E13 106 E3
Phillimore Gdns KENS W8 119 K2
WLSDN NW10 82 A6
Phillimore Gardens Cl
KENS W8 119 K3
Phillimore Pl KENS W8 119 K2
Phillimore Ter KENS W8 * 119 K3
Phillimore Wk KENS W8 119 K3
Phillipp St IS N1 7 H1
Phillips Cl DART DA1 170 E1
Philpot La FENCHST EC3M 13 G5
Philpot St WCHPL E1 * 104 D5
Phineas Pett Rd
ELTH/MOT SE9 146 D4
Phipp's Bridge Rd MTCM CR4 178 C6
Phipps Hatch La ENC/FH EN2 23 J1
Phipp's Ms BGVA SW1W 15 J5
Phipp St SDTCH EC2A 7 G6
Phoebeth Rd LEW SE13 144 D6
Phoenix Cl HACK E8 * 86 B6
NTHWD HA6 26 D6
WALTH E17 51 H5
WWKM BR4 199 G6
Phoenix Ct BTFD TW8 117 F5
POP/IOD E14 124 D4
Phoenix Dr HAYES BR2 215 H2
Phoenix Pk BTFD TW8 * 116 E5
Phoenix Pl DART DA1 171 G2
FSBYW WC1X 5 H6
Phoenix Rd CAMTN NW1 4 C4
PGE/AN SE20 181 K2
Phoenix St LSQ/SEVD WC2H 10 D4
Phoenix Wy HEST TW5 114 C6
Phoenix Wharf Rd STHWK SE1 19 K3
Phyllis Av NWMAL KT3 192 E2
Physic Pl CHEL SW3 120 E6
Picardy Manorway BELV DA17 129 J3
Picardy Rd BELV DA17 129 H5
Picardy St BELV DA17 129 H3
Piccadilly MYFR/PICC W1J 15 K1
Piccadilly Ar MYFR/PICC W1J 10 A7
Piccadilly Circ MYFR/PICC W1J 10 B6
Pickard Cl STHGT/OAK N14 34 D3
Pickard St FSBYE EC1V 6 B4
Pickering Av EHAM E6 108 A1
Pickering Gdns
FBAR/BDGN N11 48 A2
SNWD SE25 197 G3
Pickering Pl STJS SW1Y * 16 B1
Pickering St IS N1 85 H6
Pickets Cl BUSH WD23 28 D3
Pickets St BAL SW12 161 F2
Pickett Cft STAN HA7 43 K4
Pickett's Lock La ED N9 37 F4
Pickford Cl BXLYHN DA7 149 F3
Pickford La BXLYHN DA7 149 F3
Pickford Rd BXLYHN DA7 149 F4
Pickfords Whf IS N1 * 6 C3
Pickhurst Gn HAYES BR2 199 J4
Pickhurst La HAYES BR2 199 J3
Pickhurst Md HAYES BR2 199 J4
Pickhurst Pk HAYES BR2 199 H3
Pickhurst Ri WWKM BR4 199 G5
Pickwick Cl HSLWW TW4 134 D6
Pickwick Ms UED N18 50 A1
Pickwick Pl HRW HA1 60 E4
Pickwick Rd DUL SE21 162 E2
Pickwick St STHWK SE1 18 C3
Pickwick Wy CHST BR7 185 H2
Pickworth Cl VX/NE SW8 * 141 K1
Picton Pl MBLAR W1H 9 H4
Picton St CMBW SE5 142 E1
Pied Bull Yd IS N1 6 A1
Piedmont Rd
WOOL/PLUM SE18 127 J5
Pier Head WAP E1W * 123 J1
Piermont Pl BMLY BR1 184 C5
Piermont Rd EDUL SE22 143 J6
Pierrepoint Ar IS N1 * 6 A2
Pierrepoint Rd ACT W3 98 D6
Pierrepoint Rw IS N1 6 A2
Pier Rd CAN/RD E16 126 E2
EBED/NFELT TW14 134 A6
ERITH DA8 130 B6
Pier St POP/IOD E14 125 F4
Pier Ter WAND/EARL SW18 140 A5
Pier Wy WOOL/PLUM SE18 127 J3
Pigeon La HPTN TW12 155 F6
Pigott St POP/IOD E14 105 J5
Pike Cl BMLY BR1 184 A1
Pike Rd MLHL NW7 31 F6
Pike's End PIN HA5 59 F1
Pikestone Cl YEAD UB4 * 95 J3
Pilgrimage St STHWK SE1 18 E3
Pilgrim Cl MRDN SM4 194 A4
Pilgrim Hl WNWD SE27 162 D6
Pilgrims Cl NTHLT UB5 78 C3
PLMGR N13 35 F6
Pilgrims Ct DART DA1 151 K6
Pilgrim's La HAMP NW3 83 H2
Pilgrims Ms POP/IOD E14 106 B6
Pilgrims Pl ASHF TW15 * 152 C6
Pilgrim's Ri EBAR EN4 21 J6
Pilgrim St BLKFR EC4V * 12 A4
Pilgrims Wy ARCH N19 66 D5
SAND/SEL CR2 212 B4
WBLY HA9 62 D5
Pilkington Rd ORP BR6 216 C1
PECK SE15 143 J3
Pilot Cl DEPT SE8 124 C6
Pilsden Cl WIM/MER SW19 * 159 G3
Piltdown Rd OXHEY WD19 27 H6
Pilton Pl WALW SE17 122 D5
Pimlico Rd BGVA SW1W 121 F5
Pinchbeck Rd ORP BR6 217 F4
Pinchin & Johnsons Yd
WCHPL E1 * 104 C6
Pinchin St WCHPL E1 104 C6
Pincott Pl BROCKY SE4 144 A4
Pincott Rd BXLYHS DA6 149 H6
WIM/MER SW19 178 B4
Pindar St SDTCH EC2A 13 G1
Pindock Ms MV/WKIL W9 101 F3
Pine Apple Ct WESTW SW1E * 16 A4
Pine Av SRTFD E15 88 B3
WWKM BR4 198 E5
Pine Cl LEY E10 69 J6
PGE/AN SE20 181 K4
STAN HA7 29 H6
STHGT/OAK N14 34 C2
Pine Coombe CROY/NA CR0 213 F2
Pinecrest Gdns ORP BR6 216 B2
Pinecroft KTN/HRWW/W HA3 62 B2
WELL DA16 148 B1
Pinecroft Crs BAR EN5 20 C5
Pinefield Cl POP/IOD E14 * 105 J6
Pine Gdns BRYLDS KT5 191 H3
RSLP HA4 59 F5
Pine Gld ORP BR6 215 K2
Pine Gv FSBYPK N4 66 E6
TRDG/WHET N20 32 D3
WIM/MER SW19 177 J1
Pinelands Cl BKHTH/KID SE3 * 145 J1
Pinelees Ct
MORT/ESHN SW14 * 137 K5
Pinemartin Cl CRICK NW2 82 A1
Pine Rdg CAR SM5 210 A6
Pine Rd CRICK NW2 82 A2
FBAR/BDGN N11 34 A4
Pines Cl NTHWD HA6 40 C2
Pines Rd BMLY BR1 184 D5
The Pines NRWD SE19 * 180 C2
STHGT/OAK N14 22 C6
WFD IG8 38 E5
Pine St CLKNW EC1R 5 J6
Pine Tree Cl HEST TW5 134 A2
Pine Wk BRYLDS KT5 191 H3
Pinewood Av BFN/LL DA15 167 K3
PIN HA5 42 B2
RAIN RM13 111 K3
Pinewood Cl CROY/NA CR0 213 G1
NTHWD HA6 40 E1
ORP BR6 201 J5
PIN HA5 42 B2
Pinewood Dr ORP BR6 216 E3
Pinewood Gv WEA W13 97 J5
Pinewood Ldg BUSH WD23 * 28 D3
Pinewood Ms
STWL/WRAY TW19 152 A1
Pinewood Pl BXLY DA5 170 B4
Pinewood Rd ABYW SE2 128 E6
FELT TW13 154 A5
HAYES BR2 199 K1
Pinfold Rd STRHM/NOR SW16 161 K6
Pinglestone Cl WDR/YW UB7 132 B1
Pinkcoat Cl FELT TW13 154 A5
Pinkham Wy North Circular Rd
MUSWH N10 47 K3
Pinkwell Av HYS/HAR UB3 113 G4
Pinkwell La HYS/HAR UB3 113 G4
Pinley Gdns DAGW RM9 91 H6
Pinnacle Hl BXLYHN DA7 149 J5
Pinnacle Hl North
BXLYHN DA7 149 J4
Pinnell Rd ELTH/MOT SE9 146 C5
Pinner Ct PIN HA5 60 A1
Pinner Gn PIN HA5 41 G5
Pinner Gv PIN HA5 59 J1
Pinner Hl PIN HA5 41 F3
Pinner Hill Rd PIN HA5 41 G4
Pinner Park Av
RYLN/HDSTN HA2 42 C5
Pinner Park Gdns
RYLN/HDSTN HA2 42 C5
Pinner Rd HRW HA1 60 B2
NTHWD HA6 40 D4
OXHEY WD19 27 H1
PIN HA5 59 K1
Pinner Vw RYLN/HDSTN HA2 60 C1
Pinn Wy RSLP HA4 58 B4
Pintail Cl EHAM E6 107 J4
Pintail Rd WFD IG8 53 F3
Pintail Wy YEAD UB4 95 H4
Pinto Cl BORE WD6 * 31 F1
Pinto Wy BKHTH/KID SE3 146 A5
Pioneer Cl SHB W12 99 K5
Pioneer St PECK SE15 143 H2
Pioneer Wy SHB W12 100 A5
WATW WD18 26 D1
Piper Cl HOLWY N7 85 F3
Piper Rd KUT/HW KT1 175 H6
Pipers Gdns CROY/NA CR0 198 B4
Pipers Gn CDALE/KGS NW9 62 E2
Pipers Green La EDGW HA8 30 A5
Pipewell Rd CAR SM5 194 D3
Pippin Cl CRICK NW2 81 J1
CROY/NA CR0 198 C5
Pippins Cl WDR/YW UB7 112 A3
Piquet Rd PGE/AN SE20 181 K5
Pirbright Crs CROY/NA CR0 214 A4
Pirbright Rd
WAND/EARL SW18 159 J3
Pirie St CAN/RD E16 126 A1
Pitcairn Cl ROMW/RG RM7 74 C1
Pitcairn Rd MTCM CR4 178 E3
Pitchford St SRTFD E15 88 B5
Pitfield Crs THMD SE28 128 B1
Pitfield St IS N1 7 G4
Pitfield Wy PEND EN3 24 E2
WLSDN NW10 80 E4
Pitfold Rd LEE/GVPK SE12 165 K2
Pitlake CROY/NA CR0 196 C6
Pitman St CMBW SE5 142 D1
Pitsea Pl WCHPL E1 105 F5
Pitsea St WCHPL E1 105 F5
Pitshanger La EA W5 97 H3
Pitt Crs WIM/MER SW19 160 A6
Pittman Gdns IL IG1 90 C3
Pitt Rd ORP BR6 216 C2
RYLN/HDSTN HA2 60 C6
THHTH CR7 196 D2
Pitt's Head Ms
MYFR/PKLN W1K 15 H1
Pittsmead Av HAYES BR2 199 K4
Pitt St KENS W8 119 K2
Pittville Gdns SNWD SE25 181 H6
Pixley St POP/IOD E14 105 H5
Pixton Wy CROY/NA CR0 213 H5
Place Farm Av ORP BR6 201 J5
Plaistow Gv BMLY BR1 184 A3
SRTFD E15 88 D6
Plaistow La BMLY BR1 183 K3
Plaistow Park Rd PLSTW E13 107 F1
Plaistow Rd PLSTW E13 106 E1
SRTFD E15 88 D6
Plane St SYD SE26 163 J5
Plane Tree Crs FELT TW13 154 A5
Plantagenet Cl
HOR/WEW KT19 207 F2
Plantagenet Gdns CHDH RM6 73 K4
Plantagenet Pl CHDH RM6 73 K4

Plantagenet Rd BAR EN5.....21 G5
Plantain Gdns WAN E11 *.....88 B1
Plantain Pl STHWK SE1.....18 E2
Plantation Dr STMC/STPC BR5...202 E5
Plantation La FENCHST EC3M...13 G5
Plantation Rd ERITH DA8.....150 D2
The Plantation
  BKHTH/KID SE3.....145 K3
Plashet Gv EHAM E6.....89 G6
Plashet Rd PLSTW E13.....88 E6
Plassy Rd CAT SE6.....164 E2
Platina St SDTCH EC2A.....7 F6
Plato Rd CLAP SW4.....141 K5
Platt's La HAMP NW3.....82 E1
Platts Rd PEND EN3.....24 E2
Platt St CAMTN NW1.....4 C2
Plawsfield Rd BECK BR3.....182 A4
Plaxtol Cl BMLY BR1.....184 B4
Plaxtol Rd ERITH DA8.....149 H1
Playfair St HMSMTH W6 *.....119 F5
Playfield Av CRW RM5.....56 E4
Playfield Crs EDUL SE22.....143 F6
Playfield Rd EDGW HA8.....44 E5
Playford Rd FSBYPK N4.....66 G5
Playgreen Wy CAT SE6.....164 D6
Playground Cl BECK BR3.....182 A5
Playhouse Ct STHWK SE1 *.....18 C2
Playhouse Yd BLKFR EC4V.....12 A4
Plaza Pde ALP/SUD HA0 *.....80 A4
Pleasance Rd PUT/ROE SW15..138 E3
  STMC/STPC BR5.....186 C5
The Pleasance PUT/ROE SW15.138 E5
Pleasant Gv CROY/NA CRO.....213 H1
Pleasant Pl IS N1.....85 H5
Pleasant Vw ERITH DA8.....130 B5
Pleasant Wy ALP/SUD HA0 *.....97 J4
Plender St CAMTN NW1 *.....4 A1
Pleshey Rd HOLWY N7.....84 D2
Plesman Wy WLGTN SM6 *.....210 E6
Plevna Crs SEVS/STOTM N15..68 A3
Plevna Rd ED N9.....36 C5
  HPTN TW12.....172 E4
Plevna St POP/IOD E14.....125 F3
Pleydell Av HMSMTH W6.....118 C3
  NRWD SE19.....181 G3
Pleydell Est FSBYE EC1V.....6 D5
Pleydell Gdns NRWD SE19 *..181 G2
Pleydell St EMB EC4Y.....11 K4
Plimsoll Cl POP/IOD E14.....105 K5
Plimsoll Rd FSBYPK N4.....85 H1
Plough Farm Cl RSLP HA4.....58 B3
Plough La CROY/NA CRO.....210 E2
  EDUL SE22.....163 G1
  TEDD TW11 *.....174 B1
  WIM/MER SW19.....178 B1
  WLGTN SM6.....210 E6
Plough Lane Cl WLGTN SM6.210 E3
Ploughmans Cl CAMTN NW1...84 D6
Ploughmans End ISLW TW7....135 J6
Plough Pl FLST/FETLN EC4A...11 K3
  NRWD SE19.....181 G3
Plough St BTSEA SW11.....140 C4
  HOR/WEW KT19 *.....207 F5
Plough St WCHPL E1 *.....104 C5
Plough Ter BTSEA SW11.....140 C5
Plough Wy BERM/RHTH SE16..124 A4
Plough Yd SDTCH EC2A.....7 H7
Plover Wy BERM/RHTH SE16..124 B3
  YEAD UB4.....95 H5
Plowden Blds EMB EC4Y *.....11 J5
Plowman Cl UED N18.....49 K1
Plowman Wy BCTR RM8.....73 J5
Plumbers Rw WCHPL E1.....104 C4
Plumbridge St GNWCH SE10 *.145 F2
Plum Cl FELT TW13.....153 K3
Plum Garth BTFD TW8.....116 E4
Plum La WOOL/PLUM SE18.....147 G1
Plummer La MTCM CR4.....178 E4
Plummer Rd CLAP SW4.....161 H1
Plumpton Cl NTHLT UB5.....78 A4
Plumpton Wy CAR SM5.....209 J1
Plumstead Common Rd
  WOOL/PLUM SE18.....127 H6
Plumstead High St
  WOOL/PLUM SE18.....127 J4
Plumstead Rd
  WOOL/PLUM SE18.....127 H4
Plumtree Cl DAGE RM10.....92 D4
Plumtree Ct FLST/FETLN EC4A..11 K3
  CAN/RD E16.....106 E4
Plymouth Rd BMLY BR1.....184 A4
Plymouth Wharf POP/IOD E14.125 G4
Plympton Av KIL/WHAMP NW6..82 D5
Plympton Cl BELV DA17 *.....129 F3
Plympton Pl STJWD NW8 *.....2 C7
Plympton Rd KIL/WHAMP NW6..82 D5
Plympton St STJWD NW8.....2 C7
Plymstock Rd WELL DA16.....148 D1
Pocklington Cl CDALE/KGS NW9..45 G3
Pocock Av WDR/YW UB7.....112 C3
Pocock St STHWK SE1.....18 A2
Podmore Rd
  WAND/EARL SW18.....140 B5
Poet's Rd HBRY N5.....85 K3
Poets Wy HRW HA1 *.....60 E1
Pointalls Cl FNCH N3.....47 G5
Point Cl GNWCH SE10.....145 F2
Pointer Cl THMD SE28.....109 K5
Pointers Cl POP/IOD E14.....124 E5
Point Hi GNWCH SE10.....145 F2
Point Pl WBLY HA9.....80 D5
Point Pleasant
  WAND/EARL SW18.....139 K5
Point Wharf La BTFD TW8.....136 E1
Poland St SOHO/CST W1F.....10 B3
Polebrook Rd
  BKHTH/KID SE3.....146 B4
Polecroft La CAT SE6.....164 C4
Pole Hill Rd CHING E4.....38 A2
Polesden Gdns RYNPK SW20..176 E6
Polesworth Rd DAGW RM9.....110 B1
Pollard Cl CAN/RD E16.....106 E6
  CHIG IG7.....55 G1
  HOLWY N7.....85 F3
Pollard Rd MRDN SM4.....194 C2

TRDG/WHET N20.....33 J4
Pollard Rw BETH E2.....104 C2
Pollards Crs
  STRHM/NOR SW16.....179 K6
Pollards Hi East
  STRHM/NOR SW16.....180 A6
Pollards Hi North
  STRHM/NOR SW16.....180 A6
Pollards Hi South
  STRHM/NOR SW16.....179 K6
Pollards Hi West
  STRHM/NOR SW16.....179 K6
Pollard St BETH E2 *.....104 C2
Pollards Wood Rd
  STRHM/NOR SW16.....179 K6
Pollen St CONDST W1S.....9 K4
Pollitt Dr STJWD NW8.....2 A6
Polperro Cl ORP BR6.....202 A3
Polperro Ms LBTH SE11.....17 K6
Polsted Rd CAT SE6.....164 C2
Polthorne Gv
  WOOL/PLUM SE18.....127 H4
Polworth Rd
  STRHM/NOR SW16.....179 K1
Polygon Rd CAMTN NW1 *.....4 C3
The Polygon CLAP SW4 *.....141 H5
Polytechnic St
  WOOL/PLUM SE18.....127 F4
Pomell Wy WCHPL E1.....13 K3
Pomeroy St NWCR SE14.....143 K1
Pomeroy St NWCR SE14.....143 K1
Pomfret Rd CMBW SE5.....142 C4
Pomoja La ARCH N19.....66 E6
Pond Cl BKHTH/KID SE3.....145 K2
  NFNCH/WDSP N12.....47 J2
Pond Cottage La BECK BR3...198 D5
Ponder St HOLWY N7 *.....85 F5
Pond Farm Est CLPT E5 *.....86 E1
Pondfield Rd DAGE RM10.....92 D3
  HAYES BR2.....199 H5
  ORP BR6.....216 C2
Pond Gn RSLP HA4.....58 C6
Pond Hill Gdns CHEAM SM3 *.208 C4
Pond Md DDUL SE21.....162 E1
Pond Pl CHEL SW3.....14 C7
Pond Rd BKHTH/KID SE3.....145 K4
  SRTFD E15.....106 C1
Pondside Cl HYS/HAR UB3...133 G1
Pond St HAMP NW3.....83 J3
Pond Wy TEDD TW11 *.....174 D2
Pondwood Ri ORP BR6.....201 K4
Ponler St WCHPL E1.....104 D5
Ponsard Rd WLSDN NW10.....100 A2
Ponsford St HOM E9.....86 E4
Ponsonby Pl WEST SW1P.....121 J5
Ponsonby Rd PUT/ROE SW15.158 E2
Ponsonby Ter WEST SW1P.....121 J5
Pontefract Rd BMLY BR1.....183 K1
Ponton Rd VX/NE SW8.....141 J1
Pont St KTBR SW1X.....14 E5
Pont Street Ms CHEL SW3.....14 E5
Pool Cl BECK BR3.....182 D1
  E/WMO/HCT KT8.....188 C2
Poole Cl CAT SE6.....164 D4
Poole Court Rd HEST TW5.....134 D3
Poole Rd HOM E9.....87 F4
  HOR/WEW KT19.....207 F4
Pooles Blds FSBYW WC1X.....5 J7
Pooles La WBPTN SW10 *.....140 B6
Pooles Pk FSBYPK N4.....67 G6
Poole St IS N1.....6 E1
Poole Wy YEAD UB4 *.....94 C2
Pooley Dr
  MORT/ESHN SW14.....137 K4
Poolmans St
  BERM/RHTH SE16.....124 A2
Pool Rd E/WMO/HCT KT8.....188 E2
  HRW HA1.....60 D4
Poolsford Rd CDALE/KGS NW9..63 G1
Poonah St WCHPL E1.....104 E5
Pope Cl EBED/NFELT TW14...153 J3
  WIM/MER SW19 *.....178 C2
Pope Rd HAYES BR2.....200 C2
Pope's Av WHTN TW2.....155 K4
Popes Dr FNCH N3.....46 E4
Popes Gv CROY/NA CRO.....213 H1
  WHTN TW2.....155 K4
Pope's La EA W5.....116 E3
Pope's Rd BRXN/ST SW9 *.....142 B5
Pope St STHWK SE1.....19 H3
Popham Cl FELT TW13.....154 D5
Popham Gdns
  RCH/KEW TW9 *.....137 J4
Popham Rd IS N1.....85 J6
Popham St IS N1.....6 C1
Popinjays Rw CHEAM SM3 *..208 B3
Poplar Av MTCM CR4.....178 E4
  NWDGN UB2.....115 G3
  ORP BR6.....201 G6
Poplar Bath St POP/IOD E14...105 K6
Poplar Cl HOM E9.....87 H3
  PIN HA5.....41 J3
Poplar Court Pde TWK TW1 *.156 D1
Poplar Crs HHSMTH W6 *.....119 F2
Poplar Farm Cl
  HOR/WEW KT19.....206 E4
Poplar Gdns NWMAL KT3.....176 A5
Poplar Gv FBAR/BDGN N11...48 A2
  NWMAL KT3.....176 A5
  WBLY HA9.....80 E1
Poplar High St POP/IOD E14..105 K6
Poplar Ms SHB W12 *.....119 F1
Poplar Mt BELV DA17.....129 J4
Poplar Pl BAY/PAD W2.....101 F6
  HYS/HAR UB3.....94 E6
  THMD SE28.....109 K6
Poplar Rd CHEAM SM3.....193 J5
  HNHL SE24.....142 D5
  WIM/MER SW19.....177 K5
Poplar Rd South
  WIM/MER SW19.....177 K6
Poplars Cl RSLP HA4.....58 C6
Poplars Rd WALTH E17.....69 K3

The Poplars STHGT/OAK N14...22 B6
Poplar St ROMW/RG RM7.....74 E1
Poplar Vw WBLY HA9 *.....61 K6
Poplar Wk CROY/NA CRO.....196 D6
  HNHL SE24.....142 D5
Poplar Wy BARK/HLT IG6.....54 C2
  FELT TW13.....153 K5
Poppins Ct FLST/FETLN EC4A..12 A4
Poppleton Rd WAN E11.....70 C3
Poppy Cl BELV DA17.....129 J3
  HAYES BR2.....215 G3
Poppy La CROY/NA CRO.....197 K4
Porchester Garden Ms
  BAY/PAD W2 *.....101 F5
Porchester Gdns BAY/PAD W2.101 F6
Porchester Ga BAY/PAD W2 *.101 G6
Porchester Md BECK BR3.....182 E2
Porchester Pl BAY/PAD W2...8 D4
Porchester Rd BAY/PAD W2..101 F5
  KUT/HW KT1.....175 J5
Porchester Square Ms
  BAY/PAD W2 *.....101 F5
Porchester Ter BAY/PAD W2.101 G6
Porch Wy TRDG/WHET N20....33 K3
Porcupine Cl ELTH/MOT SE9.166 D4
Porden Rd BRXS/STRHM SW2.142 A5
Porlock Av RYLN/HDSTN HA2..60 C5
Porlock Rd EN EN1.....36 A1
Porlock St STHWK SE1.....19 F2
Porrington Cl CHST BR7.....184 E4
Portal Cl RSLP HA4.....76 E2
  WNWD SE27.....162 B5
Portbury Cl PECK SE15.....143 H2
Portchester Cl CMBW SE5.....142 D5
Portcullis Lodge Rd
  ENC/FH EN2.....23 K4
Portelet Rd WCHPL E1.....105 F2
Porten Houses WKENS W14 *.119 H3
Porten Rd WKENS W14.....119 H3
Porter Rd EHAM E6.....107 K5
Porters Av DAGW RM9.....91 H4
Porter St MHST W1U.....9 F1
  STHWK SE1.....12 D7
Porters Wk WAP E1W *.....104 D6
Porters Wy WDR/YW UB7.....112 C5
Porteus Rd BAY/PAD W2.....101 G4
Portgate Cl MV/WKIL W9.....100 D3
Porthcawe Rd SYD SE26.....164 B6
Porthkerry Av WELL DA16.....148 B5
Portia Wy BOW E3.....105 H3
The Porticos WBPTN SW10 *.120 C6
Portinscale Rd PUT/ROE SW15.139 H6
Portland Av BFN/LL DA15.....168 B1
  NWMAL KT3.....192 D4
  STNW/STAM N16.....68 B5
Portland Crs ELTH/MOT SE9..166 D4
  FELT TW13.....153 G6
  GFD/PVL UB6.....96 A4
  STAN HA7.....43 K5
Portland Crs West STAN HA7..43 K6
Portland Dr ENC/FH EN2.....24 A1
Portland Gdns CHDH RM6.....73 K2
  FSBYPK N4.....67 H3
Portland Gv VX/NE SW8.....142 A2
Portland Ms SOHO/CST W1F..10 B4
Portland Pl CAVSQ/HST W1G..9 J2
  SNWD SE25.....197 H1
Portland Ri FSBYPK N4.....67 H5
Portland Rd ASHF TW15.....152 B5
  BMLY BR1.....166 B6
  KUT/HW KT1.....175 F6
  MTCM CR4.....178 D5
  NTGHL W11.....100 C6
  NWDGN UB2.....114 E3
  SEVS/STOTM N15.....68 A1
  SNWD SE25.....197 J1
  YEAD UB4.....94 C2
Portland Sq WAP E1W.....123 J1
Portland St WALW SE17.....122 E5
Portland Ter RCH/KEW TW9 *.136 E5
Portman Av
  MORT/ESHN SW14.....138 A4
Portman Cl BXLY DA5.....170 B3
  BXLYHN DA7.....148 E4
  MBLAR W1H *.....9 F3
Portman Dr WFD IG8.....53 H5
Portman Gdns CDALE/KGS NW9..45 F4
Portman Ms South MBLAR W1H.9 F4
Portman Rd KUT/HW KT1.....175 G5
Portman Sq MBLAR W1H.....9 F3
Portman St MBLAR W1H.....9 F4
Portman Towers MBLAR W1H..9 F3
Portmeadow Wk ABFW SE2...128 E2
Portmeers Cl WALTH E17 *.....69 H3
Portnall Rd MV/WKIL W9.....100 D2
Portobello Ct NTGHL W11 *.....100 D6
Portobello Ms NTGHL W11 *..100 D6
Portobello Rd NKENS W10.....100 C4
Portpool La FSBYW WC1X.....11 J1
Portree Cl POP/IOD E14 *.....106 E5
Portree St POP/IOD E14.....106 B5
Portsea Ms BAY/PAD W2.....8 D4
Portsea Pl BAY/PAD W2.....8 D4
Portside Rd VX/NE SW8.....141 H3
Portsmouth Av THDIT KT7.....190 B4
Portsmouth Rd
  ESH/CLAY KT10.....204 A4
  KUT/HW KT1.....174 E6
  PUT/ROE SW15.....158 E3
Portsmouth St LINN WC2A.....11 H3
Portsoken St TWRH EC3N.....13 J5
Portugal Gdns WHTN TW2 *..155 H4
Portugal St LINN WC2A.....11 H4
Portway RAIN RM13.....93 J2
  SRTFD E15.....88 E6
Portway Crs EW KT17.....207 J6

Portway Gdns
  WOOL/PLUM SE18.....146 C2
Postern Gn ENC/FH EN2.....23 G3
The Postern BARB EC2Y *.....12 D2
Post La WHTN TW2.....155 J5
Postmill Cl CROY/NA CRO.....212 E1
Post Office Ap FSTGT E7.....89 F3
Post Rd NWDGN UB2.....115 G3
Postway Ms IL IG1 *.....90 B1
Potier St STHWK SE1.....19 F5
Potter Cl MTCM CR4.....179 G5
  WAN E11.....70 B5
The Potteries BAR EN5 *.....20 E6
Potterne Cl WIM/MER SW19..159 G2
Potters Cl CROY/NA CRO.....198 B5
Potters Fld EN EN1 *.....24 A5
Potters Gv NWMAL KT3.....191 K1
Potters Heights Cl PIN HA5...41 F3
Potter's La BAR EN5.....20 E5
  STRHM/NOR SW16 *.....179 J2
Potter's Rd BAR EN5.....21 F5
  FUL/PGN SW6.....140 B3
Potter St NTHWD HA6.....40 E4
Pottery Cl SNWD SE25.....197 J1
Pottery La NTGHL W11.....119 H1
Pottery Rd BTFD TW8.....117 F6
  BXLY DA5.....169 K4
Pottery St BERM/RHTH SE16 *..123 J2
Pott St BETH E2.....104 D2
Poulett Gdns TWK TW1.....156 A4
Poulett Rd EHAM E6.....107 K1
Poulter Pk MTCM CR4.....194 D5
Poulters Wd HAYES BR2.....215 H3
Poulton Av SUT SM1.....209 H1
Poulton Cl HACK E8.....86 D4
Poultry LOTH EC2R.....12 E4
Pound Cl ORP BR6.....201 J6
  SURB KT6.....190 D5
Pound Court Dr ORP BR6.....201 J6
Pound Farm La
  ESH/CLAY KT10.....189 J5
Pound La WLSDN NW10.....81 J5
Pound Park Rd CHARL SE7.....126 C4
Pound Pl ELTH/MOT SE9.....167 F1
Pound St CAR SM5.....209 K3
Pountney Rd BTSEA SW11.....141 F4
Poverest Rd STMC/STPC BR5..202 A2
Powder Mill La DART DA1.....171 H4
  WHTN TW2.....154 E3
Powell Cl EDGW HA8.....44 B2
Powell Gdns DAGE RM10.....92 C2
Powell Rd BKHH IG9.....39 G2
  CLPT E5.....86 D1
Power Rd CHSWK W4.....117 H4
Powers Ct TWK TW1.....156 E1
Powerscroft Rd CLPT E5.....86 E2
  SCUP DA14.....186 D2
Powis Cl BUSH WD23 *.....28 D5
Powis Gdns GLDGN NW11.....64 D4
  NTGHL W11.....100 D5
Powis Ms NTGHL W11.....100 D5
Powis Pl BMSBY WC1N.....5 F7
Powis Rd BOW E3.....105 K2
Powis Sq NTGHL W11.....100 D5
Powis St WOOL/PLUM SE18..127 F3
Powlett Pl CAMTN NW1 *.....84 B5
Pownall Gdns HSLW TW3.....135 G5
Pownall Rd HACK E8.....86 C6
  HSLW TW3.....135 G5
Pownsett Ter IL IG1 *.....90 C3
Powster Rd BMLY BR1.....183 K1
Powys Cl BXLYHN DA7.....128 E6
Powys La PLMGR N13.....34 E6
Poynders Rd CLAP SW4.....161 H2
Poynings Cl ORP BR6.....202 D6
Poynings Rd ARCH N19.....84 C1
Poynings Wy
  NFNCH/WDSP N12.....46 E1
Poyntell Crs CHST BR7.....185 J4
Poynter Rd EN EN1.....24 B6
Poynton Rd TOTM N17.....50 C5
Poyntz Rd BTSEA SW11.....140 E3
Poyser St BETH E2.....104 D1
Praed Ms BAY/PAD W2.....8 B3
Praed St BAY/PAD W2.....8 B3
Pragel St PLSTW E13.....107 F1
Pragnell Rd LEE/GVPK SE12..166 A4
Prague Pl BRXS/STRHM SW2..141 K6
Prah Rd FSBYPK N4.....67 G6
Prairie St VX/NE SW8.....141 F3
Pratt Ms CAMTN NW1 *.....4 A1
Pratt St CAMTN NW1.....4 A1
Pratt Wk LBTH SE11.....17 H6
Prayle Gv CRICK NW2.....64 B5
Prebend Gdns CHSWK W4....118 C4
Prebend St IS N1.....6 C1
Precinct Rd HYS/HAR UB3.....94 E6
Premiere Pl POP/IOD E14.....105 J6
Premier Park Rd WLSDN NW10..98 D1
Prendergast Rd
  BKHTH/KID SE3.....145 H3
Prentis Rd STRHM/NOR SW16.161 K6
Prentiss Ct CHARL SE7.....126 C4
Presburg Rd NWMAL KT3.....192 B2
Presburg St CLPT E5 *.....87 F1
Prescelly Pl EDGW HA8.....44 B4
Prescot St WCHPL E1.....13 K5
Prescott Av STMC/STPC BR5..201 G3
Prescott Cl EMPK RM11.....75 K5
Prescott Pl CLAP SW4.....141 J4
Presentation Ms
  BRXS/STRHM SW2.....162 A4
Presidents Dr WAP E1W.....123 J1
President St FSBYE EC1V *.....6 C4
Press Rd WLSDN NW10.....81 F1
Prestage Wy POP/IOD E14 *..106 A6
Prestbury Rd FSTGT E7.....89 G5
Prestbury Sq ELTH/MOT SE9..166 E6
Prested Rd BTSEA SW11.....140 D5
Preston Av CHING E4.....52 B2
Preston Cl STHWK SE1 *.....19 G6
  WHTN TW2.....155 K5
Preston Dr BXLYHN DA7.....148 E1
  HOR/WEW KT19.....207 G4

WAN E11.....71 G5
Preston Gdns IL IG1.....71 J5
  WLSDN NW10 *.....81 J4
Preston Hi KTN/HRWW/W HA3..62 A4
Preston Pl RCHPK/HAM TW10..137 F6
  WLSDN NW10.....81 J4
Preston Rd
  KTN/HRWW/W HA3.....62 A4
  NRWD SE19.....180 C2
  RYNPK SW20.....176 D3
  WAN E11.....70 C2
Prestons Rd HAYES BR2.....214 E1
  POP/IOD E14.....106 A6
Preston Vls KUT/HW KT1 *.....175 G5
Preston Waye
  KTN/HRWW/W HA3.....62 A5
Prestwich Ter CLAP SW4 *.....141 J6
Prestwick Cl NWDGN UB2....114 C5
Prestwick Rd OXHEY WD19 *..27 J4
Prestwood OXHEY WD19 *.....27 J4
Prestwood Av
  KTN/HRWW/W HA3.....61 H1
Prestwood Cl
  KTN/HRWW/W HA3.....61 H1
  WOOL/PLUM SE18 *.....128 C6
Prestwood Dr CRW RM5.....56 E1
Prestwood Gdns
  CROY/NA CRO.....196 D4
Prestwood St IS N1 *.....6 D3
Pretoria Av WALTH E17.....69 G1
Pretoria Crs CHING E4.....38 A3
Pretoria Pde LEW SE13 *.....144 D5
Pretoria Rd CAN/RD E16.....106 D2
  CHING E4.....38 A3
  IL IG1.....90 B2
  ROMW/RG RM7.....74 E1
  STRHM/NOR SW16.....179 G2
  TOTM N17.....42 B5
  WAN E11.....70 B6
Pretoria Rd North UED N18.....50 B2
Prevost Rd FBAR/BDGN N11..34 A4
Price Cl MLHL NW7.....32 A6
  TOOT SW17.....160 E5
Price Rd CROY/NA CRO.....211 H3
Price's St STHWK SE1.....18 B1
Pricklers Hl BAR EN5.....21 F5
Prickley Wd HAYES BR2.....199 J5
Priddy's Yd CROY/NA CRO *..196 D6
Prideaux Pl ACT W3.....99 F6
  FSBYW WC1X.....5 H4
Prideaux Rd BRXN/ST SW9...141 K4
Pridham Rd THHTH CR7.....196 E1
Priestfield Rd FSTH SE23.....164 B5
Priestlands Park Rd
  BFN/LL DA15.....168 A5
Priestley Cl STNW/STAM N16 *..68 B4
Priestley Gdns CHDH RM6.....73 H3
Priestley Rd MTCM CR4.....179 F5
Priestley Wy CRICK NW2.....63 J5
  WALTH E17.....57 F1
Priest Park Av
  RYLN/HDSTN HA2.....60 A6
Priests Av ROM RM1.....57 H3
Priests Br MORT/ESHN SW14..138 B5
Prima Rd BRXN/ST SW9.....142 B1
Primrose Av ENC/FH EN2.....23 K2
  GDMY/SEVK IG3.....73 G4
Primrose Cl BOW E3.....105 J1
  CAT SE6.....183 F1
  RYLN/HDSTN HA2.....59 K4
  WLGTN SM6.....195 G5
Primrose Dr WDR/YW UB7...112 A4
Primrose Gdns BUSH WD23...28 B2
  HAMP NW3.....83 J4
  RSLP HA4.....77 G3
Primrose Hl EMB EC4Y.....11 K4
Primrose Hill Rd HAMP NW3...83 J4
Primrose Hill Studios
  CAMTN NW1 *.....84 A6
Primrose La CROY/NA CRO....197 K5
Primrose Ms CAMTN NW1 *...83 K5
Primrose Pl ISLW TW7 *.....136 A3
Primrose Rd LEY E10.....69 K5
  SWFD E18.....53 F5
Primrose Sq HOM E9.....86 E5
Primrose St SDTCH EC2A.....13 G1
Primrose Wk EW KT17.....207 H5
  NWCR SE14 *.....144 B1
Primrose Wy ALP/SUD HA0 *..97 K1
Primula St SHB W12.....99 J5
Prince Albert Rd CAMTN NW1..3 G1
  STJWD NW8.....2 C2
Prince Arthur Rd HAMP NW3..83 H3
Prince Charles Dr HDN NW4..64 A4
Prince Charles Rd
  BKHTH/KID SE3.....145 J2
Prince Charles Wy
  WLGTN SM6.....195 G5
Prince Consort Dr CHST BR7..185 J4
Prince Consort Rd SKENS SW7.14 A4
Princedale Rd NTGHL W11....119 H1
Prince Edward Rd HOM E9....87 H4
Prince George Av
  STHGT/OAK N14.....22 C6
Prince George Rd
  STNW/STAM N16.....86 A2
Prince George's Av
  RYNPK SW20.....177 F5
Prince George's Rd
  WIM/MER SW19.....178 C3
Prince Henry Rd CHARL SE7..146 C1
Prince Imperial Rd CHST BR7..185 F4
  WOOL/PLUM SE18.....146 E2
Prince John Rd ELTH/MOT SE9.146 D6
Princelet St WCHPL E1.....13 K1
Prince of Orange La
  GNWCH SE10 *.....145 F2
Prince of Wales Cl HDN NW4..63 K1
Prince of Wales Dr
  BTSEA SW11.....140 E2
Prince of Wales Ga
  SKENS SW7.....14 C2
Prince of Wales Pas
  CAMTN NW1 *.....4 A5

Prince of Wales Rd
BKHTH/KID SE3 145 J2
CAN/RD E16 107 G5
KTTN NW5 84 A4
SUT SM1 194 C6
Prince of Wales Ter
CHSWK W4 118 B5
KENS W8 * 120 A2
Prince Regent La PLSTW E13 107 G3
Prince Regent Ms CAMTN NW1 4 A5
Prince Regent Rd HSLW TW3 135 H4
Prince Rd SNWD SE25 197 F2
Prince Rupert Rd
ELTH/MOT SE9 146 E5
Princes Ar MYFR/PICC W1J 10 B7
Princes Av ACT W3 117 H3
CAR SM5 209 K5
CDALE/KGS NW9 62 C1
FNCH N3 47 F4
MUSWH N10 48 B6
PLMGR N13 49 G1
STMC/STPC BR5 201 K2
SURB KT6 191 H6
WDGN N22 48 D4
WFD IG8 39 F6
Princes Cl CDALE/KGS NW9 62 C1
EDGW HA8 44 C1
HPTN TW12 155 J6
SCUP DA14 168 E5
Princes Ct WBLY HA9 80 A3
Princes Dr HRW HA1 42 E6
Princes Gdns ACT W3 98 C5
EA W5 97 J3
SKENS SW7 14 B4
Prince's Ga SKENS SW7 14 C3
Princes Gate Ct SKENS SW7 14 A3
Princes Gate Ms SKENS SW7 14 B4
Princes La MUSWH N10 48 A6
Prince's Ms BAY/PAD W2 100 E6
HMSMTH W6 * 118 E5
IS N1 85 F6
Princes Pde GLDGN NW11 * 64 C3
Princes Pk RAIN RM13 93 J5
Princes Park Av GLDGN NW11 64 C3
HYS/HAR UB3 94 B6
Princes Park Cir HYS/HAR UB3 94 B6
Princes Park Cl HYS/HAR UB3 94 B6
Princes Park La HYS/HAR UB3 94 B6
Princes Park Pde HYS/HAR UB3 94 B6
Princes Pl NTGHL W11 119 H1
Prince's Pln HAYES BR2 200 D4
Princes Ri LEW SE13 145 F3
Princes Riverside Rd
BERM/RHTH SE16 124 A1
Princes Rd BARK/HLT IG6 72 D1
BKHH IG9 39 G4
DART DA1 170 E2
DART DA1 171 J3
FELT TW13 153 J5
KUTN/CMB KT2 175 H4
MORT/ESHN SW14 138 A4
PGE/AN SE20 182 A2
RCH/KEW TW9 137 G2
RCHPK/HAM TW10 137 G6
ROM RM1 75 J2
TEDD TW11 155 J6
UED N18 36 E6
WEA W13 116 C1
WIM/MER SW19 177 K2
Princess Alice Wy THMD SE28 127 J2
Princess Av WBLY HA9 62 A6
Princess Crs FSBYPK N4 67 H6
Princesses Pde DART DA1 * 150 C6
Princess La RSLP HA4 58 C5
Princess Louise Cl BAY/PAD W2 8 B1
Princess May Rd
STNW/STAM N16 86 A2
Princess Ms HAMP NW3 83 H4
Princess Pde ORP BR6 * 216 A1
Prince's Sq BAY/PAD W2 100 E6
Princess Rd CAMTN NW1 84 A6
CROY/NA CR0 196 D3
KIL/WHAMP NW6 100 E1
Princess St BXLYHN DA7 149 G4
STHWK SE1 18 B5
Princes St CONDST W1S 9 K4
LOTH EC2R 12 E4
RCH/KEW TW9 137 F5
SUT SM1 209 H2
TOTM N17 50 A2
Prince's Ter PLSTW E13 89 F6
Prince St DEPT SE8 124 C6
Princes Vw DART DA1 171 K3
Princes Wy BKHH IG9 39 G4
CROY/NA CR0 211 F3
RSLP HA4 77 J2
WIM/MER SW19 159 H3
WWKM BR4 214 D2
Prince's Yd NTGHL W11 119 H1
Princethorpe Rd SYD SE26 164 A6
Princeton St GINN WC1R 11 G2
Pringle Gdns
STRHM/NOR SW16 161 H6
Printers Inn Ct
FLST/FETLN EC4A 11 J3
Printinghouse La
HYS/HAR UB3 113 H2
Printing House Yd BETH E2 * 7 H5
Priolo Rd CHARL SE7 126 B5
Prior Av BELMT SM2 209 J5
Prior Bolton St IS N1 85 H4
Prioress Rd WNWD SE27 162 C5
Prioress St STHWK SE1 19 G5
Prior Rd IL IG1 90 A1
Priors Cft WALTH E17 51 G5
Priors Fld NTHLT UB5 77 J4
Priorsford Av STMC/STPC BR5 202 B1
Priors Gdns RSLP HA4 77 G3
Priors Md EN EN1 24 A2
Prior St GNWCH SE10 145 F1
Priory Av ALP/SUD HA0 79 F2
CEND/HSY/T N8 66 D1
CHEAM SM3 208 B2
CHING E4 37 H5
CHSWK W4 118 B3
STMC/STPC BR5 201 J3
WALTH E17 69 J2
Priory Cl ALP/SUD HA0 79 F2
BECK BR3 182 B6
BMLY BR1 184 E4
CHING E4 37 H5
DART DA1 151 F6
HPTN TW12 172 E4
HYS/HAR UB3 95 F6
RSLP HA4 58 D5
STAN HA7 29 F5
STHGT/OAK N14 22 B6
SWFD E18 52 E4
TRDG/WHET N20 32 D2
WIM/MER SW19 * 178 A4
Priory Ct BLKFR EC4V * 12 B4
VX/NE SW8 141 J2
WALTH E17 51 H6
Priory Crs ALP/SUD HA0 79 G1
CHEAM SM3 208 B2
NRWD SE19 180 D3
Priory Dr ABYW SE2 128 E5
STAN HA7 29 F5
Priory Field Dr EDGW HA8 30 D6
Priory Gdns ALP/SUD HA0 79 G2
BARN SW13 138 C4
CHSWK W4 * 118 B4
DART DA1 151 G6
HGT N6 66 B3
HPTN TW12 172 E4
SNWD SE25 197 G1
Priory Green Est IS N1 5 G2
Priory Gv CLAP SW4 141 K2
Priory Hl ALP/SUD HA0 79 G2
DART DA1 171 G1
Priory La E/WMO/HCT KT8 189 F1
PUT/ROE SW15 138 C6
Priory Leas ELTH/MOT SE9 * 166 D3
Priory Ms EMPK RM11 75 K5
Priory Pk BKHTH/KID SE3 145 J4
Priory Park Rd ALP/SUD HA0 79 G2
KIL/WHAMP NW6 82 D6
Priory Pl DART DA1 171 G1
Priory Rd BARK IG11 90 D5
CHEAM SM3 208 B2
CHSGTN KT9 206 A1
CHSWK W4 118 A3
CROY/NA CR0 196 B4
DART DA1 151 G5
EHAM E6 89 H6
HPTN TW12 172 E3
HSLW TW3 135 H6
KIL/WHAMP NW6 83 F5
MUSWH N10 66 C1
RCH/KEW TW9 117 H6
Priory St BOW E3 105 K2
Priory Ter KIL/WHAMP NW6 83 F6
The Priory BKHTH/KID SE3 145 J4
CROY/NA CR0 * 211 G1
ORP BR6 * 202 C4
Priory Vw BUSH WD23 28 E2
Priory Vls FBAR/BDGN N11 * 47 K2
Priory Wk WBPTN SW10 120 B5
Priory Wy NWDGN UB2 114 C3
RYLN/HDSTN HA2 60 B1
WDR/YW UB7 112 B6
Pritchard's Rd BETH E2 104 C1
Priter Rd BERM/RHTH SE16 * 123 H3
Private Rd EN EN1 23 K6
Probert Rd BRXS/STRHM SW2 142 B6
Probyn Rd BRXS/STRHM SW2 162 C4
Procter St GINN WC1R 11 G2
Proctor Cl MTCM CR4 179 F4
Proctors Cl EBED/NFELT TW14 153 K3
Progress Wy CROY/NA CR0 196 A6
EN EN1 24 C6
WDGN N22 49 G4
Promenade Approach Rd
CHSWK W4 138 B1
The Promenade CHSWK W4 138 B2
EDGW HA8 * 44 C1
Prospect Cl BELV DA17 129 H4
HEST TW5 134 E2
RSLP HA4 59 H4
SYD SE26 163 J6
Prospect Cottages
WAND/EARL SW18 139 K5
Prospect Crs WHTN TW2 155 H1
Prospect Hl WALTH E17 69 K1
Prospect Pl CHSWK W4 118 A5
CRICK NW2 82 D1
DART DA1 171 H1
EFNCH N2 65 H1
HAYES BR2 184 A6
ROMW/RG RM7 56 E5
RYNPK SW20 176 E3
WAP E1W 123 K1
Prospect Rd BAR EN5 20 E5
CRICK NW2 82 D1
SURB KT6 190 D3
WFD IG8 53 G1
Prospect St BERM/RHTH SE16 123 J2
Prospect V WOOL/PLUM SE18 126 D4
Prospero Rd ARCH N19 66 D5
Protea Cl CAN/RD E16 106 D3
Prothero Gdns HDN NW4 63 K2
Prothero Rd FUL/PGN SW6 139 H1
Prout Gv WLSDN NW10 81 G2
Prout Rd CLPT E5 86 D1
Providence Cl HOM E9 * 87 F6
Providence Ct MYFR/PKLN W1K 9 H5
Providence La HYS/HAR UB3 133 G1
Providence Pl IS N1 6 A1
ROMW/RG RM7 56 B4
Providence Rd WDR/YW UB7 112 B1
Providence Row Cl BETH E2 104 D2
Providence Sq STHWK SE1 19 G2
Providence Yd BETH E2 * 104 C2
Provincial Ter PGE/AN SE20 * 182 A3
Provost Est IS N1 6 E4
Provost Rd HAMP NW3 83 K5
Provost St FSBYE EC1V 6 E5
Prowse Av BUSH WD23 28 C4
Prowse Pl CAMTN NW1 84 C5
Pruden Cl STHGT/OAK N14 * 34 C4
Prusom St WAP E1W 123 J1
Pudding La MON EC3R 13 F5
Pudding Mill La SRTFD E15 87 K6
Puddle Dock BLKFR EC4V 12 B5
Puffin Cl BARK IG11 109 H2
CROY/NA CR0 198 A2
Pulborough Rd
WAND/EARL SW18 159 J2
Pulborough Wy HSLWW TW4 134 B5
Pulford Rd SEVS/STOTM N15 67 K3
Pulham Av EFNCH N2 65 G1
Puller Rd BAR EN5 20 C3
Pulleyns Av EHAM E6 107 J2
Pullman Gdns PUT/ROE SW15 159 F1
Pullman Ms LEE/GVPK SE12 166 A5
Pullman Pl ELTH/MOT SE9 146 D6
Pulross Rd BRXN/ST SW9 142 A4
Pulteney Cl BOW E3 87 H6
ISLW TW7 136 B4
Pulteney Rd SWFD E18 53 F6
Pulton Pl FUL/PGN SW6 139 K1
Puma Ct WCHPL E1 13 J1
Pump Aly BTFD TW8 136 E1
Pump Cl NTHLT UB5 96 A1
Pump Ct EMB EC4Y * 11 J4
Pump House Cl HAYES BR2 183 J5
Pump House Ms WCHPL E1 * 104 C6
Pumping Station Rd
CHSWK W4 138 B1
Pump La HYS/HAR UB3 113 K2
NWCR SE14 143 K1
Punderson's Gdns BETH E2 104 D2
Purbeck Av NWMAL KT3 192 C3
Purbeck Dr CRICK NW2 64 B6
Purbeck Rd EMPK RM11 75 J4
Purbrook St STHWK SE1 19 H4
Purcell Crs FUL/PGN SW6 * 119 G6
Purcell Ms WLSDN NW10 * 81 G5
Purcell Rd GFD/PVL UB6 96 B4
Purcells Av EDGW HA8 44 C1
Purcell St IS N1 7 G2
Purcers Cross Rd
FUL/PGN SW6 139 J2
Purchese St CAMTN NW1 4 C2
Purdy St BOW E3 105 K3
Purelake Ms LEW SE13 * 145 G4
Purland Cl BCTR RM8 74 B5
Purland Rd THMD SE28 128 A2
Purleigh Av WFD IG8 53 J2
Purley Av CRICK NW2 64 C6
Purley Cl CLAY IG5 54 A5
Purley Pl IS N1 85 H5
Purley Rd ED N9 35 K5
SAND/SEL CR2 211 K5
Purley Wy CROY/NA CR0 196 A5
CROY/NA CR0 211 G2
Purneys Rd ELTH/MOT SE9 146 C5
Purrett Rd WOOL/PLUM SE18 128 A5
Pursers Cross Rd
FUL/PGN SW6 * 139 J2
Pursewardens Cl WEA W13 116 D1
Pursley Rd MLHL NW7 45 K3
Purves Rd WLSDN NW10 99 K2
Putney Br PUT/ROE SW15 139 H4
Putney Bridge Ap
PUT/ROE SW15 139 H4
Putney Bridge Rd
PUT/ROE SW15 139 H5
Putney Common
PUT/ROE SW15 139 F4
Putney Ex PUT/ROE SW15 * 139 G5
Putney Heath PUT/ROE SW15 158 E1
Putney Heath La
PUT/ROE SW15 159 G1
Putney High St
PUT/ROE SW15 139 H5
Putney Hl PUT/ROE SW15 159 G2
Putney Park Av
PUT/ROE SW15 138 D5
Putney Park La
PUT/ROE SW15 138 E5
Puttenham Cl OXHEY WD19 27 G5
Pycombe Cnr
NFNCH/WDSP N12 32 D6
Pycroft Wy ED N9 36 C6
Pylbrook Rd SUT SM1 208 E1
Pym Cl EBAR EN4 21 H6
Pymers Md DUL SE21 162 D3
Pymmes Brook Trail EBAR EN4 33 K2
PLMGR N13 34 E6
Pymmes Cl PLMGR N13 49 F1
TOTM N17 50 D4
Pymmes Gdns North ED N9 36 B5
Pymmes Gdns South ED N9 36 B5
Pymmes Green Rd
FBAR/BDGN N11 34 B6
Pymmes Rd PLMGR N13 48 E2
Pymms Brook Dr EBAR EN4 21 J5
Pyne Rd SURB KT6 191 H5
Pynham Cl ABYW SE2 128 B3
Pynnacles Cl STAN HA7 43 H1
Pyrland Rd HBRY N5 85 K3
RCHPK/HAM TW10 157 G1
Pyrmont Gv WNWD SE27 162 C5
Pyrmont Rd CHSWK W4 117 H6
Pytchley Crs NRWD SE19 180 D2
Pytchley Rd EDUL SE22 143 F4

Q

The Quadrangle BAY/PAD W2 8 C3
HNHL SE24 * 142 D6
WBPTN SW10 * 140 B2
Quadrant Ar REGST W1B 10 B6
Quadrant Cl HDN NW4 * 63 K2
Quadrant Gv HAMP NW3 83 K3
Quadrant Rd RCH/KEW TW9 136 E5
THHTH CR7 196 C1
The Quadrant BELMT SM2 209 G4
BXLYHN DA7 148 E1
EDGW HA8 * 44 C2
NKENS W10 * 100 B2
RCH/KEW TW9 136 E6
RYLN/HDSTN HA2 * 42 D6
RYNPK SW20 177 H4
Quad Rd WBLY HA9 * 79 K1
Quaggy Wk BKHTH/KID SE3 145 K5
Quainton St WLSDN NW10 81 F1
Quaker La NWDGN UB2 115 F3
Quakers Course
CDALE/KGS NW9 45 H4
Quakers Pl FSTGT E7 89 H3
Quaker St WCHPL E1 7 J7
Quakers Wk WCHMH N21 35 K1
Quality Ct FLST/FETLN EC4A 11 J3
Quantock Cl HYS/HAR UB3 133 G1
Quantock Gdns CRICK NW2 * 64 B6
Quantock Ms PECK SE15 143 H3
Quantock Rd BXLYHN DA7 150 B3
Quarles Cl CRW RM5 56 C3
Quarles Park Rd CHDH RM6 73 H3
Quarrendon St FUL/PGN SW6 139 K2
Quarr Rd CAR SM5 194 C3
Quarry Ms PUR RM19 131 K4
Quarry Park Rd SUT SM1 208 D4
Quarry Ri SUT SM1 208 D4
Quarry Rd WAND/EARL SW18 160 B1
Quartermile La LEY E10 87 K2
Quatre Ports CHING E4 * 52 B1
Quay House POP/IOD E14 * 124 D2
Quebec Ms MBLAR W1H 9 F4
Quebec Rd GNTH/NBYPK IG2 72 C4
YEAD UB4 95 G6
Quebec Wy BERM/RHTH SE16 124 A2
Queen Adelaide Rd
PGE/AN SE20 181 K2
Queen Anne Av HAYES BR2 183 K6
Queen Anne Dr
ESH/CLAY KT10 204 E5
Queen Anne Ga BXLYHN DA7 148 E4
Queen Anne Ms
CAVSQ/HST W1G 9 K2
Queen Anne Rd HOM E9 87 F4
Queen Annes Cl WHTN TW2 155 J5
Queen Anne's Gdns
CHSWK W4 118 B3
EA W5 117 F2
EN EN1 36 A1
MTCM CR4 * 178 E6
Queen Anne's Ga STJSPK SW1H 16 C3
Queen Anne's Gv CHSWK W4 118 B3
EA W5 117 F2
EN EN1 35 K2
Queen Anne's Pl EN EN1 36 A1
Queen Anne St
CAVSQ/HST W1G 9 J2
Queen Anne Ter WAP E1W * 104 D6
Queenborough Gdns
CHST BR7 185 J2
GNTH/NBYPK IG2 72 A1
Queen Caroline Est
HMSMTH W6 119 F5
Queen Caroline St
HMSMTH W6 119 F5
Queen Elizabeth Buildings
EMB EC4Y * 11 J5
Queen Elizabeth Gdns
MRDN SM4 193 K1
Queen Elizabeth Rd
KUTN/CMB KT2 175 G5
WALTH E17 51 G6
Queen Elizabeth's Cl
STNW/STAM N16 67 K6
Queen Elizabeth's Dr
STHGT/OAK N14 34 E3
Queen Elizabeth St
STHWK SE1 19 J2
Queen Elizabeth's Wk
STNW/STAM N16 67 K6
WLGTN SM6 210 D2
Queen Elizabeth Wk
BARN SW13 138 D2
Queenhithe BLKFR EC4V 12 D6
Queen Margaret's Gv IS N1 86 A3
Queen Mary Av MRDN SM4 193 G2
Queen Mary Cl CHSGTN KT9 206 C1
ROM RM1 75 H3
Queen Mary Rd NRWD SE19 180 C2
Queen Mary's Av CAR SM5 209 K5
Queen Mother Ga BAY/PAD W2 15 H1
Queens Acre CHEAM SM3 208 B5
Queens Av FELT TW13 154 B6
FNCH N3 47 G3
GFD/PVL UB6 96 B5
KTN/HRWW/W HA3 43 H6
MUSWH N10 48 A6
TRDG/WHET N20 33 H4
WCHMH N21 35 H3
WFD IG8 53 F1
Queensberry Ms West
SKENS SW7 * 14 A6
Queensberry Pl FSTGT E7 89 H3
SKENS SW7 14 A6
Queensberry Wy SKENS SW7 * 14 A6
Queensborough Ms
BAY/PAD W2 * 101 G6
Queensborough Ter
BAY/PAD W2 101 F6
Queensbridge Pk ISLW TW7 155 J1
Queensbridge Rd HACK E8 86 B5
Queensbury Rd
CDALE/KGS NW9 63 F4
WLSDN NW10 98 B1
Queensbury Station Pde
EDGW HA8 44 B6
Queensbury St IS N1 85 J5
Queens Circ VX/NE SW8 141 G1
Queen's Cl EDGW HA8 44 C1
ESH/CLAY KT10 * 204 B2
WLGTN SM6 210 B3
Queens Club Gdns
WKENS W14 119 H6
Queens Club Ter
WKENS W14 * 119 J6
Queenscourt WBLY HA9 80 A2
Queen's Crs KTTN NW5 84 A4
RCHPK/HAM TW10 137 G6
Queenscroft Rd
ELTH/MOT SE9 146 C6
Queensdale Crs NTGHL W11 119 G1
Queensdale Pl NTGHL W11 119 H1
Queensdale Rd NTGHL W11 119 G1
Queensdale Wk NTGHL W11 119 H1
Queens Down Rd CLPT E5 86 D2
Queens Dr BRYLDS KT5 191 H4
EA W5 98 B5
FSBYPK N4 67 H6
LEY E10 69 J4
THDIT KT7 190 B3
Queen's Elm Sq CHEL SW3 120 C5
Queen's Gdns BAY/PAD W2 101 G6
EA W5 97 J4
HDN NW4 64 A2
HEST TW5 134 D2
RAIN RM13 111 F1
Queens Garth FSTH SE23 * 163 K4
Queen's Ga SKENS SW7 120 B2
Queens Gate Gdns CHST BR7 185 J4
SKENS SW7 120 B3
Queensgate Gdns
PUT/ROE SW15 138 E5
Queen's Gate Ms SKENS SW7 120 B3
Queensgate Pl
KIL/WHAMP NW6 82 E5
Queen's Gate Pl SKENS SW7 120 B3
Queen's Gate Place Ms
SKENS SW7 120 B3
Queen's Gate Ter SKENS SW7 120 B3
Queen's Gv STJWD NW8 2 A1
Queen's Grove Rd CHING E4 38 B3
Queen's Head St IS N1 6 B1
Queens Keep TWK TW1 * 156 D1
Queensland Av UED N18 49 J2
WIM/MER SW19 178 A4
Queensland Cl WALTH E17 51 H5
Queensland Pl HOLWY N7 85 G2
Queensland Rd HOLWY N7 85 G3
Queens La MUSWH N10 48 B6
Queens Md EDGW HA8 44 B2
Queensmead STJWD NW8 83 H6
Queen's Mead Rd HAYES BR2 183 J5
Queensmere Cl
WIM/MER SW19 159 G4
Queensmere Rd
WIM/MER SW19 159 G4
Queensmill Rd FUL/PGN SW6 139 G1
Queens Pde CEND/HSY/T N8 * 67 H1
CRICK NW2 * 82 A4
EA W5 * 98 B5
FBAR/BDGN N11 * 47 K1
FBAR/BDGN N11 * 48 E3
HDN NW4 * 63 K2
Queens Parade Cl
FBAR/BDGN N11 47 K1
Queens Park Gdns FELT TW13 153 J5
Queen's Pl MRDN SM4 193 K1
Queens Prom KUT/HW KT1 190 E1
Queen Sq BMSBY WC1N 5 F7
Queen's Ride BARN SW13 138 E4
Queen's Ri RCHPK/HAM TW10 157 G1
Queens Rd BAR EN5 20 B4
BARK IG11 90 C5
BECK BR3 182 B5
BKHH IG9 39 F4
BMLY BR1 183 K5
CHST BR7 185 G2
CROY/NA CR0 196 C3
EA W5 98 A5
ED N9 36 D4
EN EN1 24 A5
ERITH DA8 130 B6
FBAR/BDGN N11 48 E3
FELT TW13 154 A3
FNCH N3 47 G4
HDN NW4 64 A2
HPTN TW12 155 G6
HSLW TW3 135 G4
HYS/HAR UB3 94 C5
KUTN/CMB KT2 175 H3
MORT/ESHN SW14 138 A4
MRDN SM4 193 K1
MTCM CR4 178 C6
NWDGN UB2 114 C2
NWMAL KT3 192 C1
PECK SE15 143 K2
PLSTW E13 89 F6
RCHPK/HAM TW10 157 G1
TEDD TW11 174 A2
THDIT KT7 190 A2
TWK TW1 156 A3
WALTH E17 69 H3
WAN E11 70 C4
WDR/YW UB7 112 C2
WELL DA16 148 C3
WIM/MER SW19 177 K2
WLGTN SM6 210 B3
Queen's Rd West PLSTW E13 106 E1
Queens Rw WALW SE17 122 E6
Queens Ter ISLW TW7 136 B5
PLSTW E13 89 F6
STJWD NW8 2 A1
THDIT KT7 * 190 B3
WCHPL E1 * 104 E3
Queensthorpe Ms SYD SE26 * 164 A6
Queensthorpe Rd SYD SE26 164 A6
Queens Town Gdns
RAIN RM13 111 H2
Queenstown Rd CHEL SW3 121 G6
Queen St BXLYHN DA7 149 G4
CROY/NA CR0 211 J2
ERITH DA8 * 130 B6
MANHO EC4N 12 D4
MYFR/PICC W1J 9 J7
ROMW/RG RM7 75 F3
TOTM N17 50 A2
Queen Street Pl CANST EC4R 12 D6
Queensville Rd CLAP SW4 161 J2
Queens Wk ASHF TW15 152 A6
CDALE/KGS NW9 62 E6
CHING E4 38 B3

EA W5 ....97 J3
HRW HA1 ....60 E1
RSLP HA4 ....77 G1
Queens Walk Ter RSLP HA4 * 77 G1
The Queens Wk STHWK SE1 ......13 H7
Queens Wy FELT TW13 ....154 B6
HDN NW4 ....64 A2
Queensway BAY/PAD W2 ....101 F6
CROY/NA CR0 ....211 F4
PEND EN3 ....24 E5
STMC/STPC BR5 ....201 H2
SUN TW16 ....172 A5
WWKM BR4 ....214 E2
Queens Well Av
TRDG/WHET N20 ....33 J6
Queen's Whf HMSMTH W6 ....119 F5
Queenswood Av HEST TW5.......134 E3
HPTN TW12 ....173 G2
THHTH CR7 ....196 B2
WALTH E17 ....52 A4
WLGTN SM6 ....210 D2
Queenswood Gdns WAN E11 .....70 E5
Queenswood Pk FNCH N3 ....46 C5
Queenswood Rd BFN/LL DA15 ..148 A5
FSTH SE23 ....168 B5
Queen's Wood Rd HGT N6 ....66 B3
Queen's Yd FITZ W1T 4 B7
Queen Victoria Av
ALP/SUD HA0 ....79 K5
Queen Victoria St BLKFR EC4V ...12 A5
Queen Victoria Ter WAP E1W *...104 D6
Quemerford Rd HOLWY N7 ....85 F3
Quentin Pl LEW SE13 ....145 H4
Quentin Rd LEW SE13 ....145 H4
Quernmore Cl BMLY BR1 ....183 K2
Quernmore Rd BFN/LL DA15 .....183 K2
FSBYPK N4 ....67 G3
Querrin St FUL/PGN SW6 ....140 B3
Questor DART DA1 ....171 J4
Quex Ms KIL/WHAMP NW6 ....82 E6
Quex Rd KIL/WHAMP NW6 ....82 E6
Quick Rd CHSWK W4 ....118 A5
Quicks Rd WIM/MER SW19 ....178 A3
Quick St IS N1 ....6 B3
Quicksword Rd CLKNW EC1R * 5 J7
Quiet Nook HAYES BR2...............215 H1
Quill St EA W5 ....98 A2
FSBYPK N4 ....85 G1
Quilp St STHWK SE1.....................18 C2
Quilter Rd STMC/STPC BR5 ....202 D5
Quilter St BETH E2 ....104 C2
WOOL/PLUM SE18 ....128 A5
Quince Rd LEW SE13 ....144 E3
Quintin Av RYNPK SW20 ....177 H4
Quinton Cl BECK BR3 ....183 F6
HEST TW5 ....134 A1
WLGTN SM6 ....210 B2
Quinton Rd THDIT KT7 ....190 B5
Quinton St WAND/EARL SW18...160 B4
Quixley St POP/IOD E14 ....106 B6
Quorn Rd EDUL SE22 ....143 F5

R

Rabbit Rw KENS W8 * 119 K1
Rabbits Rd MNPK E12 ....89 J2
Rabournemead Dr RSLP HA4 .....77 J3
Raby Rd NWMAL KT3 ....192 A1
Raby St POP/IOD E14 * 105 G5
Raccoon Wy HSLWW TW4 ....134 B5
Rachel Cl BARK/HLT IG6 ....72 C1
Rackham Cl WELL DA16 ....148 C3
Rackham Ms
STRHM/NOR SW16...................179 H2
Racton Rd FUL/PGN SW6 ....119 K6
Radbourne Av EA W5 ....116 D4
Radbourne Cl CLPT E5.................87 F2
Radbourne Crs
KTN/HRWW/W HA3 * 61 H3
Radbourne Crs WALTH E17 ....52 B6
Radbourne Rd BAL SW12 ....161 H2
Radcliffe Av ENC/FH EN2.............23 J2
WLSDN NW10 ....99 J1
Radcliffe Gdns CAR SM5............209 J5
Radcliffe Rd CROY/NA CR0 ....197 G6
KTN/HRWW/W HA3 ....43 G5
STHWK SE1 ....19 H3
WCHMH N21 ....35 H5
Radcliffe Wy NTHLT UB5 ....95 H2
Radcot St LBTH SE11 ....122 B5
Raddington Rd NKENS W10 ......100 C4
Radfield Wy ELTH/MOT SE9 ....167 J2
Radford Est WLSDN NW10 * 99 G2
Radford Rd LEW SE13 ....165 F1
Radford Wy BARK IG11...............109 F2
Radipole Rd FUL/PGN SW6 ....139 J2
Radius Pk EBED/NFELT TW14 * ...133 J5
Radland Rd CAN/RD E16 ....106 E5
Radlet Av SYD SE26 ....163 J5
Radlett Cl FSTGT E7 ....88 D4
Radlett Pl STJWD NW8 ....2 C1
Radley Av GDMY/SEVK IG3 ....91 F2
Radley Cl EBED/NFELT TW14 .....153 J3
Radley Ct BERM/RHTH SE16 .....124 A2
Radley Gdns
KTN/HRWW/W HA3 * 62 A1
Radley Ms KENS W8 * 119 K3
Radley Rd TOTM N17 ....50 A5
Radley's La SWFD E18 *...............52 E5
Radleys Md DAGE RM10.............92 D4
Radley Sq CLPT E5 * 68 E6
Radley Ter CAN/RD E16 * 106 D4
Radlix Rd LEY E10 ....69 J5
Radnor Av HRW HA1...................60 E2
WELL DA16 ....148 C6
Radnor Cl CHST BR7 ....185 K2
MTCM CR4 ....195 K2
Radnor Crs REDBR IG4.................71 K2
WOOL/PLUM SE18 ....148 B1

Radnor Gdns EN EN1 ....24 A2
TWK TW1 ....156 A4
Radnor Ms BAY/PAD W2 ....8 B4
Radnor Pl BAY/PAD W2 ....8 C4
Radnor Rd HRW HA1...................60 C2
KIL/WHAMP NW6 ....82 C6
PECK SE15 ....143 H1
TWK TW1 ....156 A4
Radnor St FSBYE EC1V 6 D5
Radnor Ter WKENS W14...............119 J4
Radnor Wk CHEL SW3 ....120 D5
CROY/NA CR0 ....198 B4
Radnor Wy WLSDN NW10 ....98 D3
Radstock Av
KTN/HRWW/W HA3 ....43 G6
Radstock Cl FBAR/BDGN N11 .....48 A1
Radstock St BTSEA SW11 ....140 D1
Raeburn Av BRYLDS KT5 ....191 J3
DART DA1 ....150 E6
Raeburn Cl EFNCH N2...................65 J1
KUT/HW KT1 ....174 E3
Raeburn Rd BFN/LL DA15 ....167 K1
EDGW HA8 ....44 C5
YEAD UB4 ....94 B1
Raeburn St BRXS/STRHM SW2 ...141 K5
Rafford Wy BMLY BR1 ....184 A5
Ragglesword CHST BR7...............185 F4
Raglan Cl HSLWW TW4 ....134 D6
Raglan Ct CROY/NA CR0.............211 H3
Raglan Gdns OXHEY WD19...........27 F3
Raglan Rd BELV DA17 ....129 G4
EN EN1 ....36 A2
HAYES BR2 ....200 B1
WALTH E17 ....70 A2
WOOL/PLUM SE18 ....127 H5
Raglan St KTTN NW5 ....84 B4
Raglan Ter RYLN/HDSTN HA2 * ...78 B2
Raglan Wy NTHLT UB5 ....78 C4
Ragley Cl ACT W3 ....117 K2
Raider Cl ROMW/RG RM7 ....56 D4
Railey Ms KTTN NW5...................84 C3
Railshead Rd ISLW TW7 ....136 C5
Railton Rd HNHL SE24 ....142 B6
Railway Ap HRW HA1 ....61 F1
STHWK SE1 ....12 E7
TWK TW1 ....156 B2
WLGTN SM6 * 210 B4
Railway Av BRXN/ST SW9 * 142 B5
Railway Av BERM/RHTH SE16 ...123 K2
Railway Gv NWCR SE14 ....144 C1
Railway Pl BELV DA17.................129 H5
Railway Ri EDUL SE22 ....143 F5
Railway Side BARN SW13............138 B4
Railway Station Whf LEY E10 * ...69 G5
Railway St BCTR RM8 ....73 J5
IS N1 ....5 F3
Railway Ter FELT TW13 ....153 K3
LEW SE13 * 144 E5
WALTH E17 ....52 A4
Rainborough Cl WBLY HA9 ....80 E4
Rainbow Av POP/IOD E14 ....124 E5
Rainbow Ct OXHEY WD19...........27 G1
Rainbow St CMBW SE5...............143 F1
Raine St WAP E1W 123 J1
Rainham Cl BTSEA SW11 ....160 D1
ELTH/MOT SE9...........................167 K1
Rainham Rd RAIN RM13...............93 H5
WLSDN NW10 ....100 A3
Rainham Rd North DAGE RM10 ...74 D6
Rainham Rd South DAGE RM10 ...92 E2
Rainhill Wy BOW E3 ....105 J2
Rainsborough Av DEPT SE8 ....124 B4
Rainsford Rd WLSDN NW10...98 D2
Rainsford St BAY/PAD W2 ....8 C3
Rainsford Wy HCH RM12.............75 J5
Rainton Rd CHARL SE7 ....125 K5
Rainville Rd HMSMTH W6 ....119 F6
Raisins Hl PIN HA5 ....41 G6
Raith Av STHGT/OAK N14...........34 D5
Raleana Rd POP/IOD E14...........125 F1
Raleigh Av WLGTN SM6 ....210 D2
YEAD UB4 ....95 F4
Raleigh Cl ERITH DA8 ....130 C6
HDN NW4 ....64 A2
PIN HA5 ....59 H4
RSLP HA4 ....58 C6
Raleigh Dr BRYLDS KT5..............191 K5
ESH/CLAY KT10..........................204 D3
TRDG/WHET N20 ....33 J5
Raleigh Gdns
BRXS/STRHM SW2 ....162 A1
MTCM CR4 ....178 E6
Raleigh Ms IS N1 ....6 B1
ORP BR6 ....217 F4
Raleigh Rd CEND/HSY/T N8 ....67 G1
ENC/FH EN2 ....23 K5
FELT TW13 ....153 J4
NWDGN UB2 ....114 D3
PGE/AN SE20 ....182 A3
RCH/KEW TW9 ....137 G4
Raleigh St IS N1 ....6 B1
Raleigh Wy FELT TW13 ....172 B1
STHGT/OAK N14 ....34 D3
Ralph Perring Ct BECK BR3 ....198 D1
Ralston St CHEL SW3 ....120 E5
Ralston Wy OXHEY WD19...........27 H4
Rama Cl STRHM/NOR SW16 ....179 K3
Ramac Wy CHARL SE7................125 K4
Rambler Cl STRHM/NOR SW16 ...161 H6
Rame Cl TOOT SW17 ....179 F1
Ramilles Cl BRXS/STRHM SW2 ...161 K1
Ramillies Pl SOHO/CST W1F 10 A4
Ramillies Rd BFN/LL DA15 ....168 C1
CHSWK W4 ....118 A3
MLHL NW7 ....31 G4
Ramillies St SOHO/CST W1F 10 A4
Ramones Ter MTCM CR4 * 195 H1
Rampart St WCHPL E1................104 D5
Ram Pas KUT/HW KT1................174 E5
Rampayne St PIM SW1V..............121 J5
Rampton Cl CHING E4..................37 J5
Ramsay Gdns GPK RM2...............57 K4

Ramsay Rd ACT W3 ....117 K3
FSTGT E7 ....88 E1
Ramscroft Cl ED N9 ....36 A2
Ramsdale Rd TOOT SW17...179 F1
Ramsden Cl STMC/STPC BR5...202 D5
Ramsden Dr CRW RM5................56 C1
Ramsden Rd BAL SW12 * 161 F2
ERITH DA8 ....150 A1
FBAR/BDGN N11 ....47 K1
ORP BR6 ....202 C4
Ramsey Cl CDALE/KGS NW9 .....63 H3
GFD/PVL UB6 ....78 E3
Ramsey Rd THHTH CR7 ....196 A3
Ramsey St BETH E2 ....104 C3
Ramsey Wy STHGT/OAK N14...34 C2
Ramsgate St HACK E8 * 86 B4
Ramsgill Ap GNTH/NBYPK IG2...73 F1
Ramsgill Dr GNTH/NBYPK IG2 ...73 F2
Rams Gv CHDH RM6 ....74 A1
Ram St WAND/EARL SW18 ....140 A6
Ramulis Dr YEAD UB4 ....95 J3
Ramus Wood Av ORP BR6...216 E3
Rancliffe Gdns ELTH/MOT SE9 ...146 D5
Rancliffe Rd EHAM E6 ....107 J1
Randall Av CRICK NW2 ....63 G6
Randall Cl BTSEA SW11 ....140 D2
ERITH DA8 ....129 K6
Randall Pl GNWCH SE10 ....145 F1
Randall Rd LBTH SE11 ....122 A5
Randall Rw LBTH SE11 ....17 G7
Randell's Rd IS N1 ....84 E6
Randisbourne Gdns CAT SE6 * ...164 E5
Randle Rd RCHPK/HAM TW10...156 D6
Randlesdown Rd CAT SE6 ....164 E5
Randolph Ap CAN/RD E16...107 G5
Randolph Av MV/WKIL W9 ....101 F1
Randolph Cl BXLYHN DA7 ....149 K4
KUTN/CMB KT2 * 175 F1
Randolph Gdns
KIL/WHAMP NW6 ....101 F1
Randolph Gv CHDH RM6 * ...73 J2
Randolph Ms MV/WKIL W9 ....101 G3
Randolph Rd HAYES BR2 ....200 E5
MV/WKIL W9 ....101 G3
STHL UB1 * 114 E2
WALTH E17 ....69 K2
Randon Cl PIN HA5 ....42 B5
Ranelagh Av BARN SW13...138 D3
FUL/PGN SW6 ....139 J4
Ranelagh Cl EDGW HA8 ....30 C6
Ranelagh Dr EDGW HA8.............30 C6
TWK TW1 ....136 C5
Ranelagh Gdns CHSWK W4 ......137 K1
FUL/PGN SW6 ....139 H4
IL IG1 ....72 A5
WAN E11 ....71 G2
Ranelagh Gv BGVA SW1W 121 F5
Ranelagh Pl NWMAL KT3 ....192 B2
Ranelagh Rd ALP/SUD HA0 ....79 K3
EA W5 ....116 E2
EHAM E6 ....90 A5
PIM SW1V 121 H5
STHL UB1 ....114 C1
TOTM N17 ....50 A6
WAN E11 ....88 C2
WDGN N22 ....49 F4
WLSDN NW10 ....99 H2
Ranfurly Rd SUT SM1..................193 K6
Rangefield Rd BMLY BR1...183 H1
Rangers Rd BKHH IG9................38 E2
Rangeworth Pl BFN/LL DA15...168 A5
Rangoon St TWRH EC3N * 13 J4
Rankin Cl CDALE/KGS NW9 ....45 G6
Ranleigh Gdns BXLYHN DA7 ......149 G1
Ranmere St BAL SW12................161 G3
Ranmoor Cl HRW HA1.................60 D1
Ranmoor Gdns HRW HA1 ...60 D1
Ranmore Av CROY/NA CR0 ....212 B1
Ranmore Pth STMC/STPC BR5...202 B1
Ranmore Rd BELMT SM2 ....208 B6
Rannoch Cl EDGW HA8...............30 D4
Rannoch Rd HMSMTH W6 ....119 F6
Rannock Av CDALE/KGS NW9 ...63 F4
Ransom Cl OXHEY WD19...........27 G2
Ransom Rd CHARL SE7 * 126 B5
Ranston St CAMTN NW1 ....8 C1
Ranulf Rd CRICK NW2 ....82 D2
Ranwell Cl BOW E3 * 87 H6
Ranworth Cl ERITH DA8 ....150 B3
Ranworth Rd ED N9 ....36 E4
Ranyard Cl CHSGTN KT9 ....206 B1
Raphael Av ROM RM1.................57 H6
Raphael Dr THDIT KT7 ....190 A5
Raphael St SKENS SW7 ....14 E3
Rapier Cl PUR RM19...................131 J4
Rasper Rd TRDG/WHET N20 ...33 G4
Rastell Av BRXS/STRHM SW2 ...161 J4
Ratcliffe Cl LEE/GVPK SE12 ....165 K2
Ratcliffe Cross St WCHPL E1 * ...105 F5
Ratcliffe La POP/IOD E14...........105 G5
Ratcliff Rd FSTGT E7 ....89 G3
Rathbone Pl FITZ W1T 10 C2
Rathbone Sq CROY/NA CR0 * ...211 J2
Rathbone St CAN/RD E16 ....106 D4
FITZ W1T 10 B2
Rathcoole Av CEND/HSY/T N8 ...67 F2
Rathcoole Gdns
CEND/HSY/T N8 ....67 F2
Rathfern Rd CAT SE6 ....164 C3
Rathgar Av WEA W13..................116 C1
Rathgar Cl FNCH N3 ....46 D5
Rathgar Rd BRXN/ST SW9 ....142 C4
Rathmell Dr CLAP SW4...............161 J1
Rathmore Rd CHARL SE7 ....126 A5
Rattray Rd BRXS/STRHM SW2 ...142 B5
Raul Rd PECK SE15 ....143 H3
Raveley St KTTN NW5.................84 C2
Raven Cl CDALE/KGS NW9 ...45 H5
Ravencroft Crs ELTH/MOT SE9 ...166 E5
Ravenet St BTSEA SW11 ....141 G2
Ravenfield Rd TOOT SW17 ....160 E5
Ravenhill Rd PLSTW E13 ...89 G6

Ravenna Rd PUT/ROE SW15 ...139 G6
Ravenoak Wy CHIG IG7...............54 E1
Ravenor Park Rd GFD/PVL UB6 ...96 B2
Raven Rd SWFD E18 ....53 G5
Raven Rw WCHPL E1..................104 D4
Ravens Ait SURB KT6 * 190 E2
Ravensbourne Av HAYES BR2 ...183 G6
STWL/WRAY TW19...................152 B5
Ravensbourne Gdns CLAY IG5 ...54 A4
WEA W13 ....97 H4
Ravensbourne Pk
BROCKY SE4 ....164 D2
Ravensbourne Park Crs
CAT SE6 ....164 C2
Ravensbourne Pl DEPT SE8 ......144 E5
Ravensbourne Rd BMLY BR1 ....183 K6
CAT SE6 ....164 C2
DART DA1 ....150 D4
Ravens Cl CDALE/KGS NW9 ......45 G5
EN EN1 ....24 A3
HAYES BR2 ....183 J5
Ravenscourt Av HMSMTH W6 ...118 D4
Ravenscourt Cl RSLP HA4 ....58 A4
Ravenscourt Gdns
HMSMTH W6 ....118 C4
Ravenscourt Pk HMSMTH W6 ...118 D4
Ravenscourt Pl HMSMTH W6 ...118 E4
Ravenscourt Rd HMSMTH W6 ...118 E4
STMC/STPC BR5 ....186 B6
Ravenscourt Sq HMSMTH W6 ...118 D3
Ravenscraig Rd
FBAR/BDGN N11 ....34 B6
Ravenscroft Av GLDGN NW11...64 D4
WBLY HA9 ....62 A5
Ravenscroft Cl CAN/RD E16 ......106 E4
Ravenscroft Pk BAR EN5.............20 B5
Ravenscroft Rd BECK BR3 ....181 K5
CAN/RD E16 ....106 E4
CHSWK W4 ....117 K4
Ravenscroft St BETH E2 ....7 K3
Ravensdale Av
NFNCH/WDSP N12 ....33 G6
Ravensdale Gdns NRWD SE19 ...180 E3
Ravensdale Rd HSLWW TW4 .....134 D4
STNW/STAM N16 ....68 B4
Ravensdon St LBTH SE11 ....122 B5
Ravensfield DAGW RM9...............91 K2
Ravensfield Gdns
HOR/WEW KT19........................207 G3
Ravenshaw St
KIL/WHAMP NW6 ....82 D3
Ravenshill CHST BR7..................185 G4
Ravenshurst Av HDN NW4...........64 A1
Ravenside Cl UED N18 ....51 F1
Ravenslea Rd BAL SW12 ....160 E2
Ravensmead Rd HAYES BR2 .....183 G3
Ravensmede Wy CHSWK W4 ...118 C4
Ravens Ms BKHTH/KID SE3 * ...145 H2
Ravenstone Rd
CDALE/KGS NW9 ....63 H3
CEND/HSY/T N8 ....49 F6
Ravenstone St BAL SW12 ....161 F3
Ravens Wy LEE/GVPK SE12 ......145 K6
Ravenswood BXLY DA5...............169 F3
Ravenswood Av SURB KT6 ....191 G5
WWKM BR4 ....199 F5
Ravenswood Cl CRW RM5 ....56 D1
Ravenswood Ct
KUTN/CMB KT2 ....175 K2
Ravenswood Crs
RYLN/HDSTN HA2 ....59 K6
WWKM BR4 ....199 F5
Ravenswood Gdns ISLW TW7 ...135 K2
Ravenswood Pk NTHWD HA6 ...40 E2
Ravenswood Rd BAL SW12 ....161 G2
CROY/NA CR0 ....211 H1
WALTH E17 ....70 A1
Ravensworth Rd
ELTH/MOT SE9 ....166 E6
WLSDN NW10 * 99 K2
Ravey St SDTCH EC2A 7 G6
Ravine Gv WOOL/PLUM SE18 ...127 K6
Rav Pinter Cl STNW/STAM N16...68 A4
Rawlings Cl BECK BR3 ....199 F2
Rawlings Crs WBLY HA9.............80 D1
Rawlings St CHEL SW3 ....14 E6
Rawlins Cl FNCH N3 ....46 C6
SAND/SEL CR2 ....213 H5
Rawnsley Av MTCM CR4 ....194 C2
Rawreth Wk IS N1 * 85 J6
Rawson St BTSEA SW11 * 141 G2
Rawsthorne Cl CAN/RD E16 ......126 C1
Rawstone Pl FSBYE EC1V *...........6 A4
Rawstorne St FSBYE EC1V 6 A4
Ray Bell Ct BROCKY SE4 *...144 C3
Raydean Rd BAR EN5.................20 E6
Raydons Gdns DAGW RM9...92 A2
Raydons Rd DAGW RM9.............92 A3
Raydon St ARCH N19 ....66 B6
Rayfield Cl HAYES BR2 ....200 D3
Rayford Av LEE/GVPK SE12 ......165 J2
Rayford Cl DART DA1...................151 F6
Ray Gdns BARK IG11...................109 G1
STAN HA7 ....43 H1
Ray Lamb Wy ERITH DA8...........130 E6
Rayleas Cl WOOL/PLUM SE18 ...147 G2
Rayleigh Av TEDD TW11 ....173 K2
Rayleigh Cl PLMGR N13 ....35 K5
Rayleigh Ct KUT/HW KT1 ...175 H5
Rayleigh Ri SAND/SEL CR2 ......212 A4
Rayleigh Rd CAN/RD E16 ....126 A1
PLMGR N13 ....35 J5
WFD IG8 ....53 G3

WIM/MER SW19 ....177 J6
Ray Lodge Rd WFD IG8 ...53 G2
Raymead Av THHTH CR7 ...196 B2
Raymere Gdns
WOOL/PLUM SE18 ....147 J1
Raymond Av SWFD E18...............52 D6
Raymond Av EA W5 ....116 D3
SWFD E18 ....52 D6
Raymond Buildings
GINN WC1R * 11 H1
Raymond Cl SYD SE26 ....181 K5
Raymond Rd BECK BR3 ....198 B1
GNTH/NBYPK IG2 ....72 D4
PLSTW E13 ....89 G5
WIM/MER SW19 ....177 J2
Raymond Wy
ESH/CLAY KT10 * 205 G4
Raymouth Rd
BERM/RHTH SE16 ....123 J4
Rayne Ct SWFD E18 ....70 D1
Rayners Cl ALP/SUD HA0 ...79 K3
Rayners Gdns NTHLT UB5 ...95 F2
Rayners La PIN HA5 ....59 K3
RYLN/HDSTN HA2 ....60 A5
Rayner's Rd PUT/ROE SW15 ...139 H6
Raynes Av WAN E11 ....71 G4
Raynham Av UED N18 ....50 C1
Raynham Rd HMSMTH W6 ....118 E4
UED N18 ....50 C1
Raynham Ter UED N18 ....50 C1
Raynor Cl STHL UB1....................114 E1
Raynor Pl IS N1 ....85 J6
Raynton Cl RYLN/HDSTN HA2 ...59 H4
YEAD UB4 ....94 D3
Raynton Dr YEAD UB4 ....94 C1
Ray Rd CRW RM5........................56 D1
E/WMO/HCT KT8........................189 G2
Rays Av UED N18........................36 E6
Rays Rd UED N18 ....36 E6
WWKM BR4 ....199 F4
Ray St CLKNW EC1R 5 K7
Ray Street Br CLKNW EC1R * ...5 K7
Raywood Cl WDR/YW UB7 ....133 F1
Reachview Cl CAMTN NW1 ...84 C5
Reading La HACK E8 ....86 D6
Reading Rd NTHLT UB5 ....78 B3
SUT SM1 ....209 G3
Reads Cl IL IG1 ....90 B1
Reapers Cl CAMTN NW1 ....84 D6
Reapers Wy ISLW TW7 ....135 J6
Reardon Pth WAP E1W...............123 J1
Reardon St WAP E1W 123 J1
Reaston St NWCR SE14...............143 K1
Reckitt Rd CHSWK W4 ....118 B5
Record St PECK SE15 ....123 K6
Recovery St TOOT SW17............178 D1
Recreation Av ROMW/RG RM7 ...74 E2
Recreation Rd HAYES BR2 ....183 J5
NWDGN UB2 ....114 D4
SYD SE26 ....164 A6
Recreation Wy MTCM CR4 ....179 K6
Rectar Pl ALPERTON...................66 B6
Rector St IS N1 ....6 C1
Rectory Cl CHING E4 ....37 J5
DART DA1 ....150 B5
FNCH N3 ....46 D4
RYNPK SW20 ....177 F5
SCUP DA14 ....168 C6
STAN HA7 ....43 H2
SURB KT6 ....190 D5
Rectory Crs WAN E11..................71 G3
Rectory Field Crs CHARL SE7 ...146 B1
Rectory Gdns BECK BR3 * ...182 D4
CEND/HSY/T N8 ....66 E1
CHST BR7 ....185 H4
NTHLT UB5 ....77 K6
Rectory Gn BECK BR3 ....182 C4
Rectory Gv CLAP SW4 ....141 H4
CROY/NA CR0 ....196 C6
FELT TW13 ....154 E6
Rectory La EDGW HA8 ....44 C2
SCUP DA14 ....168 C6
STAN HA7 ....43 H1
SURB KT6 ....190 D5
TOOT SW17 ....179 F1
WLGTN SM6 ....210 C2
Rectory Orch WIM/MER SW19 ...159 H6
Rectory Park Av NTHLT UB5 ...95 K2
Rectory Pl CHST BR7 * 185 H4
WOOL/PLUM SE18 ....127 F4
Rectory Rd BARN SW13...............138 D3
BECK BR3 ....182 D4
DAGE RM10 ....92 C4
HAYES BR2 ....215 H5
HEST TW5 ....134 B3
HYS/HAR UB3 ....94 C5
MNPK E12 ....89 K3
NWDGN UB2 ....114 C3
STNW/STAM N16 ....68 B6
SUT SM1 ....208 E1
WALTH E17 ....69 K1
Rectory Sq WCHPL E1................105 F4
Reculver Ms UED N18.................36 C6
Reculver Rd
BERM/RHTH SE16 ....124 A4
Red Anchor Cl CHEL SW3 * ...120 C6
Redan Pl BAY/PAD W2 * 101 F5
Redan St WKENS W14 ....119 G3
Redan Ter CMBW SE5.................142 C3
Red Barracks Rd
WOOL/PLUM SE18 ....126 E4
Redberry Gv SYD SE26...............163 K5
Redbourne Av FNCH N3 ....46 E4
Redbourne Dr THMD SE28 ....109 K5
Redbridge Gdns CMBW SE5...143 F1
Redbridge La East REDBR IG4 ...71 J3
Redbridge La West WAN E11 ...71 F3
Redburn St CHEL SW3 ....120 E6
Redcar Cl RAIN RM13..................111 K3
Redcar St CMBW SE5 ....142 D1
Redcastle Cl WCHPL E1 ....104 E6
Red Cedars Rd ORP BR6 ...201 K4
Redchurch St BETH E2 ....7 J6
Redcliffe Cl ECT SW5..................120 A5
Redcliffe Gdns IL IG1...................72 A5

WBPTN SW10 ...120 A5
Redcliffe Ms WBPTN SW10 ...120 A5
Redcliffe Rd WBPTN SW10 ...120 A5
Redcliffe Sq WBPTN SW10 ...120 B5
Redcliffe Sq WBPTN SW10 * ...120 A5
Redcliffe Rd EHAM E6 ...89 G6
Redcross Rd STHL UB1 ...84 A6
Redcross Wy STHWK SE1 ...18 D2
Reddings Cl MLHL NW7 ...31 H6
The Reddings MLHL NW7 ...31 H5
Reddington Cl SAND/SEL CR2 ...211 K6
Reddons Rd PECK SE15 ...143 H1
Reddons Rd BECK BR3 ...182 A3
Reddy Rd ERITH DA8 ...130 C6
Rede Pl BAY/PAD W2 ...100 E5
Redesdale Gdns ISLW TW7 ...136 B1
Redesdale St CHEL SW3 ...120 G6
Redfern Av HSLWW TW4 ...155 F2
Redfern Rd CAT SE6 ...165 F2
WLSDN NW10 ...81 G5
Redfield La ECT SW5 ...119 K4
Redfield Ms ECT SW5 ...119 K4
Redford Av THHTH CR7 ...196 A1
WLGTN SM6 ...210 E4
Redford Cl FELT TW13 ...153 J4
Redford Wk IS N1 * ...85 H6
Redgate Dr HAYES BR2 ...200 A6
Redgate Ter PUT/ROE SW15 ...159 G1
Redgrave Cl CROY/NA CR0 ...197 G3
Redgrave Rd PUT/ROE SW15 ...139 G5
Redgrave Ter BETH E2 * ...104 C2
Redhall Ter EA W5 * ...98 C6
Red Hi CHST BR7 ...185 F1
Redhill Dr EDGW HA8 ...44 E5
Redhill St CAMTN NW1 ...3 K4
Red House La BXLYHS DA6 ...148 E5
Red House Rd CROY/NA CR0 ...195 J3
Red House Sq IS N1 * ...85 J5
Redington Gdns HAMP NW3 ...83 F1
Redington Rd HAMP NW3 ...83 F1
Redland Gdns
E/WMO/HCT KT8 * ...188 E1
Redlands Rd PEND EN3 ...25 G2
Redlands Wy
BRXS/STRHM SW2 ...161 K2
Red La ESH/CLAY KT10 ...205 G4
Redleaf Cl BELV DA17 ...129 H6
Redlees Cl ISLW TW7 ...136 B5
Red Lion Cl STMC/STPC BR5 ...202 D3
WALW SE17 * ...122 E6
Red Lion Ct FLST/FETLN EC4A ...11 K3
HSLW TW3 * ...135 G4
Red Lion Hl EFNCH N2 ...47 H5
Red Lion Pde PIN HA5 * ...41 J6
Red Lion Pl
WOOL/PLUM SE18 * ...147 F2
Red Lion Rd SURB KT6 ...191 G6
Red Lion Rw WALW SE17 ...122 D6
Red Lion Sq BMSBY WC1N ...11 G2
WAND/EARL SW18 * ...139 K6
Red Lion St GINN WC1R ...11 G2
RCHPK/HAM TW10 ...156 E6
Red Lion Yd MYFR/PKLN W1K *...9 H7
Red Lodge Crs BXLY DA5 ...170 A5
Red Lodge Rd BXLY DA5 ...170 A5
WWKM BR4 ...199 F5
Redman Cl NTHLT UB5 ...95 G1
Redman's Rd WCHPL E1 ...104 E4
Redmead La WAP E1W * ...123 H1
Redmead Rd HYS/HAR UB3 ...113 H4
Redmore Rd HMSMTH W6 ...118 E4
Red Oak Cl ORP BR6 ...216 B1
Red Pl MYFR/PKLN W1K * ...9 G5
Redpoll Wy ERITH DA18 ...128 E3
Red Post Hl HNHL SE24 ...142 E6
Redriffe Rd PLSTW E13 ...106 D1
Redriff Rd BERM/RHTH SE16 ...124 B3
ROMW/RG RM7 ...56 D5
Redroofs Cl BECK BR3 ...182 E4
Redruth Cl WDGN N22 ...49 F3
Redruth Rd HOM E9 ...86 E6
Redstart Cl EHAM E6 ...107 J4
NWCR SE14 * ...144 B1
Redston Rd CEND/HSY/T N8 ...66 D1
Redvers Rd WDGN N22 ...49 G5
Redvers St IS N1 ...7 H4
Redwald Rd CLPT E5 ...87 F2
Redway Dr WHTN TW2 ...155 H2
Redwing Ms CMBW SE5 ...142 D3
Redwing Rd WLGTN SM6 ...210 E5
Red Wood Cl BERM/RHTH SE16...128 A1
BFN/LL DA15 ...168 A5
BOW E3 ...105 J1
OXHEY WD19 ...27 G6
STHGT/OAK N14 ...34 C2
Redwood Gdns CHING E4 * ...37 K2
Redwood Wy BAR EN5 ...20 B6
Reece Ms SKENS SW7 ...14 A6
Reed Av ORP BR6 ...216 E1
Reed Cl CAN/RD E16 ...106 E4
LEE/GVPK SE12 ...145 K6
Reede Wy DAGE RM10 ...92 D4
Reedham Cl TOTM N17 ...68 C3
Reedham St PECK SE15 * ...143 H3
Reedholm Vis STNW/STAM N16 ...85 K2
Reed Pond Wk GPK RM2 ...57 H5
Reed Pl CLAP SW4 ...141 J5
Reed Rd TOTM N17 ...50 B6
Reedsfield Cl ASHF TW15 ...152 E5
Reedsfield Rd ASHF TW15 ...152 D6
Reedworth St LBTH SE11 ...17 K7
Reenglass Rd STAN HA7 ...29 K6
Rees Dr STAN HA7 ...30 A6
Rees Gdns CROY/NA CR0 ...197 G3
Reesland Cl MNPK E12 ...90 A4
Rees St IS N1 ...6 E1
Reets Farm Cl CDALE/KGS NW9 ...63 G3
Reeves Av CDALE/KGS NW9 ...63 F4
Reeves Cnr CROY/NA CR0 ...196 C6
Reeves Ms MYFR/PKLN W1K *...9 G6

Reeves Rd BOW E3 ...105 K3
WOOL/PLUM SE18 ...127 G6
Reform Rw TOTM N17 ...50 B5
Reform St BTSEA SW11 ...140 E3
Regal Cl EA W5 ...97 K4
WCHPL E1 ...104 C4
Regal Crs WLGTN SM6 ...210 B1
Regal Dr FBAR/BDGN N11 ...48 B1
Regal La CAMTN NW1 ...3 H1
Regal Wy KTN/HRWW/WS HA3 ...62 A3
IS N1 * ...7 G3
Regarder Rd CHIG IG7 ...55 H1
Regarth Av ROM RM1 ...75 G6
Regatta Cl CHIG IG7 ...54 C1
EA W5 ...98 A5
HPTN TW12 ...172 E1
Regency Ct EN EN1 ...23 K6
Regency Dr RSLP HA4 ...58 C5
Regency Gdns WOT/HER KT12 ...188 C5
Regency Lawn KTTN NW5 * ...84 B1
Regency Ms BECK BR3 ...183 F4
WLSDN NW10 ...81 J4
Regency Pde HAMP NW3 * ...83 H5
Regency Pl WEST SW1P * ...16 C6
Regency St WEST SW1P ...16 C6
Regency Ter HGT N6 * ...65 K3
SEVS/STOTM N15 ...68 A2
SKENS SW7 * ...120 C5
Regency Wk CROY/NA CR0 ...198 B5
Regency Wy BXLYHN DA7 ...148 E4
Regeneration Rd
BERM/RHTH SE16 * ...124 A4
Regent Cl HEST TW5 ...134 A2
KTN/HRWW/W HA3 ...62 A3
NFNCH/WDSP N12 ...47 G1
Regent Gdns GDMY/SEVK IG3 ...73 G5
Regent Pde BELMT SM2 * ...209 G4
STNW/STAM N16 * ...68 B4
Regent Pl WIM/MER SW19 ...178 B1
HNHL SE24 ...142 E6
Regents Av PLMGR N13 ...49 G1
Regents Bridge Gdns
KIL/WHAMP NW6 * ...101 F1
Regent Sq BELV DA17 ...129 J4
BOW E3 ...105 K2
STPAN WC1H ...5 F5
Regent's Rw HACK E8 ...86 C6
Regent St CHSWK W4 ...117 H5
CONDST W1S ...10 A4
WLSDN NW10 ...100 B2
Regents Whf IS N1 * ...5 G2
Reginald Rd DEPT SE8 ...144 D1
FSTGT E7 ...88 E5
NTHWD HA6 ...40 D4
Reginald Sq DEPT SE8 ...144 D1
Regina Rd FSBYPK N4 ...67 F5
NWDGN UB2 ...114 D4
SNWD SE25 ...181 H6
WEA W13 ...116 B1
Regina Ter WEA W13 ...116 B1
Regis Rd KTTN NW5 ...84 B3
Regnart Buildings CAMTN NW1 ...4 B5
Reidi Cl PIN HA5 ...40 E6
Reidhaven Rd
WOOL/PLUM SE18 ...127 K4
Reigate Av CHEAM SM3 ...193 K6
Reigate Rd BMLY BR1 ...165 K4
GDMY/SEVK IG3 ...73 F6
Reigate Wy WLGTN SM6 ...210 E3
Reighton Rd CLPT E5 ...86 C1
Reizel Cl STNW/STAM N16 ...68 B5
Relay Rd SHB W12 ...100 A6
Relf Rd PECK SE15 ...143 H4
Reliance Ar BRXN/ST SW9 ...142 B5
Relton Ms SKENS SW7 ...14 C4
Rembrandt Cl BGVA SW1W *...121 F5
POP/IOD E14 ...125 G3
Rembrandt Ct
HOR/WEW KT19 ...207 H4
Rembrandt Rd EDGW HA8 * ...44 C5
LEW SE13 ...145 H5
Rembrandt Wy
WOT/HER KT12 ...188 A6
Remington Rd EHAM E6 ...107 J5
SEVS/STOTM N15 ...67 K3
Remington St IS N1 ...6 C3
Remnant St HOL/ALD WC2B ...11 G3
Remus Rd BOW E3 ...87 J5
Rendle Cl CROY/NA CR0 ...197 G2
Rendlesham Rd CLPT E5 ...86 C2
ENC/FH EN2 ...23 H2
Renforth St BERM/RHTH SE16 ...123 K2
Renfrew Cl EHAM E6 ...108 A6
Renfrew Rd HEST TW5 ...134 C3
KUTN/CMB KT2 ...175 J3
LBTH SE11 ...18 A6
Renmuir St TOOT SW17 ...178 E2
Rennell St LEW SE13 ...145 F4
Renness Rd WALTH E17 ...51 G6
Rennets Cl ELTH/MOT SE9 ...147 J6
Rennets Wood Rd
ELTH/MOT SE9 ...147 J6
Rennie Cl ASHF TW15 ...152 A5
Rennie Est BERM/RHTH SE16 ...123 J4
Rennie St STHWK SE1 ...11 K7
Renown Cl CROY/NA CR0 ...196 C5
ROMW/RG RM7 ...56 C4
Rensburg Rd WALTH E17 ...69 F2
Rensburg Vis WALTH E17 * ...69 F2

Renshaw Cl BELV DA17 ...129 G6
Renters Av HDN NW4 ...64 A3
Renton Cl BRXS/STRHM SW2 * ...162 A1
Renton Dr STMC/STPC BR5 ...202 E4
Renwick Rd BARK IG11 ...109 H3
Repens Wy YEAD UB4 ...95 H3
Rephidim St STHWK SE1 ...19 F5
Replingham Rd
WAND/EARL SW18 ...159 J3
Reporton Rd FUL/PGN SW6 ...139 H1
Repository Rd
WOOL/PLUM SE18 ...126 E6
Repton Av ALP/SUD HA0 ...79 J2
GPK RM2 ...57 J6
HYS/HAR UB3 ...113 G4
Repton Cl SUT SM1 ...209 J3
Repton Ct BECK BR3 ...182 E4
Repton Dr GPK RM2 ...75 J1
Repton Gdns GPK RM2 ...57 J6
Repton Gv CLAY IG5 ...53 K4
Repton Rd
KTN/HRWW/W HA3 ...62 B1
ORP BR6 ...217 G2
Repton St POP/IOD E14 ...105 G5
Repulse Cl ROMW/RG RM7 ...56 D4
Reservoir Cl THHTH CR7 ...180 E6
Reservoir Rd BROCKY SE4 ...144 B3
RSLP HA4 ...58 A2
STHGT/OAK N14 ...22 C6
Resolution Wy DEPT SE8 ...144 D1
Restell Cl BKHTH/KID SE3 ...125 H6
Restmor Wy WLGTN SM6 ...195 F6
Reston Pl SKENS SW7 ...14 A4
Restons Crs ELTH/MOT SE9 ...167 J1
Reston Vw CAN/RD E16 ...107 H6
Retford St BETH E2 ...7 J4
Retingham Wy CHING E4 ...37 K4
Retreat Cl KTN/HRWW/W HA3 ...61 J2
Retreat Pl HOM E9 ...86 E4
Retreat Rd RCH/KEW TW9 ...136 E6
The Retreat BARN SW13 ...138 D4
BRYLDS KT5 ...191 G3
CDALE/KGS NW9 ...63 F2
ORP BR6 ...217 H4
RYLN/HDSTN HA2 ...60 A4
THHTH CR7 ...196 E1
WPK KT4 ...207 K1
Reunion Rw WAP E1W * ...104 D6
Reveley Sq BERM/RHTH SE16 ...124 B2
Revell Rd WOOL/PLUM SE18 ...128 A6
Revell Rd KUT/HW KT1 ...175 J5
SUT SM1 ...208 D4
Revelon Rd BROCKY SE4 ...144 B4
Revelstoke Rd
WAND/EARL SW18 ...159 K4
Reventlow Rd ELTH/MOT SE9 ...167 H3
Reverdy Rd STHWK SE1 ...123 H4
Reverend Ct RYLN/HDSTN HA2 ...78 B1
Revesby Rd CAR SM5 ...194 C3
Review Rd CRICK NW2 ...81 H1
DAGE RM10 ...110 D1
Rewell St FUL/PGN SW6 * ...140 B1
Rewley Rd CAR SM5 ...194 C3
Rex Pl MYFR/PKLN W1K * ...9 H7
Reydon Av WAN E11 ...71 G3
Reynard Cl BMLY BR1 ...185 F6
Reynard Dr NRWD SE19 ...181 G3
Reynard Pl NWCR SE14 * ...124 B6
Reynardson Rd TOTM N17 ...49 J3
Reynolds Av CHDH RM6 ...73 J4
CHSGTN KT9 ...206 A5
MNPK E12 ...90 A3
Reynolds Cl CAR SM5 ...194 E6
GLDGN NW11 ...65 F4
WIM/MER SW19 ...178 C4
Reynolds Dr EDGW HA8 ...44 B6
Reynolds Pl BKHTH/KID SE3 ...146 A1
RCHPK/HAM TW10 ...157 G1
Reynolds Rd CHSWK W4 ...117 K3
NWMAL KT3 ...192 A4
PECK SE15 ...143 K6
YEAD UB4 ...95 H3
Reynolds Wy CROY/NA CR0 ...212 A2
Rheidol Ms IS N1 ...6 C2
Rheidol Ter IS N1 ...6 C2
Rheingold Wy WLGTN SM6 ...210 E6
Rheola Cl TOTM N17 ...50 B4
Rhoda St BETH E2 ...7 J6
Rhodes Av WDGN N22 ...48 C4
Rhodesia Rd BRXN/ST SW9 ...141 K3
WAN E11 ...70 B6
Rhodes St HOLWY N7 ...85 F3
Rhodeswell Rd BOW E3 ...105 G4
Rhodrons Av CHSGTN KT9 ...206 A3
Rhondda Gv BOW E3 ...105 G2
Rhyl Rd GFD/PVL UB6 ...97 F1
Rhyl St KTTN NW5 ...84 A4
Rhys Av FBAR/BDGN N11 ...48 D3
Rialto Rd MTCM CR4 ...179 F5
Ribble Cl WFD IG8 ...53 G2
Ribblesdale Av
FBAR/BDGN N11 ...47 K2
NTHLT UB5 ...78 B4
Ribblesdale Rd CEND/HSY/T N8 ...67 F1
STRHM/NOR SW16 ...179 G1
Ribbon Dance Ms CMBW SE5 ...142 E2
Ribchester Av GFD/PVL UB6 ...97 F1
Ribston Cl HAYES BR2 ...200 E5
Ricardo Pde POP/IOD E14 ...105 K5
Ricards Rd WIM/MER SW19 ...177 J1
Rice Pde STMC/STPC BR5 ...201 J2
Richard House Dr CAN/RD E16 ...107 H5
Richards Av ROMW/RG RM7 ...74 E2
Richards Cl BUSH WD23 ...28 D1
HRW HA1 ...61 F2
HYS/HAR UB3 ...113 G4
Richard's Pl CHEL SW3 ...14 D6
WALTH E17 ...51 J3
Richard St WCHPL E1 ...104 D5
Richbell Pl BMSBY WC1N ...11 G1

Richborne Ter VX/NE SW8 ...142 A1
Richborough Cl
STMC/STPC BR5 ...202 E1
Richborough Rd CRICK NW2 ...82 B2
Richens Cl HSLW TW3 ...135 J3
Riches Rd IL IG1 ...72 C6
Richfield Rd BUSH WD23 ...28 C3
Richford Ga HMSMTH W6 * ...119 F3
Richford Rd SRTFD E15 ...88 D6
Richford St SHB W12 ...119 F2
Richlands Av EW KT17 ...207 J2
Richmer Rd ERITH DA8 ...150 D1
Richmond Av CHING E4 ...52 B1
EBED/NFELT TW14 ...153 H1
IS N1 ...85 F6
RYNPK SW20 ...177 H4
WLSDN NW10 ...81 K4
Richmond Buildings
SOHO/CST W1F ...10 C4
Richmond Cl WALTH E17 ...69 H3
Richmond Crs CHING E4 ...38 C1
ED N9 ...36 C3
IS N1 ...85 F6
Richmond Dr WFD IG8 ...53 J3
Richmond Gdns HDN NW4 ...63 J3
KTN/HRWW/W HA3 ...43 F3
Richmond Gn CROY/NA CR0 ...210 E1
Richmond Gv IS N1 ...85 H5
Richmond Hl
RCHPK/HAM TW10 ...157 F1
Richmond Ms SOHO/CST W1F...10 C4
Richmond Pde TWK TW1 * ...156 D1
Richmond Park Rd
KUTN/CMB KT2 ...175 F3
MORT/ESHN SW14 ...137 K6
Richmond Pl
WOOL/PLUM SE18 ...127 H4
Richmond Rd BAR EN5 ...21 G6
CHING E4 ...38 B3
EA W5 ...117 F2
EFNCH N2 ...47 G5
FBAR/BDGN N11 ...48 E2
FSTGT E7 ...89 F3
HACK E8 ...86 C5
IL IG1 ...90 C2
ISLW TW7 ...136 B5
KUTN/CMB KT2 ...174 E1
ROM RM1 ...75 H3
RYNPK SW20 ...176 E4
SEVS/STOTM N15 ...68 A3
TWK TW1 ...156 C1
WALTH E17 ...51 G3
WAN E11 ...70 B6
WDGN N22 ...48 C4
WHALL SW1A ...16 E2
WIM/MER SW19 ...178 A2
Richmond St PLSTW E13 ...106 E1
Richmond Ter WHALL SW1A ...16 E2
Richmond Vls WALTH E17 * ...51 K4
Richmond Wy SHB W12 ...119 G2
WAN E11 ...70 E6
Richmount Gdns
BKHTH/KID SE3 ...145 K4
Rich St POP/IOD E14 ...105 H6
Rickard Cl BRXS/STRHM SW2 ...162 B3
HDN NW4 ...63 J1
Rickards Cl SURB KT6 ...191 F6
Rickett St FUL/PGN SW6 ...119 K6
Rickman St WCHPL E1 ...104 E3
Rickmansworth Rd
NTHWD HA6 ...40 B3
PIN HA5 ...41 F5
Rick Roberts Wy SRTFD E15 ...88 B6
Rickthorne Rd ARCH N19 ...66 E6
Ridding La GFD/PVL UB6 ...79 F3
Riddons Rd LEE/GVPK SE12 ...166 C5
Rideout St WOOL/PLUM SE18 ...126 E4
Rider Cl BFN/LL DA15 ...167 K2
The Ride BTFD TW8 ...116 C5
PEND EN3 ...24 E4
Ridgdale St BOW E3 ...105 J1
Ridge Av DART DA1 ...170 C1
WCHMH N21 ...35 J2
Ridgebrook Rd
BKHTH/KID SE3 ...146 B5
Ridge Cl CDALE/KGS NW9 ...63 F1
HDN NW4 ...46 B5
THMD SE28 ...127 J2
Ridge Crest ENC/FH EN2 ...23 F2
Ridgecroft Cl BXLY DA5 ...169 K3
Ridge Hl GLDGN NW11 ...64 C5
Ridgemead Cl STHGT/OAK N14...34 E4
Ridgemont Gdns EDGW HA8 ...30 E5
Ridgemount Av CROY/NA CR0 ...198 A6
Ridge Rd CEND/HSY/T N8 ...67 F3
CHEAM SM3 ...193 J4
CRICK NW2 ...82 D1
MTCM CR4 ...179 G3
Ridge Ter WCHMH N21 * ...35 J2
The Ridge BAR EN5 * ...20 D6
BXLY DA5 ...169 G2
ORP BR6 ...201 J6
WHTN TW2 ...155 J2
Ridgeview Rd
TRDG/WHET N20 ...33 F5
Ridge Wy DART DA1 ...170 C1
FELT TW13 ...154 D5
Ridgeway HAYES BR2 ...199 K6
WFD IG8 ...39 G6
Ridgeway Av EBAR EN4 ...33 K1
Ridgeway Crs ORP BR6 ...216 E1
Ridgeway Crescent Gdns
ORP BR6 ...201 K6
Ridgeway Dr BMLY BR1 ...166 A6
Ridgeway East BFN/LL DA15 ...148 A6
Ridgeway Gdns REDBR IG4 ...71 J2
IS N1 ...85 J5
Ridgeway Rd ISLW TW7 ...135 K1
Ridgeway Rd North ISLW TW7 ...135 K1
The Ridgeway ACT W3 ...117 H3
CDALE/KGS NW9 ...63 G2
CHING E4 ...38 A3
CROY/NA CR0 ...210 E1

ENC/FH EN2 ...23 G2
FBAR/BDGN N11 ...33 K6
FNCH N3 ...47 F3
GLDGN NW11 ...64 D5
GPK RM2 ...75 J1
KTN/HRWW/W HA3 ...61 K3
MLHL NW7 ...31 K6
RSLP HA4 ...58 E4
RYLN/HDSTN HA2 ...60 A6
STAN HA7 ...43 J2
STHGT/OAK N14 ...34 E4
Ridgeway West BFN/LL DA15 ...147 K6
Ridgewell Cl DAGE RM10 ...92 D6
IS N1 ...6 E1
SYD SE26 ...164 C6
Ridgmount Gdns GWRST WC1E ...10 C1
Ridgmount Rd
WAND/EARL SW18 ...140 A6
Ridgmount St GWRST WC1E ...10 C1
Ridgway RCHPK/HAM TW10 * ...157 F1
WIM/MER SW19 ...177 F3
Ridgway Gdns
WIM/MER SW19 ...177 G3
Ridgway Pl WIM/MER SW19 ...177 H2
Ridgway Rd BRXN/ST SW9 ...142 C4
The Ridgway BELMT SM2 ...209 H6
Ridgwell Rd CAN/RD E16 ...107 G4
Riding House St GTPST W1W ...9 K2
REGST W1B * ...9 K2
Ridings Av WCHMH N21 ...23 H5
The Ridings BRYLDS KT5 ...191 H2
EA W5 ...98 B3
EBAR EN4 ...21 J4
EW KT17 ...207 K4
The Riding GLDGN NW11 ...64 D4
Ridler Rd EN EN1 ...24 A1
Ridley Av WEA W13 ...116 C3
Ridley Cl HARH RM3 ...57 K4
Ridley Rd FSTGT E7 ...89 G2
HACK E8 ...86 B3
HAYES BR2 ...183 J6
WELL DA16 ...148 C2
WIM/MER SW19 ...178 A3
WLSDN NW10 ...99 J1
Ridsdale Rd PGE/AN SE20 ...181 J4
Riefield Rd ELTH/MOT SE9 ...147 J5
Riesco Dr CROY/NA CR0 ...212 E4
Riffel Rd CRICK NW2 ...82 A3
Rifle Pl NTGHL W11 ...119 G1
Rifle Range La HRW HA1 ...61 F5
Rifle St POP/IOD E14 ...105 K4
Rigault Rd FUL/PGN SW6 ...139 H3
Rigby Cl CROY/NA CR0 ...211 G1
Rigby La HYS/HAR UB3 ...113 G2
Rigby Ms IL IG1 ...72 A6
Rigden St POP/IOD E14 ...105 K5
Rigeley Rd WLSDN NW10 ...99 J2
Rigg Ap LEY E10 ...69 F5
Rigge Pl CLAP SW4 ...141 J5
Right Side STHGT/OAK N14 * ...34 D3
Riley Rd PEND EN3 ...25 J1
STHWK SE1 ...19 J4
Riley St WBPTN SW10 ...140 C1
Rinaldo Rd BAL SW12 ...161 G2
Ring Cl BMLY BR1 ...184 A3
Ringcroft St HOLWY N7 ...85 F3
Ringers Rd BMLY BR1 ...183 K6
Ringford Rd
WAND/EARL SW18 ...139 J6
Ringlet Cl CAN/RD E16 ...107 F4
Ringmer Av FUL/PGN SW6 ...139 H2
Ringmer Pl WCHMH N21 ...23 K6
Ringmer Wy BMLY BR1 ...200 E2
Ringmore Ri FSTH SE23 ...163 J2
Ringsend Rd CHST BR7 ...186 B6
Ringslade Rd WDGN N22 ...49 F5
Ringstead Rd CAT SE6 ...164 E2
SUT SM1 ...209 H2
Ring Wy FBAR/BDGN N11 ...48 C2
Ringway NWDGN UB2 ...114 D5
Ringwood Av CROY/NA CR0 ...195 K4
EFNCH N2 ...47 K6
Ringwood Cl PIN HA5 * ...41 G6
Ringwood Gdns
PUT/ROE SW15 ...158 D4
Ringwood Rd WALTH E17 ...69 H5
Ringwood Wy HPTN TW12 ...155 G2
WCHMH N21 ...35 H2
Ripley Cl BMLY BR1 ...200 E2
CROY/NA CR0 ...214 A4
Ripley Gdns
MORT/ESHN SW14 ...138 A4
Ripley Ms WAN E11 ...70 C5
Ripley Rd BELV DA17 ...129 H4
CAN/RD E16 ...107 G5
GDMY/SEVK IG3 ...73 F6
HPTN TW12 ...173 F3
IL IG1 ...72 E6
Ripley Vls WEA W13 * ...97 G6
Ripon Cl NTHLT UB5 ...78 A3
Ripon Gdns CHSGTN KT9 ...205 K3
IL IG1 ...71 J3
Ripon Rd ED N9 ...36 D2
TOTM N17 ...49 K6
WOOL/PLUM SE18 ...127 G6
Rippersley Rd WELL DA16 ...148 B2
Ripple Rd BARK IG11 ...90 C5
BARK IG11 ...91 F6
DAGW RM9 ...110 A1
Ripplevale Gv IS N1 ...85 F5
Rippolson Rd
WOOL/PLUM SE18 ...128 A5
Risborough Cl MUSWH N10 * ...48 B6
Risborough Dr WPK KT4 ...192 D4
Risborough St STHWK SE1 ...18 C2
Risdon St BERM/RHTH SE16 ...123 K2
Risedale Rd BXLYHN DA7 ...149 J4
Riseldine Rd FSTH SE23 ...164 B1
Rise Park Bvd ROM RM1 ...57 H4
Rise Park Pde ROM RM1 ...57 G5

The Rise BKHH IG9 39 H3
BXLY DA5 168 D2
DART DA1 150 C5
EDGW HA8 44 D1
GFD/PVL UB6 79 G3
MLHL NW7 45 H2
PLMGR N13 35 G6
SAND/SEL CR2 212 E6
WAN E11 70 E2
WLSDN NW10 81 F1
Rising Hill Cl NTHWD HA6 * 40 A2
Risinghill St IS N1 5 J2
Risingholme Cl BUSH WD23 28 B2
KTN/HRWW/W HA3 42 E4
Risingholme Rd
KTN/HRWW/W HA3 42 E5
The Risings WALTH E17 70 B1
Risley Av TOTM N17 49 J4
Rita Rd VX/NE SW8 141 K1
Ritches Rd SEVS/STOTM N15 67 J2
Ritchie Rd CROY/NA CR0 197 J3
Ritchie St IS N1 5 K2
Ritchings Av WALTH E17 69 G1
Ritherdon Rd TOOT SW17 161 F4
Ritson Rd HACK E8 86 B4
Ritter St WOOL/PLUM SE18 127 F6
Rivaz Pl HOM E9 86 E4
Rivenhall Gdns SWFD E18 70 D1
River Av PLMGR N13 35 H5
THDIT KT7 190 B4
Riverbank E/WMO/HCT KT8 173 K6
River Bank THDIT KT7 190 A2
WCHMH N21 35 J2
Riverbank Rd BMLY BR1 165 K5
Riverbank Wy BTFD TW8 116 D6
River Barge Cl POP/IOD E14 125 F2
River Cl NWDGN UB2 115 H2
RAIN RM13 111 K4
RSLP HA4 58 D3
WAN E11 71 G3
Rivercourt Rd HMSMTH W6 118 E4
Riverdale Dr
WAND/EARL SW18 160 A3
Riverdale Gdns TWK TW1 136 D6
Riverdale Rd BXLY DA5 169 G2
ERITH DA8 129 J5
FELT TW13 154 D6
TWK TW1 156 D1
WOOL/PLUM SE18 128 A5
Riverdene EDGW HA8 30 E6
Riverdene Rd IL IG1 90 A1
River Front EN EN1 23 K4
River Gdns CAR SM5 195 F6
EBED/NFELT TW14 134 A6
River Grove Pk BECK BR3 182 C4
Riverhead Cl WALTH E17 51 F5
Riverholme Dr
HOR/WEW KT19 207 F6
River La RCHPK/HAM TW10 156 E3
Rivermead E/WMO/HCT KT8 173 H6
SURB KT6 * 190 E2
Rivermead Cl TEDD TW11 174 C1
Rivermead Rd UED N18 * 51 F1
River Meads Av WHTN TW2 155 G5
Rivernook Cl WOT/HER KT12 188 B2
Riverpark Gdns HAYES BR2 183 G3
River Park Rd WDGN N22 49 F5
River Park Vw ORP BR6 202 C4
River Pl IS N1 85 J5
River Reach TEDD TW11 174 D2
River Rd BARK IG11 108 E1
BKHH IG9 39 J3
Riversdale Rd CRW RM5 56 D3
HBRY N5 85 H1
THDIT KT7 190 B2
Riversfield Rd EN EN1 24 A4
Riverside CHARL SE7 126 A3
HDN NW4 63 K4
SUN TW16 * 172 C5
TWK TW1 156 C3
Riverside Av E/WMO/HCT KT8 189 J2
Riverside Cl CLPT E5 68 E5
HNWL W7 96 E3
KUT/HW KT1 190 E1
STMC/STPC BR5 186 D5
WLGTN SM6 210 B1
Riverside Ct CHING E4 * 37 K1
Riverside Dr CHSWK W4 138 B1
ESH/CLAY KT10 204 A2
GLDGN NW11 * 64 C3
MTCM CR4 194 D2
RCHPK/HAM TW10 156 C5
Riverside Gdns ALP/SUD HA0 98 A1
ENC/FH EN2 23 J3
HMSMTH W6 118 E5
Riverside Ms CROY/NA CR0 * 210 E1
Riverside Pl FBAR/BDGN N11 * 34 C5
STWL/WRAY TW19 152 A1
Riverside Rd IL IG1 90 B1
OXHEY WD19 27 F1
SCUP DA14 169 F5
SEVS/STOTM N15 68 C3
SRTFD E15 106 A1
STWL/WRAY TW19 132 A6
TOOT SW17 160 A6
The Riverside
E/WMO/HCT KT8 * 173 J6
Riverside Vls SURB KT6 * 190 D3
Riverside Wk ISLW TW7 135 K4
KUT/HW KT1 174 E5
Riverside Wy DART DA1 151 H6
Riverside Yd TOOT SW17 160 A5
Riverstone Cl RYLN/HDSTN HA2 60 D6
River St CLKNW EC1R 5 J4
River Ter HMSMTH W6 119 F5
Riverton Cl MV/WKIL W9 * 100 D2
Riverview Gdns BARN SW13 118 E6
River View Gdns TWK TW1 156 A4
Riverview Pk CAT SE6 164 D4
Riverview Rd CHSWK W4 137 J1
HOR/WEW KT19 206 E2
River Wk SUN TW16 172 C5
River Wy FELT TW13 155 G4
GNWCH SE10 125 J3
HOR/WEW KT19 207 F3
Riverway PLMGR N13 49 G1
River Whf BELV DA17 * 130 A2
Riverwood La CHST BR7 185 J5
Rivington Av WFD IG8 53 H5
Rivington Crs CDALE/KGS NW9 45 G3
Rivington Pl SDTCH EC2A 7 H5
Rivington St SDTCH EC2A 7 H5
Rivington Wk HACK E8 86 C6
Rivulet Rd TOTM N17 49 J3
Rixon St HOLWY N7 85 G1
Rixsen Rd MNPK E12 89 J3
Roach Rd BOW E3 87 J5
Roads Pl FSBYPK N4 66 E6
Roan St GNWCH SE10 125 F6
Robarts Cl PIN HA5 59 F2
Robb Rd STAN HA7 43 G2
Robert Adam St MBLAR W1H 9 G3
Roberta St BETH E2 104 C2
Robert Cl CHIG IG7 55 F1
MV/WKIL W9 101 G3
Robert Keen Cl PECK SE15 143 H2
Robert Lowe Cl NWCR SE14 144 A1
Roberton Dr BMLY BR1 184 B5
Robertsbridge Rd CAR SM5 194 B4
Roberts Cl CHEAM SM3 208 B5
ELTH/MOT SE9 167 J3
HARH RM3 57 K4
STMC/STPC BR5 202 D2
THHTH CR7 180 E6
WDR/YW UB7 112 B1
Roberts Ct CHSGTN KT9 * 205 K3
WLSDN NW10 81 G4
Roberts House
WOOL/PLUM SE18 146 D2
Roberts Ms KTBR SW1X * 15 G5
Robertson Rd SRTFD E15 88 A6
Robertson St VX/NE SW8 141 G4
Robert's Pl CLKNW EC1R * 5 K6
Robert Sq LEW SE13 145 F5
Roberts Rd BELV DA17 129 H5
MLHL NW7 46 C1
WALTH E17 51 K4
Robert St CAMTN NW1 3 K5
CHCR WC2N 11 F6
CROY/NA CR0 211 J1
WOOL/PLUM SE18 127 J5
Robeson St BOW E3 105 H4
Robina Cl BXLYHS DA6 148 E5
NTHWD HA6 40 D5
Robin Cl CRW RM5 57 F3
HPTN TW12 172 D1
MLHL NW7 31 G5
Robin Gv BTFD TW8 116 D6
HGT N6 66 A6
KTN/HRWW/W HA3 62 B3
Robin Hill Dr CHST BR7 184 D2
Robinhood Cl MTCM CR4 195 H1
Robin Hood Dr
KTN/HRWW/W HA3 43 F3
Robin Hood Gdns
POP/IOD E14 * 106 A6
Robin Hood Gn
STMC/STPC BR5 202 B2
Robin Hood La BXLYHS DA6 149 F6
Robinhood La MTCM CR4 179 H6
Robin Hood La POP/IOD E14 106 A6
PUT/ROE SW15 158 B5
SUT SM1 208 E3
Robin Hood Rd
PUT/ROE SW15 158 B6
Robin Hood Wy GFD/PVL UB6 79 F4
PUT/ROE SW15 158 B6
Robin Hood Wy (Kingston By-Pass)
PUT/ROE SW15 158 B6
Robinia Cl BARK/HLT IG6 54 E2
PGE/AN SE20 181 H4
Robinia Crs LEY E10 69 K6
Robins Gv WWKM BR4 214 E1
Robinson Cl HCH RM12 93 K5
WAN E11 88 C1
Robinson Crs BUSH WD23 28 C3
Robinson Rd BETH E2 104 E1
DAGE RM10 92 C2
WIM/MER SW19 178 D2
Robinson's Cl WEA W13 97 G4
Robinson St CHEL SW3 120 E6
Robin Wy STMC/STPC BR5 186 C6
Robinwood Pl
RCHPK/HAM TW10 158 A6
Robsart St BRXN/ST SW9 142 A3
Robson Av WLSDN NW10 81 J6
Robson Cl EHAM E6 107 J5
ENC/FH EN2 23 H3
Robson Rd WNWD SE27 162 C5
Rocastle Rd BROCKY SE4 144 B6
Roch Av EDGW HA8 44 B5
Rochdale Rd ABYW SE2 128 C5
WALTH E17 69 J4
Rochdale Wy DEPT SE8 144 D1
Rochelle Cl BTSEA SW11 140 C5
Rochelle St BETH E2 7 J5
Rochemont Wk HACK E8 * 7 K1
Roche Rd STRHM/NOR SW16 179 K4
Rochester Av BMLY BR1 184 A5
FELT TW13 153 J4
PLSTW E13 89 G6
Rochester Cl BFN/LL DA15 168 C1
EN EN1 24 A2
STRHM/NOR SW16 * 179 K3
Rochester Dr BXLY DA5 169 H1
PIN HA5 59 H2
Rochester Gdns CROY/NA CR0 212 A1
IL IG1 71 K4
Rochester Ms CAMTN NW1 84 C5
EA W5 * 116 D4
Rochester Pde FELT TW13 * 153 K5
Rochester Pl CAMTN NW1 84 C4
Rochester Rd CAMTN NW1 84 C4
CAR SM5 209 K2
DART DA1 171 K2
NTHWD HA6 40 D6
Rochester Rw WEST SW1P 16 B6
Rochester Sq CAMTN NW1 84 C5
Rochester St WEST SW1P 16 C5
Rochester Ter CAMTN NW1 84 C4
Rochester Wk STHWK SE1 * 12 E7
Rochester Wy BKHTH/KID SE3 146 A2
DART DA1 170 B2
ELTH/MOT SE9 146 E4
Rochester Wy Relief Rd
ELTH/MOT SE9 146 D6
Roche Wk MRDN SM4 194 C3
Rochford Av CHDH RM6 73 J2
Rochford Cl EHAM E6 107 H1
HCH RM12 93 K4
Rochford Wk HACK E8 * 86 C5
Rochford Wy CROY/NA CR0 195 K3
Rock Av MORT/ESHN SW14 138 A4
Rockbourne Rd FSTH SE23 164 A3
Rock Cl MTCM CR4 178 C5
Rockell's Pl EDUL SE22 163 J1
Rockford Av GFD/PVL UB6 97 H1
Rock Grove Wy
BERM/RHTH SE16 123 H4
Rockhall Rd CRICK NW2 82 B2
Rockhampton Rd
SAND/SEL CR2 212 A4
STRHM/NOR SW16 162 B6
Rock Hl SYD SE26 163 G6
Rockingham Av EMPK RM11 75 K3
Rockingham Cl
PUT/ROE SW15 138 C5
Rockingham Ga BUSH WD23 28 C1
Rockingham St STHWK SE1 18 C5
Rockland Rd PUT/ROE SW15 139 H5
Rocklands Dr
KTN/HRWW/W HA3 43 H5
Rockley Rd SHB W12 119 G2
Rockmount Rd NRWD SE19 180 E2
WOOL/PLUM SE18 128 A5
Rocks La BARN SW13 138 D4
Rock St FSBYPK N4 67 G6
Rockware Av GFD/PVL UB6 78 E6
Rockways BAR EN5 31 H1
Rockwell Gdns NRWD SE19 163 F6
Rockwell Rd DAGE RM10 92 D3
Rocliffe St IS N1 6 B3
Rocombe Crs FSTH SE23 * 163 K2
Rocque La BKHTH/KID SE3 145 J4
Rodborough Rd GLDGN NW11 64 E5
Roden Gdns CROY/NA CR0 197 F3
Rodenhurst Rd CLAP SW4 161 H2
Roden St HOLWY N7 85 F1
IL IG1 90 A1
Rodeo Cl ERITH DA8 150 E2
Roderick Rd HAMP NW3 83 K2
Rodgers Cl BORE WD6 29 K1
Roding Gdns LOU IG10 39 J1
Roding La BKHH IG9 39 J3
Roding La North WFD IG8 53 J5
Roding La South REDBR IG4 71 H2
Roding Ms WAP E1W 123 H1
Roding Rd CLPT E5 87 F2
EHAM E6 108 B4
Rodings Rw BAR EN5 * 20 C5
Roding Vw BKHH IG9 39 H3
Rodmarton St MHST W1U 9 F2
Rodmell Cl YEAD UB4 95 J3
Rodmell Slope
NFNCH/WDSP N12 46 D1
Rodmere St GNWCH SE10 125 H5
Rodmill La BRXS/STRHM SW2 161 K2
Rodney Cl NWMAL KT3 192 B2
PIN HA5 59 J4
WOT/HER KT12 * 188 B5
Rodney Gdns PIN HA5 59 G2
WWKM BR4 214 E2
Rodney Pl STHWK SE1 18 D6
WALTH E17 51 G5
WIM/MER SW19 178 B4
Rodney Rd HSLW TW3 155 F1
MTCM CR4 178 D5
NWMAL KT3 192 B2
WALW SE17 18 D7
WAN E11 71 F1
WOT/HER KT12 188 B6
Rodney St IS N1 5 H2
Rodney Wy ROMW/RG RM7 56 D4
Rodway Rd BMLY BR1 184 A4
PUT/ROE SW15 158 D2
Rodwell Cl RSLP HA4 * 59 G5
Rodwell Rd EDUL SE22 163 G1
Roebuck Cl FELT TW13 154 A6
Roebuck La BKHH IG9 39 G3
Roebuck Rd BARK/HLT IG6 55 H2
CHSGTN KT9 206 C3
Roedean Av PEND EN3 24 E2
Roedean Cl ORP BR6 217 H2
PEND EN3 24 E2
Roedean Crs PUT/ROE SW15 158 B1
Roe End CDALE/KGS NW9 62 E1
Roe Gn CDALE/KGS NW9 62 E2
Roehampton Cl
PUT/ROE SW15 138 D5
Roehampton Dr CHST BR7 185 H2
Roehampton Ga
PUT/ROE SW15 158 B1
Roehampton High St
PUT/ROE SW15 158 D2
Roehampton La
PUT/ROE SW15 138 D6
Roehampton V
PUT/ROE SW15 158 C5
Roe La CDALE/KGS NW9 62 E1
Roe Wy WLGTN SM6 210 E5
Rofant Rd NTHWD HA6 40 C2
Roffey St POP/IOD E14 125 F2
Rogers Gdns DAGE RM10 92 C3
Rogers Rd CAN/RD E16 106 D5
DAGE RM10 92 C3
TOOT SW17 160 C6
Rogers Ruff NTHWD HA6 40 A4
Roger St BMSBY WC1N 5 H7
Rogers Wk NFNCH/WDSP N12 33 F5
Rojack Rd FSTH SE23 164 A3
Rokeby Gdns WFD IG8 52 E4
Rokeby Pl RYNPK SW20 176 E3
Rokeby Rd BROCKY SE4 * 144 C3
Rokeby St SRTFD E15 88 C6
Rokesby Cl WELL DA16 147 J3
Rokesby Pl ALP/SUD HA0 79 K3
Rokesly Av CEND/HSY/T N8 66 E2
Roland Gdns SKENS SW7 120 B5
Roland Ms WCHPL E1 * 105 F4
Roland Rd WALTH E17 70 B1
Roland Wy WALW SE17 122 E5
WBPTN SW10 120 B5
WPK KT4 192 C6
Roles Gv CHDH RM6 73 K1
Rolfe Cl EBAR EN4 21 J5
Rolinsden Wy HAYES BR2 215 H2
Rollesby Rd CHSGTN KT9 206 C4
Rollesby Wy THMD SE28 109 J6
Rolleston Av STMC/STPC BR5 201 G3
Rolleston Cl STMC/STPC BR5 201 G4
Rolleston Rd SAND/SEL CR2 211 K5
Roll Gdns GNTH/NBYPK IG2 72 A2
Rollins St NWCR SE14 123 K6
Rollit Crs HSLW TW3 135 F6
Rollit St HOLWY N7 85 G3
Rolls Buildings
FLST/FETLN EC4A 11 J3
Rollscourt Av HNHL SE24 142 D6
Rolls Park Av CHING E4 51 J2
Rolls Park Rd CHING E4 51 K1
Rolls Rd STHWK SE1 123 G5
Rolls Royce Cl WLGTN SM6 210 E5
Rolt St DEPT SE8 124 B6
Rolvenden Gdns BMLY BR1 184 C4
Rolvenden Pl TOTM N17 50 C4
Roman Cl ACT W3 117 J2
EBED/NFELT TW14 134 B6
RAIN RM13 111 F1
Romanfield Rd
BRXS/STRHM SW2 162 A2
Romanhurst Av HAYES BR2 199 H1
Romanhurst Gdns BECK BR3 199 H1
Roman Ri NRWD SE19 180 E2
Roman Rd BETH E2 105 F1
BOW E3 87 H6
CHSWK W4 118 B4
EHAM E6 107 J3
IL IG1 90 B4
MUSWH N10 48 B3
Roman Sq THMD SE28 128 B1
Roman Wy CROY/NA CR0 196 C6
DART DA1 150 B6
EN EN1 24 B6
HOLWY N7 85 F4
Romany Gdns CHEAM SM3 193 K4
Romany Ri STMC/STPC BR5 201 H5
Roma Rd WALTH E17 51 G6
Romberg Rd TOOT SW17 161 F5
Romborough Gdns LEW SE13 145 F6
Romborough Wy LEW SE13 145 F6
Rom Crs ROMW/RG RM7 75 G4
Romeland BORE WD6 29 K1
Romero Sq BKHTH/KID SE3 146 B5
Romeyn Rd
STRHM/NOR SW16 162 A5
Romford Rd CHDH RM6 55 K2
CRW RM5 56 A3
MNPK E12 90 A1
SRTFD E15 88 D4
Romford St WCHPL E1 104 C4
Romilly Dr OXHEY WD19 27 J6
Romilly Rd FSBYPK N4 67 H6
Romilly St SOHO/SHAV W1D 10 D5
Rommany Rd WNWD SE27 162 E6
Romney Cl CHSGTN KT9 206 A2
GLDGN NW11 65 G5
RYLN/HDSTN HA2 60 A4
TOTM N17 50 D4
Romney Dr BMLY BR1 184 C3
RYLN/HDSTN HA2 60 A4
Romney Gdns BXLYHN DA7 149 G2
Romney Rd GNWCH SE10 125 F6
NWMAL KT3 192 A3
WOOL/PLUM SE18 127 H3
YEAD UB4 94 B1
Romney Rw CRICK NW2 * 64 B6
Romney St WEST SW1P 16 D5
Romola Rd BRXS/STRHM SW2 162 C3
Romsey Cl ORP BR6 216 C2
Romsey Rd DAGW RM9 91 K6
WEA W13 * 97 G6
Rom Valley Wy
ROMW/RG RM7 75 G3
Ronald Av SRTFD E15 106 C2
Ronald Cl BECK BR3 198 C2
Ronalds Rd BMLY BR1 183 K4
HBRY N5 85 H3
Ronaldstone Rd BFN/LL DA15 167 K1
Rona Rd HAMP NW3 84 A2
Ronart St KTN/HRWW/W HA3 43 F6
Rona Wk IS N1 85 K4
Rondu Rd CRICK NW2 82 C3
Ronelean Rd SURB KT6 191 G6
Roneo Cnr ROMW/RG RM7 75 H5
Roneo Link HCH RM12 75 H5
Ronfearn Av STMC/STPC BR5 202 E2
Ron Green Cl ERITH DA8 130 A5
Ron Leighton Wy EHAM E6 89 J6
Ronnie La BCTR RM8 73 J6
Ronver Rd LEE/GVPK SE12 165 K3
Rood La FENCHST EC3M 13 G5
Rookby Ct WCHMH N21 35 H4
Rook Cl WBLY HA9 80 D1
Rookeries Cl FELT TW13 154 A5
Rookery Dr CHST BR7 185 F4
Rookery Gdns
STMC/STPC BR5 202 D2
Rookery La HAYES BR2 200 C3
Rookery Rd CLAP SW4 141 H5
The Rookery
STRHM/NOR SW16 * 180 A2
Rookery Wy CDALE/KGS NW9 63 H2
Rookesley Rd STMC/STPC BR5 202 E4
Rookfield Av MUSWH N10 66 C1
Rookfield Cl MUSWH N10 66 C1
Rookley Cl BELMT SM2 209 F6
Rooks Ter WDR/YW UB7 * 112 B2
Rookstone Rd TOOT SW17 178 E1
Rookwood Av NWMAL KT3 192 D1
WLGTN SM6 210 D2
Rookwood Gdns CHING E4 * 38 D4
Rookwood Rd
STNW/STAM N16 68 B3
Roosevelt Wy DAGE RM10 93 F4
Rootes Dr NKENS W10 100 B3
Ropemaker Rd
BERM/RHTH SE16 124 B2
Ropemaker's Flds
POP/IOD E14 * 105 H6
Ropemaker St BARB EC2Y 12 E1
Roper La STHWK SE1 19 H3
Ropers Av CHING E4 52 A1
Ropers Orch CHEL SW3 * 120 D6
Roper St ELTH/MOT SE9 146 E6
Roper Wy MTCM CR4 179 F5
Ropery St BOW E3 105 H3
Rope St BERM/RHTH SE16 124 B3
Ropewalk Gdns WCHPL E1 104 C5
Ropewalk Ms HACK E8 * 86 B5
Rope Yd Rails
WOOL/PLUM SE18 127 G3
Ropley St BETH E2 104 C1
Rosa Alba Ms HBRY N5 85 J2
Rosa Av ASHF TW15 152 D6
Rosaline Rd FUL/PGN SW6 139 H1
Rosaline Ter FUL/PGN SW6 * 139 H1
Rosamond St SYD SE26 163 J5
Rosamond Vls
MORT/ESHN SW14 * 138 A5
Rosamund Cl SAND/SEL CR2 211 K2
Rosary Cl HSLW TW3 134 D3
Rosary Gdns ASHF TW15 152 E6
BUSH WD23 28 E2
SKENS SW7 120 B4
Rosary Ga BTSEA SW11 141 G1
Rosaville Rd FUL/PGN SW6 139 J1
Roscoe St STLK EC1Y 6 D7
Roscoff Cl EDGW HA8 44 D4
Roseacre Cl WEA W13 97 H4
Roseacre Rd WELL DA16 148 C4
Rose Aly STHWK SE1 12 D7
Roseary Cl WDR/YW UB7 112 A4
Rose Av MRDN SM4 194 B2
MTCM CR4 178 E4
SWFD E18 53 F5
Rosebank PGE/AN SE20 181 J3
Rosebank Av HRW HA1 79 F2
Rose Bank Cl
NFNCH/WDSP N12 47 J1
Rosebank Cl TEDD TW11 174 B2
Rosebank Est BOW E3 105 H1
Rosebank Gdns ACT W3 * 99 F5
BOW E3 * 105 G1
Rosebank Gv WALTH E17 51 H6
Rosebank Rd HNWL W7 115 K2
WALTH E17 69 J3
Rosebank Wk CAMTN NW1 * 84 D5
Rosebank Wy ACT W3 99 F5
Rose Bates Dr CDALE/KGS NW9 62 C1
Roseberry Gdns DART DA1 171 F2
FSBYPK N4 67 H3
ORP BR6 216 E1
Roseberry Pl HACK E8 86 B4
Roseberry St
BERM/RHTH SE16 123 J4
Rosebery Av BFN/LL DA15 167 K2
CLKNW EC1R 5 J7
MNPK E12 89 J4
NWMAL KT3 176 C5
RYLN/HDSTN HA2 77 J2
THHTH CR7 180 D5
TOTM N17 50 C5
Rosebery Cl MRDN SM4 193 G3
Rosebery Ct CLKNW EC1R 5 J6
Rosebery Gdns
CEND/HSY/T N8 * 66 E2
SUT SM1 209 F2
WEA W13 97 G5
Rosebery Ms MUSWH N10 48 C5
Rosebery Pde EW KT17 * 207 H5
Rosebery Rd BUSH WD23 28 B3
CLAP SW4 161 K1
ED N9 36 C5
HSLW TW3 135 H6
KUT/HW KT1 175 J5
MUSWH N10 48 C5
SUT SM1 208 D4
Rosebine Av WHTN TW2 155 J2
Rosebriars ESH/CLAY KT10 204 C3
Rosebury Rd FUL/PGN SW6 140 A3
Rosebury Sq WFD IG8 54 A3
Rosebury V RSLP HA4 58 E6
Rose Ct WCHPL E1 13 J2
Rosecourt Rd CROY/NA CR0 196 A3
Rosecroft Av HAMP NW3 82 E1
Rosecroft Cl STMC/STPC BR5 202 D3
Rosecroft Ct NTHWD HA6 * 40 A2
Rose Croft Gdns CRICK NW2 81 J1
Rosecroft Gdns WHTN TW2 155 J3
Rosecroft Rd STHL UB1 96 A3
Rosecroft Wk ALP/SUD HA0 79 K3
PIN HA5 59 H2
Rose & Crown Yd STJS SW1Y * 16 B1
Rose Dl ORP BR6 201 G6
Rosedale Av HYS/HAR UB3 94 B4
Rosedale Cl ABYW SE2 128 C3
HNWL W7 116 A2
STAN HA7 43 H2
Rosedale Gdns DAGW RM9 91 H5
Rosedale Rd DAGW RM9 91 H5
EW KT17 207 J3
FSTGT E7 89 G3
RCH/KEW TW9 137 F5
ROM RM1 56 E6
Rosedene Av CROY/NA CR0 195 K4
GFD/PVL UB6 96 A2
MRDN SM4 193 K2
STRHM/NOR SW16 162 A5
Rosedene Cl DART DA1 171 F2
Rosedene Gdns
GNTH/NBYPK IG2 72 A1
Rosedene Ter LEY E10 69 K6
Rosedew Rd HMSMTH W6 119 G6
Rose End WPK KT4 193 G5
Rosefield POP/IOD E14 105 J6

osefield Cl CAR SM5 ....209 J3
osefield Gdns POP/IOD E14 ....105 J6
ose Garden Cl EDGW HA8 ....44 A2
ose Gdns EA W5 ....116 E3
  FELT TW13 ....153 K4
  STHL UB1 ....96 A3
  STWL/WRAY TW19 ....152 A2
ose Gin CDALE/KGS NW9 ....63 F1
  ROMW/RG RM7 ....75 C5
oseheart Ms NTGHL W11 ....100 D6
osehatch Av CHDH RM6 ....55 K6
oseheath Rd HSLWW TW4 ....134 E6
osehill CDALE/KGS KT10 ....205 G4
  HPTN TW12 ....173 F4
ose HI SUT SM1 ....194 A6
osehill Av SUT SM1 ....194 B5
osehill Court Pde
  MRDN SM4 * 194 B4
osehill Gdns GFD/PVL UB6 .....79 F3
  SUT SM1 ....194 A6
ose Hill Pk West SUT SM1 ....194 B5
osehill Rd WAND/EARL SW18 ...160 B1
oseland Cl TOTM N17 ....49 K3
ose La CHDH RM6 ....74 A1
ose Lawn BUSH WD23 ....28 C3
oseleigh Av HBRY N5 ....85 H2
oseleigh Cl TWK TW1 ....156 E1
osemary Av
  MORT/ESHN SW14 ....137 K4
  ED N9 ....36 D3
  ENC/FH EN2 ....23 K2
  FNCH N3 ....47 F5
  HSLWW TW4 ....134 C3
  ROM RM1 ....57 H6
osemary Cl CROY/NA CRO 195 K4
osemary Dr POP/IOD E14 ......106 B5
  REDBR IG4 ....71 H2
osemary Gdns BCTR RM8 ....74 B5
  CHSGTN KT9 ....206 A2
osemary La
  MORT/ESHN SW14 ....137 K4
osemary Rd PECK SE15 ....143 G1
  TOOT SW17 ....160 A5
  WELL DA16 ....148 A2
osemary St N1 ....85 K6
osemead CDALE/KGS NW9 ....63 H4
osemead Av FELT TW13 ....153 J4
  MTCM CR4 ....179 H6
  WBLY HA9 ....80 A3
osemont Av
  NFNCH/WDSP N12 ....47 G2
osemont Rd ACT W3 ....98 D6
  HAMP NW3 ....83 H4
  NWMAL KT3 ....175 K6
  RCHPK/HAM TW10 ....157 F1
osemoor St CHEL SW3 ....14 E7
osemount Cl WFD IG8 ....53 K2
osemount Dr BMLY BR1 ....200 E1
osemount Rd ALP/SUD HA0 ......80 A6
  WEA W13 ....97 G6
osenau Crs BTSEA SW11 ....140 E2
osenau Rd BTSEA SW11 ....140 D2
osendale Rd HNHL SE24 ....162 D2
oseneath Av WCHMH N21 ....35 H3
osenthal Pl
  STRHM/NOR SW16 ....162 B6
oseneath Rd BTSEA SW11 ......161 F1
oseneath Wk EN EN1 ....24 A5
osenheath Cl ORP BR6 ....217 H5
osens Wk EDGW HA8 ....30 D5
osenthal Rd CAT SE6 ....164 E1
ose Park Cl YEAD UB4 ....95 G5
oserton St POP/IOD E14 ......125 F2
he Rosery CROY/NA CRO 198 A3
ose Sq CHEL SW3 ....120 C5
he Roses WFD IG8 * 52 D3
osetree St COVGDN WC2E 10 D5
osethorn Cl BAL SW12 ....161 J2
osetta Cl VX/NE SW8 ....141 K1
oseveare Rd LEE/GVPK SE12 ...166 B6
oseville Av HSLW TW3 ....135 F6
oseville Rd HYS/HAR UB3 .....113 K5
osevine Rd RYNPK SW20 ....177 F5
ose Wk BRYLDS KT5 ....191 J2
  WWKM BR4 ....199 G6
oseway DUL SE21 ....162 E1
  EDGW HA8 ....30 E6
ose Wy LEE/GVPK SE12 ....145 K6
osewarne Cl PGE/AN SE20 .....181 J5
osewood RDART DA2 ....170 B6
osewood Av GFD/PVL UB6 ....79 G3
  HCH RM12 ....93 J3
osewood Cl SCUP DA14 ....168 D5
osewood Ct KUTN/CMB KT2 ....175 H3
osewood Gv SUT SM1 ....194 B6
osewood Ter PGE/AN SE20 * ...181 K5
osher Cl SRTFD E15 ....88 B5
osina St HOM E9 ....87 F4
oskell Rd PUT/ROE SW15 .....139 G4
oslin Rd ACT W3 ....117 J3
oslin Wy BMLY BR1 ....184 E5
oslyn Cl MTCM CR4 ....178 C5
oslyn Gdns GPK RM2 ....57 H5
oslyn Ms SEVS/STOTM N15 .....68 A2
oslyn Rd SEVS/STOTM N15 .....67 K2
osmead Rd NTGHL W11 ....100 C6
osoman Pl CLKNW EC1R 5 K6
osoman St CLKNW EC1R 5 K5
ossall Cl CLNPK NW11 ....75 J1
ossall Crs WLSDN NW10 ....98 R2
oss Av BCTR RM8 ....74 B6
  MLHL NW7 ....46 C1
oss Cl HYS/HAR UB3 ....113 G4
  KTN/HRWW/W HA3 ....42 C5
  NTHLT UB5 ....78 D2
ossdale SUT SM1 ....209 J3
  ED N9 ....36 E1
ossdale Rd CDALE/KGS NW9 ....62 E5
ossendale St CLPT E5 ....86 E1
ossendale Wy CAMTN NW1 ......84 B5
ossetti Rd BERM/RHTH SE16 ..123 J5
oss House WOOL/PLUM SE18 ...146 D2

Rossignol Gdns CAR SM5 ......195 F6
Rossindel Rd HSLW TW3 ....135 F6
Rossington Cl EN EN1 ....24 D1
Rossington St CLPT E5 * 68 D6
Rossiter Flds BAR EN5 ....32 C1
Rossiter Rd BAL SW12 ....161 G3
Rossland Cl BXLYHS DA6 ......149 H6
Rosslyn Av BARN SW13 ....138 B4
  BCTR RM8 ....74 B4
  CHING E4 ....38 D4
  EBAR EN4 ....33 J1
  EBED/NFELT TW14 ....153 K1
Rosslyn Cl HYS/HAR UB3 ....94 B4
  WWKM BR4 ....214 D1
Rosslyn Crs HRW HA1 ....61 F1
  WBLY HA9 ....80 A1
Rosslyn Hl HAMP NW3 ....83 H3
Rosslyn Park Ms HAMP NW3 ....83 H3
Rosslyn Rd BARK IG11 ....90 D5
  TWK TW1 ....156 D1
  WALTH E17 ....70 A1
Rossmore Cl STJWD NW8 * 2 D7
Rossmore Rd STJWD NW8 ....2 D6
Ross Pde WLGTN SM6 ....210 B4
Ross Rd DART DA1 ....170 D1
  SNWD SE25 ....181 F6
  WHTN TW2 ....155 H5
Ross Wy ELTH/MOT SE9 ....146 D4
  NTHWD HA6 ....26 D6
Rosswood Gdns WLGTN SM6 ....210 B4
Rostella Rd TOOT SW17 ....160 C6
Rostrever Gdns HYS/HAR UB3 .113 H1
Rostrevor Av
  SEVS/STOTM N15 ....68 B3
Rostrevor Gdns NWDGN UB2 ...114 B3
Rostrevor Rd FUL/PGN SW6 ...139 J2
  WIM/MER SW19 ....177 K1
Rotary St STHWK SE1 ....18 A4
Rothbury Av RAIN RM13 ....111 K4
Rothbury Cottages
  GNWCH SE10 ....125 K5
Rothbury Gdns ISLW TW7 .....136 B1
Rothbury Rd HOM E9 ....87 H5
Rotherfield Rd CAR SM5 .....210 A2
Rotherfield St N1 ....85 J5
Rotherham Wk STHWK SE1 * 18 B1
Rotherhill Av
  STRHM/NOR SW16 ....179 J2
Rotherhithe New Rd
  BERM/RHTH SE16 ....123 K4
Rotherhithe Old Rd
  BERM/RHTH SE16 ....124 A4
Rotherhithe St
  BERM/RHTH SE16 ....123 K2
Rotherhithe Tnl
  BERM/RHTH SE16 ....123 K2
Rothermere Rd CROY/NA CRO ..211 F3
Rotherwick HI EA W5 ....98 B3
Rotherwick Rd GLDGN NW11 ....64 E4
Rotherwood Cl
  WIM/MER SW19 ....177 H4
Rotherwood Rd
  PUT/ROE SW15 ....139 G4
Rothery St IS N1 * 85 H6
Rothery Ter BRXN/ST SW9 * ..142 C1
Rothesay Av GFD/PVL UB6 .....78 C4
  RCHPK/HAM TW10 ....137 J5
  RYNPK SW20 ....177 H5
Rothesay Rd SNWD SE25 ......196 E1
Rothsay Rd FSTGT E7 ....89 G5
Rothsay St STHWK SE1 ....19 G4
Rothschild Rd CHSWK W4 .....117 K4
Rothschild St DWND SE27 ....162 C6
Rothwell Gdns DAGW RM9 ......91 J5
Rothwell Rd DAGW RM9 ....91 J6
Rothwell St CAMTN NW1 ....84 A5
Rotterdam Dr POP/IOD E14 ...125 F3
Rouel Rd BERM/RHTH SE16 ....123 H4
Rougemont Av MRDN SM4 ......193 K3
The Roughs NTHWD HA6 ....26 C5
Roundaway Rd CLAY IG5 ....53 K5
Roundel Cl BROCKY SE4 ......144 C5
Round Gv CROY/NA CRO 198 A4
Roundhay Cl FSTH SE23 ......164 A4
Roundhedge Wy ENC/FH EN2 ...23 F1
Round HI SYD SE26 ....163 J4
Roundhill Dr ENC/FH EN2 ....23 F5
Roundlyn Gdns
  STMC/STPC BR5 ....202 C1
Roundtable Rd BMLY BR1 .....165 K5
Roundtree Rd ALP/SUD HA0 ...79 H5
Roundways RSLP HA4 ....76 D1
The Roundway
  ESH/CLAY KT10 ....205 F4
  TOTM N17 ....49 K4
  WATW WD18 ....26 D2
Roundwood CHST BR7 ....185 G5
Roundwood Av STKPK UB11 ....113 F2
Roundwood Cl RSLP HA4 * 58 B4
Roundwood Pk WLSDN NW10 ....81 J6
Roundwood Rd WLSDN NW10 ....81 G4
Roundwood Ter
  STNW/STAM N16 ....68 B1
Rounton Rd BOW E3 ....105 J3
Roupell Rd BRXS/STRHM SW2 ..161 K3
Roupell St STHWK SE1 ....17 K1
Rousden St CAMTN NW1 ....84 C5
Rouse Gdns DUL SE21 ....163 F6
Rous Rd BKHH IG9 ....39 J3
Routemaster Cl PLSTW E13 ...107 F2
Routh Rd WAND/EARL SW18 ...160 D2
Routh St EHAM E6 ....107 K4
Rover Av BARK/HLT IG6 ....55 F2
Rowallan Rd FUL/PGN SW6 ...139 H1
Rowan Av CHING E4 ....51 H2
Rowan Cl ALP/SUD HA0 ....79 G1
  EA W5 ....117 F2
  IL IG1 ....90 D3
  KTN/HRWW/W HA3 ....43 F2
  NWMAL KT3 ....176 B5
  STRHM/NOR SW16 ....179 H4
Rowan Crs DART DA1 ....170 C1
  STRHM/NOR SW16 ....179 H4
Rowan Dr CDALE/KGS NW9 .....45 J6

Rowan Gdns CROY/NA CRO 212 B1
Rowan PI HYS/HAR UB3 ....94 D6
Rowan Rd BTFD TW8 ....136 C1
  BXLYHN DA7 ....149 F4
  HMSMTH W6 ....119 G4
  STRHM/NOR SW16 ....179 H5
  WDR/YW UB7 ....112 A4
The Rowans PLMGR N13 ....35 J5
Rowan Ter PGE/AN SE20 * 181 H4
Rowan Wy ROMW/RG RM7 ....74 C1
Rowantree Cl WCHMH N21 ......35 K3
Rowantree Ms ENC/FH EN2 .....23 H3
Rowantree Rd ENC/FH EN2 .....23 H3
  WCHMH N21 ....35 K3
Rowan Wk EFNCH N2 ....65 G3
  HAYES BR2 ....215 K1
  NKENS W10 * 100 C3
Rowanwood Av BFN/LL DA15 ..168 B3
Rowben Cl TRDG/WHET N20 .....33 F3
Rowberry Cl FUL/PGN SW6 ...139 G1
Rowcross St STHWK SE1 ......123 G5
Rowdell Rd NTHLT UB5 ....78 A6
Rowden Pde CHING E4 * 51 J2
Rowden Rd BECK BR3 ....182 B4
  CHING E4 ....51 K2
  HOR/WEW KT19 ....206 E2
Rowditch La BTSEA SW11 .....141 F3
Rowdon Av WLSDN NW10 ....81 K5
Rowdown Crs CROY/NA CRO 214 B6
Rowdowns Rd DAGW RM9 ....92 B6
Rowe Gdns BARK IG11 ....109 F1
Rowe La HOM E9 ....86 E3
Rowena Crs BTSEA SW11 .....140 D3
Rowe Wk RYLN/HDSTN HA2 .....77 J4
Rowfant Rd TOOT SW17 ......161 F4
Rowhill Rd CLPT E5 ....86 D2
Rowington Cl BAY/PAD W2 ...101 F4
Rowland Av
  KTN/HRWW/W HA3 ....43 J6
Rowland Gv SYD SE26 ....163 J5
Rowland HII Av TOTM N17 ....49 K3
Rowland Hill St HAMP NW3 ...83 J3
Rowland Rd NTHWD HA6 * 40 C3
Rowlands Av PIN HA5 ....42 A2
Rowlands Cl HGT N6 ....66 A3
  MLHL NW7 ....45 H3
Rowlands Rd BCTR RM8 ....74 B6
Rowland Wy WIM/MER SW19 ...178 A4
Rowlatt Cl RDART DA2 ......171 F6
Rowley Av BFN/LL DA15 .....168 C2
Rowley Cl ALP/SUD HA0 ....80 B5
  OXHEY WD19 ....27 J1
Rowley Gdns FSBYPK N4 ....67 J4
Rowley La BAR EN5 ....32 A5
Rowley Wy STJWD NW8 ....83 G6
Rowlls Rd KUT/HW KT1 ....175 G6
Rowney Gdns DAGW RM9 ....91 H4
Rowney Rd DAGW RM9 ....91 H4
Rowntree Cl KIL/WHAMP NW6 * .82 E4
Rowntree Rd WHTN TW2 ......155 K3
Rowse Cl SRTFD E15 ....88 A6
Rowsley Av HDN NW4 ....46 A6
Rowstock Gdns HOLWY N7 .....84 D4
Rowton Rd WOOL/PLUM SE18 ..147 H1
Rowzill Rd STMC/STPC BR5 ..186 C4
Roxborough Av HRW HA1 ......60 D4
  ISLW TW7 ....136 A1
Roxborough Pk HRW HA1 ......60 D3
Roxborough Rd HRW HA1 ......60 D2
Roxbourne Cl NTHLT UB5 .....77 H4
Roxburgh Rd WNWD SE27 ....180 C1
Roxburn Wy RSLP HA4 ....76 D1
Roxby PI FUL/PGN SW6 ......119 K6
Roxeth Green Av
  RYLN/HDSTN HA2 ....78 B1
Roxeth Gv RYLN/HDSTN HA2 ..60 D6
Roxley Rd LEW SE13 ....164 E1
Roxton Gdns CROY/NA CRO ...213 H4
Roxwell Rd BARK IG11 ....109 G1
  SHB W12 ....118 D2
Roxwell Wy WFD IG8 ....53 G3
Roxy Av CHDH RM6 ....73 J4
Royal Albert Rd EHAM E6 ...108 A6
Royal Albert Wy CAN/RD E16 .107 H4
Royal Ar CONDST W1S 10 A5
Royal Arsenal West
  WOOL/PLUM SE18 * 127 F5
Royal Av CHEL SW3 ....15 F7
  WPK KT4 ....192 B6
Royal Botanic Gdns
  RCH/KEW TW9 ....137 H1
Royal Circ WNWD SE27 ......162 B5
Royal Ct DEPT SE8 ....124 C6
  GDMY/SEVK IG3 ....73 F4
  ORP BR6 ....216 E2
Royal College St
  CAMTN NW1 ....84 C5
Royal Ct BANK EC3V 13 F4
  ELTH/MOT SE9 ....166 E3
  EN EN1 * 24 E5
Royal Crs GNTH/NBYPK IG2 ...72 D5
  NTGHL W11 ....119 G1
  RSLP HA4 ....77 J2
Royal Crescent Ms NTGHL W11 .119 G2
Royal Docks Rd EHAM E6 ....108 D5
Royal HI GNWCH SE10 ....145 F1
Royal Hospital Rd CHEL SW3 .120 E6
Royal Ms BAL SW12 * 161 H3
Royal Mint Ct TWRH EC3N 13 K5
Royal Mint St TWRH EC3N 13 K5
Royal Naval PI NWCR SE14 ..144 C1
Royal Oak PI EDUL SE22 ....163 J1
Royal Oak Rd BXLYHS DA6 ..149 G6
  HACK E8 ....86 D4
Royal Oak Yd STHWK SE1 .....19 G3
Royal Opera Ar STJS SW1Y * .10 C7
Royal Orchard Cl
  WAND/EARL SW18 ....159 H2

Royal Pde BKHTH/KID SE3 ....145 J2
  CHST BR7 ....185 H3
  FUL/PGN SW6 * 139 H1
Royal Pl GNWCH SE10 ....145 F1
Royal Rd CAN/RD E16 ....107 H5
  SCUP DA14 ....168 C5
  TEDD TW11 ....173 J1
  WALW SE17 ....122 C6
Royal Route WBLY HA9 ....80 A2
Royal St STHWK SE1 ....17 H4
Royal Victor PI BOW E3 ....105 F1
Roycraft Av BARK IG11 ......109 F1
Roycroft Cl
  BRXS/STRHM SW2 * 162 B3
  EHAM E6 ....53 F4
Roydene Rd
  WOOL/PLUM SE18 ....127 K6
Roydon Cl LOU IG10 ....39 J2
Roy Gdns GNTH/NBYPK IG2 ...72 E1
Roy Gv HPTN TW12 ....173 G2
Royle Cl GPK RM2 ....75 K2
Royle Crs WEA W13 ....97 G3
Roy Rd NTHWD HA6 ....40 D3
Roy Sq POP/IOD E14 ....105 G6
Royston Av CHING E4 ....51 J1
  SUT SM1 ....209 H1
  WLGTN SM6 ....210 D2
Royston Cl HEST TW5 ....134 A2
Royston Gdns IL IG1 ....71 H3
Royston Gv PIN HA5 ....41 K2
Royston Park Rd PIN HA5 ...41 K2
Royston Rd DART DA1 ....170 C1
  PGE/AN SE20 ....182 A4
  RCHPK/HAM TW10 ....137 F6
The Roystons BRYLDS KT5 ...191 J2
Royston St BETH E2 ....104 E1
Rozel Rd CLAP SW4 ....141 H3
Rubastic Rd NWDGN UB2 ....114 B3
Rubens Rd NTHLT UB5 ....95 G1
Rubens St CAT SE6 ....164 C4
Ruby Ms WALTH E17 * 51 J6
Ruby Rd WALTH E17 ....51 J6
Ruby St PECK SE15 ....123 J6
Ruby Triangle PECK SE15 * .123 J6
Ruckholt Cl LEY E10 ....87 K1
Ruckholt Rd LEY E10 ....87 K2
Rucklidge Av WLSDN NW10 ...99 H1
Rudall Crs HAMP NW3 ....83 H2
Ruddington Cl CLPT E5 .....87 G2
Ruddock Cl EDGW HA8 ....44 E3
Ruddstreet Cl
  WOOL/PLUM SE18 ....127 G4
Rudgwick Ter STJWD NW8 * 2 E1
Rudland Rd BXLYHN DA7 .....149 J4
Rudloe Rd BAL SW12 ....161 H2
Rudolf PI VX/NE SW8 ....121 K6
Rudolph Rd BUSH WD23 ......28 A1
  KIL/WHAMP NW6 ....100 E1
  PLSTW E13 ....88 D2
Rudyard Gv EDGW HA8 ....44 E2
The Ruffetts SAND/SEL CR2 .212 D5
Ruffle Cl WDR/YW UB7 ......112 B2
Rufford Cl HRW HA1 ....61 G3
Rufford St IS N1 ....84 E6
Rufus Cl RSLP HA4 ....77 H1
Rufus St IS N1 ....7 G5
Rugby Av ALP/SUD HA0 ....79 J2
  ED N9 ....36 B3
  GFD/PVL UB6 ....78 D4
Rugby Cl HRW HA1 ....60 E1
Rugby Gdns DAGW RM9 ....91 J5
Rugby La BELMT SM2 ....208 B6
Rugby Rd CDALE/KGS NW9 ....62 C1
  CHSWK W4 ....118 B2
  DAGW RM9 ....91 H5
  WHTN TW2 ....155 K1
Rugby St BMSBY WC1N 5 G7
Rugg St POP/IOD E14 ....105 J6
Ruislip Cl GFD/PVL UB6 .....96 B5
Ruislip Ct RSLP HA4 * 58 D6
Ruislip Rd GFD/PVL UB6 .....96 B3
  NTHLT UB5 ....95 G1
Ruislip Rd East GFD/PVL UB6 .96 C3
  HNWL W7 ....96 C3
Ruislip St TOOT SW17 ......160 E6
Rumbold Rd FUL/PGN SW6 ...140 A1
Rum Cl WAP E1W 104 D6
Rumsey Cl HPTN TW12 ......172 E2
Rumsey Rd BRXN/ST SW9 ....142 A4
Runbury Cir CDALE/KGS NW9 .63 G6
Runcorn Cl TOTM N17 ....68 D1
Runcorn PI NTGHL W11 ......100 C6
Rundell Crs HDN NW4 ....63 K2
Runes Ct MTCM CR4 ....194 C1
Runnelfield HRW HA1 ....78 E1
Runnymede
  WIM/MER SW19 ....178 C4
Runnymede Cl WHTN TW2 ....155 G1
Runnymede Crs
  STRHM/NOR SW16 ....179 J4
Runnymede Gdns
  GFD/PVL UB6 ....96 D1
  WHTN TW2 ....155 G1
Runnymede Rd HSLW TW3 ....155 G1
Rupack St BERM/RHTH SE16 * .123 K2
Rupert Av WBLY HA9 ....80 A3
Rupert Ct E/WMO/HCT KT8 * .189 F1
  SOHO/SHAV W1D 10 C5
Rupert Gdns BRXN/ST SW9 ..142 C3
Rupert Rd ARCH N19 ....84 D1
  CHSWK W4 ....118 B3
  KIL/WHAMP NW6 ....100 D1
Rupert St SOHO/SHAV W1D ...10 C5
Rural Cl EMPK RM11 ....75 K4
Rural Wy STRHM/NOR SW16 ..179 G3
Rusbridge Cl HACK E8 ......86 C3
Ruscoe Rd CAN/RD E16 .....106 D5
Ruscombe Wy
  EBED/NFELT TW14 ....153 J2
Rusham Rd BAL SW12 ....160 E1
Rushbrook Crs WALTH E17 ...51 H4
Rushbrook Rd ELTH/MOT SE9 .167 H4
Rush Common Ms
  BRXS/STRHM SW2 ....161 K2

Rushcroft Rd
  BRXS/STRHM SW2 ....142 B5
  CHING E4 ....51 K3
Rushden Cl NRWD SE19 ......180 E3
Rushdene ABYW SE2 ....128 D3
Rushdene Av EBAR EN4 ....33 J2
Rushdene Cl NTHLT UB5 .....95 G1
Rushdene Crs NTHLT UB5 ....95 F5
Rushdene Rd PIN HA5 ....59 G3
Rushden Gdns CLAY IG5 .....54 A6
  MLHL NW7 ....45 J2
Rushdon Cl ROM RM1 ....75 J2
Rushet Rd STMC/STPC BR5 ..186 A5
Rushett Cl THDIT KT7 .....190 C5
Rushett Rd THDIT KT7 .....190 C4
Rushey Cl NWMAL KT3 ......192 A1
Rushey Gn CAT SE6 ....164 E2
Rushey Hl ENC/FH EN2 ......23 F5
Rushey Md BROCKY SE4 .....144 D6
Rushford Rd BROCKY SE4 ...164 C1
Rush Green Gdns
  ROMW/RG RM7 ....74 E5
Rush Green Rd
  ROMW/RG RM7 ....74 E5
Rushgrove Av
  CDALE/KGS NW9 ....63 H1
Rushgrove Pde
  CDALE/KGS NW9 * 63 H1
Rushgrove St
  WOOL/PLUM SE18 ....126 E4
Rush Hill Ms BTSEA SW11 ..141 F4
Rush Hill Rd BTSEA SW11 ..141 F4
Rushley Cl HAYES BR2 .....215 H4
Rushmead BETH E2 ....104 D2
The Rushmead
  RCHPK/HAM TW10 ....156 C5
Rushmead Cl CROY/NA CRO ..212 B2
Rushmere Ct WPK KT4 ......192 D6
Rushmere PI WIM/MER SW19 .177 G1
Rushmon PI CHEAM SM3 * ...208 C4
Rushmon Vis NWMAL KT3 * ..192 C1
Rushmoor Cl PIN HA5 ....59 F1
Rushmore Cl BMLY BR1 ....184 D6
Rushmore Rd CLPT E5 ....86 E2
Rusholme Av DAGW RM9 ......92 C1
Rusholme Gv NRWD SE19 ...181 F1
Rusholme Rd PUT/ROE SW15 .159 G1
Rushout Av KTN/HRWW/W HA3 .61 H3
Rushton St IS N1 ....7 F2
Rushworth St STHWK SE1 ....18 B2
Rushy Meadow La CAR SM5 ..194 D6
Ruskin Av EBED/NFELT TW14 .153 J2
  MNPK E12 ....89 K4
  RCH/KEW TW9 ....137 H1
  WELL DA16 ....148 B3
Ruskin Cl GLDGN NW11 ......65 F3
Ruskin Dr WELL DA16 ......148 B4
  WPK KT4 ....192 E6
Ruskin Gdns EA W5 * 97 K5
  HARH RM3 ....57 K4
  KTN/HRWW/W HA3 ....62 B2
Ruskin Gv DART DA1 ....151 K6
  WELL DA16 ....148 B3
Ruskin Rd BELV DA17 ......129 H4
  CAR SM5 ....209 K3
  CROY/NA CRO 196 C6
  ISLW TW7 ....136 A3
  STHL UB1 ....95 J6
  TOTM N17 ....50 B4
Ruskin Wk ED N9 ....36 C4
  HAYES BR2 ....200 D3
  HNHL SE24 ....162 D1
Ruskin Wy WIM/MER SW19 ...178 C4
Rusland Av ORP BR6 ....216 D1
Rusland Park Rd HRW HA1 ...60 E1
Rusper Cl CRICK NW2 ....82 A1
  STAN HA7 ....29 J6
Rusper Rd DAGW RM9 ....91 J4
  WDGN N22 ....49 H5
Russel Cl BECK BR3 ....182 E6
Russell Av WDGN N22 ....49 H5
Russell Cl BXLYHN DA7 ....149 H5
  CHARL SE7 * 146 B1
  DART DA1 ....150 D4
  NTHWD HA6 ....40 A1
  RSLP HA4 ....59 G2
  WLSDN NW10 ....80 E5
Russell Ct BAR EN5 * 21 G5
  WHALL SW1A * 16 B1
Russell Dr STWL/WRAY TW19 .152 A1
Russell Gdns GLDGN NW11 ...64 C4
  RCHPK/HAM TW10 ....156 D4
  TRDG/WHET N20 ....33 J4
  WDR/YW UB7 ....112 D5
  WKENS W14 ....119 H3

Russell Gardens Ms
  WKENS W14 ....119 H2
Russell Gv BRXN/ST SW9 ...142 B2
  MLHL NW7 ....45 G1
Russell Kerr Cl CHSWK W4 .137 K1
Russell La TRDG/WHET N20 ..33 J4
Russell Pde GLDGN NW11 * ..64 C3
Russell PI HAMP NW3 ....83 J3
  SAND/SEL CR2 ....212 B6
Russell Rd BKHH IG9 ....39 G3
  CAN/RD E16 ....106 E5
  CEND/HSY/T N8 ....66 D3
  CHING E4 ....37 H6
  EN EN1 ....24 B1
  LEY E10 ....70 A3
  MTCM CR4 ....178 D6
  NTGHL W11 ....119 H3
  NTHLT UB5 ....78 A4
  NTHWD HA6 ....26 A5
  SEVS/STOTM N15 ....68 A2
  WALTH E17 ....51 H6
  WDGN N22 ....49 G5
  WHTN TW2 ....156 A1
  WIM/MER SW19 ....177 K3
  WLSDN NW10 ....81 F5
Russell Sq GWRST WC1E 4 D7
Russell St COVGDN WC2E 11 F5
Russell Wy OXHEY WD19 * 27 F2

SUT SM1 209 F3
Russet Cl *HGDN/ICK* UB10 94 A3
Russet Crs *HOLWY* N7 * 85 F3
Russet Dr *CROY/NA* CR0 198 B5
Russets Cl *CHING* E4 38 B6
Russett Cl *ORP* BR6 217 H3
Russia Dock Rd
BERM/RHTH SE16 * 124 B1
Russia La *BETH* E2 104 E1
Russia Rw *CITYW* EC2V 12 D4
Rusthall Av *CHSWK* W4 118 A3
Rusthall Cl *CROY/NA* CR0 197 K3
Rustic Av *STRHM/NOR* SW16 179 G3
Rustic Pl *ALP/SUD* HA0 79 K2
Rustington Wk *MRDN* SM4 193 J4
Ruston Av *BRYLDS* KT5 191 J4
Ruston Ms *NTGHL* W11 * 100 C5
Ruston Rd *WOOL/PLUM* SE18 126 D3
Ruston St *BOW* E3 87 H6
Rust Sq *CMBW* SE5 142 E1
Rutford Rd *STRHM/NOR* SW16 179 K1
Ruth Cl *KTN/HRWW/W* HA3 62 B1
Rutherford Cl *BELMT* SM2 209 H4
Rutherford St *WEST* SW1P 16 C6
Rutherford Wy *BUSH* WD23 28 D3
WBLY HA9 80 C1
Rutherglen Rd *ABYW* SE2 128 B6
Rutherwyke Cl *EW* KT17 207 J4
Ruthin Cl *CDALE/KGS* NW9 63 G3
Ruthin Rd *BKHTH/KID* SE3 125 K6
Ruthven St *HOM* E9 87 F6
Rutland Av *BFN/LL* DA15 168 B2
Rutland Cl *BXLY* DA5 168 E3
DART DA1 171 G2
MORT/ESHN SW14 137 J4
Rutland Ct *CHST* BR7 185 F4
SKENS SW7 14 D3
Rutland Dr *MRDN* SM4 193 K4
RCHPK/HAM TW10 156 E3
Rutland Gdns *BCTR* RM8 91 J3
CROY/NA CR0 212 A2
FSBYPK N4 67 H3
SKENS SW7 14 D3
WEA W13 * 97 G4
Rutland Ga *BELV* DA17 129 J5
HAYES BR2 199 J1
SKENS SW7 14 C4
Rutland Gate Ms *SKENS* SW7 * 14 C3
Rutland Gv *HMSMTH* W6 118 E5
Rutland Ms *STJWD* NW8 * 83 F6
Rutland Ms South *SKENS* SW7 * 14 C4
Rutland Pk *CAT* SE6 164 C4
CRICK NW2 82 A4
Rutland Pl *BUSH* WD23 * 28 D3
FARR EC1M * 12 B1
Rutland Rd *FSTGT* E7 89 H5
HOM E9 87 F6
HRW HA1 60 C3
HYS/HAR UB3 113 G4
IL IG1 90 B2
STHL UB1 96 A3
WALTH E17 69 J3
WAN E11 71 F2
WHTN TW2 155 J4
WIM/MER SW19 178 D3
Rutland St *SKENS* SW7 14 D4
Rutland Wk *CAT* SE6 164 C4
Rutland Wy *STMC/STPC* BR5 202 D3
Rutley Cl *LBTH* SE11 122 C6
Rutlish Rd *WIM/MER* SW19 177 K4
Rutter Gdns *MTCM* CR4 194 C1
Rutters Cl *WDR/YW* UB7 112 D2
Rutt's Ter *NWCR* SE14 144 A2
The Rutts *BUSH* WD23 28 D3
Ruvigny Gdns
PUT/ROE SW15 139 G4
Ruxley Cl *HOR/WEW* KT19 206 D3
SCUP DA14 186 E2
Ruxley Crs *ESH/CLAY* KT10 205 H5
Ruxley La *HOR/WEW* KT19 206 E3
Ruxley Ms *HOR/WEW* KT19 206 D3
Ruxley Rdg *ESH/CLAY* KT10 205 G5
Ruxley Towers
ESH/CLAY KT10 * 205 G5
Ryan Cl *BKHTH/KID* SE3 146 A5
RSLP HA4 59 F5
Ryan Ct *OXHEY* WD19 * 27 J2
Ryan Dr *BTFD* TW8 116 B6
Ryarsh Crs *ORP* BR6 216 E2
Rycroft Wy *TOTM* N17 * 50 B6
Ryculff Sq *BKHTH/KID* SE3 145 J3
Rydal Cl *HDN* NW4 46 C4
Rydal Crs *GFD/PVL* UB6 97 H2
Rydal Dr *BXLYHN* DA7 149 H2
WWKM BR4 199 H6
Rydal Gdns *CDALE/KGS* NW9 63 G2
HSLW TW3 155 G1
PUT/ROE SW15 176 B1
WBLY HA9 61 J5
Rydal Mt *HAYES* BR2 * 199 J1
Rydal Rd *STRHM/NOR* SW16 179 J1
Rydal Wy *PEND* EN3 36 E1
RSLP HA4 77 G2
Rydens Av *WOT/HER* KT12 188 B6
Rydens Cl *WOT/HER* KT12 188 B6
Rydens Pk *WOT/HER* KT12 188 C6
Ryde Pl *TWK* TW1 156 D1
Ryder Cl *BUSH* WD23 28 B1
Ryder Dr *BERM/RHTH* SE16 123 J5
Ryder Gdns *RAIN* RM13 93 H4
Ryder St *STJS* SW1Y 10 B7
Ryde Vale Rd *BAL* SW12 161 G4
Rydston Cl *HOLWY* N7 85 F5
Rye Cl *BXLY* DA5 169 J1
Ryecotes Md *DUL* SE21 163 F3
Rye Crs *STMC/STPC* BR5 202 E5
Ryecroft Av *CLAY* IG5 54 B5
WHTN TW2 155 G3
Ryecroft Rd *LEW* SE13 145 F6
STMC/STPC BR5 201 J3
STRHM/NOR SW16 180 B2
Ryecroft St *FUL/PGN* SW6 140 A2
Ryedale *EDUL* SE22 163 J1
Ryefield Av *HGDN/ICK* UB10 76 A6
Ryefield Crs *PIN* HA5 * 40 E5
Ryefield Pde *NTHWD* HA6 * 40 E5
Ryefield Rd *NRWD* SE19 180 D2
Rye Hill Pk *PECK* SE15 143 K5
Ryelands Crs *LEE/GVPK* SE12 166 B1
Rye La *PECK* SE15 143 H2
Rye Rd *PECK* SE15 144 A5
The Rye *STHGT/OAK* N14 34 C2
Rye Wk *PUT/ROE* SW15 139 G6
Rye Wy *EDGW* HA8 44 B2
Ryfold Rd *WIM/MER* SW19 159 K5
Ryhope Rd *FBAR/BDGN* N11 34 B6
Ryland Cl *FELT* TW13 153 J6
Rylandes Rd *CRICK* NW2 81 J1
SAND/SEL CR2 212 D6
Ryland Rd *KTTN* NW5 * 84 B4
Rylett Crs *SHB* W12 118 C3
Rylett Rd *SHB* W12 118 C2
Rylston Rd *FUL/PGN* SW6 119 J6
PLMGR N13 35 K5
Rymer Rd *CROY/NA* CR0 197 F4
Rymer St *HNHL* SE24 162 C1
Rymill St *CAN/RD* E16 127 F1
Rysbrack St *CHEL* SW3 14 E4
Rythe Cl *CHSGTN* KT9 205 J5
Rythe Ct *THDIT* KT7 190 B4
Rythe Rd *ESH/CLAY* KT10 204 D3

S

Sabbarton St *CAN/RD* E16 106 D5
Sabine Rd *BTSEA* SW11 140 E4
Sable Cl *HSLWW* TW4 134 B4
Sable St *IS* N1 85 H5
Sach Rd *CLPT* E5 68 D6
Sackville Av *HAYES* BR2 199 K5
Sackville Cl *RYLN/HDSTN* HA2 78 D1
Sackville Est S
TRHM/NOR SW16 161 K5
Sackville Gdns *IL* IG1 71 K5
Sackville Rd *BELMT* SM2 208 E5
DART DA1 171 G4
Sackville St *MYFR/PICC* W1J 10 B6
Saddlers Cl *PIN* HA5 42 A1
Saddlers Ms *KUT/HW* KT1 * 174 D4
Saddlescombe Wy
NFNCH/WDSP N12 46 E1
Sadler Cl *MTCM* CR4 178 E5
Sadlers Ride *E/WMO/HCT* KT8 173 H5
Saffron Av *POP/IOD* E14 106 B6
Saffron Cl *CROY/NA* CR0 195 K3
GLDGN NW11 64 D2
Saffron Hl *HCIRC* EC1N 11 K2
Saffron Rd *CRW* RM5 57 F5
Saffron St *FARR* EC1M 11 K1
Saffron Wy *SURB* KT6 190 E5
Sage Cl *EHAM* E6 107 K4
Sage St *WCHPL* E1 104 E6
Sage Wy *FSBYW* WC1X 5 G5
Sage Yd *SURB* KT6 * 191 G5
Saigasso Cl *CAN/RD* E16 107 H5
Sail St *LBTH* SE11 17 H6
Sainfoin Rd *TOOT* SW17 161 F4
Sainsbury Rd *NRWD* SE19 181 F1
St Agatha's Dr *KUTN/CMB* KT2 175 G2
St Agatha's Gv *CAR* SM5 194 E5
St Agnes Cl *HOM* E9 * 86 E6
St Agnes Pl *CMBW* SE5 122 C6
St Agnes Well *STLK* EC1Y 7 F6
St Aidan's Rd *EDUL* SE22 163 J1
WEA W13 116 C2
St Albans Av *CHSWK* W4 118 A3
EHAM E6 107 K2
FELT TW13 172 C1
St Albans Crs *WDGN* N22 49 G4
St Albans Farm *HSLWW* TW4 * 134 B6
St Alban's Gdns *TEDD* TW11 174 B1
St Alban's Gv *CAR* SM5 194 D4
KENS W8 120 A3
St Albans La *GLDGN* NW11 64 E5
St Alban's Ms *BAY/PAD* W2 8 B1
St Alban's Pl *IS* N1 6 A1
St Albans Rd *BAR* EN5 20 C2
DART DA1 171 J1
GDMY/SEVK IG3 73 F5
KTTN NW5 84 A1
KUTN/CMB KT2 175 F2
SUT SM1 208 D2
WFD IG8 52 E3
WLSDN NW10 81 G6
St Alban's St *STJS* SW1Y 10 C6
St Albans Ter *HMSMTH* W6 119 H6
St Alfege Rd *CHARL* SE7 126 C6
St Alphage Gdn *BARB* EC2Y 12 D2
St Alphage Gdns *BARB* EC2Y * 12 D2
St Alphage Highwalk
BARB EC2Y 12 D2
St Alphage Wk *EDGW* HA8 * 44 E5
St Alphege Rd *ED* N9 36 E2
St Alphonsus Rd *CLAP* SW4 141 H5
St Amunds Cl *CAT* SE6 164 D6
St Andrews Av *ALP/SUD* HA0 79 G2
HCH RM12 93 H3
St Andrews Cl
BERM/RHTH SE16 * 123 J5
CRICK NW2 * 81 K1
NFNCH/WDSP N12 * 33 G6
RSLP HA4 59 H6
STAN HA7 * 43 J5
THDIT KT7 190 C5
THMD SE28 109 K5
St Andrew's Ct
WAND/EARL SW18 160 B4
St Andrews Dr *ORP* BR6 202 C3
STAN HA7 43 J4
St Andrew's Gv
STNW/STAM N16 67 K5
St Andrew's Hl *BLKFR* EC4V 12 B5
St Andrews Ms *BAL* SW12 161 J3
STNW/STAM N16 * 68 A4
St Andrew's Pl *CAMTN* NW1 3 J6
St Andrew's Rd *ACT* W3 99 G5
CAR SM5 209 J1
CDALE/KGS NW9 63 F5
CROY/NA CR0 211 J2
ED N9 36 E2
EN EN1 23 K4
GLDGN NW11 64 D3
HNWL W7 115 K2
IL IG1 71 K4
PLSTW E13 107 F2
ROMW/RG RM7 75 F3
SCUP DA14 168 E5
SURB KT6 190 E3
WALTH E17 51 F5
WAN E11 70 C3
WKENS W14 119 H6
WLSDN NW10 81 K4
St Andrew's Sq *NTGHL* W11 * 100 C5
SURB KT6 190 E3
St Andrews Ter *OXHEY* WD19 * 41 G1
St Andrew St *HCIRC* EC1N 11 K2
St Andrews Wy *BOW* E3 105 K3
St Anna Rd *BAR* EN5 * 20 B6
St Anne's Av
STWL/WRAY TW19 152 A2
St Anne's Cl *HGT* N6 84 A1
OXHEY WD19 27 G6
St Annes Ct *SOHO/CST* W1F 10 C4
St Annes Gdns *WLSDN* NW10 98 B2
St Anne's Pas *POP/IOD* E14 * 105 H5
St Anne's Rd *ALP/SUD* HA0 79 K3
LEY E10 70 B6
St Anne's Rw *POP/IOD* E14 105 H5
St Anne St *POP/IOD* E14 105 H5
St Ann's *BARK* IG11 90 C6
St Anns Ct *HDN* NW4 * 45 K6
St Ann's Crs *WAND/EARL* SW18 160 A1
St Ann's Gdns *HAMP* NW3 84 A4
St Ann's Hl *WAND/EARL* SW18 140 A6
St Ann's Park Rd
WAND/EARL SW18 160 B1
St Ann's Rd *BARK* IG11 90 C6
BARN SW13 * 138 C3
ED N9 36 B4
HRW HA1 60 E3
NTGHL W11 100 B6
SEVS/STOTM N15 67 K2
St Ann's St *WEST* SW1P 16 D5
St Ann's Ter *STJWD* NW8 2 B2
St Ann's Vls *NTGHL* W11 119 G1
St Ann's Wy *CROY/NA* CR0 211 H4
St Anselm's Pl *MYFR/PKLN* W1K 9 J5
St Anselms Rd *HYS/HAR* UB3 113 J2
St Anthony's Av *WFD* IG8 53 G2
St Anthonys Cl *TOOT* SW17 160 D4
WAP E1W * 123 H1
St Anthony's Ct *HAYES* BR2 201 G5
St Anthony's Wy
EBED/NFELT TW14 133 J5
St Antony's Rd *FSTGT* E7 89 F5
St Arvans Cl *CROY/NA* CR0 212 A1
St Asaph Rd *BROCKY* SE4 144 A4
St Aubyn's Av *HSLW* TW3 135 F6
WIM/MER SW19 177 J1
St Aubyns Cl *ORP* BR6 217 F1
St Aubyns Gdns *ORP* BR6 202 A6
St Aubyn's Rd *NRWD* SE19 181 G2
St Audrey Av *BXLYHN* DA7 149 H3
St Augustine's Av *BMLY* BR1 200 D2
EA W5 98 A1
SAND/SEL CR2 211 J5
WBLY HA9 80 A1
St Augustine's Rd *BELV* DA17 129 G4
CAMTN NW1 84 D5
St Austell Cl *EDGW* HA8 44 B5
St Austell Rd *BKHTH/KID* SE3 145 F3
St Awdry's Rd *BARK* IG11 90 D5
St Barnabas Cl *BECK* BR3 183 F5
St Barnabas' Gdns
E/WMO/HCT KT8 189 F2
St Barnabas Rd *MTCM* CR4 179 F3
SUT SM1 209 H3
SWFD E18 53 F4
WALTH E17 69 J3
St Barnabas St *BGVA* SW1W 121 F5
St Barnabas Ter *HOM* E9 87 F3
St Barnabas Vls *VX/NE* SW8 141 K2
St Bartholomew's Cl *SYD* SE26 163 K6
St Bartholomew's Rd *EHAM* E6 89 J6
St Benets Cl *TOOT* SW17 * 160 D4
St Benet's Gv *MRDN* SM4 194 B4
St Benjamins Dr *ORP* BR6 217 J6
St Bernards *CROY/NA* CR0 212 A1
St Bernards Cl *WNWD* SE27 162 E6
St Bernard's Rd *EHAM* E6 89 H6
St Blaise Av *BMLY* BR1 184 A5
St Botolph St *HDTCH* EC3A 13 J3
St Bride's Av *EDGW* HA8 44 B4
St Brides Cl *ERITHM* DA18 128 E2
St Bride St *FLST/FETLN* EC4A 11 K3
St Catherines Cl *CHSGTN* KT9 205 K4
TOOT SW17 * 160 D4
St Catherines Ct *FELT* TW13 153 K3
St Catherine's Dr *NWCR* SE14 144 A3
St Catherines Ms *CHEL* SW3 14 E6
St Catherines Rd *CHING* E4 37 J4
RSLP HA4 58 A2
St Chads Cl *SURB* KT6 190 D4
St Chad's Gdns *CHDH* RM6 74 A4
St Chad's Pl *FSBYW* WC1X 5 F4
St Chad's Rd *CHDH* RM6 74 A3
St Chad's St *STPAN* WC1H 5 F4
St Charles Pl *NKENS* W10 100 C4
St Charles Sq *NKENS* W10 100 C4
St Christopher's Cl *ISLW* TW7 135 K2
St Christophers Dr
HYS/HAR UB3 95 F6
St Christopher's Ms
WLGTN SM6 210 C3
St Christopher's Pl *MHST* W1U 9 H4
St Clair Cl *CLAY* IG5 53 K5
St Clair Dr *WPK* KT4 207 K1
St Clair Rd *PLSTW* E13 107 F1
St Clair's Rd *CROY/NA* CR0 197 F6
St Clare St *TWRH* EC3N 13 J4
St Clements Ct *PUR* RM19 131 K4
St Clement's La *LINN* WC2A 11 H4
St Clements St *HOLWY* N7 85 G5
St Clements Yd *EDUL* SE22 * 143 G6
St Cloud Rd *WNWD* SE27 162 D6
St Crispins Cl *HAMP* NW3 83 J2
STHL UB1 95 K5
St Cross St *HCIRC* EC1N 11 K1
St Cuthberts Gdns *PIN* HA5 * 41 K3
St Cuthbert's Rd *CRICK* NW2 82 D4
PLMGR N13 49 G2
St Cyprian's St *TOOT* SW17 160 E6
St Davids Cl
BERM/RHTH SE16 * 123 J5
WBLY HA9 80 E1
WWKM BR4 198 E4
St David's Dr *EDGW* HA8 44 B4
St Davids Ms *BOW* E3 105 G2
St David's Pl *HDN* NW4 63 K4
St Davids Sq *POP/IOD* E14 124 E5
St Denis Rd *WNWD* SE27 162 E6
St Dionis Rd *FUL/PGN* SW6 139 J3
St Donatt's Rd *NWCR* SE14 144 C2
St Dunstan's Av *ACT* W3 99 F6
St Dunstans Cl *HYS/HAR* UB3 113 J4
St Dunstan's Gdns *ACT* W3 99 F6
St Dunstan's Hl *MON* EC3R * 13 G6
SUT SM1 208 C2
St Dunstan's La *MON* EC3R * 13 G6
St Dunstan's Rd *FELT* TW13 153 J5
FSTGT E7 89 F4
HMSMTH W6 119 G5
HNWL W7 115 K2
HSLWW TW4 134 A3
SNWD SE25 197 G1
St Edmunds Av *RSLP* HA4 58 B3
St Edmunds Cl *ABYW* SE2 128 E2
STJWD NW8 2 E1
TOOT SW17 160 D4
St Edmunds Dr *STAN* HA7 43 G4
St Edmund's La *WHTN* TW2 155 G2
St Edmunds Rd *DART* DA1 151 J5
ED N9 36 C2
IL IG1 71 K3
St Edmunds Sq *BARN* SW13 119 F6
St Edmund's Ter *STJWD* NW8 2 D2
St Edward's Cl *GLDGN* NW11 64 E3
St Edwards Wy *ROM* RM1 75 G1
St Egberts Wy *CHING* E4 38 A3
St Elmo Rd *ACT* W3 118 C2
St Elmos Rd *BERM/RHTH* SE16 124 B2
St Erkenwald Ms *BARK* IG11 90 D6
St Erkenwald Rd *BARK* IG11 90 D6
St Ervans Rd *NKENS* W10 100 C4
St Faith's Cl *ENC/FH* EN2 23 J2
St Faith's Rd *HNHL* SE24 162 C3
St Fidelis' Rd *ERITH* DA8 130 A4
St Fillans Rd *CAT* SE6 165 F3
St Francis Cl *ORP* BR6 201 K3
OXHEY WD19 27 F3
St Francis Rd *EDUL* SE22 143 F5
St Francis Wy *IL* IG1 90 D2
St Gabriel's Cl *WAN* E11 71 F5
St Gabriels Rd *CRICK* NW2 82 B3
St George's Av
CDALE/KGS NW9 62 E1
EA W5 116 E2
FSTGT E7 89 F5
HOLWY N7 84 D2
STHL UB1 95 K6
St George's Circ *STHWK* SE1 18 A3
St Georges Cl *ALP/SUD* HA0 79 G1
GLDGN NW11 64 D3
THMD SE28 109 K5
VX/NE SW8 141 H2
St George's Dr *OXHEY* WD19 27 J5
PIM SW1V 121 G5
St Georges Flds *BAY/PAD* W2 8 D5
St George's Gdns *SURB* KT6 191 J6
St George's Gv *TOOT* SW17 160 C5
St George's La *MON* EC3R * 13 F5
St Georges Ms
BERM/RHTH SE16 124 C4
CAMTN NW1 83 K5
CHSWK W4 * 117 K6
St Georges Pde *CAT* SE6 * 164 C4
St George's Rd *BECK* BR3 182 E4
BMLY BR1 184 E5
CHSWK W4 118 A2
DAGW RM9 92 B2
ED N9 36 C5
EN EN1 24 B1
FELT TW13 154 C6
FSTGT E7 89 F5
GLDGN NW11 64 D3
HNWL W7 116 A1
IL IG1 71 K4
KUTN/CMB KT2 175 H3
LEY E10 88 A1
MTCM CR4 179 G6
PLMGR N13 35 F5
RCH/KEW TW9 137 G4
SCUP DA14 186 E2
STHWK SE1 18 A5
STMC/STPC BR5 201 J3
TWK TW1 136 C6
WIM/MER SW19 177 J2
WLGTN SM6 210 B3
St Georges Rd West
BMLY BR1 184 D5
St George's Ct *STP* EC4M * 12 A3
St George's Sq *FSTGT* E7 89 F5
NWMAL KT3 * 176 B6
PIM SW1V 121 J5
St George's Square Ms
PIM SW1V 121 J5
St George's Ter *CAMTN* NW1 83 K5
PECK SE15 * 143 H1
St George St *CONDST* W1S 9 K5
St George's Wk *CROY/NA* CR0 196 D6
St George's Wy *PECK* SE15 123 F6
St Gerards Cl *CLAP* SW4 141 H6
St German's Pl *BKHTH/KID* SE3 145 K3
St German's Rd *FSTH* SE23 164 B3
St Giles Av *DAGE* RM10 92 D5
HGDN/ICK UB10 76 A2
St Giles Churchyard
BARB EC2Y * 12 D2
St Giles Circ *SOHO/SHAV* W1D 10 D3
St Giles Cl *DAGE* RM10 92 D5
ORP BR6 216 D3
St Giles Ct *LSQ/SEVD* WC2H 10 D3
St Giles High St
LSQ/SEVD WC2H 10 D3
St Giles Pas *LSQ/SEVD* WC2H 10 D4
St Giles Rd *CMBW* SE5 143 F1
St Gothard Rd *WNWD* SE27 162 E6
St Gregory Cl *RSLP* HA4 77 G2
St Helena Rd
BERM/RHTH SE16 124 A4
St Helena St *FSBYW* WC1X * 5 J5
St Helena Ter *RCH/KEW* TW9 * 136 E6
St Helens *THDIT* KT7 * 189 K4
St Helen's Crs
STRHM/NOR SW16 180 A4
St Helen's Gdns *NKENS* W10 100 B5
St Helen's Pl *OBST* EC2N 13 G3
St Helens Rd *ERITHM* DA18 128 E2
IL IG1 71 K3
STRHM/NOR SW16 180 A5
WEA W13 116 C1
St Helier Av *MRDN* SM4 194 B4
St Heliers Av *HSLWW* TW4 135 F6
St Helier's Rd *LEY* E10 69 K3
St Hildas Cl *KIL/WHAMP* NW6 * 82 B6
TOOT SW17 160 D4
St Hilda's Rd *BARN* SW13 118 E6
St Hughes Cl *TOOT* SW17 * 160 D4
St Hugh's Rd *PGE/AN* SE20 181 J4
St Ivians Dr *GPK* RM2 57 J6
St James Av *SUT* SM1 208 E3
TRDG/WHET N20 33 J5
WEA W13 116 B1
St James' Cl *NWMAL* KT3 192 C2
RSLP HA4 59 G6
STJWD NW8 2 E2
TRDG/WHET N20 33 J5
St James' Ct *WESTW* SW1E * 16 B4
St James' Gdns *ALP/SUD* HA0 79 K5
GNTH/NBYPK IG2 73 H1
St James Ms *POP/IOD* E14 * 125 F3
St James Pl *DART* DA1 171 G1
St James Rd *CAR* SM5 209 J1
EBAR EN4 21 H4
ED N9 36 D4
FSTGT E7 88 D3
MTCM CR4 179 F3
SURB KT6 190 E3
SUT SM1 208 E4
St James's *NWCR* SE14 144 B2
St James's Av *BECK* BR3 182 B6
BETH E2 104 E1
HPTN TW12 173 H1
St James's Chambers
STJS SW1Y * 10 B7
St James's Cl *TOOT* SW17 * 160 E4
TOOT SW17 * 179 F1
WOOL/PLUM SE18 127 H5
St James's Ct *KUT/HW* KT1 * 175 F6
WESTW SW1E 16 B4
St James's Crs *BRXN/ST* SW9 142 B4
St James's Dr *BAL* SW12 160 E3
St James's Gdns *CAMTN* NW1 * 4 A5
NTGHL W11 119 H1
St James's Gv *BTSEA* SW11 * 140 E3
St James's La *MUSWH* N10 66 B1
St James's Ms *WALTH* E17 69 G2
St James's Pk *CROY/NA* CR0 196 D4
St James's Pl *WHALL* SW1A 16 A1
St James Sq *SURB* KT6 190 D4
St James's Rd
BERM/RHTH SE16 123 H3
CROY/NA CR0 196 E5
HPTN TW12 173 G1
KUT/HW KT1 174 E5
St James's Rw *CHSGTN* KT9 * 205 K4
St James's Sq *STJS* SW1Y 10 C7
St James's St *WALTH* E17 69 G2
WHALL SW1A 10 A7
St James's Ter *STJWD* NW8 2 E2
St James's Terrace Ms
STJWD NW8 2 E1
St James St *HMSMTH* W6 119 F5
St James Ter *BAL* SW12 * 161 F3
ORP BR6 * 217 J6
St James Wk *CLKNW* EC1R 6 A6
St James Wy *BXLY* DA5 169 H2
SCUP DA14 187 F1
St Jerome's Gv *HYS/HAR* UB3 94 A5
St Joan's Rd *ED* N9 36 B4
St John Cl *FUL/PGN* SW6 * 139 K1
St John's Av *FBAR/BDGN* N11 47 K1
PUT/ROE SW15 139 G6
WLSDN NW10 81 H6
St John's Church Rd *HOM* E9 * 86 E3
St John's Cl *FUL/PGN* SW6 * 139 K1
RAIN RM13 93 J5
STHGT/OAK N14 34 C1
TRDG/WHET N20 * 33 G4
WBLY HA9 80 A3
St John's Ct *BKHH* IG9 39 F3
ISLW TW7 136 A3
St John's Crs *BRXN/ST* SW9 142 B4
St John's Dr *WAND/EARL* SW18 160 A3
WOT/HER KT12 188 B5
St John's Est *IS* N1 7 F3
STHWK SE1 19 J2
St John's Gdns *NTGHL* W11 100 D6
St John's Gv *ARCH* N19 66 C6
BARN SW13 * 138 C3
RCH/KEW TW9 * 137 F5
St John's Hl *BTSEA* SW11 140 D5
St John's Hill Gv *BTSEA* SW11 140 C5
St John's La *FARR* EC1M 6 A7
St Johns Pde *SCUP* DA14 * 168 C6
WEA W13 * 116 C1
St John's Pk *BKHTH/KID* SE3 145 K1
St John's Pl *FARR* EC1M 6 A7
St John's Rd *BARK* IG11 90 E6
BTSEA SW11 140 D5
CAN/RD E16 106 E5

CAR SM5 209 J1
CHING E4 37 K5
CROY/NA CR0 211 H1
CRW RM5 56 E1
E/WMO/HCT KT8 189 J1
EHAM E6 89 J6
ERITH DA8 130 A5
FELT TW13 154 E6
GLDGN NW11 64 D3
GNTH/NBYPK IG2 72 E4
HRW HA1 61 F3
ISLW TW7 136 A3
KUT/HW KT1 174 D5
NWDGN UB2 114 D3
NWMAL KT3 175 K6
PGE/AN SE20 181 K3
RCH/KEW TW9 137 F5
SCUP DA14 168 C6
SEVS/STOTM N15 68 A3
STMC/STPC BR5 201 J3
SUT SM1 193 K6
WALTH E17 51 K5
WBLY HA9 79 K2
WELL DA16 148 C4
WIM/MER SW19 177 H3
John's Sq FARR EC1M 6 A7
John's Ter FSTGT E7 89 F4
NKENS W10 100 B3
WOOL/PLUM SE18 127 H6
John St FSBYE EC1V 5 K3
John's V DEPT SE8 144 D3
John's Vls ARCH N19 66 D6
KENS W8 120 A3
John's Wy ARCH N19 66 D5
John's Wood High St
STJWD NW8 2 B3
John's Wood Pk STJWD NW8 2 A1
John's Wood Rd STJWD NW8 2 A6
John's Wood Ter
STJWD NW8 2 C2
Josephs Cl NKENS W10 100 C4
ORP BR6 217 F2
Joseph's Dr STHL UB1 114 D1
Josephs Gv HDN NW4 63 K1
Joseph's Rd ED N9 36 D2
Joseph's St VX/NE SW8 * 141 G2
Joseph's V BKHTH/KID SE3 145 H4
Jude's Rd BETH E2 104 D1
Jude St STNW/STAM N16 86 A3
Julian's Cl
STRHM/NOR SW16 * 162 B6
Julian's Farm Rd
WNWD SE27 162 B6
Julian's Rd
KIL/WHAMP NW6 82 D5
Justin Cl STMC/STPC BR5 186 E6
Katharine's Prec
CAMTN NW1 * 3 J2
Katharine's Wy TWRH EC3N 13 K7
Katherines Rd
ERITHM DA18 128 E2
Katherines Wk
NTGHL W11 * 100 B6
Keverne Rd ELTH/MOT SE9 166 D6
Kilda Rd ORP BR6 202 A5
WEA W13 116 B2
Kilda's Rd HRW HA1 60 E3
STNW/STAM N16 67 K5
Kitts Ter NRWD SE19 181 F1
Laurence Cl
STMC/STPC BR5 186 E6
Laurence's Cl
KIL/WHAMP NW6 82 B6
Lawrence Cl EDGW HA8 44 B3
Lawrence Dr PIN HA5 59 F2
Lawrence St POP/IOD E14 125 F1
Lawrence Ter NKENS W10 100 C4
Lawrence Wy
BRXN/ST SW9 * 142 B3
Leonard's Av CHING E4 52 B2
KTN/HRWW/W HA3 61 J2
Leonards Cl WELL DA16 148 B4
Leonard's Gdns HEST TW5 134 D1
IL IG1 90 C3
Leonards Ri ORP BR6 216 E2
Leonard's Rd CROY/NA CR0 211 H1
ESH/CLAY KT10 205 F4
MORT/ESHN SW14 137 K4
POP/IOD E14 106 A5
SURB KT6 190 E2
THDIT KT7 190 B3
WEA W13 97 J6
WLSDN NW10 99 F3
Leonards Sq KTTN NW5 84 A4
Leonard's St BOW E3 105 K2
Leonard's Ter CHEL SW3 120 E5
Leonard's Wk
STRHM/NOR SW16 180 A3
Leonards Wy EMPK RM11 75 K5
Loo Av CHEL SW3 120 D6
Louis Rd WNWD SE27 162 D6
Loy's Rd TOTM N17 50 A5
Lucia Dr SRTFD E15 88 D6
Luke's Av CLAP SW4 141 J5
ENC/FH EN2 23 K1
IL IG1 90 B3
Luke's Cl SNWD SE25 197 J3
Luke's Est FSBYE EC1V 6 E6
Luke's Ms NTGHL W11 100 D5
Luke's Rd NTGHL W11 100 D4
Lukes's Cl FSBYE EC1V 6 D6
Luke's Sq CAN/RD E16 106 D5
Luke's St CHEL SW3 120 D5
Lukes Yd MV/WKIL W9 * 100 D1
Malo Av ED N9 36 E5
Margarets BARK IG11 90 D6
RCHPK/HAM TW10 * 175 K1
Margarets Av BFN/LL DA15 167 J5
CHEAM SM3 208 C1
RYLN/HDSTN HA2 78 C1
SEVS/STOTM N15 67 H1
TRDG/WHET N20 33 G3
Margarets Cl ORP BR6 217 H2
Margarets Ct
PUT/ROE SW15 * 138 E5
St Margaret's Crs
PUT/ROE SW15 * 138 E6
St Margaret's Dr TWK TW1 136 C6
St Margaret's Gv TWK TW1 156 B1
WAN E11 88 D1
WOOL/PLUM SE18 127 H6
St Margarets La KENS W8 * 120 A3
St Margarets Ms
RCHPK/HAM TW10 * 175 K1
St Margaret's Rd BROCKY SE4 144 C5
EDGW HA8 44 D1
HNWL W7 115 K2
MNPK E12 71 G6
RSLP HA4 58 B3
TOTM N17 50 A6
TWK TW1 136 C5
WLSDN NW10 100 A2
St Margaret's Ter
WOOL/PLUM SE18 127 H5
St Margaret St WEST SW1P 16 E3
St Mark's Cl BAR EN5 21 F4
FUL/PGN SW6 139 K2
St Mark's Crs CAMTN NW1 * 84 A6
St Marks Ga HOM E9 87 H5
St Mark's Gv WBPTN SW10 140 A1
St Mark's Hl SURB KT6 191 F3
St Mark's Pl NTGHL W11 100 C5
WIM/MER SW19 * 177 J2
St Mark's Ri HACK E8 86 B3
St Mark's Rd EA W5 117 F1
EN EN1 36 B1
HAYES BR2 184 A6
HNWL W7 115 K2
MTCM CR4 178 E5
NKENS W10 100 B5
SNWD SE25 197 H1
TEDD TW11 174 C3
St Mark's Sq CAMTN NW1 84 A6
St Mark St WCHPL E1 13 K4
St Marks Vls FSBYPK N4 * 67 F6
St Martins NTHWD HA6 40 B1
St Martin's Ap RSLP HA4 58 C4
St Martin's Av EHAM E6 107 H1
St Martin's Cl CAMTN NW1 84 C6
EN EN1 24 D2
ERITHM DA18 128 E2
OXHEY WD19 27 G6
St Martins Ct LSQ/SEVD WC2H 10 E5
St Martin's La BECK BR3 198 E2
CHCR WC2N 10 E5
St Martin's Le Grand STBT EC1A 12 C3
St Martin's Pl LSQ/SEVD WC2H 10 E6
St Martin's Rd BRXN/ST SW9 142 A3
DART DA1 171 J1
ED N9 36 D4
St Martin's St LSQ/SEVD WC2H * 10 D6
St Martin's Wy TOOT SW17 160 B5
St Mary Abbot's Pl KENS W8 119 J3
St Mary Abbots Ter
WKENS W14 * 119 J3
St Mary At Hl MON EC3R 13 G6
St Mary Av WLGTN SM6 210 A1
St Mary Axe HDTCH EC3A 13 G4
St Marychurch St
BERM/RHTH SE16 123 K2
St Mary Graces Ct
TWRH EC3N * 13 K6
St Mary Newington Cl
WALW SE17 * 123 F5
St Mary Rd WALTH E17 69 K1
St Marys BARK IG11 108 D1
St Mary's Ap MNPK E12 89 K3
St Mary's Av FNCH N3 46 C5
HAYES BR2 183 H6
NTHWD HA6 40 C1
NWDGN UB2 115 G4
STWL/WRAY TW19 152 A2
TEDD TW11 * 174 A2
WAN E11 71 F3
St Mary's Cl CHSGTN KT9 206 B5
EW KT17 207 H5
STMC/STPC BR5 186 C5
TOTM N17 * 50 B5
St Marys Ct SHB W12 * 118 C3
St Mary's Crs HDN NW4 45 K6
HYS/HAR UB3 94 D6
ISLW TW7 135 J1
STWL/WRAY TW19 152 A2
St Mary's Dr
EBED/NFELT TW14 153 F2
St Marys Est
BERM/RHTH SE16 * 123 K2
St Mary's Gdns LBTH SE11 17 K6
St Mary's Ga KENS W8 120 A3
St Mary's Gn EFNCH N2 47 G6
St Mary's Gv BARN SW13 138 E4
CHSWK W4 117 J6
IS N1 85 H4
RCH/KEW TW9 137 G5
St Mary's Ms
KIL/WHAMP NW6 * 83 F5
St Mary's Pth IS N1 * 85 H6
WCHPL E1 * 104 C5
St Mary's Pl EA W5 116 E2
KENS W8 120 A3
St Mary's Rd BXLY DA5 169 K3
CEND/HSY/T N8 * 66 E1
E/WMO/HCT KT8 189 J2
EA W5 116 E2
EBAR EN4 33 K2
ED N9 36 E3
GLDGN NW11 64 C4
HYS/HAR UB3 94 D6
IL IG1 72 C6
LEY E10 88 A1
PECK SE15 143 K3
PLSTW E13 107 F1
SNWD SE25 181 F6
SURB KT6 190 E3
WIM/MER SW19 177 H1
WLSDN NW10 81 G6
WPK KT4 192 B6
St Mary's Sq BAY/PAD W2 8 A1
EA W5 * 116 E2
St Mary's Ter BAY/PAD W2 8 A1
BORE WD6 * 29 K1
St Mary St WOOL/PLUM SE18 126 E4
St Marys Vw
KTN/HRWW/W HA3 61 J2
St Mary's Wk HYS/HAR UB3 94 D6
LBTH SE11 17 K6
St Marys Wy CHIG IG7 54 A1
St Matthew's Av SURB KT6 191 F5
St Matthews Cl OXHEY WD19 27 H1
RAIN RM13 93 J5
St Matthews Ct SRTFD E15 88 D5
St Matthews Dr BMLY BR1 184 E6
St Matthew's Rd
BRXS/STRHM SW2 142 A6
EA W5 117 F1
St Matthew's Rw BETH E2 104 C2
St Matthew St WEST SW1P 16 C4
St Matthias Cl CDALE/KGS NW9 63 H2
St Maur Rd FUL/PGN SW6 139 J2
St Meddens CHST BR7 * 185 J3
St Mellion Cl THMD SE28 109 K5
St Merryn Cl
WOOL/PLUM SE18 147 J1
St Michael's Aly BANK EC3V 13 F4
St Michaels Av ED N9 36 E2
WBLY HA9 80 C4
St Michaels Cl BMLY BR1 184 D6
CAN/RD E16 107 H4
ERITHM DA18 * 128 E2
FNCH N3 46 D5
NFNCH/WDSP N12 47 J1
WOT/HER KT12 188 B6
WPK KT4 192 C6
St Michaels Ct GLDGN NW11 * 64 D4
St Michael's Crs PIN HA5 59 J3
St Michael's Gdns NKENS W10 100 C4
St Michaels Ri WELL DA16 * 148 C2
St Michael's Rd BRXN/ST SW9 142 A3
CRICK NW2 82 A2
CROY/NA CR0 196 D5
WELL DA16 148 C4
WLGTN SM6 210 C4
St Michael's St BAY/PAD W2 8 B3
St Michaels Ter HGT N6 * 66 A5
WDGN N22 48 E5
St Mildred's Ct LOTH EC2R * 12 E4
St Mildreds Rd CAT SE6 165 H2
St Nicholas Av HCH RM12 93 J1
St Nicholas Cl BORE WD6 29 K1
St Nicholas Glebe TOOT SW17 179 F2
St Nicholas Rd SUT SM1 209 F3
THDIT KT7 190 A3
WOOL/PLUM SE18 128 A5
St Nicholas St DEPT SE8 144 C2
St Nicholas Wy SUT SM1 209 F2
St Nicolas La CHST BR7 184 D4
St Ninian's Ct TRDG/WHET N20 33 K5
St Norbert Rd BROCKY SE4 144 B5
St Olaf's Rd FUL/PGN SW6 139 H1
St Olave's Rd EHAM E6 90 A6
St Olave's Wk
STRHM/NOR SW16 179 H5
St Onge Pde EN EN1 * 23 K4
St Oswald's Pl LBTH SE11 122 A5
St Oswald's Rd
STRHM/NOR SW16 180 C4
St Oswulf St WEST SW1P * 16 D7
St Pancras Gdns CAMTN NW1 4 D1
St Pancras Wy CAMTN NW1 84 D6
St Paul's Av
BERM/RHTH SE16 * 124 A1
CRICK NW2 81 K4
KTN/HRWW/W HA3 62 B2
St Paul's Church Yd
BLKFR EC4V * 12 B4
St Paul's Cl CAR SM5 194 D4
CHARL SE7 126 C5
CHSGTN KT9 205 K2
EA W5 117 G2
HSLW TW3 134 E3
HYS/HAR UB3 113 G5
St Paul's Cray Rd CHST BR7 185 J4
St Pauls Crs CAMTN NW1 84 D5
HDN NW4 * 46 A6
St Paul's Dr SRTFD E15 88 B3
St Pauls Ms CAMTN NW1 84 D5
St Paul's Pl IS N1 85 K4
St Pauls Ri PLMGR N13 49 H2
St Pauls Rd BARK IG11 90 C6
BTFD TW8 116 E6
ERITH DA8 149 K1
IS N1 85 H4
RCH/KEW TW9 137 G4
THHTH CR7 180 D6
TOTM N17 50 C3
St Pauls Ter WALW SE17 * 122 C6
St Paul St IS N1 6 C1
St Paul's Wy FNCH N3 47 F3
POP/IOD E14 105 H4
St Paul's Wood Hl
STMC/STPC BR5 185 K5
St Peter's Av BETH E2 104 C1
UED N18 36 C6
WALTH E17 70 C1
St Petersburgh Ms
BAY/PAD W2 * 101 F6
St Petersburgh Pl
BAY/PAD W2 101 F6
St Peter's Cl BETH E2 104 C1
BUSH WD23 28 D3
CHST BR7 185 J3
GNTH/NBYPK IG2 72 E1
RSLP HA4 59 H6
TOOT SW17 160 D4
St Peters Ct E/WMO/HCT KT8 189 F1
HDN NW4 * 64 A2
LEE/GVPK SE12 * 145 J6
St Peter's Gdns WNWD SE27 162 B5
St Peter's Gv HMSMTH W6 118 D4
St Peters Ms FSBYPK N4 * 67 H2
St Peters Pl MV/WKIL W9 101 F3
St Peter's Rd CROY/NA CR0 211 K2
E/WMO/HCT KT8 189 F1
ED N9 36 D3
HMSMTH W6 * 118 D5
KUT/HW KT1 175 H5
STHL UB1 96 A4
TWK TW1 136 C6
St Peter's Sq BETH E2 * 104 C1
HMSMTH W6 118 D4
St Peter's St IS N1 6 B1
SAND/SEL CR2 211 K3
St Peter's Ter FUL/PGN SW6 139 H1
St Peter's Vls HMSMTH W6 118 D4
St Peter's Wy EA W5 97 K4
HYS/HAR UB3 113 G5
IS N1 * 86 A5
St Philip's Av WPK KT4 192 E6
St Philip Sq VX/NE SW8 * 141 G3
St Philip's Rd HACK E8 86 C4
SURB KT6 190 E3
St Philip St VX/NE SW8 141 G3
St Philip's Wy IS N1 85 J6
St Quentin Rd WELL DA16 148 A4
St Quintin Av NKENS W10 100 A4
St Quintin Rd PLSTW E13 107 F2
St Raphael's Wy WLSDN NW10 80 E3
St Regis Cl MUSWH N10 48 B5
St Ronans Cl EBAR EN4 21 H1
St Ronans Crs WFD IG8 52 E3
St Rule St VX/NE SW8 141 H3
St Saviours Ct WDGN N22 48 D5
St Saviour's Est STHWK SE1 19 J4
St Saviour's Rd
BRXS/STRHM SW2 142 A6
CROY/NA CR0 196 D3
Saints Cl WNWD SE27 162 C6
Saints Dr FSTGT E7 89 H3
St Silas Pl KTTN NW5 84 A4
St Simon's Av PUT/ROE SW15 139 F6
St Stephen's Av SHB W12 118 E2
WALTH E17 70 A2
WEA W13 97 H5
St Stephens Cl KTTN NW5 * 83 K3
STHL UB1 96 A4
STJWD NW8 2 C1
WALTH E17 69 K2
St Stephen's Crs BAY/PAD W2 100 E5
THHTH CR7 180 B6
St Stephen's Gdns
BAY/PAD W2 100 E5
TWK TW1 156 D1
St Stephen's Gv LEW SE13 145 F4
St Stephen's Ms BAY/PAD W2 100 E4
St Stephens Pde WHALL SW1A 16 E2
St Stephens Rd BAR EN5 20 B6
BOW E3 87 G6
EHAM E6 89 G5
HSLW TW3 155 F1
WALTH E17 69 K2
WDR/YW UB7 112 A1
WEA W13 97 H5
St Stephens Ter VX/NE SW8 * 141 K1
St Stephen's Wk SKENS SW7 * 120 B4
St Swithin's La MANHO EC4N 12 E5
St Swithun's Rd LEW SE13 * 145 G6
St Theresa's Rd
EBED/NFELT TW14 133 J5
St Thomas Cl SURB KT6 191 G5
St Thomas Ct BXLY DA5 169 H2
St Thomas' Dr PIN HA5 41 J4
STMC/STPC BR5 201 H5
St Thomas Gdns IL IG1 90 C4
St Thomas Rd BELV DA17 129 K2
CAN/RD E16 106 E5
CHSWK W4 137 K1
STHGT/OAK N14 34 D2
St Thomas's Gdns HAMP NW3 84 A4
St Thomas's Pl HOM E9 * 86 E5
St Thomas's Rd FSBYPK N4 67 G6
WLSDN NW10 81 G6
St Thomas's Sq HACK E8 86 D5
St Thomas St STHWK SE1 19 F1
St Thomas's Wy FUL/PGN SW6 139 J1
St Ursula Gv PIN HA5 59 H2
St Ursula Rd STHL UB1 96 A5
St Vincent Cl WNWD SE27 180 C1
St Vincent Rd WHTN TW2 155 H1
St Vincents Av DART DA1 151 K6
St Vincents La MLHL NW7 46 A1
St Vincents Rd DART DA1 171 K1
St Vincent St MHST W1U 9 H2
St Wilfrid's Cl EBAR EN4 * 21 J6
St Wilfrid's Rd EBAR EN4 21 H6
St Winefride's Av MNPK E12 89 K3
St Winifred's Cl CHIG IG7 54 C1
St Winifred's Rd TEDD TW11 174 C2
Saladin Dr PUR RM19 131 K4
Salamanca Pl LBTH SE11 17 G7
Salamanca St LBTH SE11 17 G7
Salamander Cl KUTN/CMB KT2 174 D1
Salamander Quay KUT/HW KT1 * 174 E4
Salamons Wy RAIN RM13 111 G5
Salcombe Dr CHDH RM6 74 B3
MRDN SM4 193 G5
Salcombe Gdns MLHL NW7 46 A2
Salcombe Rd ASHF TW15 152 B6
STNW/STAM N16 86 B3
WALTH E17 69 H4
Salcombe Wy RSLP HA4 58 E6
Salcott Rd BTSEA SW11 140 E6
CROY/NA CR0 210 E1
Salehurst Cl KTN/HRWW/W HA3 62 A2
Salehurst Rd BROCKY SE4 164 C1
Salem Pl CROY/NA CR0 211 J1
Sale Pl BAY/PAD W2 8 C2
Sale St BETH E2 104 C3
Salford Rd BRXS/STRHM SW2 161 J3
Salhouse Cl THMD SE28 109 J5
Salisbury Av BARK IG11 90 D5
FNCH N3 46 D5
SUT SM1 208 D4
Salisbury Cl WALW SE17 18 E6
WPK KT4 207 H1
Salisbury Ct EMB EC4Y 11 K4
FLST/FETLN EC4A 12 A4
Salisbury Gdns
WIM/MER SW19 * 177 H3
Salisbury Pavement
FUL/PGN SW6 * 139 K1
Salisbury Pl BRXN/ST SW9 142 C1
MBLAR W1H 8 E1
Salisbury Prom
CEND/HSY/T N8 * 67 H2
Salisbury Rd BAR EN5 20 C4
BXLY DA5 169 H3
CAR SM5 209 K4
CHING E4 37 J5
CROY/NA CR0 197 H3
DAGE RM10 92 D4
ED N9 36 C5
FELT TW13 154 B3
FSBYPK N4 67 H2
FSTGT E7 88 E4
GDMY/SEVK IG3 72 E6
GPK RM2 75 K2
HAYES BR2 200 D2
HOR/WEW KT19 207 F2
HRW HA1 60 D2
HSLWW TW4 134 B4
MNPK E12 89 H3
NWDGN UB2 * 114 D4
NWMAL KT3 176 A6
PIN HA5 58 E1
RCH/KEW TW9 137 F5
WALTH E17 70 A2
WDGN N22 49 H5
WEA W13 116 C2
WIM/MER SW19 177 H3
Salisbury Sq EMB EC4Y * 11 K4
Salisbury St ACT W3 117 K2
STJWD NW8 2 C7
Salisbury Ter PECK SE15 143 K4
Salix Cl SUN TW16 172 A3
Sally Murray Cl MNPK E12 90 A2
Salmen Rd PLSTW E13 106 D1
Salmon La POP/IOD E14 105 G5
Salmon Ms KIL/WHAMP NW6 * 82 E3
Salmon Rd BELV DA17 129 H5
DART DA1 151 J4
Salmons Rd CHSGTN KT9 206 A4
ED N9 36 C3
Salmon St CDALE/KGS NW9 62 E4
POP/IOD E14 * 105 H5
Salomons Rd PLSTW E13 107 G4
Salop Rd WALTH E17 69 F3
Saltash Cl SUT SM1 208 D2
Saltash Rd BARK/HLT IG6 54 D3
WELL DA16 148 D2
Saltcoats Rd CHSWK W4 118 B2
Saltcote Cl DART DA1 170 B1
Saltcroft Cl WBLY HA9 62 D5
Salter Cl RYLN/HDSTN HA2 77 K1
Salterford Rd TOOT SW17 179 F2
Salter Rd BERM/RHTH SE16 124 B2
Salters' Hall Ct MANHO EC4N * 12 E5
Salter's Hl NRWD SE19 180 E1
Salters Rd NKENS W10 100 B3
WALTH E17 70 B1
Salters Rw IS N1 * 85 K4
Salter St POP/IOD E14 105 J6
WLSDN NW10 99 J2
Salterton Rd HOLWY N7 84 E1
Saltford Cl ERITH DA8 130 B5
Saltley Cl EHAM E6 107 J5
Saltoun Rd BRXS/STRHM SW2 142 B5
Saltram Crs MV/WKIL W9 100 D2
Saltwell St POP/IOD E14 105 J6
Saltwood Cl ORP BR6 217 J2
Saltwood Gv WALW SE17 * 122 E5
Salusbury Rd KIL/WHAMP NW6 82 C6
Salvador TOOT SW17 178 D1
Salvia Gdns GFD/PVL UB6 97 G1
Salvin Rd PUT/ROE SW15 139 G4
Salway Cl WFD IG8 52 E3
Salway Pl SRTFD E15 88 B4
Salway Rd SRTFD E15 88 B4
Samantha Cl WALTH E17 69 H4
Sam Bartram Cl CHARL SE7 126 B5
Samels Ct HMSMTH W6 118 D5
Samford St STJWD NW8 2 C7
Samos Rd PGE/AN SE20 181 J5
Sampson Av BAR EN5 20 B6
Sampson Cl BELV DA17 128 E3
Sampson St WAP E1W * 123 H1
Samson St PLSTW E13 107 G1
Samuel Cl HACK E8 86 B6
NWCR SE14 124 A6
WOOL/PLUM SE18 126 D4
Samuel Gray Gdns
KUTN/CMB KT2 174 E4
Samuel St PECK SE15 143 G1
WOOL/PLUM SE18 126 E4
Sancroft Cl CRICK NW2 81 K1
Sancroft Rd
KTN/HRWW/W HA3 43 F5
Sancroft St LBTH SE11 122 B5
Sanctuary Cl DART DA1 171 F1
Sanctuary Rd
STWL/WRAY TW19 152 D1
Sanctuary St STHWK SE1 18 D3
The Sanctuary BXLY DA5 168 E1
WEST SW1P 16 D4
Sandall Cl EA W5 98 A3
Sandall Rd EA W5 98 A3
KTTN NW5 84 C4
Sandal Rd NWMAL KT3 192 B1
UED N18 50 C1
Sandal St SRTFD E15 88 C6
Sandalwood Cl WCHPL E1 105 G3
Sandalwood Dr RSLP HA4 58 A4
Sandalwood Rd FELT TW13 154 A5
Sandbach Pl
WOOL/PLUM SE18 127 H5
Sandbourne Av
WIM/MER SW19 178 A6
Sandbourne Rd BROCKY SE4 144 B3
Sandbrook Cl MLHL NW7 45 F2
Sandbrook Rd
STNW/STAM N16 86 A1
Sandby Gn ELTH/MOT SE9 146 D4
Sandcliff Rd ERITH DA8 130 A4
Sandcroft Cl PLMGR N13 49 H2
Sandell's Av ASHF TW15 153 F6
Sandell St STHWK SE1 17 J2

Sanders Cl HPTN TW12 .....173 H1
Sanders La MLHL NW7 .....46 B3
Sanderson Cl KTTN NW5 * 84 E2
Sanders Pde
  STRHM/NOR SW16 * 179 K2
Sanderstead Av CRICK NW2 .....64 C6
Sanderstead Cl CLAP SW4 .....161 H2
Sanderstead Rd LEY E10 .....69 G5
  SAND/SEL CR2 .....211 K5
  STMC/STPC BR5 .....202 C3
Sandfield Gdns THHTH CR7 .....180 C6
Sandfield Pl THHTH CR7 .....180 C6
Sandfield Rd THHTH CR7 .....180 C6
Sandford Av WDGN N22 .....49 H4
Sandford Rd BXLYHS DA6 .....149 F5
  EHAM E6 .....107 K2
  HAYES BR2 .....199 K1
Sandford Rw WALW SE17 .....122 C5
Sandford St FUL/PGN SW6 .....140 A1
Sandgate Cl ROMW/RG RM7 .....74 E4
Sandgate La
  WAND/EARL SW18 .....160 D3
Sandgate Rd WELL DA16 .....148 D1
Sandgate St PECK SE15 .....123 J6
Sandhills WLGTN SM6 .....210 D2
The Sandhills WBPTN SW10 * 120 B6
Sandhurst Av BRYLDS KT5 .....191 J4
  RYLN/HDSTN HA2 .....60 B3
Sandhurst Cl CDALE/KGS NW9 .....44 C5
  SAND/SEL CR2 .....212 A6
Sandhurst Dr GDMY/SEVK IG3 .....91 F2
Sandhurst Pde CAT SE6 * 165 F3
Sandhurst Rd BFN/LL DA15 .....168 A5
  BXLY DA5 .....148 E6
  CAT SE6 .....165 G3
  CDALE/KGS NW9 .....44 C5
  ED N9 .....36 E1
  ORP BR6 .....217 F5
Sandhurst Wy SAND/SEL CR2 .....212 A5
Sandifer Dr CRICK NW2 .....82 B1
Sandiford Rd CHEAM SM3 .....193 J6
Sandiland Crs HAYES BR2 .....199 J6
Sandilands CROY/NA CR0 .....212 C1
Sandilands Rd FUL/PGN SW6 .....140 A2
Sandison St PECK SE15 .....143 G4
Sandland St GINN WC1R 11 H2
Sandling Ri ELTH/MOT SE9 .....167 F5
Sandlings Cl PECK SE15 .....143 J3
Sandmartin Wy WLGTN SM6 .....195 G5
Sandmere Rd CLAP SW4 .....141 K5
Sandon Cl ESH/CLAY KT10 .....189 J4
Sandow Crs HYS/HAR UB3 .....113 J3
Sandown Av DAGE RM10 .....92 E4
  ESH/CLAY KT10 .....204 C3
Sandown Cl HEST TW5 .....133 J1
Sandown Ct BELMT SM2 * 209 F5
  DAGE RM10 .....92 E4
  SYD SE26 .....163 J5
Sandown Ga ESH/CLAY KT10 .....189 J6
Sandown Rd ESH/CLAY KT10 .....204 A4
  SNWD SE25 .....197 J2
Sandown Wy NTHLT UB5 .....77 J3
Sandpiper Cl
  BERM/RHTH SE16 .....124 C2
  WALTH E17 .....51 F3
Sandpiper Rd SUT SM1 .....208 D3
Sandpiper Ter CLAY IG5 * 54 B6
Sandpiper Wy
  STMC/STPC BR5 .....202 E1
Sandpit Pl CHARL SE7 .....126 D5
Sandpit Rd BMLY BR1 .....183 H1
  DART DA1 .....151 J5
Sandpits Rd CROY/NA CR0 .....213 F2
  RCHPK/HAM TW10 .....156 E4
Sandra Cl HSLW TW3 .....135 G6
  WDGN N22 .....49 J4
Sandridge Cl HRW HA1 .....60 E2
Sandridge St ARCH N19 .....66 C6
Sandringham Av RYNPK SW20 .....177 H4
Sandringham Cl EN EN1 .....24 A3
  WIM/MER SW19 * 159 G3
Sandringham Crs
  RYLN/HDSTN HA2 .....78 A1
Sandringham Dr ASHF TW15 .....152 A6
  BXLY DA5 .....170 B4
  WELL DA16 .....147 K3
Sandringham Gdns
  BARK/HLT IG6 .....54 C6
  CEND/HSY/T N8 .....66 E3
  E/WMO/HCT KT8 .....189 H1
  HEST TW5 .....133 K2
  NFNCH/WDSP N12 .....47 H2
Sandringham Ms HPTN TW12 .....172 E3
Sandringham Rd BARK IG11 .....91 F4
  BMLY BR1 .....183 K1
  CRICK NW2 .....81 K3
  CROY/NA CR0 .....196 D2
  FSTGT E7 .....89 G3
  GLDGN NW11 .....64 C4
  HACK E8 .....86 C3
  HTHAIR TW6 .....132 B6
  LEY E10 .....70 A5
  NTHLT UB5 .....78 A5
  WDGN N22 .....49 J6
  WPK KT4 .....207 J1
Sandrock Pl CROY/NA CR0 .....213 F2
Sandrock Rd LEW SE13 .....144 D4
Sands End La FUL/PGN SW6 .....140 A2
Sandstone La CAN/RD E16 .....107 G6
Sandstone Pl ARCH N19 .....66 B6
Sandstone Rd LEE/GVPK SE12 .....166 A4
Sandtoft Rd CHARL SE7 .....126 A6
Sandway Rd STMC/STPC BR5 .....202 D2
Sandwell Crs KIL/WHAMP NW6 .....82 E4
Sandwich St STPAN WC1H 4 E5
Sandwick Cl MLHL NW7 .....45 J3
Sandy Bury ORP BR6 .....216 D1

Sandy Dr EBED/NFELT TW14 .....153 H3
Sandy Hill Av
  WOOL/PLUM SE18 .....127 G5
Sandy Hill La
  WOOL/PLUM SE18 .....127 G4
Sandyhill Rd IL IG1 .....90 B2
Sandy Hill Rd WLGTN SM6 .....210 C6
  WOOL/PLUM SE18 .....127 G5
Sandy La BELMT SM2 .....208 C6
  KTN/HRWW/W HA3 .....62 B3
  MTCM CR4 .....195 H4
  NTHWD HA6 .....26 D4
  ORP BR6 .....202 B4
  RCHPK/HAM TW10 .....156 D4
  STMC/STPC BR5 .....186 E3
  TEDD TW11 .....174 B3
  WOT/HER KT12 .....188 B5
Sandy La North WLGTN SM6 .....210 D3
Sandy La South WLGTN SM6 .....210 C6
Sandy Ldg PIN HA5 * 42 A2
Sandy Lodge Ct NTHWD HA6 * 40 C1
Sandy Lodge La NTHWD HA6 .....26 B4
Sandy Lodge Wy NTHWD HA6 .....40 C2
Sandymount Av STAN HA7 .....43 J1
Sandy Rdg CHST SE7 .....185 F2
Sandy Rd HAMP NW3 .....65 F6
Sandy's Rw WCHPL E1 .....13 H2
Sandy Wy CROY/NA CR0 .....213 H1
Sanford La STNW/STAM N16 .....68 B6
Sanford St NWCR SE14 .....124 B6
Sanford Ter STNW/STAM N16 .....86 B1
Sanger Av CHSGTN KT9 .....206 B3
Sangley Rd CAT SE6 .....164 E3
  SNWD SE25 .....197 F1
Sangora Rd BTSEA SW11 .....140 C5
Sansom Rd WAN E11 * 70 C6
Sansom St CMBW SE5 .....142 E1
Sans Wk CLKNW EC1R 6 A6
Santley St BRXS/STRHM SW2 .....141 K5
Santos Rd PUT/ROE SW15 .....139 K6
Saperton Wk LBTH SE11 .....17 H6
Saphora Ct ORP BR6 .....216 D3
Sapphire Cl BCTR RM8 .....73 J5
  EHAM E6 .....108 A5
Sapphire Rd DEPT SE8 .....124 B4
Saracen Cl CROY/NA CR0 .....196 E3
Saracen St POP/IOD E14 .....105 J5
Sarah St BETH E2 .....7 H4
Saratoga Rd CLPT E5 .....86 E2
Sardinia St HOL/ALD WC2B 11 G4
Sarita Cl KTN/HRWW/W HA3 .....42 D5
Sark Cl HEST TW5 .....135 F1
Samesfield Rd ENC/FH EN2 * 23 K5
Sarre Rd KIL/WHAMP NW6 .....82 D3
Sarsen Av HSLW TW3 .....134 E3
Sarsfeld Rd BAL SW12 .....160 E3
Sarsfield Rd GFD/PVL UB6 .....97 H1
Sartor Rd PECK SE15 .....144 A5
Sarum Ter BOW E3 * 105 H3
Satanita Cl CAN/RD E16 .....107 H5
Satchell Md CDALE/KGS NW9 .....45 H4
Satchwell Rd BETH E2 .....104 C2
Sattar Ms STNW/STAM N16 * 85 K1
Sauls Gn WAN E11 .....88 C1
Saunders Cl POP/IOD E14 * 105 H6
Saunders Ness Rd
  POP/IOD E14 .....125 G4
Saunders Rd
  WOOL/PLUM SE18 .....128 A5
Saunders St LBTH SE11 .....17 J6
Saunders Wy DART DA1 .....171 J4
  THMD SE28 .....109 H6
Saunderton Rd ALP/SUD HA0 .....79 H3
Saunton Av HYS/HAR UB3 .....133 J1
Saunton Rd HCH RM12 .....75 J6
Savage Gdns EHAM E6 .....107 K5
  TWRH EC3N 13 H5
Savanah Cl PECK SE15 .....143 G1
Savernake Ct STAN HA7 .....43 J2
Savernake Rd ED N9 .....36 C1
  HAMP NW3 .....83 K2
Savery Dr SURB KT6 .....190 D4
Savile Cl NWMAL KT3 .....192 B2
Savile Rw CONDST W1S 10 A5
Saville Rd CAN/RD E16 .....126 D1
  CHDH RM6 .....74 B3
  CHSWK W4 .....118 A3
  TWK TW1 .....156 A3
Saville Rw HAYES BR2 .....199 J5
Savill Gdns RYNPK SW20 .....176 D6
Savill Rw WFD IG8 .....52 D2
Savona Cl WIM/MER SW19 .....177 G3
Savona St VX/NE SW8 .....141 H1
Savoy Av HYS/HAR UB3 .....113 H5
Savoy Cl EDGW HA8 .....44 C1
  SRTFD E15 .....88 C6
Savoy Ct TPL/STR WC2R * 11 F6
Savoy Hl TPL/STR WC2R * 11 G6
Savoy Ms CLAP SW4 .....141 K4
Savoy Pde EN EN1 * 24 A4
Savoy Pl CHCR WC2N 11 F6
Savoy Rw DART DA1 .....151 F6
Savoy Rw TPL/STR WC2R 11 G5
Savoy Steps TPL/STR WC2R * 11 G6
Savoy St TPL/STR WC2R 11 G6
Savoy Wy TPL/STR WC2R 11 G6
Sawbill Cl YEAD UB4 .....95 H4
Sawkins Cl WIM/MER SW19 .....159 G4
Sawley Rd SHB W12 .....118 D1
Sawtry Cl CAR SM5 .....194 C4
Sawyer Ct IO PIN 36 C4
Sawyer's Hl
  RCHPK/HAM TW10 .....157 G2
Sawyers Lawn WEA W13 .....97 F5
Sawyer St STHWK SE1 .....18 C2
Saxby Rd BRXS/STRHM SW2 .....161 K2
Saxham Rd BARK IG11 .....90 E6
Saxlingham Rd CHING E4 .....38 B5
Saxon Av FELT TW13 .....154 E4
Saxonbury Av SUN TW16 .....172 A6
Saxonbury Cl MTCM CR4 .....178 C6
Saxonbury Gdns SURB KT6 .....190 D5
Saxon Cl SURB KT6 .....190 E5
  WALTH E17 .....69 J4

Saxon Dr ACT W3 .....98 D5
Saxonfield Cl
  BRXS/STRHM SW2 .....162 A2
Saxon Rd BMLY BR1 .....183 J5
  BOW E3 .....105 H1
  CROY/NA CR0 .....196 C5
  EHAM E6 .....107 K3
  IL IG1 .....90 B3
  KUTN/CMB KT2 .....175 F4
  RDART DA2 .....171 H6
  STHL UB1 .....95 J6
  WBLY HA9 .....80 E3
  WDGN N22 .....49 H4
Saxon Wy STHGT/OAK N14 .....34 D1
Saxony Pde HYS/HAR UB3 .....94 A4
Saxton Cl LEW SE13 .....145 G4
Saxville Rd STMC/STPC BR5 .....186 C6
Sayesbury La UED N18 .....50 C1
Sayes Court Rd
  STMC/STPC BR5 .....186 B6
Sayes Court St DEPT SE8 .....124 C6
Scadbury Gdns
  STMC/STPC BR5 .....186 B5
Scads Hill Cl ORP BR6 .....202 A3
Scala St FITZ W1T 10 B1
Scales Rd TOTM N17 .....50 B6
Scammell Wy WATW WD18 .....26 D1
Scampston Ms NKENS W10 .....100 B5
Scampton Rd HTHAIR TW6 .....152 C1
Scandrett St WAP E1W * 123 J1
Scarba Wk IS N1 * 85 K4
Scarborough Rd ED N9 .....36 E2
  FSBYPK N4 .....67 G4
  HTHAIR TW6 .....153 F1
  WAN E11 .....70 B5
Scarborough St WCHPL E1 .....13 K4
Scarbrook Rd CROY/NA CR0 .....211 J1
Scarle Rd ALP/SUD HA0 .....79 K4
Scarlet Cl STMC/STPC BR5 .....202 C1
Scarlet Rd CAT SE6 .....165 H5
Scarsbrook Rd BKHTH/KID SE3 .....146 C4
Scarsdale Pl KENS W8 .....120 A3
Scarsdale Rd RYLN/HDSTN HA2 .....78 C1
Scarsdale Vls KENS W8 .....119 K3
Scarth Rd BARN SW13 .....138 C4
Scawen Cl CAR SM5 .....210 A2
Scawen Rd DEPT SE8 .....124 B5
Scawfell St BETH E2 .....7 K3
Scaynes La
  NFNCH/WDSP N12 .....32 E6
Sceptre Rd BETH E2 .....104 E2
Scholars Rd BAL SW12 .....161 H3
  CHING E4 .....38 A3
Scholefield Rd ARCH N19 .....66 D5
Schonfeld Sq STNW/STAM N16 .....67 K6
School Cl DART DA1 .....150 C5
School House La TEDD TW11 .....174 C3
Schoolhouse La WAP E1W * 105 F6
School La BUSH WD23 .....28 B3
  KUT/HW KT1 .....174 D4
  PIN HA5 * 59 J1
  SURB KT6 .....191 H5
  WELL DA16 .....148 C4
School Pas KUT/HW KT1 .....175 G5
  STHL UB1 .....114 F1
School Rd CHST BR7 .....185 H4
  DAGE RM10 .....92 C6
  E/WMO/HCT KT8 .....189 J1
  HPTN TW12 .....173 H2
  HSLW TW3 .....135 H4
  KUT/HW KT1 * 174 D4
  MNPK E12 .....89 K2
  WDR/YW UB7 .....112 A6
  WLSDN NW10 .....99 F3
School Road Av HPTN TW12 .....173 H2
School Wy BCTR RM8 .....91 H1
Schoolway NFNCH/WDSP N12 .....47 H2
Schooner Cl BARK IG11 .....109 H2
  POP/IOD E14 .....125 G3
  PUT/ROE SW15 .....139 J6
Sclater St WCHPL E1 .....7 J6
Scoresby St STHWK SE1 .....18 A1
Scorton Av GFD/PVL UB6 .....97 G1
Scotch Common WEA W13 .....97 G4
Scot Gv PIN HA5 .....41 H3
Scotia Rd BRXS/STRHM SW2 .....162 A2
Scotland Gn TOTM N17 .....50 B5
Scotland Green Rd PEND EN3 .....25 F6
Scotland Green Rd North
  PEND EN3 .....25 F5
Scotland Rd BKHH IG9 .....39 G3
Scotney Cl ORP BR6 .....216 A2
Scots Cl STWL/WRAY TW19 .....152 A3
Scotsdale Cl BELMT SM2 .....208 D5
  CHST BR7 .....201 K1
Scotsdale Rd LEE/GVPK SE12 .....146 A6
Scotswood Cl CLKNW EC1R * 5 K6
Scotswood Wk TOTM N17 * 50 D3
Scott Cl HOR/WEW KT19 .....207 H6
  STRHM/NOR SW16 .....180 A4
  WDR/YW UB7 .....112 C4
Scott Crs ERITH DA8 .....150 C2
  RYLN/HDSTN HA2 .....60 B5
Scott Ellis Gdns STJWD NW8 .....2 A5
Scottes La BCTR RM8 .....73 K5
Scott Farm Cl THDIT KT7 .....190 C5
Scott Gdns HEST TW5 .....134 C1
Scott Lidgett Crs
  BERM/RHTH SE16 .....123 H2
Scotts Dr HPTN TW12 .....173 G3
Scotts Farm Rd
  HOR/WEW KT19 .....206 E4
Scott's La HAYES BR2 .....183 G6
Scotts Pas WOOL/PLUM SE18 * 127 G4
Scotts Rd BMLY BR1 .....165 K6
  LEY E10 .....70 A5
  NWDGN UB2 .....114 B3
  SHB W12 .....118 E2
Scott St WCHPL E1 .....104 D3
Scott Trimmer Wy HEST TW5 .....134 C3
Scottswell Dr CDALE/KGS NW9 .....63 H2

Scoulding Rd CAN/RD E16 .....106 D5
Scouler St POP/IOD E14 .....106 B6
Scout La CLAP SW4 .....141 H4
Scout Wy MLHL NW7 .....31 F6
Scovell Crs STHWK SE1 * 18 C3
Scovell Rd STHWK SE1 .....18 C3
Scrattons Ter BARK IG11 .....109 K1
Scriven St HACK E8 .....86 B6
Scrooby St CAT SE6 .....164 E1
Scrubs La WLSDN NW10 .....99 J2
Scrutton St SDTCH EC2A 7 G6
Scutari Rd EDUL SE22 .....143 J6
Scylla Crs HTHAIR TW6 .....152 E2
Scylla Rd HTHAIR TW6 .....152 E1
  PECK SE15 .....143 J4
Seabright St BETH E2 .....104 D2
Seabrook Dr WWKM BR4 .....199 H6
Seabrook Gdns ROMW/RG RM7 .....74 C4
Seabrook Rd BCTR RM8 .....91 K1
Seaburn Cl RAIN RM13 .....111 G2
Seacole Cl ACT W3 .....99 F5
Seacourt Rd ABYW SE2 .....128 E2
Seacroft Gdns OXHEY WD19 .....27 H5
Seafield Rd FBAR/BDGN N11 .....34 D6
Seaford Cl RSLP HA4 .....58 B6
Seaford Rd EN EN1 .....24 A6
  HTHAIR TW6 .....132 A6
  SEVS/STOTM N15 .....67 K2
  WEA W13 .....116 C1
  WLSDN NW10 .....81 H6
Seaforth Av NWMAL KT3 .....192 E2
Seaforth Crs HBRY N5 .....85 J3
Seaforth Gdns
  HOR/WEW KT19 .....207 H2
  WCHMH N21 .....35 F2
  WFD IG8 .....53 G1
Seagrave Cl WCHPL E1 * 105 F4
Seagrave Rd FUL/PGN SW6 .....119 K6
Seagry Rd WAN E11 .....70 E3
Seagull La CAN/RD E16 .....106 E6
Sealand Rd HTHAIR TW6 .....152 D1
Seal St HACK E8 .....86 B2
Searles Cl BTSEA SW11 .....140 D1
Searles Dr EHAM E6 .....108 B4
Searles Rd STHWK SE1 .....19 F6
Sears St CMBW SE5 .....142 E1
Seasprite Cl NTHLT UB5 .....95 H2
Seaton Cl LBTH SE11 .....122 C5
  PLSTW E13 .....106 E3
  PUT/ROE SW15 .....158 E2
  WHTN TW2 .....155 J1
Seaton Dr ASHF TW15 .....152 B4
Seaton Gdns RSLP HA4 .....76 E1
Seaton Rd ALP/SUD HA0 .....98 A1
  DART DA1 .....170 C2
  HYS/HAR UB3 .....113 G4
  MTCM CR4 .....178 D5
  WELL DA16 .....148 D1
  WHTN TW2 .....155 H1
Seaton St UED N18 .....50 C1
Sebastian St FSBYE EC1V 6 B5
Sebastopol Rd ED N9 .....36 C6
Sebbon St IS N1 .....85 H5
Sebergham Gv MLHL NW7 .....45 J3
Sebert Rd FSTGT E7 .....89 G2
Sebright Rd BAR EN5 .....20 B3
Secker Crs KTN/HRWW/W HA3 .....42 C4
Secker St STHWK SE1 .....17 J1
Second Av ACT W3 .....118 C1
  CHDH RM6 .....73 J2
  DAGE RM10 .....110 D1
  EN EN1 .....24 B6
  HDN NW4 .....46 B6
  HYS/HAR UB3 .....113 J1
  MNPK E12 .....89 J2
  MORT/ESHN SW14 .....138 B4
  NKENS W10 .....100 C3
  PLSTW E13 .....106 E2
  UED N18 .....36 E6
  WALTH E17 .....69 J2
  WBLY HA9 .....61 K6
  WOT/HER KT12 .....188 B3
Second Cl E/WMO/HCT KT8 .....189 G1
Second Cross Rd WHTN TW2 .....155 J4
Second Wy WBLY HA9 .....80 D2
Sedcombe Cl SCUP DA14 .....168 C5
Sedcote Rd PEND EN3 .....24 E6
Sedding St KTBR SW1X 15 G6
Seddon Rd MRDN SM4 .....194 C2
Seddon St FSBYW WC1X 5 G5
Sedgebrook Rd BKHTH/KID SE3 .....146 C3
Sedgecombe Av
  KTN/HRWW/W HA3 .....61 J2
Sedgeford Rd SHB W12 .....118 C1
Sedgehill Rd CAT SE6 .....182 D1
Sedgemere Av EFNCH N2 .....47 G6
Sedgemere Rd ABYW SE2 .....128 D3
Sedgemoor Dr DAGE RM10 .....92 C2
Sedge Rd TOTM N17 .....50 E3
Sedgeway CAT SE6 .....165 J3
Sedgewood Cl HAYES BR2 .....199 J4
Sedgmoor Pl CMBW SE5 .....143 F1
Sedgwick Rd LEY E10 .....70 A6
Sedgwick St HOM E9 .....87 F3
Sedleigh Rd WAND/EARL SW18 .....159 J1
Sedlescombe Rd
  FUL/PGN SW6 .....119 J6
Sedley Cl EN EN1 .....24 D1
Sedley Pl MYFR/PKLN W1K 9 J4
Sednem Ct DECK SE15 .....143 H5
Sedum Cl CDALE/KGS NW9 .....62 D2
Seeley Dr DUL SE21 .....163 F6
Seelig Av CDALE/KGS NW9 .....63 J4
Seely Rd TOOT SW17 .....179 F2
Seething La TWRH EC3N 13 H5
Seething Wells La SURB KT6 .....190 D3
Sefton Av KTN/HRWW/W HA3 .....42 D5
  MLHL NW7 .....45 F1

Sefton Cl STMC/STPC BR5 .....202 A1
Sefton St ENC/FH EN2 * 23 H2
Sefton Rd CROY/NA CR0 .....197 H6
  STMC/STPC BR5 .....202 A1
Sefton St PUT/ROE SW15 .....139 F3
Sekforde St CLKNW EC1R 6 A7
Sekhon Ter FELT TW13 .....155 F5
Selah Dr SWLY BR8 .....187 K4
Selan Gdns YEAD UB4 .....95 G4
Selbie Av WLSDN NW10 .....81 H4
Selborne Av BXLY DA5 .....169 F3
  MNPK E12 .....90 A2
Selborne Gdns GFD/PVL UB6 .....97 G1
  HDN NW4 .....63 J3
Selborne Rd CMBW SE5 .....142 E4
  CROY/NA CR0 .....212 A1
  IL IG1 .....72 A6
  NWMAL KT3 .....176 B5
  SCUP DA14 .....168 C6
  STHGT/OAK N14 .....34 E5
  WALTH E17 .....69 H2
  WDGN N22 .....49 F4
Selbourne Av SURB KT6 .....191 G6
Selby Cha RSLP HA4 .....59 F4
Selby Cl CHSGTN KT9 .....206 A5
  CHST BR7 .....185 F2
Selby Gdns STHL UB1 .....96 A4
Selby Gn CAR SM5 .....194 D4
Selby Rd CAR SM5 .....194 D4
  EA W5 .....97 H3
  PGE/AN SE20 .....181 H5
  PLSTW E13 .....107 F4
  TOTM N17 .....50 A2
  WAN E11 .....88 B1
Selby St WCHPL E1 .....104 D3
Selden Rd PECK SE15 .....143 K3
Selhurst Cl WIM/MER SW19 .....159 G3
Selhurst New Rd SNWD SE25 .....197 F3
Selhurst Pl CROY/NA CR0 .....197 F3
Selhurst Rd ED N9 .....35 K5
  SNWD SE25 .....197 G2
Selinas La BCTR RM8 .....74 A4
Selkirk Dr ERITH DA8 .....150 B2
Selkirk Rd TOOT SW17 .....160 D6
  WHTN TW2 .....155 H4
Sellers Hall Cl FNCH N3 .....46 E3
Sellincourt Rd TOOT SW17 .....178 D2
Sellindge Cl BECK BR3 .....182 C3
Sellons Av WLSDN NW10 .....81 H6
Sellwood Dr BAR EN5 .....20 B6
Selsdon Av SAND/SEL CR2 .....211 K4
  SURB KT6 .....191 F2
Selsdon Cl CRW RM5 .....56 E4
Selsdon Park Rd
  SAND/SEL CR2 .....213 G6
Selsdon Rd ADL/WDHM KT15 .....88 C1
  CRICK NW2 .....63 H6
  PLSTW E13 .....89 G5
  SAND/SEL CR2 .....211 K3
  WAN E11 .....70 E6
  WNWD SE27 .....162 C5
Seldon Wy POP/IOD E14 .....124 E3
Selsea Pl STNW/STAM N16 .....86 A3
Selsey Crs WELL DA16 .....148 E2
Selsey St POP/IOD E14 .....105 J4
Selvage La MLHL NW7 .....45 F1
Selway Cl PIN HA5 .....58 E1
Selwood Pl SKENS SW7 .....120 C5
Selwood Rd CHEAM SM3 .....193 J5
  CHSGTN KT9 .....205 K2
  CROY/NA CR0 .....197 H6
Selwood Ter SKENS SW7 * 120 C5
Selworthy Cl WAN E11 .....71 F2
Selworthy Rd CAT SE6 .....164 C5
Selwyn Av CHING E4 .....52 A2
  GDMY/SEVK IG3 .....73 F2
  RCH/KEW TW9 .....137 G4
Selwyn Cl HSLWW TW4 .....134 D5
Selwyn Ct EDGW HA8 .....44 D3
Selwyn Crs WELL DA16 .....148 C5
Selwyn Rd BOW E3 .....105 H1
  NWMAL KT3 .....192 A2
  PLSTW E13 .....89 F6
  WLSDN NW10 .....81 G5
Semley Pl BGVA SW1W 15 H6
Semley Rd STRHM/NOR SW16 .....179 K5
Senate St PECK SE15 .....143 K3
Seneca Rd THHTH CR7 .....196 D1
Senga Rd WLGTN SM6 .....195 G1
Senhouse Rd CHEAM SM3 .....208 B1
Senior St BAY/PAD W2 .....101 F4
Senlac Rd LEE/GVPK SE12 .....166 A3
Sennen Rd EN EN1 .....36 C1
Senrab St WCHPL E1 .....105 F5
Sentinel Cl NTHLT UB5 .....95 J3
September Wy STAN HA7 .....43 H2
Sequoia Cl BUSH WD23 .....28 D3
Sequoia Pk PIN HA5 .....42 B2
Serbin Cl LEY E10 .....70 A4
Serenaders Rd BRXN/ST SW9 .....142 B3
Serjeant's Inn EMB EC4Y * 11 K4
Serle St LINN WC2A 11 H3
Sermon Dr SWLY BR8 .....187 K6
Sermon La BLKFR EC4V 12 C4
Serpentine Rd BAY/PAD W2 .....14 F1
Service Route No 1 SRTFD E15 .....88 B5
Service Route No 2 SRTFD E15 .....88 B5
Service Route No 3 SRTFD E15 .....88 B5
Servidem Dr BRXH E4 .....184 C2
Servite Ct SE4 STHWK SE1 * 19 H2
Setchell Rd STHWK SE1 .....19 J7
Setchell Wy STHWK SE1 .....19 J7
Seton Gdns DAGW RM9 .....91 J5
Settles St WCHPL E1 .....104 C4
Settrington Rd FUL/PGN SW6 .....140 A3
Seven Acres CAR SM5 .....194 D6
  NTHWD HA6 .....40 D2
Seven Dials LSQ/SEVD WC2H 10 E4
Sevenex Pde WBLY HA9 * 80 A3
Seven Kings Rd
  GDMY/SEVK IG3 .....73 F1
Seven Kings Wy
  KUTN/CMB KT2 .....174 E4
Sevenoaks Rd BROCKY SE4 .....164 C1
  ORP BR6 .....217 F4

Sevenoaks Wy
STMC/STPC BR5 ....186 D6
Seven Sisters Rd HOLWY N7 ...85 F1
SEVS/STOTM N15 ....67 K3
Seven Stars Yd WCHPL E1 ......13 K1
Seventh Av HYS/HAR UB3 ......113 K1
MNPK E12 ....197 G3
Severnake Cl POP/IOD E14 ....124 D4
Severn Av GPK RM2 ....51 K6
NKENS W10 ....100 C2
Severn Dr EN EN1 ....24 C1
ESH/CLAY KT10 ....190 B6
WOT/HER KT12 ....188 C6
Severn Wy WLSDN NW10 ....81 H3
Severus Rd BTSEA SW11 ....140 D5
Seville Ms IS N1 ....86 A5
Seville St KTBR SW1X 15 F3
Sevington Rd HDN NW4 ....63 K3
Sevington St MV/WKIL W9 .....101 F3
Seward Rd BECK BR3 ....182 A5
HNWL W7 ....116 B2
Sewardstone Rd BETH E2 ......104 E1
CAN/RD E16 ....25 K5
Seward St FSBYE EC1V 6 B6
Sewdley St CLPT E5 ....87 F1
Sewell Rd ABYW SE2 ....128 B3
Sewell St PLSTW E13 ....106 E2
Sextant Av POP/IOD E14 ......125 G4
Sexton Cl RAIN RM13 ....93 J1
Seymer Rd ROM RM1 ....57 F6
Seymour Av EW KT17 ....207 K6
MRDN SM4 ....193 G4
TOTM N17 ....50 C5
Seymour Cl E/WMO/HCT KT8 ...189 J3
LOU IG10 ....39 J1
PIN HA5 ....41 K4
Seymour Dr HAYES BR2 ....200 E5
Seymour Gdns BROCKY SE4 ....144 A4
BRYLDS KT5 ....191 G2
FELT TW13 ....154 A6
IL IG1 ....71 K5
RSLP HA4 ....59 H5
TWK TW1 ....156 A1
Seymour Ms MBLAR W1H 9 G3
Seymour Pl MBLAR W1H 8 E2
SNWD SE25 ....197 J1
Seymour Rd CAR SM5 ....210 A3
CEND/HSY/T N8 ....37 K3
CHING E4 ....37 K3
CHSWK W4 ....117 K4
E/WMO/HCT KT8 ....189 J3
ED N9 ....36 D4
EHAM E6 ....89 H6
FNCH N3 ....47 F3
HPTN TW12 ....173 H1
KUT/HW KT1 ....174 E4
LEY E10 ....69 H5
MTCM CR4 ....195 F4
WAND/EARL SW18 ....159 J2
WIM/MER SW19 ....159 C5
Seymour St MBLAR W1H 8 E4
WOOL/PLUM SE18 ....127 H4
Seymour Ter PGE/AN SE20 .....181 J4
Seymour Vls PGE/AN SE20 .....181 J4
Seymour Wy WBPTN SW10 ......120 E4
Seyssel St POP/IOD E14 ......125 F4
Shaa Rd ACT W3 ....118 E1
Shacklegate La TEDD TW11 ....155 K6
Shackleton Cl FSTH SE23 .....163 J4
Shackleton Rd STHL UB1 ......95 K6
Shacklewell La HACK E8 ....86 B3
Shacklewell Rd
STNW/STAM N16 ....86 B2
Shacklewell Rw HACK E8 ....86 B2
Shacklewell St BETH E2 ....7 K6
Shadbolt Av CHING E4 ....51 G1
Shadbolt Cl WPK KT4 ....192 C6
Shad Thames STHWK SE1 ....19 K2
Shadwell Dr NTHLT UB5 ....95 F2
Shadwell Gdns WCHPL E1 * 104 E6
Shadwell Pierhead WAP E1W ...104 E6
Shady Bush Cl BUSH WD23 .....28 C2
Shaef Wy TEDD TW11 ....174 B3
Shafter Rd DAGE RM10 ....92 E4
Shaftesbury Av BAR EN5 ....21 G5
EBED/NFELT TW14 ....153 K1
KTN/HRWW/W HA3 ....61 K3
MYFR/PICC W1J 10 C5
NWDGN UB2 ....115 F4
PEND EN3 ....25 F3
RYLN/HDSTN HA2 ....60 C5
Shaftesbury Cir
RYLN/HDSTN HA2 * 60 C5
Shaftesbury Gdns
WLSDN NW10 ....99 G3
Shaftesbury Ms KENS W8 ......119 K3
Shaftesbury Pde
RYLN/HDSTN HA2 * 60 C5
Shaftesbury Pl BARB EC2Y * ...12 C2
Shaftesbury Rd ARCH N19 ......66 E5
BECK BR3 ....182 C5
CAR SM5 ....194 C4
CHING E4 ....38 B3
FSTGT E7 ....89 G5
RCH/KEW TW9 ....137 F4
ROM RM1 ....75 H3
UED N18 ....50 A1
WALTH E17 ....69 K2
The Shaftesburys BARK IG11 ..108 C1
Shaftesbury St IS N1 ....6 E2
Shaftesbury Ter
HMSMTH W6 * 119 F5
Shaftesbury Wy WHTN TW2 ....155 J5
Shaftesbury Waye YEAD UB4 ...95 F4
Shafton Ms KTBR SW1X 14 E6
Shafton Rd HOM E9 ....87 F6
Shakespeare Av
EBED/NFELT TW14 ....153 K1
FBAR/BDGN N11 ....48 C1
HLSDN NW10 ....81 F6
Shakespeare Crs MNPK E12 ....89 K5
Shakespeare Dr
KTN/HRWW/W HA3 ....62 B1

Shakespeare Gdns EFNCH N2...65 K1
Shakespeare Rd ACT W3 ......117 K1
BXLYHN DA7 ....149 F2
DART DA1 ....151 K5
FNCH N3 ....46 E4
HNHL SE24 ....142 C6
HNWL W7 ....97 F6
MLHL NW7 ....31 J6
ROM RM1 ....75 H5
WALTH E17 ....51 F5
WLSDN NW10 ....81 F6
Shakespeare Ter
RCH/KEW TW9 * 137 H4
Shakespeare Wy FELT TW13 ...154 B6
Shakspeare Ms
STNW/STAM N16 ....86 A2
Shakspeare Wk
STNW/STAM N16 ....86 A2
Shalbourne Sq HOM E9 ....87 H4
Shalcomb St WBPTN SW10 .....120 B6
Shalden Dr MRDN SM4 ....193 H2
RSLP HA4 ....77 G1
Shaldon Rd EDGW HA8 ....44 B5
Shalfleet Dr NKENS W10 ......100 B6
Shalford Cl ORP BR6 ....216 C2
Shalford Ct IS N1 ....6 A2
Shalimar Gdns ACT W3 ....98 E6
Shalimar Rd ACT W3 ....98 E6
Shallons Rd ELTH/MOT SE9 ...167 G6
Shalstone Rd
MORT/ESHN SW14 ....137 J4
Shalston Vis SURB KT6 ....191 G3
Shamrock Rd CROY/NA CRO 196 A3
Shamrock St CLAP SW4 ....141 J4
Shamrock Wy STHGT/OAK N14 ..34 B3
Shandon Rd CLAP SW4 ....161 H1
Shand St STHWK SE1 ....19 H2
Shandy St WCHPL E1 ....105 F4
Shalimar Gdns OXHEY WD19 ....27 G6
Shanklin Rd CEND/HSY/T N8 ...66 D2
SEVS/STOTM N15 ....68 C1
Shannon Cl CRICK NW2 ....82 B1
HEST TW5 ....114 C5
Shannon Gv BRXN/ST SW9 ....142 A5
Shannon Pl STJWD NW8 ....2 D2
Shannon Wy BECK BR3 ....182 E2
Shap Crs CAR SM5 ....194 E5
Shapland Wy PLMCR N13 ....49 F1
Shapwick Cl FBAR/BDGN N11 ...47 K1
Shardcroft Av HNHL SE24 ....142 C6
Shardeloes Rd BROCKY SE4 ...144 C3
Shard's Sq PECK SE15 ....123 H6
Sharland Cl THHTH CR7 ......196 B3
Sharman Ct SCUP DA14 ....168 B6
Sharnbrooke Cl WELL DA16 ...148 D4
Sharon Cl SURB KT6 ....190 D5
Sharon Gdns HOM E9 ....86 E6
Sharon Rd CHSWK W4 ....118 A5
PEND EN3 ....25 G3
Sharples Hall St CAMTN NW1 ..83 K5
Sharps La RSLP HA4 ....58 B5
Sharp Wy DART DA1 ....151 J4
Sharratt St PECK SE15 ....123 K6
Sharsted St WALW SE17 ......122 C5
Sharvel La NTHLT UB5 ....76 E6
Shavers Pl MYFR/PICC W1J ...10 C6
Shaw Av BARK IG11 ....110 A1
Shawbrooke Rd
ELTH/MOT SE9 ....146 C5
Shawbury Rd EDUL SE22 ......143 F5
Shaw Cl BUSH WD23 ....28 E4
EMPK RM11 ....75 K5
THMD SE28 ....128 C1
Shaw Crs POP/IOD E14 ....105 G5
Shaw Dr WOT/HER KT12 ....188 B4
Shawfield Pk BMLY BR1 ......184 C5
Shawfield St CHEL SW3 ......120 C5
Shawford Rd HOR/WEW KT19 ..207 F4
Shaw Gdns BARK IG11 ....110 A1
Shaw Rd BMLY BR1 ....165 J5
EDUL SE22 ....143 F5
PEND EN3 ....25 F2
Shaw's Cottages FSTH SE23 ..164 B5
Shaw Sq WALTH E17 ....51 G4
The Shaw CHST BR7 ....185 H3
Shaw Wy WLGTN SM6 ....210 E6
Shaxton Crs CROY/NA CRO 214 A6
Shearing Dr MRDN SM4 ....194 B4
Shearling Wy HOLWY N7 ....84 E4
Shearman Rd BKHTH/KID SE3 ..145 J5
Shearwater Cl BARK IG11 ....109 G2
Shearwater Rd SUT SM1 ......208 D3
Shearwater Wy YEAD UB4 ......95 H5
Shearwood Crs DART DA1 .....150 C4
Sheaveshill Av CDALE/KGS NW9 .45 G4
Sheaveshill Pde
CDALE/KGS NW9 * 63 G1
Sheaveshill Pde
CDALE/KGS NW9 * 63 G1
Sheen Common Dr
RCHPK/HAM TW10 ....137 H5
Sheen Court Rd
RCHPK/HAM TW10 ....137 H5
Sheendale Rd RCH/KEW TW9 ..137 F4
Sheenewood SYD SE26 ....181 J1
Sheen Gate Gdns
MORT/ESHN SW14 ....137 K5
Sheen Gv IS N1 ....85 G6
Sheen La MORT/ESHN SW14 ...137 K5
Sheen Pk RCH/KEW TW9 ....137 F4
Sheen Rd RCHPK/HAM TW10 ...137 F5
STMC/STPC BR5 ....202 A1
Sheen Wy WLGTN SM6 ....211 F3
Sheen Wd MORT/ESHN SW14 ...137 K6
Sheepcote Cl HEST TW5 ......133 K1
Sheepcote La BTSEA SW11 ....140 E3
STMC/STPC BR5 ....203 H1
Sheepcote Rd HRW HA1 ....61 F3
Sheephouse Wy NWMAL KT3 ...192 B4
Sheep La HACK E8 ....86 D6
Sheep Walk Ms
WIM/MER SW19 ....177 G2
Sheerwater Rd CAN/RD E16 ...107 H4
Sheffield Rd HTHAIR TW6 .....153 F1
Sheffield St LINN WC2A * 11 G4

Sheffield Ter KENS W8 ....119 K2
Sheffield Wy HTHAIR TW6 ....133 G6
Shefton Ri NTHWD HA6 ....40 E3
Sheila Rd CRW RM5 ....56 D3
Shelbourne Cl PIN HA5 ....41 K6
Shelbourne Rd TOTM N17 ......50 D4
Shelburne Dr HSLWW TW4 ....155 F1
Shelburne Rd HOLWY N7 ....85 F2
Shelbury Cl SCUP DA14 ......168 B5
Shelbury Rd EDUL SE22 ......143 J6
Sheldon Av CLAY IG5 ....54 B5
HGT N6 ....65 H6
Sheldon Cl LEE/GVPK SE12 ...146 A6
PGE/AN SE20 ....181 J4
Sheldon Rd BXLYHN DA7 ......149 G2
CRICK NW2 ....82 B2
DAGW RM9 ....92 A5
UED N18 ....36 A6
Sheldon St CROY/NA CRO 211 J1
Sheldrake Cl CAN/RD E16 ....126 E1
Sheldrake Pl KENS W8 ....119 J2
Sheldrick Cl MTCM CR4 ......178 C5
Shelduck Cl FSTGT E7 ....89 G2
Sheldwich Ter HAYES BR2 * ..200 D5
Shelford Pl STNW/STAM N16 ...85 K1
Shelford Ri NRWD SE19 ......181 F3
Shelford Rd BAR EN5 ....32 A1
Shelgate Rd BTSEA SW11 ....140 D6
Shell Cl HAYES BR2 ....200 D5
Shellduck Cl CDALE/KGS NW9 ..45 G5
Shelley Av GFD/PVL UB6 ....96 D2
HCH RM12 ....75 H6
MNPK E12 ....89 K5
Shelley Cl EDGW HA8 ....30 C5
GFD/PVL UB6 ....96 D2
NTHWD HA6 ....40 D1
ORP BR6 ....216 E1
YEAD UB4 ....94 E4
Shelley Crs HEST TW5 ....134 C2
STHL UB1 ....95 K5
Shelley Dr WELL DA16 ....147 K2
Shelley Gdns ALP/SUD HA0 ....61 J6
Shelley Rd WLSDN NW10 ....81 F6
Shelley Wy WIM/MER SW19 ...178 C2
Shellgrove Rd
STNW/STAM N16 * 86 A3
Shelliness Rd CLPT E5 ....86 D5
Shell Rd LEW SE13 ....144 E4
Shellwood Rd BTSEA SW11 ...140 E3
Shelmerdine Cl BOW E3 ......105 J4
Shelson Av FELT TW13 ....153 J6
Shelton Rd WIM/MER SW19 ...177 K4
Shelton St LSO/SEVD WC2H * ..10 E4
Shenfield Rd WFD IG8 ....53 F3
Shenfield St IS N1 ....7 H5
Shenley Av RSLP HA4 ....58 D1
Shenley Rd CMBW SE5 ....143 F2
DART DA1 ....171 K1
HEST TW5 ....134 D2
Shepherd Cl FELT TW13 .....154 D6
Shepherdess Pl FSBYE EC1V 6 D4
Shepherdess Wk IS N1 ....6 D3
Shepherd's Bush Gn SHB W12 .119 F2
Shepherd's Bush Market
SHB W12 ....119 F2
Shepherd's Bush Pl SHB W12 *.119 G2
Shepherd's Bush Rd
HMSMTH W6 ....119 F4
Shepherds Cl CHDH RM6 ....73 K2
HGT N6 ....66 B5
ORP BR6 ....217 F1
STAN HA7 ....43 J2
Shepherds Gn CHST BR7 ......185 J3
Shepherd's Hi HGT N6 ....66 B3
Shepherds La DART DA1 ......170 C2
HOM E9 ....87 F3
THMD SE28 ....127 K1
Shepherd's Leas
ELTH/MOT SE9 ....147 J5
Shepherds Pl MYFR/PKLN W1K ..9 G3
Shepherds Rd WATW WD18 .....26 E1
Shepherds Wk BUSH WD23 .....28 B4
CRICK NW2 ....63 J6
HAMP NW3 ....83 H3
Shepherds Wy SAND/SEL CR2 .213 F5
Shepiston La WDR/YW UB7 ....112 A4
Shepley Cl CAR SM5 ....210 A1
Shepley Ms PEND EN3 ....25 J1
Sheppard Cl EN EN1 ....24 C3
SURB KT6 ....191 F1
Sheppard Dr
BERM/RHTH SE16 ....123 J5
Sheppard St CAN/RD E16 .....106 D3
Shepperton Rd IS N1 ....85 K6
STMC/STPC BR5 ....201 H4
Sheppey Cl ERITH DA8 ....150 E1
Sheppey Gdns DAGW RM9 ......91 J5
Sheppey Rd DAGW RM9 ....91 H5
Sheppey Wk IS N1 * 85 J5
Shepton Houses BETH E2 * ...104 E2
Sherard Rd ELTH/MOT SE9 ...146 D5
Sherborne Av NWDGN UB2 ....115 F4
PEND EN3 ....24 E3
Sherborne Cl YEAD UB4 ....95 G5
Sherborne Crs CAR SM5 .....194 D4
Sherborne Gdns
CDALE/KGS NW9 ....44 C6
WEA W13 ....97 H5
Sherborne La MANHO EC4N 12 E5
Sherborne Pl NTHWD HA6 .....40 B2
Sherborne Rd CHEAM SM3 ....193 K6
CHSGTN KT9 ....206 A3
EBED/NFELT TW14 ....153 G3
STMC/STPC BR5 ....202 A2
Sherborne St IS N1 ....85 K6
Sherborne Vls WEA W13 * 97 H4
Sherboro Rd SEVS/STOTM N15 ..68 B3
Sherbrooke Cl BXLYHN DA7 ...149 H5
Sherbrooke Rd FUL/PGN SW6 .139 H1
Sherbrook Gdns WCHMH N21 ...35 H2

Shere Cl CHSGTN KT9 ....205 K3
Sheredan Rd CHING E4 ....52 B1
Shere Rd GNTH/NBYPK IG2 .....72 A2
Sherfield Cl NWMAL KT3 .....191 J1
Sherfield Gdns PUT/ROE SW15 .158 C1
Sheridan Cl HARH RM3 ....57 K3
Sheridan Ct DART DA1 ....151 K5
HSLWW TW4 ....134 D6
Sheridan Crs CHST BR7 ......185 G6
Sheridan Gdns
KTN/HRWW/W HA3 ....61 K3
Sheridan Pl HPTN TW12 ......173 G4
Sheridan Rd BELV DA17 ......129 H4
BXLYHN DA7 ....149 F4
FSTGT E7 ....88 D1
RCHPK/HAM TW10 ....156 D5
WIM/MER SW19 ....177 J4
Sheridan St WCHPL E1 ....104 D5
Sheridan Ter NTHLT UB5 * 78 B5
Sheridan Wk CAR SM5 ....209 K3
GLDGN NW11 ....64 E3
Sheridan Wy BECK BR3 ....182 C4
Sheringham Av MNPK E12 ......89 K2
ROMW/RG RM7 ....74 D3
STHGT/OAK N14 ....22 C6
Sheringham Dr BARK IG11 ....91 F3
Sheringham Rd HOLWY N7 .....85 F4
PGE/AN SE20 ....181 J5
Sherington Av PIN HA5 ....42 A3
Sherington Rd CHARL SE7 ....126 A6
Sherland Rd TWK TW1 ....156 A3
Sherlies Av ORP BR6 ....201 K6
Sherlock Ms MHST W1U 9 G1
Sherman Gdns CHDH RM6 ......73 J3
Sherman Rd BMLY BR1 ....183 K4
Shernhall St WALTH E17 ......52 A6
Sherrard Rd FSTGT E7 ....89 G4
Sherrards Wy BAR EN5 ....20 E6
Sherrick Green Rd
WLSDN NW10 ....81 J3
Sherriff Rd KIL/WHAMP NW6 ...82 E4
Sherringham Av FELT TW13 ..153 K5
TOTM N17 ....50 C5
Sherrock Gdns HDN NW4 ....63 J1
Sherry Ms BARK IG11 ....90 D5
Sherwin Rd NWCR SE14 ......144 A2
Sherwood SURB KT6 ....190 D6
Sherwood Av GFD/PVL UB6 .....78 E4
RSLP HA4 ....58 C3
STRHM/NOR SW16 ....179 J3
SWFD E18 ....53 F2
YEAD UB4 ....95 F5
Sherwood Cl BXLY DA5 ......168 D1
WALTH E17 ....51 H5
WEA W13 ....116 C1
Sherwood Ct MBLAR W1H 8 D5
Sherwood Gdns BARK IG11 ....90 D5
POP/IOD E14 ....124 D4
STHWK SE1 ....19 H5
Sherwood House
RYLN/HDSTN HA2 * 78 C1
Sherwood Park Av
BFN/LL DA15 ....168 B2
Sherwood Park Rd MTCM CR4 .195 H5
SUT SM1 ....208 E3
Sherwood Rd BARK/HLT IG6 ...72 C1
CROY/NA CRO 197 J4
HDN NW4 ....46 A6
HPTN TW12 ....173 H1
RYLN/HDSTN HA2 ....60 C6
WELL DA16 ....147 K4
WIM/MER SW19 ....177 J3
Sherwoods Rd OXHEY WD19 ....27 J2
Sherwood St SOHO/SHAV W1D ..10 B5
TRDG/WHET N20 ....33 J1
Sherwood Ter TRDG/WHET N20 .33 H5
Sherwood Wy WWKM BR4 ......199 F6
Shetland Cl BORE WD6 ....31 F1
Shetland Rd BOW E3 ....105 H1
Shield Dr BTFD TW8 ....116 C6
Shield St ABYW SE2 ....128 D4
Shield Rd ASHF TW15 ....153 F6
Shillaker Ct ACT W3 ....118 C1
Shilliber Pl MBLAR W1H 8 D1
Shillingford Cl MLHL NW7 .....46 B3
Shillingford St IS N1 * 85 H6
Shilling Pl HNWL W7 * 116 B1
Shinfield St SHB W12 ....100 A5
Shinglewell Rd ERITH DA8 ...149 H1
Shinners Cl SNWD SE25 ......197 H2
Shipka Rd BAL SW12 ....161 G3
Ship La MORT/ESHN SW14 ....137 K4
Shipman Rd CAN/RD E16 .....107 F5
FSTH SE23 ....164 A4
Ship & Mermaid Rw
STHWK SE1 * 19 F2
Ship St DEPT SE8 ....144 D2
Ship Tavern Pas BANK EC3V ...13 G5
Shipton Cl BCTR RM8 ....91 K1
Shipton St BETH E2 ....7 K4
Shipwright Rd
BERM/RHTH SE16 ....124 B2
Shipwright Sq STHWK SE1 * ...19 G1
Shirburn Cl FSTH SE23 ......163 K2
Shirbutt St POP/IOD E14 ....105 K6
Shirebrook Rd BKHTH/KID SE3 .146 C4
Shire Cl EW KT17 ....207 H5
Shirehall Cl HDN NW4 ....64 B3
Shirehall Gdns HDN NW4 ......64 B3
Shirehall La HDN NW4 ....64 B3
Shirehall Pk HDN NW4 ....64 B3
Shire Horse Wy ISLW TW7 ...136 A4
Shire La ORP BR6 ....215 K5
ORP BR6 ....216 A6
The Shires RCHPK/HAM TW10 .157 F6
Shirland Ms MV/WKIL W9 .....100 D2
Shirland Rd MV/WKIL W9 ....100 E3
Shirley Av BXLY DA5 ....168 E2
CROY/NA CRO 197 K5
SUT SM1 ....209 H3
Shirley Church Rd
CROY/NA CRO 213 F1

Shirley Cl DART DA1 ....151 F5
HSLW TW3 ....135 H6
WALTH E17 * 51 K6
Shirley Crs BECK BR3 ....198 B1
Shirley Dr HSLW TW3 ....135 H6
Shirley Gdns BARK IG11 ......90 E5
HNWL W7 ....116 A1
Shirley Hills Rd CROY/NA CRO .213 F3
Shirley Oaks Rd CROY/NA CRO .198 A5
Shirley Park Rd CROY/NA CRO .197 J5
Shirley Rd BFN/LL DA15 .....167 K5
CHSWK W4 ....118 A2
CROY/NA CRO 197 K6
EN EN1 ....23 J4
SRTFD E15 ....88 C5
WLGTN SM6 ....210 C6
Shirley Rw SNWD SE25 * 181 H5
Shirley St CAN/RD E16 ......106 C5
Shirley Wy CROY/NA CRO 213 H1
Shirlock Rd HAMP NW3 ....83 K2
Shirwell Cl MLHL NW7 ....46 B3
Shobden Rd TOTM N17 ....49 K4
Shobroke Cl CRICK NW2 ....82 A1
Shoebury Rd EHAM E6 ....89 K6
Shoe La FLST/FETLN EC4A 11 K3
STBT EC1A 12 A2
Sholden Gdns STMC/STPC BR5 .202 D2
Shooters Av
KTN/HRWW/W HA3 ....61 J1
Shooters Hi WOOL/PLUM SE18 .146 E2
Shooters Hill Rd
BKHTH/KID SE3 ....145 H2
Shooters Rd ENC/FH EN2 ......23 G1
Shoot-up Hi CRICK NW2 ....82 C4
Shore Cl EBED/NFELT TW14 ..153 K2
HPTN TW12 ....172 D1
Shoreditch High St BETH E2 ....7 H5
WCHPL E1 ....13 H1
Shoreham Cl BXLY DA5 ....168 E2
CROY/NA CRO 197 K3
WAND/EARL SW18 ....140 A6
Shoreham Rd STMC/STPC BR5 .186 C4
Shoreham Rd (East)
HTHAIR TW6 ....132 B6
Shoreham Rd (West)
HTHAIR TW6 ....132 B6
Shoreham Wy HAYES BR2 .....199 K3
Shore Pl HNWL W7 * 86 E6
Shore Rd HOM E9 ....86 E5
Shorncliffe Rd STHWK SE1 ...123 G5
Shorndean St CAT SE6 ......165 F3
Shorne Cl BFN/LL DA15 .....168 C1
STMC/STPC BR5 ....202 E1
Shornefield Cl BMLY BR1 ....185 F6
Shorrolds Rd FUL/PGN SW6 ..139 K1
Shortcroft Rd EW KT17 .....207 H5
Shortcrofts Rd DAGW RM9 ....92 B4
Shorter St WCHPL E1 ....13 J5
Shortgate NFNCH/WDSP N12 ...32 D6
Shortlands HMSMTH W6 ....119 G4
HYS/HAR UB3 ....113 G6
Shortlands Cl BELV DA17 ....129 G3
UED N18 ....36 A3
Shortlands Gdns HAYES BR2 .183 H5
Shortlands Gv HAYES BR2 ...183 G6
Shortlands Rd HAYES BR2 ...183 G6
KUTN/CMB KT2 ....175 G3
LEY E10 ....69 K4
Short La STWL/WRAY TW19 ...152 C2
Short Rd CHSWK W4 ....118 B6
STWL/WRAY TW19 ....152 B1
WAN E11 ....70 C6
Shorts Cft CDALE/KGS NW9 ....62 D1
Shorts Gdns LSO/SEVD WC2H * .10 E4
Shorts Rd CAR SM5 ....209 J2
Short St STHWK SE1 ....17 K2
Shortway ELTH/MOT SE9 .....167 F3
Short Wy NFNCH/WDSP N12 ....47 J2
WHTN TW2 ....155 H2
Shotfield WLGTN SM6 ....210 B4
Shott Cl SUT SM1 ....209 G3
Shottendane Rd
FUL/PGN SW6 * 139 K2
Shottery Cl ELTH/MOT SE9 ..166 D5
Shottfield Av
MORT/ESHN SW14 ....138 B5
Shoulder of Mutton Aly
POP/IOD E14 ....105 G6
Shouldham St MBLAR W1H 8 D2
Showers Wy HYS/HAR UB3 ....113 K1
Shrapnel Cl WOOL/PLUM SE18 .146 D1
Shrapnel Rd ELTH/MOT SE9 ..146 E4
Shrewsbury Av
KTN/HRWW/W HA3 ....62 A1
MORT/ESHN SW14 ....137 K5
Shrewsbury Crs WLSDN NW10 ..81 F6
Shrewsbury La
WOOL/PLUM SE18 ....147 G2
Shrewsbury Ms BAY/PAD W2 ..100 E5
Shrewsbury Rd BAY/PAD W2 ..100 E5
BECK BR3 ....182 B6
CAR SM5 ....194 D4
FBAR/BDGN N11 ....48 D2
HTHAIR TW6 ....133 F1
MNPK E12 ....89 H4
Shrewsbury St NKENS W10 ...100 A3
Shrewton Rd TOOT SW17 * ...178 E3
Shroffold Rd BMLY BR1 ......165 H6
Shropshire Cl MTCM CR4 ....195 K4
Shropshire Rd WDGN N22 .....49 F3
Shroton St CAMTN NW1 ....8 C1
The Shrubberies CHIG IG7 ....54 E1
SWFD E18 ....52 E5
Shrubbery Gdns WCHMH N21 ...35 H2
Shrubbery Rd ED N9 ....36 C5
STHL UB1 ....95 K6
STRHM/NOR SW16 ....161 K6
The Shrubbery SURB KT6 * ...191 F5
Shrubland Cl TRDG/WHET N20 .33 H4
Shrubland Gv WPK KT4 ....208 A1
Shrubland Rd HACK E8 ....86 C6
WALTH E17 ....51 J6

Shrublands Av CROY/NA CR0 ...213 J2
Shrublands Cl CHIG IG7 ...54 C2
SYD SE26 ...
Shrubsall Cl ELTH/MOT SE9 ...166 D5
Shuna Wk IS N1 * ...85 K4
Shurland Av EBAR EN4 ...33 H1
Shurland Gdns PECK SE15 * ...143 G1
Shurlock Dr ORP BR6 ...216 C2
Shuters Sq WKENS W14 ...119 J5
Shuttle Cl BFN/LL DA15 ...168 A2
Shuttlemead BXLY DA5 ...169 G2
Shuttle Rd DART DA1 ...150 D4
Shuttle St WCHPL E1 ...104 C3
Shuttleworth Rd BTSEA SW11 ...140 C3
Sibella Rd CLAP SW4 ...141 J3
Siddons La ... Sibley Cl BXLYHS DA6 ...149 F6
Sibley Ct UX/CGN UB8 ...94 A4
Sibley Gv MNPK E12 ...89 J5
Sibthorpe Rd LEE/GVPK SE12 ...166 B2
Sibthorp Rd MTCM CR4 * ...178 E5
Sibton Rd CAR SM5 ...194 D4
Sicilian Av NOXST/BSQ WC1A * ...11 J2
Sidbury St FUL/PGN SW6 ...139 H2
Sidcup By-Pass Rd SCUP DA14 ...167 K6
Sidcup Hi SCUP DA14 ...186 C1
Sidcup Hill Gdns SCUP DA14 * ...186 D1
Sidcup Pl SCUP DA14 ...186 B1
Sidcup Rd ELTH/MOT SE9 ...166 A6
LEE/GVPK SE12 ...146 A6
Siddeley Dr HSLWW TW4 ...134 D4
Siddons La CAMTN NW1 * ...3 F7
Siddons Rd CROY/NA CR0 ...211 G1
FSTH SE23 ...164 B4
TOTM N17 ...50 C4
Side Rd WALTH E17 ...69 H2
Sidewood Rd ELTH/MOT SE9 ...167 J3
Sidford Pl STHWK SE1 ...17 H5
The Sidings LOU IG10 ...39 J1
WAN E11 ...70 A5
Sidmouth Av ISLW TW7 ...135 K5
Sidmouth Cl OXHEY WD19 ...27 F4
Sidmouth Dr RSLP HA4 ...76 E1
Sidmouth Pde CRICK NW2 * ...82 A5
Sidmouth Rd LEY E10 ...88 A1
PECK SE15 ...143 G2
STMC/STPC BR5 ...202 C2
WELL DA16 ...148 C6
WLSDN NW10 ...82 A5
Sidmouth St STPAN WC1H ...5 F5
Sidney Av PLMGR N13 ...49 F2
Sidney Elson Wy EHAM E6 ...108 A1
Sidney Gdns BTFD TW8 ...116 E6
Sidney Gv FSBYE EC1V ...6 A3
Sidney Rd BECK BR3 ...182 B5
BRXN/ST SW9 ...142 A3
FSTGT E7 ...88 E1
RYLN/HDSTN HA2 ...42 C6
SNWD SE25 ...197 H2
TWK TW1 ...156 A1
WDGN N22 ...49 F3
Sidney Sq WCHPL E1 * ...104 E4
Sidney St WCHPL E1 ...104 D5
Sidworth St HACK E8 ...86 D5
Siebert Rd BKHTH/KID SE3 ...125 K6
Siemens Rd WOOL/PLUM SE18 ...126 C3
Sienna Ter CRICK NW2 * ...63 J6
Sierra Dr DAGW RM9 ...110 E1
Sigdon Rd HACK E8 ...86 C3
The Sigers RSLP HA4 ...59 F3
Signmakers Yd CAMTN NW1 * ...3 K1
Sigrist Sq KUTN/CMB KT2 ...175 F4
Silbury Av MTCM CR4 ...178 D4
Silbury St IS N1 * ...6 E4
Silchester Rd NKENS W10 ...100 B5
Silecroft Rd BXLYHN DA7 ...149 H2
Silesia Buildings HACK E8 ...86 D5
Silex St STHWK SE1 ...18 B3
Silk Cl LEE/GVPK SE12 ...145 K5
Silkfield Rd CDALE/KGS NW9 ...63 G2
Silk Mill Rd OXHEY WD19 ...27 F2
Silk Mills Pth LEW SE13 ...145 F4
Silkstream Pde EDGW HA8 * ...44 E4
Silkstream Rd EDGW HA8 ...44 E4
Silk St BARB EC2Y ...12 D1
Silsoe Rd WDGN N22 ...49 F5
Silver Birch Av CHING E4 ...51 H1
Silver Birch Cl CAT SE6 ...164 C5
FBAR/BDGN N11 ...48 A2
RDART DA2 ...170 B6
THMD SE28 ...109 H6
Silver Birch Ms BARK/HLT IG6 ...54 C2
Silverbirch Wk HAMP NW3 * ...83 K4
Silvercliffe Gdns EBAR EN4 ...21 J5
Silver Cl KTN/HRWW/W HA3 ...42 D3
NWCR SE14 ...144 B1
Silver Crs CHSWK W4 ...117 J4
Silverdale CAMTN NW1 * ...4 A5
ENC/FH EN2 ...22 E5
FSTH SE23 ...164 A6
SYD SE26 ...163 K6
Silverdale Cl HNWL W7 ...115 K1
NTHLT UB5 ...77 K3
SUT SM1 ...208 D2
Silverdale Dr ELTH/MOT SE9 ...166 D4
HCH RM12 ...93 K4
SUN TW16 ...172 A5
Silverdale Gdns HYS/HAR UB3 ...113 K2
Silverdale Rd BXLYHN DA7 ...149 J3
CHING E4 ...52 B2
HYS/HAR UB3 ...113 K2
STMC/STPC BR5 ...186 B6
Silverdene
NFNCH/WDSP N12 * ...47 F2
Silver Dene PUT/ROE SW15 * ...139 F6
Silver Hall St ISLW TW7 ...136 B4
Silverholme Cl
KTN/HRWW/W HA3 ...62 A4
Silver La WWKM BR4 ...199 G6
Silverleigh Rd THHTH CR7 ...196 A1
Silvermere Av CRW RM5 ...56 D2
Silvermere Dr UED N18 * ...51 F4
Silvermere Rd LEW SE13 ...164 D1
Silvermere Wy SNWD SE25 * ...181 H5
Silver Pl SOHO/CST W1F ...10 B5
Silver Rd SHB W12 ...100 B6

Silver Spring Cl ERITH DA8 ...129 J6
Silverston Wy STAN HA7 ...43 J2
Silver St EN EN1 ...23 K4
UED N18 ...35 K6
Silverthorne Rd VX/NE SW8 ...141 G3
Silverthorn Gdns CHING E4 ...37 J4
Silverton Rd HMSMTH W6 ...119 G6
Silvertown Wy CAN/RD E16 ...106 D6
Silvertree La GFD/PVL UB6 ...96 D2
Silver Wk BERM/RHTH SE16 ...124 C1
Silver Wy ROMW/RG RM7 ...56 D6
Silverwood Cl BECK BR3 ...182 D3
CROY/NA CR0 ...213 H6
NTHWD HA6 ...40 A4
Silvester Rd EDUL SE22 ...143 G6
Silvester St STHWK SE1 ...18 E3
Silwood Estate Regeneration
Area DEPT SE8 ...124 A5
Silwood St BERM/RHTH SE16 ...124 A5
Simmil Rd ESH/CLAY KT10 ...204 E3
Simmons Dr BCTR RM8 ...92 A2
Simmons La CHING E4 ...38 B4
Simmons Rd
WOOL/PLUM SE18 ...127 G5
Simmons' Wy TRDG/WHET N20 ...33 J4
Simms Cl CAR SM5 ...194 D6
Simms Gdns EFNCH N2 ...47 G5
Simms Rd STHWK SE1 ...123 H4
Simnel Rd LEE/GVPK SE12 ...166 A2
Simon Cl NTGHL W11 ...100 D6
Simonds Rd LEY E10 ...69 J6
Simone Cl BMLY BR1 ...184 C4
Simons Wk SRTFD E15 ...88 B3
Simpson Cl WCHMH N21 ...23 F6
Simpson Dr ACT W3 ...99 F5
Simpson Rd HSLWW TW4 ...134 E1
RAIN RM13 ...93 H4
RCHPK/HAM TW10 ...156 D6
Simpson's Rd HAYES BR2 ...183 K6
POP/IOD E14 ...105 K6
Simpson St BTSEA SW11 ...140 D3
Simpson Wy SURB KT6 ...190 D3
Sims Cl ROM RM1 ...75 H1
Sinclair Dr BELMT SM2 ...209 F6
Sinclair Gdns WKENS W14 ...119 G2
Sinclair Gv GLDGN NW11 ...64 B4
Sinclair Rd CHING E4 ...51 H1
WKENS W14 ...119 H3
Sinclare Cl EN EN1 ...24 B2
Singapore Rd HNWL W7 ...116 B1
Singer St FSBYE EC1V ...7 F5
Singleton Cl CROY/NA CR0 ...196 D4
HCH RM12 ...93 H2
WIM/MER SW19 ...178 E3
Singleton Rd DAGW RM9 ...92 B3
Singleton Scarp
NFNCH/WDSP N12 ...46 E1
Sinnott Rd WALTH E17 ...51 F4
Sion Rd TWK TW1 ...156 C3
Sipson Cl WDR/YW UB7 ...112 D6
Sipson La HYS/HAR UB3 ...113 F6
WDR/YW UB7 ...112 E6
Sipson Rd WDR/YW UB7 ...112 C3
Sir Alexander Cl ACT W3 ...118 C1
Sir Cyril Black Wy
WIM/MER SW19 ...177 J3
Sirdar Rd MTCM CR4 ...179 F2
NTGHL W11 ...100 B6
WDGN N22 ...49 J5
Sir John Kirk Cl CMBW SE5 ...142 D1
Sir Thomas Moore Est
CHEL SW3 ...120 C6
Sirus Rd NTHWD HA6 ...40 E1
Sise La MANHO EC4N * ...12 E4
Sisley Rd BARK IG11 ...90 E6
Sispara Gdns
WAND/EARL SW18 ...159 J1
Sissinghurst Cl BMLY BR1 ...183 H1
Sissinghurst Rd CROY/NA CR0 ...197 H4
Sister Mabels Wy PECK SE15 ...143 H1
Sisters Av BTSEA SW11 ...140 E5
Sistova Rd BAL SW12 ...161 G3
Sisulu Pl BRXN/ST SW9 ...142 B4
Sittingbourne Av EN EN1 ...35 K1
Sitwell Gv STAN HA7 ...43 F1
Siverst Cl NTHLT UB5 ...78 B4
Siviter Wy DAGE RM10 ...92 D5
Siward Rd HAYES BR2 ...184 A1
TOOT SW17 ...160 B5
WDGN N22 ...49 K4
Sixth Av HYS/HAR UB3 ...113 J1
MNPK E12 ...89 K2
NKENS W10 ...100 C2
Sixth Cross Rd WHTN TW2 ...155 H5
Skardu Rd CRICK NW2 ...82 C3
Skeena Hi WAND/EARL SW18 ...159 H2
Skeet Hill La STMC/STPC BR5 ...203 G6
Skeffington Rd EHAM E6 ...89 K6
Skeffington St
WOOL/PLUM SE18 ...127 H3
Skelbrook St
WAND/EARL SW18 ...160 A4
Skelgill Rd PUT/ROE SW15 ...139 J5
Skelley Rd SRTFD E15 ...88 D5
Skelton Cl HACK E8 * ...86 B4
Skelton Rd FSTGT E7 ...88 E4
Skelton's La LEY E10 ...69 K4
Skelwith Rd HMSMTH W6 ...119 F6
Skenfrith Ho PECK SE15 * ...123 J6
Skerne Rd KUTN/CMB KT2 ...174 E4
Skerne Wk KUTN/CMB KT2 ...174 E4
Sketchley Gdns
BERM/RHTH SE16 ...124 A5
Sketty Rd EN EN1 ...24 B5
Skiers St SRTFD E15 ...88 C6
Skiffington Cl
BRXS/STRHM SW2 ...162 B3
Skinner Pl BGVA SW1W * ...15 G7
Skinners La BLKFR EC4V ...12 D5
HEST TW5 ...135 G2
Skinner St CLKNW EC1R ...6 A6
Skipsea Av EHAM E6 ...107 K2
Skipton Cl FBAR/BDGN N11 ...48 A2

Skipton Dr HYS/HAR UB3 ...113 F3
Skipworth Rd HOM E9 ...86 E6
Skylines Village
POP/IOD E14 * ...125 F2
Sky Peals Rd WFD IG8 ...52 B4
Skyport Dr WDR/YW UB7 ...132 A1
Sladebrook Rd
BKHTH/KID SE3 ...146 C4
Sladedale Rd
WOOL/PLUM SE18 ...127 K5
Slade Gdns ERITH DA8 ...150 C2
Slade Green Rd ERITH DA8 ...150 C2
Sladen Pl CLPT E5 ...86 D2
Slades Cl ENC/FH EN2 ...23 G4
Slades Dr CHST BR7 ...167 H6
Slades Gdns ENC/FH EN2 ...23 G4
Slades Hi ENC/FH EN2 ...23 G4
Slades Ri ENC/FH EN2 ...23 G4
The Slade WOOL/PLUM SE18 ...127 K6
Slade Wk WALW SE17 ...122 C6
Slagrove Pl LEW SE13 ...144 D6
Slaidburn St WBPTN SW10 ...120 B6
Slaithwaite Rd LEW SE13 ...145 F5
Slaney Pl HOLWY N7 ...85 G3
Slaney Rd ROM RM1 ...75 G2
Slattery Rd FELT TW13 ...154 B3
Sleaford Gn OXHEY WD19 ...27 H5
Sleaford St VX/NE SW8 ...141 H1
Slievemore Cl CLAP SW4 ...141 J4
Slingsby Pl COVGDN WC2E ...10 E5
Slippers Pl BERM/RHTH SE16 ...123 J3
Sloane Av CHEL SW3 ...14 D7
Sloane Ct East CHEL SW3 ...121 F5
Sloane Ct West CHEL SW3 ...121 F5
Sloane Gdns BGVA SW1W ...15 G7
ORP BR6 ...216 C1
Sloane Sq BGVA SW1W ...15 F7
Sloane St KTBR SW1X ...15 F3
Sloane Ter KTBR SW1X ...15 F6
Sloane Wk CROY/NA CR0 ...198 C3
Slocum Cl THMD SE28 ...109 J6
Slough La CDALE/KGS NW9 ...62 E3
Sly St WCHPL E1 * ...104 D5
Smaldon Cl WDR/YW UB7 ...112 D5
Smallberry Av ISLW TW7 ...136 A3
Smallbrook Ms BAY/PAD W2 ...8 A4
Smalley Cl STNW/STAM N16 ...86 B1
Smallwood Rd TOOT SW17 ...160 C6
Smarden Cl BELV DA17 ...129 H5
Smart St BETH E2 ...105 F2
Smart's Pl HHOL WC1V ...11 F3
UED N18 ...50 C1
Smeaton Cl CHSGTN KT9 ...205 K4
Smeaton Rd WAND/EARL SW18 ...159 K2
WFD IG8 ...53 K1
Smeaton St WAP E1W ...123 J1
Smedley St VX/NE SW8 ...141 J3
Smeed Rd BOW E3 ...87 J5
Smiles Pl LEW SE13 ...145 F3
Smith Cl BERM/RHTH SE16 ...124 A1
Smithfield St STBT EC1A ...12 A2
Smithies Rd ABYW SE2 ...128 C4
Smith's Ct SOHO/SHAV W1D * ...10 C5
Smithson Rd TOTM N17 ...49 K4
Smith Sq WEST SW1P ...16 E5
Smith St BRYLDS KT5 ...191 G5
CHEL SW3 ...120 E5
Smith Ter CHEL SW3 ...120 E5
Smithwood Cl
WIM/MER SW19 ...159 H4
Smithy St WCHPL E1 ...104 E4
Smugglers Wy
WAND/EARL SW18 ...140 A5
Smyrks Rd WALW SE17 ...123 F5
Smyrna Rd KIL/WHAMP NW6 ...82 E5
Smythe St POP/IOD E14 ...105 K6
Snakes La EBAR EN4 ...22 A4
Snakes La East WFD IG8 ...53 G2
Snakes La West WFD IG8 ...52 E2
Snakey La FELT TW13 ...153 K6
Snaresbrook Dr STAN HA7 ...29 K6
Snaresbrook Rd WAN E11 ...70 D1
Snarsgate St NKENS W10 ...100 A4
Sneath Av GLDGN NW11 ...64 D4
Snell's Pk UED N18 ...50 B2
Sneyd Rd CRICK NW2 ...82 A3
Snipe Cl ERITH DA8 ...150 E1
Snowbury Rd FUL/PGN SW6 ...140 A3
Snowden Dr CDALE/KGS NW9 ...63 G3
Snowdon Crs HYS/HAR UB3 ...113 F3
Snowdon Rd West
HTHAIR TW6 ...153 F1
Snowdown Cl PGE/AN SE20 ...181 K4
Snowdrop Cl HPTN TW12 ...173 F2
Snow Hi STBT EC1A ...12 A1
Snowsfields STHWK SE1 ...19 F2
Snowshill Rd MNPK E12 ...89 J3
Snowy Fielder Waye
ISLW TW7 ...136 C3
Soames St PECK SE15 ...143 G4
Soames Wk NWMAL KT3 ...176 B4
Soho Sq SOHO/SHAV W1D ...10 C4
Soho St SOHO/SHAV W1D ...10 C3
Sojourner Truth Cl HACK E8 * ...86 D4
Solander Gdns WCHPL E1 ...104 D6
Solebay St WCHPL E1 ...105 G3
Solent Ri PLSTW E13 ...106 E2
Solent Rd KIL/WHAMP NW6 ...82 E3
HTHAIR TW6 ...152 C1
Solna Av PUT/ROE SW15 ...139 F6
Solna Rd WCHMH N21 ...35 K3
Solomon Av UED N18 ...36 C6
Solomon's Pas PECK SE15 ...143 J5
Solon New Rd CLAP SW4 ...141 K5
Solon Rd BRXS/STRHM SW2 ...141 K6
Solway Cl HACK E8 ...86 B4
HSLWW TW4 ...134 D4
Solway Rd EDUL SE22 ...143 H5
WDGN N22 ...49 H4
Somaford Gv EBAR EN4 ...33 H1
Somali Rd CRICK NW2 ...82 D2
Somerby Rd BARK IG11 ...90 D5
Somercotes Cl EBAR EN4 ...21 J4
Somerden Rd STMC/STPC BR5 ...202 E4
Somerfield Rd FSBYPK N4 ...67 H6

Somerfield St
BERM/RHTH SE16 ...124 A5
Somerford Cl PIN HA5 ...58 E1
Somerford Gv STNW/STAM N16 ...86 B2
Somerford St WCHPL E1 * ...104 D3
Somerford Wy
BERM/RHTH SE16 ...124 B2
Somerhill Av BFN/LL DA15 ...168 C2
Somerhill Rd WELL DA16 ...148 C3
Somerleyton Rd
BRXN/ST SW9 ...142 B5
Somersby Gdns REDBR IG4 ...71 K2
Somers Cl CAMTN NW1 * ...4 C2
Somers Crs BAY/PAD W2 ...8 C4
Somerset Av CHSGTN KT9 ...205 K2
RYNPK SW20 ...176 E5
WELL DA16 ...148 A6
Somerset Cl NWMAL KT3 ...192 B3
TOTM N17 ...49 K5
WFD IG8 ...52 E3
Somerset Gdns HGT N6 ...66 A4
LEW SE13 ...144 E3
STRHM/NOR SW16 ...180 A6
TEDD TW11 ...173 K1
TOTM N17 ...50 B6
Somerset Rd BAR EN5 ...21 F6
BTFD TW8 ...116 D6
CHSWK W4 ...118 A3
DART DA1 ...170 E1
HDN NW4 ...46 A1
HRW HA1 ...60 C3
KUT/HW KT1 ...175 G5
ORP BR6 ...202 B4
PEND EN3 ...25 J1
STHL UB1 ...95 K4
TEDD TW11 ...173 K1
TOTM N17 ...50 B6
UED N18 ...50 B1
WALTH E17 ...69 J2
WEA W13 ...116 C1
WIM/MER SW19 ...159 H5
Somerset Sq WKENS W14 * ...119 H3
Somerset Sq Little TWRH EC3N ...13 J4
Somerset Waye HEST TW5 ...114 D6
Somersham Rd BXLYHN DA7 ...149 F3
Somers Pl BRXS/STRHM SW2 ...162 A1
Somers Rd BRXS/STRHM SW2 ...162 A1
WALTH E17 ...69 H1
Somers Wy BUSH WD23 ...28 C2
Somerton Av RCH/KEW TW9 ...137 J4
Somerton Rd CRICK NW2 ...82 B2
PECK SE15 ...143 J5
Somertrees Av
LEE/GVPK SE12 ...166 A4
Somervell Rd RYLN/HDSTN HA2 ...77 K3
Somerville Av BARN SW13 ...119 F6
Somerville Rd CHDH RM6 ...73 J2
DART DA1 ...171 J1
PGE/AN SE20 ...182 A3
Sonderburg Rd HOLWY N7 ...67 F6
Sondes St WALW SE17 ...122 E6
Songhurst Cl CROY/NA CR0 ...196 A3
Sonia Cl OXHEY WD19 ...27 G2
Sonia Gdns CRICK NW2 ...81 H2
HEST TW5 ...114 E6
NFNCH/WDSP N12 ...33 G6
Sonning Gdns HPTN TW12 ...172 D2
Sonning Rd CROY/NA CR0 ...197 H3
Soper Cl CHING E4 ...51 H1
FSTH SE23 ...164 A3
Soper Ms PEND EN3 ...25 J1
Sophia Cl HOLWY N7 ...85 F4
Sophia Rd CAN/RD E16 ...107 F5
LEY E10 ...69 K5
Sophia Sq BERM/RHTH SE16 ...105 G6
Sopwith Av CHSGTN KT9 ...206 A3
Sopwith Cl KUTN/CMB KT2 ...175 G1
Sopwith Rd HEST TW5 ...134 B1
Sopwith Wy KUTN/CMB KT2 ...175 F4
VX/NE SW8 ...141 J1
Sorrel Bank CROY/NA CR0 ...213 G6
Sorrel Cl THMD SE28 ...128 B1
Sorrel Gdns EHAM E6 ...107 J4
Sorrel La POP/IOD E14 ...106 B5
Sorrell Cl BRXN/ST SW9 ...142 B3
NWCR SE14 ...144 B1
Sorrel Wk ROM RM1 ...57 H6
Sorrento Rd SUT SM1 ...209 F1
Sotheby Rd HBRY N5 ...85 J1
Sotheran Cl HACK E8 ...86 C6
Soudan Rd BTSEA SW11 ...140 E2
Souldern Rd WKENS W14 * ...119 G3
Sounds Ldg SWLY BR8 ...203 K3
South Access Rd LEY E10 ...69 F4
Southacre Wy PIN HA5 ...41 G4
South Africa Rd NKENS W10 ...100 A6
SHB W12 ...99 K6
Southall Cl STHL UB1 ...95 K6
Southall La HEST TW5 ...114 A5
Southall Pl STHWK SE1 ...18 E3
Southampton Buildings
LINN WC2A * ...11 J2
Southampton Gdns
MTCM CR4 ...195 K2
Southampton Ms CAN/RD E16 ...126 A1
Southampton Pl
NOXST/BSQ WC1A ...11 F2
Southampton Rd HAMP NW3 ...83 K3
HTHAIR TW6 ...152 C1
Southampton Rw RSQ WC1B ...11 F1
Southampton St
COVGDN WC2E ...11 F5
Southampton Wy CMBW SE5 ...142 E1
Southam St NKENS W10 ...100 C3
South Audley St
MYFR/PKLN W1K ...9 H6
South Av CAR SM5 ...210 A5
CHING E4 ...37 K2
RCH/KEW TW9 ...137 H3
South Avenue Gdns STHL UB1 ...95 K6
South Bank STHWK SE1 ...11 K6
SURB KT6 ...191 F3

Southbank THDIT KT7 ...190 C4
South Bank Ter SURB KT6 * ...191 F3
South Birkbeck Rd WAN E11 ...88 B1
South Black Lion La
HMSMTH W6 ...118 D5
South Bolton Gdns
WBPTN SW10 ...120 A5
Southborough Cl SURB KT6 ...190 E5
Southborough La HAYES BR2 ...200 E2
Southborough Rd BMLY BR1 ...184 D6
HOM E9 ...86 E6
SURB KT6 ...191 F5
Southborough Rd (The Lane)
SURB KT6 ...191 F5
Southbourne HAYES BR2 ...199 K4
Southbourne Av
CDALE/KGS NW9 ...44 E5
Southbourne Cl PIN HA5 ...59 J4
Southbourne Crs HDN NW4 ...64 C1
Southbourne Gdns IL IG1 ...90 C3
LEE/GVPK SE12 ...146 A4
RSLP HA4 ...59 F5
Southbridge Pl CROY/NA CR0 ...211 J2
Southbridge Rd
CROY/NA CR0 ...211 J2
Southbridge Wy NWDGN UB2 ...114 D2
Southbrook Rd LEW SE13 ...165 H1
STRHM/NOR SW16 ...179 K4
Southbury Av EN EN1 ...24 B5
Southbury Rd EN EN1 ...24 B5
South Carriage Dr KTBR SW1X ...15 F2
SKENS SW7 ...14 C3
Southchurch Ct PLMGR N13 ...49 F1
Southchurch Rd EHAM E6 ...107 K1
South Cl BAR EN5 ...20 D4
BXLYHS DA6 ...148 E5
DAGE RM10 ...92 C6
FELT TW13 ...155 F5
HGT N6 ...66 B3
MRDN SM4 ...193 K3
PIN HA5 ...59 K4
WDR/YW UB7 ...112 C3
The South Colonnade
POP/IOD E14 ...124 D1
Southcombe St WKENS W14 ...119 H4
Southcote Av BRYLDS KT5 ...191 J4
FELT TW13 ...153 K4
Southcote Rd ARCH N19 ...84 C2
SNWD SE25 ...197 J2
WALTH E17 ...69 F2
South Countess Rd WALTH E17 ...51 H3
South Crs CAN/RD E16 ...106 B4
Southcroft Av WELL DA16 ...147 K4
WWKM BR4 ...199 F1
Southcroft Rd ORP BR6 ...216 E1
STRHM/NOR SW16 ...179 G2
South Cross Rd BARK/HLT IG6 ...72 C2
South Croxted Rd DUL SE21 ...162 E5
Southdean Gdns
WIM/MER SW19 ...159 J4
South Dene MLHL NW7 ...31 F5
Southdown Av HNWL W7 ...116 B3
Southdown Crs
GNTH/NBYPK IG2 ...72 E2
RYLN/HDSTN HA2 ...60 C5
Southdown Dr RYNPK SW20 ...177 G3
Southdown Rd CAR SM5 ...210 A6
EMPK RM11 ...75 K4
RYNPK SW20 ...177 G3
Southdown Vls
SEVS/STOTM N15 * ...67 H2
South Ealing Rd EA W5 ...116 E2
South Eastern Av ED N9 ...36 B5
South Eaton Pl BGVA SW1W ...15 H6
South Eden Park Rd
BECK BR3 ...198 E1
South Edwardes Sq KENS W8 ...119 J3
South End CROY/NA CR0 ...211 J3
KENS W8 * ...120 A3
Southend Cl ELTH/MOT SE9 ...167 F1
Southend Crs ELTH/MOT SE9 ...167 F1
Southend La CAT SE6 ...164 D6
South End Rd HAMP NW3 ...83 J2
RAIN RM13 ...93 J6
Southend Rd BECK BR3 ...182 D4
EHAM E6 ...89 K5
REDBR IG4 ...71 H4
South End Rd (North Circular)
SWFD E18 ...52 E5
WALTH E17 ...52 D5
South End Rw KENS W8 ...120 A3
Southern Av
EBED/NFELT TW14 ...153 K3
SNWD SE25 ...181 G6
Southern Down Rd FELT TW13 * ...154 B3
Southern Gv BOW E3 ...105 H2
Southern Perimeter Rd
HTHAIR TW6 ...152 E1
Southern Rd EFNCH N2 ...65 K1
PLSTW E13 ...107 F1
Southern St IS N1 ...5 G2
Southern Wy CHDH RM6 ...74 C5
GNWCH SE10 ...125 J5
Southern Esk Rd FSTGT E7 ...89 F4
Southey Rd BRXN/ST SW9 ...142 B2
SEVS/STOTM N15 ...68 A2
WIM/MER SW19 ...177 K3
Southey St PGE/AN SE20 ...182 A3
Southfield BAR EN5 ...32 B1
Southfield Gdns TWK TW1 ...156 A6
Southfield Pk
RYLN/HDSTN HA2 ...60 B1
Southfield Rd CHST BR7 ...186 A6
CHSWK W4 ...118 B3
PEND EN3 ...36 E1
Southfields E/WMO/HCT KT8 ...189 K1
HDN NW4 ...45 K3
Southfields Ms
WAND/EARL SW18 * ...159 K1

Southfields Rd
WAND/EARL SW18 159 K1
Southfleet Rd ORP BR6 216 E1
South Gdns WBLY HA9 * 62 C6
WIM/MER SW19 178 C3
South Gate Av FELT TW13 153 G6
Southgate Gv IS N1 85 K5
Southgate Rd IS N1 85 K6
South Gipsy Rd WELL DA16 148 E4
South Gv HGT N6 66 A5
SEVS/STOTM N15 67 K2
WALTH E17 69 H2
South Hall Dr RAIN RM13 111 K4
South Hl CHST BR7 184 E2
NTHWD HA6 * 40 C4
South Hill Av RYLN/HDSTN HA2 78 C1
South Hill Gv HRW HA1 78 E2
South Hill Pk HAMP NW3 83 J2
South Hill Park Gdns
HAMP NW3 83 J2
South Hill Rd HAYES BR2 183 H6
Southholme Cl NRWD SE19 181 F4
Southill La PIN HA5 58 E1
Southill Rd CHST BR7 184 D3
Southill St POP/IOD E14 105 K5
South Island Pl BRXN/ST SW9 142 A1
South Kensington Station Ar
SKENS SW7 14 B6
South Lambeth Pl VX/NE SW8 121 K6
South Lambeth Rd VX/NE SW8 121 K6
Southland Rd
WOOL/PLUM SE18 148 A1
Southlands Av ORP BR6 216 E2
Southlands Dr
WIM/MER SW19 159 G4
Southlands Gv BMLY BR1 184 D6
Southlands Rd HAYES BR2 200 C1
Southland Wy HSLW TW3 135 J6
South La KUT/HW KT1 174 E6
NWMAL KT3 192 A1
South La West NWMAL KT3 192 A1
South Lodge Av MTCM CR4 195 K1
South Lodge Crs ENC/FH EN2 22 D5
South Lodge Dr
STHGT/OAK N14 22 E6
South Md CDALE/KGS NW9 45 H4
HOR/WEW KT19 207 H5
Southmead Rd
WIM/MER SW19 159 H3
South Molton La
MYFR/PKLN W1K 9 J4
South Molton Rd
CAN/RD E16 106 E5
South Molton St
MYFR/PKLN W1K 9 J4
Southmont Rd ESH/CLAY KT10 189 K6
Southmoor Wy HOM E9 87 H4
South Mt TRDG/WHET N20 * 33 G4
South Norwood Hl
SNWD SE25 181 F5
South Oak Rd
STRHM/NOR SW16 162 A6
Southold Ri ELTH/MOT SE9 166 E5
Southolm St VX/NE SW8 141 G2
Southover BMLY BR1 183 K1
NFNCH/WDSP N12 32 E6
South Pde CHEL SW3 120 C5
CHSWK W4 118 A4
EDGW HA8 * 44 C5
WLGTN SM6 * 210 C4
South Park Crs CAT SE6 165 H3
IL IG1 90 D1
South Park Dr IL IG1 90 E1
South Park Gv NWMAL KT3 191 K1
South Park Hill Rd
SAND/SEL CR2 211 K3
South Park Ms FUL/PGN SW6 140 A4
South Park Rd IL IG1 90 D1
WIM/MER SW19 177 K2
South Park Ter IL IG1 90 D1
South Park Wy RSLP HA4 77 G4
South Pl BRYLDS KT5 191 G4
LVPST EC2M 13 F2
PEND EN3 24 E6
South Place Ms LVPST EC2M 13 F2
Southport Rd
WOOL/PLUM SE18 127 J4
Southridge Pl RYNPK SW20 177 G3
South Ri BAY/PAD W2 * 8 D5
CAR SM5 209 J6
South Rd CHDH RM6 73 J2
EA W5 116 E4
ED N9 36 C3
EDGW HA8 44 D4
ERITH DA8 130 C6
FELT TW13 172 C1
FSTH SE23 164 A4
NWDGN UB2 114 E2
WDR/YW UB7 112 D3
WHTN TW2 155 J5
WIM/MER SW19 178 C2
South Rw BKHTH/KID SE3 145 K3
Southsea Rd KUT/HW KT1 191 F1
South Sea St
BERM/RHTH SE16 124 C3
South Side HMSMTH W6 118 C3
SEVS/STOTM N15 * 68 B1
Southside Common
WIM/MER SW19 177 G2
Southspring ELTH/MOT SE9 167 J2
South Sq GINN WC1R 11 J2
GLDGN NW11 64 E3
South St BMLY BR1 183 K5
ISLW TW7 136 B4
MYFR/PKLN W1K 9 H7
PEND EN3 25 F6
RAIN RM13 110 E1
ROM RM1 75 G2
South Tenter St WCHPL E1 13 K5
South Ter SKENS SW7 14 C6
SURB KT6 191 F3
WDGN N22 48 E5
South V HRW HA1 78 E2
NRWD SE19 181 F2
Southvale Rd BKHTH/KID SE3 145 H3
South Vale Rd SURB KT6 191 F6
South Vw BMLY BR1 184 B5
Southview Av WLSDN NW10 81 H3
South View Cl BXLY DA5 169 G1
Southview Cl TOOT SW17 179 F1
South View Ct NRWD SE19 * 180 D3
South View Crs
GNTH/NBYPK IG2 72 B3
Southview Dr SWFD E18 53 F6
Southview Gdns WLGTN SM6 210 C5
Southview Rd BMLY BR1 165 G6
South View Rd
CEND/HSY/T N8 48 D6
LOU IG10 39 K1
PIN HA5 41 F2
RDART DA2 171 G5
Southviews SAND/SEL CR2 213 F6
South Vls CAMTN NW1 84 D4
Southville VX/NE SW8 141 J2
Southville Cl
EBED/NFELT TW14 153 H2
HOR/WEW KT19 207 F6
Southville Crs
EBED/NFELT TW14 153 H3
Southville Rd
EBED/NFELT TW14 153 H3
THDIT KT7 190 B4
South Wk WWKM BR4 214 C1
Southwark Br CANST EC4R 12 D6
Southwark Bridge Rd
STHWK SE1 18 B4
Southwark Park Est
BERM/RHTH SE16 * 123 J4
Southwark Park Rd
BERM/RHTH SE16 19 K6
Southwark Pl BMLY BR1 184 E6
Southwark St STHWK SE1 12 B7
Southwater Cl BECK BR3 182 E3
South Wy CROY/NA CR0 213 G1
FBAR/BDGN N11 48 C2
RYLN/HDSTN HA2 60 A1
WBLY HA9 80 C3
Southway GLDGN NW11 65 F3
HAYES BR2 199 K4
RYNPK SW20 193 G1
TRDG/WHET N20 32 E4
WLGTN SM6 210 C2
Southwell Av NTHLT UB5 78 A4
Southwell Gdns SKENS SW7 120 B4
Southwell Grove Rd WAN E11 70 C6
Southwell Rd CMBW SE5 142 D4
CROY/NA CR0 196 B3
KTN/HRWW/W HA3 61 K3
South Western Rd TWK TW1 156 B1
Southwest Rd WAN E11 70 B5
South Wharf Rd BAY/PAD W2 8 A3
Southwick Ms BAY/PAD W2 8 B3
Southwick Pl BAY/PAD W2 8 C4
Southwick St BAY/PAD W2 8 C3
Southwick Yd BAY/PAD W2 * 8 D4
Southwold Dr BARK IG11 91 G3
Southwold Rd BXLY DA5 169 J1
CLPT E5 68 D6
Southwood Av HGT N6 66 B4
KUTN/CMB KT2 175 K4
Southwood Cl BMLY BR1 200 E1
WPK KT4 193 G5
Southwood Dr BRYLDS KT5 191 K4
Southwood Gdns
BARK/HLT IG6 72 B1
ESH/CLAY KT10 205 G1
Southwood La HGT N6 66 A4
Southwood Lawn Rd HGT N6 66 B4
Southwood Pk HGT N6 * 66 B4
Southwood Rd ELTH/MOT SE9 167 G4
THMD SE28 128 C1
South Worple Wy
MORT/ESHN SW14 138 A4
Southy Ms CAN/RD E16 125 K1
Sovereign Cl EA W5 97 J4
RSLP HA4 58 C5
WAP E1W 104 D6
Sovereign Ct E/WMO/HCT KT8 188 E1
Sovereign Crs
BERM/RHTH SE16 105 G6
Sovereign Gv ALP/SUD HA0 79 K1
Sovereign Ms BETH E2 * 7 J2
Sovereign Pk WLSDN NW10 * 98 D3
Sovereign Pl HRW HA1 61 F2
Sovereign Rd BARK IG11 109 J2
Sowerby Cl ELTH/MOT SE9 146 E6
Sowrey Av RAIN RM13 93 H4
Space Waye
EBED/NFELT TW14 133 K6
Spa Cl NRWD SE19 181 F4
Spafield St CLKNW EC1R 5 J6
Spa Green Est CLKNW EC1R * 5 K4
Spa Hl THHTH CR7 180 E4
Spalding Cl EDGW HA8 45 G3
Spalding Rd HDN NW4 64 A3
TOOT SW17 179 G1
Spanby Rd BOW E3 105 J3
Spaniards Cl GLDGN NW11 65 G5
Spaniards End GLDGN NW11 65 G5
Spaniards Rd HAMP NW3 65 G6
Spanish Pl MHST W1U * 9 H3
Spanish Rd WAND/EARL SW18 140 B6
Sparkbridge Rd HRW HA1 60 E1
Sparke Ter CAN/RD E16 * 106 D5
Sparkford Gdns
FBAR/BDGN N11 48 A1
Sparks Cl ACT W3 99 F5
BCTR RM8 73 K6
HAYES BR2 200 A1
HPTN TW12 172 D2
Spa Rd BERM/RHTH SE16 19 J5
Sparrow Cl HPTN TW12 172 D2
Sparrow Dr STMC/STPC BR5 201 H5
Sparrow Farm Dr
EBED/NFELT TW14 154 C2
Sparrow Farm Rd EW KT17 207 J2
Sparrow Gn DAGE RM10 92 D1
Sparrows Herne BUSH WD23 28 B2
Sparrows La ELTH/MOT SE9 167 H3
Sparrows Wy BUSH WD23 * 28 C2
Sparrows Wick BUSH WD23 * 28 C3
Sparsholt Rd ARCH N19 67 F5
BARK IG11 90 E6
Sparta St GNWCH SE10 145 F2
Speakers Ct CROY/NA CR0 * 196 E5
Spearman St
WOOL/PLUM SE18 * 127 F6
Spear Ms ECT SW5 119 K4
Spears Rd ARCH N19 66 E5
Speart La HEST TW5 134 D1
Spectrum Pl WALW SE17 122 E5
Spedan Cl HAMP NW3 83 F1
Speedwell St DEPT SE8 144 D1
Speer Rd THDIT KT7 190 A3
Speirs Cl NWMAL KT3 192 C3
Spekehill ELTH/MOT SE9 166 E5
Speke Rd THHTH CR7 180 E5
Speldhurst Cl HAYES BR2 199 J2
Speldhurst Rd CHSWK W4 118 A3
HOM E9 87 F5
Spellbrook Wk IS N1 * 85 J6
Spelman St WCHPL E1 104 C4
Spence Cl BERM/RHTH SE16 124 C2
Spencer Av PLMGR N13 49 F2
YEAD UB4 94 E4
Spencer Cl FNCH N3 46 D5
ORP BR6 201 K6
WFD IG8 53 G1
WLSDN NW10 98 B2
Spencer Dr EFNCH N2 65 G3
Spencer Gdns
MORT/ESHN SW14 137 K6
Spencer Hl WIM/MER SW19 177 H2
Spencer Hill Rd
WIM/MER SW19 177 H3
Spencer House SURB KT6 * 191 F2
Spencer Ms HMSMTH W6 119 H6
Spencer Pk WAND/EARL SW18 140 C6
Spencer Pl CROY/NA CR0 196 E4
IS N1 85 H5
WEST SW1P 16 B5
Spencer Ri KTTN NW5 84 B2
Spencer Rd ACT W3 117 K1
ALP/SUD HA0 61 J6
BMLY BR1 183 J3
BTSEA SW11 140 C5
CEND/HSY/T N8 67 F2
CHSWK W4 137 K1
E/WMO/HCT KT8 189 H1
EHAM E6 89 H6
FBAR/BDGN N11 34 B6
GDMY/SEVK IG3 73 F5
ISLW TW7 135 J2
KTN/HRWW/W HA3 42 E5
MTCM CR4 194 E4
RAIN RM13 111 F2
RYNPK SW20 176 E4
SAND/SEL CR2 212 A3
TOTM N17 50 C4
WALTH E17 52 A5
WHTN TW2 155 K5
Spencer St FSBYE EC1V 6 A5
NWDGN UB2 114 C3
Spencer Wk PUT/ROE SW15 139 G5
Spenser Gv STNW/STAM N16 86 A2
Spenser Ms DUL SE21 162 E3
Spenser Rd HNHL SE24 142 C6
Spenser St WEST SW1E 16 B4
Spensley Wk STNW/STAM N16 85 K1
Speranza St
WOOL/PLUM SE18 128 A5
Sperling Rd TOTM N17 50 B5
Spert St POP/IOD E14 105 G6
Speyside STHGT/OAK N14 34 C1
Spey St POP/IOD E14 106 A4
Spey Wy ROM RM1 57 G3
Spezia Rd WLSDN NW10 99 J1
Spicer Cl CMBW SE5 142 C3
WOT/HER KT12 188 B3
Spices Yd CROY/NA CR0 211 J2
Spielman Rd DART DA1 151 J5
Spigurnell Rd TOTM N17 49 K4
Spikes Bridge Rd STHL UB1 95 J5
Spilsby Cl CDALE/KGS NW9 45 G5
Spindle Cl WOOL/PLUM SE18 126 D3
Spindlewood Gdns
CROY/NA CR0 211 K2
Spindrift Av POP/IOD E14 124 E4
Spinel Cl WOOL/PLUM SE18 128 A5
Spinnaker Cl BARK IG11 109 H2
Spinnells Rd RYLN/HDSTN HA2 59 K5
Spinney Cl BECK BR3 198 E1
NWMAL KT3 192 B2
RAIN RM13 111 G1
WPK KT4 207 H1
Spinney Dr EBED/NFELT TW14 153 F2
Spinney Gdns DAGW RM9 92 A3
NRWD SE19 181 G1
Spinney Oak BMLY BR1 184 D5
The Spinneys BMLY BR1 184 E5
The Spinney ALP/SUD HA0 79 G1
BARN SW13 * 118 E6
CHEAM SM3 208 A2
NFNCH/WDSP N12 * 47 G3
SCUP DA14 187 F1
STAN HA7 30 A6
STRHM/NOR SW16 161 H5
WCHMH N21 35 G2
The Spires DART DA1 171 G4
Spirit Quay WAP E1W 123 H1
Spital Sq WCHPL E1 13 H1
Spital St DART DA1 171 G1
WCHPL E1 104 C4
Spital Yd WCHPL E1 * 13 H1
Spitfire Est HEST TW5 * 114 B5
Spitfire Wy HEST TW5 114 B5
Spode Wk KIL/WHAMP NW6 * 83 F3
Spondon Rd SEVS/STOTM N15 68 C1
Spoonbill Wy YEAD UB4 95 H4
Spooner Wk WLGTN SM6 210 D3
Sportsbank St CAT SE6 165 F2
Spottons Gv TOTM N17 49 J4
Spout Hl CROY/NA CR0 213 J3
Spratt Hall Rd WAN E11 70 E3
Spray St WOOL/PLUM SE18 127 G4
Spreighton Rd
E/WMO/HCT KT8 189 G1
Sprimont Pl CHEL SW3 120 E5
Springall St PECK SE15 143 J1
Springbank WCHMH N21 35 F1
Springbank Rd LEW SE13 165 H1
Springbank Wk CAMTN NW1 84 D5
Springbourne Ct BECK BR3 183 F4
Spring Bridge Rd EA W5 97 K6
Spring Cl BAR EN5 20 B6
BCTR RM8 73 K5
Springclose La CHEAM SM3 208 C4
Spring Cnr FELT TW13 * 153 K5
Spring Court Rd ENC/FH EN2 23 G1
Springcroft Av EFNCH N2 47 K6
Springdale Rd STNW/STAM N16 85 K2
Spring Dr PIN HA5 58 E3
Springfield BUSH WD23 28 D3
CLPT E5 68 D5
Springfield Av HPTN TW12 173 G2
MUSWH N10 48 C6
RYNPK SW20 177 J6
Springfield Cl
NFNCH/WDSP N12 47 F1
STAN HA7 29 G5
Springfield Dr GNTH/NBYPK IG2 72 C2
Springfield Gdns BMLY BR1 200 E1
CDALE/KGS NW9 63 F2
CLPT E5 68 D5
RSLP HA4 59 F5
WFD IG8 53 G3
WWKM BR4 198 E6
Springfield Gv CHARL SE7 126 B6
Springfield La KIL/WHAMP NW6 82 E6
Springfield Mt CDALE/KGS NW9 63 G2
Springfield Pl NWMAL KT3 191 K1
Springfield Ri SYD SE26 163 J6
Springfield Rd BMLY BR1 200 E1
BXLYHN DA7 149 J4
CHING E4 38 C3
EHAM E6 89 K5
FBAR/BDGN N11 48 C1
HNWL W7 115 K1
HRW HA1 60 E3
HYS/HAR UB3 114 B1
KUT/HW KT1 191 F1
SEVS/STOTM N15 68 C1
SRTFD E15 * 106 C2
STJWD NW8 83 G6
SYD SE26 181 J1
TEDD TW11 174 B1
THHTH CR7 180 D4
WALTH E17 69 H3
WELL DA16 148 C4
WHTN TW2 155 F3
WIM/MER SW19 177 J1
WLGTN SM6 210 B3
Springfield Wk
KIL/WHAMP NW6 83 F6
Springfield Wy
STMC/STPC BR5 186 D6
Spring Gdns E/WMO/HCT KT8 189 H2
HBRY N5 85 J3
HCH RM12 93 K2
ORP BR6 217 H4
ROMW/RG RM7 74 E2
WFD IG8 53 G3
WHALL SW1A 10 E7
WLGTN SM6 210 C3
Spring Gv CHSWK W4 117 H5
HPTN TW12 173 G4
LOU IG10 39 H1
MTCM CR4 179 F4
Spring Grove Crs HEST TW5 135 H2
Spring Grove Rd HSLW TW3 135 H2
RCHPK/HAM TW10 137 G6
Springhead Rd ERITH DA8 130 C6
Spring Hl CLPT E5 68 C4
SYD SE26 163 K6
Springhurst Cl CROY/NA CR0 213 H2
Spring Lake STAN HA7 29 H6
Spring La CLPT E5 68 D5
MUSWH N10 48 A6
SNWD SE25 197 J3
Spring Ms MHST W1U * 9 F1
Spring Park Av CROY/NA CR0 198 A6
Springpark Dr BECK BR3 183 F6
FSBYPK N4 67 J5
Spring Park Rd CROY/NA CR0 198 A6
Spring Pl FNCH N3 46 E5
KTTN NW5 84 A3
Springpond Rd DAGW RM9 92 A3
Springrice Rd LEW SE13 165 F1
Spring Rd FELT TW13 153 J5
Spring Shaw Rd
STMC/STPC BR5 186 B4
Spring St BAY/PAD W2 8 A4
EW KT17 207 H6
Spring Tide Cl PECK SE15 * 143 H2
Spring V BXLYHN DA7 149 J5
Springvale Av BTFD TW8 116 E5
Spring V North DART DA1 171 G2
Spring V South DART DA1 * 171 G2
Springvale Ter WKENS W14 119 G3
Spring Villa Rd EDGW HA8 44 C3
Spring Vls WEA W13 * 116 C1
Spring Wk WCHPL E1 104 C4
Springwater Cl
WOOL/PLUM SE18 * 147 F2
Springwell Av WLSDN NW10 81 H6
Springwell Rd HEST TW5 134 C2
STRHM/NOR SW16 162 B6
Springwood Crs EDGW HA8 30 E4
Springwood Wy ROM RM1 75 J2
Sprowston Ms FSTGT E7 88 E4
Sprowston Rd FSTGT E7 88 E3
Sprucedale Gdns
CROY/NA CR0 213 F2
PUR/KEN CR8 210 E6
Spruce Hills Rd WALTH E17 51 K5
Sprules Rd BROCKY SE4 144 B3
Spurfield E/WMO/HCT KT8 173 G6
Spurgeon Av NRWD SE19 180 E4
Spurgeon Rd NRWD SE19 180 E3
Spurgeon St STHWK SE1 18 E5
Spurling Rd DAGW RM9 92 B4
EDUL SE22 * 143 G5
Spurrell Av RDART DA2 170 A6
Spur Rd BARK IG11 108 C2
EBED/NFELT TW14 134 A6
EDGW HA8 30 A6
ISLW TW7 136 B1
ORP BR6 202 B6
SEVS/STOTM N15 * 67 K1
STHWK SE1 17 J2
WHALL SW1A 16 A3
Spurstowe Rd HACK E8 86 D4
Spurstowe Ter HACK E8 86 C3
The Square CAR SM5 210 A3
HMSMTH W6 119 F5
IL IG1 72 A4
RCHPK/HAM TW10 137 F6
STKPK UB11 113 G1
WFD IG8 52 E1
Squarey St TOOT SW17 160 B5
Squire Gdns STJWD NW8 2 A5
Squires Ct WIM/MER SW19 159 K6
Squires La FNCH N3 47 G4
Squire's Mt HAMP NW3 83 H1
Squires Wy RDART DA2 170 A6
Squires Wood Dr CHST BR7 * 184 E3
Squirrel Cl HSLWW TW4 134 B4
Squirrel Ms HNWL W7 * 97 G6
Squirrels Cl NFNCH/WDSP N12 33 G6
Squirrels Gn WPK KT4 192 C6
Squirrel's Heath Av GPK RM2 57 K6
The Squirrels BUSH WD23 28 D1
LEW SE13 145 G4
PIN HA5 41 K6
Squirries St BETH E2 104 C2
Stable Cl KUTN/CMB KT2 175 G2
NTHLT UB5 96 A1
Stable Ms WNWD SE27 180 D1
Stables End ORP BR6 216 C1
Stables Wy LBTH SE11 122 B5
Stable Wk EFNCH N2 * 47 H4
IS N1 5 F2
Stable Wy NKENS W10 100 A5
Stable Yard Rd WHALL SW1A 16 B2
Stacey Av UED N18 36 E6
Stacey Cl LEY E10 70 B2
Stacey St HOLWY N7 85 G1
LSQ/SEVD WC2H 10 D4
Stackhouse St KTBR SW1X 14 E4
Stacy Pth CMBW SE5 * 143 F1
Staddon Cl BECK BR3 198 B1
Staddon Ct BECK BR3 198 B1
Stadium Rd WOOL/PLUM SE18 146 E1
Stadium St WBPTN SW10 140 B1
Stadium Wy DART DA1 170 B1
WBLY HA9 80 B2
Staffa Rd LEY E10 69 G5
Stafford Cl CHEAM SM3 208 C4
KIL/WHAMP NW6 100 E2
STHGT/OAK N14 22 C6
WALTH E17 69 H3
Stafford Gdns CROY/NA CR0 211 F3
Stafford Pl RCHPK/HAM TW10 157 G2
WESTW SW1E 16 A4
Stafford Rd BOW E3 105 H1
CROY/NA CR0 211 G2
FSTGT E7 89 G5
KIL/WHAMP NW6 100 E2
KTN/HRWW/W HA3 42 C3
NWMAL KT3 175 K6
RSLP HA4 76 D2
SCUP DA14 167 K6
WLGTN SM6 210 C4
Staffordshire St PECK SE15 143 H2
Stafford St MYFR/PICC W1J 10 A7
Stafford Ter KENS W8 119 K3
Stag Cl EDGW HA8 44 D5
Staggart Gn BARK/HLT IG6 55 F1
Stag La BKHH IG9 39 F4
CDALE/KGS NW9 44 E6
PUT/ROE SW15 158 C5
Stag Pl WESTW SW1E 16 A4
Stags Wy ISLW TW7 116 A6
Stainbank Rd MTCM CR4 179 G6
Stainby Cl WDR/YW UB7 112 B3
Stainby Rd TOTM N17 50 B6
Stainer St STHWK SE1 19 F1
Staines Av CHEAM SM3 193 G6
Staines Rd EBED/NFELT TW14 153 G2
HSLWW TW4 134 C6
IL IG1 90 D2
WHTN TW2 155 H5
Staines Rd East SUN TW16 172 B5
Stainforth Rd GNTH/NBYPK IG2 72 D4
WALTH E17 69 J1
Staining La CITYW EC2V 12 D3
Stainmore Cl CHST BR7 185 J4
Stainsbury St BETH E2 104 E1
Stainsby Pl POP/IOD E14 * 105 J5
Stainsby Rd POP/IOD E14 105 J5
Stainton Rd LEW SE13 165 G2
PEND EN3 24 E2
Stalbridge St CAMTN NW1 8 D1
Stalham St BERM/RHTH SE16 123 J3
Stalham Wy WFD IG8 54 B4
Stambourne Wy NRWD SE19 181 F3
WWKM BR4 214 A1
Stamford Brook Av
HMSMTH W6 118 C3
Stamford Brook Gdns
HMSMTH W6 118 C3
Stamford Brook Rd
HMSMTH W6 118 C3
Stamford Cl
KTN/HRWW/W HA3 42 E3
SEVS/STOTM N15 68 C1
STHL UB1 96 A6
Stamford Dr HAYES BR2 199 J1
Stamford Gdns DAGW RM9 91 J5
Stamford Gv East
STNW/STAM N16 68 C5
Stamford Gv West
STNW/STAM N16 68 C5
Stamford Hl STNW/STAM N16 68 B5
Stamford Rd DAGW RM9 91 H5

EHAM E6.................................89 J6
IS N1....................................86 A5
SEVS/STOTM N15........................68 C2
Stamford St STHWK SE1..............11 J7
Stamp PI BETH E2.......................7 J3
Stanborough HACK E8..................86 B4
Stanborough CI HPTN TW12...........172 E2
Stanborough Rd HSLW TW3...........135 J4
Stanbridge PI WCHMH N21............35 H4
Stanbridge Rd PUT/ROE SW15.......139 F4
Stanbrook Rd ABYW SE2..............128 C2
Stanbury Ct HAMP NW3.................83 K4
Stanbury Rd PECK SE15...............143 J2
Stancroft CDALE/KGS NW9.............45 G3
Standale Gv RSLP HA4..................58 A2
Standard PI SDTCH EC2A...............7 H5
Standard Rd BELV DA17..............129 H5
BXLYHS DA6............................149 F5
HSLWW TW4............................134 D4
PEND EN3................................25 G1
WLSDN NW10.............................98 E3
Standen Rd WAND/EARL SW18......159 K2
Standfield Rd DAGE RM10.............92 C3
Standish Rd HMSMTH W6............118 D4
Stane CI WIM/MER SW19..............178 A3
Stanfield Rd BOW E3...................105 G1
Stanford CI HPTN TW12...............172 E2
ROMW/RG RM7..........................74 D3
RSLP HA4................................58 A3
WFD IG8..................................53 J1
Stanford PI STHWK SE1................19 G7
Stanford Rd FBAR/BDGN N11..........47 K1
KENS W8.................................120 A3
STRHM/NOR SW16.....................179 K5
Stanford St WEST SW1P..............16 C7
Stanford Wy
STRHM/NOR SW16.....................179 J5
Stangate Gdns STAN HA7...............29 H6
Stanger Rd SNWD SE25...............197 H1
Stanham PI DART DA1.................150 D5
Stanham Rd DART DA1.................151 F6
Stanhope Av FNCH N3..................46 D6
HAYES BR2...............................199 K5
KTN/HRWW/W HA3......................42 D4
Stanhope CI
BERM/RHTH SE16 *.....................124 A2
Stanhope Gdns FSBYPK N4............67 H5
HGT N6....................................66 B3
IL IG1......................................71 K5
MLHL NW7...............................45 H1
SKENS SW7..............................120 B4
Stanhope Ga BECK BR3...............15 H1
MYFR/PKLN W1K.........................15 H1
Stanhope Gv BECK BR3...............198 C2
Stanhope Ms East SKENS SW7.......120 B4
Stanhope Ms South
SKENS SW7..............................120 B4
Stanhope Ms West
SKENS SW7..............................120 B4
Stanhope Pde CAMTN NW1.............3 K4
Stanhope Park Rd
GFD/PVL UB6.............................96 C3
Stanhope PI BAY/PAD W2...............8 E4
Stanhope Rd BAR EN5..................32 B1
BCTR RM8................................74 B6
BFN/LL DA15.............................168 B6
BXLYHN DA7............................149 F5
CAR SM5.................................210 A4
CROY/NA CRO...........................212 A1
GFD/PVL UB6.............................96 C4
HGT N6....................................66 C3
NFNCH/WDSP N12.......................47 G1
RAIN RM13...............................111 J1
Stanhope Rw MYFR/PICC W1J........15 J1
Stanhope St CAMTN NW1...............4 A4
Stanhope Ter BAY/PAD W2..............8 B5
TWK TW1.................................156 C2
Stanier CI WKENS W14................119 J5
Stanlake Rd SHB W12.................119 F1
Stanlake Vis SHB W12.................119 F1
Stanley Av ALP/SUD HA0...............80 A5
BARK IG11...............................109 7 2
BCTR RM8................................74 B5
BECK BR3................................183 F6
GFD/PVL UB6.............................78 C6
GPK RM2...................................75 J1
NWMAL KT3..............................192 D2
Stanley CI ALP/SUD HA0................80 A5
GPK RM2...................................75 J1
Stanley Crs NTGHL W11...............100 D6
Stanleycroft CI ISLW TW7.............135 K2
Stanley Gdns ACT W3.................118 B2
CRICK NW2...............................82 A3
MTCM CR4 *..............................179 F7
NTGHL W11.............................100 D6
WLGTN SM6.............................210 C4
Stanley Gardens Rd
TEDD TW11...............................173 K1
Stanley Gv THHTH CR7...............196 B3
VX/NE SW8..............................141 F3
Stanley Park Dr ALP/SUD HA0.........80 B5
Stanley Park Rd CAR SM5............209 K5
WLGTN SM6.............................210 B5
Stanley Pas CAMTN NW1................4 E3
Stanley Rd ACT W3.....................117 J5
BELMT SM2..............................209 F4
CAR SM5.................................210 A5
CHING E4..................................38 B3
CROY/NA CRO...........................196 B4
EN EN1.....................................36 B5
EFNCH N2.................................65 H1
EN EN1.....................................24 A4
HAYES BR2..............................184 D6
HSLW TW3...............................135 H5
IL IG1......................................72 D6
MRPK E12.................................89 J3
MORT/ESHN SW14.....................137 J5
MRDN SM4...............................193 K1
MTCM CR4...............................179 F3
MUSWH N10...............................48 B4
NTHWD HA6...............................40 E4
ORP BR6..................................202 A5
RYLN/HDSTN HA2.......................60 C6

SCUP DA14...............................168 B5
SEVS/STOTM N15.......................67 H1
SRTFD E15.................................88 B6
STHL UB1.................................95 J6
SWFD E18.................................52 D4
TEDD TW11...............................173 K1
WALTH E17...............................69 K3
WBLY HA9.................................80 B4
WHTN TW2...............................155 J5
WIM/MER SW19.........................177 K3
Stanley Rd North RAIN RM13.........93 G6
Stanley Rd South RAIN RM13.......111 H1
Stanley Sq CAR SM5...................209 K6
Stanley St DEPT SE8..................144 C1
Stanley Ter ARCH N19 *................66 E6
BXLYHS DA6 *............................149 H5
Stanley Wy STMC/STPC BR5........202 C2
Stanmer St BTSEA SW11.............140 D2
Stanmore Gdns
RCH/KEW TW9...........................137 G4
SUT SM1.................................209 G1
Stanmore HI STAN HA7................29 H6
Stanmore Rd BELV DA17..............129 K4
RCH/KEW TW9...........................137 G4
SEVS/STOTM N15.......................67 H1
WAN E11....................................70 D5
Stanmore St IS N1........................5 F3
Stanmore Ter BECK BR3...............182 D5
Stannard Ms HACK E8 *................86 C4
Stannard Rd HACK E8..................86 C4
Stannary PI LBTH SE11...............122 B5
Stannary St LBTH SE11...............122 B6
Stannet Wy WLGTN SM6..............210 C2
Stansbury Sq NKENS W10.............100 C2
Stansfeld Rd CAN/RD E16...........107 H5
Stansfield Rd BRXN/ST SW9.........142 A4
HSLWW TW4............................134 A3
Stansgate Rd DAGE RM10.............74 C6
Stanstead CI HAYES BR2.............199 J2
Stanstead Gv CAT SE6.................164 C3
Stanstead Rd FSTH SE23...............164 B3
WAN E11....................................71 F2
Stansted CI RAIN RM12.................93 K4
Stansted Crs BXLY DA5...............168 E5
Stansted Rd HTHAIR TW6.............132 C5
Stanswood Gdns CMBW SE5.........143 F1
Stanthorpe CI
STRHM/NOR SW16 *...................179 K1
Stanthorpe Rd
STRHM/NOR SW16 *...................179 K1
Stanton Av TEDD TW11...............173 K2
Stanton CI HOR/WEW KT19...........206 D3
STMC/STPC BR5........................202 D4
WPK KT4.................................193 G5
Stanton Rd BARN SW13...............138 C3
CROY/NA CRO...........................196 D4
RYNPK SW20.............................177 G5
Stanton St PECK SE15 *..............143 H2
Stanton Wy SYD SE26.................164 C6
Stanway CI CHIG IG7.....................54 E1
Stanway Gdns ACT W3................117 H1
EDGW HA8................................44 E2
Stanway St IS N1..........................7 H2
Stanwell Cl STWL/WRAY TW19.....152 A1
Stanwell Gdns
STWL/WRAY TW19.....................152 A1
Stanwell Rd ASHF TW15..............152 B6
EBED/NFELT TW14......................152 E2
Stanwick Rd WKENS W14.............119 J4
Stanworth St STHWK SE1.............19 J3
Stanwyck Gdns HARH RM3............57 K1
Stapenhill Rd ALP/SUD HA0...........79 H1
Staple CI BXLY DA5....................170 A5
Staplefield CI
BRXS/STRHM SW2 *...................161 K3
PIN HA5...................................41 J3
Stapleford Av GNTH/NBYPK IG2......72 E2
Stapleford CI CHING E4.................38 A5
KUT/HW KT1.............................175 H5
WIM/MER SW19.........................159 H2
Stapleford Gdns CRW RM5............56 C2
Stapleford Rd ALP/SUD HA0...........79 K5
Stapleford Wy BARK IG11............109 H2
Staplehurst Rd CAR SM5.............209 J5
LEW SE13................................145 G6
Staple Inn HHOL WC1V.................11 J2
Staple St STBERM/RHTH SE16......124 B1
Stapleton Crs RAIN RM13..............93 J4
Stapleton Gdns CROY/NA CRO......211 G3
Stapleton Hall Rd FSBYPK N4........67 F4
Stapleton Rd BXLYHN DA7...........149 G1
ORP BR6.................................217 F1
TOOT SW17..............................161 F5
Stapleton Vls
STNW/STAM N16 *......................86 A2
Stapley Rd BELV DA17................129 H5
Staplyton Rd BAR EN5..................20 C4
Starbeck CI ELTH/MOT SE9..........167 F2
Starboard Wy POP/IOD E14.........124 D3
Starch House La BARK/HLT IG6.......54 D5
Starcross St CAMTN NW1...............4 B5
Starfield Rd SHB W12.................118 D2
Star & Garter HI
RCHPK/HAM TW10.....................157 F3
Star HI DART DA1.......................150 E6
Star La CAN/RD E16...................106 C3
STMC/STPC BR5........................202 E1
Starling CI BKHH IG9....................38 E3
PIN HA5...................................41 G6
Starling Rd CROY/NA CRO...........198 B3
Starmans CI DAGW RM9................92 A6
Star Rd HGDN/ICK UB10................94 A3
ISLW TW7................................135 J3
WKENS W14.............................119 J6
Star St BAY/PAD W2......................8 B3
Starts CI ORP BR6......................216 A1
Starts Hill Av ORP BR6...............216 B3
Starts Hill Rd ORP BR6...............216 B1
Starveall CI WDR/YW UB7.............112 E3
Star Yd LINN WC2A......................11 J3
State Farm Av ORP BR6...............216 A2
Staten Gdns TWK TW1................156 A3
Statham Gv STNW/STAM N16.........85 K1
UED N18...................................50 A1

Station Ap ALP/SUD HA0................79 H4
BAR EN5..................................21 G5
BECK BR3................................182 D4
BELMT SM2..............................208 C5
BKHH IG9 *................................39 H6
BKHTH/KID SE3.........................146 A4
BXLYHN DA7............................149 F5
BXLYHN DA7............................149 K5
CAMTN NW1 *.............................4 B3
CAT SE6..................................182 C1
CHING E4..................................38 C2
CHING E4..................................52 B2
CHST BR7................................184 D2
CHST BR7................................185 F4
CROY/NA CRO *.........................196 E6
DART DA1................................171 H1
ESH/CLAY KT10.........................205 F1
FBAR/BDGN N11.........................48 B1
FSTGT E7 *................................89 F2
FUL/PGN SW6 *.........................139 H4
GFD/PVL UB6............................78 C5
GLDGN NW11 *...........................64 B4
HAYES BR2..............................199 K5
HOR/WEW KT19........................207 H3
HPTN TW12..............................173 F4
HYS/HAR UB3............................113 J3
KUT/HW KT1.............................175 H5
NTHWD HA6.............................40 C5
ORP BR6.................................202 A6
ORP BR6.................................217 H5
OXHEY WD19.............................27 H5
PIN HA5...................................41 J6
RCH/KEW TW9..........................137 H2
RSLP HA4................................58 E5
RSLP HA4................................77 F3
SAND/SEL CR2...........................211 K6
STMC/STPC BR5........................202 C1
STRHM/NOR SW16......................179 J1
SWFD E18 *...............................53 F5
WALTH E17................................69 J2
WAN E11....................................70 E2
WAN E11 *.................................88 C2
WDR/YW UB7.............................112 B1
WELL DA16..............................148 B3
WFD IG8 *..................................53 G2
WLSDN NW10.............................99 H2
Station Approach Rd
CHSWK W4...............................137 K1
Station Ar CTPST W1W *................3 K7
Station Av HOR/WEW KT19...........207 G6
NWMAL KT3.............................176 B6
Station Buildings HAYES BR2 *.....199 K5
Station Chambers EA W5 *............98 C5
Station Crs ALP/SUD HA0..............79 H4
ASHF TW15..............................152 A6
BKHTH/KID SE3.........................125 K5
SEVS/STOTM N15.......................67 K1
Stationers Hall Ct STP EC4M *.......12 B4
Station Est BECK BR3..................198 A1
Station Estate Rd
EBED/NFELT TW14......................154 A3
Station Garage Ms
STRHM/NOR SW16 *...................179 J2
Station Gdns CHSWK W4..............137 K1
Station Gv ALP/SUD HA0................80 A4
Station HI HAYES BR2..................199 K6
Station House Ms ED N9...............36 C6
Station Pde ACT W3 *...................98 C5
BAL SW12 *...............................61 G5
BARK IG11................................90 C5
BECK BR3 *..............................198 A1
BELMT SM2..............................209 G4
BMLY BR1 *..............................183 K4
BXLYHN DA7 *...........................149 F5
CHSWK W4 *............................117 K4
CLPT E5 *..................................68 D3
CRICK NW2...............................82 A4
CHSWK W4 *............................118 A3
EA W5 *...................................117 G1
EBAR EN4 *................................22 A5
EBED/NFELT TW14 *...................154 A2
EHAM E6 *.................................89 K7
EHAM E6 *.................................89 J5
FNCH N3 *.................................46 E4
HCH RM12.................................93 K2
KTN/HRWW/W HA3 *....................43 H5
NTHLT UB5 *.............................78 A5
NTHLT UB5 *.............................78 B3
RCH/KEW TW9 *.........................137 H2
ROM RM1 *................................75 G3
RSLP HA4 *................................58 A6
STHGT/OAK N14..........................34 D3
Station Pas PECK SE15................143 K2
SWFD E18.................................53 F5
Station PI FSBYPK N4....................67 G6
Station Ri WNWD SE27 *..............162 C4
Station Rd ASHF TW15................152 C6
BAR EN5..................................21 F6
BARK/HLT IG6...........................54 D6
BARN SW13.............................138 D4
BCTR RM8................................73 K6
BELV DA17...............................129 H3
BFN/LL DA15.............................168 B4
BMLY BR1................................183 K4
BXLYHN DA7............................149 F4
CAR SM5.................................209 K2
CHING E4..................................51 K6
CHSGTN KT9.............................206 A3
CROY/NA CRO...........................196 D5
DART DA1................................170 C1
EA W5.....................................98 B5
EDGW HA8................................44 C2
ESH/CLAY KT10.........................189 J6
FBAR/BDGN N11........................48 B1
FNCH N3 *.................................46 E4
GPK RM2...................................75 K1
HAYES BR2..............................183 H5
HNWL W7................................115 K1
HOLWY N7 *..............................84 C1
HPTN TW12..............................173 G4
HRW HA1..................................61 F1
HYS/HAR UB3...........................113 J2
HYS/HAR UB3...........................113 J5

IL IG1..90 B1
KUT/HW KT1.............................174 E4
KUTN/CMB KT2.........................174 D2
LEW SE13................................145 F4
MLHL NW7.................................45 G2
MNPK E12................................89 H2
NRWD SE19..............................181 H2
NWMAL KT3.............................192 E2
ORP BR6.................................202 A6
RYLN/HDSTN HA2.......................60 B2
SCUP DA14...............................168 B5
SNWD SE25..............................197 G1
STMC/STPC BR5........................202 D1
TEDD TW11...............................174 B2
THDIT KT7................................190 A4
TOTM N17.................................50 C6
TWK TW1.................................156 A3
WALTH E17................................69 G3
WCHMH N21...............................35 H5
WDGN N22................................48 E5
WIM/MER SW19.........................178 B4
WLSDN NW10.............................99 H1
WWKM BR4..............................199 F5
Station Rd North BELV DA17.........129 J3
Station Sq STMC/STPC BR5.........201 H2
Station St SRTFD E15....................88 B5
Station Ter CMBW SE5................142 D2
WLSDN NW10.............................100 D1
Station Vw GFD/PVL UB6..............78 D6
Station Wy BKHH IG9....................39 H6
CHEAM SM3.............................208 C4
Station Yd ASHF TW15 *..............152 C6
RSLP HA4 *................................77 F1
STHL UB1 *..............................114 E2
TWK TW1.................................156 B2
Staunton Rd KUTN/CMB KT2.........175 C3
Staunton St DEPT SE8.................124 C6
Staveley CI HOLWY N7 *................84 E2
PECK SE15 *..............................143 J2
Staveley Gdns CHSWK W4...........138 A2
Staveley Rd CHSWK W4..............117 K6
Staverton Rd CRICK NW2..............82 A5
Stave Yard Rd
BERM/RHTH SE16......................124 B1
Stavordale Rd CAR SM5..............194 B4
HBRY N5...................................85 G2
Stayner's Rd WCHPL E1..............105 F3
Stayton Rd SUT SM1..................208 E1
Steadfast Rd KUT/HW KT1...........174 E4
Stead St WALW SE17....................18 E7
Steam Farm La
EBED/NFELT TW14......................133 J5
Stean St HACK E8........................86 B6
Stebbing Wy BARK IG11..............109 G1
Stebondale St POP/IOD E14.........125 F5
Stedly SCUP DA14 *....................168 B6
Stedman CI BXLY DA5................170 B5
Steed CI EMPK RM11....................75 K5
Steedman St WALW SE17.............18 C7
Steeds Rd MUSWH N10................47 K4
Steeds Wy LOU IG10....................39 J1
Steel Ap BARK IG11.....................109 H1
Steele Rd CHSWK W4..................117 K3
ISLW TW7................................136 B5
TOTM N17.................................49 J2
WAN E11....................................88 C2
WLSDN NW10.............................98 E1
Steele's Ms North HAMP NW3 *.......83 K4
Steele's Ms South HAMP NW3........83 K4
Steele's Rd HAMP NW3.................83 K4
Steel's La WCHPL E1..................104 E5
Steelyard Pas CANST EC4R *.........12 E6
Steep CI ORP BR6.......................217 F4
Steep HI CROY/NA CRO................212 A2
STRHM/NOR SW16......................161 J5
Steeplands BUSH WD23................28 B2
Steeple CI FUL/PGN SW6.............139 H4
WIM/MER SW19.........................159 H6
Steeplestone CI UED N18..............49 J1
Steeple Wk IS N1 *......................85 J6
Steerforth St
WAND/EARL SW18.....................160 A4
Steering CI ED N9..........................36 E4
Steers Md MTCM CR4..................178 E4
Steers Wy BERM/RHTH SE16........124 B2
Stella Rd TOOT SW17..................178 E2
Stelling Rd ERITH DA8.................150 A1
Stellman CI CLPT E5.....................86 C1
Stembridge Rd PGE/AN SE20........181 J3
Stephan CI HACK E8.....................86 C6
Stephen Av RAIN RM13.................93 J4
Stephen CI ORP BR6...................217 F1
Stephendale Rd FUL/PGN SW6......140 A4
Stephen Ms FITZ W1T...................10 C2
Stephen Rd BXLYHN DA7.............149 K4
Stephenson Rd HNWL W7..............97 F5
WALTH E17 *..............................69 G2
WHTN TW2...............................155 F2
Stephenson St CAN/RD E16..........106 C4
WLSDN NW10.............................99 G2
Stephenson Wy CAMTN NW1...........4 B6
Stephen's Rd SRTFD E15..............88 C6
Stephen St FITZ W1T....................10 C3
Stepney Cswy WCHPL E1.............105 F5
Stepney Gn WCHPL E1................104 E4
Stepney High St WCHPL E1...........105 F4
Stepney Wy WCHPL E1................104 E4
Sterling Av EDGW HA8..................30 C6
Sterling CI WLSDN NW10...............81 J5
Sterling Gdns NWCR SE14...........124 B6
Sterling PI BTFD TW8..................117 F4
Sterling Rd ENC/FH EN2................23 K2
Sterling Wy (North Circular)
UED N18...................................49 K1
Stern CI BARK IG11....................109 J1
Sterndale Rd DART DA1................171 J2
WKENS W14.............................119 G3
Sterne St SHB W12....................119 G2
Sternhall La PECK SE15...............143 H4
Sternhold Av
BRXS/STRHM SW2......................161 K4
Sterry Crs DAGE RM10..................92 C3
Sterry Dr HOR/WEW KT19............207 G2

THDIT KT7................................189 K3
Sterry Gdns DAGE RM10...............92 C4
Sterry Rd BARK IG11...................91 F6
DAGE RM10..............................92 B2
Sterry St STHWK SE1....................18 E3
Steucers La FSTH SE23...............164 B3
Steve Biko La CAT SE6...............164 E6
Steve Biko Rd HOLWY N7..............85 G1
Steve Biko Wy HSLW TW3...........135 F4
Stevedale Rd WELL DA16.............148 D3
Stevedore St WAP E1W...............123 J1
Stevenage Rd EHAM E6.................90 A2
FUL/PGN SW6..........................139 G2
Stevens Av HOM E9......................86 E4
Stevens CI BECK BR3..................182 D2
BXLY DA5................................170 A6
HPTN TW12..............................172 E2
PIN HA5...................................59 G2
Stevens Gn BUSH WD23................28 C3
Stevens' La ESH/CLAY KT10.........205 G5
Stevens CI BAR EN5......................33 H1
Stevenson Cr
BERM/RHTH SE16......................123 H5
Stevens Rd BCTR RM8..................73 H6
Stevens St STHWK SE1................19 H4
Steventon Rd SHB W12................99 H6
Steward St WCHPL E1..................13 H1
Stewart CI CDALE/KGS NW9 *.......62 E5
CHST BR7................................185 G1
HPTN TW12..............................172 D2
Stewart Rd WAN E11.....................88 B2
Stewartsby CI UED N18.................49 J1
Stewart's Gv CHEL SW3...............120 C5
Stewart's La VX/NE SW8..............141 G1
Stewart's Rd VX/NE SW8..............141 H2
Stewart St POP/IOD E14...............125 F2
Stew La BLKFR EC4V.....................12 C5
Steyne Rd ACT W3......................117 K1
Steyning Gv ELTH/MOT SE9..........166 E5
Steynings Wy
NFNCH/WDSP N12.......................46 E1
Steyning Wy HSLWW TW4............134 B5
Steynton Av BXLY DA5................169 F4
Stickland Rd BELV DA17..............129 H4
Stickleton CI GFD/PVL UB6............96 B2
Stilecroft Gdns ALP/SUD HA0.........79 H1
Stile Hall Gdns CHSWK W4............117 H5
Stiles CI ERITH DA8....................129 J5
HAYES BR2..............................200 E3
Stillingfleet Rd BARN SW13.........138 D1
Stillington St WEST SW1P.............16 B6
Stillness Rd FSTH SE23...............164 B1
Stipularis Dr YEAD UB4................95 H3
Stirling Av PIN HA5........................59 H4
WLGTN SM6.............................210 E5
Stirling CI RAIN RM13.................111 K2
SCUP DA14...............................168 A6
STRHM/NOR SW16......................179 H3
Stirling Dr ORP BR6....................217 H3
Stirling Gv HSLW TW3.................135 H5
Stirling Rd ACT W3......................117 J5
BRXN/ST SW9............................141 K3
HYS/HAR UB3............................95 F6
KTN/HRWW/W HA3......................43 F6
PLSTW E15..............................107 F1
TOTM N17.................................50 C4
WALTH E17................................51 G6
WDGN N22................................49 H4
WHTN TW2...............................155 F2
Stirling Wk BRYLDS KT5..............191 J3
Stirling Wy BORE WD6..................31 F1
Stiven Crs RYLN/HDSTN HA2.........77 K1
Stockbury Rd CROY/NA CRO.........197 K3
Stockdale Rd BCTR RM8...............74 B5
Stockdove Wy GFD/PVL UB6..........97 F2
Stocker Gdns DAGW RM9..............91 J5
Stockfield Rd ESH/CLAY KT10.......204 E5
STRHM/NOR SW16......................162 A5
Stockholm Rd
BERM/RHTH SE16......................123 K5
Stockholm Wy WAP E1W *............123 H1
Stockhurst CI PUT/ROE SW15.......139 F3
Stockingswater La PEND EN3.........25 G4
Stockland Rd ROMW/RG RM7.........75 F3
Stock La RDART DA1...................171 F6
Stockley CI WDR/YW UB7.............112 E2
Stockley Farm Rd
WDR/YW UB7.............................112 E3
Stockley Rd WDR/YW UB7.............112 E3
Stock Orchard Crs
HOLWY N7 *..............................85 F2
Stock Orchard St HOLWY N7..........85 F3
Stockport Rd
STRHM/NOR SW16......................179 J4
Stocksfield Rd WALTH E17 *...........52 A6
Stocks PI POP/IOD E14................105 H6
Stock St PLSTW E15....................106 E1
Stockton CI BAR EN5....................21 G5
Stockton Gdns MLHL NW7.............31 F5
UED N18...................................49 J3
Stockton Rd TOTM N17.................49 J3
UED N18...................................50 C2
Stockwell Av BRXN/ST SW9.........142 A4
Stockwell CI BMLY BR1................184 A5
Stockwell Gdns BRXN/ST SW9......142 A2
Stockwell Gn BRXN/ST SW9.........142 A3
Stockwell La BRXN/ST SW9..........142 A3
Stockwell Park Crs
BRXN/ST SW9............................142 A3
Stockwell Park Rd
BRXN/ST SW9............................142 B2
Stockwell Park Wk
BRXN/ST SW9............................142 A4
Stockwell Rd BRXN/ST SW9.........142 A3
Stockwell St GNWCH SE10...........125 F6
Stodart Rd PGE/AN SE20..............181 K4
Stoford CI WIM/MER SW19...........159 H3
Stokenchurch St
FUL/PGN SW6.............................140 A2
Stoke Newington Church St
STNW/STAM N16........................85 K1

Stoke Newington Common
STNW/STAM N16..........86 B1
Stoke Newington High St
STNW/STAM N16..........86 B1
Stoke Newington Rd
STNW/STAM N16..........86 B3
Stoke Pl WLSDN NW10..........99 H2
Stoke Rd KUTN/CMB KT2..........175 K5
Stokesby Rd CHSGTN KT9..........206 B4
Stokesley St SHB W12..........99 H5
Stokes Rd CROY/NA CRO..........198 A5
EHAM E6..........107 J3
Stoll Cl CRICK NW2..........82 A1
Stonard Rd BCTR RM8..........91 H3
PLMGR N13..........35 G5
Stonards HI LOU IG10..........39 K1
Stondon Pk FSTH SE23..........164 B2
Stonebridge Pk WLSDN NW10..........81 F5
Stonebridge Rd
SEVS/STOTM N15..........68 A2
Stonebridge Wy WBLY HA9..........80 D4
Stonechat Sq EHAM E6..........107 J4
Stone Cl BCTR RM8..........74 C6
CLAP SW4..........141 H3
WDR/YW UB7..........112 C1
Stonecot Cl MRDN SM4..........193 H5
Stonecot HI MRDN SM4..........193 H5
Stone Crs EBED/NFELT TW14..........153 J2
Stonecroft Rd ERITH DA8..........149 K1
Stonecroft Wy CROY/NA CRO..........195 K4
Stonecutter St
FLST/FETLN EC4A..........12 A3
Stonefield Cl BXLYHN DA7..........149 H4
RSLP HA4..........77 J3
Stonefield St IS N1..........85 G6
Stonefield Wy CHARL SE7..........146 C1
RSLP HA4..........77 H3
Stonegate Cl STMC/STPC BR5..........186 D6
Stone Gv EDGW HA8..........30 A6
Stonegrove Gdns EDGW HA8..........30 A6
Stonehall Av IL IG1..........71 J3
Stone Hall Gdns KENS W8 *..........120 A3
Stone Hall Pl KENS W8 *..........120 A3
Stone Hall Rd WCHMH N21..........35 F2
Stoneham Rd FBAR/BDGN N11..........48 C1
Stonehill Cl MORT/ESHN SW14..........138 A6
Stonehill Rd CHSWK W4..........117 H5
MORT/ESHN SW14..........137 K6
Stonehills Ct DUL SE21..........163 F5
Stonehouse Broadway
EW KT17..........207 J3
Stonehouse Rd HDTCH EC3A..........15 H5
Stone House Ct HDTCH EC3A..........15 H5
Stonehouse La ORP BR6..........217 K6
Stonehouse Rd ORP BR6..........217 K6
Stoneleigh Av EN EN1..........24 D1
WPK KT4..........207 J1
Stoneleigh Broadway
EW KT17..........207 J3
Stoneleigh Crs
HOR/WEW KT19..........207 J3
Stoneleigh Park Av
CROY/NA CRO..........198 A3
Stoneleigh Park Rd
HOR/WEW KT19..........207 H4
Stoneleigh Pl NTGHL W11..........100 B6
Stoneleigh Rd CAR SM5..........194 D4
CLAY IG5..........53 J6
TOTM N17..........50 B5
Stoneleigh St NTGHL W11..........100 B6
Stoneleigh Ter ARCH N19..........66 B6
Stonell's Rd TOOT SW17..........160 E5
Stonemasons Cl
SEVS/STOTM N15 *..........67 K1
Stonenest St FSBYPK N4..........67 F5
Stone Park Av BECK BR3..........198 D1
Stone Pl WPK KT4..........192 D6
Stone Rd HAYES BR2..........199 J2
Stones Cross Rd SWLY BR8..........203 K2
Stones End St STHWK SE1..........18 C3
Stonewall EHAM E6..........108 A4
Stonewood Rd ERITH DA8..........130 B5
Stoneyard La POP/IOD E14..........105 K6
Stoneycroft Cl LEE/GVPK SE12..........165 J2
Stoneycroft Rd WFD IG8..........53 J2
Stoneydown WALTH E17..........69 G1
Stoneyfields Gdns EDGW HA8..........30 E6
Stoneyfields La EDGW HA8..........30 E5
Stoney La HDTCH EC3A..........13 H5
NRWD SE19..........181 G2
Stoney St STHWK SE1..........12 E7
Stonhouse St CLAP SW4..........141 H4
Stonnell's Rd BTSEA SW11..........140 E6
Stonor Rd WKENS W14..........119 J4
Stonycroft Cl PEND EN3..........25 G5
Stopes St PECK SE15..........143 G1
Stopford Rd PLSTW E13..........88 E6
WALW SE17..........122 C5
Store Rd CAN/RD E16..........127 F2
Storers Quay POP/IOD E14..........125 G4
Store St GWRST WC1E..........10 C2
SRTFD E15..........88 B3
Storey Rd HGT N6..........65 K3
WALTH E17..........69 H1
Storey's Ga STJSPK SW1H..........16 D3
Stories Ms CMBW SE5 *..........143 F3
Stories Rd CMBW SE5..........143 F4
Stork Rd FSTGT E7..........88 D4
Storksmead Rd EDGW HA8..........45 G3
Storks Rd BERM/RHTH SE16 *..........123 H3
Stormont Rd BTSEA SW11..........141 F5
HGT N6..........65 K4
Stormont Wy CHSGTN KT9..........205 J3
Stormount Dr HYS/HAR UB3..........113 F2
Storrington Rd CROY/NA CRO..........197 G5
Story St IS N1..........85 F5
Stothard St WCHPL E1..........104 E3
Stott Cl WAND/EARL SW18..........160 C1
Stoughton Av CHEAM SM3..........208 B3
Stoughton Cl LBTH SE11..........17 H7
PUT/ROE SW15..........158 D3
Stour Av NWDGN UB2..........115 F3

Stourcliffe St BAY/PAD W2..........8 E4
Stour Cl HAYES BR2..........215 G2
Stourhead Cl WIM/MER SW19..........159 G2
Stourhead Gdns RYNPK SW20..........176 D6
Stour Rd BOW E3..........87 J5
DAGE RM10..........74 C6
DART DA1..........150 D4
Stourton Av FELT TW13..........154 E6
Stowage DEPT SE8..........124 E6
The Stowage DEPT SE8..........124 D6
Stow Crs WALTH E17..........51 G4
Stowe Gdns ED N9..........36 B3
Stowe Pl SEVS/STOTM N15..........50 A6
Stowe Rd ORP BR6..........217 H2
SHB W12..........118 E2
Stowting Rd ORP BR6..........216 E2
Stox Md KTN/HRWW/W HA3..........42 D4
Stracey Rd WLSDN NW10..........81 F6
Strachan Pl RYNPK SW20..........177 F2
Stradbroke Dr CHIG IG7..........54 B2
Stradbroke Gv BKHH IG9..........39 H5
CLAY IG5..........53 J6
Stradbroke Pk CHIG IG7..........54 B2
Stradbroke Rd HBRY N5..........85 J2
Stradbrook Cl
RYLN/HDSTN HA2..........77 K1
Stradella Rd HNHL SE24..........162 D1
Strafford Av CLAY IG5..........54 A5
Strafford Rd ACT W3..........117 K2
BAR EN5..........20 C4
HSLW TW3..........134 E4
TWK TW1..........156 B2
Strafford St POP/IOD E14..........124 D2
Strahan Rd BOW E3..........105 G2
Straight Rd HARH RM3..........57 K1
Straightsmouth GNWCH SE10..........145 F1
The Straight NWDGN UB2..........114 C2
Strait Rd EHAM E6..........107 J6
Straker's Rd EDUL SE22..........143 J5
Strand TPL/STR WC2R..........11 F6
Strand Dr RCH/KEW TW9..........137 J1
Strandfield Cl
WOOL/PLUM SE18..........127 K5
Strand-on-the-Green
CHSWK W4..........117 H6
Strand Pl UED N18..........36 A6
Strangways Ter WKENS W14..........119 J3
Stranraer Wy IS N1..........84 E6
Strasburg Rd BTSEA SW11..........141 F2
Stratfield Park Cl WCHMH N21..........35 H2
DAGE RM10..........92 E5
Stratford Ct NWMAL KT3..........192 A1
Stratford Gv PUT/ROE SW15..........139 G5
Stratford House Av BMLY BR1..........184 D6
Stratford Pl MHST W1U..........9 J4
Stratford Rd HTHAIR TW6..........152 E1
KENS W8..........119 K4
NWDGN UB2..........114 D4
PLSTW E13..........88 E6
THHTH CR7..........196 B1
YEAD UB4..........95 F3
Stratford Vls CAMTN NW1..........84 C5
Strathan Cl WAND/EARL SW18..........159 H1
Strathaven Rd LEE/GVPK SE12..........166 A1
Strathblaine Rd BTSEA SW11..........140 C5
Strathbrook Rd
STRHM/NOR SW16..........162 A6
Strathcona Rd WBLY HA9..........61 K6
Strathdale STRHM/NOR SW16..........180 A1
Strathdon Dr TOOT SW17..........160 C5
Strathearn Av HYS/HAR UB3..........133 J1
WHTN TW2..........155 H3
Strathearn Pl BAY/PAD W2..........8 C5
Strathearn Rd SUT SM1..........208 E3
WIM/MER SW19..........177 K1
Stratheden Rd BKHTH/KID SE3..........145 K2
Strathfield Gdns BARK IG11..........90 D4
Strathleven Rd
BRXS/STRHM SW2..........141 K6
Strathmore Gdns EDGW HA8..........44 D5
FNCH N3..........47 F4
HCH RM12..........75 H5
KENS W8..........119 K1
Strathmore Rd CROY/NA CRO..........196 D4
TEDD TW11..........155 K6
WIM/MER SW19..........159 K5
Strathnairn St STHWK SE1..........123 H4
Strathray Gdns HAMP NW3 *..........83 J4
Strath Ter BTSEA SW11..........140 D5
Strathville Rd
WAND/EARL SW18..........159 K4
Strathyre Av
STRHM/NOR SW16..........180 B6
Stratton Av ENC/FH EN2..........23 K1
Stratton Cl BXLYHN DA7..........149 F4
EDGW HA8..........44 B2
HEST TW5..........134 D1
WIM/MER SW19..........177 J5
WOT/HER KT12 *..........188 B5
Strattondale St POP/IOD E14..........125 F3
Stratton Dr BARK IG11..........90 E3
Stratton Gdns STHL UB1..........95 K5
Stratton Rd BXLYHN DA7..........149 F4
WIM/MER SW19..........177 K5
Stratton St MYFR/PICC W1J..........9 K7
Strauss Rd CHSWK W4..........118 A2
Strawberry Hill Rd TWK TW1..........156 A5
Strawberry La CAR SM5..........209 K1
Strawberry Ter MUSWH N10 *..........47 K4
Strawberry V EFNCH N2..........47 H4
TWK TW1..........156 A5
Streakes Field La CRICK NW2..........63 J6
Streamdale ABYW SE2..........128 C6
Streamline Ms EDUL SE22..........163 J5
Streamside Cl ED N9..........36 B3
HAYES BR2..........199 K2
Stream Wy BELV DA17..........129 H6
Streatfeild Av EHAM E6..........89 K6
Streatfield Rd
KTN/HRWW/W HA3..........43 J6
Streatham Cl
STRHM/NOR SW16 *..........161 K4
Streatham Common
STRHM/NOR SW16..........179 J3

Streatham Common North
STRHM/NOR SW16..........180 A1
Streatham Common South
STRHM/NOR SW16..........179 K2
Streatham Ct
STRHM/NOR SW16..........161 K5
Streatham Gn
STRHM/NOR SW16 *..........161 K6
Streatham High Rd
BRXS/STRHM SW2..........161 K3
Streatham Hl
BRXS/STRHM SW2..........161 K5
Streatham Pl
BRXS/STRHM SW2..........161 K2
Streatham Rd MTCM CR4..........179 G3
Streatham St
NOXST/BSQ WC1A..........10 E3
Streatham V
STRHM/NOR SW16..........179 H4
Streathbourne Rd TOOT SW17..........161 F4
Streatleigh Pde
STRHM/NOR SW16 *..........161 K4
Streatley Pl HAMP NW3..........83 H2
Streatley Rd KIL/WHAMP NW6..........82 D5
Streeters La WLGTN SM6..........210 D1
Streetfield Ms BKHTH/KID SE3..........145 K3
Streimer Rd SRTFD E15..........106 A1
Strelley Wy ACT W3..........99 G6
Stretton Rd CROY/NA CRO..........197 F4
RCHPK/HAM TW10..........156 D4
Strickland Av DART DA1..........151 J5
Strickland Rw
WAND/EARL SW18..........160 C2
Strickland St DEPT SE8..........144 D3
Stride Rd PLSTW E13..........106 D1
Strimon Cl ED N9..........36 E4
Stripling Wy WATW WD18..........26 E1
Strode Cl MUSWH N10..........48 A5
Strode Rd FSTGT E7..........88 E2
FUL/PGN SW6..........139 G1
TOTM N17..........50 A5
WLSDN NW10..........81 J4
Strone Rd FSTGT E7..........89 G4
MNPK E12..........89 J4
Strone Wy YEAD UB4..........95 J3
Strongbow Crs ELTH/MOT SE9..........146 E6
Strongbow Rd ELTH/MOT SE9..........146 E6
Strongbridge Cl
RYLN/HDSTN HA2..........60 A5
Stronsa Rd SHB W12..........118 C2
Strood Av ROMW/RG RM7..........75 F5
Stroud Crs PUT/ROE SW15..........158 C5
Stroudes Cl WPK KT4..........192 C4
Stroud Fld NTHLT UB5..........77 J4
Stroud Ga RYLN/HDSTN HA2..........78 B2
Stroud Green Rd FSBYPK N4..........67 F5
Stroud Green Wy
CROY/NA CRO..........197 K3
Stroud Rd SNWD SE25..........197 H5
WIM/MER SW19..........159 K5
Strouds Cl CHDH RM6..........73 J2
Strout's Pl BETH E2..........7 J3
Strutton Gnd WEST SW1P..........16 C4
Strype St WCHPL E1..........13 J2
Stuart Av CDALE/KGS NW9..........63 J4
EA W5..........117 G2
HAYES BR2..........199 K5
RYLN/HDSTN HA2..........59 K2
WOT/HER KT12..........188 B5
Stuart Ct BORE WD6 *..........29 K1
Stuart Crs CROY/NA CRO..........213 H1
HYS/HAR UB3..........94 A5
WDGN N22..........49 F4
Stuart Evans Cl WELL DA16..........148 D4
Stuart Gv TEDD TW11..........173 K1
Stuart Mantle Wy ERITH DA8..........150 A1
Stuart Pl MTCM CR4..........178 E4
Stuart Rd ACT W3..........117 K1
BARK IG11..........91 G5
KIL/WHAMP NW6..........100 D2
NRWD SE19..........181 F3
PECK SE15..........143 K5
RCHPK/HAM TW10..........156 C4
THHTH CR7..........196 C1
WALTH E17..........51 F6
WAND/EARL SW18..........139 K5
WIM/MER SW19..........159 K5
Stubbs Cl CDALE/KGS NW9..........62 E2
Stubbs Dr BERM/RHTH SE16 *..........123 J5
Stubbs Wy WIM/MER SW19..........178 C4
Stucley Pl CAMTN NW1 *..........84 B5
Stucley Rd ISLW TW7..........135 H1
Studd St IS N1..........85 H6
Studdridge St FUL/PGN SW6..........139 K3
Studholme Ct HAMP NW3 *..........82 E2
Studholme St PECK SE15..........143 J1
Studio Pl KTBR SW1X *..........15 F3
The Studios BUSH WD23..........28 A1
Studland Cl BFN/LL DA15..........168 A5
Studland Rd HNWL W7..........96 D5
KUTN/CMB KT2..........174 E2
SYD SE26..........182 A1
Studland St HMSMTH W6..........118 E4
Studley Av CHING E4..........52 B3
Studley Cl CLPT E5..........87 H3
Studley Ct SCUP DA14..........186 D5
Studley Dr REDBR IG4..........71 H3
Studley Grange Rd HNWL W7..........115 K3
Studley Rd CLAP SW4..........141 J3
DAGE RM9..........91 K5
FSTGT E7..........89 F4
Stukeley Rd FSTGT E7..........89 F5
Stukeley St HOL/ALD WC2B..........11 F3
Stumps Hill La BECK BR3..........182 D2
Sturdy Rd PECK SE15..........143 J3
Sturge Av WALTH E17..........52 A5
Sturgeon Rd WALW SE17..........122 D5
Sturges Fld CHST BR7..........185 J2
Sturgess Av HDN NW4..........63 K4
Sturge St STHWK SE1..........18 C3
Sturmer Wy HOLWY N7..........85 F3

Sturminster Cl YEAD UB4..........95 G5
Sturrock Cl SEVS/STOTM N15..........67 K1
Sturry St POP/IOD E14..........105 K5
Sturt St IS N1..........6 D3
Stutfield St WCHPL E1..........104 C5
Styles Gdns BRXN/ST SW9..........142 C4
Styles Wy BECK BR3..........199 F1
Sudbourne Rd
BRXS/STRHM SW2..........141 K6
Sudbrooke Rd BAL SW12..........160 E1
Sudbrook Gdns
RCHPK/HAM TW10..........157 F5
Sudbrook La
RCHPK/HAM TW10..........157 F3
Sudbury EHAM E6..........108 A5
Sudbury Av ALP/SUD HA0..........79 J1
WBLY HA9..........79 J2
Sudbury Ct ALP/SUD HA0..........79 G1
BMLY BR1..........183 K1
Sudbury Court Dr HRW HA1..........60 E5
Sudbury Court Rd
ALP/SUD HA0..........79 G1
Sudbury Crs ALP/SUD HA0..........79 F2
BMLY BR1..........183 K1
Sudbury Crt Av ALP/SUD HA0..........79 F2
Sudbury Gdns CROY/NA CRO..........212 A2
Sudbury Heights Av
GFD/PVL UB6..........79 F3
Sudbury Hill ALP/SUD HA0..........79 F1
Sudbury Hill Cl ALP/SUD HA0..........79 F2
Sudbury Rd BARK IG11..........91 F3
Sudeley St IS N1..........6 B3
Sudlow Rd WAND/EARL SW18..........139 K5
Sudrey St STHWK SE1..........18 C3
Suez Av GFD/PVL UB6..........97 F1
Suez Rd PEND EN3..........25 G5
Suffield Rd CHING E4..........37 K5
PGE/AN SE20..........181 K5
SEVS/STOTM N15 *..........68 B2
Suffolk La CANST EC4R..........12 E5
Suffolk Park Rd WALTH E17..........69 G1
Suffolk Rd BARK IG11..........90 D5
BARN SW13..........138 C1
DAGE RM10..........92 E4
DART DA1..........171 H1
GDMY/SEVK IG3..........72 E3
PEND EN3..........25 F1
PLSTW E13..........106 D2
RYLN/HDSTN HA2..........59 K5
SCUP DA14..........186 D2
SEVS/STOTM N15..........67 K3
SNWD SE25..........197 G1
WLSDN NW10..........81 G5
WPK KT4..........192 C6
Suffolk St FSTGT E7..........88 E3
STJS SW1Y..........10 D7
Sugar House La SRTFD E15..........106 A1
Sugar Loaf Wk BETH E2 *..........104 E2
Sugden Rd BTSEA SW11..........141 F4
THDIT KT7..........190 B5
Sugden Wy BARK IG11..........109 F1
Sulgrave Gdns SHB W12..........119 F2
Sulgrave Rd SHB W12..........119 F2
Sulina Rd BRXS/STRHM SW2..........161 K2
Sulivan Ct FUL/PGN SW6..........139 K3
Sulivan Rd FUL/PGN SW6..........139 K4
Sullivan Av CAN/RD E16..........107 H4
Sullivan Cl BTSEA SW11..........140 D4
DART DA1..........170 E1
E/WMO/HCT KT8..........173 F6
Sullivan Rd LBTH SE11..........17 K6
Sullivan Wy BORE WD6..........29 J1
Sultan Rd WAN E11..........71 F1
Sultan St BECK BR3..........182 A5
CMBW SE5..........142 D1
Sumatra Rd KIL/WHAMP NW6..........82 E4
Sumburgh Rd BAL SW12..........161 F1
Summer Av E/WMO/HCT KT8..........189 J2
Summercourt Rd WCHPL E1..........104 E5
Summerene Cl
STRHM/NOR SW16..........179 H5
Summerfield Av
KIL/WHAMP NW6..........100 C1
NFNCH/WDSP N12..........32 D6
Summerfield La SURB KT6..........190 E6
Summerfield Rd LOU IG10..........39 H1
WEA W13..........97 H5
Summerfield St
LEE/GVPK SE12..........165 J2
Summer Gdns
E/WMO/HCT KT8..........189 K2
Summer Gv BORE WD6..........29 K1
Summer Hl CHST BR7..........185 F5
Summerhill Cl ORP BR6..........216 E1
Summerhill Gv EN EN1..........36 A1
Summerhill Rd DART DA1..........171 G2
SEVS/STOTM N15..........67 K1
Summerhill Wy MTCM CR4..........179 F4
Summerhouse Av HEST TW5..........134 D2
Summerhouse La
WDR/YW UB7..........112 A6
Summerhouse Rd
STNW/STAM N16..........68 A6
Summerland Gdns
MUSWH N10..........48 B6
Summerlands Av ACT W3..........98 E6
Summerlee Av EFNCH N2..........65 K1
Summerlee Gdns EFNCH N2..........65 K1
Summerley St
WAND/EARL SW18..........160 A4
Summer Pl WATW WD18 *..........26 D1
Summer Rd E/WMO/HCT KT8..........189 K2
THDIT KT7..........190 A3
Summersby Rd HGT N6..........66 B3
Summers Cl BELMT SM2..........208 E5
WBLY HA9..........62 D5
Summerskille Cl ED N9..........36 D4
Summers La NFNCH/WDSP N12..........47 H1
Summers Rw
NFNCH/WDSP N12..........47 J2
Summers St CLKNW EC1R..........5 J7
Summerstown TOOT SW17..........160 B5
Summerton Wy THMD SE28..........109 K6
Summer Trees SUN TW16..........172 A4
Summerville Gdns SUT SM1..........208 D4

Summerwood Rd ISLW TW7..........156 A1
Summit Av CDALE/KGS NW9..........63 F3
Summit Cl CDALE/KGS NW9..........63 F1
EDGW HA8..........44 C3
STHGT/OAK N14..........34 C4
Summit Dr WFD IG8..........53 H5
Summit Est STNW/STAM N16 *..........68 C4
Summit Rd NTHLT UB5..........78 A5
WALTH E17..........69 K1
Summit Wy NRWD SE19..........181 F3
STHGT/OAK N14..........34 B4
Sumner Av PECK SE15..........143 G2
Sumner Cl ORP BR6..........216 C2
Sumner Gdns CROY/NA CRO..........196 B5
Sumner Pl SKENS SW7..........14 B7
Sumner Place Ms SKENS SW7 *..........14 B7
Sumner Rd CROY/NA CRO..........196 C5
HRW HA1..........60 C4
PECK SE15..........123 G6
Sumner Rd South
CROY/NA CRO..........196 B5
Sumner St STHWK SE1..........12 C7
Sumpter Cl HAMP NW3..........83 G4
Sunbeam Crs NKENS W10..........100 A3
Sunbeam Rd WLSDN NW10..........98 E3
Sunbury Av MLHL NW7..........45 F1
MORT/ESHN SW14..........138 A5
Sunbury Ct BAR EN5..........20 C5
SUN TW16..........172 C5
Sunbury Court Rd SUN TW16..........172 B5
Sunbury Gdns MLHL NW7..........45 E1
Sunbury La BTSEA SW11..........140 C2
Sunbury Rd CHEAM SM3..........208 B1
FELT TW13..........153 K4
Sunbury St WOOL/PLUM SE18..........126 E3
Sunbury Wy FELT TW13..........172 B1
Sun Ct ERITH DA8..........150 C3
Suncroft Pl SYD SE26..........163 K5
Sunderland Mt FSTH SE23 *..........164 A4
Sunderland Rd EA W5..........116 E3
FSTH SE23..........164 A3
Sunderland Ter BAY/PAD W2 *..........101 F5
Sunderland Wy MNPK E12..........71 H6
Sundew Av SHB W12..........99 J6
Sundial Av SNWD SE25..........181 G5
Sundorne Rd CHARL SE7..........126 A5
Sundra Wk WCHPL E1 *..........105 F3
Sundridge Av BMLY BR1..........184 C4
WELL DA16..........147 J3
Sundridge Cl DART DA1..........171 J1
Sundridge Pde BMLY BR1 *..........184 A3
Sundridge Pl CROY/NA CRO *..........197 H5
Sunfields Pl BKHTH/KID SE3..........146 A1
Sun in Sands Rbt
BKHTH/KID SE3..........146 A1
Sunken Rd CROY/NA CRO..........212 E3
Sunkist Wy WLGTN SM6..........210 E6
Sunland Av BXLYHS DA6..........149 F5
Sun La BKHTH/KID SE3..........146 A1
Sunleigh Rd ALP/SUD HA0..........80 A6
Sunley Gdns GFD/PVL UB6..........97 G1
Sunlight Cl WIM/MER SW19 *..........178 B2
Sunlight Sq BETH E2..........104 D2
Sunna Gdns SUN TW16..........172 A5
Sunningdale Av ACT W3..........99 G6
BARK IG11..........90 D6
FELT TW13..........154 D4
RAIN RM13..........111 K3
RSLP HA4..........59 G5
Sunningdale Cl
BERM/RHTH SE16 *..........123 J5
STAN HA7..........43 G3
SURB KT6..........191 F6
THMD SE28..........110 A5
Sunningdale Gdns
CDALE/KGS NW9..........62 E2
KENS W8 *..........119 K3
Sunningdale Ldg EDGW HA8 *..........44 B1
Sunningdale Rd HAYES BR2..........200 D1
RAIN RM13..........93 J5
SUT SM1..........208 D1
Sunningfields Crs HDN NW4..........45 K4
Sunningfields Rd HDN NW4..........45 K5
Sunninghill Ct ACT W3 *..........117 K2
Sunninghill Rd LEW SE13..........144 E3
Sunny Bank SNWD SE25..........181 H6
Sunny Crs WLSDN NW10..........80 D5
Sunny Gdns Rd HDN NW4..........45 K3
Sunnycroft Rd HSLW TW3..........135 G3
SNWD SE25..........181 H6
STHL UB1..........96 A4
Sunnydale ORP BR6..........201 F6
Sunnydale Gdns MLHL NW7..........45 F2
Sunnydale Rd LEE/GVPK SE12..........146 A6
Sunnydene Av CHING E4..........52 B1
RSLP HA4..........58 E5
Sunnydene Gdns ALP/SUD HA0..........79 J4
Sunnydene St SYD SE26..........164 B6
Sunnyfield MLHL NW7..........31 H5
Sunny HI HDN NW4..........45 K4
Sunnyhill Cl CLPT E5..........87 G2
Sunnyhill Rd
STRHM/NOR SW16..........161 K6
Sunnyhurst Cl SUT SM1..........208 E1
Sunny Ms CRW RM5..........56 E3
Sunny Nook Gdns
SAND/SEL CR2 *..........211 K4
Sunny Pl HDN NW4..........64 A1
The Sunny Rd PEND EN3..........25 F2
Sunnyside CAT SE6 *..........164 C2
CRICK NW2..........82 D1
WIM/MER SW19..........177 G2
WOT/HER KT12..........188 B2
Sunnyside Dr CHING E4..........38 A2
Sunnyside Rd ARCH N19..........66 D4
EA W5..........116 E3
IL IG1..........90 C1

LEY E10 .....69 J5
TEDD TW11 .....155 J6
Sunnyside Rd East ED N9 .....36 C5
Sunnyside Rd North ED N9 .....36 B5
Sunnyside Rd South ED N9 .....36 B5
Sunny Vw CDALE/KGS NW9 .....63 F2
Sunny Wy NFNCH/WDSP N12 .....47 J1
Sun Pas BERM/RHTH SE16 .....123 H5
Sunray Av BRYLDS KT5 .....191 J6
   CMBW SE5 .....142 E5
   HAYES BR2 .....200 D3
   WDR/YW UB7 .....112 A2
Sunrise CI FELT TW13 .....154 E5
Sun Rd WKENS W14 .....119 J5
Sunset Av CHING E4 .....37 K3
   WFD IG8 .....52 E1
Sunset CI ERITH DA8 .....150 E1
Sunset Gdns NRWD SE19 .....181 F5
Sunset Rd CMBW SE5 .....142 D5
   THMD SE28 .....128 B2
   WALW SE17 * 176 E1
Sunset Vw BAR EN5 .....20 C3
Sunshine Wy MTCM CR4 .....178 E5
Sun St SDTCH EC2A 13 H7
Superior Dr ORP BR6 .....217 F4
Surbiton Ct SURB KT6 .....190 D5
Surbiton Crs SURB KT6 .....191 F1
Surbiton Hall CI KUT/HW KT1 .....191 F1
Surbiton Hill Pk BRYLDS KT5 .....191 G2
Surbiton Hill Rd SURB KT6 .....191 F1
Surlingham CI THMD SE28 .....109 K6
Surma CI WCHPL E1 .....104 C3
Surmans CI DAGW RM9 .....91 J6
Surrendale PI MV/WKIL W9 .....100 E3
Surrey Canal Rd
   BERM/RHTH SE16 .....123 K6
Surrey Crs CHSWK W4 .....117 H5
Surrey Gdns FSBYPK N4 .....67 J3
Surrey Gv SUT SM1 .....209 H1
   WALW SE17 .....123 F5
Surrey Ms WNWD SE27 .....163 F6
Surrey Quays Rd
   BERM/RHTH SE16 .....123 K3
Surrey Rd BARK IG11 .....90 E5
   DAGE RM10 .....92 E3
   HRW HA1 .....48 C4
   PECK SE15 .....144 A6
   WWKM BR4 .....198 E5
Surrey Rw STHWK SE1 .....18 A2
Surrey St CROY/NA CR0 .....211 J1
   PLSTW E13 .....107 F2
   TPL/STR WC2R 11 H5
Surrey Ter WALW SE17 .....19 H7
Surrey Water Rd
   BERM/RHTH SE16 .....124 A1
Surridge Gdns NRWD SE19 .....180 E2
Sury Basin KUTN/CMB KT2 .....175 F4
Susan CI ROMW/RG RM7 .....56 E6
Susannah St POP/IOD E14 .....105 K5
Susan Rd BKHTH/KID SE3 .....146 A3
Susan Wd CHST BR7 .....185 F4
Sussex Av ISLW TW7 .....135 K4
Sussex CI ARCH N19 * 66 E6
   NWMAL KT3 .....192 B1
   REDBR IG4 .....71 K3
   TWK TW1 .....156 C1
Sussex Crs NTHLT UB5 .....78 A4
Sussex Gdns BAY/PAD W2 .....8 B5
   CHSGTN KT9 .....205 K4
   EFNCH N2 .....65 K2
   FSBYPK N4 .....67 J2
Sussex Ga EFNCH N2 * 65 K1
Sussex Ms East BAY/PAD W2 * 8 B5
Sussex Ms West BAY/PAD W2 .....8 B6
Sussex PI BAY/PAD W2 .....8 B5
   CAMTN NW1 * 2 E1
   HMSMTH W6 .....119 F5
   NWMAL KT3 .....192 B1
Sussex Rd CAR SM5 .....209 K4
   DART DA1 .....171 F1
   EHAM E6 .....108 A1
   ERITH DA8 .....149 J1
   HCDN/ICK UB10 .....76 A2
   HRW HA1 .....60 C2
   MTCM CR4 * 195 K4
   NWDGN UB2 .....114 C3
   NWMAL KT3 .....192 B1
   SAND/SEL CR2 .....211 K4
   SCUP DA14 .....186 C1
   STMC/STPC BR5 .....202 D5
   WWKM BR4 .....198 E5
Sussex Ring NFNCH/WDSP N12 .....46 E1
Sussex Sq BAY/PAD W2 .....8 B5
Sussex St PIM SW1V 121 G5
   PLSTW E13 .....107 F2
Sussex Ter PGE/AN SE20 * 181 K3
Sussex Wy ARCH N19 .....66 E6
   EBAR EN4 .....22 B6
Sutcliffe CI GLDGN NW11 .....65 F2
Sutcliffe Rd WELL DA16 .....148 D3
   WOOL/PLUM SE18 .....127 K6
Sutherland Av HYS/HAR UB3 .....113 K4
   MV/WKIL W9 .....100 E3
   STMC/STPC BR5 .....202 A3
   WEA W13 .....97 H5
   WELL DA16 .....147 J5
Sutherland CI BAR EN5 .....20 C5
Sutherland Ct CDALE/KGS NW9 .....62 D1
Sutherland Dr
Sutherland Gdns
   MORT/ESHN SW14 .....138 B4
   WPK KT4 .....192 E5
Sutherland Gv TEDD TW11 .....173 K1
   WAND/EARL SW18 .....159 G2
Sutherland PI BAY/PAD W2 .....100 E5
Sutherland Rd BELV DA17 .....129 H3
   BOW E3 .....105 H1
   CHSWK W4 .....118 A6
   CROY/NA CR0 .....196 B4

ED N9 .....36 D5
   PEND EN3 .....37 F1
Sutherland Rw PIM SW1V * 121 G5
Sutherland Sq WALW SE17 .....122 D5
Sutherland St PIM SW1V 121 G5
Sutherland Vis WEA W13 * 97 G6
Sutherland Wk WALW SE17 .....122 D5
Sutlej Rd CHARL SE7 .....146 B1
Sutterton St HOLWY N7 .....85 F4
Sutton CI BECK BR3 .....182 E4
   CHSWK W4 .....117 K6
   PIN HA5 .....58 E4
Sutton Common Rd
   CHEAM SM3 .....193 J4
   SUT SM1 .....193 K6
Sutton Ct BELMT SM2 .....209 G5
   CHSWK W4 .....117 K6
   EA W5 * 98 B4
Sutton Court Rd CHSWK W4 .....117 K6
   PLSTW E13 .....107 G2
   SUT SM1 .....209 G4
Sutton Crs BAR EN5 .....20 B6
Sutton Dene HSLW TW3 .....135 G2
Sutton Dwelling Est
   CHEL SW3 .....120 D5
Sutton Est IS N1 * 85 H5
The Sutton Est IS N1 * 85 H5
Sutton Gdns CROY/NA CR0 .....197 G2
   SUT SM1 .....209 H3
Sutton Gv SUT SM1 .....209 H3
Sutton Hall Rd HEST TW5 .....135 F1
Sutton La CHSWK W4 .....117 K5
   FSBYE EC1V * 6 B7
   HSLW TW3 .....134 E3
Sutton La South CHSWK W4 .....117 K6
Sutton Park Rd SUT SM1 .....209 F4
Sutton PI HOM E9 .....86 E3
Sutton Rd BARK IG11 .....108 E1
   HEST TW5 * 135 F2
   MUSWH N10 .....48 A4
   PLSTW E13 .....106 D3
   WALTH E17 .....51 F4
Sutton Row SOHO/SHAV W1D 10 C5
Sutton Sq HEST TW5 .....134 E2
   HOM E9 * 86 E3
Sutton St WCHPL E1 .....104 E5
Sutton Wy HEST TW5 .....134 E2
   NKENS W10 .....100 A4
Swaby Rd WAND/EARL SW18 .....160 B4
Swaffield Rd
   WAND/EARL SW18 .....160 B2
Swain CI STRHM/NOR SW16 .....179 G2
Swain Rd THHTH CR7 .....196 D2
Swains CI WDR/YW UB7 .....112 B2
Swain's La HGT N6 .....66 A5
Swains Rd MTCM CR4 .....178 E5
Swainson Rd ACT W3 .....118 C2
Swains Rd MTCM CR4 .....178 E5
Swain St STJWD NW8 .....2 C6
Swaisland Dr DART DA1 .....150 E6
Swaislands Dr DART DA1 .....150 C6
Swaledale CI FBAR/BDGN N11 .....48 A2
Swallands Rd CAT SE6 .....164 D5
Swallow CI BUSH WD23 .....28 B3
   BXLYHN DA7 .....150 B2
   NWCR SE14 .....143 K2
Swallow Ct RSLP HA4 * 59 G5
Swallowdale SAND/SEL CR2 .....213 F6
Swallow Dr NTHLT UB5 .....96 A1
   WLSDN NW10 .....81 F4
Swallowfield Rd CHARL SE7 .....126 A5
Swallowfield Wy
   HYS/HAR UB3 .....113 G2
Swallow Gdns
   STRHM/NOR SW16 .....179 J1
Swallow PI CONDST W1S 9 K4
Swallow St CONDST W1S 10 B6
   EHAM E6 .....107 J4
Swallowtail CI
   STMC/STPC BR5 .....202 E1
Swanage Rd DART DA1 .....151 J6
   WAND/EARL SW18 .....160 B1
Swanage Wy HAYES UB4 .....95 G5
Swan And Pike Rd PEND EN3 .....25 J1
Swan Ap EHAM E6 .....107 J4
Swanbridge Rd BXLYHN DA7 .....149 H2
Swan CI CROY/NA CR0 * 197 F4
   FELT TW13 .....154 D6
   STMC/STPC BR5 .....186 B6
Swandon Wy
   WAND/EARL SW18 .....140 A5
Swan Dr CDALE/KGS NW9 .....45 G5
Swanfield St BETH E2 .....7 J5
Swan Island TWK TW1 * 156 B5
Swan La CANST EC4R 13 F6
   DART DA1 .....170 C2
   LOU IG10 .....39 J1
   TRDG/WHET N20 .....33 G5
Swanley Rd WELL DA16 .....148 D2
Swan Md STHWK SE1 .....19 G5
Swan Ms BRXN/ST SW9 .....142 A3
Swan Pas WCHPL E1 * 13 K4
Swan PI BARN SW13 .....138 C3
Swan Rd BERM/RHTH SE16 .....123 K2
   FELT TW13 .....154 D6
   GFD/PVL UB6 .....96 B5
   WDR/YW UB7 .....112 A2
   WOOL/PLUM SE18 .....126 C3
Swanscombe Rd CHSWK W4 .....118 B5
   NTGHL W11 .....119 G1
Swansea Rd HTHAIR TW6 .....153 F1
   PEND EN3 .....24 E5
Swanston Pth OXHEY WD19 .....27 G5
Swan St ISLW TW7 .....136 C4
   STHWK SE1 .....18 D5
Swanton Gdns
   WIM/MER SW19 .....159 G3
Swanton Rd ERITH DA8 .....149 H1
Swan Wk CHEL SW3 .....120 E6

Swan Wy PEND EN3 .....25 F3
Swanwick CI PUT/ROE SW15 .....158 C2
Swan Yd IS N1 .....85 H4
Sward Rd STMC/STPC BR5 .....202 B3
Swaton Rd BOW E3 .....105 J3
Swaylands Rd BELV DA17 .....129 H6
Swaythling CI UED N18 .....36 D6
Swedenbourg Gdns
   WCHPL E1 .....104 C6
Sweden Ga BERM/RHTH SE16 .....124 B4
Sweeney Crs STHWK SE1 .....19 K3
Sweeps La STMC/STPC BR5 .....202 E2
Sweet Briar Gn ED N9 .....36 B5
Sweet Briar Gv ED N9 .....36 B5
Sweet Briar Wk UED N18 .....36 B6
Sweetmans Av PIN HA5 .....41 H6
Sweets Wy TRDG/WHET N20 .....33 H4
Swete St PLSTW E13 .....106 E1
Sweyn PI BKHTH/KID SE3 .....145 K3
Swift CI CRYLN/HDSTN HA2 .....60 B6
   THMD SE28 .....109 H5
   WALTH E17 .....51 G5
   YEAD UB4 .....94 D5
Swift Rd FELT TW13 .....154 D5
   NWDGN UB2 .....114 E3
Swiftsden Wy BMLY BR1 .....183 H2
Swift St FUL/PGN SW6 .....139 H2
Swinbrook Rd NKENS W10 .....100 C4
Swinburne Crs CROY/NA CR0 .....197 K3
Swinburne Rd PUT/ROE SW15 .....138 D5
Swinderby Rd ALP/SUD HA0 .....80 A4
Swindon CI GDMY/SEVK IG3 .....72 E6
Swindon Rd HTHAIR TW6 .....153 F1
Swindon St SHB W12 .....118 E1
Swinfield CI FELT TW13 .....154 D6
Swinford Gdns BRXN/ST SW9 .....142 C4
Swingate La
   WOOL/PLUM SE18 .....147 K1
Swinnerton St HOM E9 .....87 G3
Swinton CI WBLY HA9 .....62 D5
Swinton PI FSBYW WC1X 5 G4
Swinton St FSBYW WC1X 5 G4
Swires Shaw HAYES BR2 .....215 H2
Swithland Gdns
   ELTH/MOT SE9 .....166 E6
Swyncombe Av BTFD TW8 .....116 C4
Swynford Gdns HDN NW4 .....63 J1
Sybil Phoenix CI DEPT SE8 .....124 A5
Sybourn St WALTH E17 .....69 H4
Sycamore Av BFN/LL DA15 .....168 A1
   BOW E3 .....87 H6
   EA W5 .....116 E3
   HYS/HAR UB3 .....94 C6
Sycamore CI ACT W3 .....118 B1
   CAR/RD E16 .....106 C3
   CAR SM5 .....209 K2
   EBAR EN4 .....33 H1
   ED N9 .....36 C6
   EDGW HA8 .....30 E6
   FELT TW13 .....153 K5
   NTHLT UB5 .....77 J6
   SAND/SEL CR2 .....211 J3
Sycamore Ct CAT SE6 .....165 F1
   CDALE/KGS NW9 .....62 E4
   NWMAL KT3 .....176 B6
   PGE/AN SE20 .....181 H4
Sycamore Gdns MTCM CR4 .....178 C5
   SHB W12 .....118 E2
Sycamore Ms CLAP SW4 .....141 H4
Sycamore Rd DART DA1 .....171 G2
   WIM/MER SW19 .....177 F2
Sycamore St FSBYE EC1V 6 C7
Sycamore Wk NKENS W10 .....100 C3
Sycamore Wy TEDD TW11 .....174 D2
Sydcote DUL SE21 * 162 D4
Sydenham Av LEW SE26 .....181 J1
   WCHMH N21 .....23 F6
Sydenham CI ROM RM1 .....75 H1
Sydenham Hill FSTH SE23 .....163 K3
Sydenham Pk SYD SE26 .....163 K5
Sydenham Park Rd FSTH SE23 .....163 J4
Sydenham Rd CROY/NA CR0 .....196 E5
   SYD SE26 .....182 A1
Sydenham Station Ap
   SYD SE26 .....163 K6
Sydmons Ct FSTH SE23 * 163 K2
Sydney CI SKENS SW7 .....14 B7
Sydney Gv HDN NW4 .....64 A2
Sydney Ms SKENS SW7 .....14 B7
Sydney PI SKENS SW7 .....14 B7
Sydney Rd ABYW SE2 .....128 E3
   BARK/HLT IG6 .....54 C5
   BXLYHS DA6 .....148 E5
   CEND/HSY/T N8 .....49 F3
   EBED/NFELT TW14 .....153 K3
   ENC/FH EN2 .....23 K3
   MUSWH N10 .....48 A4
   RCH/KEW TW9 .....137 G5
   RYNPK SW20 .....177 G5
   SCUP DA14 .....167 K6
   SUT SM1 .....208 E2
   TEDD TW11 .....174 A1
   WAN E11 .....71 F2
   WEA W13 .....116 B1
   WFD IG8 .....39 F6
Sydney St CHEL SW3 .....120 D5
Sydney Ter ESH/CLAY KT10 * 205 F4
Sylvan Av CHDH RM6 .....73 K3
   MLHL NW7 .....45 G2
   WCHMH N21 .....35 H2
   WDGN N22 .....49 F2
Sylvan Gdns SURB KT6 .....190 E4
Sylvan Gv CRICK NW2 .....82 B2
   PECK SE15 .....123 J6
Sylvan HI NRWD SE19 .....181 F4
Sylvan Rd FSTGT E7 .....88 E4
   IL IG1 .....72 C6
   NRWD SE19 .....181 F4
   WALTH E17 * 69 J2
   WAN E11 .....70 E1
Sylvan Ter PECK SE15 * 143 J1
Sylvan Wy BCTR RM8 .....91 H1

WWKM BR4 .....214 C2
Sylverdale Rd CROY/NA CR0 .....211 H1
Sylvester Av CHST BR7 .....184 E2
Sylvester Pth HACK E8 * 86 D4
Sylvester Rd ALP/SUD HA0 .....79 J3
   EFNCH N2 .....47 G5
   HACK E8 * 86 D4
   WALTH E17 .....69 H4
Sylvia Av PIN HA5 .....41 K2
Sylvia Gdns WBLY HA9 .....80 D5
Symes Ms CAMTN NW1 .....4 A2
Symington Ms HOM E9 * 87 F3
Symister Ms IS N1 * 7 G5
Symons St BCVA SW1W 15 G7
Syon Ga Wy BTFD TW8 .....136 C1
Syon La ISLW TW7 .....136 B1
   ISLW TW7 .....116 B6
Syon Pk ISLW TW7 * 136 C4
Syon Park Gdns ISLW TW7 .....136 A1

T

Tabard Garden Est STHWK SE1 .....18 E2
Tabard St STHWK SE1 .....18 D3
Tabernacle Av PLSTW E13 .....106 E3
Tabernacle St SDTCH EC2A 7 F7
Tableer Av CLAP SW4 .....141 H6
Tabley Rd HOLWY N7 .....84 E2
Tabor Gdns CHEAM SM3 .....208 D4
Tabor Gv WIM/MER SW19 .....177 H3
Tabor Rd HMSMTH W6 .....118 E3
Tachbrook Rd
   EBED/NFELT TW14 .....153 J2
   NWDGN UB2 .....114 C4
Tachbrook St PIM SW1V 16 B7
Tack Ms BROCKY SE4 .....144 D4
Tadema Rd WBPTN SW10 .....140 B1
Tadmor St SHB W12 .....119 G1
Tadworth Av NWMAL KT3 .....192 C1
Tadworth Pde HCH RM12 .....93 K2
Tadworth Rd CRICK NW2 .....63 J6
Taeping St POP/IOD E14 .....124 E4
Taffy's How MTCM CR4 .....178 D6
Taft Rd CROY/NA CR0 .....197 F4
Takeley CI CRW RM5 .....57 F5
Talacre Rd KTTN NW5 .....84 A4
Talbot Av EFNCH N2 .....47 H6
   OXHEY WD19 .....27 H1
Talbot CI SEVS/STOTM N15 .....68 B1
Talbot Ct BANK EC3V * 13 F5
Talbot Crs HDN NW4 .....63 J2
Talbot Gdns GDMY/SEVK IG3 .....73 G6
Talbot PI BKHTH/KID SE3 .....145 H2
Talbot Rd ALP/SUD HA0 .....79 K3
   CAR SM5 .....210 A3
   DAGW RM9 .....92 B5
   EDUL SE22 .....143 F5
   EHAM E6 .....107 K1
   FSTGT E7 .....88 E2
   HGT N6 .....66 A4
   ISLW TW7 .....136 B5
   KTN/HRWW/W HA3 .....43 F5
   NTGHL W11 .....100 D5
   NWDGN UB2 .....114 D4
   SEVS/STOTM N15 .....68 B1
   THHTH CR7 .....196 E1
   WDGN N22 .....48 D5
   WEA W13 * 97 G6
   WHTN TW2 .....155 K3
Talbot Sq BAY/PAD W2 .....8 A4
Talbot Wk NTGHL W11 .....100 C5
   WLSDN NW10 * 81 G4
Talbot Yd STHWK SE1 .....18 E1
Talcott Pth
   BRXS/STRHM SW2 * 162 B3
Talfourd PI PECK SE15 .....143 G2
Talfourd Rd PECK SE15 .....143 G2
Talgarth Rd HMSMTH W6 .....119 G5
Talisman CI GDMY/SEVK IG3 .....73 J6
Talisman Sq SYD SE26 .....163 H6
Talisman Wy WBLY HA9 .....80 B1
Tallack Rd LEY E10 .....69 H5
Tall Elms CI HAYES BR2 .....199 J2
Tallis CI CAN/RD E16 .....107 F5
Tallis Gv CHARL SE7 .....146 A6
Tallis St EMB EC4Y 11 K5
Tallis Vw WLSDN NW10 .....81 F4
Tallow Rd BTFD TW8 .....136 D1
Tall Trees STRHM/NOR SW16 .....180 A6
Talma Gdns WHTN TW2 .....155 K2
Talmage CI FSTH SE23 * 163 K2
Talman Gv STAN HA7 .....43 K2
Talma Rd BRXS/STRHM SW2 .....142 B5
Talwin St BOW E3 .....105 K2
Tamar CI BOW E3 * 87 H6
Tamarind Yd WAP E1W 123 H1
Tamarisk Sq SHB W12 .....99 H6
Tamar St WOOL/PLUM SE18 .....126 D4
Tamesis Gdns WPK KT4 .....192 B6
Tamian Wy HSLWW TW4 .....134 B5
Tamworth Av WFD IG8 .....52 C2
Tamworth La MTCM CR4 .....179 G6
Tamworth Pk MTCM CR4 .....195 H1
Tamworth Rd CROY/NA CR0 .....196 C6
Tamworth St FUL/PGN SW6 .....119 K6
Tancred Rd FSBYPK N4 .....67 H3
Tandridge Dr ORP BR6 .....201 J5
Tandridge PI ORP BR6 * 201 J4
Tanfield Av CRICK NW2 .....81 H2
Tanfield Rd CROY/NA CR0 .....211 J2
Tangier Rd RCHPK/HAM TW10 .....137 J4
Tangleberry CI BMLY BR1 .....200 E1
Tangle Tree CI FNCH N3 .....47 F5
Tanglewood CI CROY/NA CR0 .....212 E1
Tanglewood Wy FELT TW13 .....154 A5
Tangley Gv PUT/ROE SW15 .....158 C2
Tangley Park Rd HPTN TW12 * 172 E1

Tangmere Crs HCH RM12 .....93 K4
Tangmere Gdns NTHLT UB5 .....95 G1
Tangmere Gv KUTN/CMB KT2 .....174 E1
Tangmere Wy CDALE/KGS NW9 .....45 G5
Tanhouse Fld KTTN NW5 .....84 D3
Tankerton Houses
   STPAN WC1H * 5 F5
Tankerton Rd SURB KT6 .....191 G6
Tankerton St STPAN WC1H 5 F5
Tankerton Ter CROY/NA CR0 * 196 A4
Tankerville Rd
   STRHM/NOR SW16 .....179 J3
Tank Hill Rd PUR RM19 .....131 K4
Tank La PUR RM19 .....131 K4
Tankridge Rd CRICK NW2 .....63 K6
The Tanneries WCHPL E1 * 104 E3
Tanners CI WOT/HER KT12 .....188 A3
Tanners End La UED N18 .....36 A1
Tanner's HI DEPT SE8 .....144 D2
Tanners La BARK/HLT IG6 .....54 C6
Tanners Ms DEPT SE8 .....144 C2
Tanner St BARK IG11 .....90 C4
   STHWK SE1 .....19 H3
Tannery CI CROY/NA CR0 .....198 A2
   DAGE RM10 .....92 D2
Tannington Ter FSBYPK N4 * 85 G1
Tannsfeld Rd SYD SE26 .....182 A1
Tansley CI HOLWY N7 * 84 D3
Tanswell St STHWK SE1 * 17 J3
Tansy CI EHAM E6 .....108 A5
Tantallon Rd BAL SW12 .....161 F3
Tant Av CAN/RD E16 .....106 D5
Tantony Gv CHDH RM6 .....55 K6
Tanworth CI NTHWD HA6 .....40 A2
Tanworth Gdns PIN HA5 .....41 F5
Tan Yard La BXLY DA5 * 169 H2
Tanza Rd HAMP NW3 .....83 K2
Tapestry CI BELMT SM2 .....209 F5
Taplow Ct MTCM CR4 .....194 D1
Taplow Rd PLMGR N13 .....35 J6
Taplow St IS N1 .....6 D3
Tappesfield Rd PECK SE15 .....143 K4
Tapping CI KUTN/CMB KT2 * 175 H3
Tapp St BETH E2 * 104 D5
Tapster St BAR EN5 .....20 D4
Taransay Wk IS N1 * 85 K4
Tara Ter BROCKY SE4 * 144 B4
Tarbert Rd EDUL SE22 .....143 F6
Tarbert Wk WCHPL E1 .....104 E6
Target CI EBED/NFELT TW14 .....153 H1
Tariff Rd UED N18 .....50 C2
Tarleton Gdns FSTH SE23 .....163 J3
Tarling CI SCUP DA14 .....168 C5
Tarling Rd CAN/RD E16 .....106 D5
   EFNCH N2 .....47 G5
Tarling St WCHPL E1 .....104 D5
Tarnbank ENC/FH EN2 .....22 E6
Tarn St STHWK SE1 .....18 C5
Tarnwood Pk ELTH/MOT SE9 .....166 E3
Tarragon CI NWCR SE14 .....144 B1
Tarragon Gv SYD SE26 .....182 A2
Tarrant PI MBLAR W1H 8 E2
Tarriff Crs DEPT SE8 .....124 C4
Tarrington CI
   STRHM/NOR SW16 .....161 J6
Tarver Rd WALW SE17 .....122 C5
Tarves Wy GNWCH SE10 .....144 E1
Tash PI FBAR/BDGN N11 * 48 B1
Tasker CI HYS/HAR UB3 .....133 F1
Tasker Rd HAMP NW3 .....83 K3
Tasmania Ter UED N18 .....49 J2
Tasman Rd BRXN/ST SW9 .....141 K4
Tasso Rd HMSMTH W6 .....119 H6
Tate Gdns BUSH WD23 .....28 E1
Tate Rd CAN/RD E16 .....126 E1
   SUT SM1 .....208 E3
Tatnell Rd FSTH SE23 .....164 B1
Tattersall CI ELTH/MOT SE9 .....146 D6
Tatton Crs STNW/STAM N16 .....68 B4
Tatum St WALW SE17 .....19 F7
Tauheed CI FSBYPK N4 .....67 J6
Taunton Av HSLW TW3 .....135 H3
   RYNPK SW20 .....176 E5
Taunton CI BARK/HLT IG6 .....37 F6
   BXLYHN DA7 .....150 A4
   CHEAM SM3 .....193 K5
Taunton Dr EFNCH N2 .....47 G5
   ENC/FH EN2 .....23 G4
Taunton Ms CAMTN NW1 * 2 E7
Taunton PI CAMTN NW1 .....2 E6
Taunton Rd GFD/PVL UB6 .....78 B5
   LEW SE13 * 144 E4
Taunton Wy STAN HA7 .....44 A6
Tavern CI CAR SM5 .....194 D4
Taverners CI NTGHL W11 .....119 H1
Taverner Sq HBRY N5 * 85 J2
Taverners Wy CHING E4 .....38 C3
Tavistock Av GFD/PVL UB6 .....97 F1
   MLHL NW7 .....46 B3
   WALTH E17 .....51 F6
Tavistock CI STNW/STAM N16 * 86 A3
Tavistock Crs MTCM CR4 .....195 K1
   NTGHL W11 .....100 D4
Tavistock Gdns GDMY/SEVK IG3 .....90 E2
Tavistock Gv CROY/NA CR0 .....196 E4
Tavistock Ms NTGHL W11 * 100 D5
Tavistock PI STHGT/OAK N14 * 34 B1
   STPAN WC1H 5 F6
Tavistock Rd CAR SM5 .....194 C6
   CROY/NA CR0 .....196 E5
   EDGW HA8 .....44 C4
   FSBYPK N4 .....67 K3
   HAYES BR2 .....199 K1
   HCDN/ICK UB10 .....94 B1
   NTGHL W11 .....100 D4
   SWFD E18 .....52 E6
   WAN E11 .....70 B6
   WDR/YW UB7 .....112 A1
   WELL DA16 .....148 D2
   WLSDN NW10 .....99 H1
Tavistock Sq STPAN WC1H 4 D6
Tavistock St COVGDN WC2E 11 F5
Tavistock Ter ARCH N19 .....84 D1

Taviton St *STPAN* WC1H * 4 C6
Tavy Br *ABYW* SE2 .....128 D2
Tavy Cl *LBTH* SE11 .....122 B5
Tawney Rd *THMD* SE28 .....109 H6
Tawny Cl *FELT* TW15 .....153 K5
　　WEA W13 .....116 C1
Tawny Wy *BERM/RHTH* SE16 .....124 A4
Tayben Av *WHTN* TW2 .....155 K1
Taybridge Rd *BTSEA* SW11 .....141 F4
Tayburn Cl *POP/IOD* E14 .....106 A5
Tayfield Cl *HGDN/ICK* UB10 .....76 A1
Taylor Av *RCH/KEW* TW9 .....137 J3
Taylor Cl *CRW* RM5 .....56 C3
　　DEPT SE8 .....124 C6
　　HPTN* TW12 .....173 H1
　　HSLW TW3 .....135 H2
　　ORP BR6 .....217 F2
　　TOTM N17 .....50 C3
Taylor Rd *WIM/MER* SW19 .....178 D3
　　WLGTN* SM6 .....210 B3
Taylor Rw *RDART* DA2 .....171 F5
Taylor's Buildings
　　WOOL/PLUM SE18 .....127 G4
Taylors Cl *SCUP* DA14 .....168 A6
Taylors Ct *FELT* TW13 .....153 K4
Taylor's Gn *ACT* W3 * 99 G5
Taylor's La *BAR* EN5 .....20 D2
　　SYD SE26 .....163 J6
　　WLSDN NW10 .....81 G5
Taylors Md *MLHL* NW7 * 45 J1
Taymount Ri *FSTH* SE23 .....163 K4
Tayport Cl *IS* N1 .....85 F5
Tayside Dr *EDGW* HA8 .....30 D5
Tay Wy *ROM* RM1 .....57 H4
Taywood Rd *STHL* UB1 .....95 K2
Teak Cl *BERM/RHTH* SE16 .....124 B1
Teal Av *STMC/STPC* BR5 .....202 E1
Teal Cl *CAN/RD* E16 .....107 H4
Teal Dr *NTHWD* HA6 .....40 A3
Teale St *BETH* E2 .....104 C1
Tealing Dr *HOR/WEW* KT19 .....207 F2
Teasel Cl *CROY/NA* CR0 .....198 A5
Teasel Crs *THMD* SE28 .....127 K1
Teasel Wy *SRTFD* E15 .....106 C2
Tebworth Rd *TOTM* N17 .....50 B3
Technology Pk
　　CDALE/KGS NW9 * 45 F6
Teck Cl *ISLW* TW7 .....136 B3
Tedder Cl *CHSGTN* KT9 .....205 J3
Tedder Rd *SAND/SEL* CR2 .....213 F5
Teddington Pk *TEDD* TW11 .....174 A1
Teddington Park Rd
　　TEDD TW11 .....156 A6
Tedworth Gdns *CHEL* SW3 .....120 E5
Tedworth Sq *CHEL* SW3 .....120 E5
Tees Av *GFD/PVL* UB6 .....96 E1
Teesdale Av *ISLW* TW7 .....136 B2
Teesdale Cl *BETH* E2 .....104 C1
Teesdale Gdns *ISLW* TW7 .....136 B2
　　SNWD SE25 .....181 F5
Teesdale Rd *WAN* E11 .....70 D3
Teesdale St *BETH* E2 .....104 D1
Teesdale Yd *BETH* E2 * 104 D1
Tee The *ACT* W3 .....99 G5
Teevan Cl *CROY/NA* CR0 .....197 H4
Teevan Rd *CROY/NA* CR0 .....197 H4
Teignmouth Cl *CLAP* SW4 .....141 J5
　　EDGW HA8 .....44 B5
Teignmouth Gdns
　　GFD/PVL UB6 .....97 G1
Teignmouth Rd *CRICK* NW2 .....82 B3
　　WELL DA16 .....148 D3
Telcote Wy *RSLP* HA4 * 59 G4
Telegraph La *ESH/CLAY* KT10 .....205 F2
Telegraph Ms *GDMY/SEVK* IG3 .....73 F5
Telegraph Pas
　　BRXS/STRHM SW2 .....161 K2
Telegraph Pl *POP/IOD* E14 .....124 E4
Telegraph Rd *PUT/ROE* SW15 .....158 E2
Telegraph St *LOTH* EC2R 12 E3
Telephone Pl *WKENS* W14 * 119 J6
Telferscot Rd *BAL* SW12 .....161 J3
Telford Av *BAL* SW12 .....161 H3
Telford Cl *NRWD* SE19 .....181 G2
　　WALTH E17 .....69 G4
Telford Dr *WOT/HER* KT12 .....188 B4
Telford Rd *CDALE/KGS* NW9 .....63 J3
　　CHST BR7 .....167 J4
　　NKENS W10 .....100 C4
　　STHL UB1 .....96 B6
　　WHTN TW2 .....155 F2
Telford Rd North Circular Rd
　　UED N18 * 48 C2
Telfords Yd *WAP* E1W * 104 C6
Telford Ter *PIM* SW1V * 121 H6
Telford Wy *ACT* W3 .....99 G4
　　YEAD UB4 .....95 J4
Telham Rd *EHAM* E6 .....108 A1
Tell Gv *EDUL* SE22 .....143 G5
Tellisford *ESH/CLAY* KT10 .....204 B2
Telscan Av *WOOL/PLUM* SE18 .....146 C2
Telscombe Cl *ORP* BR6 .....201 K6
Temeraire Pl *BTFD* TW8 .....117 G5
Temeraire St
　　BERM/RHTH SE16 .....123 K2
Tempelhof Av *HDN* NW4 .....64 A4
Temperley Rd *BAL* SW12 .....161 F2
Tempest Wy *RAIN* RM13 .....93 J4
Templar Dr *THMD* SE28 .....109 K5
Templar Pl *HPTN* TW12 .....173 F3
Templars Av *GLDGN* NW11 .....64 D3
Templars Ct *DART* DA1 * 151 K6
Templars Crs *FNCH* N3 .....46 E5
Templars Dr
　　KTN/HRWW/W HA3 * 42 D2
Templar St *CMBW* SE5 .....142 C3
Temple Av *BCTR* RM8 .....74 C5
　　EMB EC4Y 11 K5
　　CROY/NA CR0 .....213 J1
　　WFD/WHT N20 .....33 H2
Temple Cl *FNCH* N3 .....46 D5
　　THHTH CR7 * 196 C2
　　WALTH E17 .....51 H4
Templecombe Rd *HOM* E9 .....86 E6

Templecombe Wy *MRDN* SM4 .....193 G2
Temple Fortune Hl
　　GLDGN NW11 .....64 E2
Temple Fortune La
　　GLDGN NW11 .....64 D3
Temple Gdns *BCTR* RM8 .....91 K1
　　EMB EC4Y * 11 J5
　　GLDGN NW11 .....64 D3
　　WCHMH N21 * 35 H4
Temple Gv *ENC/FH* EN2 .....23 H4
　　GLDGN NW11 .....64 E3
Temple Hl *DART* DA1 .....151 J6
Temple Hill Sq *DART* DA1 .....151 J6
Temple La *EMB* EC4Y 11 K4
Templeman Rd *HNWL* W7 .....97 F4
Templemead Cl *ACT* W3 .....99 G5
Temple Mead Cl *STAN* HA7 .....43 H2
Temple Mills La *LEY* E10 .....87 K2
　　SRTFD E15 .....88 A3
Temple Pde *BAR* EN5 * 33 H1
Temple Pl *TPL/STR* WC2R 11 H5
Temple Rd *CEND/HSY/T* N8 .....67 F1
　　CHSWK W4 .....117 K3
　　CRICK NW2 .....82 A2
　　CROY/NA CR0 .....211 K2
　　EA W5 .....116 E3
　　EHAM E6 .....89 J6
　　HSLW TW3 .....135 G5
　　RCH/KEW TW9 .....137 G3
Temple Sheen Rd
　　MORT/ESHN SW14 .....137 K5
Temple Ter *WDGN* N22 * 104 D1
Templeton Av *CHING* E4 .....37 J6
Templeton Cl
　　STNW/STAM N16 * 86 A3
　　THHTH CR7 .....180 E4
Templeton Pl *ECT* SW5 .....119 K4
Templeton Rd *FSBYPK* N4 .....67 K3
Temple Wy *SUT* SM1 .....209 H1
Templewood *WEA* W13 .....97 H4
Templewood Av *HAMP* NW3 .....83 F1
Templewood Gdns *HAMP* NW3 .....83 F1
Temple Yd *BETH* E2 * 104 D1
Tempsford Cl *ENC/FH* EN2 .....23 J3
Temsford Ct *RYLN/HDSTN* HA2 .....42 C5
Tenbury Cl *FSTGT* E7 .....89 H3
Tenbury Ct *BRXS/STRHM* SW2 * 161 J3
Tenby Av *KTN/HRWW/W* HA3 .....43 H5
Tenby Cl *CHDH* RM6 .....74 A3
　　SEVS/STOTM N15 .....68 B1
Tenby Gdns *NTHLT* UB5 .....78 A4
Tenby Rd *CHDH* RM6 .....74 A3
　　EDGW HA8 .....44 B4
　　PEND EN3 .....24 E4
　　WALTH E17 .....69 G2
　　WELL DA16 .....148 E2
Tench St *WAP* E1W * 123 J1
Tenda Rd *BERM/RHTH* SE16 .....123 J4
Tendring Wy *CHDH* RM6 .....73 J2
Tenham Av *BRXS/STRHM* SW2 .....161 J4
Tenniel Cl *BAY/PAD* W2 .....101 G5
Tennison Av *SNWD* SE25 .....197 G1
Tennis St *STHWK* SE1 .....18 E2
Tenniswood Rd *EN* EN1 .....24 B2
Tennyson Av *CDALE/KGS* NW9 .....44 E6
　　MNPK E12 .....89 J5
　　NWMAL KT3 .....192 E2
　　TWK TW1 .....156 A3
　　WAN E11 .....70 E4
Tennyson Cl
　　EBED/NFELT TW14 .....153 K1
　　PEND EN3 .....25 F6
　　WELL DA16 .....147 K2
Tennyson Rd *DART* DA1 .....151 K6
　　HNWL W7 .....97 F1
　　HSLW TW3 .....135 H3
　　KIL/WHAMP NW6 .....82 D6
　　MLHL NW7 .....45 H1
　　PGE/AN SE20 .....182 A3
　　SRTFD E15 .....88 C5
　　WALTH E17 .....69 H3
　　WIM/MER SW19 .....178 B1
Tennyson St *VX/NE* SW8 .....141 G3
Tennyson Wy *HCH* RM12 .....75 H5
Tensing Rd *NWDGN* UB2 .....115 F3
Tentelow La *NWDGN* UB2 .....115 G5
Tenterden Cl *ELTH/MOT* SE9 .....166 E6
　　HDN NW4 .....46 B6
Tenterden Dr *HDN* NW4 .....46 B6
Tenterden Gdns *CROY/NA* CR0 .....197 H4
　　HDN NW4 .....46 B6
Tenterden Gv *HDN* NW4 .....64 A1
Tenterden Rd *BCTR* RM8 .....74 B6
　　CROY/NA CR0 .....197 H4
　　TOTM N17 .....50 B3
Tenterden St *CONDST* W1S 9 K4
Tenter Gnd *WCHPL* E1 .....13 J2
Tent Peg La *STMC/STPC* BR5 .....201 H2
Tenter St *WCHPL* E1 .....104 D3
Teredo St *LEW* SE13 .....144 E5
Terling Cl *WAN* E11 .....88 D1
Terling Rd *BCTR* RM8 .....74 C6
Terling Wk *IS* N1 * 85 J6
Terminus Pl *PIM* SW1V 15 K5
Terrace Gdns *BARN* SW13 .....138 C3
Terrace La *RCHPK/HAM* TW10 .....157 F1
Terrace Rd *HOM* E9 .....87 F5
　　PLSTW E13 .....106 E1
　　WOT/HER KT12 .....188 A4
The Terrace *BARN* SW13 .....138 B3
　　BETH E2 * 104 E2
　　CHING E4 * 38 C5
　　EBAR EN4 * 124 C4
　　EFNCH N2 * 65 H1
　　FNCH N3 * 46 D5
　　FSTH SE23 * 164 B2
　　KIL/WHAMP NW6 .....82 B6
Terrace Vls *HMSMTH* W6 * 118 D5
Terrace Wk *DAGW* RM9 .....92 A5
Terrac St *RCH/KEW* TW9 .....137 G5
Terrapin Rd *TOOT* SW17 .....161 G5
Terretts Pl *IS* N1 * 85 H5
Terrick Rd *WDGN* N22 .....48 E4
Terrick St *SHB* W12 .....99 K5
Terrilands *PIN* HA5 .....41 K6

Terront Rd *SEVS/STOTM* N15 .....67 J2
Tessa Sanderson Wy
　　GFD/PVL UB6 .....78 D5
Testerton Rd *NTGHL* W11 * 100 B6
Testerton Wk *NTGHL* W11 * 100 B6
Tetbury Pl *IS* N1 .....6 A1
Tetcott Rd *WBPTN* SW10 .....140 B1
Tetherdown *MUSWH* N10 .....48 A6
Tetty Wy *HAYES* BR2 .....183 K5
Teversham La *VX/NE* SW8 .....141 K2
Teviot Cl *WELL* DA16 .....148 C2
Teviot St *POP/IOD* E14 .....106 A4
Tewkesbury Av *FSTH* SE23 .....163 J3
　　PIN HA5 .....59 J2
Tewkesbury Cl *LOU* IG10 .....39 J1
Tewkesbury Gdns
　　CDALE/KGS NW9 .....44 D6
Tewkesbury Rd *CAR* SM5 .....194 C5
　　SEVS/STOTM N15 .....67 K4
　　WEA W13 .....116 B1
Tewkesbury Ter
　　FBAR/BDGN N11 .....48 C2
Tewson Rd *WOOL/PLUM* SE18 .....127 K5
Teynham Av *EN* EN1 .....35 K1
Teynham Gn *HAYES* BR2 .....199 K2
Teynton Ter *TOTM* N17 .....49 J4
Thackeray Av *TOTM* N17 .....50 C5
Thackeray Cl *ISLW* TW7 .....136 B3
　　RYLN/HDSTN HA2 .....60 A5
　　WIM/MER SW19 .....177 G3
Thackeray Dr *CHDH* RM6 .....73 H4
Thackeray Ms *HACK* E8 * 86 C4
Thackeray Rd *EHAM* E6 .....107 H1
　　VX/NE SW8 .....141 G3
Thackeray St *KENS* W8 .....120 A3
Thakeham Cl *SYD* SE26 .....181 J1
Thalia Cl *GNWCH* SE10 .....125 H6
Thame Rd *BERM/RHTH* SE16 .....124 A2
Thames Av *DAGW* RM9 .....110 E2
　　GFD/PVL UB6 .....97 H2
　　WBPTN SW10 .....140 B2
Thames Bank
　　MORT/ESHN SW14 .....137 K3
Thamesbank Pl *THMD* SE28 .....109 J4
Thames Cir *POP/IOD* E14 .....124 D4
Thames Cl *HPTN* TW12 .....173 G5
　　RAIN RM13 .....111 K3
Thames Down Link
　　CHSGTN KT9 .....206 E2
　　WPK KT4 .....207 F1
Thames Dr *RSLP* HA4 .....58 A3
Thames Eyot *TWK* TW1 * 156 A4
Thames Ga *DART* DA1 .....151 K6
Thamesgate Cl
　　RCHPK/HAM TW10 .....156 C6
Thameside *TEDD* TW11 .....174 E3
Thames Meadow
　　E/WMO/HCT KT8 .....173 F6
Thamesmere Dr *THMD* SE28 .....109 G6
Thames Pth *BERM/RHTH* SE16 .....124 C3
　　BOW E3 .....106 A1
　　CHSWK W4 .....138 C2
　　CLPT E5 .....87 F1
　　LBTH SE11 .....121 K5
　　RCH/KEW TW9 .....13 H7
　　TWRH EC3N 13 H7
　　WEST SW1P 172 D6
　　WOT/HER KT12 .....172 B6
Thames Pl *PUT/ROE* SW15 .....139 G4
Thamespoint *TEDD* TW11 * 174 E3
Thames Quay *WBPTN* SW10 * 140 B2
Thames Reach *KUT/HW* KT1 * 174 E4
Thames Rd *BARK* IG11 .....109 G2
　　CAN/RD E16 .....126 C1
　　CHSWK W4 .....137 J1
　　DART DA1 .....150 D4
Thames Side *KUTN/CMB* KT2 .....174 E4
　　THDIT KT7 .....190 C5
Thames St *GNWCH* SE10 .....124 E6
　　HPTN TW12 .....173 G4
　　KUT/HW KT1 .....174 E5
　　SUN TW16 .....172 A6
Thameswalk Cl *HSLW* TW5 .....135 F3
Thames Village *CHSWK* W4 .....137 K2
Thamley *PUR* RM19 .....131 K4
Thanescroft Gdns
　　CROY/NA CR0 .....212 A1
Thanet Dr *HAYES* BR2 .....215 H1
Thanet Pl *CROY/NA* CR0 .....211 J2
Thanet Rd *BXLY* DA5 .....169 H2
　　ERITH DA8 .....150 B1
Thanet St *STPAN* WC1H 4 F6
Thant Cl *LEY* E10 .....87 K2
Tharp Rd *WLGTN* SM6 .....210 D3
Thatcham Gdns
　　TRDG/WHET N20 .....33 G2
Thatchers Wy *ISLW* TW7 .....135 J6
Thatches Gv *CHDH* RM6 .....74 A1
Thaxted Pl *RYNPK* SW20 .....177 G3
Thaxted Rd *BKHH* IG9 .....39 J2
　　ELTH/MOT SE9 .....167 H4
Thaxton Rd *WKENS* W14 .....119 J6
Thayers Farm Rd *BECK* BR3 .....182 B4
Thayer St *MHST* W1U 9 H3
Theatre Sq *SRTFD* E15 .....88 B4
Theatre St *BTSEA* SW11 .....140 E4
Theberton St *IS* N1 .....85 G6
The Beverly *MRDN* SM4 .....193 G5
The Courtyard *HAYES* BR2 .....215 J4
Theed St *STHWK* SE1 .....17 J1
The Green *WIM/MER* SW19 .....177 G1
Thelma Gv *TEDD* TW11 .....174 B2
Theobald Crs
　　KTN/HRWW/W HA3 .....42 B4
Theobald Rd *CROY/NA* CR0 .....196 C6
　　WALTH E17 .....69 H4
Theobald's Rd *FSBYW* WC1X 11 G1
Theobald St *STHWK* SE1 .....19 F5
Theodora Wy *PIN* HA5 .....40 D6
Theodore Rd *LEW* SE13 .....165 G1
Therapia La *CROY/NA* CR0 .....195 K4
Therapia Rd *EDUL* SE22 .....163 K1
Theresa Rd *HMSMTH* W6 .....118 D4
Theresa's Wk *SAND/SEL* CR2 .....211 K6

Thermopylae Ga
　　POP/IOD E14 .....124 E4
Theseus Wk *IS* N1 .....6 B1
Thesiger Rd *PGE/AN* SE20 .....182 A3
Thessaly Rd *VX/NE* SW8 .....141 J2
Thetford Cl *PLMGR* N13 .....49 H2
Thetford Rd *ASHF* TW15 .....152 B6
　　DAGW RM9 .....91 K6
　　NWMAL KT3 .....192 B3
Theydon Gdns *RAIN* RM13 .....93 G5
Theydon Gv *WFD* IG8 .....53 G2
Theydon Rd *CLPT* E5 .....68 E6
Theydon St *WALTH* E17 .....69 H4
Thicket Crs *SUT* SM1 .....209 G2
Thicket Gv *DAGW* RM9 .....91 J4
　　PGE/AN SE20 .....181 H5
Thicket Rd *PGE/AN* SE20 .....181 J5
　　SUT SM1 .....209 G2
Thicket Ter *PGE/AN* SE20 * 181 J5
Third Av *ACT* W3 .....118 C1
　　CHDH RM6 .....92 A1
　　DAGE RM10 .....92 D6
　　EN EN1 .....36 B1
　　HYS/HAR UB3 .....113 J1
　　MNPK E12 .....89 J2
　　NKENS W10 .....100 C2
　　PLSTW E13 .....106 E2
　　WALTH E17 .....69 J2
　　WBLY HA9 .....61 K6
Third Cl *E/WMO/HCT* KT8 .....189 G1
Third Cross Rd *WHTN* TW2 .....155 J4
Third Wy *WBLY* HA9 .....62 D1
Thirkleby Rd *EDGW* HA8 * 44 D4
　　WEST SW1P 16 B5
Thirlmere Av *GFD/PVL* UB6 .....97 J2
Thirlmere Gdns *WBLY* HA9 .....61 J5
Thirlmere Ri *BMLY* BR1 .....183 J2
Thirlmere Rd *BXLYHN* DA7 .....149 K3
　　MUSWH N10 .....48 A4
　　STRHM/NOR SW16 .....161 J6
Thirsk Cl *NTHLT* UB5 .....78 A4
Thirsk Rd *BTSEA* SW11 .....141 F4
　　MTCM CR4 .....179 F3
　　SNWD SE25 .....196 E1
Thirza Rd *DART* DA1 .....171 J1
Thistlefield Cl *BXLY* DA5 .....168 E3
Thistlebrook *ABYW* SE2 .....128 D3
Thistlecroft Gdns *STAN* HA7 .....43 K4
Thistledene *THDIT* KT7 .....189 K3
Thistledene Av *RYLN/HDSTN* HA2 .....59 J1
　　RYLN/HDSTN HA2 .....77 J1
Thistle Gv *WBPTN* SW10 * 120 B5
Thistlemead *CHST* BR7 .....185 G5
Thistlewaite Rd *CLPT* E5 .....86 D1
Thistlewood Cl *HOLWY* N7 .....67 F6
Thistleworth Cl *ISLW* TW7 .....135 J1
Thistley Cl *NFNCH/WDSP* N12 .....47 J2
Thomas a Beckett Cl
　　ALP/SUD HA0 .....79 F2
Thomas Baines Rd
　　BTSEA SW11 .....140 C4
Thomas Cribb Ms *EHAM* E6 .....107 K5
Thomas Dean Rd *SYD* SE26 * 164 C6
Thomas Dinwiddy Rd
　　LEE/GVPK SE12 .....166 A4
Thomas Doyle St *STHWK* SE1 .....18 B4
Thomas' La *CAT* SE6 .....164 E2
Thomas Moore St *WAP* E1W * 104 C6
Thomas More Wy *EFNCH* N2 .....47 G6
Thomas North Ter
　　CAN/RD E16 * 106 D4
Thomas Rd *POP/IOD* E14 .....105 J5
Thomas Wall Cl *SUT* SM1 .....209 F3
Thompson Av *RCH/KEW* TW9 .....137 J4
Thompson Cl *CHEAM* SM3 .....193 K5
　　IL IG1 .....90 B3
Thompson Rd *DAGW* RM9 .....92 B1
　　EDUL SE22 .....143 G6
　　HSLW TW3 .....135 G5
Thompson's Av *CMBW* SE5 .....142 D1
Thomson Crs *CROY/NA* CR0 .....196 B5
Thomson Rd
　　KTN/HRWW/W HA3 .....42 E6
Thorburn Sq *STHWK* SE1 .....123 H4
Thorburn Wy
　　WIM/MER SW19 .....178 C4
Thoresby St *IS* N1 .....6 D4
Thorkhill Gdns *THDIT* KT7 .....190 C5
Thorkhill Rd *THDIT* KT7 .....190 C5
Thornaby Gdns *UED* N18 .....50 C2
Thorn Av *BUSH* WD23 .....28 A2
Thornbury Av *ISLW* TW7 .....135 J1
Thornbury Cl *STNW/STAM* N16 .....86 A3
　　ISLW TW7 .....135 J1
Thornbury Rd *CLAP* SW4 .....161 K1
Thornby Rd *CLPT* E5 .....86 E1
Thorncliffe Rd *CLAP* SW4 .....161 K1
　　NWDGN UB2 .....114 E5
Thorn Cl *HAYES* BR2 .....201 F3
　　NTHLT UB5 .....95 K2
Thorncombe Rd *EDUL* SE22 .....143 F6
Thorn Ct *BELMT* SM2 * 209 F5
Thorncroft *EMPK* RM11 .....75 K3
Thorncroft St *VX/NE* SW8 .....141 K1
Thorndean St
　　WAND/EARL SW18 .....160 B4
Thorndene Av *TRDG/WHET* N20 .....33 F5
Thorndike Av *NTHLT* UB5 .....77 H6
Thorndike Cl *WBPTN* SW10 .....140 B1
Thorndike Rd *IS* N1 .....85 K4
Thorndike St *PIM* SW1V 16 C7
Thorndon Cl *STMC/STPC* BR5 .....186 A5
Thorndon Gdns
　　HOR/WEW KT19 .....207 G3
Thorndon Rd *STMC/STPC* BR5 .....186 A5
Thorndyke Ct *PIN* HA5 * 41 J4
Thorne Cl *CAN/RD* E16 .....106 E5
　　ERITH DA8 .....129 K5
　　WAN E11 .....88 D1
Thornell Wy *RYLN/HDSTN* HA2 .....60 A1
Thorne Rd *VX/NE* SW8 .....141 K1
Thorne's Cl *BECK* BR3 .....183 F6

Thorne St *BARN* SW13 .....138 B4
Thornet Wood Rd *BMLY* BR1 .....185 H6
Thorney Crs *BTSEA* SW11 * 140 C1
Thorneycroft Cl
　　WOT/HER KT12 .....188 B3
Thorneycroft Dr *PEND* EN3 .....25 H1
Thorney Hedge Rd *CHSWK* W4 * 117 J4
Thorney St *WEST* SW1P 16 E6
Thornfield Av *MLHL* NW7 .....46 C4
Thornfield Rd *SHB* W12 .....118 E2
Thornford Rd *LEW* SE13 .....145 F6
Thorngate Rd *MV/WKIL* W9 .....100 E3
Thorngrove Rd *PLSTW* E13 .....89 F6
Thornham Gv *SRTFD* E15 .....88 B3
Thornham St *GNWCH* SE10 .....124 E6
Thornhill Av *SURB* KT6 .....191 F6
　　WOOL/PLUM SE18 .....147 K1
Thornhill Bridge Whf *IS* N1 .....5 H1
Thornhill Crs *IS* N1 .....85 G5
Thornhill Gdns *BARK* IG11 .....90 E6
　　LEY E10 .....69 K6
Thornhill Gv *IS* N1 .....85 F5
Thornhill Rd *CROY/NA* CR0 .....196 D4
　　IS N1 .....85 G5
　　LEY E10 .....69 K6
　　NTHWD HA6 .....26 A6
　　SURB KT6 .....191 F6
Thornhill Sq *IS* N1 .....85 F5
Thornlaw Rd *WNWD* SE27 .....162 B6
Thornley Cl *TOTM* N17 .....50 C5
Thornley Dr *RYLN/HDSTN* HA2 .....60 B6
Thornsbeach Rd *CAT* SE6 .....165 F3
Thornsett Pl *PGE/AN* SE20 .....181 J5
Thornsett Rd *PGE/AN* SE20 .....181 J5
　　WAND/EARL SW18 .....160 A4
Thornsett Ter *PGE/AN* SE20 * 181 J5
Thornton Av *BRXS/STRHM* SW2 .....161 K3
　　CHSWK W4 .....118 B4
　　CROY/NA CR0 .....196 A3
　　WDR/YW UB7 .....112 C3
Thornton Cl *WDR/YW* UB7 .....112 C3
Thornton Dene *BECK* BR3 .....182 D5
Thornton Gdns *BAL* SW12 .....161 J3
Thornton Gv *PIN* HA5 .....42 A2
Thornton Hl *WIM/MER* SW19 .....177 H3
Thornton Pl *MBLAR* W1H 8 E1
Thornton Rd *BAL* SW12 .....161 J2
　　BAR EN5 .....20 C4
　　BELV DA17 * 129 J4
　　BMLY BR1 .....183 K1
　　CAR SM5 .....194 D4
　　IL IG1 .....90 B2
　　MORT/ESHN SW14 .....138 A4
　　THHTH CR7 .....196 A3
　　UED N18 .....36 E5
　　WAN E11 .....70 B6
　　WIM/MER SW19 .....177 G2
Thornton Rw *THHTH* CR7 .....196 B2
Thorntons Farm Av
　　ROMW/RG RM7 .....74 E6
Thornton St *STNW* SW9 .....142 B3
Thornton Wy *GLDGN* NW11 .....65 F2
Thorntree Rd *CHARL* SE7 .....126 C5
Thornville Gv *MTCM* CR4 .....178 B5
Thornville St *DEPT* SE8 .....144 D2
Thornwood Cl *SWFD* E18 .....53 F5
Thornwood Rd *LEW* SE13 .....145 H6
Thorogood Gdns *SRTFD* E15 .....88 C3
Thorogood Wy *RAIN* RM13 .....93 G3
Thorold Rd *IL* IG1 .....72 B6
　　WDGN N22 .....48 E3
Thorparch Rd *VX/NE* SW8 .....141 J2
Thorpebank Rd *SHB* W12 .....118 D1
Thorpe Cl *NKENS* W10 .....100 C5
　　ORP BR6 .....201 K6
　　SYD SE26 .....164 A6
Thorpe Ct *TOOT* SW17 .....160 C6
Thorpe Crs *OXHEY* WD19 .....27 F2
　　WALTH E17 .....51 H5
Thorpedale Gdns
　　GNTH/NBYPK IG2 .....72 A1
Thorpedale Rd *FSBYPK* N4 .....66 E5
Thorpe Hall Rd *WALTH* E17 .....52 A4
Thorpe Rd *BARK* IG11 .....90 D5
　　EHAM E6 .....89 K6
　　FSTGT E7 .....88 E1
　　KUTN/CMB KT2 .....175 F3
　　SEVS/STOTM N15 .....68 A3
　　WALTH E17 .....52 A5
Thorpewood Av *SYD* SE26 .....163 J4
Thorpland Av *HGDN/ICK* UB10 .....76 A1
Thorsden Wy *NRWD* SE19 * 181 F1
Thorverton Rd *CRICK* NW2 .....82 C1
Thoydon Rd *BOW* E3 .....105 G1
Thrale Rd *STRHM/NOR* SW16 .....179 H1
Thrale St *STHWK* SE1 .....18 D1
Thrasher Cl *HACK* E8 * 86 B6
Thrawl St *WCHPL* E1 .....13 J2
Threadneedle St *LOTH* EC2R 13 F4
Three Colts La *BETH* E2 .....104 D3
Three Colt St *POP/IOD* E14 * 105 H6
Three Corners *BXLYHN* DA7 .....149 J3
Three Kings Yd
　　MYFR/PKLN W1K 9 J5
Three Meadows Ms
　　KTN/HRWW/W HA3 .....43 F4
Three Mill La *BOW* E3 .....106 A2
Three Oak La *STHWK* SE1 .....19 J2
Threshers Pl *NTGHL* W11 .....100 C6
Thriftwood *FSTH* SE23 .....163 K5
Thrigby Rd *CHSGTN* KT9 .....206 B4
Throckmorten Rd
　　CAN/RD E16 .....107 F5
Throgmorton Av *OBST* EC2N 13 H3
Throgmorton St *LOTH* EC2R 13 F3
Throwley Cl *ABYW* SE2 .....128 D3
Throwley Rd *SUT* SM1 .....209 F3
Throwley Wy *SUT* SM1 .....209 F2
Thrupp Cl *MTCM* CR4 .....179 G5
Thrush Gn *RYLN/HDSTN* HA2 .....60 A1
Thrush St *WALW* SE17 .....122 D5
Thunderer Rd *DAGW* RM9 .....110 A3
Thurbarn Rd *CAT* SE6 .....182 K1

Thurland Rd
 BERM/RHTH SE16 ....123 H3
Thurlby Cl WFD IG8 ....53 K2
Thurlby Rd ALP/SUD HA0 ......79 K4
 WNWD SE27 ....162 B6
Thurleigh Av BAL SW12 ....161 H1
Thurleigh Rd BAL SW12 ....160 E1
Thurleston Av MRDN SM4 ......195 H2
Thurlestone Av GDMY/SEVK IG3...91 F2
 NFNCH/WDSP N12 ....47 K2
Thurlestone Rd WNWD SE27 ...162 B5
Thurloe Cl SKENS SW7 ....14 C6
Thurloe Gdns ROM RM1 ....75 G3
Thurloe Pl SKENS SW7 ....14 C5
Thurloe Place Ms SKENS SW7 *..14 B6
Thurloe Sq SKENS SW7 ....14 C6
Thurloe St SKENS SW7 ....14 B6
Thurlow Cl CHING E4 ....51 K2
Thurlow Gdns ALP/SUD HA0 *...79 K3
 CHIG IG7 ....54 D2
Thurlow Hl DUL SE21 ....162 D5
Thurlow Park Rd DUL SE21 .....162 C4
Thurlow Rd HAMP NW3 ....83 H5
 HNWL W7 ....116 B2
Thurlow St WALW SE17 ....123 F5
Thurlow Ter KTTN NW5 ....83 K3
Thurlston Rd RSLP HA4 ....76 E1
Thursland Rd SCUP DA14 ....187 F1
Thursley Crs CROY/NA CRO 214 B5
Thursley Gdns
 WIM/MER SW19 ....159 G4
Thursley Rd ELTH/MOT SE9 ....166 E5
Thurso St TOOT SW17 ....160 C6
Thurstan Rd RYNPK SW20 ......176 E3
Thurston Rd DEPT SE8 ....144 E3
 STHL UB1 ....95 K5
Thurtle Rd BETH E2 ....7 K1
Thwaite Cl ERITH DA8 ....129 K6
Thyer Cl ORP BR6 ....216 C2
Thyra Gv NFNCH/WDSP N12 ....47 F2
Tibbatt's Rd BOW E3 ....105 K3
Tibbenham Pl CAT SE6 ....164 E3
Tibberton Sq IS N1 * 85 J5
Tibbets Cl WIM/MER SW19 ......159 G3
Tibbet's Ride PUT/ROE SW15 ...159 G2
Tiber Gdns IS N1 ....5 F1
Ticehurst Cl STMC/STPC BR5 ...186 B3
Ticehurst Rd FSTH SE23 ....164 B4
Tickford Cl ABYW SE2 ....128 D2
Tidal Basin Rd CAN/RD E16 ....106 D6
Tidenham Gdns CROY/NA CRO ...212 A1
Tideswell Rd CROY/NA CRO 213 J1
 PUT/ROE SW15 ....139 F5
Tideway Cl RCHPK/HAM TW10 ...156 C6
Tideway Wk VX/NE SW8 * 121 H6
Tidey St BOW E3 ....105 J4
Tidford Rd WELL DA16 ....148 A3
Tidworth Rd BOW E3 ....105 J3
Tiepigs La WWKM BR4 ....199 H6
Tierney Rd BRXS/STRHM SW2 ..161 K3
Tierney Ter
 BRXS/STRHM SW2 * 161 K3
Tiger La HAYES BR2 ....200 A1
Tiger Wy CLPT E5 ....86 D2
Tigres Cl ED N9 ....36 E4
Tilbrook Rd BKHTH/KID SE3 ...146 B4
Tilbury Cl PECK SE15 ....143 G1
 STMC/STPC BR5 ....186 C5
Tilbury Rd EHAM E6 ....107 K1
 LEY E10 ....70 A4
Tildesley Rd PUT/ROE SW15 ....159 F1
Tile Farm Rd ORP BR6 ....216 D1
Tilehurst Rd CHEAM SM3 ....208 C3
 WAND/EARL SW18 ....160 C5
Tile Kiln La BXLY DA5 ....170 B5
 HGT N6 ....66 B5
 PLMGR N13 ....49 J1
Tileyard Rd HOLWY N7 ....84 E5
Tilford Av CROY/NA CRO 214 A5
Tilford Gdns WIM/MER SW19 ...159 G3
Tilia Cl SUT SM1 ....208 D5
Tilia Rd CLPT E5 ....86 D2
Tiller Rd POP/IOD E14 ....124 D3
Tillett Cl WLSDN NW10 ....80 E4
Tillet Wy BETH E2 ....104 C2
Tilley Rd FELT TW13 ....153 K3
Tillingbourne Gdns FNCH N3 ...46 D6
Tillingbourne Gn
 STMC/STPC BR5 ....202 B2
Tillingbourne Wy
 GLDGN NW11 ....64 D1
Tillingham Wy
 NFNCH/WDSP N12 ....32 E6
Tilling Rd CRICK NW2 ....63 K5
Tilling Wy WBLY HA9 * 79 K1
Tilman St WCHPL E1 ....104 D5
Tiloch St IS N1 * 85 F5
Tilloston Rd ED N9 ....36 B4
 IL IG1 ....72 A4
 KTN/HRWW/W HA3 ....42 B3
Tilney Gdns IS N1 ....85 K4
Tilney Rd DAGW RM9 ....92 B4
 NWDGN UB2 ....114 B4
Tilney St MYFR/PKLN W1K 9 H7
Tilson Cl CMBW SE5 ....143 F1
Tilson Gdns BRXS/STRHM SW2 ..161 K2
Tilson Rd TOTM N17 ....50 C4
Tilson Cl WAN E11 ....88 D1
Tilston St FUL/PGN SW6 ....119 H6
The Tiltwood ACT W3 ....98 E6
Tilt Yard Rd ELTH/MOT SE9 ....166 E1
Timber Cl CHST BR7 ....185 F5
Timbercroft HOR/WEW KT19 ...207 G2
Timbercroft La
 WOOL/PLUM SE18 ....127 K6
Timberdene Av BARK/HLT IG6 ..54 C4
Timberland Cl PECK SE15 * 143 H1
Timberland Rd WCHPL E1 * 104 D5
Timber Mill Wy CLAP SW4 ....141 J4
Timber Pond Rd
 BERM/RHTH SE16 ....124 A2
Timberslip Dr WLGTN SM6 ......210 D6
The Timbers CHEAM SM3 ....208 C4
Timber St FSBYE EC1V * 6 C6

Timberwharf Rd
 SEVS/STOTM N15 ....68 C3
Time Sq HACK E8 * 86 B3
Times Sq SUT SM1 * 209 F5
Timms Cl BMLY BR1 ....200 E1
Timothy Cl BXLYHS DA6 ....149 F6
Timothy Rd POP/IOD E14 ....105 H4
Tindal St BRXN/ST SW9 ....142 C2
Tine Rd CHIG IG7 ....54 E1
Tinniswood Cl HOLWY N7 * 85 G3
Tinsley Cl SNWD SE25 ....181 J6
Tinsley Rd WCHPL E1 ....104 E4
Tintagel Crs EDUL SE22 ....143 G5
Tintagel Dr STAN HA7 ....43 K1
Tintagel Rd CROY/NA CRO 196 D6
Tintern Av CDALE/KGS NW9 .....44 D4
Tintern Cl PUT/ROE SW15 ....139 H6
 WIM/MER SW19 ....178 B5
Tintern Gdns WCHMH N21 ....34 C2
Tintern Rd CAR SM5 ....194 C5
 WDGN N22 ....49 J4
Tintern St CLAP SW4 ....141 K5
Tintern Wy RYLN/HDSTN HA2 ...60 B5
Tinto Rd CAN/RD E16 ....106 E4
Tinwell St LBTH SE11 ....121 K5
Tippetts Cl ENC/FH EN2 ....23 J2
Tipthorpe Rd BTSEA SW11 ....141 F4
Tiptree Dr CROY/NA CRO 212 A2
Tiptree Cl CHING E4 ....38 B5
Tiptree Crs CLAY IG5 ....54 A6
Tiptree Dr ENC/FH EN2 ....23 K5
Tiptree Rd RSLP HA4 ....77 F2
Tirlemont Rd SAND/SEL CR2 ...211 J5
Tirrell Rd CROY/NA CRO 196 C5
Tisbury Rd STRHM/NOR SW16 ..179 K5
Tisdall Pl WALW SE17 ....19 F7
Titan Ct BTFD TW8 ....117 G5
Titchborne Rw BAY/PAD W2 ....8 A4
Titchfield Rd CAR SM5 ....194 C5
 STJWD NW8 ....2 D1
Titchfield Wk CAR SM5 ....194 C4
Titchwell Rd
 WAND/EARL SW18 ....160 C2
Tite St CHEL SW3 ....120 E6
The Barn La KUTN/CMB KT2 ....175 G4
Tithe Barn Wy NTHLT UB5 ....95 F1
Tithe Cl MLHL NW7 ....45 J4
 WOT/HER KT12 ....188 A5
 YEAD UB4 ....94 B2
The Ct HDN NW4 * 45 J4
The Farm Av
 RYLN/HDSTN HA2 ....78 A1
Tithe Farm Cl RYLN/HDSTN HA2..78 A1
Tithe Wk MLHL NW7 ....45 J4
Titian Av BUSH WD23 ....28 E2
Titley Cl CHING E4 ....51 J1
Titmus Av THMD SE28 ....109 H6
Titmuss St SHB W12 * 118 E2
Tiverton Av CLAY IG5 ....54 A6
Tiverton Cl CROY/NA CRO 197 G4
Tiverton Rd ELTH/MOT SE9 ......167 H3
 EDGW HA8 ....44 B5
 HSLW TW3 ....135 G3
 RSLP HA4 ....76 B1
 SEVS/STOTM N15 ....67 K3
 UED N18 ....50 A1
 WLSDN NW10 ....82 B6
Tiverton St STHWK SE1 ....18 C4
Tiverton Wy CHSGTN KT9 ....205 J3
Tivoli Gdns WOOL/PLUM SE18 ...126 D4
Tivoli Rd CEND/HSY/T N8 ....66 D2
 HSLWW TW4 ....134 D5
 WNWD SE27 ....180 D1
Toad La HSLWW TW4 ....134 E5
Tobago St POP/IOD E14 ....124 D2
Tobin Cl HAMP NW3 ....83 J5
Toby Wy SURB KT6 ....191 J6
Todhouse Yd LOTH EC2R * 12 E3
Tokyngton Av WBLY HA9 ....80 C4
Toland Sq PUT/ROE SW15 ....138 D6
Tolcarne Dr PIN HA5 ....40 E5
Toley Av KTN/HRWW/W HA3 .....62 A3
Tollbridge Cl NKENS W10 ....88 C3
Tollesbury Gdns BARK/HLT IG6 ...54 D6
Tollet St WCHPL E1 ....105 F3
Tollgate Dr DUL SE21 ....163 F4
 YEAD UB4 ....95 H6
Tollgate Gdns
 KIL/WHAMP NW6 * 100 E1
Tollgate Rd EHAM E6 ....107 J4
Tollhouse La WLGTN SM6 ....210 C6
Tollhouse Wy ARCH N19 ....66 C6
Tollington Pk FSBYPK N4 ....67 F6
Tollington Pl FSBYPK N4 ....67 F6
Tollington Rd HOLWY N7 ....85 F2
Tollington Wy HOLWY N7 ....84 E1
Tolpits La WATW WD18 ....26 B2
Tolpuddle Av PLSTW E13 ....89 G6
Tolpuddle St IS N1 ....5 J3
Tolsford Rd CLPT E5 ....86 D3
Tolson Rd ISLW TW7 ....136 B4
Tolverne Rd RYNPK SW20 ....177 F4
Tolworth Broadway
 SURB KT6 ....191 J5
Tolworth Cl SURB KT6 ....191 J5
Tolworth Gdns CHDH RM6 ....73 K2
Tolworth Park Rd SURB KT6 .....191 G6
Tolworth Ri North
 BRYLDS KT5 ....191 K4
Tolworth Ri South
 BRYLDS KT5 ....191 K5
Tolworth Rd SURB KT6 ....191 F6
Tom Cribb Rd
 WOOL/PLUM SE18 ....127 H3
Tom Jenkinson Rd
 CAN/RD E16 ....125 K1
Tomlins Gv BOW E3 ....105 J2
Tomlinson Cl BETH E2 * 7 J5
 CHSWK W4 ....117 J5
Tomlins Orch BARK IG11 ....90 C6
Tomlin's Ter POP/IOD E14 ....105 G5
Tom Mann Cl BARK IG11 ....90 E6

Tom Nolan Cl SRTFD E15 ....106 C7
Tompion St FSBYE EC1V 6 A5
Tomswood Hl BARK/HLT IG6 ......54 C4
Tomswood Rd CHIG IG7 ....54 A2
Tonbridge Crs
 KTN/HRWW/W HA3 ....62 A1
Tonbridge Rd
 E/WMO/HCT KT8 ....188 D1
Tonbridge St STPAN WC1H 4 E5
Tonbridge St CHEAM SM5 ....193 J5
Tonsley Hl WAND/EARL SW18 ...140 A6
Tonsley Pl WAND/EARL SW18 ...140 A6
Tonsley Rd WAND/EARL SW18 ...140 A6
Tonsley St WAND/EARL SW18 ...140 A6
Tonstall Rd MTCM CR4 ....179 F5
Tooke Cl PIN HA5 ....41 J4
Tookey Cl WBLY HA9 ....62 B4
Took's Ct FLST/FETLN EC4A 11 J3
Tooley St STHWK SE1 ....13 F7
Toorack Rd KTN/HRWW/W HA3 ..42 D5
Tooting Bec Gdns
 STRHM/NOR SW16 ....161 J6
Tooting Bec Rd TOOT SW17 ......161 F5
Tooting Gv TOOT SW17 ....178 D1
Tooting High St TOOT SW17 .....160 D6
Tootswood Rd HAYES BR2 ....199 H2
Topcliffe Dr ORP BR6 ....216 D2
Topham Sq TOTM N17 ....49 J4
Topham St CLKNW EC1R * 5 J6
Top House Ri CHING E4 ....38 A2
Topiary Sq RCH/KEW TW9 ....137 G4
Topley St ELTH/MOT SE9 ....146 B5
Topmast Point POP/IOD E14 * ...124 D2
Top Pk BECK BR3 ....199 H2
Topsfield Pde
 CEND/HSY/T N8 * 66 E2
Topsfield Rd CEND/HSY/T N8 .....66 E2
Topsham Rd TOOT SW17 ....160 E5
Torbay Rd KIL/WHAMP NW6 ......82 D5
 RYLN/HDSTN HA2 ....59 J6
Torbay St CAMTN NW1 * 84 B5
Torbridge Cl EDGW HA8 ....44 A3
Torcross Dr FSTH SE23 ....163 K4
Torcross Rd RSLP HA4 ....77 F1
Tor Gdns KENS W8 ....119 K2
Tor Gv THMD SE28 ....127 K1
Tormead Cl SUT SM1 ....208 E4
Tormount Rd
 WOOL/PLUM SE18 ....127 K6
Toronto Av MANHO E12 ....89 K2
Toronto Rd IL IG1 ....72 B5
Torquay Gdns REDBR IG4 ....71 H1
Torquay St BAY/PAD W2 ....101 F4
Torrens Rd BRXS/STRHM SW2 ...142 A6
 SRTFD E15 ....88 D4
Torrens Sq SRTFD E15 ....88 D4
Torrens St FSBYE EC1V 6 A3
Torrey Dr BRXN/ST SW9 ....142 B3
Torriano Av KTTN NW5 ....84 D3
Torriano Ms HOLWY N7 ....84 C3
Torridge Gdns PECK SE15 ....143 K5
Torridge Rd THHTH CR7 ....196 C2
Torridon Rd CAT SE6 ....165 G3
Torrington Av
 NFNCH/WDSP N12 ....47 H1
Torrington Cl ESH/CLAY KT10 ...204 A5
Torrington Dr
 RYLN/HDSTN HA2 ....78 B2
Torrington Gdns
 FBAR/BDGN N11 ....48 C2
 GFD/PVL UB6 ....79 J6
Torrington Gv
 NFNCH/WDSP N12 ....47 J1
Torrington Pk
 NFNCH/WDSP N12 ....33 H6
Torrington Pl FITZ W1T 10 B1
 WAP E1W 123 H1
Torrington Rd BCTR RM8 ....74 B5
 ESH/CLAY KT10 ....204 E4
 GFD/PVL UB6 ....79 J6
 RSLP HA4 ....76 E1
Torrington Sq CROY/NA CRO * ...196 E4
 STPAN WC1H * 4 C7
Torrington Wy MRDN SM4 ....193 K4
Tor Rd WELL DA16 ....148 D2
Torr Rd PGE/AN SE20 ....182 A3
Torver Rd HRW HA1 ....60 E1
Torver Wy ORP BR6 ....216 D1
Torwood Rd PUT/ROE SW15 ......138 D6
Tothill St STJSPK SW1H 16 C3
Totnes Rd WELL DA16 ....148 C1
Totnes Vls FBAR/BDGN N11 * 48 C1
Totnes Wk EFNCH N2 ....65 H1
Tottan Ter WCHPL E1 * 105 F5
Tottenhall Rd PLMGR N13 ....49 G1
Tottenham Court Rd FITZ W1T 4 B7
Tottenham East
 SEVS/STOTM N15 ....68 A1
Tottenham La CEND/HSY/T N8 ...66 E2
Tottenham Ms FITZ W1T * 10 B1
Tottenham Rd IS N1 ....86 A4
Tottenham South Side
 SEVS/STOTM N15 ....68 B1
Totterdown St TOOT SW17 ....160 E6
Totteridge Common
 TRDG/WHET N20 ....31 J4
Totteridge La TRDG/WHET N20 ...32 E4
Totteridge Village
 TRDG/WHET N20 ....32 D3
Totternhoe Cl
 KTN/HRWW/W HA3 ....61 J2
Totton Rd THHTH CR7 ....180 B6
Toulmin St STHWK SE1 ....18 C3
Toulon St CMBW SE5 ....142 D1
Tournay Rd FUL/PGN SW6 ....139 J1
Toussaint Wk
 BERM/RHTH SE16 ....123 H3
Tovil Cl PGE/AN SE20 ....181 H5
Towcester Rd BOW E3 ....105 K3
Tower Br TWRH EC3N 13 J7
Tower Bridge Ap TWRH EC3N 13 K6
Tower Bridge Ms HRW HA1 ....79 F2
Tower Bridge Rd STHWK SE1 .....19 G5

Tower Buildings WAP E1W * 123 J1
Tower Cl CHIG IG7 ....54 B2
 HAMP NW3 ....83 H3
 ORP BR6 ....202 A6
 PGE/AN SE20 ....181 J3
Tower Ct LSQ/SEVD WC2H * 10 E4
Tower Gdns Rd TOTM N17 ....49 J4
Tower Gardens Rd TOTM N17 .....49 J4
Tower Hamlets Rd FSTGT E7 ......88 D2
 WALTH E17 ....51 K4
Tower Hl TWRH EC3N 13 J6
Tower Hill Ter MON EC3R * 13 H6
Tower La WBLY HA9 * 79 K1
Tower Ms CLPT E5 * 87 G3
Tower Mill Rd PECK SE15 ....143 F6
Tower Park Rd DART DA1 ....150 C6
Tower Pl MON EC3R * 13 H6
Tower Ri RCH/KEW TW9 * 137 F6
Tower Rd BELV DA17 ....129 K4
 BXLYHN DA7 ....149 J5
 DART DA1 ....171 F2
 ORP BR6 ....202 A6
 WHTN TW2 ....155 K5
 WLSDN NW10 ....81 J5
Tower Royal MANHO EC4N * 12 D5
Towers Av HGDN/ICK UB10 ....94 A2
Towers Ct HGDN/ICK UB10 * 94 A2
Towers Pl RCHPK/HAM TW10 ...137 F6
Towers Rd PIN HA5 ....41 J4
 STHL UB1 ....96 A3
Tower St LSQ/SEVD WC2H 10 E4
Tower Ter WDGN N22 ....49 F5
Tower Vw CROY/NA CRO 198 B5
Towfield Rd FELT TW13 ....154 E4
Towncourt Crs
 STMC/STPC BR5 ....201 J3
Towncourt La STMC/STPC BR5...201 J4
Towncourt Pth FSBYPK N4 ....67 J5
Town End Pde KUT/HW KT1 * 174 E6
Towney Md NTHLT UB5 ....95 K1
Town Farm Wy
 STWL/WRAY TW19 * 152 A2
Townfield Rd HYS/HAR UB3 ....113 H1
Townfield Sq HYS/HAR UB3 ......113 J1
Town Field Wy ISLW TW7 ....136 B3
Town Hall Approach Rd
 SEVS/STOTM N15 ....68 B1
Townhall Av CHSWK W4 * 118 A4
Town Hall Pde
 BRXS/STRHM SW2 * 142 A5
Townholm Crs HNWL W7 ....116 A3
Town La STWL/WRAY TW19 ....152 A2
Townley Ct SRTFD E15 ....88 D4
Townley Rd BXLYHS DA6 ....149 H5
 EDUL SE22 ....143 F6
Townley St WALW SE17 ....122 E5
Town Meadow BTFD TW8 ....136 E1
Town Quay BARK IG11 ....90 B6
 RCH/KEW TW9 ....137 J3
Town Rd ED N9 ....36 D4
Townsend Av STHGT/OAK N14 ...34 C5
Townsend La CDALE/KGS NW9 ...63 F4
Townsend Ms
 WAND/EARL SW18 ....160 B4
Townsend Rd SEVS/STOTM N15 ...68 B2
 STHL UB1 ....114 D1
 WOOL/PLUM SE18 ....127 G3
Townsend St WALW SE17 ....19 F7
Townsend Wy NTHWD HA6 ....40 D3
Townsend Yd HGT N6 ....66 B5
Townshend Cl SCUP DA14 ....186 C2
Townshend Rd CHST BR7 ....185 G1
 RCH/KEW TW9 ....137 G5
 STJWD NW8 ....2 C2
Townshend Ter
 RCH/KEW TW9 ....137 G5
Townson Av NTHLT UB5 ....95 F1
Townson Wy NTHLT UB5 ....94 E1
Town Whf ISLW TW7 * 136 C4
Towpath Rd UED N18 ....51 F1
Towpath Wy CROY/NA CRO 197 G3
Towton Rd WNWD SE27 ....162 D4
Toynbec Cl CHST BR7 ....167 G6
Toynbee Rd RYNPK SW20 ....177 H1
Toynbee St WCHPL E1 ....13 J2
Toyne Wy HGT N6 * 65 K3
Tracey Av CRICK NW2 ....82 A3
Trade Cl PLMGR N13 ....35 G6
Trader Rd EHAM E6 ....108 B5
Tradescant Rd VX/NE SW8 ....141 K1
Trading Estate Rd
 WLSDN NW10 ....98 E3
Trafalgar Av PECK SE15 ....123 H6
 TOTM N17 ....50 A2
 WPK KT4 ....193 F5
Trafalgar Chambers
 CHEL SW3 * 120 C5
Trafalgar Gdns KENS W8 ....120 A3
 WCHPL E1 ....105 F4
Trafalgar Gv GNWCH SE10 ....125 G6
Trafalgar Rd DART DA1 ....150 D5
 GNWCH SE10 ....125 H5
 RAIN RM13 ....93 H6
 WHTN TW2 ....155 J4
 WIM/MER SW19 ....178 A3
Trafalgar Sq CHCR WC2N * 10 D7
Trafalgar St WALW SE17 ....122 E5
Trafalgar Wy CROY/NA CRO 196 E4
 POP/IOD E14 ....125 F1
Trafford Cl SRTFD E15 ....88 A3
Trafford Rd THHTH CR7 ....196 A2
Trahorn Cl WCHPL E1 ....104 C3
Tramway Av ED N9 ....36 D2
 SRTFD E15 ....88 C5
Tramway Pth MTCM CR4 ....194 D1
Tramway Rd BTFD TW8 ....116 B5
Tranby Ms HOM E9 * 87 F3
Tranmere Rd ED N9 ....36 B2
 WAND/EARL SW18 ....160 B4
 WHTN TW2 ....155 G2
Tranquil Ri ERITH DA8 ....130 B5

Tranquil V BKHTH/KID SE3 ....145 J3
Transept St CAMTN NW1 ....8 D2
Transmere Rd
 STMC/STPC BR5 ....201 H3
Transom Sq POP/IOD E14 ....124 E5
Tranton Rd BERM/RHTH SE16 ...123 J3
Traps La NWMAL KT3 ....176 B5
Travellers Site WALTH E17 * 51 H5
Travellers Wy HEST TW5 ....134 B3
Travers Cl WALTH E17 ....51 F4
Travers Rd HOLWY N7 ....85 G1
Treacy Cl BUSH WD23 ....28 C4
Treadgold St NTGHL W11 ....100 B6
Treadway St BETH E2 ....104 D1
Treaty St IS N1 ....5 J1
Trebeck St MYFR/PICC W1J * 9 J7
Treboulr Rd ECT SW5 ....119 K5
Treby St BOW E3 ....105 H3
Trecastle Wy HOLWY N7 * 84 D2
Tredegar Ms BOW E3 * 105 J1
Tredegar Rd BOW E3 ....105 H2
 FBAR/BDGN N11 ....48 D3
 RDART DA2 ....171 H5
Tredegar Sq BOW E3 ....105 H2
Trederwen Rd HACK E8 ....86 C6
Tredown Rd SYD SE26 ....181 K1
Tredwell Cl HAYES BR2 ....200 C1
Tredwell Rd WNWD SE27 ....162 C6
Tredwon Rd THMD SE28 ....109 K5
Treen Av BARN SW13 ....138 B4
Tree Rd CAN/RD E16 ....107 G5
Treeside Cl WDR/YW UB7 ....112 A4
Treetops Cl ABYW SE2 ....129 F5
 NTHWD HA6 ....40 B1
Treetops Vw LOU IG10 ....39 H6
Tree View Cl NRWD SE19 ....181 F4
Treewall Gdns BMLY BR1 ....166 A6
Trefgarne Rd DAGE RM10 ....74 C1
Trefoil Rd WAND/EARL SW18 ...140 B6
Tregaron Av CEND/HSY/T N8 ......66 E4
Tregarvon Rd BTSEA SW11 ....141 F5
Tregenna Av RYLN/HDSTN HA2 ...78 A2
Tregenna Cl STHGT/OAK N14 .....22 C6
Tregony Rd ORP BR6 ....217 F2
Trego Rd HOM E9 ....87 J5
Tregothnan Rd BRXN/ST SW9 ...141 K4
Tregunter Rd WBPTN SW10 ....120 B6
Treham Rd BARK/HLT IG6 ....54 D5
Treherne Ct BRXN/ST SW9 * 142 C2
Trehern Rd MORT/ESHN SW14 ...138 A4
Trehurst St CLPT E5 ....87 G3
Trelawney Est HOM E9 * 86 E4
Trelawney Rd BARK/HLT IG6 ....54 D5
Trelawn Rd BRXS/STRHM SW2 ...142 B6
 WAN E11 ....88 A1
Trelawny Cl WALTH E17 ....69 K1
Treloar Gdns NRWD SE19 ....180 E2
Trelwney Est HOM E9 * 86 E4
Tremadoc Rd CLAP SW4 ....141 J5
Tremaine Cl BROCKY SE4 ....144 D3
Tremaine Rd PGE/AN SE20 ....181 J5
Tremlett Gv ARCH N19 ....84 C1
Tremlett Ms ARCH N19 * 84 C1
Trenance Gdns GDMY/SEVK IG3 ...91 G1
Trenance Av RSLP HA4 ....77 F3
Trenchard Cl CDALE/KGS NW9 ...45 G4
 STAN HA7 ....43 H2
Trenchard St GNWCH SE10 ....125 G5
Trenchold St VX/NE SW8 * 121 K6
Trenear Cl ORP BR6 ....217 G2
Trenholme Rd PGE/AN SE20 ......181 J3
Trenholme Ter PGE/AN SE20 .....181 J3
Trenmar Gdns WLSDN NW10 .....99 K2
Trent Av EA W5 ....116 D4
Trentbridge Cl BARK/HLT IG6 .....55 F2
Trent Ct WAN E11 * 70 E2
Trent Gdns STHGT/OAK N14 ....34 B1
Trentham St STMC/STPC BR5 ...202 B3
Trentham St
 WAND/EARL SW18 ....159 K3
Trent Pk EBAR EN4 * 22 C3
Trent Rd BKHH IG9 ....39 F3
 BRXS/STRHM SW2 ....142 A6
Trent Wy WPK KT4 ....208 A1
 YEAD UB4 ....94 D2
Trentwood Side ENC/FH EN2 ....22 E4
Treport St WAND/EARL SW18 ...160 A2
Tresco Cl BMLY BR1 ....183 H2
Tresco Gdns CRW RM5 ....56 E1
 IL IG1 ....90 E2
Tresco Rd PECK SE15 ....143 J5
Tresham Crs STJWD NW8 ....2 C4
Tresham Rd BARK IG11 ....91 F5
Tresilian Av WCHMH N21 ....23 F6
Tressell Cl IS N1 ....85 H5
Tressillian Crs BROCKY SE4 .....144 D4
Tressillian Rd BROCKY SE4 ......144 D4
Trestis Cl YEAD UB4 ....95 H3
Treswell Rd DAGW RM9 ....92 A6
Tretawn Gdns MLHL NW7 ....31 G6
Tretawn Pk MLHL NW7 ....31 G6
Trevanion Rd WKENS W14 * 119 H5
Treve Av HRW HA1 ....60 C4
Trevelyan Av MNPK E12 ....89 K2
Trevelyan Crs
 KTN/HRWW/W HA3 ....62 A3
Trevelyan Gdns WLSDN NW10 * ...82 A6
Trevelyan Rd SRTFD E15 ....88 D2
 TOOT SW17 ....178 D2
Treveris St STHWK SE1 ....18 B1
Treverton St NKENS W10 ....100 B3
Treves Cl WCHMH N21 ....23 F5
Trevithick Cl PUT/ROE SW15 .....158 E2
Treviso Rd FSTH SE23 ....164 A4
Trevithick Cl
 EBED/NFELT TW14 ....153 J3
Trevithick Dr DART DA1 ....151 J5
Trevithick St DEPT SE8 ....124 D6
Trevone Gdns PIN HA5 ....59 J3
Trevor Cl EBAR EN4 * 21 H1
 HAYES BR2 ....199 J4
 ISLW TW7 ....136 A6

KTN/HRWW/W HA3 ... **43** F3
NTHLT UB5 ... **95** G1
Trevor Crs *RSLP* HA4 ... **76** D2
Trevor Gdns *EDGW* HA8 ... **45** F4
Trevor Pl *SKENS* SW7 ... **14** D3
Trevor Rd *EDGW* HA8 ... **45** F4
HYS/HAR UB3 ... **113** H2
WFD IG8 ... **52** E3
WIM/MER SW19 ... **177** H3
Trevor Sq *SKENS* SW7 ... **14** D3
Trevor St *SKENS* SW7 ... **14** D3
Trevose Rd *WALTH* E17 ... **52** B4
Trevose Wy *OXHEY* WD19 ... **27** G5
Trewenna Dr *CHSGTN* KT9 ... **205** K3
Trewince Rd *RYNPK* SW20 ... **177** F4
Trewint St *WAND/EARL* SW18 ... **160** B4
Trewsbury Rd *SYD* SE26 ... **182** A1
Triandra Wy *YEAD* UB4 ... **95** H4
Triangle Est *LBTH* SE11 * ... **122** A5
Triangle Pas *BAR* EN5 * ... **21** G5
Triangle Pl *CLAP* SW4 ... **141** J5
Triangle Rd *HACK* E8 ... **86** D6
The Triangle *BFN/LL* DA15 * ... **168** B2
NWMAL KT3 ... **175** K5
Trident Pl *CHEL* SW3 * ... **120** C6
Trident St *BERM/RHTH* SE16 ... **124** A4
Trident Wy *NWDGN* UB2 ... **114** A3
Trig La *BLKFR* EC4V ... **12** C5
Trigon Rd *VX/NE* SW8 ... **142** A1
Trilby Rd *FSTH* SE23 ... **164** A4
Trim St *NWCR* SE14 ... **124** C6
Trinder Rd *ARCH* N19 ... **66** E5
BAR EN5 ... **20** A6
Tring Av *EA* W5 ... **117** G1
STHL UB1 ... **95** K5
WBLY HA9 ... **80** C4
Tring Cl *BARK/HLT* IG6 ... **72** C2
Trinidad Gdns *DAGE* RM10 ... **93** F5
Trinidad St *POP/IOD* E14 ... **105** H6
Trinity Av *EFNCH* N2 ... **47** H6
EN EN1 ... **36** B1
Trinity Buoy Whf
POP/IOD E14 * ... **106** B4
Trinity Church Rd *BARN* SW13 ... **118** E6
Trinity Church Sq *STHWK* SE1 ... **18** D4
Trinity Cl *CLAP* SW4 * ... **141** H5
HACK E8 * ... **86** B4
HAYES BR2 ... **200** D5
HSLWW TW4 ... **134** D5
LEW SE13 ... **145** G5
NTHWD HA6 ... **40** C2
SAND/SEL CR2 ... **212** A6
WAN E11 ... **70** C6
Trinity Ct *ELTH/MOT* SE9 ... **167** G1
Trinity Crs *TOOT* SW17 ... **160** E4
Trinity Gdns *BRXN/ST* SW9 ... **142** A5
CAN/RD E16 ... **106** D4
DART DA1 ... **171** G1
Trinity Gn *WCHPL* E1 * ... **104** E4
Trinity Gv *GNWCH* SE10 ... **145** F2
Trinity Ms *PGE/AN* SE20 * ... **181** K4
Trinity Pde *HSLW* TW3 * ... **135** G4
Trinity Pk *CHING* E4 * ... **51** H2
Trinity Pl *BXLYHS* DA6 ... **149** G5
Trinity Ri *BRXS/STRHM* SW2 ... **162** C2
Trinity Rd *BARK/HLT* IG6 ... **54** C6
EFNCH N2 ... **47** H6
RCH/KEW TW9 * ... **137** G4
STHL UB1 ... **114** D1
TOOT SW17 ... **160** E4
WAND/EARL SW18 ... **160** C1
WDGN N22 ... **48** E4
WIM/MER SW19 ... **177** K2
Trinity Sq *TWRH* EC3N ... **13** H6
Trinity St *CAN/RD* E16 ... **106** D4
ENC/FH EN2 ... **23** J3
STHWK SE1 ... **18** D3
Trinity Wy *ACT* W3 ... **99** G6
CHING E4 ... **51** H2
Trio Pl *STHWK* SE1 ... **18** D3
Tristan Sq *BKHTH/KID* SE3 ... **145** H4
Tristram Cl *WALTH* E17 ... **52** B6
Tristram Dr *ED* N9 ... **36** C5
Tristram Rd *BMLY* BR1 ... **165** J6
Triton Sq *CAMTN* NW1 ... **4** A6
Tritton Av *CROY/NA* CR0 ... **210** E2
Tritton Rd *DUL* SE21 ... **162** E5
Triumph Cl *HYS/HAR* UB3 ... **133** F2
Triumph Rd *EHAM* E6 ... **107** K5
Trojan Wy *CROY/NA* CR0 ... **211** F1
Troon Cl *BERM/RHTH* SE16 * ... **123** J5
Troon St *WCHPL* E1 ... **105** G5
Trosley Rd *BELV* DA17 ... **129** H6
Trossachs Rd *EDUL* SE22 ... **143** F6
Trothy Rd *STHWK* SE1 ... **123** H4
Trott Rd *MUSWH* N10 ... **48** A3
Trott St *BTSEA* SW11 ... **140** C2
Trotwood *CHIG* IG7 ... **54** D2
Troughton Rd *CHARL* SE7 ... **126** A5
Troutbeck Rd *NWCR* SE14 ... **144** B2
Trout Rd *WDR/YW* UB7 ... **112** A1
Trouville Rd *CLAP* SW4 ... **161** H1
Trowbridge Rd *HOM* E9 ... **87** H4
Trowlock Av *TEDD* TW11 ... **174** D2
Trowlock Island *TEDD* TW11 ... **174** E2
Trowlock Wy *TEDD* TW11 ... **174** D2
Troy Ct *KENS* W8 ... **119** K3
Troy Rd *NRWD* SE19 ... **180** E2
Troy Town *PECK* SE15 ... **143** H4
Trubshaw Rd *NWDGN* UB2 ... **115** F3
Trueman Cl *EDGW* HA8 * ... **44** D3
Trulock Rd *TOTM* N17 ... **50** C3
Truman's Rd *STNW/STAM* N16 ... **86** A3
Trumpers Wy *HNWL* W7 ... **116** A3
Trumpington Rd *FSTGT* E7 ... **88** D2
Trump St *CITYW* EC2V ... **12** D4
Trundlers Wy *BUSH* WD23 ... **28** E3
Trundle St *STHWK* SE1 ... **18** C2
Trundleys Rd *DEPT* SE8 ... **124** B6
Trundley's Ter *DEPT* SE8 ... **124** A4
Truro Gdns *IL* IG1 ... **71** J4
Truro Rd *WALTH* E17 ... **69** H1
WDGN N22 ... **48** E3
Truro St *KTTN* NW5 ... **84** A4
Truro Wy *YEAD* UB4 ... **94** C2
Trusedale Rd *EHAM* E6 ... **107** K5
Truslove Rd *WNWD* SE27 ... **180** B1
Trussley Rd *HMSMTH* W6 ... **119** F3
Trustons Gdns *EMPK* RM11 ... **75** J4
Tryfan Cl *REDBR* IG4 ... **71** H2
Tryon Crs *HOM* E9 ... **86** E6
Tryon St *CHEL* SW3 ... **120** E5
Trystings Cl *ESH/CLAY* KT10 ... **205** G4
Tuam Rd *WOOL/PLUM* SE18 ... **127** J6
Tubbenden Cl *ORP* BR6 ... **201** K6
Tubbenden Dr *ORP* BR6 ... **216** D2
Tubbenden La *ORP* BR6 ... **216** D2
Tubbenden La South *ORP* BR6 ... **216** D3
Tubbs Rd *WLSDN* NW10 ... **99** H1
Tuck Rd *RAIN* RM13 ... **93** J4
Tudor Av *GPK* RM2 ... **57** J6
HPTN TW12 ... **173** F2
WPK KT4 ... **207** K1
Tudor Cl *ASHF* TW15 ... **152** A6
BRXS/STRHM SW2 * ... **162** A1
CDALE/KGS NW9 ... **62** E6
CHEAM SM3 ... **208** B3
CHSGTN KT9 ... **206** A3
CHST BR7 ... **184** E4
DART DA1 ... **170** E1
HAMP NW3 ... **83** J3
HGT N6 ... **66** C4
HPTN TW12 ... **173** H1
MLHL NW7 ... **45** J2
PIN HA5 ... **58** E2
WFD IG8 ... **53** F1
WLGTN SM6 ... **210** C5
Tudor Ct *ELTH/MOT* SE9 * ... **146** D5
SWLY BR8 ... **203** K4
WALTH E17 ... **69** H4
Tudor Ct North *WBLY* HA9 ... **80** C3
Tudor Ct South *WBLY* HA9 ... **80** C3
Tudor Crs *BARK/HLT* IG6 ... **54** C2
ENC/FH EN2 ... **23** J2
Tudor Dr *GPK* RM2 ... **75** J1
KUTN/CMB KT2 ... **175** F1
MRDN SM4 ... **193** G3
WOT/HER KT12 ... **188** C5
Tudor Est *WLSDN* NW10 * ... **98** D1
Tudor Gdns *ACT* W3 ... **98** C5
BARN SW13 ... **138** B4
CDALE/KGS NW9 ... **62** E6
GPK RM2 ... **75** J1
TWK TW1 ... **156** A3
WWKM BR4 ... **214** A1
Tudor Gv *HOM* E9 ... **86** E5
Tudor Pde *ELTH/MOT* SE9 * ... **146** D5
Tudor Pl *NRWD* SE19 * ... **181** G3
WIM/MER SW19 ... **178** D3
Tudor Rd *BAR* EN5 ... **20** E4
BARK IG11 ... **91** F5
BECK BR3 ... **183** F6
CHING E4 ... **51** K2
ED N9 ... **36** D2
EHAM E6 ... **89** G6
HACK E8 ... **86** D6
HPTN TW12 ... **173** F3
HSLW TW3 ... **135** J5
HYS/HAR UB3 ... **94** B5
KTN/HRWW/W HA3 ... **42** D5
KUTN/CMB KT2 ... **175** H3
NRWD SE19 ... **181** G3
PIN HA5 ... **41** G5
SNWD SE25 ... **197** J2
STHL UB1 ... **95** J6
Tudor Sq *HYS/HAR* UB3 ... **94** B4
Tudor St *EMB* EC4Y ... **11** K5
Tudor Wy *ACT* W3 ... **117** H2
STHGT/OAK N14 ... **34** D3
STMC/STPC BR5 ... **201** J3
Tudor Well Cl *STAN* HA7 ... **43** H1
Tudway Rd *BKHTH/KID* SE3 ... **146** B5
Tufnail Rd *DART* DA1 ... **171** J1
Tufnell Park Rd *HOLWY* N7 ... **84** D2
Tufter Rd *CHIG* IG7 ... **55** F1
Tufton Gdns *E/WMO/HCT* KT8 ... **173** G5
Tufton Rd *CHING* E4 ... **37** J6
Tufton St *WEST* SW1P ... **16** E5
Tugboat St *THMD* SE28 ... **127** K2
Tugela Rd *CROY/NA* CR0 ... **196** E3
Tugela St *CAT* SE6 ... **164** C4
Tugmutton Cl *ORP* BR6 ... **216** B2
Tulip Cl *CROY/NA* CR0 ... **198** A5
EHAM E6 ... **107** J4
HPTN TW12 ... **172** E2
NWDGN UB2 ... **115** H2
Tulip Gdns *CHING* E4 ... **38** B5
IL IG1 ... **90** B4
Tulip Wy *WDR/YW* UB7 ... **112** A4
Tull St *MTCM* CR4 ... **194** E4
Tulse Cl *BECK* BR3 ... **183** F6
Tulse Hl *BRXS/STRHM* SW2 ... **162** C3
Tulsemere Rd *WNWD* SE27 ... **162** D4
Tummons Gdns *SNWD* SE25 ... **181** F5
Tuncombe Rd *UED* N18 ... **36** A6
Tunis Rd *SHB* W12 ... **119** F1
Tunley Gn *POP/IOD* E14 ... **105** H4
Tunley Rd *BAL* SW12 ... **161** F4
WLSDN NW10 ... **81** G6
Tunmarsh La *PLSTW* E13 ... **107** G2
Tunnan Leys *EHAM* E6 ... **108** A5
Tunnel Av *GNWCH* SE10 ... **125** H3
Tunnel Gdns *FBAR/BDGN* N11 ... **48** C3
Tunnel Link Rd *HTHAIR* TW6 ... **132** D6
Tunnel Rd *BERM/RHTH* SE16 ... **123** K2
Tunnel Rd East *WDR/YW* UB7 ... **132** E1
Tunnel Rd West *WDR/YW* UB7 ... **132** D2
Tunstall Av *BARK/HLT* IG6 ... **55** G2
Tunstall Cl *ORP* BR6 ... **216** E2
Tunstall Rd *BRXN/ST* SW9 ... **142** A5
CROY/NA CR0 ... **197** F5
Tunstock Wy *BELV* DA17 ... **129** F3
Tunworth Cl *CDALE/KGS* NW9 ... **62** E3
Tunworth Crs *PUT/ROE* SW15 ... **158** C1
Tupelo Rd *LEY* E10 ... **69** K6
Tuppy St *WOOL/PLUM* SE18 ... **127** H3
Turene Cl *BTSEA* SW11 ... **140** B5
Turin Rd *ED* N9 ... **36** E2
Turin St *BETH* E2 ... **104** C2
Turkey Oak Cl *NRWD* SE19 ... **181** F4
Turks Rw *CHEL* SW3 ... **120** E5
Turle Rd *FSBYPK* N4 * ... **67** F6
STRHM/NOR SW16 ... **179** K5
Turlewray Cl *FSBYPK* N4 ... **67** F5
Turley Cl *SRTFD* E15 ... **88** C6
Turnagain La *STP* EC4M * ... **12** A3
Turnage Rd *BCTR* RM8 ... **74** A5
Turnant Rd *TOTM* N17 ... **49** J4
Turnberry Cl
BERM/RHTH SE16 * ... **123** J5
Turnberry Ct *OXHEY* WD19 * ... **27** G5
Turnberry Wy *ORP* BR6 ... **201** J5
Turnbury Cl *THMD* SE28 ... **109** K5
Turner Av *MTCM* CR4 ... **178** E4
SEVS/STOTM N15 ... **68** A1
WHTN TW2 ... **155** H5
Turner Cl *ALP/SUD* HA0 ... **79** K3
CMBW SE5 ... **142** C2
GLDGN NW11 ... **65** F3
Turner Ct *CMBW* SE5 * ... **142** E5
DART DA1 ... **151** F6
Turner Dr *GLDGN* NW11 ... **65** F3
Turner Ms *BELMT* SM2 ... **209** F5
Turner Rd *EDGW* HA8 ... **44** A5
NWMAL KT3 ... **192** A4
WALTH E17 ... **70** A1
Turners Meadow Wy *BECK* BR3 ... **182** C4
Turner's Rd *POP/IOD* E14 ... **105** H4
Turner St *CAN/RD* E16 ... **106** D5
WCHPL E1 ... **104** D4
Turners Wy *CROY/NA* CR0 ... **196** B6
Turner's Wd *GLDGN* NW11 ... **65** G5
Turneville Rd *WKENS* W14 ... **119** J6
Turney Rd *DUL* SE21 ... **162** D2
Turnham Green Ter *CHSWK* W4 ... **118** B4
Turnham Rd *BROCKY* SE4 ... **144** B6
Turnmill St *FARR* EC1M ... **5** K7
Turnpike Cl *DEPT* SE8 ... **144** C1
Turnpike Dr *ORP* BR6 ... **217** J6
Turnpike La *CEND/HSY/T* N8 ... **67** G1
SUT SM1 ... **209** G3
Turnpike Link *CROY/NA* CR0 ... **197** F6
Turnpike Ms *CEND/HSY/T* N8 * ... **49** G6
Turnpike Pde
CEND/HSY/T N8 * ... **49** H6
Turnpike Wy *ISLW* TW7 ... **136** B2
Turnstone Cl *CDALE/KGS* NW9 * ... **45** G5
PLSTW E13 ... **106** E2
Turnstone Ter *WEA* W13 * ... **97** F3
Turpentine La *PIM* SW1V ... **121** G5
Turpin Av *CRW* RM5 ... **56** C3
Turpin Cl *WAP* E1W ... **105** F6
Turpington Cl *HAYES* BR2 ... **200** D3
Turpington La *HAYES* BR2 ... **200** D2
Turpin La *ERITH* DA8 ... **130** D6
Turpin Rd *EBED/NFELT* TW14 ... **153** J1
Turpin's La *WFD* IG8 ... **53** K1
Turpins Yd *CRICK* NW2 * ... **63** K6
Turpin Wy *WLGTN* SM6 ... **210** B5
Turquand St *WALW* SE17 ... **18** D7
Turret Gv *CLAP* SW4 ... **141** H4
Turton Rd *ALP/SUD* HA0 ... **80** A3
Turville St *BETH* E2 ... **7** J6
Tuscan Rd *WOOL/PLUM* SE18 ... **127** J5
Tuskar St *GNWCH* SE10 ... **125** H5
Tweeddale Gv *HGDN/ICK* UB10 ... **76** A1
Tweeddale Rd *CAR* SM5 ... **194** C5
Tweedmouth Rd *PLSTW* E13 ... **107** F1
Tweed Wy *ROM* RM1 ... **57** F3
Tweedy Rd *BMLY* BR1 ... **183** K4
Twelvetrees Crs *BOW* E3 ... **106** A3
Twentyman Cl *WFD* IG8 ... **52** E1
Twickenham Br *TWK* TW1 ... **136** E6
Twickenham Cl *CROY/NA* CR0 ... **211** F1
Twickenham Gdns
GFD/PVL UB6 ... **79** G3
KTN/HRWW/W HA3 ... **42** E3
Twickenham Rd *FELT* TW13 ... **154** E5
ISLW TW7 ... **136** A6
TEDD TW11 ... **156** B6
WAN E11 ... **70** B6
Twig Folly Cl *BOW* E3 ... **105** F1
Twig Folly Whf *BETH* E2 * ... **105** F1
Twigg Cl *ERITH* DA8 ... **150** B1
Twilley St *WAND/EARL* SW18 ... **160** A2
Twine Cl *BARK* IG11 ... **109** H2
Twine Ct *WCHPL* E1 ... **104** E6
Twineham Gn
NFNCH/WDSP N12 ... **32** E6
Twine Ter *BOW* E3 * ... **105** H3
Twining Av *WHTN* TW2 ... **155** H5
Twinn Rd *MLHL* NW7 ... **46** C2
Twin Tumps Wy *THMD* SE28 ... **109** G6
Twisden Rd *KTTN* NW5 ... **84** B2
Twisleton Ct *DART* DA1 ... **171** G1
Twybridge Wy
WLSDN NW10 ... **80** E5
Twyford Abbey Rd
WLSDN NW10 ... **98** B2
Twyford Av *ACT* W3 ... **98** C6
EFNCH N2 ... **47** K6
Twyford Crs *ACT* W3 ... **117** H1
Twyford Rd *CAR* SM5 ... **194** C5
IL IG1 ... **90** C3
RYLN/HDSTN HA2 ... **60** B4
Twyford St *IS* N1 ... **85** F6
Tyas Rd *CAN/RD* E16 ... **106** D3
Tybenham Rd
WIM/MER SW19 ... **177** K6
Tyberry Rd *PEND* EN3 ... **24** D4
Tyburn La *HRW* HA1 ... **60** E4
Tyburn Wy *MBLAR* W1H ... **9** F5
Tye La *ORP* BR6 ... **216** C3
Tyers Ga *STHWK* SE1 ... **19** G3
Tyers St *LBTH* SE11 ... **122** A5
Tyers Ter *LBTH* SE11 ... **122** A5
Tyeshurst Cl *ABYW* SE2 ... **129** F5
Tylecroft Rd
STRHM/NOR SW16 ... **179** K5
Tylehurst Gdns *IL* IG1 ... **90** C3
Tyler Cl *BETH* E2 ... **7** J2
Tylers Ga *KTN/HRWW/W* HA3 ... **62** A3
Tylers Green Rd *SWLY* BR8 ... **203** K3
Tyler St *GNWCH* SE10 ... **125** H5
Tylney Av *NRWD* SE19 ... **181** G1
Tylney Rd *BMLY* BR1 ... **184** C5
FSTGT E7 ... **89** G2
Tynan Cl *EBED/NFELT* TW14 ... **153** K3
Tyndale La *IS* N1 ... **85** H5
Tyndale Ter *IS* N1 ... **85** H5
Tyndall Rd *LEY* E10 ... **70** A6
WELL DA16 ... **148** A4
Tyneham Cl *BTSEA* SW11 * ... **141** F4
Tyneham Rd *BTSEA* SW11 ... **141** F3
Tynemouth Cl *EHAM* E6 ... **108** B5
Tynemouth Dr *EN* EN1 ... **24** C1
Tynemouth Rd *MTCM* CR4 ... **179** F3
SEVS/STOTM N15 ... **68** B1
WOOL/PLUM SE18 ... **127** K5
Tynemouth St
FUL/PGN SW6 ... **140** B3
Tynemouth Ter
SEVS/STOTM N15 * ... **68** B1
Tyne St *WCHPL* E1 ... **13** K3
Tynsdale Rd *WLSDN* NW10 ... **81** G4
Type St *BETH* E2 ... **105** F1
Tyrawley Rd *FUL/PGN* SW6 ... **140** A2
Tyre La *CDALE/KGS* NW9 * ... **63** G1
Tyrell Cl *HRW* HA1 ... **78** E2
Tyrone Rd *EHAM* E6 ... **107** K1
Tyron Wy *SCUP* DA14 ... **167** K6
Tyrrell Av *WELL* DA16 ... **148** B6
Tyrrell Rd *EDUL* SE22 ... **143** H5
Tyrrel Wy *CDALE/KGS* NW9 ... **63** H4
Tyrwhitt Rd *LEW* SE13 ... **144** D4
Tysoe St *CLKNW* EC1R ... **5** K5
Tyson Gdns *FSTH* SE23 * ... **163** K2
Tyson Rd *FSTH* SE23 ... **163** K2
Tyssen Rd *STNW/STAM* N16 * ... **86** B1
Tyssen St *HACK* E8 ... **86** B4
Tytherton Rd *ARCH* N19 ... **84** D1

U

Uamvar St *POP/IOD* E14 ... **105** K4
Uckfield Gv *MTCM* CR4 ... **179** F4
Udall Gdns *CRW* RM5 ... **56** C2
Udall St *WEST* SW1P ... **16** B7
Udney Park Rd *TEDD* TW11 ... **174** B1
Uffington Rd *WLSDN* NW10 ... **81** J6
WNWD SE27 ... **162** B6
Ufford Cl *KTN/HRWW/W* HA3 ... **42** B3
Ufford Rd *KTN/HRWW/W* HA3 ... **42** B3
Ufford St *STHWK* SE1 ... **17** K2
Ufton Rd *IS* N1 ... **86** A5
Uhura Sq *STNW/STAM* N16 * ... **86** A1
Ullathorne Rd *S*
TRHM/NOR SW16 ... **161** H6
Ulleswater Rd *PLMGR* N13 ... **34** E6
Ulleswater Vls *PLMGR* N13 * ... **34** E6
Ullin St *POP/IOD* E14 ... **106** A4
Ullswater Cl *BMLY* BR1 ... **183** H2
KUTN/CMB KT2 * ... **158** A6
YEAD UB4 ... **94** C1
Ullswater Ct
RYLN/HDSTN HA2 * ... **60** A4
Ullswater Crs *PUT/ROE* SW15 ... **158** A6
Ullswater Rd *BARN* SW13 ... **138** D1
WNWD SE27 ... **162** C5
Ullswater Wy *HCH* RM12 ... **93** J3
Ulster Gdns *PLMGR* N13 ... **35** J6
Ulster Pl *CAMTN* NW1 ... **3** J7
Ulundi Rd *BKHTH/KID* SE3 ... **125** H6
Ulva Rd *PUT/ROE* SW15 ... **139** G5
Ulverscroft Rd *EDUL* SE22 ... **143** H6
Ulverston Rd *WALTH* E17 ... **52** B5
Ulysses Rd *KIL/WHAMP* NW6 ... **82** D3
Umberston St *WCHPL* E1 * ... **104** C5
Umbria St *PUT/ROE* SW15 ... **158** D1
Umfreville Rd *FSBYPK* N4 ... **67** H3
Undercliff Rd *LEW* SE13 ... **144** D4
Underhill *BAR* EN5 ... **20** E6
Underhill Ct *BAR* EN5 * ... **20** E6
Underhill Rd *EDUL* SE22 ... **143** H6
Underhill St *CAMTN* NW1 ... **3** K1
Underne Av *STHGT/OAK* N14 ... **34** B4
Undershaft *HDTCH* EC3A ... **13** G4
Undershaw Rd *BMLY* BR1 ... **165** H5
Underwood *CROY/NA* CR0 ... **214** A4
Underwood Rd *CHING* E4 ... **51** K1
WCHPL E1 ... **104** C3
WFD IG8 ... **53** H3
Underwood Rw *IS* N1 ... **6** D4
Underwood St *IS* N1 ... **6** D4
The Underwood
ELTH/MOT SE9 ... **166** E4
Undine Rd *POP/IOD* E14 ... **124** E4
Undine St *TOOT* SW17 ... **178** E1
Uneeda Dr *GFD/PVL* UB6 ... **78** D6
Union Cl *WAN* E11 ... **88** B2
Union Ct *CLAP* SW4 ... **141** K3
Union Dr *WCHPL* E1 * ... **105** G3
Union Gv *VX/NE* SW8 ... **141** J3
Union Rd *ALP/SUD* HA0 ... **80** A4
CROY/NA CR0 ... **196** D4
FBAR/BDGN N11 ... **48** D2
HAYES BR2 ... **200** C2
NTHLT UB5 ... **96** A1
VX/NE SW8 ... **141** J3
Union Sq *IS* N1 ... **6** C1
Union St *BAR* EN5 ... **20** C5
KUT/HW KT1 ... **174** E5
SRTFD E15 ... **88** B6
STHWK SE1 ... **18** B1
Union Wk *BETH* E2 ... **7** J4
Unity Cl *CROY/NA* CR0 ... **213** K6
WLSDN NW10 ... **81** J4
WNWD SE27 ... **180** D1
Unity Ms *CAMTN* NW1 ... **4** C2
Unity Wy *WOOL/PLUM* SE18 ... **126** C3
University Cl *CDALE/KGS* NW9 ... **45** H3
University Gdns *BXLY* DA5 ... **169** G2
University Rd *WIM/MER* SW19 ... **178** C2
University St *FITZ* W1T ... **4** B7
University Wy *DART* DA1 ... **151** G4
EHAM E6 ... **108** A6
Unwin Av *EBED/NFELT* TW14 ... **133** G6
Unwin Cl *PECK* SE15 ... **123** H6
Unwin Rd *ISLW* TW7 ... **135** K4
SKENS SW7 ... **14** B4
Upbrook Ms *BAY/PAD* W2 ... **101** G5
Upcerne Rd *WBPTN* SW10 ... **140** B1
Upcroft Av *EDGW* HA8 ... **44** E1
Updale Rd *SCUP* DA14 ... **168** A6
Upfield *CROY/NA* CR0 ... **197** J6
Upfield Rd *HNWL* W7 ... **97** F3
Uphall Rd *IL* IG1 ... **90** B3
Upham Park Rd *CHSWK* W4 ... **118** B4
Uphill Dr *CDALE/KGS* NW9 ... **62** E2
MLHL NW7 ... **45** G1
Uphill Gv *MLHL* NW7 ... **31** G6
Uphill Rd *MLHL* NW7 ... **31** G6
Upland Rd *BELMT* SM2 ... **209** H5
BXLYHN DA7 ... **149** G4
EDUL SE22 ... **143** H6
PLSTW E13 ... **106** E3
SAND/SEL CR2 ... **211** K3
Uplands *BECK* BR3 ... **182** D5
Uplands Av *WALTH* E17 ... **51** F6
Uplands Cl *MORT/ESHN* SW14 ... **137** J6
Uplands Park Rd *ENC/FH* EN2 ... **23** G3
Uplands Rd *CEND/HSY/T* N8 ... **67** F2
CHDH RM6 ... **55** K6
EBAR EN4 ... **34** A3
ORP BR6 ... **202** C5
WFD IG8 ... **53** J3
The Uplands *RSLP* HA4 ... **58** E5
Uplands Wy *WCHMH* N21 ... **23** G6
Upminster Rd South
RAIN RM13 ... **111** J3
Upney La *BARK* IG11 ... **91** F5
Upnor Wy *WALW* SE17 ... **123** F5
Uppark Dr *GNTH/NBYPK* IG2 ... **72** C3
Upper Abbey Rd *BELV* DA17 ... **129** G4
Upper Addison Gdns
WKENS W14 ... **119** H2
Upper Bank St *POP/IOD* E14 ... **124** E1
Upper Bardsey Wk *IS* N1 * ... **85** J4
Upper Belgrave St *KTBR* SW1X ... **15** H4
Upper Berenger Wk
WBPTN SW10 * ... **140** C1
Upper Berkeley St *BAY/PAD* W2 ... **8** E4
Upper Beulah Hl *NRWD* SE19 ... **181** F4
Upper Blantyre Wk
WBPTN SW10 * ... **140** C1
Upper Brighton Rd *SURB* KT6 ... **190** E3
Upper Brockley Rd
BROCKY SE4 ... **144** C4
Upper Brook St
MYFR/PKLN W1K ... **9** G5
Upper Butts *BTFD* TW8 ... **116** D6
Upper Caldy Wk *IS* N1 * ... **85** J4
Upper Camelford Wk
NTGHL W11 * ... **100** C5
Upper Cheyne Rw *CHEL* SW3 ... **120** D6
Upper Clapton Rd *CLPT* E5 ... **68** D6
Upper Clarendon Wk
NTGHL W11 * ... **100** C5
Upper Dartrey Wk
WBPTN SW10 * ... **140** B1
Upper Dengie Wk *IS* N1 * ... **85** J6
Upper Elmers End Rd
BECK BR3 ... **198** B1
Upper Farm Rd
E/WMO/HCT KT8 ... **188** E1
Upper Gn East *MTCM* CR4 ... **178** E5
Upper Gn West *MTCM* CR4 ... **178** E5
Upper Grosvenor St
MYFR/PKLN W1K ... **9** G6
Upper Grotto Rd *TWK* TW1 ... **156** A4
Upper Gnd *STHWK* SE1 ... **11** J7
Upper Gv *SNWD* SE25 ... **197** F1
Upper Grove Rd *BELV* DA17 ... **129** G6
Upper Gulland Wk *IS* N1 * ... **85** J4
Upper Ham Rd
RCHPK/HAM TW10 ... **156** E6
Upper Handa Wk *IS* N1 * ... **85** K4
Upper Harley St *CAMTN* NW1 ... **3** H7
Upper Hawkwell Wk *IS* N1 * ... **85** J6
Upper Hitch *OXHEY* WD19 ... **27** J3
Upper Holly Hill Rd *BELV* DA17 ... **129** J5
Upper John St *REGST* W1B ... **10** B5
Upper Lismore Wk *IS* N1 * ... **85** J4
Upper Ldg *KENS* W8 * ... **120** A1
Upper Ml *HMSMTH* W6 ... **118** D5
Upper Marsh *STHWK* SE1 ... **17** H4
Upper Montagu St *MBLAR* W1H ... **8** E1
Upper Mulgrave Rd
BELMT SM2 ... **208** C5
Upper North St *POP/IOD* E14 ... **105** K5
Upper Paddock Rd
OXHEY WD19 ... **27** J1
Upper Park Rd *BELV* DA17 ... **129** J4
BMLY BR1 ... **184** A4
FBAR/BDGN N11 ... **48** B1
HAMP NW3 ... **83** K4
KUTN/CMB KT2 ... **175** H2
Upper Phillimore Gdns
KENS W8 * ... **119** K2
Upper Rainham Rd *HCH* RM12 ... **75** H5
Upper Ramsey Wk *IS* N1 ... **85** K4
Upper Rawreth Wk *IS* N1 * ... **85** J6
Upper Richmond Rd
PUT/ROE SW15 ... **138** E5
Upper Richmond Rd West
RCHPK/HAM TW10 ... **137** H5
Upper Rd *PLSTW* E13 ... **106** E2
WLGTN SM6 ... **210** D3
Upper St Martin's La
LSQ/SEVD WC2H ... **10** E4
Upper Selsdon Rd
SAND/SEL CR2 ... **212** B6
Upper Sheppey Wk *IS* N1 ... **85** J4
Upper Sheridan Rd *BELV* DA17 ... **129** H4
Upper Shirley Rd
CROY/NA CR0 ... **212** E1
Upper Sq *ISLW* TW7 ... **136** B4
Upper St *IS* N1 ... **5** K3
Upper Sunbury Rd
HPTN TW12 ... **172** E4

Upper Sutton La *HEST* TW5 ....135 F2
Upper Tachbrook St *PIM* SW1V ...16 A6
Upper Tail *OXHEY* WD19 ....27 J5
Upper Talbot Wk
  NTGHL W11 * 100 C5
Upper Teddington Rd
  KUT/HW KT1 ....174 D4
Upper Ter *HAMP* NW3 ....83 G1
Upper Thames St *BLKFR* EC4V 12 C5
Upper Tollington Pk
  FSBYPK N4 ....67 G5
Upperton Rd *SCUP* DA14 ....186 A1
Upperton Rd East *PLSTW* E13 ...107 G2
Upperton Rd West *PLSTW* E13...107 G2
Upper Tooting Pk *TOOT* SW17 ...160 E4
Upper Tooting Rd *TOOT* SW17 ...160 E6
Upper Town Rd *GFD/PVL* UB6 ....96 B3
Upper Tulse HI
  BRXS/STRHM SW2 ....162 A2
Upper Vernon Rd *SUT* SM1 ....209 H3
Upper Walthamstow Rd
  WALTH E17 ....70 B1
Upper Whistler Wk
  WBPTN SW10 * 140 B1
Upper Wickham La
  WELL DA16 ....148 C3
Upper Wimpole St
  CAVSQ/HST W1G * 9 H1
Uppingham Av *STAN* HA7 ....43 J6
Upsdell Av *PLMGR* N13 ....49 G2
Upstall St *CMBW* SE5 ....142 C2
Upton Av *FSTGT* E7 ....88 E5
Upton CI *BXLY* DA5 ....169 G1
  CRICK NW2 ....82 C1
Upton Dene *BELMT* SM2 ....209 F5
Upton Gdns *KTN/HRWW/W* HA3...61 J3
Upton La *FSTGT* E7 ....89 F4
Upton Lodge CI *BUSH* WD23 ....28 C2
Upton Park Rd *FSTGT* E7 ....89 F5
Upton Rd *BXLYHS* DA6 ....149 F5
  HSLW TW3 ....135 F4
  THHTH CR7 ....180 E5
  UED N18 ....50 C1
  WOOL/PLUM SE18 ....127 H6
Upton Rd South *BXLY* DA5 ....169 G1
Upway *NFNCH/WDSP* N12 ....47 J3
Upwood Rd *LEE/GVPK* SE12 ......165 K1
  STRHM/NOR SW16 ....179 K4
Urlwin St *CMBW* SE5 ....122 D6
Urnwin Wk *BRXN/ST* SW9 ....142 B2
Urmston Dr *WIM/MER* SW19 .....159 H3
Ursula Ms *FSBYPK* N4 ....67 H5
Ursula St *BTSEA* SW11 ....140 D2
Urswick Rd *DAGW* RM9 ....92 A5
  HOM E9 ....86 E3
Usborne Ms *VX/NE* SW8 ....142 A1
Usher Rd *BOW* E3 ....87 J1
Usk Rd *BTSEA* SW11 ....140 B5
Usk St *BETH* E2 ....105 F2
Uvedale Rd *DAGE* RM10 ....92 C1
  ENC/FH EN2 ....23 K6
Uverdale Rd *WBPTN* SW10 ....140 B1
Uxbridge Rd EA W5 ....85 J6
  FELT TW13 ....154 C4
  HGDN/ICK UB10.........................94 A3
  HPTN TW12 ....155 F6
  SHB W12 ....118 D1
  STHL UB1 ....115 F1
  STHL UB1 ....96 E6
  WEA W13 ....116 C1
  YEAD UB4 ....94 E5
Uxbridge Rd (Harrow Weald)
  KTN/HRWW/W HA3 ....42 B3
Uxbridge Rd (Hatch End)
  ....41 J4
Uxbridge Rd High St
  STHL UB1 ....115 K1
Uxbridge Rd (Pinner) *PIN* HA5 ...41 H5
Uxbridge Rd (Stanmore)
  STAN HA7 ....43 G1
Uxbridge Rd The Broadway
  YEAD UB4 ....95 H6
Uxbridge St *KENS* W8 ....119 K1
Uxendon Crs *WBLY* HA9 ....62 A5
Uxendon HI *WBLY* HA9 ....62 B5

V

Valance Av *CHING* E4 ....38 D3
Valan Leas *HAYES* BR2 ....183 H6
Vale CI *EFNCH* N2 ....47 K6
  MV/WKIL W9 ....101 G2
  ORP BR6 ....216 A2
  TWK TW1 * 156 E5
Vale Cottages
  WAND/EARL SW18 ....159 J1
Vale Ct *ACT* W3 * 4 A4
Vale Crs *PUT/ROE* SW15 ....158 B6
Vale Cft *ESH/CLAY* KT10 ....205 F5
  PIN HA5 ....59 J2
Vale Dr *BAR* EN5 ....20 D5
Vale End *EDUL* SE22 ....143 G5
Vale Gv *ACT* W3 ....118 A1
  FSBYPK N4 ....67 J4
Vale La *ACT* W3 ....98 C4
Valence Av *BCTR* RM8 ....73 K5
Valence Circ *BCTR* RM8 ....91 K1
Valence Rd *ERITH* DA8 ....150 A1
Valence Wood Rd *BCTR* RM8 ....91 K1
Valencia Rd *STAN* HA7 ....29 J5
Valency CI *NTHWD* HA6 ....26 D6
Valentia PI *BRXN/ST* SW9 ....142 B5
Valentine Av *BXLY* DA5 ....169 F4
Valentine PI *STHWK* SE1 ....18 A2
Valentine Rd *HOM* E9 * 87 F4
  RYLN/HDSTN HA2 ....78 B1
Valentines Rd *IL* IG1 ....72 B5
Valentines Wy *DAGE* RM10 ....75 C6
Vale of Health *HAMP* NW3 ....83 G1
Valerian Wy *SRTFD* E15 ....106 C2
Vale Ri *GLDGN* NW11 ....64 D5

Vale Rd *BMLY* BR1 ....185 F5
  DART DA1 ....170 E3
  ESH/CLAY KT10 ....204 E6
  FSBYPK N4 ....67 J4
  FSTGT E7 ....89 F4
  HOR/WEW KT19 ....207 H2
  MTCM CR4 ....179 J6
  SUT SM1 ....209 F2
Vale Rd North *SURB* KT6 ....191 F6
Vale Rw *HBRY* N5 ....85 H1
Vale Royal *HOLWY* N7 ....84 E5
Vale St *WNWD* SE27 ....162 E5
Valeswood Rd *BMLY* BR1 ....183 J1
Vale Ter *FSBYPK* N4 ....67 J3
The Vale *ACT* W3 ....118 A1
  CHEL SW3 ....120 D6
  CRICK NW2 ....82 B1
  CROY/NA CR0 ....198 A6
  EBED/NFELT TW14 ....154 A1
  FELT TW13 ....154 A1
  HEST TW5 ....114 D6
  MUSWH N10 ....48 A4
  RSLP HA4 ....77 G2
  STHGT/OAK N14 ....34 E2
  WFD IG8 ....52 E3
Valetta Gv *PLSTW* E13 ....106 E1
Valetta Rd *ACT* W3 ....118 B2
Valette St *HACK* E8 * 86 D4
Valiant CI *NTHLT* UB5 ....95 H2
  ROMW/RG RM7 ....56 C5
Valiant Wy *EHAM* E6 ....107 K4
Vallance Rd *WCHPL* E1 ....104 C3
  WDGN N22 ....48 B5
Vallentin Rd *WALTH* E17 ....70 A1
Valley Av *NFNCH/WDSP* N12 ....33 H6
Valley CI *DART* DA1 ....170 C1
  LOU IG10 ....39 K1
  PIN HA5 ....41 F5
Valleyfield Rd
  STRHM/NOR SW16 ....180 A1
Valley Fields Crs *ENC/FH* EN2 ....23 G3
Valley Gdns *ALP/SUD* HA0 ....80 B5
  WIM/MER SW19 ....178 C5
Valley Gv *CHARL* SE7 ....126 B5
Valley HI *LOU* IG10 ....39 K1
Valley Pk *WATW* WD18 * 26 A2
Valley Rd *DART* DA1 ....170 C1
  ERITH DA8 ....129 K4
  HAYES BR2 ....183 H5
  STMC/STPC BR5 ....186 C4
  STRHM/NOR SW16 ....162 A6
Valley Side *CHING* E4 ....37 J3
Valley Vw *BAR* EN5 ....32 C1
Valley Wk *CROY/NA* CR0 ....197 K6
Valliere Rd *WLSDN* NW10 ....99 J2
Valliers Wood Rd
  BFN/LL DA15 ....167 K3
Vallis Wy *CHSGTN* KT9 ....205 K2
  WEA W13 ....97 G4
Valmar Rd *CMBW* SE5 ....142 D2
Valnay St *TOOT* SW17 ....178 E1
Valognes Av *WALTH* E17 ....51 G4
Valonia Gdns
  WAND/EARL SW18 ....159 J1
Vambery Rd
  WOOL/PLUM SE18 ....127 H6
Vanbrough Crs *NTHLT* UB5 ....95 G1
Vanbrugh Dr *WOT/HER* KT12 ....188 B4
Vanbrugh Flds
  BKHTH/KID SE3 ....125 J6
Vanbrugh HI *GNWCH* SE10 ....125 H5
Vanbrugh Pk *BKHTH/KID* SE3 ...145 K1
Vanbrugh Park Rd
  BKHTH/KID SE3 ....145 J1
Vanbrugh Park Rd West
  BKHTH/KID SE3 ....145 J1
Vanbrugh Rd *CHSWK* W4 ....118 A3
Vanbrugh Ter *BKHTH/KID* SE3 ...145 J2
Vanburgh CI *CAN/RD* E16 ....107 H4
  ORP BR6 ....201 K5
Vancouver CI *ORP* BR6 ....217 G2
Vancouver Man *EDGW* HA8 * 44 D4
Vancouver Rd *EDGW* HA8 ....44 D4
  FSTH SE23 ....164 B4
  RCHPK/HAM TW10 ....156 D6
  YEAD UB4 ....95 F3
Vanderbilt Rd
  WAND/EARL SW18 ....160 A3
Vanderbilt Vis *SHB* W12 * 119 G2
Vanderville Gdns *EFNCH* N2 ....47 G5
Vandome CI *CAN/RD* E16 ....107 F5
Vandon St *STJSPK* SW1H 16 B4
Van Dyck Av *NWMAL* KT3 ....192 A4
Vandyke CI *PUT/ROE* SW15 ....159 G1
Vandyke Cross *ELTH/MOT* SE9 ..146 D6
Vandy St *SDTCH* EC2A * 7 G7
Vane CI *HAMP* NW3 ....83 H3
  KTN/HRWW/W HA3 ....62 B3
Vanessa CI *BELV* DA17 ....129 H5
Vanessa Wy *BXLY* DA5 ....170 A5
Vanguard CI *CDALE/KGS* NW9 *..45 G3
Vanguard CI *CAN/RD* E16 ....106 E4
  CROY/NA CR0 ....196 C5
  ROMW/RG RM7 ....56 D5
  THHTH CR7 ....196 C1
Vanguard St *DEPT* SE8 ....144 D2
Vanguard Wy *CROY/NA* CR0 .....212 D2
  HTHAIR TW6 ....133 H3
  WLGTN SM6 ....210 E5
Vanneck Sq *PUT/ROE* SW15 *...138 D6
Vanoc Gdns *BMLY* BR1 ....165 K6
Vansittart Rd *FSTGT* E7 ....88 E2
Vansittart St *NWCR* SE14 ....144 B1
Vanston PI *FUL/PGN* SW6 ....139 K1
Vantage HI *KENS* W8 ....11 K3
Vant Rd *TOOT* SW17 ....178 E1
Varcoe Rd *BERM/RHTH* SE16 ....123 J5
Vardens Rd *BTSEA* SW11 ....140 C5
Vardon CI *STHGT* N12 * 47 J1
Varden St *WCHPL* E1 ....104 D5
Varley Dr *TWK* TW1 ....136 D5
Varley Rd *CAN/RD* E16 ....107 F5
Varley Wy *MTCM* CR4 ....178 C5
Varna Rd *FUL/PGN* SW6 ....139 H1
  HPTN TW12 * 173 G4

Varndell St *CAMTN* NW1 ....4 A4
Varsity Dr *TWK* TW1 * 136 A6
  WHTN TW2 ....135 K6
Varsity Rw *MORT/ESHN* SW14 ..137 K3
Vartry Rd *SEVS/STOTM* N15 ....68 A3
Vassall Rd *BRXN/ST* SW9 ....142 B1
Vauban Est *BERM/RHTH* SE16 ....19 K5
Vauban St *BERM/RHTH* SE16 ......19 K5
Vaughan Av *HDN* NW4 ....63 J2
  HMSMTH W6 ....118 C4
Vaughan Est *BETH* E2 * 7 J4
Vaughan Gdns *IL* IG1 ....71 K4
Vaughan Rd *CMBW* SE5 ....142 D3
  HRW HA1 ....60 C4
  SRTFD E15 ....88 D2
  THDIT KT7 ....190 C4
  WELL DA16 ....148 A3
Vaughan St *BERM/RHTH* SE16 ..124 C2
Vaughan Wy *WAP* E1W 104 C6
Vaughan Williams CI
  DEPT SE8 ....144 D1
Vauxhall Br *VX/NE* SW8 ....121 K5
Vauxhall Bridge Rd *PIM* SW1V 16 A6
Vauxhall Gdns *SAND/SEL* CR2 ...211 J4
Vauxhall Gv *VX/NE* SW8 ....122 A6
Vauxhall PI *DART* DA1 ....171 H2
Vauxhall St *LBTH* SE11 ....122 A5
Vauxhall Wk *LBTH* SE11 ....122 A5
Vawdrey CI *WCHPL* E1 ....104 E3
Veals Md *MTCM* CR4 ....178 D4
Vectis Gdns *TOOT* SW17 ....179 G2
Vectis Rd *TOOT* SW17 ....179 G2
Veda Rd *LEW* SE13 ....144 D5
Vega Crs *NTHWD* HA6 ....40 D1
Vega Rd *BUSH* WD23 ....28 C2
Veldene Wy *RYLN/HDSTN* HA2 ...77 K1
Vellum Dr *CAR* SM5 ....210 A1
Venables CI *DAGE* RM10 ....92 D2
Venables St *STJWD* NW8 ....8 B7
Vencourt PI *HMSMTH* W6 ....118 D5
Venetian Rd *CMBW* SE5 ....142 D3
Venetia Rd EA W5 ....116 E2
  FSBYPK N4 ....67 H3
Venette CI *RAIN* RM13 ....111 K4
Venner Rd *SYD* SE26 ....181 K2
Venners CI *BXLYHN* DA7 ....150 B3
Venn St *CLAP* SW4 ....141 H5
Ventnor Av *STAN* HA7 ....43 H4
Ventnor Dr *NFNCH/WDSP* N12 ...33 F5
Ventnor Gdns *BARK* IG11 ....90 E4
Ventnor Rd *BERM/RHTH* SE16 ...123 K2
  NWCR SE14 ....144 A1
Ventnor Ter *SEVS/STOTM* N15 ...68 C1
Venture CI *BXLY* DA5 ....169 F2
Venue St *POP/IOD* E14 ....105 K4
Venus Rd *WOOL/PLUM* SE18 ....126 E3
Vera Av *WCHMH* N21 ....23 G5
Vera Ct *OXHEY* WD19 * 27 H1
Vera Lynn CI *FSTGT* E7 ....88 E2
Vera Rd *FUL/PGN* SW6 ....139 H2
Verbena CI *CAN/RD* E16 ....106 D3
  WDR/YW UB7 ....112 A5
Verbena Gdns *HMSMTH* W6 .....118 D5
Verdant La *CAT* SE6 ....165 H3
Verdayne Av *CROY/NA* CR0 ......198 A5
Verderers Rd *CHIG* IG7 ....55 G1
Verdun Rd *BARN* SW13 ....138 D1
  WOOL/PLUM SE18 ....128 A5
Vereker Rd *WKENS* W14 * 119 H5
Vere St *MHST* W1U 9 J4
Vermont CI *ENC/FH* EN2 ....23 H5
Vermont Rd *NRWD* SE19 ....180 E2
  SUT SM1 ....209 F1
  WAND/EARL SW18 ....160 A1
Verney Gdns *DAGW* RM9 ....92 A2
Verney Rd *BERM/RHTH* SE16 ....123 J5
  DAGW RM9 ....92 A3
Verney St *WLSDN* NW10 ....80 E1
Verney Wy *BERM/RHTH* SE16 ...123 J5
Vernham Rd
  WOOL/PLUM SE18 ....127 H6
Vernon Av *MNPK* E12 ....89 K2
  RYNPK SW20 ....177 F6
  WFD IG8 ....53 F2
Vernon CI *HOR/WEW* KT19 ....206 E4
  STMC/STPC BR5 ....186 C6
Vernon Crs *EBAR* EN4 ....22 A6
Vernon Dr *STAN* HA7 ....43 G4
Vernon Ms *BMSBY* WC1N 11 F2
Vernon Ri *FSBYW* WC1X 5 H6
  GFD/PVL UB6 ....78 D3
Vernon Rd *BOW* E3 ....105 H1
  CEND/HSY/T N8 * 49 G6
  CRW RM5 ....56 E1
  FELT TW13 ....153 J4
  GDMY/SEVK IG3 ....73 F5
  MORT/ESHN SW14 ....138 A4
  SRTFD E15 ....88 C5
  SUT SM1 ....209 G3
  WALTH E17 ....69 H1
  WAN E11 ....70 C5
Vernon Sq *FSBYW* WC1X 5 H4
Vernon Yd *NTGHL* W11 ....100 D6
Veroan Rd *BXLYHN* DA7 ....149 F3
Verona Dr *SURB* KT6 ....191 F6
Veronica Gdns *MTCM* CR4 ....179 H4
Veronica Rd *TOOT* SW17 ....161 G5
Veronique Gdns
  CNTH/NBYPK IG2 ....72 C2
Verran Rd *BAL* SW12 * 161 G2
Versailles Rd *PGE/AN* SE20 ......181 H5
Verulam Av *WALTH* E17 ....69 H4
Verulam Buildings *CLKNW* WC1X *.5 J7
Verulam Rd *GFD/PVL* UB6 ....96 A3
Verulam St *FSBYW* WC1X 11 J1
Verwood Dr *EBAR* EN4 ....21 K4
Verwood Rd *RYLN/HDSTN* HA2 ...42 C4
Veryan CI *STMC/STPC* BR5 ....202 D1
Vesage Ct *HCIRC* EC1N * 11 K2
Vesta Rd *BROCKY* SE4 ....144 B3
Vestris Rd *FSTH* SE23 ....164 A4
Vestry Rd *CMBW* SE5 ....143 F2
  WALTH E17 ....69 K1
Vestry St *IS* N1 ....6 E4

Vevey St *FSTH* SE23 ....164 C4
Viaduct Rd *BETH* E2 ....104 D2
Viaduct Rd *EFNCH* N2 ....47 H5
Viaduct St *BETH* E2 ....104 D2
The Viaduct *MUSWH* N10 * 66 B1
  SWFD E18 ....52 E5
Vian St *LEW* SE13 ....144 E4
Vibart Gdns *BRXS/STRHM* SW2 ..162 A2
Vibart Wk *IS* N1 * 84 E6
Vibia Ct *STWL/WRAY* TW19 ......152 A2
Vicarage CI *ERITH* DA8 ....129 K6
  NTHLT UB5 ....77 K6
  RSLP HA4 ....58 B4
  WPK KT4 ....192 B5
Vicarage Ct *BECK* BR3 * 182 B6
Vicarage Crs *BTSEA* SW11 ....140 C5
Vicarage Dr *BARK* IG11 ....90 C5
  BECK BR3 ....182 D4
  MORT/ESHN SW14 ....138 A6
Vicarage Farm Rd *HEST* TW5 ...134 D2
Vicarage Flds *WOT/HER* KT12 ...188 B3
  CROY/NA CR0 ....211 G1
Vicarage Ga *KENS* W8 ....120 A2
Vicarage Gv *CMBW* SE5 ....142 E2
Vicarage La *EHAM* E6 ....107 K2
  IL IG1 ....72 D5
  SRTFD E15 ....88 C4
Vicarage Ms *CHSWK* W4 * 118 B6
Vicarage Pde
  SEVS/STOTM N15 * 67 J7
Vicarage Pk
  WOOL/PLUM SE18 ....127 H5
Vicarage Rd *BXLY* DA5 ....169 J3
  CROY/NA CR0 ....211 G1
  DAGE RM10 ....92 D5
  E/WMO/HCT KT8 ....174 D4
  EMPK RM11 ....75 J5
  HDN NW4 ....63 J3
  LEY E10 ....69 K4
  MORT/ESHN SW14 ....138 A6
  SRTFD E15 ....88 D5
  SUT SM1 ....208 E2
  TEDD TW11 ....174 B1
  TOTM N17 ....50 C3
  WATW WD18 ....26 E2
  WHTN TW2 ....155 H1
  WHTN TW2 ....155 K4
  WOOL/PLUM SE18 ....127 H5
Vicarage Wk *BTSEA* SW11 * 140 C2
Vicarage Wy *RYLN/HDSTN* HA2 ...60 A4
  WLSDN NW10 ....81 F1
Vicars Bridge CI *ALP/SUD* HA0 ...98 A1
Vicar's CI *EN* EN1 ....24 A3
  HACK E8 ....86 E6
  SRTFD E15 ....88 E6
Vicars HI *LEW* SE13 ....144 E5
Vicar's Moor La *WCHMH* N21 ......35 G2
Vicars Oak Rd *NRWD* SE19 ....181 F2
Vicar's Rd *KTTN* NW5 ....84 A3
Viceroy CI *EFNCH* N2 * 65 J1
Viceroy Pde *EFNCH* N2 * 47 J5
Viceroy Rd *VX/NE* SW8 ....141 K2
Vickers CI *CROY/NA* CR0 ....211 F5
Vickers Rd *ERITH* DA8 ....130 A5
Victor Gv *ALP/SUD* HA0 ....80 A5
Victoria Av *CRW* RM5 ....56 D2
  E/WMO/HCT KT8 ....188 E1
  EHAM E6 ....89 H6
  FNCH N3 ....46 D2
  HSLW TW3 ....135 F6
  SURB KT6 ....190 E5
  WBLY HA9 ....80 D4
  WLGTN SM6 ....210 A1
Victoria CI *E/WMO/HCT* KT8 ......173 F6
  EBAR EN4 ....21 H5
  HRW HA1 * 61 F3
  HYS/HAR UB3 ....94 D6
Victoria Cottages
  RCH/KEW TW9 ....137 G2
Victoria CI *WBLY* HA9 ....80 C4
Victoria Crs *NRWD* SE19 ....180 E2
  SEVS/STOTM N15 ....68 A2
  WIM/MER SW19 ....177 J3
Victoria Dock Rd *CAN/RD* E16 ...106 E6
Victoria Dr *WIM/MER* SW19 ......159 G3
Victoria Emb *TPL/STR* WC2R 11 G6
  EMB EC4Y 11 K4
Victoria Gdns *HEST* TW5 ....134 D1
  NTGHL W11 ....119 K1
Victoria Ga *BAY/PAD* W2 ....8 B5
Victoria Gv *KENS* W8 ....120 B3
  NFNCH/WDSP N12 ....47 H1
Victoria Grove Ms
  BAY/PAD W2 ....101 G6
Victoria La *HYS/HAR* UB3 ....113 G5
  WAND/EARL SW18 ....160 B3
Victorian Gv *STNW/STAM* N16 ....86 A1
Victorian Rd *STNW/STAM* N16 ....86 B1
Victoria Pde *RCH/KEW* TW9 * 137 H2
Victoria Park Rd *HOM* E9 ....87 F5
Victoria Park Sq *BETH* E2 ....104 E2
Victoria Pas *RCHPK/HAM* TW10 ..136 E6
Victoria PI *RCH/KEW* TW9 ....136 E6
Victoria Ri *CLAP* SW4 ....141 G4
Victoria Rd *BARK* IG11 ....90 B4
  BFN/LL DA15 ....168 B3
  BKHH IG9 ....39 H4
  BUSH WD23 ....28 B3
  BXLYHS DA6 ....149 H6
  CHING E4 ....38 C3
  CHST BR7 ....185 F1
  DAGE RM10 ....92 E3
  DART DA1 ....171 H4
  EA W5 ....98 E5
  ED N9 ....36 B5
  ERITH DA8 ....130 B6
  FELT TW13 ....154 A3
  FSBYPK N4 ....67 F4
  HDN NW4 ....64 A1
  KENS W8 ....120 B3
  KIL/WHAMP NW6 ....100 D1
  KUT/HW KT1 ....175 G5

  MLHL NW7 ....45 H1
  MORT/ESHN SW14 ....138 A4
  MTCM CR4 ....178 D5
  NWDGN UB2 ....114 E3
  PLSTW E13 ....106 E1
  ROM RM1 ....75 H2
  RSLP HA4 ....77 F1
  SEVS/STOTM N15 * 68 C1
  SURB KT6 ....190 E5
  SUT SM1 ....209 H3
  SWFD E18 ....53 F2
  TEDD TW11 ....174 B2
  TWK TW1 ....156 C2
  WALTH E17 ....52 A5
  WAN E11 ....88 A1
  WDGN N22 ....48 D4
  WEA W13 ....97 G1
  WLSDN NW10 ....99 G1
Victoria Sq *BGVA* SW1W 15 K4
Victoria St *BELV* DA17 ....129 G5
  PIM SW1V 16 A5
  SRTFD E15 ....88 C6
  WEST SW1P 16 B5
Victoria Ter *EA* W5 ....116 E1
  FSBYPK N4 ....67 G4
  HRW HA1 ....60 E5
Victoria Vis *RCH/KEW* TW9 * 137 G2
Victoria Wy *CHARL* SE7 ....126 A5
  WOOL/PLUM SE18 ....104 C5
Victor Rd *PGE/AN* SE20 ....182 A3
  RYLN/HDSTN HA2 ....42 C6
  TEDD TW11 ....173 K1
  WLSDN NW10 ....99 K2
Victors Dr *HPTN* TW12 * 172 D1
Victors Wy *BAR* EN5 ....20 D4
Victor Vls *UED* N18 * 35 K5
Victory Av *MRDN* SM4 ....194 B2
Victory Pk *WBLY* HA9 * 79 K1
Victory PI *NRWD* SE19 * 181 F2
  WALW SE17 ....18 D6
Victory Rd *RAIN* RM13 ....111 J1
  WAN E11 ....71 G1
  WIM/MER SW19 ....178 B3
Victory Wy *BERM/RHTH* SE16 ....124 B2
  HEST TW5 ....114 B5
  ROMW/RG RM7 ....56 E5
Vienna CI *CLAY* IG5 ....53 H5
Viewfield CI *KTN/HRWW/W* HA3 ...62 A4
Viewfield Rd *BFN/LL* DA15 ....168 D3
  WAND/EARL SW18 ....159 J1
Viewland Rd
  WOOL/PLUM SE18 ....128 A5
View Rd *HGT* N6 ....65 K4
The View *ABYW* SE2 ....129 F5
Vigo Rd *WCHMH* N21 ....35 J2
Vigilant CI *SYD* SE26 ....163 H6
Vignoles Rd *ROMW/RG* RM7 .....74 C4
Vigo St *MYFR/PICC* W1J 10 A6
Viking Gdns *EHAM* E6 ....107 J3
Viking PI *LEY* E10 ....69 H5
Viking Rd *STHL* UB1 ....95 J6
Viking Wy *BELV* DA17 ....129 K3
Villacourt Rd
  WOOL/PLUM SE18 ....148 B1
Village Ar *CHING* E4 * 38 B3
Village CI *CHING* E4 * 38 A2
  HAMP NW3 * 83 H3
Village Green Rd *DART* DA1 ......150 D5
Village Ms *CDALE/KGS* NW9 * 63 F6
Village Mt *HAMP* NW3 * 83 G2
Village Park CI *EN* EN1 ....36 A1
  EN EN1 ....35 K1
The Village Rd *EN* EN1 ....46 C5
The Village *CHARL* SE7 ....126 B6
  HAMP NW3 * 83 H1
Village Wy *ASHF* TW15 ....152 C6
  BARK/HLT IG6 ....54 C6
  BECK BR3 ....182 D6
  NHNL SE24 ....162 C6
  PIN HA5 ....59 K4
  WLSDN NW10 ....81 F2
Village Wy East
  RYLN/HDSTN HA2 ....59 K4
Villa Rd *BRXN/ST* SW9 ....142 B4
Villas Rd *WOOL/PLUM* SE18 .....127 H4
Villa St *WALW* SE17 ....19 F8
Villers Av *BRYLDS* KT5 ....191 G2
  WHTN TW2 ....154 E3
Villiers CI *BRYLDS* KT5 ....191 G1
  LEY E10 ....69 J6
Villiers Gv *BELMT* SM2 ....208 B6
Villiers Rd *BECK* BR3 ....182 A5
  CRICK NW2 ....81 J4
  ISLW TW7 ....135 K3
  KUT/HW KT1 ....175 G5
  OXHEY WD19 ....27 J1
  STHL UB1 ....114 E1
Villiers St *CHCR* WC2N 11 F7
Vincent CI *BFN/LL* DA15 ....167 K1
  BAR EN5 ....20 E3
  EBAR EN4 ....54 D2
  ESH/CLAY KT10 ....204 B3
  HAYES BR2 ....200 A1
  WDR/YW UB7 ....112 D6
Vincent Gdns *CRICK* NW2 ....81 H1
Vincent Pde *FSBYPK* N4 * 66 E5
Vincent Rd *ACT* W3 ....117 K3
  ALP/SUD HA0 ....80 C6
  CHING E4 ....52 A2
  CROY/NA CR0 ....197 F4
  DAGW RM9 ....92 A5
  HSLWW TW4 ....134 C4
  ISLW TW7 ....135 J2
  KUT/HW KT1 ....175 H6
  SEVS/STOTM N15 ....67 H1
  WDGN N22 ....48 D5
  WOOL/PLUM SE18 ....127 G4
Vincent Rw *HPTN* TW12 ....173 H2

Vincents Cl BERM/RHTH SE16......124 B2
Vincent Sq WDGN N22 * 49 G5
WEST SW1P 16 B6
Vincent St CAN/RD E16 ......106 E4
WEST SW1P 16 C6
Vincent Ter IS N1......6 A2
Vincent Vls
SEVS/STOTM N15 * 67 J1
Vince St FSBYE EC1V......7 F5
Vine Cl BRYLDS KT5 ......191 G3
SUT SM1 ......209 G1
WDR/YW UB7 ......112 D4
Vine Ct KTN/HRWW/W HA3 ......62 A3
WCHPL E1 ......104 C4
Vine Gdns IL IG1 ......90 C3
Vinegar St WAP E1W......123 J1
Vinegar Yd STHWK SE1......19 G2
Vine Hl CLKNW EC1R 5 J7
Vine La STHWK SE1 ......19 H1
Vine Pl HSLW TW3 ......135 G5
Vineries Bank MLHL NW7 ......45 K1
Vineries Cl WDR/YW UB7 ......112 D6
The Vineries CAT SE6 * 164 D3
EN EN1 ......24 A4
STHGT/OAK N14 ......34 C1
Vine Rd BARN SW13 ......138 C4
E/WMO/HCT KT8......189 H1
ORP BR6 ......217 F4
SRTFD E15 ......88 D5
Vine Rw RCHPK/HAM TW10 * 137 F6
Viners Cl WOT/HER KT12 ......188 B3
Vines Av FNCH N3 ......47 F4
Vine Sq WKENS W14 * 119 J5
Vine St CONDST W1S......10 B6
ROMW/RG RM7 ......74 E2
TWRH EC3N 13 J4
Vine Street Br FARR EC1M......5 K7
Vine Street Crs TWRH EC3N 13 J5
Vine Yd STHWK SE1......18 D2
Vineyard Av MLHL NW7 ......46 C3
Vineyard Cl CAT SE6 ......164 D3
KUT/HW KT1 ......175 G6
Vineyard Gv FNCH N3......47 F4
Vineyard Hill Rd
WIM/MER SW19 ......159 K6
Vineyard Ms CLKNW EC1R * 5 J6
Vineyard Pth
MORT/ESHN SW14 ......138 A4
Vineyard Rd FELT TW13 ......153 K5
Vineyard Rw E/WMO/HCT KT8 ......174 D4
The Vineyard
RCHPK/HAM TW10 ......136 E6
Vineyard Wk CLKNW EC1R......5 J6
Viney Bank CROY/NA CR0 ......213 H6
Viney Rd LEW SE13 ......144 E4
Vining St BRXN/ST SW9 ......142 B5
Vinson Cl ORP BR6 ......202 B5
Vintry Ms WALTH E17 ......69 J1
Viola Av ABYW SE2 ......128 C4
EBED/NFELT TW14 ......154 B1
STWL/WRAY TW19 ......152 B4
Viola Sq SHB W12 ......99 H6
Violet Av ENC/FH EN2 ......23 K1
Violet Cl CAN/RD E16 ......106 C3
CHEAM SM3 ......193 H5
DEPT SE8 ......124 C6
WLGTN SM6 ......195 F5
Violet Gdns CROY/NA CR0 ......211 H3
Violet Hl STJWD NW8 ......101 G1
Violet La CROY/NA CR0......211 H3
Violet Rd BOW E3 ......105 K3
SWFD E18......53 F5
WALTH E17......69 J3
Violet St BETH E2 ......104 D3
Virgil St STHWK SE1......17 H4
Virginia Cl CRW RM5 ......56 E3
NWMAL KT3 ......191 K1
Virginia Gdns BARK/HLT IG6 ......54 D5
Virginia Rd BETH E2 ......7 K4
THHTH CR7......180 D4
Virginia St WAP E1W * 104 C6
Viscount Cl FBAR/BDGN N11......48 A1
Viscount Dr EHAM E6......107 K4
Viscount Gv NTHLT UB5 ......95 H2
Viscount Rd
STWL/WRAY TW19 ......152 A2
Viscount St STLK EC1Y 6 C7
Viscount Wy HTHAIR TW6 ......133 H5
Vista Av PEND EN3 ......25 F3
Vista Dr REDBR IG4 ......71 H2
The Vista CHING E4 ......38 B2
ELTH/MOT SE9......166 D2
Vista Wy KTN/HRWW/W HA3 ......62 A3
Viveash Cl HYS/HAR UB3 ......113 J3
Vivian Av HDN NW4 ......63 K2
WBLY HA9......80 C4
Vivian Cl OXHEY WD19 ......26 E4
Vivian Gdns OXHEY WD19 ......26 E3
WBLY HA9......80 C3
Vivian Rd BOW E3 ......105 G1
Vivian Sq PECK SE15......143 J4
Vivian Wy EFNCH N2 ......65 H2
Vivien Cl CHSGTN KT9 ......206 A5
Vivienne Cl TWK TW1 ......156 E1
Vixen Ms HACK E8 *......86 B6
Voce Rd WOOL/PLUM SE18......147 J1
Voewood Cl NWMAL KT3 ......192 C3
Voltaire Rd CLAP SW4......141 J4
Volt Av WLSDN NW10......99 F2
Volta Wy CROY/NA CR0 ......196 A5
Voluntary Pl WAN E11 ......70 E3
Vorley Rd ARCH N19......66 C6
Voss Ct STRHM/NOR SW16 ......179 K2
Voss St BETH E2......104 C2
Voyagers Cl THMD SE28......109 J5
Vulcan Cl EHAM E6 ......108 A5
Vulcan Ga ENC/FH EN2......23 G3
Vulcan Rd BROCKY SE4......144 C3
Vulcan Ter BROCKY SE4 ......144 C3
Vulcan Wy HOLWY N7 ......85 F4
WLGTN SM6 ......210 E6
Vyner Rd ACT W3......99 F6
Vyner St BETH E2 ......104 D1
The Vyne BXLYHN DA7 ......149 J4
Vyse Cl BAR EN5 ......20 A5

W

Wadding St WALW SE17......18 E7
Waddington Cl EN EN1 ......24 A5
Waddington Rd SRTFD E15......88 B3
Waddington St SRTFD E15 ......88 B4
Waddington Wy NRWD SE19 ......180 D4
Waddon Cl CROY/NA CR0 ......211 G1
Waddon Court Rd
CROY/NA CR0 ......211 G2
Waddon Marsh Wy
CROY/NA CR0 ......196 A5
Waddon New Rd
CROY/NA CR0 ......211 H1
Waddon Park Av
CROY/NA CR0 ......211 G2
Waddon Rd CROY/NA CR0......211 G1
Waddon Wy CROY/NA CR0 ......211 G4
Wade Av STMC/STPC BR5 ......202 E4
Wade House STHWK SE1 * 123 H2
Wade Rd CAN/RD E16......107 G5
Wade's Gv WCHMH N21......35 G2
Wade's Hl WCHMH N21 ......35 G1
Wade's La TEDD TW11 ......174 B1
Wadeson St BETH E2 ......104 D1
Wade's Pl POP/IOD E14 ......105 K6
Wadeville Av CHDH RM6 ......74 A3
Wadeville Cl BELV DA17 ......129 H5
Wadham Av CHING E4 ......51 K3
Wadham Gdns GFD/PVL UB6 ......78 D4
HAMP NW3 ......83 J5
Wadham Rd CHING E4 ......51 K3
PUT/ROE SW15 ......139 H5
Wadhurst Cl PGE/AN SE20......181 J5
Wadhurst Rd CHSWK W4......118 A3
Wadley Rd WAN E11......70 C4
Wadsworth Cl GFD/PVL UB6......97 J1
PEND EN3......25 F6
Wadsworth Rd GFD/PVL UB6 ......97 H1
Wager St BOW E3 ......105 H3
Waghorn Rd
KTN/HRWW/W HA3 ......43 K6
PLSTW E13......89 G6
Waghorn St PECK SE15 ......143 H4
Wagner St PECK SE15......143 K1
Wagstaff Gdns DAGW RM9 ......91 J5
Wagtail Cl CDALE/KGS NW9......45 G5
EN EN1 ......24 D2
Wagtail Wk BECK BR3 ......199 F2
Wagtail Wy STMC/STPC BR5 ......202 E1
Waid Cl DART DA1 ......171 J1
Waights Ct KUTN/CMB KT2 ......175 F4
Wainfleet Av CRW RM5 ......56 E5
Wainford Cl WIM/MER SW19 ......159 G3
Wainwright Gv ISLW TW7 ......135 J5
Waite Davies Rd
LEE/GVPK SE12 ......165 J2
Waite St PECK SE15......123 G6
Wakefield Gdns IL IG1......71 J3
NRWD SE19 ......181 F3
Wakefield Ms STPAN WC1H......5 F5
Wakefield Rd
FBAR/BDGN N11 ......48 D1
RCHPK/HAM TW10 ......136 E6
SEVS/STOTM N15 ......68 B2
Wakefield St BMSBY WC1N......5 F6
EHAM E6......89 J6
UED N18......50 C1
Wakehams Hl PIN HA5 ......41 K6
Wakeham St IS N1 ......85 K4
Wakehurst Rd BTSEA SW11......140 E6
Wakeling La ALP/SUD HA0 ......79 H1
Wakeling Rd HNWL W7 ......97 F4
Wakeling St WCHPL E1 * 105 G5
Wakelin Rd SRTFD E15 ......106 C1
Wakeman Rd WLSDN NW10 ......100 A2
Wakemans Hill Av
CDALE/KGS NW9 ......63 F2
Wakering Rd BARK IG11......90 C5
Wakerly Cl EHAM E6......107 K5
Wakley St FSBYE EC1V 6 A4
Walberswick St VX/NE SW8 ......141 K1
Walbrook MANHO EC4N......12 E5
Walburgh St WCHPL E1 ......104 D5
Walcorde Av WALW SE17......18 D7
Walcot Rd PEND EN3 ......25 H3
Walcot Sq LBTH SE11 ......17 K6
Walcott St WEST SW1P * 16 B6
Waldeck Gv WNWD SE27 ......162 C5
Waldeck Rd CHSWK W4 ......117 H6
DART DA1 ......171 J2
MORT/ESHN SW14 ......137 K4
SEVS/STOTM N15 ......49 H6
WEA W13 ......97 H5
Waldegrave Gdns TWK TW1 ......156 A4
Waldegrave Pk TWK TW1 ......156 A6
Waldegrave Rd BCTR RM8 ......73 J6
BMLY BR1......200 D2
CEND/HSY/T N8 * 49 G6
EA W5 ......98 B6
NRWD SE19 ......181 G3
TWK TW1 ......156 A6
Waldegrove CROY/NA CR0 ......212 B1
Waldemar Av FUL/PGN SW6 ......139 H2
WEA W13 ......116 D1
Waldemar Rd
WIM/MER SW19 ......177 K1
Walden Av CHST BR7 ......166 E6
PLMGR N13 ......35 J6
RAIN RM13 ......111 F1
Walden Cl BELV DA17 ......129 G5
Walden Gdns THHTH CR7 ......196 A1
Waldenhurst Rd
STMC/STPC BR5 ......202 E4
Walden Pde CHST BR7 *......184 E2
Walden Rd CHST BR7 ......184 E2
TOTM N17 ......49 K4
Waldens Cl STMC/STPC BR5 ......202 E4
Waldenshaw Rd FSTH SE23......163 K3
Waldens Rd STMC/STPC BR5......203 F3
Walden St WCHPL E1 * 104 D5
Walden Wy BARK/HLT IG6 ......54 E3
MLHL NW7 ......46 B2
Waldo Cl CLAP SW4......141 H6
Waldo Pl WIM/MER SW19 ......178 D3
Waldorf Cl SAND/SEL CR2 ......211 H6
Waldo Rd BMLY BR1......184 B6
WLSDN NW10......99 K2
Waldram Crs FSTH SE23......163 K3
Waldram Park Rd FSTH SE23 ......164 A3
Waldrist Wy ERITHM DA18 ......129 G2
Waldron Gdns HAYES BR2......183 G6
Waldronhyrst CROY/NA CR0......211 H2
Waldron Ms CHEL SW3......120 C6
Waldron Rd HRW HA1 ......60 E5
WAND/EARL SW18 ......160 B5
The Waldrons CROY/NA CR0......211 J2
Waldron's Yd RYLN/HDSTN HA2......60 D6
Waldstock Rd THMD SE28......109 G6
Waleran Cl STAN HA7 ......43 F2
Walerand Rd LEW SE13 ......145 F3
Wales Av CAR SM5......209 K3
Wales Cl PECK SE15......143 J1
Wales Farm Rd ACT W3 ......99 F4
Waleton Acres WLGTN SM6 * 210 C4
Waley St WCHPL E1 * 105 F4
Walfield Av TRDG/WHET N20 ......33 F2
Walford Rd STNW/STAM N16 ......86 A2
Walfrey Gdns DAGW RM9 ......92 A5
Walham Green Ct
FUL/PGN SW6 * 140 A1
Walham Gv FUL/PGN SW6......139 K1
Walham Ri WIM/MER SW19 ......177 H2
Walham Yd FUL/PGN SW6......139 K1
Walkden Rd CHST BR7 ......167 F6
Walker Cl DART DA1 ......150 C4
EBED/NFELT TW14 ......153 J2
FBAR/BDGN N11 ......34 C6
HNWL W7 ......115 K1
HPTN TW12 ......172 E2
WOOL/PLUM SE18 ......127 H4
Walker's Ct SOHO/CST W1F......10 C5
Walkerscroft Md CAT SE6 ......164 E4
DUL SE21 ......162 D3
Walker's Pl PUT/ROE SW15 *......139 H5
Walkley Rd DART DA1......150 E6
The Walks EFNCH N2 ......47 H6
The Walk PLMGR N13 * 35 G5
Wallace Cl THMD SE28 ......109 K6
Wallace Crs CAR SM5 ......209 K3
Wallace Rd IS N1 ......85 J4
Wallace Wy ROM RM1 ......57 F4
Wallbutton Rd BROCKY SE4 ......144 B3
Wallcote Av CRICK NW2......64 B5
Wall End Rd EHAM E6......90 A5
Wallenger Av GPK RM2 ......57 K6
Waller Dr NTHWD HA6 ......40 E5
Waller Rd NWCR SE14......144 A3
Wallers Cl DAGW RM9 ......92 A6
WFD IG8 ......53 K2
Wallflower St SHB W12 ......99 H6
Wallgrave Rd ECT SW5......120 A4
Wallingford Av NKENS W10 ......100 B4
Wallington Cl RSLP HA4......58 A3
Wallington Rd GDMY/SEVK IG3......73 F4
Wallis Cl BTSEA SW11 ......140 C4
EMPK RM11 ......75 K5
RDART DA2......170 D5
Wallis Rd HOM E9 ......87 H4
STHL UB1 ......96 B5
Wallorton Gdns
MORT/ESHN SW14 ......138 A5
Wallside BARB EC2Y * 12 D2
Wall St IS N1......85 K4
Wallwood Rd WAN E11 ......70 B4
Wallwood St POP/IOD E14 ......105 H4
Walmar Cl EBAR EN4 ......21 H2
Walmer Cl CHING E4 ......37 K4
ORP BR6......216 D2
ROMW/RG RM7......56 D5
Walmer Gdns HNWL W7......116 B2
Walmer Rd NTGHL W11 ......100 C6
Walmer Ter WOOL/PLUM SE18......127 H4
Walmgate Rd GFD/PVL UB6 ......79 H6
Walmington Fold
NFNCH/WDSP N12 ......46 E2
Walm La CRICK NW2 ......82 B4
Walney Wk IS N1 * 85 J4
Walnut Av WDR/YW UB7 ......112 D3
Walnut Cl BARK/HLT IG6......72 C1
CAR SM5 ......209 K3
DEPT SE8 ......124 C6
HYS/HAR UB3 ......94 C6
Walnut Ct EA W5 * 117 F2
Walnut Gdns SRTFD E15 ......88 C3
Walnut Gv EN EN1......23 K6
Walnut Ms BELMT SM2......209 G5
Walnut Rd LEY E10 ......69 J6
Walnuts Rd ORP BR6 ......202 B5
Walnut Tree Av DART DA1......171 H4
MTCM CR4 *......178 D6
Walnut Tree Cl BARN SW13 ......138 C2
CHST BR7 ......185 H4
Walnut Tree Rd BCTR RM8 ......73 K6
BTFD TW8......117 F6
ERITH DA8 ......130 B5
GNWCH SE10 * 125 H5
HEST TW5 * 114 E6
Walnut Tree Wk LBTH SE11......17 J6
Walnut Wy BKHH IG9 ......39 H5
RSLP HA4 ......77 G4
Walpole Av RCH/KEW TW9 ......137 G3
Walpole Cl PIN HA5......42 A3
WEA W13 ......116 D2
Walpole Crs TEDD TW11......174 A1
Walpole Gdns CHSWK W4 ......117 K5
WHTN TW2......155 K4
Walpole Ms STJWD NW8 ......2 A1
Walpole Pl TEDD TW11......174 A1
Walpole Rd CROY/NA CR0 ......196 E6
EHAM E6......89 G5
HAYES BR2 ......200 C2
SURB KT6 ......191 F4
SWFD E18......52 D4
TEDD TW11 ......174 A1
TOTM N17 ......49 J5
WALTH E17......69 G1
WHTN TW2 ......155 K4
WIM/MER SW19 ......178 C2
Walpole St CHEL SW3 ......120 E5
Walrond Av WBLY HA9......80 A3
Walsham Cl STNW/STAM N16 ......68 C5
THMD SE28 ......109 K6
Walsham Rd EBED/NFELT TW14......154 A2
NWCR SE14 ......144 A3
Walsingham Gdns
HOR/WEW KT19 ......207 G2
Walsingham Pk CHST BR7......185 J5
Walsingham Rd CLAP SW4 ......161 F1
CLPT E5......86 C1
ENC/FH EN2......23 K5
MTCM CR4 ......194 E2
STMC/STPC BR5 ......186 C4
WEA W13 * 116 B1
Walsingham Wk BELV DA17 ......129 H6
Walters Rd PEND EN3 ......24 E6
SNWD SE25 ......197 F1
Walter St BETH E2......105 F2
KUTN/CMB KT2 * 175 F4
Walters Wy FSTH SE23 ......164 A1
Walters Yd BMLY BR1......183 K5
Walter Ter WCHPL E1 ......105 F5
Walterton Rd MV/WKIL W9......100 D3
Walter Wk EDGW HA8 ......44 E2
Waltham Av
CDALE/KGS NW9 ......62 C3
HYS/HAR UB3 ......113 F3
Waltham Cl DART DA1 ......170 D1
STMC/STPC BR5 ......202 E5
Waltham Dr EDGW HA8 ......44 C5
Waltham Pk WALTH E17 ......51 J3
Waltham Rd CAR SM5......194 C5
NWDGN UB2......114 D3
WFD IG8 ......53 J2
Walthamstow Av CHING E4 ......51 J3
Walthamstow Av (North Circular)
CHING E4 ......51 G1
Waltham Wy CHING E4 ......37 H5
Waltheof Av TOTM N17 ......49 K4
Waltheof Gdns TOTM N17......49 K4
Walton Av CHEAM SM3 ......208 D1
NWMAL KT3 ......192 C1
RYLN/HDSTN HA2 ......77 K3
WBLY HA9......80 D1
Walton Cl CRICK NW2 ......63 K6
HRW HA1 ......60 D1
VX/NE SW8......141 K1
Walton Dr HRW HA1 ......60 D1
WLSDN NW10......81 F4
Walton Gdns ACT W3 ......98 D4
FELT TW13 ......153 J6
WBLY HA9......62 A6
Walton Gn CROY/NA CR0......213 K6
Walton Pk WOT/HER KT12......188 C6
Walton Park La
WOT/HER KT12 ......188 D6
Walton Pl CHEL SW3 ......14 E4
Walton Rd CRW RM5 ......56 B3
HRW HA1 ......60 D1
MNPK E12 ......90 A2
PLSTW E13 ......107 G1
SCUP DA14......168 C5
SEVS/STOTM N15 * 68 B1
WOT/HER KT12 ......188 C2
Walton St CHEL SW3......14 D6
ENC/FH EN2......23 K2
Walton Vls IS N1 * 86 A5
Walton Wy ACT W3......98 D4
MTCM CR4 ......195 H1
Walt Whitman Cl HNHL SE24 * 142 C5
Walverns Cl OXHEY WD19 ......27 G1
Walworth Pl WALW SE17 ......122 D5
Walworth Rd WALW SE17 ......18 C6
Walwyn Av BMLY BR1 ......184 C6
Wanborough Dr
PUT/ROE SW15 ......158 E3
Wanderer Dr BARK IG11......109 H2
Wandle Bank CROY/NA CR0 ......210 E1
WIM/MER SW19 ......178 C2
Wandle Ct HOR/WEW KT19 ......206 E2
Wandle Court Gdns
CROY/NA CR0 ......210 E1
Wandle Rd CROY/NA CR0 ......210 E1
CROY/NA CR0 ......211 J1
MRDN SM4......194 C2
TOOT SW17......160 D4
WLGTN SM6 ......195 G6
Wandle Side CROY/NA CR0 ......211 F1
WLGTN SM6 ......210 B1
Wandle Wy MTCM CR4 ......194 E2
WAND/EARL SW18 ......160 A3
Wandon Rd FUL/PGN SW6......140 A1
Wandsworth Br
WAND/EARL SW18 ......140 B4
Wandsworth Bridge Rd
FUL/PGN SW6 ......140 A2
Wandsworth Common
West Side
WAND/EARL SW18 ......140 B6
Wandsworth High St
WAND/EARL SW18 ......139 K6
Wandsworth Pln
WAND/EARL SW18 ......140 A6
Wandsworth Rd CLAP SW4......141 G4
VX/NE SW8......121 K6
Wangey Rd CHDH RM6......73 K4
Wanless Rd HNHL SE24 ......142 D4
Wanley Rd CMBW SE5 ......142 E5
Wanlip Rd PLSTW E13......107 F3
Wannock Gdns BARK/HLT IG6......54 B3
Wansbeck Rd HOM E9 ......87 H5
Wansdown Pl FUL/PGN SW6......140 A1
Wansey St WALW SE17......18 D7
Wansford Rd WFD IG8 ......53 G4
Wanstead Cl BMLY BR1 ......184 B5
Wanstead La IL IG1 ......71 J3
Wanstead Park Av MNPK E12 ......71 H6
Wanstead Park Rd IL IG1......71 J5
Wanstead Pl WAN E11 ......70 E3
Wanstead Rd BMLY BR1 ......184 B5
Wansunt Rd BXLY DA5......169 K3
Wantage Rd LEE/GVPK SE12......145 J6
Wantz La RAIN RM13 ......111 K3
Wantz Rd DAGE RM10 ......92 D2
Wapping Dock St WAP E1W * 123 J1
Wapping High St WAP E1W......123 H1
Wapping La WAP E1W 104 D6
Wapping Wall WAP E1W 123 K1
Warbank La KUTN/CMB KT2 ......176 C3
Warbeck Rd SHB W12 ......118 E1
Warberry Rd WDGN N22 ......49 F5
Warboys Ap KUTN/CMB KT2 ......175 J2
Warboys Crs CHING E4......52 A1
Warboys Rd KUTN/CMB KT2 ......175 J2
Warburton Cl IS N1......86 A4
KTN/HRWW/W HA3 ......42 D2
Warburton Rd HACK E8......86 D6
WHTN TW2......155 G3
Warburton St HACK E8......86 D6
Warburton Ter WALTH E17 ......51 K5
Wardalls Gv NWCR SE14 * 143 K1
Ward Cl ERITH DA8 ......130 A6
SAND/SEL CR2......212 A3
Wardell Cl CDALE/KGS NW9......45 G3
Warden Av CRW RM5 ......56 E1
RYLN/HDSTN HA2 ......59 J5
Warden Rd KTTN NW5 ......84 A4
Wardens Gv STHWK SE1......18 C1
Wardle St HOM E9......87 F3
Wardley St WAND/EARL SW18 ......160 A2
Wardo Av FUL/PGN SW6 ......139 H2
Wardour Ms SOHO/CST W1F......10 B4
Wardour St SOHO/CST W1F......10 B3
Ward Rd ARCH N19......84 C2
SRTFD E15 * 88 B6
Wardrobe Pl BLKFR EC4V * 12 B4
The Wardrobe
RCH/KEW TW9 * 136 E6
Wards Rd GNTH/NBYPK IG2......72 D4
Wareham Cl HSLW TW3 ......135 G5
Waremead Rd
GNTH/NBYPK IG2 ......72 B2
Warepoint Dr THMD SE28 ......127 J2
Warfield Rd
EBED/NFELT TW14 ......153 H2
HPTN TW12 ......173 G4
WLSDN NW10......100 B2
Warfield Yd WLSDN NW10 * 100 B2
Wargrave Av SEVS/STOTM N15 ......68 C3
Wargrave Rd RYLN/HDSTN HA2 ......78 C1
Warham Rd FSBYPK N4......67 G2
KTN/HRWW/W HA3 ......43 F6
SAND/SEL CR2......211 J3
Warham St CMBW SE5......142 C1
Waring Cl ORP BR6......217 F4
Waring Dr ORP BR6 ......217 F4
Waring Rd SCUP DA14 ......186 D2
Waring St WNWD SE27......162 D6
Warkworth Gdns ISLW TW7 ......136 B1
Warkworth Rd TOTM N17......49 K3
Warland Rd WOOL/PLUM SE18......147 J1
Warley Av ROMW/RG RM7 ......74 B4
YEAD UB4......94 E5
Warley Rd CLAY IG5......54 A4
ED N9 ......36 E4
WFD IG8 ......53 F3
YEAD UB4......94 E5
Warley St BETH E2 ......105 F2
Warlingham Rd THHTH CR7 ......196 C1
Warlock Rd MV/WKIL W9......100 D3
Warlters Cl HOLWY N7 *......84 E2
Warlters Rd HOLWY N7 ......84 E2
Warltersville Rd ARCH N19 ......66 E4
Warming Cl CLPT E5 *......87 F1
Warmington Rd HNHL SE24 ......162 D1
Warmington St PLSTW E13......106 E3
Warminster Rd SNWD SE25......181 H5
Warminster Sq SNWD SE25......181 H5
Warminster Wy MTCM CR4......179 G4
Warndon St BERM/RHTH SE16......123 K4
Warneford Pl OXHEY WD19......27 J1
Warneford Rd
KTN/HRWW/W HA3 ......43 K6
Warneford St HOM E9 ......86 D6
Warne Pl BFN/LL DA15 ......168 C1
Warner Av CHEAM SM3 ......193 H6
Warner Cl CDALE/KGS NW9 ......63 H4
HPTN TW12 ......172 E1
HYS/HAR UB3 ......133 G1
SRTFD E15 ......88 C3
Warner Pl BETH E2 ......104 C1
Warner Rd BMLY BR1......183 J3
CEND/HSY/T N8 ......66 D1
CMBW SE5 ......142 D2
WALTH E17......69 G1
Warner St CLKNW EC1R 5 J7
Warner Ter POP/IOD E14 * 105 J4
Warner Yd CLKNW EC1R......5 J7
Warnford Rd ORP BR6......217 F3
Warnham Court Rd CAR SM5 ......209 K5
Warnham Rd
NFNCH/WDSP N12 ......47 H1
Warple Ms ACT W3 * 118 B2
Warple Wy ACT W3......118 B2
Warren Av BMLY BR1......183 H3
ORP BR6......217 F3
RCHPK/HAM TW10 ......137 J5
SAND/SEL CR2......213 F5
WAN E11 * 88 B1
Warren Cl BXLYHS DA6......149 H6
ED N9 ......37 F2
ESH/CLAY KT10 ......204 C2
WBLY HA9......61 K6
YEAD UB4......95 G4
Warren Ct CHARL SE7 ......126 B5
Warren Crs ED N9......36 B2
Warren Cutting
KUTN/CMB KT2 ......176 A3
Warrender Rd ARCH N19......84 C1
Warrender Wy RSLP HA4......58 E4
Warren Dr GFD/PVL UB6 ......96 B3
HCH RM12 ......93 J1
ORP BR6......217 H3
RSLP HA4 ......59 H4
Warren Dr North BRYLDS KT5......191 J5
Warren Dr South BRYLDS KT5 ......191 K5
The Warren Dr WAN E11 ......71 G4
Warren Flds STAN HA7 * 29 J6

Warren Gdns ORP BR6 ....217 G3
Warren La STAN HA7 ....29 G4
WOOL/PLUM SE18 ....127 G5
Warren Ms GTPST W1W 4 A7
Warren Pk KUTN/CMB KT2 ....175 K2
Warren Park Rd KUTN/CMB KT2 ...209 H4
Warren Ri NWMAL KT3 ....176 A4
Warren Rd BARK/HLT IG6 ....72 D2
BUSH WD23 ....28 C3
BXLYHS DA6 ....149 H6
CHING E4 ....38 A4
CRICK NW2 ....62 A5
CROY/NA CRO 197 F5
DART DA1 ....171 H5
HAYES BR2 ....199 K6
KUTN/CMB KT2 ....175 K2
LEY E10 ....88 A1
ORP BR6 ....217 F3
SCUP DA14 ....168 D5
WAN E11 ....71 J5
WHTN TW2 ....155 J1
WIM/MER SW19 ....178 D2
Warrens Shawe La EDGW HA8 .....30 D4
Warren St FITZ W1T 4 A7
The Warren CAR SM5 ....209 H6
HEST TW5 ....134 E1
HOR/WEW KT19 ....207 F2
MNPK E12 ....89 J2
YEAD UB4 ....94 E5
Warren Wy MLHL NW7 ....46 C2
Warren Wood Cl HAYES BR2 ....199 K6
Warriner Dr ED N9 ....36 C5
Warriner Gdns BTSEA SW11 ....140 E2
Warrington Crs MV/WKIL W9 ......101 G3
Warrington Gdns
MV/WKIL W9 ....101 G3
Warrington Pl POP/IOD E14 * 125 F1
Warrington Rd BCTR RM8 ....73 K6
CROY/NA CRO 211 H1
HRW HA1 ....60 E2
RCHPK/HAM TW10 ....136 E6
Warrington Sq BCTR RM8 ....73 K6
Warrior Sq MNPK E12 ....90 A2
Warsaw Cl RSLP HA4 ....77 F4
Warspite Rd
WOOL/PLUM SE18 ....126 D3
Warton Rd SRTFD E15 ....88 A6
Warwall EHAM E6 ....108 B5
Warwick Av EDGW HA8 ....30 C5
MV/WKIL W9 ....101 G4
RYLN/HDSTN HA2 ....77 K2
Warwick Chambers
KENS W8 * 119 K3
Warwick Cl BUSH WD23 ....28 E2
BXLY DA5 ....169 G2
EBAR EN4 ....21 H6
HPTN TW12 ....173 H3
ORP BR6 ....217 G1
Warwick Ct HHOL WC1V 11 H2
Warwick Crs BAY/PAD W2 ....101 G4
YEAD UB4 ....94 D3
Warwick Dene ACT W3 ....117 F1
Warwick Dr BARN SW13 ....138 C4
Warwick Gdns FSBYPK N4 ....67 J2
IL IG1 ....72 B5
THDIT KT7 ....190 A2
THHTH CR7 * 196 B1
WKENS W14 ....119 J3
Warwick Gv BRYLDS KT5 ....191 G4
CLPT E5 ....68 D5
Warwick House St STJS SW1Y 10 D7
Warwick La STP EC4M 12 B3
Warwick Pde
KTN/HRWW/W HA3 * 43 H5
Warwick Pl EA W5 ....116 E2
MV/WKIL W9 ....101 G4
THDIT KT7 * 190 B3
Warwick Pl North PIM SW1V * 16 A7
Warwick Rd BAR EN5 ....21 F5
CHING E4 ....51 J1
EA W5 ....117 F1
FBAR/BDGN N11 ....34 B6
FSTGT E7 ....88 D4
HSLWW TW4 ....134 A4
KUT/HW KT1 ....174 D4
MNPK E12 ....89 J3
NWDGN UB2 ....114 E3
NWMAL KT3 ....175 K6
PGE/AN SE20 ....181 J6
SCUP DA14 ....186 C1
SUT SM1 ....209 G3
THDIT KT7 ....190 A2
THHTH CR7 ....180 B6
UED N18 ....36 A6
WALTH E17 ....51 K5
WAN E11 ....71 F2
WDR/YW UB7 ....112 B1
WELL DA16 ....148 C3
WHTN TW2 ....155 K3
WKENS W14 ....119 J4
Warwick Rw WESTW SW1E 16 A4
Warwickshire Pth DEPT SE8 ....144 C1
Warwick Sq PIM SW1V 16 A7
STP EC4M 12 B3
Warwick Square Ms PIM SW1V 16 A7
Warwick St REGST W1B 10 B5
Warwick Ter WALTH E17 * 70 D2
WOOL/PLUM SE18 ....127 J6
Warwick Wy DART DA1 ....171 H4
PIM SW1V 121 G5
Warwick Yd STLK EC1Y * 6 D7
Washington Av MNPK E12 ....89 J2
Washington Cl BOW E3 ....105 K2
Washington Rd BARN SW13 ....138 D1
EHAM E6 ....89 G5
KUT/HW KT1 ....175 H5
SWFD E18 ....53 F1
WPK KT4 ....192 E6
Wastdale Rd FSTH SE23 ....164 A3
Watchfield Ct CHSWK W4 * 117 K5
The Watch NFNCH/WDSP N12 * ...33 G6
Watcombe Rd SNWD SE25 ....197 J2
Waterbank Rd CAT SE6 ....164 E5
Waterbeach Rd DAGW RM9 ....91 J4

Water Brook La HDN NW4 * 64 A2
Watercress Pl IS N1 ....86 A5
Waterdale Rd ABYW SE2 ....128 B6
Waterden Rd SRTFD E15 ....87 J5
Waterer Ri WLGTN SM6 ....210 D4
Waterfall Cottages
WIM/MER SW19 ....178 C2
Waterfall Rd FBAR/BDGN N11 ......34 B6
WIM/MER SW19 ....178 C2
Waterfall Ter TOOT SW17 ....178 D2
Waterfield Cl BELV DA17 ....129 H3
THMD SE28 ....128 C1
Waterfield Gdns SNWD SE25 .....197 F1
Waterford Rd FUL/PGN SW6 ......140 A2
Waterford Wy WLSDN NW10 ....81 K3
The Waterfront BORE WD6 * 29 H1
Water Gdns STAN HA7 ....43 H2
The Water Gdns BAY/PAD W2 ....8 C3
Watergate St DEPT SE8 ....124 D6
The Watergate OXHEY WD19 ....27 H4
Waterhall Av CHING E4 ....38 C6
Waterhall Cl WALTH E17 ....51 F4
Waterhead Cl ERITH DA8 ....150 D1
Waterhouse Cl HAMP NW3 ....83 H3
Wateringbury Cl
STMC/STPC BR5 ....186 C6
Water La CAMTN NW1 ....4 B2
ED N9 ....36 D5
GDMY/SEVK IG3 ....91 F1
KUT/HW KT1 ....174 E4
NWCR SE14 ....143 K1
PUR RM19 ....131 K4
RCH/KEW TW9 ....136 E6
SCUP DA14 ....169 G5
SRTFD E15 ....88 C4
TWK TW1 ....156 B3
Water Lily Cl NWDGN UB2 ....115 H2
Waterloo Br STHWK SE1 ....11 H6
Waterloo Cl
EBED/NFELT TW14 ....153 J5
HOM E9 ....86 E3
Waterloo Gdns BETH E2 ....104 E1
ROMW/RG RM7 ....75 F3
RCH/KEW TW9 ....117 H6
STJS SW1Y 11 H7
Waterloo Rd BARK/HLT IG6 ....54 C5
CRICK NW2 ....63 J6
EHAM E6 ....88 D3
FSTGT E7 ....88 D3
LEY E10 ....69 J4
ROMW/RG RM7 ....75 F2
STHWK SE1 ....11 H7
SUT SM1 ....209 H3
Waterloo Ter IS N1 ....85 H5
Waterlow Rd ARCH N19 ....66 C5
Waterman Cl OXHEY WD19 ....27 F1
Watermans Cl
KUTN/CMB KT2 ....175 F2
Watermans Ms EA W5 ....98 A6
Waterman Sq PGE/AN SE20 ....181 K3
Waterman Sq PUT/ROE SW15 .....139 G4
Waterman Wy WAP E1W 123 J1
Waterman La
EBED/NFELT TW14 ....153 H3
Watermead La MTCM CR4 ....194 E3
Watermeadow Cl ERITH DA8 ....150 E1
Watermeadow La
FUL/PGN SW6 ....140 B3
Watermead Rd CAT SE6 ....165 G4
Watermead Wy TOTM N17 ....50 D5
Watermens Sq PGE/AN SE20 * 181 K3
Water Ms PECK SE15 ....143 K5
Watermill Cl
RCHPK/HAM TW10 ....156 D5
Watermill La UED N18 ....50 A1
Water Mill Wy FELT TW13 ....154 E4
Watermill Wy WIM/MER SW19 ....178 B4
Watermint Cl STMC/STPC BR5 ....202 E1
Watermint Quay
STNW/STAM N16 ....68 C4
Water Rd ALP/SUD HA0 ....80 B6
Water's Edge FUL/PGN SW6 * 139 G2
Watersedge HOR/WEW KT19 ......206 E2
Watersfield Wy EDGW HA8 ....43 J3
Waterside DART DA1 ....150 B6
WALTH E17 ....69 F3
Waterside Av BECK BR3 ....198 E2
Waterside Cl BARK IG11 ....91 G2
BERM/RHTH SE16 ....123 H2
HOM E9 ....87 H6
NTHLT UB5 ....95 K2
SURB KT6 ....191 H5
Waterside Dr LEW SE13 ....65 J1
Waterside Dr WOT/HER KT12 .....188 A2
Waterside Rd NWDGN UB2 ....115 F3
Waterside Wy TOOT SW17 ....160 B6
Watersmeet Wy THMD SE28 ......109 K5
Waterson St BETH E2 * 7 H4
Watersplash Cl KUT/HW KT1 ....175 F6
Watersplash La HEST TW5 ....114 A5
Waters Rd CAT SE6 ....165 H5
KUT/HW KT1 ....175 J6
Waters Sq KUT/HW KT1 ....175 J6
Water St TPL/STR WC2R 11 J5
Water Tower Hl CROY/NA CRO 211 K2
Water Tower Pl IS N1 ....5 K1
Waterworks La CLPT E5 ....69 F6
Waterworks Rd
BRXS/STRHM SW2 ....161 K1
Watery La HYS/HAR UB3 ....113 G5
NTHLT UB5 ....95 G1
RYNPK SW20 ....177 J5
SCUP DA14 ....186 C2
Wates Wy MTCM CR4 ....194 E3
Wateville Rd TOTM N17 ....49 J4
Watford Cl BTSEA SW11 ....140 D2
Watford Heath OXHEY WD19 ....27 H2
Watford Heath Farm
OXHEY WD19 * 27 J1
Watford Rd BORE WD6 ....29 J1
CAN/RD E16 ....106 E4
HRW HA1 ....61 G6
NTHWD HA6 ....40 D3

Watford Wy HDN NW4 ....45 J5
Watford Wy (Barnet By-Pass)
MLHL NW7 ....31 C6
ERITH DA8 ....150 E1
Watkin Rd WBLY HA9 ....80 D1
Watkinson Rd HOLWY N7 ....85 F4
Watkins Wy BXLY DA5 ....170 A4
Watling Av EDGW HA8 ....44 E4
Watling Ct STP EC4M 12 D4
Watlings Cl CROY/NA CRO 198 B5
Watling St BXLYHS DA6 ....149 K6
PECK SE15 ....123 F6
STP EC4M 12 C4
Watlington Gv SYD SE26 ....182 B1
Watney Market WCHPL E1 * 104 D5
Watney Rd MORT/ESHN SW14 ...137 K4
Watneys Rd MTCM CR4 ....195 J2
Watney St WCHPL E1 ....104 D5
Watson Av CHEAM SM3 ....193 H6
EHAM E6 ....90 A5
Watson Cl STNW/STAM N16 ....85 K5
WIM/MER SW19 ....178 D2
Watson's Ms MBLAR W1H 8 D2
Watsons Rd WDGN N22 ....49 F4
Watson's St DEPT SE8 ....144 D1
Wattisfield Rd CLPT E5 ....86 E1
Watts Cl SEVS/STOTM N15 ....68 A2
Watts Gv BOW E3 ....105 J4
Watt's La CHST BR7 ....185 F1
TEDD TW11 ....174 B1
Watts Rd THDIT KT7 ....190 B4
Watts St WAP E1W 123 J1
Wat Tyler Rd BKHTH/KID SE3 .....145 F3
Wauthier Cl PLMGR N13 ....49 H1
Wavel Pl BFN/LL DA15 ....167 K1
Wavell Dr BFN/LL DA15 ....167 K1
Wavel Ms KIL/WHAMP NW6 ....83 F5
Wavel Pl SYD SE26 ....163 G6
Wavendon Av CHSWK W4 ....118 A5
Waveney Av PECK SE15 ....143 J5
Waveney Cl WAP E1W 123 H1
Waverley Av BRYLDS KT5 ....191 J5
CHING E4 ....37 G6
SUT SM1 ....194 A6
WALTH E17 ....52 B6
WBLY HA9 ....80 B3
WHTN TW2 ....154 E3
Waverley Cl E/WMO/HCT KT8 .....189 F2
HAYES BR2 ....200 C2
HYS/HAR UB3 ....113 G4
Waverley Crs
WOOL/PLUM SE18 ....127 J6
Waverley Gdns BARK IG11 ....108 E1
BARK/HLT IG6 ....54 C5
EHAM E6 ....107 J4
NTHWD HA6 ....40 E4
Waverley Gv HDN NW4 ....46 A6
Waverley Pl FSBYPK N4 * 67 H5
ST/JWD NW8 ....2 A3
Waverley Rd CEND/HSY/T N8 ....66 D3
ENC/FH EN2 ....23 K3
EW KT17 ....207 K5
RAIN RM13 ....111 K2
RYLN/HDSTN HA2 ....59 J4
SNWD SE25 ....197 J1
STHL UB1 ....96 A6
STHGT/OAK N14 ....34 D3
TOTM N17 ....50 D3
WALTH E17 ....52 A6
WAP E1W 127 H5
Waverley Wy CAR SM5 ....209 J4
Waverton Rd
WAND/EARL SW18 ....160 B2
Waverton St MYFR/PICC W1J 9 J7
Wavertree Rd
BRXS/STRHM SW2 ....162 A3
SWFD E18 ....52 E5
Waxlow Crs STHL UB1 ....96 A5
Waxlow Rd WLSDN NW10 ....98 E1
Waxwell La PIN HA5 ....41 H6
Wayborne Gv RSLP HA4 * 58 A3
Waye Av HEST TW5 ....133 K2
Wayfarer Rd NTHLT UB5 ....95 J2
Wayford St BTSEA SW11 ....140 D3
Wayland Av HACK E8 ....86 C3
Waylands HYS/HAR UB3 ....94 B4
Waylett Pl ALP/SUD HA0 ....79 K2
WNWD SE27 ....162 C5
Wayne Cl ORP BR6 ....217 F1
Wayneflete Tower Av
ESH/CLAY KT10 ....204 A1
Wayneflete Av CROY/NA CRO 211 H1
Waynflete Sq NKENS W10 ....100 B6
Waynflete St
WAND/EARL SW18 ....160 B4
Wayside CRICK NW2 ....64 C5
CROY/NA CRO 213 K4
MORT/ESHN SW14 ....137 K5
Wayside Av BUSH WD23 ....28 D1
Wayside Cl ROM RM1 ....57 H6
STHGT/OAK N14 ....34 C1
Wayside Ct TWK TW1 ....156 D1
Wayside Gdns DAGE RM10 ....92 C3
Wayside Gv CHST BR7 ....166 E6
Wayside Ms GNTH/NBYPK IG2 .....72 A3
Weald Cl BERM/RHTH SE16 ....123 J5
HAYES BR2 ....200 D6
Weald La KTN/HRWW/W HA3 ....42 D5
Weald Ri KTN/HRWW/W HA3 ....43 F3
Weald Sq CLPT E5 * 68 D6
Wealdstone Rd CHEAM SM3 ....193 H6
The Weald CHST BR7 ....184 E2
Weald Wy ROMW/RG RM7 ....74 D3
YEAD UB4 ....94 C2
Wealdwood Gdns PIN HA5 * 42 B2
Weale Rd CHING E4 ....38 B5
Weardale Gdns ENC/FH EN2 ....23 K2
Weardale Rd LEW SE13 ....145 G5
Wear Pl BETH E2 ....104 D2
Wearside Rd LEW SE13 ....144 E5
Weaver Cl EHAM E6 ....108 B6
Weavers Cl ISLW TW7 ....135 K5
Weavers La STHWK SE1 ....19 H1
Weavers Ter FUL/PGN SW6 * 119 K6
Weaver St WCHPL E1 ....104 C3
Weaver Wk WNWD SE27 ....162 C6

Webb Cl NKENS W10 ....100 A3
ERITH DA8 ....150 E1
Webber Cl BORE WD6 ....29 K1
Webber Rw STHWK SE1 ....17 K2
Webber St STHWK SE1 ....17 K2
Webb Est CLPT E5 * 68 C4
Webb Pl WLSDN NW10 ....99 H2
Webb Rd BKHTH/KID SE3 ....125 J6
Webbs Rd BTSEA SW11 ....140 E6
Webbscroft Rd DAGE RM10 ....92 D2
YEAD UB4 ....94 E2
Webb St STHWK SE1 ....19 G5
Webster Gdns EA W5 ....116 E1
Webster Rd BERM/RHTH SE16 ....123 H5
WAN E11 ....88 A1
Wedderburn Rd BARK IG11 ....90 D6
HAMP NW3 ....83 H3
Wedgewood Cl NTHWD HA6 * 40 A3
Wedgwood Wk
KIL/WHAMP NW6 * 83 F5
Wedgwood Wy NRWD SE19 ....180 D3
Wedlake St NKENS W10 ....100 C3
Wedmore Av CLAY IG5 ....54 A4
Wedmore Gdns ARCH N19 ....66 E6
Wedmore Ms ARCH N19 ....84 D1
Wedmore St ARCH N19 ....84 D1
Weech Rd KIL/WHAMP NW6 ....82 E2
Weedington Rd KTTN NW5 ....84 A3
Weekley Sq BTSEA SW11 * 140 C4
Weigall Rd LEE/GVPK SE12 ....145 K5
Weighhouse St MYFR/PKLN W1K ...9 H5
Weighton Rd
KTN/HRWW/W HA3 ....42 D4
PGE/AN SE20 ....181 J5
Weihurst Gdns SUT SM1 ....209 H5
Weimar St PUT/ROE SW15 ....139 H4
Weirdale Av TRDG/WHET N20 ......33 K4
Weir Hall Av UED N18 ....49 K2
Weir Hall Gdns UED N18 ....49 K1
Weir Hall Rd UED N18 ....49 K2
Weir Rd BAL SW12 ....161 H5
BXLY DA5 ....169 J2
WIM/MER SW19 ....160 A5
Weirside Gdns WDR/YW UB7 ......112 A1
Weirs Pas CAMTN NW1 ....4 D4
Weiss Rd PUT/ROE SW15 ....139 G5
Welbeck Av BFN/LL DA15 ....168 B3
WAN E11 ....71 F2
Welbeck Cl BFN/LL DA15 * 165 K6
BMLY BR1 ....184 A4
YEAD UB4 ....95 F3
Welbeck Cl EW KT17 ....207 J5
NWMAL KT3 ....192 C2
Welbeck Rd EBAR EN4 ....21 J2
EHAM E6 ....107 H2
RYLN/HDSTN HA2 ....60 B5
SUT SM1 ....194 D6
Welbeck St MHST W1U 9 J3
Welbeck Vls WCHMH N21 * 35 J3
Welbeck Wy MHST W1U 9 J3
Welby St CMBW SE5 ....142 C2
Welch Pl PIN HA5 * 41 G4
Weldon Cl RSLP HA4 ....77 F4
Weldon Dr E/WMO/HCT KT8 ....188 E1
Weld Pl FBAR/BDGN N11 ....48 B1
Welfare Rd SRTFD E15 ....88 C5
Welford Cl CLPT E5 * 87 F1
Welford Pl WIM/MER SW19 ....159 H6
Welham Rd TOOT SW17 ....179 F1
Welhouse Rd CAR SM5 ....194 D5
Wellacre Rd
KTN/HRWW/W HA3 ....61 H5
Welland Cl BFN/LL DA15 * 54 C6
Welland Gdns GFD/PVL UB6 ....97 F1
Welland Ms WAP E1W 123 H1
Wellands Cl BMLY BR1 ....184 E5
Welland St GNWCH SE10 ....125 F6
Well Ap BAR EN5 ....20 A6
Wellbrook Rd ORP BR6 ....216 A2
Wellby Cl ED N9 ....36 C3
Well Cl RSLP HA4 ....77 J1
STRHM/NOR SW16 ....162 A6
Wellclose Sq WAP E1W 104 C6
Wellclose St WAP E1W 104 C6
Wellcome Av DART DA1 ....151 H5
Well Cottage Cl WAN E11 ....71 G4
Well Ct MANHO EC4N 12 D4
Welldon Crs HRW HA1 ....60 E3
Weller Ct STHWK SE1 ....18 C2
Wellesley Av HMSMTH W6 ....118 E3
NTHWD HA6 ....40 D1
Wellesley Cl CHARL SE7 * 126 B5
CEND/HSY/T N8 * 66 D1
Wellesley Court Rd
CROY/NA CRO * 196 E6
Wellesley Crs WHTN TW2 ....155 K4
Wellesley Gv CROY/NA CRO 196 E5
Wellesley Park Ms ENC/FH EN2 ...23 H5
Wellesley Pl CAMTN NW1 * 4 C5
KTTN NW5 ....84 A3
Wellesley Rd BELMT SM2 ....209 G4
CHSWK W4 ....117 H5
CROY/NA CRO 196 D5
HRW HA1 ....60 E2
IL IG1 ....72 B6
KTTN NW5 ....83 K3
WALTH E17 ....69 J3
WAN E11 ....71 F1
WHTN TW2 ....155 J5
Wellesley St WCHPL E1 ....105 F4
Wellesley Ter IS N1 ....6 E4
Wellfield Av MUSWH N10 ....48 B6
Wellfield Gdns CAR SM5 ....209 J6
Wellfield Rd
STRHM/NOR SW16 ....161 K6
Wellfit St HNHL SE24 ....142 C4
Wellgarth GFD/PVL UB6 ....79 H4
Wellgarth Rd GLDGN NW11 ....65 F5
Well Gv TRDG/WHET N20 ....33 G3
Well Hall Pde ELTH/MOT SE9 ......146 E5
Well Hall Rd ELTH/MOT SE9 ....146 E5
Wellhouse La BAR EN5 ....20 A5
Wellhouse Rd BECK BR3 ....198 C1
Wellhurst Cl ORP BR6 ....217 F5
Welling High St WELL DA16 ....148 C4

Wellington Av BFN/LL DA15 ....168 B1
CHING E4 ....37 J4
ED N9 ....36 D5
HSLW TW3 ....135 F6
PIN HA5 ....41 J3
SEVS/STOTM N15 ....68 A1
WPK KT4 ....208 A1
Wellington Cl DAGE RM10 ....100 E5
NTCHL W11 ....100 E5
NWCR SE14 ....144 A2
OXHEY WD19 ....27 H1
Wellington Crs NWMAL KT3 ....175 K6
Wellington Dr DAGE RM10 ....100 E5
Wellington Gdns CHARL SE7 ......126 B5
HPTN TW12 ....155 J6
Wellington Ms HOLWY N7 * 85 F4
Wellington Pde BFN/LL DA15 * ...148 B6
Wellington Park Est
CRICK NW2 ....62 J3
Wellington Pl EFNCH N2 * 65 J2
ST/JWD NW8 ....2 B3
Wellington Rd BELV DA17 ....129 G5
BXLY DA5 ....168 E1
CROY/NA CRO 196 C5
DART DA1 ....171 F1
EA W5 ....116 E4
EBED/NFELT TW14 ....133 H6
EHAM E6 ....89 J6
EN EN1 ....24 A6
FSTGT E7 ....88 D2
HAYES BR2 ....200 B1
HPTN TW12 ....155 J6
KTN/HRWW/W HA3 ....42 D4
LEY E10 ....69 G5
PIN HA5 ....41 K4
ST/JWD NW8 ....2 B3
STMC/STPC BR5 ....202 C3
WALTH E17 ....51 F2
WAN E11 ....70 E2
WIM/MER SW19 ....159 K4
WLSDN NW10 * 100 B3
Wellington Rd North
HSLWW TW4 ....134 E4
Wellington Rd South
HSLWW TW4 ....134 E5
Wellington Rw BETH E2 ....7 K4
Wellington St CHCR WC2R 11 F5
Wellington Ter BFN/LL DA15 * 11 F5
WOOL/PLUM SE18 ....127 F4
Wellington Ter
CEND/HSY/T N8 * 49 G6
HRW HA1 ....60 D6
NTCHL W11 * 100 D6
WAP E1W * 123 J1
Wellington Wy BOW E3 ....105 J2
Welling Wy ELTH/MOT SE9 ....147 K4
Well La MORT/ESHN SW14 ....137 K6
Wellmeadow Rd HNWL W7 ....116 B4
LEW SE13 ....165 H1
Well Rd BAR EN5 ....20 A6
HAMP NW3 ....83 H1
Wells Cl NTHLT UB5 * 95 G2
SAND/SEL CR2 ....212 A3
Wells Dr CDALE/KGS NW9 ....63 F5
RAIN RM13 ....93 J4
Wells House Rd WLSDN NW10 .....99 G4
Wellside Cl BAR EN5 ....20 A5
Wellside Gdns
MORT/ESHN SW14 ....137 K5
Wells Ms FITZ W1T * 10 B2
Wellsmoor Gdns BMLY BR1 ....185 F6
Wells Park Rd SYD SE26 ....163 H6
Wells Pl CMBW SE5 ....143 F1
WAND/EARL SW18 ....160 B2
Wells Ri ST/JWD NW8 ....2 C1
Wells Rd BMLY BR1 ....184 E5
SHB W12 ....119 F2
Wells Sq FSBYW WC1X * 5 G4
Wellstead Av ED N9 ....37 F1
Wellstead Rd EHAM E6 ....108 A1
Wells Ter FSBYPK N4 ....67 G6
The Wells STHGT/OAK N14 ....34 D3
Wells Wy CMBW SE5 ....122 E6
SKENS SW7 ....14 A5
Well Wk HAMP NW3 ....83 H1
Wellwood Rd GDMY/SEVK IG3 ......73 G5
Welsford St STHWK SE1 ....123 H5
Welsh Cl PLSTW E13 ....106 E2
Welshpool St HACK E8 *.................86 D6
Welshside Wk CDALE/KGS NW9 * ...63 G3
Welstead Wy CHSWK W4 ....118 C3
Weltje Rd HMSMTH W6 ....118 D5
Welton Rd WOOL/PLUM SE18 .....148 A1
Welwyn Av EBED/NFELT TW14 ....133 J1
Welwyn St BETH E2 ....104 E2
Welwyn Wy YEAD UB4 ....94 C3
Wembley Hill Rd WBLY HA9 ....80 B3
Wembley Park Dr WBLY HA9 ....80 A2
Wembley Rd HPTN TW12 ....173 F4
Wembley Wy WBLY HA9 ....80 D4
Wemborough Rd STAN HA7 ....43 J3
Wembury Rd HGT N6 ....66 B4
Wemyss Rd BKHTH/KID SE3 ....145 J3
Wendela Ct HRW HA1 ....78 E1
Wendell Rd SHB W12 ....118 C2
Wendling Rd CAR SM5 ....194 C5
Wendon St BOW E3 ....87 H6
Wendover Cl YEAD UB4 * 95 H3
Wendover Dr NWMAL KT3 ....192 C3
Wendover Rd ELTH/MOT SE9 ......146 C4
HAYES BR2 ....200 A1
WLSDN NW10 ....99 H1
Wendover Wy BUSH WD23 ....28 C1
ORP BR6 ....202 B3
WELL DA16 ....148 B6
Wendy Cl EN EN1 ....36 B1
Wendy Wy ALP/SUD HA0 ....80 A6
Wenlock Gdns HDN NW4 * 63 J1
Wenlock Rd EDGW HA8 ....44 D4
IS N1 ....6 C3

Wenlock St IS N1 ...6 D3
Wennington Rd BOW E3 ...105 H1
RAIN RM13 ...111 K1
Wensley Av WFD IG8 ...52 E3
Wensley Cl CRW RM5 ...56 C1
ELTH/MOT SE9 ...166 E1
FBAR/BDGN N11 ...48 A2
Wensleydale Av CLAY IG5 ...53 J5
Wensleydale Gdns
HPTN TW12 ...173 G3
Wensleydale Rd HPTN TW12 ...173 H4
Wensley Rd UED N18 ...50 D2
Wentland Cl CAT SE6 ...165 G4
Wentland Rd CAT SE6 ...165 G4
Wentworth Av FNCH N3 ...46 E1
Wentworth Cl ASHF TW15 ...152 E6
FNCH N3 ...47 F3
HAYES BR2 * ...199 K6
MRDN SM4 ...193 K4
ORP BR6 ...216 E3
SURB KT6 ...190 E6
THMD SE28 ...109 K5
Wentworth Crs HYS/HAR UB3 ...113 G3
PECK SE15 ...143 H1
Wentworth Dr DART DA1 ...170 D2
PIN HA5 ...58 E2
Wentworth Gdns
PLMGR N13 ...35 H5
Wentworth HI WBLY HA9 ...62 B5
Wentworth Pk FNCH N3 ...47 F3
Wentworth Pl STAN HA7 * ...43 H1
Wentworth Rd BAR EN5 ...20 B5
CROY/NA CR0 ...196 B4
GLDGN NW11 ...64 D3
MNPK E12 ...89 H2
NWDGN UB2 ...114 B4
Wentworth St WCHPL E1 ...13 K2
Wentworth Wy PIN HA5 ...59 H1
RAIN RM13 ...111 H3
Wenvoe Av BXLYHN DA7 ...149 J3
Wepham Cl YEAD UB4 ...95 H4
Wernbrook St
WOOL/PLUM SE18 ...127 H6
Werndee Rd SNWD SE25 ...197 H1
Werneth Hall Rd CLAY IG5 ...53 K6
Werrington St CAMTN NW1 ...4 C3
Werter Rd PUT/ROE SW15 ...139 H5
Wesleyan Pl KTTN NW5 ...84 B2
Wesley Av CAN/RD E16 ...125 K1
HSLW TW3 ...134 D3
WLSDN NW10 ...98 E2
Wesley Cl HOLWY N7 ...67 F6
RYLN/HDSTN HA2 ...60 C5
STMC/STPC BR5 ...186 D6
WALW SE17 ...18 B7
Wesley Rd EFNCH N2 ...47 J5
HYS/HAR UB3 ...94 E6
LEY E10 ...70 A4
WLSDN NW10 ...80 E6
Wesley Sq NTGHL W11 ...100 B5
Wesley St CAVSQ/HST W1G ...9 H2
Wessex Av WIM/MER SW19 ...177 K5
Wessex Cl ESH/CLAY KT10 ...190 A6
CDMY/SEVK IG3 ...73 H2
KUTN/CMB KT2 ...175 J4
Wessex Ct BECK BR3 * ...182 B4
Wessex Dr ERITH DA8 ...150 B3
PIN HA5 ...41 J3
Wessex Gdns CRICK NW2 ...64 C5
Wessex La GFD/PVL UB6 ...96 D1
Wessex St BETH E2 ...104 E2
Wessex Ter MTCM CR4 * ...194 D2
Wessex Wy BXLY DA5 ...170 A4
Wesson Md CMBW SE5 * ...142 D1
Westacott YEAD UB4 ...94 C4
Westacott Cl ARCH N19 ...66 D5
West Ap STMC/STPC BR5 ...201 H2
West Arbour St WCHPL E1 ...105 F5
West Av FNCH N3 ...46 E2
HDN NW4 ...64 B2
HYS/HAR UB3 ...94 D6
PIN HA5 ...59 K4
STHL UB1 ...95 K6
WALTH E17 ...69 K2
WLGTN SM6 ...210 E3
West Avenue Rd WALTH E17 ...69 J1
West Bank BARK IG11 ...90 B6
ENC/FH EN2 ...23 J4
STNW/STAM N16 ...68 A3
Westbank Rd HPTN TW12 ...173 H2
West Barnes La NWMAL KT3 ...192 E2
RYNPK SW20 ...176 E6
Westbeech Rd WDGN N22 ...49 G6
Westbere Dr STAN HA7 ...43 K1
Westbere Rd CRICK NW2 ...82 C2
Westbourne Av ACT W3 ...99 F5
CHEAM SM3 ...193 H6
Westbourne Cl YEAD UB4 ...95 G3
Westbourne Crs BAY/PAD W2 ...8 A5
Westbourne Crescent Ms
BAY/PAD W2 ...8 A5
Westbourne Dr FSTH SE23 ...164 A4
Westbourne Gdns
BAY/PAD W2 ...101 F5
Westbourne Ga BAY/PAD W2 ...8 B4
Westbourne Grove Ms
NTGHL W11 * ...100 E5
Westbourne Grove Ter
BAY/PAD W2 ...101 F5
Westbourne Park Rd
BAY/PAD W2 ...100 E5
BAY/PAD W2 ...101 F4
Westbourne Pl ED N9 ...36 D5
Westbourne Rd BXLYHN DA7 ...148 E1
CROY/NA CR0 ...197 G3
FELT TW13 ...153 J5
HOLWY N7 ...85 G4
SYD SE26 ...182 A2
Westbourne St
BAY/PAD W2 ...8 A5
Westbourne Ter
BAY/PAD W2 ...101 G5
Westbourne Terrace Ms
BAY/PAD W2 ...101 G5

Westbourne Terrace Rd
BAY/PAD W2 ...101 G4
Westbridge Cl SHB W12 ...118 D1
Westbridge Rd BTSEA SW11 ...140 C2
Westbrook Av HPTN TW12 ...172 E5
Westbrook Cl EBAR EN4 ...21 H4
Westbrook Crs EBAR EN4 ...21 H4
Westbrook Dr
STMC/STPC BR5 ...202 E5
Westbrooke Crs WELL DA16 ...148 D4
Westbrooke Rd BFN/LL DA15 ...167 J4
WELL DA16 ...148 C3
Westbrook Rd BKHTH/KID SE3 ...145 K2
HEST TW5 ...134 E1
THHTH CR7 ...180 E4
Westbury Ar WDGN N22 * ...49 H6
Westbury Av ALP/SUD HA0 ...80 A5
ESH/CLAY KT10 ...205 F4
STHL UB1 ...95 K4
WDGN N22 ...49 H6
Westbury Cl RSLP HA4 ...58 E4
Westbury Gv FNCH N3 ...46 E2
Westbury La BKHH IG9 ...39 G4
Westbury Lodge Cl PIN HA5 ...41 H6
Westbury Pl BTFD TW8 ...116 E6
Westbury Rd ALP/SUD HA0 ...80 A5
BARK IG11 ...90 D6
BKHH IG9 ...39 G3
BMLY BR1 ...184 C4
CROY/NA CR0 ...196 E5
EA W5 ...98 A5
FBAR/BDGN N11 ...48 E2
FELT TW13 ...154 C3
FSTGT E7 ...89 F5
IL IG1 ...72 A6
NFNCH/WDSPK N12 ...46 E2
NTHWD HA6 ...26 C6
NWMAL KT3 ...192 A1
PGE/AN SE20 ...182 A4
WALTH E17 ...69 J1
Westbury Ter FSTGT E7 ...89 F4
West Carriage Dr BAY/PAD W2 ...8 B6
West Central St
NOXST/BSQ WC1A ...10 E3
West Chantry
RYLN/HDSTN HA2 ...42 B4
Westchester Dr HDN NW4 ...46 B6
Westcliffe Vls KUT/HW KT1 * ...175 G5
West Cl ASHF TW15 ...152 B6
EBAR EN4 ...34 A1
ED N9 ...36 B5
GFD/PVL UB6 ...96 C2
RAIN RM13 ...111 K3
WBLY HA9 ...62 B5
Westcombe Av CROY/NA CR0 ...195 K3
Westcombe Dr BAR EN5 ...20 E6
Westcombe HI BKHTH/KID SE3 ...125 K6
Westcombe Park Rd
BKHTH/KID SE3 ...125 H6
West Common Rd HAYES BR2 ...199 K6
Westcoombe Av RYNPK SW20 ...176 C4
Westcote Ri STRHM/NOR SW16 ...179 H1
Westcott Cl BMLY BR1 ...200 D2
CROY/NA CR0 ...213 K6
SEVS/STOTM N15 ...68 B3
Westcott Crs HNWL W7 ...96 E4
Westcott House
POP/IOD E14 * ...105 J6
Westcott Rd WALW SE17 ...122 C6
West Ct ALP/SUD HA0 ...61 J6
Westcroft Cl CRICK NW2 ...82 C2
PEND EN3 ...24 E1
Westcroft Gdns MRDN SM4 ...177 J6
Westcroft Ms HMSMTH W6 * ...118 D4
Westcroft Rd CAR SM5 ...210 A2
Westcroft Sq HMSMTH W6 ...118 D4
Westcroft Wy CRICK NW2 ...82 C2
West Cromwell Rd ECT SW5 ...119 K4
West Cross Route NTGHL W11 ...100 B6
West Cross Wy BTFD TW8 ...116 C6
Westdale Rd
WOOL/PLUM SE18 ...127 G6
Westdean Av LEE/GVPK SE12 ...166 A3
Westdean Cl
WAND/EARL SW18 ...160 A1
Westdown Rd CAT SE6 ...164 D6
SRTFD E15 ...88 B3
West Drayton Park Av
WDR/YW UB7 ...112 B3
West Dr BELMT SM2 ...208 B6
KTN/HRWW/W HA3 ...42 D2
TOOT SW17 ...161 G2
West Drive Gdns
KTN/HRWW/W HA3 ...42 D2
West Eaton Pl KTBR SW1X ...15 G5
West Eaton Place Ms
KTBR SW1X ...15 G6
West Ella Rd WLSDN NW10 ...81 G5
West End Av PIN HA5 ...59 H1
WALTH E17 ...52 A4
West End Cl WLSDN NW10 ...80 E5
West End Ct PIN HA5 ...59 H1
West End Gdns NTHLT UB5 ...95 G1
West End La BAR EN5 ...20 B5
HYS/HAR UB3 ...133 F1
KIL/WHAMP NW6 ...82 E4
PIN HA5 ...41 H6
West End Rd RSLP HA4 ...76 E2
RSLP HA4 ...77 F3
STHL UB1 ...114 D1
Westerdale Rd GNWCH SE10 ...125 K5
Westerfield Rd
SEVS/STOTM N15 ...68 B2
Westergate Rd ABYW SE2 ...129 F6
Westerham Av UED N18 ...35 K5
Westerham Dr BFN/LL DA15 ...168 D1
Westerham Rd HAYES BR2 ...215 H4
LEY E10 ...69 K5
Westerley Crs SYD SE26 * ...182 C1
Western Av DAGE RM10 ...92 E4
EA W5 ...98 B3
GFD/PVL UB6 ...97 F2
GLDGN NW11 ...64 B3

NTHLT UB5 ...77 F5
Western Ct FNCH N3 * ...46 E2
Western Gdns EA W5 ...98 D6
Western Gtwy CAN/RD E16 ...106 E6
Western La BAL SW12 ...161 F2
Western Man BAR EN5 * ...21 F6
Western Ms MV/WKIL W9 ...100 D3
Western Pde BAR EN5 ...20 D6
Western Rd BRXN/ST SW9 ...142 04
EA W5 ...97 K6
EFNCH N2 ...47 K6
MTCM CR4 ...178 D4
NWDGN UB2 ...114 B4
PLSTW E13 ...89 F6
ROM RM1 ...75 H2
SUT SM1 ...208 E3
WALTH E17 ...70 A2
WDGN N22 ...49 F5
WLSDN NW10 ...98 E5
Western Ter HMSMTH W6 * ...118 D5
Western Vw HYS/HAR UB3 ...113 J2
Westerville Gdns
GNTH/NBYPK IG2 ...72 C4
Western Wy BAR EN5 ...32 E1
THMD SE28 ...127 K2
Westferry Circ POP/IOD E14 ...124 C1
Westferry Rd POP/IOD E14 ...105 J6
Westfield Cl CDALE/KGS NW9 ...44 E6
FUL/PGN SW6 * ...140 B1
PEND EN3 ...25 G4
SUT SM1 ...208 D2
Westfield Dr
KTN/HRWW/W HA3 ...61 K2
Westfield Gdns CHDH RM6 ...73 J5
KTN/HRWW/W HA3 ...61 K1
Westfield La
KTN/HRWW/W HA3 ...61 K1
Westfield Pk PIN HA5 ...41 K3
Westfield Park Dr WFD IG8 ...53 J2
Westfield Rd BECK BR3 ...182 C5
BXLYHN DA7 ...150 A4
CROY/NA CR0 ...196 C5
DAGW RM9 ...92 A2
MLHL NW7 ...31 F5
MTCM CR4 ...178 D5
SURB KT6 ...190 E4
SUT SM1 ...208 C3
WEA W13 ...116 B1
WOT/HER KT12 ...188 D4
Westfields Av BARN SW13 ...138 C4
Westfields Rd ACT W3 ...98 D4
Westfield St
WOOL/PLUM SE18 ...126 C3
Westfield Wy RSLP HA4 ...76 C1
PIM SW1V ...121 G5
West Gdns WAP E1W ...104 D6
WIM/MER SW19 ...178 D2
West Ga EA W5 ...98 A2
Westgate Est
EBED/NFELT TW14 * ...152 E3
Westgate Rd BECK BR3 ...183 F4
DART DA1 ...171 G1
SNWD SE25 ...197 J1
Westgate St HACK E8 ...86 D6
Westgate Ter WBPTN SW10 ...120 B5
Westglade Ct
KTN/HRWW/W HA3 ...61 K2
West Green Pl GFD/PVL UB6 ...78 D6
West Green Rd S
EVS/STOTM N15 ...67 K1
West Gv GNWCH SE10 ...145 F2
WFD IG8 ...53 G2
Westgrove La GNWCH SE10 ...145 F2
West Halkin St KTBR SW1X ...15 G4
West Hallowes ELTH/MOT SE9 ...166 C2
West Hall Rd RCH/KEW TW9 ...137 J2
West Ham La SRTFD E15 ...88 C5
West Hampstead Ms
KIL/WHAMP NW6 ...83 F4
West Harding St
FLST/FETLN EC4A * ...11 K3
West Hatch Mnr RSLP HA4 ...58 D5
Westhay Gdns
MORT/ESHN SW14 ...137 J6
West Heath Av GLDGN NW11 ...64 E5
West Heath Cl DART DA1 ...170 C1
HAMP NW3 ...82 E1
West Heath Dr GLDGN NW11 ...64 E5
West Heath Gdns HAMP NW3 ...64 E5
West Heath Rd BXLYHN DA7 ...128 C3
DART DA1 ...170 C1
HAMP NW3 ...64 E6
West HI DART DA1 ...171 F1
HGT N6 ...66 A5
WAND/EARL SW18 ...159 G2
WIM/MER SW19 ...159 G2
Westholm GLDGN NW11 ...65 F1
Westholme ORP BR6 ...201 K4
Westholme Gdns RSLP HA4 ...58 E5
Westhorne Av ELTH/MOT SE9 ...146 A6
Westhorpe Gdns HDN NW4 ...46 A6
Westhorpe Rd PUT/ROE SW15 ...139 F4
West House Cl
WIM/MER SW19 ...159 H3
Westhurst Dr CHST BR7 ...185 G1
West India Av POP/IOD E14 ...124 D1
West India Dock Rd
POP/IOD E14 ...105 H5
Westlake Cl PLMGR N13 ...35 G5
YEAD UB4 ...95 J3
Westland Cl
STWL/WRAY TW19 * ...152 B1
Westland Dr HAYES BR2 ...199 J4
Westland Pl FSBYE EC1V ...6 E4
Westlands Cl HYS/HAR UB3 ...113 K4

Westlands Ter BAL SW12 ...161 H1
West La BERM/RHTH SE16 ...123 J2
West Lea HNWL W7 ...116 B3
Westleigh Av PUT/ROE SW15 ...139 F6
Westleigh Dr BMLY BR1 ...184 D5
West Links ALP/SUD HA0 ...97 K2
Westlinton Cl MLHL NW7 ...46 C2
West Lodge Av ACT W3 ...117 H1
West Lodge Ct ACT W3 * ...117 H1
Westmacott Dr
EBED/NFELT TW14 ...153 K3
West Ml KENS W8 * ...119 K1
West Malling Wy HCH RM12 ...93 K3
West Md HOR/WEW KT19 ...207 G4
RSLP HA4 ...77 G2
Westmead PUT/ROE SW15 ...158 E2
Westmead Rd SUT SM1 ...209 H2
Westmede BARK/HLT IG6 ...54 C2
Westmere Dr MLHL NW7 ...31 F5
Westminster Av THHTH CR7 ...180 C5
Westminster Br HWST SW1P ...17 F3
Westminster Bridge Rd
STHWK SE1 ...17 G3
Westminster Cl
EBED/NFELT TW14 ...153 K3
TEDD TW11 ...174 B1
Westminster Dr PLMGR N13 ...48 E1
Westminster Gdns BARK IG11 ...108 E1
BARK/HLT IG6 ...54 D5
CHING E4 ...38 C3
Westminster Rd ED N9 ...36 D3
HNWL W7 ...115 K1
SUT SM1 ...194 C6
Westmoat Cl BECK BR3 ...183 F3
Westmont Rd ESH/CLAY KT10 ...189 K6
Westmoor Gdns PEND EN3 ...25 F3
Westmoor Rd PEND EN3 ...25 F3
Westmoor St CHARL SE7 ...126 C3
Westmoreland Av WELL DA16 ...147 K4
Westmoreland Dr BELMT SM2 ...209 F6
Westmoreland Pl EA W5 ...97 K4
HAYES BR2 ...183 K6
PIM SW1V ...121 G6
Westmoreland Rd BARN SW13 ...138 C2
CDALE/KGS NW9 ...62 B1
HAYES BR2 ...199 H2
WALW SE17 ...122 C6
Westmoreland St
CAVSQ/HST W1G ...9 H2
Westmoreland Ter
PGE/AN SE20 ...181 J3
PIM SW1V ...121 G5
Westmorland Cl MNPK E12 ...71 H3
TWK TW1 ...156 C1
Westmorland Rd HRW HA1 ...60 B2
WALTH E17 ...69 J3
Westmorland Wy MTCM CR4 ...195 J1
WELL DA16 * ...148 C3
Westmount Ct EA W5 * ...98 B4
Westmount Rd ELTH/MOT SE9 ...146 E3
West Oak BECK BR3 ...183 G4
Weston Av E/WMO/HCT KT8 ...188 D1
ESH/CLAY KT10 ...189 K4
Weston Dr KTN/HRWW/W HA3 ...43 J5
STAN HA7 ...43 H4
Weston Gdns ISLW TW7 ...135 J2
Weston Gn DAGW RM9 ...92 A2
THDIT KT7 ...189 K6
Weston Green Rd
ESH/CLAY KT10 ...189 J5
Weston Gv BMLY BR1 ...183 J3
Weston Pk CEND/HSY/T N8 ...66 E3
KUT/HW KT1 ...175 F5
THDIT KT7 ...189 K6
Weston Park Cl THDIT KT7 * ...189 K5
Weston Ri FSBYW WC1X ...5 H3
Weston Rd BMLY BR1 ...183 J4
CHSWK W4 ...117 K3
DAGW RM9 ...92 A2
EN EN1 ...23 K3
ESH/CLAY KT10 ...189 K5
Weston St STHWK SE1 ...19 G3
Weston Wk HACK E8 * ...86 D6
Westover HI HAMP NW3 ...64 E6
Westover Rd
WAND/EARL SW18 ...160 B1
Westow HI NRWD SE19 ...181 F2
Westow St NRWD SE19 ...181 F2
West Pk ELTH/MOT SE9 ...166 D4
West Park Av RCH/KEW TW9 ...137 J2
West Park Cl CHDH RM6 ...73 K2
HEST TW5 ...114 E6
West Park Rd NWDGN UB2 ...115 J1
RCH/KEW TW9 ...137 H2
West Parkside GNWCH SE10 ...125 J2
West Pl NWDGN UB2 * ...115 G4
WIM/MER SW19 ...177 F1
Westpole Av EBAR EN4 ...22 B5
Westport Rd PLSTW E13 ...107 F4
Westport St WCHPL E1 ...105 F5
West Poultry Av FARR EC1M ...12 A2
West Quarters SHB W12 ...99 J5
West Quay Dr YEAD UB4 ...95 J4
West Ridge Gdns GFD/PVL UB6 ...96 C2

West Side Common
WIM/MER SW19 ...177 F2
West Smithfield STBT EC1A ...12 B2
West Sq LBTH SE11 ...18 A5
West St BETH E2 ...104 D1
BMLY BR1 ...183 K4
BXLYHN DA7 ...149 G5
CAR SM5 ...209 K2
CROY/NA CR0 ...211 J3
ERITH DA8 ...130 A4
HRW HA1 ...60 D5
LSQ/SEVD WC2H ...10 D4
SUT SM1 ...209 F3
WALTH E17 ...69 J1
West Street La CAR SM5 ...209 K2
West Street Pl CROY/NA CR0 * ...211 J3
West Temple Sheen
MORT/ESHN SW14 ...137 J6
West Tenter St WCHPL E1 ...13 K4
West Twrs PIN HA5 ...59 H5
West Vw EBED/NFELT TW14 ...153 F3
Westview HNWL W7 ...96 E5
Westview Cl NKENS W10 ...100 A5
WLSDN NW10 ...81 H5
Westview Crs ED N9 ...36 A2
Westview Dr WFD IG8 ...53 H5
West View Gdns BORE WD6 ...29 K1
West View Rd DART DA1 ...171 J1
Westville Rd SHB W12 ...118 D3
West Wk EBAR EN4 ...34 A3
HYS/HAR UB3 ...113 K1
Westward Rd CHING E4 ...51 H1
Westward Wy
KTN/HRWW/W HA3 ...62 A3
West Warwick Pl PIM SW1V * ...16 E7
West Wy CROY/NA CR0 ...198 B6
EDGW HA8 ...44 D1
HEST TW5 ...134 E2
PIN HA5 ...59 H1
RSLP HA4 ...58 D5
STMC/STPC BR5 ...201 J2
WLSDN NW10 ...81 F2
WWKM BR4 ...199 J6
Westway NTGHL W11 ...100 D4
RYNPK SW20 ...192 E4
SHB W12 ...99 J6
West Wy GI RYNPK SW20 ...176 E6
West Way Gdns CROY/NA CR0 ...198 A6
Westways HOR/WEW KT19 ...207 H2
Westwell Cl STMC/STPC BR5 ...202 E5
Westwell Rd
STRHM/NOR SW16 ...179 K2
Westwell Road Ap
STRHM/NOR SW16 ...179 K2
Westwick Gdns HEST TW5 ...134 A3
WKENS W14 ...119 G2
Westwood Av NRWD SE19 ...180 D4
RYLN/HDSTN HA2 ...78 B2
Westwood Cl BMLY BR1 ...184 C6
ESH/CLAY KT10 ...204 C1
Westwood Gdns BARN SW13 ...138 C6
Westwood HI SYD SE26 ...181 H1
Westwood La WELL DA16 ...148 B5
Westwood Pk FSTH SE23 ...163 H2
Westwood Pl SYD SE26 ...181 H1
Westwood Rd BARN SW13 ...138 C4
CAN/RD E16 ...126 A1
GDMY/SEVK IG3 ...73 F5
West Woodside BXLY DA5 ...169 F3
Wetheral Dr STAN HA7 ...43 H4
Wetherby Cl NTHLT UB5 ...78 B4
Wetherby Gdns ECT SW5 ...120 B4
Wetherby Ms ECT SW5 ...120 A5
Wetherby Pl ECT SW5 ...120 B4
Wetherby Rd ENC/FH EN2 ...23 J2
Wetherden St WALTH E17 ...69 H4
Wetherell Rd HOM E9 ...87 F6
Wetherill Rd MUSWH N10 ...47 K6
Wexford Rd BAL SW12 ...160 E2
Weybourne St
WAND/EARL SW18 ...160 B4
Weybridge Ct STHWK SE1 * ...123 J5
Weybridge Rd THHTH CR7 ...196 B1
Wey Ct HOR/WEW KT19 ...206 E4
Weydown Cl WIM/MER SW19 ...159 H3
Weyhill Rd WCHPL E1 * ...104 C5
Weylond Rd BCTR RM8 ...92 B2
Weyman Rd BKHTH/KID SE3 ...146 B2
Weymouth Av EA W5 ...116 D3
MLHL NW7 ...45 G1
Weymouth Ct EHAM E6 ...108 B5
Weymouth Ct BELMT SM2 * ...209 F5
Weymouth Rd YEAD UB4 ...94 C2
Weymouth St CAVSQ/HST W1G ...9 J1
Weymouth Ter BETH E2 ...7 K2
Weymouth Vls FSBYPK N4 * ...67 F6
Weymouth Wk STAN HA7 ...43 G2
Whadcoat St FSBYPK N4 ...67 G6
Whalebone Av CHDH RM6 ...74 B3
Whalebone Gv CHDH RM6 ...74 B3
Whalebone La North
CHDH RM6 ...56 A3

Whalebone La South
BCTR RM8 ...74 B5
Whales Yd SRTFD E15 * ...88 C5
Wharf Bridge Rd ISLW TW7 ...136 C4
Wharfdale Cl
FBAR/BDGN N11 ...48 A2
Wharfdale Rd IS N1 ...5 F2
Wharfedale Gdns
STRHM/NOR SW16 ...196 A1
Wharfedale St WBPTN SW10 ...120 A5
Wharf La TWK TW1 ...156 B3
Wharf Pl BETH E2 ...86 C6
Wharf Rd IS N1 ...6 C3
PEND EN3 ...37 G1
SRTFD E15 ...88 B6
Wharfside Cl ERITH DA8 ...130 C5
Wharfside Rd CAN/RD E16 ...106 C5

Wharf St CAN/RD E16................106 C4
Wharf Ter PUT/ROE SW15.........194 A4
Wharncliffe Dr STHL UB1............115 J1
Wharncliffe Gdns SNWD SE25....181 F5
Wharncliffe Rd SNWD SE25.......180 E5
Wharton Cl WLSDN NW10............81 G4
Wharton Rd BMLY BR1................184 A4
Wharton St FSBYW WC1X..............5 H5
Whateley Rd DUL SE22..............143 G6
PGE/AN SE20....................182 A5
Whatley Av RYNPK SW20............177 G6
Whatman Rd FSTH SE23.............164 A2
Wheastone Rd NKENS W10 *.......100 C4
Wheatfields PEND EN3..................25 G2
Wheatfield Wy KUT/HW KT1........175 F6
Wheathill Rd PGE/AN SE20........181 J5
Wheatland's HEST TW5..............115 F6
Wheatlands Rd TOOT SW17........161 F5
Wheatley Cl HDN NW4...................45 J5
Wheatley Crs HYS/HAR UB3..........94 E6
Wheatley Gdns ED N9.................49 G4
Wheatley Rd ISLW TW7..............136 A4
Wheatley St CAVSQ/HST W1G.........9 H2
Wheatley Terrace Rd
ER.TH DA8...........................130 C6
Wheat Sheaf Cl POP/IOD E14.....124 D4
Wheatsheaf Cl RSLP HA4.............77 J5
Wheatsheaf La FUL/PGN SW6....139 F1
VX/NE SW8...........................141 K1
Wheatsheaf Rd ROM RM1..............75 H3
Wheatsheaf Ter
FUL/PGN SW6....................139 J1
Wheatstone Cl
WIM/MER SW19...................178 C4
Wheatstone Rd NKENS W10.......100 C4
Wheeler Gdns IS N1....................84 E6
Wheeler La WCHPL E1...................13 J1
Wheeler Pl HAYES BR2...............200 A1
Wheelers Cross BARK IG11.........108 D1
Wheelers Dr RSLP HA4................58 A3
Wheel Farm Dr DAGE RM10...........92 E1
Wheelock Cl ERITH DA8.............149 J1
Wheelright Cl BARN WD23............28 B1
Wheelwright St HOLWY N7............85 F5
Whelan Wy WLGTN SM6.............210 D1
Wheler St WCHPL E1.....................7 J7
Whellock Rd CHSWK W4............118 B3
Whenman Av BXLY DA5..............169 K4
Whetstone Cl TRDG/WHET N20.....33 H4
Whetstone Pk LINN WC2A...........11 G3
Whetstone Rd BKHTH/KID SE3...146 B3
Whewell Rd BRXN N19..................66 E6
Whichcote St STHWK SE1 *...........17 J1
Whidborne Cl DEPT SE8.............144 D3
Whidborne St STPAN WC1H...........5 F5
Whimbrel Wy YEAD UB4................95 H5
Whinchat Rd THMD SE28.............127 J3
Whinfell Cl STRHM/NOR SW16...179 J1
Whinyates Rd ELTH/MOT SE9.....146 D4
Whippendell Cl
STMC/STPC BR5..................186 C4
Whippendell Wy
STMC/STPC BR5..................186 C4
Whipps Cross Rd WAN E11.........70 C2
Whiskin St CLKNW EC1R...............6 A5
Whistler Gdns EDGW HA8............44 B5
Whistlers Av BTSEA SW11 *.......140 C1
Whistler St HBRY N5....................85 H2
Whistler Wk WBPTN SW10 *.....140 B1
Whiston Rd BETH E2......................7 J2
Whitacre Ms LBTH SE11.............122 B5
Whitbread Cl TOTM N17................50 C4
Whitbread Rd BROCKY SE4........144 B5
Whitburn Rd LEW SE13..............144 E6
Whitby Av WLSDN NW10...............98 D2
Whitby Gdns CDALE/KGS NW9.....44 C6
SUT SM1...............................194 C6
Whitby Pde RSLP HA4 *................59 G6
Whitby Rd RSLP HA4....................77 F1
RYLN/HDSTN HA2.................78 C1
SUT SM1..............................194 C6
WOOL/PLUM SE18..................126 E4
Whitby St WCHPL E1.....................7 J6
Whitcher Cl NWCR SE14.............124 B6
Whitcher Pl KTTN NW5................84 C4
Whitchurch Av EDGW HA8...........44 B3
Whitchurch Cl EDGW HA8...........44 B2
Whitchurch Gdns EDGW HA8.......44 B3
Whitchurch La EDGW HA8...........43 J3
Whitchurch Pde EDGW HA8 *......44 C3
Whitchurch Rd NTGHL W11.........100 B6
Whitcomb St SOHO/SHAV W1D....10 C5
Whitcome Ms RCH/KEW TW9.....137 J2
Whitear Wk SRTFD E15...............88 B4
Whitebarn La DAGE RM10..........110 C1
Whitebeam Av HAYES BR2..........201 H4
Whitebeam Cl BRXN/ST SW9 *...142 A1
White Bear Pl HAMP NW3 *..........83 H2
White Bridge Av MTCM CR4........194 C1
White Bridge Cl
EBED/NFELT TW14................153 J1
White Butts Rd RSLP HA4............77 H1
Whitechapel High St WCHPL E1...13 K3
Whitechapel Rd WCHPL E1.........104 C5
White City Cl SHB W12...............100 A6
White City Rd SHB W12................99 K6
White Conduit St IS N1..................5 K1
Whitecote Rd STHL UB1...............96 C5
White Craig Cl PIN HA5.................42 A1
Whitecroft Cl BECK BR3..............199 G1
Whitecroft Wy BECK BR3............199 F1
Whitecross St STLK EC1Y..............6 D7
Whitefield Av CRICK NW2.............64 A6
Whitefield Cl STMC/STPC BR5...186 D6
WAND/EARL SW18..................159 H1
Whitefoot La CAT SE6................165 G6
Whitefoot Ter BMLY BR1............165 J5
Whitefriars Dr
KTN/HRWW/W HA3..............42 E5
Whitefriars St EMB EC4Y.............12 A4
White Gate Gdns
KTN/HRWW/W HA3..............42 E3
Whitehall WHALL SW1A................16 E1
Whitehall Ct WHALL SW1A...........16 E1
Whitehall Crs CHSGTN KT9........205 K3
Whitehall Gdns ACT W3..............117 H1
CHING E4................................38 B3
CHSWK W4...........................117 J6
WHALL SW1A.........................16 E1
Whitehall La BKHH IG9................38 E4
ERITH DA8...........................150 C3
Whitehall Pk ARCH N19...............66 C5
Whitehall Park Rd CHSWK W4...117 J6
Whitehall Pl CAR SM5.................210 B2
WHALL SW1A.........................16 E1
Whitehall Rd CHING E4.................38 C4
HAYES BR2..........................200 C2
HNWL W7.............................116 B2
HRW HA1...............................60 E4
THHTH CR7..........................196 B2
Whitehall St TOTM N17................50 B3
White Hart Barn SW11A..............138 B5
ROMW/RG RM7......................56 C4
WDGN N22.............................49 G4
White Hart Rd ORP BR6..............202 B4
WOOL/PLUM SE18..................127 K4
White Hart St LBTH SE11...........122 B5
White Hart Ter TOTM N17 *...........50 B5
White Hart Yd STHWK SE1...........18 E1
Whitehaven Cl HAYES BR2..........199 K2
Whitehaven St STJWD NW8...........2 C7
Whitehead Cl RDART DA2...........171 F5
UED N18.................................49 K1
WAND/EARL SW18.................160 B2
Whiteheads Gv CHEL SW3............14 D7
White Heart Av UX/CGN UB8........94 A4
Whiteheath Av RSLP HA4.............58 A4
White Heron Ms TEDD TW11 *....174 A2
Whitehill Rd DART DA1...............150 D6
Whitehorse La SNWD SE25........197 F1
White Horse La WCHPL E1...........105 F3
White Horse Rd EHAM E6............107 K2
WCHPL E1.............................105 G5
Whitehorse Rd CROY/NA CRO....196 D4
WCHPL E1.............................105 G4
White House Dr STAN HA7............29 J6
White House La ENC/FH EN2........23 J2
Whitehouse Wy
STHGT/OAK N14......................34 B4
Whitehurst Dr UED N18 *..............51 F1
Whitelands Crs
WAND/EARL SW18................159 H2
White Kennett St WCHPL E1.........13 H3
White Ledges WEA W13................97 J5
Whitelegg Rd PLSTW E13...........106 D1
Whiteley Rd NRWD SE19............180 E1
Whiteleys Wy FELT TW13............155 F5
White Lion Cl BANK EC3V............13 G4
PECK SE15 *...........................13 K6
White Lion Hl BLKFR EC4V...........12 C5
White Lion St IS N1.......................5 J3
White Ldg NRWD SE19...............180 C3
White Lodge Cl BELMT SM2.......209 G5
EFNCH N2...............................65 J1
ISLW TW7.............................136 B5
The White Ldg BAR EN5 *............20 C4
White Lyon Ct BARB EC2Y..........12 C1
White Oak Dr BECK BR3.............183 F5
White Oak Gdns BFN/LL DA15...168 A2
Whiteoaks La GFD/PVL UB6.........96 D1
White Orchards STAN HA7............43 G1
TRDG/WHET N20....................32 D2
White Post La HOM E9.................87 J5
White Post St PECK SE15............143 K1
White Rd SRTFD E15....................88 C5
Whites Av GNTH/NBYPK IG2.........72 E5
White's Grounds STHWK SE1.......19 H2
Whites Grounds Est STHWK SE1...19 H2
Whites Meadow BMLY BR1 *.......201 F1
White's Rw WCHPL E1..................13 J2
White's Sq CLAP SW4.................141 J5
Whitestile Rd BTFD TW8.............116 D5
Whitestone La HAMP NW3...........83 G1
Whitestone Wk HAMP NW3 *........83 G1
White St NWDGN UB2................114 C2
Whitethorn Gdns
CROY/NA CRO.......................197 J6
ENC/FH EN2...........................23 K6
Whitethorn St BOW E3...............105 J3
Whitewebbs Wy
STMC/STPC BR5..................186 A4
Whitfield Pl FITZ W1T *..................4 A7
Whitfield Rd BXLYHN DA7..........149 G1
EHAM E6................................89 G5
GNWCH SE10.........................145 G2
Whitfield St FITZ W1T...................10 B2
Whitford Gdns MTCM CR4..........178 E6
Whitgift Av BELMT/SEL CR2.......211 J3
Whitgift St CROY/NA CRO...........211 J1
LBTH SE11.............................17 G6
Whitings Rd BAR EN5...................20 A6
Whitings Wy EHAM E6................108 A4
Whitland Rd CAR SM5................194 C6
Whitley Cl STWL/WRAY TW19....152 B1
Whitley Rd TOTM N17..................50 A5
Whitlock Dr WAND/EARL SW18...159 H2
Whitman Rd BOW E3..................105 G3
Whitmead Cl SAND/SEL CR2.......211 K4
Whitmore Cl FBAR/BDGN N11.....48 B1
Whitmore Est IS N1........................7 H1
Whitmore Gdns WLSDN NW10...100 A1
Whitmore Rd BECK BR3.............182 C6
HRW HA1................................60 C4
IS N1......................................7 H1
Whitnell Wy PUT/ROE SW15 *....139 F6
Whitney Av REDBR IG4..................71 H1
Whitney Rd LEY E10......................69 J4
Whitney Wk SCUP DA14.............187 F2
Whitstable Cl BECK BR3..............182 C4
Whitstable Pl CROY/NA CRO.......211 J2
Whitstone La BECK BR3..............198 E2
Whittaker Av RCH/KEW TW9 *....136 E6
Whittaker Rd CHEAM SM3..........208 D1
EHAM E6................................89 G5
Whittaker St BGVA SW1W...........15 G7

Whitta Rd MNPK E12....................89 H2
Whittell Gdns SYD SE26.............163 K5
Whittingstall Rd
FUL/PGN SW6......................139 J2
Whittington Av BANK EC3V...........13 G4
YEAD UB4...............................94 D4
Whittington Ms
NFNCH/WDSP N12.................33 G6
Whittington Rd WDGN N22..........48 E3
Whittington Wy PIN HA5...............59 J2
Whittlebury Cl CAR SM5.............209 K5
Whittle Cl GFD/PVL UB6..............96 B5
WALTH E17.............................69 G3
Whittle Rd HEST TW5.................134 B1
NWDGN UB2..........................115 G2
Whittlesea Rd
KTN/HRWW/W HA3................42 C3
Whittlesey St STHWK SE1...........17 K1
Whitton Av East GFD/PVL UB6.....79 F3
Whitton Av West NTHLT UB5.......78 B5
Whitton Cl GFD/PVL UB6..............79 H4
Whitton Dene HSLW TW3...........135 G6
Whitton Dr GFD/PVL UB6.............79 G4
Whitton Manor Rd ISLW TW7.....135 G6
Whitton Rd HSLW TW3...............135 G6
WHTN TW2............................155 K1
Whitton Wave HSLW TW3...........155 J1
Whitwell Rd PLSTW E13.............106 E2
Whitworth Rd SNWD SE25.........181 F6
WOOL/PLUM SE18..................147 F1
Whitworth St GNWCH SE10.......125 H5
Whorlton Rd PECK SE15.............143 H4
Whybridge Cl RAIN RM13.............93 G6
Whymark Av WDGN N22..............49 G6
Whytecroft HEST TW5................134 C1
Whyteville Rd FSTGT E7...............89 F4
Wichling Cl STMC/STPC BR5......202 E5
Wickersley Rd BTSEA SW11.......141 F4
Wickers Oake NRWD SE19 *.......163 G6
Wicker St WCHPL E1 *...............104 C5
Wicket Rd GFD/PVL UB6..............97 G2
The Wickets ASHF TW15............152 B6
Wickets Wy BARK/HLT IG6...........55 F2
The Wicket CROY/NA CRO..........213 J3
Wickford St WCHPL E1...............104 E3
Wickford Wy WALTH E17..............69 F1
Wickham Av CHEAM SM3...........208 A3
CROY/NA CRO.......................198 B6
Wickham Cha WWKM BR4..........199 G4
Wickham Cl ELTH/MOT SE9........166 C6
PEND EN3................................24 D4
Wickham Ct WWKM BR4 *..........214 B2
Wickham Court Rd
WWKM BR4...........................199 F6
Wickham Crs WWKM BR4...........199 F6
Wickham Gdns BROCKY SE4......144 C4
Wickham La ABYW SE2...............128 C5
Wickham Ms BROCKY SE4..........144 C3
Wickham Rd BECK BR3..............182 E6
BROCKY SE4........................144 C4
CHING E4................................52 A3
CROY/NA CRO.......................198 C5
KTN/HRWW/W HA3................42 D1
Wickham St LBTH SE11..............122 A5
WELL DA16............................147 K3
Wickham Wy BECK BR3..............199 F1
Wick La BOW E3..........................87 J6
Wickliffe Av FNCH N3...................46 C5
Wickliffe Gdns WBLY HA9............62 C1
Wicklow St STPAN WC1X..............5 G4
Wick Rd HOM E9..........................87 F4
TEDD TW11...........................174 C3
Wicksteed Cl BXLY DA5.............170 A5
Wickwood St CMBW SE5.............142 C3
Widdenham Rd HOLWY N7...........85 F2
Widdenham Rd
RYLN/HDSTN HA2...................59 J6
Widdin St SRTFD E15.................88 B5
Widecombe Gdns REDBR IG4.......71 J1
Widecombe Rd
ELTH/MOT SE9......................166 D5
Widecombe Wy EFNCH N2...........65 H2
Widegate St WCHPL E1................13 H2
Widenham Cl PIN HA5..................59 G2
Wide Wy STRHM/NOR SW16.......179 J6
Widgeon Cl CAN/RD E16............107 F5
Widgeon Rd ERITH DA8..............150 E1
Widley Rd MV/WKIL W9..............100 E2
Widmore Lodge Rd BMLY BR1...184 C5
Widmore Rd BMLY BR1..............184 B5
Wieland Rd NTHWD HA6...............40 E3
Wigeon Wy YEAD UB4..................95 H5
Wiggins Md CDALE/KGS NW9.......45 H5
Wigginton Av WBLY HA9..............80 E4
Wightman Rd CEND/HSY/T N8.....67 G1
Wigley Rd FELT TW13.................154 C4
Wigmore Pl CAVSQ/HST W1G *.....9 J3
Wigmore St MHST W1U...............9 H4
Wigram Rd WAN E11....................71 G3
Wigram Sq WALTH E17.................52 A6
Wigston Cl UED N18......................50 A1
Wigston Rd PLSTW E13..............107 F3
Wigton Gdns STAN HA7...............44 A4
Wigton Pl LBTH SE11..................122 B5
Wigton Rd WALTH E17..................51 H4
Wilberforce Ms CLAP SW4.........141 J5
Wilberforce Rd
CDALE/KGS NW9...................63 H2
FSBYPK N4............................85 H1
Wilberforce Wy
WIM/MER SW19....................177 G2
Wilbraham Pl KTBR SW1X...........15 G6
Wilbury Av BELMT SM2...............208 D6
Wilbury Wy UED N18....................49 K1
Wilby Ms NTGHL W11................100 D6
Wilcot Av OXHEY WD19................27 J2
Wilcot Cl OXHEY WD19................27 J2
Wilcox Cl VX/NE SW8.................141 K1
Wilcox Rd SUT SM1....................209 F2
TEDD TW11...........................156 B5
VX/NE SW8...........................141 K1
Wildacres NTHWD HA6.................26 D6
Wild Ct HOL/ALD WC2B...............11 G3
Wildcroft Gdns STAN HA7............43 G2

Wildcroft Rd PUT/ROE SW15......159 F2
Wilde Cl HACK E8........................86 C6
Wilde Pl PLMGR N13....................49 H2
Wilder Ct RSLP HA4......................59 F5
Wilderness Rd CHST BR7...........185 G3
The Wilderness
E/WMO/HCT KT8...................189 H2
HPTN TW12 *........................155 C6
Wilde Rd ERITH DA8...................149 K2
Wilderton Rd STNW/STAM N16.....68 A4
Wildfell Rd CAT SE6...................164 E2
Wild Goose Dr PECK SE15..........143 K2
Wild Hatch GLDGN NW11.............64 E3
Wild Oaks Cl NTHWD HA6............40 D2
Wild's Rents STHWK SE1.............19 G4
Wild St HOL/ALD WC2B................11 F4
Wildwood NTHWD HA6.................40 B2
Wildwood Cl LEE/GVPK SE12.....165 J2
Wildwood Gv HAMP NW3..............65 G5
Wildwood Ri GLDGN NW11...........65 G5
Wildwood Rd GLDGN NW11..........65 F3
Wilford Cl ENC/FH EN2 *..............23 K4
NTHWD HA6...........................40 B3
Wilfred Av RAIN RM13.................111 J4
Wilfred St WESTW SW1E...............16 A4
Wilfrid Gdns ACT W3....................98 E4
Wilkes Rd BTFD TW8...................117 F6
Wilkie Wy EDUL SE22 *..............143 H5
Wilkins Cl HYS/HAR UB3.............113 J5
MTCM CR4............................178 D4
Wilkinson Gdns NRWD SE19......181 F4
Wilkinson Rd CAN/RD E16..........107 G5
Wilkinson St VX/NE SW8............142 A1
Wilkinson Wy CHSWK W4...........118 A2
Wilkin St KTTN NW5.....................84 A4
Wilkin Street Ms KTTN NW5 *......84 B4
Wilks Gdns CROY/NA CRO..........198 B5
Wilks Pl IS N1...............................7 H3
Willan Rd TOTM N17....................49 K5
Willan Wall CAN/RD E16.............106 D6
Willard St VX/NE SW8.................141 G4
Willcocks Cl CHSGTN KT9..........206 A1
Willcott Rd ACT W3.....................117 J1
Will Crooks Gdns
ELTH/MOT SE9......................146 C5
Willenhall Av BAR EN5..................33 G1
Willenhall Dr HYS/HAR UB3..........94 C6
Willenhall Rd
WOOL/PLUM SE18..................127 G5
Willerfield Rd WLSDN NW10.........98 E2
Willersley Av BFN/LL DA15..........168 A3
ORP BR6...............................216 D1
Willersley Cl BFN/LL DA15..........168 A3
Willesden La KIL/WHAMP NW6.....82 B5
Willes Rd KTTN NW5....................84 B4
Willett Cl NTHLT UB5 *.................95 G2
STMC/STPC BR5..................201 K3
Willett Pl THHTH CR7.................196 B2
Willett Wy STMC/STPC BR5.......201 J2
William Barefoot Dr
ELTH/MOT SE9......................167 F4
William Bonney Est CLAP SW4 *...141 J5
William Booth Rd
PGE/AN SE20........................181 H4
William Carey Wy HRW HA1.........60 E3
William Cl CRW RM5.....................56 E4
FNCH N3................................47 H5
LEW SE13.............................145 F4
NWDGN UB2.........................115 H2
William Covell Cl ENC/FH EN2 *...23 F1
William Dr STAN HA7....................43 G2
William Ellis Wy
BERM/RHTH SE16 *..............123 H3
William Gdns PUT/ROE SW15....138 E6
William Guy Gdns BOW E3..........105 K2
William IV St CHCR WC2N............10 E6
William Margrie Cl
PECK SE15 *.........................143 H3
William Ms KTBR SW1X................15 F3
William Morley Cl EHAM E6..........89 H6
William Morris Cl WALTH E17.......51 H6
William Morris Wy
FUL/PGN SW6......................140 B4
William Petty Wy
STMC/STPC BR5..................202 D5
William Rd CAMTN NW1.................4 A5
SUT SM1..............................209 G3
WIM/MER SW19....................177 H3
Williams Av WALTH E17.................51 H4
William's Buildings BETH E2 *....104 E3
Williams Cl CEND/HSY/T N8 *......66 D5
FUL/PGN SW6......................139 H1
Williams Gv SURB KT6...............190 D3
WDGN N22..............................49 G4
Williams La MORT/ESHN SW14...137 K4
MRDN SM4...........................194 B3
Williamson Cl GNWCH SE10.......125 J5
Williamson Rd FSBYPK N4...........67 H3
Williamson St HOLWY N7 *..........84 E2
Williamson Wy MLHL NW7............46 C2
Williams Ter CROY/NA CRO.........211 G4
Williams Wy RDART DA2.............170 D4
WEA W13 *............................116 B1
Willifield Wy GLDGN NW11..........64 E2
Willingdon Rd WDGN N22.............49 H5
Willingham Cl KTTN NW5..............84 C3
Willingham Ter KTTN NW5 *.........84 C3
Willington Ct HOM E9 *................87 H4
Willington Rd BRXN/ST SW9.......141 K4
Willis Av SUT SM1.......................209 J4
Willis Rd CROY/NA CRO..............196 D4
ERITH DA8...........................129 K4
SRTFD E15............................106 D1
Willis St POP/IOD E14.................105 K5
Willmore End WIM/MER SW19....178 A4
Willoughby Av CROY/NA CRO......211 F2
Willoughby Dr RAIN RM13............93 G5
Willoughby Gv TOTM N17.............50 D3

Willoughby La TOTM N17..............50 D3
Willoughby Ms TOTM N17............50 D3
Willoughby Park Rd TOTM N17.....50 D3
Willoughby Rd
CEND/HSY/T N8.....................49 G6
HAMP NW3............................83 H2
KUTN/CMB KT2....................175 F4
TWK TW1.............................136 D6
Willoughby Wy CHARL SE7.........126 A4
Willow Av BARN SW13................138 C3
BFN/LL DA15........................168 B1
Willow Bridge Rd IS N1...............85 J4
Willow Cl ADL/WDHM KT15 *......143 C6
BTFD TW8.............................116 D6
BXLY DA5.............................169 G1
HAYES BR2..........................200 C2
HCH RM12............................93 J3
STMC/STPC BR5..................202 C3
Willow Ct STAN HA7 *..................43 K5
Willowcourt Av
KTN/HRWW/W HA3................61 H2
Willow Dean PIN HA5....................41 H5
Willow Dene BUSH WD23..............28 C2
Willowdene HGT N6......................65 K4
Willow Dene PIN HA5....................41 H5
Willowdene Cl WHTN TW2..........155 H2
Willow Dr BAR EN5.......................20 C5
Willow End NTHWD HA6...............40 E2
TRDG/WHET N20....................33 F5
Willowfields Cl
WOOL/PLUM SE18..................127 K5
Willow Gdns HEST TW5 *............135 F2
RSLP HA4...............................58 D6
Willow Gv CHST BR7..................185 F2
RSLP HA4...............................58 D6
Willowhayne Dr
WOT/HER KT12.....................188 A4
Willowhayne Gdns WPK KT4......208 A2
Willow La MTCM CR4..................194 E2
Willowmead Cl EA W5...................97 K4
Willowmere ESH/CLAY KT10.......204 C2
Willow Mt CROY/NA CRO............212 A2
Willow Pl WEST SW1P...................16 B7
Willow Rd CHDH RM6...................73 K3
DART DA1............................171 F3
EA W5.................................117 F2
EN EN1...................................24 B2
ERITH DA8...........................150 C2
HAMP NW3............................83 H2
NWMAL KT3.........................191 K1
WLGTN SM6.........................210 B5
Willow Rd WMRDN SM4.............194 A2
Willows Cl PIN HA5.......................41 G5
The Willows BECK BR3 *.............182 D4
EBAR EN4 *............................33 J1
ESH/CLAY KT10....................204 E4
GVW D19...............................27 F2
Willow St CHING E4.......................38 B2
ROMW/RG RM7.....................74 E1
SDTCH EC2A...........................7 G5
Willow Ter PGE/AN SE20 *..........181 J4
FNCH N3................................47 J3
HOR/WEW KT19...................207 H4
NTGHL W11..........................100 E6
SYD SE26..............................163 J5
WHTN TW2............................155 J1
Willow Tree Cl BOW E3 *............105 J1
Willow Tree La YEAD UB4...........160 A5
Willow Tree Wk BMLY BR1..........184 A4
Willowtree Wy
STRHM/NOR SW16...............187 F2
SHB W12 *.............................99 G6
Willow Vw WIM/MER SW19........178 C4
Willow Wk CHEAM SM3.............208 D1
DART DA1 *..........................151 H6
ORP BR6..............................216 B1
SEVS/STOTM N15...................67 K3
STHWK SE1............................19 H6
WALTH E17 *..........................51 H1
WCHMH N21............................35 F1
Willow Wy ASHF/SUD HA0 *........79 J4
FNCH N3................................47 H5
HOR/WEW KT19...................207 F4
NTGHL W11..........................100 E6
SYD SE26..............................163 J5
WHTN TW2............................155 J1
Willow Wood Crs SNWD SE25....197 F3
Willow Wren Whf
NWDGN UB2 *.......................114 A4
Will Rd KTTN NW5........................84 B4
Willrose Crs ABYW SE2.............128 C5
Wills Crs HSLW TW3...................155 G5
Wills Gv MLHL NW7......................45 J1
Willshaw St NWCR SE14............144 D2
Wilman Gv HACK E8....................86 C5
Wilmar Cl YEAD UB4.....................94 B3
Wilmar Gdns WWKM BR4...........198 E5
Wilmer Cl RCHPK/HAM TW10....175 G1
Wilmer Crs RCHPK/HAM TW10...175 G1
Wilmer Gdns IS N1........................7 H1
Wilmer Lea Cl SRTFD E15............88 A5
Wilmer Pl STNW/STAM N16.........68 B5
Wilmer Wy STHGT/OAK N14.......48 E1
Wilmington Av CHSWK W4.........138 A1
ORP BR6..............................202 D6
Wilmington Court Rd
RDART DA2...........................170 D5
Wilmington Gdns BARK IG11.......90 D5
Wilmington Sq FSBYW WC1X.......5 J5
Wilmington St FSBYW WC1X........5 J5
Wilmot Cl PECK SE15.................143 H1
Wilmot Pl CAMTN NW1................84 C5
HNWL W7.............................115 K1
Wilmot Rd CAR SM5 *................209 K3
DART DA1.............................151 F5
LEY E10...................................69 K6
TOTM N17..............................49 K6
Wilmot St BETH E2.....................104 D3

Wilmount St
  WOOL/PLUM SE18 ....127 G4
Wilna Rd *WAND/EARL* SW18 ......160 B2
Wilsham St *NTGHL* W11 ....119 C1
Wilsmere Dr
  KTN/HRWW/W HA3 ....42 E5
  NTHLT UB5 ....77 J4
Wilson Av *MTCM* CR4 ....178 D5
Wilson Cl *SAND/SEL* CR2 ....211 K3
  WBLY HA9 ....62 B4
Wilson Dr *WBLY* HA9 ....62 B4
Wilson Gdns *HRW* HA1 ....60 C4
Wilson Gv *BERM/RHTH* SE16 ......123 J2
Wilson Rd *CHSGTN* KT9 ....206 B4
  CMBW SE5 ....142 E2
  IL IG1 ....71 K4
  PLSTW E13 ....107 H2
Wilson's Av *POP/IOD* E14 ....105 H5
Wilson's Rd *HMSMTH* W6 ....119 G5
Wilson St *SDTCH* EC2A 13 F1
  WALTH E17 ....70 A2
  WCHMH N21 ....35 G2
Wilthorne Gdns *DAGE* RM10 ....92 D5
Wilstone Cl *NTHLT* UB5 ....95 J6
Wilton Av *CHSWK* W4 ....118 C4
Wilton Cl *WDR/YW* UB7 ....112 A6
Wilton Dr *CRW* RM5 ....56 E3
Wilton Est *HACK* E8 *..............86 C4
Wilton Gdns *E/WMO/HCT* KT8 * 173 F6
  WOT/HER KT12 ....188 C5
Wilton Gv *NWMAL* KT3 ....177 J3
  WIM/MER SW19 ....177 J2
Wilton Ms *HACK* E8 * 86 D4
  KTBR SW1X 15 H4
Wilton Pl *KTBR* SW1X 15 G3
Wilton Rd *ABYW* SE2 ....128 D3
  EBAR EN4 ....21 K5
  HSLWW TW4 ....134 C4
  MUSWH N10 ....48 A5
  PIM SW1V 16 A6
  WIM/MER SW19 ....178 D3
Wilton Rw *KTBR* SW1X 15 G3
Wilton Sq *IS* N1 ....85 K6
Wilton St *KTBR* SW1X 15 J4
Wilton Ter *KTBR* SW1X 15 G4
Wilton Vls *IS* N1 *...................6 E1
Wilton Wk *FELT* TW13 * 154 A4
Wiltshire Cl *CHEL* SW3 ....14 D7
  MLHL NW7 * 45 J1
Wiltshire Gdns *FSBYPK* N4 ....67 J3
  WHTN TW2 ....155 H3
Wiltshire La *PIN* HA5 ....58 E1
  RSLP HA4 ....40 D6
Wiltshire Rd *BRXN/ST* SW9 ....142 B4
  ORP BR6 ....202 B4
  THHTH CR7 ....180 B6
Wilverley Crs *NWMAL* KT3 ....192 B3
Wimbart Rd
  BRXS/STRHM SW2 * 162 A2
Wimbledon Br
  WIM/MER SW19 ....177 J3
Wimbledon Hill Rd
  WIM/MER SW19 ....177 H2
Wimbledon Park Rd
  WIM/MER SW19 ....159 H5
Wimbledon Park Side
  WIM/MER SW19 ....158 E2
Wimbledon Rd *TOOT* SW17 ....160 B6
Wimbolt St *BETH* E2 ....104 C2
Wimborne Av *NWDGN* UB2 ....115 F4
  STMC/STPC BR5 ....186 A6
  YEAD UB4 ....95 F5
Wimborne Cl *BKHH* IG9 ....39 G4
  LEE/GVPK SE12 ....145 J6
  WPK KT4 ....193 F5
Wimborne Dr *CDALE/KGS* NW9 ...44 C6
  PIN HA5 ....59 H4
Wimborne Gdns *WEA* W13 ....97 H4
Wimborne Rd *ED* N9 ....36 C4
  TOTM N17 ....50 A5
Wimborne Av *BECK* BR3 ....182 A6
Wimbourne St *IS* N1 ....6 E2
Wimpole Cl *HAYES* BR2 ....200 B2
  KUT/HW KT1 ....175 G5
Wimpole Ms *CAVSQ/HST* W1G 9 J1
Wimpole Rd *WDR/YW* UB7 ....112 A1
Wimpole St *CAVSQ/HST* W1G 9 J3
Wimshurst Cl *CROY/NA* CR0 ......195 K5
Winans Wk *BRXN/ST* SW9 ....142 B3
Wincanton Rd
  WAND/EARL SW18 ....159 J2
Wincanton Gdns *BARK/HLT* IG6 ...54 B6
Wincanton Rd
  WAND/EARL SW18 ....159 J2
Winchcombe Gdns
  ELTH/MOT SE9 ....146 D4
Winchcombe Rd *CAR* SM5 ....194 C4
Winchcomb Gdns
  ELTH/MOT SE9 ....146 D4
Winchelsea Av *BXLYHN* DA7 ......149 G1
Winchelsea Cl *PUT/ROE* SW15 ....139 G6
Winchelsea Rd *FSTGT* E7 ....88 E2
  TOTM N17 ....50 A6
  WLSDN NW10 ....81 F6
Winchelsey Ri *SAND/SEL* CR2 .....212 B4
Winchendon Rd *FUL/PGN* SW6 ...139 J1
  TEDD TW11 ....155 J6
Winchester Av *CDALE/KGS* NW9 ..44 B6
  HEST TW5 ....114 E6
  KIL/WHAMP NW6 ....82 D6
Winchester Cl *EN* EN1 * 24 A6
  ESH/CLAY KT10 ....204 A2
  HAYES BR2 ....183 J6
  KUTN/CMB KT2 ....175 J3
  LBTH SE11 * 17 G7
Winchester Dr *PIN* HA5 ....59 H2
Winchester Pk *HAYES* BR2 ....183 J6
Winchester Pl *HACK* E8 ....86 B3
  HGT N6 ....66 B5
Winchester Rd *BXLYHN* DA7 ......148 E3

Winchester Sq *STHWK* SE1 ....12 E7
Winchester St *ACT* W3 ....117 K1
  PIM SW1V 121 C5
Winchester Wk *STHWK* SE1 ....12 E7
Winchfield Cl
  KTN/HRWW/W HA3 ....61 J3
Winchfield Rd *SYD* SE26 ....182 B1
Winchilsea Crs
  E/WMO/HCT KT8 ....173 H5
Winchmore Hill Rd
  STHGT/OAK N14 ....34 E2
Winckley Cl *KTN/HRWW/W* HA3 ...62 B2
Wincott St *LBTH* SE11 ....17 K6
Wincrofts Dr *ELTH/MOT* SE9 .....147 J5
Windall Cl *NRWD* SE19 ....181 H4
Windborough Rd *CAR* SM5 ....210 A5
Windermere Av *FNCH* N3 ....46 E6
  HCH RM12 ....93 J5
  KIL/WHAMP NW6 ....82 C6
  RSLP HA4 ....59 G4
  WBLY HA9 ....61 J5
  WIM/MER SW19 ....178 A6
Windermere Cl *DART* DA1 ....170 E3
  EBED/NFELT TW14 ....153 H5
  ORP BR6 ....216 B1
  STWL/WRAY TW19 ....152 A4
Windermere Gdns *REDBR* IG4 .....71 J2
Windermere Gv *WBLY* HA9 ....61 J5
Windermere Hall *EDGW* HA8 * 44 B1
Windermere Rd *ARCH* N19 * 66 C6
  BXLYHN DA7 ....149 K3
  CROY/NA CR0 ....197 G5
  EA W5 ....116 D3
  MUSWH N10 ....48 B4
  PUT/ROE SW15 ....158 D4
  STHL UB1 ....95 K4
  STRHM/NOR SW16 ....179 H4
  WWKM BR4 ....199 H6
Winders Rd *BTSEA* SW11 ....140 D3
Windfield Cl *SYD* SE26 ....164 A6
Windham Rd *RCH/KEW* TW9 .....137 G4
Winding Wy *BCTR* RM8 ....91 J1
Windlass Pl *DEPT* SE8 ....124 B4
Windlesham Gv
  WIM/MER SW19 ....159 G3
Windley Cl *FSTH* SE23 ....163 K4
Windmill Cl
  BERM/RHTH SE16 ....123 H4
  LEW SE13 * 145 F3
  SURB KT6 ....190 D5
Windmill Dr *CLAP* SW4 ....141 G6
  HAYES BR2 ....215 G2
Windmill Gdns *ENC/FH* EN2 ......23 J3
Windmill Gv *CROY/NA* CR0 ....196 D4
Windmill Hl *ENC/FH* EN2 ....23 H4
  HAMP NW3 * 83 G1
  RSLP HA4 ....58 D5
Windmill La *BAR* EN5 ....31 H1
  BUSH WD23 ....28 D1
  GFD/PVL UB6 ....96 C4
  ISLW TW7 ....115 K4
  SRTFD E15 ....88 B4
  THDIT KT7 ....190 C4
Windmill Pas *CHSWK* W4 * 118 B4
Windmill Ri *KUTN/CMB* KT2 ......175 J3
Windmill Rd *CHSWK* W4 ....118 B4
  CROY/NA CR0 ....196 D4
  EA W5 ....116 D4
  HPTN TW12 ....173 G1
  MTCM CR4 ....195 H2
  UED N18 ....35 K6
  WAND/EARL SW18 ....160 C1
  WIM/MER SW19 ....176 E1
Windmill Rw *LBTH* SE11 * 122 B5
Windmill St *BUSH* WD23 ....28 E3
  FITZ W1T 10 C2
Windmill Wk *STHWK* SE1 * 17 K1
Windover Av *CDALE/KGS* NW9 ...45 F3
Windrose Cl *BERM/RHTH* SE16 ...124 A3
Windrush *NWMAL* KT3 ....191 J1
Windrush Cl *BTSEA* SW11 * 140 C5
  CHSWK W4 ....137 K1
Windrush La *FSTH* SE23 ....164 A5
Windrush Rd *WLSDN* NW10 ......81 F6
Windsor Av *CHEAM* SM3 ....208 C1
  E/WMO/HCT KT8 ....173 F6
  EDGW HA8 ....30 D6
  NWMAL KT3 ....191 K2
  WALTH E17 ....51 F4
  WIM/MER SW19 ....178 B4
Windsor Cl *CHST* BR7 ....185 G1
  FNCH N3 ....46 C5
  NTHWD HA6 ....40 D5
  RYLN/HDSTN HA2 ....78 A1
  WNWD SE27 ....162 D6
Windsor Crs *RYLN/HDSTN* HA2 ...78 A1
  WBLY HA9 ....62 C6
Windsor Dr *ASHF* TW15 ....152 A6
  DART DA1 ....170 D1
  EBAR EN4 ....33 K1
  ORP BR6 ....217 G4
Windsor Gv *WNWD* SE27 ....162 D6
Windsor Ms *CAT* SE6 ....165 F3
Windsor Park Rd
  HYS/HAR UB3 ....133 J1
Windsor Rd *BAR* EN5 ....32 B1

  BCTR RM8 ....92 A1
  BXLYHN DA6 ....149 F5
  CHING E4 ....51 J4
  CRICK NW2 ....81 K4
  EA W5 ....98 A6
  FNCH N3 ....47 F6
  FSTGT E7 ....89 F3
  HOLWY N7 ....84 E1
  HSLWW TW4 ....134 A3
  IL IG1 ....90 C2
  KTN/HRWW/W HA3 ....42 C4
  KUTN/CMB KT2 ....175 F3
  LEY E10 ....69 K6
  NWDGN UB2 ....114 E3
  RCH/KEW TW9 ....137 G3
  TEDD TW11 ....173 J1
  THHTH CR7 ....180 C5
  TOTM N17 ....50 C5
  WALTH E17 ....70 E5
  WPK KT4 ....207 J1
Windsor Ter *IS* N1 ....6 D4
Windsor Wk *WKENS* W14 ....119 G4
Windspoint Dr *PECK* SE15 * 123 H6
Windus Rd *STNW/STAM* N16 .....68 B5
Windy Rdg *BMLY* BR1 ....184 D4
Windy Ridge Cl
  WIM/MER SW19 ....177 G1
Wine Cl *WAP* E1W 104 E6
Winery La *KUT/HW* KT1 ....175 G6
Winey Cl *CHSGTN* KT9 ....205 J5
Winforton St *GNWCH* SE10 ....145 F2
Winfrith Rd *WAND/EARL* SW18 ..160 B2
Wingate Crs *CROY/NA* CR0 ....195 K3
Wingate Rd *HMSMTH* W6 ....118 E3
  IL IG1 ....90 B5
  SCUP DA14 ....186 D3
Wingfield Ct *WATW* WD18 * 26 B1
Wingfield Ms *PECK* SE15 * 143 H4
Wingfield Rd *KUTN/CMB* KT2 .....175 G2
  SRTFD E15 ....88 C3
  WALTH E17 ....69 K2
Wingfield St *PECK* SE15 ....143 H4
Wingfield Wy *RSLP* HA4 ....77 F4
Wingford Rd
  BRXS/STRHM SW2 ....161 K1
Wingmore Rd *HNHL* SE24 ....142 D4
Wingrave Rd *HMSMTH* W6 ......119 F6
Wingrove Rd *CAT* SE6 ....165 H1
Wings Cl *SUT* SM1 ....208 E2
Winifred Cl *BARK* IG11 ....108 D1
Winifred Gv *BTSEA* SW11 ....140 E5
Winifred Pl *NFNCH/WDSP* N12 ...47 G1
Winifred Rd *BCTR* RM8 ....74 A6
  DART DA1 ....150 B4
  ERITH DA8 ....130 B5
  HPTN TW12 ....155 F6
  WIM/MER SW19 ....177 K4
Winifred St *CAN/RD* E16 ....126 E1
  EN EN1 ....36 B2
Winifred Ter *EN* EN1 * 36 B2
Winkfield Rd *WDGN* N22 ....49 G4
Winkley St *BETH* E2 ....104 D1
Winlaton Rd *BMLY* BR1 ....165 G6
Winmill Rd *BCTR* RM8 ....92 B1
Winn Bridge Cl *WFD* IG8 ....53 H4
Winn Common Rd
  WOOL/PLUM SE18 ....127 K6
Winnett St *SOHO/SHAV* W1D 10 C5
Winnings St *EFNCH* N2 ....65 H3
Winnington Cl *EFNCH* N2 ....65 H4
Winnington Rd *EFNCH* N2 ....65 H4
  PEND EN3 ....24 E1
Winnipeg Dr *ORP* BR6 ....217 F4
Winnock Rd *WDR/YW* UB7 ......112 A1
Winn Rd *LEE/GVPK* SE12 ....165 K3
Winns Av *WALTH* E17 ....51 H5
Winns Ms *SEVS/STOTM* N15 .....68 A1
Winns Ter *WALTH* E17 ....51 J5
Winsbeach *WALTH* E17 *..........52 B6
Winscombe Crs *EA* W5 ....97 K3
Winscombe St *KTTN* NW5 ....84 B1
Winsford Rd *CAT* SE6 ....164 C5
Winsford Ter *UED* N18 * 49 K1
Winsham Gv *BTSEA* SW11 ....141 F6
Winslade Rd
  BRXS/STRHM SW2 ....141 K6
Winsland Ms *BAY/PAD* W2 ....8 A3
Winsland St *BAY/PAD* W2 ....8 A3
Winsley St *GTPST* W1W 10 A3
Winslow *CI* PIN* HA5 ....59 F3
  WLSDN NW10 ....81 G1
Winslow Gv *CHING* E4 ....38 C4
Winslow Rd *HMSMTH* W6 ....119 F6
Winslow Wy *FELT* TW13 ....154 C5
Winsor Ter *EHAM* E6 ....108 B4
Winstanley Rd *BTSEA* SW11 .....140 C4
Winstead Gdns *DAGE* RM10 ....92 E3
Winston Av *CDALE/KGS* NW9 .....63 G4
Winston Cl *KTN/HRWW/W* HA3 ...43 F2
  ROMW/RG RM7 ....74 E2
Winston House *SURB* KT6 * 191 F2
Winston Rd *STNW/STAM* N16 .....85 K2
Winston Wy *IL* IG1 ....90 B1
Winter Av *EHAM* E6 ....89 J6
Winterborne Av *ORP* BR6 ....216 D1
Winterbourne Rd *BCTR* RM8 ......73 J6
  CAT SE6 ....164 C3
  THHTH CR7 ....196 B1
Winter Box Wk
  RCHPK/HAM TW10 ....137 G6
Winterbrook Rd *HNHL* SE24 .....162 D1
Winterfold Cl *WIM/MER* SW19 ...159 H4
Winters Rd *THDIT* KT7 ....190 C4
Winterstoke Rd *CAT* SE6 ....164 C3
Winterton Pl *WBPTN* SW10 ......120 B6
Winterwell Rd
  BRXS/STRHM SW2 ....141 K6
Winterthorpe Rd *PUT/ROE* SW15 ..139 H5
Winterthorpe St *WCHPL* E1 ......104 D4
Winthrop St *WCHPL* E1 ....104 D4
Winton Av *FBAR/BDGN* N11 ......48 C3

Winton Cl *ED* N9 ....37 F2
Winton Gdns *EDGW* HA8 ....44 B3
Winton Rd *ORP* BR6 ....216 B2
The Wintons *BUSH* WD23 * 28 D3
Wirral Wood Cl *CHST* BR7 ....185 F2
Wisbeach Rd *CROY/NA* CR0 ......196 E2
Wisborough Rd *SAND/SEL* CR2 ..212 B6
Wisdons Cl *DAGE* RM10 ....74 D5
Wise La *MLHL* NW7 ....45 J2
  WDR/YW UB7 ....112 A4
Wiseman Rd *LEY* E10 ....69 J6
Wise Rd *SRTFD* E15 ....88 A6
Wiseton Rd *TOOT* SW17 ....160 D3
Wishart Rd *BKHTH/KID* SE3 ......146 D2
Wisley Rd *BTSEA* SW11 ....141 F6
  STMC/STPC BR5 ....186 B5
Wistaria Cl *ORP* BR6 ....201 G6
  IL IG1 ....90 B3
Wisteria Rd *LEE* SE13 ....145 G5
Witan St *BETH* E2 ....104 D2
Witham Cl *LOU* IG10 ....39 H1
Witham Rd *DAGE* RM10 ....92 C3
  GPK RM2 ....75 K2
  ISLW TW7 ....135 J2
  PGE/AN SE20 ....181 K6
  WEA W13 ....116 B2
Witherby Cl *SAND/SEL* CR2 .....212 A3
Witherington Rd *HBRY* N5 * 85 G3
Withers Md *CDALE/KGS* NW9 .....45 H5
Witherston Wy *ELTH/MOT* SE9 ..167 F4
Withey La *RSLP* HA4 ....58 A2
Withy Md *CHING* E4 ....38 C4
Witley Crs *CROY/NA* CR0 ....214 A4
Witley Gdns *NWDGN* UB2 ....114 E4
Witley Rd *ARCH* N19 ....66 C6
Witney Cl *PIN* HA5 ....41 K2
Witney Pth *FSTH* SE23 ....164 A5
Wittenham Wy *CHING* E4 ....38 B5
Wittering Cl *KUTN/CMB* KT2 .....174 E1
Wittersham Rd *BMLY* BR1 ....183 J1
Wivenhoe Cl *PECK* SE15 ....143 H4
Wivenhoe Ct *HSLW* TW3 ....134 C5
Wivenhoe Rd *BARK* IG11 ....109 G1
Wiverton Rd *SYD* SE26 ....181 K2
Wix Rd *DAGE* RM9 ....91 K6
Wix's La *CLAP* SW4 ....141 G5
Woburn Av *HCH* RM12 ....93 J2
Woburn Cl *BUSH* WD23 ....28 C1
  WIM/MER SW19 ....178 B2
Woburn Pth *STPAN* WC1H 4 D5
Woburn Rd *CAR* SM5 ....194 D5
  CROY/NA CR0 ....196 D5
Woburn Sq *STPAN* WC1H 4 C6
Woburn Wk *STPAN* WC1H 4 D5
Wodeham Gdns *WCHPL* E1 ....104 C4
Wodehouse Av *PECK* SE15 ....143 G2
Wodehouse Rd *DART* DA1 ....151 K5
Woffington Cl
  E/WMO/HCT KT8 ....174 D1
Woking Cl *PUT/ROE* SW15 ....138 C5
Woldham Pl *HAYES* BR2 ....200 B2
Woldham Rd *HAYES* BR2 ....200 B1
Wolds Dr *ORP* BR6 ....216 A2
Wolfe Cl *HAYES* BR2 ....199 K3
  YEAD UB4 ....95 G3
Wolfe Crs *CHARL* SE7 ....126 C5
Wolferton Rd *MNPK* E12 ....89 K2
Wolffe Gdns *SRTFD* E15 ....88 D4
Wolfington Rd *WNWD* SE27 .....162 C6
Wolfram Cl *LEW* SE13 ....145 H6
Wolfrencroft Cl *BTSEA* SW11 ....140 D4
Wollaston Cl *WALW* SE17 ....18 C6
Wolmer Cl *EDGW* HA8 ....30 C5
Wolmer Gdns *EDGW* HA8 ....30 C4
Wolseley Av
  WAND/EARL SW18 ....159 K4
Wolseley Gdns *CHSWK* W4 ......117 J6
Wolseley Rd *CEND/HSY/T* N8 ....66 D3
  CHSWK W4 ....117 K4
  FSTGT E7 ....89 F5
  KTN/HRWW/W HA3 ....42 E6
  MTCM CR4 ....195 F4
  ROMW/RG RM7 ....74 E4
  WDGN N22 ....49 F4
Wolseley St *STHWK* SE1 ....19 K3
Wolsey Av *EHAM* E6 ....108 A2
  WALTH E17 ....51 H3
Wolsey Cl *HSLW* TW3 ....135 H5
  KUTN/CMB KT2 ....175 J4
  NWDGN UB2 ....114 C3
  RYNPK SW20 ....176 E3
  WPK KT4 ....207 J2
Wolsey Ct *ELTH/MOT* SE9 * 166 E1
  KUTN/CMB KT2 ....175 J4
Wolsey Crs *MRDN* SM4 ....193 J4
Wolsey Dr *KUTN/CMB* KT2 ....175 F1
  WOT/HER KT12 ....188 C5
Wolsey Gdns *BARK/HLT* IG6 ......54 C2
Wolsey Gv *EDGW* HA8 ....45 F3
  ESH/CLAY KT10 ....204 C3
  ORP BR6 ....202 B2
Wolsey Ms *KTTN* NW5 ....84 C4
  ORP BR6 ....217 F3
Wolsey Rd *ASHF* TW15 ....152 A6
  E/WMO/HCT KT8 ....189 J1
  EN EN1 ....24 C2
  ESH/CLAY KT10 ....204 B2
  HPTN TW12 ....173 G2
  IS N1 ....85 K3
  RKW/CH/CXG WD3 ....26 A5
  SUN TW16 ....172 C4
Wolsey St *WCHPL* E1 ....104 E4
Wolsey Wy *CHSGTN* KT9 ....206 C3
Wolstonbury *NFNCH/WDSP* N12 ..46 E1
Wolvercote Rd *ABYW* SE2 ....128 E2
Wolverley St *BETH* E2 ....104 D2
Wolverton Av *KUTN/CMB* KT2 ...175 H4
Wolverton Gdns *EA* W5 ....98 B6
  HMSMTH W6 ....119 G4
Wolverton Rd *STAN* HA7 ....43 H2
Wolverton Wy *STHGT/OAK* N14 ..22 C6
Wolves La *WDGN* N22 ....49 G3
Womersley Rd *CEND/HSY/T* N8 ...67 F3

Wonersh Wy *BELMT* SM2 ....208 B6
Wonford Cl *NWMAL* KT3 ....176 B4
Wontner Cl *IS* N1 * 85 J5
Wontner Rd *BAL* SW12 ....160 E4
Woodall Cl *CHSGTN* KT9 ....205 J5
Woodall Rd *PEND* EN3 ....25 F6
Woodbank Rd *BMLY* BR1 ....165 J5
Woodbastwick Rd *SYD* SE26 .....182 A2
Woodberry Av
  RYLN/HDSTN HA2 ....60 C1
  WCHMH N21 ....35 G4
Woodberry Cl *MLHL* NW7 ....46 B3
Woodberry Crs *MUSWH* N10 ......48 B6
Woodberry Down *FSBYPK* N4 ....67 J5
Woodberry Gdns
  NFNCH/WDSP N12 ....47 G2
Woodberry Gv *BXLY* DA5 ....170 A5
  FSBYPK N4 ....67 J4
  NFNCH/WDSP N12 ....47 G2
Woodberry Wy *CHING* E4 ....38 A3
  NFNCH/WDSP N12 ....47 G2
Woodbine Cl *WHTN* TW2 ....155 J4
Woodbine Gv *ENC/FH* EN2 ....23 K1
  PGE/AN SE20 ....181 J3
Woodbine La *WPK* KT4 ....207 K1
Woodbine Pl *WAN* E11 ....71 F1
Woodbine Rd *BFN/LL* DA15 ......167 K3
Woodbines Av *KUT/HW* KT1 .....174 E6
Woodbine Ter *HOM* E9 * 86 E4
Woodborough Rd
  PUT/ROE SW15 ....138 E5
Woodbourne Av
  STRHM/NOR SW16 ....161 J5
Woodbourne Dr
  ESH/CLAY KT10 ....205 F4
Woodbridge Cl *HOLWY* N7 ....67 F6
  WLGTN SM6 ....210 B5
Woodbridge Rd *BARK* IG11 ....91 F3
Woodbridge St *CLKNW* EC1R 6 A6
Woodbrook Rd *ABYW* SE2 ....128 B6
Woodburn Cl *HDN* NW4 ....64 B2
Woodbury Cl *CROY/NA* CR0 ......197 G6
  WAN E11 ....71 F1
Woodbury Gdns *BMLY* BR1 ......165 J5
Woodbury Park Rd *WEA* W13 ......97 H3
Woodbury Rd *WALTH* E17 ....69 K1
Woodbury St *TOOT* SW17 ....178 D1
Woodchester Sq *BAY/PAD* W2 ...101 F4
Woodchurch Cl *BFN/LL* DA15 ....167 J3
Woodchurch Dr *BMLY* BR1 ....184 C3
Woodchurch Rd
  KIL/WHAMP NW6 ....82 E5
Wood Cl *BETH* E2 ....104 C3
  BXLY DA5 ....170 B5
  CDALE/KGS NW9 ....63 F4
  HRW HA1 ....60 D4
Woodclyffe Dr *CHST* BR7 ....185 F5
Woodcock Ct
  KTN/HRWW/W HA3 ....62 A4
Woodcock Dell Av
  KTN/HRWW/W HA3 ....61 J3
Woodcock Hl
  KTN/HRWW/W HA3 ....61 J2
Woodcombe Crs *FSTH* SE23 .....163 K3
Woodcot Cl *PEND* EN3 ....36 E1
Woodcote Av *HCH* RM12 ....93 J2
  MLHL NW7 ....46 A2
  THHTH CR7 ....196 C2
  WLGTN SM6 ....210 B6
Woodcote Cl *KUTN/CMB* KT2 ....175 G1
  PEND EN3 ....36 E1
Woodcote Dr *ORP* BR6 ....201 J4
Woodcote Gn *WLGTN* SM6 ......210 C6
Woodcote Ms *LOU* IG10 ....39 H2
  WLGTN SM6 ....210 B4
Woodcote Pl *WNWD* SE27 * 180 C1
Woodcote Rd *WAN* E11 ....70 E4
  WLGTN SM6 ....210 B4
Wood Crest *BELMT* SM2 * 209 G5
Woodcroft *ELTH/MOT* SE9 ....166 E5
  GFD/PVL UB6 ....79 H4
  WCHMH N21 ....35 F3
Woodcroft Av *MLHL* NW7 ....45 G3
  STAN HA7 ....43 G4
Woodcroft Crs *THHTH* CR7 ......196 C2
Woodcroft Ms *DEPT* SE8 ....124 B4
Woodcroft Rd *THHTH* CR7 ....196 C2
Woodedge Cl *CHING* E4 ....38 D3
Wooden Bridge Ter
  WNWD SE27 * 162 C5
Wood End *HYS/HAR* UB3 ....94 E5
  SWLY BR8 ....203 K1
Wood End Av
  RYLN/HDSTN HA2 ....78 B2
Wood End Cl *NTHLT* UB5 ....78 E3
Woodend Gdns *ENC/FH* EN2 ......22 E5
Wood End Gdns *NTHLT* UB5 ......78 C3
Wood End Gn *YEAD* UB4 ....94 D4
Wood End Green Rd
  HYS/HAR UB3 ....94 B4
Wood End La *NTHLT* UB5 ....78 B4
Wood End Rd *HRW* HA1 ....78 D5
Woodend Rd *WALTH* E17 ....52 A5
The Wood End *WLGTN* SM6 ....210 B6
Wood End Wy *NTHLT* UB5 ....78 C3
Wooder Gdns *FSTGT* E7 ....88 E2
Wooderson Cl *SNWD* SE25 ......197 F1
Woodfall Av *BAR* EN5 ....20 D6
Woodfall Dr *DART* DA1 ....150 C5
Woodfall Rd *FSBYPK* N4 ....67 G5
Woodfall St *CHEL* SW3 ....120 E5
Woodfarrs *CMBW* SE5 ....142 E5
Wood Fld *HAMP* NW3 * 83 K3
Woodfield Av *ALP/SUD* HA0 ......79 J1
  CAR SM5 ....210 A4
  CDALE/KGS NW9 ....45 G3
  EA W5 ....97 J3
  NTHWD HA6 ....40 B5
  STRHM/NOR SW16 ....161 J5
Woodfield Cl *EN* EN1 ....24 A5

NRWD SE19 ...... 180 D3
Woodfield Crs EA W5 ...... 97 K3
Woodfield Dr EBAR EN4 ...... 34 A3
GPK RM2 ...... 75 J1
Woodfield Gdns NWMAL KT3 ...192 C2
Woodfield Gv
  STRHM/NOR SW16 ...... J5
Woodfield Pl MV/WKIL W9 ...100 D4
Woodfield Ri BUSH WD23 ...... 28 D2
Woodfield Rd EA W5 ...... 97 J3
  ESH/CLAY KT10 ...... 190 A6
  HSLWW TW4 ...... 134 A3
  MV/WKIL W9 ...... 100 D4
Woodfield Wy FBAR/BDGN N11 ....48 D3
Woodford Bridge Rd
  REDBR IG4 ...... 53 H6
Woodford Crs PIN HA5 ...... 40 G5
Woodford New Rd WALTH E17 ...70 C1
Woodford Pl WBLY HA9 ...... 62 A5
Woodford Rd FSTGT E7 ...... 89 E3
  SWFD E18 ...... 70 E1
Woodgate Av CHSGTN KT9 ...205 K3
Woodgate Crs EL EHAM E6 ...... 40 E2
Woodgate Dr
  STRHM/NOR SW16 ...... 179 J3
Woodgate Gdns LD EHAM E6 ...119 F2
Woodgate Ct EHAM E6 ...... 107 J5
Woodgrange Av EA W5 ...... 117 C1
  EN EN1 ...... 36 C1
  KTN/HRWW/W HA3 ...... 61 J2
  NFNCH/WDSP N12 ...... 47 H2
Woodgrange Cl
  KTN/HRWW/W HA3 ...... 61 K2
Woodgrange Gdns EN EN1 ...... 36 C1
Woodgrange Rd FSTGT E7 ...... 88 E3
Woodgrange Ter EN EN1 * 36 C1
Woodhall Av DUL SE21 ...163 G5
  PIN HA5 ...... 41 J4
Woodhall Dr DUL SE21 ...163 G5
  PIN HA5 ...... 41 H4
Woodhall Ga PIN HA5 ...... 41 H3
Woodhall La OXHEY WD19 ...... 27 H5
Woodham Ct SWFD E18 ...... 70 D1
Woodham Rd CAT SE6 ...165 F5
Woodhatch Cl EHAM E6 ...... 107 J4
Woodhaven Gdns
  BARK/HLT IG6 ...... 72 C1
Woodhayes Rd RYNPK SW20 ...177 F5
Woodhead Dr ORP BR6 ...216 E1
Woodheyes Rd WLSDN NW10 ....81 G3
Woodhill WOOL/PLUM SE18 ...126 D4
Woodhill Crs
  KTN/HRWW/W HA3 ...... 61 K3
Woodhouse Av GFD/PVL UB6 ....97 F1
Woodhouse Cl EDUL SE22 ...143 H5
  GFD/PVL UB6 ...... 97 F1
  HYS/HAR UB3 ...113 H5
Woodhouse Eaves NTHWD HA6 ..40 E1
Woodhouse Gv MNPK E12 ...... 89 J4
Woodhouse Rd
  NFNCH/WDSP N12 ...... 47 G2
  WAN E11 ...... 88 D1
Woodhurst Av
  STMC/STPC BR5 ...... 201 H3
Woodhurst Rd ABYW SE2 ...128 B5
  ACT W3 ...... 117 K1
Woodington Cl ELTH/MOT SE9 ..167 F1
Woodison St BOW E3 ...105 G3
Woodknoll Dr CHST BR7 ...184 E4
Woodland Ap GFD/PVL UB6 ......79 G4
Woodland Cl CDALE/KGS NW9 ...62 E3
  HOR/WEW KT19 * 207 G4
  NRWD SE19 ...... 181 F2
  WFD IG8 ...... 39 F5
Woodland Ct GLDGN NW11 * 64 C2
Woodland Crs CNWCH SE10 ...125 H5
  Woodland Gdns ISLW TW7 ...135 K4
  MUSWH N10 ...... 66 B2
Woodland Gv CROY/NA CRO ...211 G5
  GNWCH SE10 ...125 H5
Woodland Hl NRWD SE19 ...181 F2
Woodland Ms
  STRHM/NOR SW16 ...161 K5
Woodland Ri CFD/PVL UB6 ......79 G4
  MUSWH N10 ...... 66 B1
Woodland Rd CHING E4 ...... 38 A3
  FBAR/BDGN N11 ...... 48 B1
  NRWD SE19 ...... 181 F1
  THHTH CR7 ...196 B1
Woodlands GLDGN NW11 * 64 C2
  RYLN/HDSTN HA2 ...... 60 A1
  RYNPK SW20 ...193 F1
Woodlands Av ACT W3 ...... 117 J1
  BFN/LL DA15 ...167 K3
  CHDH RM6 ...... 74 A3
  FNCH N3 ...... 47 F3
  NWMAL KT3 ...176 A4
  RSLP HA4 ...... 59 G5
  WAN E11 ...... 71 F5
  WPK KT4 ...192 C6
Woodlands Cl BMLY BR1 ...184 E5
  ESH/CLAY KT10 ...205 F5
  GLDGN NW11 ...... 64 C2

WAN E11 * 70 C6
Woodlands St LEW SE13 ...165 G2
Woodlands Ter SWLY BR8 * ...203 K3
The Woodlands CMBW SE5 * ...142 C1
  ESH/CLAY KT10 ...189 H6
  HRW HA1 * 60 E6
  ISLW TW7 ...136 A3
  LEW SE13 ...165 G2
  NRWD SE19 ...180 D3
  ORP BR6 ...217 H4
  STAN HA7 * 34 H1
  STHGT/OAK N14 ...... 34 B3
  WLGTN SM6 ...210 B6
Woodland St HACK E8 ...... 86 B4
Woodlands Wy
  PUT/ROE SW15 ...139 J6
Woodland Ter CHARL SE7 ...126 D4
Woodland Wk HAMP NW5 ......83 J3
  HOR/WEW KT19 ...206 C4
Woodland Wy ABYW SE2 ...128 E4
  BRYLDS KT5 ...191 J6
  CROY/NA CRO ...198 B5
  MLHL NW7 ...... 45 G2
  MRDN SM4 ...193 J1
  MTCM CR4 ...179 F3
  STMC/STPC BR5 ...201 H1
  WCHMH N21 ...... 35 G4
  WFD IG8 ...... 39 F5
  WWKM BR4 ...214 A1
Wood La CDALE/KGS NW9 ......63 F4
  DAGE RM10 ...... 74 C6
  HCH RM12 ...... 93 J3
  HGT N6 ...... 66 B3
  ISLW TW7 ...115 K6
  RSLP HA4 ...... 58 C6
  SHB W12 ...100 A5
  STAN HA7 ...... 28 D1
  WFD IG8 ...... 52 D1
Woodlawn Cl PUT/ROE SW15 ...139 J6
Woodlawn Crs WHTN TW2 ...155 G4
Woodlawn Dr FELT TW13 ...154 C4
Woodlawn Rd FUL/PGN SW6 ...139 F1
Woodlea Dr HAYES BR2 ...199 H2
Woodlea Gv NTHWD HA6 ...... 40 A2
Woodlea Rd STNW/STAM N16 ...86 A1
Woodleigh Av
  NFNCH/WDSP N12 ...... 47 J2
Woodleigh Gdns
  STRHM/NOR SW16 ...161 K5
Woodley Cl TOOT SW17 ...178 E3
Woodley La SUT SM1 ...209 J1
Wood Lodge Gdns BMLY BR1 ...184 D5
Wood Lodge La WWKM BR4 ...214 A1
Woodman Ms RCH/KEW TW9 ...137 J2
Woodman Pth BARK/HLT IG6 ....54 E1
Woodmans Gv WLSDN NW10 ....81 H3
Woodmansterne Rd
  STRHM/NOR SW16 ...179 H3
Woodman St CAN/RD E16 ...127 F1
Wood Ms TOTM N17 * 50 C2
Woodmere ELTH/MOT SE9 ...166 E2
Woodmere Av CROY/NA CRO ...198 A4
Woodmere Cl BTSEA SW11 ...141 F4
Woodmere Gdns
  CROY/NA CRO ...198 A4
Woodnook Rd
  STRHM/NOR SW16 ...179 G1
Woodpecker Cl BUSH WD23 ....28 C3
  ED N9 ...... 36 D1
  KTN/HRWW/W HA3 ...... 43 H4
Woodpecker Ms LEW SE13 ...145 G5
Woodpecker Mt CROY/NA CRO ...213 G6
Woodpecker Rd THMD SE28 ...109 J6
Woodquest Av HNHL SE24 ...142 C6
Wood Ride EBAR EN4 ...... 21 H2
  STMC/STPC BR5 ...201 J1
Woodridge Cl ENC/FH EN2 * ...23 G2
Woodridge Wy NTHWD HA6 ....40 C2
Woodridings Av PIN HA5 ...... 41 K4
Woodridings Cl PIN HA5 ...... 41 K3
Woodriffe Rd WAN E11 ...... 70 B4
Wood Ri PIN HA5 ...... 58 E2
Wood Rd WLSDN NW10 ...... 80 E5
Woodrow WOOL/PLUM SE18 ...126 D4
Woodrow Cl GFD/PVL UB6 ......79 H5
Woodrow Ct TOTM N17 ...... 50 E6
Woodrush Cl NWCR SE14 ...144 B1
Woodrush Wy CHDH RM6 ......73 K1
Woodseer St WCHPL E1 ...... 13 K1
Woodsford Sq WKENS W14 ...119 H2
Woodshire Rd DAGE RM10 ....92 E1
Woodside BKHH IG9 ...... 39 G4
  GLDGN NW11 ...... 64 E2
  ORP BR6 ...217 G3
  WIM/MER SW19 ...177 J1
Woodside Av ALP/SUD HA0 ......80 A6
  CHST BR7 ...185 H1
  ESH/CLAY KT10 ...189 K4
  HGT N6 ...... 65 K2
  NFNCH/WDSP N12 ...... 33 G6
  SNWD SE25 ...197 J3
Woodside Cl ALP/SUD HA0 ......80 A6
  BRYLDS KT5 ...191 K4
  BXLYHN DA7 ...150 A5
  RSLP HA4 ...... 58 B3
  STAN HA7 ...... 43 G1
Woodside Ct EA W5 * 117 F1
  CROY/NA CRO ...197 H4
Woodside Court Rd
  CROY/NA CRO ...197 H4
Woodside Crs BFN/LL DA15 ...167 K3
Woodside End ALP/SUD HA0 ....80 A6
Woodside Gdns CHING E4 ...... 51 K1
  TOTM N17 ...... 50 B5
Woodside Grange Rd
  NFNCH/WDSP N12 ...... 33 F6
Woodside Gn SNWD SE25 ...197 H3
Woodside Gv
  NFNCH/WDSP N12 ...... 33 G5
Woodside La BXLY DA5 ...168 E1
  NFNCH/WDSP N12 ...... 33 F5

Woodside Pde
  BFN/LL DA15 * ...167 K5
Woodside Pk SNWD SE25 ...197 H5
Woodside Park Av WALTH E17 ..70 B1
Woodside Park Rd
  NFNCH/WDSP N12 ...... 33 F6
Woodside Pl ALP/SUD HA0 ......80 A6
Woodside Rd BFN/LL DA15 ...167 K5
  BMLY BR1 ...200 D2
  BXLYHN DA7 ...150 A5
  KUTN/CMB KT2 ...175 F1
  NTHWD HA6 ...... 40 D3
  NWMAL KT3 ...176 A5
  PLSTW E13 ...107 G3
  SNWD SE25 ...197 J3
  SUT SM1 ...209 G1
  WDGN N22 ...... 49 G5
  WFD IG8 ...... 38 E6
Woodside Wy CROY/NA CRO ...197 K3
  MTCM CR4 ...179 G4
Wood's Ms MYFR/PKLN W1K 9 F5
Woodson Rd KTTN NW5 ...... 84 A1
Wood's Pl STHWK SE1 ...... 19 H5
Woodspring Rd
  WIM/MER SW19 ...159 H4
Wood's Rd PECK SE15 ...143 J2
The Woods NTHWD HA6 ...... 40 E1
Woodstock Av CHEAM SM3 ...193 J4
  GLDGN NW11 ...... 64 C5
  HNWL W7 ...116 B3
  ISLW TW7 ...136 B6
  STHL UB1 ...... 95 K2
Woodstock Cl BXLY DA5 ...169 G3
  STAN HA7 ...... 44 A5
Woodstock Crs ED N9 ...... 36 D1
Woodstock Gdns BECK BR3 ...182 E4
  GDMY/SEVK IG3 ...... 73 G6
  YEAD UB4 ...... 94 D4
Woodstock Gra EA W5 * ...117 F1
Woodstock La SHB W12 ...119 G2
Woodstock La North
  SURB KT6 ...190 D6
Woodstock La South
  ESH/CLAY KT10 ...205 H3
Woodstock Ms CAVSQ/HST W1G ..9 H2
Woodstock Ri CHEAM SM3 ...193 J5
Woodstock Rd ALP/SUD HA0 ....80 A6
  BUSH WD23 ...... 28 E2
  CAR SM5 ...210 A3
  CHSWK W4 ...118 B4
  CROY/NA CRO ...211 K1
  FNCH N3 ...... 47 G1
  FSTGT E7 ...... 89 G5
  GLDGN NW11 ...... 64 D4
  WALTH E17 ...... 52 B5
Woodstock St CAN/RD E16 ...106 C5
  MYFR/PKLN W1K 9 J4
Woodstock Ter POP/IOD E14 ...105 K6
Woodstock Wy MTCM CR4 ...179 H5
Woodstone Av EW KT17 ...207 J5
Wood St BAR EN5 ...... 20 A5
  CAN/RD E16 ...107 F6
  CHSWK W4 ...118 B5
  CITYW EC2V 12 D3
  KUT/HW KT1 ...174 E5
  MTCM CR4 ...195 F4
  WALTH E17 ...... 52 A6
Woodsyre SYD SE26 ...163 G6
Wood Ter CRICK NW2 * 63 H6
Woodthorpe Rd
  PUT/ROE SW15 ...138 E5
Woodthorne Cl HDN NW4 ...... 46 A5
Wood V FSTH SE23 ...163 J3
  MUSWH N10 ...... 66 C2
Woodvale Av SNWD SE25 ...181 G6
Woodvale Wy CRICK NW2 ...... 82 B1
Woodvale Gv CHING E4 ...... 38 A6
Woodview Cl KUTN/CMB KT2 ...158 A6
  ORP BR6 ...201 H6
Woodview Wy SWLY BR8 ...187 K5
Woodville Cl LEE/GVPK SE12 ...145 K6
  TEDD TW11 ...156 B6
Woodville Gdns BARK/HLT IG6 ..54 B6
  EA W5 ...... 98 A5
  RSLP HA4 ...... 58 A4
  SURB KT6 * ...190 E4
Woodville Gv WELL DA16 * ...148 B4
Woodville Rd BAR EN5 ...... 21 F4
  EA W5 ...... 98 A5
  GLDGN NW11 ...... 64 B4
  KIL/WHAMP NW6 * ...100 D1
  MRDN SM4 ...193 K1
  RCHPK/HAM TW10 ...156 C5
  STNW/STAM N16 ...... 86 A3
  SWFD E18 ...... 53 F5
  THHTH CR7 ...180 E6
  WALTH E17 ...... 69 G1
  WAN E11 ...... 70 D5

Woollaston Rd FSBYPK N4 ......67 H3
Woollett Cl DART DA1 ...150 D3
Woolmead Av CDALE/KGS NW9 ..63 J4
Woolmer Gdns UED N18 ...... 50 C2
Woolmer Rd UED N18 ...... 50 C1
Woolmore St POP/IOD E14 ...106 A6
Woolneigh St FUL/PGN SW6 ...140 A4
Woolridge Wy HOM E9 * 86 E5
Wool Rd RYNPK SW20 ...176 E2
Woolstaplers Wy
  BERM/RHTH SE16 ...123 H5
Woolston Cl WALTH E17 ...... 51 F5
Woolstone Rd FSTH SE23 ...164 B4
Woolwich Church St
  CHARL SE7 ...126 C4
Woolwich Common
  WOOL/PLUM SE18 ...127 F6
Woolwich Foot Tnl
  CAN/RD E16 ...127 F2
Woolwich High St
  WOOL/PLUM SE18 ...127 F3
Woolwich Manor Wy
  CAN/RD E16 ...127 G1
Woolwich Manorway
  EHAM E6 ...108 A6
Woolwich Manor Wy
  EHAM E6 ...... 107 K3
Woolwich New Rd
  WOOL/PLUM SE18 ...127 F6
Woolwich Rd ABYW SE2 ...128 E6
  BXLYHN DA7 ...149 H4
  CHARL SE7 ...126 B4
  GNWCH SE10 ...125 K5
Wooster Gdns POP/IOD E14 ...106 B5
Wootton Gv FNCH N3 ...... 46 E4
Wootton St STHWK SE1 ...... 17 K2
Worbeck Rd PGE/AN SE20 ...181 J5
Worcester Av TOTM N17 ...... 50 C3
  CROY/NA CRO ...198 C6
  MTCM CR4 ...179 F5
Worcester Cl CRICK NW2 ...... 81 J1
Worcester Cl WOT/HER KT12 ...188 B6
Worcester Crs MLHL NW7 ...... 31 G5
  WFD IG8 ...... 53 F1
Worcester Dr CHSWK W4 ...118 B3
Worcester Gdns GFD/PVL UB6 ...78 C4
  IL IG1 ...... 71 J4
  WPK KT4 ...207 G1
Worcester Ms KIL/WHAMP NW6 ..83 F4
Worcester Park Rd WPK KT4 ...206 E1
  MNPK E12 ...... 89 K1
  WALTH E17 ...... 51 F5
  WIM/MER SW19 ...177 J1
Worcesters Av EN EN1 ...... 24 C1
Wordsworth Av GFD/PVL UB6 ...96 D1
  MNPK E12 ...... 89 J5
  SWFD E18 ...... 70 D1
Wordsworth Dr CHEAM SM3 ...208 A2
Wordsworth Pde
  CEND/HSY/T N8 * 67 H1
Wordsworth Pl HAMP NW3 ......83 K3
Wordsworth Rd FELT TW13 ...154 E6
  PGE/AN SE20 ...182 A3
  STHWK SE1 ...... 19 J7
  STNW/STAM N16 ...... 85 K5
  WELL DA16 ...147 K1
  WLGTN SM6 ...210 C4
Wordsworth Wk GLDGN NW11 ...64 D1
Wordsworth Wy DART DA1 ...151 K5
  WDR/YW UB7 ...112 B4
Worfield St BTSEA SW11 ...140 D1
Worgan St BERM/RHTH SE16 ...124 A3
  LBTH SE11 ...122 A5
Worland Rd SRTFD E15 ...... 88 C5
Worlds End Est
  WBPTN SW10 * ...140 C1
Worlds End La ORP BR6 ...217 G5
Worlds End Pas
  WBPTN SW10 * ...140 C1
Worleys Dr ORP BR6 ...216 D2
Worlidge St HMSMTH W6 ...119 F5
Worlingham Rd EDUL SE22 ...143 G5
Wormholt Ter SHB W12 * ...118 D1
Wormwood St LVPST EC2M ...13 G3
Wornington Rd NKENS W10 ...100 C4
Woronzow Rd STJWD NW8 ......2 B1
Worple Av ISLW TW7 ...136 B6
  WIM/MER SW19 ...177 G2
Worple Cl RYLN/HDSTN HA2 ....59 J5
Worple Rd ISLW TW7 ...136 B5
  RYNPK SW20 ...177 G4
Worple Road Ms
  WIM/MER SW19 ...177 H2
Worple St MORT/ESHN SW14 ...138 A4
Worple Wy RCHPK/HAM TW10 ..137 F6
  RYLN/HDSTN HA2 ...... 59 K5
Worship St SDTCH EC2A 7 G7
Worslade Rd TOOT SW17 ...160 C6
Worsley Bridge Rd CAT SE6 ...182 C1
Worsley Gv CLPT E5 ...... 86 C2
Worsley Rd WAN E11 ...... 88 C2
Worsopp Dr CLAP SW4 ...141 H6
Worth Cl ORP BR6 ...216 E2
Worthfield Cl HOR/WEW KT19 ...207 F5
Worth Gv WALW SE17 * ...122 E5
Worthing Cl SRTFD E15 ...... 88 C6
Worthing Rd HEST TW5 ...114 E6
Worthington Cl MTCM CR4 ...195 G1
Worthington Rd SURB KT6 ...191 G5
  EHAM E6 ...... 89 H5
Worton Gdns ISLW TW7 ...135 J3
Worton Rd ISLW TW7 ...136 A4
Worton Wy ISLW TW7 ...135 J2
Wotton Ct STMC/STPC BR5 ...202 E2
Wotton Rd CRICK NW2 ...... 82 A2
Wouldham Rd CAN/RD E16 ...106 D5
Wouldham Ter
  STMC/STPC BR5 * ...186 C6
Wragby Rd WAN E11 ...... 88 C1
Wrampling Pl ED N9 ...... 36 C3
Wray Av CLAY IG5 ...... 54 A6

Wray Crs FSBYPK N4 ...... 66 G5
Wrayfield Rd CHEAM SM3 ...208 B1
Wray Rd BELMT SM2 ...208 D6
Wraysbury Cl HSLWW TW4 ...134 D6
Wrekin Rd WOOL/PLUM SE18 ...147 H1
Wren Av CRICK NW2 ...... 82 A3
  NWDGN UB2 ...114 E4
Wren Cl CAN/RD E16 ...106 D5
  ED N9 ...... 37 F3
  STMC/STPC BR5 ...186 E6
Wren Crs BUSH WD23 ...... 28 C3
Wren Dr WDR/YW UB7 ...112 A3
Wren Gdns DAGW RM9 ...... 91 K3
  HCH RM12 ...... 93 J5
Wren Ms LEW SE13 * ...145 H5
Wren Rd CMBW SE5 ...142 E2
  DAGW RM9 ...... 91 K3
  SCUP DA14 ...168 C5
Wren St FSBYW WC1X 5 H6
Wrentham Av WLSDN NW10 ...100 B1
Wrenthorpe Rd BMLY BR1 ...165 H6
Wrenwood Wy PIN HA5 ...... 59 F1
Wren Rd BOW E3 ...... 105 J1
Wrexham Gdns
  BKHTH/KID SE3 ...146 B2
Wrigglesworth St NWCR SE14 ..144 A1
Wright Cl LEW SE13 ...145 G5
Wright Rd HEST TW5 ...114 B6
Wright Cl DAGE RM10 ...... 92 C2
Wrights La KENS W8 ...119 K3
Wrights Pl WLSDN NW10 * 80 E4
Wright's Rd BOW E3 ...105 H1
  SNWD SE25 ...181 F6
Wright's Rw CAR SM5 ...210 B2
Wrigley Cl CHING E4 ...... 52 B1
Wrotham Rd BAR EN5 ...... 20 C3
  CAMTN NW1 * 84 C5
  WEA W13 ...116 C1
  WELL DA16 ...148 D2
Wrottesley Rd WLSDN NW10 ...99 K1
  WOOL/PLUM SE18 ...127 H6
Wroughton Rd BTSEA SW11 ...160 E1
Wroughton Ter HDN NW4 * 63 K1
Wroxall Rd DAGW RM9 ...... 91 J4
Wroxham Gdns
  FBAR/BDGN N11 ...... 48 C3
Wroxham Rd THMD SE28 ...109 K6
Wroxton Rd PECK SE15 ...143 J3
Wrythe Gn CAR SM5 ...209 K1
Wrythe Green Rd CAR SM5 ...209 K1
Wrythe La CAR SM5 ...194 C5
Wulfstan St SHB W12 ...... 99 H5
Wyatt Cl BUSH WD23 ...... 28 E2
  FELT TW13 ...154 C3
Wyatt Dr BARN SW13 ...118 E6
Wyatt Park Rd
  BRXS/STRHM SW2 ...162 A4
Wyatt Rd DART DA1 ...150 C4
  FSTGT E7 ...... 88 E4
  HBRY N5 ...... 85 J1
Wyatt's La WALTH E17 ...... 52 A6
Wyborne Wy WLSDN NW10 ....80 E5
Wybourn Av BAR EN5 ...... 20 D4
Wyche Gv SAND/SEL CR2 ...211 J5
Wycherley Cl BKHTH/KID SE3 ...145 J1
Wycherley Crs BAR EN5 ...... 33 F1
Wychwood Av EDGW HA8 ...... 43 K2
  THHTH CR7 ...180 C6
Wychwood Cl EDGW HA8 ...... 43 K2
Wychwood End HGT N6 ...... 66 C4
Wychwood Gdns CLAY IG5 ...... 71 K1
Wychwood Wy NTHWD HA6 ....40 C2
Wycliffe Cl WELL DA16 ...148 A2
Wycliffe Rd BTSEA SW11 ...141 F4
  WIM/MER SW19 ...178 A2
Wyclif St FSBYE EC1V 6 A5
Wycombe Gdns CRICK NW2 ....64 D6
Wycombe Pl
  WAND/EARL SW18 ...160 B1
Wycombe Rd ALP/SUD HA0 ......80 C6
  GNTH/NBYPK IG2 ...... 71 K2
  TOTM N17 ...... 50 C4
Wycombe Sq KENS W8 ...119 J1
Wydell Cl MRDN SM4 ...193 F3
Wydenhurst Rd CROY/NA CRO ...197 H4
Wydeville Manor Rd
  LEE/GVPK SE12 ...166 A6
Wye Cl ASHF TW15 ...152 E6
  ORP BR6 ...202 A4
  RSLP HA4 ...... 58 B3
Wyemead Crs CHING E4 ...... 38 C4
Wye St BTSEA SW11 ...140 C4
Wyfields CLAY IG5 ...... 54 B4
Wyfold Rd FUL/PGN SW6 ...139 H2
Wyke Cl ISLW TW7 ...116 A5
Wykeham Av DAGW RM9 ......91 J4
Wykeham Cl WDR/YW UB7 ...112 D6
Wykeham Gn DAGW RM9 ......91 J4
Wykeham Hi WBLY HA9 ...... 62 B5
Wykeham Ri TRDG/WHET N20 ..32 C3
Wykeham Rd HDN NW4 ...... 64 A2
  KTN/HRWW/W HA3 ...... 61 H1
Wyke Rd BOW E3 ...... 87 J5
  RYNPK SW20 ...177 F5
Wylchin Cl PIN HA5 ...... 58 E1
Wyldes Cl GLDGN NW11 ...... 65 G5
Wyldfield Gdns ED N9 ...... 36 B4
Wyld Wy WBLY HA9 ...... 80 D4
Wyleu St FSTH SE23 ...164 B2
Wylie Rd NWDGN UB2 ...115 F3
Wyllen Cl WCHPL E1 ...104 E3
Wylo Dr BAR EN5 ...... 31 J1
Wymark Cl RAIN RM13 ...111 H1
Wymering Rd MV/WKIL W9 ...100 E2
Wymond St PUT/ROE SW15 ...139 F4
Wynan Rd POP/IOD E14 ...124 E5
Wynaud Ct WDGN N22 ...... 49 F2
Wynchgate KTN/HRWW/W HA3 ..42 E3
  STHGT/OAK N14 ...... 34 E2

Wyncote Wy SAND/SEL CR2 .....213 F6
Wyncroft Cl BMLY BR1......184 E6
Wyndale Av CDALE/KGS NW9 ....62 C5
Wyndcliff Rd CHARL SE7 .....126 A6
Wyndcroft Cl ENC/FH EN2 ....23 H4
Wyndham Crs HSLWW TW4....154 C1
  KTTN NW5 .....
Wyndham Ms MBLAR W1H 8 E5
Wyndham Pl MBLAR W1H 8 E2
Wyndham Rd CMBW SE5 .....142 D1
  EBAR EN4 .....33 K3
  EHAM E6....89 H5
  KUTN/CMB KT2 .....175 G3
  WEA W13 ....116 C3
Wyndham St MBLAR W1H 8 E1
Wyndhurst Cl SAND/SEL CR2 ....211 H5
Wynell Rd FSTH SE23 .....164 A5
Wynford Gv STMC/STPC BR5 ....186 C6
Wynford Pl BELV DA17.....129 H6
Wynford Rd IS N1 .....5 G2
Wynford Wy ELTH/MOT SE9 ....166 E5
Wynlie Gdns PIN HA5 .....41 F5
Wynndale Rd SWFD E18 .....53 F4
Wynne Rd BRXN/ST SW9 .....142 B3
Wynn's Av BFN/LL DA15 .....148 B6
Wynnstay Gdns KENS W8 * 119 K3
Wynter St BTSEA SW11 .....140 B5
Wynton Gdns SNWD SE25 .....197 F2
Wynton Pl ACT W3 .....98 D5
Wynyard Ter LBTH SE11 * 122 A5
Wynyatt St FSBYE EC1V 6 A4
Wyre Gv EDGW HA8 .....30 E5
  HYS/HAR UB3 .....113 K4
Wyresdale Crs GFD/PVL UB6....97 F2
Wyteleaf Cl RSLP HA4 .....58 A5
Wythburn Pl MBLAR W1H 8 E4
Wythenshawe Rd DAGE RM10 ....92 C1
Wythes Cl BMLY BR1 .....184 E5
Wythes Rd CAN/RD E16 .....126 D1
Wythfield Rd ELTH/MOT SE9 ....166 E1
Wyvenhoe Rd
  RYLN/HDSTN HA2 .....78 C1

Wyvern Cl DART DA1 .....171 F2
  ORP BR6.....217 H1
Wyvern Est NWMAL KT3 * 176 D6
Wyvil Rd VX/NE SW8.....141 K1
Wyvis St POP/IOD E14 .....105 K4

Y

Yabsley St POP/IOD E14 .....125 F1
Yalding Gv STMC/STPC BR5.....202 E1
Yalding Rd BERM/RHTH SE16.....123 H3
Yale Cl HSLWW TW4 .....134 E6
Yale Wy HCH RM12 .....93 J2
Yarborough Rd
  WIM/MER SW19 .....178 C4
Yardley Cl CHING E4 .....25 K6
Yardley La CHING E4 .....25 K6
Yardley St FSBYW WC1X.....5 J5
Yarmouth Crs TOTM N17.....68 D2
Yarmouth Pl MYFR/PICC W1J....15 J1
Yarnton Wy ABYW SE2 .....128 D2
  ERITHM DA18.....129 G3
Yarrow Crs EHAM E6.....107 J4
Yateley St WOOL/PLUM SE18 ....126 C3
Yeading Av RSLP HA4 .....59 J6
Yeading Fk YEAD UB4 .....95 G4
Yeading Gdns YEAD UB4 .....95 F4
Yeading La YEAD UB4 .....95 F5
Yeames Cl WEA W13.....97 C5
Yeate St IS N1.....85 K5
Yeatman Rd HGT N6 .....65 K3
Yeats Cl LEW SE13 * 145 G3
  WLSDN NW10.....81 G4
Ye Cnr BUSH WD23 .....27 H1
Yeend Cl E/WMO/HCT KT8.....189 F1
Yeldham Rd HMSMTH W6 * 119 G5
Yeldham Vls HMSMTH W6 * 119 G5
Yelverton Rd BTSEA SW11.....140 C3
Yenston Cl MRDN SM4.....193 K3
Yeoman Cl EHAM E6.....108 B6
Yeoman Rd NTHLT UB5.....77 J5

Yeomans Acre RSLP HA4 .....58 E3
Yeoman's Rw CHEL SW3 .....14 D5
Yeoman St BERM/RHTH SE16....124 B4
Yeomans Wy PEND EN3 * 24 D5
Yeomans Wy BARK/HLT IG6 .....54 C2
Yeo St BOW E3.....105 K4
Yeovil Cl ORP BR6.....201 K6
Yeovilton Pl KUTN/CMB KT2 .....174 E1
Yerbury Rd ARCH N19.....84 D1
Yester Dr CHST BR7.....184 D3
Yester Pk CHST BR7.....184 E3
Yester Rd CHST BR7.....184 E3
Yew Cl BKHH IG9.....39 H4
Yewdale Cl BMLY BR1.....183 H2
Yewfield Rd WLSDN NW10 .....81 H5
Yew Gv CRICK NW2.....82 B2
The Yews ASHF TW15 *.....152 E6
Yewtree Cl RYLN/HDSTN HA2 ....60 B1
Yew Tree Cl WCHMH N21.....35 G2
  WELL DA16 .....148 B2
  WPK KT4 .....192 B5
Yew Tree Ct BORE WD6 .....29 K1
Yew Tree Gdns CHDH RM6 .....74 A2
  ROMW/RG RM7 .....75 F2
Yewtree Rd BECK BR3.....182 C6
Yew Tree Rd SHB W12 .....99 H6
Yew Tree Wk HSLWW TW4....134 E6
Yew Wk HRW HA1 .....60 E5
Yoakley Rd STNW/STAM N16 ....68 A6
Yoke Cl HOLWY N7.....84 E4
Yolande Gdns ELTH/MOT SE9 ....146 D6
Yonge Pk HOLWY N7.....85 G1
York Av BFN/LL DA15.....167 K4
  HNWL W7 ....115 K1
  HYS/HAR UB3 .....94 A5
  KTN/HRWW/W HA3.....43 H4
  MORT/ESHN SW14.....137 K6
York Br CAMTN NW1 .....3 G6
York Buildings CHCR WC2N.....11 F6
York Cl CMBW SE5 * 142 D3
  EHAM E6.....107 K5
  HNWL W7 .....115 K1
  MRDN SM4.....194 A1
York Gdns WOT/HER KT12.....188 C6
York Ga CAMTN NW1 .....3 H7
  STHGT/OAK N14.....34 C2

York Gv PECK SE15.....143 K2
York Hl STRHM/NOR SW16.....162 C5
York House Pl KENS W8 * 120 A2
Yorkland Av WELL DA16.....148 A5
York Ms IL IG1.....72 A6
  KTTN NW5.....84 B5
York Pde BTFD TW8 *.....116 E5
  CDALE/KGS NW9 *.....63 J5
York Pl BTSEA SW11.....140 B4
  IL IG1 ....72 A6
York Ri KTTN NW5.....84 B1
  ORP BR6.....201 K5
York Rd ACT W3.....98 E5
  BAR EN5.....21 G6
  BELMT SM2.....208 E4
  BTSEA SW11.....140 B5
  CHING E4.....51 J1
  CROY/NA CRO.....196 B4
  DART DA1.....151 J6
  EA W5....116 D3
  FBAR/BDGN N11.....48 D2
  FSTGT E7.....88 E4
  HSLW TW3.....135 G4
  IL IG1 ....90 A1
  KUTN/CMB KT2.....175 G3
  LEY E10.....88 A1
  NTHWD HA6.....40 E5
  RAIN RM13.....93 F5
  RCHPK/HAM TW10.....137 G6
  STHWK SE1.....17 H2
  TEDD TW11.....155 K6
  UED N18....50 D1
  WALTH E17.....69 F2
  WCHMH N21.....35 K2
  WIM/MER SW19.....178 A2
Yorkshire Cl STNW/STAM N16....86 A1
Yorkshire Gdns UED N18.....50 D1
Yorkshire Grey Yd HHOL WC1V *....11 G2
Yorkshire Rd MTCM CR4.....195 K2
  POP/IOD E14 .....105 G5
York Sq POP/IOD E14 * 105 G5
York St BARK IG11.....90 B6
  MBLAR W1H 8 E2
  MHST W1U.....9 F4
  TWK TW1 .....156 B3

York St Chambers MHST W1U * 9 F1
York Ter ENC/FH EN2 .....23 J1
  ERITH DA8.....149 K2
York Ter East CAMTN NW1.....3 H7
York Ter West CAMTN NW1.....3 G7
Yorkton St BETH E2.....104 C1
York Wy CHSGTN KT9.....205 K5
  FELT TW13.....154 E5
  IS N1 .....5 F2
  TRDG/WHET N20.....33 K5
York Way Ct IS N1.....5 F2
York Way Est HOLWY N7.....84 E4
Youngmans Cl ENC/FH EN2.....23 J2
Young Rd CAN/RD E16.....107 G5
Youngs Rd GNTH/NBYPK IG2.....72 D2
Young St KENS W8.....120 A2
Yoxley Ap GNTH/NBYPK IG2.....72 C3
Yoxley Dr GNTH/NBYPK IG2.....72 C3
Yukon Rd BAL SW12.....161 G2
Yuletide Cl WLSDN NW10.....81 G4
Yunus Khan Cl WALTH E17.....69 J2

Z

Zambezie Dr ED N9.....36 E5
Zampa Rd BERM/RHTH SE16....123 K5
Zander Ct BETH E2.....104 C2
Zangwill Rd BKHTH/KID SE3.....146 C2
Zealand Av WDR/YW UB7.....132 A1
Zealand Rd BOW E3.....105 G1
Zelah Rd STMC/STPC BR5.....202 C4
Zennor Rd BAL SW12.....161 H3
Zenoria St EDUL SE22.....143 G5
Zermatt Rd THHTH CR7.....196 D1
Zetland St POP/IOD E14.....106 A4
Zion Pl THHTH CR7.....196 E1
Zion Rd THHTH CR7.....196 E1
Zoar St STHWK SE1.....12 C7
Zoffany St ARCH N19.....66 D6

Index - featured places

22 Jermyn Street Hotel
  STJS SW1Y 10 B6
AAIS
  DART DA1 .....171 H2
Aarotya Medical Centre
  TOTM N17 .....67 J1
Abbey Business Centre
  VX/NE SW8 .....141 K2
The Abbey Clinic
  BELV DA17.....129 C5
Abbey College London
  BAY/PAD W2.....100 E5
The Abbey Court Townhouse
  Hotel BAY/PAD W2.....100 E6
Abbey Industrial Estate
  ALP/SUD HA0.....80 B6
  MTCM CR4.....194 D2
Abbey Lane Commercial
  Estate SRTFD E15.....106 B1
Abbey Medical Centre
  STJWD NW8.....83 F6
Abbey Mills
  WIM/MER SW19.....178 B4
Abbey Park Industrial Estate
  BARK IG11.....90 C6
Abbey Primary School
  ABYW SE2.....128 D3
  MRDN SM4.....193 K4
Abbey (rems of)
  ABYW SE2 .....128 C6
Abbey Road Health Centre
  SRTFD E15.....88 C6
Abbey Road Studios
  STJWD NW8.....101 G1
Abbey School for the English
  Language STJWD NW8.....101 G1
Abbey Sports Centre
  BARK IG11.....90 C6
Abbey Trading Estate
  SYD SE26.....182 B1
Abbey Wharf Industrial Estate
  BARK IG11.....108 D2
Abbey Wood School
  ABYW SE2.....128 B3
Abbotsbury Primary School
  MRDN SM4.....193 K2
ABC Cinema
  CAT SE6.....164 E3
  HAMP NW3.....83 J3
  PUT/ROE SW15.....139 H4
Abercorn School
  MBLAR W1H.....8 E2
  STJWD NW8.....101 G1
Abercorn Trading Estate
  ALP/SUD HA0.....79 K6
Aberdeen Wharf WAP
  E1W.....123 J1
Abergden Industrial Estate
  HYS/HAR UB3.....113 G2
Abney Park Cemetery
  STNW/STAM N16.....68 A4
Acacia Business Centre
  WAN E11.....88 C1
The Academy at Peckham
  PECK SE15.....143 G2
The Academy School
  HAMP NW3.....83 H2
Acland Burghley School
  KTTN NW5.....84 B2

Acorn Industrial Park
  DART DA1.....170 C1
Acorn Medical Centre
  TWK TW1.....156 B3
Acre Road Health Clinic
  KUTN/CMB KT2.....175 G3
Acton Business Centre
  WLSDN NW10.....99 F3
Acton Central
  Industrial Estate
  ACT W3.....98 D6
Acton Health Centre
  ACT W3.....117 K1
Acton High School
  ACT W3.....117 H2
Acton Hospital
  ACT W3.....117 H2
Acton Lane Medical Centre
  CHSWK W4.....118 A2
Acton Park Industrial Estate
  ACT W3.....118 C1
  CHSWK W4.....118 A2
Acton Swimming Baths
  ACT W3.....117 K1
Acton & West London College
  ACT W3.....117 J1
Acumen (Anglo School)
  NRWD SE19.....181 F4
Adams Bridge Business Centre
  WBLY HA9.....80 D3
Adamsrill Primary School
  FSTH SE23.....164 B5
Adath Yisroel Cemetery
  EN N1.....24 B2
Addey & Stanhope School
  NWCR SE14.....144 C2
The Addington Golf Club
  CROY/NA CRO.....213 H6
Addington Palace Golf Club
  CROY/NA CRO.....213 G4
Addiscombe CC
  CROY/NA CRO.....212 C1
Addison Primary School
  WKENS W14.....119 G3
Adelphi Theatre
  COVGDN WC2E.....11 F6
Adler Industrial Estate
  HYS/HAR UB3.....113 G2
Admiral Hyson Industrial
  Estate BERM/RHTH SE16 ....123 J4
Admiralty Arch
  STJS SW1Y.....10 D7
ADT Technology College
  PUT/ROE SW15.....139 J6
The Adult College of Barking
  & Dagenham BARK IG11.....90 E4
Adult Education Centre
  DART DA1.....171 J2
  POP/IOD E14.....125 F3
Aerodrome Hotel
  CROY/NA CRO.....211 G4
Africa Centre
  COVGDN WC2E.....11 F5
Agora Shopping Centre
  PECK SE15.....143 H3
Ainslie Wood Primary School
  CHING E4.....51 K1
Airbase Unity Elementary
  School HGDN/ICK UB10....58 A6

Airbus Coach Station
  HTHAIR TW6.....132 C4
Air Call Business Centre
  CDALE/KGS NW9.....45 F6
Airedale Physiotherapy Clinic
  CHSWK W4.....118 C5
Airlinks Golf Club
  NWDGN UB2.....114 B4
Air Links Industrial Estate
  HEST TW5.....114 B5
Airport Gate
  Business Centre
  WDR/YW UB7.....132 C1
Aksaray Sports Club
  STNW/STAM N16.....85 K2
Albany Centre & Theatre
  DEPT SE8.....144 C1
Albany Clinic
  BFN/LL DA15.....168 B6
  WIM/MER SW19.....178 A5
The Albany College
  HDN NW4.....63 K2
Albany Park Canoe &
  Sailing Centre
  KUTN/CMB KT2.....174 E2
Albany School Grant
  Maintained PEND EN3.....25 F1
The Albany School
  HCH RM12.....75 K6
Albemarle Independent
  College BAY/PAD W2 *.....101 F6
Albemarle Primary School
  WIM/MER SW19.....159 H4
Albert Memorial
  SKENS SW7.....14 A2
Albery Theatre
  CHCR WC2N.....10 E5
Albion Health Centre
  WCHPL E1.....104 D4
Albion J & I School
  BERM/RHTH SE16.....123 K2
Albion Street Health Centre
  BERM/RHTH SE16.....123 K2
Albright Industrial Estate
  RAIN RM13.....111 H4
The Alchemy Gallery
  CLKNW EC1R.....5 J6
Alderbrook Primary School
  BAL SW12.....161 G2
Aldersbrook County
  Secondary School
  MNPK E12.....71 G5
Aldersbrook Primary School
  WAN E11.....71 F5
Alderwood Primary School
  ELTH/MOT SE9.....167 J1
Aldgate Bus Station
  HDTCH EC3A.....13 J3
Aldwych Theatre
  HOL/ALD WC2B.....11 G4
Alexander Mcleod Primary
  School ABYW SE2.....128 C5
Alexandra Avenue Clinic
  RYLN/HDSTN HA2.....59 K6
Alexandra Business Centre
  PEND EN3.....25 F5
Alexandra Infant School
  KUTN/CMB KT2.....175 H3
  PGE/AN SE20.....182 A3

Alexandra Junior School
  HSLW TW3.....135 G3
  SYD SE26.....182 A2
Alexandra Palace
  WDGN N22.....48 D6
Alexandra Palace Ice Rink
  WDGN N22.....48 D5
Alexandra Park School
  FBAR/BDGN N11.....48 B5
Alexandra Primary School
  WDGN N22.....49 F5
Alfred Salter Primary School
  BERM/RHTH SE16.....124 A2
Alfreds Way Industrial Estate
  BARK IG11.....91 G6
Allenby Primary School
  STHL UB1.....96 A5
Allen Edwards
  Primary School
  CLAP SW4.....141 K2
The All England Lawn Tennis
  & Croquet Club
  WIM/MER SW19.....159 G5
Allergy Clinic
  CAVSQ/HST W1G.....9 J2
Alleyns School
  EDUL SE22.....143 F6
Allfarthing JMI School
  WAND/EARL SW18.....160 B1
Alma Primary School
  BERM/RHTH SE16.....123 H4
  PEND EN3.....25 G6
Almeida Theatre
  IS N1.....85 H5
Al Sadiq & Al-Zahra High
  School KIL/WHAMP NW6....82 C6
Al Saints Benhilton CE
  Primary School SUT SM1.....209 F1
All Saints Catholic School
  BCTR RM8.....74 C5
All Saints CE Junior School
  NRWD SE19.....181 F4
All Saints CE Primary School
  BKHTH/KID SE3.....145 H3
  CRICK NW2.....82 D1
  FUL/PGN SW6.....139 H5
  PUT/ROE SW15.....139 H4
  TRDG/WHET N20.....33 H4
  WIM/MER SW19.....178 B5
All Souls CE Primary School
  GTPST W1W.....10 A2
Alium Medical Centre
  WAN E11.....70 B4

Alpine Business Centre
  EHAM E6.....108 A4
Alscot Road
  Industrial Estate
  STHWK SE1.....19 K6
Altmore Infant School
  EHAM E6.....89 K5
The Alton School
  PUT/ROE SW15.....158 C2
Amber Primary School
  FSBYPK N4.....85 H1
Ambleside Junior School
  WOT/HER KT12.....188 B5
AMC Business Centre
  WLSDN NW10.....98 D2
American Intercontinental
  University MHST W1U.....9 H2
American School in London
  STJWD NW8.....83 G6
Amherst Primary School
  HACK E8.....86 C3
Ampthill Square Medical
  Centre CAMTN NW1 ..... 4 A3
Anchorage Point
  Industrial Estate
  CHARL SE7.....126 B3
Anchor Bay Industrial
  Estate
  ERITH DA8.....150 C1
Anchor Retail Park
  WCHPL E1.....104 E3
Andover Medical Centre
  HOLWY N7.....85 F1
The Andrew Ewing Primary
  School HEST TW5.....134 E1
Andrew Sketchley Theatre
  WCHPL E1.....104 C4
Anerley School
  PGE/AN SE20.....181 H4
Angel Centre
  DART DA1.....171 H1
Angerstein Business Park
  GNWCH SE10.....125 K4
Anglian Industrial Estate
  BARK IG11.....109 F5
Animal Cemetery
  REDBR IG4.....53 H6
Annexmount School
  EFNCH N2.....65 G3
Annunciation RC Infant
  School EDGW HA8.....45 F4
The Annunciation RC Junior
  School MLHL NW7.....45 F2
Anson Primary School
  CRICK NW2.....82 B3
Ante Natal Clinic
  MUSWH N10.....48 A6
Antonys RC Primary
  School WFD IG8.....38 E6
Apex Industrial Estate
  WLSDN NW10.....99 H3
Apex Retail Park
  FELT TW13.....154 E5
Apollo Theatre
  SOHO/SHAV W1D.....10 C5
Apollo Victoria Theatre
  PIM SW1V.....16 A5

Apostolic Nuncio
WIM/MER SW19 ....159 F5
Applegarth Primary School
CROY/NA CR0 ....213 K4
Apsley House,
The Wellington Museum
BAY/PAD W2 ....15 G2
Aquarius Business Park
CRICK NW2 ....63 J5
Aquarius Golf Club
PECK SE15 ....143 K6
Aragon Primary School
MRDN SM4 ....193 H4
Arcadia Shopping Centre
EA W5 ....97 K6
The Archbishop Lanfranc
School CROY/NA CR0 ....195 K3
Archbishop Michael Ramsey
School CMBW SE5 ....142 C1
Archbishop Summers CE
Primary School LBTH SE11 ...17 K7
Archbishop Tenisons CE
School CROY/NA CR0 ....212 B1
Archbishop Tenison's School
VX/NE SW8 ....122 A6
Archdale Business Centre
RYLN/HDSTN HA2 ....60 C6
Archdeacon Cambridge's CE
Primary School
WHTN TW2 ....155 K4
Arches Business Centre
NWDGN UB2 ....114 E2
Arches Leisure Centre
CNWCH SE10 ....125 G6
Archgate Business Centre
NFNCH/WDSP N12 ....33 G6
Archway Business Centre
ARCH N19 ....84 D1
Archway Leisure Centre
ARCH N19 ....66 C6
Arena Estate
FSBYPK N4 ....67 H3
Argyle Primary School
STPAN WC1H 5 F5
Arklow Trading Estate
NWCR SE14 ....124 B6
Armourers & Braziers' Hall
LOTH EC2R 12 E3
Arndale Health Centre
WAND/EARL SW18 ....159 K1
Arnhem Wharf Primary
School POP/IOD E14 ....124 C3
Arnold House School
STJWD NW8 ....2 A2
Arnos Pool
FBAR/BDGN N11 ....48 D1
Arnot Abbey
FARR EC1M 12 A1
Arsenal FC (Highbury)
HBRY N5 ....85 G1
Arts Centre
BMLY BR1 ....184 C4
HAMP NW3 ....83 F5
Art School
BECK BR3 ....198 B2
The Arts Educational School
CHSWK W4 ....118 B4
Arts Theatre
LSO/SEVD WC2H 10 D5
PUT/ROE SW15 ....139 G5
Ashbourne College
KENS W8 ....120 A2
Ashburnham Primary School
WBPTN SW10 ....140 C1
Ashburton Community
School CROY/NA CR0 ....197 J4
Ashburton Primary School
CROY/NA CR0 ....197 J3
Ashby Mill School
CLAP SW4 ....141 K6
Ashfield Junior School
BUSH WD23 ....28 B2
Ashford Clinic
ASHF TW15 ....152 B5
Ashford High School
ASHF TW15 ....152 B5
Ashford Hospital A & E
ASHF TW15 ....152 B4
Ashford Industrial Estate
ASHF TW15 ....155 F6
Ashford Sports Club
ASHF TW15 ....152 A6
STWL/WRAY TW19 ....152 C3
Ashgrove College
WALTH E17 ....51 J6
Ashgrove Trading Estate
BMLY BR1 ....183 G2
Ashleigh Commercial Estate
CHARL SE7 ....126 B4
Ashmead Primary School
DEPT SE8 ....144 D3
Ashmole Centre
STHGT/OAK N14 ....34 C3
Ashmole Primary School
VX/NE SW8 ....122 A6
Ashmole School
STHGT/OAK N14 ....34 C3
Ashmount Primary School
ARCH N19 ....66 D4
Ashton House School
ISLW TW7 ....135 J2
Ashton Playing Fields Track
WFD IG8 ....53 J2
Aspen House School
CMBW SE5 ....122 C6
Aspen House Secondary &
Primary School
BRXS/STRHM SW2 ....161 K3
Asquith Court School
HPTN TW12 ....173 G4
KTN/HRWW/WS HA3 ....61 H3
Asquith School
PEND EN3 ....24 E5
Assembly Rooms
KUT/HW KT1 ....191 F1

Associated Newspapers
BERM/RHTH SE16 ....124 A3
Aston Clinic
NWMAL KT3 ....192 B1
Aston House School
EA W5 ....97 K5
Asylum Medical Centre
CEND/HSY/T N8 ....49 G6
Atfoulks Lynch College
FLST/FETLN EC4A 12 A3
Atheley Primary School
CAT SE6 ....164 D5
Athelstan House School
HPTN TW12 ....173 F4
Athenaeum Hotel
MYFR/PICC W1J 15 J1
Athena Medical Centre
CLPT E5 ....86 E2
Atherton Leisure Centre
FSTGT E7 ....88 D4
Athlone House Hospital
HGT N6 ....65 K5
Athlon Industrial Estate
ALP/SUD HA0 ....97 K1
Atkinson Morley Hospital
RYNPK SW20 ....176 E3
Atlas Business Centre
CRICK NW2 ....63 K6
Atlas Transport Estate
BTSEA SW11 ....140 B3
Attlee Youth &
Community Centre
WCHPL E1 ....13 J2
Auriol Junior School
HOR/WEW KT19 ....207 H2
Australia House
HOL/ALD WC2B 11 H4
Aveling Park School
WALTH E17 ....51 J5
Avenue House School
WEA W13 ....97 H5
Avenue Industrial Estate
CHING E4 ....51 H2
Avenue Primary School
KIL/WHAMP NW6 ....82 C5
MNPK E12 ....89 J2
Avigdor Primary School
STNW/STAM N16 ....67 K6
Avondale Park Primary School
NTGHL W11 ....100 B6
Avon House School
WFD IG8 ....38 E6
Avon Trading Estate
WKENS W14 ....119 J4
Axis Business Centre
SRTFD E15 ....87 K6
The Aylesham Centre
PECK SE15 ....143 H2
Ayloff Primary School
HCH RM12 ....93 K2
Aylward F & M Schools
STAN HA7 ....43 K1
Aylward School
UED N18 ....35 K6
Aylwin Secondary School
BERM/RHTH SE16 ....19 K6
BAA Heathrow Visitor
Centre
HTHAIR TW6 ....132 E2
Babington House School
CHST BR7 ....184 E2
Back Care Clinic
WPK KT4 ....192 D5
Bacon's College
BERM/RHTH SE16 ....124 B1
Baden Powell House
SKENS SW7 ....120 B4
Baden Powell Primary
School CLPT E5 ....86 D1
Bakers Hall
MON EC3R 13 H6
Balaam Leisure Centre
PLSTW E13 ....106 E3
Balfour Business Centre
NWDGN UB2 ....114 C3
Balgowan Primary School
BECK BR3 ....182 B5
Balham Health Centre
BAL SW12 ....161 G4
Balham Leisure Centre
TOOT SW17 ....161 F4
Balmoral Trading
BARK IG11 ....109 F4
Baltic Exchange
HDTCH EC3A 13 H3
Bancrofts School
WFD IG8 ....38 E5
Bandon Hill Cemetery
WLGTN SM6 ....210 D3
Bandon Hill Primary School
WLGTN SM6 ....210 D4
Bangabandhu Primary
School BETH E2 ....104 E2
Bank of England
LOTH EC2R 12 E4
Bank of England Extension
STP EC4M 12 C4
Bankside Gallery
STHWK SE1 ....12 B6
Bankside Jetty
STHWK SE1 ....12 C6
Bankside Park Industrial
Estate BARK IG11 ....109 G2
Bannister Stadium
KTN/HRWW/WS HA3 ....42 C2
Bannockburn Primary
School WOOL/PLUM SE18 ...128 A4
Banqueting House
WHALL SW1A 16 E1
Barber Surgeons' Hall
BARB EC2Y 12 D2
Barbican Cinema
BARB EC2Y 12 C1
The Barbican
BARB EC2Y 12 C1

Barbican Theatre
BARB EC2Y 12 D1
Barclay J & I School
LEY E10 ....70 B3
Barham Primary School
ALP/SUD HA0 ....79 J4
Baring Primary School
LEE/GVPK SE12 ....165 K2
Baring Road Medical Centre
LEE/GVPK SE12 ....165 K1
Barkantine Clinic
POP/IOD E14 ....124 D2
Barking Abbey Comprehensive
School (Lower) BARK IG11 .....90 D3
Barking Abbey Comprehensive
School (Upper) BARK IG11 .....91 F4
Barking Abbey Industrial Estate
BARK IG11 ....90 B6
Barking Abbey Leisure Centre
BARK IG11 ....91 G4
Barking College
ROMW/RG RM7 ....75 F6
Barking FC
BCTR RM8 ....91 H3
Barking Hospital
BARK IG11 ....91 F5
Barking industrial Park
BARK IG11 ....91 F6
Barking RUFC
DAGW RM9 ....91 K6
Barkingside Cemetery
BARK/HLT IG6 ....54 B6
Barkingside FC
BARK/HLT IG6 ....72 D1
Barlby Primary School
NKENS W10 ....100 B3
Barley Lane Primary School
GDMY/SEVK IG3 ....73 G4
Barnabas Medical Centre
NTHLT UB5 ....78 C4
Barn Croft Primary School
WALTH E17 ....69 G3
Barnehurst Primary School
BXLYHN DA7 ....149 K2
Barnehurst Public Pay & Play
Golf Club BXLYHN DA7 ....150 A4
Barn Elms Athletics Track
BARN SW13 ....138 E3
Barn Elms Water Sports Centre
BARN SW13 ....139 F3
Barnes Clay Primary School
DART DA1 ....150 D5
Barnes Hospital
MORT/ESHN SW14 ....138 B4
Barnes Primary School
BARN SW13 ....138 B4
Barnes Sports Club
BARN SW13 ....138 C2
Barnet College
BAR EN5 ....20 D5
CDALE/KGS NW9 ....45 H4
NFNCH/WDSP N12 ....47 G1
Barnet Copthall Pool
HDN NW4 ....45 K3
Barnet Copthall Stadium
HDN NW4 ....46 A4
Barnet County Court
BAR EN5 ....21 G5
FNCH N3 ....46 E4
Barnet FC (Underhill)
BAR EN5 ....20 E6
Barnet General Hospital
BAR EN5 ....20 B5
Barnet Health Centre
BAR EN5 ....20 E6
Barnet Hill JMI School
BAR EN5 ....20 D6
Barnet Hospital Chest Clinic
BAR EN5 ....20 B5
Barnet Magistrates Court
BAR EN5 ....20 D5
Barnet Museum
BAR EN5 ....20 C5
Barnet Trading Estate
BAR EN5 ....20 D4
Barnfield Primary School
EDGW HA8 ....44 E4
Barnhill Community High
School YEAD UB4 ....95 F2
Barn Hotel
RSLP HA4 ....58 C6
Barnsbury School for Girls
IS N1 ....85 G4
Barons Court Theatre
WKENS W14 ....119 H5
Barratt Industrial Park
BOW E3 ....106 A3
Barrett Industrial Park
STHL UB1 ....115 F1
Barrett Way Industrial Estate
HRW HA1 ....42 D6
Barrington Primary School
BXLYHN DA7 ....148 E3
Barrow Hedges Primary
School CAR SM5 ....209 J5
Barrow Hill Junior School
STJWD NW8 ....2 C3
Barton House Health Centre
STNW/STAM N16 ....85 K1
Barwell Business Park
CHSGTN KT9 ....205 K5
Basil Street Hotel
KTBR SW1X 14 E3
Bassett House School
NKENS W10 ....100 B5
Baston School
HAYES BR2 ....200 A6
Bath Factory Estate
HNHL SE24 ....162 D1
Battersea Business Centre
BTSEA SW11 ....141 F4
Battersea Dogs' Home
VX/NE SW8 ....141 G1
Battersea Power Station
(disused) VX/NE SW8 ....121 G6

Battersea Sports Centre
BTSEA SW11 ....140 C4
Battersea
Technology College
BTSEA SW11 ....140 E2
Battersea Tutorial College
LEE/GVPK SE12 ....161 F4
BBC Broadcasting House
REGST W1B 9 K2
BBC Studios
MV/WKIL W9 ....101 F3
BBC Television Centre
SHB W12 ....100 A6
BBC White City
SHB W12 ....100 A6
BBC Worldwide
SHB W12 ....100 A5
Beal High School
REDBR IG4 ....53 J6
Beam Primary School
DAGE RM10 ....110 E1
Beatrice Tate School
BETH E2 ....104 D2
Beatrix Potter Primary
School
WAND/EARL SW18 ....160 B3
Beauclerc Infant School
SUN TW16 ....172 B6
The Beaufort Hotel
CHEL SW3 ....14 E5
Beaumont Primary School
LEY E10 ....69 K4
Beaver College
BAY/PAD W2 ....100 E6
The Beavers Comm Primary
School HSLWW TW4 ....134 B4
Beaverwood School for Girls
CHST BR7 ....185 K2
Beckenham Business Centre
BECK BR3 ....182 B2
Beckenham Crematorium
SNWD SE25 ....181 K6
Beckenham CC
BECK BR3 ....182 E5
Beckenham Hospital
BECK BR3 ....182 C5
Beckenham Leisure Centre
BECK BR3 ....182 C5
Beckenham Place Park Golf
Course BECK BR3 ....182 B4
Beckenham RFC
BECK BR3 ....198 B1
Beckenham Town FC
BECK BR3 ....198 D2
Becket Sports Centre
DART DA1 ....171 F1
Beckford Primary School
KIL/WHAMP NW6 ....82 D3
Beckmead School
BECK BR3 ....198 D5
The Beck Theatre
HYS/HAR UB3 ....94 D5
Beckton Ski Centre
EHAM E6 ....108 A3
Beckton Special School
CAN/RD E16 ....107 H4
Beckton Triangle Retail Park
EHAM E6 ....108 B2
Becontree Day Hospital
BCTR RM8 ....74 A6
Becontree Primary School
BCTR RM8 ....91 H1
Bective House Clinic
PUT/ROE SW15 ....139 J5
Beddington Infants School
WLGTN SM6 ....210 C1
Beddington Medical Centre
CROY/NA CR0 ....210 E2
Beddington Park Primary
School CROY/NA CR0 ....210 D1
Beddington Trading Estate
CROY/NA CR0 ....195 K5
Bedelsford School
KUT/HW KT1 ....175 F6
Bedensfield Clinic
SCUP DA14 ....187 F1
Bedfont Health Centre
EBED/NFELT TW14 ....153 H2
Bedfont Industrial Park
FELT TW13 ....153 G5
Bedfont J & I School
EBED/NFELT TW14 ....153 H1
Bedfont Lakes Country Park
EBED/NFELT TW14 ....153 F4
Bedington Infant School
WLGTN SM6 ....210 C2
Bedonwell Clinic
ABYW SE2 ....128 E3
Bedonwell Medical Centre
BELV DA17 ....129 G5
Bedonwell Primary School
BELV DA17 ....129 F5
Beecholme Primary School
MTCM CR4 ....179 G4
Beechwood School
STRHM/NOR SW16 ....161 K4
Beechwood Preparatory School
REDBR IG4 ....71 K1
The Beehive School
ARCH N19 ....66 D4
Beis Rochel D'Satmar Girls
School
STNW/STAM N16 ....68 A4
Beis Trana Girls School
STNW/STAM N16 ....68 A4
Beis Yaakov Primary School
CDALE/KGS NW9 ....45 F6
Bellamy's Wharf
BERM/RHTH SE16 ....124 A1
Bellenden Primary School
PECK SE15 ....143 H4
Bellenden Road Business
Centre PECK SE15 ....143 G3
Bellenden Road Retail Park
PECK SE15 ....143 G2

Belleville Primary School
BTSEA SW11 ....140 E6
Belle Vue Cinema
WLSDN NW10 ....81 K5
Bell Industrial Estate
CHSWK W4 ....117 K4
Bellingham Trading Estate
CAT SE6 ....164 E5
Bell Lane JMI School
HDN NW4 ....64 B1
Belmont F & M School
KTN/HRWW/W HA3 ....43 F5
Belmont J & I School
WDGN N22 ....49 J6
Belmont (Mill Hill Junior School)
MLHL NW7 ....31 J5
Belmont Park School
LEY E10 ....70 A3
Belmore Primary School
BXLYHN DA7 ....149 H1
Belmore School
NTHLT UB5 ....95 F2
Belvedere Day Hospital
WLSDN NW10 ....81 J6
Belvedere Industrial Estate
BELV DA17 ....130 A1
Belvedere Link Business Centre
BELV DA17 ....129 K3
Belvedere Primary School
BELV DA17 ....129 J4
Belvue Business Centre
NTHLT UB5 ....78 B5
Belvue School
NTHLT UB5 ....78 A6
Benedict House
Preparatory School
BFN/LL DA15 ....168 A6
Benedict Primary School
MTCM CR4 ....178 C6
Benhurst JMI School
HCH RM12 ....93 K1
Ben Jonson Primary School
WCHPL E1 ....105 G3
Bensham Manor School
THHTH CR7 ....196 D2
Benson Primary School
CROY/NA CR0 ....213 G1
Bentall Shopping Centre
KUT/HW KT1 ....174 E5
Benthal Primary School
STNW/STAM N16 ....86 C1
Bentley Wood Girls School
STAN HA7 ....43 F1
Bentworth Primary School
SHB W12 ....99 K5
Beormund School
STHWK SE1 ....18 E3
Berger Primary School
HOM E9 ....87 F4
Berjaya Eden Park Hotel
BAY/PAD W2 ....101 F6
The Berkeley Hotel
KTBR SW1X 15 G2
Berkeley Primary School
HEST TW5 ....114 C6
Berlitz Schools of Languages
LINN WC2A 11 J2
Bermondsey Town Hall
STHWK SE1 ....19 K5
Bermondsey Trading Estate
BERM/RHTH SE16 ....123 K4
Berrymede Infant School
ACT W3 ....117 J2
Berrymede Junior School
ACT W3 ....117 J2
Bertram House School
TOOT SW17 ....161 F4
Bessemer Grange J & I School
EDUL SE22 ....145 F3
Bessemer Park Industrial
Estate BRXN/ST SW9 ....142 C5
Best Western Cumberland
Hotel HRW HA1 ....61 F3
Best Western Hotel
HAMP NW3 ....83 H5
Best Western
Master Robert Hotel
HEST TW5 ....134 E2
Beth Jacob Grammar School
HDN NW4 ....64 A1
Bethlem Royal Hospital
BECK BR3 ....198 D4
Bethnal Green Museum of
Childhood BETH E2 ....104 D2
Bethnal Green Technology
College BETH E2 ....7 K5
Beths Grammar School
for Boys BXLY DA5 ....169 H1
Beulah Infant School
THHTH CR7 ....180 D5
Beverley School
NWMAL KT3 ....192 D2
Beverley Trading Estate
MRDN SM4 ....193 G4
Bevington Primary School
NKENS W10 ....100 C4
Bexley College
ERITH DA8 ....129 K4
Bexley CC
BXLY DA5 ....169 H3
Bexley Grammar School
WELL DA16 ....148 C5
Bexleyheath Centre
BXLYHS DA6 ....149 F5
Bexleyheath Golf Club
BXLYHS DA6 ....149 F6
Bexleyheath Marriott Hotel
BXLYHS DA6 ....149 J5
Bexleyheath School
BXLYHN DA7 ....149 G4
Bexley Hospital
BXLY DA5 ....170 B4
Bexley RFC
BXLY DA5 ....169 H2

BFI London IMAX Cinema *STHWK* SE1 ...17 H1
Bickley Park CC *BMLY* BR1 ...184 D5
Bickley Park Preparatory School *BMLY* BR1 ...184 C6
Bickley Park School *BMLY* BR1 ...184 D5
Big Ben *WEST* SW1P ...17 F3
Bigland Green Primary School *WCHPL* E1 ...104 D6
Billingsgate Fish Market *POP/IOD* E14 ...124 E1
Bingham Hotel *RCHPK/HAM* TW10 ...157 F1
Birbeck College *RSQ* WC1B ...10 D2
Birchmere Business Park *THMD* SE28 ...128 A2
Birchwood Park Golf Club *RDART* DA2 ...187 K3
Bird College *SCUP* DA14 ...168 D5
Birkbeck College *STPAN* WC1H ...4 D7
Birkbeck Primary School *SCUP* DA14 ...168 C5
Bishop Challoner RC School *WCHPL* E1 ...104 E6
Bishop Challoner Girls School *WCHPL* E1 ...104 C6
Bishop Challoner School *HAYES* BR2 ...183 G5
Bishop Douglas RC School *EFNCH* N2 ...47 G5
Bishop Gilpin Primary School *WIM/MER* SW19 ...177 J1
Bishop John Robinson CE Primary School *THMD* SE28 ...109 J6
Bishop Justus CE (Secondary) School *HAYES* BR2 ...200 D4
Bishop Perrin CE Primary School *WHTN* TW2 ...155 G2
Bishop Ramsey CE School (Upper) *RSLP* HA4 ...58 E4
Bishop Ramsey CE School *RSLP* HA4 ...58 D4
Bishopsgate Institute *WCHPL* E1 ...13 H2
Bishop Stopford's School *EN* EN1 ...24 C3
Bishop Thomas Grant School *STRHM/NOR* SW16 ...180 A1
Bishop Winnington-Ingram CE Primary School *RSLP* HA4 ...58 B3
Blackburn Trading Estate *STWL/WRAY* TW19 ...152 C1
Blackfen School for Girls *BFN/LL* DA15 ...168 B1
Blackfriars Millennium Pier *EMB* EC4Y ...11 K5
Blackfriars Pier *BLKFR* EC4V ...12 B5
Blackheath Bluecoat CE School *BKHTH/KID* SE3 ...146 A1
Blackheath Business Estate *CNWCH* SE10 ...145 F2
The Blackheath Clinic *BKHTH/KID* SE3 ...145 H4
Blackheath High School GDST *BKHTH/KID* SE3 ...145 J3
Blackheath High Senior School *BKHTH/KID* SE3 ...145 J4
Blackheath Hospital *BKHTH/KID* SE3 ...145 J4
Blackheath Preparatory School *BKHTH/KID* SE3 ...145 K2
Blackheath RFC (The Rectory Field) *BKHTH/KID* SE3 ...146 A1
Blackwall Trading Estate *POP/IOD* E14 ...106 B4
Blair Peach Primary School *STHL* UB1 ...114 C1
Blake College *GTPST* W1W ...10 A1
Blanche Nevile Special School *TOTM* N17 ...49 K2
Blanche Nevile School *MUSWH* N10 ...48 A6 / ...49 G4
Blenheim Business Centre *MTCM* CR4 ...178 E4
Blenheim Primary School *ORP* BR6 ...202 E6
Blenheim Shopping Centre *PGE/AN* SE20 ...181 K3
Blessed Dominic RC Primary School *CDALE/KGS* NW9 ...45 G5
Blessed John Roche Catholic School *POP/IOD* E14 ...105 H5
Blessed Sacrament RC Primary School *IS* N1 ...5 F1
Blood Transfusion Centre *EDGW* HA8 ...44 D3
Bloomfield Clinic Guys *STHWK* SE1 ...19 F2
Bloomsbury College *FUL/PGN* SW6 ...139 K1
Bloomsbury Theatre *STPAN* WC1H ...4 C7
Blossom House School *RYNPK* SW20 ...176 E3
Blossoms Inn Medical Centre *CITYW* EC2V ...12 D5
Blue Gate Fields Primary School *WCHPL* E1 ...104 E6
The Blue School *ISLW* TW7 ...136 B4
Blyth's Wharf *POP/IOD* E14 ...105 G6

BMI Medical Centre *CAVSQ/HST* W1G ...9 H2
Bnois Jerusalem School *STNW/STAM* N16 ...67 K4
The Bob Hope Theatre *ELTH/MOT* SE9 ...166 E1
Bodywise Natural Health Centre *BETH* E2 ...104 E2
Boleyn Cinema *EHAM* E6 ...107 H1
Bolingbroke Hospital *BTSEA* SW11 ...140 D6
Bolingbroke Primary School *BTSEA* SW11 ...140 C2
Bond First School *MTCM* CR4 ...178 E5
Bond Primary School *MTCM* CR4 ...178 E5
Bonner Primary School *BETH* E2 ...105 F1
Bonneville Primary School *CLAP* SW4 ...161 H1
The Bonnington in Bloomsbury Hotel *RSQ* WC1B ...11 F1
Bonus Pastor School *BMLY* BR1 ...165 H6
Boones Industrial Estate *RAIN* RM13 ...111 H3
Booster Cushion Theatre *WDGN* N22 ...49 F5
Borough Market *STHWK* SE1 ...12 E7
Boston Business Park *HNWL* W7 ...115 K3
Boston University *SKENS* SW7 ...120 B4
Botwell RC Primary School *HYS/HAR* UB3 ...113 J2
Boundary Business Park *MTCM* CR4 ...178 C5
Bounds Green Health Centre *FBAR/BDGN* N11 ...48 D3
Bounds Green Industrial Estate *FBAR/BDGN* N11 ...48 C2
Bounds Green Primary School *FBAR/BDGN* N11 ...48 E3
Bourne CP School *RSLP* HA4 ...77 G3
Bourne Hall Health Centre *EW* KT17 ...207 H6
Bourne Hall Museum *EW* KT17 ...207 H6
Bourne Road Industrial Park *DART* DA1 ...150 A6
Bourneside Sports Club *STHGT/OAK* N14 ...34 E3
Bousfield Primary School *ECT* SW5 ...120 A5
Boutcher CE Primary School *STHWK* SE1 ...19 J5
Bowater House *SKENS* SW7 ...14 E3
Bow County Court *BOW* E3 ...88 C4
Bowden House Clinic *HRW* HA1 ...60 E6
Bower Park School *ROM* RM1 ...57 G2
Bowes Primary School *FBAR/BDGN* N11 ...48 D1
Bowes Road Clinic *FBAR/BDGN* N11 ...48 C1
Bow Industrial Park *SRTFD* E15 ...87 J5
Bowling Alley
 ACT W3 ...98 C4
 BERM/RHTH SE16 ...124 A3
 BRXS/STRHM SW2 ...161 K4
 BXLYHS DA6 ...149 G5
 DAGE RM10 ...110 D1
 EHAM E6 ...108 A4
 FELT TW13 ...154 A4
 KUTN/CMB KT2 ...175 F5
 LEW SE13 ...145 F4
 NTHWD HA6 ...40 C3
 ORP BR6 ...202 B5
 ROM RM1 ...75 G2
 RYLN/HDSTN HA2 ...60 B2
 SURB KT6 ...191 J6
 SUT SM1 ...209 F3
Bowman Trading Estate *CDALE/KGS* NW9 ...44 C6
Bow Secondary School *BOW* E3 ...105 J1
Bow Street Magistrates Court *HOL/ALD* WC2B ...11 F4
Bow Triangle Business Centre *BOW* E3 ...105 J3
Boxgrove Primary School *ABYW* SE2 ...128 D3
Boys' Club *EDGW* HA8 ...44 C3
Brackenbury Health Centre *HMSMTH* W6 ...118 E3
Brackenbury Primary School *HMSMTH* W6 ...118 E3
Bracken Industrial Estate *BARK/HLT* IG6 ...55 F3
Brady Recreation Centre *WCHPL* E1 ...104 C4
Braeside Senior School *BKHH* IG9 ...39 F3
Braincroft Primary School *CRICK* NW2 ...81 H1
Braintree Road Industrial Estate *RSLP* HA4 ...77 F2
Bramah's Tea & Coffee Museum *STHWK* SE1 ...18 D1
Brampton Manor School *PLSTW* E13 ...107 H3
Brampton Primary School *BXLYHN* DA7 ...148 E3 / *EHAM* E6 ...107 J2
Brandlehow Primary School *PUT/ROE* SW15 ...139 J5

Branollys Health Centre *PLSTW* E13 ...106 E3
Breakspear Crematorium *RSLP* HA4 ...58 A2
Breaside Preparatory School *BMLY* BR1 ...184 B4
Breaside Pre Preparatory School *BMLY* BR1 ...183 K3
Brecknock Primary School *HOLWY* N7 ...84 D4
Bredinghurst School *PECK* SE15 ...143 K5
Brent Adult College *WLSDN* NW10 ...81 F6
Brent Arts Council *CRICK* NW2 ...81 J1
Brent Child & Family Clinic *WLSDN* NW10 ...81 H3
Brent Cross Shopping Centre *HDN* NW4 ...64 A4
Brentfield Medical Centre *WLSDN* NW10 ...81 F4
Brentfield Primary School *WLSDN* NW10 ...81 F4
Brentford Business Centre *BTFD* TW8 ...136 D1
The Brentford Clinic *BTFD* TW8 ...117 F6
Brentford County Court *BTFD* TW8 ...136 E1
Brentford FC London Broncos RLFC (Griffin Park) *BTFD* TW8 ...116 E6
Brentford Fountain Leisure Centre *CHSWK* W4 ...117 G5
Brentford Health Centre *BTFD* TW8 ...116 E6
Brentford Medical Centre *BTFD* TW8 ...136 E1
Brentford School for Girls *BTFD* TW8 ...116 E6
Brent Knoll School *FSTH* SE23 ...164 A5
Brent Magistrates Court House *WLSDN* NW10 ...81 G4
Brent Park Industrial Estate *NWDGN* UB2 ...114 A3
Brentside First School *HNWL* W7 ...96 E3
Brentside High School *HNWL* W7 ...96 E3
Brentside Primary School *HNWL* W7 ...96 E3
Brent Trading Estate *WLSDN* NW10 ...81 G3
Brent Valley Golf Club *HNWL* W7 ...96 E6
Brentwaters Business Park *BTFD* TW8 ...136 D1
Brewers' Hall *CITYW* EC2V ...12 D2
Brewery Industrial Estate *IS* N1 ...6 C3
Brewery Mews Business Centre *ISLW* TW7 ...136 A4
Brick Lane Music Hall *CAN/RD* E16 ...126 C1
Brick Lane Music House *WCHPL* E1 ...7 K7
Bricklayer Arms Industrial Estate *STHWK* SE1 ...19 J7
The Bridewell Theatre *EMB* EC4Y ...12 A4
The Bridge Business Centre *NWDGN* UB2 ...115 F2
The Bridge Hotel *GFD/PVL* UB6 ...96 C1
Bridge Lane Theatre *BTSEA* SW11 ...140 D2
The Bridge Leisure Centre *SYD* SE26 ...182 C1
Bridge Park Business & Leisure Centre *WLSDN* NW10 ...80 D5
The Bridge School *ARCH* N19 ...66 C6 / *CLKNW* EC1R ...6 A6
Brigham Young University *BAY/PAD* W2 ...100 A3
Bright Sparks Montessori School *WKENS* W14 ...119 G2
Brigstock Medical Centre *THHTH* CR7 ...196 C2
Brimsdown Industrial Estate *PEND* EN3 ...24 E3
Brimsdown Primary School *PEND* EN3 ...25 F4
Brindishe Primary School *LEE/GVPK* SE12 ...145 J6
Britain and London Visitor Centre *STJS* SW1Y ...10 C7
Britannia Business Centre *CRICK* NW2 ...82 B2
Britannia Leisure Centre *IS* N1 ...7 F1
Britannia Sports Ground *WALTH* E17 ...51 J3
Britannia Village Primary School *CAN/RD* E16 ...126 A1
British Airways London Eye *STHWK* SE1 ...17 G2
British Cartoon Centre *BMSBY* WC1N ...5 F7
British Dental Association *CAVSQ/HST* W1G ...9 J2
British Library *CAMTN* NW1 ...4 D4
British Library Newspaper *CDALE/KGS* NW9 ...45 G6
British Medical Association *STPAN* WC1H ...4 D6
British Museum *RSQ* WC1B ...10 E2

British Telecom Tower *GTPST* W1W ...10 A1
BRIT School for Performing Arts *SNWD* SE25 ...196 E5
Brittons School Technology College *RAIN* RM13 ...93 H5
Brixton Academy *BRXN/ST* SW9 ...142 B4
Brixton College for Further Education *BRXS/STRHM* SW2 ...142 A6
Brixton Recreation Centre *BRXN/ST* SW9 ...142 B4
Broadfields Infant School *EDGW* HA8 ...30 C4
Broadfields Junior School *EDGW* HA8 ...30 C4
Broadgate *LVPST* EC2M ...13 F1
Broadgate Ice Arena *LVPST* EC2M ...13 G2
Broadhurst School *KIL/WHAMP* NW6 ...83 G5
Broadmead Primary School *CROY/NA* CR0 ...196 E3
Broadwalk Shopping Centre *EDGW* HA8 ...44 C2
Broadwater Farm Primary School *TOTM* N17 ...49 K5
Broadwater Primary School *TOOT* SW17 ...160 C6
Broadway Clinic *EDGW* HA8 ...44 D4
Broadway Retail Park *CRICK* NW2 ...82 B2
Broadway Shopping Centre *BXLYHS* DA6 ...149 H5 / *HMSMTH* W6 ...119 F5
Broadway Square Shopping Centre *BXLYHN* DA7 ...149 H5
Broadway Squash & Fitness Centre *HMSMTH* W6 ...119 G4
Brocklebank Health Centre *WAND/EARL* SW18 ...160 A2
Brocklebank Industrial Estate *GNWCH* SE10 ...125 K4
Brockley Cross Business Centre *BROCKY* SE4 ...144 B4
Brockley Primary School *BROCKY* SE4 ...144 C6
Brockwell Lido *HNHL* SE24 ...162 C1
Bromet Primary School *OXHEY* WD19 ...27 H2
Bromley Cemetery *BMLY* BR1 ...183 J3
Bromley College of Further & Higher Education *BMLY* BR1 ...183 K4 / *HAYES* BR2 ...200 C5
Bromley County Court *BMLY* BR1 ...183 K4
Bromley Court Hotel *BMLY* BR1 ...183 H2
Bromley FC *BMLY* BR1 ...200 A2
Bromley Golf Club *HAYES* BR2 ...200 D4
Bromley High School GDST *BMLY* BR1 ...201 F1
Bromley Hospitals NHS Trust *ORP* BR6 ...217 F2
Bromley Industrial Centre *BMLY* BR1 ...184 C6
Bromley Mall Indoor Market *BMLY* BR1 ...183 K5
Bromley Museum *ORP* BR6 ...202 C4
Bromley Road Infant School *BECK* BR3 ...182 E4
Bromley Road Retail Park *CAT* SE6 ...164 E4
Bromley Tennis Centre *ORP* BR6 ...216 D1
Brompton Cemetery *WBPTN* SW10 ...120 A6
Brompton Medical Centre *WBPTN* SW10 ...120 A5
Brompton Oratory *SKENS* SW7 ...14 C5
Bromyard Leisure Centre *ACT* W3 ...118 B1
Brondesbury College for Boys *KIL/WHAMP* NW6 ...82 B5
Brooke Trading Estate *ROM* RM1 ...75 H4
Brookfield Primary School *CHEAM* SM3 ...193 H5 / *HGT* N6 ...66 B6
Brook House FC *YEAD* UB4 ...94 D2
Brook Industrial Estate *YEAD* UB4 ...114 C1
Brook Industrial Park *STMC/STPC* BR5 ...202 D1
Brookland Primary School *GLDGN* NW11 ...65 F1
Brooklands Primary School *BKHTH/KID* SE3 ...145 K4
Brook Lane Business Centre *BTFD* TW8 ...116 E5
Brookmarsh Trading Estate *DEPT* SE8 ...144 E1
Brookmead Industrial Estate *MTCM* CR4 ...195 H5
Brookside Primary School *YEAD* UB4 ...95 G2
Broomfield House School *RCH/KEW* TW9 ...137 G2
Broomfield School *STHGT/OAK* N14 ...48 D1
Broomsleigh Business Park *CAT* SE6 ...182 C1
Broomwood Hall *STRHM/NOR* SW16 ...161 H6

Broomwood Hall School *BAL* SW12 ...161 F1
Brothwick Wharf *DEPT* SE8 ...124 D5
Brownlow Medical Centre *FBAR/BDGN* N11 ...48 E1
Brown's Hotel *MYFR/PICC* W1J ...9 K6
Bruce Castle Museum *TOTM* N17 ...50 A4
Bruce Grove Primary School *TOTM* N17 ...50 B5
Brunel Engine House *BERM/RHTH* SE16 ...123 K2
Brunel University *GLDGN* NW11 ...64 B5 / *ISLW* TW7 ...135 K1 / *TWK* TW1 ...136 C5
Brunel University (Osterley Campus) Track *ISLW* TW7 ...135 K1
Brunswick Health Centre *FBAR/BDGN* N11 ...34 A4
Brunswick Housing & Shopping Centre *BMSBY* WC1N ...5 F6
Brunswick Industrial Park *FBAR/BDGN* N11 ...34 B6
Brunswick Medical Centre *BMSBY* WC1N ...4 E6
Brunswick Park JMI School *FBAR/BDGN* N11 ...34 A3
Brunswick Park Primary School *CMBW* SE5 ...142 E1
BT Centre *STBT* EC1A ...12 C3
Buckhurst Hill FC *BKHH* IG9 ...39 J3
Buckhurst Hill Primary School *BKHH* IG9 ...39 J4
Buckingham College Preparatory School *PIN* HA5 ...59 K3
Buckingham College School *HRW* HA1 ...60 E2
Buckingham Palace *WHALL* SW1A ...15 K3
Buckingham Primary School *HPTN* TW12 ...172 E1
Buckingham Road Cemetery *IL* IG1 ...72 D6
Buckland Infant School *CHSGTN* KT9 ...206 B3
Building Centre *GWRST* WC1E ...10 C2
Building Crafts College *SRTFD* E15 ...88 A5
Bullers Wood School *CHST* BR7 ...184 E4
Bullsbridge Industrial Estate *NWDGN* UB2 ...114 A4
The Bull Theatre *BAR* EN5 ...20 D5
Bupa Roding Hospital *REDBR* IG4 ...53 H6
Burbage School *IS* N1 ...7 G2
Burdett Coutts CE Primary School *WEST* SW1P ...16 C5
Burgess Business Park *CMBW* SE5 ...142 E1
Burgess Park Tennis Centre *CMBW* SE5 ...122 D6
Burlington Danes School *SHB* W12 ...99 K4
Burlington Infant School *NWMAL* KT3 ...192 C1
Burnham Trading Estate *DART* DA1 ...151 G5
Burnhill Business Centre *BECK* BR3 ...182 D4
Burnley Road Clinic *WLSDN* NW10 ...81 J3
Burns Hotel *ECT* SW5 ...120 A4
Burnside Industrial Estate *BARK/HLT* IG6 ...55 H1
Burnt Ash Infant School *BMLY* BR1 ...183 K1
Burnt Ash School *BMLY* BR1 ...183 J1
Burnt Oak Junior School *BFN/LL* DA15 ...168 B3
Burntwood School *TOOT* SW17 ...160 C4
Bursted Wood Primary School *BXLYHN* DA7 ...149 J3
Burwell Industrial Estate *LEY* E10 ...69 G5
Burwood School *ORP* BR6 ...202 E6
Bushey Golf & Country Club *BUSH* WD23 ...28 A1
Bushey Hall School *BUSH* WD23 ...27 K1
Bushey Health Centre *BUSH* WD23 ...28 B3
Bushey Heath Primary School *BUSH* WD23 ...28 D3
Bushey Museum & Art Gallery *BUSH* WD23 ...28 A1
Bush Hill Park Golf Club *WCHMH* N21 ...23 J6
Bush Hill Park Medical Centre *EN* EN1 ...36 B1
Bush Hill Park Primary School *EN* EN1 ...24 C6
Bush House (BBC) *HOL/ALD* WC2B ...11 G4
Bush Industrial Estate *ARCH* N19 ...84 C1 / *WLSDN* NW10 ...99 F5
The Business Academy Bexley *ERITHM* DA18 ...129 F2

The Business Design Centre
IS N1 ....5 K1
Bute House Preparatory
School for Girls
HMSMTH W6 ....119 F4
Butlers Wharf
STHWK SE1 ....19 K1
Butler's Wharf Business Centre
STHWK SE1 ....19 K2
Butler's Wharf Pier
STHWK SE1 ....19 K1
Butterfly House
BTFD TW8 ....136 C2
Butterfly Sports Club
ELTH/MOT SE9 ....167 G1
Buxlow Preparatory School
WBLY HA9 ....80 A1
Buzzard Creek Industrial
Estate *BARK* IG11 ....109 F2
Byam Shaw School of Art
ARCH N19 ....66 C6
Byfleet Industrial Estate
WATW WD18 ....26 A3
Bygrove JMI School
POP/IOD E14 ....105 K5
Byron Court Primary School
ALP/SUD HA0 ....61 J6
Cabinet War Rooms
WHALL SW1A 16 D2
Cabot Place
POP/IOD E14 ....124 D1
The Cadogan Hotel
KTBR SW1X 15 F5
Cadogan Pier
CHEL SW3 ....120 D6
Calder House School
BTSEA SW11 ....140 E2
Caledonian Market
STHWK SE1 ....19 H4
Cally Pool
IS N1 ....85 F6
Calverton Primary School
CAN/RD E16 ....107 H5
Cambell Primary School
DAGW RM9 ....91 K5
Camberwell Business Centre
CMBW SE5 ....142 E1
Camberwell College of Arts
CMBW SE5 ....143 F2
Camberwell Leisure Centre
CMBW SE5 ....142 E2
Camberwell New Cemetery
FSTH SE23 ....164 A1
Camberwell Trading Estate
CMBW SE5 ....142 C3
Cambridge Park Bowling &
Sports Club
TWK TW1 ....156 D1
Cambridge School
HMSMTH W6 ....118 E4
Cambridge Theatre
LSQ/SEVD WC2H 10 E4
Camden House Clinic
BKHTH/KID SE3 ....145 H3
Camden Junior School
CAR SM5 ....209 K2
Camden Market
CAMTN NW1 ....84 A5
Camden Mews Day Hospital
KTTN NW5 ....84 C4
Camden Peoples Theatre
CAMTN NW1 ....4 A5
Camden School for Girls
KTTN NW5 ....84 C4
Camden Theatre
CAMTN NW1 ....4 A2
Camden Town Hall &
St Pancras Library
CAMTN NW1 ....4 E4
Camelot Primary School
PECK SE15 ....143 J1
Cameron House School
CHEL SW3 ....120 C6
Camperdown House
WCHPL E1 ....13 K4
Campion House College
ISLW TW7 ....135 J1
Campsbourne J & I School
CEND/HSY/T N8 ....48 E6
Canada House
STJS SW1Y 10 D7
Canada House Business Centre
RSLP HA4 ....59 G5
Canada Place
POP/IOD E14 ....124 E1
Canada Square
POP/IOD E14 ....124 E1
Canada Water Retail Park
BERM/RHTH SE16 ....124 A3
Canada Wharf Museum
BERM/RHTH SE16 ....124 C1
Canal Cafe Theatre
BAY/PAD W2 ....101 G4
Canary Riverside
POP/IOD E14 ....124 C1
Canary Wharf Pier
POP/IOD E14 ....124 C1
Canary Wharf Tower
POP/IOD E14 ....124 D1
Canberra Primary School
SHB W12 ....99 K6
Canbury 2000 Business Park
KUTN/CMB KT2 ....175 F4
Canbury Business Centre
KUTN/CMB KT2 ....175 F4
Canbury Medical Centre
KUTN/CMB KT2 ....175 G4
Canbury School
RCHPK/HAM TW10 ....175 J2
C&L Golf & Country Club
NTHLT UB5 ....77 F5
C&L Leisure Centre
NTHLT UB5 ....77 F5
Cann Hall Primary School
WAN E11 ....88 D1

The Canning School
KENS W8 ....119 K3
Cannizaro House Hotel
WIM/MER SW19 ....177 F2
Cannon Hill Clinic
STHGT/OAK N14 ....34 E5
Cannon Lane Primary School
PIN HA5 ....59 H3
Cannon Sports Club
CANST EC4R 12 D5
Cannon Trading Estate
WBLY HA9 ....80 D2
Cannon Wharf Business Centre
DEPT SE8 ....124 B4
Canon Barnett Primary School
WCHPL E1 ....13 K3
Canonbury Business Centre
IS N1 ....85 J6
Canonbury Primary School
IS N1 ....85 H4
Canon Palmer RC High School
IL IG1 ....72 E5
Canons High School
EDGW HA8 ....44 B5
The Canons Leisure Centre
MTCM CR4 ....194 E1
Canterbury Industrial Estate
NWCR SE14 ....124 A6
Cantium Retail Park
STHWK SE1 ....123 H6
Capital Business Centre
ALP/SUD HA0 ....97 K1
MTCM CR4 ....194 E2
SAND/SEL CR2 ....211 K4
Capital City Academy
WLSDN NW10 ....81 K6
The Capital Hotel
CHEL SW3 ....14 E3
Capital Industrial Estate
BELV DA17 ....129 J4
BELV DA17 ....129 K1
Capital Radio
LSQ/SEVD WC2H 10 D6
Capital Wharf
WAP E1W 123 H1
Capitol Industrial Park
CDALE/KGS NW9 ....44 E6
Caplan Estate
MTCM CR4 ....179 H4
Cardiff Road Industrial
Estate *WATW* WD18 ....27 F1
Cardinal Hinsley High School
WLSDN NW10 ....81 J6
Cardinal Pole RC Secondary
Lower School
HOM E9 ....87 G4
Cardinal Pole RC Secondary
School *HOM* E9 ....87 F5
Cardinal Road Infant School
FELT TW13 ....154 A3
The Cardinal Vaughan
Memorial School
WKENS W14 ....119 H2
Cardinal Wiseman RC School
CFD/PVL UB6 ....96 C4
Cardwell Primary School
WOOL/PLUM SE18 ....126 E4
Carew Manor School
WLGTN SM6 ....210 D1
Carlisle Infant School
HPTN TW12 ....173 G2
Carlton Gate Development
MV/WKIL W9 ....100 E4
Carlton House
STJS SW1Y 16 C1
The Carlton Mitre Hotel
E/WMO/HCT KT8 ....173 K6
Carlton Primary School
KTTN NW5 ....84 A3
The Carlton Tower Hotel
KTBR SW1X 15 F4
Carlton Vale Infant School
KIL/WHAMP NW6 ....100 D2
Carlyle's House (NT)
CHEL SW3 ....120 D6
Carnwath Road Industrial
Estate *FUL/PGN* SW6 ....140 A4
Carpenters Park Cemetery
OXHEY WD19 ....27 K6
Carpenters Business Park
SRTFD E15 ....87 J4
Carpenters' Hall
LVPST EC2M 13 F2
Carpenters Primary School
SRTFD E15 ....88 A4
Carshalton AFC
SUT SM1 ....209 J1
Carshalton College of FE
CAR SM5 ....209 K1
Carshalton High School
for Boys *CAR* SM5 ....194 C6
Carshalton High School
for Girls *CAR* SM5 ....209 J1
Carshalton War Memorial
Hospital *CAR* SM5 ....209 K3
Carterhatch Primary School
EN EN1 ....24 D2
Caryl Thomas Clinic
HRW HA1 ....60 E1
The Cassel Hospital
RCHPK/HAM TW10 ....156 E6
Cassidy Medical Centre
FUL/PGN SW6 ....139 K1
Castilion Primary School
THMD SE28 ....109 J5
Castlebar Special School
WEA W13 ....97 G4
Castlecombe Primary School
ELTH/MOT SE9 ....184 D1
Castle Hill Primary School
CROY/NA CRO 214 A4
Castle Industrial Estate
WALW SE17 ....18 C6
Caterham High School
CLAY IG5 ....53 K5

Catford Cricket & Sports Club
CAT SE6 ....164 E3
Catford Cyphers CC
CAT SE6 ....164 C4
Catford Girls School
CAT SE6 ....165 G5
Catford Trading Estate
CAT SE6 ....164 E4
Catford Wanderers Sports Club
CAT SE6 ....165 F6
Cathal Leisure Centre
WAN E11 ....88 B1
Cator Park School for Girls
BECK BR3 ....182 B3
Cavendish College
FITZ W1T 10 C2
Cavendish Primary School
CHSWK W4 ....138 B1
The Cavendish School
CAMTN NW1 ....84 B6
Cavendish Special School
HNWL W7 ....97 F5
Caxton Hall
STJSPK SW1H 16 C4
Caxton Trading Estate
HYS/HAR UB3 ....113 H2
Cayley Primary School
POP/IOD E14 ....105 G4
Cecil Park Clinic
PIN HA5 ....59 J1
The Cedar School
FSTGT E7 ....89 G4
Cedars F & M School
KTN/HRWW/W HA3 ....42 C4
The Cedars Primary School
HEST TW5 ....133 K1
Cedar Way Industrial Estate
CAMTN NW1 ....84 D5
Cenotaph
WHALL SW1A 16 E2
Centaurs Business Centre
BTFD TW8 ....116 B6
Centaurs RFC
ISLW TW7 ....116 A6
Central Business Centre
WLSDN NW10 ....81 G3
Central Criminal Court
STP EC4M 12 A3
Centrale Shopping Centre
CROY/NA CRO 196 D6
Central Foundation
Boys School *SDTCH* EC2A 7 F6
Central Foundation
Girls School *BOW* E3 ....105 G2
Central Hall
STJSPK SW1H 16 D3
Central Hendon Clinic
HDN NW4 ....63 K1
Central London County Court
CAVSQ/HST W1G 3 J7
Central London Golf Club
TOOT SW17 ....160 C4
Central London Markets
FARR EC1M 12 A2
Central Medical Centre
MRDN SM4 ....194 B1
Central Middlesex Hospital
WLSDN NW10 ....98 E2
Central Park Arena
DART DA1 ....171 H3
Central Park Primary School
EHAM E6 ....107 H1
Central St Martins Coll of
Art & Design *BMSBY* WC1N ...11 G2
Central School of Ballet
CLKNW EC1R 5 K7
Central School of Fashion
CTPST W1W 10 A2
Central School of Speech
& Drama *CAMTN* NW1 ....4 C1
Central School of Speech
HAMP NW3 ....83 H5
Central Square Shopping
Centre *ALP/SUD* HA0 ....79 K4
Centre Court Shopping Centre
WIM/MER SW19 ....177 J2
Centre Point
LSQ/SEVD WC2H 10 D3
Chace Community School
EN EN1 ....24 A2
Chadwell Heath Industrial Park
BCTR RM8 ....74 A5
Chadwell Heath Leisure Centre
CHDH RM6 ....73 K3
Chadwell Heath School
CHDH RM6 ....73 H3
Chadwell Infant & Primary
School *CHDH* RM6 ....73 J4
Chaffinch Business Park
BECK BR3 ....182 A6
Chailey Industrial Estate
HYS/HAR UB3 ....113 K2
Chalcot School
CAMTN NW1 ....84 B4
Chalgrove Primary School
FNCH N3 ....46 C6
Chalkhill Primary School
WBLY HA9 ....80 D1
The Chamberlain Hotel
TWRH EC3N 13 J5
Chambers Business Park
WDR/YW UB7 ....112 D6
Chambers Wharf
BERM/RHTH SE16 ....123 H2
Chandlers Field Primary
School *E/WMO/HCT* KT8 ...189 F2
Chandos Business Centre
WLGTN SM6 ....210 C4
Channelsea Business Centre
SRTFD E15 ....106 B1
Channing School
HGT N6 ....66 B5
Chapel End Infant School
WALTH E17 ....51 K4
Chapel End Junior School
WALTH E17 ....51 K4

Chapman Park Industrial
Estate *WLSDN* NW10 ....81 H4
Charing Cross Hospital
HMSMTH W6 ....119 G6
Chessington Golf Club
CHSGTN KT9 ....205 G5
Charles Dickens Primary
School *STHWK* SE1 ....18 C3
Charles Edward Brook School
CMBW SE5 ....142 C2
Charles Edward Brook School
Upper School *CMBW* SE5 ...142 C2
Charles Lamb Primary
School *IS* N1 ....85 J6
Charlotte Sharman Primary
School *LBTH* SE11 ....18 A5
Charlotte Turner Primary
School *DEPT* SE8 ....124 D6
Charlton Athletic FC
(The Valley) *CHARL* SE7 ...126 B5
Charlton Health & Fitness
Centre *CHARL* SE7 ....126 B5
Charlton House
CHARL SE7 ....126 C6
Charlton Manor Junior School
CHARL SE7 ....146 C1
Charlton RFC
ELTH/MOT SE9 ....167 G2
Charlton School
CHARL SE7 ....120 E5
Charville Primary School
YEAD UB4 ....94 C1
Charter Clinic
CHEL SW3 ....120 D5
Charterhouse
FARR EC1M 6 A7
Charteris Road Sports Centre
KIL/WHAMP NW6 ....82 D6
Charter Nightingale Hospital &
Counselling Centre
CAMTN NW1 ....8 D1
The Charter School
EDUL SE22 ....142 E6
Chartfield School
PUT/ROE SW15 ....138 E6
Chartwell Business Centre
BMLY BR1 ....184 C6
Chase Bridge Primary School
WHTN TW2 ....155 K1
Chase Farm Hospital
ENC/FH EN2 ....23 G1
Chase Lane Primary School
CHING E4 ....37 H6
Chase Lodge Hotel
KUT/HW KT1 ....174 D4
Chase Road Trading Estate
WLSDN NW10 ....99 F3
Chase Side Primary School
ENC/FH EN2 ....23 J3
Chaseville Clinic
WCHMH N21 ....35 F1
Chatsworth Infant School
BFN/LL DA15 ....168 B3
Chatsworth & I School
HSLW TW3 ....135 H5
Chaucer Clinic
NWDGN UB2 ....115 J2
Cheam Common J & I School
WPK KT4 ....192 E6
Cheam Fields Primary School
CHEAM SM3 ....208 C3
Cheam High School
CHEAM SM3 ....208 C2
Cheam Leisure Centre
CHEAM SM3 ....208 B2
Cheam Park Farm Junior
School *CHEAM* SM3 ....208 C1
Cheam Sports Club
BELMT SM2 ....208 B5
Chelsea Barracks
BCVA SW1W 121 F5
Chelsea Bridge
Business Centre
VX/NE SW8 ....141 G1
Chelsea Centre & Theatre
WBPTN SW10 ....140 C1
Chelsea Cinema
CHEL SW3 ....120 D5
The Chelsea Club
Leisure Centre
FUL/PGN SW6 ....120 A6
Chelsea College of
Art & Design *CHEL* SW3 ...120 D5
FUL/PGN SW6 ....140 D3
Chelsea College of
Art & Design *CHEL* SW3 ...121 J5
Chelsea FC (Stamford Bridge)
FUL/PGN SW6 ....140 A1
Chelsea Fields Industrial
Estate *WIM/MER* SW19 ...178 C4
Chelsea Leisure Centre
CHEL SW3 ....120 D5
Chelsea Old Town Hall
CHEL SW3 ....120 D5
Chelsea Physic Garden
CHEL SW3 ....120 E6
Chelsea Village Hotel
WBPTN SW10 ....140 A1
Chelsea & Westminster
Hospital *WBPTN* SW10 ....120 B6
Chelsea Wharf
WBPTN SW10 ....140 C1
Chennestone Community
School *SUN* TW16 ....172 A6
Cherington House Health
Centre *HNWL* W7 ....116 A1
Cherry Garden Pier
BERM/RHTH SE16 ....123 J2
Cherry Garden School
BERM/RHTH SE16 ....123 H4
Cherry Lane Primary School
WDR/YW UB7 ....112 C4
Cherry Orchard Primary
School *CHARL* SE7 ....126 B1
Chessington CC
CHSGTN KT9 ....205 J5

Chessington Community
College & Sports Centre
CHSGTN KT9 ....205 K5
Chessington Golf Club
CHSGTN KT9 ....205 K5
The Chesterfield Mayfair
Hotel *MYFR/PICC* W1J 9 J7
Chesterton Primary School
BTSEA SW11 ....141 F2
Chestnut Grove School
BAL SW12 ....161 F3
Cheyne Centre
CHEL SW3 ....120 D6
Chicken Shed Theatre
STHGT/OAK N14 ....22 B4
Chigwell Golf Club
CHIG IG7 ....54 A1
Childeric Primary School
NWCR SE14 ....144 B1
Childs Hill Clinic
CRICK NW2 ....64 D6
Childs Hill Primary School
CRICK NW2 ....82 C1
Childs Welfare Clinic
DAGW RM9 ....91 J3
Chiltonian Industrial Estate
LEE/GVPK SE12 ....165 J1
Chimnocks Wharf
POP/IOD E14 ....105 G6
Chingford CE Infant School
CHING E4 ....38 B3
Chingford CE Junior School
CHING E4 ....38 B3
Chingford Foundation School
CHING E4 ....37 K3
Chingford Hall Primary School
CHING E4 ....51 H2
Chingford Health Centre
CHING E4 ....37 H6
Chingford Industrial Centre
CHING E4 ....51 G1
Chingford RFC
CHING E4 ....37 J3
Chisenhale Primary School
BOW E3 ....105 G1
Chislehurst Caves
CHST BR7 ....185 F4
Chislehurst Cemetery
CHST BR7 ....185 K1
Chislehurst Golf Club
CHST BR7 ....185 G3
Chislehurst Natural
Health Centre *CHST* BR7 ...185 G2
Chislehurst & Sidcup
GRM School *BFN/LL* DA15 ...168 C3
Chiswick & Bedford Park
Preparatory School
CHSWK W4 ....118 B4
Chiswick Business Park
CHSWK W4 ....117 J4
Chiswick Community School
CHSWK W4 ....138 A1
Chiswick House
CHSWK W4 ....118 A6
Chrisp Street Health Centre
POP/IOD E14 ....105 K5
Christ Church Bentinck
CE Primary School
CAMTN NW1 ....8 C1
Christ Church Brondesbury
CE J & I School
KIL/WHAMP NW6 ....82 D6
Christ Church CE Infant
School *NWMAL* KT3 ....176 B6
Christ Church CE Junior
School *NWMAL* KT3 ....176 A6
Christ Church CE Primary
School
BAR EN5 ....20 B3
BRXN/ST SW9 ....142 B3
BRXS/STRHM SW2 ....162 A3
BRYLDS KT5 ....191 H5
CHEL SW3 ....120 E6
FSTH SE23 ....164 A4
WOOL/PLUM SE18 ....147 F2
Christchurch CE
Primary School
HAMP NW3 ....83 H1
WCHPL E1 ....13 K2
Christ Church CE Middle School
EA W5 ....97 K6
Christchurch Industrial Centre
STHWK SE1 ....12 A7
Christ Church Primary School
ERITH DA8 ....130 A6
Christ Church School
CAMTN NW1 ....3 K3
Christ Church Secondary
School *NFNCH/WDSP* N12 ...47 H1
Christian Meeting Hall
BECK BR3 ....182 D4
Christine King 6th Form
College *LEW* SE13 ....145 G4
Christopher Hatton
Primary School
FSBYW WC1X 5 J7
Christ's College Finchley
EFNCH N2 ....47 F6
Christs College School
EFNCH N2 ....47 F6
Christs School
RCHPK/HAM TW10 ....157 F2
Christ the King RC First
School *STWL/WRAY* TW19 ...152 A1
Christ the King RC Primary
School *FSBYPK* N4 ....67 F6
Chrysalis Theatre
BAL SW12 ....161 F3
Chrysanthemum Clinic
CHSWK W4 ....137 K1
Chrysolyte Independent
Christian School
STHWK SE1 ....19 F4
Church Down Adult School
LEE/GVPK SE12 ....165 K4

Church End Medical Centre WLSDN NW10 ...81 G4
Church Farm House Museum HDN NW4 ...45 K6
Church Farm Swimming Pool EBAR EN4 ...33 K3
Churchfield Primary School ED N9 ...36 B3
Churchfield School WOOL/PLUM SE18 ...128 A4
Churchfields J & I School SWFD E18 ...52 E4
Churchfields Primary School BECK BR3 ...182 A6
Church Hill Primary School EBAR EN4 ...33 K2
Church House WEST SW1P ...16 D4
Churchill Clinic STHWK SE1 ...17 K4
Churchill College RYNPK SW20 ...177 F5
Churchill Gardens Primary School PIM SW1V ...121 H5
Churchill Theatre HAYES BR2 ...183 K5
Church Mead Infant School LEY E10 ...69 J5
Church Mead Junior School LEY E10 ...69 J5
The Church School BTFD TW8 ...117 F6
Church Stairs WAP E1W ...123 J2
Church Trading Estate ERITH DA8 ...150 D1
Cineworld Cinema BXLYHS DA6 ...149 J5 / FELT TW13 ...154 A4 / WDGN N22 ...49 G5
City Banking College STHWK SE1 ...19 F2
City Business Centre BERM/RHTH SE16 ...123 K2
City Business College FSBYE EC1V ...6 B5
City Central Estate FSBYE EC1V ...6 C5
City College of Higher Education IS N1 ...7 F4
City & Guilds of London-Art School LBTH SE11 ...122 C5
City Health Centre IS N1 ...6 E6
City Inn WEST SW1P ...16 E6
City & Islington 6th Form College HOLWY N7 ...85 F2
City & Islington College FSBYE ...6 D5 / FSBYPK N4 ...67 H6 / HOLWY N7 ...84 E2 / IS N1 ...85 J6 / STLK EC1Y ...7 G1
The City Literary Institute HOL/ALD WC2B ...11 F3
The City of London Academy EDUL SE22 ...143 H6 / STHWK SE1 ...123 H5
City of London Cemetery MNPK E12 ...71 J6
City of London Club OBST EC2N ...13 G3
City of London College WCHPL E1 ...104 C5
City of London Crematorium MNPK E12 ...89 H1
City of London Magistrates Court MANHO EC4N ...12 E4
City of London Polytechnic Sports Ground ELTH/MOT SE9 ...166 B4
City of London School BLKFR EC4V ...12 B5
City of London School for Girls BARB EC2Y ...12 C1
City of Westminster Cemetery HNWL W7 ...116 A1
City of Westminster College BAY/PAD W2 ...8 A1 / MV/WKIL W9 ...100 D2
City of Westminster Vehicle Pound BAY/PAD W2 ...9 F6
City Technology Colleges Trust WHALL SW1A ...10 E7
City University FSBYE EC1V ...6 A4 / FSBYE EC1V ...6 B5
City University Business School BARB EC2Y ...12 D1
Civic Centre & Bromley Palace BMLY BR1 ...184 A5
Civic Medical Centre HRW HA1 ...60 E2
Civil Service Recreation Centre WEST SW1P ...16 D5
Civil Service Sports Ground ELTH/MOT SE9 ...166 B1
Clapham Common Clinic CLAP SW4 ...141 J5
Clapham Manor Primary School CLAP SW4 ...141 H4
Clapham Manor Street Public Baths CLAP SW4 ...141 J4
Clapham North Business Centre CLAP SW4 ...141 K4
Clapham Park Estate CLAP SW4 ...141 J6
Clapham Picture House CLAP SW4 ...141 H5
Clapton Girls Technology College CLPT E5 ...86 E2
Clapton Jewish Boys School STNW/STAM N16 ...68 B4

Clara Grant Primary School BOW E3 ...105 J3
Claredon Hotel BKHTH/KID SE3 ...145 J3
Clare House Primary School BECK BR3 ...183 F5
Claremont Clinic FSTGT E7 ...89 F3
Claremont Fan Court School ESH/CLAY KT10 ...204 B4
Claremont High School & Performing Arts College KTN/HRWW/W HA3 ...62 A2
Claremont Way Industrial Estate CRICK NW2 ...64 A5
Clarence House WHALL SW1A ...16 B2
Clarendon Primary School ASHF TW15 ...152 C5
Clarendon Special School HPTN TW12 ...173 G2
Claridge's Hotel MYFR/PKLN W1K ...9 J5
Claverings Industrial Estate ED N9 ...36 E4
Claygate Primary School ESH/CLAY KT10 ...204 E5
Clayhall Clinic CLAY IG5 ...53 J6
Clayponds Hospital WHALL SW1A ...117 F4
Cleeve Park School SCUP DA14 ...168 D5
Clementine Churchill Hospital HRW HA1 ...78 E1
Cleopatra's Needle CHCR WC2N ...11 G7
Clerkenwell County Court IS N1 ...6 A2
Clerkenwell Heritage Centre FARR EC1M ...6 A7
Clerkenwell Parochial CE Primary School CLKNW EC1R ...5 J5
Cleveland Primary School IL IG1 ...90 B2
Cleves Primary School EHAM E6 ...89 H6
Clifton Lodge School EA W5 ...97 K6
Clifton Primary School NWDGN UB2 ...114 D4
Clink Exhibition STHWK SE1 ...12 E7
Clissold Leisure Centre STNW/STAM N16 ...85 K1
Clissold Park Natural Health Centre STNW/STAM N16 ...68 A6
Clitterhouse Primary School CRICK NW2 ...64 B6
Clockhouse Industrial Estate EBED/NFELT TW14 ...152 E3
Clockhouse Primary School CRW RM5 ...56 D2
Clock Museum CITYW EC2V ...12 D3
Cloisters Business Centre VX/NE SW8 ...141 G1
Clore Gallery WEST SW1P ...16 E7
Clore Tikva School BARK/HLT IG6 ...54 C5
Clothworkers' Hall FENCHST EC3M ...13 H5
Clouster's Green WAP E1W ...123 H1
Coach & Horses Hotel RCH/KEW TW9 ...137 G1
Cobden Centre WLSDN NW10 ...81 H4
Cobourg Primary School CMBW SE5 ...123 G5
Cochrane Theatre GINN WC1R ...11 G2
Cockfosters Sports Ground EBAR EN4 ...21 K4
The Cockpit Theatre STJWD NW8 ...2 C7
Coldharbour Industrial Estate CMBW SE5 ...142 D5
Coldharbour Leisure Centre ELTH/MOT SE9 ...166 E4
Coldharbour Sports Ground ELTH/MOT SE9 ...167 F4
Colebrooke Primary School IS N1 ...6 A2
Colegrave School SRTFD E15 ...88 B3
Coleraine Park Primary School TOTM N17 ...50 D4
Coleridge Primary School HGT N6 ...66 D4
Colfes Prep School LEE/GVPK SE12 ...166 A1
Colindale Business Park CDALE/KGS NW9 ...44 E6
Colindale Hospital CDALE/KGS NW9 ...45 G6
Colindale Primary School CDALE/KGS NW9 ...63 H1
Coliseum Theatre CHCR WC2N ...10 E6
College Fields Business Centre WIM/MER SW19 ...178 D4
College of Arms BLKFR EC4V ...12 C4
College of Central London SDTCH EC2A ...7 F6
College of Fuel Technology HGT N6 ...66 A3
College of Law FLST/FETLN EC4A ...11 J3 / GWRST WC1E ...10 C1

College of North East London CEND/HSY/T N8 ...67 G1 / FBAR/BDGN N11 ...48 C4 / SEVS/STOTM N15 ...68 B1
College of North West London KIL/WHAMP NW6 ...82 E6 / WBLY HA0 ...80 C1 / WLSDN NW10 ...81 H3
College of Organists STBT EC1A ...11 K2
College Park School WBLY HA9 ...80 B3
Collier Row Clinic ROMW/RG RM7 ...56 D4
Collier Row FC ROMW/RG RM7 ...56 B4
Collingwood Business Centre ARCH N19 ...84 E1
Collingwood Preparatory School WLGTN SM6 ...210 B3
Collis Primary School TEDD TW11 ...174 C2
Coinbrook School OXHEY WD19 ...27 G4
Colonia Convent Girls School CROY/NA CR0 ...213 F1
Colonnades Leisure Park CROY/NA CR0 ...211 G4
The Colonnades Shopping Centre BGVA SW1W ...15 J6
Colours Sports Club SUT SM1 ...209 G3
Columbia Primary School BETH E2 ...7 K4
Colvestone Primary School HACK E8 ...86 B3
Colville Primary School NTGHL W11 ...100 D5
Colvers Lane Medical Centre ERITH DA8 ...150 A2
Colyers Primary School ERITH DA8 ...150 A3
Comber Grove Primary School CMBW SE5 ...142 D1
Comedy Theatre STJS SW1Y ...10 C6
Comelle House Trading Estate DEPT SE8 ...124 B5
Comfort Inn HYS/HAR UB3 ...113 H5 / KENS W8 ...119 K4 / VX/NE SW8 ...141 K1
Commonwealth Institute KENS W8 ...119 J5
Community Arts Centre GNWCH SE10 ...144 E1
Community Care Centre ENC/FH EN2 ...23 K2
Community Centre (Island History Trust) POP/IOD E14 ...125 F4
Compass Theatre HGDN/ICK UB10 ...76 A1
Complementary Health Centre LEW SE13 ...165 H1
Compton Leisure Centre NTHLT UB5 ...77 J6
The Compton School NFNCH/WDSP N12 ...47 J2
Compton Sports Centre NFNCH/WDSP N12 ...47 J2
Concord Business Centre ACT W3 ...98 D4
Coney Hill School HAYES BR2 ...199 J6
Connaught Business Centre CDALE/KGS NW9 ...63 H2 / CROY/NA CR0 ...211 F4 / MTCM CR4 ...194 E2
Connaught Girls School Language College WAN E11 ...70 C5
The Connaught Hotel MYFR/PKLN W1K ...9 H6
Connaught House School BAY/PAD W2 ...8 A4
Conrad Hotel WBPTN SW10 ...140 B2
Consort Clinic PECK SE15 ...143 J4
Consulate General of Monaco SKENS SW7 ...14 A6
Consulate of Burkina Faso BTSEA SW11 ...140 B4
Consulate of Chile CAVSQ/HST W1G ...3 J7
Consulate of Colombia GTPST W1W ...10 A3
Consulate of Eritrea IS N1 ...5 K2
Consulate of Guinea MYFR/PKLN W1K ...9 G6
Consulate of Panama MYFR/PICC W1J ...15 J1
Control Tower HTHAIR TW6 ...132 E4
Convent of Jesus & Mary Infant School CRICK NW2 ...82 A4
Convent of Jesus & Mary Language College WLSDN NW10 ...81 H6
Conway Hall FSBYW WC1X ...11 G1
Conway Medical Centre WOOL/PLUM SE18 ...127 J4
Conway Primary School WOOL/PLUM SE18 ...127 K4
Coombe Girls School NWMAL KT3 ...176 A5
Coombe Hill Golf Club KUTN/CMB KT2 ...176 A3
Coombe Hill J & I School NWMAL KT3 ...176 A4

Coombe Wood Golf Club KUTN/CMB KT2 ...175 J3
Coopers' Hall LVPST EC2M ...13 H2
Coopers Lane Primary School LEE/GVPK SE12 ...165 K4
Coopers Technology College CHST BR7 ...185 H4
Copenhagen Primary School IS N1 ...5 F1
Copland Community School & Technology Centre WBLY HA9 ...80 B3
Coppermill Primary School WALTH E17 ...69 F2
Coppetts Wood Hospital MUSWH N10 ...47 K4
Coppetts Wood Primary School MUSWH N10 ...48 A4
Coppice Primary School CHIG IG7 ...55 G1
Copthall School MLHL NW7 ...45 K2
Copthorne Tara Hotel KENS W8 ...119 K3
Cordwainers College HOM E9 ...86 E5
Corinthian Casuals FC CHSGTN KT9 ...206 C1
Coronet Cinema NTGHL W11 ...119 K1 / SEVS/STOTM N15 ...49 H6
Corpus Christi RC Primary School BRXS/STRHM SW2 ...142 A6
Corus Hotel BAY/PAD W2 ...8 A5
Cosmopolitan College IS N1 ...5 G3
Coston Secondary Modern Girls School GFD/PVL UB6 ...96 C1
Coteford Infant School RSLP HA4 ...58 E2
The County Hotel WFD IG8 ...52 C5
Courtauld Institute HOL/ALD WC2B ...11 G5
Court Farm Industrial Estate STWL/WRAY TW19 ...152 C1
Courtfield Medical Centre ECT SW5 ...120 A4
Courtland JMI School MLHL NW7 ...31 G4
Covent Garden Flower Market VX/NE SW8 ...121 J6
Covent Garden Medical Centre LSO/SEVD WC2H ...11 F4
CPFC Soccer & Sports Centre BRXN/ST SW9 ...142 A4
Crafts Council IS N1 ...5 K3
Crampton Primary School WALW SE17 ...18 B7
Cranbrook College IL IG1 ...72 A6
Cranford Community College HEST TW5 ...114 A6
Cranford Infant School HSLWW TW4 ...133 K3
Cranford Junior School HSLWW TW4 ...134 A3
Cranford Park Junior School HYS/HAR UB3 ...113 J4
Cranford Park Primary School HYS/HAR UB3 ...113 J2
Cranleigh Gardens Industrial Estate STHL UB1 ...95 K4
Cranley Townhouse Hotel ECT SW5 ...120 B5
Cranmer Primary School MTCM CR4 ...194 E1
The Craven Clinic HMSMTH W6 ...118 E4
Craven Park Health Centre WLSDN NW10 ...81 F6
Craven Park Medical Centre WLSDN NW10 ...81 F6
Craven Park Primary School SEVS/STOTM N15 ...68 C3
Crawford Primary School CMBW SE5 ...142 D2
Crayfield Industrial Park STMC/STPC BR5 ...186 D5
Crayfields Business Park STMC/STPC BR5 ...186 D4 / STMC/STPC BR5 ...202 D2
Crayford Commercial Centre DART DA1 ...150 B6
Crayford Industrial Estate DART DA1 ...150 C6
Crayford Leisure Centre & Greyhound Stadium DART DA1 ...170 B1
Crayford Medical Centre DART DA1 ...150 D4
Crayside Industrial Estate DART DA1 ...150 D4
Cray Valley Golf Club STMC/STPC BR5 ...187 F4
Creekmouth Industrial Estate BARK IG11 ...109 F3
Creek Road Health Centre DEPT SE8 ...124 D6
Creek Road Industrial Estate DEPT SE8 ...124 E6
Cremer Business Centre BETH E2 ...7 J3
Crewe House MYFR/PICC W1J ...9 J7
Cricket Green School MTCM CR4 ...178 D6
Cricket Pavilion WEST SW1P ...16 C6
Cricklefield Stadium IL IG1 ...72 E6

Cricklewood Trading Estate CRICK NW2 ...82 C1
Crispin Industrial Centre UED N18 ...50 E1
Criterion Theatre MYFR/PICC W1J ...10 B6
Crockenhill Primary School SWLY BR8 ...203 K3
Crofton Leisure Centre BROCKY SE4 ...164 D1
Crofton School BROCKY SE4 ...164 D1
Croham Hurst Golf Club SAND/SEL CR2 ...212 B4
Cromer Road Primary School BAR EN5 ...21 F4
Cromwell Business Centre BARK IG11 ...108 E2
Cromwell Hospital KENS W8 ...120 A4
Crook Log Primary School BXLYHS DA6 ...148 E5
Crook Log Sports Centre WELL DA16 ...148 E4
Crossways Academy Sixth Form BROCKY SE4 ...144 B3
Crouch End Art School CEND/HSY/T N8 ...66 E2
Crouch End Health Centre CEND/HSY/T N8 ...66 E2
Crouch Hill Recreation Centre ARCH N19 ...66 E4
Crowland Primary School SEVS/STOTM N15 ...68 B2
Crowlands Primary School ROMW/RG RM7 ...74 E3
Crown Business Centre WDGN N22 ...112 C1
Crown Close Business Centre BOW E3 ...87 J6
Crown Court at the Borough STHWK SE1 ...18 B2
Crowndale Health Centre CAMTN NW1 ...4 B2
Crowne Plaza Hotel WDR/YW UB7 ...112 D4
Crownfield Primary School ROMW/RG RM7 ...56 C5
Crown Lane Clinic STNGT/OAK N14 ...34 C3
Crown Lane Primary School WNWD SE27 ...162 D6
Crown Moran Hotel CRICK NW2 ...82 B2
Crown Trading Centre HYS/HAR UB3 ...113 H2
Crown Woods School ELTH/MOT SE9 ...147 H6
Croydon Airport Industrial Estate CROY/NA CR0 ...211 G5
Croydon Cemetery THHTH CR7 ...196 A2
Croydon Clocktower Cinema CROY/NA CR0 ...211 J1
Croydon College CROY/NA CR0 ...211 K1
Croydon Fairfield Halls Cinema CROY/NA CR0 ...211 K1
Croydon FC SNWD SE25 ...197 K2
Croydon indoor Bowling Club SAND/SEL CR2 ...211 J5
Croydon Road Industrial Estate SNWD SE25 ...197 K1
Croydon Sports Arena SNWD SE25 ...197 K2
Crusader Industrial Estate FSBYPK N4 ...67 J3
Crusoe House School IS N1 ...6 E4
Crystal Palace FC (Selhurst Park) SNWD SE25 ...197 F1
Crystal Palace Museum NRWD SE19 ...181 G2
Cuaco Sports Ground BECK BR3 ...182 D2
Cubitt Town Primary School POP/IOD E14 ...125 F3
Cuddington Cemetery WPK KT4 ...192 E6
Cuddington CP School HOR/WEW KT19 ...207 H1
Culloden Primary School POP/IOD E14 ...106 B5
Culvers House Primary School MTCM CR4 ...195 F5
Cumberland Business Park WLSDN NW10 ...98 D2
Cumberland Comprehensive School CAN/RD E16 ...106 D4
Cumberland Park Industrial Estate WLSDN NW10 ...99 J2
Cumnor House School SAND/SEL CR2 ...211 H6
Curwen Primary School PLSTW E13 ...106 E1
Curzon Mayfair Cinema MYFR/PICC W1J ...15 J1
Curzon Soho Cinema SOHO/SHAV W1D ...10 D5
Custom House MON EC3R ...13 G6
Cutlers' Hall STP EC4M ...12 B3
Cutty Sark Clipper Ship GNWCH SE10 ...125 F6
Cygnet Clinic Beckton EHAM E6 ...108 B4
Cygnus Business Centre WLSDN NW10 ...81 H3
Cypress Infant School SNWD SE25 ...181 F5

Cypress Junior School
 SNWD SE25 ....181 F5
Cyprus College of Art
 WNWD SE27 ....162 C6
Cyril Jackson Primary
 School
 POP/IOD E14 ....105 H6
Dagenham Chest Clinic
 BCTR RM8 ....92 B1
Dagenham Civic Centre
 DAGE RM10 ....74 D6
Dagenham Priory Comp
 Perforing Arts College
 DAGE RM10 ....92 D5
Dagenham & Redbridge FC
 BCTR RM8 ....92 D3
Dagenham Swimming Pool
 BCTR RM8 ....74 B6
Daiglen School
 BKHH IG9 ....39 G3
Daily Mirror Office
 FLST/FETLN EC4A 11 K2
Daily Telegraph
 POP/IOD E14 ....124 D3
Dairy Meadow Primary
 School NWDGN UB2 ....114 E3
D'Albiac House
 HTHAIR TW6 ....132 D3
Dali Universal Exhibition
 STHWK SE1 ....17 G2
Dallington School
 FSBYE EC1V 6 B6
Dalmain Primary School
 FSTH SE23 ....164 B3
Daniola Taylor Centre
 PECK SE15 ....143 G1
Danecroft School
 EBAR EN4 ....33 J1
Danesfield Manor School
 WOT/HER KT12 ....188 A6
Danetree School
 HOR/WEW KT19 ....206 E5
Danson Primary School
 RCH/KEW TW9 ....137 H4
Danson Watersports Centre
 WELL DA16 ....148 C5
Darell Primary School
 BXLYHS DA6 ....148 D6
Darent Industrial Park
 ERITH DA8 ....131 G5
Darrick Wood Primary School
 ORP BR6 ....216 B2
Darrick Wood School
 ORP BR6 ....216 B1
Darrick Wood Sports Centre
 ORP BR6 ....216 C1
Darrick Wood
 Swimming Pool
 ORP BR6 ....216 B1
Dartford County Court
 DART DA1 ....171 H1
Dartford Golf Club
 DART DA1 ....170 E4
Dartford Grammar School
 for Boys DART DA1 ....171 F1
Dartford Grammar School
 for Girls DART DA1 ....171 F2
Dartford Magistrates Court
 DART DA1 ....171 G1
Dartford Museum & Library
 DART DA1 ....171 H2
Dartford Natural Health
 Centre DART DA1 ....171 H2
Dartford Technology College
 DART DA1 ....171 F2
Dartford West Health Centre
 DART DA1 ....171 F1
Darwin Centre
 SKENS SW7 ....14 A5
Datapoint Business Centre
 CAN/RD E16 ....106 B3
Daubeney Primary School
 CLPT E5 ....87 G2
David Game College
 NTGHL W11 ....119 K1
David Livingstone Primary
 School THHTH CR7 ....180 D4
David Lloyd Leisure Centre
 KENS W8 ....120 A4
David Lloyd Sports Centre
 EN EN1 ....24 C3
David Lloyd Tennis Centre
 SCUP DA14 ....186 D1
Davidson J & I School
 CROY/NA CR0 ....197 G4
Davies Laing & Dick College
 BAY/PAD W2 ....100 E6
Davies Lane Infant School
 WAN E11 ....70 D6
Davies's College
 STHWK SE1 ....18 D2
Dawlish Primary School
 LEY E10 ....70 A6
Days Inn
 STHWK SE1 ....17 J5
Days Lane Primary School
 BFN/LL DA15 ....168 A1
Deanesfield Primary School
 RSLP HA4 ....77 H2
Deansbrook Primary School
 MLHL NW7 ....44 E2
Deansfield Primary School
 ELTH/MOT SE9 ....147 F4
De Beauvoir Infants School
 IS N1 ....86 A4
De Bohun Primary School
 STHGT/OAK N14 ....22 B6
Deimere Hotel
 BAY/PAD W2 ....8 B4
Delta Wharf
 GNWCH SE10 ....125 G2
Denmead School
 HPTN TW12 ....173 F3
Denvale Trade Centre
 STMC/STPC BR5 ....202 C2

Denver Industrial Estate
 RAIN RM13 ....111 H4
Department for Environment,
 Food & Rural Affairs
 WHALL SW1A 10 E7
Department for Transport
 WEST SW1P 10 E7
Department of Education
 STJSPK SW1H 16 D3
Department of Health
 WHALL SW1A 16 E2
Department of Trade &
 Industry STJSPK SW1H 16 D3
Deptford Business Centre
 DEPT SE8 ....124 A5
Deptford Green School
 NWCR SE14 ....144 C1
Deptford Park Business
 Centre DEPT SE8 ....124 B5
Deptford Park Primary
 School DEPT SE8 ....124 B5
Deptford Trading Estate
 DEPT SE8 ....124 B5
Dersingham Infant School
 MNPK E12 ....89 K3
Derwentwater Primary
 School
 ACT W3 ....117 K1
Design Museum
 STHWK SE1 ....19 K1
Deutsche Schule
 RCHPK/HAM TW10 ....156 E3
De Vere Cavendish Hotel
 STJS SW1Y 10 B7
Devonshire Hospital
 MHST W1U 9 H1
Devonshire House
 Preparatory School
 HAMP NW3 ....83 H3
Devonshire House School
 HAMP NW3 ....83 G3
Devonshire Primary School
 BELMT SM2 ....209 G5
Diamond College
 SOHO/SHAV W1D 10 D3
Diana Fountain
 E/WMO/HCT KT8 ....174 A5
Diana Princess of
 Wales Fountain
 BAY/PAD W2 ....14 B1
Diane Matthews Clinic
 ROM/RW RM7 ....75 F1
Dilloway Industrial Estate
 NWDGN UB2 ....114 D2
Discovery Business Park
 BERM/RHTH SE16 ....123 H3
Docklands Medical Centre
 POP/IOD E14 ....124 D4
Docklands Sailing Centre
 POP/IOD E14 ....124 D3
Docklands Sailing &
 Watersports Centre
 POP/IOD E14 ....124 C3
Dockley Road Industrial
 Estate BERM/RHTH SE16 ...123 H3
Dockmaster's House
 POP/IOD E14 ....105 J6
Dockwell's Industrial Estate
 EBED/NFELT TW14 ....134 A6
Dockyard Industrial Estate
 WOOL/PLUM SE18 ....126 D3
Dog Kennel Hill Primary
 School CMBW SE5 ....143 F4
Dokal Industrial Estate
 NWDGN UB2 ....114 D2
Dollis Infant School
 MLHL NW7 ....46 A3
Dollis Junior School
 MLHL NW7 ....46 A3
The Dolphin Leisure Centre
 ROM RM1 ....75 H1
Dolphin School
 BTSEA SW11 ....140 E6
Dolphin Square Hotel
 PIM SW1V 121 H5
Dome GNWCH SE10 ....125 H1
Dominion Business Park
 ED N9 ....37 F4
Dominion Theatre
 SOHO/SHAV W1D 10 D3
Donmar Warehouse Theatre
 LSQ/SEVD WC2H 10 E4
Donnington Primary School
 WLSDN NW10 ....81 K5
The Dorchester Hotel
 MYFR/PKLN W1K 9 H7
Dorchester Primary School
 WPK KT4 ....193 F5
Dorma Trading Park
 LEY E10 ....69 F5
Dormers Wells High School
 STHL UB1 ....96 A5
Dormers Wells Leisure Centre
 STHL UB1 ....96 B5
Dormers Wells Medical Centre
 STHL UB1 ....96 A5
Dormers Wells Junior School
 STHL UB1 ....96 B6
Dorothy Barley Primary School
 BCTR RM8 ....91 H3
Dorset Road Infant School
 ELTH/MOT SE9 ....166 D4
Douay Martyrs RC School
 HGDN/ICK UB10 ....76 A2
Douglas Bader Foundation
 PUT/ROE SW15 ....158 D1
Dovers Corner Industrial
 Estate RAIN RM13 ....111 H2
Downderry Primary School
 BMLY BR1 ....165 H6
Downe Manor
 Primary School
 NTHLT UB5 ....95 F2
Downham Health Centre
 BMLY BR1 ....165 H6

Downhills Primary School
 TOTM N17 ....67 K1
Downsell Primary School
 WAN E11 ....88 B2
Downshall Primary School
 CNTH/NBYPK IG2 ....72 E4
Downsview Primary School
 NRWD SE19 ....180 D3
Downsview School
 CLPT E5 ....86 D2
Drapers Hall
 LOTH EC2R 13 F3
Drapers Sports Ground
 SRTFD E15 ....88 A2
The Draycott Hotel
 CHEL SW3 ....15 F6
Drayton Green
 Primary School
 WEA W13 ....97 G6
Drayton Manor High School
 HNWL W7 ....97 F6
Drayton Park Primary School
 HBRY N5 ....85 G3
DRCA Business Centre
 BTSEA SW11 ....141 F2
Drew Primary School
 CAN/RD E16 ....126 D1
Driving School & Road
 Safety Centre
 KTN/HRWW/W HA3 ....43 G6
Dr Johnson's House
 FLST/FETLN EC4A 11 K4
Dr Triplets CE J & I School
 HYS/HAR UB3 ....94 D5
Drury Way Industrial Estate
 WLSDN NW10 ....81 F2
Duchess Theatre
 COVGDN WC2E 11 G5
Duff Miller College
 SKENS SW7 ....120 B3
Duke of York Column
 STJS SW1Y 16 D1
Duke of York's HQ
 CHEL SW3 ....15 F7
Duke of York Theatre
 CHCR WC2N 10 E6
Dukes Head Hotel
 CAR SM5 ....210 B2
Dulverton Primary School
 BFN/LL DA15 ....167 J4
Dulwich College
 DUL SE21 ....163 F3
Dulwich College
 Preparatory School
 DUL SE21 ....163 F5
Dulwich College Track
 DUL SE21 ....163 F4
Dulwich Hamlet FC
 EDUL SE22 ....143 F5
Dulwich Hamlet
 Junior School
 DUL SE21 ....162 E1
Dulwich Hospital
 EDUL SE22 ....143 F5
Dulwich Leisure Centre
 EDUL SE22 ....143 H5
Dulwich Medical Centre
 EDUL SE22 ....143 H6
Dulwich Picture Gallery
 DUL SE21 ....162 E2
Dulwich & Sydenham
 Hill Golf Club
 DUL SE21 ....163 H4
Dulwich Village CE
 Infant School
 DUL SE21 ....163 F1
Dunbar Wharf
 POP/IOD E14 ....105 H6
Duncombe Primary School
 ARCH N19 ....66 E5
Dundee Wharf
 POP/IOD E14 ....105 H6
Dundonald Primary School
 WIM/MER SW19 ....177 J3
Dunningford Primary School
 RAIN RM12 ....93 H3
Dunraven School &
 Upper School
 STRHM/NOR SW16 ....162 A5
Duppas Junior School
 CROY/NA CR0 ....211 H3
Durand Primary School
 BRXN/ST SW9 ....142 A2
Durands Wharf
 BERM/RHTH SE16 ....124 C2
Durants School
 PEND EN3 ....24 E2
Durdans Park Primary School
 STHL UB1 ....95 K4
Durston House School
 EA W5 ....97 K5
Dysart School
 KUTN/CMB KT2 ....156 E6
 SURB KT6 ....191 F4
Dyslexia Teaching Centre
 ECT SW5 ....120 A5
 KENS W8 ....120 A5
Eaglesfield School
 WOOL/PLUM SE18 ....147 F2
Eagle Trading Estate
 MTCM CR4 ....194 E3
Ealdham Primary School
 ELTH/MOT SE9 ....146 B5
Ealing Abbey
 EA W5 ....97 J5
Ealing Abbey Scriptorium
 WEA W13 ....97 J5
The Ealing Broadway Centre
 EA W5 ....97 K6
Ealing Central Sports Ground
 GFD/PVL UB6 ....97 G1
Ealing Civic Centre
 EA W5 ....97 J6
Ealing College Upper School
 WEA W13 ....97 H5

Ealing CC
 EA W5 ....98 A5
Ealing Film Studios
 EA W5 ....116 D1
Ealing Golf Club
 GFD/PVL UB6 ....97 H2
Ealing Hospital
 NWDGN UB2 ....115 J2
Ealing Northern Sports Centre
 GFD/PVL UB6 ....78 D2
Ealing Park Health Centre
 EA W5 ....116 E4
Ealing Road Trading Estate
 BTFD TW8 ....116 E5
Ealing Sports Centre
 EA W5 ....98 A6
Ealing Tertiary College
 EA W5 ....116 D1
 STHL UB1 ....114 D2
Ealing Tutorial College
 EA W5 ....97 J6
Eardley Primary School
 STRHM/NOR SW16 ....179 H2
Earlham J & I School
 WDGN N22 ....49 G3
Earlham Primary School
 FSTGT E7 ....88 D5
Earl's Court Exhibition Centre
 ECT SW5 ....119 K5
Earlsfield Primary School
 WAND/EARL SW18 ....160 B4
Earlsmead F & M School
 RYLN/HDSTN HA2 ....77 K2
Earlsmead Primary School
 SEVS/STOTM N15 ....68 B1
Earth Gallery
 SKENS SW7 ....14 B5
East Acton Primary School
 ACT W3 ....99 G6
East Barking Centre
 BARK IG11 ....91 J3
East Barnet Health Centre
 EBAR EN4 ....21 H6
East Barnet School
 EBAR EN4 ....21 H4
East Beckton District Centre
 EHAM E6 ....107 K5
Eastbrook Comprehensive
 School DAGE RM10 ....92 E2
Eastbrook End Cemetery
 DAGE RM10 ....93 G1
Eastbrookend Country Park
 DAGE RM10 ....93 F2
Eastbury Comprehensive
 School BARK IG11 ....91 F6
Eastbury Farm JMI School
 NTHWD HA6 ....26 D6
Eastbury Infant School
 BARK IG11 ....91 F5
Eastcote CC
 PIN HA5 ....59 F2
Eastcote Health Centre
 PIN HA5 ....59 G4
Eastcote Industrial Estate
 RSLP HA4 ....59 G4
Eastcote Lane Cemetery
 RYLN/HDSTN HA2 ....78 B1
Eastcote Primary School
 ELTH/MOT SE9 ....147 J4
Eastcourt Independent
 School
 GDMY/SEVK IG3 ....73 G5
Eastern Business Park
 HTHAIR TW6 ....133 J3
Eastfield Primary School
 PEND EN3 ....25 F1
East Finchley Cemetery
 EFNCH N2 ....47 F6
East Finchley Medical Centre
 EFNCH N2 ....65 J1
East Finchley School of
 English EFNCH N2 ....47 J6
Eastgate Business Park
 LEY E10 ....69 G5
East Greenwich Christ Church
 CE Primary School
 GNWCH SE10 ....125 H4
East Ham Industrial Estate
 CAN/RD E16 ....107 H3
East Ham Jewish Cemetery
 EHAM E6 ....107 J2
East Ham Leisure Centre
 EHAM E6 ....89 K6
East Ham Memorial Hospital
 FSTGT E7 ....89 H5
East Ham Nature Reserve
 EHAM E6 ....107 K3
East Lane Business Park
 WBLY HA9 ....79 K1
Eastlea Community Centre
 CAN/RD E16 ....106 D3
Eastlea Community School
 CAN/RD E16 ....106 C3
East London Business College
 WAN E11 ....70 C5
East London Cemetery
 PLSTW E13 ....106 D2
East London Crematorium
 PLSTW E13 ....106 C2
East London RFC
 EHAM E6 ....107 K4
East London RUFC
 PLSTW E13 ....106 D1
Eastman Dental Hospital
 FSBYW WC1X 5 G6
East Molesey CC
 E/WMO/HCT KT8 ....173 H6
East Sheen Cemetery
 RCHPK/HAM TW10 ....137 H6
East Sheen Primary School
 MORT/ESHN SW14 ....138 B5
East Thamesmead Business
 Park ERITHM DA18 ....129 G2
East Wickham Primary
 School WELL DA16 ....148 A2

Eaton Manor RFC
 WAN E11 ....71 G2
Eaton Square Preparatory
 School BGVA SW1W 15 J6
Eaton Square School
 PIM SW1V 16 A7
Ecclesbourne Primary School
 THHTH CR7 ....196 D2
Eckerd College
 GWRST WC1E 10 C1
Ecole de Mime Corporel Dramatique
 & Theatre de l'Ange Fou
 FSBYPK N4 ....66 E6
Eden College
 STHWK SE1 ....18 B4
Edenham High School
 CROY/NA CR0 ....198 B4
Eden Medical Centre
 WKENS W14 ....119 J4
Edenvale Child Health Clinic
 TOOT SW17 ....179 F3
Eden Walk Shopping Centre
 KUT/HW KT1 ....175 F5
Edes Business Park
 WLGTN SM6 ....195 F6
Edgebury Primary School
 CHST BR7 ....167 H6
Edge Business Centre
 CRICK NW2 ....63 K6
Edgwarebury Cemetery
 EDGW HA8 ....30 C4
Edgwarebury Hotel
 BORE WD6 ....30 A2
Edgware Clinic
 EDGW HA8 ....44 C2
Edgware College
 HAMP NW3 ....83 G4
Edgware Community Hospital
 EDGW HA8 ....44 C3
Edgware FC & Wealdstone FC
 EDGW HA8 ....44 C3
Edgware Infant School
 EDGW HA8 ....44 C2
Edgware Junior School
 EDGW HA8 ....44 C2
The Edgware School
 EDGW HA8 ....30 B6
Edinburgh Primary School
 WALTH E17 ....69 H2
Edith Neville Primary School
 CAMTN NW1 ....4 C4
Edmonton Cemetery
 ED N9 ....35 K4
Edmonton County Court
 UED N18 ....50 C1
Edmonton Green Shopping
 Centre ED N9 ....36 D4
Edmonton Leisure Centre
 ED N9 ....36 C5
Edmonton Upper School
 EN EN1 ....36 B2
Edmund Waller Primary
 School
 NWCR SE14 ....144 A3
Education Centre
 WOOL/PLUM SE18 ....127 G5
Edward Betham CE Primary
 School GFD/PVL UB6 ....96 D2
Edward Pauling School
 FELT TW13 ....153 H4
Edward Wilson Primary School
 BAY/PAD W2 ....101 F4
Edwin Lambert School
 EMPK RM11 ....75 J3
Effra Road Retail Park
 BRXS/STRHM SW2 ....142 B6
Effra Site (St George Wharf,
 under re-development)
 VX/NE SW8 ....121 K5
Eglinton Junior School
 WOOL/PLUM SE18 ....127 G6
Eglinton Primary School
 WOOL/PLUM SE18 ....147 F1
Elbourne Trading Estate
 BELV DA17 ....129 J3
Eldenwall Industrial Estate
 BCTR RM8 ....74 A5
Eldon JMI School
 ED N9 ....36 D3
Eleanor Palmer Primary School
 KTTN NW5 ....84 C2
Eleanor Smith Special School
 PLSTW E13 ....106 E1
Electrical Trades Union College
 ESH/CLAY KT10 ....204 A2
Electric Centre
 NTCHL W11 ....100 D5
Elephant & Castle Leisure Centre
 LBTH SE11 ....18 B6
Elephant & Castle Shopping
 Centre STHWK SE1 ....18 B5
Elers Clinic
 HYS/HAR UB3 ....113 G4
Elfrida Primary School
 CAT SE6 ....164 E6
Eliot Bank Primary School
 FSTH SE23 ....163 J4
Elizabeth Garrett Anderson
 Hospital CAMTN NW1 ....4 D5
Elizabeth Garrett Anderson
 School IS N1 ....5 H1
Elizabeth Selby Infant School
 BETH E2 ....92 C2
Elizabeth Trading Estate
 NWCR SE14 ....124 A6
Ellen Wilkinson Primary School
 EHAM E6 ....107 H4
Ellen Wilkinson School for
 Girls ACT W3 ....98 B5
Ellerslie Square
 Industrial Estate
 BRXS/STRHM SW2 ....141 K5
Ellingham Primary School
 CHSGTN KT9 ....205 K4

Elmbridge Leisure Centre
WOT/HER KT12 ......188 A2
Elin Court School
WNWD SE27 ......162 C4
Elmgrove F & M School
KTN/HRWW/W HA3 ......61 G1
Elmhurst Primary School
FSTGT E7 ......89 F5
Elmhurst School
CROY/NA CRO 211 K2
Elm Lea Trading Estate
TOTM N17 ......50 C3
Elmwood Primary School
CROY/NA CRO 196 C4
Elm Wood Primary School
WNWD SE27 ......162 C5
Eisdale Street Health Centre
HOM E9 ......86 E5
Elsley Primary School
WBLY HA9 ......80 B4
Elsley School
BTSEA SW11 ......141 F4
Eltham Bus Station
ELTH/MOT SE9 ......146 E6
Eltham Cemetery
ELTH/MOT SE9 ......147 H5
Eltham CE Primary School
ELTH/MOT SE9 ......146 E6
Eltham College Junior School
ELTH/MOT SE9 ......166 C3
Eltham College Senior School
ELTH/MOT SE9 ......166 C4
Eltham Crematorium
ELTH/MOT SE9 ......147 J5
Eltham Green School
ELTH/MOT SE9 ......166 C1
Eltham Health Clinic
ELTH/MOT SE9 ......146 D6
Eltham Health & Fitness
Centre ELTH/MOT SE9 ......167 F1
Eltham Hill Tech College
ELTH/MOT SE9 ......166 D1
Eltham Palace (remains)
ELTH/MOT SE9 ......166 D2
Eltham Pools
ELTH/MOT SE9 ......146 D6
Eltham Warren Golf Club
ELTH/MOT SE9 ......147 G6
Eithorne Park High School
HNWL W7 ......116 A3
Eithorne Sports Centre
HNWL W7 ......116 A3
Elystan Business Centre
HYS/HAR UB3 ......95 G6
Emanuel School
WAND/EARL SW18 ......140 C6
Embankment Pier
CHCR WC2N 11 G7
Embassy of Afghanistan
SKENS SW7 ......14 A3
Embassy of Albania
BGVA SW1W 15 K5
Embassy of Algeria
NTGHL W11 ......119 H1
Embassy of Angola
MYFR/PKLN W1K 9 G6
Embassy of Argentina
KENS W8 ......9 J5
Embassy of Armenia
KENS W8 ......120 A3
Embassy of Austria
KTBR SW1X 15 G4
Embassy of Bahrain
SKENS SW7 ......120 B3
Embassy of Belarus
KENS W8 ......120 A2
Embassy of Belgium
KTBR SW1X 15 H5
Embassy of Bolivia
KTBR SW1X 15 H5
Embassy of Bosnia-
Herzegovina
CAVSO/HST W1G 9 K3
Embassy of Brazil
MYFR/PKLN W1K 9 G5
Embassy of Bulgaria
SKENS SW7 ......120 B5
Embassy of Cameroon
NTGHL W11 ......119 H1
Embassy of China
CAVSO/HST W1G 9 J1
Embassy of Costa Rica
BAY/PAD W2 ......101 G6
Embassy of Cote d'Ivoire
KTBR SW1X 15 K4
Embassy of Croatia
GTPST W1W 3 K7
Embassy of Cuba
LSQ/SEVD WC2H 10 E3
Embassy of Democratic
Republic of the Congo
KTBR SW1X 15 F5
Embassy of Denmark
KTBR SW1X 14 E4
Embassy of
Dominican Republic
BAY/PAD W2 ......101 F5
Embassy of Ecuador
KTBR SW1X 14 E4
Embassy of Egypt
MYFR/PICC W1J 9 J7
Embassy of Estonia
SKENS SW7 ......120 B2
Embassy of Ethiopia
SKENS SW7 ......14 B3
Embassy of Finland
KTBR SW1X 15 G4
Embassy of France
KTBR SW1X 15 G4
Embassy of Georgia
KENS W8 ......120 A2
Embassy of Germany
KTBR SW1X 15 G4
Embassy of Ghana
HGT N6 ......66 B5

Embassy of Greece
KENS W8 ......119 J1
Embassy of Guatemala
WBPTN SW10 ......120 A6
Embassy of Holy See
WIM/MER SW19 ......159 F5
Embassy of Honduras
MBLAR W1H 9 F1
Embassy of Hungary
KTBR SW1X 15 H5
Embassy of Iceland
KTBR SW1X 15 G6
Embassy of Indonesia
MYFR/PKLN W1K 9 H6
Embassy of Iran
SKENS SW7 ......14 B3
Embassy of Iraq
SKENS SW7 ......120 B3
Embassy of Ireland
KTBR SW1X 15 J5
Embassy of Israel
KENS W8 ......120 A2
Embassy of Italy
MYFR/PKLN W1K 9 H5
Embassy of Japan
MYFR/PICC W1J 15 K1
Embassy of Jordan
KENS W8 ......119 K2
Embassy of Korea
WESTW SW1E 16 B4
Embassy of Krygyzstan
MBLAR W1H 8 E2
Embassy of Kuwait
KTBR SW1X 15 F2
Embassy of Latvia
CAMTN NW1 ......3 G7
Embassy of Lebanon
KENS W8 ......120 A1
Embassy of Liberia
BAY/PAD W2 ......100 E6
Embassy of Lithuania
MBLAR W1H 8 E1
Embassy of Luxembourg
KTBR SW1X 15 G3
Embassy of Mexico
MYFR/PICC W1J 15 J1
Embassy of Mongolia
KENS W8 ......120 A2
Embassy of Morocco
SKENS SW7 ......120 B4
Embassy of Mozambique
FITZ W1T 4 A7
Embassy of Myanmar
MYFR/PICC W1J 9 J7
Embassy of Nepal
KENS W8 ......120 A1
Embassy of Netherlands
SKENS SW7 ......120 B2
Embassy of Norway
KTBR SW1X 15 H4
Embassy of Oman
SKENS SW7 ......120 B3
Embassy of Paraguay
KENS W8 ......120 A3
Embassy of Peru
KTBR SW1X 15 F4
Embassy of Philippines
KENS W8 ......120 A1
Embassy of Poland
CAVSO/HST W1G 9 J1
Embassy of Portugal
KTBR SW1X 15 G3
Embassy of Qatar
MYFR/PKLN W1K 9 H7
Embassy of
Republic of Gabon
SKENS SW7 ......120 B3
Embassy of
Republic of Senegal
CRICK NW2 ......82 A5
Embassy of Romania
KENS W8 ......120 A2
Embassy of Russian Federation
KENS W8 ......120 A1
Embassy of Saudi Arabia
MYFR/PICC W1J 9 J7
Embassy of Slovak Republic
KENS W8 ......120 A1
Embassy of Slovenia
CAVSO/HST W1G 9 J3
Embassy of Spain
KTBR SW1X 15 H4
Embassy of Sudan
WHALL SW1A 16 A1
Embassy of Sweden
MBLAR W1H 8 E2
Embassy of Switzerland
MBLAR W1H 8 E2
Embassy of Syria
KTBR SW1X 15 G3
Embassy of Thailand
SKENS SW7 ......120 B3
Embassy of Tunisia
SKENS SW7 ......14 B3
Embassy of Turkey
KTBR SW1X 15 H3
Embassy of Turkmenistan
FITZ W1T 10 B2
Embassy of Ukraine
NTGHL W11 ......119 H1
Embassy of
United Arab Emirates
SKENS SW7 ......14 B2
Embassy of Uruguay
SKENS SW7 ......14 D4
Embassy of USA
MYFR/PKLN W1K 9 G5
Embassy of Uzbekistan
NTGHL W11 ......119 J1
Embassy of Venezuela
SKENS SW7 ......14 B5
Embassy of Yemen
SKENS SW7 ......14 A6
Ember Sports Club
ESH/CLAY KT10 ......189 H5

Embroidery World Business
Centre WFD IG8 ......53 H5
EMD Walthamstow Cinema
WALTH E17 ......69 J1
Emery Theatre
POP/IOD E14 ......105 K5
Emmanuel CE Primary
School
KIL/WHAMP NW6 ......82 E3
Empire Cinema
LSQ/SEVD WC2H 10 D5
Endsleigh Industrial Estate
NWDGN UB2 ......114 D4
Enfield Business Centre
PEND EN3 ......24 E3
Enfield Chace Lower School
ENC/FH EN2 ......24 A1
Enfield College
PEND EN3 ......24 E4
Enfield County Upper School
ENC/FH EN2 ......23 K4
Enfield CC
EN EN1 ......24 A5
Enfield FC
ED N9 ......36 E4
Enfield Golf Club
ENC/FH EN2 ......23 H5
Enfield Grammar School
(Upper) ENC/FH EN2 ......23 K4
Enfield Hotel
ENC/FH EN2 ......23 H3
Enfield Lower Grammar
School ENC/FH EN2 ......23 K3
English Language Institute
STHWK SE1 ......17 J1
English Martyrs RC
Primary School
WALW SE17 ......18 E7
WCHPL E1 ......13 K4
Ennersdale Primary School
LEW SE13 ......145 G6
Ensham Secondary School
TOOT SW17 ......178 E1
Enterprise Business Park
POP/IOD E14 ......124 E2
Enterprise Industrial Estate
BERM/RHTH SE16 ......123 K5
Epsom & Ewell High School
HOR/WEW KT19 ......206 E6
Eric Liddell Sports Centre
ELTH/MOT SE9 ......166 C4
Eridge House Preparatory
School FUL/PGN SW6 ......139 J3
Erith Cemetery
BELV DA17 ......129 J6
Erith & District Hospital
ERITH DA8 ......130 A6
Erith Health Centre
ERITH DA8 ......130 A6
Erith Library & Museum
ERITH DA8 ......130 B5
Erith School
ERITH DA8 ......149 K1
Erith School Community
Sports Centre
ERITH DA8 ......149 K1
Erith Small Business Centre
ERITH DA8 ......130 C6
Erith Sports Centre
ERITH DA8 ......130 B6
Erith Stadium
ERITH DA8 ......130 B6
Erith Theatre Guild
ERITH DA8 ......130 A6
Ernest Bevin School
TOOT SW17 ......160 D5
Eros MYFR/PICC W1J 10 C6
Esher CE High School
ESH/CLAY KT10 ......204 A1
Esher Church School (Primary)
ESH/CLAY KT10 ......204 C4
Esher College
THDIT KT7 ......189 K4
Esher RFC
WOT/HER KT12 ......188 D6
Essendine Primary School
KIL/WHAMP NW6 ......100 E2
Essex Primary School
MNPK E12 ......89 J4
Ethelburga GM School
BTSEA SW11 ......140 D2
Ethel Davis School
CHDH RM6 ......73 H2
Euro Business Centre
SRTFD E15 ......88 D6
Eurolink Business Centre
BRXS/STRHM SW2 ......142 B5
Europa Trading Estate
ERITH DA8 ......130 A5
European Business Centre
CDALE/KGS NW9 ......45 F6
European School of Economics
KTBR SW1X 15 H3
European Vocational College
HDTCH EC3A 13 H4
Euro Way School
CEND/HSY/T N8 ......49 G6
Euro Way School London
FSBYPK N4 ......67 H4
Euston Centre
CAMTN NW1 ......4 A6
Euston Tower
CAMTN NW1 ......4 A6
Evans Business Centre
CRICK NW2 ......81 J1
Eveline Lowe Primary School
STHWK SE1 ......123 H5
Evendine College
SOHO/SHAV W1D 10 C3
Eversley Medical Centre
THHTH CR7 ......196 B3
Eversley Primary School
WCHMH N21 ......22 E6
Everyman Cinema
HAMP NW3 ......83 G2

Evolution House
RCH/KEW TW9 ......137 F3
Ewell Athletics Track
HOR/WEW KT19 ......207 F4
Ewell Castle Junior School
EW KT17 ......207 H6
Ewell Castle School
EW KT17 ......207 J6
Ewell Grove Infant School
HOLWY N7 ......84 E4
EW Fact/Emile Woolf Colleges
HOLWY N7 ......84 E4
ExCeL Exhibition Centre
CAN/RD E16 ......107 F6
Exchange Square
SDTCH EC2A 13 G1
The Exchange
IL IG1 ......72 B6
Exhibition Halls
STLK EC1Y 12 D1
Express by Holiday Inn
ALP/SUD HA0 ......80 C6
BKHH IG9 ......39 F4
CAN/RD E16 ......106 C5
CHING E4 ......51 J3
CROY/NA CRO 196 D6
FSBYE EC1V 5 J2
GNWCH SE10 ......125 J3
HMSMTH W6 ......118 E4
PIM SW1V 121 H5
SRTFD E15 ......105 K1
STHWK SE1 ......12 B7
WAND/EARL SW18 ......140 A5
WIM/MER SW19 ......178 C3
Eye Clinic
LSQ/SEVD WC2H 10 D3
Faircharm Trading Estate
DEPT SE8 ......144 E1
IS N1 ......5 G2
The Faircross Complementary
Medical Centre
BARK IG11 ......90 E4
Fairfield Clinic
BKHH IG9 ......39 F3
Fairfield Pool & Leisure Centre
DART DA1 ......171 H2
Fairfield Trade Park
KUT/HW KT1 ......175 G6
Fairholme Primary School
EBED/NFELT TW14 ......153 G3
Fairlawn Primary School
FSTH SE23 ......163 K2
Fairley House School
WEST SW1P 16 C7
Fairlop Primary School
BARK/HLT IG6 ......54 C4
Fairview Industrial Centre
DAGW RM9 ......111 F5
Fairview Industrial Estate
HYS/HAR UB3 ......113 J2
Fairview Medical Centre
STRHM/NOR SW16 ......179 K4
Fairway Primary School
MLHL NW7 ......31 F4
Fairways Business Park
LEY E10 ......69 G6
Falconbrook Primary School
BTSEA SW11 ......140 C3
Falcon Business Centre
BTSEA SW11 ......140 D5
Falcon Park Industrial Estate
WLSDN NW10 ......81 G3
The Falcon School for Girls
EA W5 ......117 G1
Falkner House School
SKENS SW7 ......120 B5
Family Records Centre
FSBYE EC1R 5 J5
Fanmakers' Hall
LVPST EC2M 13 G3
Fan Museum
GNWCH SE10 ......145 F1
Faraday Building
BLKFR EC4V 12 B4
Farm Lane Trading Estate
FUL/PGN SW6 ......119 K6
Farnborough Primary School
ORP BR6 ......216 D3
Farnell House Medical Centre
HSLW TW3 ......135 G2
Farnham Green Primary
School GDMY/SEVK IG3 ......73 G3
Farrington & Stratford
House School CHST BR7 ......185 J3
Fashion & Textile
Design Museum STHWK SE1 ......19 H3
Featherstone High School
NWDGN UB2 ......114 C4
Featherstone Industrial Estate
NWDGN UB2 ......114 D2
Featherstone Road Health
Clinic NWDGN UB2 ......114 D3
Felnex Trading Estate
WLGTN SM6 ......195 F6
Feltham Airparcs Leisure
Centre FELT TW13 ......154 C4
Feltham Athletics Arena
EBED/NFELT TW14 ......153 K2
Felthambrook Industrial
Estate FELT TW13 ......154 A5
Feltham Community College
FELT TW13 ......154 B4
Feltham Hill Infant School
FELT TW13 ......153 J5
Feltham Hill Junior School
FELT TW13 ......153 J5
Feltham & Hounslow Boro FC
EBED/NFELT TW14 ......153 K2
Fenstanton J & I School
BRXS/STRHM SW2 ......162 B3
Fenton House
HAMP NW3 ......83 G1
Ferrier Industrial Estate
WAND/EARL SW18 ......140 A5

Ferry Island Retail Park
TOTM N17 ......50 B6
Ferry Lane Industrial Estate
RAIN RM13 ......111 J4
WALTH E17 ......50 E6
Ferry Lane Primary School
TOTM N17 ......68 D1
Festival Pier
STHWK SE1 ......11 H7
Field End Primary School
RSLP HA4 ......77 H1
Fielding Primary School
WEA W13 ......116 C3
Film House Cinema
STHWK SE1 ......136 E6
Financial Times
POP/IOD E14 ......106 A5
STHWK SE1 ......12 D7
Finchley Catholic High
School
NFNCH/WDSP N12 ......33 G5
Finchley CC
FNCH N3 ......47 F5
Finchley Golf Club
MLHL NW7 ......46 D2
Finchley Industrial Centre
NFNCH/WDSP N12 ......33 G6
Finchley Lido
NFNCH/WDSP N12 ......47 H3
Finchley Manor Lawn
Tennis & Squash Club
FNCH N3 ......46 C4
Finchley Memorial Hospital
FNCH N3 ......47 G3
Finchley Youth Theatre
EFNCH N2 ......47 J6
Fine Arts College
HAMP NW3 ......83 J4
Finsbury Circus Medical Centre
LVPST EC2M 13 F2
Finsbury Health Centre
CLKNW EC1R 5 J6
Finsbury Leisure Centre
FSBYE EC1V 6 D5
Finsbury Park Track
FSBYPK N4 ......67 H4
Finton House School
TOOT SW17 ......160 E4
Fircroft Primary School
TOOT SW17 ......160 E4
Fire Brigade Museum
STHWK SE1 ......18 C2
Firepower
(Museum of Artillery)
WOOL/PLUM SE18 ......127 G3
Firs Farm Primary School
PLMGR N13 ......35 K5
First Steps Montessori School
NTHLT UB5 ......77 H6
Fisher Athletic FC
BERM/RHTH SE16 ......124 A1
Fishmonger's Hall
CANST EC4R 12 E6
Fitness Unlimited Leisure
Centre BOW E3 ......105 J1
Fitzjohns Primary School
HAMP NW3 ......83 H3
Fitzrovia Medical Centre
GTPST W1W 4 A7
Fitzroy Nuffield Hospital
MBLAR W1H 8 E3
Five Bridges
LBTH SE11 ......122 A5
Five Elms Primary School
DAGW RM9 ......92 B1
Five Ways Business Centre
FELT TW13 ......154 A5
Flamsteed House Museum
GNWCH SE10 ......145 G1
Flaxman Sports Centre
CMBW SE5 ......142 D3
Fleecefield Primary School
ED N9 ......36 C4
Fleet Primary School
HAMP NW3 ......83 K3
Fleetway Business Park
GFD/PVL UB6 ......97 H1
Fleming Lab School
BAY/PAD W2 ......8 B3
Flora Gardens Primary School
HMSMTH W6 ......118 E4
Florence Nightingale Museum
STHWK SE1 ......17 G3
Florida State University
BMSBY WC1N 10 D2
Flutters Leisure Centre
FUL/PGN SW6 ......139 K1
FOB School
STNW/STAM N16 ......68 C4
Follys End Christian High
School SNWD SE25 ......197 F3
The Foot Clinic
WIM/MER SW19 ......177 H1
Fordbridge Medical Centre
ASHF TW15 ......152 C2
The Ford College
CONDST W1S 9 K4
Fordgate Business Park
BELV DA17 ......129 K2
Ford Industrial Park
DAGW RM9 ......110 D3
Fordview Industrial Estate
RAIN RM13 ......111 F2
Foreign & Commonwealth
Office WHALL SW1A 16 D2
Foreland Medical Centre
NTGHL W11 ......100 C6
Forest Business Park
WALTH E17 ......69 F4
Forestdale Primary School
CROY/NA CRO 213 G6
Foresters Primary School
WLGTN SM6 ......210 D4
Forest Gate Community
School FSTGT E7 ......88 E3

Forest Hill Business Centre
FSTH SE23 ....163 K4
Forest Hill Industrial Estate
FSTH SE23 ....163 K4
Forest Hill Pools
FSTH SE23 ....164 A5
Forest Hills Pools
FSTH SE23 ....163 K4
Forest House Business Centre
WAN E11 ....70 D4
Forest Industrial Park
BARK/HLT IG6 ....54 E3
Forest Park
Cemetery & Crematorium
CHIG IG7 ....55 J1
Forest Road Medical Centre
WALTH E17 ....51 H6
Forest School
WALTH E17 ....70 C1
Forest Trading Estate
WALTH E17 ....51 F6
Forge Close Clinic
HAYES BR2 ....199 K5
Forge Lane Primary School
FELT TW13 ....172 D2
The Former Health Centre
CHARL SE7 ....126 C4
Forster Park Primary School
CAT SE6 ....165 H5
Fortismere School
EFNCH N2 ....47 K5
Fortune Theatre
HOL/ALD WC2B 11 F4
The Forum
EDGW HA8 ....44 C2
Fossdene Primary School
CHARL SE7 ....126 A5
Fosters Primary School
WELL DA16 ....148 D3
Foster's Primary School
WELL DA16 ....148 D3
Foulds School
BAR EN5 ....20 B4
The Foundling Museum
BMSBY WC1N 5 F7
Fountayne Business Centre
SEVS/STOTM N15 ....68 C1
Fountayne Road Health
Centre *CLPT* E5 ....68 C6
Four Seasons Hotel
MYFR/PICC W1J 15 J2
POP/IOD E14 ....124 C1
Foxfield Primary School
WOOL/PLUM SE18 ....127 H5
Fox Primary School
KENS W8 ....119 K1
Frances Bardsley School for
Girls *ROM* RM1 ....75 J2
Franciscan Primary School
TOOT SW17 ....161 F6
Francis Holland School
BGVA SW1W 15 H7
CAMTN NW1 ....2 E7
Frank Barnes Primary School
STJWD NW8 ....83 H5
Franklin Industrial Estate
PGE/AN SE20 ....181 K4
Freehold Industrial Centre
HSLWW TW4 ....134 B6
Free Trade Wharf
WAP E1W 105 F6
Fresh Wharf Estate
BARK IG11 ....90 B6
Freuchen Medical Centre
WLSDN NW10 ....99 H1
Freud Museum
HAMP NW3 ....83 H4
Friars Primary Foundation
School *STHWK* SE1 ....18 A2
Friends House
CAMTN NW1 ....4 C5
Friends of Bar Ilan University
GLDGN NW11 ....64 E5
Friends of the Hebrew
University
CAMTN NW1 ....3 J1
Friern Barnet School
FBAR/BDGN N11 ....47 K1
Friern Bridge Retail Park
FBAR/BDGN N11 ....48 B2
Frithwood Primary School
NTHWD HA6 ....40 D2
Froebel College
PUT/ROE SW15 ....158 D1
Frogmore Industrial Estate
HBRY N5 ....85 J2
HYS/HAR UB3 ....113 H2
WLSDN NW10 ....98 E2
Fryent Country Park
WBLY HA9 ....62 C4
Fryent Medical Centre
CDALE/KGS NW9 ....62 E4
Fryent Primary School
CDALE/KGS NW9 ....62 E4
Fulham Clinic
FUL/PGN SW6 ....119 J6
Fulham Cross School
FUL/PGN SW6 ....139 G1
Fulham FC (Craven Cottage)
BARN SW13 ....139 F2
Fulham Medical Centre
FUL/PGN SW6 ....140 A1
Fulham Palace
FUL/PGN SW6 ....139 H3
Fulham Preparatory School
FUL/PGN SW6 ....139 H3
Fulham Primary School
FUL/PGN SW6 ....119 K6
Fulham & South Kensington
Institute *WBPTN* SW10 ......120 B5
Fuller Smith & Turner
Sports Club *CHSWK* W4 ....138 C1
Fullwell Cross
Health Centre
BARK/HLT IG6 ....54 C5

Fullwell Cross Swimming
Pool & Recreation Centre
BARK/HLT IG6 ....54 C5
Fullwood Primary School
BARK/HLT IG6 ....72 C1
Fulwell Golf Club
HPTN TW12 ....155 J6
Furzedown Primary School
TOOT SW17 ....179 G2
Furze Infant School
CHDH RM6 ....74 A3
Future Business College
CONDST W1S 9 K4
Gainsborough Clinic
PLMGR N13 ....35 F6
Gainsborough Primary School
HOM E9 ....87 H4
SRTFD E15 ....106 C2
Galleywall Primary School
BERM/RHTH SE16 ....123 J4
Galliard Primary School
ED N9 ....36 C1
Gallions Mount Primary
School *WOOL/PLUM* SE18 ...128 A5
Gallions Primary School
EHAM E6 ....108 B5
Gallions Reach
Shopping Park *EHAM* E6 ....108 B4
Gants Hill Medical Centre
GNTH/NBYPK IG2 ....72 A3
Gardener Industrial Estate
BECK BR3 ....182 B1
Garden House Boys School
KTBR SW1X 14 E5
Garden Primary School
MTCM CR4 ....179 J6
Garden Suburb Primary School
GLDGN NW11 ....64 D2
Garfield Primary School
FBAR/BDGN N11 ....48 B1
WIM/MER SW19 ....178 B2
Garratt Park Secondary
Special School
WAND/EARL SW18 ....160 A5
Garrick Industrial Centre
CDALE/KGS NW9 ....63 H2
Garrick Theatre
LSQ/SEVD WC2H 10 E6
The Garth Hotel
CRICK NW2 ....64 C6
The Garth School
MRDN SM4 ....194 C2
The Garth Road Industrial
Centre *MRDN* SM4 ....193 H4
Gascoigne Primary School
BARK IG11 ....90 C6
Gate Cinema
NTGHL W11 ....119 K1
Gatehouse School
BETH E2 ....105 F1
The Gatehouse Theatre
HGT N6 ....66 A5
Gate Theatre
NTGHL W11 ....100 E6
Gateway Business Centre
BECK BR3 ....182 B2
WOOL/PLUM SE18 ....127 H3
Gateway Industrial Estate
WLSDN NW10 ....99 H2
Gateway Primary School
STJWD NW8 ....2 B1
Gayhurst Primary School
HACK E8 ....86 C5
Gearies Infant School
GNTH/NBYPK IG2 ....72 A2
Gearies Junior School
GNTH/NBYPK IG2 ....72 B2
Geffrye Museum
BETH E2 ....7 H3
Gemini Business Estate
NWCR SE14 ....124 A5
General Medical Clinics
WCHPL E1 ....13 J1
Genesis Cinema
WCHPL E1 ....104 E3
Geoffrey Chaucer School
Technology College
STHWK SE1 ....18 E5
The Geoffrey Lloyd
Foulkes Clinic
IL IG1 ....72 A6
Geoffrey Whitworth Theatre
DART DA1 ....150 D5
George Eliot J & I School
STJWD NW8 ....83 G6
George Green School
POP/IOD E14 ....125 F5
George Lowe Court
BAY/PAD W2 ....101 F4
George Mitchell School
LEY E10 ....69 K5
George Spicer Primary School
EN EN1 ....24 B4
George Tomlinson Primary
School *WAN* E11 ....70 C5
Germal College
FSBYPK N4 ....67 G5
Gibson Business Centre
TOTM N17 ....50 B2
The Gibson Business Centre
TOTM N17 ....50 B3
Gidea Park College
GPK RM2 ....57 J6
Gidea Park Primary School
GPK RM2 ....75 H1
The Gielgud Theatre
SOHO/SHAV W1D 10 C5
Giffin Business Centre
DEPT SE8 ....144 D1
Gilbert Collection
TPL/STR WC2R 11 G5
Gilbert Colvin Primary School
CLAY IG5 ....54 A4

Gilbert Scott Primary School
SAND/SEL CR2 ....213 G6
Gillespie Primary School
FSBYPK N4 ....85 H1
Girdlers' Hall
CITYW EC2V 12 D2
Glade Primary School
CLAY IG5 ....53 K4
Gladesmore Community School
SEVS/STOTM N15 ....68 C2
The Glades Shopping Centre
BMLY BR1 ....183 K5
Gladstone Medical Centre
CRICK NW2 ....81 H2
Gladstone Park Primary
School *WLSDN* NW10 ....81 J3
Glaziers/Scientific
Instrument Makers Hall
STHWK SE1 ....12 E7
Glebe F & M School
KTN/HRWW/W HA3 ....61 K1
Glebe Primary School
HGDN/ICK UB10 ....76 B2
Glebe School
WWKM BR4 ....199 G5
Gleen Lecky Health Centre
PUT/ROE SW15 ....139 G5
Glenbrook Primary School
CLAP SW4 ....161 J1
Glencairn Sports Club
FBAR/BDGN N11 ....48 C3
Glendower Preparatory School
SKENS SW7 ....120 B4
Glenham College
IL IG1 ....72 B6
Glenlyn Medical Centre
E/WMO/HCT KT8 ....189 H2
Glenthorne High School
CHEAM SM5 ....193 K5
Globe Primary School
BETH E2 ....104 E2
Globe Wharf
BERM/RHTH SE16 ....105 F6
Gloucester Primary School
PECK SE15 ....143 F1
Godolphin & Latymer School
HMSMTH W6 ....118 E4
Godwin Junior School
FSTGT E7 ....89 F2
Golborne Medical Centre
NKENS W10 ....100 D3
Goldbeaters Primary School
EDGW HA8 ....45 F4
Golden Hinde Educational
Museum *STHWK* SE1 ....12 E6
Golders Green Crematorium
GLDGN NW11 ....64 E4
Golders Green Health Centre
GLDGN NW11 ....65 F5
Golders Hill Health Centre
EFNCH N2 ....65 G3
Golders Hill School
GLDGN NW11 ....64 E4
Goldhawk Industrial Estate
SHB W12 ....118 E3
Goldsmiths College
BROCKY SE4 ....144 C4
DEPT SE8 ....124 D6
LEW SE13 ....145 H5
NWCR SE14 ....144 C2
Goldsmiths College
Sports Ground *SCUP* DA14 ..169 G5
Goldsmiths Hall
STBT EC1A 12 C3
Goldsmith University of
London *NWCR* SE14 ....144 C2
Gonville Primary School
THHTH CR7 ....196 A2
Goodinge Health Centre
HOLWY N7 ....84 E4
Goodmayes Retail Park
CHDH RM6 ....73 H4
Goodrich J & I School
EDUL SE22 ....163 H1
Good Shepherd RC
Primary School
BMLY BR1 ....165 J6
CROY/NA CR0 ....213 K5
The Good Shepherd RC
Primary School
SHB W12 ....118 C2
Goodwyn School
MLHL NW7 ....45 J1
Goose Green Primary School
EDUL SE22 ....143 G5
Goose Green Trading Estate
EDUL SE22 ....143 H5
Gordonbrock Primary School
BROCKY SE4 ....144 D6
Gordon Hospital
WEST SW1P 16 C7
Gordon House Health Centre
WEA W13 ....116 D1
Gordon Infant School
IL IG1 ....90 D1
Gordon Primary School
ELTH/MOT SE9 ....146 E5
Goresbrook Leisure Centre
DAGW RM9 ....91 K6
Goresbrook Sports Centre
DAGW RM9 ....91 K6
The Goring Hotel
BGVA SW1W 15 K4
Gorringe Park Primary School
MTCM CR4 ....179 F4
Gosai Cinema
WEA W13 ....116 C1
Gosbury Hill Health Centre
CHSGTN KT9 ....206 A2
Gosford Primary School
REDBR IG4 ....71 K2
Gove Farm Retail Park
CHDH RM6 ....73 J4
Gower House School
CDALE/KGS NW9 ....62 E6

Grace Business Centre
MTCM CR4 ....194 E3
Grace Theatre at the
Latchmere *BTSEA* SW11 ...140 E3
Graduate School of
Management *TOTM* N17 .....50 B4
Grafton Primary School
BCTR RM8 ....74 A6
HOLWY N7 ....84 E1
Grahame Park Health Centre
CDALE/KGS NW9 ....45 G4
Grahame Park J & I School
CDALE/KGS NW9 ....45 G4
Granard Business Centre
EDGW HA8 ....45 G2
Granard Primary School
PUT/ROE SW15 ....158 E1
Granby Sports Club
ELTH/MOT SE9 ....184 D1
Grand Avenue Primary
School *BRYLDS* KT5 ....191 K4
Grand Vitesse Industrial
Centre *STHWK* SE1 ....18 B1
Grand Union Industrial
Estate *WLSDN* NW10 ....98 D1
Grange Blooms Hotel
RSQ WC1B 10 C1
Grange F & M School
RYLN/HDSTN HA2 ....60 D2
Grange Fitzrovia Hotel
GTPST W1W 9 K1
Grange Holborn Hotel
RSQ WC1B 11 F2
Grange Infant School
CAN/RD E16 ....106 D3
Grange Langham Court Hotel
GTPST W1W 9 K2
The Grange Museum
CRICK NW2 ....81 H2
Grange Park Clinic
YEAD UB4 ....94 D3
Grange Park Preparatory
School *WCHMH* N21 ....35 H1
Grange Park Primary School
ENC/FH EN2 ....23 G5
YEAD UB4 ....94 D3
Grange Primary School
EA W5 ....116 E2
STHWK SE1 ....19 G5
Grange Rochester Hotel
WEST SW1P 16 C6
Grange Whitehall Hotel
RSQ WC1B 10 E2
Grangewood Independent
School *FSTGT* E7 ....89 H1
Grangewood School
RSLP HA4 ....58 E2
Granton Primary School
STRHM/NOR SW16 ....179 H3
Granville Road Industrial
Estate *CRICK* NW2 ....64 D6
Grasmere Primary School
STNW/STAM N16 ....85 K2
Grasshoppers RFC
ISLW TW7 ....116 A6
Grassroots School
HPTN TW12 ....173 F4
Grasvenor Avenue Infant
School *BAR* EN5 ....32 E1
Gravel Hill Primary School
BXLYHS DA6 ....149 J6
Graveney School
TOOT SW17 ....179 G2
Graves Yard Industrial Estate
WELL DA16 ....148 B3
Grays Farm Primary School
STMC/STPC BR5 ....186 C4
Grazebrook Primary School
STNW/STAM N16 ....68 A6
Great Cambridge Industrial
Estate *EN* EN1 ....24 D0
Great Chapel Street
Medical Centre
SOHO/SHAV W1D 10 C3
Great Eastern Hotel
LVPST EC2M 13 G2
Great Jubilee Wharf
WAP E1W 123 K1
Great Scotland Yard
WHALL SW1A 10 E7
Great Western
Industrial Park
NWDGN UB2 ....115 G2
Great West Trading Estate
BTFD TW8 ....116 C6
Greencares Primary School
ELTH/MOT SE9 ....167 F4
The Green CE Primary School
TOTM N17 ....50 B6
Green Dragon Primary School
BTFD TW8 ....117 F5
Greenfield Medical Centre
CRICK NW2 ....82 C1
Greenfield Primary School
OXHEY WD19 ....41 G1
Greenfields Junior School
SHB W12 ....99 H6
Greenfields Special School
MUSWH N10 ....47 K6
Greenford Avenue Medical
Centre *HNWL* W7 ....96 E4
Greenford Green Clinic
GFD/PVL UB6 ....78 C3
Greenford High School
GFD/PVL UB6 ....96 A2
Greenford Industrial Estate
GFD/PVL UB6 ....78 B6
Greenford Park Cemetery
GFD/PVL UB6 ....96 B4
Greenford Road Medical
Centre *GFD/PVL* UB6 ....96 D1
Greenford Sports Centre
STHL UB1 ....96 A2
Greengate Medical Centre
PLSTW E13 ....107 F2

Greengrove College
STHGT/OAK N14 ....34 E4
Greenheath Business Centre
BETH E2 ....104 D2
Greenhill College
HRW HA1 ....61 F2
Greenhill Park Medical Centre
WLSDN NW10 ....81 G6
Greenland Pier
BERM/RHTH SE16 ....124 C3
Green Lane Business Park
ELTH/MOT SE9 ....167 F4
Green Lane Primary School
WPK KT4 ....192 E4
Greenleaf Primary School
WALTH E17 ....51 H6
Greenmead Primary School
PUT/ROE SW15 ....138 E6
The Green School for Girls
ISLW TW7 ....136 B1
Greenshaw High School
SUT SM1 ....194 B6
Greenshields Industrial Estate
CAN/RD E16 ....125 K1
Greenside Primary School
SHB W12 ....118 D2
Greenslade Primary School
WOOL/PLUM SE18 ....127 J6
Green Street Green Primary
School *ORP* BR6 ....217 F4
Greenvale School
FSTH SE23 ....164 B5
Greenwich Centre Business
Park *DEPT* SE8 ....144 E1
Greenwich Cinema
GNWCH SE10 ....145 F1
Greenwich College
GNWCH SE10 ....145 H6
Greenwich Community
College *GNWCH* SE10 ....145 F1
WOOL/PLUM SE18 ....127 G4
WOOL/PLUM SE18 ....127 J6
Greenwich Industrial Estate
CHARL SE7 ....126 A4
GNWCH SE10 ....144 E1
Greenwich Natural Health
Centre *GNWCH* SE10 ....145 F1
Greenwich Pier
GNWCH SE10 ....125 F5
Greenwich Theatre &
Art Gallery *GNWCH* SE10 ..145 G1
Greenwood Primary School
GFD/PVL UB6 ....78 C3
Greenwood Theatre
STHWK SE1 ....19 F2
Green Wrythe Primary School
CAR SM5 ....194 C3
Greig City Academy
CEND/HSY/T N8 ....67 F1
Gresham College
FLST/FETLN EC4A 11 J2
The Gresham
Hyde Park Hotel
BAY/PAD W2 ....101 G6
Gresham Way Industrial
Estate *WIM/MER* SW19 ....160 A5
Grey Coat Hospital School
WEST SW1P 16 C5
The Greycoat Hospital
WEST SW1P 16 C7
Grey Court School
RCHPK/HAM TW10 ....156 E5
Greyhound Hotel
CAR SM5 ....209 K3
Griffen Manor School
WOOL/PLUM SE18 ....147 K2
Grimsdyke F & M School
PIN HA5 ....41 K2
Grims Dyke Golf Club
PIN HA5 ....28 A6
Grim's Dyke Hotel
KTN/HRWW/W HA3 ....42 D1
Grinling Gibbons Primary
School *DEPT* SE8 ....124 C6
Grist Memorial Sports Club
E/WMO/HCT KT8 ....189 K2
Grocers' Hall
CITYW EC2V 12 E4
Grosvenor Hospitals
HDN NW4 ....63 K2
Grosvenor House Hotel
MYFR/PKLN W1K 9 G6
The Grosvenor House Hotel
GTPST W1W 10 B3
The Grove Health Centre
SHB W12 ....118 E2
Grove House (Frobel College)
PUT/ROE SW15 ....158 C1
Grovelands Priory Hospital
STHGT/OAK N14 ....34 C3
Grovelands School
WOT/HER KT12 ....188 A3
Grove Medical Centre
DEPT SE8 ....124 B4
The Grove Medical Centre
ARCH N19 ....66 D6
Grove Park Industrial Estate
CDALE/KGS NW9 ....63 F1
Grove Park Primary School
CHSWK W4 ....117 K6
Grove Park School
CDALE/KGS NW9 ....62 E1
Grove Primary School
CHDH RM6 ....73 H2
Grove Road Primary School
HSLW TW3 ....135 F5
The Groves Medical Centre
NWMAL KT3 ....176 B6
Grove Village Medical Centre
EBED/NFELT TW14 ....153 H1
Guardian Angels RC
Primary School
BOW E3 ....105 G3
Guardian Newspapers
POP/IOD E14 ....124 E2

Guards' Chapel & Museum
WHALL SW1A 16 C3
Guildhall Art Gallery
CITYW EC2V 12 D3
Guildhall School of
Music & Drama *BARB* EC2Y ..12 D2
STLK EC1Y 6 D7
Guildhall University
WCHPL E1 ....104 C5
Gumley House Convent School
ISLW TW7 ....136 B4
Gunnersbury Catholic School
BTFD TW8 ....116 D5
Gunnersbury Park Museum
ACT W5 ....117 H3
Gurnell Leisure Centre
WEA W13 ....97 F2
Guru Gobind Singh
Khalsa College *CHIG* IG7 ..39 K3
Guru Nanak Medical Centre
STHL UB1 ....114 C1
Guru Nanak Sikh Primary &
Secondary School
HYS/HAR UB3 ....114 B1
Guys Hospital
STHWK SE1 ....19 F1
Gwyn Jones Primary School
WAN E11 ....70 B4
Gypsy Moth IV
GNWCH SE10 ....125 F6
Haberdasher's Aske's Hatcham
College *NWCR* SE14 ..144 A3
Haberdashers' Hall
STBT EC1A 12 A2
Hackbridge Primary School
WLCTN SM6 ....195 F5
Hackney Business Centre
HACK E8 ....86 D4
Hackney Community College
IS N1 ....7 G3
Hackney Empire
Variety Theatre *HACK* E8 ..86 D4
Hackney Free &
Parochial CE School
HOM E9 ....86 E4
The Hackney Museum
HACK E8 ....86 D4
Hackney Sports Centre
HOM E9 ....87 J2
Hadley Wood Golf Club
EBAR EN4 ....21 J2
Hadley Wood Primary School
EBAR EN4 ....21 G1
The Haelan Clinic
CEND/HSY/T N8 ....66 E3
Haggerston School
BETH E2 ....7 K2
Haggerston Swimming Pool
BETH E2 ....7 K1
Hague Primary School
BETH E2 ....104 D3
Hailey Road Business Park
ERITHM DA18 ....129 H2
Haimo Primary School
ELTH/MOT SE9 ....146 C6
Hainault Business Park
BARK/HLT IG6 ....55 J1
Hainault Forest Golf Club
CHIG IG7 ....55 K2
Hainault Forest High School
& the Learning Centre
BARK/HLT IG6 ....55 G1
Hakim Qureshi Clinic
NWDGN UB2 ....114 D3
The Hale Clinic
REGST W1B 3 K7
Half Moon Theatre
WCHPL E1 ....105 F3
Haling Manor High School
CROY/NA CR0 ....211 H5
The Halkin Hotel
KTBR SW1X 15 H3
Halley Primary School
POP/IOD E14 ....105 G4
Hallfield Clinic
BAY/PAD W2 ....101 G5
Hallfield Primary School
BAY/PAD W2 ....101 G5
The Hall Junior School
HAMP NW3 ....83 H4
Hallmark Trading Estate
WBLY HA9 ....80 E2
Hall Place
BXLY DA5 ....169 K1
Halls Business Centre
HYS/HAR UB3 ....113 K3
The Hall School
WIM/MER SW19 ....158 D5
Hall School Wimbledon
RYNPK SW20 ....177 G4
The Hall Senior School
HAMP NW3 ....83 H4
Hallsville Primary School
CAN/RD E16 ....106 E5
Halstow Primary School
GNWCH SE10 ....125 J5
Hambrough Primary School
STHL UB1 ....114 D1
Hamer Indoor Market
BOW E3 ....105 H1
Ham Health Clinic
RCHPK/HAM TW10 ....156 D5
Ham House (NT)
RCHPK/HAM TW10 ....156 D3
Hamilton House Hotel
GNWCH SE10 ....145 G2
Hamilton Road Industrial
Estate *WNWD* SE27 ....162 E6
Hamlet International
Industrial Estate
ERITH DA8 ....130 A5
Hammersmith Apollo
HMSMTH W6 ....119 F5
Hammersmith Cemetery
HMSMTH W6 ....119 G5

The Hammersmith Hospitals
SHB W12 ....99 J5
Hammersmith Industrial
Estate *HMSMTH* W6 ....119 F6
Hammersmith New Cemetery
RCH/KEW TW9 ....137 J3
Hammersmith Palais
HMSMTH W6 ....119 F4
Hammersmith Physio &
Sports Injury Clinic
HMSMTH W6 ....119 F4
Hammersmith & West London
College
WKENS W14 ....119 G4
Hampden Gurney School
MBLAR W1H 8 D3
Ham & Petersham CC
RCHPK/HAM TW10 ....156 E6
The Hampshire School
(Knightsbridge)
SKENS SW7 ....14 C5
Hampstead CC
KIL/WHAMP NW6 ....83 F3
Hampstead Golf Club
EFNCH N2 ....65 G4
Hampstead Hill School
HAMP NW3 ....83 K2
Hampstead Medical Centre
HAMP NW3 ....83 G2
Hampstead Parochial CE
School *HAMP* NW3 ....83 G2
Hampstead School
CRICK NW2 ....82 C2
Hampstead School of English
KIL/WHAMP NW6 ....82 E2
Hampstead Theatre
HAMP NW3 ....83 H5
Hampton Cemetery
HPTN TW12 ....173 F3
Hampton Community College
HPTN TW12 ....173 F1
Hampton Court Palace
E/WMO/HCT KT8 ....174 A6
Hampton Court Palace
Golf Club
E/WMO/HCT KT8 ....190 D2
Hampton Farm Industrial
Estate *FELT* TW13 ....154 D5
Hampton FC
HPTN TW12 ....173 G4
Hampton Hill Junior School
HPTN TW12 ....173 H1
Hampton Infant School
HPTN TW12 ....172 E3
Hampton Junior School
HPTN TW12 ....173 F4
The Hampton Medical Centre
HPTN TW12 ....173 F3
Hampton Open Air Pool
HPTN TW12 ....173 H3
Hampton Road Industrial Park
CROY/NA CR0 ....196 D3
Hampton School
HPTN TW12 ....173 F1
Hampton Wick Infants School
KUT/HW KT1 ....174 D3
Handel House Museum
MYFR/PKLN W1K 9 J5
Handsworth Health Clinic
CHING E4 ....52 B2
Handsworth Primary School
CHING E4 ....52 B2
Hanover Primary School
IS N1 ....6 B2
Hanover Trading Estate
HOLWY N7 ....84 E3
Hanover West Industrial Estate
WLSDN NW10 ....98 E2
Hanworth Trading Estate
FELT TW13 ....154 D5
Harbinger Primary School
POP/IOD E14 ....124 D4
Harborough School
ARCH N19 ....66 D6
Harenc School
SCUP DA14 ....186 D1
Hargrave Park Primary School
ARCH N19 ....66 C6
Haringey Arts Council
ED N9 ....36 C4
Haringey Community Health
Clinic *SEVS/STOTM* N15 ....68 B1
Haringey Magistrates Court
HGT N6 ....66 A3
Harlesden Primary School
WLSDN NW10 ....99 G1
Harley Medical Centre
CAVSQ/HST W1G 9 K3
The Harley Medical Centre
CANST EC4R 12 D5
Harley Street Clinic
CAVSQ/HST W1G 9 J2
Harlington Community School
WDR/YW UB7 ....113 G4
Harlyn Primary School
PIN HA5 ....41 F6
The Harold Macmillan Medical
Centre *HRW* HA1 ....60 D4
Harp Business Centre
CRICK NW2 ....63 J6
Harpley School
WCHPL E1 ....104 E3
Harrington Hall Hotel
SKENS SW7 ....120 B4
Harrington Hill
Primary School
CLPT E5 ....68 D5
Harris City Technology College
NRWD SE19 ....181 G4
Harrodian School
BARN SW13 ....138 C1
Harrods Store
CHEL SW3 ....14 E4
Harrovian Business Village
HRW HA1 ....60 D4

Harrow Arts Centre
PIN HA5 ....42 A3
Harrow Borough FC
RYLN/HDSTN HA2 ....78 A2
Harrow College
HRW HA1 ....60 E4
KTN/HRWW/W HA3 ....42 E2
Harrow CC
HRW HA1 ....78 E2
Harrow Crown Courts
HRW HA1 ....42 D6
Harrow Heritage Museum
RYLN/HDSTN HA2 ....42 C6
Harrow High School
HRW HA1 ....61 G3
Harrow Leisure Centre
KTN/HRWW/W HA3 ....43 F6
Harrow Magistrates Court
HRW HA1 ....61 F1
Harrow RFC
STAN HA7 ....29 H5
Harrow Road Health Centre
BAY/PAD W2 ....100 E4
Harrow School
HRW HA1 ....60 E4
RYLN/HDSTN HA2 ....60 E4
Harrow Town CC
RYLN/HDSTN HA2 ....60 A5
Harrow Weald Cemetery
KTN/HRWW/W HA3 ....42 E2
Harry Gosling
Primary School
WCHPL E1 ....104 C5
Hartley Primary School
EHAM E6 ....89 J6
Hartscourt Golf &
Country Club *BUSH* WD23 ..28 C4
Hartsbourne JMI School
BUSH WD23 ....28 D4
Harvington School
EA W5 ....97 J5
Haselbury Infant School
ED N9 ....36 A5
Haseltine Primary School
CAT SE6 ....164 C6
Haslemere Business Centre
EN EN1 ....24 D5
Haslemere Industrial Estate
EBED/NFELT TW14 ....133 K6
WAND/EARL SW18 ....160 A4
Haslemere Primary School
MTCM CR4 ....178 C5
Hasmonean High School
Boys Site *HDN* NW4 ....46 B5
Hasmonean High School
Girls Site *MLHL* NW7 ....45 J4
Hasmonean Primary School
HDN NW4 ....64 B2
Haste Hill Golf Club
NTHWD HA6 ....40 C5
Hastings Clinic
BRXS/STRHM SW2 ....142 A6
Hastingwood Trading
Estate
UED N18 ....51 G2
Hatcham Mews Business
Centre *NWCR* SE14 ....144 A1
Hatch End High School
KTN/HRWW/W HA3 ....42 B3
Hatch End Swimming Pool
PIN HA5 ....42 A3
Hatfeild Primary School
MRDN SM4 ....193 H3
Hathaway Primary School
WEA W13 ....97 F4
Hatton School
REDBR IG4 ....53 H6
Havelock Primary School
HYS/HAR UB3 ....114 E3
Haven Green Clinic
EA W5 ....97 K5
Havering College of Further &
Higher Education
EMPK RM11 ....75 K4
Havering Magistrates Court
ROM RM1 ....75 G1
Haverstock School
CAMTN NW1 ....84 A4
Hawes Down Clinic
WWKM BR4 ....199 G6
Hawes Down Primary School
WWKM BR4 ....199 G5
The Hawker Centre
KUTN/CMB KT2 ....174 E1
Hawkesdown House School
KENS W8 ....119 K1
Hawkeswood School
CHING E4 ....38 C4
Hawkins Clinic
PUT/ROE SW15 ....139 G5
RYNPK SW20 ....176 C4
Hawksmoor Primary School
THMD SE28 ....109 H6
Hawley Infant School
CAMTN NW1 ....84 B5
Haydon School
PIN HA5 ....40 D4
Hayes Bridge Middle School
NWDGN UB2 ....114 D2
Hayes Bridge Primary School
YEAD UB4 ....114 C1
Hayes Bridge Retail Park
HYS/HAR UB3 ....95 G6
Hayes CC
HYS/HAR UB3 ....94 D6
Hayes FC
HYS/HAR UB3 ....94 D6
Hayes Grove Priory Hospital
HAYES BR2 ....199 K6
The Hayes Manor School
HYS/HAR UB3 ....94 B5
Hayes Park J & I School
YEAD UB4 ....94 D3
Hayes Pool
HYS/HAR UB3 ....113 J1

Hayes Primary School
HAYES BR2 ....200 A5
Hayes School
HAYES BR2 ....200 A6
Hayes Social & Sports Club
HYS/HAR UB3 ....94 D6
Hayes Stadium Sports Centre
HYS/HAR UB3 ....94 B5
Hay Lane School
CDALE/KGS NW9 ....62 E1
Hays Galleria
STHWK SE1 ....13 G7
Hayward Gallery
STHWK SE1 ....17 H1
Hazeldene Medical Centre
WBLY HA9 ....80 D4
Hazelwood Infant School
PLMGR N13 ....35 H5
Hazelwood Junior School
PLMGR N13 ....35 C6
Headstart Montessori School
TOOT SW17 ....160 B5
Health Service Clinic
CHDH RM6 ....56 A6
Healy Medical Centre
CLPT E5 ....68 D5
The Heart Hospital
CAVSQ/HST W1G 9 H2
Heathbrook Primary School
VX/NE SW8 ....141 H3
Heath Business Centre
HSLW TW3 ....135 H5
Heathfield College
HAYES BR2 ....215 G4
Heathfield Primary School
WHTN TW2 ....155 F3
Heathfield School (Senior)
PIN HA5 ....59 H3
Heath House Preparatory
School *BKHTH/KID* SE3 ..145 J3
The Heartland School
HSLWW TW4 ....154 E1
Heathmere Primary School
PUT/ROE SW15 ....158 D3
Heathpark Golf Club
WDR/YW UB7 ....112 D3
Heathrow Airport
HTHAIR TW6 ....132 E3
Heathrow Airport Central
Bus & Coach Station
HTHAIR TW6 ....132 D4
Heathrow International
Trading Estate
HSLWW TW4 ....134 A4
Heathrow Medical Centre
HYS/HAR UB3 ....113 G5
Heathrow Primary School
WDR/YW UB7 ....112 C6
Heathrow World Cargo Centre
HTHAIR TW6 ....132 C6
Heathside Preparatory School
HAMP NW3 ....83 G2
Heathway Industrial Estate
DAGE RM10 ....92 D2
Heathway Medical Centre
DAGW RM9 ....92 B2
Heavers Farm Primary
School
SNWD SE25 ....197 G2
Heber Primary School
EDUL SE22 ....163 G1
Heckford Street Business
Centre *WAP* E1W 105 F6
Hedges & Butler Estate
SRTFD E15 ....106 A1
Hedgewood School
YEAD UB4 ....94 C2
Helena Road Clinic
WLSDN NW10 ....81 K2
Heliport Industrial Estate
BTSEA SW11 ....140 C3
Hellenic College of London
KTBR SW1X 14 E5
Helston Court Business
Centre
WIM/MER SW19 ....176 E1
Henderson Hospital
BELMT SM2 ....208 E6
Hendon Cemetery
HDN NW4 ....46 B4
Hendon Crematorium
HDN NW4 ....46 B3
Hendon FC
CRICK NW2 ....64 B6
Hendon Golf Club
HDN NW4 ....46 A3
Hendon Preparatory School
HDN NW4 ....46 B6
Hendon School
HDN NW4 ....64 B2
Hendon Secretarial College
HDN NW4 ....64 A2
Hendon Youth Sports Centre
CRICK NW2 ....64 B4
Henry Cavendish Primary
School *BAL* SW12 ....161 H3
Henry Compton School
FUL/PGN SW6 ....139 G2
Henry Fawcett
Primary School
LBTH SE11 ....122 B6
Henry Green Primary School
BCTR RM8 ....73 K5
Henry Maynard Junior School
WALTH E17 ....70 A2
Henwick Primary School
ELTH/MOT SE9 ....146 C4
Herbert Morrison Primary
School *VX/NE* SW8 ....141 K1
Hereward House School
HAMP NW3 ....83 J4
Her Majestys' Theatre
STJS SW1Y 10 D7

Hermitage Primary School
WAP E1W 123 H1
Herne Hill School
HNHL SE24 ....142 D6
Herne Hill Stadium
(Cycle Centre) *DUL* SE21 ..162 E1
Heron Industrial Estate
SRTFD E15 ....105 K1
Heronsgate Primary School
THMD SE28 ....127 J3
Heron Trading Estate
ACT W3 ....98 D4
Hersham Trading Estate
WOT/HER KT12 ....188 D6
Heston Community School
HEST TW5 ....135 F1
Heston Community
Sports Hall
HEST TW5 ....135 F1
Heston Industrial Mall
HEST TW5 ....134 E1
Heston Infant School
HEST TW5 ....135 F1
Heston Junior School
HEST TW5 ....115 F6
Heston Park CC
HEST TW5 ....114 E6
Heston Swimming Baths
HEST TW5 ....114 E6
HGS Institute Centre
GLDGN NW11 ....65 F2
Higgs Industrial Estate
BRXN/ST SW9 ....142 C4
Highams Lodge Business
Centre *WALTH* E17 ....51 F6
Highams Park School
CHING E4 ....52 B2
Highbury Corner
Magistrates Court
HOLWY N7 ....85 G4
Highbury Fields School
HBRY N5 ....85 H2
Highbury Grove School
HBRY N5 ....85 J3
Highbury Park Clinic
HBRY N5 ....85 H1
Highbury Pool
HBRY N5 ....85 H4
Highbury Quadrant
Primary School
HBRY N5 ....85 J2
High Commission of Angola
MYFR/PKLN W1K 9 H5
High Commission of
Antigua & Barbuda
MHST W1U 9 G3
High Commission of Bahamas
MYFR/PICC W1J 9 H7
High Commission of
Bangladesh *SKENS* SW7 ..120 B3
High Commission of
Barbados *FITZ* W1T 10 C3
High Commission of Belize
CAVSQ/HST W1G 9 J3
High Commission of Botswana
MHST W1U 9 J4
High Commission of Brunei
KTBR SW1X 15 G4
High Commission of Cyprus
MYFR/PKLN W1K 9 G5
High Commission of Dominica
ECT SW5 ....120 A4
High Commission of Fiji
KTBR SW1X 120 B2
High Commission of Gambia
KENS W8 ....120 A2
High Commission of Grenada
ECT SW5 ....120 A5
High Commission of Guyana
NTGHL W11 ....101 F6
High Commission of Jamaica
SKENS SW7 ....14 A3
High Commission of Kenya
CAVSQ/HST W1G 9 J1
High Commission of Lesotho
KTBR SW1X 15 G4
High Commission of Malawi
MYFR/PKLN W1K 9 J5
High Commission of Malaysia
KTBR SW1X 15 H3
High Commission of Maldives
MHST W1U 9 G1
High Commission of Malta
MYFR/PICC W1J 10 B6
High Commission of Namibia
CAVSQ/HST W1G 9 K2
High Commission of
New Zealand
STJS SW1Y 10 C7
High Commission of Nigeria
CHCR WC2N 10 E7
EMB EC4Y 11 K4
High Commission of Pakistan
KTBR SW1X 15 F4
High Commission of
Papua New Guinea
STJS SW1Y 10 B7
High Commission of St Lucia
KENS W8 ....120 A2
High Commission of Seychelles
MBLAR W1H 9 F1
High Commission of
Sierra Leone
REGST W1B 10 A3
High Commission of Singapore
KTBR SW1X 15 F3
High Commission of
South Africa *CHCR* WC2N ..10 E7
High Commission of Sri Lanka
BAY/PAD W2 ....8 B5
High Commission of
Swaziland
WESTW SW1E 16 A4
High Commission of Tonga
MBLAR W1H 8 D2

High Commission of Trinidad & Tobago *KTBR* SW1X ...15 G4
High Commission of Uganda *STJS* SW1Y ...10 D7
High Commission of Zambia *BAY/PAD* W2 ...120 B2
High Commission of Zimbabwe *CHCR* WC2N ...10 E6
High Cross Centre *SEVS/STOTM* N15 ...68 C1
High Elms Country Park *ORP* BR6 ...216 C5
High Elms Golf Club *ORP* BR6 ...216 C5
Highfield Infant School *HAYES* BR2 ...199 H1
Highfield Junior School *HAYES* BR2 ...199 H1
Highfield Primary School *WCHMH* N21 ...35 H3
Highfield School *WAND/EARL* SW18 ...160 D2
Highgate Cemetery *HGT* N6 ...66 A5
Highgate Golf Club *HGT* N6 ...65 J3
Highgate Junior School *HGT* N6 ...65 K4
Highgate Pre-Preparatory School *HGT* N6 ...65 K4
Highgate Primary School *HGT* N6 ...65 K3
Highgate Private Hospital *HGT* N6 ...65 K3
Highgate School *HGT* N6 ...65 K4
Highgate Wood School *CEND/HSY/T* N8 ...66 C2
Highgrove Pool *RSLP* HA4 ...58 E4
Highlands J & I School *IL* IG1 ...71 K5
Highlands Primary School *IL* IG1 ...71 K5
Highshore School *PECK* SE15 ...143 G2
High View Primary School *BTSEA* SW11 ...140 C5
Highview Primary School *WLGTN* SM6 ...210 E3
The Highway Primary School *ORP* BR6 ...217 J3
The Highway Trading Centre *WCHPL* E1 ...105 F6
Hillbrook Primary School *TOOT* SW17 ...160 E6
Hillcroft College *SURB* KT6 ...191 F3
Hillcross Primary School *MRDN* SM4 ...193 J1
Hill House International Junior School *CHEL* SW3 ...14 E5
Hill House Preparatory School *CHEL* SW3 ...120 D6
Hill Mead Infant School *BRXN/ST* SW9 ...142 C5
Hillmead Primary School *BRXN/ST* SW9 ...142 C5
Hills Grove Primary School *WELL* DA16 ...148 D1
Hillside Primary School *NTHWD* HA6 ...40 E3
STMC/STPC BR5 ...202 D4
Hillyfield Primary School *WALTH* E17 ...51 G6
Hilly Fields Medical Centre *BROCKY* SE4 ...144 D6
Hilton Docklands Pier *BERM/RHTH* SE16 ...124 C1
The Hiltongrove Business Centre *WALTH* E17 ...69 J1
Hinchley Wood Primary School *THDIT* KT7 ...190 B6
Hinchley Wood School & Sixth Form Centre *THDIT* KT7 ...190 B6
Hinley Clinic *LBTH* SE11 ...17 K7
Hispaniola *WHALL* SW1A ...17 F1
Hitherfield Primary School *STRHM/NOR* SW16 ...162 B4
Hither Green Cemetery *CAT* SE6 ...165 J4
Hither Green Primary School *LEW* SE13 ...165 G1
HM Prison *BRXS/STRHM* SW2 ...161 K1
HOLWY N7 ...84 E2
SHB W12 ...99 J5
THMD SE28 ...127 K3
WAND/EARL SW18 ...160 C1
HMS Belfast *STHWK* SE1 ...13 H7
HMS President *EMB* EC4Y ...11 K5
HM Young Offender Institution *FELT* TW13 ...153 J6
Hobbayne F & M School *HNWL* W7 ...97 F5
Hobbayne Primary School *HNWL* W7 ...96 E5
Hogarth Business Park *CHSWK* W4 ...118 B6
The Hogarth Hotel *ECT* SW5 ...120 A4
Hogarth Industrial Estate *WLSDN* NW10 ...99 J3
Hogarth's House *CHSWK* W4 ...118 A6
Holbeach Primary School *CAT* SE6 ...164 D2

Holborn College *WKENS* W14 ...119 H6
WOOL/PLUM SE18 ...126 C4
Holborn College Independent School *HMSMTH* W6 ...119 F5
Holborn Medical Centre *BMSBY* WC1N ...5 G7
Holborn Town Hall *HHOL* WC1V ...11 F3
Holbury Centre *ERITH* DA8 ...150 D1
Holiday Inn *BMSBY* WC1N ...4 E7
BXLY DA5 ...169 J1
CAMTN NW1 ...84 B5
CRICK NW2 ...64 A5
EA W5 ...98 A2
FSBYW WC1X ...5 H5
GTPST W1W ...3 J3
HAMP NW3 ...83 J5
HYS/HAR UB3 ...133 C2
MYFR/PICC W1J ...9 K6
SKENS SW7 ...120 B4
SUT SM1 ...209 F4
WDR/YW UB7 ...112 D5
Holland House *KENS* W8 ...119 J2
Holland House School *EDGW* HA8 ...30 C4
Holland Park School *KENS* W8 ...119 J2
Holland Park Theatre *WKENS* W14 ...119 J2
Holland Street Clinic *KENS* W8 ...119 K2
Hollickwood JMI School *MUSWH* N10 ...48 B3
Holloway School *HOLWY* N7 ...84 D3
Hollydale Primary School *PECK* SE15 ...143 K3
The Hollyfield School *SURB* KT6 ...191 F2
Holly House Private Hospital *BKHH* IG9 ...39 F4
Hollymount Primary School *RYNPK* SW20 ...177 F4
Holly Park JMI School *FBAR/BDGN* N11 ...48 A1
The Holme *CAMTN* NW1 ...3 F5
Holmleigh Primary School *STNW/STAM* N16 ...68 B5
Holy Cross Preparatory School *KUTN/CMB* KT2 ...175 K3
Holy Cross RC Convent School *NWMAL* KT3 ...192 A1
Holy Cross RC Primary School *CAT* SE6 ...165 F3
Holy Family RC Primary School *BKHTH/KID* SE3 ...146 A5
POP/IOD E14 ...105 J6
Holy Family Technology College *WALTH* E17 ...69 K1
Holy Ghost RC Primary School *BAL* SW12 ...160 E2
Holy Innocents C Primary School *ORP* BR6 ...217 F1
Holy Trinity CE Junior School *WLGTN* SM6 ...210 C2
Holy Trinity CE Primary School *BGVA* SW1W ...15 G6
BRXS/STRHM SW2 ...162 A2
DART DA1 ...151 F6
EFNCH N2 ...47 H6
FSTH SE23 ...163 K4
KIL/WHAMP NW6 ...83 G4
NTHWD HA6 ...40 A2
RCHPK/HAM TW10 ...137 H5
Holy Trinity College *BMLY* BR1 ...184 B4
Holy Trinity in St Silas *CAMTN* NW1 ...84 B5
Holy Trinity Lamorbey CE Primary School *BFN/LL* DA15 ...168 B3
Holy Trinity Primary School *HACK* E8 ...86 A4
WIM/MER SW19 ...177 K2
Holy Trinity School *CHEL* SW3 ...15 F6
Holywell School *WATW* WD18 ...26 D1
Homefield Preparatory School *SUT* SM1 ...208 E3
Homerton College of Technology *HOM* E9 ...86 E3
Homerton Hospital *CLPT* E5 ...87 F3
Homoeopathic Health Centre *MLHL* NW7 ...45 H1
PLSTW E13 ...106 C3
Honeypot Business Centre *STAN* HA7 ...44 A4
Honeypot Lane Centre *STAN* HA7 ...43 K4
Honeypot Medical Centre *STAN* HA7 ...44 A5
Honeywell Primary School *BTSEA* SW11 ...160 E1
Honor Oak Crematorium *FSTH* SE23 ...144 A6
Honor Oak Gallery *FSTH* SE23 ...164 A1
Honor Oak Health Centre *BROCKY* SE4 ...144 B5
Honourable Artillery Company HQ *STLK* EC1Y ...6 E7
Hook Lane Primary School *WELL* DA16 ...148 B4
Hook Rise South Industrial Park *CHSGTN* KT9 ...206 A3
Horizon Business Centre *ED* N9 ...37 F4

Horizon Industrial Estate *PECK* SE15 ...123 H6
Horizon Project Children with Special Needs *RCH/KEW* TW9 ...137 G2
Horizon School *STNW/STAM* N16 ...86 A2
The Horniman Museum & Gardens *FSTH* SE23 ...163 J3
Horniman Primary School *FSTH* SE23 ...163 J3
Horn Park Primary School *LEE/GVPK* SE12 ...166 A2
Hornsby House School *BAL* SW12 ...161 F3
Hornsey Central Hospital *CEND/HSY/T* N8 ...66 C2
Hornsey Rise Health Centre *CEND/HSY/T* N8 ...66 D4
Hornsey School for Girls *CEND/HSY/T* N8 ...67 F2
Horn Stairs *BERM/RHTH* SE16 ...124 C1
Horseferry Road Magistrates Court *WEST* SW1P ...16 D5
Horse Guards Parade *WHALL* SW1A ...16 D1
Horsenden Hill Golf Club *GFD/PVL* UB6 ...79 H4
Horsenden Primary School *GFD/PVL* UB6 ...78 E4
Horton Country Park *HOR/WEW* KT19 ...206 C6
Horton Industrial Park *WDR/YW* UB7 ...112 C1
Horton Park Golf & Country Club *HOR/WEW* KT19 ...206 E5
Hortus Cemetery *NWDGN* UB2 ...114 E2
Hospital of St John & St Elizabeth *STJWD* NW8 ...2 A5
Hotel Ibis *BARK* IG11 ...90 B6
CAMTN NW1 ...4 B5
GNWCH SE10 ...125 F6
HYS/HAR UB5 ...133 H2
POP/IOD E14 ...106 A6
SRTFD E15 ...88 C4
WBLY HA9 ...80 C3
Hotham Primary School *PUT/ROE* SW15 ...139 G5
Hotspur Industrial Estate *TOTM* N17 ...50 D2
Houndsfield Primary School *ED* N9 ...36 C2
Hounslow Business Park *HSLW* TW3 ...135 F5
Hounslow CC *HSLW* TW3 ...134 C3
Hounslow Cemetery *HSLW* TW4 ...134 E2
Hounslow College Independent School *FELT* TW13 ...154 C6
Hounslow Heath Golf Club *HSLWW* TW4 ...134 C6
Hounslow Heath Infant School *HSLWW* TW4 ...134 D4
Hounslow Heath Junior School *HSLWW* TW4 ...134 D4
Hounslow Manor School *HSLW* TW3 ...135 G4
Hounslow Manor Sports Hall *HSLW* TW3 ...135 G4
Hounslow Town Primary School *HSLW* TW3 ...135 H4
House of Detention *CLKNW* EC1R ...5 K6
House of St Barnabas *SOHO/SHAV* W1D ...10 C4
Houses of Parliament *WEST* SW1P ...17 F3
Houston Business Park *YEAD* UB4 ...114 B1
Howard Primary School *CROY/NA* CR0 ...211 J2
Howland Quay *BERM/RHTH* SE16 ...124 A3
Hoxton Hall Community Theatre *IS* N1 ...7 G2
HQS Wellington (Master Mariners) *TPL/STR* WC2R ...11 J6
HSBC Sports Club *BECK* BR3 ...182 B2
HSBC Tower *POP/IOD* E14 ...124 E1
Hubbinet Industrial Estate *ROMW/RG* RM7 ...56 E6
Hugh Myddelton Primary School *CLKNW* EC1R ...5 K5
The Humana Wellington Hospital *STJWD* NW8 ...2 B4
Humber Trading Estate *CRICK* NW2 ...63 K6
Hungerford Primary School *HOLWY* N7 ...84 D4
Hunters Hall Primary School *DAGE* RM10 ...92 D3
Hunter Street Health Centre *STPAN* WC1H ...4 E6
Huntsman Sports Club *BKHTH/KID* SE3 ...145 K5
Hurlingham Business Park *FUL/PGN* SW6 ...139 K4
Hurlingham & Chelsea School *FUL/PGN* SW6 ...139 K4
Hurlingham House *FUL/PGN* SW6 ...139 J4
Hurlingham Private School *PUT/ROE* SW15 ...139 J3
Huron University *GWRST* WC1E ...10 E1

Hurricane Trading Centre *CDALE/KGS* NW9 ...45 H4
Hurstmere School *BFN/LL* DA15 ...168 C5
Hurst Park Primary School *E/WMO/HCT* KT8 ...173 F6
Hurst Primary School *BXLY* DA5 ...168 E3
Hyatt Carlton Tower Hotel *KTBR* SW1X ...15 F5
The Hyde Industrial Estate *CDALE/KGS* NW9 ...63 H2
The Hyde School *CDALE/KGS* NW9 ...63 H2
Hyland House School *WALTH* E17 ...52 B5
Hyleford Leavers Unit School *BARK/HLT* IG6 ...54 D5
Hyleford School *IL* IG1 ...72 D1
Hythe Road industrial Estate *WLSDN* NW10 ...99 J3
Ian Mikardo High School *BOW* E3 ...105 K2
Ibstock Place School *PUT/ROE* SW15 ...158 B1
ICA Cinema *STJS* SW1Y ...10 D7
Ichthus Primary School *CMBW* SE5 ...143 F1
Ickburgh School *CLPT* E5 ...86 D1
Ickenham Clinic *HGDN/ICK* UB10 ...76 A1
Ihlara Sport FC *HBRY* N5 ...85 J2
IKEA Store Brent Park *WLSDN* NW10 ...81 F3
IKEA Store Croydon *CROY/NA* CR0 ...196 A5
IKEA Store Edmonton *UED* N18 ...50 E2
Ikra Primary School *STNW/STAM* N16 ...86 A2
Ilderton Primary School *BERM/RHTH* SE16 ...123 K6
Ilford County Court *IL* IG1 ...72 D6
Ilford County High School *BARK/HLT* IG6 ...54 C5
Ilford Golf Club *IL* IG1 ...71 K5
Ilford Jewish Primary School *BARK/HLT* IG6 ...54 D6
Ilford Medical Centre *IL* IG1 ...90 B1
Ilford Preparatory School *GDMY/SEVK* IG3 ...73 F5
Ilford Retail Park *IL* IG1 ...72 C6
Ilford Swimming Pool *IL* IG1 ...72 D6
Imber Court Trading Estate *E/WMO/HCT* KT8 ...189 J3
Immanuel CE Primary School *STRHM/NOR* SW16 ...179 K2
Immanuel College *BUSH* WD23 ...28 E2
Immanuel School *ROM* RM1 ...57 G2
Imperial College *PUT/ROE* SW15 ...139 G3
SKENS SW7 ...14 A4
SKENS SW7 ...120 C5
Imperial College Athletic Ground *WDR/YW* UB7 ...113 F6
Imperial College of Science *FUL/PGN* SW6 ...119 K6
Imperial College of Science & Technology *SKENS* SW7 ...14 B3
Imperial College School of Medicine *PIM* SW1V ...16 C7
Imperial War Museum *STHWK* SE1 ...17 K5
Imperial War Museum Annexe *STHWK* SE1 ...17 K5
Independent Industrial Estate *WDR/YW* UB7 ...112 C1
Independent Jewish School *HDN* NW4 ...64 B2
India House *HOL/ALD* WC2B ...11 G5
Infant College *IL* IG1 ...72 K6
Innellan House School *PIN* HA5 ...41 J6
Inner London Sessions House (Crown Court) *STHWK* SE1 ...18 C4
Innholders Hall *CANST* EC4R ...12 D5
Innkeeper's Lodge *BECK* BR3 ...198 D3
NTHLT UB5 ...78 A4
SAND/SEL CR2 ...211 J4
SAND/SEL CR2 ...211 J6
STHGT/OAK N14 ...34 E4
Inns of Court & Chancery *TPL/STR* WC2R ...11 J4
Inns of Court School of Law *GINN* WC1R ...11 H1
Institut Francais *SKENS* SW7 ...14 A6
Intercontinental London *MYFR/PICC* W1J ...15 H2
Intercontinental The Churchill London *MBLAR* W1H ...9 F3
International Community School *CAMTN* NW1 ...3 G7
International School of Havana *STJS* SW1Y ...10 D7
International School of London *ACT* W3 ...117 H4

International School of Moscow *WHALL* SW1A ...16 E2
International Trading Estate *NWDGN* UB2 ...114 A3
Invicta Industrial Estate *SRTFD* E15 ...106 C2
Invicta Primary School *BKHTH/KID* SE3 ...125 K6
Invicta Sports Club *DART* DA1 ...151 G6
Inwood Business Centre *HSLW* TW3 ...135 G5
IQRA Independent School *BRXN/ST* SW9 ...142 B4
Ironmonger Row Baths *FSBYE* EC1V ...6 C5
Ironmongers Hall *STBT* EC1A ...12 C2
Islamia Girls School *KIL/WHAMP* NW6 ...82 C6
Islamic College for Advanced Study *WLSDN* NW10 ...81 K5
The Islamic Grammar School *WAND/EARL* SW18 ...159 J2
Island Clinic *POP/IOD* E14 ...125 F2
Isleworth Cemetery *ISLW* TW7 ...136 B3
Isleworth Recreation Centre *ISLW* TW7 ...136 A5
Isleworth & Syon School for Boys *ISLW* TW7 ...135 K1
Isleworth Town Primary School *ISLW* TW7 ...136 A3
Islington Arts & Media School *FSBYPK* N4 ...67 G3
Islington Business Centre *IS* N1 ...85 J6
Islington Crematorium *EFNCH* N2 ...47 J4
Islington Green Medical Centre *IS* N1 ...6 B1
Islington Green School *IS* N1 ...6 B1
Islington Tennis Centre *HOLWY* N7 ...84 D4
Islington Town Hall *IS* N1 ...85 H5
Ismaili Centre *SKENS* SW7 ...14 B6
Italia Conti Academy of Theatre Arts *BRXN/ST* SW9 ...141 K4
Italian Hospital *WEST* SW1P ...16 A6
Ithaca College *SKENS* SW7 ...120 B4
Ivybridge Primary School *ISLW* TW7 ...156 A1
Ivybridge Retail Park *ISLW* TW7 ...136 A6
Ivydale Primary School *BROCKY* SE4 ...144 A5
Jack & Jill School *HPTN* TW12 ...173 F2
TWK TW1 ...155 K4
Jack Taylor School *KIL/WHAMP* NW6 ...83 G6
Jack Tizard School *FUL/PGN* SW6 ...139 G2
Jacques Prevert School *WKENS* W14 ...119 G4
Jamahiriya School *CMBW* SE5 ...120 D6
James Allens Preparatory Girls School *EDUL* SE22 ...142 E6
James Dixon Primary School *PGE/AN* SE20 ...181 H4
Jamestown Mental Health Centre *HAMP* NW3 ...83 K5
James Wolfe Primary School *GNWCH* SE10 ...144 E1
Jamiatul Ummah School *WCHPL* E1 ...104 D5
Janet Adegoke Leisure Centre *SHB* W12 ...99 J6
The Japanese School *ACT* W3 ...98 B4
Japan Green Medical Centre *ACT* W3 ...117 J1
Jenner Health Centre *FSTH* SE23 ...164 B3
Jenny Hammond Primary School *WAN* E11 ...88 C2
Jermyn Street Theatre *MYFR/PICC* W1J ...10 B6
Jessop Primary School *HNHL* SE24 ...142 C5
Jewel Tower *WEST* SW1P ...16 E4
Jewish Cemetery *GLDGN* NW11 ...64 E3
Jewish Community Theatre *CMBW* SE5 ...142 E4
Jewish Free School *KTTN* NW5 ...84 D4
The Jewish Museum *CAMTN* NW1 ...3 J1
FNCH N3 ...46 E5
Jews College London *HDN* NW4 ...64 B1
The Joe Richardson Community School *DAGW* RM9 ...91 K6
Johanna Primary School *STHWK* SE1 ...17 J3
John Ball Primary School *BKHTH/KID* SE3 ...145 H3
John Betts Primary School *HMSMTH* W6 ...118 D3
John Bramston Primary School *BARK/HLT* IG6 ...55 G2
John Burns Primary School *BTSEA* SW11 ...141 F3

John Chilton School
NTHLT UB5 ....77 J5
John Dixon Clinic
BERM/RHTH SE16 ....123 J3
John Donne Primary School
PECK SE15 ....143 J2
John F Kennedy Special
School *SRTFD* E15 ....88 B6
John Keble CE Primary
School *WLSDN* NW10 ....99 H1
John Kelly Boys & Girls
Technology College
CRICK NW2 ....81 H1
The John Loughborough
School *TOTM* N17 ....50 B5
John Lyon School
RYLN/HDSTN HA2 ....60 D5
John Milton Primary School
VX/NE SW8 ....141 H1
John Nightingale School
E/WMO/HCT KT8 ....172 E6
John Orwell Sports Centre
WAP E1W 123 H1
John Paul II RC School
WIM/MER SW19 ....159 G2
John Perryn Primary School
ACT W3 ....99 G5
John Perry Primary School
DAGE RM10 ....93 F4
John Roan Lower School
BKHTH/KID SE3 ....145 J1
John Roan School
BKHTH/KID SE3 ....145 H1
John Ruskin College
SAND/SEL CR2 ....213 G5
John Ruskin Primary School
WALW SE17 ....122 D6
John Scott Health Centre
FSBYPK N4 ....67 J5
John Scurr Primary School
WCHPL E1 ....104 E3
John Smith House
WALW SE17 ....18 C7
Johnsons Industrial Estate
HYS/HAR UB3 ....113 K3
John Stainer Primary School
BROCKY SE4 ....144 B4
Joseph Clarke Special School
CHING E4 ....52 B2
Joseph Hood Primary School
RYNPK SW20 ....177 H5
Joseph Lancaster Primary
School *STHWK* SE1 ....18 C5
Joydens Wood Infant School
RDART DA2 ....170 B6
Joydens Wood Junior
School
BXLY DA5 ....170 B6
Jubilee Country Park
HAYES BR2 ....201 G1
Jubilee Market
COVGDN WC2E 11 F5
Jubilee Primary School
BRXS/STRHM SW2 ....162 B1
THMD SE28 ....109 J6
Jubilee Sports Ground
CHING E4 ....38 B6
Julians Primary School
STRHM/NOR SW16 ....162 B6
Juno Way Ind Est
NWCR SE14 ....124 A4
Jurys Clifton-Ford Hotel
MHST W1U 9 H2
Jurys Great Russell Street
RSQ WC1B 10 D3
Jury's Inn Hotel
CROY/NA CR0 ....196 D6
Jurys Kensington Hotel
SKENS SW7 ....14 A7
JVC Business Park
CRICK NW2 ....63 J5
Kaizen Primary School
PLSTW E13 ....107 F3
Kangley Business Centre
SYD SE26 ....182 C1
Katella Trading Estate
BARK IG11 ....108 E2
Katherine Road Medical
Centre *FSTGT* E7 ....89 G4
Keats House Museum
HAMP NW3 ....83 H2
Keble Preparatory School
WCHMH N21 ....35 G2
Keen Students
Supplementary School
WCHPL E1 ....104 C4
Keir Hardie Primary School
CAN/RD E16 ....106 E4
Keith Davis Cue Sports Club
DAGW RM9 ....91 K5
Kelmscott Community Centre
WALTH E17 ....69 H3
Kelmscott Leisure Centre
WALTH E17 ....69 H3
Kelmscott School
WALTH E17 ....69 H3
Kelsey Park School
BECK BR3 ....182 D6
Kelvin Industrial Estate
GFD/PVL UB6 ....78 B6
GFD/PVL UB6 ....96 D2
Kemnal Technology College
STMC/STPC BR5 ....186 C3
Kempton Park Racecourse
SUN TW16 ....172 A3
Ken Barrington Centre
LBTH SE11 ....122 A6
Kender Primary School
NWCR SE14 ....143 K2
Kenmont Primary School
WLSDN NW10 ....99 J2
Kenmore Park Middle School
KTN/HRWW/W HA3 ....43 K6
Kenneth More Theatre
IL IG1 ....90 C1

Kensal Green Cemetery
WLSDN NW10 ....99 K2
Kensal Rise Primary School
WLSDN NW10 ....100 B1
Kensington Av Primary School
THHTH CR7 ....180 B4
Kensington Business Centre
SKENS SW7 ....14 D4
Kensington & Chelsea College
NKENS W10 ....100 C4
WBPTN SW10 ....140 D1
Kensington & Chelsea
Town Hall *KENS* W8 ......119 K2
Kensington House Hotel
KENS W8 ....120 B2
Kensington Leisure Centre
NTGHL W11 ....100 B6
Kensington Market
KENS W8 ....120 A2
Kensington Palace
KENS W8 ....120 A1
Kensington Park Hotel
REGST W1B 9 K1
Kensington Preparatory
School *FUL/PGN* SW6 ....139 J2
Kensington Primary School
MNPK E12 ....89 K4
Kensington School of
Business *HCIRC* EC1N 11 K1
Kensington Wharf
WBPTN SW10 ....140 C1
Kensit Memorial College
FNCH N3 ....46 C5
Kentish Town CE Primary
School *KTTN* NW5 ....84 C3
Kentish Town Health Centre
KTTN NW5 ....84 C4
Kentish Town Industrial
Estate *KTTN* NW5 ....84 B3
Kentish Town Sports
Centre
KTTN NW5 ....84 A4
Kenton Clinic
KTN/HRWW/W HA3 ....62 A2
Kenton CC
KTN/HRWW/W HA3 ....61 J1
Kent Park Industrial Estate
PECK SE15 ....123 J6
Kenwood House
HGT N6 ....65 J5
Kerem House School
EFNCH N2 ....65 J5
The Kerem School
EFNCH N2 ....65 H2
Keston CE Primary School
HAYES BR2 ....215 H3
Kew Bridge Steam Museum
BTFD TW8 ....117 G5
Kew College
RCH/KEW TW9 ....137 H1
Kew Gardens
(Royal Botanic Gardens)
RCH/KEW TW9 ....137 F2
Kew Palace
RCH/KEW TW9 ....137 F1
Kew Retail Park
RCH/KEW TW9 ....137 J2
Kew Riverside Primary School
RCH/KEW TW9 ....137 J3
Keyplan & Roxburghe College
FITZ W1T 4 B7
Keyworth Primary School
WALW SE17 ....122 C5
Khalsa College London
HRW HA1 ....61 F3
Kidbrooke Park Primary
School *BKHTH/KID* SE3 ..146 B3
Kidbrooke School
BKHTH/KID SE3 ....146 C3
Kilburn Park Junior School
KIL/WHAMP NW6 ....100 D2
Killick Street Medical Centre
IS N1 ....5 C2
Kilmorie Primary School
FSTH SE23 ....164 B4
Kimberley Industrial Estate
WALTH E17 ....51 H3
Kimpton Industrial Estate
CHEAM SM3 ....193 J6
King Alfred School
GLDGN NW11 ....65 F5
King Athelstan Primary School
KUT/HW KT1 ....175 G6
King Edwards Road Clinic
HACK E8 ....86 B5
King Edward VII Hospital
for Officers *MHST* W1U 9 H1
King Fahad Academy
(Boys School & Girls
Lower School) *ACT* W3 ......99 G6
King Fahad Academy
(Girls Upper School)
EA W5 ....116 D4
The Kingfisher Medical
Centre *DEPT* SE8 ....124 C6
The Kingfisher Sports Centre
KUT/HW KT1 ....175 F5
King George Hospital
GDMY/SEVK IG3 ....73 C2
Kingham Industrial Estate
WLSDN NW10 ....99 F2
King & Queen Wharf
WAP E1W 105 F6
Kings Avenue Medical Centre
GFD/PVL UB6 ....96 C5
Kings Avenue School
CLAP SW4 ....141 K6
Kingsbury Green Primary
School *CDALE/KGS* NW9 ..62 D2
Kingsbury High School
CDALE/KGS NW9 ....62 D1
Kingsbury Hospital
CDALE/KGS NW9 ....62 C1
Kingsbury Tamil School
CDALE/KGS NW9 ....44 D6

Kingsbury Trading Estate
CDALE/KGS NW9 ....62 E3
King's College Hospital
CMBW SE5 ....142 D4
Kings College London
CMBW SE5 ....142 E3
HAMP NW3 ....82 E2
HMSMTH W6 ....119 K2
LSQ/SEVD WC2H 11 F4
STHWK SE1 ....12 B7
STHWK SE1 ....18 C1
TPL/STR WC2R 11 H5
WEST SW1P 16 B6
Kings College School of
Medicine & Dentistry
CMBW SE5 ....142 D3
Kings College Senior School
WIM/MER SW19 ....177 F2
Kings College Sports Ground
RSLP HA4 ....58 C3
Kingsdale School
DUL SE21 ....163 F5
Kings Estate
HCH RM12 ....93 J2
Kingsford Community School
PLSTW E15 ....107 G5
Kingsgate Business Centre
KUTN/CMB KT2 ....175 F4
Kingsgate Primary School
KIL/WHAMP NW6 ....82 E5
Kings Hall Leisure Centre
CLPT E5 ....86 E3
Kings Head Theatre
IS N1 ....85 G6
Kings House School
RCHPK/HAM TW10 ....137 G6
Kingsland Health Centre
HACK E8 ....86 B5
Kingsland School
HACK E8 ....86 B3
Kingsland Shopping Centre
CROY/NA CR0 ....196 A5
Kings Mall Shopping Centre
HMSMTH W6 ....119 F4
Kingsmeadow Athletics
Centre *KUT/HW* KT1 ......175 H6
Kingsmead Primary School
CLPT E5 ....87 G2
Kingsmead School
EN EN1 ....24 C5
The Kings Oak Private
Hospital
ENC/FH EN2 ....23 G1
Kings Solomon High School
BARK/HLT IG6 ....54 D5
Kings Private Clinic
GDMY/SEVK IG3 ....73 F5
MHST W1U 9 G1
Kings School of English
BECK BR3 ....182 C5
Kings Stairs
BERM/RHTH SE16 ....123 J2
Kingston Business Centre
CHSGTN KT9 ....206 A1
Kingston College of FE
KUT/HW KT1 ....175 F6
Kingston College Theatre
KUT/HW KT1 ....174 E6
Kingston Crematorium
KUT/HW KT1 ....175 H6
Kingston Crown Court
KUT/HW KT1 ....174 E6
Kingston Grammar School
KUT/HW KT1 ....175 G5
Kingston Hospital
KUTN/CMB KT2 ....175 H4
Kingstonian FC
NWMAL KT3 ....175 J6
Kingston Lodge Hotel
KUTN/CMB KT2 ....175 J3
Kingston University
BRYLDS KT5 ....191 H2
KUT/HW KT1 ....175 F6
KUTN/CMB KT2 ....176 A1
King Street College
HMSMTH W6 ....119 F4
Kingsway Business Park
HPTN TW12 ....172 E4
Kingsway College
KTTN NW5 ....84 B4
STPAN WC1H 5 G5
Kingswood Primary School
WNWD SE27 ....162 E6
Kisharon School
GLDGN NW11 ....64 D3
Kite of Ealing Montessori
School *EA* W5 ....97 J4
KLC School of Design
WBPTN SW10 ....140 B2
Knightsbridge Barracks
SKENS SW7 ....14 D3
Knightsbridge
Medical Centre
KTBR SW1X 15 F4
Knollmead Primary School
WPK KT4 ....191 K6
Knowledge Point School
HOLWY N7 ....85 F4
Kobi Nazrul Primary School
WCHPL E1 ....104 C5
KP Estate
RAIN RM13 ....111 G6
Kubrick Business Estate
FSTGT E7 ....89 F2
Laban Centre
DEPT SE8 ....144 E1
Laburnum Health Centre
DAGE RM10 ....74 C6
Lady Bankes Primary School
RSLP HA4 ....58 E5

The Lady Eleanor Holles
School *HPTN* TW12 ....173 C1
Lady Margaret Primary
School *STHL* UB1 ....95 K4
Lady Margaret School
FUL/PGN SW6 ....139 K2
Ladywell Arena
LEW SE13 ....164 E1
Ladywell Cemetery
BROCKY SE4 ....144 C6
Ladywell Leisure Centre
LEW SE13 ....145 F6
Lake Business Centre
TOTM N17 ....50 C2
Laker Industrial Estate
BECK BR3 ....182 C1
Lambeth Cemetery
TOOT SW17 ....178 B1
Lambeth College
CLAP SW4 ....141 H6
STHWK SE1 ....19 H1
Lambeth College
(Vauxhall Centre)
VX/NE SW8 ....141 J2
Lambeth Crematorium
TOOT SW17 ....160 B6
Lambeth Education
LBTH SE11 ....122 B6
Lambeth Palace
STHWK SE1 ....17 G5
Lambs Court
POP/IOD E14 ....105 G6
Lamont Business Centre
CROY/NA CR0 ....195 K4
Lamorbey Swimming Centre
BFN/LL DA15 ....168 B4
Lampton School
HEST TW5 ....135 F2
The Lanark Medical Centre
MV/WKIL W9 ....101 F2
Lancaster House
WHALL SW1A 16 A2
Lancasterian Primary School
TOTM N17 ....50 A4
Lancaster Road
Industrial Estate
EBAR EN4 ....21 H6
Lancelot Medical Centre
ALP/SUD HA0 ....79 K3
The Landmark Hotel
CAMTN NW1 ....8 E1
The Lanesborough Hotel
KTBR SW1X 15 G2
Lanford Obesity Clinic
ED N9 ....36 D2
Langbourne Primary School
DUL SE21 ....163 F5
Langdon Down Centre
TEDD TW11 ....174 D3
Langdon Park School
POP/IOD E14 ....105 K5
Langdon School
EHAM E6 ....108 B1
The Langham School
FUL/PGN SW6 ....140 A3
The Langham Hotel
SEVS/STOTM N15 ....67 J1
Langhedge Lane Industrial
Estate *UED* N18 ....50 B2
Langley Park Girls School
& Sports Centre
BECK BR3 ....198 E2
Langley Park Golf Club
BECK BR3 ....199 G3
Langley Park School
for Boys
BECK BR3 ....198 E3
Langthorne Health Centre
WAN E11 ....88 B1
Langthorne Hospital
WAN E11 ....88 B2
Lansbury Lawrence
Primary School
POP/IOD E14 ....105 K5
Lansdowne College
BAY/PAD W2 ....101 F6
Lansdowne School
BRXN/ST SW9 ....142 A4
La Retraite RC Girls School
BAL SW12 ....161 H2
Lark Hall Primary School
CLAP SW4 ....141 J3
Larkshall Business Centre
CHING E4 ....38 B4
Larmenier Infant School
HMSMTH W6 ....119 G4
La Sainte Union Convent
School *KTTN* NW5 ....84 A1
La Salette RC
Primary School
RAIN RM13 ....111 J2
Latchmere J & I School
KUTN/CMB KT2 ....175 G2
Latchmere Leisure Centre
BTSEA SW11 ....140 E3
Lathom Junior School
EHAM E6 ....89 J5
Latymer All Saints CE
Primary School *ED* N9 ......36 B4
The Latymer School
ED N9 ....36 A4
Latymer Upper School
HMSMTH W6 ....118 D4
Launcelot Primary School
BMLY BR1 ....165 K6
Laurel Clinic
EA W5 ....116 D4
Laurence Haines School
WATW WD18 ....26 E1
Lauriston Primary School
HOM E9 ....87 F6
Lavender Primary School
ENC/FH EN2 ....23 K1
Lawdale Junior School
BETH E2 ....104 C2

Lawrence Trading Estate
GNWCH SE10 ....125 H4
Lawrence Wharf
BERM/RHTH SE16 ....124 C1
Laycock Primary School
IS N1 ....85 G4
Lazards Sports Club
SUN TW16 ....172 A4
Leadenhall Market
BANK EC3V 13 G4
Lea Park Trading Estate
LEY E10 ....69 H4
Leaside Business Centre
PEND EN3 ....25 H3
Leathermarket Gardens
STHWK SE1 ....19 G3
Leathersellers Sports Ground
ELTH/MOT SE9 ....166 B2
Leathers Hall
HDTCH EC3A 13 G3
Lea Valley Primary School
TOTM N17 ....50 C3
Lea Valley Trading Estate
UED N18 ....36 E6
UED N18 ....51 F2
L'Ecoles des Petits School
FUL/PGN SW6 ....140 A3
Lee Manor Primary School
LEW SE13 ....165 H1
Leeside Court
BERM/RHTH SE16 ....124 A1
Leeside Trading Estate
TOTM N17 ....50 E3
Leesons Primary School
STMC/STPC BR5 ....186 B6
Lee Valley Campsite
CHING E4 ....25 K3
Lee Valley Ice Centre
LEY E10 ....69 F6
Lee Valley Leisure Centre
Camping & Caravan
ED N9 ....37 F3
Lee Valley Leisure Golf Club
ED N9 ....37 G2
Lee Valley Watersports
Centre
CHING E4 ....51 G2
The Leigh City Technology
College *DART* DA1 ....171 K3
The Leigh Technology
College (West Campus)
DART DA1 ....171 K3
Leigh Close Industrial Estate
NWMAL KT3 ....192 A1
Leighton House Museum &
Art Gallery *WKENS* W14 ..119 J3
Le Meridien Piccadilly Hotel
CONDST W1S 10 B6
Le Meridien Russell Hotel
RSQ WC1B 4 E7
Le Meridien Waldorf
HOL/ALD WC2B 11 G5
Lemuel Findlay
Supplementary School
SEVS/STOTM N15 ....68 B1
Lena Gardens Primary School
HMSMTH W6 ....119 F3
Leopold Primary School
WLSDN NW10 ....81 H5
Leopold Street Clinic
BOW E3 ....105 H4
Lesnes Abbey
ABYW SE2 ....128 E4
Lessness Heath Primary
School *BELV* DA17 ....129 H5
Lewin Mead Community
Mental Health Centre
STRHM/NOR SW16 ....179 J2
Lewis Clinic
CAR SM5 ....210 A2
Lewisham Bridge Primary
School *LEW* SE13 ....144 E4
Lewisham Business Centre
NWCR SE14 ....124 A6
Lewisham Centre
LEW SE13 ....145 F4
Lewisham College
DEPT SE8 ....144 D2
Lewisham Crematorium
CAT SE6 ....165 J4
Lewisham Police Station
LEW SE13 ....145 F5
The Leys Primary School
DAGE RM10 ....92 E5
Leyton Business Centre
LEY E10 ....69 H6
Leyton Cross
DART DA1 ....170 D4
Leyton FC
LEY E10 ....69 H5
Leyton Industrial Village
LEY E10 ....69 F4
Leyton-Lee Valley Ice
Centre *LEY* E10 ....69 F6
Leyton Leisure Centre
LEY E10 ....69 K4
Leyton Orient FC
(Matchroom Stadium)
LEY E10 ....87 K1
Leytonstone School
WAN E11 ....70 C3
Leyton VI Form College
LEY E10 ....70 B3
Leyton Youth Sports Ground
LEY E10 ....69 K5
The Liberty City Clinic
SDTCH EC2A 7 G6
Liberty II Centre
ROM RM1 ....75 G1
Liberty Middle School
MTCM CR4 ....178 D5
The Liberty
ROM RM1 ....75 G2
Library & Community Centre
BTSEA SW11 ....140 C4

Lillian Baylis School
LBTH SE11 ...... 17 H7
VX/NE SW8 ...... 121 K6
Lillian Baylis Technology
School LBTH SE11 ...... 122 A5
Lillian Baylis Theatre
FSBYE EC1V 6 A4
Lillian Bishop School of
English SKENS SW7 ...... 14 A6
Limehouse Hole Stairs
POP/IOD E14 ...... 124 C1
Limes Farm Primary School
CHIG IG7 ...... 54 D2
Lime Trees Park Golf Club
NTHLT UB5 ...... 77 G6
Lincoln Road Clinic
EN EN1 ...... 24 C6
Lincoln's Inn
LINN WC2A 11 H3
The Lindal Hotel
HRW HA1 ...... 60 E2
Linden Bridge School
WPK KT4 ...... 207 G1
Linden Lodge School
WIM/MER SW19 ...... 159 H3
Lindon Bennett School
FELT TW13 ...... 172 C1
Linford Christie Stadium
SHB W12 ...... 99 J4
The Link Day Primary School
CROY/NA CR0 ...... 210 E2
The Link Secondary School
CROY/NA CR0 ...... 211 F2
Links Primary School
TOOT SW17 ...... 179 F2
Linley Sambourne House
KENS W8 ...... 119 J2
Linnet House Clinic
BGVA SW1W 2 C5
Linton Mead Primary School
THMD SE28 ...... 109 H6
Lionel Road Primary School
BTFD TW8 ...... 117 F4
Liongate Hotel
E/WMO/HCT KT8 ...... 174 A6
Lion House School
PUT/ROE SW15 ...... 139 G5
Lismarine Industrial Park
BORE WD6 ...... 29 H1
Lisson Grove Health Centre
STJWD NW8 ...... 2 C6
Lister Community School
Performing Arts College
PLSTW E13 ...... 107 F1
The Lister Hospital
BGVA SW1W 121 G5
Lister House Clinic
CAVSQ/HST W1G 9 J3
Little Danson Welfare Clinic
WELL DA16 ...... 148 B5
Little Eden & Eden High
School FELT TW15 ...... 154 C6
Little Furze JMI School
OXHEY WD19 ...... 27 F5
Little Hands Theatre
HDN NW4 ...... 64 A1
Little Heath School
CHDH RM6 ...... 73 H1
Little Ilford School
MNPK E12 ...... 89 K3
Little St Helens School
NTHWD HA6 ...... 40 C2
Little Stanmore F & M School
EDGW HA8 ...... 44 A4
Little Venice Medical Centre
STJWD NW8 ...... 2 A7
Little Wandsworth School
TOOT SW17 ...... 161 F4
Livesey Museum for Children
PECK SE15 ...... 123 J6
Livingstone Hospital
DART DA1 ...... 171 J2
Livingstone Primary School
EBAR EN4 ...... 21 H4
The Livity School
BRXS/STRHM SW2 ...... 141 K6
Lloyd Park Centre
WALTH E17 ...... 51 J5
Lloyds Register CC
DUL SE21 ...... 162 E3
Locks View Court
POP/IOD E14 ...... 105 G6
Lockwood Industrial Park
TOTM N17 ...... 50 D6
Lombard Business Centre
BTSEA SW11 ...... 140 C3
Lombard Business Park
CROY/NA CR0 ...... 196 A4
WAND/EARL SW18 ...... 160 C1
WIM/MER SW19 ...... 178 B5
Lombard Trading Estate
CHARL SE7 ...... 126 A4
Lombardy Retail Park
HYS/HAR UB3 ...... 95 F6
London Academy of Music
& Dramatic Art
HMSMTH W6 ...... 119 G5
KENS W8 ...... 119 K4
London Aquarium
STHWK SE1 ...... 17 G3
London Area Terminal
Control Centre
WDR/YW UB7 ...... 112 C2
London Arena
POP/IOD E14 ...... 124 E3
London Bible College
NTHWD HA6 ...... 40 B2
London Bridge City Pier
STHWK SE1 ...... 13 G7
London Bridge Hospital
STHWK SE1 ...... 13 F7
London Bridge Hotel
STHWK SE1 ...... 18 E1
London Bridge Sports Centre
CANST EC4R 12 E6

London Business School
CAMTN NW1 ...... 2 E6
The London Canal Museum
IS N1 ...... 5 F2
London Capital College
CAMTN NW1 ...... 84 B6
London Chest Hospital
BETH E2 ...... 104 E1
London City Airport
CAN/RD E16 ...... 126 D1
London City College
STHWK SE1 ...... 11 J7
London City Mission
STHWK SE1 ...... 19 H2
The London Clinic
MHST W1U 3 H7
London College of Business
& Computing
BETH E2 ...... 104 D1
London College of Business
& Computing Services
CLAP SW4 ...... 141 J5
London College of
Communication (University
of the Arts) LBTH SE11 ...... 18 A5
London College of Fashion
CAVSQ/HST W1G 9 J4
MHST W1U 9 H4
SDTCH EC2A 7 H6
London College of
Further Education
LBTH SE11 ...... 18 A7
London College of
Higher Education
CLAP SW4 ...... 141 G4
London College of
International Business
Studies HHOL WC1V 11 F2
The London College
KENS W8 ...... 119 K1
London Commodity Exchange
TWRH EC3N 13 K6
London Cornish RFC
PUT/ROE SW15 ...... 158 C5
London Dungeon
STHWK SE1 ...... 13 G6
London Electronics College
ECT SW5 ...... 119 K5
London Eye Clinic
CAVSQ/HST W1G 9 J2
London Fields Primary School
HACK E8 ...... 86 D6
London Foot Hospital
FITZ W1T 4 A7
London Gender Clinic
HDN NW4 ...... 63 K3
London Group Business Park
CRICK NW2 ...... 63 H5
London Guildhall University
LVPST EC2M 13 F2
TWRH EC3N 13 J4
London Guildhall University
Sports Ground
LEE/GVPK SE12 ...... 166 B4
London Heart Clinic
CAVSQ/HST W1G 9 J2
The London Industrial Estate
EHAM E6 ...... 108 A4
London Industrial Park
EHAM E6 ...... 108 B4
The London institute
WEST SW1P 121 K5
London International Film School
LSO/SEVD WC2H 10 E4
The London Irish Youth
Theatre HCT N6 ...... 66 B5
London Islamic
School/Madrasah
WCHPL E1 ...... 104 D5
London Ladies & Girls FC
CAT SE6 ...... 182 E1
London Lane Clinic
BMLY BR1 ...... 183 J3
London Lighthouse
NTGHL W11 ...... 100 C5
London Living Theatre
SYD SE26 ...... 164 A6
London Marriott Hotel
Park Lane MYFR/PKLN W1K 9 F5
London Marriott Hotel
HAMP NW3 ...... 83 J5
STHWK SE1 ...... 17 G2
London Metropolitan University
(North London Campus)
HOLWY N7 ...... 85 G3
London Metropolitan Archives
CLKNW EC1R 5 K6
London Metropolitan
University HOLWY N7 ...... 85 G2
London Metropolitan
University
(London City Campus)
WCHPL E1 ...... 13 J3
London Nautical School
STHWK SE1 ...... 11 K7
London Open College
FSBYE EC1V 6 B4
London Oratory School
FUL/PGN SW6 ...... 139 K1
London Pavilion
REGST W1B 10 C2
London Road Medical Centre
THHTH CR7 ...... 196 B3
London School of Economics
LINN WC2A 11 H4
LSO/SEVD WC2H 10 E3
STHWK SE1 ...... 12 C7
London School of Hygiene &
Tropical Medicine
(University of London)
GWRST WC1E 10 D1
London Scottish Golf Club
WIM/MER SW19 ...... 158 E5
London Silver Vaults
LINN WC2A 11 J2

The London Television
Centre (LWT) STHWK SE1 ...... 11 J7
London Tourist Board &
Convention Centre
BGVA SW1W 15 J4
London Toy & Model Museum
BAY/PAD W2 ...... 101 G6
London Transport Bus Depot
BXLYHN DA7 ...... 149 J4
London Transport Museum
COVGDN WC2E 11 F5
London Underwriting Centre
MON EC3R 13 H5
London Weather Centre
CLKNW EC1R 11 J1
The London Welbeck Hospital
MHST W1U 9 H1
London Welsh FC
RCH/KEW TW9 ...... 137 F4
London West Crematorium
WLSDN NW10 ...... 99 K3
London Wetland Centre
BARN SW13 ...... 138 E2
London Zoo
CAMTN NW1 ...... 3 G2
Lonesome Primary School
MTCM CR4 ...... 194 B4
Long Ditton County Infant
School SURB KT6 ...... 190 D5
Longfield Primary School
RYLN/HDSTN HA2 ...... 60 A3
Longford Community School
EBED/NFELT TW14 ...... 153 J2
Longford Industrial Estate
HPTN TW12 ...... 173 G2
Longlands Primary School
BFN/LL DA15 ...... 167 K5
Long Lane AFC
BKHTH/KID SE3 ...... 146 B5
Longmead Primary School
WDR/YW UB7 ...... 112 A4
Longshaw Primary School
CHING E4 ...... 38 B5
Lord Lister Health Centre
FSTGT E7 ...... 88 E2
Lordship Lane Clinic
TOTM N17 ...... 50 A5
Lordship Lane Primary School
WDGN N22 ...... 49 J4
Lord's Tour & MCC Museum
STJWD NW8 ...... 2 A5
Lorimar Business Centre
RAIN RM13 ...... 111 G5
Loughborough Primary
School CMBW SE5 ...... 142 C3
Lovelace Primary School
CHSGTN KT9 ...... 205 J3
Lovell's Wharf
GNWCH SE10 ...... 125 G5
Lower Clapton Health Centre
CLPT E5 ...... 86 E3
Lower Place Business Centre
WLSDN NW10 ...... 98 E1
Lower Sydenham Industrial
Estate CAT SE6 ...... 182 C1
Lowfield Medical Centre
DART DA1 ...... 171 H2
Low Hall Sports Ground
WALTH E17 ...... 69 F3
The Lowndes Hotel
KTBR SW1X 15 F4
Lowther Primary School
BARN SW13 ...... 118 D6
Loxford School of Science &
Technology IL IG1 ...... 90 D3
Loyola Preparatory School
BKHH IG9 ...... 39 G3
LPR Sports Club
BARK/HLT IG6 ...... 55 F4
LSE Sports Club
BARK/HLT IG6 ...... 192 A3
LT Lost Property Office
CAMTN NW1 ...... 3 F7
Lubavitch House School
STNW/STAM N16 ...... 68 B4
Lucas Vale Primary School
DEPT SE8 ...... 144 D2
Lucie Clayton College
KENS W8 ...... 120 B3
Lutomer House Business
Centre POP/IOD E14 ...... 124 E1
Lux Cinema
IS N1 ...... 7 G5
Lycee Francais
SKENS SW7 ...... 14 A6
The Lyceum Theatre
TPL/STR WC2R 11 G5
Lyndean Industrial Estate
ABYW SE2 ...... 128 D3
Lyndhurst House
Preparatory School
HAMP NW3 ...... 83 H3
Lyndhurst Primary School
CMBW SE5 ...... 142 E3
Lyon Business Park
BARK IG11 ...... 108 E1
Lyon Park J & I School
ALP/SUD HA0 ...... 80 B5
Lyonsdown School
BAR EN5 ...... 21 G6
Lyric Theatre
SOHO/SHAV W1D 10 C5
Lyric Theatre Hammersmith
HMSMTH W6 ...... 119 F4
Mabwin Supplementary
School ED N9 ...... 36 D4
Macaulay CE Primary School
CLAP SW4 ...... 141 G5
Madame Tussaud's &
The London Planetarium
CAMTN NW1 ...... 3 F7
Madeira Grove Clinic
WFD IG8 ...... 53 F1
Madni Girls School
WCHPL E1 ...... 104 D5

Mahatma Gandhi Industrial
Estate BRXN/ST SW9 ...... 142 C4
Maida Vale Hospital
STJWD NW8 ...... 101 G2
Maida Vale Medical Centre
MV/WKIL W9 ...... 101 F2
Malcolm Primary School
PGE/AN SE20 ...... 181 K3
The Malden Centre
NWMAL KT3 ...... 192 C1
Malden Golf Club
NWMAL KT3 ...... 176 B5
Malden Manor Junior School
NWMAL KT3 ...... 192 B4
Malden Parochial Primary
School WPK KT4 ...... 192 B5
Malden Road Baths
CHEAM SM3 ...... 208 B2
Malham Road Industrial
Estate FSTH SE23 ...... 164 A3
Mall Galleries
STJS SW1Y 10 D7
The Mall School
WHTN TW2 ...... 155 J5
Malmesbury Primary School
MRDN SM4 ...... 194 B4
Malorees J & I School
KIL/WHAMP NW6 ...... 82 B5
Malory School
BMLY BR1 ...... 165 K6
Mandarin Oriental Hotel
KTBR SW1X 15 F2
Mander Portman Woodward
SKENS SW7 ...... 120 B4
The Mandeville Hotel
MHST W1U 9 H3
Mandeville Primary School
CLPT E5 ...... 87 G1
Mandeville Special School
NTHLT UB5 ...... 77 K4
Manford Industrial Estate
ERITH DA8 ...... 130 E6
Manford Way Health Centre
BARK/HLT IG6 ...... 55 F2
Manor Brook Medical Centre
BKHTH/KID SE3 ...... 146 A3
Manor Drive Health Centre
WPK KT4 ...... 192 C5
Manorfield Primary School
POP/IOD E14 ...... 105 K4
Manor House School
HNWL W7 ...... 96 B6
Manor Infant School
BARK IG11 ...... 91 F4
Manor Oak Primary School
STMC/STPC BR5 ...... 202 C2
Manor Park Cemetery
FSTGT E7 ...... 89 H2
Manor Park Crematorium
FSTGT E7 ...... 89 G2
Manor Park Methodist School
MNPK E12 ...... 89 J2
Manor Park Primary School
SUT SM1 ...... 209 G3
Manor Primary School
SRTFD E15 ...... 106 C1
The Manor Primary School
ROM RM1 ...... 75 H2
Manorside Primary School
FNCH N3 ...... 47 F4
Manor Special School
WLSDN NW10 ...... 100 B1
Manor Way Business Centre
RAIN RM13 ...... 111 F4
Mansion House
MANHO EC4N 12 E4
Mapledown School
CRICK NW2 ...... 64 B4
Maple Grove Business Centre
HSLWW TW4 ...... 134 B5
Maple House Independent
Montessori
THHTH CR7 ...... 196 D1
Maple House School
THHTH CR7 ...... 180 D6
Maple Industrial Estate
FELT TW13 ...... 153 K4
Maple Infant School
SURB KT6 ...... 190 E2
Maples Business Centre
IS N1 ...... 85 G5
Marble Arch
BAY/PAD W2 ...... 9 F5
Marble Hill House
TWK TW1 ...... 156 D2
Maria Fidelis Convent
Lower School CAMTN NW1 ...... 4 C4
Maria Fidelis Convent
Senior School CAMTN NW1 ...... 4 C4
Marion Richardson
Primary School WCHPL E1 ...... 105 F5
Marion Vian Primary School
BECK BR3 ...... 198 A2
Maritime Industrial Estate
CHARL SE7 ...... 126 A4
Maritime Museum
GNWCH SE10 ...... 125 H4
The Marjory Kinnon School
EBED/NFELT TW14 ...... 133 H6
Market Trading Estate
NWDGN UB2 ...... 114 A4
Marks Gate Junior School
CHDH RM6 ...... 56 A6
Marlborough CC
DUL SE21 ...... 163 H3
Marlborough Day Hospital
STJWD NW8 ...... 101 G1
Marlborough F & M School
HRW HA1 ...... 60 E1
Marlborough House
STJS SW1Y 16 B1
Marlborough Park School
BFN/LL DA15 ...... 168 B3
Marlborough Primary School
CHEL SW3 ...... 14 D7

ISLW TW7 ...... 136 C1
Marlborough Trading Estate
RCH/KEW TW9 ...... 137 J2
Marlowe Business Centre
NWCR SE14 ...... 144 B1
Marner Primary School
BOW E3 ...... 105 K3
Marriott Hotel
HTHAIR TW6 ...... 133 G2
KIL/WHAMP NW6 ...... 101 F1
MBLAR W1H 8 D3
MYFR/PKLN W1K 9 H5
Marshalls Park School
ROM RM1 ...... 57 G5
Marshall Street Leisure Centre
SOHO/CST W1F 10 B4
Marsh Gate Business Centre
SRTFD E15 ...... 106 A1
Marshgate Primary School
RCHPK/HAM TW10 ...... 137 G6
Marshgate Trading Estate
SRTFD E15 ...... 87 K5
Marsh Green School
DAGW RM9 ...... 110 C1
Martan College
HOL/ALD WC2B 11 F3
Martinbridge Industrial Estate
EN EN1 ...... 24 C6
Martindale Industrial Estate
EN EN1 ...... 24 A6
Martin Infant School
EFNCH N2 ...... 47 J5
Marvels Lane Primary School
LEE/GVPK SE12 ...... 166 B6
Mary Boone School
WKENS W14 ...... 119 H4
Maryland Industrial Estate
SRTFD E15 ...... 88 C3
Maryland Primary School
SRTFD E15 ...... 88 C3
Marylebone Health Centre
MHST W1U 3 H7
Marylebone Magistrates Court
CAMTN NW1 ...... 8 D1
Marymount International
School
KUTN/CMB KT2 ...... 175 K2
Mary Wallace Theatre
TWK TW1 ...... 156 B3
Maswell Park Health Centre
HSLW TW3 ...... 135 H6
Matilda Marks School
MLHL NW7 ...... 45 F1
Matrix Business Centre
DART DA1 ...... 151 H6
The Maudsley Hospital
CMBW SE5 ...... 142 E3
Maughan Library
(Kings College)
FLST/FETLN EC4A 11 J3
Mawbrey Brough Health
RCH/KEW TW9 ...... 141 K1
The Mawney School
ROMW/RG RM7 ...... 75 F2
Mayday University Hospital
THHTH CR7 ...... 196 C3
Mayesbrook Park Arena
BARK IG11 ...... 91 G3
Mayespark Primary School
GDMY/SEVK IG3 ...... 91 G1
Mayfair Medical Centre
MYFR/PKLN W1K 9 H4
Mayfield Primary School
PIN HA5 ...... 41 J6
Mayfield School & College
BCTR RM8 ...... 73 J5
Mayflower Primary School
POP/IOD E14 ...... 105 J5
Maypole Primary School
BXLY DA5 ...... 170 B4
Maytime School
IL IG1 ...... 90 A1
Mayville J & P School
WAN E11 ...... 88 C1
Mazenod RC Primary School
KIL/WHAMP NW6 ...... 82 E5
McEntee School
WALTH E17 ...... 51 H4
Mackay Trading Estate
NKENS W10 ...... 100 C3
McMillan Clinic
HYS/HAR UB3 ...... 94 A6
MDO Majidiah (UK)
IL IG1 ...... 104 D6
The Mead Infant School
HOR/WEW KT19 ...... 207 H1
Meadlands Primary School
RCHPK/HAM TW10 ...... 156 D6
Meadowgate School
BROCKY SE4 ...... 144 A4
Meadowside Leisure
Centre
BKHTH/KID SE3 ...... 146 B5
The Meadow Special School
STMC/STPC BR5 ...... 186 B3
Mead Road Infant School
CHST BR7 ...... 185 H2
Mednurs Clinic
SEVS/STOTM N15 ...... 67 K3
Melcombe Primary School
HMSMTH W6 ...... 119 G6
Melia White House Hotel
CAMTN NW1 ...... 3 K6
Melish Industrial Estate
WOOL/PLUM SE18 ...... 126 C3
Mellow Lane School
YEAD UB4 ...... 94 A3
Melrose Special School
MTCM CR4 ...... 178 D6
Memorial Hospital
WOOL/PLUM SE18 ...... 147 F5

The Menorah Foundation
School EDGW HA8 ....44 E3
Menorah Grammar School
GLDGN NW11 ....64 C6
Menorah Primary School
GLDGN NW11 ....64 C6
Menzies Prince Regent Hotel
HCIRC IG8 ....53 K2
Mercers' Hall
CITYW EC2V 12 D4
The Merchant Taylors Hall
BANK EC3V 13 F4
Merchant Taylors School
NTHWD HA6 ....26 C5
Mercure London City Bankside
STHWK SE1 ....18 C1
Meridian Clinic
BRXN/ST SW9 ....142 A4
Meridian Locality Mental
Health Centre CHARL SE7 ..126 B6
Meridian Primary School
GNWCH SE10 ....125 G5
Meridian Sports Club
CHARL SE7 ....146 D1
Meridian Trading Estate
CHARL SE7 ....126 A4
Merlin Primary School
BMLY BR1 ....165 K5
Merlin School
PUT/ROE SW15 ....139 G6
Mermaid Theatre
BLKFR EC4V 12 B5
Merrielands Retail Park
DAGW RM9 ....92 B6
Merryhills Clinic
ENC/FH EN2 ....23 F4
Merryhills Primary School
ENC/FH EN2 ....23 F5
Merton Abbey Primary School
WIM/MER SW19 ....178 A4
Merton Adult College
RYNPK SW20 ....177 H6
Merton College
MRDN SM4 ....193 J5
Merton Court Preparatory
School SCUP DA14 ....168 D6
Merton Industrial Park
WIM/MER SW19 ....178 B4
Merton Park Primary School
WIM/MER SW19 ....177 J5
Merton Road Industrial Estate
WAND/EARL SW18 ....159 K2
Metro Business Centre
SYD SE26 ....182 C2
The Metro Golf Centre
HDN NW4 ....46 A4
Metro Industrial Centre
ISLW TW7 ....135 K3
Metropolitan Business Centre
IS N1 ....86 A5
Metropolitan Hospital
STHWK SE1 ....17 K4
Metropolitan Police FC
E/WMO/HCT KT8 ....189 J3
Metropolitan Police Hayes
Sports Club
HAYES BR2 ....199 J6
Metropolitan Police (Hendon)
Track CDALE/KGS NW9 .....45 H6
Metropolitan Police Training
School, Hendon
CDALE/KGS NW9 ....45 H6
Metropolitan Tabernacle
LBTH SE11 ....18 A6
Metro Trading Centre
WBLY HA9 ....80 D2
Michael Faraday Primary
School WALW SE17 ....122 E5
Michael Manley Industrial
Estate VX/NE SW8 ....141 H3
Michael Sobell Sinai School
KTN/HRWW/W HA3 ....62 C5
The Michael Tippett School
LBTH SE11 ....17 K7
Midas Business Centre
DAGE RM10 ....92 C2
Midas Industrial Estate
DAGE RM10 ....92 C2
Middle Park Primary School
ELTH/MOT SE9 ....166 C2
Middle Row Primary School
NKENS W10 ....100 C3
Middlesex School Team
ROM RM1 ....75 H3
Middlesex Business Centre
NWDGN UB2 ....115 F2
Middlesex CCC
(Lord's Cricket Ground)
STJWD NW8 ....2 B4
Middlesex Guildhall
WEST SW1P 16 D5
Middlesex Hospital
GTPST W1W 10 B2
Middlesex Hospital Medical
School FITZ W1T 10 B2
Middlesex Hospital Nurses
Home GTPST W1W 10 A1
Middlesex Hospital School of
Physiotherapy
FITZ W1T 10 B2
Middlesex Hospital Sports
Ground CHST BR7 ....186 A1
Middlesex University
EBAR EN4 ....34 A1
GLDGN NW11 ....65 F5
TOTM N17 ....50 A2
WDGN N22 ....49 H3
Middlesex University
Business School HDN NW4 ..63 K1
Middle Temple Hall
TPL/STR WC2R 11 J5
Midfield Primary School
CHST BR7 ....186 B3
Midway Mission Hospital
BETH E2 ....7 J5

Milbourne Lodge Junior School
ESH/CLAY KT10 ....204 C3
Milbourne Lodge School
ESH/CLAY KT10 ....204 C3
Mile End & Bow Business
Centre WCHPL E1 ....104 D4
Mile End Hospital
WCHPL E1 ....105 F2
Mile End Stadium
POE E3 ....105 G4
Milehams Industrial Estate
PUR RM19 ....131 K3
Miles Coverdale Primary
School SHB W12 ....119 F2
Milestone Hotel &
Apartments Townhouse
KENS W8 ....120 A2
Millbank Millennium Pier
WEST SW1P 16 E7
Millbank Primary School
WEST SW1P 16 D7
Millbank Tower
WEST SW1P 16 E7
Millennium Arena
BTSEA SW11 ....141 F1
Millennium Bailey's Hotel
SKENS SW7 ....120 B4
Millennium Balloon
STHWK SE1 ....19 H1
Millennium Gloucester Hotel
SKENS SW7 ....14 B4
Millennium Harbour
Development POP/IOD E14 ..124 C2
Millennium Hotel
KTBR SW1X 15 F3
Millennium Hotel London
Mayfair MYFR/PKLN W1K ...9 H6
The Millennium Primary
School GNWCH SE10 ....125 J3
Millennium Quay
DEPT SE8 ....124 E6
Millennium Wharf
Development
POP/IOD E14 ....125 G3
Mill Farm Business Park
HSLWW TW4 ....154 D2
Millfields J & I School
CLPT E5 ....86 E2
Millfield Theatre
UED N18 ....35 K6
Mill Green Business Park
MTCM CR4 ....194 E4
Mill Hill Cemetery
MLHL NW7 ....46 A2
Mill Hill County High School
MLHL NW7 ....31 G4
The Mill Hill CC
MLHL NW7 ....32 A5
Mill Hill Golf Club
MLHL NW7 ....31 G4
Mill Hill Industrial Estate
MLHL NW7 ....45 H2
Mill Hill School
MLHL NW7 ....31 K6
Mill Lane Medical Centre
KIL/WHAMP NW6 ....82 E3
Mill Lane Trading Estate
CROY/NA CR0 ....211 F1
Mill River Trading Estate
PEND EN3 ....25 G5
Millside Industrial Estate
DART DA1 ....151 G5
Mill Street Clinic
STHWK SE1 ....19 K2
Mill Trading Estate
WLSDN NW10 ....98 D1
Millwall FC (The New Den)
BERM/RHTH SE16 ....123 K5
Milmead Industrial Estate
TOTM N17 ....50 D5
Milton Natural Health Centre
HGT N6 ....66 C4
Minet Clinic
HYS/HAR UB3 ....113 K1
Minet J & I School
HYS/HAR UB3 ....114 A1
Ministry of Defence
WHALL SW1A 11 H7
Mint Business Park
CAN/RD E16 ....106 E4
Mirravale Trading Estate
BCTR RM8 ....74 A4
Mission Grove Primary School
WALTH E17 ....69 H2
Mitcham CC
MTCM CR4 ....194 D1
Mitcham Golf Club
MTCM CR4 ....195 F2
Mitcham Industrial Estate
MTCM CR4 ....179 F4
Mitcham Road Crematorium
THHTH CR7 ....195 K2
Mitcham Vale High School
MTCM CR4 ....179 G5
STRHM/NOR SW16 ....179 H5
Mitchell Brook Primary
School WLSDN NW10 ....81 F4
Mitre Bridge Industrial Park
WLSDN NW10 ....99 K3
Moatbridge School
ELTH/MOT SE9 ....166 C1
Moberly Sports & Education
Centre NKENS W10 ....100 B2
Molesey Hospital
E/WMO/HCT KT8 ....189 F2
Molesey Lock
E/WMO/HCT KT8 ....173 K6
Mollison Drive Health Centre
WLGTN SM6 ....210 E5
Monega Primary School
MNPK E12 ....89 H3
Monken Hadley CE Primary
School EBAR EN4 ....20 E2
Monkfrith Primary School
EBAR EN4 ....34 A2

Monks Hill Sports Centre
SAND/SEL CR2 ....213 F5
Monks Orchard Primary
School CROY/NA CR0 ....198 A2
Monson Primary School
NWCR SE14 ....144 A1
The Montague on the
Gardens Hotel RSQ WC1B ..10 E1
Montbelle School
ELTH/MOT SE9 ....167 F6
Montbelle Primary School
ELTH/MOT SE9 ....167 G5
Montcalm-Hotel Nikko
MBLAR W1H 9 F4
Monteagle Primary School
DAGW RM9 ....91 H6
Montem Primary School
HOLWY N7 ....85 F1
Montpelier Primary School
EA W5 ....97 K4
The Monument
CANST EC4R 13 F5
Moore Place Golf Club
ESH/CLAY KT10 ....204 A3
Moorfields Eye Hospital
FSBYE EC1V 6 E5
Moorfields Primary School
STLK EC1Y 6 E6
Moor Lane Junior School
CHSGTN KT9 ....206 B3
Moor Park Industrial Estate
WATW WD18 ....26 A2
Morden Cemetery
MRDN SM4 ....193 F3
Morden College Homes
BKHTH/KID SE3 ....145 K3
Morden First School
MRDN SM4 ....193 K2
Morden Hall Medical Centre
WIM/MER SW19 ....178 A6
Morden Hall Park NT
WIM/MER SW19 ....194 B1
Morden Mount Primary
School LEW SE13 ....144 E3
Morden Park Pool
MRDN SM4 ....193 J2
Morden Road Clinic
WIM/MER SW19 ....178 A6
Moreland Primary School
FSBYE EC1V 6 B6
Moriah Jewish Day School
PIN HA5 ....59 J5
Morley College
STHWK SE1 ....17 K4
Morningside Primary School
HOM E9 ....86 E4
Mornington Sports &
Fitness Centre
CAMTN NW1 ....84 B2
Morpeth School
BETH E2 ....104 E2
Mortimer Road Clinic
WLSDN NW10 ....100 A2
Mortimer School
STRHM/NOR SW16 ....161 J4
Mortlake Cemetery
MORT/ESHN SW14 ....138 B4
Mortlake Crematorium
RCH/KEW TW9 ....137 J3
Moselle School
TOTM N17 ....50 A1
Mosiah Foundation
Supplementary School
STNW/STAM N16 ....68 A5
Mossford Green Primary
School BARK/HLT IG6 ....54 C5
Moss Hall Primary School
FNCH N3 ....47 F2
Mostyn Hotel
MBLAR W1H 9 F4
The Mother & Baby Clinic
HOM E9 ....86 E4
Mottingham Community
Health Clinic
ELTH/MOT SE9 ....166 D6
Mottingham Primary School
ELTH/MOT SE9 ....166 E5
Mount Carmel RC Primary
School EA W5 ....116 D3
Mount Carmel RC
Technology College
for Girls
ARCH N19 ....66 D5
The Mount Infant School
NWMAL KT3 ....175 J4
Mount Medical Centre
FELT TW13 ....154 D4
Mount School
MLHL NW7 ....45 K1
Mount Stewart Primary
School KTN/HRWW/W HA3 ..61 K3
Mowlem Primary School
BETH E2 ....104 E1
Mowlem Trading Estate
TOTM N17 ....50 E5
MS Business Centre
PIN HA5 ....41 H6
MSP Business Centre
WBLY HA9 ....80 D2
Mudchute City Farm
POP/IOD E14 ....125 F4
Mudlands Estate
RAIN RM13 ....111 G2
Mulberry Business Centre
BERM/RHTH SE16 ....124 A2
Mulberry House School
CRICK NW2 ....82 C3
Mulberry School for Girls
WCHPL E1 ....104 D5
The Mulberry School
TOTM N17 ....50 B5

Mulgrave Primary School
WOOL/PLUM SE18 ....127 F4
Munroe Centre
STHWK SE1 ....19 F2
Murky Puddle Theatre
NWMAL KT3 ....176 C6
Murray Business Centre
STMC/STPC BR5 ....186 C6
Muschamp Primary School
CAR SM5 ....194 D6
Museum in Docklands
POP/IOD E14 ....105 J6
Museum of Domestic Design
& Architecture
EBAR EN4 ....21 K6
Museum of Fulham Palace
FUL/PGN SW6 ....139 G3
Museum of Garden History
STHWK SE1 ....17 F5
Museum of London
STBT EC1A 12 C2
Museum of London
(Archaeological Research
Centre)
IS N1 ....6 D1
Museum of Richmond
RCH/KEW TW9 ....136 E6
Museum of Rugby &
Twickenham Stadium Tours
WHTN TW2 ....155 K1
Museum of the Order
of St John FARR EC1M 6 B7
Museums of the Royal
College of Surgeons
LINN WC2A 11 H3
Musical Museum
BTFD TW8 ....117 F6
Muswell Hill Bowling Club
MUSWH N10 ....48 A6
Muswell Hill Golf Club
FBAR/BDGN N11 ....48 B4
Muswell Hill Primary School
MUSWH N10 ....48 B5
Myatt Garden Primary School
BROCKY SE4 ....144 C3
Myatts Field Clinic
BRXN/ST SW9 ....142 C2
N1 Shopping Centre
IS N1 ....5 K2
Nags Business Centre
ALP/SUD HA0 ....97 K1
Nags Head Shopping Centre
HOLWY N7 ....85 F2
Naima Jewish Preparatory
School KIL/WHAMP NW6 ..101 F1
The National Archives
RCH/KEW TW9 ....137 J1
National Army Museum
CHEL SW3 ....120 E6
National Film Theatre
STHWK SE1 ....11 H7
National Gallery
LSQ/SEVD WC2H 10 D6
National Hospital for
Neurology & Neurosurgery
BMSBY WC1N 4 E7
National Hospital for Sick
Children (Great Ormond St)
BMSBY WC1N 4 E7
National Maritime Museum
GNWCH SE10 ....125 G6
National Physical Laboratory
TEDD TW11 ....173 K2
National Portrait Gallery
LSQ/SEVD WC2H 10 D6
National Sports Centre
NRWD SE19 ....181 H2
National Temperance Hospital
CAMTN NW1 ....4 A4
National Youth Theatre of GB
HOLWY N7 ....84 E1
Natural History Museum
SKENS SW7 ....14 A5
Natural Therapy Clinic
TOOT SW17 ....179 G1
Nature Reserve
WALTH E17 ....68 E4
Natwest Sports Club
BECK BR3 ....182 C2
Navigation College
CANST EC4R 12 D5
NEC Harlequins RFC (The Stoop
Memorial Ground)
WHTN TW2 ....155 K2
Negus 6th Form Centre
WOOL/PLUM SE18 ....127 J6
Nelson Dock Museum
BERM/RHTH SE16 ....124 C1
Nelson Hospital
WIM/MER SW19 ....177 J5
Nelson Primary School
EHAM E6 ....108 A1
WHTN TW2 ....155 G1
Nelson's Column
CHCR WC2N 10 D7
Nelson Trading Estate
WIM/MER SW19 ....178 A4
Neo Clinic
PIM SW1V 16 A6
The New Ambassadors Theatre
LSQ/SEVD WC2H 10 D4
New Atlas Wharf Development
POP/IOD E14 ....124 C3
New Brentford Cemetery
HSLW TW3 ....134 E3
Newbury Park Health Centre
GNTH/NBYPK IG2 ....72 D3
The New Business Centre
WLSDN NW10 ....99 H2
New Caledonian Wharf
BERM/RHTH SE16 ....124 C3
New Chiswick Pool
CHSWK W4 ....138 B1
New City Primary School
PLSTW E13 ....107 G2

New Connaught Rooms
HOL/ALD WC2B 11 F3
New Covent Garden Market
VX/NE SW8 ....141 J1
New Crane Wharf
WAP E1W 123 K1
New Cross Sports Arena
NWCR SE14 ....144 B1
New End Primary School
HAMP NW3 ....83 G2
New End Theatre
HAMP NW3 ....83 G1
New England Industrial Estate
BARK IG11 ....108 C1
Newfield Primary School
WLSDN NW10 ....81 H5
The New Furness Primary
School WLSDN NW10 ....99 J1
Newham College of
Further Education
EHAM E6 ....107 K1
SRTFD E15 ....88 C5
Newham Community College
CAN/RD E16 ....106 C3
Newham General Hospital
PLSTW E13 ....107 G3
Newham Leisure Centre
PLSTW E13 ....107 G4
Newham Medical Centre
PLSTW E13 ....107 G3
Newham Sixth Form College
PLSTW E13 ....107 F3
New Health Centre
TOTM N17 ....50 A4
Newington Court
Business Centre
STHWK SE1 ....18 C5
Newington Green Primary
School STNW/STAM N16 .....86 A3
Newington Industrial Estate
WALW SE17 ....18 B7
New Kings Primary School
FUL/PGN SW6 ....139 J3
Newland House School
TWK TW1 ....156 A6
New London Theatre
LSQ/SEVD WC2H 11 F3
Newnham J & I School
RSLP HA4 ....59 G5
Newport J & I School
LEY E10 ....70 A6
New River Sports Centre
WDGN N22 ....49 H3
New River Village
CEND/HSY/T N8 ....49 F6
New Rush Hall School
IL IG1 ....72 C6
New School
FUL/PGN SW6 ....139 J2
New Scotland Yard
STJSPK SW1H 16 C4
News International
WAP E1W 104 D6
New Southgate Cemetery
FBAR/BDGN N11 ....34 B5
New Southgate Crematorium
FBAR/BDGN N11 ....34 B5
New Southgate Industrial
Estate FBAR/BDGN N11 ....48 C1
New Southgate Pain Clinic
& Medical Centre
FBAR/BDGN N11 ....48 C1
New Spitalfields Market
LEY E10 ....87 J1
Newstead Wood School
for Girls ORP BR6 ....216 D1
Newton Farm F & M School
RYLN/HDSTN HA2 ....59 K6
Newton Industrial Estate
CHDH RM6 ....73 K1
Newton Medical Centre
BAY/PAD W2 ....101 F5
Newton Preparatory School
VX/NE SW8 ....141 G1
Newtons Primary School
RAIN RM13 ....111 F1
New Victoria Hospital
KUTN/CMB KT2 ....176 B3
New Woodlands School
BMLY BR1 ....165 H6
SYD SE26 ....163 J5
Nightingale Clinic
PLSTW E13 ....107 G1
Nightingale Primary School
CLPT E5 ....86 C2
SWFD E18 ....71 G1
WDGN N22 ....48 E4
WOOL/PLUM SE18 ....127 C6
Nightingale School
TOOT SW17 ....160 D4
The Nightingale School
STHWK SE1 ....17 G3
Nineacres School
WOOL/PLUM SE18 ....127 J5
No 41 Hotel
WESTW SW1E 15 K4
Noam Primary School
KTN/HRWW/W HA3 ....47 F1
Noel Park Primary School
WDGN N22 ....49 H5
Nonsuch High School for Girls
EW KT17 ....208 B5
Nonsuch Primary School
EW KT17 ....207 K3
Noor Ul Islam School
LEY E10 ....70 A6
Norbury Complementary
Therapy Clinic
STRHM/NOR SW16 ....180 A4
Norbury F & M School
STRHM/NOR SW16 ....180 A5
Norbury Health Centre
HRW HA1 ....60 E2
Norbury Manor Primary School
STRHM/NOR SW16 ....179 K4

Norbury Manor Secondary
Girls School
STRHM/NOR SW16 ....180 A4
Norbury Trading Estate
STRHM/NOR SW16 ....180 A5
Norfolk House School
MUSWH N10 ....48 B5
Norland Place School
NTGHL W11 ....119 H1
Norlington School
WAN E11 ....70 B5
Normand Croft Community
School *WKENS* W14 ....119 J6
Normandy Primary School
ERITH DA8 ....150 A2
Normanhurst School
CHDH E4 ....38 B2
Norman Park Athletics Track
HAYES BR2 ....200 A3
Norman Shaw Building
(MP's Offices) *WHALL* SW1A ...16 E2
North Acton Business Park
ACT W3 ....99 F5
North Beckton Primary School
EHAM E6 ....107 K3
North Bridge House
HAMP NW3 ....83 G4
North Bridge House School
HAMP NW3 ....83 H4
North Bridge House Senior
School *CAMTN* NW1 ....3 J1
Northbrook CE School
LEW SE13 ....145 H6
Northbury Primary School
BARK IG11 ....90 B4
North Clinic
BMLY BR1 ....183 K4
North Croydon Medical
Centre *THHTH* CR7 ....196 C3
North Ealing Primary School
WEA W13 ....97 H3
North East Surrey
Crematorium *NWMAL* KT3 ...193 F3
Northend Primary School
ERITH DA8 ....150 C2
North End Trading Estate
ERITH DA8 ....150 B1
North Feltham
Trading Estate
EBED/NFELT TW14 ....134 A5
Northfields Industrial Estate
ALP/SUD HA0 ....80 C6
Northfields Prospect
Business Centre
WAND/EARL SW18 ....139 J5
Northgate Business Centre
EN EN1 ....24 D4
Northgate Clinic
CDALE/KGS NW9 ....63 G3
Northgate Industrial Park
ROMW/RG RM7 ....56 B5
North Harringey Primary
School *CEND/HSY/T* N8 .....67 G1
North Havering College of
Adult Education
ROM RM1 ....75 G1
North London Collegiate School
EDGW HA8 ....44 A2
The North London Hospice
NFNCH/WDSP N12 ....33 F5
North London School of
Physiotherapy
ARCH N19 ....66 C5
North London Tutorial College
HDN NW4 ....64 A3
North Middlesex Golf Club
TRDG/WHET N20 ....33 H5
North Middlesex Hospital
UED N18 ....50 A1
Northolt Aerodrome
RSLP HA4 ....76 E4
Northolt High School
NTHLT UB5 ....77 K4
Northolt Primary School
NTHLT UB5 ....77 H5
Northolt Road Clinic
RYLN/HDSTN HA2 ....78 C1
Northolt Swimarama
NTHLT UB5 ....78 A4
North Primary School
STHL UB1 ....95 K6
Northside Primary School
NFNCH/WDSP N12 ....47 G1
The North Street Health
Centre *CLAP* SW4 ....141 H4
Northumberland Heath
Medical Centre
ERITH DA8 ....150 A1
Northumberland Heath
Primary School
ERITH DA8 ....149 J1
Northumberland Park
Industrial Estate
TOTM N17 ....50 D2
Northumberland Park School
TOTM N17 ....50 C3
Northview Primary School
WLSDN NW10 ....81 G2
Northway School
MLHL NW7 ....30 E5
North West Kent College
DART DA1 ....171 F4
North West London
Jewish J & I School
CRICK NW2 ....82 C5
North West London Medical
Centre *MV/WKIL* W9 ....101 G2
North Westminster
Community School
BAY/PAD W2 ....8 A2
North Westminster Community
School
MV/WKIL W9 ....100 E3
North Weylands Industrial
Estate *WOT/HER* KT12 .....188 D6

Northwick Park Hospital &
Clinical Research Centre
HRW HA1 ....61 H4
Northwold Primary School
CLPT E5 ....68 C6
Northwood Cemetery
NTHWD HA6 ....40 D5
Northwood College
NTHWD HA6 ....40 B3
Northwood FC
NTHWD HA6 ....40 D5
Northwood Golf Club
NTHWD HA6 ....40 B3
Northwood & Pinner
Community Hospital
NTHWD HA6 ....40 E4
Northwood Preparatory
School *RKW/CH/CXG* WD3 ...26 A4
Northwood Primary
School *ERITHM* DA18 ....129 F3
Northwood School
NTHWD HA6 ....41 F4
Northwood Sports Centre
PIN HA5 ....41 F4
Norwegian/British Monument
BAY/PAD W2 ....8 C7
The Norwegian School
WIM/MER SW19 ....177 F3
Norwood Green Infant School
NWDGN UB2 ....114 D5
Norwood Green Junior School
NWDGN UB2 ....114 D5
Norwood Heights Shopping
Centre *NRWD* SE19 ....181 F2
Norwood School
WNWD SE27 ....180 D1
Notre Dame RC Girls School
STHWK SE1 ....18 A4
Notre Dame RC Primary
School
WOOL/PLUM SE18 ....127 G6
Notre Dame University
LSQ/SEVD WC2H 10 D6
Notting Hill & Ealing High
School *WEA* W13 ....97 H4
Novotel
CAMTN NW1 ....4 D5
STHWK SE1 ....18 D1
TWRH EC3N 13 H5
WDR/YW UB7 ....112 D4
Novotel London Waterloo
STHWK SE1 ....18 B1
Novotel London West
HMSMTH W6 ....119 G5
Nower Hill High School
PIN HA5 ....60 A1
NTGB Sports Ground
EHAM E6 ....90 A4
Nuffield Hospital
ENC/FH EN2 ....23 G3
Nugent Industrial Park
STMC/STPC BR5 ....202 D1
Nutrition Clinic
MHST W1U 9 G1
O2 Centre *HAMP* NW3 ......83 G4
Oakdale Infant School
SWFD E18 ....53 F5
Oakdale Junior School
SWFD E18 ....53 G5
Oakfield Preparatory School
DUL SE21 ....162 E4
Oakfield Primary School
DART DA1 ....171 G4
Oakfield Road Industrial Estate
PGE/AN SE20 ....181 J3
Oak Hill Health Centre
SURB KT6 ....191 F3
Oakhill Primary School
WFD IG8 ....52 C2
Oakington Manor School
WBLY HA9 ....80 D3
Oakland CP School
EBAR EN4 ....33 K1
Oaklands Primary School
HNWL W7 ....116 A2
Oaklands School
ISLW TW7 ....135 J4
Oaklands Secondary School
BETH E2 ....104 C2
Oak Lane Cemetery
TWK TW1 ....156 B2
Oak Lane Medical Centre
TWK TW1 ....156 C2
Oakleigh School
TRDG/WHET N20 ....33 J5
Oak Lodge Hotel
EN EN1 ....36 A1
Oak Lodge JMI School
WWKM BR4 ....198 E4
Oak Lodge Medical Centre
EDGW HA8 ....44 D3
Oak Lodge School
BAL SW12 ....160 E2
FNCH N2 ....47 G6
Oakthorpe Primary School
PLMGR N13 ....49 J1
Oak Tree Medical Centre
GDMY/SEVK IG3 ....72 E6
Oakwood Business Park
WLSDN NW10 ....99 F2
Oakwood Medical Centre
STHGT/OAK N14 ....22 C6
Oasis Sports Centre
LSQ/SEVD WC2H 10 D3
Obstetrics Hospital
CROY/NA CR0 ....211 K1
Occupational Health Centre
CROY/NA CR0 ....211 K1
Odeon Cinema
ARCH N19 ....84 E1
EBAR EN5 ....20 E6
BECK BR3 ....182 D5
CAMTN NW1 ....84 B6
ELTH/MOT SE9 ....146 D5
ESH/CLAY KT10 ....204 B2

FITZ W1T 10 C2
GNTH/NBYPK IG2 ....72 A3
HAYES BR2 ....183 K5
KENS W8 ....119 J5
KIL/WHAMP NW6 ....83 H5
KUTN/CMB KT2 ....175 F5
LSQ/SEVD WC2H 10 D6
MBLAR W1H 9 F4
MUSWH N10 ....66 A1
RCHPK/HAM TW10 ....136 E6
ROM RM1 ....75 H2
STJS SW1Y 10 C6
STRHM/NOR SW16 ....161 K5
SWFD E18 ....52 E5
WIM/MER SW19 ....177 K3
Odeon Covent Garden Cinema
LSQ/SEVD WC2H 10 D4
Odeon Wardour Street Cinema
SOHO/SHAV W1D 10 C5
Odessa Infant School
FSTGT E7 ....88 E3
Odyssey Business Park
RSLP HA4 ....77 F3
Old Actonians Sports Club
EA W5 ....117 G2
Old Admiralty
WHALL SW1A 16 D1
Old Bancroftians FC
BKHH IG9 ....39 H6
Old Barnes Cemetery
BARN SW13 ....138 E3
Old Beckenhamian RFC
WWKM BR4 ....214 B1
Old Bellgate Wharf
Development *POP/IOD* E14 ...124 C3
Old Bexley Business Park
BXLY DA5 ....169 J2
Old Bexley CE Primary School
BXLY DA5 ....169 G5
Old Brockleians
Sports Ground
ELTH/MOT SE9 ....166 B1
Old Bromlians CC
HAYES BR2 ....200 A2
Old Cemetery
EDUL SE22 ....163 J1
Oldchurch Hospital
ROMW/RG RM7 ....75 F3
Old Colfeian Sports Club
LEE/GVPK SE12 ....145 K6
Old Curiosity Shop
LINN WC2A 11 G3
Old Elthamians Sports Club
CHST BR7 ....185 K2
Oldfield House Special
School
HPTN TW12 ....172 E4
Oldfield Primary School
CHSWK W4 ....96 D1
Oldfields Trading Estate
SUT SM1 ....208 E1
Old Fold Manor Golf Club
BAR EN5 ....20 C2
Old Ford Primary School
BOW E3 ....105 H1
Oldhill Medical Centre
STNW/STAM N16 ....68 B5
Old Jamaica Business Estate
BERM/RHTH SE16 ....19 K4
Old Lyonian Sports Ground
RYLN/HDSTN HA2 ....60 C2
Old Millhillians Sports Ground
PIN HA5 ....42 A4
Old Netley J & I School
CAMTN NW1 ....3 K5
Old Oak Primary School
SHB W12 ....99 H5
Old Operating Theatre &
Herb Garret Museum
STHWK SE1 ....18 E1
Old Owens Sports Ground
TRDG/WHET N20 ....33 H3
Old Palace Primary School
BOW E3 ....105 K2
Old Palace School
CROY/NA CR0 ....211 H1
Old Royal Naval College
GNWCH SE10 ....125 G5
Old Royal Observatory
Greenwich *GNWCH* SE10 ...145 G1
Old Spitalfields Market Hall
WCHPL E1 ....13 J1
Old Station Museum
CAN/RD E16 ....127 F2
Old Sun Wharf
POP/IOD E14 ....105 G6
Old Tiffinians Sports Ground
E/WMO/HCT KT8 ....189 K2
Old Treasury
WHALL SW1A 16 E2
Old Vicarage School
RCHPK/HAM TW10 ....157 F1
Old Vic Theatre
STHWK SE1 ....17 K2
Old War Office
WHALL SW1A 16 E1
Old Wilsonians Sports Club
WWKM BR4 ....199 H5
Oliver Business Park
BOW E3 ....105 G1
Oliver Goldsmith Primary
School *CDALE/KGS* NW9 ....63 F2
CMBW SE5 ....143 G2
Olympia
WKENS W14 ....119 H3
Olympia Industrial Estate
WDGN N22 ....49 F5
Olympic Industrial Estate
WBLY HA9 ....80 D2
Olympic Retail Park
WBLY HA9 ....80 C2
Olympic Trading Estate
WBLY HA9 ....80 D2

One Aldwych Hotel
COVGDN WC2E 11 G5
The One Stanley Medical
Centre *ALP/SUD* HA0 ....80 A5
On Sai Clinic
ECT SW5 ....120 A4
Open Air Theatre
CAMTN NW1 ....3 G5
The Open University
FSBYW WC1X 5 G4
HAMP NW3 ....82 E2
Ophaboom Theatre
WLSDN NW10 ....99 K1
Optimax Laser Eye Clinic
HAMP NW3 ....83 G4
Orange Tree Theatre
RCH/KEW TW9 ....137 F5
Oratory RC Primary School
CHEL SW3 ....121 D5
Orchard Business Centre
SYD SE26 ....182 C1
The Orchard Health Centre
BARK IG11 ....108 C1
Orchard Hill College of
Further Education
CAR SM5 ....209 K6
Orchard House School
CHSWK W4 ....118 A4
Orchard J & I School
HOM E9 ....86 E5
Orchard Primary School
SCUP DA14 ....186 C1
The Orchard School
E/WMO/HCT KT8 ....189 J2
Orchard Shopping Centre
DART DA1 ....171 H1
The Orchard Theatre
DART DA1 ....171 H1
Orchard Way Primary
School
CROY/NA CR0 ....198 B4
Oriel Primary School
FELT TW13 ....154 D5
Orient Industrial Park
LEY E10 ....69 J6
Orion Business Centre
BERM/RHTH SE16 ....124 A5
Orleans House Gallery
TWK TW1 ....156 C3
Orleans Infant School
TWK TW1 ....156 C2
Orley Farm School
HRW HA1 ....78 D1
Orpington College of FE
ORP BR6 ....202 B5
The Orpington Halls
ORP BR6 ....202 B6
Orpington Mental Health
Centre *ORP* BR6 ....217 F1
Orpington Retail Park
STMC/STPC BR5 ....202 D1
Osidge JMI School
STHGT/OAK N14 ....34 C3
Osmani Primary School
WCHPL E1 ....104 C4
Osteopathic Clinic
HOR/WEW KT19 ....207 F3
Osterley Four Pillars Hotel
ISLW TW7 ....136 A1
Osterley RFC
NWDGN UB2 ....115 G3
Our Lady Immaculate RC
Primary School
BRYLDS KT5 ....191 J5
Our Lady of Dolours RC
Primary School
BAY/PAD W2 ....101 F2
Our Lady of Grace RC
Junior School
CRICK NW2 ....81 K1
Our Lady of Grace RC Primary
School *CHARL* SE7 ....126 A6
Our Lady of Lourdes RC Primary
School
FBAR/BDGN N11 ....48 C1
FNCH N3 ....47 G3
LEW SE13 ....145 G4
WAN E11 ....70 D5
WLSDN NW10 ....80 E6
Our Lady of Muswell RC
Primary School
MUSWH N10 ....48 A5
Our Lady of the Assumption
RC Infant School
BETH E2 ....104 E1
Our Lady of the Rosary RC
School *BFN/LL* DA15 ....167 K1
Our Lady of the Sacred
Heart School *HOLWY* N7 ...85 F3
Our Lady of the Visitation RC
Combined Primary School
GFD/PVL UB6 ....96 C3
Our Lady of Victories RC
Primary School
PUT/ROE SW15 ....139 G5
SKENS SW7 ....120 B4
Our Lady Queen of Heaven RC
Primary School
WIM/MER SW19 ....159 G2
Our Lady RC Primary School
POP/IOD E14 ....105 H5
Our Lady & St Johns RC
Primary School
BTFD TW8 ....116 D5
Our Lady & St Joseph
Primary School *IS* N1 ....86 A4
Our Lady & St Philip Neri
Infant School *FSTH* SE23 ...164 A5
Our Lady & St Phillip
Neri Junior School
SYD SE26 ....164 B6
Our Ladys Cath Primary
School *DART* DA1 ....171 G1

Our Ladys RC Primary School
WDGN WC2E 84 C6
Oval Business Centre
LBTH SE11 ....122 A5
Oval House Theatre
LBTH SE11 ....122 B6
Oval Primary School
CROY/NA CR0 ....197 F5
Overton Grange School
BELMT SM2 ....209 F6
Oxford Gardens Primary
School *NKENS* W10 ....100 B5
Oxford House College
SOHO/SHAV W1D 10 C3
Oxhey Infant School
BUSH WD23 ....27 J1
Oxhey Park Golf Centre
OXHEY WD19 ....27 H3
Oxhey Wood Primary School
OXHEY WD19 ....27 G5
Oxo Tower Wharf
STHWK SE1 ....11 K6
Paddington Bowling &
Sports Club *MV/WKIL* W9 ...101 F3
Paddington Green
Primary School
BAY/PAD W2 ....2 A7
Paddington Recreation
Ground Athletics Track
MV/WKIL W9 ....100 E2
Paddock School
PUT/ROE SW15 ....138 C5
Pain Relief Clinic
HDN NW4 ....63 K3
Paint Pots Montessori School
WBPTN SW10 ....120 B6
Pakeman Primary School
HOLWY N7 ....85 F1
Palace Gardens Shopping
Centre *ENC/FH* EN2 ....23 K4
Palace of Westminster
WEST SW1P 17 F3
Palace Theatre
SOHO/SHAV W1D 10 C5
Palladium Theatre
REGST W1B 10 A4
Palmers Green High School
WCHMH N21 ....35 G4
Palmerston Business Centre
SUT SM1 ....209 G3
Palm House
RCH/KEW TW9 ....137 G2
Panorama Pier
STHWK SE1 ....12 B6
Paradise Swimming Pools
MLHL NW7 ....45 G1
Paragon Hotel
FUL/PGN SW6 ....119 K6
Paray House School
FUL/PGN SW6 ....139 J3
Parayhouse School
WBPTN SW10 ....140 B1
Parchmore Medical Centre
THHTH CR7 ....180 D6
Pardes House &
Beis Yaakov School *FNCH* N3 ...46 D4
Pardes House Grammar
School
FNCH N3 ....46 D5
Parent Infant Clinic
HAMP NW3 ....83 G3
Parish CE Primary School
BMLY BR1 ....183 K3
Parish Church CE Primary
School *CROY/NA* CR0 ....211 H1
Park Business Centre
KIL/WHAMP NW6 ....100 E2
Parkes Townhouse Hotel
CHEL SW3 ....14 D4
Parkfield Industrial Estate
BTSEA SW11 ....141 F3
Parkfield JMI School
HDN NW4 ....63 K4
Parkgate House School
BTSEA SW11 ....141 F5
Park Hall Trading Estate
WNWD SE27 ....162 D5
Park High School
STAN HA7 ....43 K5
Park Junior School
CROY/NA CR0 ....211 K1
Parkhill Primary School
CLAY IG5 ....53 K6
Park Hill School
KUTN/CMB KT2 ....175 H5
Park House Medical Centre
KIL/WHAMP NW6 ....100 C1
Park House RFC
HAYES BR2 ....200 B6
Park Infants School
SRTFD E15 ....88 C5
The Park Inn Heathrow
WDR/YW UB7 ....132 E1
Parklands Primary School
ROM RM1 ....57 F6
Park Lane Primary School
WBLY HA9 ....80 A3
Park Medical Centre
BERM/RHTH SE16 ....124 A4
Park Mews Small Business
Centre *HNHL* SE24 ....162 D1
Park Road Clinic
CEND/HSY/T N8 ....66 D2
Park Road Swimming Centre
CEND/HSY/T N8 ....66 D2
Park School for Girls
IL IG1 ....72 A6
Parkside Business Estate
DEPT SE8 ....124 C6
Parkside Clinic
NTGHL W11 ....100 D5
Parkside Health
NTGHL W11 ....100 C5

Parkside Hospital
WIM/MER SW19 ....159 G5
Park Walk Primary School
WBPTN SW10 ....120 C6
Parkway Primary School
ERTHM DA18 ....129 F3
Parkway Trading Estate
HEST TW5 ....114 B6
Parkwood Primary School
FSBYPK N4 ....67 H6
Parliament Hill Fields
Athletics Track KTTN NW5 ....83 K2
Parliament Hill Lido
KTTN NW5 ....84 A2
Parliament Hill School
KTTN NW5 ....84 A2
Parmiter Industrial Centre
BETH E2 ....104 D1
Parnells Sports Ground
KTN/HRWW/W HA3 ....62 B3
Parsloes Primary School
DAGW RM9 ....92 B4
Parsons Green Health Clinic
FUL/PGN SW6 ....139 K2
Passport Language Schools
BMLY BR1 ....184 A4
The Patrick Doody Clinic &
Health Centre
WIM/MER SW19 ....177 K3
Pattinson Clinic
RCHPK/HAM TW10 ....136 E6
The Paul Robeson Theatre
HSLW TW3 ....135 G4
Pavilion Barclays Sports
Ground EA W5 ....98 A4
The Pavilion Leisure Centre
BMLY BR1 ....183 K5
Pavilion Restaurant
RCH/KEW TW9 ....137 F3
Paxton Primary School
NRWD SE19 ....181 G2
PDSA Hospital
REDBR IG4 ....53 H6
Peace Pagoda
BTSEA SW11 ....140 E1
Peacock Estate
TOTM N17 ....50 B2
Peacock Industrial Estate
TOTM N17 ....50 B3
The Peacock Theatre
HOL/ALD WC2B 11 G4
Peall Road Industrial Estate
CROY/NA CRO 196 A3
Peckham Park Primary
School PECK SE15 ....143 H1
Peckham Pulse Healthy
Living Centre
PECK SE15 ....143 H2
Peckham Rye Primary School
PECK SE15 ....143 J4
Pelham Primary School
BXLYHN DA7 ....149 G4
WIM/MER SW19 ....177 K3
Pembridge Court Hotel
NTGHL W11 ....100 E6
Pembridge Hall
BAY/PAD W2 ....100 E6
Pendragon Secondary School
BMLY BR1 ....165 K5
Pentavia Retail Park
MLHL NW7 ....45 H3
Penwortham Primary
School
STRHM/NOR SW16 ....179 G2
Percival David Foundation
of Chinese Art
STPAN WC1H 4 D6
Perivale Industrial Park
GFD/PVL UB6 ....79 G6
Perivale New Business Centre
GFD/PVL UB6 ....97 J1
Perivale Park Athletics Track
GFD/PVL UB6 ....96 E2
Perivale Park Golf Course
GFD/PVL UB6 ....96 E2
Perivale Primary School
GFD/PVL UB6 ....97 J1
Perrin Road Clinic
ALP/SUD HA0 ....79 H2
Perry Hall Primary School
ORP BR6 ....202 A3
Perrymount Primary School
FSTH SE23 ....164 A4
Peterborough
Primary School
FUL/PGN SW6 ....139 K3
Peterborough &
St Margaret's High School
STAN HA7 ....28 E5
Peter Hills School
BERM/RHTH SE16 ....124 A1
Peter James Business Centre
HYS/HAR UB3 ....113 K2
Peterley Business Centre
BETH E2 ....104 D1
Peter Pan Statue
BAY/PAD W2 ....8 A7
Petrie Museum of Egyptian
Archaeology GWRST WC1E 4 C7
Pett's Hill Primary School
NTHLT UB5 ....78 B3
Pewterers' Hall
CITYW EC2V 12 D2
Phoenix Business Centre
POP/IOD E14 ....105 J4
Phoenix Cinema
EFNCH N2 ....65 J1
Phoenix College
MRDN SM4 ....194 A2
Phoenix High School
SHB W12 ....99 J6
Phoenix Industrial Estate
HRW HA1 ....61 F1
Phoenix Leisure Centre
CAT SE6 ....164 E2

Phoenix School
HAMP NW3 ....83 H4
Phoenix Secondary &
Primary School BOW E3 ....105 H2
Phoenix Theatre
LSO/SEVD WC2H 11 F4
Phoenix Trading Estate
GFD/PVL UB6 ....79 J6
Physical Energy Statue
BAY/PAD W2 ....14 A1
Piccadilly Theatre
SOHO/SHAV W1D 10 C5
Pickford Lane Medical Centre
BXLYHN DA7 ....149 F2
Pickhurst Infant School
HAYES BR2 ....199 H5
Pickhurst Junior School
HAYES BR2 ....199 H5
Picture House Cinema
SRTFD E15 ....88 B4
Pilgrims Way J & I School
PECK SE15 ....123 K6
Pilot Industrial Centre
WLSDN NW10 ....99 G3
Pilton Estate
CROY/NA CRO 196 C6
Pimlico Clinic
PIM SW1V 121 H5
Pinewood Primary School
CRW RM5 ....56 D1
Pinkwell Primary School
WDR/YW UB7 ....113 F4
Pinnacles Cricket &
Squash Club SUT SM1 ....208 E4
Pinner Hill Golf Club
PIN HA5 ....41 F2
Pinner Medical Centre
PIN HA5 ....59 J1
Pinner Park Primary School
RYLN/HDSTN HA2 ....42 B6
Pinner View Medical Centre
HRW HA1 ....60 C2
Pinner Wood Primary
School
PIN HA5 ....41 G4
Pioneers Industrial Park
CROY/NA CRO 195 K5
Pippins School
ASHF TW15 ....152 C6
Pitshanger Manor Museum
EA W5 ....116 D1
Plaisterers Hall
CITYW EC2Y 12 C2
Plaistow Hospital
PLSTW E13 ....107 F1
Plaistow Primary School
PLSTW E13 ....89 G6
Plantation House
Medical Centre
LOTH EC2R 13 F3
Plashet Jewish Cemetery
MNPK E12 ....89 H4
Plashet Road Medical Centre
FSTGT E7 ....89 F5
Plashet School
EHAM E6 ....89 J4
Players Theatre
CHCR WC2N 10 E7
The Playhouse
CHCR WC2N 11 F7
Plaza Business Centre
PEND EN3 ....25 H3
Pleasance Theatre
HOLWY N7 ....84 E4
Plumcroft Primary School
WOOL/PLUM SE18 ....127 H6
Plumstead Leisure Centre
WOOL/PLUM SE18 ....128 A5
Plumstead Manor School
WOOL/PLUM SE18 ....127 J5
The Pointer School
BKHTH/KID SE3 ....145 K2
Police Cadet School
WAN E11 ....70 E5
The Polish Institute &
Sikorski Museum
SKENS SW7 ....14 B3
Polka Theatre for Children
WIM/MER SW19 ....178 A2
Ponders End Industrial Estate
PEND EN3 ....25 H5
Pooles Park Primary School
FSBYPK N4 ....67 F6
Pools in the Park
RCH/KEW TW9 ....136 E5
Pope John Primary School
SHB W12 ....99 K6
Pope's Grotto Hotel
TWK TW1 ....156 B4
Pop In Business Centre
WBLY HA9 ....80 D3
Poplar Business Park
POP/IOD E14 ....106 A6
Poplar Primary School
WIM/MER SW19 ....177 K6
Pop Up Theatre
IS N1 ....5 K3
Porchester Leisure Centre
BAY/PAD W2 ....101 F5
Portcullis House
WHALL SW1A 17 F3
The Portland Hospital
REGST W1B 3 K7
Portland House Medical Centre
GFD/PVL UB6 ....96 B3
Portland Medical Centre
SNWD SE25 ....197 J2
Portland Place School
REGST W1B 9 K1
The Portman Clinic
HAMP NW3 ....83 H4
Portobello Market
NKENS W10 ....100 C5
Portobello Medical Centre
NTGHL W11 ....100 C5

Portway Primary School
SRTFD E15 ....88 E6
Posthouse
KENS W8 ....120 A3
Pound Park Nursery School
CHARL SE7 ....126 C5
The Pountney Clinic
HSLW TW3 ....135 F4
Poverest Primary School
STMC/STPC BR5 ....202 B2
Powergate Business Park
WLSDN NW10 ....99 F2
Power Industrial Estate
ERITH DA8 ....150 C2
Premier Cinema
PECK SE15 ....143 H3
Premier Lodge
BARK IG11 ....90 B6
CHDH RM6 ....74 A2
CROY/NA CRO 211 G4
EDGW HA8 ....44 C3
HOR/WEW KT19 ....207 G3
STHWK SE1 ....12 D7
WBLY HA9 ....80 C1
WHTN TW2 ....155 H5
Premier Travel Inn
IS N1 ....5 F3
Prendergast School
BROCKY SE4 ....144 D5
Preston Manor School
WBLY HA9 ....62 B6
Preston Medical Centre
WBLY HA9 ....80 A1
Preston Park Primary School
WBLY HA9 ....61 K5
PR for Schools
SYD SE26 ....163 K5
Priestmead F & M Schools
KTN/HRWW/W HA3 ....43 H6
Primrose Hill Clinic
CAMTN NW1 ....84 A6
Primrose Montessori School
HBRY N5 ....85 J1
Prince Charles Cinema
SOHO/SHAV W1D 10 D5
Prince Edward Theatre
SOHO/SHAV W1D 10 C4
Prince of Wales Theatre
STJS SW1Y 10 C6
Princes College
NOXST/BSQ WC1A 10 E3
Princes Court Business Centre
WAP E1W 104 D6
Princess Avenue School
MUSWH N10 ....48 B6
Princess Frederica CE
J & I School WLSDN NW10 ....99 K1
Princess Grace Hospital
MHST W1U 3 G7
Princess Louise Hospital
NKENS W10 ....100 A4
Princess May Primary School
STNW/STAM N16 ....86 A3
Princess of Wales
Conservatory
RCH/KEW TW9 ....137 G1
The Princess Royal
Distribution Centre
WLSDN NW10 ....80 D6
The Princess Royal University
Hospital ORP BR6 ....216 A1
Prior Western Primary School
STLK EC1Y 6 D7
Priory CE Primary School
STMC/STPC BR5 ....178 A1
Priory House School
CAT SE6 ....164 E3
Priory Leisure Centre
STMC/STPC BR5 ....202 D5
Priory Retail Park
WIM/MER SW19 ....178 C3
Priory School
STMC/STPC BR5 ....202 D5
Priory Shopping Centre
DART DA1 ....171 G1
Priory Special School
SNWD SE25 ....197 G1
The Priory
ORP BR6 ....202 C4
Privy Council
STJS SW1Y 16 C1
Privy Council Office
WHALL SW1A 16 E1
Progress Business Park
CROY/NA CRO 196 A6
Pronto Trading Estate
YEAD UB4 ....94 C2
Prospect House School
PUT/ROE SW15 ....159 G2
Prospect of Whitby
WAP E1W 123 K1
Proud Gallery
CHCR WC2N 10 E6
Providence Road School
WDR/YW UB7 ....112 B1
Provident Industrial Estate
HYS/HAR UB3 ....113 K2
Psychiatric Home
BRXN/ST SW9 ....141 K4
Pump House
BERM/RHTH SE16 ....124 B1
Pump Lane Industrial Estate
HYS/HAR UB3 ....114 A2
The Purcell School
HRW HA1 ....78 D1
Purdy Hicks Gallery
STHWK SE1 ....12 A7
Purfleet Industrial Park
PUR RM19 ....131 J1
Purfleet Primary School
PUR RM19 ....131 K4
Purley Oaks Primary School
SAND/SEL CR2 ....211 K5
Pursuit Centre
WAP E1W 104 E6

Putney Animal Hospital
PUT/ROE SW15 ....139 G5
Putney Exchange Shopping
Centre PUT/ROE SW15 ....139 G5
Putney High School
PUT/ROE SW15 ....139 G6
Putney Hospital
PUT/ROE SW15 ....139 F4
Putney Leisure Centre
PUT/ROE SW15 ....139 F5
Putney Lower Common
Cemetery PUT/ROE SW15 ....138 E3
Putneymead Medical Centre
PUT/ROE SW15 ....139 F5
Putney Park School
PUT/ROE SW15 ....138 E5
Putney School of Art
PUT/ROE SW15 ....139 H5
Putney Vale Cemetery
PUT/ROE SW15 ....158 D4
Putney Vale Crematorium
PUT/ROE SW15 ....158 D4
Pylon Trading Estate
CAN/RD E16 ....106 B3
Quadrant Business Park
KIL/WHAMP NW6 ....82 C6
Quality Hotel
HRW HA1 ....60 D3
PIM SW1V 15 K7
WBLY HA9 ....80 C2
Quebec Industrial Estate
BERM/RHTH SE16 ....124 B2
Queen Charlotte's Cottage
RCH/KEW TW9 ....137 G1
Queen Charlotte's Hospital
SHB W12 ....99 K5
Queen Elizabeth Centre
BAR EN5 ....20 D5
Queen Elizabeth Conference
Centre WEST SW1P 16 D3
Queen Elizabeth Hall
STHWK SE1 ....11 G7
Queen Elizabeth Hospital
CHARL SE7 ....126 E6
Queen Elizabeth II School
MV/WKIL W9 ....100 D3
Queen Elizabeth Museum
CHING E4 ....38 D2
Queen Elizabeths Boys School
BAR EN5 ....20 B4
Queen Elizabeths Girls School
BAR EN5 ....20 D5
Queen Elizabeth Stadium
EN EN1 ....24 B3
Queenhithe Stairs
BLKFR EC4V 12 C6
Queen Mary's Hospital
HAMP NW3 ....83 G1
SCUP DA14 ....186 B1
Queen Mary's Hospital
for Children SUT SM1 ....194 B5
Queen Mary's University
Hospital PUT/ROE SW15 ....158 D1
Queen Mary & Westfield
College SWFD E18 ....52 E4
WCHPL E1 ....105 F3
Queen Mother Moore School
CLAP SW4 ....141 J5
Queen Mother Sports Centre
PIM SW1V 16 A6
Queensbridge Infant School
HACK E8 ....86 B5
Queensbridge Sports Centre
HACK E8 ....86 B5
Queen's Building
HTHAIR TW6 ....132 E4
The Queens CE Primary
School RCH/KEW TW9 ....137 G1
Queen's Club
WKENS W14 ....119 H5
Queens College London
CAVSQ/HST W1G 9 J2
Queen's Gallery
WHALL SW1A 15 K3
Queens Gate School
SKENS SW7 ....14 A5
The Queens House
GNWCH SE10 ....125 G6
Queens Ice Skating Club
BAY/PAD W2 ....101 F6
Queens Manor Primary School
FUL/PGN SW6 ....139 F1
Queensmead School
RSLP HA4 ....77 H2
Queensmead Sports Centre
RSLP HA4 ....77 H3
Queens Medical Centre
RCHPK/HAM TW10 ....137 G6
Queensmill School
FUL/PGN SW6 ....139 K3
Queens Park Community
School KIL/WHAMP NW6 ....82 A6
Queens Park Health Centre
NKENS W10 ....100 C2
Queens Park Primary School
NKENS W10 ....100 C2
Queens Park Rangers FC
(Loftus Rd Stadium)
SHB W12 ....118 E1
Queen's Road Cemetery
CROY/NA CRO 196 D3
Queens Road Practice
NWCR SE14 ....144 B2
Queens Theatre
SOHO/SHAV W1D 10 C5
Queensway Business Centre
PEND EN3 ....24 E5
Queenswell Infant School
TRDG/WHET N20 ....33 H4
Queen Victoria Memorial
WHALL SW1A 16 A3
The Questors Theatre
EA W5 ....97 J6
Radcliffe College
SOHO/CST W1F 10 A4

Radisson Edwardian Berkshire
Hotel OXSTW W1C 9 J4
Radisson Edwardian Grafton
Hotel CAMTN NW1 ....4 A6
Radisson Edwardian
Hampshire Hotel
SOHO/SHAV W1D 10 D6
Radisson Edwardian Hotel
HYS/HAR UB3 ....133 F1
Radisson Edwardian
Kenilworth Hotel
RSQ WC1B 10 D2
Radisson Edwardian
Marlborough Hotel
RSQ WC1B 10 D2
Radisson Edwardian
Mayfair Hotel
MYFR/PICC W1J 9 K6
Radisson Edwardian
Mountbatten Hotel
LSO/SEVD WC2H 10 E4
Radisson Edwardian
Pastoria Hotel
LSO/SEVD WC2H 10 D6
Radisson Edwardian
Vanderbilt Hotel
SKENS SW7 ....120 B4
Radisson SAS Portman Hotel
MBLAR W1H 9 F3
Raglan Infant School
EN EN1 ....36 A1
Raglan Junior School
EN EN1 ....36 A2
Raglan Primary School
HAYES BR2 ....200 B1
Railton Road Clinic
BRXN/ST SW9 ....142 C6
Rainbow Industrial Estate
RYNPK SW20 ....176 E5
Rainbow Quay
BERM/RHTH SE16 ....124 B3
Raines Foundation School
BETH E2 ....104 D2
Rainham Hall NT
RAIN RM13 ....111 J3
Rainham Trading Estate
RAIN RM13 ....111 G2
Rainham Village Primary
School RAIN RM13 ....111 J3
Ramac Industrial Estate
CHARL SE7 ....125 K5
Ramada Encore London
West Hotel ACT W3 ....99 F3
Ram Brewery & Visitor Centre
WAND/EARL SW18 ....140 A6
Rams Episcopal Primary
School HACK E8 ....86 E3
Randal Cremer Primary
School BETH E2 ....7 J2
Ranelagh Gardens (site of
Chelsea Flower Show)
CHEL SW3 ....121 F6
Ranelagh Primary School
SRTFD E15 ....106 C1
Rangefield Primary School
BMLY BR1 ....183 H1
Ransomes Dock Business
Centre BTSEA SW11 ....140 D7
Raphael Independent School
EMPK RM11 ....75 J3
Rathbow Clinic
BAY/PAD W2 ....2 B7
Rathfern Primary School
CAT SE6 ....164 C3
Ravenor Primary School
GFD/PVL UB6 ....96 A3
Ravensbourne College of
Design & Communication
CHST BR7 ....185 F1
The Ravensbourne School
HAYES BR2 ....200 C1
Ravenscourt Park
Preparatory School
HMSMTH W6 ....118 D4
Ravenscroft Medical Centre
GLDGN NW11 ....64 D4
Ravenscroft Primary School
PLSTW E13 ....106 E3
Ravenscroft School
TRDG/WHET N20 ....32 D2
Ravenside Retail Park
UED N18 ....51 F1
Ravensquay Business Centre
STMC/STPC BR5 ....202 C2
Ravenstone Primary School
NWCR SE14 ....161 F3
Ravenswood Industrial Estate
WALTH E17 ....70 A1
Ravens Wood School
HAYES BR2 ....215 H3
Ray Lodge Primary School
WFD IG8 ....53 H2
Raynes Park High School
NWMAL KT3 ....176 E6
Raynes Park Sports Ground
RYNPK SW20 ....176 D5
Raynes Park Vale FC
RYNPK SW20 ....193 G2
Raynham Primary School
UED N18 ....50 C1
RCA SKENS SW7 ....120 B3
RCA Sculpture School
BTSEA SW11 ....140 D1
Reay Primary School
BRXN/ST SW9 ....142 A1
Rectory Business Centre
SCUP DA14 ....168 C6
Rectory Paddock School
STMC/STPC BR5 ....186 D5
Redbridge College
CHDH RM6 ....73 H2
Redbridge Museum
IL IG1 ....90 B1
Redbridge Primary School
REDBR IG4 ....71 J2

Redbridge Sports Centre
BARK/HLT IG6 ....54 D4
Redbridge Tuition Service
GNTH/NBYPK IG2 ....72 D5
Redburn Industrial Estate
PEND EN3 ....37 F1
Redcliffe School
WBPTN SW10 ....120 B6
Redifford School
PIN HA5 ....59 J1
Redford Lodge Psychiatric
Hospital ED N9 ....36 C4
Red Gates School
CROY/NA CR0 ....211 G3
Redhill Junior School
CHST BR7 ....185 G1
Redlands Primary School
WCHPL E1 ....104 E4
Red Lion Business Park
SURB KT6 ....191 G6
Rediff Primary School
BERM/RHTH SE16 ....124 B2
Red Rose Trading Estate
EBAR EN4 ....21 H6
Regent Business Centre
HYS/HAR UB3 ....114 A2
Regent Clinic
CAVSQ/HST W1G 9 J2
Regent College London
PIN HA5 ....59 K4
Regent's College & European
Business School
CAMTN NW1 ....3 F6
Regent's Park Barracks
CAMTN NW1 ....3 J3
Regents Park Clinic
CAMTN NW1 ....2 E6
Regents Park Hotel
CAMTN NW1 ....2 E7
Regents Park Medical Centre
CAMTN NW1 ....2 E2
Regent's Park Track
CAMTN NW1 ....2 E2
Regina Coeli RC Primary School
CROY/NA CR0 ....211 H5
The Rembrandt Hotel
SKENS SW7 ....14 C5
Renaissance Chancery
Court Hotel HHOL WC1V ...11 G2
The Renaissance Hotel
HTHAIR TW6 ....133 F2
Renoir Cinema
BMSBY WC1N 5 F6
Renwick Industrial Estate
BARK IG11 ....109 H1
Rewards Centre
HSLW TW3 ....135 H4
Reynard Mills Trading Estate
BTFD TW8 ....116 D5
Reynolds Sports Centre
EA W5 ....117 H2
Rhodes Avenue Primary
School FBAR/BDGN N11 ...48 C4
Rhodes Farm Clinic
MLHL NW7 ....32 A6
Rhyl Primary School
KTTN NW5 ....84 A4
RIBA Library Drawings &
Manuscript Collection
MBLAR W1H 9 F5
Ricards Lodge High School
WIM/MER SW19 ....159 J6
Richard Alibon Primary School
DAGE RM10 ....92 C3
Richard Atkins Primary School
BRXS/STRHM SW2 ....161 J2
Richard Cloudesley School
STLK EC1Y 6 C7
Richard Cobden Primary
School CAMTN NW1 ....4 B1
Rich Industrial Estate
PECK SE15 ....123 J6
STHWK SE1 ....19 H5
Richmond Adult &
Community College
RCH/KEW TW9 ....136 E5
Richmond American
International University
RCHPK/HAM TW10 ....157 F1
The Richmond Clinic
RCHPK/HAM TW10 ....137 G5
Richmond College
KENS W8 ....120 A3
Richmond Community
College TWK TW1 ....156 A3
Richmond FC
RCH/KEW TW9 ....136 E5
The Richmond Gate Hotel
RCHPK/HAM TW10 ....157 F2
The Richmond Golf Club
RCHPK/HAM TW10 ....157 F4
The Richmond Green
Medical Centre
RCH/KEW TW9 ....136 E6
The Richmond Hill Hotel
RCHPK/HAM TW10 ....157 F2
Richmond House School
HPTN TW12 ....172 E1
Richmond Lock
RCH/KEW TW9 ....136 D5
Richmond Magistrates Court
RCH/KEW TW9 ....136 E5
Richmond Park Golf Club
PUT/ROE SW15 ....158 B2
Richmond Road Medical
Centre KUTN/CMB KT2 ...175 F3
Richmond Theatre
RCH/KEW TW9 ....136 E5
Richmond upon Thames
College
WHTN TW2 ....155 K2
Ridge House Clinic
WCHMH N21 ....35 K2
Ridgeway Primary School
SAND/SEL CR2 ....212 A6

Rio Cinema
HACK E8 ....86 B3
Ripple J & I School
BARK IG11 ....90 D6
Risebridge Golf Club
ROM RM1 ....57 H3
Rise Park Primary School
ROM RM1 ....57 H3
Risley Avenue Primary School
TOTM N17 ....50 A4
The Ritz Hotel
MYFR/PICC W1J 10 A7
Ritzy Cinema
BRXN/ST SW9 ....142 B5
River Brent Business Park
WWDGN UB2 ....115 K3
River Gardens
Business Centre
EBED/NFELT TW14 ....134 A5
River Mole Business Park
ESH/CLAY KT10 ....189 F5
River Place Health Centre
IS N1 ....85 J5
River Road Business Park
BARK IG11 ....108 E2
Riversdale Primary School
WAND/EARL SW18 ....159 K3
Riverside Business Centre
WAND/EARL SW18 ....160 A3
Riverside Community
Health Care WKENS W14 ...119 G3
Riverside Golf Club
THMD SE28 ....110 A5
Riverside Industrial Estate
BARK IG11 ....109 G2
DART DA1 ....151 H6
ED N9 ....37 G1
Riverside Primary School
BERM/RHTH SE16 ....123 H2
Riverside Quarter
WAND/EARL SW18 ....139 K5
Riverside Studios Cinema
BARN SW13 ....118 E5
Riverside Swimming Centre
ERITH DA8 ....130 B5
Riverside Wandle
Trading Estate MTCM CR4 ...194 E4
Riverston School
LEE/GVPK SE12 ....145 K6
Riverview CE Primary School
HOR/WEW KT19 ....206 E2
The RJ Mitchell Primary
School HCH RM12 ....93 K4
RNLI Lifeboat Station
TWRH EC3N 13 H7
Roan Industrial Estate
MTCM CR4 ....178 D4
Robert Blair Primary School
HOLWY N7 ....84 E4
Robert Browning Primary
School WALW SE17 ....122 E5
Robert Clack School
BCTR RM8 ....74 B5
Robin Hood Infant School
SUT SM1 ....208 E3
Robin Hood Junior School
SUT SM1 ....209 F3
Robin Hood Lane Health
Centre
SUT SM1 ....208 E3
Robin Hood Primary School
KUTN/CMB KT2 ....176 A1
Robinsfield Infant School
STJWD NW8 ....2 B2
Roxbourne Medical Centre
RYLN/HDSTN HA2 ....60 B6
Rockliffe Manor Primary
School WOOL/PLUM SE18 ...128 A6
Rockmount Primary School
NRWD SE19 ....180 D2
Rockware Business Centre
GFD/PVL UB6 ....78 D6
Roding Primary School
BCTR RM8 ....91 J2
WFD IG8 ....53 J3
The Roebuck Hotel
BKHH IG9 ....39 J1
Roebuck Road Trading Estate
BARK/HLT IG6 ....55 H2
Roe Green J & I School
CDALE/KGS NW9 ....62 D1
Roehampton Church School
PUT/ROE SW15 ....158 E2
Roehampton Golf Club
PUT/ROE SW15 ....138 C5
Roehampton Institute
PUT/ROE SW15 ....138 C6
WAND/EARL SW18 ....159 H1
The Roehampton Priory
Hospital PUT/ROE SW15 ...138 C5
Roehampton Recreation
Centre PUT/ROE SW15 ...158 D2
Roger Ascham Primary
School WALTH E17 ....51 H4
Roger Bannister Sports Ground
KTN/HRWW/W HA3 ....42 C2
Rokeby School
KUTN/CMB KT2 ....175 K3
SRTFD E15 ....88 B5
Rokesly Primary School
CEND/HSY/T N8 ....66 E2
Roman Bath
TPL/STR WC2R 11 H5
Roman Industrial Estate
CROY/NA CR0 ....197 F4
Roman Road Primary School
EHAM E6 ....107 H3
Roman Wall Remains
BARB EC2Y 12 C2
Romford Cemetery
ROMW/RG RM7 ....74 E4
Romford Clinic
ROM RM1 ....75 H1

Romford County Court
ROM RM1 ....75 H1
Romford Golf Club
GPK RM2 ....57 J6
Romford Ice Rink
ROMW/RG RM7 ....75 G4
Romford Shopping Hall
ROM RM1 ....75 G1
Ronald Rose Primary School
WIM/MER SW19 ....159 G2
Rood Lane Medical Centre
FENCHST EC3M 13 G5
Rooks Heath School
RYLN/HDSTN HA2 ....78 A1
Roosevelt Memorial
MYFR/PKLN W1K 9 H5
Ropery Business Park
CHARL SE7 ....126 B4
Rosary Priory High School
BUSH WD23 ....28 E1
Rosary RC Infant School
HEST TW5 ....114 E6
The Rosary RC Primary School
HAMP NW3 ....83 J3
Rosebery Industrial Park
TOTM N17 ....50 D5
Rose Bruford College
BFN/LL DA15 ....168 C3
DEPT SE8 ....124 E6
Roselands Clinic
NWMAL KT3 ....191 K1
Rosemary School (Primary)
IS N1 ....85 J6
Rose McAndrew Clinic
BRXN/ST SW9 ....142 A3
Rosemead Preparatory
School DUL SE21 ....162 D4
Rosendale Primary School
DUL SE21 ....162 D2
Rose of Kingston (Kingston Theatre)
KUT/HW KT1 ....174 E5
Rose Theatre Exhibition
STHWK SE1 ....12 C7
Rosetta Primary School
CAN/RD E16 ....107 F4
Rosewood Medical Centre
HCH RM12 ....93 K3
Rosh Pinah Primary School
EDGW HA8 ....30 D4
Rosslyn Park RFC
PUT/ROE SW15 ....138 C5
Rotherfield Primary School
IS N1 ....85 J6
Rotherhithe Civic Centre
BERM/RHTH SE16 ....123 K2
Rotherhithe Primary School
BERM/RHTH SE16 ....123 K4
The Rotunda
KUT/HW KT1 ....175 F5
The Roundhouse Theatre
CAMTN NW1 ....84 A5
Roundshaw J & I School
WLGTN SM6 ....210 E5
Roundwood Park Medical
Centre WLSDN NW10 ....81 J5
Rowan High School
CLAP SW4 ....161 J1
Rowan Preparatory School
ESH/CLAY KT10 ....205 F5
Rowans School
RYNPK SW20 ....176 D3
Rowhill School
RDART DA2 ....171 F6
Rowley Industrial Park
ACT W3 ....117 J3
Roxbourne Medical Centre
RYLN/HDSTN HA2 ....60 B6
Roxbourne Middle School
RSLP HA4 ....59 H6
Roxeth F & M School
RYLN/HDSTN HA2 ....60 D6
Roxeth Manor First School
RYLN/HDSTN HA2 ....78 A1
Roxeth Mead School
RYLN/HDSTN HA2 ....60 D6
Roxwell Trading Park
WALTH E17 ....51 F4
Royal Academy of Arts
MYFR/PICC W1J 10 A6
Royal Academy of
Dramatic Art GWRST WC1E ...4 D7
Royal Academy of Music
CAMTN NW1 ....3 H7
Royal Air Force Museum
CDALE/KGS NW9 ....45 J5
Royal Albert Hall
SKENS SW7 ....14 A3
Royal Arsenal
WOOL/PLUM SE18 ....127 G3
Royal Ballet School
LSQ/SEVD WC2H 11 F4
The Royal Ballet School
RCHPK/HAM TW10 ....158 A3
Royal Blackheath Golf Club
ELTH/MOT SE9 ....166 E2
Royal Botanic Gardens
Kew School
RCH/KEW TW9 ....137 G1
Royal Brompton &
National Heart Hospitals
CHEL SW3 ....120 C5
Royal Chace Hotel
ENC/FH EN2 ....23 F1
Royal College of
Anaesthetists
RSQ WC1B 10 E1
Royal College of Art
SKENS SW7 ....120 B2
Royal College of Music
SHB W12 ....118 D3
SKENS SW7 ....14 A4
Royal College of Nursing
CAMTN NW1 ....4 B6
CAVSQ/HST W1G 9 K5
IS N1 ....6 A1

Royal College of Obstetricians
& Gynaecologists
CAMTN NW1 ....2 E6
Royal College of
Ophthalmologists
CAMTN NW1 ....3 G7
Royal College of
Paediatrics & Child Health
GTPST W1W 9 K1
The Royal College of Pathology
STJS SW1Y 16 C1
Royal College of Physicians
CAMTN NW1 ....3 J6
Royal College of Surgeons
CAMTN NW1 ....11 H3
Royal Courts of Justice
LINN WC2A 11 H4
Royal Court Theatre
BCVA SW1W 15 G7
Royal Court Young
Peoples Theatre
NKENS W10 ....100 C4
The Royal Dock
Community School
CAN/RD E16 ....107 G5
Royal Docks Medical Centre
EHAM E6 ....108 A5
Royal Epping Forest Golf Club
CHING E4 ....38 C2
Royal Exchange
LOTH EC2R 13 F4
Royal Festival Hall
STHWK SE1 ....17 G1
Royal Free Hospital School of
Medicine
HAMP NW3 ....83 J3
Royal Free University
College Medical School
HAMP NW3 ....83 J3
Royal Garden Hotel
KENS W8 ....120 A2
Royal Geographical Society
SKENS SW7 ....14 A3
The Royal Horseguards
WHALL SW1A 17 F1
Royal Horticultural Society
New Hall WEST SW1P 16 C5
Royal Horticultural Society
Old Hall WEST SW1P 16 C6
Royal Hospital
RCH/KEW TW9 ....137 F4
Royal Hospital Chelsea
CHEL SW3 ....120 C5
Royal Hospital for
Neuro-Disability
WAND/EARL SW18 ....159 H1
Royal Hospital & Home
PUT/ROE SW15 ....158 E2
Royal Hospital Museum
CHEL SW3 ....121 F5
Royal Institute of
British Architects
REGST W1B 9 K1
Royal Institution's
Faraday Museum
MYFR/PICC W1J 9 K6
Royal Lancaster Hotel
BAY/PAD W2 ....8 B6
The Royal London Estate
TOTM N17 ....50 D3
Royal London
Homeopathic Hospital
BMSBY WC1N 11 F1
Royal Marsden Hospital
CHEL SW3 ....120 C5
The Royal Mews
WHALL SW1A 15 J4
Royal Mid-Surrey Golf Club
RCH/KEW TW9 ....136 E4
Royal Military School of Music
WHTN TW2 ....155 J1
Royal Mint Court
TWRH EC3N 13 K6
Royal National Orthopaedic
Hospital GTPST W1W 3 K7
STAN HA7 ....29 H3
Royal National Theatre
CMBW SE5 ....142 B1
STHWK SE1 ....11 J7
Royal National Throat,
Nose & Ear Hospital
FSBYW WC1X 5 G4
Royal Observatory Greenwich
GNWCH SE10 ....125 G6
Royal Opera House
COVGDN WC2E 11 F4
The Royal Park Hotel
BAY/PAD W2 ....8 A4
Royal Park Primary School
SCUP DA14 ....169 F5
Royal Russell School
CROY/NA CR0 ....212 D4
The Royal School
HAMP NW3 ....83 H2
Royal Society of Arts
CHCR WC2N 11 F6
Royal Society of Medicine
CAVSQ/HST W1G 9 J3
Royal Veterinary College
CAMTN NW1 ....4 B1
Royal Victoria Docks
Watersports Centre
CAN/RD E16 ....106 E6
Royal Wimbledon Golf Club
WIM/MER SW19 ....176 C4
Royston Primary School
BECK BR3 ....182 A4
RSPCA Animal Hospital
HOLWY N7 ....67 F6
The Rubens at the Palace
Hotel WESTW SW1E 15 K4
Rudolph Steiner Hall
CAMTN NW1 ....2 E6
Rufus Business Centre
WAND/EARL SW18 ....160 A4

Ruislip Gardens Primary School
HGDN/ICK UB10 ....76 C2
Ruislip Golf Club
RSLP HA4 ....58 A6
Ruislip Manor FC
RSLP HA4 ....58 D6
Ruislip RFC
RSLP HA4 ....58 B6
Ruislip Woods National
Nature Reserve NTHWD HA6 ...40 A6
RSLP HA4 ....58 C2
Rush Croft School
CHING E4 ....51 K3
Rushey Green Primary School
CAT SE6 ....164 E3
Rush Green Junior School
IL IG1 ....71 K6
Rush Green Primary School
ROMW/RG RM7 ....75 F5
Rushmore Junior School
CLPT E5 ....86 E2
Ruskin House School
HNHL SE24 ....142 D6
The Russell JMI School
RCHPK/HAM TW10 ....156 E5
The Russell School
RCHPK/HAM TW10 ....156 E5
Russet House School
EN EN1 ....24 D2
Ruthlin School
RYNPK SW20 ....177 J5
Ruxley Corner Industrial
Estate SCUP DA14 ....186 E2
Ruxley Park Golf Centre
STMC/STPC BR5 ....186 E4
Ryde College
WATW WD18 ....26 C1
Ryefield Primary School
HGDN/ICK UB10 ....76 B6
Ryelands Primary School
SNWD SE25 ....197 J2
Saatchi Gallery
STHWK SE1 ....17 G2
Sacred Heart C Primary
School PUT/ROE SW15 ...138 D6
Sacred Heart High School
HMSMTH W6 ....119 F4
Sacred Heart High School
for Girls KTN/HRWW/W HA3 ...42 E5
Sacred Heart Junior School
HMSMTH W6 ....119 G4
Sacred Heart RC Infant School
BTSEA SW11 ....140 D3
Sacred Heart RC Junior &
Middle School
BTSEA SW11 ....140 D4
Sacred Heart RC Primary
School NWMAL KT3 ....192 D1
OXHEY WD19 ....27 K1
RSLP HA4 ....58 C6
TEDD TW11 ....174 C3
Sacred Heart RC School
CMBW SE5 ....142 D2
Sacred Heart School
HOLWY N7 ....85 F3
Saddlers Hall
CITYW EC2V 12 D3
Sadler's Wells Theatre
CLKNW EC1R 5 K4
Safari Cinema
CROY/NA CR0 ....196 C5
Safari Cinema & Bingo
HRW HA1 ....61 F2
Sai Medical Centre
POP/IOD E14 ....125 F1
St Agathas RC Primary School
KUTN/CMB KT2 ....175 G2
St Agnes RC Primary School
BOW E3 ....105 J2
CRICK NW2 ....82 C1
St Aidans Primary School
FSBYPK N4 ....67 G4
St Aidans RC Primary School
IL IG1 ....72 D5
St Albans CE Primary School
KTTN NW5 ....84 A1
St Albans Health Clinic
KTTN NW5 ....84 A1
St Albans RC Aided
Primary School
E/WMO/HCT KT8 ....189 G2
St Albans RC Church
& School Presbytery
HCH RM12 ....93 J3
St Albans RC JMI School
HCH RM12 ....93 K5
St Albans Road Infant School
DART DA1 ....171 J1
St Alfege with St Peter CE
Primary School
GNWCH SE10 ....125 F6
St Aloysius College
ARCH N19 ....66 C5
St Aloysius RC Infant School
CAMTN NW1 ....4 C4
St Aloysius RC Junior School
CAMTN NW1 ....4 B3
St Andrew & Francis CE
Jm & I School CRICK NW2 ...81 J4
St Andrews CE JMI School
TRDG/WHET N20 ....32 D4
St Andrews CE Primary School
EN EN1 ....23 K3
STHGT/OAK N14 ....34 C2
St Andrews CE School
CROY/NA CR0 ....211 H2
St Andrews Greek School
CAMTN NW1 ....84 B4
St Andrews Hospital
BOW E3 ....105 K3
St Andrews Primary School
BRXN/ST SW9 ....142 A3
St Andrews School
RYLN/HDSTN HA2 ....60 B2

WLSDN NW10 ....81 K5
St Angelas Ursuline
Convent School FSTGT E7 ...89 F4
St Annes Catholic High
School PLMGR N13 ....35 G6
St Anne CE Primary School
WAND/EARL SW18 ....140 A6
St Annes Convent School
EN EN1 ....23 K5
St Annes County Primary
School STWL/WRAY TW19 ...152 B2
St Annes RC Primary School
LBTH SE11 ....122 A6
WCHPL E1 ....104 C3
St Annes Special School
MRDN SM4 ....194 A2
St Anne's Trading Estate
POP/IOD E14 ....105 H5
St Anns CE Primary School
SEVS/STOTM N15 ....67 K2
St Ann's General Hospital
SEVS/STOTM N15 ....67 J2
St Anns Hospital
HNWL W7 ....115 K1
St Ann's Shopping Centre
HRW HA1 ....60 E3
St Anselms RC Primary School
DART DA1 ....151 K6
HRW HA1 ....60 E4
NWDGN UB2 ....114 C5
TOOT SW17 ....161 F5
St Anthonys Hospital
WPK KT4 ....193 G5
St Anthony's Preparatory
School HAMP NW3 ....83 H2
St Anthonys RC Primary
School EDUL SE22 ....163 G1
PGE/AN SE20 ....181 J4
St Anthony's School
HAMP NW3 ....83 G3
St Antonys RC Primary
School
FSTGT E7 ....88 E5
St Aubyns School
WFD IG8 ....52 D3
St Augustines CE School
KIL/WHAMP NW6 ....100 E1
St Augustines Primary School
BELV DA17 ....129 G3
KIL/WHAMP NW6 ....101 F1
St Augustines Priory School
EA W5 ....98 A4
St Augustines Infant
School GNTH/NBYPK IG2 ...72 E2
St Augustines RC Primary
School CAT SE6 ....182 E1
GNTH/NBYPK IG2 ....72 B2
WKENS W14 ....119 H6
St Bartholomews CE
Primary School SYD SE26 ...163 K6
St Bartholomews Hospital
FSTGT EC1A 6 D7
St Bartholomews Medical
School FARR EC1M 6 B7
St Bartholomews & Royal
London School of Medicine
FARR EC1M 12 C1
St Bartholomew's the Great
STBT EC1A 12 B2
St Barts and the Royal
London Hospital
WCHPL E1 ....104 D4
St Barts Hospital Sports
Ground CHST BR7 ....185 J2
St Bedes CE Infant School
BAL SW12 ....161 J3
St Bedes RC Primary School
CHDH RM6 ....73 J2
St Benedicts Junior School
EA W5 ....97 J4
St Benedicts School
EA W5 ....97 K4
St Bernadettes RC Primary
School
KTN/HRWW/W HA3 ....62 A1
St Bonaventures School
FSTGT E7 ....88 E5
St Boniface RC Primary School
TOOT SW17 ....178 E1
St Catherines RC Girls School
BXLYHS DA6 ....149 J6
St Catherines RC J & I School
YEAD/YW UB7 ....112 A2
St Catherines School
TWK TW1 ....156 A4
St Cecilia's CE Primary School
WAND/EARL SW18 ....159 H2
St Cecilias RC Primary School
WPK KT4 ....193 G6
St Chads RC Primary School
SNWD SE25 ....197 F2
St Charles Hospital
NKENS W10 ....100 B4
St Charles RC Primary School
NKENS W10 ....100 B4
St Christinas Preparatory
School STJWD NW8 ....2 D2
St Christopher House
STHWK SE1 ....12 C7
St Christophers School
BECK BR3 ....183 F5
HAMP NW3 ....83 H3
WBLY HA0 ....80 B1
St Clare Business Park
HPTN TW12 ....173 H2
St Clement Danes CE
Primary School
HOL/ALD WC2B 11 G4
St Clement & St James CE
Primary School
NTGHL W11 ....119 H1
St Clements Hospital
BOW E3 ....105 H2
St Clements Primary School
EW KT17 ....207 H6

St Columbas RC Boys School
BXLYHS DA6 ....149 J6
St Cuthbert with St Mattias
CE Primary School
ECT SW5 ....120 A5
St Cyprians Greek Orthodox
Primary School
THHTH CR7 ....180 D5
St Davids College
WWKM BR4 ....198 E4
St Davids Health Centre
STWL/WRAY TW19 ....152 A2
St Davids School
ASHF TW15 ....152 C5
St Dominics 6th Form College
HRW HA1 ....60 E6
St Dominics RC Primary School
HRW NW3 ....83 K3
St Dunstans CE Primary School
CHEAM SM3 ....208 C4
St Dunstans College
CAT SE6 ....164 C3
St Ebba's Hospital
HOR/WEW KT19 ....206 E6
St Edmunds RC Primary School
ED N9 ....36 D3
POP/IOD E14 ....124 D4
WHTN TW2 ....155 G2
St Edwards CE
Comprehensive School
CHDH RM6 ....74 C3
St Edwards CE Primary School
ROM RM1 ....75 F1
St Edwards RC JMI School
STJWD NW8 ....2 C7
St Elizabeths RC Primary
School RCHPK/HAM TW10 ...157 G1
St Elphéges RC Primary
School WLGTN SM6 ....210 E4
St Faiths CE School
WAND/EARL SW18 ....140 A6
St Fidelis Catholic Primary
School ERITH DA8 ....129 K6
St Francesca Cabrini Primary
School FSTH SE23 ....163 K1
St Francis de Sales RC Junior
School TOTM N17 ....50 A3
St Francis of Assisi Primary School
NTCHL W11 ....100 B6
St Francis RC Primary School
PECK SE15 ....123 H6
SRTFD E15 ....88 C3
St Francis Xavier College
BAL SW12 ....161 G1
St Gabriels CE Primary School
PIM SW1V 121 H5
St George's Cathedral
STHWK SE1 ....17 K4
St Georges Cathedral RC
Primary School STHWK SE1 ...18 A4
St Georges CE Primary School
BMLY BR1 ....184 B5
PECK SE15 ....143 F1
VX/NE SW8 ....141 H2
St Georges College
HOLWY N7 ....85 G1
St Georges Elizabethan Theatre
KTTN N1 ....84 D2
St Georges Hanover Square CE
Primary School
MYFR/PKLN W1K 9 H6
St Georges Hospital
TOOT SW17 ....178 D1
St Georges Industrial Estate
KUTN/CMB KT2 ....174 E1
WDGN N22 ....49 H3
St Georges Medical Centre
HDN NW4 ....45 K6
St Georges RC Primary School
ENC/FH EN2 ....23 K3
HRW HA1 ....79 F1
St Georges RC School
MV/WKIL W9 ....101 F1
St Georges Shopping
Centre & Cinema
BMSBY WC1N 5 G7
St George the Martyr CE
Primary School
BMSBY WC1N 5 G7
St Gildas RC Junior School
CEND/HSY/T N8 ....66 E2
St Giles College London Central
RSQ WC1B 11 F1
St Giles School
CROY/NA CRO 211 H4
St Gregorys High School
KTN/HRWW/W HA3 ....61 K2
St Gregorys RC Primary School
HRW HA1 ....97 J3
St Helens Catholic Infant
School WALTH E17 ....70 A2
St Helens Junior School
for Girls NTHWD HA6 ....40 C2
St Helens RC Primary School
BRXN/ST SW9 ....142 B4
PLSTW E13 ....106 D5
St Hellier Hospital
SUT SM1 ....194 B5
St Hildas School
BUSH WD23 ....28 B2
St Ignatius RC Primary School
SEVS/STOTM N15 ....68 A3
St James Boys Junior School
WKENS W14 ....119 H4
St James CE J & I School
BERM/RHTH SE16 ....123 H3
St James CE Primary School
MUSWH N10 ....66 A1
NWCR SE14 ....144 B2
PEND EN3 ....24 E3
St James CE Junior School
FSTGT E7 ....88 D5
St James Independent School
TWK TW1 ....156 A4
WKENS W14 ....119 H4

St James Medical Centre
CROY/NA CRO 196 E4
St James & Michaels CE
Primary School
BAY/PAD W2 ....101 G6
St James RC Primary School
HAYES BR2 ....201 G2
WHTN TW2 ....155 K5
St James's Health Centre
WALTH E17 ....69 G2
St James's Palace
WHALL SW1A 16 B1
St James the Great RC Primary
School
PECK SE15 ....143 G2
THHTH CR7 ....180 C5
St Joachims RC Primary
School CAN/RD E16 ....107 G5
St Joan of Arc RC Primary
School HBRY N5 ....85 H2
St John Fisher RC F & M
School RYLN/HDSTN HA2 ....60 A1
St John Fisher RC Primary
School ERITH DA18 ....129 F3
GFD/PVL UB6 ....97 J2
NWMAL KT3 ....192 D1
St John of Jerusalem CE
Primary School
HOM E9 ....86 E5
St Johns and St James CE
School UED N18 ....50 B1
St Johns Angell Town CE
Primary School
BRXN/ST SW9 ....142 C3
St Johns CE First School
STAN HA7 ....29 G6
St Johns CE Middle School
STAN HA7 ....29 G6
St Johns CE Primary School
BETH E2 ....104 E1
BKHH IG9 ....39 F3
CROY/NA CRO 213 F1
FBAR/BDGN N11 ....33 K6
KUT/HW KT1 ....175 H6
PGE/AN SE20 ....181 K3
TRDG/WHET N20 ....33 G4
St Johns CE School
CDALE/KGS NW9 ....63 G2
St John's CE Walham Green
FUL/PGN SW6 ....139 H2
St Johns CE Infant School
HDN NW4 ....63 K2
St John's Concert Hall
WEST SW1P 16 E5
St Johns Highbury Vale CE
Primary School
HBRY N5 ....85 H2
St John's Hospital
SOHO/SHAV W1D 10 D5
St John's Hospital Day Centre
BTSEA SW11 ....140 C5
St John's Lodge
CAMTN NW1 ....3 G4
St Johns Primary School
WEA W13 ....116 C2
St Johns RC Primary School
BERM/RHTH SE16 ....124 B2
St Johns RC Special School
WFD IG8 ....54 A1
St Johns & St Clements CE
J & I School
PECK SE15 ....143 H4
St Johns School
ENC/FH EN2 ....23 G3
NTHWD HA6 ....41 F2
St Johns Upper Holloway CE
Primary School
ARCH N19 ....84 D1
St Johns Walworth CE
Primary School
WALW SE17 ....18 C7
St Johns Way Medical Centre
ARCH N19 ....66 D5
St Johns Wood School
STJWD NW8 ....2 C4
St Johns Wood Synagogue
STJWD NW8 ....2 A3
St John the Baptist CE
Junior School KUT/HW KT1 ...174 E3
St John the Baptist CE
Primary School CAT SE6 .....165 F6
IS N1 ....7 G3
St John the Baptist School
BETH E2 ....104 E1
St John the Divine CE
Primary School CMBW SE5 ...142 C1
St John the Evangelist
RC Primary School IS N1 ....6 A2
St John Vianney RC
Primary School
SEVS/STOTM N15 ....67 H1
St Josephs Academic RC
School RKHTH/KID SE3 ......145 H4
St Joseph's Annexe
ABYW SE2 ....128 D6
St Josephs Catholic
Infant School LEY E10 ....69 H5
NRWD SE19 ....180 D2
St Josephs Catholic
Primary School BMLY BR1 ...184 B3
St Josephs College
STRHM/NOR SW16 ....180 C2
St Josephs Convent School
WAN E11 ....70 E3
St Josephs Primary School
HDN NW4 ....63 K1
PUT/ROE SW15 ....139 K6
St Joseph's RC College
MLHL NW7 ....31 H6
St Josephs RC
F & M School
KTN/HRWW/W HA3 ....43 G5
St Josephs RC Junior School
CMBW SE5 ....142 D1
LEY E10 ....69 K5

NRWD SE19 ....180 D2
WBLY HA9 ....80 B3
St Josephs RC Primary School
ARCH N19 ....66 B5
BARK IG11 ....90 C6
BERM/RHTH SE16 ....123 K3
CHEL SW3 ....14 E7
DAGW RM9 ....92 B2
DART DA1 ....150 A5
DEPT SE8 ....144 D1
GNWCH SE10 ....125 H5
HNWL W7 ....115 K1
HOL/ALD WC2B 11 F3
KUT/HW KT1 ....175 F5
OXHEY WD19 ....27 F5
STHWK SE1 ....18 D2
STHWK SE1 ....13 H2
WLSDN NW10 ....81 G5
St Judes CE Primary School
HNHL SE24 ....162 C1
STHWK SE1 ....18 A5
St Judes & Pauls CE
Primary School IS N1 ....86 A3
St Katharine Pier
TWRH EC3N 13 K7
St Lawrence Business Centre
FELT TW13 ....154 A4
St Lawrence Catholic School
FELT TW13 ....154 A4
St Lawrence Junior School
E/WMO/HCT KT8 ....173 J6
St Lawrence University
FSBYW WC1X 5 H7
St Leonards CE Primary School
STRHM/NOR SW16 ....179 J1
St Leonards Hospital
IS N1 ....7 H2
St Lukes CE Primary School
CAN/RD E16 ....106 D5
FSBYE EC1V 6 D5
KUTN/CMB KT2 ....175 G4
MV/WKIL W9 ....100 E2
POP/IOD E14 ....125 G4
WNWD SE27 ....180 D1
St Luke's Health Centre
CAN/RD E16 ....106 D5
St Lukes Hospital for
the Clergy FITZ W1T 4 A7
St Lukes School
THHTH CR7 ....196 B1
St Lukes Woodside Hospital
MUSWH N10 ....66 A1
St Margaret Clitherow
RC Primary School
THMD SE28 ....128 C1
St Margaret Lee CE
Primary School
LEW SE13 ....145 H5
St Margarets Business Centre
TWK TW1 ....156 B2
St Margarets Clitherow RC
Primary School WOOL/PLUM SE18 ...127 H6
St Margarets Primary School
BARK IG11 ....90 B6
St Margarets School
BUSH WD23 ....28 A2
HAMP NW3 ....83 F2
St Marks Catholic School
HSLW TW3 ....134 E4
St Marks CE Primary School
ARCH N19 ....66 E6
HAYES BR2 ....183 K6
LBTH SE11 ....122 B6
SNWD SE25 ....197 H1
St Marks Industrial Estate
CAN/RD E16 ....126 C1
St Marks Primary School
MTCM CR4 ....178 E5
NWDGN UB2 ....115 K2
St Marthas Senior School
EBAR EN4 ....20 E2
St Martin in the Fields
High School
BRXS/STRHM SW2 ....162 C3
St Martin of Pores RC
Primary School
FBAR/BDGN N11 ....48 C2
St Martins Hospital
BAY/PAD W1K 9 G5
St Martins-in-the-Fields
CHCR WC2N 10 E6
St Martins Medical Centre
RSLP HA4 ....58 C4
St Martins
Pre Preparatory School
NTHWD HA6 ....40 D7
St Martins School
MLHL NW7 ....45 J1
St Martins School of Art
SOHO/SHAV W1D 10 D4
St Martins Theatre
LSO/SEVD WC2H 10 D5
St Mary Abbots CE
Primary School KENS W8 .....120 A2
The St Marylebone CE
Girls School MHST W1U 9 H1
St Marylebone Crematorium
EFNCH N2 ....47 F6
St Mary Magdalene CE Primary
School
BAT/PAD W2 ....101 J2
WOOL/PLUM SE18 ....126 E4
St Mary Magdalene Peckham CE
Primary School
PECK SE15 ....143 J3
St Mary Magdalene
Primary School HOLWY N7 ...85 G4
St Mary Magdalen's
Primary School BROCKY SE4 ...144 B5
MORT/ESHN SW14 ....138 A4
St Marys Magdalen's RC
Junior School CRICK NW2 .....81 K4

St Mary of the Angels RC
Primary School
BAY/PAD W2 ....100 E5
St Marys Abbey
MLHL NW7 ....31 J5
St Mary & St Joseph
Catholic School SCUP DA14 ...186 A1
St Mary & St Michael RC
Primary School WCHPL E1 ...104 E5
St Mary & St Peters CE
Primary School
TEDD TW11 ....173 K1
St Marys Bryanston Sq CE
Primary School
MBLAR W1H 8 E2
St Mary's Catholic
Primary School CHING E4 .....38 D3
HCH HM12 ....75 J5
St Mary's CE J & I School
CEND/HSY/T N8 ....66 D3
St Marys CE Junior School
CEND/HSY/T N8 ....66 E1
STWL/WRAY TW19 ....152 B1
THDIT KT7 ....190 C5
St Mary's Cemetery
BTSEA SW11 ....140 D6
St Marys CE Primary School
CHSGTN KT9 ....206 A4
EBAR EN4 ....33 J1
FNCH N3 ....46 D4
IS N1 ....85 H5
LEW SE13 ....144 E6
PUT/ROE SW15 ....139 G4
TWK TW1 ....156 B2
WALTH E17 ....69 K1
WLSDN NW10 ....81 G4
St Marys Greek Cathedral
WDGN N22 ....49 F4
St Mary's High School
CROY/NA CRO 196 D5
St Marys Hospital
BAY/PAD W2 ....8 B3
St Marys Hospital Medical
School BAY/PAD W2 ....8 B3
St Marys Infant School
CAR SM5 ....209 J2
St Mary's Junior School
TWK TW1 ....156 C2
St Marys Kilburn
Primary School
KIL/WHAMP NW6 ....82 E6
St Marys Primary School
WKENS W14 ....119 G3
St Marys RC Infant School
CAR SM5 ....209 K5
St Marys RC J & I School
CROY/NA CRO 196 C5
St Marys RC Junior School
WALTH E17 ....52 A6
St Marys RC Primary School
BECK BR3 ....183 F3
CHSWK W4 ....118 B5
CLAP SW4 ....141 H6
ELTH/MOT SE9 ....147 F6
ISLW TW7 ....136 B4
KIL/WHAMP NW6 ....100 E1
NKENS W10 ....100 C3
PEND EN3 ....25 F5
St Mary's RC Primary School
SEVS/STOTM N15 ....67 K2
St Marys RC Primary School
VX/NE SW8 ....141 G2
WIM/MER SW19 ....177 K3
St Marys School
CEND/HSY/T N8 ....67 F2
HAMP NW3 ....83 G3
St Marys Stoke Newington CE
Primary School
STNW/STAM N16 ....67 K6
St Matthews CE Primary
School PEND EN3 ....24 E6
RYNPK SW20 ....176 D4
SURB KT6 ....191 F4
WDR/YW UB7 ....112 B1
St Matthews CE School
WEST SW1P 16 D4
St Matthias CE Primary School
BETH E2 ....7 K6
STNW/STAM N16 ....86 A3
St Meryl JMI School
OXHEY WD19 ....27 J5
St Michael At Bowes Junior
School PLMGR N13 ....49 G2
St Michaels and St Martins RC
Primary School
HSLWW TW4 ....134 E4
St Michaels Catholic
Grammar School
NFNCH/WDSP N12 ....47 F1
St Michaels CE Primary School
ENC/FH EN2 ....23 J2
HGT N6 ....66 A4
WAND/EARL SW18 ....159 J2
WDGN N22 ....49 F4
St Michaels CE Aided
Primary School Hall
WELL DA16 ....148 D2
St Michaels RC Primary School
EHAM E6 ....107 K1
St Michaels RC Secondary
School BERM/RHTH SE16 ...123 H2
St Michaels Sydenham CE
Primary School
SYD SE26 ....164 B6
St Monicas RC Primary School
IS N1 ....7 G4
STNGT/OAK N14 ....34 E5
SUT SM1 ....209 J3
St Nicholas Centre
SUT SM1 ....209 F3
St Nicholas Preparatory School
CDALE/KGS NW9 ....62 E6
SKENS SW7 ....14 B3
St Nicholas School
BORE WD6 ....30 A1

CHST BR7 ....185 H3
St Olaves Grammar School
  ORP BR6 ....217 H1
St Olaves Preparatory School
  ELTH/MOT SE9 ....167 G4
St Pancras Hospital
  CAMTN NW1 ....4 C1
St Pancras & Islington
  Cemetery EFNCH N2 ....47 J4
St Patricks Church School
  STHWK SE1 ....17 J1
St Patricks Infants School
  WAP E1W 123 J1
St Patricks International
  School SOHO/CST W1F 10 B3
St Patricks Primary School
  KTTN NW5 ....84 B4
St Patricks RC JMI School
  ROMW/RG RM7 ....56 D4
St Patricks RC Primary School
  WALTH E17 ....69 C1
  WOOL/PLUM SE18 ....127 J4
St Paul & All Hallows
  Junior School ED N9 ....36 D2
St Paulinus CE Primary School
  DART DA1 ....150 B5
St Pauls & All Hallows
  Infant School TOTM N17 ....50 C3
St Paul's Cathedral
  STP EC4M 12 C4
St Pauls Cathedral School
  STP EC4M 12 C4
St Pauls CE JMI School
  MLHL NW7 ....31 K6
St Pauls CE Primary School
  BTFD TW8 ....116 E6
  CHSGTN KT9 ....206 A2
  FBAR/BDGN N11 ....48 A1
  HAMP NW3 ....83 J5
  WALW SE17 ....122 C5
  WCHMH N21 ....35 H2
  WCHPL E1 ....104 C6
St Pauls CE Junior School
  KUTN/CMB KT2 ....175 H3
St Pauls Cray CE Primary
  School STMC/STPC BR5 ....186 D6
St Pauls Cray Health Clinic
  STMC/STPC BR5 ....186 B5
St Pauls Girls School
  HMSMTH W6 ....119 C4
St Pauls Preparatory School
  BARN SW13 ....118 D5
St Paul's Primary School
  HMSMTH W6 ....119 F5
St Pauls RC Primary School
  THDIT KT7 ....189 K4
  WDGN N22 ....49 F5
St Pauls RC School
  WOOL/PLUM SE18 ....128 B6
St Pauls Road Medical Centre
  IS N1 ....85 H4
St Pauls Steiner School
  IS N1 ....85 K4
St Pauls Way School BOW E3 ....105 J3
St Pauls with St Lukes CE
  Primary School BOW E3 ....105 H4
St Paul's with St Michaels CE
  Primary School HACK E8 ....86 C6
St Peter Chanel RC Primary
  School DAGA DA14 ....186 D1
St Peter & Paul RC Primary
  School CHST BR7 ....185 K5
St Peter & Pauls Primary
  School FSBYE EC1V 6 A6
St Peters Catholic Primary
  School ROM RM1 ....57 F6
St Peters CE Primary School
  HMSMTH W6 ....118 D5
  MV/WKIL W9 ....100 E3
  WALW SE17 ....122 E5
  WAP E1W 123 K1
St Peters Eaton Square CE
  Primary School
  BGVA SW1W 15 J5
St Peter's Hospital
  COVGDN WC2E 11 F5
St Peters Primary School
  SAND/SEL CR2 ....211 K4
St Peters RC Primary School
  DAGW RM9 ....92 B6
  WOOL/PLUM SE18 ....127 C5
St Philips School
  CHSGTN KT9 ....205 K4
  SKENS SW7 ....120 B4
St Phillips Infant School
  SYD SE26 ....163 J6
St Philomenas Catholic
  High School CAR SM5 ....209 J5
St Philomenas RC Primary
  School STMC/STPC BR5 ....202 D4
St Quintins Health Centre
  NKENS W10 ....100 A4
St Raphaels Hospice
  WPK KT4 ....193 G6
St Raphaels RC Primary School
  NTHLT UB5 ....95 F1
St Raphaels Way Medical Centre
  WBLY HA9 ....80 E3
St Richards with St Andrews CE
  Primary School
  RCHPK/HAM TW10 ....156 C5
St Robert Southwell RC
  Primary School
  CDALE/KGS NW9 ....62 E3
St Savior & St Mary Overie
  STHWK SE1 ....18 D2
St Saviour & St Olaves School
  STHWK SE1 ....19 F5
St Saviours CE Primary School
  HNHL SE24 ....142 D4
  MV/WKIL W9 ....101 F3
  POP/IOD E14 ....105 K4
  WALTH E17 ....69 H4
St Saviours CE Infant School
  EA W5 ....116 E1

St Saviours RC Primary School
  LEW SE13 ....145 F5
St Scholasticas RC
  Primary School
  STNW/STAM N16 ....86 C1
St Stephens CE Junior School
  TWK TW1 ....156 B1
St Stephens CE Primary School
  BAY/PAD W2 ....100 E4
  DEPT SE8 ....144 D3
  SHB W12 ....119 F1
St Stephens CE School
  VX/NE SW8 ....141 K1
St Stephens Primary School
  EHAM E6 ....89 G5
St Stephens RC Primary School
  WELL DA16 ....148 B4
St Swithun Wells RC Primary
  School RSLP HA4 ....77 C1
St Teresa RC Primary School
  BCTR RM8 ....91 J2
St Teresas RC School
  KTN/HRWW/W HA3 ....42 C4
St Theresas RC Primary School
  FNCH N3 ....46 E6
St Thomas a' Becket RC
  Primary School
  ABYW SE2 ....128 B3
St Thomas Becket RC Primary
  School SNWD SE25 ....197 H3
St Thomas CE Primary School
  NKENS W10 ....100 C3
St Thomas' Hospital
  STHWK SE1 ....17 G6
St Thomas More RC Primary
  School BXLYHN DA7 ....149 G3
  ELTH/MOT SE9 ....146 D4
St Thomas More RC School
  CHEL SW3 ....14 E7
  ELTH/MOT SE9 ....167 F1
St Thomas More School
  WDGN N22 ....49 F3
St Thomas of Canterbury
  Primary School
  MTCM CR4 ....179 F6
St Thomas of Canterbury RC
  Primary School
  FUL/PGN SW6 ....139 J1
St Thomas the Apostle
  College PECK SE15 ....143 K2
St Ursulas Convent School
  GNWCH SE10 ....145 C1
St Ursulas RC Infant School
  HARH RM3 ....57 K2
St Ursulas RC Junior School
  HARH RM3 ....57 K2
St Vincent de Paul RC Primary
  School WEST SW1P 16 A5
St Vincents Catholic Primary
  School ELTH/MOT SE9 ....166 D6
St Vincents Hospital
  RSLP HA4 ....40 C4
St Vincents RC Primary School
  ACT W3 ....98 D6
  BCTR RM8 ....73 J4
  MLHL NW7 ....31 K6
St Vincent's RC Primary School
  MHST W1U 9 G2
St Walter & St John Sports
  Ground TOOT SW17 ....160 D3
St William of York Primary
  School FSTH SE23 ....164 B3
St Winefrides Catholic Primary
  School MNPK E12 ....89 K3
St Winifreds Catholic Junior
  School LEE/GVPK SE12 ....165 J1
St Winifreds RC Infant School
  LEW SE13 ....145 H6
Salcombe Preparatory School
  STHGT/OAK N14 ....34 D2
Samuel Jones Industrial Estate
  PECK SE15 ....143 F1
Samuel Rhodes School
  IS N1 ....85 G6
Sanderstead Junior School
  SAND/SEL CR2 ....211 K6
Sandgate Trading Estate
  BERM/RHTH SE16 ....123 J5
Sandhurst Primary School
  CAT SE6 ....165 H2
Sandown Industrial Park
  ESH/CLAY KT10 ....189 F6
Sandown Park Racecourse
  ESH/CLAY KT10 ....204 B1
Sandown Sports Club & Ski
  Centre ESH/CLAY KT10 ....204 B1
Sandringham Primary School
  FSTGT E7 ....89 F4
Sandy Lodge Golf Club
  NTHWD HA6 ....26 B4
Sapcote Trading Centre
  WLSDN NW10 ....81 H3
Sarah Bonnell School
  SRTFD E15 ....88 C4
Sarum Hall School
  HAMP NW3 ....83 J5
Satmer Trust School
  STNW/STAM N16 ....68 C6

The Savoy Hotel
  COVGDN WC2E 11 F5
Savoy Pier
  TPL/STR WC2R 11 G6
Savoy Theatre
  TPL/STR WC2R 11 G6
Saxon Business Centre
  WIM/MER SW19 ....178 B5
Sayer Clinic
  CROY/NA CRO 211 F2
Sayer Clinics
  MBLAR W1H 9 F4
Schiller International School
  STHWK SE1 ....17 J1
Schomberg House
  STJS SW1Y 16 B1
School of Art
  RCH/KEW TW9 ....137 F5
School of Creative
  Technologies PLMGR N13 ....49 F1
School of English
  GLDGN NW11 ....64 E5
The School of Pharmacy
  BMSBY WC1N 5 F6
The School of St David &
  St Katharine
  CEND/HSY/T N8 ....66 E1
Science Museum IMAX
  Cinema SKENS SW7 ....14 A5
The Science Museum Library
  SKENS SW7 ....14 A4
Scotts Park Primary School
  BMLY BR1 ....184 B4
Scott Wilkie Primary School
  CAN/RD E16 ....107 G5
Screen on Baker Street
  Cinema MHST W1U 9 F1
Screen on the Green
  Cinema IS N1 ....6 A1
Screen on the Hill Cinema
  HAMP NW3 ....83 J3
Sebright Primary School
  BETH E2 ....104 C1
Seconde Centre
  SUT SM1 ....208 E3
Sedgehill School
  CAT SE6 ....182 E1
Sedgewick Centre
  WCHPL E1 ....13 K3
Selborne Primary School
  GFD/PVL UB6 ....97 F1
Selhurst High School for Boys
  SNWD SE25 ....196 E3
The Selhurst Medical Centre
  SNWD SE25 ....197 F3
Sellincourt School
  TOOT SW17 ....178 D2
Selsdon Primary School
  SAND/SEL CR2 ....213 F5
Selsdon Primary School
  SAND/SEL CR2 ....212 E6
Selsdon Road Industrial
  Estate SAND/SEL CR2 ....211 K5
Selwyn Primary School
  CHING E4 ....52 A2
  PLSTW E13 ....88 E6
Sergeant Industrial Estate
  WAND/EARL SW18 ....160 A1
Serpentine Gallery
  BAY/PAD W2 ....14 B1
Servite RC Primary School
  WBPTN SW10 ....120 B6
Seven Islands Leisure Centre
  BERM/RHTH SE16 ....123 K3
Seven Kings Health Centre
  GDMY/SEVK IG3 ....72 E5
Seven Kings High School
  Technology College
  GNTH/NBYPK IG2 ....72 D4
Seven Mills Primary School
  POP/IOD E14 ....124 D2
Sevenoaks Way Industrial
  Estate STMC/STPC BR5 ....186 D6
Seven Sisters Primary
  School SEVS/STOTM N15 ....67 K2
Seymour Gardens Medical
  Centre IL IG1 ....71 K5
Seymour Leisure Centre
  MBLAR W1H 8 E2
Shaare Zedek Medical Centre
  GLDGN NW11 ....64 D3
Shacklewell Primary School
  STNW/STAM N16 ....86 B2
Shadwell Dock Stairs
  WAP E1W 105 F6
Shaftesbury High School
  KTN/HRWW/W HA3 ....42 B4
Shaftesbury Hospital
  LSQ/SEVD WC2H 10 E4
Shaftesbury Medical Centre
  RYLN/HDSTN HA2 ....60 C5
Shaftesbury Park Primary
  School BTSEA SW11 ....141 F4
Shaftesbury Primary School
  FSTGT E7 ....89 G5
Shaftesbury Theatre
  LSQ/SEVD WC2H 10 E3
Shahjalal Medical Centre
  WCHPL E1 ....104 C5
Shakespeare Business Centre
  BRXN/ST SW9 ....142 C4
Shakespeare's Globe Theatre
  STHWK SE1 ....12 B6
The Shamrock Sports Club
  ACT W3 ....98 E5
Shannon Corner Retail Park
  NWMAL KT3 ....192 D1
Shapla J & I School
  WCHPL E1 ....104 C6
Sharp Sports Centre
  EDGW HA8 ....44 C2
Shawcroft School
  STMC/STPC BR5 ....203 F2
Sheen Mount International School
  MORT/ESHN SW14 ....138 B5

Sheen Lane Health Centre
  MORT/ESHN SW14 ....137 K4
Sheen Lawn Tennis &
  Squash Club
  MORT/ESHN SW14 ....137 K6
Sheen Mount Primary School
  RCHPK/HAM TW10 ....137 J6
Sheen Sports Centre
  MORT/ESHN SW14 ....138 B5
Shell Centre
  STHWK SE1 ....17 H1
Shelley School
  CLAP SW4 ....141 H4
Shenstone School
  DART DA1 ....150 A6
Shepherd's Bush CC
  ACT W3 ....99 G6
Shepherd's Bush Empire
  SHB W12 ....119 F2
Shepherds Community School
  BROCKY SE4 ....144 C4
Sheraton Belgravia Hotel
  KTBR SW1X 15 G5
Sheraton Business Centre
  GFD/PVL UB6 ....97 J1
Sheraton Park Tower Hotel
  KTBR SW1X 15 F2
Sheraton Skyline Hotel
  HYS/HAR UB3 ....133 C1
Sheringdale Primary School
  WAND/EARL SW18 ....159 J5
Sheringham Junior School
  MNPK E12 ....89 K2
Sherington Primary School
  CHARL SE7 ....126 A6
Sherlock Holmes Hotel
  MHST W1U 9 F1
Sherlock Holmes Museum
  CAMTN NW1 ....3 F7
Sherwood Park Primary
  School BFN/LL DA15 ....168 C1
Sherwood Park School
  WLGTN SM6 ....210 D1
Sherwood School
  MTCM CR4 ....195 H1
Shirley Clinic
  CROY/NA CRO 197 K5
Shirley High School
  CROY/NA CRO 213 F1
Shirley Oaks Hospital
  CROY/NA CRO 197 K4
Shirley Park Golf Club
  CROY/NA CRO 197 J6
Shirley Wanderers RFC
  WWKM BR4 ....214 A2
Shooters Hill Golf Club
  WOOL/PLUM SE18 ....147 H2
Shooters Hill Post 16 Campus
  WOOL/PLUM SE18 ....147 F1
Shooting Star House
  (Childrens Hospice)
  HPTN TW12 ....172 E2
Shopping City
  WDGN N22 ....49 F5
The Shopping Hall
  EHAM E6 ....89 J6
Shore Business Centre
  HOM E9 ....86 E5
Shoreditch Comprehensive
  School IS N1 ....7 H3
Shoreditch County Court
  STLK EC1Y 7 F6
Shotfield Health Clinic
  WLGTN SM6 ....210 B4
Showcase Cinema
  WDGN N22 ....49 G5
Showcase Newham Cinema
  BARK IG11 ....108 C2
Shrewsbury House School
  SURB KT6 ....190 E6
Shrewsbury Road Health
  Centre FSTGT E7 ....89 H5
Sidcup Cemetery
  BXLY DA5 ....168 E4
Sidcup Golf Club
  BFN/LL DA15 ....168 B4
Sidcup Health Centre
  SCUP DA14 ....168 B5
Sidcup Sports Club
  SCUP DA14 ....168 A6
Sidney Russell School
  DAGW RM9 ....92 A2
Silicon Business Centre
  GFD/PVL UB6 ....97 J1
Silverdale Industrial Estate
  HYS/HAR UB3 ....113 K1
Silver Industrial Estate
  TOTM N17 ....50 B5
Silver Street Medical Centre
  UED N18 ....36 A6
Silver Wing Industrial Estate
  CROY/NA CRO 211 F4
Simon Marks Jewish
  Primary School
  STNW/STAM N16 ....68 B5
Sinclair House School
  FUL/PGN SW6 ....139 J2
Singlegate Primary School
  WIM/MER SW19 ....178 C3
Sion College
  EMB EC4Y 11 K5
Sion Manning RC Girls School
  NKENS W10 ....100 B4
Sir Francis Drake Primary
  School DEPT SE8 ....124 B5
Sir George Monoux College
  WALTH E17 ....51 K5
Sir James Barrie School
  VX/NE SW8 ....141 J2
Sir John Cass Foundation/
  Redcoat School WCHPL E1 ....105 F4
Sir John Cass Foundation
  School HDTCH EC3A 13 H4
Sir John Lillie Primary School
  HMSMTH W6 ....119 H6

Sir John Soane's Museum
  LINN WC2A 11 G3
Sir Thomas Abney Primary
  School STNW/STAM N16 ....67 K4
Sir Thomas Lipton Memorial
  Hospital STHGT/OAK N14 ....34 B2
Sir William Burrough Primary
  School POP/IOD E14 ....105 G5
Site of Greenwich Hospital
  GNWCH SE10 ....125 J5
Six Bridges Trading Estate
  STHWK SE1 ....123 H5
The Sixth Form College
  CLPT E5 ....86 D1
Skillion Business Park
  BARK IG11 ....109 F2
Skinners Co Lower Girls School
  CLPT E5 ....68 C5
Skinners Companys School
  For Girls STNW/STAM N16 ....68 A4
Ski Slope
  STMC/STPC BR5 ....186 E4
Slade Gallery
  ERITH DA8 ....150 E2
Slade Green Primary School
  ERITH DA8 ....150 D1
Slade School of Fine Art
  STPAN WC1H 4 D5
Sleaford Industrial Estate
  VX/NE SW8 ....141 H1
Sloane Hospital
  BECK BR3 ....183 G2
Smallberry Green Primary
  School ISLW TW7 ....136 B3
Smallwood Primary School
  TOOT SW17 ....160 C6
SMA Medical Centre
  LEY E10 ....69 K4
Smithy Street School
  WCHPL E1 ....104 E4
Snaresbrook College
  SWFD E18 ....52 E5
Snaresbrook Crown Court
  WAN E11 ....70 D2
Snaresbrook Primary School
  SWFD E18 ....70 E1
Snooker Club
  WEA W13 ....116 C1
Snowsfields Primary School
  STHWK SE1 ....19 G2
SOAS
  STPAN WC1H 4 E7
Sobell Leisure Centre
  HOLWY N7 ....85 F1
Sobell Medical Centre
  HOLWY N7 ....85 G2
Sofitel St James London Hotel
  STJS SW1Y 10 C7
Soho Parish CE Primary
  School SOHO/CST W1F 10 C5
Solent Road Health Centre
  KIL/WHAMP NW6 ....82 E4
Somerset House
  TPL/STR WC2R 11 G5
Somers Town Community
  Sports Centre
  CAMTN NW1 ....4 B3
Sorsby Health Centre
  CLPT E5 ....87 F2
South Bank Business Centre
  VX/NE SW8 ....121 J6
Southbank International
  School HAMP NW3 ....83 G4
Southbank International
  School Kensington
  NTCHL W11 ....100 D6
Southbank University
  STHWK SE1 ....18 A3
  STHWK SE1 ....18 C4
Southborough Primary School
  HAYES BR2 ....201 F2
Southborough Primary School
  SURB KT6 ....206 A1
Southbury Primary School
  PEND EN3 ....24 D5
South Camden Community
  School CAMTN NW1 ....4 B2
South Chelsea College
  BRXN/ST SW9 ....142 A5
South Croydon Medical
  Centre SAND/SEL CR2 ....211 J6
South Croydon Sports Club
  SAND/SEL CR2 ....212 A3
South Eastern University
  HOLWY N7 ....85 F1
Southern Road Primary
  School PLSTW E13 ....107 F1
Southfield F & M School
  CHSWK W4 ....118 B2
Southfield Medical Centre
  CHSWK W4 ....118 A2
The Southfields Clinic
  WAND/EARL SW18 ....159 J5
Southfields Community
  School WAND/EARL SW18 ....159 K3
Southgate Cemetery
  STHGT/OAK N14 ....34 C4
Southgate College
  STHGT/OAK N14 ....34 C4
Southgate Compton CC
  EBAR EN4 ....21 K5
Southgate Leisure Centre
  STHGT/OAK N14 ....34 D2
Southgate Road Medical
  Centre IS N1 ....85 K5
Southgate School
  EBAR EN4 ....22 B6
South Grove Primary School
  WALTH E17 ....69 G3
South Hampstead CC
  CRICK NW2 ....82 A5
South Hampstead High School
  HAMP NW3 ....83 H4
South Haringa J & I School
  FSBYPK N4 ....67 H2

South Herts Golf Club
TRDC/WHET N20 ....32 E3
Southlake Primary School
ABYW SE2 ....128 E2
Southlands College
PUT/ROE SW15 ....138 C5
South Lewisham Health
Centre *CAT* SE6 ....165 F6
South London Crematorium
MTCM CR4 ....179 H5
South London Gallery
CMBW SE5 ....143 F2
The South London Natural
Health Centre
CLAP SW4 ....141 H5
South London Tamil School
CROY/NA CR0 ....196 D4
South London Theatre
WNWD SE27 ....162 D5
Southmead Primary School
WIM/MER SW19 ....159 H3
South Norwood Country Park
SNWD SE25 ....197 K1
South Norwood Hill Medical
Centre *SNWD* SE25 ....181 F5
South Norwood Medical
Centre *SNWD* SE25 ....197 F1
South Norwood Pools &
Fitness Centre
SNWD SE25 ....197 H2
South Norwood Primary
School *SNWD* SE25 ....197 H2
South Park Business Centre
IL IG1 ....72 E6
South Park Clinic
IL IG1 ....90 E2
South Park Hotel
SAND/SEL CR2 ....212 A2
South Park Primary School
GDMY/SEVK IG3 ....90 E1
South Quay Plaza
POP/IOD E14 ....124 E2
South Rise Primary School
WOOL/PLUM SE18 ....127 J5
Southside Industrial Estate
VX/NE SW8 ....141 H1
South Thames College
TOOT SW17 ....178 D1
WAND/EARL SW18 ....140 A6
South Thames College/
Wandsworth Adult College
PUT/ROE SW15 ....158 C1
Southville Infant School
EBED/NFELT TW14 ....153 J3
Southwark Bridge Business
Centre *STHWK* SE1 ....18 D1
Southwark Bridge Stairs
BLKFR EC4V 12 C6
Southwark Cathedral
STHWK SE1 ....12 E7
Southwark College
BERM/RHTH SE16 ....123 J3
CMBW SE5 ....143 F1
STHWK SE1 ....18 A2
STHWK SE1 ....19 H4
Southwark Crown Court
STHWK SE1 ....13 G7
Southwark Park Primary
School *BERM/RHTH* SE16 ....123 J3
Southwark Park Sports Centre
BERM/RHTH SE16 ....123 K4
Southwark Sports Ground
DUL SE21 ....163 G3
South West Middlesex
Crematorium *FELT* TW13 ....154 D3
Southwold Primary School
CLPT E5 ....68 E6
South Woodford Health
Centre *SWFD* E18 ....52 E4
Southwood Hospital
HGT N6 ....66 A4
Sovereign Primary School
DAGW RM9 ....92 A2
Sovereign Business Centre
PEND EN3 ....25 H4
The Space Arts Centre Cinema
POP/IOD E14 ....124 C4
The Spanish School
NKENS W10 ....100 C4
Sparrow Farm Community
Junior School *EW* KT17 ....207 K3
Sparrow Farm Infant School
EBED/NFELT TW14 ....154 B2
Sparrow Farm Junior School
EBED/NFELT TW14 ....154 B2
Speakers Corner
BAY/PAD W2 ....9 F5
Spectators Viewing Area
HTHAIR TW6 ....132 E4
Speedway Industrial Estate
HYS/HAR UB3 ....113 G2
Speke's Monument
BAY/PAD W2 ....120 B1
Spelthorne Sixth Form
College *ASHF* TW15 ....152 C6
Spencer House
WHALL SW1A 16 A1
The Spires Shopping Centre
BAR EN5 ....20 C4
Spiritualist University
WLSDN NW10 ....81 J5
Spitalfields Community Farm
BETH E2 ....104 C3
Spitalfields Health Centre
WCHPL E1 ....13 K2
Splashworld Swimming
Centre *WELL* DA16 ....148 L6
Sports Ground Pavilion
HGDN/ICK UB10 ....94 B1
Springfield Christian School
CAT SE6 ....164 C5
Springfield Hospital
TOOT SW17 ....160 D5

Springfield Primary School
VX/NE SW8 ....141 J1
Spring Grove Primary School
ISLW TW7 ....135 J3
Springhallow School
HNWL W7 ....97 F5
Spring Park Primary School
CROY/NA CR0 ....213 J1
Springvale Retail Park
STMC/STPC BR5 ....186 D6
STMC/STPC BR5 ....202 E2
Springwell Infant School
HEST TW5 ....134 D1
Springwell Junior School
HEST TW5 ....134 D1
Squirrels Heath Junior School
GPK RM2 ....75 K2
Squirrels Trading Estate
HYS/HAR UB3 ....113 J3
SS Angelas & Bonaventures
6th Form *FSTGT* E7 ....89 F4
SS Mary & Pancras CE
Primary School *CAMTN* NW1 ....4 C3
SS Peter & Paul RC
Primary School *MTCM* CR4 ....194 E1
SS Peter & Pauls RC Primary
School *IL* IG1 ....90 D1
The Stables Gallery &
Art Centre *CRICK* NW2 ....81 J2
Stadium Business Centre
WBLY HA9 ....80 D1
Stadium Industrial Estate
WBLY HA9 ....80 D3
Stadium Retail Park
WBLY HA9 ....80 C1
Stafford Cross Business
Park *CROY/NA* CR0 ....211 F3
The Stafford Hotel
MAYL SW1A 16 A1
Stag Lane Medical Centre
CDALE/KGS NW9 ....44 E6
Stag Lane Primary School
EDGW HA8 ....44 C5
Stamford Clinic
HMSMTH W6 ....118 D4
Stamford Hill Primary School
SEVS/STOTM N15 ....67 K3
Stamford House Secure Unit
HMSMTH W6 ....118 C3
Stanburn Middle School
STAN HA7 ....43 J3
Standard Industrial Estate
CAN/RD E16 ....126 C2
Stanford Primary School
STRHM/NOR SW16 ....179 J4
Stanhope Primary School
GFD/PVL UB6 ....96 C3
Stanley Infant School
TEDD TW11 ....155 K6
Stanley Junior School
TEDD TW11 ....155 K6
Stanley Park High School
CAR SM5 ....210 A4
Stanley Park Junior School
CAR SM5 ....209 K5
Stanley Technical
High School
SNWD SE25 ....181 G6
Stanmore College
STAN HA7 ....43 H2
Stanmore Golf Club
STAN HA7 ....43 H3
Stanton School of English
BAY/PAD W2 ....101 F5
Stanton Square Industrial
Estate *CAT* SE6 ....164 C6
Staple Inn Buildings
HHOL WC1V 11 J2
Staples Corner Business Park
CRICK NW2 ....63 J5
Star Business Centre
DAGW RM9 ....111 F4
Star Primary School
CAN/RD E16 ....106 C3
Stationers Hall
STP EC4M 12 B4
Stationery Office
HOL/ALD WC2B 11 G3
Stebon Primary School
POP/IOD E14 ....105 H4
Stephen Hawking Primary
School *POP/IOD* E14 ....105 G5
Stepney Day Hospital
WCHPL E1 ....104 E5
Stepney Greencoat CE
Primary School
POP/IOD E14 ....105 H5
Stepney Green School
WCHPL E1 ....105 F4
Ster Century Cinema
ROM RM1 ....75 G2
Sterling Industrial Estate
DAGE RM10 ....92 D2
Sterling Way Clinic
UED N18 ....50 B1
Stewart Fleming Primary
School *PGE/AN* SE20 ....181 K6
Stewart Headlam Primary
School *WCHPL* E1 ....104 D3
Stillness Primary School
BROCKY SE4 ....164 B1
Stirling Retail Park
BORE WD6 ....31 F1
Stirling Way Industrial Estates
CROY/NA CR0 ....195 K4
Stock Exchange
STP EC4M 12 B3
Stockley Park Business Centre
STKPK UB11 ....113 F1
Stockley Park Golf Club
STKPK UB11 ....94 A6
Stockwell Park School
BRXN/ST SW9 ....142 A2
Stockwell Primary School
BRXN/ST SW9 ....142 A4

The Stonebridge Primary
School *WLSDN* NW10 ....80 E6
Stonebridge Shopping
Centre *WLSDN* NW10 ....81 F6
Stonehill Business Centre
UED N18 ....51 F2
Stonehill Business Park
UED N18 ....51 F1
Stone Lake Retail Park
CHARL SE7 ....126 B4
Stoneydown Park Primary
School *WALTH* E17 ....69 G1
Storey Primary School
CAN/RD E16 ....127 F1
Stormont House School
CLPT E5 ....86 D2
Stowford College
BELMT SM2 ....209 G5
Strand on the Green
J & I School *CHSWK* W4 ....117 H6
Strand Palace Hotel
TPL/STR WC2R 11 F5
Strand Theatre
HOL/ALD WC2B 11 G5
Stratford Magistrates Court
SRTFD E15 ....88 B5
Stratford School
FSTGT E7 ....88 E5
Stratford Shopping Centre
SRTFD E15 ....88 B5
Strathmore School
RCHPK/HAM TW10 ....156 E3
Strawberry Fields School
BAY/PAD W2 ....100 C5
Strawberry Hill Golf Club
WHTN TW2 ....155 K5
Streatham Cemetery
TOOT SW17 ....160 D5
Streatham & Clapham
High School
STRHM/NOR SW16 ....161 H5
Streatham & Clapham
High School (Prep)
BRXS/STRHM SW2 ....162 A3
Streatham & Croydon RFC
THHTH CR7 ....196 B2
Streatham Ice Rink
STRHM/NOR SW16 ....179 K1
Streatham Leisure Centre
STRHM/NOR SW16 ....161 K4
Streatham Modern School
STRHM/NOR SW16 ....179 K2
Streatham Park Cemetery
MTCM CR4 ....179 H5
Streatham Swimming Pool
STRHM/NOR SW16 ....179 K1
Streatham Vale Sports Club
STRHM/NOR SW16 ....179 H3
Streatham Wells Primary
School *BRXS/STRHM* SW2 ....162 A4
Stroud Green Primary School
FSBYPK N4 ....67 G5
Studholme Medical Centre
ASHF TW15 ....152 C6
The Study Preparatory
School *WIM/MER* SW19 ....177 G1
The Study School
NWMAL KT3 ....192 B2
Sudbourne Primary School
BRXS/STRHM SW2 ....142 A6
Sudbury Court Sports Club
ALP/SUD HA0 ....79 J1
Sudbury Golf Club
GFD/PVL UB6 ....79 J4
Sudbury Primary School
ALP/SUD HA0 ....79 H2
Suffolks Primary School
EN EN1 ....24 D3
Sulivan Primary School
FUL/PGN SW6 ....139 K3
Summerside JMI School
NFNCH/WDSP N12 ....47 H2
Sunbury Court
SUN TW16 ....172 C5
Sunbury Lock
WOT/HER KT12 ....172 A6
Sundridge Park Golf Club
BMLY BR1 ....184 B2
Sun Life Trading Estate
EBED/NFELT TW14 ....133 K4
Sunnyfields Primary School
HDN NW4 ....45 K6
Sunnyhill Primary School
STRHM/NOR SW16 ....162 A6
Sunshine House School
NTHWD HA6 ....40 B2
Surbiton Business Centre
SURB KT6 ....190 E3
Surbiton Cemetery
BRYLDS KT5 ....191 H1
Surbiton Golf Club
ESH/CLAY KT10 ....205 H2
Surbiton High School
KUT/HW KT1 ....191 F1
Surbiton Hospital
SURB KT6 ....191 F3
Surbiton Natural Health
Centre *SURB* KT6 ....191 F3
Surrey CCC (The Oval)
LBTH SE11 ....122 A6
Surrey Docks Farm
BERM/RHTH SE16 ....124 C2
Surrey Docks Health
Centre
BERM/RHTH SE16 ....124 B2
Surrey Docks Watersports
Centre *BERM/RHTH* SE16 ....124 B3
Surrey Quays Leisure Park
BERM/RHTH SE16 ....124 A3
Surrey Quays Shopping
Centre *BERM/RHTH* SE16 ....124 A3
Surrey Square J & I School
WALW SE17 ....122 E5
Sussex House Preparatory
School *KTBR* SW1X 14 E6

Sutcliffe Park Athletics Track
ELTH/MOT SE9 ....146 A6
Sutton Alternative Health
Centre *SUT* SM1 ....209 F3
Sutton Arena
CAR SM5 ....194 C4
Sutton Bowling Club
BELMT SM2 ....208 E6
Sutton Cemetery
CHEAM SM3 ....193 J6
Sutton Civic Centre
SUT SM1 ....209 F3
Sutton College of Learning
for Adults *SUT* SM1 ....209 F3
Sutton Grammar School
for Boys *SUT* SM1 ....209 G3
Sutton High Junior School
SUT SM1 ....209 F4
Sutton High School for
Girls GDST *SUT* SM1 ....209 F3
Sutton House
HOM E9 ....86 E3
Suttons Business Park
RAIN RM13 ....111 F2
Sutton United FC
SUT SM1 ....208 E2
Sutton West Centre
SUT SM1 ....208 E3
Swaffield Primary School
WAND/EARL SW18 ....160 B1
Swakeleys School
HGDN/ICK UB10 ....94 A1
Swaminarayan School
WLSDN NW10 ....81 F4
Swan Business Centre
CHSWK W4 ....118 A4
Swan Business Park
DART DA1 ....151 G5
Swan Lane Pier
CANST EC4R 12 E6
Swanlea School
WCHPL E1 ....104 D3
Swansmere School
WOT/HER KT12 ....188 B5
Swedish School
BARN SW13 ....118 D6
Swiss Cottage Leisure Centre
HAMP NW3 ....83 H5
Swiss Cottage School
HAMP NW3 ....83 H6
Swissotel London,
The Howard *TPL/STR* WC2R ...11 H5
Swiss Re-Insurance Tower
HDTCH EC3A 13 H4
Sybil Elgar School
EA W5 ....98 A6
NWDGN UB2 ....114 E3
Sybourn Infant School
LEY E10 ....69 G5
Sybourn Junior School
WALTH E17 ....69 H4
Sydenham Girls School
SYD SE26 ....163 J5
Sydenham High School Junior
Department
SYD SE26 ....163 J6
Sydenham High School
(Secondary) *SYD* SE26 ....181 J1
Sydenham High School
Sports Ground *BECK* BR3 ....182 D1
Sydney Russell
Comprehensive School
DAGW RM9 ....91 K3
Syon House
BTFD TW8 ....136 D2
Syon Park
BTFD TW8 ....136 D3
Syon Park School
ISLW TW7 ....136 C2
Syracuse University London
Centre *NTGHL* W11 ....100 D5
Tabard Theatre
CHSWK W4 ....118 B4
Taberner House
CROY/NA CR0 ....211 J1
TA Centre
HDN NW4 ....44 D3
HRW HA1 ....61 F2
NFNCH/WDSP N12 ....47 H4
Tait Road Industrial Estate
CROY/NA CR0 ....196 E4
Talmud Torah School
STNW/STAM N16 ....67 K4
Tamian Industrial Estate
HSLWW TW4 ....134 B5
Tamworth Manor High School
STRHM/NOR SW16 ....179 J6
Tandem Centre
WIM/MER SW19 ....178 C4
Tate Britain
WEST SW1P 16 E7
Tate Modern
STHWK SE1 ....12 B7
Tavistock Clinic
HAMP NW3 ....83 H4
TAVR Centre
KUT/HW KT1 ....190 E1
Tavy Clinic
ABYW SE2 ....128 D2
Tawhid Boys School
STNW/STAM N16 ....68 B6
Teddington Business Park
TEDD TW11 ....174 A1
Teddington Cemetery
TEDD TW11 ....155 K6
Teddington Clinic
TEDD TW11 ....173 K2
Teddington Lock
TEDD TW11 ....156 C6
Teddington Memorial Hospital
TEDD TW11 ....173 K2
Teddington Pool & Fitness
Centre *TEDD* TW11 ....174 B1
Teddington School
TEDD TW11 ....174 B2

The Teddington Theatre Club
E/WMO/HCT KT8 ....189 J3
Telferscot Primary School
BAL SW12 ....161 H3
Temperate House
RCH/KEW TW9 ....137 G3
Temple Hill Primary School
DART DA1 ....151 K6
Temple of Bacchus
CMBW SE5 ....142 D3
Temple of Mithras
MANHO EC4N 12 E4
Tenby Road Clinic
EDGW HA8 ....44 B5
Tennis Centre
CHIG IG7 ....39 K3
Tennis Club
HAYES BR2 ....200 A1
STAN HA7 ....43 F1
Tenterden Sports Club
KTN/HRWW/W HA3 ....62 A4
Terence McMillan Stadium
PLSTW E13 ....107 G3
Tetherdown Primary School
MUSWH N10 ....66 A1
Thames Barrier
CAN/RD E16 ....126 C2
Thames Barrier Information
& Learning Centre
WOOL/PLUM SE18 ....126 C3
Thames Christian College
BTSEA SW11 ....140 C4
Thames Ditton Infant School
THDIT KT7 ....190 A3
Thames Ditton Junior
School *THDIT* KT7 ....190 A4
Thameside Industrial Estate
CAN/RD E16 ....126 C1
Thames Magistrates Court
BOW E3 ....105 J2
Thamesmead Leisure Centre
THMD SE28 ....109 G6
Thamesmead Shopping
Centre *THMD* SE28 ....109 G6
Thames Valley University
EA W5 ....116 E1
Thamesview Business Centre
RAIN RM13 ....111 G4
Thames View Clinic
BARK IG11 ....109 F1
Thames View J & I School
BARK IG11 ....109 G1
Thames Water Tower
NTGHL W11 ....119 G2
Thatched House Hotel
SUT SM1 ....208 D4
Theatre Centre
BECK BR3 ....182 E5
Theatre for Mankind
FSBYPK N4 ....67 F5
Theatre Museum Library &
Archive *COVGDN* WC2E 11 F5
Theatre of the Dispossessed
WIM/MER SW19 ....159 J4
Theatre Royal
HOL/ALD WC2B 11 F4
SRTFD E15 ....88 B4
Theatre Royal Haymarket
STJS SW1Y 10 D6
Theodore McLeary
Primary School *EDUL* SE22 ....143 G5
Therapia Trading Estate
CROY/NA CR0 ....195 J4
Thistlebrook Industrial Estate
ABYW SE2 ....128 C3
Thomas Arnold Primary
School *DAGW* RM9 ....92 B5
Thomas Buxton Primary
School *WCHPL* E1 ....104 C3
Thomas Fairchild Primary
School *IS* N1 ....6 E2
Thomas Francis Academy
BRXN/ST SW9 ....142 C5
Thomas Gamuel Primary
School *WALTH* E17 ....69 J3
Thomas Jones Primary School
NTGHL W11 ....100 C5
Thomas London
Independent Day School
KENS W8 ....120 A3
Thomas Preparatory School
BTSEA SW11 ....140 E6
Thomas Road Industrial
Estate *POP/IOD* E14 ....105 J4
Thomas's Preparatory
School *BTSEA* SW11 ....140 C2
Thomas Tallis School
BKHTH/KID SE3 ....146 A4
Thornhill Primary School
IS N1 ....85 G5
Thornton Heath Health
Centre *THHTH* CR7 ....196 D1
Thornton Heath Pools
& Fitness Centre
THHTH CR7 ....196 D1
Thornton Road Industrial
Estate *CROY/NA* CR0 ....195 K3
Thornton Primary School
CHARL SE7 ....126 C5
Thorpe Hall Primary School
WALTH E17 ....52 A4
Three Bridges Business
Centre *NWDGN* UB2 ....115 H2
Three Bridges Primary
School *NWDGN* UB2 ....115 G3
Three Mills Heritage Centre
SRTFD E15 ....106 A2
Thurlow Park School
WNWD SE27 ....162 C4
Thurston Industrial Estate
LEW SE13 ....144 E4
Tidemill Primary School
DEPT SE8 ....144 D1

Tideway Industrial Estate
 VX/NE SW8 ....121 H6
Tiffin Girls School
 KUTN/CMB KT2 ....175 F2
Tiffin School
 KUTN/CMB KT2 ....175 G5
Tiller Centre (Swimming
 Baths) POP/IOD E14 ....124 D3
Tiller Leisure Centre
 POP/IOD E14 ....124 D3
Timbercroft Primary School
 WOOL/PLUM SE18 ....147 K1
Timbers Clinic
 KTN/HRWW/W HA3 ....42 D2
Times Square Shopping
 Centre SUT SM1 ....209 F3
Tiverton Primary School
 SEVS/STOTM N15 ....67 K3
Tobacco Dock
 WAP E1W 104 D6
Tokyngton Community
 Centre WBLY HA9 ....80 D3
Toldos School
 STNW/STAM N16 ....67 K5
Tolgate Primary School
 CROY/NA CRO 197 K3
 PLSTW E13 ....107 G3
Tolworth CP School
 SURB KT6 ....191 G5
Tolworth Girls School
 SURB KT6 ....206 B1
Tolworth Recreation Centre
 CHSGTN KT9 ....206 B1
Tolworth Tower
 SURB KT6 ....191 J5
Tom Hood School
 WAN E11 ....88 D1
Tooting Bec Athletics Track
 TOOT SW17 ....161 G6
Tooting Leisure Centre
 TOOT SW17 ....161 F6
Tooting & Mitcham United FC
 MTCM CR4 ....179 F4
Torah Temimah Primary
 School CRICK NW2 ....81 K2
Torah Vodaas
 GLDGN NW11 ....64 D6
Torriano J & I School
 KTTN NW5 ....84 C3
Torridon Primary School
 CAT SE6 ....165 G4
Torrington Clinic
 NFNCH/WDSP N12 ....47 G1
Torrington Park Health Centre
 NFNCH/WDSP N12 ....33 G6
Total Health Clinic
 SHB W12 ....118 E2
Tottenhall Infants School
 PLMGR N13 ....49 G2
Tottenham Green Leisure
 Centre SEVS/STOTM N15 ......68 A1
Tottenham Hale Retail Park
 SEVS/STOTM N15 ....68 C1
Tottenham Hotspur FC
 (White Hart Lane)
 TOTM N17 ....50 B3
Tottenham Park Cemetery
 ED N9 ....36 D5
Tottenham Sports Centre
 TOTM N17 ....50 B4
Totteridge CC
 TRDG/WHET N20 ....32 E4
Tower 42
 OBST EC2N 13 G3
The Tower Bridge Exhibition
 STHWK SE1 ....19 H1
Tower Bridge Primary School
 STHWK SE1 ....19 J2
Tower Bridge Wharf
 WAP E1W 123 H1
Tower Hamlets College
 POP/IOD E14 ....105 K6
 WCHPL E1 ....104 E4
Tower Industrial Estate
 SNWD SE25 ....197 H1
Tower Medical Centre
 WCHPL E1 ....104 C5
Tower Millennium Pier
 MON EC3R 13 H7
Tower of London
 TWRH EC3N 13 J6
Tower Retail Park
 DART DA1 ....150 C6
Towers Business Park
 WBLY HA9 ....80 D2
Tower Stairs
 MON EC3R 13 G6
Town Farm Primary School
 STWL/WRAY TW19 ....152 A2
Townley Grammar School
 for Girls BXLYHS DA6 ....169 G1
Townmead Business Centre
 FUL/PGN SW6 ....140 B4
Townsend Industrial Estate
 WLSDN NW10 .... —
Townsend Primary School
 WALW SE17 ....19 F6
Toynbee Hall & Curtain
 Theatre WCHPL E1 ....13 J3
Trabzon Spor FC
 STNW/STAM N16 ....85 K2
Trade Union Congress
 NOXST/BSQ WC1A 10 D3
Trafalgar Business Centre
 BARK IG11 ....109 F3
Trafalgar Primary & Infant
 School WHTN TW2 ....155 J4
Trafalgar Square
 CHCR WC2N 10 D7
Trafalgar Trading Estate
 PEND EN3 ....25 H5
Tramshed Theatre
 WOOL/PLUM SE18 ....127 G4
Trans Atlantic College
 BETH E2 ....7 J2

Transport House
 WEST SW1P 16 E5
Travel Inn
 CAN/RD E16 ....107 H6
 ECT SW5 ....120 A4
 FUL/PGN SW6 ....139 H4
 GFD/PVL UB6 ....97 H2
 HTHAIR TW6 ....133 H2
 KTN/HRWW/W HA3 ....61 H3
 PUR RM19 ....131 J5
 REDBR IG4 ....71 H2
 ROM RM1 ....75 H2
 SAND/SEL CR2 ....212 C3
 STHWK SE1 ....17 G2
 STPAN WC1H 4 D5
 YEAD UB4 ....95 F5
Travelodge
 ACT W3 ....98 C3
 BTSEA SW11 ....140 B4
 HEST TW5 ....114 B6
 HEST TW5 ....114 D6
 POP/IOD E14 ....106 B5
 REDBR IG4 ....71 G2
 ROM RM1 ....75 G2
 STPAN WC1H 5 F4
 WCHPL E1 ....13 J5
Treasury
 WHALL SW1A 16 E3
The Treaty Centre
 HSLW TW3 ....135 G4
The Treehouse School
 BMSBY WC1N 5 G6
Trent CE Primary School
 EBAR EN4 ....21 K5
Trent Country Park
 EBAR EN4 ....22 A3
Trent Park Cemetery
 EBAR EN4 ....22 A4
Trent Park Golf Club
 EBAR EN4 ....22 C5
Trevor Roberts School
 HAMP NW3 ....83 H5
Tricycle Cinema
 KIL/WHAMP NW6 ....82 D5
Trident Business Centre
 TOOT SW17 ....178 E1
Trinity Business Centre
 BERM/RHTH SE16 ....124 C2
Trinity Catholic Lower
 High School WFD IG8 ....38 E6
Trinity College Centre
 PECK SE15 ....143 F1
Trinity College of Music
 CNWCH SE10 ....125 F6
 CNWCH SE10 ....9 H2
Trinity Hospital
 CNWCH SE10 ....125 G5
Trinity House
 TWRH EC3N 13 H5
Trinity RC High School
 (Upper) WFD IG8 ....38 E6
Trinity St Marys Primary
 School BAL SW12 ....161 F3
Trinity School
 CROY/NA CRO 197 K6
 DAGE RM10 ....92 C1
Trinity School Belvedere
 BELV DA17 ....129 K4
Trinity Trading Estate
 HAYES BR2 ....113 K3
Tripcock Point Development
 Site THMD SE28 ....109 F6
Triumph Trading Estate
 TOTM N17 ....50 C2
Trocadero Centre
 MYFR/PICC W1J 10 C6
Trojan Business Centre
 WLSDN NW10 ....81 H4
Troy Industrial Estate
 HRW HA1 ....61 F2
True Buddha School
 IS N1 ....5 G1
Tudor Lodge Health Centre
 WIM/MER SW19 ....159 G2
Tudor Lodge Hotel
 PIN HA5 ....59 F3
Tudor Primary School
 FNCH N3 ....47 G4
 STHL UB1 ....95 J6
Tufnell Park Primary School
 HOLWY N7 ....84 D2
Tuke School
 PECK SE15 ....143 J2
Tulloch Clinic
 SHB W12 ....119 G1
Tunnel Avenue Trading
 Estate CNWCH SE10 ....125 G2
Turney School
 DUL SE21 ....162 D2
Turnham Primary School
 BROCKY SE4 ....144 B5
Turtle Key Arts Centre
 FUL/PGN SW6 ....119 K6
TV Studios
 WBLY HA9 ....80 C1
Tweeddale Primary School
 CAR SM5 ....194 C4
Twenty Nevern Square Hotel
 ECT SW5 ....119 K5
Twickenham Cemetery
 WHTN TW2 ....155 G3
Twickenham Golf Club
 FELT TW13 ....155 F5
Twickenham Park Health
 Centre TWK TW1 ....156 D1
Twickenham Stadium
 WHTN TW2 ....155 K1
Twickenham Trading Estate
 TWK TW1 ....156 A1
Two Bridges Business Park
 SAND/SEL CR2 ....211 K4
Twyford CE High School
 ACT W3 ....117 H1
Twyford Sports Centre
 ACT W3 ....117 J1

Tynemouth Road Health
 Centre SEVS/STOTM N15 ....68 B1
The Type Museum
 BRXN/ST SW9 ....142 A2
Tyssen Primary School
 STNW/STAM N16 ....68 C5
UCI Cinema
 BAY/PAD W2 ....101 F6
 BERM/RHTH SE16 ....124 A5
 ED N9 ....37 F2
 STPAN WC1H 209 F3
UCI Empire Cinema
 LSQ/SEVD WC2H 10 D6
UCI Filmworks Cinema
 CNWCH SE10 ....125 J4
UCI Hospitals
 FITZ W1T 4 B7
UGC Cinema
 CHEL SW3 ....120 C6
 CRICK NW2 ....63 K5
 EA W5 ....97 K6
 EN EN1 ....24 C5
 HMSMTH W6 ....118 E4
 SOHO/SHAV W1D 10 C5
Underhill J & I School
 BAR EN5 ....20 C6
Unicorn Primary School
 BECK BR3 ....198 E2
Unicorn School
 RCH/KEW TW9 ....137 G2
United Medical & Dental
 Schools STHWK SE1 ....17 G4
United Services Sports
 Ground CHSWK W4 ....138 B2
Unity College
 KTTN NW5 ....84 B2
Unity Trading Estate
 WFD IG8 ....53 H6
University Church of
 Christ the King
 STPAN WC1H 4 C7
University College Hospital
 GWRST WC1E 4 B7
 HAMP NW3 ....83 H4
University College Junior
 School HAMP NW3 ....83 G2
University College London
 FITZ W1T 10 B1
 GWRST WC1E 4 C7
 STPAN WC1H 4 C7
University College London,
 Astor College FITZ W1T 10 B1
University College London,
 Department of Clinical
 Haematology GWRST WC1E ...4 C7
University College London
 Medical School
 FITZ W1T 10 A1
University College School
 HAMP NW3 ....83 G3
University Hospital Lewisham
 LEW SE13 ....144 E6
University of California
 WHALL SW1A 16 A1
University of East London
 EHAM E6 ....108 A6
 PLSTW E13 ....107 F2
 SRTFD E15 ....88 A5
 SRTFD E15 ....88 C4
University of East London
 Institute BCTR RM8 ....91 G3
University of Greenwich
 DART DA1 ....171 J4
 ELTH/MOT SE9 ....167 J1
 CNWCH SE10 ....125 G5
 WOOL/PLUM SE18 ....127 F5
University of Greenwich
 (Mansion Site)
 ELTH/MOT SE9 ....167 H1
University of Greenwich
 Sports Ground
 ELTH/MOT SE9 ....146 D5
 ELTH/MOT SE9 ....167 H2
University of London
 BAY/PAD W2 ....8 A4
 BMSBY WC1N 5 F7
 CLKNW EC1R 5 K6
 FITZ W1T 10 D1
 GWRST WC1E 10 D1
 NWCR SE14 ....144 B2
 STPAN WC1H 4 D6
University of London
 Athletics Ground
 NWMAL KT3 ....192 D2
University of Middlesex
 EBAR EN4 ....22 C3
 PEND EN3 ....24 D6
University of North London
 HOLWY N7 ....85 F5
University of Westminster
 CAMTN NW1 ....4 A6
 CHSWK W4 ....137 K2
 GTPST W1W 9 K1
 HGT N6 ....66 B5
 HRW HA1 ....61 G4
 MHST W1U 9 G1
Uphall Primary School
 IL IG1 ....90 B3
Upland Primary School
 BXLYHN DA7 ....149 G4
Uplands Business Park
 WALTH E17 ....51 F5
Upper Montagu Street Clinic
 MBLAR W1H 8 E1
Upper Tooting Independent
 High School
 TOOT SW17 ....160 D4
Upton Cross Primary School
 PLSTW E13 ....89 F6
Upton Day Hospital
 BXLYHS DA6 ....149 F5
Upton Lane Medical Centre
 FSTGT E7 ....89 F4
Upton Primary School
 BXLY DA5 ....149 F6

Upton Road School
 BXLYHS DA6 ....149 F6
The Undang Academy
 LSQ/SEVD WC2H 10 E4
Ursuline High School
 IL IG1 ....72 B6
 RYNPK SW20 ....177 G3
Ursuline Preparatory School
 WIM/MER SW19 ....177 G3
Uxbridge College
 HYS/HAR UB3 ....94 E6
Uxbridge County Court
 YEAD UB4 ....94 C4
Uxendon Manor JMI School
 KTN/HRWW/W HA3 ....62 A2
Vale Farm Sports Centre
 ALP/SUD HA0 ....79 H2
Vale Industrial Estate
 WATW WD18 ....26 A3
The Vale Medical Centre
 FSTH SE23 ....164 B4
Valence House Museum &
 Library BCTR RM8 ....73 K6
Valence Junior School
 BCTR RM8 ....73 K6
Valentine High School
 IL IG1 ....72 A3
Valentines High Lower School
 GNTH/NBYPK IG2 ....72 B2
Vale Park Industrial
 ACT W3 ....118 B2
The Vale School
 SKENS SW7 ....120 B3
Valley Primary School
 HAYES BR2 ....183 J5
Valmar Trading Estate
 CMBW SE5 ....142 D2
Vanbrugh Theatre
 GWRST WC1E 4 C7
Vanguard Trading Estate
 SRTFD E15 ....88 A6
Vaudeville Theatre
 COVGDN WC2E 11 F5
Vaughan F & M School
 RYLN/HDSTN HA2 ....60 C3
Vauxhall Primary School
 LBTH SE11 ....122 A5
Vencourt Hotel
 HMSMTH W6 ....118 D4
Vernon House Special School
 WLSDN NW10 ....80 E3
Vestry Hall
 MTCM CR4 ....178 E6
Vestry House Museum
 WALTH E17 ....69 K1
Vicarage Fields Health Clinic
 BARK IG11 ....90 C5
The Vicarage Field Shopping
 Centre BARK IG11 ....90 C5
Vicarage Primary School
 EHAM E6 ....107 K2
Vicars Green Primary School
 GFD/PVL UB6 ....97 J1
VI Components Industrial
 Park
 ERITH DA8 ....130 B5
Vicoria Hall
 FNCH N3 ....46 E5
Victoria & Albert Museum
 SKENS SW7 ....14 B5
Victoria Business Centre
 WELL DA16 ....148 B3
Victoria Bus Station
 PIM SW1V 15 K5
Victoria Chiropractic Clinic
 CHEL SW3 ....14 E3
Victoria Coach Station
 BGVA SW1W 15 J7
Victoria Industrial Estate
 ACT W3 ....99 F4
Victoria Industrial Park
 DART DA1 ....151 G6
Victoria Junior School
 FELT TW13 ....154 A3
Victoria Medical Centre
 PIM SW1V 16 B7
Victoria Palace Theatre
 WESTW SW1E 15 K5
Victoria Park Industrial
 Centre HOM E9 ....87 H5
Victoria Park Plaza Hotel
 PIM SW1V 16 A6
Victoria Place
 Shopping Centre
 PIM SW1V 15 K6
Victoria Rail/Air Terminal
 PIM SW1V 15 K6
Victoria Retail Park
 RSLP HA4 ....77 H3
Victoria Wharf
 POP/IOD E14 ....105 G6
Victoria West Industrial
 Estate DEPT SE8 ....124 C5
Victor Seymour Infant
 School CAR SM5 ....209 K1
Victory Business Centre
 ISLW TW7 ....136 A5
Victory Primary School
 WALW SE17 ....18 D6
Viking Business Centre
 ROMW/RG RM7 ....57 H5
Viking Primary School
 NTHLT UB5 ....95 H2
Village Infant School
 DAGE RM10 ....92 C5
The Village School
 HAMP NW3 ....83 K4
Villiers High School
 STHL UB1 ....115 F1
The Vine Clinic
 KUTN/CMB KT2 ....175 F2
Vine Medical Centre
 E/WMO/HCT KT8 ....173 H6
The Vines School
 BTSEA SW11 ....141 F5

The Vineyard Primary School
 RCHPK/HAM TW10 ....157 F1
Vinopolis, City of Wine
 STHWK SE1 ....12 D7
Vinters' Hall
 BLKFR EC4V 12 C5
VIP Trading Estate
 CHARL SE7 ....126 B4
Virginia Primary School
 BETH E2 ....7 J5
Virgo Fidelis Convent Schools
 NRWD SE19 ....180 D2
Vittoria Primary School
 IS N1 ....5 H1
Voyager Business Estate
 BERM/RHTH SE16 ....123 H3
VUE Cinema
 ACT W3 ....98 C3
 CROY/NA CRO 196 A6
 DAGW RM9 ....92 A6
 FUL/PGN SW6 ....139 K1
 HAMP NW3 ....83 G4
 HRW HA1 ....60 E3
 SHB W12 ....119 G2
VUE Finchley Lido
 Cinema NFNCH/WDSP N12 ...47 H3
VUE West End
 Cinema SOHO/SHAV W1D 10 D5
Vulcan Business Centre
 CROY/NA CRO 214 C6
Waddon Clinic
 CROY/NA CRO 211 G3
Waddon Infant School
 CROY/NA CRO 211 G3
Wadham Lodge Sports
 Centre WALTH E17 ....51 K4
Wadsworth Business Centre
 GFD/PVL UB6 ....97 J1
The Waldegrave Clinic
 TEDD TW11 ....174 A1
Waldegrave Girls School
 WHTN TW2 ....155 J5
Waldo Industrial Estate
 BMLY BR1 ....184 B6
Waldorf School of SW London
 STRHM/NOR SW16 ....161 H4
Waldorf Steiner School
 of SW London
 STRHM/NOR SW16 ....161 J6
Walker Primary School
 STHGT/OAK N14 ....34 D4
The Wallace Centre
 DEPT SE8 ....124 E6
The Wallace Collection
 MHST W1U 9 G3
Wallbrook Business Centre
 HSLWW TW4 ....134 A4
Wallington County Grammar
 School WLGTN SM6 ....210 B1
Wallington High School for
 Girls WLGTN SM6 ....210 B6
Walmer Road Clinic
 NTGHL W11 ....100 C6
Walm Lane Clinic
 CRICK NW2 ....82 B3
Walnut Leisure Centre
 ORP BR6 ....202 B5
Walnuts Shopping Centre
 ORP BR6 ....202 B5
Walnut Tree Walk Primary
 School LBTH SE11 ....17 J6
Waltham Forest College
 WALTH E17 ....50 E6
 WALTH E17 ....51 K6
Waltham Forest Magistrates
 Court WALTH E17 ....51 K6
Waltham Forest Theatre
 WALTH E17 ....51 H6
Waltham Forest Pool &
 Track WALTH E17 ....51 K5
Walthamstow Business
 Centre WALTH E17 ....52 A5
Walthamstow Greyhound
 Stadium CHING E4 ....51 K3
Walthamstow School for Girls
 WALTH E17 ....69 K1
Walton Business Centre
 WOT/HER KT12 ....188 A4
Walton Casuals FC
 WOT/HER KT12 ....188 A2
Walton Community Hospital
 WOT/HER KT12 ....188 A6
Walton Swimming Pool
 WOT/HER KT12 ....188 A5
Walworth Lower School
 WALW SE17 ....122 E5
Walworth Town Hall
 WALW SE17 ....18 C7
Walworth Upper School
 WALW SE17 ....123 F5
Wandle Primary School
 WAND/EARL SW18 ....160 A3
Wandle Recreation Centre
 WAND/EARL SW18 ....160 A1
Wandle Trading Estate
 MTCM CR4 ....194 E4
Wandle Valley School
 CAR SM5 ....194 D4
Wandsworth Adult College
 BTSEA SW11 ....141 F2
 TOOT SW17 ....160 D4
Wandsworth Cemetery
 WAND/EARL SW18 ....160 B3
Wandsworth County Court
 PUT/ROE SW15 ....139 G5
Wandsworth Trading Estate
 WAND/EARL SW18 ....160 A2
Wanstead CC
 WAN E11 ....71 F4
Wanstead CE Primary School
 WAN E11 ....70 E2
Wanstead Golf Club
 WAN E11 ....71 F4
Wanstead High School
 WAN E11 ....71 G3

Wanstead Hospital
WAN E11 ....71 F1
Wanstead Leisure Centre
WAN E11 ....71 G3
Wapping Sports Centre
WAP E1W 123 J1
Wapping Wharf
WAP E1W 123 K1
Warehouse Theatre
CROY/NA CR0 ....196 E6
War Memorial Sports Ground
WAP E1W 209 J2
Warnford Industrial Estate
HYS/HAR UB3 ....113 H2
Warren Comprehensive
School *CHDH* RM6 ....74 B2
Warren Dell Primary School
OXHEY WD19 ....27 G5
Warrender School
RSLP HA4 ....58 D4
Warren Junior School
CHDH RM6 ....74 B2
The Warren Medical Centre
YEAD UB4 ....95 F5
Warren Road Primary School
ORP BR6 ....217 F2
Warren Sports Centre
CHDH RM6 ....74 B2
Warwick Dubbing Theatre
SOHO/CST W1F 10 C1
Warwick Estate
BAY/PAD W2 ....101 F4
Warwick Leadlay Gallery
GNWCH SE10 ....125 F6
Warwick School for Boys
WALTH E17 ....70 A1
The Washington Mayfair Hotel
MYFR/PICC W1J 9 K7
Waterfront Leisure Centre
WOOL/PLUM SE18 ....127 F3
Watergate School
CAT SE6 ....182 E1
LEW SE13 ....144 E5
Waterloo Health Centre
STHWK SE1 ....17 J3
Watermans Arts, Cinema &
Theatre Centre *BTFD* TW8 .....117 F6
The Watermans Hall
MON EC3R 13 C6
Watermeads High School
MRDN SM4 ....194 C3
Watermill Business Centre
PEND EN3 ....25 H5
Water Rats Theatre
STPAN WC1H 5 F4
Waterside Business Centre
ISLW TW7 ....136 C5
The Waterside
Trading Centre
HNWL W7 ....115 K3
Watersports Centre
FSBYPK N4 ....67 J5
Waterways Business Centre
PEND EN3 ....25 H1
Watling Clinic
EDGW HA8 ....45 F3
Watling Medical Centre
EDGW HA8 ....44 E4
Wavelengths Leisure Pool &
Library *DEPT* SE8 ....144 D1
Waverley Industrial Estate
HRW HA1 ....42 D6
Waverley Lower Secondary
School *EDUL* SE22 ....143 J6
Waverley School
PECK SE15 ....143 K6
PEND EN3 ....24 E5
Waxchandlers' Hall
CITYW EC2V 12 D3
Weald F & M School
KTN/HRWW/W HA3 ....43 F5
Webber Douglas Academy
of Dramatic Art
SKENS SW7 ....120 B4
Wedgwood Special School
WKENS W14 ....119 J5
Welbeck Clinic
CRICK NW2 ....82 E1
Welbourne Primary School
TOTM N17 ....68 C1
Welcome Lodge
MLHL NW7 ....31 F5
Wellcome Institute
CAMTN NW1 ....4 C6
Welldon Park Middle School
RYLN/HDSTN HA2 ....78 C2
The Welling Clinic
WELL DA16 ....148 B5
Welling Medical Centre
WELL DA16 ....148 A5
Welling Arch
WELL DA16 ....148 C2
Wellington Arch
MYFR/PICC W1J 15 H2
Wellington Barracks
STJSPK SW1H 16 B3
Wellington Primary School
BOW E3 ....105 J2
HSLW TW5 ....134 E5
Welling United FC
WELL DA16 ....148 D4
Wells Primary School
WFD IG8 ....39 F6
Wembley Arena
WBLY HA9 ....80 C2
Wembley Commercial Centre
WBLY HA9 ....61 K6
Wembley Conference Centre
WBLY HA9 ....80 B2
Wembley FC
ALP/SUD HA0 ....79 H2
Wembley High School
ALP/SUD HA0 ....79 J1
Wembley Hospital
ALP/SUD HA0 ....79 K4

Wembley Manor Primary
School *WBLY* HA9 ....80 A1
Wembley Park Business
Centre *WBLY* HA9 ....80 D1
Wembley Stadium Industrial
Estate *WBLY* HA9 ....80 C1
Wembley Stadium
(under development)
WBLY HA9 ....80 C2
Wendell Park Primary School
SHB W12 ....118 C2
Wentworth Tutorial College
GLDGN NW11 ....64 B3
The Wernher Collection at
Ranger's House
GNWCH SE10 ....145 G2
Wesley's Chapel, House &
Museum *STLK* EC1Y 6 E6
Wessex Gardens Primary
School *CRICK* NW2 ....64 C5
West 12 Shopping & Leisure
Centre *WKENS* W14 ....119 G2
West Acton Primary School
ACT W3 ....98 D5
West Beckton Health Centre
CAN/RD E16 ....107 G4
Westbourne Green Sports
Complex *BAY/PAD* W2 ....100 E4
Westbourne Primary School
SUT SM1 ....208 E1
Westbridge College
BTSEA SW11 ....140 D2
Westbrooke School
WELL DA16 ....148 E4
The Westbury Hotel
MYFR/PICC W1K 9 K5
Westbury Medical Centre
WDGN N22 ....49 J5
Westcott Leisure Centre
CAR SM5 ....210 A2
West Drayton Primary School
WDR/YW UB7 ....112 B2
West Ealing Business Centre
WEA W13 ....97 G6
Western Avenue Business
Park *ACT* W3 ....98 D3
Western International Market
NWDGN UB2 ....114 A4
Western Trading Estate
WLSDN NW10 ....98 E3
West Ewell Infant School
HOR/WEW KT19 ....207 F3
Westfields Primary School
BARN SW13 ....138 C3
Westgate Business Centre
NKENS W10 ....100 C3
Westgate Primary School
DART DA1 ....171 G2
West Green Primary School
SEVS/STOTM N15 ....67 J1
West Grove Primary School
STHGT/OAK N14 ....34 D2
West Ham Church Primary
School *SRTFD* E15 ....88 D6
West Ham Lane Clinic
SRTFD E15 ....88 C6
West Hampstead Clinic
KIL/WHAMP NW6 ....82 E5
West Ham United FC
EHAM E6 ....107 H1
West Hatch High School
CHIG IG7 ....53 K1
West Hendon Clinic
CDALE/KGS NW9 ....63 H3
West Hill Primary School
DART DA1 ....171 F1
WAND/EARL SW18 ....139 K6
West India Pier
POP/IOD E14 ....124 C2
West India Shopping Centre
POP/IOD E14 ....124 D1
Westland Heliport
BTSEA SW11 ....140 C4
West Lea School
ED N9 ....36 A5
West Lodge Park Hotel
EBAR EN4 ....21 K1
West Lodge Preparatory
School *BFN/LL* DA15 ....168 A5
West Lodge Primary School
PIN HA5 ....59 H1
West London Academy
NTHLT UB5 ....77 H6
West London County Court
WKENS W14 ....119 H4
West London Magistrates
Court *HMSMTH* W6 ....119 G5
West London Tamil School
WLSDN NW10 ....99 H1
West Mead Clinic
RSLP HA4 ....77 G1
West Middlesex Golf Club
STHL UB1 ....96 C6
West Middlesex University
Hospital *ISLW* TW7 ....136 B3
Westminster Abbey
WEST SW1P 16 E4
Westminster Abbey Choir
School *WEST* SW1P 16 D4
Westminster Business
Square *LBTH* SE11 ....122 A5
Westminster Cathedral
WEST SW1P 16 A5
Westminster Cathedral Choir
School *WEST* SW1P 16 A5
Westminster Cathedral RC
Primary School *PIM* SW1V 121 J5
Westminster City Hall
WESTW SW1E 16 B4
Westminster City School
WESTW SW1E 16 B4
Westminster College
SOHO/SHAV W1D 10 B5
Westminster Industrial Estate
WOOL/PLUM SE18 ....126 C3

Westminster Kingsway
College *BTSEA* SW11 ....141 F2
Westminster Natural
Health Centre *PIM* SW1V 16 A7
Westminster Pier
WHALL SW1A 17 F3
Westminster School
WEST SW1P 16 E4
Westminster Technical
College *WEST* SW1P 16 B6
Westminster Theatre
WESTW SW1E 16 A4
Westminster Tutors
SKENS SW7 ....14 A7
Westminster Under School
WEST SW1P 16 C7
Westmoor Community Clinic
PUT/ROE SW15 ....158 D2
West Norwood Clinic
WNWD SE27 ....162 D4
West Norwood Crematorium
WNWD SE27 ....162 D5
West One Shopping Centre
MYFR/PKLN W1K 9 H4
Weston Green School
THDIT KT7 ....189 K5
Weston Park Clinic
CEND/HSY/T N8 ....66 E2
Weston Park Primary School
CEND/HSY/T N8 ....67 F2
Westpoint Trading Estate
ACT W3 ....98 D4
West Ramp Coach Park
WDR/YW UB7 ....132 D2
West Ruislip Elementary
School *HGDN/ICK* UB10 ....76 A1
West Thames College
ISLW TW7 ....135 K2
West Thamesmead Business
Park *THMD* SE28 ....128 A3
West Thornton Primary
School *CROY/NA* CR0 ....196 A4
West Twyford Primary
School *WLSDN* NW10 ....98 C1
Westway Business Centre
BAY/PAD W2 ....101 F4
Westway Sports Centre
NKENS W10 ....100 B5
West Wickham Swimming
Baths *WWKM* BR4 ....199 F5
West Wimbledon Primary
School *RYNPK* SW20 ....176 E6
Westwood College
WELL DA16 ....147 J5
Westwood Language College
for Girls *RRWD* SE19 ....180 D3
Westwood School
BUSH WD23 ....28 D4
Whaddon House Clinic
CMBW SE5 ....143 F4
Whipps Cross Hospital
LEY E10 ....70 B3
White Bridge Primary School
LOU IG10 ....39 J4
Whitechapel Art Gallery
WCHPL E1 ....13 K3
Whitechapel Sports Centre
WCHPL E1 ....104 C3
Whitefield School
CRICK NW2 ....64 B4
Whitefield School & Leisure
Centre *WALTH* E17 ....52 B4
Whitefriars F & M School
KTN/HRWW/W HA3 ....42 E5
Whitefriars Trading Estate
KTN/HRWW/W HA3 ....42 D5
Whitehall Primary School
CHING E4 ....38 C4
Whitehall Theatre
WHALL SW1A 10 D7
White Hart Lane School
WDGN N22 ....49 H3
Whiteheath Junior School
RSLP HA4 ....58 A3
Whitehorse Manor Primary
School *THHTH* CR7 ....196 V1
White House Preparatory
& Kindergarten *BAL* SW12 ....161 J3
Whitehouse Preparatory
School *BAL* SW12 ....161 H3
Whitelands College
PUT/ROE SW15 ....158 D2
Whiteleys Shopping Centre
BAY/PAD W2 ....101 F5
Whiterose Trading Estate
EBAR EN4 ....33 J2
Whitgift School
SAND/SEL CR2 ....211 J3
Whitgift Shopping Centre
CROY/NA CR0 ....196 D6
Whitings Hill Primary School
BAR EN5 ....20 A6
Whitmore High School
RYLN/HDSTN HA2 ....60 C5
Whitmore Primary School
IS N1 ....7 F2
Whittingham Community
Primary School
WALTH E17 ....51 G4
Whittington Hospital
ARCH N19 ....66 B6
Whitton Health Centre
WHTN TW2 ....155 H3
Whitton Health Clinic
WHTN TW2 ....155 H3
Whitton School
WHTN TW2 ....155 G4
Whitton Sports & Fitness
Centre *WHTN* TW2 ....155 G4
Whybridge Infant School
RAIN RM13 ....93 J6
Whybridge Junior School
RAIN RM13 ....93 H6

Wickham Court School
WWKM BR4 ....214 B2
Wickham Theatre
WWKM BR4 ....214 B1
Wide Way Health Clinic
MTCM CR4 ....179 J6
Widmore Centre
BMLY BR1 ....184 B5
Wigmore Hall
MHST W1U 9 J3
Wilberforce Primary School
NKENS W10 ....100 C2
Wilbury Primary School
UED N18 ....49 K1
Willesden Community Hospital
WLSDN NW10 ....81 J5
Willesden County Court
WLSDN NW10 ....99 G1
Willesden Medical Centre
WLSDN NW10 ....81 K4
Willesden Sports Centre
WLSDN NW10 ....81 K6
Willesden Sports Stadium
WLSDN NW10 ....81 K6
William Bellamy J & I School
DAGE RM10 ....74 C6
William Byrd School
HYS/HAR UB3 ....113 F6
William C Harvey Special
School *TOTM* N17 ....49 K5
William Davies Primary School
FSTGT E7 ....89 H4
William Ellis School
KTTN NW5 ....84 A1
William Ellis Sports Ground
EDGW HA8 ....44 C4
William Ford CE Junior School
DAGE RM10 ....92 C5
William Hogarth School
CHSWK W4 ....118 B6
William Morris Academy
HMSMTH W6 ....119 G5
William Morris Gallery
WALTH E17 ....51 J6
William Morris School
WALTH E17 ....51 G4
William Patten Primary School
STNW/STAM N16 ....68 B6
William Torbitt J & I School
GNTH/NBYPK IG2 ....72 E2
William Tyndale Primary
School *IS* N1 ....85 H5
Willington School
WIM/MER SW19 ....177 J2
Willow Business Centre
MTCM CR4 ....194 E2
Willow Business Park
SYD SE26 ....163 K5
Willowfield Adult Education
Centre *WALTH* E17 ....51 F6
Willowfield School
HNHL SE24 ....142 D5
WALTH E17 ....51 G6
The Willows Clinic
CHST BR7 ....185 F2
The Willows
YEAD UB4 ....95 H3
Willow Tree Primary School
NTHLT UB5 ....77 J4
Wilmington Boys Grammar
School *RDART* DA2 ....170 E5
Wilmington Grammar School
for Girls *RDART* DA2 ....170 E4
Wilmington Hall School
RDART DA2 ....170 D5
Wilmington Primary School
RDART DA2 ....170 D5
Wilson's School
WLGTN SM6 ....210 E4
Wimbledon Chase
Primary School
RYNPK SW20 ....177 H4
Wimbledon College-
Preparatory School
WIM/MER SW19 ....177 G3
Wimbledon Common Golf
Club *WIM/MER* SW19 ....176 E1
Wimbledon Common
Pre-Preparatory School
WIM/MER SW19 ....177 F2
Wimbledon (Gap Road)
Cemetery
WIM/MER SW19 ....160 A6
Wimbledon High School
WIM/MER SW19 ....177 H2
Wimbledon House School
WIM/MER SW19 ....177 J4
Wimbledon Magistrates
Court *WIM/MER* SW19 ....177 K2
Wimbledon Park Athletics
Track *WIM/MER* SW19 ....159 J4
Wimbledon Park Golf Club
WIM/MER SW19 ....159 J5
Wimbledon Park Primary
School *WIM/MER* SW19 ....159 K4
Wimbledon Recreation
Centre *WIM/MER* SW19 ....178 A2
Wimbledon RFC
RYNPK SW20 ....176 C3
Wimbledon School of Art
WIM/MER SW19 ....177 H4
Wimbledon School of English
WIM/MER SW19 ....177 H2
Wimbledon Squash &
Badminton Club
WIM/MER SW19 ....177 H3
Wimbledon Stadium
TOOT SW17 ....160 A6
Wimbledon Stadium
Business Centre
WIM/MER SW19 ....160 A5
Wimbledon Theatre
WIM/MER SW19 ....177 K3

Winchcombe Business Centre
PECK SE15 ....123 F6
Winchmore Hill Clinic
WCHMH N21 ....35 H4
Winchmore Hill CC
WCHMH N21 ....35 J3
Winchmore School
WCHMH N21 ....35 J4
Windmill Business Centre
NWDGN UB2 ....115 H1
The Windmill on the
Common Hotel *CLAP* SW4 ....141 G2
Windmill School
BRXS/STRHM SW2 ....161 K1
Windmill Trading Estate
MTCM CR4 ....195 H2
Windrush Primary School
THMD SE28 ....128 C1
Winfield House
CAMTN NW1 ....2 D4
Wingate & Finchley FC
NFNCH/WDSP N12 ....47 H3
Wingate Trading Estate
TOTM N17 ....50 B3
Wingfield Primary School
BKHTH/KID SE3 ....145 K4
Winns Primary School
WALTH E17 ....51 H5
Winsor Primary School
EHAM E6 ....108 A5
Winston Churchill's Britain
at War Experience
STHWK SE1 ....19 F1
Winterbourne Infant School
THHTH CR7 ....196 B1
Winton Primary School
IS N1 ....5 G3
Witley Industrial Estate
NWDGN UB2 ....114 E4
Witnitz School
STNW/STAM N16 ....68 B5
Wix Primary School
CLAP SW4 ....141 G4
Wolf Fields Primary School
NWDGN UB2 ....114 E4
Wolfson Hillel Primary School
STHGT/OAK N14 ....34 D1
Wolfson Medical Centre
RYNPK SW20 ....176 D3
Wolsey Business Park
WATW WD18 ....26 B2
Wolsey Junior School
CROY/NA CR0 ....214 E5
The Women's Library
WCHPL E1 ....13 J3
The Woodberry Clinic
MUSWH N10 ....48 B6
Woodbridge High School &
Language College
WFD IG8 ....53 F3
Woodbrook School
BECK BR3 ....182 C4
Woodbury Down Primary
School *FSBYPK* N4 ....67 J4
Woodcroft Primary School
EDGW HA8 ....45 F3
Wood End J & I Schools
GFD/PVL UB6 ....78 D3
Wood End Park Junior School
HYS/HAR UB3 ....94 A6
Woodentops School
BAL SW12 ....161 J5
Woodfield School
CDALE/KGS NW9 ....63 G5
Woodford County High School
WFD IG8 ....52 D2
Woodford Golf Club
WFD IG8 ....52 D1
Woodford Green
Preparatory School
WFD IG8 ....52 E2
Woodford Green Primary
School *WFD* IG8 ....52 D1
Woodford Trading Estate
WFD IG8 ....53 G5
Woodgrange Infant School
FSTGT E7 ....89 F2
Woodgrange Park Cemetery
FSTGT E7 ....89 H3
Wood Green Crown Court
WDGN N22 ....49 G4
Wood Green Health Centre
WDGN N22 ....49 F4
Wood Green Old Boys FC
WDGN N22 ....49 G3
Woodhall School
OXHEY WD19 ....27 J6
Woodhill Primary School
CHARL SE7 ....126 D4
Woodhouse College
NFNCH/WDSP N12 ....47 H2
Woodlands F & M School
KTN/HRWW/W HA3 ....42 C3
Woodlands J & I School
IL IG1 ....90 D2
Woodlands Medical Centre
LEW SE13 ....165 G1
Woodlands Park Primary
School *SEVS/STOTM* N15 ....67 J2
Woodlane High School
SHB W12 ....99 K5
Wood Lane Medical Centre
RSLP HA4 ....58 C5
Wood Lane School
FUL/PGN SW6 ....140 B2
Wood Lane Sports Centre
BCTR RM8 ....74 C5
Woodmansterne Primary
School *STRHM/NOR* SW16 ....179 J4
Woodridge Primary School
NFNCH/WDSP N12 ....32 D5
Woodside Health Centre
SNWD SE25 ....197 J2
Woodside Infants School
CROY/NA CR0 ....197 H4

Acknowledgements

The Post Office is a registered trademark of Post Office Ltd. in the UK and other countries.

Schools address data provided by Education Direct.

Petrol station information supplied by Johnsons

One-way street data provided by © Tele Atlas N.V. Tele Atlas

Garden centre information provided by

Garden Centre Association   Britains best garden centres

Wyevale Garden Centres

The boundary of the London congestion charging zone supplied by Transport for London

The statement on the front cover of this atlas is sourced, selected and quoted from a reader comment and feedback form received in 2004

Notes

Notes

 **Street by Street** QUESTIONNAIRE

Dear Atlas User
Your comments, opinions and recommendations are very important to us.
So please help us to improve our street atlases by taking a few minutes
to complete this simple questionnaire.

You do not need a stamp (unless posted outside the UK). If you do not want to remove this page from your street atlas, then photocopy it or write your answers on a plain sheet of paper.

Send to: The Editor, AA Street by Street, FREEPOST SCE 4598,
Basingstoke RG21 4GY

ABOUT THE ATLAS...

Which city/town/county did you buy?

Are there any features of the atlas or mapping that you find particularly useful?

Is there anything we could have done better?

Why did you choose an AA Street by Street atlas?

Did it meet your expectations?

Exceeded ☐   Met all ☐   Met most ☐   Fell below ☐

Please give your reasons

Where did you buy it?

For what purpose? (please tick all applicable)

To use in your own local area ☐   To use on business or at work ☐

Visiting a strange place ☐   In the car ☐   On foot ☐

Other (please state)

LOCAL KNOWLEDGE...

Local knowledge is invaluable. Whilst every attempt has been made to make the information contained in this atlas as accurate as possible, should you notice any inaccuracies, please detail them below (if necessary, use a blank piece of paper) or e-mail us at *streetbystreet@theAA.com*

ABOUT YOU...

Name (Mr/Mrs/Ms)

Address

                                                            Postcode

Daytime tel no

E-mail address

Which age group are you in?

Under 25 ☐   25-34 ☐   35-44 ☐   45-54 ☐   55-64 ☐   65+ ☐

Are you an AA member?   YES ☐   NO ☐

Do you have Internet access?   YES ☐   NO ☐

Thank you for taking the time to complete this questionnaire. Please send it to us as soon as possible, and remember, you do not need a stamp (unless posted outside the UK).

We may want to contact you about other products and services provided by us, or our partners (by mail, telephone) but please tick the box if you DO NOT wish to hear about such products and services from us by mail or telephone. ☐

ML38